American Reference Books Annual

1997 VOLUME 28

AMERICAN REFERENCE BOOKS ANNUAL

1997 VOLUME 28

Bohdan S. Wynar EDITOR IN CHIEF
Ed Volz ASSOCIATE EDITOR

EDITORIAL ASSISTANT
Melissa R. Root

Comprehensive annual reviewing service for
reference books published in the United States and Canada

1997

LIBRARIES UNLIMITED
ENGLEWOOD, COLORADO

Copyright © 1997 Libraries Unlimited, Inc.
All Rights Reserved
Printed in the United States of America

No part of this publication may be reproduced, stored in a retrieval system, or transmitted, in any form or by any means, electronic, mechanical, photocopying, recording, or otherwise, without the prior written permission of the publisher.

LIBRARIES UNLIMITED, INC.
P.O. Box 6633
Englewood, CO 80155-6633
1-800-237-6124
www.lu.com

Library of Congress Cataloging-in-Publication Data

American reference books annual, 1970-
  Englewood, Colo., Libraries Unlimited.

    v. 19x26 cm.

Indexes:
    1970-74. 1v.
    1975-79. 1v.
    1980-84. 1v.
    1985-89. 1v.
    1990-94. 1v.

    I. Reference books--Bibliography--Periodicals.
I. Wynar, Bohdan S. II. Volz, Ed. III. Root, Melissa R.
Z1035.1.A55 011'.02
ISBN 1-56308-554-2(1997 edition)
ISSN 0065-9959

Contents

Introduction xiii
Contributors xv
Journals Cited xxvii

Part I
GENERAL REFERENCE WORKS

1—General Reference Works

Acronyms and Abbreviations 3
Almanacs 4
Bibliography 6
  Bibliographic Guides 5
  National and Trade Bibliography 10
    International 10
    United States 11
    Canada 11
Biography 12
  International 12
  United States 17
  Canada 19
  Great Britain 19
Catalogs and Collections 20
Chronology 21
Dictionaries and Encyclopedias 22
Directories 26
Government Publications 28
Handbooks and Yearbooks 29
Indexes 30
Museums 33
Periodicals and Serials 33
Quotation Books 35

Part II
SOCIAL SCIENCES

2—Social Sciences in General

Social Sciences in General 41

3—Area Studies

General Works 45
United States 46
  General Works 46
  California 47
  Florida 47
  New York 48
  Ohio 48
  Texas 49
Africa 50
  General Works 50
  Algeria 51
  Botswana 51
  Congo (Brazzaville) 52
  Côte d'Ivoire 52
  Guinea 53
  Kenya 53
  Mali 53
  Mauritania 54
  South Africa 54
  Tanzania 55
  Togo 55
  Uganda 56
  Western Sahara 56
Asia 56
  Afghanistan 56
  China 57
  India 57
  Japan 58
  Mongolia 59
Australia 59
Europe 60
  Albania 60
  Eastern Europe 60
  France 61
  Great Britain 61
  Iceland 62
  Luxembourg 62
  Romania 63
  San Marino 63
  Slovenia 64
  Soviet Union 64
Indian Ocean Area 66
  Punjab 66
Latin America and the Caribbean 66
  General Works 66
  Cayman Islands 69
  Cuba 69
  Falkland Islands 69
  Mexico 70
Middle East 70
  General Works 70
  Kuwait 72
  Syria 73
Oceania 73
West Indies 74

4—Economics and Business

General Works 75
   Atlases 75
   Bibliography 75
   Bio-bibliography 76
   Biography 77
   Dictionaries and Encyclopedias 78
   Directories 79
   Handbooks and Yearbooks 88
   Thesauri 89
Accounting 89
Business Services and Investment Guides . . . 90
   Directories 90
   Handbooks and Yearbooks 91
Consumer Education 93
Finance and Banking 94
Industry and Manufacturing 95
Insurance 98
International Business 99
   General Works 99
      Dictionaries and Encyclopedias 99
      Directories 101
      Handbooks and Yearbooks 106
   Africa 109
   Arab Countries 110
   Asia 110
   Australia 112
   Europe 112
      General Works 112
      Eastern Europe 115
   Latin America and the Caribbean 115
   North America 116
Labor 117
   Bibliography 117
   Dictionaries and Encyclopedias 118
   Directories 118
   Handbooks and Yearbooks 120
Management 123
Marketing and Trade 124
Real Estate 129

5—Education

General Works 131
   Bibliography 131
   Dictionaries and Encyclopedias 132
   Quotation Books 133
Alternative Education 134
Computer Resources 135
Elementary and Secondary Education . . . 136
   Bibliography 136
   Dictionaries and Encyclopedias 137
   Directories 137
   Handbooks and Yearbooks 138
Higher Education 139
   Bibliography 139
   Directories 140
**International Exchange Programs and
  Opportunities** 143
Nonprint Materials and Resources 144

6—Ethnic Studies and Anthropology

Anthropology and Ethnology 147
Ethnic Studies 149
   General Works 149
   Asian Americans 151
   Blacks 152
   Filipino Americans 154
   German Americans 154
   Hispanic Americans 155
   Indians of North America 157
      Bibliography 157
      Biography 157
      Dictionaries and Encyclopedias 158
      Handbooks and Yearbooks 158
      Quotation Books 160
   Irish Americans 160
   Jews 161
   Latin Americans 161

7—Genealogy

Genealogy 163
   Bibliography 163
   Dictionaries and Encyclopedias 164
   Directories 165
   Handbooks and Yearbooks 165
   Indexes 169
Personal Names 169

8—Geography and Travel Guides

Geography 171
   General Works 171
      Atlases 171
       United States, 171; *International*, 171
      Dictionaries and Encyclopedias 174
Place-Names 175
Travel Guides 176
   General Works 176
   United States 177
   Australia 179
   Canada 180
   Europe 180
      Great Britain 180
      Italy 180
      Spain 181

9—History

Archaeology 183
American History 184
   Almanacs 184
   Archives 185
   Atlases 186
   Bibliography 186
   Biography 188
   Chronology 190
   Dictionaries and Encyclopedias 190
   Handbooks and Yearbooks 194
African History 196
Asian History 197
   General Works 197
   Indic 197
   Korean 198
   Philippines 198
   Vietnamese 199
European History 200
   General Works 200
   British 201
   Eastern Europe 203
   French 204
   Greek 204
   Spanish 205
Latin American and Caribbean
  History 206
Middle Eastern History 207
World History 208
   Atlases 208
   Bibliography 209
   Biography 210
   Chronology 211
   Dictionaries and Encyclopedias 212
   Handbooks and Yearbooks 216

10—Law

General Works 217
   Bibliography 217
   Biography 219
   Dictionaries and Encyclopedias 219
   Handbooks and Yearbooks 221
Criminology 225
   Bibliography 225
   Biography 226
   Dictionaries and Encyclopedias 226
   Handbooks and Yearbooks 228
Environmental Law 230
Human Rights 231
Intellectual Property 233

11—Library and Information Science and Publishing and Bookselling

Library and Information Science 235
   General Works 235
     Bibliography 235
     Catalogs and Collections 235
     Dictionaries and Encyclopedias 237
     Handbooks and Yearbooks 238
   Cataloging and Classification 240
   Information Technology 242
   Intellectual Freedom and Censorship . . . 244
   Research 245
   School Libraries 245
   Special Libraries and Collections 246
   Storytelling 248
   University and College Libraries 248
Publishing and Bookselling 249
   General Works 249
     Bibliography 249
     Dictionaries and Encyclopedias 249
     Directories 250

12—Military Studies

General Works 251
   Atlases 251
   Bibliography 252
   Biography 253
   Dictionaries and Encyclopedias 254
   Directories 255
   Handbooks and Yearbooks 256
Air Force 257
Navy 258
Weapons 259

13—Political Science

General Works 263
Politics and Government 264
   United States 264
     Bibliography 264
     Biography 265
     Dictionaries and Encyclopedias 267
     Directories 270
     Handbooks and Yearbooks 270
   Europe 272
     General Works 272
     British 274
   Latin America and Caribbean 274
   Russian Federation 275
   South Africa 275
Ideologies 276
International Organizations 277

13—Political Science (continued)

International Relations 279
Public Policy and Administration 280

14—Psychology and Parapsychology

Psychology 283
   Bibliography 283
   Dictionaries and Encyclopedias 284
Parapsychology 286

15—Recreation and Sports

General Works 291
   Almanacs 291
   Biography 291
   Chronology 292
   Dictionaries and Encyclopedias 293
Baseball 294
Basketball 297
Football 298
Hockey 299
Martial Arts 300
Olympics 300
Skiing 301
Track-Athletics 302

16—Sociology

Abortion 303
Aging 304
Disabled 305
Family, Marriage, and Divorce 306
Gay and Lesbian Studies 307
Philanthropy 309
   Bibliography 309
   Directories 310
   Handbooks and Yearbooks 317
Sex Studies 318
Social Welfare and Social Work 319
Substance Abuse 320
Youth and Child Development 321

17—Statistics, Demography, and Urban Studies

Demography 323
Statistics 324
Urban Studies 328

18—Women's Studies

Bibliography 331
Biography 334

Dictionaries and Encyclopedias 335
Directories 336
Handbooks and Yearbooks 337
Indexes 339
Periodicals and Serials 340

Part III
HUMANITIES

19—Humanities in General

Humanities in General 343

20—Communication and Mass Media

General Works 345
Authorship 346
   General Works 346
   Handbooks and Yearbooks 347
   Style Manuals 348
Newspapers and Magazines 350
Radio, Television, Audio, and Video . . . 351
   Biography 351
   Catalogs and Collections 352
   Dictionaries and Encyclopedias 352
   Directories 353
   Handbooks and Yearbooks 355

21—Decorative Arts

Collecting 357
   Autographs 357
   Books 357
   Clocks 358
   Coins (and Paper Money) 358
   Dolls 359
   Firearms 360
   Folk Art 360
   Glass 360
   Marbles 361
Crafts 361
Design 362
Photography 362

22—Fine Arts

General Works 363
   Bibliography 363
   Biography 365
   Catalogs and Collections 365
   Dictionaries and Encyclopedias 366
   Directories 367
Architecture 368
Painting 369

23—Language and Linguistics

General Works 373
   Bibliography 373
   Dictionaries and Encyclopedias 374
   Handbooks and Yearbooks 375
English-Language Dictionaries 377
   General Usage 377
   Abridged 378
   Eponyms 379
   Etymology 380
   Euphemisms 381
   Foreign Words and Phrases 382
   Historical 382
   Idioms, Colloquialisms, and Special
      Usage 383
   Obsolete Words 386
   Other English-Speaking Countries 386
   Rhetoric 386
   Slang 387
   Unabridged 388
Non-English-Language Dictionaries . . . 388
   Armenian 388
   Delaware 389
   French 389
   German 390
   Greek 392
   Hebrew 392
   Hungarian 394
   Italian 394
   Japanese 394
   Lao 395
   Lithuanian 396
   Māori 397
   Polish 397
   Romanian 398
   Russian 398
   Sanskrit 399
   Shan 399
   Sign Language 400
   Siksika 401
   Spanish 401
   Turkish 403
   Vietnamese 403
   Yiddish 404
   Yoruba 404

24—Literature

General Works 405
   Bibliography 405
   Biography 408
   Dictionaries and Encyclopedias 409
   Handbooks and Yearbooks 412

Children's and Young Adult
   Literature 424
   General Works 424
      Bibliography 424
      Biography 425
      Handbooks and Yearbooks 426
   Children's Literature 426
      Bibliography 426
      Biography 427
      Dictionaries and Encyclopedias 428
      Handbooks and Yearbooks 429
      Indexes 430
   Young Adult Literature 430
Drama 431
Fiction 431
   General Works 431
   Crime and Mystery 433
   Science Fiction, Fantasy, and Horror . . . 433
   Short Stories 436
National Literature 437
   American Literature 437
      General Works 437
         Bibliography, 437; *Biography*, 438;
         Dictionaries and Encyclopedias, 440;
         Handbooks and Yearbooks, 440
      Individual Authors 442
         Isaac Asimov, 442; *Edgar Rice
         Burroughs*, 442; *T. S. Eliot*, 443; *Allen
         Ginsberg*, 444; *James Michener*, 445;
         Marjorie Kinnan Rawlings, 445; *John
         Steinbeck*, 446; *Thomas Wolfe*, 446
   British Literature 447
      General Works 447
         Biography, 447; *Dictionaries and
         Encyclopedias*, 450
      Drama 450
      Individual Authors 452
         Jane Austen, 452; *Geoffrey Chaucer*,
         452; *Samuel Taylor Coleridge*, 453;
         William Congreve, 453; *Charles Dickens*,
         453; *Samuel Johnson*, 455; *D. H.
         Lawrence*, 455; *W. Somerset Maugham*,
         456; *John Milton*, 456; *Ann Radcliffe*,
         456; *William Shakespeare*, 457
      Poetry 457
   African Literature 458
   Australian Literature 458
   Canadian Literature 459
   German Literature 460
   Irish Literature 460
   Italian Literature 462
   Latin American and Caribbean
      Literature 462

24—Literature (continued)

National Literature (continued)
   Oceanian Literature 463
   Spanish Literature 464
Poetry 464

25—Music

General Works 467
   Bibliography 467
   Biography 469
   Chronology 469
   Dictionaries and Encyclopedias 470
   Directories 471
   Discography 471
   Indexes 472
Children's 473
Composers 473
Conductors 479
Instruments 480
Musical Forms 481
   Choral 481
   Classical 482
   Popular 484
      General Works 484
      Big Band 488
      Blues 489
      Folk 489
      Jazz 491
      Musicals 491
      Rhythm and Blues 492
      Rock 492
   Sacred 495

26—Mythology, Folklore, and Popular Culture

Folklore 497
Mythology 498
Popular Culture 499

27—Performing Arts

General Works 501
   Bio-bibliography 501
   Biography 501
   Handbooks and Yearbooks 502
Dance 502
Film, Television, and Video 504
   Bibliography 504
   Biography 505
   Catalogs and Collections 506
   Dictionaries and Encyclopedias 507
   Filmography 509

   Handbooks and Yearbooks 514
   Indexes 520
   Videography 521
Theater 522
   Bibliography 522
   Biography 523
   Chronology 523
   Dictionaries and Encyclopedias 524
   Directories 524
   Handbooks and Yearbooks 525
   Indexes 526

28—Philosophy and Religion

Philosophy 527
   Bibliography 527
   Biography 528
   Dictionaries and Encyclopedias 528
Religion 532
   General Works 532
      Atlases 532
      Bibliography 532
      Biography 535
      Dictionaries and Encyclopedias 535
      Directories 538
      Handbooks and Yearbooks 538
   Bible Studies 539
      Bibliography 539
      Dictionaries and Encyclopedias 543
      Handbooks and Yearbooks 545
   Buddhism 546
   Christianity 546
      Almanacs 546
      Bibliography 547
      Biography 548
      Dictionaries and Encyclopedias 549
      Directories 552
      Handbooks and Yearbooks 552
   Islam 553
   Judaism 554
   Sikhism 555
   Taoism 556

Part IV
SCIENCE AND TECHNOLOGY

29—Science and Technology in General

Bibliography 559
Biography 560
Catalogs and Collections 562
Chronology 562
Dictionaries and Encyclopedias 563

Directories 565
Handbooks and Yearbooks 565
Indexes 566

30—Agricultural Sciences

General Works 567
Food Sciences and Technology 568
Horticulture 571
Veterinary Science 573

31—Biological Sciences

General Works 575
Biology 576
Botany 579
   General Works 579
   Flowering Plants 580
   Fungi 581
   Herbs 583
   Trees and Shrubs 583
Natural History 586
Zoology 586
   Birds 586
   Domestic Animals 588
   Mammals 589
   Marine Animals 590

32—Engineering

General Works 591
Aeronautical Engineering 592
Architectural Engineering 592
Astronautical Engineering 593
Automotive Engineering 594
Civil Engineering 595
Electric Engineering and Electronics . . . 595
Industrial Engineering 596
Materials Science 596
Mechanical Engineering 597
Plant Engineering 597

33—Health Sciences

General Works 599
   Atlases 599
   Bibliography 599
   Dictionaries and Encyclopedias 600
   Directories 602
   Handbooks and Yearbooks 604
Medicine 606
   General Works 606
      Dictionaries and Encyclopedias 606
      Handbooks and Yearbooks 608
   Alternative Medicine 610

Dentistry 614
Endocrinology 614
Nursing 615
Pediatrics 615
Psychiatry 616
Sports Medicine 617
Pharmacy and Pharmaceutical Sciences . . . 617

34—High Technology

General Works 619
Computing 620
   General Works 620
   Microcomputing 622
   Software 623
Telecommunications 624

35—Physical Sciences and Mathematics

Physical Sciences 627
   Chemistry 627
      Dictionaries and Encyclopedias 627
      Directories 628
      Handbooks and Yearbooks 629
      Indexes 631
   Earth and Planetary Sciences 631
      General Works 631
      Astronomy and Space Sciences 632
      Climatology and Meteorology 633
      Geology 634
      Paleontology 636
   Physics 638
Mathematics 640

36—Resource Sciences

Energy Resources 643
   Directories 643
   Handbooks and Yearbooks 645
Environmental Science 646
   Bibliography 646
   Dictionaries and Encyclopedias 647
   Directories 648
   Handbooks and Yearbooks 650

37—Transportation

General Works 653
Air 653
Ground 655
Water 657

Author/Title Index 659

Subject Index 687

Introduction

PURPOSE AND SCOPE

American Reference Books Annual, a far-reaching reviewing service for reference books, is now in its 28th volume. The 1,449 books and CD-ROMs reviewed in this volume cover imprints from 1996 and some from 1995 that were received too late to be reviewed in the previous volume. The number of reviews in ARBA 97 is approximately 400 fewer than in ARBA 96. Changes in office hardware and software consumed a considerable amount of time, causing this year's shortage. Now that the ARBA database is running on improved software, the production process is more streamlined and efficient. Titles not reviewed this year will be picked up in ARBA 98. We apologize for any inconvenience. In the 28 volumes of ARBA published since 1970, a total of 48,547 titles have been reviewed. Five cumulative indexes for ARBA cover the years 1970-1974, 1975-1979, 1980-1984, 1985-1989, and 1990-1994. These indexes expedite the use of the annual volumes.

ARBA differs significantly from other reviewing media in its basic purpose, which is to provide comprehensive coverage of English-language reference books published in the United States and Canada during a single year. The categories of reference books reviewed in ARBA and the policy regarding them can be summarized as follows: (1) Dictionaries, encyclopedias, indexes, directories, bibliographies, guides, concordances, atlases, gazetteers, and other types of ready-reference tools are routinely reviewed in each volume of ARBA; coverage of this category of reference materials is nearly complete. (2) General encyclopedias that are updated annually, yearbooks, almanacs, indexing and abstracting services, and other annuals or serials are usually reviewed at intervals of three, four, or five years. The first review of such works generally provides an appropriate historical background. Subsequent reviews of these publications attempt to point out changes in scope, editorial policy, and similar matters. (3) New editions of reference books are ordinarily reviewed with appropriate comparisons to the older editions. (4) Traditionally, foreign reference titles have been reviewed only if they had an exclusive distributor in the United States. In 1987 coverage was expanded to include Canadian publications that do not have U.S. distributors. Prices for such titles are in Canadian dollars unless otherwise indicated. Substantial coverage of Canadian reference publications has been achieved and will continue until it is as complete for Canada as it is for the United States. Other foreign title coverage is restricted to English-language publications from Great Britain, as well as a few select sources from Australia and other countries. (5) Government publications are reviewed on a highly selected basis because other Libraries Unlimited works, *Government Reference Books* and *Government Reference Serials*, provide the library professional with comprehensive coverage of government reference publications. In ARBA 97 only Library of Congress publications and international publications, such as those of the United Nations, are covered. (6) Reprints are reviewed in ARBA on a selective basis as they often are produced in limited quantities. (7) Titles produced for the mass market in the areas of collectibles, travel guides, and genealogy receive selective coverage.

Certain categories of reference books are usually not reviewed in ARBA: those of fewer than 48 pages, those produced by vanity presses or by the author as publisher, and those generated by library staffs for internal use. Highly specialized reference works printed in a limited number of copies and that do not appeal to the general library audience ARBA serves may also be omitted.

Because there has been a significant increase and interest in electronic publishing, ARBA has begun reviewing this medium. More than 45 CD-ROMs receive comprehensive and lengthy evaluations in this edition. Future volumes will continue to include reviews of these state-of-the-art information storage devices in a variety of subject areas.

REVIEWING POLICY

To ensure well-written and erudite reviews, the ARBA staff maintains a roster of more than 400 scholars, practitioners, and library educators in all subject specialties at libraries and universities throughout the United States and Canada. Because ARBA is not a selective reviewing source, such as *Choice* or *Library Journal*, the reviews are generally longer and more critical, to detail the strengths and weaknesses of important reference works. Reviewers are asked to examine books and provide well-documented critical comments, both positive and negative. Coverage usually includes the usefulness of a given work; organization, execution, and pertinence of contents; prose style; format; availability of supplementary materials (e.g., indexes, appendixes); and similarity to other works and previous editions. Reviewers are encouraged to address the intended audience but not necessarily to give specific recommendations for purchase. An adequate description and evaluation of the reference book are sufficient. All reviews in ARBA are signed.

ARRANGEMENT

ARBA 97 consists of 37 chapters, an author/title index, and a subject index. It is divided into four alphabetically arranged parts: "General Reference Works," "Social Sciences," "Humanities," and "Science and Technology." "General Reference Works" is subdivided by form: bibliography, biography, catalogs and collections, dictionaries and encyclopedias, handbooks and yearbooks, indexes, and so on. Within the remaining three parts, chapters are organized by topic. Thus, under "Social Sciences" the reader will find chapters titled "Economics and Business," "Education," "History," "Law," and "Sociology."

Each chapter is subdivided to reflect the arrangement strategy of the entire volume. There is a section on general works followed by a topical breakdown. For example, in the chapter titled "Performing Arts," "General Works" is followed by "Dance" and "Film, Television, and Video." The latter is divided into sections by format, which include "Biography" and "Filmography." Subdivisions are based on the amount of material available on a given topic and vary from year to year.

ACKNOWLEDGMENTS

In closing, we wish to express our gratitude to the many talented contributors without whose support this volume of ARBA could not have been compiled. We would also like to thank the members of our staff who were instrumental in its preparation: G. Kim Dority, Pamela J. Getchell, Shannon M. Graff, Stephen Haenel, Lori D. Kranz, Patricia B. Lutz, Ron Maas, Judy Gay Matthews, and Kay Minnis.

Bohdan S. Wynar, Editor in Chief

Editorial Staff

Bohdan S. Wynar, Editor in Chief
Melissa R. Root, Assistant Editor

Contributors

Stephen H. Aby, Education Bibliographer, Bierce Library, Univ. of Akron, Ohio.
January Adams, Asst. Director in Charge of Adult Services, Franklin Township Public Library, N.J.
Laural L. Adams, Reference Librarian —Business, Univ. Library, New Mexico State Univ., Las Cruces.
Sandra Adell, Asst. Professor, Dept. of Afro-American Studies, Univ. of Wisconsin, Madison.
Walter C. Allen, Assoc. Professor Emeritus, Graduate School of Library and Information Science, Univ. of Illinois, Urbana.
Donald Altschiller, Reference Librarian, Boston Univ.
Mary Jo Aman, Education Librarian, Golda Meir Library, Univ. of Wisconsin, Milwaukee.
Elizabeth L. Anderson, Part-time Instructor, Lansing Community College, Mich.
Frank J. Anderson, Librarian Emeritus, Sandor Teszler Library, Wofford College, Spartanburg, S.C.
James D. Anderson, Assoc. Dean and Professor, School of Communication, Information, and Library Studies, Rutgers Univ., New Brunswick, N.J.
Robert T. Anderson, Professor, Religious Studies, Michigan State Univ., East Lansing.
Charles R. Andrews, Dean of Library Services, Hofstra Univ., Hempstead, N.Y.
Hermina G. B. Anghelescu, Fulbright Doctoral Student/Teaching Assistant, Graduate School of Library and Information Science, Univ. of Texas, Austin.
Susan B. Ardis, Head, McKinney Engineering Library, Univ. of Texas, Austin.
Henry T. Armistead, Adult Reference Librarian, Free Library of Philadelphia, Pa.
Melvin S. Arrington Jr., Assoc. Professor of Modern Languages, Univ. of Mississippi, University.
Susan C. Awe, Arvada Branch Manager, Jefferson County Public Library, Colo.
Susan D. Baird-Joshi, Database Programmer/Analyst, Rho, Redmond, Wash.
Jan Bakker, Resource Center Director, North Central Regional Educational Laboratory, Oak Brook, Ill.
Jack Bales, Reference Librarian, Mary Washington College Library, Fredericksburg, Va.
JoAnn Balingit, Library Media Specialist, Bancroft Intermediate School, Wilmington, Del.
Robert M. Ballard, Professor, School of Library and Information Science, North Carolina Central Univ., Durham.
Gary D. Barber, Head of Reference, Daniel A. Reed Library, State Univ. of New York, Fredonia.
Helen M. Barber, Reference Librarian, New Mexico State Univ., Las Cruces.
Suzanne I. Barchers, Author/Consultant, Denver, Colo.
Donald A. Barclay, Reference Librarian, Univ. Libraries, Univ. of Houston, Tex.
David Bardack, Professor, Dept. of Biological Sciences, Univ. of Illinois, Chicago.
Craig W. Beard, Reference Librarian, Mervyn H. Sterne Library, Univ. of Alabama, Birmingham.
Sandra E. Belanger, Reference Librarian, San Jose State Univ. Library, Calif.
Carol Willsey Bell, Head, Local History and Genealogy Dept., Warren-Trumbull County Public Library, Warren, Ohio.

George H. Bell, Assoc. Librarian, Daniel E. Noble Science and Engineering Library, Arizona State Univ., Tempe.

Adrienne Antink Bendel, Medical Group Management Association, Lakewood, Colo.

Kenneth W. Berger, Team Leader, Reference/ILL Home Team, Perkins Library, Duke Univ., Durham, N.C.

Bernice Bergup, Humanities Reference Librarian, Davis Library, Univ. of North Carolina, Chapel Hill.

John B. Beston, Professor of English, Nazareth College of Rochester, N.Y.

Barbara M. Bibel, Reference Librarian, Science/Business/Sociology Dept., Main Library, Oakland Public Library, Calif.

David Bickford, Information Specialist, Univ. of Phoenix, Ariz.

Terry D. Bilhartz, Assoc. Professor of History, Sam Houston State Univ., Huntsville, Tex.

James E. Bird, Head, Science and Engineering Dept., Raymond H. Folger Library, Univ. of Maine, Orono.

John D. Blackwell, Co-ordinator of Information Services, Arthur A. Wishart Library, Algoma Univ. College, Sault Ste. Marie,, Ont.

Ron Blazek, Professor, School of Library Science, Florida State Univ., Tallahassee.

Richard Bleiler, Reference Librarian, Univ. of Connecticut, Storrs.

Laura K. Blessing, Personnel Librarian, Univ. of Texas, Arlington.

Daniel K. Blewett, Reference Librarian, Cudahy Library, Loyola Univ., Chicago.

Edna M. Boardman, Library Media Specialist, Minot High School, Magic City Campus, N.D.

George S. Bobinski, Dean and Professor, School of Information and Library Studies, State Univ. of New York, Buffalo.

Bobray Bordelon, Social Science Reference Center, Firestone Library, Princeton Univ. Libraries, N.J.

Mary J. Bowman, Reference Librarian, Noel Memorial Library, Louisiana State Univ., Shreveport.

James K. Bracken, Head, Second Floor Main Library Information Services, Ohio State Univ., Columbus.

William Bright, Research Associate in Linguistics, Univ. of Colorado, Boulder.

Georgia Briscoe, Assoc. Director and Head of Technical Services, Law Library, Univ. of Colorado, Boulder.

Simon J. Bronner, Distinguished Professor of Folklore and American Studies, Capitol College, Pennsylvania State Univ., Middletown.

Natalie Brower-Kirton, Staff, Libraries Unlimited, Inc.

Barbara E. Brown, (formerly) Head, General Cataloguing Section, Library of Parliament, Ottawa, Ont.

Judith M. Brugger, Books/Journals Team, Library, Los Alamos National Laboratory, N.Mex.

Patrick J. Brunet, Library Manager, Western Wisconsin Technical College, La Crosse.

Betty Jo Buckingham, (retired) Consultant, Iowa Dept. of Education, Des Moines.

Robert H. Burger, Head, Slavic and East European Library, Univ. of Illinois, Urbana-Champaign.

Joanna M. Burkhardt, Head Librarian, College of Continuing Education Library, Univ. of Rhode Island, Providence.

Ingrid Schierling Burnett, Reference Librarian, Univ. of Southern Colorado Library, Pueblo.

Lois J. Buttlar, Assoc. Professor, School of Library and Information Science, Kent State Univ., Ohio.

Hans E. Bynagle, Library Director and Professor of Philosophy, Whitworth College, Spokane, Wash.

Diane M. Calabrese, Research Associate for Planning and Eisenhower Grant Programs, Coordinating Board for Higher Education, Jefferson City, Mo.

John Lewis Campbell, Online Services Coordinator, Univ. of Georgia Libraries, Athens.

Luiz Alberto Cardoso, D.D.S., Governors Park Dental Group, Denver, Colo.

Ruth A. Carr, Chief, U.S. History, Local History and Genealogy Div., New York Public Library.
Joseph Cataio, Manager, Booklegger's Bookstore, Chicago.
Jo A. Cates, (formerly) Head, Transportation Library, Northwestern Univ. Library, Chicago.
G. A. Cevasco, Assoc. Professor of English, St. John's Univ., Jamaica, N.Y.
Bert Chapman, Government Publications Coordinator, Purdue Univ., West Lafayette, Ind.
Boyd Childress, Reference Librarian, Ralph B. Draughon Library, Auburn Univ., Ala.
Dene L. Clark, Reference Librarian, Auraria Library, Denver, Colo.
Paul F. Clark, Assoc. Professor, Pennsylvania State Univ., University Park.
Stella T. Clark, Professor, Foreign Languages, California State Univ., San Marcos.
Gail Clement, Science/Information Services Librarian, Florida International Univ., Miami.
Barbara E. Clotfelter, Head, Business Dept., Birmingham Public Library, Ala.
Harriette M. Cluxton, (formerly) Director of Medical Library Services, Illinois Masonic Medical Center, Chicago.
Gary R. Cocozzoli, Director of the Library, Lawrence Technological Univ., Southfield, Mich.
Joshua Cohen, Director for Outreach and Continuing Education, Mid-Hudson Library System, Poughkeepsie, N.Y.
Donald E. Collins, Assoc. Professor, Dept. of Library and Information Studies, East Carolina Univ., Greenville, N.C.
Kay O. Cornelius, formerly Teacher and Magnet School Lead Teacher, Huntsville City Schools, Ala.
Paul B. Cors, Catalog Librarian, Univ. of Wyoming, Laramie.
Angelo Costanzo, Professor of English, Shippensburg Univ., Pa.
Brian E. Coutts, Head, Dept. of Library Public Services, Helm-Cravens Library, Western Kentucky Univ., Bowling Green.
Bob Craigmile, Reference Librarian, Pitts Theology Library, Emory Univ., Atlanta, Ga.
Kathleen W. Craver, Head Librarian, National Cathedral School, Washington, D.C.
Milton H. Crouch, Asst. Director for Reader Services, Bailey/Howe Library, Univ. of Vermont, Burlington.
George M. Cumming Jr., Librarian III, Adult Services, Boston Public Library.
Gregory Curtis, Director, Northern Maine Technical College, Presque Isle.
Mark Cyzyk, Reference Librarian, Albert S. Cook Library, Towson State Univ., Md.
William J. Dane, Supervising Librarian, Special Libraries, Newark Public Library, N.J.
Elizabeth D'Antonio-Gan, Instructor/Reference Librarian, Auraria Library, Denver, Colo.
Joseph W. Dauben, Professor of History and History of Science, City Univ. of New York.
Anthony J. Dedrick, Coordinator, Access Services, Auraria Library, Denver, Colo.
Dominique-René de Lerma, Professor, Conservatory of Music, Lawrence Univ., Appleton, Wis.
Barbara Delzell, Vancouver, Wash.
Elie M. Dick, President, Mintra, Inc., Woodbury, Minn.
Donald C. Dickinson, Professor, Graduate Library School, Univ. of Arizona, Tucson.
John B. Dillon, European Humanities Bibliographer, Memorial Library, Univ of Wisconsin, Madison.
David Dodd, Cataloger and Archivist, Univ. of Colorado, Colorado Springs.
Carol A. Doll, Asst. Professor, Graduate School of Library and Information Science, Univ. of Washington, Seattle.
David A. Doman, PAC Instruction Specialist, Pikes Peak Library District, Colorado Springs, Colo.
Margaret F. Dominy, Head, Mathematics-Physics-Astronomy Library, Univ. of Pennsylvania, Philadelphia.

G. Kim Dority, Assoc. Director/Project Manager, The Library, National Cable Television Center and Museum, Denver, Colo.

Lamia Doumato, Head of Reader Services, National Gallery of Art, Washington, D.C.

John A. Drobnicki, Librarian, Queens Library, Jamaica, N.Y.

Joe P. Dunn, Charles A. Dana Professor of History and Politics, Converse College, Spartanburg, S.C.

David Eggenberger, Freelance Writer and Editor, Vienna, Va.

Owen H. Ellard, San Antonio, Tex.

Marie Ellis, English and American Literature Bibliographer, Univ. of Georgia Libraries, Athens.

Jean Engler, Reference Librarian, Koelbel Public Library, Englewood, Colo.

Edward Erazo, Reference/Outreach Librarian, New Mexico State Univ., Las Cruces.

Jonathon Erlen, Curator, History of Medicine, Univ. of Pittsburgh, Pa.

G. Edward Evans, Univ. Librarian, Charles Von der Ahe Library, Loyola Marymount Univ., Los Angeles, Calif.

Andrew Ezergailis, Professor of History, Ithaca College, N.Y.

Ian Fairclough, Coe Library, Laramie, Wyo.

Kathleen Farago, Reference Librarian, Lakewood Public Library, Ohio.

Evan Ira Farber, College Librarian Emeritus, Earlham College, Richmond, Ind.

Megan S. Farrell, Collection Development Librarian and Asst. Professor, Dupre Library, Univ. of Southwestern Louisiana, Lafayette.

Eleanor Ferrall, Librarian Emerita, Arizona State Univ., Tempe.

Ken Feser, Systems Librarian, Cleveland Museum of Art, Ohio.

Judith J. Field, Senior Lecturer, Program for Library and Information Science, Wayne State Univ., Detroit, Mich.

Joan B. Fiscella, Bibliographer for Professional Studies, Library, Univ. of Illinois, Chicago.

Virginia S. Fischer, Reference/Documents Librarian, Univ. of Maine, Presque Isle.

Patricia Fleming, Professor, Faculty of Library and Information Science, Univ. of Toronto.

Michael Florman, Staff, Libraries Unlimited, Inc.

Michael A. Foley, Honors Director, Marywood College, Scranton, Pa.

Harold O. Forshey, Assoc. Dean, Miami Univ., Oxford, Ohio.

Lynne M. Fox, Assoc. Professor/Reference Librarian, Univ. of Northern Colorado, Greeley.

A. David Franklin, Professor of Music, Winthrop Univ., Rock Hill, S.C.

David K. Frasier, Asst. Librarian, Reference Dept., Indiana Univ., Bloomington.

Susan J. Freiband, Assoc. Professor, Graduate School of Librarianship, Univ. of Puerto Rico, San Juan.

David O. Friedrichs, Professor, Univ. of Scranton, Pa.

Ronald H. Fritze, Assoc. Professor, Dept. of History, Lamar Univ., Beaumont, Tex.

Paula Frosch, Assoc. Museum Librarian, Thomas J. Watson Library, Metropolitan Museum of Art, New York.

Sandra E. Fuentes, Student, Graduate School of Library and Information Science, Univ. of Texas, Austin.

Monica Fusich, Reference and Instruction Librarian, Henry Madden Library, Fresno, Calif.

Ahmad Gamaluddin, Professor, School of Library Science, Clarion State College, Pa.

Vera Gao, Catalog Librarian, Auraria Library, Univ. of Colorado, Denver.

Zev Garber, Professor and Chair, Jewish Studies, Los Angeles Valley College, Calif.

Joan Garner, Staff, Libraries Unlimited, Inc.

Gregg S. Geary, Music Librarian, Sinclair Library, Univ. of Hawaii, Honolulu.

Tommie Brett Geer, Investment Advisor, Denver, Colo.

Pamela J. Getchell, Staff, Libraries Unlimited, Inc.

Gerald L. Gill, Assoc. Professor/Business Reference Librarian, James Madison Univ., Harrisburg, Va.

Elizabeth A. Ginno, Coordinator of Library Computer Information Resources, Univ. Library, California State Univ., Hayward.

Edwin S. Gleaves, State Librarian and Archivist, Tennessee State Library and Archives, Nashville.

Barbara B. Goldstein, Media Specialist, Magothy River Middle School, Arnold, Md.

Anthony Gottlieb, Psychiatrist, Kaiser Permanente Health Care, Denver.

Allie Wise Goudy, Professor, Western Illinois Univ., Macomb.

M. Patrick Graham, Director, Pitts Theology Library, Emory Univ., Atlanta, Ga.

Marilynn Green, Librarian, NASA Johnson Space Center, Scientific and Technical Information Center, Houston, Tex.

Stephen W. Green, Coordinator, Reference and Instruction Services, Auraria Library, Denver, Colo.

Richard W. Grefrath, Reference Librarian, Univ. of Nevada, Reno.

Arthur Gribben, Professor, Union Institute, Los Angeles, Calif.

Margarete Gross, Librarian, Chicago Public Library.

Laurel Grotzinger, Professor, Univ. Libraries, Western Michigan Univ., Kalamazoo.

Leonard Grundt, Professor, A. Holly Patterson Library, Nassau Community College, Garden City, N.Y.

Kwabena Gyimah-Brempong, Professor of Economics, College of Business Administration, Univ. of South Florida, Tampa.

Stephen Haenel, Staff, Libraries Unlimited, Inc.

Susan B. Hagloch, Director, Tuscarawas County Public Library, New Philadelphia, Ohio.

Blaine H. Hall, English Language and Literature Librarian, Harold B. Lee Library, Brigham Young Univ., Provo, Utah.

L. Hallewell, Visiting Professor, UNESP, Marilia, Brazil.

Deborah Hammer, Head, History, Travel and Biography Div., Queens Borough Public Library, Jamaica, N.Y.

Gary Handman, Head, Media Resources Center, Univ. of California, Berkeley.

Joseph Hannibal, Curator of Invertebrate Paleontology, Cleveland Museum of Natural History, Ohio.

Constance Hardesty, Twenty-first Century Communications, Denver, Colo.

Roberto P. Haro, Director and Professor, San Francisco State Univ., Calif.

Chauncy D. Harris, Samuel N. Harper Distinguished Service Professor Emeritus of Geography, Univ. of Chicago.

Ann Hartness, Asst. Head Librarian, Benson Latin American Collection, Univ. of Texas, Austin.

Ralph Hartsock, Senior Music Catalog Librarian, Univ. of North Texas, Denton.

Karen D. Harvey, Assoc. Dean for Academic Affairs, Univ. College, Univ. of Denver, Colo.

Joy Hastings, Manager, Technical Library, Hunt-Wesson, Inc., Fullerton, Calif.

Robert J. Havlik, Librarian Emeritus and Exhibit Coordinator, Univ. of Notre Dame, Ind.

Fred J. Hay, Librarian of the W. L. Eury Appalachian Collection and Assoc. Professor, Center for Appalachian Studies, Appalachian State Univ., Boone, N.C.

James S. Heller, Director of the Law Library and Assoc. Professor of Law, Marshall-Wythe Law Library, College of William and Mary, Williamsburg, Va.

Mary Hemmings, Technical Services Librarian, Law Library, Univ. of Calgary, Alta.

David Henige, African Studies Bibliographer, Memorial Library, Univ. of Wisconsin, Madison.

Carol D. Henry, Librarian, Lyons Township High School, LaGrange, Ill.

Mark Y. Herring, Dean of Libraries, Oklahoma Baptist Univ., Shawnee.

Susan Davis Herring, Reference Librarian, Univ. of Alabama Library, Huntsville.

Christopher J. Hoeppner, Reference Instruction Librarian, DePaul Univ., Chicago.

Richard E. Holl, Asst. Professor, History Dept., Lees College, Jackson, Ky.

Paul L. Holmer, Reference Librarian, Buley Library, Southern Connecticut State Univ., New Haven.

Curtis D. Holmes, Aurora Hinkley High School, Colo.

Shirley L. Hopkinson, Professor, Div. of Library and Information Science, San Jose State Univ., Calif.

Renee B. Horowitz, Professor, Dept. of Technology, College of Engineering, Arizona State Univ., Tempe.

Clay Housholder, Reference and Technical Associate, Main Library, Indiana Univ., Bloomington.

C. D. Hurt, Director, Graduate Library School, Univ. of Arizona, Tucson.

Jonathan F. Husband, Program Chair of the Library/Reader Services Librarian, Henry Whittemore Library, Framingham State College, Mass.

Ludmila N. Ilyina, (retired) Professor, Natural Resources Institute, Winnipeg, Man.

David Isaacson, Asst. Head of Reference and Humanities Librarian, Waldo Library, Western Michigan Univ., Kalamazoo.

Barbara Ittner, Staff, Libraries Unlimited, Inc.

John A. Jackman, Extension Entomologist, Texas A & M Univ., College Station.

Eugene B. Jackson, Professor Emeritus, Graduate School of Library and Information Sciences, Univ. of Texas, Austin.

Peggy Jobe, Government Publications Librarian for International Documents, Univ. of Colorado, Boulder.

D. Barton Johnson, Professor Emeritus of Russian, Univ. of California, Santa Barbara.

Richard D. Johnson, Director of Libraries, James M. Milne Library, State Univ. College, Oneonta, N.Y.

Marie F. Jones, Reference and Bibliographic Instruction Librarian, Muskingum College, New Concord, Ohio.

Marjorie H. Jones, Educational Media Specialist, Bryan Senior High School, Omaha, Neb.

Kelly M. Jordan, Engineering Reference Librarian, Pennsylvania State Univ., University Park.

Jane Jurgens, Reference Librarian, St. Cloud State Univ., Minn.

Elaine F. Jurries, Coordinator of Serials Services, Auraria Library, Denver, Colo.

Sue Kamm, Head, Audio-Visual and Stack Maintenance Divisions, Inglewood Public Library, Calif.

Thomas A. Karel, Assoc. Director for Public Services, Shadek-Fackenthal Library, Franklin and Marshall College, Lancaster, Pa.

John Laurence Kelland, Reference Bibliographer for Life Sciences, Univ. of Rhode Island Library, Kingston.

Dean H. Keller, Assoc. Dean of Libraries, Kent State Univ., Ohio.

Barbara E. Kemp, Asst. Director, Dewey Graduate Library, State Univ. of New York, Albany.

Caroline M. Kent, Head of Research Services, Widener Library, Harvard Univ., Cambridge, Mass.

Jackson Kesler, Professor of Theatre and Dance, Western Kentucky Univ., Bowling Green.

Sung Ok Kim, Senior Asst. Librarian/Social Sciences Cataloging Librarian, Cornell Univ., Ithaca, N.Y.

Norman L. Kincaide, Citation Editor, Shepard's/McGraw-Hill, Inc., Colorado Springs, Colo.

Christine E. King, Reference—Music Library, State Univ. of New York, Stony Brook.

John Kirton, Pilot, First Officer, Scenic Airlines, Las Vegas, Nev.

Janet J. Kosky, Mukwonago Community Library, Wis.

Lori D. Kranz, Freelance Editor; Assoc. Editor, *The Bloomsbury Review*, Denver, Colo.

Betsy J. Kraus, Librarian/Technical Editor, Environmental Evaluation Group, Albuquerque, N.Mex.

Linda A. Krikos, Head, Women's Studies Library, Ohio State Univ., Columbus.

Marlene M. Kuhl, Library Manager, Baltimore County Public Library, Reisterstown Branch, Md.

Colby H. Kullman, Assoc. Professor and Editor, *Studies in American Drama*, Univ. of Mississippi, University.

Natalie Kupferberg, Health Sciences Library Coordinator, Ferris State Univ., Big Rapids, Mich.

Robert V. Labaree, Reference/Public Services Librarian, Von KleinSmid Library, Univ. of Southern California, Los Angeles.

Linda L. Lam-Easton, Assoc. Professor, Dept. of Religious Studies, California State Univ., North Ridge.

Mary Larsgaard, Asst. Head, Map and Imagery Laboratory Library, Univ. of California, Santa Barbara.

Binh P. Le, Reference Librarian, Abington College, Pennsylvania State Univ., University Park.

Brad R. Leach, Records Manager, Northern Colorado Water Conservancy District, Loveland.

Patricia M. Leach, Editorial Technician Training Leader, Group Publishing, Loveland, Colo.

Hwa-Wei Lee, Dean of Libraries, Ohio Univ., Athens.

Joann H. Lee, (formerly) Head of Reader Services, Lake Forest College, Ill.

R. S. Lehmann, Rocky Mountain BankCard System, Colorado National Bank, Denver.

Richard A. Leiter, Director, Law Library, Howard Univ., Washington, D.C.

John A. Lent, Drexel Hill, Pa.

Tze-chung Li, Professor, Graduate School of Library and Information Science, Rosary College, River Forest, Ill.

Charlotte Lindgren, Professor Emerita of English, Emerson College, Boston.

John T. Lloyd, Asst. Biology Librarian, Univ. of Illinois, Urbana-Champaign.

Larry Lobel, Virtuoso Keyboard Services, Petaluma, Calif.

Koraljka Lockhart, Publications Editor, San Francisco Opera, Calif.

Robert Logsdon, Assoc. Director/Public Services, Indiana State Library, Indianapolis.

Jeffrey E. Long, Interlibrary Loan/Photocopy Services Library Assistant, Lamar Soutter Library/Univ. of Massachusetts Medical Center, Worcester

Jeffrey R. Luttrell, Leader, Humanities Cataloging Team, Princeton Univ. Library, N.J.

Marit S. MacArthur, Reference Librarian, Auraria Libraries, Univ. of Colorado, Denver.

Sara R. Mack, Professor Emerita, Dept. of Library Science, Kutztown Univ., Pa.

Theresa Maggio, Head of Public Services, Southwest Georgia Regional Library, Bainbridge.

Linda Main, Assoc. Professor, San Jose State Univ., Calif.

Kelly Malone, Ph.D Candidate, Univ. of North Carolina, Chapel Hill.

Kay Mariea, Staff, Libraries Unlimited, Inc.

S. D. Markman, Professor Emeritus, Art Dept., Duke Univ., Durham, N.C.

Judith A. Matthews, Physics-Astronomy/Science Reference Librarian, Main Library, Michigan State Univ., East Lansing.

Judy Gay Matthews, Staff, Libraries Unlimited, Inc.

George Louis Mayer, (formerly) Senior Principal Librarian, New York Public Library and Part-Time Librarian, Adelphi, Manhattan Center and Brooklyn College.

James R. McDonald, Professor of Geography, Eastern Michigan Univ., Ypsilanti.

Christopher Michael McDonough, Lecturer, Dept. of Classics, Princeton Univ., N.J.

Dana McDougald, Lead Media Specialist, Learning Resources Center, Cedar Shoals High School, Athens, Ga.

Robert B. McKee, Professor, Mechanical Engineering, Univ. of Nevada, Reno.

Susan V. McKimm, Business Reference Specialist, Cuyahoga County Library System, Maple Heights, Ohio.

T. McKimmie, Reference Librarian, New Mexico State Univ., Las Cruces.

Marian B. McLeod, Professor of Speech Communication and Theater, Trenton State College, N.J.

Maria O'Neil McMahon, (deceased) Professor, School of Social Work, East Carolina Univ., Greenville, N.C.

Jean C. McManus, Asst. Reference Librarian, Tisch Library, Tufts Univ., Medford, Mass.

Warren L. Meinhardt, Assoc. Professor of Spanish, Southern Illinois Univ., Carbondale.

Sue Lyon Mertl, President, Lyon Consulting Group, Inc., Marietta, Ga.

Lillian R. Mesner, Technical Services Librarian, Agricultural Library, Univ. of Kentucky, Lexington.

G. Douglas Meyers, Chair, Dept. of English, Univ. of Texas, El Paso.

George A. Meyers, Chairman, National Labor Commission, Baltimore, Md.

Robert Michaelson, Head Librarian, Seeley G. Mudd Library for Science and Engineering, Northwestern Univ., Evanston, Ill.

Bogdan Mieczkowski, Professor of Economics, Ithaca College, N.Y.

Seiko Mieczkowski, Hobart & William Smith Colleges, Geneva, N.Y.

Bill Miller, Director of Libraries, Florida Atlantic Univ., Boca Raton.

Richard A. Miller, Professor of Economics, Wesleyan Univ., Middletown, Conn.

Carol L. Mitchell, Southeast Asian Bibliographic Services Librarian, General Library System, Univ. of Wisconsin, Madison.

James Moffet, Head, Reference Dept, Baldwin Public Library, Birmingham, Mich.

Terry Ann Mood, Humanities Bibliographer, Univ. of Colorado, Denver.

Gerald D. Moran, Director, McCartney Library, Geneva College, Beaver Falls, Pa.

K. Mulliner, Asst. to the Director of Libraries, Ohio Univ. Library, Athens.

Walt Mundkowsky, Freelance Film and Music Critic, Beverly Hills, Calif.

Paul M. Murphy III, NREMT-Paramedic, Paramedic Div., EMS, Denver General Hospital, Colo.

James M. Murray, Director, East Bonner County Library, Sandpoint, Idaho.

Charles Neuringer, Professor of Psychology and Theatre and Film, Univ. of Kansas, Lawrence.

John Newman, Univ. Archivist, Colorado State Univ., Fort Collins.

Danuta A. Nitecki, Assoc. Univ. Librarian, Yale Univ., New Haven, Conn.

Eric R. Nitschke, Reference Librarian, Robert W. Woodruff Library, Emory Univ., Atlanta, Ga.

Christopher W. Nolan, Head, Reference Services, Maddux Library, Trinity Univ., San Antonio, Tex.

Carol L. Noll, Plano, Tex.

O. Gene Norman, Head, Reference Dept., Indiana State Univ. Libraries, Terre Haute.

Marilyn Strong Noronha, Reference Librarian, Harleigh B. Trecker Library, Univ. of Connecticut, West Hartford.

Marshall E. Nunn, Professor, Dept. of History, Glendale Community College, Calif.

Herbert W. Ockerman, Professor, Ohio State Univ., Columbus.

Barbara J. O'Hara, Adult Services Librarian, Free Library of Philadelphia, Pa.

Ray Olszewski, Computer Systems Specialist, Nueva School, Hillsborough, Calif.

Berniece M. Owen, Coordinator, Library Technical Services, Portland Community College, Oreg.

John Howard Oxley, Halifax, N.S.

Joseph W. Palmer, Assoc. Professor, School of Information and Library Studies, State Univ. of New York, Buffalo.

Robert Palmieri, Professor Emeritus, School of Music, Kent State Univ., Ohio.

Penny Papangelis, Health Sciences Librarian, Western Kentucky Univ., Bowling Green.

J. Carlyle Parker, Librarian and Univ. Archivist Emeritus, Library, California State Univ., Turlock.

Maureen Pastine, Director, Central Libraries, Southern Methodist Univ., Dallas, Tex.

Elizabeth Patterson, Head, Reference and Computer Reference Services, Robert W. Woodruff Library, Emory Univ., Atlanta, Ga.

Gari-Anne Patzwald, Freelance Editor and Indexer, Lexington, Ky.

Harry E. Pence, Professor of Chemistry, State Univ. of New York, Oneonta.

Karin Pendle, Professor of Musicology, Univ. of Cincinnati, Ohio.

Kevin W. Perizzolo, Staff, Libraries Unlimited, Inc.

Glenn Petersen, Professor of Anthropology and International Affairs, Graduate Center and Baruch College, City Univ. of New York.

Phillip P. Powell, Asst. Reference Librarian, Robert Scott Small Library, College of Charleston, S.C.

Carl Pracht, Reference Librarian, Southeast Missouri State Univ., Cape Girardeau.

Randall Rafferty, Reference Librarian, Mississippi State Univ. Library, Mississippi State.

Varadaraja V. Raman, Professor of Physics and Humanities, Rochester Institute of Technology, N.Y.

Kristin Ramsdell, Assoc. Librarian, California State Univ., Hayward.

Lisé Rasmussen, Reference Librarian, Dowling College, Oakdale, N.Y.

Jack Ray, Asst. Director, Loyola/Notre Dame Library, Baltimore, Md.

James Rettig, Asst. Univ. Librarian for Reference and Information Services, Swem Library, College of William and Mary, Williamsburg, Va.

Diane B. Rhodes, Life Sciences and Agriculture Librarian, Arizona State Univ., Tempe.

Jo Anne H. Ricca, Staff, Libraries Unlimited, Inc.

Robert B. Marks Ridinger, Head, Electronic Information Resources Management Dept., Univ. Libraries, Northern Illinois Univ., De Kalb.

Alice Robbin, Asst. Professor, School of Information Studies, Florida State Univ., Tallahassee.

Anne F. Roberts, Adjunct Professor, School of Education, State Univ. of New York, Albany.

William B. Robison, Asst. Professor, History, Southeastern Louisiana Univ., Hammond.

John M. Robson, Institute Librarian, Rose-Hulman Institute of Technology, Terre Haute, Ind.

Ilene F. Rockman, Assoc. Dean of Library Services, California Polytechnic State Univ., San Luis Obispo.

Anne C. Roess, Librarian, Peoples Gas, Light & Coke Co., Chicago.

JoAnn V. Rogers, Professor, College of Library and Information Science, Univ. of Kentucky, Lexington.

Deborah V. Rollins, Reference Librarian, Univ. of Maine, Orono.

John B. Romeiser, Professor of French and Dept. Head, Univ. of Tennessee, Knoxville.

James E. Root Jr., Arvada, Colo.

Melissa Rae Root, Staff, Libraries Unlimited, Inc.

Samuel Rothstein, Professor Emeritus, School of Librarianship, Univ. of British Columbia, Vancouver.

Michele Russo, Head of Public Services, Franklin D. Schurz Library, Indiana Univ., South Bend.

Kenneth I. Saichek, President, Saichek/Vail Associates and C.E.O., Kybercom, Wauwatosa, Wis.

Nadine Salmons, Technical Services Librarian, Fort Carson's Grant Library, Colo.

Edmund F. SantaVicca, Librarian, Information Commons, Estrella Mountain Community College Center, Litchfield Park, Ariz.

Frederick A. Schlipf, Executive Director, Urbana Free Library and Adjunct Professor, Graduate School of Library and Information Science, Univ. of Illinois.

Diane Schmidt, Asst. Biology Librarian, Univ. of Illinois, Urbana.

Steven J. Schmidt, Assoc. Librarian, Indiana Univ./Purdue Univ. at Indianapolis Libraries.
Willa Schmidt, Reference Librarian, Univ. of Wisconsin, Madison.
John P. Schmitt, Head of Reference, Univ. of Wyoming Libraries, Laramie.
Deborah K. Scott, Asst. Librarian, Employer's Reinsurance Corp., Overland Park, Kans.
Ralph Lee Scott, Assoc. Professor, East Carolina Univ. Library, Greenville, N.C.
Robert A. Seal, Univ. Librarian, Texas Christian Univ., Fort Worth.
Margretta Reed Seashore, Professor of Genetics and Pediatrics, Yale Univ. School of Medicine, New Haven, Conn.
Ravindra Nath Sharma, Library Director, West Virginia State College, Institute.
Bruce A. Shuman, Adjunct Professor, Univ. of South Florida, Tampa.
Robert Skinner, Technology Development Librarian, Central Univ. Libraries, Southern Methodist Univ., Dallas, Tex.
Robert M. Slade, Independent Consultant, North Vancouver, B.C.
Jeanette C. Smith, Head, Government Documents, New Mexico State Univ. Library, Las Cruces.
Nathan M. Smith, Director, School of Library and Information Sciences, Brigham Young Univ., Provo, Utah.
Mary Ellen Snodgrass, Freelance Writer, Charlotte, N.C.
Howard Spring, Asst. Professor, Univ. of Guelph, Ontario.
Karen Y. Stabler, Head of Information Services, New Mexico State Univ. Library, Las Cruces.
Allen E. Staver, Assoc. Professor, Dept. of Geography, Northern Illinois Univ., De Kalb.
Lillian Jane Steele, Historian, Old Salem, Inc, Winston-Salem, N.C.
Norman D. Stevens, Director Emeritus, Univ. of Connecticut Libraries, Storrs.
John P. Stierman, Reference Librarian, Western Illinois Univ., Macomb.
John W. Storey, Professor of History, Lamar Univ., Beaumont, Tex.
William C. Struning, Professor, Seton Hall Univ., South Orange, N.J.
Bruce Stuart, Assoc. Professor of Health Administration, Pennsylvania State Univ., University Park.
Timothy E. Sullivan, Asst. Professor of Economics, Towson State Univ., Md.
Richard H. Swain, Reference Librarian, West Chester Univ., Pa.
James H. Sweetland, Assoc. Professor, School of Library and Information Science, Univ. of Wisconsin, Milwaukee.
Nigel Tappin, (formerly) General Librarian, North York Public Library, Ont.
Deborah A. Taylor, Staff, Libraries Unlimited, Inc.
Glynys R. Thomas, Library Director, Ligature, Inc., Boston.
Katherine Margaret Thomas, (formerly) Biologist, Long Point Bird Observatory, Toronto.
Paul H. Thomas, Head, Catalog Dept., Hoover Institution Library, Stanford Univ., Calif.
Sharon Thomerson, Patron Services Librarian, Villa Library, Jefferson County Public Library, Lakewood, Colo.
Christine E. Thompson, Head, Catalog Dept. and Assoc. Professor, Univ. of Alabama Libraries, Tuscaloosa.
Mary Ann Thompson, Asst. Professor of Nursing, Saint Joseph College, West Hartford, Conn.
Angela Marie Thor, Information Consultant, Syracuse, N.Y.
Peter Thorpe, Professor Emeritus (Retired), Univ. of Colorado, Denver.
Bruce H. Tiffney, Assoc. Professor of Geology and Biological Sciences, Univ. of California, Santa Barbara.
Andrew G. Torok, Assoc. Professor, Northern Illinois Univ., De Kalb.
Gregory M. Toth, Reference Librarian, State Univ. of New York, Brockport.

Carol Truett, Assoc. Professor, Appalachian State Univ., Boone, N.C.

Dean Tudor, Professor, School of Journalism, Ryerson Polytechnical Institute, Toronto.

Elias H. Tuma, Professor of Economics, Univ. of California, Davis.

Diane J. Turner, Science/Engineering Liaison, Auraria Library, Univ. of Colorado, Denver.

Robert L. Turner Jr., Librarian and Asst. Professor, Radford Univ., Va.

Arthur R. Upgren, Professor of Astronomy and Director, Van Vleck Observatory, Wesleyan Univ., Middletown, Conn.

Judith A. Valdez, Instructor/Reference Librarian, Auraria Library, Univ. of Colorado, Denver.

Vandelia L. VanMeter, Assoc. Professor, Library Director, Spalding Univ., Louisville, Ky.

Debra S. Van Tassel, Reference Librarian, Univ. of Colorado, Boulder.

Dario J. Villa, Reference Librarian/Bibliographer, Ronald Williams Library, Northeastern Illinois Univ., Chicago.

Kathleen J. Voigt, Head, Reference Dept., Carlson Library, Univ. of Toledo, Ohio.

Bridget D. Volz, Freelance Librarian and Weaver, Denver, Colo.

Ed Volz, Staff, Libraries Unlimited, Inc.

David V. Waller, Asst. Professor of Sociology, Dept. of Sociology and Anthropology, Univ. of Texas, Arlington.

Jeff Wanser, Coordinator, Reference and Government Documents, Hiram College Library, Ohio.

J. E. Weaver, Dept. of Economics, Drake Univ., Des Moines, Iowa.

Jean Weihs, Principal Consultant, Technical Services Group, Toronto.

Michael Weinberg, Reference Librarian, Ronald Williams Library, Northeastern Illinois Library, Chicago.

Lynda Welborn, Director of Libraries, Colorado Academy, Denver.

Emily L. Werrell, Reference/Instructional Services Librarian, Northern Kentucky Univ., Highland Heights.

Lee Weston, Reference Services Manager, James A. Michener Library, Univ. of Northern Colorado, Greeley.

Carol Wheeler, Government Documents Reference Librarian, Univ. of Georgia Libraries, Athens.

Cathy Seitz Whitaker, (formerly) Social Work Librarian, Hillman Library, Univ. of Pittsburgh, Pa.

David L. White, Professor, History Dept., Appalachian State Univ., Boone, N.C.

Marilyn Domas White, Assoc. Professor, College of Library and Information Services, Univ. of Maryland, College Park.

Molly White, Librarian, Physics-Math-Astronomy Library, Univ. of Texas, Austin.

Robert L. Wick, Asst. Professor and Fine Arts Bibliographer, Auraria Library, Univ. of Colorado, Denver.

William H. Wiese, Science and Reference Librarian, Parks Library, Iowa State Univ., Ames.

Lorna A. Wiggins, Business Librarian, Social Sciences Dept., R. B. Draughon Library, Auburn Univ., Ala.

Albert Wilhelm, Professor of English, Tennessee Technological Univ., Cookeville.

Lynn F. Williams, Professor, Div. of Writing, Literature, and Publishing, Emerson College, Boston.

Wiley J. Williams, Professor Emeritus, School of Library Science, Kent State Univ., Ohio.

Frank L. Wilson, Professor and Head, Dept. of Political Science, Purdue Univ., West Lafayette, Ind.

Mark A. Wilson, Professor of Geology, College of Wooster, Ohio.

William G. Wilson, Lecturer, Univ. of Maryland, College Park.

Glenn R. Wittig, Director of Library Services, Criswell College, Dallas, Tex.

Raymund F. Wood, Editor, *The Westerners*, Encino, Calif.

Bohdan S. Wynar, Staff, Libraries Unlimited, Inc.

Eveline L. Yang, Manager, Information Delivery Programs, Auraria Library, Univ. of Colorado, Denver.

Hope Yelich, Reference Librarian, Earl Gregg Swem Library, College of William and Mary, Williamsburg, Va.

A. Neil Yerkey, Assoc. Professor, School of Information and Library Studies, State Univ. of New York, Buffalo.

Henry E. York, Head, Collection Management, Cleveland State Univ., Ohio.

Arthur P. Young, Director, Northern Illinois Libraries, Northern Illinois Univ., De Kalb.

Louis G. Zelenka, Public Services Librarian, Satilla Regional Library, Douglas, Ga.

Susan Zernial, Staff, Libraries Unlimited, Inc.

L. Zgusta, Professor of Linguistics and the Classics and Member of the Center for Advance Study, Univ. of Illinois, Urbana.

Anita Zutis, Adjunct Librarian, Queensborough Community College, Bayside, N.Y.

Journals Cited

FORM OF CITATION	JOURNAL TITLE
BL	Booklist
BR	Book Report
Choice	Choice
C&RL	College & Research Libraries
EL	Emergency Librarian
JAL	Journal of Academic Librarianship
LJ	Library Journal
RBB	Reference Books Bulletin
RQ	RQ
SLJ	School Library Journal
SLMQ	School Library Media Quarterly
VOYA	Voice of Youth Advocates

Part I
GENERAL REFERENCE WORKS

1 General Reference Works

ACRONYMS AND ABBREVIATIONS

1. **Acronyms, Initialisms, & Abbreviations Dictionary 1997.** 21st ed. Mary Rose Bonk and others, eds. Detroit, Gale, 1996. 3v. $285.00/PC. ISBN 0-8103-2219-6. ISSN 0270-4404.

Having grown 301 pages from its 16th edition (see ARBA 93, entry 1), Gale's multivolume set remains indispensable and easy to use. Distinctions among the terms are made in prefatory comments, although their definitions sometimes overlap: An *acronym* is read or spoken as a word (RADAR); *initialisms* are like acronyms, but with each letter verbalized (RPM); an *abbreviation* is a shortened form of a word or words (Ph.D.). Topical coverage is comprehensive, while the geographic scope characteristically favors the United States, England, and Canada. Foreign terms that are common to U.S. publications are included, but it is Gale's *International Acronyms, Initialisms, and Abbreviations Dictionary* (see ARBA 86, entry 1) that thoroughly chronicles non-English-language terms.

Each entry provides some or all of the following elements: a definition, an English translation (if necessary), the language (if foreign), the source code, the place of origin, a subject category, and a sponsoring entity. Entries are arranged letter by letter. Where there are several meanings for a single entry—a frequent occurrence—they are listed alphabetically. In the interest of history, entries for obsolete terms are retained indefinitely.

Given the extent to which acronyms, abbreviations, and initialisms permeate our careers and private lives, all but the smallest libraries are mandated to own a source of this type. Its usefulness is manifold: from an interlibrary loan staff member identifying an OCLC code, to a history student verifying outdated abbreviations, to an entrepreneur researching potential competitors. This is a set worthy of its status as one of Gale's flagship publications. Even the quality of its binding is impressive.—**Ed Volz**

2. Fox, Franklin W., III, comp. **The Gobbledygook Book: Dictionary of Acronyms, Abbreviations, Initializations, & Esoteric Terminology.** Troy, Mich., Momentum Books, 1996. 324p. $9.95pa. ISBN 1-879094-50-9.

Ever wonder what country a car with a "CH" on the back comes from? (Switzerland.) Did you know that the word *Gestapo* came from the German "Geheime Staatspolizei"? Can you distinguish between NMR and MRI? The "gobbledygook" of the title is of various kinds: general (mostly acronyms and initialisms); legal (primarily Latin terminology); criminological (police talk); cyberspace-related; medical; and numerical. The numerical section, which gives the meanings of number-containing phrases such as "1-A" and "401(k)," is a useful contribution to the abbreviations reference literature not offered by the 3-volume *Acronyms, Initialisms & Abbreviations Dictionary* (see entry 1).

The section on medicine contains errors. For example, *placenta* is listed as the "organ that contains the fetus during pregnancy" (p. 300), when this is the definition of the uterus, not the placenta. The author commits a different kind of error in the case of *greenstick fracture*, whose entry (p. 289) reads "part of the bone." Was the book hastily copyread? However, features that stand out are the "Legal Lingo" and the "Buzzwords from Cyberspace" sections. There are enough Latin legal phrases (*pro bono, habeas corpus, in flagrante delicto*) to justify a law student's purchasing this book and carrying it in his or her briefcase (the book measures four by seven inches). The cyberspace section goes beyond abbreviations and initialisms to define actual words, which makes the section readable (e.g., *hypertext, menu-driven*).

The Gobbledygook Book is not expensive, and not totally ephemeral. It is recommended for public, academic, and especially personal libraries.—**Penny Papangelis**

ALMANACS

3. **Canadian Almanac & Directory 1997.** Anne Marie Aldighieri and others, eds. Toronto, Canadian Almanac & Directory Publishing; distr., Detroit, Gale, 1996. 1v. (various paging). maps. index. $225.00. ISBN 1-895021-26-X.

This acclaimed directory continues to justify its position among the premier reference books on Canada (see ARBA 92, entry 98, for a review of an earlier edition). New this year is a larger, 8½-by-11 inch format. Now with 10 independently paginated sections, the almanac provides excellent contact information for a host of Canadian institutions and associations. Furnished are the contact names, postal and e-mail addresses, and telephone and fax numbers for government officials and offices, as well as the same information for financial, educational, cultural, judicial, and medical systems.

Section 1 constitutes the almanac and provides information on honors, awards, weights and measures, form of address, and vital statistics. Significant additions this year include a Website directory that lists Websites and TELNET addresses for associations, government agencies, educational institutions, and cultural organizations. This almanac and directory remains an authoritative work and an essential source for most libraries.—**Owen H. Ellard**

4. **Canadian Sourcebook, 1997: Your Sourcebook of Canadian Facts.** 32d ed. Don Mills, Ont., Southam, 1996. 1v. (various paging). index. $197.00. ISBN 0-919-217-87-7. ISSN 0823-1133.

A country-specific almanac, given the limit of its scope and the expansiveness of its capacity, can safely be expected to demonstrate eye-popping inclusiveness. The 32d edition of this general reference work passes that test. Redesigned into telephone directory dimensions, the purpose of this resource "... is to supply facts, descriptions, and addresses to general and reference library patrons, and to provide librarians and other providers of general reference facilities with a complete reference tool to be used in serving their business or public clientele" (note from the editor).

A month-by-month news update (from November 1995 through October 1996) precedes the book's 18 chapters: "General Information"; "Geography"; "Natural Resources"; "People"; "Religion"; "Education"; "Sources of Information"; "Communications"; "Transportation"; "Labour"; "Law"; "Banking, Finance & Insurance"; "Business, Industry & Trade"; "The Canadian Constitution"; "The Federal Government"; "Provincial and Territorial Governments"; "Intergovernmental Agencies"; and "Municipal Governments." A 104-page index provides workable, if not precise, access to the general text. The general index entry "Radio stations" is used, for example, but individual stations are not indexed by call letters. That is perhaps a picayune complaint about a book so wide-ranging and thorough.

This is an essential source of directory information, of business statistics, and for the names of contact people in a host of public and private sector associations. Libraries with a demand for Canadiana are directed here.—**Ed Volz**

5. **Chase's Calendar of Events 1997.** 40th ed. Chicago, Contemporary Books, 1996. 752p. illus. $49.95pa. ISBN 0-8092-3174-3. ISSN 0740-5286.

A book of days, a book of dates, a chronological list of significant events by each date in the calendar year—each of the preceding may be used to describe this work. Anyone who has ever looked for significant or trivial information for any date will probably be familiar with *Chase's Calendar of Events*. That person would also be familiar with the basic arrangement. Significant events on the particular date, past and present, are followed by names and years of birth of living celebrities born on that date. In selecting the date April 18 to compare with an earlier (1993) edition of *Chase's* and three similar works dating back to 1978, 7 of 29 events listed in the earlier edition were listed in the 1997 edition. These were all historically significant events as opposed to the special celebrations and designated days and weeks, of which the "Trolley Car Spectacular" of 1993 would be an example.

The San Francisco earthquake and Paul Revere's "Midnight Ride" were the only events for the date that were included in all the volumes perused. An omission from all but the 1978 volume is significant: April 18 is Zimbabwe Independence Day, the date of the signing of the Canadian Constitution, the date in 1521 that Martin Luther refused to recant his writings before Emperor Charles V and the imperial Diet at Worms, and the date of the death of Albert Einstein. If it is a criticism, *Chase's* has a definite North

American and United States bias. If one is looking for specifically religious holidays and celebrations, there are better sources. Yet *Chase's* is fun to use and peruse. If a favorite event is not included, users are provided with instructions for submitting it, although selection is not guaranteed.

The various "Spotlight" sections chronologically discuss significant events by topic and provide entertaining as well as informative browsing. The index is adequate, but subject knowledge is helpful. The table of contents, however, provides a useful guide to the topics or subjects included.—**Robert M. Ballard**

6. **Information Please Almanac, Atlas, & Yearbook, 1996.** 49th ed. Otto Johnson, ed. New York, Houghton Mifflin, 1995. 1024p. illus. maps. index. $24.95; $10.95pa. ISBN 0-395-75525-5; 0-395-75524-7pa. ISSN 0073-7860.

In the 1996 *Information Please Almanac*, a section entitled "Gender Issues" replaces the section on women's issues. The new section incorporates many of the significant topics that had been in the women's issues section. In this reviewer's opinion, when viewed with the section "Family Matters" that follows, "Gender Issues" gives a much better and more balanced coverage of issues of concern to women and all people. Articles on sexual harassment, the Equal Rights Amendment, and the Women's Hall of Fame with selected honorees remain. Articles about gender in the workplace, the fatherhood movement, and spousal abuse are superior to those that they replace.

As a compendium of miscellaneous facts and statistics, the *Information Please Almanac* serves its purpose well. Forty percent of the pages cover three sections alone: "Countries of the World," "U.S. States, Cities, and Statistics," and "Sports." Other sections with information exclusively on the United States include "Business and the Economy," "Consumer Resources," "U.S. History," "Presidential Elections," "Cabinet Members," "Executive Departments and Agencies," and "Presidents of the U.S. (Biographies)." Whether it be environmental issues, the topic of slavery, Native Americans, employment statistics, or birth and death rates, the almanac provides a compilation of useful and current information on the population of the United States.

The United States is the primary focus, but sections on geography, space exploration, awards including Nobel prize-winners, and current events help provide a more international orientation. The "Headline History" section provides brief summaries of human development from antiquity to the present day. The charts and tables with lists of superlatives and significant persons, places, or things are too numerous to review. References and sources can easily be verified using both print and online sources. The *Information Please Almanac* is well indexed and easy to use. Surprisingly the terms *CD-ROM*, *e-mail*, and *online* did not appear in the index. While they were defined in the section entitled "Computer Notes," they were otherwise absent from the text. The almanac would not be an ideal selection for current events of a topical nature, but it is an excellent source of current and factual information about geographic localities and significant past events and records, including athletics.—**Robert M. Ballard**

7. **The New View Almanac.** By Jenny Tesar. Bruce S. Glassman, ed. Woodbridge, Conn., Blackbirch Press, 1996. 608p. illus. maps. index. $24.95. ISBN 1-56711-123-8.

This statistical almanac of the United States is divided into 12 major subject areas, such as "Health and Nutrition," "Politics and Government," "Drugs and Crime," and "Agriculture and Natural Resources." The areas are further subdivided into shorter, more specific topics. Each of these topics is introduced by a brief narrative summary and a set of "Fingertip Facts" for understanding the upcoming group of graphs and charts. The almanac contains more than 2,000—mainly black-and-white but also some color—charts, graphs (mostly bar and pie graphs), and maps. Many outline maps of the United States are used to illustrate state data on a given topic. The book contains a detailed table of contents and a subject index.

This almanac is visually striking, including quite a few clever graphs, such as a watch shape depicting leisure time and U.S. apple production shown on an apple-shaped graph. The sources of the graphs vary from U.S. government publications to special associations to popular magazines. While sources are cited, there is not enough detail to verify the accuracy of any graph. The latest date for the data is 1993. More detail on some graphs would be welcome; when state data are given for a certain topic, they are usually for the top and bottom 5 or 10 states. The data are more useful when comparing regions of the country on any given topic. This almanac is not as comprehensive as *Statistical Abstract of the United States*

(115th ed.; see ARBA 96, entry 920), and therefore can be best used as a supplementary source in high school and public libraries. [R: BR, Sept/Oct 96, p. 58; LJ, Feb 96, p. 144; RQ, Summer 96, pp. 561-62; SLJ, Aug 96, p. 183]—**Kathleen Farago**

BIBLIOGRAPHY

Bibliographic Guides

8. **Guide to Reference Books.** 11th ed. Robert Balay and Vee Friesner Carrington, with Murray S. Martin, eds. Chicago, American Library Association, 1996. 2020p. $275.00. ISBN 0-8389-0669-9.

Currently edited by Balay et al., *Guide to Reference Books* was reviewed in *American Reference Books Annual* several times, the last review being published in ARBA 87 (see entry 17). (The 9th edition was reviewed in ARBA 77 [see entry 14] and its supplement in ARBA 81 [see entry 3], both edited by Eugene Sheehy of Columbia University.) The present edition contains 15,875 entries, approximately the same number as in the 10th edition. At the American Library Association Midwinter meeting in 1992, certain editorial discussions were held by a panel of former contributors, and in the preface readers will find an adequate summary of the discussion, editorial policy, and an outline of general principles of coverage. Among other things, it is indicated that the guide should be published in a single volume, with higher proportions of titles pertaining to non-Western cultures. In the preface one also reads that ". . . although the eleventh edition should continue to list primarily sources in printed format, those in machine readable form should be included, recognizing the increasing importance of these sources" (p. xxi).

In contrast to the previous edition, which had a limited number of contributors, the present edition lists some 50 individuals, covering a wide geographic range of U.S. universities, but not public libraries. In addition, there are some other statements in the introduction that have influenced the criteria for selection of pertinent materials. For example, it was indicated that "although the editors have had substantial reference experience, we were not in a position to select titles, to assess their usefulness, or to verify some details of bibliographic description (e.g., the contents of volumes published on continuations). By force of circumstance, we devoted most of our attention to editing annotations (usually with an eye to making them more concise), combining entries for related titles, resolving problems in entries . . ." (p. xxi). Five experienced librarians assisted the editors in reading proof pages at an early stage, advising about completeness, accuracy, balance, and so forth. In other words, approximately 50 contributors were responsible for criteria of selection and a proper balance of titles in a given section. Annotations, as in previous editions, are brief and are intended to explain a source's scope and describe its arrangement, potential audience, and purpose.

Guide to Reference Books, first published in 1907, belongs among the most important reference sources for the library profession, and for all practical purposes has not only a long tradition, but is also well executed and carefully prepared in order to achieve a much-needed balance between thousands of reference sources published every year in the United States and abroad. In general, the selection of reference sources in this edition is quite good but occasionally uneven, as is illustrated with one example. The section on philosophy was prepared by 2 librarians from Harvard University and contains 80 entries. The 10th edition contained 132 entries and was prefaced by helpful comments discussing in 2 paragraphs the structure of philosophical literature and some older but important reference sources too numerous to mention here. The arrangement of material in both editions is also quite different. For example, in the recent edition there is a so-called chronological arrangement (e.g., such subdivisions as "Ancient," "Medieval," "Renaissance," "Modern," "Nineteenth Century," and "Twentieth Century"). There are also form subdivisions. The previous edition had a separate section on individual philosophers starting with Aristotle and also sections on individual countries (e.g., Belgium, China, Colombia, France, Germany, and so on). The emphasis on non-Western countries is also open for discussion. Again, in the philosophy section one finds nothing dealing with Russian, Georgian, Armenian, or Ukrainian philosophy. The older edition had at least one entry for the Soviet Union. The coverage in philosophy was discussed at some length in the review of the 10th edition.

To ascertain the validity of the claim of balanced treatment, one can only look in the index. There are about as many entries for Uganda as Ukraine. As most students know, in the former Soviet Union Ukraine was the second republic after Russia in population, and one can expect there are more reference books published in Ukraine in comparison to Uganda. Another problem is a significant representation of rather obsolete titles published many years ago. Most of them are not "classic" and have a rather limited reference value; for example, Harmon's *Political Science Bibliographies* published by Scarecrow in two volumes during the 1970s, *Directory of European Political Scientists* published in 1985, and *Beacham's Guide to Key Lobbyists* published in 1989, or even Libraries Unlimited's *American Political Women* published in 1980. These comments are based on a random sampling using a few pages of the guide that deal with political science. Similar problems exist in many sections, and much of this depends on the knowledge and practical reference experience of individual contributors. Some centralized control, primarily in such matters as additions and removal of pertinent reference sources, would have improved the volume.

In conclusion, as it is, the *Guide* adequately maintains the long tradition of Mudge, Winchell, Sheehy, and now Balay and his associates. It should be purchased by most libraries in spite of its rather high price. One hopes the American Library Association can produce some kind of abridgment for smaller libraries that will need this new edition for general orientation. [R: Choice, June 96, pp. 1591-92; RBB, 1 May 96, p. 1526]—**Bohdan S. Wynar**

9. **Media Review Digest: The Only Complete Guide to Reviews of Non-Print Media. Volume 26, 1996.** C. Edward Wall and others, eds. Ann Arbor, Mich., Pierian Press, 1996. 1130p. index. $245.00. ISBN 0-87650-324-5.

Even now, when nonprint media have become so commonplace in libraries, good bibliographic and access information continues to be more elusive than it is for its print relatives. There is no question that the *Media Review Digest* (MDR) is an enormous and useful compilation of review and descriptive information. This index is primarily intended to help find reviews for nonprint materials that are educational or informational in nature (although feature films are included). However, MDR's entries can also be used as a purchasing aid or for cataloging copy.

This edition of the MDR contains 42,000 citations and cross-references to the following types of materials: films; videocassettes; videodiscs; filmstrips; educational and spoken-word records and tapes; CD-ROMs; and a wide variety of miscellaneous education materials such as slides, transparencies, games, illustrations, globes, media kits, and so forth. The major sections of the work include "Film & Videos," "Audio," "CD-ROM," and "Miscellaneous." The book's special features section includes "Film Awards and Prizes" and "Mediagraphics." One minor irritation was that in the "Film Awards and Prizes" section, the "Parents' Choice" entries did not indicate what title was from which media section, and to the uninitiated it may not be clear exactly what a title such as *Bananaphone* is. However, this is a minor complaint.

The major change since its last review (see ARBA 82, entry 639) is the inclusion of a CD-ROM section (1995-). This is a welcome addition, as titles in CD-ROM format continue to grow in importance for libraries. Another change is the disappearance of the former "Filmstrip" section; that medium is now folded into the "Miscellaneous" section. Indexes included are by general subject and alphabetic subject (to the newly indexed educational materials). Also provided are a reviewer index (to the feature films), a geographic index to the foreign feature films, and a producers and distributors directory.

Unfortunately, this title is expensive, and therefore is out of the price range of much of its target audience (school libraries and media centers). Pierian Press is currently working on developing network access to its databases; as of this writing, that access is only available to library consortia, but access to individual libraries is anticipated sometime in the spring of 1997. This information may be more accessible (i.e., less expensive) in that format to libraries unable to afford a print subscription.—**Caroline M. Kent**

10. Miller-Lachmann, Lyn. **Global Voices, Global Visions: A Core Collection of Multicultural Books.** New Providence, N.J., R. R. Bowker/Reed Reference Publishing, 1995. 870p. maps. index. $52.00. ISBN 0-8352-3291-3.

Aiming at "general adult readers who are interested in learning more about a particular group or culture," Miller-Lachmann has patterned the present compilation on her well-received earlier work, *Our Family, Our Friends, Our World: An Annotated Guide to Significant Multicultural Books for Children and Teenagers* (see ARBA 93, entry 1127). Four of its chapters deal with the United States, listing books on African Americans, Asian Americans, Native Americans, and Latinos; eleven more cover other areas of the world, from Canada to Latin America, Western and Eastern Europe, the Middle East, Asia, and Africa. A map and discussion of the area described introduce each chapter, followed by the list of entries subdivided into categories of literature, nonfiction, and biography. Only English-language items have been included, most of them published in the twentieth century and available in the United States. Librarians and scholars from a variety of institutions made the selections; author, title, and subject indexes provide excellent access to the 1,734 generously annotated entries.

In such an ambitious undertaking, some unevenness is inevitable. Germany's present multiculturalism, for example, cannot be accurately represented, as most works by migrant workers and other recent immigrants have not been translated into English. Likewise, the literature of India dominates the section on South Asia, as editions in English are easier to find for that country. Minority groups in places such as Canada or Australia receive attention, however, as do writings reflecting a variety of standpoints on the modern Middle East. It should be noted that *Brothers Ashkenazi*, a classic novel of Jewish life in Poland, is wrongly attributed to Isaac Bashevis Singer; it was written by his older brother, Israel. Librarians and teachers looking for an introduction to a variety of world cultures and viewpoints will find this volume a useful purchase. [R: Choice, June 96, p. 1621; RBB, 15 May 96, p. 1620]—**Willa Schmidt**

11. **The Reader's Adviser on CD-ROM.** [CD-ROM]. New York, R. R. Bowker/Reed Reference Publishing, 1996. Minimum system requirements: IBM or compatible 386. CD-ROM drive with MS-DOS CD-ROM Extensions 2.2. Windows 3.1. 4MB RAM. 2MB hard disk space. VGA monitor. $550.00.

The Reader's Adviser has provided reference and literary advisory services for more than 70 years. All the information from the 14th edition of the print volumes—*Reference Works*, *British Literature*, *American Literature*, *World Literature*, *Social Sciences*, *History*, *The Arts*, *Philosophy*, *Religion*, *Science*, *Technology*, *Medicine* (see ARBA 95, entry 13)—are available on *The Reader's Adviser on CD-ROM* (RACD). More than 55,000 titles and nearly 3,300 biographies are obtainable on the disc, which is available in Windows or Macintosh platforms. The CD-ROM can be run from either a CD-ROM drive or can be installed directly on the hard drive for faster access. Installation is a simple process. Once the product is installed, the user can browse through the "Getting Started Guide" to learn how to use it, although much of it is intuitive. The disc uses Folio VIEWS technology for ease of use.

RACD is divided into five separate "volumes." They show up on-screen as book spines complete with the contents. To access any volume, the user must only double-click on the desired book spine. A table of contents then appears, from which full records are only a double-click away. For instance, opening the philosophy and religion volume (v. 4) leads to choices of general philosophy, medieval philosophy, contemporary issues in philosophy, ancient religions and philosophies, minority religions and contemporary religious movements, and so on. Double-clicking on "Asian and African Philosophy, 1850 to the Present" brings up a general introduction to the topic and a lengthy bibliography, then moves on to more specific subjects, such as Indian philosophy and Tibetan philosophy. These are subdivided into sections on individual philosophers, complete with bibliographies of works by or about that person. Each subsection contains an introduction and an annotated bibliography.

Searching is also possible through a variety of ways. Full-text and fielded searches are available by author, title, ISBN, and keyword. Complex searches are practicable using wildcard and thesaurus options. A toolbar to the left of the screen contains buttons for templates and queries. Typing in "Toni Morrison" under the "biographies & bibliographies" field in the template yields a literary biography of Morrison, a bibliography of her works, and a bibliography of works about her. Queries work by typing in words that users wish to search in conjunction. The screen then produces hits in which the words appear together. Hitting the Next button on the toolbar forwards the cursor to the next hit in the text. Hypertext links within entries appear in blue; double-clicking on these leads to other entries. The Backtrack button will take the user back to the previous screen.

Searching through the print volumes of *Reader's Adviser* can be a tedious process. To have the same information at hand in a matter of seconds is a useful thing indeed. The price of RACD is reasonable for a CD-ROM of this magnitude. Unlimited networking is available at the same price. Libraries that answer general reference questions or questions on literature—which would include all libraries—should look into having this flexible tool at their fingertips. Graduate students in English may want to consider the disc as well. As an added bonus, customer service is available on CompuServe, the Internet, the World Wide Web, or by calling a toll-free number. [R: RBB, 1 Nov 96, p. 540]—**Melissa Rae Root**

12. **Reference Books Bulletin 1994-95: A Compilation of Evaluations September 1, 1994, Through August 1995.** By American Library Association Reference Books Bulletin Editorial Board. Sandy Whiteley, ed. Kim Dillon, comp. Chicago, Booklist/American Library Association, 1995. 160p. index. $26.00pa. ISBN 0-8389-7816-9. ISSN 8755-0962.

This annual compilation from the *Reference Books Bulletin* section of the monthly American Library Association journal *Booklist* contains reviews of more than 500 books, CD-ROMs, diskettes, and online services. The book is arranged in broad subject categories, such as "social sciences," "history," and "language." In unsigned contributions that vary in length from approximately 250 to 900 words (with CD-ROMs generally the subject of the longer pieces), each reference source is given a thorough, pertinent, and impartial analysis. The *Reference Books Bulletin* annual also regularly contains omnibus reviews—an encyclopedia update (including CD-ROMs for the first time) and selected bibliographies of materials on U.S. ethnicity, children's literature, various disability issues, the environment, and trivia books.

Public and academic library collection development staff will appreciate the convenience of this paperback anthology's configuration. It is easier to handle than the individual issues of *Booklist*, and offers format, subject, and title indexes as well. In a tool this well thought out, there must be justification for its lack of an author index, but one does not come to mind. Also, as noted in the review in ARBA 95 (see entry 14), the omnibus reviews are not indexed. However, these quirks detract little from the value and convenience found here.—**Ed Volz**

13. **The Reference Sources Handbook.** 4th ed. Peter W. Lea and Alan Day, eds. London, Library Association Publishing; distr., Lanham, Md., UNIPUB, 1996. 446p. index. $60.00pa. ISBN 1-85604-177-8.

Previously published in 1980, 1984, and 1990 under the title *Printed Reference Material* (2d ed.; see ARBA 86, entry 561), this 4th edition has a title change that reflects the increased presence of electronic publishing. There are 16 chapters in this handbook, each written by experts and covering major branches of reference publishing, and each chapter is subdivided into sections. For example, the chapter on "Encyclopedias," after a brief discussion of criteria, examines appropriate works in the following categories: "English-Language Encyclopedias," "One-Volume Encyclopedias," "Junior Encyclopedias," "Foreign-Language Encyclopedias," "Subject Encyclopedias," "Buyer's Guides," and "Multimedia Encyclopedias." The texts are informative and clearly written.

The title of each work discussed is printed in bold typeface, making it easy to locate, and there is an index to all chapters. Most chapters conclude with a list of references and citations, and many have suggestions for further reading. The works selected for discussion come mainly, but not exclusively, from British publishers.—**Dean H. Keller**

14. **Short-Title Catalogue of Hungarian Books Printed Before 1851 in the British Library.** London, British Library; distr., Toronto and Cheektowaga, N.Y., University of Toronto Press, 1995. 354p. index. $120.00. ISBN 0-7123-0313-8.

The scope of the short-title catalog is clearly defined in the introduction to this volume. The catalog lists 2 categories of Hungarian books and periodicals in the holdings of the British Library: (1) books printed in Hungary before 1851 in any language; and (2) books containing a significant amount of Hungarian (e.g., grammars, dictionaries, and the like) wherever published. The catalog lists entries in Hungarian, German, Latin, French, Romanian, and Slavonic.

The material is organized alphabetically, by author's name (when known) or by title. The main listing is followed by an appendix that mentions the books destroyed during World War II, when a wing of the building of the British Museum was affected by heavy bombing. The retrieval of the material is aided through cross-listings in a series of five indexes: a select index of titles, books printed in Hungary before 1801, books in Hungarian printed outside Hungary before 1801, false and fictitious places and publishers before 1801, and an alphabetic index of printers and publishers before 1801.

The bibliographic description of the entries gives information on author (if any), title, place and year of publication, printer, and format (e.g., quatro, octavo). If several copies of the same title are available, they are also listed. Different editions of the same title are included as well, with full description. There is no annotation regarding the content of the materials listed in the catalog. A useful feature of the entire work is that each entry provides the location of the item in the British Library's holdings.

The catalog demonstrates the wealth of the Hungarica collection of the British Library. It represents a valuable research tool for scholars interested in the history of books and printing from the advent of movable type until 1851. At the same time, this catalog stands for an inestimable finding aid to one of the largest collections of Hungarian materials in Western Europe and early materials about Hungary and the surrounding area (e.g., Transylvania).—**Hermina G. B. Anghelescu**

National and Trade Bibliography

International

15. **Anders CD-ROM Guide.** 2d ed. Brookline, Mass., Andiron Press; distr., New York, Penguin Books, 1996. 232p. index. $10.95pa. ISBN 1-888056-02-9.

This long, skinny (4-by-9-inch) guide briefly reviews about 700 popular CD-ROM titles that apparently were released in 1996, although that is not stated by the editors. The intended audience is primarily parents and PC gamers, and thus the disc descriptions focus on the experience users are likely to have (or, often, have had) with the product. Reviews are enthusiastic and written in a casual style, but do an adequate job of conveying the essence of the CD-ROM at hand. The entries are arranged alphabetically by title, and alternative access is provided by a back-of-the-book index that organizes the titles by broad subject categories. New to this edition is the listing of "Anders Medallion" winners, those titles deemed best of the year's releases, and the inclusion of technical support numbers and Websites for the publishers listed at the back of the guide.

Entries include title; publisher; subject area; platform (Windows or Macintosh); a concise, single-paragraph evaluative description; and a numerical (1-25), 4-category rating based on content, multimedia aspects, usability, and overall evaluation. Most of the descriptions are syntheses of information gathered from actual CD-ROM users and from reviews of the discs in leading publications. (Although in general this works well, occasionally the use of quotation marks becomes too distracting, as in "This 'extremely thorough' tool 'takes a little time' to learn, but the rewards are 'worth it.' ") Surprisingly, the editors have included no price information, an unusual oversight for an area where prices differ so radically and have such a major impact on what CD-ROMs families are able to afford. Because the editors indicate that this reasonably priced guide will be an annual publication, perhaps they will be able to include this information in the next edition.—**G. Kim Dority**

16. **CD-ROMs in Print 1995: An International Guide....** [CD-ROM]. Westport, Conn., Mecklermedia, 1995. Minimum system requirements: IBM or compatible PC. CD-ROM drive with Microsoft CD-ROM Extensions 2.21. DOS 3.0. Windows 3.1. 2MB RAM. 5MB hard disk space. $49.95. ISBN 0-88736-991-X.

17. **CD-ROMs in Print 1996: An International Guide....** Erin E. Holmberg and others, eds. Detroit, Gale, 1996. 1232p. index. $129.95pa. ISBN 0-7876-0803-3.

In the spirit of standard sources such as *Books in Print* (see entry 18), Gale's *CD-ROMs in Print 1996* is the resource of record for its medium. Formerly published by Mecklermedia, this massive paperback lists media aside from CD-ROMs: electronic books, CD-1s, 3DOs, MMCDs, CD32s, and other less-common platforms. Entries are listed alphabetically by title, all lumped together regardless of format. Each entry features all of the typical bibliographic/catalog data elements one hopes to find in this sort of directory: subject (from a thesaurus of 200 headings); brief content description; presence of multimedia features (e.g., audio); language(s); technical specifications; and purchasing information. Prices are given in the distributor's currency, and are not converted to U.S. dollars. The CD-ROM version has its data split into two databases, by company and by CD-ROM title. One may conduct a specific search, browse, or construct a search profile by filling in on-screen keyword boxes.

A variety of indexes is provided: company names; companies by category of service provided (consultants, hardware producers); a geographic listing of distributors; Macintosh products; all of the nonstandard CD-ROM products (e.g., CD32s); and listings by audience level (preschool to scientific) and subject category. A user's guide explains to the reader the book's organization, format, and scope. The only missing component, and few users would even look for it, is a listing of the thesaurus terms used to categorize the content of the discs.

Gale has created readable, comprehensive, and informative sources in both the print and electronic formats. The print version is bound as sturdily as can be expected for a fat paperback, but may need to be reinforced with strong tape to survive the frequent use it should receive. For acquisitions and reference librarians, this guide should become an increasingly indispensable resource, in either format, as CD-ROMs gain popularity in libraries and users' homes.—**Ed Volz**

United States

18. **Books in Print 1996-97.** 49th ed. New Providence, N.J., R. R. Bowker/Reed Reference Publishing, 1996. 9v. index. $510.00/set. ISBN 0-8352-3785-0. ISSN 0068-0214.

The first incarnation of this, the highest profile of bibliographic guides, was a simple title list in the 1948 *Publishers Trade List Annual*. That 85,000-item, 357-publisher list has become a multivolume work containing approximately 1,300,000 titles from nearly 50,000 publishers. *Books in Print* (BIP) is now consulted as much by retail bookstore end users as it is by the staff in libraries of all types and sizes. As everyone knows, it lists, by author and title, books currently available for purchase in the United States. It is some of the exclusions that are less familiar: books sold exclusively to the school market; sacred works such as the Koran, Torah, Bhagavad Gita, or Bibles; books bought by subscription; and music manuscripts. The 49th edition contains an increase of more than 230,000 titles over the 48th edition (see ARBA 96, entries 15-16). The same configuration remains: four author volumes, four title volumes, and a ninth volume that lists and indexes the corporate names of publishers included elsewhere in the set.

All post-1978 citations from *Books Out-of-Print*, which was discontinued as a volume of the BIP set in 1996, are available at no cost on the World Wide Web at http://www.reedref.com. The rationale for mounting these citations on the Web in lieu of printing them is that ". . . it would have been a disservice to devote precious resources providing information in a print volume where electronic access would suffice" (press release). This is an argument of menacing implications, limitless applicability, and spurious reasoning. At least the citations at the Website are free at present, but surely not everyone needing information about out-of-print books has (or even desires) Internet access. Despite its detractors, the book persists as the ubiquitous information medium. The increasing number of entries in each year's BIP set is evidence of that.

BIP is one of those few titles that is a regular annual purchase for all but the smallest libraries. Librarians using any but the latest edition do so with justified reluctance.—**Ed Volz**

Canada

19. **Canadian Reference Sources: An Annotated Bibliography. Ouvrages de Référence Canadiens.** Mary E. Bond, comp. and ed. Martine M. Caron, comp. Vancouver, B.C., University of British Columbia Press, 1996. 1076p. index. $225.00 (U.S.). ISBN 0-7748-0565-X.

One could imagine a reference librarian describing this title to a colleague as "Sheehy for Canada." Such a shorthand comparison would be both justified and appropriately complimentary. Reference sources about Canada, in a variety of formats, are described in 4,194 entries on 895 pages of review text. Pages are split into parallel English and French columns, at four to five titles per page. The subject spectrum is split into three broad sections: general reference works, history and related subjects (biography/genealogy/heraldry), and humanities. The last is further subdivided into arts, fine and applied arts, languages and linguistics, literature, performing arts, philosophy, and religion. The philosophy section is the shortest (3 pages); fine and applied arts is the longest (200 pages). Works that cover more than a single subject receive multiple listings as necessary. Individual entries give standard bibliographic data, such as ISBNs/ISSNs, and Dewey decimal and Library of Congress classification numbers. The brief annotations are descriptive, not evaluative, making this source similar to the American Library Association's *Guide to Reference Books* (11th ed.; see entry 8) and unlike *American Reference Books Annual*.

Several key Canadian organizations pooled their efforts on this project: the Bibliothèque Nationale du Québec, the Canadian Museum of Civilization, the Department of Indian and Northern Affairs, York University's Film Library, the University of Toronto Fine Art Library, and the Glenbow-Alberta Institute. The bibliography was compiled from September 1989 through January 1995, with new titles added up to July 1995. The current source is an updating and expansion of the 1981 Canadian Library Association publication *Canadian Reference Sources* (see ARBA 83, entry 4), commonly know by its author's last name ("Ryder").

It is somewhat unproductive to point out even the minor flaws in a reference tool such as this one, having no real competition in its subject matter and scope. Two improvements, however, could be made in future editions. The lack of blank space between the subject sections confuses the act of browsing, and the running headers need to be in a larger typeface. Such slight formatting quirks detract little from the quality and value found here. This is the preeminent source for Canadian reference bibliography; libraries with any demand for this information at last have an up-to-date resource in this volume. [R: Choice, Dec 96, p. 586]

—Ed Volz

BIOGRAPHY

International

20. **The Cambridge Biographical Dictionary.** David Crystal, ed. New York, Cambridge University Press, 1996. 495p. $16.95pa. ISBN 0-521-56780-7.

The 15,000 entries in this paperback biographical dictionary are largely derived from the previously published *Cambridge Biographical Encyclopedia* (see ARBA 95, entry 25); both titles share the same editor. Surprisingly, *The Cambridge Biographical Dictionary*, first published in 1996, is more selective than the previous book with the same title published in 1990 (see ARBA 92, entry 25) (also published as *Chambers Biographical Dictionary*), which contains 19,000 entries. After reviewing the different titles, Chambers versus Cambridge and dictionary versus encyclopedia, this reviewer became confused and questioned the reasoning behind the choice of titles.

Each entry, usually of no more than 50 words, includes the person's full name in bold typeface; year of birth (and death if relevant); place of birth; nationality; occupation; chief achievement; pronunciation (for difficult names); and, at times, cross-references to other personalities found in the book. No illustrations are provided. The scope is international, largely twentieth century, and an additional effort has been made to include often overlooked groups, such as women and African Americans. Libraries already owning any of the above titles do not need to purchase this book unless they want a more up-to-date source; otherwise, libraries wanting an easy-to-use, inexpensive, general biographical dictionary providing only brief information on a modest number of individuals would find this title useful. [R: Choice, Dec 96, p. 587]—**Carl Pracht**

21. **Dictionary of International Biography 1996: A Biographical Record of Contemporary Achievement.** 24th ed. Cambridge, England, Melrose Press; distr., Bristol, Pa., Taylor & Francis, 1995. 465p. $199.00. ISBN 0-948875-86-0.

More than 5,000 people from various professions and countries are included in this volume, which is meant to be a cumulative series. Thus, only a few entries are repeated from edition to edition. Because many world notables that one would expect to find in such a work are not included in this volume (e.g., Bill Clinton, Aung San Suu Kyi, Slobodan Milosevic), it appears that one would need to own a run of the entire series. Entries are in the standard "who's who" format, giving date/place of birth, profession, spouse name and marriage date, number of children, education, appointments, honors, memberships, publications, hobbies, and address. Cross-references are provided to 193 other collective biographies.

Although the editors adamantly state that there is no fee for inclusion, this book has the appearance of a vanity publication—83 biographees (none of whom appear in *The International Who's Who* [see ARBA 95, entry 29]) receive special "Dedications" accompanied by black-and-white photographs, and a separate "Honours List" of 172 persons follows the main section. This volume would have benefited from occupational or nationality indexes, and in the past it has *not* been indexed by *Biography and Genealogy Master Index* (see ARBA 94, entry 436, and ARBA 92, entry 392). Libraries owning *The International Who's Who* can safely pass on this expensive source.—**John A. Drobnicki**

22. Gay, Kathlyn, and Martin K. Gay. **Heroes of Conscience: A Biographical Dictionary.** Santa Barbara, Calif., ABC-CLIO, 1996. 482p. illus. index. $65.00. ISBN 0-87436-874-X.

The authors have established a definitive biographical dictionary of individuals through the late 1800s to the present day. Listed alphabetically, each entry contains a vivid description of the person's achievements through life and how they have benefited the world. A few—Clara Barton, Jimmy Carter, Albert Einstein, Jane Fonda, Mohandas Gandhi, and Edward R. Murrow—depict the variety of the individuals included.

The dictionary is international in scope, with no preference as to the geographic location or classification of their endeavor; whether it is animal rights, artistic or athletic achievements, entertainment, musicians, or politicians. Each entry is complete with references, and some also have a photograph of the individual. The work is well documented with a bibliography and a thorough index.

This dictionary contains ample information that should be expanded. It is highly recommended for academic (arts, history, public affairs, or sociology), public, and special libraries.—**Lisé Rasmussen**

23. **The Grolier Library of International Biographies.** Danbury, Conn., Grolier, 1996. 10v. illus. index. $319.00/set. ISBN 0-7172-7527-2.

This 10-volume set of biographies covers activists; athletes; entrepreneurs, inventors, and discoverers; explorers; performing artists; political and military leaders; scholars and educators; scientists; visual artists; and writers. It is a beautifully organized and well-written set for children and young adults; adults may find it useful as well. The inclusiveness of its contents speaks well for the research efforts of the editors; as they state in the introduction, the set is a "mosaic that spans time and geography while overcoming boundaries of gender, race, and class."

Entries are arranged alphabetically in each volume, sometimes including a photograph of or a quotation from the subject. The life achievements of each are placed in a historical context, and the necessary facts are summarized in a concise fashion. One of the attractive features of this set is the brevity and clarity of the writing, along with the ease of use. Appendixes include a glossary that refers to the words in bold typeface in each entry (for performers, for instance, there is a definition of *glitter rock* and *diva*; for explorers, there is *avalanche* and *malaria*). Another appendix provides a "Sources and Further Reading" list for each person profiled, and a general index includes locations, types of occupations, and people.

Whether the set is describing Italian mountaineers or Mongolian cosmonauts, French actors or African musicians, the editors succeed in supplying a well-rounded and readable addition to any library. It is highly recommended. [R: BR, Sept/Oct 96, p. 57; RBB, 1 April 96, p. 1388; SLJ, May 96, p. 145]
—**Barbara J. O'Hara**

24. **Merriam-Webster's Pocket Biographical Dictionary.** Springfield, Mass., Merriam-Webster, 1996. 372p. $3.95pa. ISBN 0-87779-507-X.

Moses's brother Aaron is the first entry; the sixteenth-century Swiss Reformation leader Huldrych Zwingli is the last. Nearly 7,000 notable people, living and dead, fit in between. There are authors and athletes, composers and heads of state. Missing is a clarification about how compilers decided who got mention and who did not. The delineator used for contemporary authors is particularly murky. Jorge Luis Borges and Gabriel García Marquez are in; A. S. Byatt, Seamus Heaney, and Vikram Seth are out. Given Byatt, Heaney, and Seth reached their pinnacles in the last decade, the explanation might be "newness." But then how did sports figures Wayne Gretzky and Michael Jordan merit spaces?

Inevitably, telegraphic synopses sometimes (and inadvertently) mislead. For example, "psychological insight" is too modern a label to hang on Jane Austen's prose. Also, the shorthand "genes sometimes behave unexpectedly inside cells" is not so much an untrue characterization of Barbara McClintock's transposon ("jumping genes") work as an uninformative one. On the whole, however, this small book is sheer fun. Those who like to test their knowledge with dense and inexpensive compendiums ought to snatch up the pocket-size volume—and keep it at arm's reach to quickly break a crossword impasse or get fast help recalling the real name of Stendhal (Marie-Henri Beyle).—**Diane M. Calabrese**

25. **The Pocket Factfile of 20th Century People.** St. Catharines, Ont., Vanwell Publishing, 1996. 208p. illus. (The Pocket Factfile Series). $10.95pa. ISBN 1-55068-083-8.

The editors state that when selecting the five hundred key figures of the twentieth century to be included in this small volume they tried to present a rounded picture of the times. Politicians form the largest group represented, followed by entertainers, business and industrial tycoons, writers, artists and musicians, and sports figures. This alphabetic arrangement of brief biographies includes photographs (some in color). The pocket size (4 by 6 inches) of this work severely limits coverage, but this type of book has appeal to individuals interested in trivia. Libraries would do better to select more traditional biographical reference tools.—**Vandelia L. VanMeter**

26. **Prominent Women of the 20th Century.** Peggy Saari, ed. Detroit, U*X*L/Gale, 1996. 4v. illus. index. $115.00/set. ISBN 0-7876-0646-4.

Until recently, history books have focused almost exclusively on the achievements of men. Although recent publications have made an effort to include women and minorities, it is still sometimes difficult to find information about female heroes. This new reference work remedies that to a great extent. Aimed at students in grades 5-12, it gives young readers a glimpse at the many facets of greatness achieved by women around the world in the past century.

The 200 alphabetically arranged biographical sketches tell the stories of such great women as Aung San Suu Kyi, the political activist and human rights advocate from Myanmar (formerly Burma); African American poet Maya Angelou; and Ida Tarbell, the American writer who exposed corrupt practices in the oil industry in the early 1900s. Many of the names are familiar—Marie Curie, Anne Frank, Madonna, Gloria Steinem, Mother Teresa, Margaret Thatcher—but others are relatively unknown. For example, the book tells the story of Annie Dodge Wauneka, the tribal leader who eradicated tuberculosis among the Navajo, and Rosalind Franklin, who codiscovered the structure of DNA.

Emphasis is on U.S. women (encompassing African American, Asian American, Hispanic American, and Native American), but the work also covers women from other countries—China, France, Germany, Japan, India, Palestine, Poland, Russia, the former Yugoslavia, and so on. There are representatives from a variety of fields, such as sports, politics, social issues, the arts, and science. A nationality/ethnicity index and an index to fields of endeavor enable readers to access specific information. The profiles (approximately 5-8 pages in length) are written in journalistic style, and what they lack in finesse is made up for with factual information. Boldfaced headlines and handsome black-and-white photographs will spark the interest of casual browsers, and lists of resources will lead them to further study.

It seems inevitable in such a work as this one that there are some obvious names missing—Angela Davis, Judy Chicago, Billie Jean King—and one might wish for less of a U.S. bias or for a more thorough index. However, this ambitious endeavor is one that should be applauded. The stories will be sources of information and inspiration to students, and the work will supplement the information offered in history textbooks and other resources. While not affordable to all school and public libraries, the price is reasonable. Those seeking a less expensive alternative that covers U.S. women throughout history may consider *Amazing American Women* (Libraries Unlimited, 1995). [R: BR, Sept/Oct 96, p. 50; RBB, 1 May 96, pp. 1534-38; SLJ, May 96, p. 146]—**Barbara Ittner**

27. **U*X*L Biographies: Biographies and Portraits of 1,500 High-Interest People.** [CD-ROM]. Detroit, U*X*L/Gale, 1996. Minimum system requirements: IBM or compatible 286 (486SX or faster recommended). ISO 9660-compatible CD-ROM drive with cables, interface card, and MS-DOS CD-ROM

Extensions 2.1 (double-speed drive or faster recommended). MS-DOS or PC-DOS 3.3. 640K RAM. 3MB hard disk space. VGA monitor and graphics card. Mouse (optional). Printer (optional). $325.00/stand-alone version; $450.00/2-8 users. ISBN 0-7876-0538-7. [Also available in Macintosh version.]

Designed for students in upper-elementary through middle school, *U*X*L Biographies* profiles 1,500 current and historical figures who represent an extremely broad range of endeavor. Although, as one would expect, there is strong representation of celebrities (especially athletes and entertainers), there are also entries for Black Elk, St. Francis of Assisi, Amelia Earhart, Vincent van Gogh, Václav Havel, Dean Koontz, Colin Powell, and Faye Wattleton. The entries range in length from 1,000 to 3,000 words and describe the individual's early years, key experiences, and adult careers. Sidebars highlight important events and provide factual summaries of each individual's career. Portraits are included with each entry, and many entries include not only other illustrations but also "fact boxes" that feature additional interesting information about the individual. Happily, the entries reflect the solid, consistent writing style found throughout the U*X*L series, and clearly are designed to engage the reader's interest. Each profile concludes with a list of sources to check for further information.

The software and search engine are simple to use and provide many options for "getting at" the kind of information students would be likely to look up. The main menu offers four search options: by name, by subject term, by personal data, and by custom search. Personal data include birth and death information; gender; nationality; ethnic group (African American, Arabic, Asian American, Hispanic American, and Native American); and occupation. Subject terms are derived from the subject term assigned to each individual based on his or her field(s) of endeavor. *U*X*L Biographies* supports use of Boolean operators and truncation, as well as offering full-text search options, printing and downloading (especially useful with the photographs and other illustrations), on-screen tutorials, and context-sensitive help buttons.

This is a well-executed, high-quality resource that belongs in every school and public library. Although an expensive purchase, it provides exceptionally strong value for its cost. It should prove to be a popular research tool for its target audience. [R: RBB, 1 Feb 96, p. 948; SLJ, Aug 96, p. 60]

—**G. Kim Dority**

28. **Who Was Who Volume IX: Who Was Who 1991-1995.** New York, St. Martin's Press, 1996. 619p. $99.95. ISBN 0-312-16246-4.

With the publication of this edition, St. Martin's Press has stepped up this necrology's publication rate, from a decennial to a quinquennial basis. As in earlier volumes (see ARBA 93, entry 46, for a review of the last decennial volume), alphabetically arranged profiles largely consist of a death date tagline appended to the subject's most recent appearance in the relevant sister publication of *Who's Who*. Cross-references remain plentiful and helpful, although some heraldic nomenclature will be an impediment for many (information on British government leader Harold Wilson is buried under the entry "Wilson of Rievaulx," for example).

Librarians on this side of the Atlantic will be pleased to find entries for Helen Hayes, Kay Boyle, Frank Capra, John Connolly, and Jonas Salk, but will be disappointed with the omission of such figures as Colleen Dewhurst, Wallace Stegner, George Abbott (New York City mayor), Robert Wagner, and Jean Mayer. The demise of such international figures as Northrop Frye and Natalia Ginzburg also is unrecorded, as is the passing of noted women Jacqueline Kennedy Onassis, Sylvia Porter, and Ginger Rogers. U.S. athletes missing from this edition's pages include Mickey Mantle, Leo Durocher, and Arthur Ashe. Given its content and price, this reference tool is optional for all but the most comprehensive of United States and Canadian biographical collections.—**Jeffrey E. Long**

29. **Who's Who in the World 1996.** 13th ed. New Providence, N.J., Marquis Who's Who/Reed Reference Publishing, 1995. 1496p. $339.95. ISBN 0-8379-1115-X.

The choice of "38,000 globally noteworthy persons" is a daunting and necessarily subjective task. Nearly every country is represented, although there are 143 Smiths, against a mere 43 Kims (only 32 from Korea), 31 Garcias (7 from the United States), 16 Singhs (4 from the United States), and 14 Zhangs (only 5 from China). Entries for librarians are overwhelmingly American. There is excellent international coverage of public officials—down to the attorney general of Western Samoa—but only of those currently in office. Immediate past presidents of Brazil, Colombia, Peru, and Venezuela, and all recent ex-prime ministers of Japan, are lacking, as are monarchical pretenders. Among businesspeople, neither Great

Britain's Richard Branson nor Brazil's José Mindlin is mentioned. Brazilian literature is represented by Jorge Amado and Nélida Piñón, but not by world best-seller Paulo Coelho. Louis Farrakhan, Vuk Stefanović Karadžić, Oliver North, Pol Pot, Raúl Salinas, O. J. Simpson, Donald Trump, and Kurt Waldheim are other interesting omissions.

The solidly factual nature of the entries determines their length. Barbara Cartland's multitudinous publications give her an entire column; President Carlos Saúl Menem gets just eight lines. Reliance on questionnaires allows such idiosyncrasies as V. S. Naipaul's entry omitting his knighthood. Most leave their religious affiliation blank. An asterisked entry shows when the Marquis Who's Who staff had to compile the entry. Cross-references are few. This reviewer nearly overlooked Gerry Adams (under "Adams, Gerard"); Sarah Ferguson (under "York"); and Afghan president Gulbuddin Hekmalyar (under his first name), while the all-through alphabetization almost lost King Juan Carlos I (following "Juana"). Nevertheless, its convenient access to basic data on so many of the world's currently prominent citizens makes this biennial standby an essential reference library purchase.—**L. Hallewell**

30. **The Who's Who of Nobel Prize Winners 1901-1995.** 3d ed. Bernard S. Schlessinger and June H. Schlessinger, eds. Phoenix, Ariz., Oryx Press, 1996. 251p. index. $49.95. ISBN 0-89774-899-9.

When Alfred Nobel invented dynamite, little did he know that his ticket to fortune would be the least explosive of his inventions. The Nobel prizes, especially in literature, have proven time and again not only to be volcanic, but also highly controversial. This new edition of those famous winners is now the most up-to-date source (barring those online) on all Nobel winners from chemistry and economics to literature, medicine, peace, and physics. Within each subject area, winners are listed chronologically. A brief vita follows, with a selected bibliography and a commentary from the award itself. Name, education, citizenship, and religion indexes follow. As sources go, this is about as pedestrian as it gets. Yet such a source, when needed, is the only thing that will suffice. Trying to locate this much information in other sources is easy; trying to find that information in the space of a few hours is humanly impossible. [R: Choice, Dec 96, p. 596]—**Mark Y. Herring**

31. **World Biographical Index. Internationaler Biographischer Index.** 2d ed. [CD-ROM]. New Providence, N.J., K. G. Saur/Reed Reference Electronic Publishing, 1995. Minimum system requirements: IBM or compatible 386. DIN/ISO 9660 CD-ROM drive with MS-DOS CD-ROM Extensions. MS-DOS 3.3. Windows 3.1. 4MB RAM. 5MB hard disk space. $1,235.00. ISBN 3-598-40257-0. (Disk is complementary for those who purchase three or more biographical archives on microfiche within a one-year time span.)

Easily installed in 5 languages (English, Spanish, French, Italian, and German), the contents of 6 biographical archives (e.g., *Archivo Biografico Italiano*) and more than 1,700 reference works from the late sixteenth to the early twentieth centuries are indexed. Approximately one million eminent individuals from North and South America and Western and Central Europe are identified, including a large concentration of some occupations (e.g., actors), a larger percentage of women than the 1st edition (1994), and few people of color. Many names were culled from Australian biographical sources.

Three search modes encourage both novice and expert searching of all fields. The Windows commands move easily between searching modes, view boxes, and lists, with more complicated Boolean searches available through the expert mode. An index option for fields retrieves either an alphabetic or a numerical list from which to search. The brief entries offer name and variations, occupation and classification code, birth and death years, and archive acronym (e.g., ABA). Person, occupation, and source entries are linked by searchable tags within entries. A gender field (f) appears only in entries for women, and the country field identifies only smaller countries (e.g., Switzerland). As retrieval of the biographies depends on use of the accompanying microfiche or original source, the location and abbreviated references are noted. A highlight for researchers is the six-language occupation thesaurus and annotation function for notetaking. Printing and downloading are relatively simple, and a handy icon for file creation and naming has improved the downloading to floppy disk function.

The abundance of data alone makes this database a valuable tool. However, its dependence on accompanying microfiche reduces its desirability for collections serving primarily undergraduates, to whom microfiche remains anathema. As collection decisions are often based on price and availability of source documents, future editions should consider the addition of full-text for indexed documents. [R: JAL, May 96, p. 247]—**Sandra E. Belanger**

United States

32. **Dictionary of American Biography. Comprehensive Index: Complete Through Supplement Ten.** New York, Scribner's/Simon & Schuster Macmillan, 1996. 1091p. $110.00. ISBN 0-684-80482-4.

Published under the auspices of the American Council of Learned Societies, the *Dictionary of American Biography* has been an indispensable and reliable source of biographical information in academic, public, and school libraries since its foundation in 1928. The original 20 volumes and its 10 double-volume reissue have been kept up-to-date with supplementary volumes. With the addition of Supplement 10 in 1995 (see ARBA 96, entry 36), this integral set now includes more than 19,000 individuals deceased prior to 1980 who made significant contributions to U.S. culture and history.

While an alphabetic index to the original set and its first seven supplements was published in 1981 (see ARBA 82, entry 122), a milestone was reached in 1990 with the publication of the single-volume *Dictionary of American Biography. Comprehensive Index: Complete Through Supplement Eight* (see ARBA 91, entry 51). The comprehensive index not only extended the coverage through supplement 8 but provided multiple access points to the biographical entries, with indexing by name, birthplace, educational institution, occupation, topic, and contributor of the entry.

At first glance, the new *Comprehensive Index* appears to offer little more than the addition of the 1,063 biographees from supplements 9 and 10. Indeed, the format is nearly identical, with the same durable binding, succinct introduction, and six main divisions. There are modest changes, however, that enhance the previously established utility of the comprehensive index. For instance, the heading for each page of the "Birthplaces" division now includes the name of the state or country, allowing the user to quickly find the desired geographic location despite the long lists of entries for such states as Massachusetts or New York. Additionally, placement of the table of contents prior to the introduction is a logical improvement over the previous index.

The editors' continued commitment to access is visible by the generous use of *see also* references. For example, the occupation of judge offers such alternatives as "chief justice," "jurist," "lawyer," and "magistrate," while the birthplace of Poland also refers the user to Silesia. The increasing dedication to diversity and inclusiveness is evident in the content. New biographical subjects include individuals (born either in the United States or in 1 of more than 60 countries) who impacted every aspect of U.S. life, from Ezra Pound and Kurt Gödel to Chet Huntley, John Lennon, and Darryl Zanuck. A wide range of new occupations—"Black Muslim Leader," "Computer Scientist," "Mediator," "Rhythm-and-Blues Musician," "Western Movie Actor," and "Zen Buddhist Philosopher"—reflects not only the passage of time but the evolution of U.S. culture.

Building on the foundation of its predecessors, this new *Comprehensive Index* is a reference tool in and of itself. Any library that seeks to maintain a complete collection of the *Dictionary of American Biography* will find this volume essential.—**Debra S. Van Tassel**

33. **Encyclopedia of American Biography.** 2d ed. John A. Garraty and Jerome L. Sternstein, eds. New York, HarperReference/HarperCollins, 1996. 1263p. $50.00. ISBN 0-06-270017-0.

First published in 1974 (see ARBA 75, entry 124), this 2d edition provides information on more than 1,000 significant and famous Americans. Each entry consists of two parts. The first section is factual, chronological information (two or three paragraphs) compiled by Columbia University graduate students. The second, much longer part, written by an expert on that person, is subjective, evaluating and interpreting the biographee's accomplishments. Although each article is signed, there is no list of contributors or indication as to the individual authors' qualifications, which may confuse general readers.

Selection criteria are questionable; for example, Ida Tarbell is included, but not Upton Sinclair. While strong on politicians, the reference is weak on entertainers—the Marx Brothers are in, but not Lucille Ball, Jack Benny, or Milton Berle. Each entry lists one or two standard biographies for further reading, but there is no index. *The Cambridge Dictionary of American Biography* (see ARBA 96, entry 35) provides less information on many more (9,000) people, and also has the benefit of name and occupational indexes. Nevertheless, this is a convenient source for both factual and critical material, although limited in scope.—**John A. Drobnicki**

34. **Notable Black American Women, Book II.** Jessie Carney Smith, ed. Detroit, Gale, 1996. 775p. illus. index. $75.00. ISBN 0-8103-9177-5.

As in the case of the 1st volume, *Notable Black American Women, Book II* focuses on the most famous and important African American women. This 2d book features more than 300 additional women, 100 of whom are historic, and the remaining 200 more contemporary. The selection is diverse, with inclusions from all geographic areas and all professional categories. Information on the individuals profiled has been collected from printed sources and the entrants and their descendants.

Each entry includes the name of the individual, birth and death dates, occupation, and a biographical sketch ranging from somewhat brief (in cases where less information is available) to extensive for better-known black women. In many cases, a black-and-white photograph is also provided. Wherever possible, the editor has supplied a list of primary sources, archival materials and where they are located, and listings of any special collections available concerning the individuals. The second volume has also added two useful features: a list of all the living biographees' addresses and a geographic index including birthplace and residence. Also provided is a detailed subject index.

The title under review is an important source of information for both historic and contemporary black women. One can learn about Alice of Dunk's Ferry (ca.1686-1802), an oral historian and slave; Mollie Ernestine Dunlap (1898-1977), a well-respected librarian and editor; and even Willie Mae (Big Mama) Thornton (1926-1984), who, of course, is a musician, blues singer, and songwriter familiar to many. The biographies are clearly written and detailed, but not overly long. In most cases, the bibliographies included provide useful sources for additional information. This work is highly recommended for all libraries, and especially for larger academic and public collections. It would also be a useful addition for secondary school libraries where information on African American women is sometimes hard to find. [R: Choice, June 96, p. 1621; RBB, 15 Feb 96, p. 1040]—**Robert L. Wick**

35. **Who's Who in Polish America.** 1996-1997 ed. Bolesław Wierzbiański and others, eds. New York, Bicentennial Publishing; distr., Hippocrene Books, 1996. 571p. index. $60.00. ISBN 0-7818-0010-1.

There are 1,962 biographies in *Who's Who in Polish America*, representing nearly 10 million Americans of Polish origin, in all walks of life. As such, the book is an important reference tool for all professionals—scholars, journalists, and librarians—in need of accurate information. The editorial work has been done over many years by Bicentennial Publishing of New York, publishers of the *Nowy Dziennik*, the largest independent Polish-language daily outside of Poland. Bicentennial also publishes *New Horizon*, a leading English-language/Polish American monthly magazine.

The candidates were selected by the publishers based on merit under the rules established by the Marquis Who's Who biographical directory series. The biographees have supplied and verified the biographical data published in the compendium. Included in each entry are date and place of birth, family members, education, career information, publications, memberships, honors, military service, languages, hobbies, and home or office address. A careful examination of the entries shows that there are some notable omissions. One hopes a future edition will include those who were not contacted or did not respond. It would also be useful in the next edition to have both geographic and occupational indexes.

This is a unique and valuable reference tool. It is especially suitable for libraries with large Slavic collections or serving communities with Polish American representation. [R: Choice, Dec 96, p. 596]

—**George S. Bobinski**

36. **Who's Who in the South and Southwest 1995-1996.** 24th ed. New Providence, N.J., Marquis Who's Who/Reed Reference Publishing, 1995. 1096p. index. $229.95. ISBN 0-8379-0825-6.

The 24th edition of this regional *Who's Who* contains 23,000 entries of individuals whose occupational stature or achievement are regionally noteworthy by the standards set by the editorial staff. Although the number of entries remains basically the same as the 23d edition (see ARBA 94, entry 26), the present work is 80 pages longer and displays a typeface that is noticeably finer. The South and Southwest are defined as those states from Virginia to Florida on the Atlantic Coast, running westward through Texas, and taking in a couple of the border states—Kentucky and West Virginia. On an extremely selective level, representatives from Puerto Rico, the United States Virgin Islands, and Mexico are included. Marquis Who's Who continues its policy of soliciting biographical information directly from qualified individuals. The amount of information to be included is at the biographee's discretion, and that variation is easily discernible and sometimes irritating.

A useful addition to this edition is the professional area index, which provides a level of access to the work not previously available. A list of professions has been established, and biographees are listed under the one that most closely applies to them. Additional detail is given by the further listing of them by state and city under the professional heading. This may be a double-edged sword for the editors regarding their inclusion policies. Such facile access allowed this reviewer to locate familiar names, and to ask himself "Why" occasionally when encountering and reading about certain names.

For a reference collection in either a southern or southwestern library, the inclusion of this work is important. The hefty price of a single volume, however, may cause libraries with tight budgets to weigh the work's merits before purchasing it. The cost rose nearly 10 percent since the 23d edition.—**Phillip P. Powell**

Canada

37. **Canadian Who's Who 1996: Volume XXXI.** Elizabeth Lumley, ed. Toronto and Buffalo, N.Y., University of Toronto Press, 1996. 1338p. $165.00 (U.S.). ISBN 0-8020-4687-8. ISSN 0068-9963.

Published by an academic press known for its reference list in Canadiana, *Canadian Who's Who* is the standard source for current biography. This edition includes entries for more than 15,000 Canadians. Each year, those already listed are twice invited to update their biographies, and questionnaires are mailed to new candidates for inclusion. More than 5,000 individuals were invited to submit new listings for the 1996 edition. Each biography follows a standard format of occupation, personal data, education, career with current position usefully picked out in capitals, publications, honors, awards, religion, recreations, clubs, and addresses. Entries vary in length from four lines to half of a three-column page.

Sample checking of musicians, writers, aboriginal and labor leaders, and even expatriates such as Peter Jennings and John Kenneth Galbraith indicates coverage that is both comprehensive and current. To measure occupational and gender inclusion, the first 50 names starting with C were examined. Of these, 11 are women, 20 work in business and finance, 10 are academics, 5 are in law, and another 5 are writers. The remaining 10 include a family planning advocate, a retired aboriginal leader, a singer, an artist, an actress, a museum curator, and a politician. Thirty-nine of the listings include a home address. Design and production are appropriate for this essential annual reference source.—**Patricia Fleming**

Great Britain

38. **The Dictionary of National Biography, 1986-1990.** C. S. Nicholls, ed. New York, Oxford University Press, 1996. 607p. index. $90.00. ISBN 0-19-865212-7.

Among the various biographical dictionaries on the market, *The Dictionary of National Biography* is unique in its content. It lists deceased Britons who had significant influence on British national life and the world. This new edition is a supplement to the dictionary, which was first published between 1885 and 1900 (a 22-volume set treats British men and women who died before 1900). Since then, 10 supplements have added a further 7,580 biographies covering those who died during the following periods: 1901-1911, 1912-1921, 1922-1930, 1931-1940, 1941-1950, 1951-1960, 1961-1970, 1971-1980, and 1981-1985, and now 1986-1990.

This supplement features 450 prominent people and is the final volume to be published in the twentieth century. Those who died after January 1, 1991, will be included in a full revision of *The New Dictionary of National Biography*, which is scheduled for publication in the twenty-first century. As usual, this supplement profiles people from many fields, such as the public figure Harold Macmillan and actor-director Laurence Olivier. Each entry provides biographical information and career summaries, focusing on successes and failures. The entries also list books or articles for further reading about each person at the end. The dictionary contains an occupational index of 23 fields, into which all 450 people are arranged (e.g., gynecologist Patrick Steptoe, who delivered the first test-tube baby in 1978, is listed in the section of "Medicine, Veterinary Science, and Dentistry"). A cumulative index lists all 8,030 names in the supplements from 1901 onward. This new supplement is a valuable contribution and is well suited for academic and public libraries.—**Sung Ok Kim**

CATALOGS AND COLLECTIONS

39. **The Printed Catalogues of the Harvard College Library, 1723-1790.** W. H. Bond and Hugh Amory, eds. Boston, The Colonial Society of Massachusetts; distr., New Castle, Del., Oak Knoll Press, 1996. 710p. index. $75.00. ISBN 0-9620737-3-3.

On the night of January 14, 1764, the building that housed the Harvard College Library was ravaged by a fire. The General Court of Massachusetts had taken up temporary quarters in the building to escape a smallpox epidemic in Boston and, in order to keep the building warm, fires remained lit throughout the night. A beam under a hearthstone caught fire, and the 5,000-plus-volume library, the largest in British North America, was devastated. Only those volumes borrowed from the library survived.

Fortunately, researchers know something about the contents of that collection because of the existence of a printed book catalog dating from 1723. This catalog, along with catalogs from 1773 and 1790, is reproduced in this new volume by the Colonial Society of Massachusetts. Amory and Bond, both formerly of Harvard College Library's Houghton Library, have done an admirable job in the reproduction of these three catalogs. The original book catalogs were used to produce digitized images that could then be manipulated to eliminate background markings, compensate for faded inks, and so forth. Amory calls this process "remastering" rather than facsimile production. The authors include an "Apparatus" section to further help in the visual interpretation of the originals. All of this has led to reproductions that are much more readable than many original publications of that century.

In their introduction, the editors carefully lay out the history and meaning of these early catalogs. The 1723 catalog (with approximately 2,900 entries) is the first library catalog published in what is now the United States. To modern eyes, it seems more like a shelf list than a catalog: The entries are arranged first by size (folio, quarto, and the like), and then in a rough author alphabetization reflecting its physical location, rather than any attempt at classification. The 1773 catalog, in fact, is not the full listing of the recovered and enhanced Harvard College collections; rather, it is the first extant listing of books recommended for "undergraduates," organized and compiled by James Winthrop. The last of the catalogs, produced in 1790, contains 9,800 entries, and, for the first time, attempts to organize the entries first by subject, and then by author. Bibliographic standards, as they are now known, were not used, and much of the organization of these collections and their catalogs was undertaken by untrained people. To help compensate for the anomalous nature of the entries, the editors have produced a useful "Index and Concordance."

Published catalogs of library collections have a variety of uses. They can assist historians in understanding what publications a particular person or population had access to at a certain time. They can assist bibliographers in determining the existence of works, as its presence in a library is factual proof of a book's existence. Private library catalogs can demonstrate the intellectual context of an individual; institutional library catalogs can demonstrate the intellectual context of an entire community. This important publication should be purchased by any university research library. In addition, any special, academic, or public library addressing the research needs of U.S. colonial or precolonial scholars should consider its purchase.—**Caroline M. Kent**

40. Simmons, R. C. **British Imprints Relating to North America, 1621-1760: An Annotated Checklist.** London, British Library; distr., Toronto and Cheektowaga, N.Y., University of Toronto Press, 1996. 395p. index. $95.00. ISBN 0-7123-0363-4.

The Britons ruled over North America during the seventeenth and eighteenth centuries. During that period, many records were kept and many books and journals relating to England and North America were published. There are many publications, including *A Short-Title Catalogue of Books Printed in England, Scotland, and Ireland* (London: Bibliographical Society, 1926), the Library of Congress's *National Union Catalog, Pre-1956 Imprints* (1968-1981), and Joseph Sabin's *Bibliotheca Americana* (Sabin, 1868-1892), which includes a majority of the publications of that period. Yet these lists are also not comprehensive. Many relatively unknown publications published in England and in North America have been left out.

Simmons has prepared a selective checklist of the British imprints relating to North America covering the period 1621-1760. The checklist is based on the above-mentioned well-known bibliographies; the card catalog of the John Carter Brown Library of Providence, Rhode Island; and catalogs of various libraries of England, Scotland, and Ireland, including the British Library, the National Library of Scotland, and the Cambridge University Library. There are only 3,212 entries included in this checklist, and all of them are relevant to North American publications appearing in the British Isles. The checklist has been arranged in chronological order and, within each year, the entries have been arranged in alphabetic order. Each entry includes full bibliographic information; author, title, place of publication, publisher, date of publication, page numbers, first edition of the imprint, and at least two known locations of British and North American libraries. The checklist does not include maps, atlases, most periodicals and magazines, editions of treaties, works relating to the Royal African Company with marginal references to North America, poetry, and dramatic works. All entries have been numbered. Many entries are annotated.

The book has an excellent introduction dealing with the history of printing in England and North America and discusses many well-known titles published during the period and listed in the book. There is a list of abbreviations and a list of library symbols for the British, Irish, European, and North American libraries provided in this book. Two excellent indexes have been furnished to help researchers. Both indexes, by titles and by authors, refer to the year of publication and the entry number in the checklist. The work is certainly an excellent reference tool for large research libraries, historians, archivists, and other scholars and researchers interested in British and North American history.—**Ravindra Nath Sharma**

CHRONOLOGY

41. Nowlan, Robert A. **Born This Day: A Book of Birthdays and Quotations of Prominent People Through the Centuries.** Jefferson, N.C., McFarland, 1996. 257p. index. $39.95. ISBN 0-7864-0166-4.

For those curious as to the famous or infamous who may have shared their birthday, Nowlan has selected seven prominent men or women—living or dead—from all places, times, and walks of life: authors, speakers, philosophers, statespeople, criminals, celebrities, anarchists, theologians, dancers, actors, athletes, and even murderers. Each entry consists of a brief capsule description of the person and a quotation, chosen to represent the person's outlook, ideas, or sense of humor. Inclusion decisions were made first on the quality of the quotation, then the prominence of the person, followed by an attempt to balance the periods of time represented. The quotations reflect universal truths, regrets, warnings, prophecies, memories, and fundamental questions, and include all subjects: love, death, freedom, sexuality, duty, right and wrong, hatreds, romance, optimism, pessimism, peace, religion, worries, fears. The statements reflect and encompass the contradictions, complexities, wisdom, humor, pleasure, and prejudices of human life. Also provided is a useful index of people, included in the calendar. Those libraries needing such a birthday book will find this a worthwhile acquisition, but much better and more extensive quotation books would be preferable if one needs a source of quotations. [R: RBB, 15 Nov 96, p. 608]—**Blaine H. Hall**

DICTIONARIES AND ENCYCLOPEDIAS

42. **The Canadian Encyclopedia Plus, 1997.** [CD-ROM]. Toronto, McClelland & Stewart, 1996. Minimum system requirements (Windows version): IBM or compatible 486DX. Double-speed CD-ROM drive. Windows 3.1. 8MB RAM. VGA 256-color monitor. 16-bit sound card. Minimum system requirements (Macintosh version): Macintosh 58040. Double-speed CD-ROM drive. System 7. 8MB RAM. 256-color, 14-inch monitor. $79.99 (U.S.). ISBN 0-7710-1970-X.

Based primarily upon the material in *The Canadian Encyclopedia* (2d ed.; see ARBA 89, entry 112), this CD-ROM extends the content with audio, video, and graphics, as well as listings from the *Gage Canadian Dictionary* (Gage Publishing, 1983), *The Columbia Encyclopedia* (5th ed.; see ARBA 95, entry 49), a French-English dictionary, and *Roget's Thesaurus* (expanded ed.; see ARBA 90, entry 1032). Together with the search engine and a relatively intuitive interface, the package is a useful and educational tool. The package will run under either Windows or Macintosh. System requirements are fairly steep, in terms of multimedia, but a great deal of the text information is still accessible without advanced graphic displays or sound cards. The disc can be run strictly from the CD-ROM drive, or an installation can be done onto the user's hard disk. (Running the encyclopedia from CD-ROM only requires a prior installation of QuickTime for access to the multimedia clips.)

A brief trawl through the topics shows the same quality as was evident in the print version of the encyclopedia. Entries taken from that source are not excerpted, but contain the full text of the original. In random checking, this reviewer could not find any entries that had not been imported to the CD-ROM, and a few have been added since the hardcopy edition. The "Expo 86" entry has not been updated since Science World was renovated, and the composer of the *Pacific Suite* could not be found. By and large, however, the material is solid and informative.

With CD-ROM-based encyclopedias, search capabilities are important. The encyclopedia section provides for four types of searching: by title, by subject, Boolean searching, and a "smart search." The Boolean search appears to do a full-text search, rather than restricting the user to canned indexes. "Smart Search" is rather interesting. It does not appear to require that all terms appear in the articles it finds, but it does seem to rank order listings on the basis of frequency of the appearance of terms. There is also a kind of thesaurus function that adds terms: A search for *Avro* and *Arrow* brought up articles with the term *CF* (the designation for Canadian fighter aircraft, of which Avro built a number). In any case, all searches are conducted quickly. A trial of the dictionary was interesting. It listed *Zamboni* (although it did not know of any synonyms), but presented the phonetic spelling by replacing the "o" with a one-half symbol and open double quotation marks, and the "i" with a paragraph mark. The disc did not like *saltchuck*, but suggested looking up *salt chuck* instead. The definitions of these and other terms were fairly terse, but accurate.—**Robert M. Slade**

43. **Encyclopedia Americana.** [CD-ROM]. Danbury, Conn., Grolier, 1996. Minimum system requirements: IBM or compatible 386SX/20MHz. CD-ROM drive with transfer speed of 150K/second and MS CD-ROM Extensions 2.21. DOS 5.0. Windows 3.1. 4MB RAM. 4MB hard disk space. 256-color SVGA monitor. Windows-supported mouse. Windows-supported printer (optional). $595.00.

The *Encyclopedia Americana* (EA) is one of the more established reference encyclopedias, a print set that was first published in 1829. EA has been published in 30 volumes for at least the last 50 years, but generally comes in at 2d place in most categories by which encyclopedias are evaluated—authority, scope, currency, accuracy, clarity, objectivity, accessibility, and special features. The most recent *American Reference Books Annual* review of EA (see ARBA 95, entry 53) is complimentary, as are other evaluation sources, yet there are criticisms of both EA and the publisher, Grolier. A 1992 *Skeptical Inquirer* article was critical of the entries. Another author/reviewer questioned EA being distributed by Amway dealers.

Briefly, EA contains more than 52,000 articles, 1,300 maps, and nearly 23,000 illustrations. To evaluate the electronic version, these comments are offered to provide a contrast between the print and CD-ROM products. EA on disc is a Windows product. For review purposes, EA was loaded on Windows 3.1 and Windows 95. Installation was simple and took approximately two minutes. The visual presentation of the Windows screen is clear—not cluttered with unnecessary icons and directive buttons. The EA

CD-ROM product is more than an encyclopedia, as it includes both a *Merriam-Webster Collegiate Dictionary* (10th ed.) and a *Chronology of World History* (Helicon), both of which add to the value of the encyclopedia. The initial screen provides immediate access to any of these three tools with a simple click on the appropriate icon. By clicking on the EA icon, an entry window appears with 10 indexes—article, full-text, synopsis, bibliography, contributor, subject, geography, article form, date, and map—as well as a user notes index created by the user. The title index is the first on the list and, for an encyclopedia, the easiest to use. A text entry box provides a space to type a term and opens the list of terms in a scroll box. Most of the indexes operate in a similar manner.

A GO button or a double click leads to the text entry box. Where applicable, one or more icons indicate appended material, such as tables, graphs, and maps; all can be accessed by a single click. A tool bar at the top of the window provides options for the advanced mode, a find feature within the textual entry, a link to other articles, FORWARD and BACK buttons, a search history option, and a PRINT button. A notes feature allows the user to create files for individual note-taking. The advanced search option is not easily mastered but, with a working knowledge of Boolean logic, can be helpful. The article title index will satisfy most encyclopedia users. One hundred searches were conducted to test the accuracy of the title index, and all but three provided direct access to the desired text. Although pull-down help screens are available at any point in the search process, the printed user guide provided the best advice for using the advanced search mode.

For the most part, entries are well written. Cross-references are provided in many instances; for example, there are 21 links directly in the text in the entry for "Music." These links are accessible by simply clicking on the word, and the history icon will easily return the user to the original text. Entries for individuals are concise and updated—O. J. Simpson was acquitted in 1995, Richard Nixon is deceased, and so forth. Most contemporary individuals have no bibliography appended. Overall, the content of the EA electronic encyclopedia compares favorably with expectations for a reference set and with other electronic products—*Microsoft Encarta* (see ARBA 95, entry 60) and *Britannica* (see ARBA 95, entry 64) were used for brief comparisons.

The printed user guide is clearly written, with appropriate illustrations showing how to use the various EA features. Starting with system requirements and installation, the guide walks the user through the indexes and special features. In a network environment, users would not have access to the guide, placing a greater emphasis on title searching. Experience suggests, however, that today's computer user will be able to navigate EA's options and screens. There are a few critical comments that warrant mention, but generally they do not detract from the quality of the product. The color and black-and-white illustrations of the print version are not included on the disc—only the maps are accessible. There are no instructions or guidelines for citing the electronic version, a feature many electronic references now include. Finally, two calls to the toll-free telephone numbers for customer service and networking information produced marginally useful responses.

EA is a good electronic encyclopedia. Information on product updates is provided, although the buyer receives discounts only on new issues. The EA can be networked rather easily without extensive additional expense (approximately $100). EA on disc is generally user friendly and for its audience—users with a high reading level and some preexisting knowledge—is an excellent encyclopedia selection. [R: RBB, 1 Nov 96, p. 530]—**Boyd Childress**

44. **Encyclopedia of the Future.** George Thomas Kurian and Graham T. T. Molitor, eds. New York, Macmillan Library Reference/Simon & Schuster Macmillan, 1996. 2v. illus. maps. index. $175.00/set. ISBN 0-02-897205-8.

The result of 5 years of planning, the advice and counsel of a 53-member advisory board, and the work of more than 400 contributors, the *Encyclopedia of the Future* is a truly stunning achievement. Its editors, noted encyclopedist Kurian and World Future Society vice president Molitor, have not produced a dry, academic tome but rather a lively, engaging compendium whose 450 articles span the multidisciplinary field known as "future studies." The work's primary goal was to provide "prediction and perspective" for what may occur in the next 25 years. Although the focus is primarily on the United States and other English-speaking countries, the broad range of articles does a good job of highlighting international influences, factors, and convergences.

The alphabetically arranged articles draw from about 40 topical areas, such as health, education, and technology. Article subjects range from advertising to artificial life, from Buddhism to business governance, from death and dying to digital communications, from weapons of mass destruction to workforce diversity. Articles run from 500 to 2,500 words in length, but the average treatment is approximately 1,500 words. Each entry concludes with a bibliography of easily located and obtained references, as well as a helpful list of related *see also* articles within the encyclopedia. Even the appendixes are of exceptional high quality and interest: The 70-page "Chronology of the Future" by David Barrett spans the beginning and end of time in a fascinating, imaginative overview, while the lists of "One Hundred Most Influential Futurists," "One Hundred Most Influential Futurist Books," and "Commissions and Work Groups on the Future" all help the interested reader follow future studies along new pathways. A detailed index concludes the work.

Encyclopedia of the Future is that marvelous achievement, a solid reference work that is intellectually challenging and eminently readable. Whether reading the thoughts of sociologist Daniel Bell, conservative William F. Buckley, *Futureshock* authors Alvin and Heidi Toffler, Nobel laureate Arno Penzias, science fiction author and visionary Arthur C. Clarke, or social philosopher Amitai Etzioni, to list but a few of the contributors, any reader with an even passing interest in the future will find something to ponder and enjoy. Although recommended for all libraries, this two-volume set may perhaps be most valuable for secondary school libraries, for it is their students who will be leading us through the future envisioned here. [R: Choice, June 96, pp. 1614-16; LJ, 1 June 96, pp. 94-96; RBB, June 96, pp. 1770-72]

—**G. Kim Dority**

45. **The Kingfisher First Encyclopedia.** New York, Larousse Kingfisher Chambers, 1996. 159p. illus. maps. index. $16.95. ISBN 0-7534-5010-0.

This first encyclopedia contains more than 80 entries that provide abundant information on a variety of subjects. Coverage includes entries on Africa, the arts, babies, computers, kings, the human body, and religion, to name a few. Each entry is enhanced by bold, bright, breathtaking illustrations. The information given is clear and concise. *See* references labeled "Find Out More" are offered for the more curious reader.

This is an excellent companion to the *Kingfisher Young World Encyclopedia*, published in 1995 (see ARBA 96, entry 50). It contains a table of contents, a glossary, and an index. This is an excellent source for seeking specific information and a great picture book for browsing. It is highly recommended for all libraries serving children. Preschools to primary schools will find this book delightfully useful. Children of all ages will appreciate it as a gift. [R: RBB, 1 Nov 96, p. 536]—**Mary J. Bowman**

46. **The Larousse Desk Reference.** James Hughes, ed. New York, Larousse Kingfisher Chambers, 1995. 800p. illus. maps. index. $39.95. ISBN 0-7523-5006-4.

The Larousse Desk Reference consists of seven thematic sections: "Earth and the Universe," "Life on Earth," "People," "History," "Science and Technology," "Arts and Culture," and "International World." Each section begins with its own table of contents. Contained in the 800 pages of densely packed text are more than 2,000 illustrations, maps, graphs, timelines, charts, and tables. Lists of prominent people grace each section, as well as definitions of important terms. Running heads with the section title and further subdivisions give the resource dictionary-like accessibility. The main text is completed by a comprehensive index (although in a minute, nearly indecipherable typeface) and other useful appendixes: a map index, conversion tables, and important global dates and festivals.

The reference combines the "comprehensiveness of an encyclopedia with the at-a-glance ease of an almanac" (jacket flap). Where else can one find in one volume principles of first aid (with detailed illustrations); a description of courtly poetry and courtly love; a breakdown of Cyprus, including area, population, per capita gross national product, and key dates; a diagram of computer networking systems; a flow chart of how a bill passes through the U.S. Congress; and identifying pictures of more than 40 herbaceous flowers? The data appear accurate and comprehensive, although one omission was noted: No mention is made in the "Telescopes and Observatories" section of the world's highest telescope, the Meyer-Womble Observatory on Mt. Evans in Colorado, which officially opened in 1996 (although the 1995 copyright could explain this).

A comparable title, *A Writer's Companion* from Louisiana State University Press (see entry 750), is divided into 19 sections consisting of definitions of all kinds of terms, from *lithograph* to *blank verse*, *Itzli* to *superego*, *quarks* to *enology*. Also included in *Companion* are details on legendary figures, popular radio shows, famous novels, great architectural works, and more. The approach of this work is more esoteric than the Larousse title and less like a reference source. For those people seeking one-stop shopping for pesky questions, *The Larousse Desk Reference* provides encyclopedia-in-a-single-volume usefulness and detail. [R: Choice, Feb 96, p. 928; SLJ, Feb 96, pp. 124-26; RBB, 1 Feb 96, p. 957]—**Melissa Rae Root**

47. **Random House Concise Encyclopedia.** New York, Random House, 1996. 727p. illus. maps. $18.00pa. ISBN 0-679-76454-2.

This is the smallest reference work called an encyclopedia that this reviewer has encountered. As people's minds are curious and there is so much information in the world, it is not a substitute for a full encyclopedia or an almanac—which is not to say that, even in the world of the Internet, the compendium is useless. The information found here is, on the whole, accurate. The entry for Latvia, covering half a page, is as good as could be expected. On the other hand, in the entry for Nicholas II, the last czar of Russia (containing only 10 lines), more than 2 of the lines are taken by the notice that he was dominated by his wife and Grigory Rasputin, a dubious contention at best. Geographic and scientific areas seem to be covered most fully and accurately. Conversely, historical entries frequently are flippant, as in the Nicholas II entry, or tend to be politicized, as in the instance that Vladimir Lenin set up a "socialist state with power in the hands of the workers" (p. 86). The encyclopedia contains no entries for Kattegat, Georgy Plekhanov, Gus Hall, Angela Davis, Michael Harrington, or Hugo von Hofmannsthal. It has an entry for Michel Foucault but none for Jacques Derrida. Hugh Hefner is in, but Eric Hoffer is out.

—**Andrew Ezergailis**

48. **The World Book Encyclopedia.** [1996 ed.] Chicago, World Book, 1996. 22v. illus. maps. index. $644.00/set. ISBN 0-7166-0096-X.

First published in 1917, *The World Book Encyclopedia* has developed a solid reputation as the premier "teaching" encyclopedia for upper-elementary and secondary school students, their families, and other adults interested in learning more about their world. The encyclopedia's 1996 iteration continues this tradition in four areas: content, currency, supporting graphics, and "learning opportunities."

Content is added, revised, or updated annually by the more than 3,000 subject specialists who comprise the encyclopedia's team of authors, consultants, and reviewers. Coverage is especially strong in the areas likely to be encountered in an upper-elementary or secondary school curriculum, for example, in math and science, history, and the social sciences. The contributors do a good job of providing a balanced overview of controversial issues; for example, coverage of the Arab-Israeli conflict, new to this year's encyclopedia, uses carefully neutral language to describe what is a highly charged topic, while the article on national health insurance does an excellent job of balancing opposing viewpoints.

The emphasis on editorial quality, authority, and reliability is further enhanced by *World Book*'s concern with readability and accessibility. Throughout, articles are written to gently lead the reader from introductory to more complex concepts, and they include many supplementary charts, illustrations, and topical sidebars to further explain challenging concepts. Advanced terms are italicized, then defined or explained within the text; a broader context is provided for many of the articles by concluding lists of related articles. Frequently, technical or scientific concepts are made more accessible by relating them to the everyday experiences of the reader; for example, the article on aerodynamics includes a great overview—with illustrations—on just how those sonic booms that shake the dining room glasses happen. Whenever topics lend themselves to a broader treatment, the goal always is for readers to understand not only the topic itself, but also its relationships and contextual significance.

Currentness is another area where the encyclopedia excels. Among the set's roughly 18,000 entries, readers will find 99 new articles (including ones on African American literature, the Internet, and 40 new biographies); 120 replaced or extensively revised articles (including updated treatments of sexuality, African Americans, and health insurance, plus coverage of the recently created elements 110 and 111); and another 1,700 articles whose revisions have been less extensive. Additionally, some 50 bibliographies have been updated to reflect more recent scholarship. Statistics are current throughout, and occasionally contain 1996 estimates and projections to 2001, where these numbers come from an authoritative source.

Nearly one-third of the encyclopedia's space is devoted to supporting graphics, including illustrations, maps, photographs, timelines, diagrams, and art. Long known for excellent supporting graphics but somewhat slow to adopt the color emphasis employed by its competitors, *World Book* remedied this situation several years ago; the result is that 80 percent of the illustrations in the 1996 edition are now in color, including most of the 70 new maps and 480 illustrations.

Reflecting its strong commitment to the needs of learners, both child and adult, *World Book* continues to offer many learning opportunities throughout its 22 volumes. Many of the encyclopedia's longer articles conclude with an outline of contents that helps students refer back to specific sections of an article; study and review questions provide good follow-up. Long articles are also accompanied by bibliographies divided into 2 sections: The first, "Level 1," lists books of an introductory nature, while the second, "Level 2," lists books more appropriate to advanced readers. Readers will also find another 1,600 reading and study guides located throughout the index, posing advanced questions, suggesting study projects, and offering the same two-tier approach to recommended reading.

Given the excellent quality and presentation of its content, its commitment to currentness, and its focus on teaching and learning, this encyclopedia remains one of the preeminent reference works of U.S. publishing. Although two competitors—*Compton's Encyclopedia* (see ARBA 95, entries 50-51) and *Academic American Encyclopedia* (see ARBA 95, entry 41)—are also highly regarded for the school and family market, *World Book* should remain the first purchase for libraries serving upper-elementary through secondary school students. [R: RBB, 15 Sept 96, p. 278]—**G. Kim Dority**

DIRECTORIES

49. **Encyclopedia of Associations: National Organizations of the U.S.** [CD-ROM]. Detroit, Gale, 1995. Minimum system requirements: IBM or compatible 286 (386 or faster recommended). ISO 9660-compatible CD-ROM drive with cables, interface card, and MS-DOS CD-ROM Extensions 2.1. MS-DOS or PC-DOS 3.3. 640K RAM (520K available). 2.5MB hard disk space. VGA monitor and graphics card (color monitor recommended). Mouse (optional). Printer (optional). $595.00/single user; $725.00/2-8 users. ISBN 0-7876-0026-1.

Consider this CD-ROM the mother of all association directories. With it, one can locate information on 23,000 U.S. national associations; 19,000 international associations; 102,000 U.S. regional, state, and local associations; and 300,000 U.S. 501(c) nonprofit organizations. Also, one can read the complete text of association membership and descriptive materials for nearly 2,000 U.S. national organizations. Entries include all the standard items researchers have come to expect from this series of publications: general contact information; founding date; number of members; paid staff size; purpose and history of the group; related regional, state, and local groups; and affiliations and budgets.

Among these nearly 444,000 associations, researchers may search by association name, by geographic area, by Standard Industrial Classification code or description, by budget figures, by number of members, and by year established. In addition, one may search in "free text" mode, which supports much broader-ranging information gathering. An advanced capability, "expert mode search," allows users to sort by publication information, by convention and meeting information, by awards bestowed, and by availability of computer and telecommunications services. As would be expected, the search options include Boolean operators and truncation. This will be a standard, and often-used, purchase for almost all libraries.—**G. Kim Dority**

50. **Gale's Ready Reference Shelf.** [CD-ROM]. Detroit, Gale, 1996. Minimum system requirements: IBM or compatible 386 (486DX or higher recommended). ISO 9660-compatible, double-speed CD-ROM drive with MS-DOS CD-ROM Extensions 2.2. DOS 5.0. Windows 3.1. 8MB RAM. 10MB hard disk space. SVGA monitor and graphics card. Windows-compatible mouse. Printer (optional). $3,500/stand-alone version. ISBN 0-7876-0622-7.

This CD-ROM provides directory information to more than 260,000 associations, products, publishers, databases, newspapers, broadcasters, newsletters, special libraries, research centers, and religious organizations. It allows simultaneous searching of 11 printed reference sources: *Encyclopedia of Associations*; *International Associations*; *Regional, State, and Local Associations* (all volumes); *Gale Directory of*

Databases (all volumes); *Publishers Directory*; *Directories in Print*; *Newsletters in Print*; *Gale Directory of Publications and Broadcast Media*; *Directory of Special Libraries and Information Centers* (excluding appendixes); *Research Centers Directory*; and the *Encyclopedia of American Religions* (excluding the religious essays).

There are three search modes, each of which opens at the click of an icon. The "Quick Search" is the easiest mode: One simply types a subject term, keyword, name of product, organization, periodical title, or personal name in the search box. Successful searches yield a results window on the right listing names of entries. A window on the left displays the full entry for each name listed. Typography and layout make these entries easier to read than in the printed sources. Boolean AND, OR, and NOT operators permit more refined searches and may be combined in the same search.

The "Extended Search" allows the user to limit a search to organizations, publications, or databases. Each of these three categories, in turn, is further subdivided (e.g., organizations include academic library, corporate library, cable television company, and national association). One can search all three categories at once or limit a search to just one subset. Once a type of entry is selected, a name search can be further limited by organization name, publication title, or personal name; a location search can be limited by city, state, zip code, country, and area code; and a details search can be limited by subject, ISSN, or full text. Both internal and external truncation with full Boolean operators permit more precision. Although not included on the demo disc, the manual indicates that one can save and recall extended searches. Although quite sophisticated searches are possible using both the quick and extended search modes, the "Expert Search" permits even further refinement. This mode permits one to use 100 different field tags either singly or in combination, as well as truncation and Boolean operators. Field tags include acronym, advertising rate budget, conventions held, discounts, languages, number of staff, printing method, sales percentage, software, vendor, and many other delimiters.

Known item name searches can be accomplished easily in the quick search mode. Rather detailed searches can be constructed in the quick mode by taking advantage of the Boolean commands. The extended search is more convenient for groups of related items—such as publishers of directories having to do with alcoholism. This reviewer had trouble constructing workable searches in the expert mode, despite reading the manual and using the Help Screen, until dialing the toll-free help number, which yielded the response that most searches could be accomplished in the quick or extended mode. Sample searches indicated that this CD-ROM was no more up-to-date than the reference books it may replace.

Annual subscriptions to the paper versions of the 11 reference books included in this CD-ROM would total $4,659. The $3,500 stand-alone database permits much faster and much more sophisticated searches. (Networking is available for an extra charge.) On the other hand, only one person can use the database at a time, while the books permit multiple use. Many of the books are keyword searchable. Most reference departments cannot function without the *Encyclopedia of Associations*. It is convenient to be able to search 10 other useful (and expensive) reference books at the same time as searching this directory. Yet it would also be difficult to justify the added cost if a library has been functioning well without some of the sources included in this CD-ROM and does not anticipate needing to perform many of the sophisticated searches this source facilitates.—**David Isaacson**

51. **National Fax Directory, 1996: How to Contact Nearly 180,000 Major Fax Users in the U.S.** Yolanda A. Johnson, ed. Detroit, Gale, 1996. 2203p. $110.00pa. ISBN 0-8103-5638-4. ISSN 1045-9499.

Gale's annual fax directory lists approximately 80,000 more corporations and organizations than the similar *FaxUSA* (see ARBA 95, entry 189). Listings are in alphabetic order and provide fax number, mailing address, and telephone number. Attended fax machines, which require a call to the operator before sending material, are indicated by an asterisk next to the number. In the subject listings section, which makes up one-third of the volume, headings are quite broad. For instance, the category "Printing/Publishing" includes directories, newspapers and periodicals, major publishing houses, and small presses. City, state, and fax number are conveniently provided here. By contrast, the subject index in Omnigraphics's *Business Phone Book USA*—which includes fax and toll-free numbers as well as some e-mail and World Wide Web addresses for more than 122,000 listings—has categories for magazines and journals, newspapers, printing, and publishers, each of which is further subdivided.

The *National Fax Directory* is not available in electronic format, which would allow the creation of targeted fax lists for use with database and direct-dial software. This may be a consideration for some business collections. Because many national business directories (e.g., *Ward's Business Directory* [see ARBA 93, entry 198, and ARBA 90, entry 182], *Directory of Corporate Affiliations* [see ARBA 91, entry 142, and ARBA 90, entry 175]) contain fax numbers, and also index by Standard Industrial Classification code, larger libraries will probably have sufficient resources without this title. Smaller institutions may consider *National Fax Directory* if fax numbers are the primary consideration, although the Omnigraphics title gives fax numbers for most of its listings and will prove more useful as a general business directory.—**Deborah V. Rollins**

52. **National 5-Digit Zip Code & Post Office Directory 1996.** Lanham, Md., Bernan Press, 1996. 2v. maps. $24.95pa./set. ISBN 0-89059-058-3.

The information one expects is here—addresses arranged alphabetically by state and city, followed by their assigned five-digit codes. Lists of main and branch post offices appear, both independently and under their respective cities and states. Post office box numbers are given for their home post offices (e.g., P.O. Box 1112 is housed in Gary, Indiana's 15th Avenue station). Rural routes, hotels and motels, apartment complexes, and large office/retail buildings are listed under entries for individual cities. A roster of new and discontinued zip codes is featured.

Unexpected information appears in this directory as well. City place-name address abbreviations are explained (for example, Cumberland Gap, Tennessee, abbreviates to "Cumb Gap"). The mechanics and rationale of zip coding are illustrated. An "addressing for success" appendix offers a primer of efficient mailing techniques for both foreign and domestic mail. Other appendixes take the mystery out of the address change service, nonstandard mail, classes of mail, special and nonmail services, metered mail, and even the organizational structure of the U.S. Postal Service itself.

More than a simple directory, these two volumes act as a consumer guide to the entity that still serves the United States as the primary document-delivery provider. Priced at about $3 a pound, libraries should skip this set only if they opt to buy the *Zip+4 Directory* (National Address Information Center, annual) instead.

—**Ed Volz**

GOVERNMENT PUBLICATIONS

53. Morehead, Joe. **Introduction to United States Government Information Sources.** 5th ed. Englewood, Colo., Libraries Unlimited, 1996. 333p. illus. index. $55.00. ISBN 1-56308-485-6.

The latest edition of this important reference work does an excellent job of describing the rapidly changing world of U.S. government information. The organization of the new edition remains similar to that of the 4th edition (see ARBA 93, entry 73), with some changes. A new chapter on public access in the electronic age opens the new edition. It ably describes the foray of the Government Printing Office (GPO) into electronic publishing, as well as the legislative and legal contexts for this venture. Other chapters cover GPO's programs and services, the depository library system, general reference sources, legislative branch information sources, the presidency, regulations and decisions, legal sources of information, statistical sources, technical report literature, and geographic information sources. Three indexes providing access by personal name, title/series title, and subject complete the work.

Most notably absent from the new edition are separate chapters on executive departments and independent agencies and on government periodicals and serials. Also missing is the useful overview of the federal budget that was previously in the chapter on statistical sources. These omissions account for approximately 140 fewer pages in the new edition. While the omitted information is available in other sources, it was useful for students and documents librarians to have it available in this textbook, which also serves as a ready-reference tool.

In spite of these omissions, this source remains an essential guide for anyone needing an understanding of the print and electronic publishing of the three branches of the U.S. government. Working in an environment where information is out-of-date before it is even published, Morehead has done an outstanding job of updating both background information and print/electronic resources in this well-organized book. [R: JAL, Nov 96, p. 477]—**Carol Wheeler**

54. Zwirn, Jerrold, comp. **Accessing U.S. Government Information: Subject Guide to Jurisdiction of the Executive and Legislative Branches.** rev. ed. Westport, Conn., Greenwood Press, 1996. 178p. index. (Bibliographies and Indexes in Law and Political Science, no.24). $59.95. ISBN 0-313-29765-7.

The revised and expanded edition of Zwirn's subject guide to federal information for the executive and legislative branches of government clarifies its focus in an enlarged and explanatory subtitle. Intended for preliminary research, its purpose is to provide subject access correlation with federal entities and to identify links between them. Although 20 pages longer than the original volume (see ARBA 91, entry 46), the revisions are more significant, reflecting the "variable nature of national issues" and consequential reorganization of government agendas and roles.

As with the original volume, the format is composed of five sections or parts, with the first part listing specific subject categories with reference to agency, committee, subunits, and funding jurisdiction. A multiple cross-reference listing completes this part. The subsequent four parts are less extensive access points derived from the information contained in the original section—general subject categories, parent agencies, congressional committees, and appropriations subcommittees. An index of abbreviations by category completes the volume. Similar to the 1st edition, although potentially useful to a broad audience of government information users, its utility will most likely be to research specialists. [R: Choice, July/Aug 96, p. 1780]—**Virginia S. Fischer**

HANDBOOKS AND YEARBOOKS

55. Giblin, Nan J., and Barbara A. Bales. **Finding Help: A Reference Guide for Personal Concerns.** Springfield, Ill., Charles C. Thomas, 1995. 211p. $49.95; $29.95pa. ISBN 0-398-05995-0; 0-398-05996-9pa.

As self-help books have become a major industry, and are presumably regularly used by many people to assist them with personal problems, the basic idea of a bibliographic guide to the best of the books in a number of major categories is a smart one. That kind of guide is exactly what Giblin and Bales have sought to produce. Their guide provides brief, and generally helpful, annotations for from roughly 6 to 10 titles in approximately 40 different areas grouped under such major headings as stress, aging, and sexual problems. Among the topics covered are burnout, career changes, divorce, menopause, sleep problems, cancer, and a variety of other ills that triumph over contemporary society.

Because the idea for this volume is such a good one, it is unfortunate that the contents are, in the end, so disappointing. Apart from the fact that there is no index and that the annotations make for dull reading in comparison to the books being annotated, the titles covered are so out-of-date as to render this guide almost worthless. In today's publishing environment, there is no excuse for publishing a bibliographic guide in 1995 that covers very few books published after 1990. The result is that not only are outstanding books such as Sherwin Nuland's *How We Die* (Alfred A. Knopf, 1994) omitted, but in many cases, especially in areas such as AIDS/HIV (where no book after 1991 is listed), so much has changed in recent years that reliance on books published in the 1980s is a dangerous mistake.—**Norman D. Stevens**

56. Langley, Andrew. **The Illustrated Book of Questions and Answers.** New York, Facts on File, 1996. 96p. illus. maps. index. $19.95. ISBN 0-8160-3561-X.

Look out DK Publishing, Facts on File is moving into your territory. Langley's compendium of questions and answers about space, the world, nature, history, and science and technology adopts the characteristic DK crayola-colors-on-white format. The reference work bursts with energy and data to cover 270 queries that a child may ask or ponder in private. Under the 5 main topics, the author pursues 45 subissues, such as great explorers, world wars, farming, sea mammals, exploring space, the Middle Ages, and habitats. Two-page spreads feature five to seven questions in bold typeface, followed by one-paragraph answers keyed to brightly colored drawings, cutaways, sidebars, maps, and multipart diagrams. A three-page index concludes the work.

Layout is the soul of Langley's work. The pacing is brisk and upbeat, and human features are lifelike. Violence is kept in perspective. Except in historical scenes, the faces tend to be Caucasian, and women play a token role in action shots. Vocabulary challenges readers to ponder such terms as *LCD*, *compound eye*, *stalagmite*, *plowshare*, *boreal forest*, *Inuit*, *Zimbabwe*, *moraine*, *lithography*, *smart card*, and *umbilical cord*. Most questions reflect a sensitivity to children's interests; for example, What is inside the earth? What is a fossil? Others sound more like editors making a hit-or-miss guess about what a youngster may want to know about a prechosen topic; for instance, What was Paris like in the fourteenth century? How did Greek culture spread? What are computer peripherals? These questions reflect what adults want children to know rather than the scope and wording of actual kid-originated questions. Overall, however, the book vibrates with charm and adventure.—**Mary Ellen Snodgrass**

57. Padwa, Lynette. **Everything You Pretend to Know and Are Afraid Someone Will Ask.** New York, Penguin Books, 1996. 232p. $9.95pa. ISBN 0-14-051322-1.

This unique little handbook is geared toward endowing its audience with cultural literacy, and makes learning an adventure. Containing such fun information as what the electoral college really is; the difference between aspirin, acetominaphen, and ibuprofen; what water filters filter out; why the Gregorians chant; what makes a virgin vestal; a definition of cyberspace; the difference between a jail, a prison, and a penitentiary; and an analysis of the Oedipus complex, this resource makes for delightful browsing or even reading cover-to-cover. The handbook is divided into 10 sections: "Deciphering Newspeak"; "Skipped History"; "Because the Founding Fathers Said So"; "Psychobabble"; "Healthy Curiosity"; "Bon Appétit, If You Dare"; "Express Yourself"; "Big Science"; "Cyberlingo"; and "Unfathomable Miscellany." The prose is informative, easy to understand, and oftentimes witty.

However, there is more, and less, to this book than meets the eye. Some of the information given is not up-to-date, explicit, or entirely objective. For example, the section on pork-barrel legislation states that a possible solution to the problem is the line-item veto, which is now a viable option. It is true that this book was published before the November 1996 election, but the entry makes no mention of the possibility of the line-item veto passing in that election. Another problem arises in the "Psychobabble" section; Sigmund Freud, the brilliant but aggravating father of psychoanalysis, predominates. True, much of psychology today is based on his efforts, but comparatively little mention is made of other important pioneering figures, such as Carl Jung and B. F. Skinner. Also, the entry on the Oedipus complex states, somewhat erroneously, that the label for the girl's complex, the Electra complex, never really caught on. On the contrary, this term is often used in literary studies. Finally, a statement in the entry on homeopathic medicine is not only misleading but potentially dangerous. The author writes, "Certainly there is little to risk in giving it [homeopathic medicine] a try" (p. 105). Homeopathic medicines are drugs just like any other medicine, and there are potential risks involved in using them. One should consult a doctor or homeopathic specialist before consuming medicines of any kind.

A last concern with this volume as a reference work concerns its lack of an index or comprehensive table of contents. The table of contents contains a few choice headlines of the entries provided under each chapter designation, but nowhere near all of them. The omission of an index severely restricts the use of this handbook as a reference tool. Many reference librarians may shout for joy at the appearance of a volume that can answer nagging reference questions; but the inability to easily access that information limits this resource's utility. Therefore, it remains a fun vade mecum for individuals but cannot be recommended as a true reference work.—**Melissa Rae Root**

INDEXES

58. **Alternative Press Index: An Index to Alternative and Radical Publications. Volume 27, January-December 1995.** Baltimore, Md., Alternative Press Center, 1996. 636p. $225.00pa./yr. ISSN 0002-662X.

This annual index with quarterly updates provides access to more than 200 alternative magazines, newspapers, and other serial publications. Arranged by topic, each entry provides a complete citation and cross-references to other topics, as appropriate. Items included for indexing are articles of five paragraphs or more (with certain exceptions, such as classifieds, calendars, and the like); bibliographies, directories, indexes, and resource listings; foreign-language articles if they are not also printed in English (with a translated title in brackets); reprints from other sources (with the source listed as the author); editorials; all reviews, interviews, obituaries, and speeches; and fiction, songs, recipes, and regular columns (with the exception of advice or gossip columns). Unfortunately, the editors have chosen not to include either poetry or letters to the editor unless they are substantial.

A separate section of abstracts from selected periodicals is also listed at the end of each volume. Abstracts are generally taken from the original article, although some are edited by the *Alternative Press Index* staff. Each volume also contains a user's guide, including citation explication; a list of periodicals indexed, along with subscription information; and a listing of new and discontinued periodicals. This title continues to be a mainstay of reference indexes, due to its unique scope and its breadth of treatment. The index is recommended for all academic libraries, and large public and school libraries.

—Edmund F. SantaVicca

59. **Current Issues SourceFile.** [CD-ROM]. Bethesda, Md., Congressional Information Service, 1996. Minimum system requirements: IBM or compatible 386 (486 or higher recommended). CD-ROM drive. Windows 3.1. 8MB RAM. 10MB hard disk space. VGA 640 x 480, 256-color monitor. $1,195.00 (single user).

Current Issues SourceFile is a logically arranged and easy-to-use CD-ROM database that provides the complete text to more than 3,000 articles on hundreds of timely and diverse issues. This is a practical and useful reference work that is updated quarterly. Users can easily find and compare alternative positions on a number of meaningful and controversial topics. The articles and reports included within this database represent a number of divergent and opposing viewpoints and are drawn from literally hundreds of sources. Entries include position papers; speeches; reports from think tanks, advocacy groups, professional and trade associations, and private and university research centers; and federal and Congressional testimonies and investigative reports. Because the articles are argumentative as well as concise and authoritative, users of varying levels of sophistication will more easily understand the contrasting positions advocated by these various groups and authors. Moreover, because this is an electronic database, additional and practical information has also been linked to various entries. Among the more useful of these links is the inclusion of source profiles that identify and describe the group or organization that sponsored or published each article. These profiles will help users better understand and evaluate the background of some of these controversial issues.

The database is organized into 10 major subject areas: criminal justice, business and economics, education, environment, government, health, international issues, population, science and technology, and social issues. It can be electronically searched in a general browse mode or in a specific search mode. Thus, users can quickly examine the collected scope of the database or search for specific words, phrases, or names across all of the subject areas. Entries are cross-referenced and include a description of the issue or issues to consider, a short summary or abstract of the article, and the full text of the report or paper that can be readily printed or saved to a file.—**Timothy E. Sullivan**

60. **Dissertation Abstracts.** [CD-ROM]. Norwood, Mass., SilverPlatter, 1990-1996. 3 discs. Minimum system requirements: IBM or compatible 386. CD-ROM drive with Microsoft CD-ROM Extensions 2.1. Windows 3.1. 4MB memory (8MB for Windows for Workgroups, Windows 95, Windows NT, and OS/2). 14MB hard disk space. VGA monitor. $14,025.00/single networked user. (Other pricing options available.)

In addition to the three *Dissertation Abstracts* discs, items received with this product include WinSPIRS setup diskettes and much documentation. Users will benefit by using a multiple-disc reader in terms of effort in changing discs; those without such capacity are provided with a one-line statement, beneath the list of search histories, identifying the disc that was searched. Searches can be repeated automatically after a disc change. One drawback to multiple-disc access is that certain commands lock up the computer for a minute or so while each disc is scanned; this can be frustrating.

Installation of the WinSPIRS software was easy, aided by the instructions provided. Once installed, the software is initially simple to use, and users can retrieve a significant amount of data with minimal technical knowledge. For both installation and usage, familiarity with general Windows techniques is assumed. Using multiple discs, or in a networked environment, the first procedure is to select the desired databases. When only a single disc is available, a *Dissertation Abstracts* opening screen is displayed; it also contains SilverPlatter information, as well as a disclaimer.

Once this stage is past, the user is presented with a search screen. It has three parts: a one-line search text entry area, a search history area, and a retrieved records area. These areas are surrounded by buttons, with a menu bar and title bar at the top. Here, the "Quick Reference Card" provided with the product can help with orienting the user (however, not all elements of the screen are labeled on it, and its flimsiness suggests it might be misplaced). Ample documentation is given in both the "Getting Started Guide" and the "User's Manual"—the latter is particularly useful for its dictionary entries. Intuitively, the experienced Windows 95 user will enter a search term and click on the "Show" button. In many cases, merely entering one word that will be encountered anywhere in the data record will retrieve the pertinent record. The search results are promptly displayed, and the search key is added to the search history screen list, which can be revisited at any time for a subsequent search or to edit the search in the search text entry area. Search keys can be removed, individually or as a block, from the search history area by using the "Clear" button.

In the retrieved records area, one can toggle between a view of "Brief Fields" and "All Fields"; many users will want all fields so as to read the abstracts. Buttons allow jumping to next and previous records and viewing of more of the record by clicking on "Full Screen." The "Limit" button allows narrowing of the search by various criteria. Clicking on it superimposes a second screen, in which specific fields (author, degree date, advisor name, language, and publications number/order number) are available; here, rather than entering a term as free text, selection is made from a list of available terms displayed in another screen area. This feature suffers in that when the list of terms is long, the scroll bar is hypersensitive and makes large jumps between entries.

Buttons at the head of the screen provide other functions. On multidisc systems, one can access other databases by clicking on "Database." Printing and downloading to disk are similarly available. The "Thesaurus" button allows one to access a list of subjects, hierarchically arranged by broad categories. The "Index" button accesses the same fields as the "Limit" button, plus a free text index that essentially duplicates the search screen's text entry area. Also available are various menus accessed from terms in the menu bar. These are too numerous to describe in detail, but mention must be made of the "Language" option under "Tools." Selecting another language will cause the software to reinitialize. Previous searches will be lost without warning. Presumably, few users will change language in mid-use, but one may also question whether users will need this facility, considering that the tool itself is entirely oriented to English speakers (abstracts of dissertations in other languages are themselves in English). The template is translated, and so is the initial disclaimer, but the text of the *Dissertation Abstracts* opening screen remains in English. What is missing from this panoply is immediate online instruction on combining the results of two search histories using Boolean logic. This is done by entering, for example, "#1 and #2" to access the intersection of 2 previously done searches.

The CD-ROMs themselves cover a substantial range of data from the print versions of several tools: *Comprehensive Dissertation Index*, *Dissertation Abstracts International*, *Masters Abstracts International*, and *American Doctoral Dissertations*. Updates amount to 4,500 citations and abstracts monthly. One temptation facing a user, unbeknownst to many, is to assume that all pertinent positive answers to a search will be retrieved. For example, the sponsor index will pull up a list of dissertations written under a person's supervision during the 15-year span. However, that list is not necessarily complete, as not all contributors of abstracts provided that information. Some of the terms in the thesaurus have a scope note indicating that the term came into use at a certain time; earlier relevant dissertations cannot be accessed using this term. One wonders, also, in cases where for reasons of space the print version contains a shorter abstract than the author originally wrote, whether more text could be included. However, the problem of space is as much an issue in CD-ROM format as in print.

Notwithstanding the mentioned criticisms, many users will welcome the enhanced search capabilities provided by the CD-ROM version of this tool. Before buying, purchasers should make provisions to receive updates and check to see if they already have access via an online service.—**Ian Fairclough**

61. **The Left Index: A Quarterly Index to Periodicals of the Left.** Santa Cruz, Calif., Reference and Research Services, 1995. 4v. $70.00/yr./institutions; $35.00/yr./individuals. ISSN 0733-2998.

In an era of increasing access to large commercial periodical indexes online, the need for continued access to the alternative perspectives provided by a core of "left" journals remains essential. Although *left* is never clearly defined, the editors promote *The Left Index* as an important source for some 100 journal titles that, by their very nature, need to be indexed collectively. Titles range from small independent press titles, such as *Against the Current* or *In These Times*, to the peer-reviewed journals of major presses, such as *Crime, Law, and Society* or *Cultural Critique*.

Perhaps the most important function of such indexes today is the knowledge and understanding the editors bring to the task of assigning relevant headings. By bringing together important sources of information that might be lost in larger databases, they provide users with needed information to help find the countervailing argument. The index is arranged into four sections: an author list, a subject list, a book review index, and a journal index, with full bibliographic citations found only in the author list and the book review index. Subject entries, although broad, are standard Library of Congress headings with *see* and *see also* headings guiding the user to the appropriate place.

Users accustomed to the ease of electronic indexes will find this print index a challenge. However, their patience will be rewarded. In this single source, one can find the recent articles by postmodern philosophers or subjects as diverse as the progressive movement in Indonesia and feminist publishing. For those seeking information that provides a particular perspective or a publication outside the mainstream, *The Left Index*, together with the *Alternative Press Index* (see entry 58) and *Women's Studies Abstracts* (Rush Publishing, quarterly), remains an essential reference tool.—**Carol L. Mitchell**

MUSEUMS

62. Danilov, Victor J. **University and College Museums, Galleries, and Related Facilities: A Descriptive Directory.** Westport, Conn., Greenwood Press, 1996. 692p. index. $99.50. ISBN 0-313-28613-2.

This lucid, competent directory fills a void in the literature and conveys reliable and useful information about 1,108 museums and galleries in academic settings in the United States. The 152 pages of introductory material amount to a cogent book on the subject. The book is entirely accessible to the nonexpert. The entries are arranged by type of facility (e.g., agricultural museums, art galleries, sculpture gardens) and then by institution within the type. The literal use of names causes some clustering around the word "university," but everything can be found, especially with the help of the excellent index. Entries include institutional history, holdings, programs, hours, services, and other pertinent information. They are written in a clear and interesting fashion. Danilov used the survey method to gather information, and that was bound to produce mixed results. Accordingly, he followed up with additional contacts and other research. The result is not only a unique reference book but also a remarkably good one. [R: Choice, Dec 96, p. 588; RBB, 15 Mar 96, pp. 1314-15]—**John Newman**

PERIODICALS AND SERIALS

63. **Annotations: A Directory of Periodicals Listed in the Alternative Press Index.** 1996 ed. By Marie F. Jones and the Alternative Press Center. Baltimore, Md., Alternative Press Center, 1996. 175p. index. $15.00pa. ISBN 0-9653894-0-5.

A valuable supplement to its parent publication, this directory provides concise profiles for each of the periodical publications included in the indexing efforts of *Alternative Press Index* (see entry 58). Entries are arranged alphabetically by title and are numbered sequentially. Each entry provides full title and subtitle followed by terms that describe the basic content of the publication. These terms are then used as the basis for the topical index that appears at the end of the volume.

Format, frequency, and publisher of the periodical are also noted, as is complete editorial information including editor, address, telephone and fax numbers, e-mail address, and World Wide Web site. Rates for subscription are also provided. The publishing history and an indication of previous or alternate titles are presented, along with the date of first inclusion in *Alternative Press Index*. Microform sources and selected reviews of the periodical are indicated, as are the ISSN and OCLC numbers. Following this are concise annotations that profile the content, ideology, history, and unique features of the publication.

This small directory can serve as either a supplement to the parent index or as a stand-alone guide to alternative periodicals. As such, it is a worthy addition to most medium and large reference collections, and a handy acquisitions tool.—**Edmund F. SantaVicca**

64. **Periodicals in Print: Australia, New Zealand, & the South Pacific 1996.** 13th ed. Port Melbourne, Australia, D. W. Thorpe/Reed Reference Australia and Toowong, Australia, ISA Australia; distr., New Providence, N.J., Reed Reference Publishing, 1996. 855p. index. $85.00pa. ISBN 1-875589-89-9. ISSN 1322-3895.

A standard title never before reviewed in ARBA, this source is commendable for its uniqueness and scope. It is a more straightforward directory than the irregularly issued *Press, Radio & TV Guide: Australia, New Zealand and the Pacific Islands* (Sydney, Australia, County Press Ltd., 1914-), which is as much a gazetteer as a serials listing. Derived from the database of the subscription agent ISA Australia, *Periodicals in Print* succeeds the less-complete *Current Australian Serials* (National Library of Australia, printed until 1975), *Australian Serials in Print* (D. W. Thorpe, 1981-1991), and *Australian Periodicals in Print* (10th ed., D. W. Thorpe, 1993). These predecessors gathered data from questionnaires sent only to identified publishers and did not include listings for Papua New Guinea and other South Pacific countries. *Periodicals in Print* can claim both comprehensiveness of scope and impressive currency (data for the 1996 edition are entered as late as March of that year).

So what does it do? It lists, for the countries included, newspapers, magazines, yearbooks, newsletters, directories, and other publications issued serially. There are more than 13,000 entries, 10 percent more than in the previous edition. The book has five sections: titles listed alphabetically, ceased titles, publisher directory data and the titles they produce, a subject classification using common terminology, and a listing by ISSN. Entries for individual titles contain 29 set fields of data, with the number of completed fields varying from title to title. Most entries provide a brief description of the serial's purpose and scope; country of origin; publisher name; personal contact name; claims information; date of first issue; subject heading(s); cost; a circulation figure; format (e.g., disk, tabloid, newsletter); and length, if fixed. Some entries have as few as five or six data fields completed, a disappointing drawback in a directory containing so much unique information. The paper binding is adequate, although the gutters are a bit narrow for easy photocopying. Libraries needing serials information for these countries will be pleased to have a source as inclusive as this; there is no directly competing title to consider for purchase.—**Ed Volz**

65. **The Standard Periodical Directory, 1997.** 20th ed. New York, Oxbridge Communications, 1996. 2152p. index. $695.00. ISBN 0-917460-76-6.

This 20th edition of the *Standard Periodical Directory* purports to be the "largest authoritative guide to United States and Canadian periodicals" and contains "information on more than 90,000 publications." Periodicals are classified by subject categories appearing in the table of contents. A cross-index to subjects for related topics is particularly useful.

Entries give comprehensive publication information and additional information, such as publisher and editor's names, circulation, art, production, promotions directors, editorial content, target audience, year established, frequency, subscription rate, ISSN, ISBN, and LC numbers. Coverage includes magazines and journals of all kinds, as well as newsletters, newspapers, newspaper magazines, and supplements. House organs, yearbooks, and transactions and proceedings of scientific societies are also listed. New to this edition is the section of "Industry Phone Numbers."

This is a useful, single-volume tool, and it is recommended as a standard reference source. *The Standard Periodical Directory* should be used in combination with *Ulrich's International Periodicals Directory* (see entry 66), which is a more comprehensive source.—**Mary J. Bowman**

66. **Ulrich's International Periodicals Directory 1997.** 35th ed. Compiled by R. R. Bowker Serials Bibliography Department. New Providence, N.J., R. R. Bowker/Reed Reference Publishing, 1996. 5v. index. $449.95/set. ISBN 0-8352-3806-7. ISSN 0000-0175.

R. R. Bowker's five-volume set continues to set the standard for serials directories. The 35th edition lists 165,000 serials, with 112,000 of those entries updates from the 34th edition (see ARBA 96, entry 88). Nearly 6,000 serials were added during the past year, and 12,000 contact names for rights and permissions services are included for the first time. More than 6,000 online (or combined online/hard copy) serials are listed, as are 2,240 CD-ROM-based titles. The document delivery services vendor list has added coverage for the Canada Institute for Scientific and Technical Information (National Research Council of Canada) and the Library of the Royal Netherlands Academy of Arts and Sciences. One now expects directories to acknowledge the prevalence of Internet access, and *Ulrich's* does list e-mail addresses (in 18,000 entries) and World Wide Web addresses (10,000 URLs). There is, however, no Website listed for either R. R. Bowker or for the title in hand. Each entry for a specific serial also provides information regarding reprinting, indexing, and abstracting services. There are 43 potential fields of information per entry, an exemplary mix of formatting efficiency and comprehensiveness.

The established *Ulrich's* arrangement is unchanged: The first three volumes list serials in a classified list, while the remaining volumes are composed of myriad indexes. Some of the indexes are by subject, by title, by ISSN, by title changes, by cessations, by serials on CD-ROM, by online serials, and by newspapers (daily and weekly). The list of ceased titles covers the preceding three years. *Ulrich's* maintains its status as a model of reliable and clear data presentation, deserving its place on the short list of must-buy reference tools.—**Ed Volz**

QUOTATION BOOKS

67. Boritt, Gabor S., Jakob B. Boritt, Deborah R. Huso, and Peter C. Vermilyea. **Of the People, by the People, for the People, and Other Quotations by Abraham Lincoln.** New York, Columbia University Press, 1996. 162p. $19.95. ISBN 0-231-10326-3.

Lincoln quotations are easily found in standard sources, such as *Bartlett's Familiar Quotations* (see ARBA 82, entry 109). *The Morrow Book of Quotations in American History* (William Morrow, 1984) by Joseph R. Conlin is strong on Lincoln quotations; *The Macmillan Dictionary of Political Quotations* (see ARBA 94, entry 724) is a major source arranged by political subjects, such as "Parties and Machines," "Managing Government," "Freedom and Liberty," and so forth.

This new compilation contains quotations arranged according to 320 subjects. Quotations are gleaned from speeches; letters; printed messages to Congress; and from Lincoln's collected works, published by Rutgers University Press. Great care is taken to provide complete citations for each quotation used; in fact, these citations are more complete than the work's bibliography (publishers are not included there). The authors' introduction includes some of their favorite quotations, included here because they are charming but cannot be traced to Lincoln's own hand. This is a book containing verified quotations, selected because of authenticity, quality of thought, wit, language, and "usefulness to the people of the twenty-first century."

The book has an attractive format and typeface; quality paper is used throughout and the binding is sufficient. Most librarians will choose to place this title in the general circulating collection.

—**Milton H. Crouch**

68. **The Columbia World of Quotations.** [CD-ROM]. New York, Columbia University Press, 1996. Minimum system requirements (Windows version): IBM or compatible 386. CD-ROM drive with MS-DOS CD-ROM Extensions 2.0. MS-DOS 5.0. Windows 3.1. 8MB RAM. Minimum system requirements (Macintosh version): Macintosh 68030. CD-ROM drive. 8MB RAM. $350.00/institutions. ISBN 0-231-10518-5.

To search *Bartlett's Familiar Quotations* (see ARBA 82, entry 109) for a simple quotation on philosophy, one must dig through an entire column of indexed references. With this new CD-ROM, it will take about five seconds. The main screen offers the three most common search types, by author, by subject, and by source title, as well as the option of searching by keywords of the forgotten quotation. The answers are returned in a scrollable list. Clicking on each individual line reveals the quotation, its origin, and brief biographical data of its author. The entire list may be organized according to quotation, subject, author, gender, or nationality. The editors boast 70,000 quotations and 150 contributors. A second screen offers an advanced search, allowing for use of Boolean logic. Here first names of authors, author's or speaker's nationality, occupation, century, gender, publication date, or even a character's name in a novel or movie may be entered.

The search engine is amazingly fast, running on a 486DX2/66MHz, Windows 3.1, and 12MB RAM. The program installed in five minutes on this machine. There is an online help manual that every user should study. Although much of the program is intuitively designed, it does contain certain peculiarities that are necessary to know. One such example is the ubiquitous use of the question mark as a wild card. One disappointment with the program was the display. This reviewer was unable to drag-and-size to fit the desktop. It covered a mere one-third. Moreover, even at a rather steep price tag, the display is rather anachronistic looking, something one would expect from an old DOS program (which is a recommended format, along with Windows and Macintosh). Some "radio buttons" would have been nice, at least. Finally, why distribute to only institutions? This would be a welcome addition to many households, but at a more reasonable price. [R: RBB, 1 Dec 96, p. 680; SLMQ, Fall 96, p. 63]—**Kenneth I. Saichek**

69. Ginsberg, Susan. **Family Wisdom: The 2,000 Most Important Things Ever Said About Parenting, Children, and Family Life.** New York, Columbia University Press, 1996. 315p. index. $19.95. ISBN 0-231-10376-X.

This is a book of 2,000 quotations about parenting, children, and family life. The quotations were taken from journal articles and books written by prominent persons in the field, well-known writers, and journalists. Most of them come from twentieth-century sources. The quotations are insightful and witty and deal with such topics as conflicts between parents and children, working mothers, television, and poverty. They reflect all aspects of family life. An index of sources lists, alphabetically by name, the persons quoted and the section in the book in which the quotation appears. Specific subject areas may be located through the table of contents, which lists four general subjects, each of which is subdivided by many specific topics along with the page numbers where they may be found.

This book is well researched and organized. It provides quotations on family relations that are not easily available elsewhere. The work is not an essential purchase for libraries, but it may be useful in collections serving populations in the human services as a source of material for speeches and research papers.
—**Marilyn Strong Noronha**

70. **The New Beacon Book of Quotations by Women.** By Rosalie Maggio. Boston, Beacon Press, 1996. 844p. index. $35.00. ISBN 0-8070-6782-2.

This volume features approximately 16,000 quotations by 2,600 women from 6 continents and from ancient times to the present. The women quoted here are writers, artists, scientists, musicians, politicians, scholars, and celebrities. The editor states that 80 percent of the quotations do not appear in other sources. The quotations are arranged by topic in nearly 1,000 subject areas that range from abortion and birth control to football, money, tea, and youth. The name index at the end of the volume enables the reader to locate quotations by specific women, and the subject/key line index allows one to quickly find desired topics. The work is comprehensive and well researched. For all quotations, the person quoted, the source of statement, and the year are given. This book belongs on all library shelves next to *Bartlett's* and will be especially welcome in libraries with extensive women's collections.—**Marilyn Strong Noronha**

71. **The Oxford Dictionary of Humorous Quotations.** Ned Sherrin, ed. New York, Oxford University Press, 1995. 543p. index. $39.95. ISBN 0-19-214244-5.

Sherrin is the presenter of BBC Radio 4's *Loose Ends*, a weekly satiric roundup of international news. This partially explains the preponderance of British authors and the fact that many of the quotations are not particularly humorous to Americans. There are a variety of persons quoted, including comedians, playwrights, actors, musicians, novelists, cartoonists, businesspeople, lawyers, soldiers, and so on. The approximately 5,000 quotations are categorized and numbered for quick access. There are author and keyword indexes, and cross-references. Front matter includes a three-page, two-column "List of Themes" to assist in locating a topical quote. The theme "Actors and Acting," with a cross-reference to "The Theatre," is typical of the way the quotations are listed. The sayings are numbered in bold typeface and are followed by the name and dates of the author and the work from which the quote came. Thus, "Actors and Acting" #32 is a quote from John Barrymore (1882-1942) reported by Eddie Cantor in *The Way I See It* (1959). The work is legibly printed and sturdily bound. No library can ever have too many books of quotations. [R: LJ, 1 June 96, p. 98; Choice, Sept 96, p. 104; SLJ, June 96, pp. 170-71]
—**Frank J. Anderson**

72. **Women's Words: The Columbia Book of Quotations by Women.** By Mary Biggs. New York, Columbia University Press, 1996. 501p. index. $24.95. ISBN 0-231-07986-9.

Quotations by women on various subjects, from abnormality to beauty contests, football to mother-daughter relationships, sex symbols to yearning, fill this 500-page volume. Biggs has strived to supply quotations on "the humblest questions and the deepest philosophical issues" (jacket flap); in short, wit and wisdom from beyond the range of so-called women's concerns (i.e., home, marriage, family) or even women's issues. She supplies the curious browser or researcher with quotations from the well known to the obscure to the anonymous. Many of the sayings have never before been anthologized; familiar maxims profiled in *Bartlett's Familiar Quotations* (see ARBA 82, entry 109) or other well-known quotation sources do not appear in *Women's Words*. This is the book to consult for insight into women's opinions, thoughts, and feelings on pertinent or merely interesting topics.

The format is similar to that of *The Columbia Dictionary of Quotations* (see ARBA 95, entry 88): Quotations are arranged under alphabetic topics. However, rather than being listed under said topics alphabetically by quoter (as in the original Columbia title), these sayings are listed in chronological order. A helpful feature in *Women's Words* not found in *Columbia* is a detailed table of contents listing each subject. This provides access to page number in addition to access by category and quotation number found in the index. While the format of the two works may be similar, the content is not. Although many categories overlap, few quotations do (at least none that this reviewer could find). This exclusivity of the work is both a plus and a minus. Lack of repetitiveness supports purchase of both works, but many interesting quotations found in *Columbia* could also have been included in *Women's Words*.

Among the 3,000-plus citations, readers will find thought-provoking insights and commentaries from such women as Susan B. Anthony, Hillary Rodham Clinton, Sojourner Truth, Golda Meir, and Queen Elizabeth I, as well as from lesser-known or even anonymous women. Each saying supplies the speaker (if known), birth and death dates, some biographical information, where and when the quotation was spoken, and the context, where applicable. Although there are quotations from women all over the world, those by Western women predominate. Despite this small criticism, *Women's Words* is a worthy acquisition for both public and personal libraries. [R: RBB, 1 Dec 96, p. 680]—**Melissa Rae Root**

Part II
SOCIAL SCIENCES

2 Social Sciences in General

SOCIAL SCIENCES IN GENERAL

73. **Dictionary of Ethics, Theology, and Society.** Paul Barry Clarke and Andrew Linzey, eds. New York, Routledge, 1996. 926p. index. $125.00. ISBN 0-415-06212-8.

This misleadingly titled book covers a hodgepodge of theological, social, and political topics in 250 brief essays varying in length from 2 to 12 pages and written by slightly more than 150 academics, mostly British or North American. Apart from a general article on ethics and a briefer one on lying, most of the treatment accorded this subject is of the applied ethics variety, with little consideration given to formal aspects of this major subdivision of philosophy. The point of view is usually liberal in one sense or another and almost always specifically Christian, so much so in fact that the absence of these terms from the title might be thought deceptive.

The editors' introduction asserts that "Western society continues to be deeply indebted to the Judeo-Christian tradition and its synthesis with political and social thought" (p. vii). On the whole, this is a fair indication of the book's tenor, although again it understates (or passes over) the two major biases indicated above. There are articles on Protestantism, Adventism, Anglicanism, Baptists, Catholicism (point of view is Roman Catholic), Lutheranism, Methodism, Quakerism, Unitarianism, and black theology (i.e., of Christian persuasion), but none on Judaism or (perhaps significantly) Calvinism. The article on black Muslims scants theological issues, and there are no articles on Islam or on Buddhism, even though each of these religions now has a significant presence in the West. The article on "Soul" does cover major world religions, and that on the Holocaust may in its breadth redeem the purely Christian cast of the one on atonement. However, these are isolated exceptions in a volume whose real theological interests are represented by such articles as "Christology," "Grace," and "Trinity."

On the social and political side, there are articles on such larger topics as business, city, culture, economy, human rights, international relations, justice, law, society, state, violence, and war, as well as on more specific ones, such as abortion, embryo research, monetarism, multinational companies, nuclear weapons, trade unions, and usury. An article entitled "Green" is almost entirely on the Greens; although there is no corresponding "Red," there is an article on Marxism. The social agenda of the editors is clear from such articles as "Apartheid," "Child Abuse," "Homophobia," "Hunting," "Political Correctness," "Rape," "Sexism," "Speciesism," and "Vivisection," while topics of perhaps greater concern to political or social conservatives seem largely absent.

All of the articles are outfitted with brief bibliographies reflecting the ideological and other limitations of their coverage. The index is helpful but by no means complete or thorough. This book is recommended for Christian (especially Protestant) high schools, colleges, universities, seminaries, and divinity schools. Some nondenominational libraries that can afford it may also find this a useful supplement, especially on topics of current social interest, to information already made available from other sources. [R: Choice, Nov 96, p. 427]—**John B. Dillon**

74. Krantz, Les, and Jim McCormick. **The Peoplepedia: The Ultimate Reference on the American People.** New York, Henry Holt, 1996. 474p. illus. index. (A Henry Holt Reference Book). $25.00. ISBN 0-8050-3727-6.

As one of the world's social, economic, and political leaders, the United States, with the third largest population of 263 million, consistently attracts international attention. People want to know who U.S. people are; where they live; how they think, work, and play; what they are interested in; how they spend their incomes; who the prominent individuals are; and so on. *The Peoplepedia* answers all these questions in a book that is the first of its kind. It accomplishes the work of *Statistical Abstract of the United States* (see ARBA 96, entry 920), *Who's Who in America* (see ARBA 96, entry 37), and the Social Issues Resources Series as if these three resources were combined into one volume. Admittedly, the entries are fewer and more abbreviated. Nevertheless, it offers an interesting self-portrait of U.S. people through brief articles, pictures, charts, and graphs.

The book is divided into three sections. Part 1, "The American Mindset," covers what U.S. citizens think about issues from morality to feminism to faith healing. Part 2, "The American Collective," is subdivided into 11 chapters, each dealing with broad areas of U.S. life, such as education, families, populations, sexuality, possessions, and more. Last, part 3 consists of short biographical entries of people who were active in their professions during the writing of this book. All charts and graphs give sources for further research. Also included are a general index and an appendix of notable people categorized by profession. This reference resource is recommended for public libraries, high school libraries, and academic libraries with an undergraduate emphasis, but would be equally appropriate on a coffee table for intriguing browsing. [R: Choice, Dec 96, pp. 590-91]—**Elizabeth D'Antonio-Gan**

75. **The Social Science Encyclopedia.** 2d ed. Adam Kuper and Jessica Kuper, eds. New York, Routledge, 1996. 923p. $99.95. ISBN 0-415-10829-2.

The difference between a companion and an encyclopedia is not entirely clear, but this volume's coverage seems more akin to that of the former than the latter. The entries are of consistently high quality, and a few are exemplary, but a reader hoping to learn a bit about backward-bending supply curves or a theme as central to geography as location theory would find little help here. Even so, it is salutary to have in a single volume thoughtful treatment of key phenomena; concepts; and influential practitioners and thinkers in the disciplines of anthropology, economics, geography, history, philosophy, politics, psychology, and sociology as well as in more applied fields, such as communications, industrial relations, and psychiatry.

Some entries are almost entirely analytic (e.g., "Authority") while others chronicle a topic's historical development (e.g., "Reason, Rationality, and Rationalism"). On the whole, the entries tend to be limited to the discussion of recent trends: "Colonialism," for instance, treats only modern European activities, saying virtually nothing about the colonial practices of Greece, Rome, China, or any other of the many expansionist powers in world history. Most of the contributors are from Great Britain, Europe, or Commonwealth nations, and they write with a degree of clarity that often eludes American social scientists. Entries include both references and suggestions for further reading, making the volume an excellent starting point for interested laypeople. [R: Choice, Oct 96, p. 258; RBB, 1 April 96, p. 1390]
—**Glenn Petersen**

76. **The Social Sciences: A Cross-Disciplinary Guide to Selected Sources.** 2d ed. Nancy L. Herron, ed. Englewood, Colo., Libraries Unlimited, 1996. 323p. index. (Library and Information Science Text Series). $43.00; $32.00pa. ISBN 1-56308-309-4; 1-56308-351-5pa.

This book seeks to be a guide to reference resources in the social sciences and a teaching tool for students who need to learn about these sources. The volume consists of 12 chapters on reference literature mainly in individual disciplines—a chapter on general reference, 7 chapters on "established" disciplines, 2 on "emerging" disciplines, and 2 on disciplines with "recognized social implications." The volume includes author, title, and subject indexes.

The inclusion of business, education, or law as social science disciplines is questionable, but is an obvious accommodation to the realities of higher education today. But what of linguistics? Why not devote separate but equal attention to fields such as women's studies or social work instead of forcing them into a field such as sociology? This kind of classificatory practice seems to reflect more an old-fashioned misunderstanding of the development of academic specialization than the progressive mantle of interdisciplinary chic.

As a reference tool, this volume lacks organizational consistency across chapters. For example, one chapter groups "current awareness tools" together, yet another similar group of resources is listed as "electronic resources." This problem is reproduced in the volume's subject index also. For a volume that claims uniqueness for its attention to these resources, this is hardly a minor complaint. Ultimately, these flaws are not fatal. This volume should be in the collections of most academic and public libraries because it is an inexpensive, handy, annotated guide to more than 1,100 sources. The innovations of this edition—updated annotations and the inclusion of electronic resources—not only make it a good replacement for the earlier edition (see ARBA 91, entry 74), but also earn it a place among other reference guides.

—David V. Waller

77. Walden, Graham R., comp. **Polling and Survey Research Methods, 1935-1979: An Annotated Bibliography.** Westport, Conn., Greenwood Press, 1996. 581p. index. (Bibliographies and Indexes in Law and Political Science, no.25). $99.50. ISBN 0-313-27790-7.

Walden has produced another excellent annotated bibliography on polling and survey research methods that serves as a retrospective to his 1990 publication, *Public Opinion Polls and Survey Research* (see ARBA 91, entry 82). The volume currently under review begins with work from the mid-1930s when Gallup and Roper began their polls. They were among the first to use scientific sampling in polling and survey research. By 1947, the American Association for Public Opinion Research was founded in response to this growing field. This bibliography provides information on 1,013 items, covering this time period until 1979. The primary disciplines treated are agriculture, economics, education, law, library science, mass media, medicine, political science, psychology, public relations, social work, and sociology.

Walden has designed this source to be of use to practitioners, researchers, students, and librarians. It will be of particular use to those interested in the history of the development of polls and surveys. All items in the bibliography can be acquired through interlibrary loan from at least one library—which is a useful feature. There are 17 major divisions of the subject (e.g., instructional material, history, design and planning, sampling, interviewing). The methodology, coverage, and explanations of the citations and annotations (descriptive, nonevaluative) are carefully explained in the introduction. There are four appendixes (acronyms, source journals, print and CD-ROM sources, and organizations) and author and selective keyword indexes. This bibliography is a well-researched, well-written volume, and it will be a valuable addition to any academic library because it covers an important aspect of so many disciplines.

—Michele Russo

78. **World Databases in Social Sciences.** C. J. Armstrong and R. R. Fenton, eds. New Providence, N.J., Bowker-Saur/Reed Reference Publishing, 1996. 793p. index. (World Databases Series). $235.00. ISBN 1-85739-116-0.

World Databases in Social Sciences represents a major effort to bring together information on electronic databases throughout the world. The directory is divided into 11 sections: social sciences/sociology, social science in general, ethnic studies/anthropology, urban and rural studies, women/children/elderly, social medicine/handicapped, substance abuse, demography, psychology, social policy and services, and opinion polls. Under each entry, the master record is fully explained, including information on type of database, year of initiation, languages, coverage, number of records, update period, update size, downloadable status, sources, and index unit. Following this information is a detailed narrative description of the database with occasional reference to third-party reviews. The various databases are described in sufficient detail for the user to determine relevance and overall structure before embarking upon a search. Four indexes round out the volume: a list of all vendor addresses, a subject index, a producer index, and a database name index. *World Databases in Social Sciences* is an essential purchase for the modern electronic library, and the editors and publisher should be complimented for a well-executed reference tool. Perhaps the next edition will appear in a digital format. [R: Choice, Nov 96, p. 440]

—Arthur P. Young

3 Area Studies

GENERAL WORKS

79. **Junior Worldmark Encyclopedia of the Nations.** Timothy L. Gall, Susan Bevan Gall, and others, eds. Detroit, U*X*L/Gale, 1996. 9v. illus. maps. index. $225.00/set. ISBN 0-7876-0741-X.

Young students will appreciate this well-organized set of information on countries of the world. The 35 numbered headings are consistent for all of the 193 entries, Afghanistan through Zimbabwe, making it possible for the user to quickly compare 2 or more countries. Headings cover geography and environment, history, population and culture, government, economy, health and education, recreation, famous people, and additional bibliographic sources for each.

Entries begin with illustrations of the national emblem and flag of the country in question; the name of the capital; and brief information about the anthem, currency, weights and measurement system, holidays, and international time difference. However, emblems and flags are displayed in black-and-white, and students must refer to a color symbol key at the beginning of the volume. This is one drawback in an otherwise excellent reference tool. The encyclopedia does not provide a heading for ethnic food, which would be helpful.

Each entry has a map of the country showing major cities and adjoining countries plus graphic presentation of some data, including a chart of social indicators comparing the country to averages for low-income and high-income countries and to the United States. More than 300 black-and-white photographs throughout the entire set reflect daily life and scenery one may expect to see in that country. All volumes end with a comprehensive glossary. Volume 9 contains an index to the full set.

This set is highly recommended for student use. The publisher also offers a companion set, four volumes of in-depth information about U.S. states and territories (*Junior Worldmark Encyclopedia of the States* [1996]) for $100. [R: RBB, 1 May 96, p. 1530; SLJ, Aug 96, p. 182]—**Jean Engler**

80. **The World Factbook 1996-97.** By the Central Intelligence Agency. McLean, Va., Brassey's (U.S.), 1996. 557p. maps. $32.95. ISBN 1-57488-014-4. ISSN 0277-1527.

This title is a direct reprint, without the colored maps, of the U.S. government publication of the same name and is a handy basic reference on the politics, economics, and general demographics of all the nations of the world. Brassey's hardcover version is priced reasonably and is physically well made. However, the following points should be kept in mind. First, contrary to the publisher's claim of a "limited audience" for this title, it is readily available. Second, as the publisher does admit on the verso of the title page, Brassey's reprints are dated later than the original, so that the present title is, in fact, the text labeled as 1995 by the government, not an updated version.

Those interested in this valuable source may find machine-readable versions via the World Wide Web (essentially free other than network charges) and in several CD-ROM and diskette formats from National Technical Information Service (NTIS) for $30 or less. Paperback copies are available in depository libraries, and may be purchased from NTIS for $29 as well. Much of the information is also available in other commercial products, notably the *Time Magazine Compact Almanac* CD-ROM. [R: BL, Aug 96, p. 1919]—**James H. Sweetland**

81. **Year Book of the Muslim World 1996: A Handy Encyclopaedia.** Mohammed Nasir Jawed, ed. New Delhi, Medialine; distr., Columbia, Mo., South Asia Books, 1996. 776p. illus. maps. $36.00. ISBN 81-86420-00-2.

This 1st edition of the *Year Book* has been published in order to inform its readers about the "latest stories and events that [have taken] place in the Muslim World" (prologue). Introductory material includes an overview of events in Bosnia; comments on flash points such as Somalia, Eritrea, and Afghanistan; essays explaining Pakistan's elections and the Kashmir situation; and an analysis of Chechnya. Thereafter, the book is divided into seven parts: information on Islam and historical information of the Islamic world, facts concerning contemporary Muslim countries, information about current Muslim societies, the economies of Muslim states, scientific and technological information about the Islamic world, and sporting achievements within the same group of states. The book concludes with a section on Palestine, including reprints of the documents signed by Israel and the new Palestine Authority in 1993.

Each section contains copious material. For example, one can find an explanation of the Islamic calendar, paragraph-length biographies of significant twentieth-century Muslims, lists of media outlets in every Muslim state, and a comparison of the armed forces (including defense expenditures) of Muslim states. However, the quality of the book's presentation detracts considerably from the volume's overall worth. For instance, some charts are not labeled; many terms are not defined for the lay reader (e.g., *Talaq* on p. 59); a chronology leaves out the period 550-750 C.E.; and there are historically inaccurate and suspect comments. For example, Dante Alighieri is described as the greatest writer in Latin. Consequently, while the volume does contain considerable information, there are probably better sources for said information.
—**David L. White**

UNITED STATES

General Works

82. **Macmillan Color Atlas of the States.** By Mark T. Mattson. New York, Macmillan Library Reference/Simon & Schuster Macmillan, 1996. 377p. illus. maps. $100.00. ISBN 0-02-864659-2.

Rich in facts and as inviting as a cornucopia, the Macmillan atlas spills out a pleasurable 4-color guided tour of the 50 states, Washington, D.C., Puerto Rico, the U.S. Virgin Islands, Guam, American Samoa, and the Northern Mariana Islands. The delightful layout and clear subheadings entice the student, teacher, parent, librarian, and general reader. Within this hefty volume are flap copy synopsizing the contents and a clever pictorial table of contents—a subdued U.S. map featuring red-lettered page numbers of entries alphabetized by state. The formal table of contents precedes acknowledgments. A surprisingly unattractive and unimaginative two-page introduction does a poor job of initiating young readers into the purpose and reference style of an atlas. Models and sidebars would help.

Each state receives a seven-page entry. The first page of the entry features the seal and motto, which is translated into English. Legal holidays and a brief history of the state flag are followed by festivals and events and a small map situating the state in its region (e.g., Colorado set among Montana, Idaho, Wyoming, Utah, Nevada, Arizona, and New Mexico). Alongside the cluster are figures comparing the other states in population and a list repeating state capitals. The right column covers revenues and expenditures and general financial data, such as per capita income and sales tax. A second map indicates the size, location, boundaries, and measurements of the state. A paragraph on facts includes the origin of the state name; the nickname; and the state song, bird, and tree. It is unusual for a quality reference work to pass up an opportunity to picture these last two details.

The second page offers a scale map featuring highways, cities, airports, lakes, state parks, welcome centers, county seats, and educational institutions. Cultural attractions are described more fully below. Additional pages cover weather, topography, land use, hydrology, history, events, population figures and projections, famous citizens, ethnicity, education, economy, and resources. A pie chart displays employment percentages. The body concludes with a handy columnar listing of facts by state. An unexplained one-page appendix discusses the environmental quality in six states.

Macmillan excels at layout and graphics. Page numbers in red are easy to spot, typefaces are clear, and maps are subtly shaded. The details are suited to young readers. Mattson has done a masterful job of using space to advantage. However, text is marred by unsubtle nuances (e.g., Arizona rejects the holiday honoring Martin Luther King Jr., frequent mention of polygamy in Mormon history); questionable priorities (e.g., biographer Katharine Anthony over Maya Angelou); and omissions (e.g., Black Hills revered as sacred ground, U.S. presidents born in North Carolina), all of which indicate the need for better editing. Historical content favors athletes, outlaws, politicians, and movie stars, and misses opportunities to pinpoint the Trail of Tears and the Long Walk and to honor great Native American speakers, philosophers, artisans, and leaders.

Overall, the writing is heavy-handed and male-centered. California's entry ignores Japanese internment at Camp Manzanar and the work of conservationist John Muir and the Sierra Club, but allots five lines to riots, two to assassination, six to earthquakes and fire, and seven to the O. J. Simpson trial. North Carolina's entry overemphasizes the utterances of Jesse Helms but omits comment on evangelist Billy Graham. A library reference work costing $100 can do better. [R: RBB, 1 Nov 96, pp. 536-38]

—Mary Ellen Snodgrass

California

83. Hansen, Gladys. **San Francisco Almanac: Everything You Want to Know About Everyone's Favorite City.** rev. ed. San Francisco, Calif., Chronicle Books, 1995. 430p. illus. maps. index. $16.95pa. ISBN 0-8118-0841-6.

This monumental collection of information can answer almost any question about San Francisco. The facts and figures are organized under 47 subjects, both historical and contemporary, arranged alphabetically from accolades to weather. The city and county of San Francisco are described in terms of governmental organization; officials, including mayors and department heads with brief biographical sketches, and lists of other officials through the years; place- and street-names; geography and geology; flora and fauna; and maritime history.

A 64-page chronology covers the period of time from the year 1510 to January 14, 1994. Charts present statistics on such topics as tallest buildings, steepest streets, earthquakes, vintage firehouses, shipwrecks, cable car specifications, and population. Black-and-white photographs, some historical, show persons, buildings, bridges, and scenic views. There are even lists of songs about San Francisco and of films photographed in and about the city. There is one map, which shows some of the major districts, but it is not accessible through the index or table of contents. Subsequent editions might have their reference value further enhanced by additional maps showing places mentioned in the text and also by a list of charts, tables, and photographs.

This will be a basic reference source for both public and academic libraries in California and in larger collections elsewhere. Historians and students of California history will appreciate this aid. Students of natural history will find the section on San Francisco's native flora and fauna to be thorough and helpful. While the work is not intended to be a tourist guide, visitors and new residents should also find it useful.—**Shirley L. Hopkinson**

Florida

84. Servies, James A., and Lana D. Servies. **A Bibliography of Florida. Volume 2: 1846-1880.** Pensacola, Fla., King & Queen Books, 1995. 488p. index. $165.00. ISBN 0-9636370-1-0.

Following publication of the first volume in 1993, this is the second in a series of chronologically arranged bibliographies designed to identify every Florida imprint (known or suspected) as well as all newspapers and periodicals issued in the state. Included here are monographs, articles, corporate and government documents, maps, and broadsides. Volume 1 treated the period from the Age of Discovery year-by-year through 1845 in sequential fashion with 3,106 entries (see ARBA 95, entry 105). Volume 2 continues the sequence beginning with entry 3107 and the year 1846, the first year of statehood, and concludes with coverage of the year 1880 (entry 6898).

Clearly, the work represents a major effort of real value to historians in setting forth the most comprehensive and complete documentation ever provided for a single state; other reviewers have suggested that it serve as a model for subsequent efforts in other states. One of the important purposes is to provide emphasis to those elusive but treasured firsthand reports and narratives written by reputable observers of their time. More remains to be accomplished as the authors' intent is to provide coverage to the end of World War II; the next volume will cover the period from 1881 to the end of the nineteenth century. Most important, the body of the work is thoroughly accessible through its well-constructed, comprehensive index, which includes names of authors, printers, and signatories of documents as well as subjects and topics. Published privately in limited edition through their own bookstore, the authors have made a real contribution to the scholarship of their adopted state. [R: Choice, Feb 96, p. 934]

—**Ron Blazek**

New York

85. Grabowski, John, and David Rhoden, comps. **Awesome Almanac—New York.** Walworth, Wis., B & B Publishing, 1995. 208p. illus. maps. index. $14.95pa. ISBN 1-880190-26-5.

Written in a breezy style that should appeal to browsers as well as students, the authors have produced a handy source for information on both famous and not-so-famous New Yorkers, from the founder of "Bible Communism" to the inventor of "xerography." Other topics covered include natural resources, the arts, population statistics, and the state government, as well as a historical overview. Because it was designed for quick reference, the subjects are by no means discussed exhaustively.

One might expect that New York City would receive the major emphasis in such a book, but this is not the case here—this treasury of facts does not ignore the rest of the state. A New York State day-by-day chronology, as well as the many lists of New Yorkers by categories (Hall of Famers in various sports, Medal of Honor recipients, and so on), should prove ideal for school assignments.

There are numerous black-and-white photographs, illustrations, and maps, but the book would have been more useful had each chapter contained references or suggestions for further reading, rather than one selected bibliography at the end. The price should allow purchase of additional copies for the circulating collection. The almanac is highly recommended for all New York libraries, and for anywhere there is an interest in the Empire State.—**John A. Drobnicki**

Ohio

86. Benson, Marjorie, comp. **Awesome Almanac—Ohio.** Walworth, Wis., B & B Publishing, 1995. 208p. illus. maps. index. $14.95pa. ISBN 1-880190-19-2.

The subtitle on the cover reads "A Treasury of Facts and Fictions, Celebrities and Celebrations, and the Weird and Wonderful!" This paperback book does indeed contain a wide variety of trivial information; for example, who knows that Don Novello (Father Guido Sarducci of *Saturday Night Live*) was born on January 1, 1943, in Ashtabula? There are 10 chapters covering sports, entertainment, business and industry, government, and so on. The chapter headings and subheadings are not very revealing and provide only minimal guidance. Because of the lack of sound organization and the miscellaneous nature of the information, use of the index is required (although the index is primarily proper names, with few subject entries). There are no cross-references or references from the individual entries to sources and the relatively few statistics buried in the text.

This text is definitely a general/popular interest item; one can imagine patrons happily browsing it to pass some time. The work does provide a chronology, photographs and drawings, outline maps, and a list of selected references. Similar almanacs currently exist or are being prepared for several other states by the same publisher. (See entries 85 and 89 for reviews of others in the series.) Primarily of interest to all types of Ohio libraries, the almanac could go in the circulating collection, due to its low price.

—**Daniel K. Blewett**

87. **The Dictionary of Cleveland Biography.** David D. Van Tassel and John J. Grabowski, eds. Cleveland, Ohio, Case Western Reserve University and the Western Reserve Historical Society and Bloomington, Ind., Indiana University Press, 1996. 545p. index. $75.00. ISBN 0-253-33055-6.

88. **The Encyclopedia of Cleveland History.** 2d ed. David D. Van Tassel and John J. Grabowski, eds. Cleveland, Ohio, Case Western Reserve University and the Western Reserve Historical Society and Bloomington, Ind., Indiana University Press, 1996. 1165p. illus. maps. index. $59.95. ISBN 0-253-33056-4.

This two-volume set is a revision and expansion of the *Encyclopedia of Cleveland History*, published in 1987 (see ARBA 88, entry 519). The new work is divided into a volume containing historic information about Cleveland and its environs, and another containing biographies. Each is alphabetically arranged. While the title refers to Cleveland, the articles include information concerning all of Cuyahoga County and its social, economic, and religious development. Cross-references to other articles in the set are indicated, and many articles are followed by bibliographic citations. The typeface and page layouts are clearer and more attractive than in the original.

The historical volume contains the original articles, revised and updated, plus almost 400 new articles. The general entries, 200 to 500 words in length, describe specific cities, organizations, churches, businesses, schools, and so forth. The signed, interpretive essays, 500 to 4,000 words in length, explore such major topics as hospitals and health planning, music, and real estate. The original maps and charts have been updated, and select photographs enhance the text. The historical volume has two indexes: a subject guide that lists each entry under a relevant subject and an alphabetic index of personal, corporate, and community names and events.

The biographical volume contains approximately 1,500 entries, 600 new to this edition. The two main criteria for inclusion were that the person must have died prior to June 1, 1995, and must have lived in the Cleveland area long enough to have contributed significantly to its development and to have been affected by it. All of the entries are about the same length. Unfortunately, this means that interesting facts found in the original volume have sometimes been cut for the sake of space, and people of greater importance are given the same space as those of lesser import. Articles written by one individual are followed by that person's initials. There are no photographs in this volume. Two indexes are supplied: a name index of individuals, places, corporations, and institutions, and a subject guide listing individuals' names under fields of endeavor, such as "education," "communication," and the like. This subject guide is, at times, poor. "Neighborhoods" has two names listed under it. Were no others involved in neighborhoods? Also, few scientists are listed under "science"; others are misidentified as being in other fields.

Both volumes are interesting to read and are useful reference tools. Each can stand on its own, but is best used in conjunction with the other. The 1st edition of the encyclopedia should be retained for the historical information that has been edited from it.—**Kathleen Farago**

Texas

89. Martin, Suzanne, comp. **Awesome Almanac—Texas.** Walworth, Wis., B & B Publishing, 1995. 208p. illus. maps. index. $14.95pa. ISBN 1-880190-22-2.

This entertaining guide to trivia and history includes information about hundreds of people, places, and things Texan. The publishers have "awesome almanacs" for more than a dozen states (see entries 85 and 86 for reviews of others in the series). The book is arranged into 10 general categories, such as sports, nature, business, and entertainment. Most entries are 100-150 words in length, but some are longer. The pages are rarely dull; each one provides a graphic, and some especially interesting entries are highlighted as "awesome." An interesting feature is the "Texas One Day at a Time" calendar of dates in Texas history or on famous Texans. The text is written in a chatty style.

Unlike other Texas almanacs, such as the *Texas Almanac and State Industrial Guide* (see ARBA 93, entry 111), the coverage in this book is limited. For those unacquainted with Texas, it may be a fun first guide suitable for browsing; but for most people, it will seem superficial. Because there are others for less money that have more than twice as much material, this book is recommended only for public and school libraries that would like an additional fun reference work on Texas.—**Edward Erazo**

AFRICA

General Works

90. Blackhurst, Hector. **East and Northeast Africa Bibliography.** Lanham, Md., Scarecrow, 1996. 301p. index. (Scarecrow Area Bibliographies, no.7). $62.50. ISBN 0-8108-3090-6.

This seventh volume in Scarecrow's Area Bibliographies series covers Djibouti, Eritrea, Ethiopia, Kenya, Somalia, Sudan, Tanzania, and Uganda. The book's excellent introduction explains its scope and arrangement, as well as listing other sources for further research. The bibliography contains 3,838 numbered entries, each for a publication of more than 40 pages in length published from 1960 on, primarily in the humanities and social sciences. Most of the books covered are in English, but some are in French, Italian, or German. Entries for each country, East Africa, and Northeast Africa are subdivided by subject headings chosen to "reflect the nature of the literature on that country rather than some predetermined scheme." Other entries are listed under people or significant events. An author index at the back refers to entry numbers.

The care and knowledge that went into this bibliography are obvious. The author's extensive expertise in East and Northeast Africa justifies his forfeiture of any standard subject headings in favor of meaningful ones of his own creation. Such headings as "Somalia—Trees" or "Tanzania—Handicrafts" make this book more useful than the usual area bibliography. Exclusion of facsimile reprints is a welcome relief. An arbitrary decision to exclude coffee-table books on wildlife and travel will hardly impinge on the serious researcher. The classic texts excluded because they were published before 1960 are made known to the reader through the bibliographies that Blackhurst discusses in the introduction. This handy volume will serve as an excellent starting place for the serious researcher, as well as a tidy single source for a more cursory study of East and Northeast Africa.—**Cathy Seitz Whitaker**

91. **The Encyclopaedia Africana Dictionary of African Biography. Volume Three: South Africa-Botswana-Lesotho-Swaziland.** L. H. Ofosu-Appiah, ed. Algonac, Mich., Reference Publications, 1995. 304p. illus. maps. index. $75.00. ISBN 0-917256-21-2.

Until recently, reliable sources on African historical events and biographies of important contributors to African development were not readily available. *Encyclopaedia Africana Dictionary of African Biography* is quickly changing the situation. Volume 3 in the series, covering South Africa, Botswana, Lesotho, and Swaziland, is an excellent retrospective biographical dictionary of southern Africa. From Abdurahman through Mohandas K. Gandhi to Zwide, the biographies are accurate, current, well written, concise, and accessible to all readers, including the professional historian and the casual reader. The coverage is balanced and encompasses the great historical African leaders (such as Shaka) and the practitioners of apartheid (such as Voster).

The book begins with a historical introduction to the peoples and countries, as well as major historical events of the region, and provides a glossary of terms at the end. These factors, together with maps of the region, make this reference work extremely user friendly to both the professional and the novice. This volume is an important contribution to the understanding of southern Africa. Unfortunately, the editors of the Encyclopaedia Africana series made a conscious decision to exclude biographies of living persons who have made and continue to make enormous contributions to the development of the region. In spite of this omission, the editors and contributors have done an excellent job in putting this volume together. This volume must be one of the first to be added to any collection of reference works on Africa.

—**Kwabena Gyimah-Brempong**

92. McIlwaine, John. **Writings on African Archives.** New Providence, N.J., published for the Standing Conference on Library Materials on Africa (SCOLMA), Hans Zell/Reed Reference Publishing, 1996. 279p. index. $75.00. ISBN 1-873836-66-X.

Writings on African Archives continues and updates the earlier compilations done by J. D. Pearson (see ARBA 73, entry 252). This current work includes Pearson's citations and supplements them with a record of publications from 1973 through 1994. The bibliography covers material written about African archives and manuscript collections located both within Africa itself and in non-African countries having significant collections.

The work is separated into two parts: Part 1, "Archives in Africa," covers the organization and management practices of archives in African countries and also the writings describing the actual collections housed in African institutions. This part contains a general section for writings covering the entire continent or significant portions of it, followed by broad regions, and is then subdivided by groups corresponding to earlier colonial empires. Each grouping or country is then split into two sections: administrative aspects of archives and records management and a guide to specific collections. Part 2, "Archives Relating to Africa Located Overseas," focuses only on actual collections held in Europe, North America, South America, and Asia. The collections located in each country are divided by general works and relevant volumes of the IGA guides, followed by separate sections for more general geographic areas, and then references to specific regions.

All African countries are represented and the vast majority of citations are post-1963 and in western languages, although all material traced is included regardless of language. Brief annotations are included as needed. A comprehensive index covering authors, titles, and subjects is provided. Overall, this book is a thorough and well-organized supplement to current bibliographic works, although the reader should keep in mind that virtually all of the research was done in British libraries. McIlwaine's work is highly recommended for major research libraries with significant African collections or graduate-level programs. [R: Choice, Nov 96, p. 432]—**Anthony J. Dedrick**

Algeria

93. Lawless, Richard I., comp. **Algeria**. rev. ed. Santa Barbara, Calif., Clio Press/ABC-CLIO, 1995. 309p. index. (World Bibliographical Series, v.19). $89.00. ISBN 1-85109-130-0.

This volume, a revised edition (see ARBA 82, entry 327, for a review of the 1st edition), resembles the nearly 200 other volumes in this series. There are a large number (886) of items divided into a number of classifications, with a plenitude of cross-referencing. As with most other entries in the series, the largest number of items is in the "History" section. Included are title and subject indexes as well as a useful listing of recent theses and dissertations on Algeria in English, in which the United Kingdom is surprisingly well represented. To start the text is a 40-page introduction orienting users to postindependence Algeria.

Also consonant with the rest of the series, English-language titles predominate, even though probably less than 10 percent of the output on Algeria is in that language. The publishers make no bones about this, pointing out that the series is "principally designed for the English speaker" (p. v). Presumably, this means that the intended market is libraries in the United States, Canada, and the British Isles, but there can never be an acceptable scholarly—as opposed to a business—argument for devising bibliographies in which the major criterion is language, especially when the language chosen is so much in a minority.

Luckily, this volume measures well against the long-established characteristics of the series in this respect. The compiler was able to exact a larger leaven of French-language titles, although a much larger proportion of useful French titles is omitted than of those in English. The bibliography compensates for its Anglocentrism by including information on several other bibliographies. Unfortunately, the invaluable *Annuaire de l'Afrique du Nord* is relegated to the section called "The Country and Its People," although cross-referenced in the former section. In sum, this bibliography is a better buy than many titles in this series, but does not provide representative entrée into the vast literature on a vast country. [R: Choice, Oct 96, p. 253]—**David Henige**

Botswana

94. Ramsay, Jeff, Barry Morton, and Fred Morton. **Historical Dictionary of Botswana**. 3d ed. Lanham, Md., Scarecrow, 1996. 321p. (African Historical Dictionaries, no.70). $64.00. ISBN 0-8108-3143-0.

Two of the authors (Fred Morton and Ramsay) of the present work also participated in the previous edition (see ARBA 91, entry 94), so readers may expect similarities in approach and content. This edition is about one-third longer than its immediate predecessor. Written by historians, which has not yet become standard operating procedure for this series, this edition contains much more on the precolonial and colonial periods than most of the African Historical Dictionaries volumes. Still, it may have been improved in a number of ways. For instance, because most of the *kgosis* (paramount rulers) of the various ethnic groups have entries, it would have been helpful for context to have provided chronological lists of these as an appendix. Conversely, the terms in the glossary may well have been integrated into the dictionary proper—only a few are—as several of them (e.g., *morafe*) require more elucidation.

The absence of an index in a work of this kind is unconscionable. While most information about a person or event is likely to be found in the relevant entry, it happens that much ancillary information occurs in other entries. For instance, instead of clustering various battles under "Battle of," an index could have done this, leaving readers to seek out details where they will expect to find them—under the name of the battle. There is an extensive, 60-page bibliography, but, oddly, the number of items under "History" has actually decreased from 345 in the previous edition to 302 in this one.

Although this work is clearly superior to its predecessors, the fact remains that libraries are being asked to purchase a historical dictionary of Botswana for the third time in 20 years. Surely it is fair to ask whether this process had to be quite so incremental. More to the point, does Scarecrow plan to recycle these dictionaries indefinitely, using libraries' standing orders as a smoke screen? To put it another way, why should libraries continue with standing orders for this series anyhow?—**David Henige**

Congo (Brazzaville)

95. Decalo, Samuel, Virginia Thompson, and Richard Adloff. **Historical Dictionary of Congo.** Lanham, Md., Scarecrow, 1996. 379p. (African Historical Dictionaries, no.69). $79.50. ISBN 0-8108-3116-3.

The 1st and 2d editions of *Historical Dictionary of Congo* (formerly titled *Historical Dictionary of the People's Republic of the Congo [Congo-Brazzaville]* [see ARBA 76, entry 250] and *Historical Dictionary of the People's Republic of the Congo* [see ARBA 86, entry 111], respectively), by Thompson and Adloff, have been indispensable sources of material to those who have studied various aspects of the Congo Republic. As good as the 2 previous editions of the book were, the 3d edition, adding Decalo to the roster, is even better and much more comprehensive in its coverage and analysis of events in Congo. Most of the topics in previous editions are retained, expanded and updated, in this edition. The volume also includes a large number of new materials, especially in the areas of politics, economics, and science.

The 316-page dictionary is a comprehensive listing of events, personalities, issues, and all things relevant to Congo. It covers the latest events of the 1990s, as well as those at the beginnings of Congo as a nation in the 1960s. The dictionary is followed by a large bibliography that is divided into 13 subject areas. The bibliography, consisting of listings in both English and French, is preceded by an introduction in which the authors highlight the most influential works in each subsection. A superb introduction to the volume is provided, which pulls together all the major strands of entries into a coherent whole. In particular, the evolution of the political and economic systems in Congo is superb. This book is an excellent addition to the Historical Dictionary series.—**Kwabena Gyimah-Brempong**

Côte d'Ivoire

96. Daniels, Morna, comp. **Côte d'Ivoire.** Santa Barbara, Calif., Clio Press/ABC-CLIO, 1996. 231p. index. (World Bibliographical Series, v.131). $92.50. ISBN 1-85109-120-3.

This work follows the pattern set for the rest of the bibliographies in this series. It is designed as an introduction for English speakers who have little or no knowledge of the Côte d'Ivoire. Its 786 entries are arranged topically, with a short but useful introduction and three indexes (by author, title, subject) appended. The compiler, librarian at the British Library, has added the usual, useful annotations describing the value of each entry. Formerly a colony of France, most of what has been written about the Côte d'Ivoire is in French, and as a result, so are many of the entries in this bibliography (although the compiler has translated their titles into English).

Because the work is introductory in nature, and due to the relative lack of material in English on the topic, the compiler has included a broad spectrum of materials that deal with Africa or West Africa in general, as well as books and journal articles specifically on the Côte d'Ivoire itself. This attempt to include as many English-language sources as possible no doubt explains why, for example, the general periodical *West Africa*, which deals primarily with English-speaking western Africa, is listed, but another general periodical, *Jeune Afrique*, which is devoted to francophone Africa, is not. This book will be a valuable contribution to libraries serving students (especially undergraduates) or that have a large Africana collection—especially because no other general bibliography on the Côte d'Ivoire directed to English speakers currently exists.—**Paul H. Thomas**

Guinea

97. Binns, Margaret, comp. **Guinea.** Santa Barbara, Calif., Clio Press/ABC-CLIO, 1996. 89p. index. (World Bibliographical Series, v.191). $64.75. ISBN 1-85109-148-3.

As noted on the cover, this work (volume 191 of the World Bibliographical Series of country profiles) is the first annotated bibliography on Guinea to be published, although it is not intended to be comprehensive. In the introduction, the compiler recounts her problems in locating publications dealing with this mineral-rich West African nation, noting that, while comparatively little writing on Guinea exists in languages other than French, special effort has been made to seek out and include English texts. Researchers will find this background a useful orientation to the subject literature. All entries are clearly and concisely annotated. The bibliography is recommended for large public libraries and academic reference collections.—**Robert B. Marks Ridinger**

Kenya

98. Coger, Dalvan, comp. **Kenya.** rev. ed. Santa Barbara, Calif., Clio Press/ABC-CLIO, 1996. 276p. index. (World Bibliographical Series, v.25). $88.00. ISBN 1-85109-257-9.

Although only 15 years have intervened since the 1st edition of this bibliography (see ARBA 83, entry 305), the appearance of this revised edition is testimony to how much is being written about Kenya. The number of titles included in this edition (840) is 276 more than in the original version. Coger, a new compiler and professor at the University of South Carolina, has replaced Robert Collison, but he has continued to follow the same basic format (entries arranged alphabetically within subject chapters) as the earlier work, including the useful annotations found with each title. Nevertheless, the table of contents shows modifications that reflect the changes in emphasis in what is being written about Kenya. For example, added chapters or significantly increased titles are found in the areas of human rights, population groups, the Mau Mau rebellion, economics, and women, while chapters on libraries and museums, printing and publishing, and library catalogs have been eliminated.

The chronology is brought up to April 1995 and the most recent publications (books and journal articles) are from 1994. The brief introduction is brought up to the early 1990s. Intended not only for beginning students of Kenya but for those intending to travel there as well, this bibliography deserves a place in most library collections—especially considering that Kenya is undoubtedly one of the most popular travel destinations in Africa for U.S. tourists. Larger collections will want to retain the earlier edition as the annotations for titles that were dropped are still useful. —**Paul H. Thomas**

Mali

99. Imperato, Pascal James. **Historical Dictionary of Mali.** 3d ed. Lanham, Md., Scarecrow, 1996. 363p. (African Historical Dictionaries, no.11). $87.50. ISBN 0-8108-3128-7.

This is the 3d edition of a work originally published in 1977, reviewed in ARBA 78 (see entry 287), and subsequently revised every 10 years by the original author, Imperato. This edition continues the trend of significant expansion and revision: It is 30 percent larger than the 2d edition (see ARBA 87, entry 99).

The principal sections consist of a historical chronology, an introduction, a dictionary, and a bibliography. These are supplemented by a limited number of maps and tables. The 48-page chronology covers primarily the eleventh century through June 1995, and more than half of the section is devoted to events since 1986. The 21-page introduction covers such general topics as agriculture, industry, and administration and has been updated where appropriate since the earlier editions. The extensive dictionary (230 pages) is inclusive, and the entries typically range from a few sentences to a page or more in length. The bibliography section is divided into 10 principal topics, most of which are further subdivided.

Although the citations are not annotated, the author does provide a useful bibliographic overview that includes evaluations of other major bibliographies and specific sources for a number of broad topics, such as culture, social issues, and science. Imperato has placed significant emphasis on recent works (post-1985). A large number of the pre-1970 citations that appeared in the earlier editions of this work have been dropped, but the author cites alternative sources containing most of the entries deleted. Because of the organization and structure of this work, an index is not included, nor is one needed. Students and scholars of Africa should find this much expanded edition useful and easy to use.—**Anthony J. Dedrick**

Mauritania

100. Pazzanita, Anthony G. **Historical Dictionary of Mauritania.** 2d ed. Lanham, Md., Scarecrow, 1996. 315p. maps. (African Historical Dictionaries, no.68). $69.50. ISBN 0-8108-3095-7.

This is a revision of a work by Alfred Gerteiny originally published in 1981 and reviewed in ARBA 82 (see entry 332). Pazzanita is a writer and lawyer who has several other publications dealing with this part of Africa. The 2d edition is more than three times the size of the original, and the format and arrangement are similar to other titles in this series. The work includes a brief but useful user's notes section, a list of abbreviations and acronyms, an eight-page chronology, two basic outline maps, an introduction, the dictionary itself, and a selected bibliography divided into subject categories. The 17-page bibliography of approximately 350 entries contains a significant number of new entries since the 1st edition.

The main dictionary is divided into five broad categories, each of which is further subdivided: general, economic, historical, political, and social. Approximately two-thirds of the citations are in English, with the remainder primarily in French. Unfortunately, the useful set of basic tables dealing with topics, such as gross domestic product and population, present in the earlier edition have been omitted in this work. Nonetheless, the core of this work, with more than 300 entries covering a wide variety of topics, is comprehensive and well written. Most academic and the larger public libraries will want to acquire this compact overview of one of the least-studied countries of Africa.—**Anthony J. Dedrick**

South Africa

101. Musiker, Reuben, and Naomi Musiker. **Southern Africa Bibliography.** Lanham, Md., Scarecrow, 1996. 287p. index. (Scarecrow Area Bibliographies, no.11). $52.00. ISBN 0-8108-3175-9.

This latest joint effort by two internationally recognized South African bibliographers presents the monographic literature pertaining to the 10 countries of the southern African region (Lesotho, Botswana, Swaziland, Malawi, Zambia, Zimbabwe, Mozambique, Angola, South Africa itself, and newly independent Namibia) issued from 1945 through early 1995. The second of the Scarecrow Area Bibliographies series to take a geographic focus, its 4,081 nonannotated entries (more than 60 percent pertaining to South Africa) are arranged alphabetically by country. Subjects included range from citations on art and archaeology, through history and politics, to literature and women's issues interfiled by author and title. The political complexities of the ending of apartheid rule are addressed through the listing of all seven major parties, from the African National Congress to Inkatha.

Language coverage is predominantly English, with selected items in Afrikaans, Portuguese, and German. Readers new to the field of African studies or unfamiliar with the literature on a specific area will find the comprehensive summaries of extant bibliographies given in the introduction an invaluable background. Indexing is provided by author only. This bibliography is essential for reference collections in all types of libraries, particularly in light of the massive changes taking place in this portion of the continent.

—**Robert B. Marks Ridinger**

Tanzania

102. Darch, Colin, comp. **Tanzania.** rev. ed. Santa Barbara, Calif., Clio Press/ABC-CLIO, 1996. 379p. index. (World Bibliographical Series, v.54). $90.00. ISBN 1-85109-219-6.

Containing mostly new or revised entries, this latest edition includes more recent and contemporary publications (see ARBA 86, entry 115, for a review of the 1st edition). Although the compiler notes his extensive use of electronic sources to obtain information, he does limit his citations to print sources. Similar to the earlier edition, the book is organized into thematic chapters, including history, population, religion, statistics, and literature among numerous other topics. The bibliography, as with the other volumes in the World Bibliographical Series, consists almost entirely of English-language sources. The annotations are particularly useful, offering both analytic and critical descriptions of the cited works. A brief introduction provides a sufficient survey of recent history, and the author, title, and subject indexes offer quick access. The work demonstrates the enormous diligence and care of the compiler, encompassing annotated entries ranging from a Tanzanian newspaper to an article on the country's housing published in a scholarly journal. This is an essential bibliography for students and scholars of this East African nation.—**Donald Altschiller**

Togo

103. Decalo, Samuel. **Historical Dictionary of Togo.** 3d ed. Lanham, Md., Scarecrow, 1996. 390p. (African Historical Dictionaries, no.9). $84.00. ISBN 0-8108-3073-6.

The first 2 editions of *Historical Dictionary of Togo* by Decalo (see ARBA 89, entry 101, and ARBA 77, entry 316) have been indispensable and authoritative reference materials for any scholar interested in the study of Togo. The much-expanded and -updated 3d edition of the dictionary is even more authoritative and contains more reference material than the previous 2 editions. Most of the entries in the earlier editions are retained in the 3d, while new topics, events, and personalities are included. In addition to covering the early, optimistic history of Togo, it contains entries about events, activities, and personalities of individuals and organizations that have dragged Togo through social, political, and ethnic conflicts and the resultant economic stagnation of the late 1980s and 1990s. While not giving short shrift to earlier events, the dictionary provides comprehensive coverage of the modern history of Togo.

The dictionary itself is followed by an expanded and comprehensive 90-page bibliography, which is as current as can be. As in other historical dictionaries edited by Decalo, the bibliography is divided into various subject areas to promote ease of use. The book also furnishes some statistical data on population, major cities, budgets for some selected years, and the international trade balance for a few years. To make these data usable to the reader, it should have been presented as a historical series as well as expanded to include data on the evolution of per capita income, price indexes, and other macroeconomic data. In spite of this shortcoming, the book will continue to be the most authoritative source of reference material on Togo, making it a must-have item on the acquisition list of every library and for researchers, policy-makers, and students interested in Africa.—**Kwabena Gyimah-Brempong**

Uganda

104. Nyeko, Balam, comp. **Uganda**. rev. ed. Santa Barbara, Calif., Clio Press/ABC-CLIO, 1996. 346p. index. (World Bibliographical Series, v.11). $85.00. ISBN 1-85109-243-9.

Nyeko—currently a professor of history at the National University of Lesotho; a native of Uganda; and author of several works, including *Swaziland*, a bibliography in this same series (rev. ed.; see ARBA 96, entry 126)—has done an expert job in maintaining the high standards set by Robert L. Collison in the 1st edition (see ARBA 83, entry 309). This revision is significantly larger than its predecessor, containing 798 annotated citations of books and journal articles, compared to 521 in the original edition. The chronology is brought up to mid-1995, as is the short but informative introduction, although the most recent publications cited appear to date from 1994.

The bibliography is arranged in the usual manner for this series: alphabetically by author (or by title if there is no author) within subject chapters, appended to which are three indexes. One curious chapter, however, was entitled "Professional Periodicals," and its contents may have been better placed in their respective subject chapters, as one wonders how many readers would find this topic helpful. As with all the bibliographies in this excellent series, this volume does not attempt to be comprehensive, but it certainly should be considered the place to start for anyone, undergraduate or otherwise, who has little or no background in Uganda. It deserves a place in any good Africana collection.—**Paul H. Thomas**

Western Sahara

105. Pazzanita, Anthony G., comp. **Western Sahara**. Santa Barbara, Calif., Clio Press/ABC-CLIO, 1996. 259p. index. (World Bibliographical Series, v.190). $64.75. ISBN 1-85109-256-0.

This latest addition to the bibliographic resources on the territory of Western Sahara is predominantly composed of materials that "address the development and progress of the armed dispute... by Mauritania, Morocco and the Polisario Front from the mid-1970s to the end of 1995." Contents reflect the expertise of the compiler in international law and a direct familiarity with the scattered literature of this complex topic. Annotations are clear, and arrangement is by author, with the exception of two sections, "Spanish Sahara and the United Nations" and "Politics and Foreign Relations," which are in chronological order due to the large number of official documents cited. Readers unfamiliar with either the region or its political past will find the introductory essay and its accompanying chronology invaluable. Indexing is provided by author, subject, and title. The compiler coedited the 2d edition of the *Historical Dictionary of Western Sahara* (see ARBA 95, entry 110). The title under review is recommended for large public libraries and academic libraries supporting degree programs in African studies, international law, and political science.—**Robert B. Marks Ridinger**

ASIA

Afghanistan

106. Adamec, Ludwig W. **Dictionary of Afghan Wars, Revolutions, and Insurgencies.** Lanham, Md., Scarecrow, 1996. 364p. illus. maps. (Historical Dictionaries of Wars, Revolution, and Civil Unrest, no.1). $48.00. ISBN 0-8108-3232-1.

Although much has been written about Afghanistan as an arena of Kipling's "great game" (one of the entries) and, in recent years, its struggle with the former Soviet Union and the subsequent civil war, this historical dictionary provides a complete overview of the seemingly unceasing wars of the Afghan people during the past two-and-a-half centuries. Written by a well-qualified specialist on Middle Eastern studies who also wrote the *Biographical Dictionary of Afghanistan* (Akademische Druck u. Verlagsanstalt,

1987) and the *Historical Dictionary of Afghanistan* (see ARBA 93, entry 121), this highly useful reference work includes an extensive introduction that presents a historical overview of the wars, revolutions, and insurgencies from past to present.

In the dictionary section, there are entries on each war, and its subheadings. Other entries cover important individuals, tactics, logistics, and weapons. A small number of illustrations are also provided. Two useful sections follow the dictionary: a chronology that lists major events from 1747 to 1996 and a bibliography that includes a representative selection of books and articles in English with just a few titles in French and German. Although the volume is 300-plus pages in length, it is a compact reference tool for readers who are interested in the military history of Afghanistan or its role as an arena in world affairs.—**Hwa-Wei Lee**

China

107. **NTC's Dictionary of China's Cultural Code Words.** By Boye Lafayette De Mente. Lincolnwood, Ill., National Textbook, 1996. 506p. $17.95. ISBN 0-8442-8480-7.

This is not a standard dictionary. The work contains interesting commentaries on Chinese culture and society and cogent cultural comparisons between China and the West, but it is not a practical guide for businesspeople, such as *Nippon Business Handbook* (see ARBA 94, entry 241). The body of the work under review consists of 305 numbered entries covering a Chinese word or phrase. Each term is given in Chinese with two romanizations (pinyin and a nonstandard "intuitive" form), and each term is followed by a one- to four-page essay discussing the cultural significance of the term.

The entries are in alphabetic order by pinyin romanization, and there is a "Guide to Cultural Themes" that lists the 305 entries under 10 general headings such as "Men, Women, and Sex"; "Culture and Customs"; "Ethics, Morality, and Education"; and so on. There is a table of contents, but this includes only the romanization and a rather fanciful title for each entry. For example, entry 2, *an* (which means "peace"), is entitled "Heaven on Earth"; entry 170, *ming yi* (which means "censorship"), is entitled "Keeping a Tight Rein"; and entry 220, *song* (which means "conflict"), is entitled "Knowing When to Run."

The author's one-page preface presents the work to "foreign visitors and businesspeople," but it is hard to imagine anyone totally unfamiliar with Chinese language, culture, and history using this work as a reference tool. The author assumes that readers have a certain general level of knowledge about Chinese culture, for example, that they know about *I Ching (Book of Changes)*. Also, he prefers the Cantonese to the Mandarin romanization for some terms on the grounds that it is "better known." Arranging the work in alphabetic order by pinyin romanization precludes its use as a reference tool. To be used as a dictionary, each essay would have to begin with a literal definition of the term in question, and there would have to be an English index listing the important concepts covered. There would also have to be a Chinese index, so that someone who knows Chinese could look up a term. Without indexes in English and Chinese, a reader must either read the work from beginning to end, browse at random, or browse according to the 10 categories provided in the "Guide." In addition to the above drawbacks, there are some editorial problems.

The dictionary would be better organized as a continuous narrative in 10 chapters corresponding to the 10 categories of the "Guide." Nonetheless, it would make an interesting addition to the general collection of any library serving foreign visitors and businesspeople in need of general works on Chinese culture.
—**Richard H. Swain**

India

108. Mansingh, Surjit. **Historical Dictionary of India.** Lanham, Md., Scarecrow, 1996. 511p. (Asian Historical Dictionaries, no.20). $78.00. ISBN 0-8108-3078-7.

India is one of the oldest countries in the world. Many excellent books have been written on the history of India, but perhaps this is the best ready-reference historical dictionary ever written on the history and current events of India. The dictionary is arranged in alphabetic order and includes entries on people, places, religion, politics, government, and other aspects of the Indian civilization. Entries range from one paragraph to five pages in length depending on the importance, space, and research material available to the author on the ancient, medieval, and modern periods of history. The book includes a list of abbreviations and acronyms, a glossary, and a chronology of Indian history covering the period 400,000 B.C.E. to 1994 C.E. There are a few useful maps of historical India and an extensive bibliography under different subject headings, such as bibliographies and dictionaries; English-language journals; culture; economy; government, politics, security, and international relations; history; modern India; science and technology; society and religion; and education. There are many subheadings under the main subject headings, and all entries have been arranged alphabetically with full bibliographic information. The book has three appendixes: listings of the chief executives in British India, heads of state of independent India, and prime ministers of India.

An added attraction in this book is an excellent introduction by the author. She has given an insightful overview of India. It deals with many aspects of the country, including geographic setting, historical background, and future of the country. The essay talks about the diversity of the nation; its history, culture, people, and different religions; the coming of foreigners to India, including Muslims and Britishers; and the impact of their rule over India and Indians. The introduction deals with the achievements, problems, population, poverty, communalism, the painful division of the country in 1947, and the progress of independent India. It is an excellent addition to the literature, and this book is highly recommended for all historians, scholars of Indian history, and all libraries interested in developing their collections on India.

—**Ravindra Nath Sharma**

Japan

109. De Mente, Boye Lafayette. **Japan Encyclopedia.** Lincolnwood, Ill., Passport Books/National Textbook, 1995. 558p. illus. index. $27.95. ISBN 0-8442-8435-1.

De Mente, who lived in Japan for more than 20 years and wrote such pioneering books as *How to Do Business with the Japanese* (National Textbook, 1987) and *Japanese Etiquette & Ethics in Business* (5th ed., National Textbook, 1987), compiled this complete, one-volume work. The concise yet comprehensive book is a useful companion for tourists, businesspeople, and students, as well as educators and librarians who need information about Japan, the Japanese people, and their culture.

The encyclopedia contains 812 entries; includes a map and 200 illustrations; and covers history, politics, business, economics, the arts, education, and customs. Of the 800-plus entries, 365 are written in English, with Japanese equivalents and phonetic pronunciations as well (e.g., Japan/Nippon (Neep-pone). Approximately 200 entries are Japanese words with phonetic pronunciations (e.g., Sushi [Sue-she]). Each entry, with an explanation ranging from 1 sentence to 15 pages, provides concise and easily understood information. Some entries direct readers to related subjects, and some provide lists for further reading. The line drawings and photographs help explain Japan's uniqueness.

Because about 200 entries are written in Japanese words, it would be helpful for readers if a subject index was provided. However, *Japan Encyclopedia* serves as a unique and comprehensive reference tool for anyone who has an interest in or would like to know more about Japan. [R: Choice, Jan 96, p. 754; RBB, Jan 96, p. 884]—**Sung Ok Kim**

110. Makino, Yasuko, and Mihoko Miki, comps. **Japan and the Japanese: A Bibliographic Guide to Reference Sources.** Westport, Conn., Greenwood Press, 1996. 157p. index. (Bibliographies and Indexes in Asian Studies, no.1). $65.00. ISBN 0-313-26311-6.

This annotated bibliography on Japan and the Japanese is designed for use by students and researchers at any level and also by librarians who develop collections. The bibliography is a useful reference tool to those who depend on English-language sources for their information. The guide consists of two parts and three indexes. Part 1 lists 131 titles for general reference works, while part 2 lists 401 titles for specific subject areas. The general reference area covers general bibliographies, dissertations, encyclopedias, biographies, serial union lists, and directories of organizations both outside and in the United States. The specific subject area covers topics ranging from art, music, and literature to economics, people and society, politics, religion, and science and technology.

A subject phrase search on "Japan—bibliography" in the Research Libraries Group's RLIN databases hits 564 clusters in monographs and 77 clusters in serials in various languages. Even though the guide limits its materials to the English language, it provides a large amount of information and relatively current materials with publication dates after 1980. The annotation of each entry in the bibliography ranges from 10 to 232 words and gives clear explanations of coverage and purpose. Numbered entries, underlined titles, and double spaces between entries and annotations also make this guide easy to use. Author, subject, and title indexes that are directed to the entry numbers are one more helpful aspect. This selected bibliography provides up-to-date information and eases searching.—**Sung Ok Kim**

Mongolia

111. Sanders, Alan J. K. **Historical Dictionary of Mongolia.** Lanham, Md., Scarecrow, 1996. 317p. (Asian Historical Dictionaries, no.19). $47.50. ISBN 0-8108-3077-9.

The Mongol Empire once comprised the biggest empire in history, but modern Mongolia is one of the countries that is largely unnoticed by many Western societies. As a result, there is a lack of knowledge about modern Mongolia. However, Sanders, one of the foremost authorities on the locale, wrote the *Historical Dictionary of Mongolia*, which is published as the 19th volume in a series of Asian historical dictionaries.

Mongolia, newly independent (since 1990) from Soviet domination, has been building its relations with other parts of the world and will require the rest of the world to learn more about them. The dictionary provides entries on the various Mongol tribes and the Communist period with a focus on the persons, institutions, events, and places important in the new Mongolia. The chronology provides information on the long history of Mongolia, from the Genghis Khan's birth in 1162 to affairs in 1994. The bibliography section, which comes after the dictionary section in the book, provides 527 materials for further reading and concentrates on twentieth-century Mongolia. It has a separate contents page, and its subjects cover general, culture, economy, history, politics, science and technology, social, Mongols, and Mongolia's neighbors.

The historical dictionary helps ameliorate the lack of knowledge about modern Mongolia. All of this material is useful for those who want to know more. However, the most important information is that about contemporary Mongolia.—**Sung Ok Kim**

AUSTRALIA

112. **Australia: A Reader's Guide.** John Arnold, Janet Baker, Peter Browne, and Elizabeth Morrison, eds. Port Melbourne, Australia, D. W. Thorpe/Reed Reference Australia and Clayton, Australia, National Centre for Australian Studies, Monash University; distr., New Providence, N.J., Reed Reference Publishing, 1996. 464p. index. $48.00. ISBN 1-875589-24-4.

This reader's guide presents 75- to 100-word annotations of 1,350-plus nonfiction books about Australia as a reference for general readers and Australian and overseas students tackling Australian topics, as well as a reference for researchers, librarians, and journalists. Some entries provide citations to other volumes that are not listed here. To be included, volumes must make a substantial and lasting contribution (even if argumentative or opinionated); as the introduction notes, they must be "survivors"; and they must be "in print, accessible in university and large public libraries [presumably in Australia] or obtainable through the secondhand book trade." The cutoff date is August 1995, and the imprint and accessibility requirements mean that most of the volumes were published in the past 25 or 30 years, although earlier "classics" are included.

The annotations are alphabetically listed within 10 categories: history and heritage (about 25 percent); arts and culture; sports and recreation; habitat; science and technology; politics, foreign relations, and law; the economy; media and communications; Australia today; and reference books. A useful eight-page chapter assists readers in "Finding Australian Books." The excellent index by author, title, and topic allows quick and easy cross-referencing among the categories. This volume is the only selected listing and critical evaluation of books about Australia available today.—**Richard A. Miller**

EUROPE

Albania

113. Hutchings, Raymond. **Historical Dictionary of Albania.** Lanham, Md., Scarecrow, 1996. 277p. (European Historical Dictionaries, no.12). $56.00. ISBN 0-8108-3107-4.

Albania, mountainous and underdeveloped, exotic and little known, is revealed in this dictionary of 450 alphabetically arranged terms. Among the subjects covered are history, politics, culture, religion, international relations, language, economics, and social customs. Main entries are in bold typeface, often followed by a descriptor in parentheses. Birth and death dates are supplied when known. Each page consists of one column in a readable typeface. No pronunciation guides are provided; generous cross-references simplify full use.

The bibliography, primarily in English and Albanian, is a boon for questing searchers looking for materials that do not enjoy wide circulation. The 10-page introduction provides information on area of boundaries; underground resources (chrome, copper, oil); language; religion; and so on. Three outline maps of Albania are included (general area, boundaries in the twentieth century, and ethnographic regions), but they are too small and have too little detail to make reference work with them likely. The six-page chronology is useful, but dated; 1993 is the latest date given, on Pope John Paul II's visit to this remote country. As with any dictionary, if one does not know the spelling of the word sought, some frustration can occur, so persistence is needed to fully access the information available.

On the whole, the dictionary will provide superficial information to the avid seeker. It will be of assistance to library employees seeking answers to general reference questions on Albania.

—Judy Gay Matthews

Eastern Europe

114. **The American Bibliography of Slavic and East European Studies for 1993.** By American Association for the Advancement of Slavic Studies. Patt Leonard and Rebecca Routh, comps. and eds. Armonk, N.Y., M. E. Sharpe, 1996. 602p. index. $100.00. ISBN 1-56324-750-X. ISSN 0094-3770.

The 6,260 entries of *The American Bibliography of Slavic and East European Studies* (ABSEES) cover citations of a wide variety of books, journal articles, government and research reports, dissertations, and book reviews published in 1993. The work includes "English-language and selected foreign-language materials published in the United States and Canada" as well as "publications produced by American institutions abroad" (p. xv). The introduction to the volume advises the researcher to consult it in conjunction with its European counterpart, *The European Bibliography of Slavic and East European Studies*.

ABSEES lists materials in the humanities and social sciences pertaining to the countries of Central and Eastern Europe and to the former republics of the Soviet Union: Albania; Armenia; Azerbaijan; Belarus; Bulgaria; Cyprus; the Czech Republic; the former East Germany; Estonia; Georgia; Greece; Hungary; Kazakhstan; Kyrgyzstan; Latvia; Lithuania; Moldova; Poland; Romania; the Russian Federation; Slovakia; Tajikistan; Turkmenistan; Ukraine; Uzbekistan; and the former Yugoslavia (Bosnia-Herzegovina, Croatia, Macedonia, Montenegro, Serbia, and Slovenia). The 19 chapters present broad subject categories: anthropology, ethnology, and archaeology; culture and the arts; economics and foreign trade; education and scholarship; geography and demography; government, law, and politics; history; international relations; language and linguistics; literature; military affairs; philosophy, political theory, and ideology; psychology; religion; science and technology; and sociology. Special chapters are dedicated to general [matters], obituaries, and reviews of books published in previous years. In its turn, each chapter has at least one level of subdivisions, most of them from a geographic, historical, or theory versus practice standpoint. The three indexes (by author, title, and subject) offer quick access to the entries. The subject index is elaborate and offers detailed and straightforward subheadings, followed by time divisions whenever possible—for example, **SOVIET UNION—CONFISCATED ART WORKS (1939-1945)**.

ABSEES is strongly recommended for scholars, researchers, and specialists in Slavic, Balkan, and Central and Eastern European Studies as an excellent starting point in their research. In order to simplify the researchers' work, the materials included provide the complete bibliographic description of the item. In case of a multiauthor monograph, the title of each chapter and its author(s) are specified along with the page range. ABSEES will also prove useful for libraries that maintain collections on Slavic and Eastern European studies. ABSEES is a must in these collections. At the same time, ABSEES should be used by acquisition librarians and Slavic bibliographers as a selection tool in their collection development work in order to build a strong collection in this area.—**Hermina G. B. Anghelescu**

France

115. Northcutt, Wayne. **The Regions of France: A Reference Guide to History and Culture.** Westport, Conn., Greenwood Press, 1996. 310p. illus. maps. index. $55.00. ISBN 0-313-29223-X.

The regional diversity of *La Belle France* is the topic of this reference guide. Organized into 22 chapters, each covers a region's geography, culture, history, politics, and economics. The introductory chapter introduces users to France as a whole, giving a historical overview, a summary of the regions, and a brief description of the images of France. Maps of the region under consideration begin each chapter, with a select bibliography completing it. Each area section is subdivided into segments on regional geography, history, recent politics, population, economy, culture (including cuisine and a recipe indigenous to that region), and architecture and noteworthy sites. Photographs found in the middle of the volume illustrate many of the places discussed in the text. Appendixes offer a timeline and a list of the rulers of France, from Hugh Capet (ruler from 987 to 996) to current president Jacques Chirac. A general bibliography at the end of the volume leads users to further resources on France, and the index provides access by name, geographic location, or topic.

Because the volume covers so many aspects of the different regions of France, it serves as a reference on many different levels. The resource could also function as a travel guide. School and public libraries will find the handbook useful; university or college libraries may also be well served by the volume, although they may want more detail and less glossing over than are provided here. For those people who think only of Paris when they think of France, this resource will illuminate the wide diversity of this intriguing country.—**Melissa Rae Root**

Great Britain

116. Creaton, Heather, comp. **London.** Santa Barbara, Calif., Clio Press/ABC-CLIO, 1996. 165p. index. (World Bibliographical Series, v.189). $67.00. ISBN 1-85109-248-X.

Anyone needing an introductory, comprehensive bibliography of London in all its aspects will welcome the appearance of Creaton's new work. The compiler, an authority on London's history at the University of London's Institute of Historical Research, begins with a brief historical survey of the city. This is followed by 25 chapters listing 600 numbered and annotated bibliographic entries. Entries in the individual chapters cover such topics as geography, guidebooks, history, finance, the arts, leisure, the media, and other bibliographies of London. Individual annotations are well written and provide useful descriptions and evaluations of the individual works, sometimes including lists of related titles. There are separate indexes for authors, titles, and subjects, and a map of greater London and its boroughs. This volume is part of ABC-CLIO's World Bibliographical Series and reflects its highest standards.—**Ronald H. Fritze**

117. Palmer, Alan. **Dictionary of the British Empire and Commonwealth.** London, John Murray; distr., North Pomfret, Vt., Trafalgar Square, 1996. 395p. index. $35.00. ISBN 0-7195-5650-3.

The British Empire once ruled nearly 25 percent of the world's population and 20 percent of its land surface (p. vii). This governmental structure encompassed nations as ethnically and culturally diverse as India, Australia, South Africa, and Jamaica. Since the Empire's dissolution, it has evolved into a commonwealth of former British colonies whose individual and collective membership influences global political, economic, and cultural trends. *Dictionary of the British Empire and Commonwealth* provides biographical information about the individuals, events, and locations contributing to the historical and contemporary development of the nations that were once part of the British Empire.

Opening with an introduction, the work then provides maps showing the British Empire's vast global coverage. The dictionary section features entries of a paragraph to one page in length on important individuals and developments in the Empire and Commonwealth history. Dictionary entries include Australia's Blue Mountains, British Columbia, diamonds, Dominica, first fleet, Hausa, imperial preference, Nelson Mandela, Qantas, railways, slave trade, Transvaal, Zambia, and many others. An appendix features 1995 Commonwealth membership as well as a selective bibliography for further reading.

Dictionary of the British Empire and Commonwealth is a helpful and reasonably priced introduction to those wanting to study the history of the British Empire and its member nations. Individual entries are succinct and informative and will, hopefully, lead readers to more detailed study and analysis of the historical and ongoing evolution of the countries that once belonged to the British Empire. [R: LJ, Aug 96, p. 64]
—**Bert Chapman**

Iceland

118. McBride, Francis R., comp. **Iceland.** rev. ed. Santa Barbara, Calif., Clio Press/ABC-CLIO, 1996. 345p. maps. index. (World Bibliographical Series, v.37). $99.00. ISBN 1-85109-237-4.

This annotated bibliography of works primarily in English covers every aspect of Iceland, including its history, geography, economy, and politics, and its people, their customs, their religion, and the social organization. The literature surveyed is analyzed critically and is intended to provide "an interpretation of [Iceland] that will express its culture, its place in the world, and the qualities and background that make it unique." Librarians and booksellers interested in finding the most recent and informative works on Iceland will find this to be a useful guide. For those wishing to visit Iceland, there is a section devoted specifically to travel guides. Emphasis is given to materials published since 1983, with a separate section on electronic resources available on the Internet. Indexes of authors, titles, and subjects are included, as well as a map identifying the more important towns and major topographic features of Iceland.—**Joseph W. Dauben**

Luxembourg

119. Barteau, Harry C. **Historical Dictionary of Luxembourg.** Lanham, Md., Scarecrow, 1996. 260p. illus. (European Historical Dictionaries, no.14). $56.00. ISBN 0-8108-3106-6.

The author served 19 years as head of the American International School of Luxembourg, so one could say that he has lived with his subject. In more than 350 entries, he provides information on the important places, people, objects, themes, and events of a small but prosperous country that is frequently overshadowed by its larger neighbors. All subject areas and time periods are touched upon, although the twentieth century naturally dominates the book. The 23-page introduction provides an overview of the Grand Duchy's history, politics, and culture. Cross-references are capitalized in the text, but there are no suggested readings at the end of entries. The dictionary is completed by a chronology; a list of acronyms and special terms; and lists of rulers, prime ministers since 1848, and U.S. units stationed in the country during the two world wars. (There was no corresponding list for German units, but this might be due to anti-German feelings left over from the wars.)

This reviewer wishes that more thematic maps were included. A section of seven black-and-white photographs of important buildings and monuments is an extra feature. There is no index, and the book is rounded out by a 40-page bibliography of more than 500 relevant materials. Fourteen titles in this series have been published so far, and libraries should have the whole series. There are few reference books available on Luxembourg, so this sturdily constructed title is most welcome for its ability to provide quick answers to questions. It is recommended for the reference collections of academic and large public libraries.
—**Daniel K. Blewett**

Romania

120. Treptow, Kurt W., and Marcel Popa. **Historical Dictionary of Romania.** Lanham, Md., Scarecrow, 1996. 311p. (European Historical Dictionaries, no.15). $64.00. ISBN 0-8108-3179-1.

The *Historical Dictionary of Romania* was written by an American specialist in Romanian studies who is a visiting professor at the University of Iasi and the director of the Center for Romanian Studies of the Romanian Cultural Foundation. The dictionary was coauthored by a Romanian scholar who is the director of the Encyclopedic Publishing House in Bucharest. The work is part of the European Historical Dictionaries, a series of dictionaries dedicated to individual countries in Europe.

The organization of the volume is meant to help the user by providing at the beginning some basic rules on spelling and pronouncing Romanian words. The chapter entitled "Historical Chronology" has as the first entry "3rd Millennium B.C." and as the last one "1995, 30 August." The chronology points out significant cultural, economic, social, and political events in the history of the three Romanian principalities: Walachia, Moldavia, and Transylvania. This is followed by the chapter called "Rulers of Romania," which lists all of the leaders of the Romanian principalities and Romania's chiefs of state. The introduction offers a brief overview on the country's geography, population, history, and economy.

The dictionary per se includes proper names of cities, provinces, vaivodes, kings, politicians, literary and artistic figures, political parties, and institutions; and events, such as wars, battles, and peace treaties. A considerable amount of entries represent Romanian concepts that are hard, if not impossible, to translate into English. Therefore, the authors decided to use the Romanian terminology as the main entry, followed by an explanation of the concept that is preceded by an English version of the term, usually a periphrasis. It is unfortunate that some prominent political figures mentioned in the chapter "Rulers of Romania" did not receive any treatment in the dictionary section (e.g., George Bibescu and Barbu Stirbe). The dictionary is very up-to-date, however. It contains entries dedicated to politicians elected after the 1989 revolutionary wave that led to the collapse of the Ceausescu regime (e.g., Ionee Roman and Nicolae Văcăroiu).

The selected bibliography is divided into several sections, such as "Reference Works and General Studies," followed by a chronological presentation of the major periods in Romania's history. Special sections are dedicated to economics and demography; language; art, literature, and folklore; and religion. The almost 1,000 items selected—both books and articles—are in English, French, German, Italian, Romanian, and Spanish. Their publication dates range from 1855 to 1995. A succinct annotation of these items would have been welcome. The "Reference Works and General Studies" section contains only 70 titles. It omits a significant work that annotates more than 1,000 items—*Ceausescu's Romania: An Annotated Bibliography* (see ARBA 95, entry 160).

The dictionary is targeted primarily to Romanianists, students, and specialists in Romanian studies. Its acquisition is essential for libraries building collections supporting Slavic, Balkan, or Eastern European studies. It is also an indispensable tool in any Romanian library or archive where English-speaking scholars conduct research.—**Hermina G. B. Anghelescu**

San Marino

121. Edwards, Adrian, and Chris Michaelides, comps. **San Marino.** Santa Barbara, Calif., Clio Press/ABC-CLIO, 1996. 100p. index. (World Bibliographical Series, v.188). $65.00. ISBN 1-85109-242-0.

The World Bibliographical Series is designed to provide research assistance to English-reading scholars and students. The current volume on San Marino is the latest in the series. San Marino is a small, landlocked country with fewer than 25,000 inhabitants. As the only Western European nation to bring a Communist government to office through free elections—and also remove it by elections a dozen years later—San Marino does have some distinction and interest that go beyond its small size. The book provides a brief introduction and historical background to the country. It also includes a chronology dating from the legendary origins of the city-state in the third century to San Marino's entry into a customs agreement with the European Union in 1992.

Most volumes in this bibliographical series stress English-language sources. San Marino's location, tucked away in the Italian foothills, means that most of what has been written on the country is in Italian. Each bibliographical entry includes an English translation of the title and a short abstract of its contents. San Marino is not likely to attract much popular attention beyond those tourists interested in accumulating passport stamps to document their international travels. However, major research libraries may find this bibliography useful in filling out their collections.—**Frank L. Wilson**

Slovenia

122. Carmichael, Cathie, comp. **Slovenia.** Santa Barbara, Calif., Clio Press/ABC-CLIO, 1996. 176p. index. (World Bibliographical Series, v.186). $85.00. ISBN 1-85109-239-0.

This is the latest in a remarkable series of bibliographies that will eventually cover every country in the world. In this, the series' 186th volume, the compiler deals with Slovenia, a country that was a part of the former Yugoslavia. Entries are exhaustive and divided into groups, including the country and its people, geography, tourism and travel guides, flora and fauna, history, languages and dialects, politics, statistics, the arts, education, economy, and more. Located in the back of the book are a general index and lists of authors and titles.

The book is aimed at English-speaking scholars of Slavic cultures, who will find it quite valuable. If there is any flaw in it, it would be the fact that it is often unclear whether an entry is published in English or Slovene or even some other language. One assumes that *Slowenien: Karte und Fuehrer* (*Slovenia: Map and Guide*), for example, is published in German only, but the bibliography does not indicate whether that is the case. The brief annotations describing each of the entries are concise, informative, and well written. This is a valuable tool for the Slavic scholar, although the somewhat steep price for such a slim volume may cause researchers to seek it out at major public libraries, colleges, and universities.

—**Koraljka Lockhart**

Soviet Union

123. Ruffin, M. Holt, Joan McCarter, and Richard Upjohn. **The Post-Soviet Handbook: A Guide to Grassroots Organizations and Internet Resources in the Newly Independent States.** Seattle, Wash., Center for Civil Society International with University of Washington Press, 1996. 393p. index. $19.95pa. ISBN 0-295-97534-2.

This book is intended for the active citizens of the world. If a person wishes to contact human rights, self-help, environmentalist, literary, consumer, scientific friendship, educational, and gay groups within the newly independent former Soviet states, there is nothing better to recommend than the volume under review. The handbook consists of three parts: U.S.-based organizations with connections inside the independent states, organizations within the independent states (save for the Baltics), and Internet resources. The larger scheme behind the intention of the authors is to document and bolster the civil society (grass roots) within ex-Communist states. Although the authors give the impression that no organization is too small to be included in the volume, one cannot easily assess the completeness of the listings. The work certainly gives an assurance that if one wants to find a like-minded group in the ex-Communist lands, this is a good place to start the search for the civil society of one's choice, even if it may not end there. One wishes that the handbook had a more comprehensive index. [R: BL, 15 Oct 96, p. 452; Choice, Dec 96, p. 594; LJ, 1 Nov 96, p. 62]—**Andrew Ezergailis**

124. Schaffner, Bradley L. **Bibliography of the Soviet Union, Its Predecessors and Successors.** Lanham, Md., Scarecrow, 1995. 569p. index. (Scarecrow Area Bibliographies, no.5). $72.50. ISBN 0-8108-2860-X.

This is volume 5 in a relatively new Scarecrow series, Scarecrow Area Bibliographies. Schaffner is currently the Russian studies librarian at the University of Kansas. The book seems to be ambitious, covering not only the former Soviet Union and now the Russian Federated Republic, but also the countries known as the Commonwealth of Independent States (Armenia, Azerbaijan, Belarus, Kazakhstan, Kyrgyzstan,

Moldova, Russia, Tajikistan, Turkmenistan, Ukraine, Uzbekistan); the Baltic States of Estonia, Latvia, and Lithuania; and Georgia. It should be noted that several countries are not members of the Commonwealth (e.g., Estonia, Latvia, and Lithuania), and others are associate members (e.g., Ukraine). As a matter of fact, the concept of the Commonwealth of Independent States has little in common with any kind of federation of the former Soviet Republics, but is instead a practical body with the aim to solve some common problems in this area, such as criminal activities, border disputes, and the like.

The table of contents is not helpful in locating certain needed materials because it has only one general listing, "bibliography," without any subdivisions. A subject index is also absent. This book lists primarily social science and humanities texts, excluding the areas of science and technology as well as fiction and criticism of specific works of literature. Most of the monographs were published in English since 1984, with some Western European languages represented only in certain sections. Works in native languages are usually excluded and this, contrary to the statement in the introduction, includes some important reference works published in Slavic languages.

In general, the coverage is highly selective, but criteria for such selection are not clearly spelled out. Books are arranged by modified Library of Congress subject headings, and monographs that belong together are not necessarily in one place. For example, in entry 33, Conquest is listed under the general heading **AGRICULTURE COLLECTIVIZATION—HISTORY**. The author, a British scholar, deals primarily with famine in Ukraine. The subject heading **ALCOHOLISM** has 2 entries, **CRIMEAN TARTARS** has 1, **DEFECTORS** has 2, **DÉTENTE** has 2, and **DISSENT** has only 10.

An examination of the section on Ukraine yielded this information: The coverage is probably adequate in terms of pure numbers, but the author copied some of the entries from sometimes unreliable sources. For example, entry 9272 lists *Encyclopedia of Ukraine*. This work was published in two volumes, the second in 1971. The spelling of the title should be *Encyclopaedia*. The University of Toronto also published during 1984 and 1993 a 6-volume set of *Encyclopaedia of Ukraine*, not mentioned by the compiler. Needless to say, there are several encyclopedias published in the Ukrainian language (e.g., a 10-volume set published abroad, and 12- and 20-volume sets published in Kiev). *Introduction to Ukrainian History* (entry 2983) is published in 3 volumes. Some entries have little scholarly value. In other words, it is desirable to examine certain books, because copying Library of Congress cards with open entries is of little help in compiling bibliographies.

So much for criticism. All in all, this bibliography is to be used with caution and will be of some assistance to the uninitiated.—**Bohdan S. Wynar**

125. **The Statistical Handbook of Social and Economic Indicators for the Former Soviet Union.** Compiled by the CIS Committee for Statistics, International Center for Human Values. New York, Norman Ross, 1996. 307p. $75.00. ISBN 0-88354-378-8.

It is not always easy to praise compilations of statistical information. At times, it almost seems that crabbed columns with poorly delineated and often multilingual headers are meant to convey a sought-after solemnity. To the sorrow of demographers, economists, and sociologists everywhere, the statistics they need are often buried in sources of this type. Fortunately, there is another class of statistical literature, with beautiful, easy-to-read tables complemented by adequate white space and informative textual commentary. The present volume falls into the second category.

One odd thing about this volume is its presentation of data not for a single year or for a continuous sweep of years but for the years 1991-1992, and then again 1985, which frames the data around the 1991 coup that changed the Soviet Union into the Commonwealth of Independent States (CIS). There is no further emphasis on the purely political. Instead, there are 307 pages of tabular data concerning basic socioeconomic indexes, population and labor resources, income, consumption, education, crime, health, maternity, transportation, communications, and environmental control. Some users may consider it a flaw that the data are broken out by the 11 members of the Commonwealth (Armenia, Azerbaijan, Belarus, Kazakhstan, Kyrgyzstan, Moldova, Russia, Tajikistan, Turkmenistan, Ukraine, and Uzbekistan) while there is no line representing the sum total of all CIS members. Moreover, despite the presence of a well-organized table of contents, there is no index.

The obvious source with which to compare this monograph would be the three pertinent volumes of the *Russia and Eurasia Facts and Figures Annual* (Academic International Press). However, a researcher may not want to do the three lookups necessary to make the kind of comparisons ready-made in the

Statistical Handbook. Also, even when he or she does, the data, while close, do not always match. The *Statistical Handbook*, for instance, records 61 kg of meat products consumed per person in 1991 (p. 110), and the *Annual* for 1991 reports 65 kg (p. 209). As discrepancies of this sort are the daily stuff of statisticians, this reviewer happily recommends that the data in this excellent volume be weighed together with other data currently available. [R: Choice, Dec 96, p. 587; LJ, 15 Sept 96, pp. 58-59]—**Judith M. Brugger**

INDIAN OCEAN AREA

Punjab

126. Tatla, Darshan Singh, and Ian Talbot, comps. **Punjab.** Santa Barbara, Calif., Clio Press/ABC-CLIO, 1995. 323p. index. (World Bibliographical Series, v.180). $80.00. ISBN 1-85109-232-3.

Punjab is the 180th volume published in the World Bibliographic Series and as such resembles previous publications in many ways. As with other volumes, this text offers an introduction, in this case a short history of Punjab and an explanation of the scope and nature of the entries in the volume. Unlike the subject of most other volumes, Punjab is not an independent state, but a rich, agricultural region lying across northeastern Pakistan and northwestern India.

This volume concentrates on books in English or English translations of Punjabi books, although there are a small number of articles and theses described. Entries within each heading are alphabetic by author and provide a useful, short paragraph description and assessment in addition to the usual bibliographic data. Many reprints of eighteenth- and nineteenth-century works are identified, but most titles date from the 1960s to the present. Subject heading topics include, among others, geography; traveler's accounts; history; postindependence Punjab (from here on entries are divided between material on East and on West Punjab); religion; health/social conditions/welfare services; politics; statistics; environment; the arts; professional periodicals; and bibliographies. Three useful indexes cross-referencing authors, titles, and subjects conclude the book, and there are two maps and a glossary. Research libraries and libraries in cities with large South Asian populations will find the book useful. [R: Choice, Mar 96, p. 1104]—**David L. White**

LATIN AMERICA AND THE CARIBBEAN

General Works

127. **Economic and Social Progress in Latin America 1995 Report: Overcoming Volatility.** Washington, D.C., Inter-American Development Bank; distr., Baltimore, Md., Johns Hopkins University Press, 1995. 308p. $18.95pa. ISBN 0-940602-97-0. ISSN 0095-2850.

Based on 1994 data, this report from the Inter-American Development Bank is an invaluable reference for the study of Latin American and Caribbean economic development, covering 26 countries in the region. Each entry has an article divided into three sections: recent economic trends, economic policies, and outlook. The entries also include two facing pages in color of exceptional note: one page of economic indicators, presented in graphs and charts of such numbers as external debt and money supply, and another with a statistical profile made from such numbers as balance of payments, exchange rates, and real gross domestic product. Finally, the entries end with a list of sources, mostly from major international and banking institutions, such as the World Bank, the International Monetary Fund, and the Organization of American States. Also cited are Latin American and Caribbean government sources.

The 2d half of the report is divided into a discussion of volatility in Latin America and the effect it has on its economy and an extensive statistical appendix that tracks 10 years of several economic indicators for its 26 countries and Latin America as a whole. The volatility of Latin America in the subtitle is explained in terms of the economic shocks and instabilities—external, fiscal, and monetary—suffered by the region and the effect these have had on economic growth. Published too early to show the effects of the major devaluation in Mexico in December 1994, the report discusses possible outcomes. The report is recommended for college, public, and special libraries with Latin American economics collections.—Edward Erazo

128. Goslinga, Marian. **A Bibliography of the Caribbean.** Lanham, Md., Scarecrow, 1996. 341p. index. (Scarecrow Area Bibliographies, no.8). $79.00. ISBN 0-8108-3097-3.

The Caribbean profiled in Goslinga's bibliography encompasses the range of islands from Bermuda in the north to Trinidad and Tobago in the south as well as the culturally and historically related mainland countries of Belize, Guyana, Suriname, and French Guiana. The book's scope is equally extended, ranging from the earliest-known publications on the Caribbean to materials published through 1992. Given the ambitiousness of this reach, the author wisely makes no claim to comprehensiveness, but suggests rather that her book be used "in conjunction with other sources."

The cultural and linguistic diversity of the Caribbean is reflected in the works cited, which include titles in English, Spanish, French, Dutch, German, and Portuguese, although emphasis is on English-language materials. Only monographs are identified among the bibliography's 3,600 items, which leaves out many materials that would interest researchers, such as journal articles, dissertations, theses, government documents, and conference papers and proceedings. The titles are organized into three sections (historical materials, reference and source materials, and contemporary works), with the majority of the book devoted to the contemporary works. This section is further subdivided into topical areas, such as "physical terrain" and "economics." Entries provide title; author; place of publication; publisher; date of publication; pagination; and when appropriate, a note regarding changes in title, edition, translations, and so on. There are no content annotations.

Although the author and title indexes are helpful, the geographic index is nearly useless, as there are no subheadings to guide the reader through the literally hundreds of entry numbers listed. For example, checking under "Cuba" in the geographic index, one finds 425 entry numbers with no differentiating indicators whatsoever. Why bother to include this index at all? In publishing, as elsewhere, the importance of adding value to content is critical; given this reality, the author may need to consider not only a vastly improved geographic index on the next go-around, but also adding annotations that take the book from a list of titles to a guide to resources.—**G. Kim Dority**

129. **Jane's Sentinel: Central America and the Caribbean Security Assessment.** 1996 ed. William Perry, ed. Alexandria, Va., Jane's Information Group, 1996. 1v. (various paging). illus. maps. index. $425.00 looseleaf w/binder. ISBN 0-7106-1326-1.

Jane's Information Group is a longtime world leader in military reference information, so perhaps with some justification they have subtitled this new global security assessment series as "The Unfair Advantage." There are 27 nations covered by this publication. Each individually numbered section includes a table of contents; a historical overview; and outlines of a nation's politics, international affairs, economy, geography, demographics, and directory of important addresses. Because much of this information can be found elsewhere, the real value of this series is in the detailed data regarding the armed forces and the outlines of the various internal and external threats that face a country. While certainly the most important information is provided, and is enough to give one an idea of a nation's strengths and weaknesses, this reviewer was disappointed that there was not more discussion or analysis of the threat situation. "Brief" and "sketchy" are the words that immediately come to mind to describe this portion of the work. However, this series is probably written for other experts or informed laypeople, and this may be all they need.

The color page at the beginning of each country's section shows where in the region the country is located, a close-up view of the country, the flag, and military aircraft markings. However, the country maps are not very detailed, with just the main cities, roads, rivers, and military bases shown. Statistical tables, charts, and graphs are included, but no outside sources are cited. "Unclassified" is printed at the top of every page; one wonders if classified information would really be printed here. Users can supplement the military information by consulting one of the many other excellent military reference books from Jane's. The subscription includes monthly newsletter updates.

Other similar printed sources that one might expect to have some kind of threat summary actually come up short. The Central Intelligence Agency's *World Factbook* (see entry 80) has little security information, and its maps are poor. *The Military Balance, 1995-1996* (London: International Institute for Strategic Studies, 1995) has more specific data on a country's armed forces, but little on threats. Its companion, *Strategic Survey, 1995-1996*, contains only a few essays on Latin America, but it does include a bit more background. *The World in Conflict: War Annual 7: Contemporary Warfare Described and Analysed* by John Laffin (Brassey's [UK], 1996) does offer more analysis of the immediate past and problems for the future, but it only has a couple of chapters relating to Latin America. The *Political Handbook of the World, 1995-1996* (SUNY Center for Social Analysis Publications, 1996) provides some discussion of the immediate past and present sticky issues. The same holds true for the *Europa World Year Book* (see ARBA 94, entry 82, and ARBA 90, entry 91) and its offspring volumes. Perhaps the title that comes closest in function to *Jane's Sentinel* is the *Political Risk Yearbook. Volume 1: North and Central America*, edited by Arthur S. Banko (Political Risk Services, 1996), which analyzes risk factors and forecasts for 18 months and 5 years and sketches possible scenarios. This service is primarily intended for business investors, so there is little military data.

This particular series from Jane's also includes volumes covering the Balkans, the Commonwealth of Independent States, the Persian Gulf, North Africa, the South China Sea, Southern Africa, and South America. The company plans to add Central Europe and the Eastern Mediterranean. This title is also available as a CD-ROM. One would expect that it would also be online soon (Jane's Internet page address is http://www.janes.com). Most libraries will be able to get by with what sources they already have, supplemented by magazines and newspapers. This expensive title is suitable for large or specialized reference collections that have a demand for current international security information.—**Daniel K. Blewett**

130. **South America, Central America, and the Caribbean 1997.** 6th ed. London, Europa; distr., Bristol, Pa., Taylor & Francis, 1996. 774p. index. $325.00. ISBN 1-85743-026-3. ISSN 0258-0661.

The 6th edition of this reference work, which began publication with its 1st edition in 1985 (see ARBA 87, entry 140), follows a pattern similar to earlier editions. It "provides a survey of the political and economic life both of the region, and of the 48 countries and territories within it" (foreword). The geographic areas listed in the title accurately reflect its coverage, although it also includes Bermuda, which is geographically part of North America. The resource is divided into three parts. The first is composed of eight essays on subjects of current regional significance, such as democratization, economies of the region, the politics of cocaine, the church and politics, and others.

Part 2, a fact-filled section entitled "Country Surveys," provides information about each country/territory through a short article summarizing its history and economy; a wide-ranging statistical survey covering area and population, agriculture, forestry, fishing, mining, industry, finance, foreign trade, transportation, communications, tourism, and education; and a directory. This latter segment gives key information about the constitution of the country; the executive, legislative, and judicial branches of its government; political organizations; diplomatic representation; religion; print and electronic media; finance; trade and industry; transportation; power; defense; tourism; and education. Names of organizations/agencies and chief executive officers, telephone numbers, and addresses are supplied. A bibliography concludes each country section. The articles in parts 1 and 2 are signed by their authors—British academics, researchers, or other professionals who are recognized specialists in the region.

Part 3, "Regional Information," serves as a directory of regional organizations; in addition to names and addresses, it describes each organization and summarizes its activities. This part also furnishes information and statistics on major commodities of the region, and lists local and foreign research institutes that study Latin America and the Caribbean. A select bibliography cites serials focusing on the region. An index of regional organizations concludes the work. Although the names, and to a lesser extent the addresses, listed in this publication become quickly outdated, it is a valuable source for quick overviews of important contemporary issues in the region, and for obtaining elusive statistics and other facts about the countries comprising it. It would be a useful addition to any reference collection needing access to basic information about this region of the world.—**Ann Hartness**

Cayman Islands

131. Boultbee, Paul G., comp. **Cayman Islands.** Santa Barbara, Calif., Clio Press/ABC-CLIO, 1996. 129p. index. (World Bibliographical Series, v.187). $65.00. ISBN 1-85109-240-4.

The Cayman Islands, discovered by Christopher Columbus in 1503 on his final voyage, have been under British control since 1734, but have been largely overlooked until 1962, when they became independent of Jamaican administration. The present population is under 26,000, and so it is astonishing that this volume's compiler has managed to locate some 447 printed items related to the islands. Some, of course, include the Caymans only incidentally in general considerations of the Caribbean or West Indies, and some of the 30 categories (such as sports and folklore) list just 2 entries. However, there are 85 entries under geology, 122 under flora and fauna, and 32 under travel guides—illustrating the change from scientific subject to tourist destination. Yet even in recent published materials, there is a clear predominance of scientific articles, some of which reveal curious facts: There are 35 species of mosquitoes, 8 of bats, but only 2 of indigenous butterflies, while there are 82 species of birds.

In view of the Caymans as an offshore banking center (30,000 companies, 500 banks, and 350 insurance companies), it is noticeable how few articles have been written on this phenomenon: Perhaps this reflects the colony's efforts to keep corporate life private. An interesting sociological study explains the prevalence of deaf-mutism as a result of interbreeding among the white population. The compiler's summaries of articles are succinct and (from those examined) fair. His search for materials has been thorough, making this the most comprehensive bibliographic sourcebook on the Cayman Islands.—**Marian B. McLeod**

Cuba

132. Stubbs, Jean, Lila Haines, and Meic F. Haines, comps. **Cuba.** Santa Barbara, Calif., Clio Press/ABC-CLIO, 1996. 337p. index. (World Bibliographical Series, v.75). $99.00. ISBN 1-85109-021-5.

The destiny of Cuba continues to generate a large volume of literature, both in favor of and against its internal and external policies. Just recently, the world media focused on the plight of freedom-seekers attempting to cross the shark-infested waters between Cuba and Key West in makeshift rafts. Many tragically lost their lives in the attempt.

With the addition of another excellent volume to the World Bibliographical Series, the scholar and student alike will benefit from this annotated bibliography. The text is composed of 1,172 entries, including numerous electronic sources, such as PAIS. The annotations are concise and range in length from several sentences to a full paragraph. Major subject areas covered include geography, tourism and travel guides, history, population studies, religion, foreign relations, and economy. One interesting and useful section is on the many aspects of revolutionary Cuban society, from the perspective of both the "insider" and "outsider."

The compilers have made an attempt to provide the reader with a well-balanced selection of the available literature, considering the vast amount of literature that the Cuban experiment has generated. The value of this reference source is enhanced by the excellent introductory essay. This work is highly recommended for all academic libraries and for public libraries serving a large population of readers.
—**Dario J. Villa**

Falkland Islands

133. Day, Alan, comp. **The Falkland Islands, South Georgia, and the South Sandwich Islands.** Santa Barbara, Calif., Clio Press/ABC-CLIO, 1996. 231p. index. (World Bibliographical Series, v.184). $69.00. ISBN 1-85109-236-6.

This work is an annotated bibliography of British territories in the South Atlantic, the Falkland Islands, and the Territory of South Georgia and the South Sandwich Islands, with a total of 693 entries in 3 sections for each of the 3 geographic locations. Entries for each geographic location, except the South Sandwich Islands, are arranged by broad subjects, and then chronologically (by date of publication or by period of coverage). The well-written annotations are informational and descriptive in nature. The section for the Falkland Islands, which occupies the lion's share of this bibliography (567 entries), covers a wide range of subjects from flora and fauna to biography and philately, and several location-specific topics, the most obvious being the 1982 war in the South Atlantic. Although the latter topic is given thorough coverage, the author limited the number of entries, keeping it in perspective in relation to other subjects.

The bibliography for South Georgia has 113 entries. The bibliography devoted to the South Sandwich Islands cites only 12 publications and does not lend itself to subject divisions, as almost all of them are about the natural characteristics of the area—geology, botany, bird life, and the like. The vast majority of books cited in this bibliography are in English, although the Falkland Islands section includes a few in Spanish in order to represent both Argentine and British views on the issue of ownership of the Falklands/Malvinas. An author, title, and subject index completes the work. The bibliography is recommended for all libraries with a need for global coverage of the geographic locations, or a clientele interested in Latin America (more specifically, Argentina), the British territories, or more general topics, such as colonialism.—**Ann Hartness**

Mexico

134. **NTC's Dictionary of Mexican Cultural Code Words.** By Boye Lafayette De Mente. Lincolnwood, Ill., National Textbook, 1996. 336p. $18.95. ISBN 0-8442-7959-5.

Although he includes a large number of essays (139) that span all facets of Mexican life, including culture, business, ethics, customs, history, language usage, politics, the sexes, and society, the author of this dictionary does not make clear the concept behind his selection of terms. A key element to a reference book is accuracy. Yet, this work has so many factual and spelling errors (including those of key terms, people, and places, in both Spanish and English) that it compromises its own reliability. The abundance and repetition of errors indicate that this goes beyond bad proofreading.

The author appears to have experience in interacting with Mexican people, especially from Mexico City, and he displays enthusiasm about life in Mexico. However, the absence of a bibliography of source material detracts from the authority to which he presumes. Quotations from acquaintances and anecdotal material fail to add substance to De Mente's general assertions. Ignoring regional differences and settling for inaccuracies, the author demonstrates that he himself has not completely surmounted the lack of understanding about the Mexican people (which in Spanish is spelled *comprensión* and not *comprensíon*, as it appears in the table of contents, or *comprención*, as in the text) of which he accuses most United States and Canadian citizens.—**Stella T. Clark**

MIDDLE EAST

General Works

135. Bosworth, Clifford Edmund. **The New Islamic Dynasties: A Chronological and Genealogical Manual.** New York, Columbia University Press, 1996. 389p. index. $45.00. ISBN 0-231-10714-5.

The word *new* in the title of this book is significant: It is the successor to *The Islamic Dynasties: A Chronological and Genealogical Handbook* (Edinburgh University Press, 1967). The present volume is much larger than the original—17 chapters covering 186 dynasties, as opposed to 10 chapters covering 82 dynasties. Almost all of the original chapters are enlarged in addition to the new dynasties added (e.g., West and East Africa, the Horn of Africa, Southeast Asia, and Indonesia).

Bosworth (professor emeritus of Arabic studies at the University of Manchester) has produced a work of high scholarship. Wherever possible, he has given dates for both the Muslim and the Christian eras. The Muslim era begins on the first day Muhammad (570-632) made his hegira from Mecca to Medina, July 16, 622. Personal names are given in full, complete with diacritical markings. Some Arabian terms seem to defy transliteration and here readers are on their own. Each region and dynasty has a chapter or subchapter with names and dates and a brief but interesting history of the particular dynasty plus a bibliography.

Of special interest is the first chapter, titled "The Caliphs." Here are the first four successors to Muhammad, called the Rightly Guided or Patriarchal Caliphs—Abu Bakr, Abu Omar, Abu Othman, and Abu Ali. In time, the Muslim community would split, with the Shia recognizing Ali (Muhammad's son-in-law) as the true successor while the Sunnis accepted Abu Bakr (Muhammad's father-in-law) as the rightful heir to the Prophet's teaching. Also of interest today are the dynasties of Al-Saud and Hashemite, which play leading roles in the Middle East. The volume under review is highly recommended, as is a helpful complementary book: Albert Hourani's *A History of the Arab Peoples* (Harvard University Press, 1991).—**David Eggenberger**

136. **Encyclopedia of the Modern Middle East.** Reeva S. Simon, Philip Mattar, and Richard W. Bulliet, eds. New York, Macmillan Library Reference/Simon & Schuster Macmillan, 1996. 4v. illus. maps. index. $350.00/set. ISBN 0-02-896011-4.

This 4-volume encyclopedia on the modern Middle East has 4,200 entries; a few genealogical trees of ruling dynasties; a list of the contributors, with minimal biographical information; a list of the biographical entries classified into 26 categories; and an index, 185 pages in length. The set covers some of the political, historical, social, and economic interactions of most of the Arab countries, Afghanistan, Iran, Israel, and Turkey.

The editors had to make difficult decisions in selecting the countries, biographical entries, contributors, and topics. They also had to decide on space allocation and the form of transliteration from the native languages into English. The selection is influenced by the apparent objective of making the Arab-Israeli conflict the central issue in the modern Middle East. However, being convinced that it is difficult to please all readers, the editors seem to have taken more liberty than is warranted in a scholarly publication. For example, they included Afghanistan but not Pakistan; they discuss the Ottoman Empire and Turkey, even though Turkey aspires to be a part of Europe; and they left out Somalia, Djibouti, and the Comoro Islands, all members of the Arab League. The editors allocated space to countries and topics according to whether they fall in one or another of various unexplained categories. It may be true that the Arab-Israeli conflict has strongly marked the history of the Middle East, but so did the middle-class revolutions, Arab socialism, the oil price revolution, the Islamic revolution in Iran, and the rise and decline of formal imperialism.

However, the most serious infraction relates to transliteration into English. Instead of applying a standard system, the editors chose to allow a mix of approaches in order to make the reference "friendly" to the reader. They also chose to omit diacritical marks and accents and the marks for *hamza* and *ayn*, which are integral to the Arabic language, rather than try to educate the reader into the intricacies of the language. This occurs side by side with the common usage of words they have adopted. The loose approach applied does little credit to the encyclopedia, and one hopes it will not be too confusing to the reader. Finally, and contrary to the editors' declared intentions, few contributors are from the Middle East. For the price to be paid and the efforts expended, Middle East scholarship and the readers deserve more rigor, explanation, consistency, and balance. [R: RBB, 15 Nov 96, p. 605]—**Elias H. Tuma**

137. **Great Dates in Islamic History.** Robert Mantran, ed. New York, Facts on File, 1996. 404p. maps. index. (Great Dates). $29.95. ISBN 0-8160-2935-0.

Great Dates in Islamic History is designed to give the reader a brief history of the Islamic world. The book covers this history from the ninth century B.C.E. to 1994. Each chapter begins with a short narrative introduction and is then divided into categories by region. The work covers the area from Morocco in the west, through North Africa to Egypt and the central areas of the Middle East, thence to Turkey and Iran, the subcontinent, and sub-Saharan Africa. Each entry is approximately one to three sentences in length. At points, the text contains two- to three-paragraph explanations of major events, movements, ideas, and items (e.g., "Ka'ba" and "The inhabitants of Mali according to Ibn Battuta"). There are charts and maps, introductory explanations of Arabic names and the Islamic calendar, a glossary, and an extensive index. However, a few entries cannot be accessed from the index (e.g., the entry on p. 25 for 778 C.E., "Border raids, thughur, organized by the Harun"), and there is at least one glaring error where the events in Palestine of May 1967 are listed under May 1966. Even given these drawbacks, the book is fairly easy to use and would find a place in libraries with an Islamic/Middle East collection.

—**David L. White**

138. Hiro, Dilip. **Dictionary of the Middle East.** New York, St. Martin's Press, 1996. 367p. index. $30.00. ISBN 0-312-12554-2.

Dictionaries on the Middle East have become a well-established genre, so it was with some lack of enthusiasm that this reviewer began an examination of yet another example. This hesitancy was misplaced. Hiro's recent effort has little in common with the cliché-driven exercises in partisanship generally encountered. To start, he has limited himself to a manageable portion of the Middle East: "the core," as he describes it. This consists of the Arab world north of the Sudan, together with Israel and Iran. Further, he demonstrates an appreciation of the region's own perspectives as well as that of the West. Finally, he is able to compress a great deal of material into succinct entries that are at once comprehensive and accessible. The page-long essay under "Phalange," for instance, begins with its Nazi inspirations and involvement in Lebanese politics of the 1960s—factors that contribute to understanding its place in the Lebanese civil war.

The dictionary offers in excess of 1,000 alphabetic entries, of which about 20 percent are cross-references. A comprehensive index, especially useful for a subject with so many foreign terms, further aids the reader. A limited number of maps is also included. Those maps of Palestine are adequate, but other areas may have been somewhat slighted. The dictionary could be improved with bibliographic notes in selected entries. Students of the Middle East at all levels will find this a useful source, and it is likely that even those with long exposure to the field will find some new insights here. Hiro's work is probably the best of the current guides to the politics of the area. [R: Choice, Dec 96, p. 589; RBB, 1 Sept 96, p. 164]
—**Paul L. Holmer**

139. **The Middle East and North Africa 1997.** 43d ed. London, Europa; distr., Detroit, Gale, 1996. 1104p. $345.00. ISBN 1-85743-030-1. ISSN 0076-8502.

As noted in ARBA 96 (see entry 160), effective formatting is the strength of this standard annual regional guide. It opens with a general survey of the area's countries, contains a directory of important international organizations, and closes with a nation-by-nation analytic commentary on each entity's geography, economics, and history. The 1997 edition features an extended essay on recent terrorist activity in the Middle East and North Africa. 1996 Israeli elections are documented and analyzed as well. A calendar of recent events (through October 1996) and a compact list of the most current Israeli and Lebanese cabinet members complete the updating from the previous edition. Libraries that maintain a collection concentration in foreign affairs have long ago made this a regular annual purchase.—**Ed Volz**

Kuwait

140. Clements, Frank A., comp. **Kuwait.** rev. ed. Santa Barbara, Calif., Clio Press/ABC-CLIO, 1996. 340p. index. (World Bibliographical Series, v.56). $97.00. ISBN 1-85109-212-9.

This is an update of the 1985 edition (see ARBA 86, entry 154). Since then, Kuwait has gone from obscurity to headline news, and this revision attempts to focus on the more recent history. The volume is part of the World Bibliographical Series, by now well known for quality, and its organization is typical of others of the set. Arrangement is by some 35 broad subject headings, within which are alphabetic entries by author or title, all of which are annotated. The focus is primarily on English materials, with only a few titles in other Western languages. Of course, the great majority of material on Kuwait comes from the Arabic press and is hence beyond the scope of this effort, but this will only increase the value to English-speaking students, although they will note the paucity of materials on certain subjects, especially literature and the arts. Librarians who already own the 1st edition will want to retain both on their shelves as much of the earlier material is not carried forward here. They will find this especially true of works dealing with Kuwait in the context of Arabia and the wider Arab world.—**Paul L. Holmer**

Syria

141. Commins, David. **Historical Dictionary of Syria.** Lanham, Md., Scarecrow, 1996. 300p. (Asian Historical Dictionaries, no.22). $49.50. ISBN 0-8108-3176-7.

This dictionary provides a detailed synopsis of Syrian history from 3500 B.C.E. to 1995 C.E. A chronology and a 14-page introduction precede the dictionary entries, providing a concise but comprehensive overview of the country's political and military history. Dictionary entries are substantial, usually at least a paragraph long, and frequently several pages. Broad topics, such as education, are covered, as are references to specific leaders, dynasties, battles, political parties, and so on. Each entry includes boldfaced links to other entries, making it easy for the user to locate additional information. An extensive bibliography, divided into 29 different categories (e.g., anthropology, economy, geology, travel guides), follows the dictionary entries. This compact reference source is a well-prepared guide to an extensive body of information.—**Ahmad Gamaluddin**

OCEANIA

142. Austin, Mary C., and Esther C. Jenkins, with Carol A. Jenkins. **Literature for Children and Young Adults About Oceania: Analysis and Annotated Bibliography with Additional Readings for Adults.** Westport, Conn., Greenwood Press, 1996. 326p. index. (Bibliographies and Indexes in World Literature, no.49). $69.50. ISBN 0-313-26643-3.

This bibliography of books for youth about Oceania is a niche publication. Yet Austin and the Jenkinses tune in so richly to the culture of the area that it is a treat for the librarian or teacher wishing to better understand and serve students who have immigrated to the United States from the islands of the Pacific, or who live there yet.

The introduction briefly describes the general geographic area of Oceania and tells the story of the movement of peoples. Then the authors break their material into three geographic sections: Australia; New Zealand; and the large island world called Melanesia, Micronesia, and Polynesia. They open for educators the indigenous literature characteristic of each area: hero tales, monster tales, numbskull tales, stories of unusual or little people, and so on. They provide, in each section, an annotated bibliography of books for children and young adults that includes information about folk, contemporary, and nonfiction literature. The authors include a list of recurring motifs and a bibliography for adults. Authors of the materials for youth are, for the most part, persons with Western names, but they draw, with the exception of clearly contemporary stories, from the native oral traditions.

District and regional libraries serving students of this background should make a copy available to their libraries. They should, in turn, inform their classroom teaching staffs of this superb overview. [R: Choice, June 96, pp. 1607-08]—**Edna M. Boardman**

143. **The Far East and Australasia 1997.** 28th ed. London, Europa; distr.; Detroit, Gale, 1996. 1191p. $395.00. ISBN 1-85743-031-X. ISSN 0071-3791.

The ARBA 96 review (see entry 167) noted the accuracy and currency of this annual regional guide. As with others in the series, this volume commences with several essays surveying issues and trends affecting the region; entries on individual countries follow, with analysis of each entity's geography, economics, and history. A directory of sociopolitical organizations ends the book. A calendar of political events (through October 1996) and a concise list of governmental changes (effective November 1996) complete the updating from the previous edition. Libraries emphasizing materials on international affairs should already have this on standing order.—**Ed Volz**

144. Jackson, Keith, and Alan McRobie. **Historical Dictionary of New Zealand.** Lanham, Md., Scarecrow, 1996. 313p. (Oceanian Historical Dictionaries, no.5). $54.00. ISBN 0-8108-3086-8.

The fifth volume in the Oceanian Historical Dictionaries series, this 8½-by-5-inch, hardcover piece is the creation of Jackson and McRobie. Both authors are political scientists with graduate degrees in history who have taught in New Zealand universities. Although entitled *Historical Dictionary of New*

Zealand, the dictionary entries themselves account for less than two-thirds of the volume. This publication also includes the standard foreword and preface, plus 6 maps, a glossary of Maori words, a 33-page chronology of salient events in New Zealand's recent history, an interesting 18-page introductory essay on New Zealand as a "Social and Economic Laboratory," a 45-page bibliography, and a brief appendix of tables of demographic and economic data.

The approximately 700 alphabetically arranged dictionary entries—from "Accident Compensation" to "Young Maori Party"—cover a wide variety of people and events throughout New Zealand's rich and colorful history. The majority of the volume, however, focuses upon the more recent past and upon New Zealand's political rather than social history. Some entries are short (only 2 sentences in length), but most contain approximately 200 words. The text is eminently readable and clearly is intended for a wide audience. Although the volume is too concise to be of great use to experts in the field, it contains an abundance of introductory information that students of New Zealand politics and culture will find interesting and entertaining. The dictionary is recommended for public libraries with Oceania area studies collections.

—**Terry D. Bilhartz**

WEST INDIES

145. Momsen, Janet Henshall, comp. **St. Lucia.** Santa Barbara, Calif., Clio Press/ABC-CLIO, 1996. 179p. index. (World Bibliographical Series, v.185). $62.00. ISBN 1-85109-136-X.

St. Lucia, the second largest of the Leeward and Windward Islands in the Lesser Antilles, is the subject of volume 185 of the World Bibliographical Series. The focus of this important reference work is on English sources, although a list of bibliographies is included that may lead the student/scholar to more extensive materials. There are a total of 531 entries with annotations ranging from a single line to short paragraphs in length. The subjects covered are numerous, and the following serves only as a sample to illustrate the extent of comprehensiveness: geography, geology and soils, history, population, language, economy, the arts, and literature. Under each one of the major subjects headings listed above are minor headings providing greater detail to the available literature. The value of this bibliography is further enhanced by the comprehensive introductory essay. Overall, this bibliography will serve a wide and varied audience, including scholars. This volume, as are others in the series, is highly recommended for academic and comprehensive public libraries.—**Dario J. Villa**

4 Economics and Business

GENERAL WORKS

Atlases

146. Charlesworth, Andrew, and others. **An Atlas of Industrial Protest in Britain, 1750-1990.** New York, St. Martin's Press, 1996. 225p. maps. $55.00. ISBN 0-312-15889-0.

This interdisciplinary scholarly work is on the cusp between geography, industrial relations, and social history. It is largely text, but extensive cartographic illustrations justify the atlas label. The work belongs in research collections on economic, social, and industrial history covering Great Britain.

The atlas is divided into four chronological parts covering the periods 1750-1850, 1850-1900, 1900-1939, and 1940-1990, respectively. Each section contains an introductory review essay on industrial unrest in the period covered. Then (with the exception of the first section, for which sources are inadequate) there is a geographic and statistical essay. Case studies on particular disputes follow. The 25 case studies cover such topics as the Luddite disturbances, the general strikes of 1842 and 1926, the coal lockout of 1893, the Winter of Discontent of 1979, the coal miners' strike of 1984-1985, and many more. Each chapter has a brief note on sources and suggestions for further reading.

There is a detailed table of contents, but no index. The contributors are history, geography, and social science academics associated with a variety of British institutions, including the universities of London, Birmingham, and Edinburgh. The cartography was done by the geography department cartographer at Queen Mary and Westfield College, London University. This is an impressive scholarly effort that deserves a place in research collections covering the relevant disciplines. It should also be considered for larger general collections where scope and client demand warrant.—**Nigel Tappin**

Bibliography

147. **Business A to Z Source Finder: A Locator Guide to Sources....** Elizabeth Louise Vandivier and Kathleen Brown, eds. Annapolis, Md., Beacon Bay Press, 1996. 590p. $85.00pa. ISBN 0-9649579-0-6.

Similar in arrangement and purpose to the *Encyclopedia of Business Information Sources* (see ARBA 93, entry 206, for a review of the 9th ed.) but covering less than half as many subjects, this locator guide appears to be directed toward the novice researcher. Each subject entry begins with a definition of the topic followed by Library of Congress (LC) subject headings, LC and Dewey call numbers, and citations to published introductions to the topic. The 500 topics, along with cross-references, are listed in a table of contents. The 2d section of the guide is devoted to listing such sources as handbooks, dictionaries, directories, bibliographies, abstracts and indexes, databases, CD-ROMs, journals and newsletters, selected books, and associations and research centers.

The editors used online catalogs, publishers' catalogs, bibliographies, and other standard sources to compile this source. One wishes they had been more selective rather than inclusive. A list of 5 recommended titles is more useful than 16 recent titles on the subject. Locator guides provide a starting point, are a great time-saver, and are well used in business collections. This is a good addition for libraries needing this type of source and unable to afford the *Encyclopedia of Business Information Sources*. [R: Choice, July/Aug 96, pp. 1768-70; RBB, June 96, p. 1764]—**Barbara E. Clotfelter**

148. King, J. E. **Post Keynesian Economics: An Annotated Bibliography.** Brookfield, Vt., Edward Elgar/Ashgate Publishing, 1995. 1v. (unpaged). index. $215.95. ISBN 1-85278-801-1.

The publication of John Maynard Keynes's classic work, *The General Theory of Employment, Interest and Money*, in 1936 (Harcourt, Brace) transformed modern economic theory and ultimately helped to reshape public policies. The book also spawned an enormous volume of literature, both pro and con. Indeed, the influence of this work has been so significant that a distinct, albeit diverse, school of economic thought has emerged and been labeled as "Post Keynesian Economics." Despite the inherent ambiguity in succinctly defining this school, economists associated with it have attempted to interpret the issues raised by the work of Keynes and to provide coherent and alternative views to neoclassical economic analysis.

This ample and informative reference work is a comprehensive view of that literature, and its 3,293 annotated entries are reasonably arranged, chronologically, by author and into 18 subject headings. Entries are organized into such subject headings as general studies; methodologies; collections and biographical studies; various interpretations of Keynes's work as well as empirical studies and the more traditional disciplinary topics of macroeconomic and microeconomic theory; labor; monetary theory; distribution and capital theory; development; growth and cycles; and international economics. The work outlines the contributions of a diverse array of scholars, including those who were contemporaries of Keynes along with the disciples and detractors of Keynesian analysis. It is a useful and thorough reference work that will increase awareness of the breadth of scholarly work carried out by various economists from the 1930s to the 1990s. [R: Choice, May 96, p. 1452]—**Timothy E. Sullivan**

149. **The Search for Economics as a Science: An Annotated Bibliography.** Lynn Turgeon, ed. Pasadena, Calif., Salem Press and Lanham, Md., Scarecrow, 1996. 428p. index. (Magill Bibliographies). $55.00. ISBN 0-8108-3120-1.

Designed as a starting point for high school or college students researching economic topics, this selective bibliography includes approximately 2,000 English-language publications—monographs, book chapters, serials, and journal articles—that represent, according to the editor, "a collection of the best in worldwide economic thinking of the past three centuries." Turgeon, who taught economics at Hofstra University for 35 years, has divided this work into 5 chapters comprising 14 sections, each section corresponding to a course frequently offered by economics and business departments at U.S. colleges and universities. Courses not covered include accounting, consumer finance, economic geography, and marketing.

The majority of bibliographic entries are for textbooks rather than primary sources or reference titles. Only one or two books published within the past five years are listed. Some publications are placed in more than one section, but when they are, different editions are frequently cited. There are no cross-references linking identical titles found in separate sections. Turgeon's annotations, which vary in length from 10 to 125 words each, lack consistency. Many are critical as well as descriptive, but many are only one or the other. Also, the author and subject indexes supplied in this volume are inadequate. Given its shortcomings, *The Search for Economics as a Science* is not recommended as a guide to the literature.—**Leonard Grundt**

Bio-bibliography

150. Cicarelli, James, and Julianne Cicarelli. **Joan Robinson: A Bio-bibliography.** Westport, Conn., Greenwood Press, 1996. 179p. index. (Bio-bibliographies in Economics, no.2). $69.50. ISBN 0-313-25844-9.

In 1975, everyone expected noted post-Keynesian economist Joan Robinson to win the Nobel prize in economics. Robinson, who is viewed by many as the greatest female economist, was denied the prize in and never won it. This biographical bibliography serves as a concise source for biographical information and provides an annotated, chronological bibliography of Robinson's works as well as a selected, annotated bibliography of works about her. The most useful feature is the chronological section highlighting major works about Robinson and her writings.

Electronic bibliographic tools make it easy to compile bibliographies. This work's strength is its carefully researched selectivity and conciseness. The biographical sketch is very brief. For more detail on Robinson's life and her influence on economic thought, one should consult such works as *The Joan Robinson Legacy* (M. E. Sharpe, 1991); *Joan Robinson and Modern Economic Theory* (New York University Press, 1989); or *The Economics of Joan Robinson* (Routledge, 1996). The index is poor and inconsistently references Robinson's works. The bio-bibliography is recommended for economic research collections only.—**Bobray Bordelon**

Biography

151. **Biographical Dictionary of European Labor Leaders.** A. Thomas Lane, ed. Westport, Conn., Greenwood Press, 1995. 2v. index. $225.00/set. ISBN 0-313-26456-2.

This 2-volume set contains more than 1,400 biographical listings of individuals connected with the labor movement in Europe from the beginnings of industrial capitalism in the nineteenth century to the present. All European countries are included. The editor has defined *labor* in broad terms and has listed individuals not only from the traditional areas, such as trade unions and labor ministers, but also from such areas as political parties, cooperatives, and what he refers to as "anarchosyndicalist" groups (introduction). Individuals from state-controlled bodies that lack any democratic procedures (e.g., the former Soviet Union and its satellites) are not discussed.

Each entry provides the name of the individual, birth and death dates, and a brief biography generally ranging between 150 and 300 words. In addition, at the end of each biography there are references to other sources where biographical information may be obtained. Also, extensive cross-references between labor leaders of different geographic areas and different intellectual viewpoints provide important links. The editor provides a number of useful appendixes, including a list of labor leaders by state or national/ethnic group, a selective bibliography, a detailed index, and a list of editors and contributors to the work.

Biographical Dictionary of European Labor Leaders is a much-needed current source of information concerning European labor leaders in general and also information on many individuals who are not generally considered in other sources on labor leaders. The dictionary is recommended for all college and university and larger public libraries. Also, it may be useful for government agencies dealing with Europeans involved in labor. [R: Choice, May 96, p. 1445]—**Robert L. Wick**

152. **Who's Who in Finance and Industry, 1996-1997.** 29th ed. New Providence, N.J., Marquis Who's Who/Reed Reference Publishing, 1995. 941p. index. $259.95. ISBN 0-8379-0330-0.

Although the entry elements and format remain the same, this biographical directory has changed since its 27th edition (see ARBA 93, entry 179). The number of biographies has shrunk from 25,400 to 21,000. Foreign coverage has significantly expanded, now constituting about one-sixth of the entries (reviewer's estimate). A "Professional Area Index," new to this edition, greatly enhances access. Biographees are categorized according to broad areas (e.g., finance, government, industry, law) that are in some cases subdivided (e.g., industry into manufacturing, service, trade, and so on); then they are divided geographically, ultimately at the city level. This arrangement usually produces a manageable number of entries under each city.

Admission to the directory is based upon the biographee's "reference value" as reflected by a position held or a significant achievement. This criterion encompasses principal officers of major corporations, high-level federal government officials, important labor leaders, significant scholars, and winners of major awards. To measure the directory's inclusion of principal officers of major corporations, this reviewer conducted a test using the *Forbes* annual rankings of the 500 largest publicly held companies by assets, sales, net income, and market value. To include truly major companies, only those present on the rankings every year, 1992-1995, were chosen. To allow sufficient time for their CEOs to become noteworthy, the CEO's tenure had to span the same four years. Of the 432 CEOs, 354, or roughly 80 percent, were in the directory. CEOs of Dow Jones, Oracle Systems, Pfizer, Rockwell International, and Tele-Communications Inc. were among those missing.

An informal test was conducted for significant people not on the *Forbes* lists but often mentioned in the business press. The success rate was fairly high. Among those missing, however, were John Bogle (chairman of Vanguard), Felix Rohatyn (investment banker), Arthur Levitt (chairman of the Securities and Exchange Commission), James Wolfensohn (president of the World Bank), and Thomas Monaghan (chairman of Domino's Pizza). Although the directory passed both of these tests with high scores, *Marquis Who's Who* should mount a more concerted effort to improve its coverage.

Entries in this directory are also available electronically as part of *The Complete Marquis Who's Who on CD-ROM* (Reed Reference Publishing, 1996), the *Marquis Who's Who* file on DIALOG, and the PEOPLE Library/EXECDR File on LEXIS/NEXIS. This directory remains an essential purchase for business reference collections.—**John Lewis Campbell**

Dictionaries and Encyclopedias

153. **Elsevier's Dictionary of Financial and Economic Terms: Spanish-English and English-Spanish.** Martha Uriona and Jose Daniel Kwacz, comps. New York, Elsevier Science, 1996. 311p. $172.00. ISBN 0-444-82256-9.

This bilingual dictionary is composed of "the most common terms and phrases used in the economic, financial and business world of today." The book is divided into four parts. The first part presents English translations of Spanish entries, followed by concise definitions in English. The second part features Spanish translations of English entries, followed by Spanish explanations. The authors have been careful in both sections to define terms and phrases plainly so that users from one field can understand definitions that fall within the scope of another. The third and fourth parts give additional word-to-word translations, but no definitions. While these are less ambiguous words and translate more clearly, it is not evident why the latter half has been separated from the former. This organization may not be obvious to users who may look up a word or phrase in the definition section but overlook the word-to-word section. A feature that would have been helpful is the inclusion of genders for Spanish words that are not clearly masculine or feminine. This slim, expensive book's strengths are its succinct and simple approach and its sturdy construction. It is especially recommended for corporate libraries, international businesses, and interpreters.

—**Laural L. Adams**

154. **English-Russian Economics Glossary.** By the Languages Service, Terminology and Technical Documentation Section. New York, United Nations, 1996. 344p. $80.00pa. ISBN 92-1-000055-2. S/N GV.R/E.96.0.12.

This glossary contains some 2,200 entries, an English index that makes it reversible into an English-Russian dictionary of economic terms, a list of national currencies in the former Soviet republics, and a bibliography. While potentially useful to foreign direct investors in Russia and possibly in some of the other former Soviet republics, the glossary is intended primarily as a help for translators of current texts on the Russian economy, with its new relevant terminology in banking, the securities markets, business law, and accounting. Old terms that are still relevant and in use are included also. Some of the terms in the glossary carry additional references to the bibliography for further explanation, something that only the most dedicated translators would be likely to seek. Some concepts, such as that of "the income elasticity of supply," have a doubtful significance as only the concept of the income elasticity of demand makes economic sense. The market for this volume seems severely limited.—**Bogdan Mieczkowski**

155. Maurer, John G., and others. **Encyclopedia of Business.** Detroit, Gale, 1995. 2v. index. $395.00/set. ISBN 0-8103-9187-2.

Comprising 700 signed, original essays written in reasonably nontechnical language by professional educators specializing in the fields covered, *Encyclopedia of Business* attempts to describe and explain the terms, phrases, and activities that make up the world of business. Seemingly all disciplines are addressed at least minimally; of topics checked, only "competitive intelligence" was found missing. The broad coverage includes all of the major business disciplines (accounting, finance, management, human relations, marketing, entrepreneurship, and so forth) plus micro- and macroeconomics terms. There are entries for domestic and international organizations, as well as separate articles on doing business in such major countries as China, Mexico, Canada, and Australia and regions such as Africa and the Arab nations. There are no biographies.

The information presented is current; for example, the "Advertising" article includes coverage of fax advertising, infomercials, online computer/Internet advertising, and "spot buys" on local cable television—all fairly recent arrivals to the advertising scene. Entries average 2,500 words, and many include graphs, charts, formulas, and tables. Unannotated lists of items for further reading frequently conclude the articles. Within entries, boldfaced cross-references lead to coverage of related terms and issues; *see* and *see also* notations further direct readers to appropriate topics. A general index and a discipline index conclude the second of the two volumes. Of these, the general index would be improved by more detailed listings under the most popular topic entries (for example, there are 31 different page listings under "Commodities," with no subtopics given), whereas the discipline index is well organized and useful.

The encyclopedia attempts to combine both a practical and theoretical approach in language that is accessible to the lay reader, and it is reasonably successful. It provides solid coverage of a broad range of business topics and does a good job of including supplementary data for clarification when necessary. However, given its purchase price of nearly $400, libraries will need to determine whether they need the generalist approach of this resource or would prefer to purchase several of the lower-priced, special-topic references in such areas as marketing, accounting, management, and the like. [R: Choice, Sept 96, p. 96; LJ, Mar 96, p. 72; RBB, June 96, p. 1769]—**G. Kim Dority**

156. Shim, Jae K., and Joel G. Siegel. **Dictionary of Economics.** New York, John Wiley, 1995. 373p. (Business Dictionary Series). $39.95. ISBN 0-471-01317-X.

Economists looking for detailed essays on classic economic terms know to consult *The New Palgrave: A Dictionary of Economics* (see ARBA 88, entry 165). Most economic dictionaries assume the user has some basic knowledge of economic terms. Shim and Siegel's new entry in John Wiley's Business Dictionary Series provides relatively jargon-free, short definitions of more than 2,200 economic terms. Slang and newer concepts, such as Clintonomics, are included. Cross-references guide the user through terminology and linkages in terms. Graphs, charts, formulas, and tables help illustrate the principles. The appendix consists of tables that give values for such items as future value, chi square, and Durbin-Watson. Unfortunately, the work fails to define Durbin-Watson and fails to meet its primary purpose of defining any term that may not be readily understood. That flaw aside, the work is useful for general reference, business, and economic collections.—**Bobray Bordelon**

Directories

157. **American Business Locations Directory.** Valerie J. Webster and Lia M. Watson, eds. Detroit, Gale, 1996. 5v. index. $575.00/set. ISBN 0-8103-8368-3. (Volumes also available individually: $150.00/v. for volumes 1-4 or $50.00/v. with purchase of v.5 [$375.00].).

The U.S. facilities (e.g., plants, offices, centers, divisions) for companies ranked within the Fortune Industrial 500 and Service 500 are identified in this directory. Intended for jobseekers, students, and sales and marketing professionals, the snapshot view of corporate holdings is arranged geographically by state and city. Entries, with as many as eight categories of information, clarify parent and location type, financial performance, and fortune ranking (for parent only); however, the number of employees is rarely noted, and the list of officers neglects position titles. Each volume has two indexes, one by Standard Industrial Classification (SIC) code and one by company name. Additional access is available through the alphabetic parent company index in volume 5.

This is potentially a useful reference tool. Its failure to meet all this reviewer's expectations results from the nature of corporate holdings, mergers, and franchises rather than volume structure or contents. An "unreal" picture of communities emerges, one in which banking dominates entries for smaller cities, and the subsidiary versus franchise option results in numerous Pizza Huts and few McDonald's in large urban areas. The publishers should consider enlarging the parent database for a more representative picture and employing the newer technologies for a format that permits downloading. Despite these limitations, a timely reference query demonstrated the directory's value as an acquisition for library business collections. [R: Choice, July/Aug 96, p. 1767; LJ, Jan 96, p. 86; RBB, Jan 96, p. 876]—**Sandra E. Belanger**

158. **America's Corporate Families 1995.** Bethlehem, Pa., Dun & Bradstreet, 1995. 3v. index. $495.00; $475.00 (libraries). ISBN 1-56203-393-X. ISSN 0890-6645.

The first two volumes of Dun & Bradstreet's *America's Corporate Families* provide information on approximately 11,000 U.S. parent companies and their 76,000 subsidiaries, branches, and divisions. Volume 1 is alphabetically arranged by parent company and supplies standard directory information, the Dun's number, annual sales figures, a narrative line of business descriptions, the net worth, the number of sites, and up to 6 Standard Industrial Classification (SIC) codes. Under each parent company one also finds the directory listing for its branches, divisions, and subsidiaries with more limited directory information. Volume 2 provides an alphabetic index to all companies; a geographic index by state, then by city; and a third index grouping companies by SIC code. Criteria used for inclusion in this set are that the parent company must have at least 2 business locations, $25 million-plus in sales, and a tangible net worth of more than $500,000. The 3d volume of the set includes information on U.S. companies and their foreign subsidiaries, information on foreign parent companies with U.S. subsidiaries, and the same types of indexes as found in volume 2.

Dun & Bradstreet's policy is to lease these volumes to libraries, which is not an inexpensive undertaking. Because Dun & Bradstreet has a family of publications, much of the information listed here can be found in other publications, such as the *Million Dollar Directory* (see ARBA 87, entry 176). This same information can also be found in National Register Publishing's *Directory of Corporate Affiliations* (see ARBA 91, entry 142, and ARBA 90, entry 175), which has as an added feature an arrangement of companies by whether they are publicly or privately held. The criteria for inclusion in this set require that the parent company have a sales volume of $10 million, thus encompassing more companies. This set is also available on CD-ROM.

There is a great deal of overlap between the National Register Publishing set and the set under review. If a library is already subscribing to other Dun & Bradstreet publications, it may decide to acquire this title. As both sets are expensive, carefully reviewing the options before selecting one over the other is important. For the occasional question concerning subsidiaries, libraries can consider using one of the online databases in this subject area.—**Judith J. Field**

159. **Business and Economic Research Directory.** London, Europa; distr., Detroit, Gale, 1996. 624p. index. $225.00. ISBN 1-85743-024-7.

This title provides the reader with an alphabetic list by country to leading business and finance research institutes. The compilers have included descriptions of approximately 2,000 research institutes located in 150 countries. There has been a serious attempt to provide complete addresses and the name of a contact person, a brief description of the institute's major research interest including founding date, and a list of its publications. The leading economic world powers are well represented, but some of the lesser economic powers have only one or two institutes listed. Part 2 is an alphabetic list of nearly 1,500 journals and periodicals that were included in the 1st section as part of the research institute description. Addresses and, in some instances, e-mail or World Wide Web addresses, a brief description of the scope of the journal, and the language in which it is published are included for each title. The index provides access by the names of research institutes. This book would be of primary interest to academic research institutions and to nonaffiliated research institutes that have personnel needing to identify research partners.—**Judith J. Field**

160. **Business Organizations, Agencies, and Publications Directory: A Guide to Approximately 30,000 New and Established Organizations....** 8th ed. Holly M. Selden and Virgil L. Burton III, eds. Detroit, Gale, 1996. 1786p. index. $375.00. ISBN 0-8103-5676-7. ISSN 0888-1413.

This most recent edition offers slightly more entries within the established topical approach (see ARBA 93, entry 190, for a review of the 6th edition). The numerous chapters, primarily alphabetic, contain standard content (e.g., name, address, telephone number) and descriptions common to most Gale publications.

Topical searches are ably served by the master name and keyword index. While some problems with past editions have been repaired, it should be noted that the limits on comprehensiveness remain, and a significant amount of the content repeats that found in other Gale or U.S. government publications.

The unwieldy size of the current iteration highlights the desirability and importance of database and Web-based formats for libraries struggling with space limitations and the provisions of the Americans with Disabilities Act. This directory remains a convenient, recommended resource for small, specialized libraries serving business clientele. Larger public and academic libraries already have these data available, albeit not as conveniently, in other publications.—**Sandra E. Belanger**

161. **Consultants & Consulting Organizations Directory 1996 Supplement: A Reference Guide....** 16th ed. Brigitte T. Darnay, ed. Detroit, Gale, 1996. 141p. index. $410.00pa. ISBN 0-7876-0297-3. ISSN 0192-091X.

This is a supplement to the 2-volume 1996 (16th) edition of *Consultants & Consulting Organizations Directory*, published annually since 1982. This supplement adds 846 listings to the 22,377 entries in the main volumes, numbered 22,378 to 24,233. They are arranged by subject in 13 chapters and are provided with geographic, consulting activities, and personal names indexes.

Each entry provides the name, address, and telephone number, along with other information, such as consulting activities, principal executive, staff, and branch offices. The index reference provides the number in the main listing. The geographic index covers first the United States firms state by state, and then the Canadian firms by province. The firms are then arranged by city under each state or province. The typeface and double-column layout are clear, and appropriate use is made of bold typeface. Useful footnotes are also provided. The work under review would be helpful for updating the 1996 edition of this directory, but is not sufficient by itself as it includes only additions and changes to the main collection.
—**Barbara E. Brown**

162. **Corporate Affiliations PLUS. Spring/Summer 1995.** [CD-ROM]. New Providence, N.J., R. R. Bowker/Reed Reference Electronic Publishing, 1995. Minimum system requirements: IBM or full MS-DOS compatible 286. ISO 9660-compatible CD-ROM drive with MS-DOS Extensions-compatible device driver and MS-DOS CD-ROM Extensions. MS-DOS or PC-DOS 3.1 (5.0 recommended). Hard disk. 535K conventional memory. Monochrome or color display. $1,995.00/yr. ISBN 0-8352-3333-2.

Although this corporate database compares favorably with other business resources as far as coverage of basic business information, it is weak in the financial information it contains, especially compared to Compact Disclosure. A complete citation contains basic contact information, parent affiliation and the percentage owned by the parent, basic financial figures, Standard Industrial Classification codes, a 10- to 50-word explanation of the company's main work, trade names, officers, board of directors, matching gift and corporate giving amounts, legal and accounting firms, registrar and transfer agent, state of incorporation, number of employees, and the year founded. One address that future editions should record is the business' World Wide Web address.

Installation was quick. While the trouble-seeking techniques in the user's guide were inadequate and inaccurate, a technical support person diagnosed the problem and provided a solution immediately. As any reference librarian knows, users need a simple, intuitive interface they can master quickly. Moreover, they need efficient user guides for reference. The database satisfies the interface requirement. Arrow keys provide access to the intuitive menus, while the Escape key performs logical functions, such as canceling file output or taking the user back to the previous screen. System designers chose text colors for the screen well; commands are in green, white, blue, and yellow on a black background, while error messages appear in red text. The blue Help screens with white messages are a nice contrast.

The publisher could provide better user guides. The bulky three-ring binder has complete instructions, but novices will not refer to large manuals when they need help. Two things would improve the database's usability for the untrained person. First, a Function and Control key template for the keyboard could tell people at a glance what to do. Second, a "cheat sheet," preferably laminated and two-sided, could explain 80 percent of the functions people use—browse, search, print, and save to disk. Because searching is one of the easiest and most intuitive tasks to do in this program, a few examples showing truncation, Boolean search logic, and skillful use of the 19 indexes would be sufficient. This database would be appropriate for high school and community college libraries.—**Susan D. Baird-Joshi**

163. **The Corporate Directory of U.S. Public Companies.** [CD-ROM]. San Mateo, Calif., Walker's Western Research, 1996. Minimum system requirements (Windows version): IBM or compatible. CD-ROM drive with MS-DOS CD-ROM Extensions 2.1. MS-DOS 3.3. Windows 3.X. 1.25MB hard disk space. 640K memory. Minimum system requirements (Macintosh version): Macintosh computer. System 6.0. 1MB RAM with Finder (or 4MB RAM with MultiFinder or System 7). Hard disk. $595.00/single user; $765.00 (with print version).

164. **The Corporate Directory of U.S. Public Companies 1996: Company Profiles and Indexes.** By Walker's. San Mateo, Calif., Walker's Western Research, 1996. 2732p. index. $320.00; $765.00 (with CD-ROM). ISBN 1-879346-27-3.

The Corporate Directory has long occupied a middle ground between the more selective number of companies covered by Hoover's titles, the briefer amount of data provided by Standard & Poor's, and the extensive but expensive coverage afforded by the multivolume sets of Dun & Bradstreet. In addition to providing data on virtually all of the roughly 10,000 publicly held companies in the United States, the directory is noteworthy for its inclusion of each company's financial ratios and balance sheet statistics and, when available, the ages and salaries of all company officers and directors, plus their total shares owned.

The companies are listed alphabetically. Entries generally give company name and contact information; general information (state in which incorporated, number of employees, and the like); stock data; a one- or two-sentence narrative description of the company's area of business; identification of officers and directors with their ages and salaries; and standard financial data (including sales, net income, and earnings-per-share for up to five years). However, information is not always complete; for example, the entry on Tele-Communications Inc., the world's largest cable television company, lists neither officers, directors, nor owners. Seven indexes help the reader locate a target company by company name, names of officers and directors, owners of five percent or more of company stock, geographic location, subsidiary or parent company relationship, Standard Industrial Classification code (listed with definitions), and stock exchange and symbol.

Although the CD-ROM adds two more years of key financials and financial ratios, a listing of recent Securities and Exchange Commission filings, the more recent auditor's report, the Fortune and Forbes rankings (if appropriate), and growth rates for sales and net income, it is in the area of access that the electronic version provides real benefits for a researcher. Going beyond the seven points provided by the print indexes, the CD-ROM version supports searching by type of business, by financial information, by keywords, by number of shares, and by number of employees. In addition, users can export selected data to their own computers to manipulate for reports, comparisons, and analysis. [R: Choice, July/Aug 96, p. 1770; LJ, 15 May 96, p. 53; RBB, June 96, p. 1766]—**G. Kim Dority**

165. **The EPM Licensing Letter Sourcebook.** 1997 ed. Martin Brochstein, ed. New York, EPM Communications, 1996. 653p. index. $295.00pa. ISBN 1-885747-06-3.

This directory provides a comprehensive source for locating information on licensing a particular property, including Larry Bird, Betty Boop, Elvis Presley, Garfield, and Purdue University. The book is arranged into six sections: licensers, licensing agents, licensees, service providers, trade associations, and cross-reference indexes. In section 1, licensers, or property owners, are divided into 13 categories, ranging from apparel and accessories to toys and games. In section 3, licensees, or manufactures, are subdivided into 17 categories, including accessories, apparel, electronics, food and beverage, and video games and software. Information provided about each licenser, licensee, and consultant includes name of company or institution, name of a major officer, address, and telephone and fax numbers. The 5 indexes in section 6 allow quick access by company name, individual name, property for licensers and agents, property for licensees, and products manufactured.

The only similar publication identified is *The International Licensing Directory* (see ARBA 88, entry 309), which is a British publication that covers 63 countries. *The EPM Licensing Letter Sourcebook* is a larger work that appears to be limited to the United States. Although it is expensive, it will be particularly helpful for licensing professionals and for business, large public, and academic libraries with a need for licensing information.—**O. Gene Norman**

166. **Hoover's Masterlist of Major U.S. Companies 1996-1997.** 3d ed. Austin, Tex., Hoover's, 1996. 946p. index. $79.95. ISBN 1-878753-83-5.

Created from a database developed by the publisher, this alphabetically arranged quick-access guide provides capsule profiles on 9,472 major public and private U.S. companies, including every publicly listed U.S. company traded on the New York Stock Exchange, the American Stock Exchange, and the NASDAQ National Market. More than 500 of the United States' largest private companies; hundreds of large enterprises (i.e., universities, foundations, and sports leagues); and many of the fastest-growing private companies are also listed. All companies on the *Forbes* list of the 500 largest private companies in the United States (e.g., insurance companies, supermarket chains, agricultural cooperatives, construction companies, and major subsidiaries of U.S. corporations) are found within the uncluttered, two-column format.

Each profile provides company name, street address, telephone and fax numbers, executives, annual sales figures and percentage change in sales from the previous year, number of employees, and what the company does. When companies failed to provide current statistics, sales figures were approximated based on the previous year's information. Estimated sales figures are clearly identified. The 144-page index lists headquarters locations, industry, and stock exchange symbol. The information contained in this hardcover edition is also available on diskette in Windows and Macintosh formats.

Because of its ease of use, timeliness, and coverage of public and private U.S. companies, this may be just what is needed by fund-raisers and salespeople for access to high-ranking business executives. Public libraries whose clients include investors, jobseekers, and executives will find its purchase worthwhile and appreciated.—**Judy Gay Matthews**

167. **Peterson's Summer Opportunities for Kids and Teenagers 1996.** 13th ed. Princeton, N.J., Peterson's Guides, 1996. 1241p. illus. index. $24.95pa. ISBN 1-56079-496-8. ISSN 0894-9417.

Thousands of sports, art, travel, and academic programs and camps that theoretically can enhance a child's development are profiled here. Some of these programs make jobs or financial aid available. Extensive indexing and tables will help users select programs that will meet their criteria, whether these be geographic, religious, special need (e.g., disabled), or residential. One criterion that is important to parents but that is not shown in the tables or indexes is price range; one must consult the individual profiles for this information. Prices vary enormously but depend largely on the length of the programs, which range from a few days to a couple of months. All programs receive brief descriptions covering interests, activities, contact information, hours, eligibility, and the like. Some 230 programs have longer 2-page descriptions written by their directors.

The book does not evaluate or rate these programs but tells users how to do so. Although parents are told to ask about American Camping Association accreditation, the book does not tell whether or not the camps included have this accreditation. (The American Camping Association has its own annual directory, *The Guide to Accredited Camps* [see ARBA 96, entry 811], which lists more than 2,000 camps.) *Peterson's* is a useful directory that will help parents find enriching experiences for their children. Information on summer programs is also available via the Internet at http://www.petersons.com. The print directory is not complete, however, and larger libraries may wish to supplement it with other reasonably priced directories.—**Susan V. McKimm**

168. **The Prentice Hall Directory of Online Business Information 1997.** By Christopher Engholm and Scott Grimes. Englewood Cliffs, N.J., Prentice Hall Career & Personal Development, 1996. 524p. illus. index. $34.95pa. ISBN 0-13-255282-5.

The two authors of *Online Business Information*, both business researchers and consultants, set out to provide an "annotated, clearly indexed, and cross-referenced businessperson's guide for really using the business tools available online like we wanted to use them." To meet this goal, they have described more than 1,000 Internet sites in 1- to 2-paragraph evaluative annotations that describe each entry's content, its value to the researcher based on professional needs and level of expertise, and how to most time-effectively use the site. When similar sites exist, the authors compare levels of usefulness. The types of sites described include academic sites; premium online services from such commercial vendors as CompuServe or Prodigy; commercial sites (i.e., "originating in the private sector") that are marketing a product or service; and "Labor of Love" sites, where (usually) a single individual with a passion for something undertakes the assemblage of every existing Internet location for information on that topic.

Topically arranged chapters cover navigational tools, general business resources, career advancement, personal finance, business services, resources by industry, international business resources, business references, and the ever-popular "fun places to go during lunch hour." The core chapters are preceded by 3 introductory chapters that provide a 10-page introduction to the Internet, how it works, and what options (e.g., e-mail) it offers; basic search strategies for business researchers; and 22 survival-tool sites for business researchers (for example, "Addresses and Phone Numbers," "Search Tools," and "U.S. Government"). Each entry notes the site's title, its Internet address, and, in cases where the service charges users a fee, pricing information. Each site is rated (one to five stars) based on content (amount and quality); ease (getting to and getting around within a site); speed (organized for fast and efficient information and retrieval?); and value (worth the time and money involved?). The annotations provide sufficient information to allow business researchers to decide whether a given site will deliver what they need, thus avoiding the dreaded "browsing" downtime. The book's margins allow for plenty of white space, encouraging lots of users' margin notes.

A terrific idea (as are most special-topic Internet directories) with solid, useful content, *Online Business Information* unfortunately lacks those touches that could make its execution as valuable as its content. There are lapses in organizational logic and access points: Edupage, a resource that is focused on educational technology and related issues, players, and companies, is listed within the "multimedia and electronic publishing" section, and has no index listing under "Education" or its *see* reference, "Training/Education." The M. I. S. Research Center, dedicated to research on the use of information technology in management (management information systems), is located under "Management, Consulting, and Human Resources" rather than in the "Information Systems Management" section, with no cross-reference either within the sections or in the index. The work suffers generally from a mediocre index with extremely poor subject indexing. For example, within the text there is a section on "Publishing and the Media" that includes entries for Interactive Age (multimedia industry), Broadcast Professional Forum (television and radio broadcasting), CBS television (television broadcasting), and Electronic Commerce Associates (online mail-order catalogs, online shopping), yet in the index the only place to find these entries is under the heading "Publishing and Media" or alphabetically by site name. A book this valuable deserves generous interchapter cross-referencing and a solid, well-thought-out index that employs useful subject terms.

Despite the need for improved cross-referencing and indexing, *Online Business Information* is nevertheless an extraordinary value for the price. The resource information is updated monthly on the World Wide Web, where one can search by key term. (However, the information offered is much scantier—one- or two-sentence versus one- or two-paragraph annotations.) Unfortunately, the Website continues the print version's occasional errors of misspelling and incorrect alphabetization. However, assuming that the next edition will do a great job of copyediting, cross-referencing, and indexing, this is a publication that one can easily recommend to all business libraries, researchers, academic libraries, and public libraries supporting business research for their communities. [R: LJ, 1 Nov 96, p. 60]—**G. Kim Dority**

169. **The Princeton Review Student Access Guide to the Best Business Schools.** 1996 ed. By Nedda Gilbert. New York, Princeton Review/Random House, 1995. 264p. index. $20.00pa. ISBN 0-679-76147-0. ISSN 1067-2141.

Aimed at prospective graduate business school applicants, this guide offers information about what admissions officers seek, what to expect during and from the master of business administration (MBA) degree program, and what characterizes the best business schools. Data for the book were drawn from surveys of more than 12,500 currently matriculated business school students, from hundreds of admission officers and administrators, and from the schools themselves.

The book is organized into three broad sections. The first three chapters are essays aimed at helping readers understand why they want an MBA, what qualities might be important for them in picking the best school for themselves, and what graduate study in business is like. The second section consists of four chapters that focus on getting accepted and includes concrete advice on writing successful application essays and a dozen examples of submitted essays, each accompanied by a detailed critique from the judging school's admission officer. The third and major portion of the guide includes alphabetically arranged profiles of 70 "best" business schools, prefaced by a ranking along 30 categories (e.g., academics, pressure, social life, facilities, and placement) of the best and worst 10 schools according to the opinions of surveyed students.

The profile for each school consists of two pages. Sidebars on each edge graphically illustrate lists of statistics on admissions, student demographics, treatment of minority and women students, specialties, degrees, tuition and housing costs, student rankings and opinions, and information on contacting the school. The text of each profile covers academics, placement and recruiting, student and campus life, and admissions. The criteria for selection of the 70 entries are not explicit, although the author addresses the use of input from annual magazine rankings, surveyed student opinions, and school administrators. All schools included offer programs accredited by the American Assembly of Collegiate Business Schools, except Rice University, which is included for its special programs and national reputation. The University of Florida and State University of New York at Albany were not included here, even though they meet the criteria of excellence, because permission to poll their students could not be obtained.

Part of the Princeton Review series, this is an easy-to-use, popular reading guide for the business school shopper, geared to the prospective student seeking the insiders' view from students already enrolled. For the price, it is a good insight but inconsistent in output data about the success or quality of the programs.—**Danuta A. Nitecki**

170. **Research Services Directory 1995: A One-Stop Guide to Commercial Research Activity.** 6th ed. Anthony L. Gerring, ed. Detroit, Gale, 1995. 931p. index. $340.00. ISBN 0-8103-7905-8. ISSN 0278-1743.

This edition lists 4,741 United States and Canadian for-profit laboratories; investigators; information brokers; engineering, market, and research firms; and organizations that provide applied, fundamental, or developmental research for other companies. Each entry may provide up to 29 data elements including name, address, telephone and fax numbers, e-mail address, company description, research or technical field, special resources and licenses, rates, affiliates, staff size, memberships, major publications, founding date, locally developed databases, library, and additional contact data (e-mail addresses are new with this edition). Published every three years, data are updated by direct mail and telephone contact.

This is one of four research directories published by Gale covering the full range of research centers, all of which are available online. The others are *Research Centers Directory* (see ARBA 96, entry 340), *Government Research Directory* (see ARBA 94, entry 740), and *International Research Centers Directory* (see ARBA 96, entry 55). As with all Gale publications, it is well indexed with company, personal, subject, and geographic names. Although printed on acid-free, recycled paper, there is no CIP information; strange from a company that relies so heavily on the library market.

Research Services Directory is recommended over R. R. Bowker's *Directory of American Research and Technology* (see ARBA 96, entry 182), an annual that lists approximately twice as many companies but has only half the data elements and half the description per entry for essentially the same price. The Gale title is a fine, standard work, highly recommended for any library needing access to serious research service.—**Patrick J. Brunet**

171. **Standard & Poor's SmallCap 600 Guide.** 1996 ed. By Standard & Poor's. New York, McGraw-Hill, 1996. 1053p. $24.95pa. ISBN 0-07-052155-7.

This guide, now in its 2d annual edition, provides investment advisory reports on the 600 companies that compose the Standard & Poor's SmallCap Index. As a group, they typify the universe of 4,800-plus small market capitalization companies and thereby serve as a benchmark against which to measure a small cap mutual fund or company's stock performance. The companies' market caps range from less than $100 million to more than $3 billion, and average $400 million. The industrial, utility, transportation, service, and financial sectors are all represented, as are the 3 major exchanges—276 from the New York Stock Exchange, 18 from the American Stock Exchange, and 306 from NASDAQ.

SmallCap 600 Guide draws 509 reports from the *Standard & Poor's Stock Reports* and 91 from the now-ceased *Standard & Poor's NASDAQ & Regional Profiles*. "Stock Reports" and "Profiles" are arranged alphabetically in separate sections. Each informative, two-page stock report contains a business description; an analysis of recent financial and stock market performance; a summary of important developments; stock performance data and a chart of price movements; earnings, dividend, and balance sheet data; and S&P's quantitative and qualitative measures. Profiles are only one-third of a page and contain a brief business description and stock and financial data. Presumably the stock reports will replace these profiles in the next edition.

Comparison of the work under review was made with well-known investment advisory tools. More than 30 percent of its companies are among those 1,600 covered by the combined *Moody's Handbook of Common Stocks* (see ARBA 93, entry 223) and *Moody's Handbook of NASDAQ Stocks* (Moody's Investors Service). Slightly more than 90 percent (reviewer's conservative estimate) of the guide's companies are among those 3,500 covered by the combined *Value Line Investment Survey, Standard Edition*, and the *Expanded Edition* (Value Line). The Value Line *Standard Edition*'s one-page reports supply more years of data but shorter business descriptions than the *SmallCap*'s stock reports. The Value Line *Expanded Edition*'s one-page reports have relatively little of *SmallCap*'s narrative financial assessment.

The decision to purchase this guide is complex. *SmallCap* is a subset of the *Standard & Poor's Stock Reports*, an expensive service, whose 3 parts cover more than 4,700 companies, with reports revised 3 or 4 times per year. Libraries subscribing to the full set of the *Stock Reports* would gain no coverage with this guide. Those who do not subscribe may find *SmallCap* and its companions, the *Standard & Poor's 500 Guide* (see ARBA 96, entry 214) and the *Standard & Poor's MidCap 400 Guide* (see ARBA 96, entry 215), which collectively cover 1,500 companies, an inexpensive alternative, if they do not mind the merely annual updating. The Value Line title extensively duplicates *SmallCap*'s company coverage and revises reports four times per year. However, libraries subscribing to it, and unable to afford the *Stock Reports*, may find the guide's different emphasis in report content complementary. Libraries owning only the Moody's handbooks would find this guide's added company coverage and report content valuable.

—John Lewis Campbell

172. **World Databases in Company Information.** C. J. Armstrong and R. R. Fenton, eds. New Providence, N.J., Bowker-Saur/Reed Reference Publishing, 1996. 1147p. index. (World Databases Series). $325.00. ISBN 1-85739-195-0.

This is the 11th title in the World Databases Series that the publisher has issued. This title attempts to provide worldwide coverage of business information databases, with special effort to identify those originating in Australasia, the Far East, Russia, and Europe. The analysis of such a compilation has to recognize the dynamic nature of the business field as the various databases continuously merge, migrate to different formats, change names, create similar but not identical databases in new formats, or simply cease being published. The editors had a formidable task in an area where the research seeks the latest information. The foreword states that the editors want this series to "become the de facto authority on electronically published databases with details of content, size, access and pricing as well as expert commentary on the major databases." They partially succeed at this goal, as the ever-changing nature of business information cannot be successfully documented in a single book. There is no indication that there will be supplements published to maintain the usefulness of this source.

Having noted this, one must also note that the book will be useful as a reference source to identify those less-familiar sources generated outside of the United States. It provides a detailed description of each database using the master record concept, which includes online hosts, CD-ROM publishers, diskette publishers, videotex hosts, and tape producers. The guide does supply some e-mail information, but not as rigorously as other information. Five sections make up the main part of this directory. The first section lists those databases that provide detailed company information; the second gives company directory information; the third segment offers product directory information; the fourth lists directories that identify individuals, and the last section furnishes a list of directories for not-for-profit organizations.

To enhance access to the vast amount of information, four indexes have been included. The first index is a directory of all the addresses referenced in the various entries. The subject index helps to identify specific subject areas within the various databases, the producer index links database names to producers serving as a guide in determining additional products that they produce, and the fourth index gives access by database names. This work is an extensive, detailed look at electronic databases providing company information, and if one uses it as a starting point when looking for information outside of their expertise, it will be of use. The contents of the book will quickly become dated as the migration to World Wide Web sites continues, but it will have value as a retrospective text. This title will be of particular value to large academic libraries and those libraries with a high demand for international trade information.

—Judith J. Field

173. **World Directory of Trade and Business Associations.** London, Euromonitor; distr., Detroit, Gale, 1996. 430p. index. $550.00pa. ISBN 0-86338-556-7.

This is an expansion of the *European Directory of Trade and Business Associations* (see ARBA 92, entry 245). There are approximately 3,900 entries encompassing international associations and those of 5 world regions and 88 countries, from all business sectors. The publisher compiled the directory through contact with associations and its own research.

The two-page introduction discusses the directory's compilation, coverage, and arrangement. Entries are clustered as follows: first, those for international associations; then, those for seven world regions (Asia, Central and South America, Eastern Europe, the rest of Europe, the Middle East and Africa, North America, and Oceania); and within each region, associations serving the whole region; followed by those of individual countries. Arrangement within sections is alphabetic. There are name and subject indexes, the latter organized into 59 business sectors.

Regional emphasis is on Europe, Asia, and North America, in that order. The top 8 countries (with their number of entries) are the United States (253), Italy (180), the United Kingdom (148), Canada (145), France (141), Japan (131), Spain (111), and Germany (107). Given the relative size of their economies, Japan and Germany seem underrepresented. Ten countries have only one entry.

Entry length varies widely, from 4 lines to half a page, with an average of 11 entries per page. Entries for some countries are typically longer than those for others. The amount of data elements also varies. In addition to address and telephone number, entries usually contain a fax number and names of chief officers. Other elements, in descending order of frequency, are membership size/composition, year established, aims, publications, activities, structure, telex number, and miscellaneous notes. The double-column page layout is attractive and legible. Names in non-roman alphabets have been translated into English. All others are in their original languages.

Some major, well-known associations are missing (e.g., American Marketing Association, Conference Board, OPEC). Occasionally, associations are listed twice. A test of the indexing for 35 entries revealed that 9 were not subject indexed and 4 not name indexed. Some entries are irritatingly alphabetized under "The." The composition and content of 20 association entries were compared with their counterparts in the *Encyclopedia of Associations International Organizations* (see ARBA 94, entry 48), hereafter abbreviated as EAIO. Both directories have many common data elements, although their content sometimes differs. The directory under review generally gives multiple officer names; EAIO gives only one. EAIO more often supplies information on aims, activities, conventions, and publications. Also, it often has two useful, unique elements: staff size and the association's languages.

Future editions of this directory should address the following: (1) significantly expand the number of entries; (2) balance country coverage better; (3) provide aims, activities, and publication information for many more associations and add staff size and official language data elements; and (4) make name and subject indexing more thorough. The publisher has produced a substantial first effort. Libraries with international business collections may wish to consider this directory, even though the price seems high.

—**John Lewis Campbell**

174. **World Directory of Trade and Business Journals.** London, Euromonitor; distr., Detroit, Gale, 1996. 378p. index. $550.00pa. ISBN 0-86338-629-6.

Euromonitor has added a new title to its distinguished series of world business directories, *World Directory of Trade and Business Journals*. This volume replaces previous editions that were limited to European journals. After listing some 60 publications with an international focus, the more than 3,000 remaining entries are distributed into 7 world regional categories. For each region, journals that cover the region are given first. These are followed by journals that are essentially national in focus, by country within each region. Entries include publisher's name and address, as well as telephone and fax numbers. With respect to the publication, information is given on year of establishment, frequency of publication, language, products/industries covered, target readership, circulation, price, and names of both the editor and the advertising manager.

The regional approach simplifies geographic searching, although the distinction in focus among world, region, and country should be taken only as a general guide. Entries are further indexed alphabetically and by business type (product or service covered). Journals serving both industrial and consumer businesses are treated, although there are more of the latter. The large number of journals listed and the broad spectrum of countries covered attest to the comprehensiveness of the volume. Euromonitor editors directly contacted publishers of journals listed to ensure a high degree of accuracy in the entries. The journal synopses are preceded by a table of contents (geographic), a brief introduction, and a list of sectors covered.

This volume can serve as a useful point of departure for obtaining further information on business firms, products, and services. It can also steer advertisers toward appropriate media to reach potential buyers or clients.—**William C. Struning**

175. **World Guide to Trade Associations.** 4th ed. Michael Zils, ed. New Providence, N.J., K. G. Saur/Reed Reference Publishing, 1995. 536p. index. (Handbook of International Documentation and Information, v.12). $395.00. ISBN 3-598-20722-0.

The 4th edition of this work contains 22,000 associations from industry, trade, craft, and service sectors from 187 countries or territories. The countries are arranged in alphabetic order according to the English-language spelling. There are also an alphabetic list of all associations' names, an index of 392 professional fields, and an index of periodical publications. This edition has been expanded to include East European and Asian countries. Chambers of industry and commerce have been left out of this edition and are scheduled to be published in a separate reference work in 1996.

Individual entries contain information, where available, on the association's name, address, telephone and fax numbers, telegram address, telefax, year founded, number of members, names of president and general secretary, area of activity, and regular publication with publication information. This oversized book contains 536 pages on average paper with average binding. The book will be extremely useful for anyone interested in an international guide to trade associations.—**Herbert W. Ockerman**

Handbooks and Yearbooks

176. **Business Statistics of the United States.** 1995 ed. Courtenay M. Slater, ed. Lanham, Md., Bernan Press, 1996. 1v. (various paging). index. $49.00pa. ISBN 0-89059-040-0.

Since 1932, the U.S. Commerce Department, Bureau of Economic Analysis's (BEA) *Business Statistics*, along with its monthly updates in the blue pages of *Survey of Current Business*, have been relied upon for their time series and industry data. *Business Statistics* and the blue pages have become casualties of government cutbacks, but the base publication has been commercially revived. Approximately 2,000 annual data time series for 1966 through 1994 and monthly data for 1991 through 1994 are provided. As with its predecessor, one still finds items such as general business indicators, commodity prices, national income and product accounts, international transactions, and background notes. Enhancements include a review of recent changes in federal programs that provide key economic indicators, charts, per capita data from national income and product accounts, and annual income and employment data for each state and region for 1959 through 1994. A standard work has been made even better. It remains a necessity for any business or economic library. [R: Choice, June 96, p. 1612]—**Bobray Bordelon**

177. **Encyclopedia of Business Information Sources Supplement: A Bibliographic Guide....** 10th ed. James Woy, ed. Detroit, Gale, 1996. 236p. $100.00pa. ISBN 0-8103-8585-6. ISSN 0071-0210.

This supplement updates the encyclopedia's 10th edition, published in 1994. Some 20 new topics are covered, and new material is presented for approximately 700 other subjects. A sample of the new topics provides an indication of the title's breadth: car wash industry, computer imaging, disability insurance, Latin American markets, multimedia, Unix, zoning. As in prior editions, subjects are presented alphabetically and listed in an "outline of contents" at the front of the volume. No index to specific sources is included.

Previously reviewed several times in ARBA (see, most recently, ARBA 93, entry 206), this work remains a useful first stop for researchers investigating a multitude of business subjects. Its importance increases as the other bibliographic work of comparable breadth, *Business Information Sources* (see ARBA 86, entry 158), becomes dated. The *Encyclopedia of Business Information Sources* continues to merit its place as a core title in a business collection of any size.—**Christopher J. Hoeppner**

Thesauri

178. Barron's Business Thesaurus. By Mary A. De Vries. Hauppauge, N.Y., Barron's Educational Series, 1996. 365p. $12.95pa. ISBN 0-8120-9327-5.

The focus of this work is to provide businesspeople with a thesaurus that meets their needs and is suitable for desktop or travel. De Vries, an author of secretarial handbooks and business communication books, has drawn the thesaurus terms from a wide variety of sources, including reports, business correspondence, news releases, periodicals, associations, and the like. Only words with five or more business-related synonyms are listed. The thesaurus contains more than 3,000 entries and 73,000 synonyms arranged in alphabetic order. The synonyms under each entry are also alphabetized.

Although entitled a "business thesaurus," the majority of the entries are in fact nonbusiness-related terms, such as *noteworthy*, *notice*, *notify*, *notion*, and *novelty*. It would be more accurate to say that this is a compact thesaurus with a business focus. Some synonyms are really more descriptive statements, such as the term *profits*, which has as one of its synonyms the phrase "income less expenses." This may be helpful as a dictionary definition but not as a thesaurus term, nor is it likely to be used as a synonym. There are also some notable absences, such as the synonyms "receivership" and "Chapter 11" under the term *bankruptcy*, or "bullish" under the term *enthusiasm*. Other major terms missing include *buyout*, *blue collar*, *mentor*, *reorganization/restructuring*, *outsource*, *proprietary*, and *shakeout*. Although the alphabetic organization of synonyms under each term is a common practice in dictionary thesauruses, it would be more helpful to place the synonyms in order of conceptual closeness to the original term.

While this thesaurus may be useful as a quick reference to businesspeople on the road, they would be better served by an up-to-date, full-length thesaurus or synonym finder. This title is not recommended for libraries.—**Gerald L. Gill**

ACCOUNTING

179. The History of Accounting: An International Encyclopedia. Michael Chatfield and Richard Vangermeersch, eds. New York, Garland, 1996. 649p. index. (Garland Reference Library of the Humanities, v.1573). $95.00. ISBN 0-8153-0809-4.

During the last century, many significant monographs have been written on the history of accounting and accounting thought. Landmark encyclopedias and handbooks on accounting also exist. The missing element has been an encyclopedia that focuses on accounting history. One of the closest attempts is R. J. Chambers's *An Accounting Thesaurus* (Elsevier Science, 1995). That work shows the etymology of accounting concepts in a manner similar to the *Oxford English Dictionary* (2d ed.; see ARBA 90, entry 1006).

The work of Chatfield and Vangermeersch is an attempt to fill the gap. Short essays on more than 400 major concepts, laws, cases, individuals, and associations provide concise summaries of the major areas of accounting. Each entry is followed by a brief bibliography. The alphabetic listing is supplemented by *see also* entries and a detailed index. This work is not intended to serve as a dictionary or handbook for the practitioner. Its purpose is to trace the history of accounting and to provide background information on important areas of accounting. As such, it is recommended for scholarly accounting and business history collections. [R: BL, July 96, p. 1845; Choice, Oct 96, p. 253]—**Bobray Bordelon**

BUSINESS SERVICES AND INVESTMENT GUIDES

Directories

180. **Bond's Franchise Guide.** 1996 ed. Oakland, Calif., Source Book Publications, 1996. 544p. index. $29.95pa. ISBN 1-887137-01-7.

Previously issued by Dow Jones-Irwin as *The Source Book of Franchise Opportunities* (see ARBA 92, entry 154; ARBA 89, entry 181; and ARBA 86, entry 222) for 7 editions, the current title was adopted in 1995 for the 8th annual publication. Previous reviews have pointed to the value of this tool as being more comprehensive and more detailed in its coverage of franchise operations in North America than any of its competitors. The guide continues as a top-drawer publication with its increased coverage due to the expanding franchise market, which today accounts for 13 percent of retail sales. Robert Bond has served as a successful consultant and has been consistent in his goal to provide the needed franchise information for "the sophisticated business person seriously interested in the process of selecting an optimal franchise opportunity."

The guide is divided into four sections. Section 1 serves as an introductory segment with 3 chapters offering technical awareness and understanding of the franchise business, including statistical tables; suggestions on how to use the data; and a useful, 23-item, annotated bibliography. Section 2 supplies the majority of the text with 2,300 franchisors listed by type in 54 chapters. (Chapter 4, "Automotive Products and Services," contains 150 business operations, while chapter 56, "Travel," identifies 21 franchises.) Just more than 1,100 of these entries are in-depth listings giving the background (history, size, geographic distribution); financial data and details; support and training information; and plans for expansion. An additional 1,200 companies are given brief listings (name, address, telephone and fax numbers, and contact persons) at the end of each of the appropriate chapters. Section 3 is an appendix providing the detailed, 40-item questionnaire from which the posted entries were derived, while section 4 furnishes a useful alphabetic listing of all franchises treated in the guide.—**Ron Blazek**

181. **Fitzroy Dearborn International Directory of Venture Capital Funds.** 2d ed. W. Keith Schilit and John T. Willig, eds. Chicago, Fitzroy Dearborn, 1996. 1417p. index. $150.00. ISBN 1-884964-51-6.

The 2d edition of this work includes a greatly enlarged list of 1,000 funds, which more than doubles the 400 entries found in the earlier text (see ARBA 96, entry 184). In addition, available e-mail addresses and mission statements are provided, along with expanded international coverage. The resource is organized in the same manner as the 1st edition. It begins with a series of nine chapters, or four more chapters than the earlier edition, that outline the essential knowledge and information required to participate in the venture capital industry. The majority of the text is once again devoted to the five broad categories of venture capital fund companies. The first four sections include U.S. companies as follows: general, high technology/medical, minority and socially useful, and strategic partners. The final section is devoted to venture capital funds available outside of the United States. Entries in each of the sections are arranged alphabetically. The text is followed by four indexes listing companies alphabetically arranged by name, fund executives, and company affiliations; funds listed by country and states (in the United States); and funds listed by investment preferences or categories.

The expanding market for venture funds makes this sourcebook valuable to investors, specialists, and researchers in the venture capital market. As a result, this work may prove useful to academic and public library reference collections when supplemented with updated information from other up-to-date print and nonprint resources.—**James M. Murray**

Handbooks and Yearbooks

182. **Cyberstocks: An Investor's Guide to Internet Companies.** Alan Chai, ed. Austin, Tex., Hoover's, 1996. 408p. index. $24.95pa. ISBN 1-57311-011-6.

The explosive growth of the Internet has created a substantial demand for books in the field. Dozens of books have already been published covering almost every aspect of the Internet. Chai's book, however, is unique. *Cyberstocks* is based on extensive research and is packed with excellent information, yet it is concise and extremely easy to read. The guide is directed to investors, but will appeal to all individuals who want to have a basic understanding of the Internet and the players shaping it.

The book consists of five parts and an index. The first four parts provide a simple, but not oversimplified, overview of the hardware, software, and services offered in the Internet market. The fifth part represents the majority of the book. It profiles some 100 companies participating in the industry. Each company profile consists of a brief history of the company, its products, its strengths and weaknesses, its sales and profits, and its future outlook. Recognizing that the fast rate of change in the industry would soon make the book out-of-date, the publishers launched a free Website in conjunction with the release of the book. The Website is updated regularly and is an excellent companion to the book.

Chai has done an excellent service to the industry. His book is highly recommended to anyone who wants to learn from and profit from the Internet.—**Elie M. Dick**

183. **The Dow Jones Averages, 1885-1995.** Phyllis S. Pierce, ed. Burr Ridge, Ill., Irwin Professional Publishing, 1996. 1v. (unpaged). $95.00. ISBN 0-7863-0974-1.

Charles Dow was a journalist who in 1884 began figuring stock performance averages on a grouping of 11 issues, mostly railroads. Industrials were separated from railroads in 1896 and the two were issued as separate indexes in the first Dow Jones listing in 1897. The current handbook was published by the company in celebration of its centennial year and as an affirmation of the continued importance and workability of its three major indexes today (industrials, utilities, transportation).

The work is simple in design, beginning with a brief introductory segment by an editor of the *Wall Street Journal*, and followed by a comprehensive graph illustrating the monthly averages for a period of 50 years, 1940 to 1990. Five separate graphs then cover the years 1991 to 1995. A chronology dating from July 3, 1884 (Dow's first publication), then traces all changes, additions, replacements, and the like, of all stocks used in each of the indexes, culminating with a 2 for 1 split of International Paper Company on September 18, 1995. The remainder of this large volume is then given to yearly and monthly charts providing daily averages, along with highs and lows for each month from 1885 to 1985.

Primarily for historians or those who love the market, the work offers the most detailed listings to date and provides awareness of such dates as the introduction of stocks not on the New York Stock Exchange and the year that transportation replaced the railroad index. The author is a professional writer with Dow Jones and has served as editor of *Irwin Investor's Handbook* (Irwin Professional Publishing) since 1977.—**Ron Blazek**

184. Ricchiuto, Steven R., and Barclays de Zoete Wedd Securities. **The Rate Reference Guide to the U.S. Treasury Market 1984-1995.** Burr Ridge, Ill., Irwin Professional Publishing, 1996. 367p. illus. $55.00. ISBN 1-55738-790-7.

The guide begins with a short overview essay and a dozen graphs charting such data series as real gross domestic product, consumer spending, employment, and prices for the period from 1971 through 1995. The book's main body comprises information on market factors affecting interest rates for the 12-year period in the title. This is done at two levels of detail. First, an annual section looks at the period on a year-by-year basis, enumerating important developments, typically 25 to 50 for each year, and cross-referencing each of these to graphs charting the yields on 3-month bills and 30-year bonds issued by the U.S. Treasury. The last and longest section of the book provides even greater detail using a monthly format. Six to twelve developments are listed and charted for each month. Monthly graphs chart the T-bill and long bond yields on a daily basis, and a third graph tracks the spread between these two yields. Finally, a table gives daily yields on Treasury securities of all maturities.

Because Treasury securities are considered risk-free, their yields serve as benchmarks for interest rates in general. Therefore, the behavior of Treasury yields is of great interest to economic and financial analysts. This book's value, unlike that of many reference works, lies not so much in its content as in its organization and presentation. The events reported in the guide all can be found summarized in such sources as business almanacs and investment newsletters. The yield data and other statistics are also readily available. No other source, however, places in such sharp relief the relationship between economic developments and interest rates. This is a highly revelatory work that merits a place in any business or economics collection.—**Christopher J. Hoeppner**

185. Williamson, Gordon K. **The 100 Best Mutual Funds You Can Buy, 1995: Includes Money Market Funds.** Holbrook, Mass., Adams Publishing, 1995. 302p. index. $12.95pa. ISBN 1-55850-440-0.

Many books are available listing mutual funds, but this one fills a void by offering concrete advice on which one to choose according to the investor's risk tolerance and investment objectives. Williamson, a Certified Professional Planner and tax attorney, has chosen the best 100 out of the approximately 5,000 mutual funds available according to 4 criteria: the number of years the manager has been there, the amount of negative market activity, the performance for the last five years, and the risk adjusted return. His approach to evaluating risk seems especially thoughtful, excluding funds that too often underperformed risk-free investment vehicles such as CD or U.S. Treasury Bills. He also covers the various kinds of funds, their particular investment strengths, dollar-cost averaging, load versus no-load, systematic withdrawal plans, big versus little funds, and includes a glossary of terms at the end. This guide, which is in its fifth year of publication, is excellent for both the beginning and the more advanced investor.—**Carol D. Henry**

186. **World Stock Exchange Fact Book: Historical Securities Data for the International Investor.** Morris Plains, N.J., Electronic Commerce, 1995. 509p. $295.00 spiralbound; $390.00 (with disk). ISBN 0-9648930-0-2.

The *Fact Book* provides information concerning stock exchanges in 42 countries, arranged in a standard format by country. The compilers indicate that all data have been gathered directly from the exchanges. The information presented is of two types: textual and statistical. The text consists mainly of bulleted lists outlining stock exchange and government regulations and practices with respect to listing and disclosure, investor protection, restrictions on foreign investments, and mergers and acquisitions. Three types of statistical information are presented: data on the exchange itself (annual trading volume and value, market capitalization, price/earnings ratios and dividend yields); data on one or more stock indexes for each exchange (monthly high, low, closing and average values); and national economic data (annual gross domestic product, balance of trade, interest and exchange rates) for each country. Additionally, the book is available with or without a 3.5-inch diskette containing Microsoft Excel spreadsheet files with all of the statistical data.

Various sources of this type are available. What distinguishes the *Fact Book*? In most cases, the work under review covers only the most prominent exchange(s) in each country—for example, in the United States, the New York and American exchanges and the NASDAQ market are covered, but the Chicago, Pacific, and other regional exchanges are not. In most cases, 20 years of statistical data are provided, much more than in other sources of this type. For most stock indexes, the *Fact Book* provides a list of the component stocks classified by industry. An appendix provides details on the various methods for computing stock indexes and other performance measures. Last but not least, the diskette adds significant value by allowing users to craft their own analyses and readily incorporate selected data into documents and presentations. These features combine to make this book a useful resource for academic and securities industry researchers seeking an analytic tool rather than a comprehensive directory of world stock markets. It is recommended for libraries with clientele of these types. [R: Choice, June 96, p. 1625; LJ, Mar 96, p. 64]—**Christopher J. Hoeppner**

CONSUMER EDUCATION

187. **Better Buys for Business: The Independent Consumer Guide to Office Equipment.** Santa Barbara, Calif., Better Buys for Business, 1996. 10v. illus. $125.00/set/yr.

Not everyone needs a copier to print a million copies per month at a speed of 135 copies per minute, but for office equipment buyers who do, *Better Buys for Business*, published since 1986, is the definitive consumer guide. Formerly known as *What to Buy for Business*, this resource is published 10 times a year, with each issue focusing on one type of office equipment. Evaluations have low-, mid-, and high-volume copiers; business telephone systems; computers; postage meter systems; fax machines; and laser and LED printers. For ease of use, issues are organized similarly into four main sections and are intended to give buyers all the facts to make the best choice.

Discussions cover a general overview of the machine; pros and cons; how to purchase the machine; the technology in plain, easy-to-understand English; hookup and networking considerations; future developments; and advance information on new machines that will be entering the market. Vendor information and profiles with company track records and comparisons of service and customer support policies should be valuable for long-term maintenance of the machines. The last section reviews specific machines and follows it with a summary chart of all models in grid format including price and features. Recommendations are made from research and analyses of the products and are unbiased.

The past 10 years have verified the trend toward more and more automation in the workplace with the advent of such machines as computers, fax machines, laptops, and color printers. One would expect there to be other guides such as this one. However, it was difficult to find any that were this comprehensive. The only book that might even compare is *The Office Equipment Adviser* by John Derrick (3d ed., What to Buy for Business, 1995), which is a condensation of the Better Buys for Business series into one paperback and does not include any price information.—**Elizabeth D'Antonio-Gan**

188. **Consumers Index to Product Evaluations and Information Sources. Volume 24, Number 2, April-June 1996.** C. Edward Wall and others, eds. Ann Arbor, Mich., Pierian Press, 1996. 163p. index. $129.00pa./yr.

Consumers Index, published quarterly and cumulated annually, is an index to articles in more than 110 periodicals, services, and World Wide Web sites. The index is geared to the general consumer and the educational/library community. It is divided into 17 main subject groupings under such headings as "Finances, Employment, Insurance and Investments," "Transportation," and "Sight and Sound." There are divisions under each of these principal headings; for example, "Sight and Sound" has subheadings for audio equipment, television, video equipment, photography, and optics. These subgroupings are further subdivided as appropriate. Articles that survey the topic as a whole appear first, followed by headings for specific products, services, or topics. Next are articles discussing alerts and warnings and articles on *National Highway Traffic Safety Administration News Releases* that detail safety recalls.

If all the sections and subdivisions give one the impression the index must be cumbersome and hard to use, such is most certainly not the case. The inside of the front cover gives a useful "how-to" explanation. This is followed by a detailed table of contents. After this is a helpful alphabetic subject index. The other indexes are by product name/manufacturer and manufacturer/product name, by recall, and by alerts and warnings. There are other periodical indexes that index product evaluation articles within a given field, but only *Readers' Guide to Periodical Literature* (see ARBA 92, entry 60) begins to offer the breadth that *Consumers Index* provides, and the *Readers' Guide* pales by comparison. The title under review is strongly recommended for public libraries of all sizes and all but the most specialized academic libraries.—**Dene L. Clark**

FINANCE AND BANKING

189. Blum, Laurie. **Free Money from the Federal Government for Small Businesses and Entrepreneurs.** 2d ed. New York, John Wiley, 1996. 358p. index. $16.95pa. ISBN 0-471-13009-5.

The majority of people in the United States are not aware of the fact that billions of government dollars are available for small businesses and entrepreneurs. These funds can be obtained from a large number of federal, state, county, and city agencies. They can be used in a wide variety of programs. The few who know about the availability of these funds do not know whom to contact and how to go about getting help.

Blum's book is an excellent attempt to help individuals and small businesses in locating the right agency to get them going. The book covers almost all types of grants in almost all fields. This includes agriculture, community development, energy, the environment, research and development, housing, and minorities. Blum ensured that addresses are complete with names of contacts and telephone and fax numbers. All entries are arranged by state and by field. Many entries are duplicated, but only to ensure simplicity and ease of use. Finally, the author goes the extra step to help the reader with instructions on how to apply and how to write winning proposals. *Free Money from the Federal Government for Small Businesses and Entrepreneurs* is highly recommended to all public libraries, university libraries, and small businesses. [R: Choice, July/Aug 96, p. 1768]—**Elie M. Dick**

190. **Fitzroy Dearborn Directory of the World's Banks.** 11th ed. Compiled and edited by Euromoney Books. Chicago, Fitzroy Dearborn, 1996. 1186p. $150.00. ISBN 1-884964-84-2.

For the past 10 years, this directory was published by *Euromoney* magazine for its subscribers. Fitzroy Dearborn has now begun publishing a hardbound annual edition, compiled by the same editors, for general distribution. The directory includes more than 10,000 financial institutions in 211 countries. The entries are organized by country and provide contact information, names of key executives, correspondent banks, subsidiaries and affiliates, ownership details, and the number of employees and branches. Indexes by bank name and by city are provided. An additional useful feature is a ranking (based on assets) of the leading 250 institutions in each of 4 regions (Europe, the Americas, Africa/Middle East, and Asia/Pacific).

The *Fitzroy Dearborn Directory* is considerably less comprehensive in coverage than are the *Thomson Bank Directory* (Thomson Financial, semiannual), *Polk's World Bank Directory* (R. L. Polk, annual), and *The Bankers' Almanac and Yearbook* (West Sussex, England: T. Skinner Directories, annual), each of which discusses in excess of 20,000 institutions. The Fitzroy Dearborn title also lacks the summarized financial data included in the Thomson and Polk directories. In fairness, it has a much lower price than these other sources. The Fitzroy Dearborn publication is apparently not primarily intended as a directory of North American financial institutions; it contains only about 100 pages of United States listings and 15 pages of Canadian listings. Finally, as in many business directories, the amount of information in the entries varies considerably. Many entries include lengthy lists of officers, subsidiaries, and corresponding institutions, while others provide contact information only. Libraries not subscribing to one of the above-named publications may want to consider this directory as a low-cost alternative for international bank information.—**Christopher J. Hoeppner**

191. Lester, Ray. **Information Sources in Finance and Banking.** New Providence, N.J., Bowker-Saur/Reed Reference Publishing, 1996. 818p. index. (Guides to Information Sources). $125.00. ISBN 1-85739-037-7.

This compendium of banking and finance resources is extremely ambitious. In its more than 800 pages, the author lists a tremendous variety of business resources from all corners of the globe and in many different media. Also included is detailed analysis of where business information originates, how value is added to it, and what form it may take as newer electronic media proliferate. Unfortunately, the result is an unwieldy tool that seems half resource directory and half library science textbook. Neither role is fulfilled adequately.

The book's most obvious problem lies in its organization. Instead of grouping information sources by such topical rubrics as "interest rates" or "money supply," the book focuses on just a few broad and ambiguous headings. Chapter names such as "approaches to structure" and "scholarly research and study" are simply not helpful to a researcher looking for a quick way to locate a source for a particular fact or statistic. The organizational problem is compounded by the book's lack of sufficient indexing. Although there are indexes of organizations and serials, there is no subject index. Hence, a researcher looking for guidance regarding industry averages of balance sheets and income data, a popularly requested business reference topic, would have to know to look in the chapter "Financial Institutions and Markets." Assuming the user was able to guess the correct chapter, he or she would then have to wade through 145 pages of text to find the entry for Robert Morris Associates's *Annual Statement Studies*.

Despite its shortcomings as a researcher's aid, this book does contain some interesting essays on the nature of information in finance and banking. However, these insightful passages are awkwardly interrupted by voluminous listings of actual information resources. As a result, using this guide as a library science textbook would be difficult as well. The limitations of this compendium seem to be inherent in the Bowker-Saur series of which it is part; other titles in this series dealing with different subject disciplines seem to have the same structural problems (see entries 1296 and 1299). The author is certainly to be commended for the extraordinarily thorough research and documentation of his work. Despite Lester's completeness, however, *Information Sources in Finance and Banking* is recommended only for special libraries in financial institutions and comprehensive academic libraries supporting a graduate-level business curriculum. For most general college and university libraries, as well as all public libraries, the amount of useful and easily retrieved information simply does not warrant the book's hefty price. [R: Choice, July/Aug 96, p. 1775]—**David Bickford**

192. **Prices and Financial Statistics in the ESCWA Region.** 13th ed. By the Economic and Social Commission for Western Asia. New York, United Nations, 1995. 178p. $42.00pa. ISBN 92-1-128155-5. ISSN 1010-6669. S/N 96.II.L.5.

This is the 13th issue of *Prices and Financial Statistics in the ESCWA Region* and contains annual figures from 1985 to 1994 in part 1, and from 1985 to 1993 in part 2. A detailed table of contents and an introductory note begin the work. Part 1 contains index numbers and prices, and part 2 financial statistics. Part 1, chapter 1 covers index numbers, and chapter 2 gives retail consumer prices of 45 items in food, beverages, and tobacco categories. In part 2, 11 countries are listed alphabetically with the following topics given under each: government revenues, government expenditures, money supply, commercial banks, assets and liabilities, central bank credit facilities, and balance of payments. A list of sources is given for each part. Two charts concerning general price indexes are also included. The typeface is clear, and the text is in English and Arabic. The page layout is portrait throughout. This book is useful for those making use of these statistics.—**Barbara E. Brown**

INDUSTRY AND MANUFACTURING

193. **CDs, Super Glue, and Salsa: How Everyday Products Are Made. Series 2.** Kathleen L. Witman, Kyung Lim Kalasky, and Neil Schlager, eds. Detroit, U*X*L/Gale, 1996. 2v. illus. index. $44.95/set. ISBN 0-7876-0870-X.

CDs, Super Glue, and Salsa, Series 2 provides explanations for how 30 products such as air bags, beepers, bungee cords, chewing gum, in-line skates, neon signs, smoke detectors, T-shirts, and zippers are manufactured. The two-volume set arranges entries alphabetically. The format for each entry details the background of the product, raw materials needed for production, design of the product and how it works, the manufacturing process, quality control, by-products, future products, and where to learn more. Step-by-step numbered guides feature what happens from start to finish. The index is extensive, with particularly helpful entries for inventors. The series includes photographs and diagrams, all black-and-white, many of poor quality.

Greater depth is provided in this series than in *The Way Things Work* by David Macaulay (Houghton Mifflin, 1988) or *What's Inside? Everyday Things* (Dorling Kindersley, 1992). This set is written for an older audience, ranging from middle schoolers through adults. However, it lacks the visual appeal and interesting style of the books for younger readers. The title, the same as *Series 1* (see ARBA 96, entry 221), is misleading because readers will not find CDs, super glue, or salsa in *Series 2*. The cover is nearly identical to the first set, causing further confusion. The set does provide information that is difficult to find, but in a rather dull package.—**Lynda Welborn**

194. **Directory of the Steel Industry and the Environment.** By the Economic Commission for Europe. New York, United Nations, 1996. 90p. $52.00pa. ISBN 92-1-116654-3. S/N E.96.II.E.22.

Sponsored by the United Nations Economic Commission for Europe (UN/ECE), the *Directory of the Steel Industry and the Environment* comprises five categories: United Nations commissions and programs; international financing organizations; international governmental organizations; international nongovernmental organizations; and governments, associations, and steelmakers of all the ECE member countries and other major steel-producing countries. This is a broad and diverse group. For example, in the last category, U.S. listings include groups within the Department of Commerce, the Environmental Protection Agency, the Department of Energy, and the International Trade Commission; the American Iron and Steel Institute, the American Welding Society, the United Steelworkers of America, and the Steel Recycling Institute; plus 12 of the nation's largest steelmakers. Generally, the entries include name, address, and telephone and fax numbers, but occasionally some of these data are absent. Some entries provide a Website or telex number, but there is no other information as to mission or history. As the author states, the directory is far from exhaustive, so it will be of interest primarily to those involved in the work done by the sponsoring organization.—**G. Kim Dority**

195. **Industrial Commodity Statistics Yearbook, 1994: Production and Consumption Statistics. Annuaire de Statistiques Industrielles par Produit.** By the Department for Economic and Social Information and Policy Analysis, Statistical Division. New York, United Nations, 1996. 067p. $110.00. ISBN 92-1-061165-9. ISSN 0257-7208. S/N E/F.96.XVII.6.

Industrial Commodity Statistics Yearbook, 1994 is an exhaustive compilation of the production and consumption of commodities from the mining, manufacturing, and power (gas and electricity) sectors. For each series, the volume reports annual production and consumption for the years 1985 to 1994 by country. The classification system used is International Standard Industrial Classification (SIC) of All Economic Activities, similar in general structure to U.S. SIC codes. The data presentation is complete and clear, with estimated substitutes for missing data and discontinuities in data series consistently indicated. The level of detail is too great for someone with only a casual interest in international economic comparisons, but for the specialist, the volume provides an essential level of detail to support planning and policy analysis.—**Ray Olszewski**

196. **International Yearbook of Industrial Statistics 1996.** By the United Nations Industrial Development Organization. Brookfield, Vt., Edward Elgar/Ashgate Publishing, 1996. 642p. $149.95. ISBN 1-85898-471-8.

This book of tables' purpose is to provide statistical indicators to assist international comparisons relating to the manufacturing sector. It covers more than 120 countries and areas. The yearbook is the second issue of the annual publication that succeeds the United Nations Industrial Development Organization's handbook of industrial statistics and replaces the *United Nations Industrial Statistics Yearbook* (annual). *International Yearbook of Industrial Statistics* is the only publication with worldwide statistics on current performance and trends in the manufacturing sector. The work allows one to analyze patterns of growth, structural changes, and industrial performance.

The yearbook is divided into areas of summary tables, manufacturing sectors, manufacturing branches, and country tables. The printing is small but readable; the paper and binding are both above average. *International Yearbook of Industrial Statistics* is a valuable library resource for industrial planning and international trade; it is a must for anyone interested in comparing industrial output from various areas of the world and in trends for these same products.—**Herbert W. Ockerman**

197. **Manufacturing Worldwide: Industry Analyses, Statistics, Products, and Leading Companies and Countries.** Arsen J. Darnay, ed. Detroit, Gale, 1995. 792p. index. $205.00. ISBN 0-8103-9681-5.

The first part of this comprehensive volume divides manufacturing into its major sectors and subsectors, presenting statistics on the products in each of these categories. Product sectors range from foods to wearing apparel. For each sector, readers find the number of establishments in the countries engaged in such manufacture, employment and compensation of employees, output, value added, capital investment, and representative companies. These statistics derive primarily from United Nations's sources: the General Industrial Statistics and the Industrial Commodity Production Statistics series. Although the product-oriented tables make up the major part of this work, the information is also summarized in country-by-country profiles for easier comparison. With its aim of providing worldwide data, the book includes information on manufacturing in 170 countries.

Because the same categories are examined in each table, comparisons are simplified. In addition, all financial data are given in U.S. dollars. The tables also calculate data as a percentage of world total to further encourage comparisons. In looking at the Republic of Turkey, for example, one finds a listing of its major employing and output sectors, the population, and the percentage of world population. The table then summarizes data from 1986 through 1991, showing statistics for the categories detailed in the paragraph above. Other areas examined include machinery and equipment per establishment, both as a number and as a dollar amount. Thus, a researcher wishing to compare Turkey's statistics with those of another country would simply turn to the appropriate table. Such ease of comparison provides a significant benefit to researchers. [R: Choice, June 96, p. 1620]—**Renee B. Horowitz**

198. **The Steel Market in 1995 and Prospects for 1996.** By the Economic Commission for Europe. New York, United Nations, 1996. 175p. $60.00pa. ISBN 92-1-116652-7. ISSN 0497-9478. S/N E.96.II.E.17.

Published annually by the secretariat of the United Nations Economic Commission for Europe (UN/ECE) since 1953, this work focuses on national and international trends in the steel market, in the iron and steel industry, and in its raw material supply situation. Statistics are based on information supplied by national governments, on market trend statements made orally or in written form by governments participating in the work of the ECE Working Party on Steel, and on other official data.

The overview consists of six chapters ("General Economic Developments in the ECE Region"; "Principal Trends in Supply and Demand in Steel"; "International Trade in Steel"; "Production Capacities, Rationalization, and Investment Activities in the Steel Industry"; "Developments in Iron and Steel Making Raw Materials"; and "National Developments") plus a one-page summary that briefly identifies the trajectory of trends documented within the text. Numerous tables and figures supplement the narrative. Although there is no index, the slim publication's table of contents and lists of tables, figures, and appendixes are sufficiently detailed to remedy that lack.—**G. Kim Dority**

199. **World Engineering Industries and Automation: Performance and Prospects 1994-1996.** By the Economic Commission for Europe. New York, United Nations, 1996. 480p. $75.00pa. ISBN 92-1-116641-1. ISSN 1020-1300. S/N E.96.II.E.5.

This statistical compilation is unusually up-to-date for a United Nations document. Most data, whether organized by industry or by country, are current up through 1994. While a two-year lag in statistical compilation always elicits groans from library customers, this book is competitive in data recency with similar U.S. government documents and similar documents from associations and commercial publishers. The scope of the industries covered is broad, given the focus on engineering in the title. In fact, almost all electronic manufacturing is included under a broad rubric of engineering. The geographic scope is primarily European. Nevertheless, data from the United States, Japan, Canada, and even Kyrgyzstan are provided in many of the tables. The tables and accompanying notes are all straightforward and relatively easy to use. This book is recommended for any library pursuing a strong international business collection. However, in light of the substantial price and specialized nature of the compilation, it would be worthwhile to check for possible redundancy of coverage with the Index to International Statistics microfiche in those libraries that subscribe to this service.—**David Bickford**

INSURANCE

200. **Glossary of Insurance and Risk Management Terms.** 6th ed. Edited by the Staff of International Risk Management Institute. Dallas, Tex., International Risk Management Institute, 1996. 161p. $18.00pa. ISBN 1-886813-23-X.

Regardless of subject, dictionaries and glossaries share many similarities. Obvious similarities include arrangement and purpose, but generally there is another unintended similarity—one source is not sufficient. Such is the case with this title. While it definitely provides clear and practical definitions, the focus is directed toward those working with the industry in a professional capacity, as evidenced by the inclusion of such terms as *factory firm*, *rainmaker*, and *30(b)6 deposition*. Unlike most dictionaries, this title frequently goes beyond the standard definition and gives a sentence or two of expert advice, highlighting advantages or disadvantages, passing along pointers, or giving warnings regarding limitations. For instance, the entry for *whole life insurance* provides a definition plus a comparison to term life. Under *flood coverage*, the entry goes on to list how coverage may be obtained.

The glossary is supplemented with a list of state insurance commissioners' addresses and telephone numbers; a directory of offices involved with workers' compensation; a list of states not permitting private insurance companies to write workers' compensation insurance and a list of states that do, along with the organization's contact information; and a list of risk management and insurance organizations. This would be a good addition to collections serving attorneys or insurance professionals.—**Barbara E. Clotfelter**

201. Rubin, Harvey W. **Dictionary of Insurance Terms.** 3d ed. Hauppauge, N.Y., Barron's Educational Series, 1995. 531p. $10.95pa. ISBN 0-8120-3379-5.

The price of the 3d edition of this useful pocket-sized insurance reference book is 10 percent higher than its predecessor, but still a bargain at $10.95. For the extra money, the reader gets a raft of new entries such as "Addendum: addition to a written policy"; "Ad infinitum: continuing on an indefinite basis"; "Adjacent: that which adjoins"; "Egress: exit, act of leaving or going out." Most entries are taken verbatim from the 2d edition (see ARBA 92, entry 210), including outdated entries (e.g., a page-and-a-half on the Medicare Catastrophic Coverage Act that was repealed in 1989). As with previous editions, the 3d edition is relatively strong in areas of life, property, and casualty insurance, and weak in health insurance.
—**Bruce Stuart**

202. **Standard & Poor's Insurance Company Ratings Guide.** 1995 ed. By Standard & Poor's. New York, McGraw-Hill, 1996. 398p. $19.95pa. ISBN 0-07-052101-8.

Standard & Poor's Insurance Company Ratings Guide is a strong addition to any consumer education collection. The goals of the book are clearly stated: to "cut through the peculiarities of accounting in this industry" and "to provide you with the highest-quality, most timely, and in-depth insurer ratings." Its strength lies in the explanatory sections preceding the actual company ratings. This information alone is worth the price of the book for consumer reference.

The contributors from McGraw-Hill and Standard & Poor's present an excellent explanation of terms and an equally excellent explanation of rating terminology and information. Due to the degree of analysis, the data are not the most timely. However, that is a technical point most valuable to the insurance industry researcher who needs the latest possible rating for a given company. For the consumer, the careful delineation of rating grades, acronyms, and relevant accounting terminology should prepare average readers for deciphering the ratings assigned to companies with whom they may consider doing business.

Parts 1 and 2 contain the "Insurance Company Rating Reports" and the "Insurance Company Rating List," respectively. Entries in part 1 provide the consumer with anecdotal and brief financial information, with up to 5 years of historical figures for 300 life, health, auto, fire, commercial, annuity, and reinsurance companies. Part 2 simply lists more than 3,000 companies alphabetically, with the most current rating as of publication. Not all consumers will find their companies of choice in part 1. However, any consumer who reads the explanatory sections will have a basic knowledge of rating criteria to apply to any insurance company report. [R: RBB, 1 April 96, p. 1390]—**Deborah K. Scott**

INTERNATIONAL BUSINESS

General Works

Dictionaries and Encyclopedias

203. Capela, John J., and Stephen W. Hartman. **Dictionary of International Business Terms.** Hauppauge, N.Y., Barron's Educational Series, 1996. 584p. (Barron's Business Guides). $12.95pa. ISBN 0-8120-9261-9.

This is an excellent, practical, and comprehensive source of information for students; practitioners in management, marketing, trade, finance, and foreign exchange; and the general public. The terms covered include specialized concepts, abbreviations and acronyms, geographic/institutional terms, military phrases, some foreign expressions, monetary units, Internet terminology, legal jargon, and so on. Cross-referencing is meticulous, the size is eminently portable, and the price is surprisingly low. Twelve appendixes provide international acronyms, Internet acronyms, contacts for major foreign markets, International Trade Commission offices, Department of Commerce information, customs information, a six-language dictionary of basic terms, weights and measures conversions, a list of currencies, and faxback services. The dictionary is highly recommended.—**Bogdan Mieczkowski**

204. **Encyclopedia of Global Industries.** Diane M. Sawinski and Wendy H. Mason, eds. Detroit, Gale, 1996. 1034p. index. $395.00. ISBN 0-8103-9767-6. ISSN 1084-8614.

This encyclopedia is a new and needed entry in the international business information field. Much of the information included in this title is available industry-by-industry in many other, far more expensive resources, so this compilation of international industry information in one volume will be seen as a welcome addition to most business reference collections. Summary information from 7 to 12 pages is provided for the 115 international industries. This includes a narrative description for each industry similar to what one would find for U.S. industries in *Standard & Poor's Industry Surveys*, brief analysis on the general outlook for the industry with projections, a general background section that provides brief descriptions of the industry in particular countries or regions, information related to research and development, and many graphs and charts used to list the major players in each industry.

Each section concludes with a reading list of industry information sources. This section could have been made more useful by referencing many of the special issues on industry outlook that trade magazines publish. These reading lists also do not always refer to the latest annual publications, and many of the general periodical articles selected do not necessarily reflect current issues. This is a minor shortcoming that one hopes will be corrected when a new edition of the title comes out. The indexes provide access to the contents by the Standard Industrial Classification (SIC) code, by the Harmonized System code, or by geographic location. Because 1997 will see the Harmonized System code replacing the SIC code, this book will not be quickly outdated.

The information here is timely and provides the reader with a useful overview of those industries with international importance. If one needs company information, other sources should be consulted, as those companies that are included are merely mentioned. This is not a shortcoming of the book, but many readers will want to do one-stop searching. This book is a valuable resource and is a must-acquisition for those libraries serving clienteles interested in international business or for academic libraries with a business administration program. [R: Choice, Oct 96, p. 250; RBB, Aug 96, p. 1924]—**Judith J. Field**

205. **Exporting to the USA and the Dictionary of International Trade.** 1996-97 ed. [CD-ROM]. San Rafael, Calif., World Trade Press, 1996. Minimum system requirements: IBM or compatible 386. CD-ROM drive. DOS 3.3. Windows 3.1. 8MB RAM. 10-20MB hard disk space. VGA 640 x 480 monitor (SVGA recommended). Windows-compatible mouse. PostScript or PCL printer and ATM or TrueType font manager (for printing). $149.00.

The CD-ROM is divided into nine parts or "books." First is the commodity index, containing an overview of import regulations and requirements for a complete range of products arranged according to the 99 chapters of the Harmonized Tariff Schedule. Next comes a section on international law, covering a wide range of legal issues. The part on international banking contains sections on banking services and letters of credit. The customs entry segment covers regulations for U.S. Customs entry and clearance. Customs forms include 30 forms from the Customs Service and other U.S. government agencies (these forms can be printed for use, but should only be used after consulting with the Customs Service). A container packing section contains a complete guide from Happag-Lloyd on how to pack shipments. Details on shipping containers include an excellent description by Happag-Lloyd on standard containers. A section on insurance provides detailed information from Insurance Company of North America (INA) and CIGNA on ocean cargo insurance. Finally, the part called "Info Lists" includes 30 sections on a range of topics, such as brokers, attorneys, General Agreement on Tariffs and Trade and the North American Free Trade Agreement. Also contained on the CD-ROM is the complete text of *Dictionary of International Trade* by Edward G. Hinkelman, which is accessible at any time from any of the books and from the main menu. The dictionary includes definitions of terms, a list of acronyms, a description of currencies of the world, an International Dialing Guide, resources for international trade, weights and measures, and a detailed table of contents.

The CD-ROM is straightforward and easy to install. The display is meant to be about 10 inches (25 cm) on the diagonal, which means that it will be smaller than most desktop or laptop screens. Nonetheless, the display is clear, distinct, and reasonably easy to read. The interface is consistent throughout all the parts of the CD-ROM, but it is somewhat cumbersome. In addition to a standard Windows pull-down menu, from the main menu one may click on an icon for any one of the nine books, or click on a button for a complete index, the dictionary, Help, or to exit the CD-ROM. After entering any one of the nine book sections, one may click on a table of contents or an index to all nine books. Also, the user always has the option to choose another book, the dictionary of terms, the dictionary of acronyms, or a list of addresses of U.S. regulatory agencies. The navigation buttons are the same within every book. Unfortunately, there is no search function allowing a user to type in a word and go to it. Instead, one must page through all the entries in an index or table of contents until coming to the desired item. In addition to the standard set of navigation buttons, there are hypertext links allowing the user to jump to related concepts.

This CD-ROM is notable for its exhaustive and authoritative coverage of importing goods into the United States. It has a serviceable interface and consistent navigation tools. This is an extremely useful source for any library serving patrons or businesses interested in importing into the United States, and the price is reasonable considering the comprehensiveness of the information provided.—**Richard H. Swain**

206. Johnston-Des Rochers, Janeen, Inés Barry, and Maguy Robert. **Export Financing and Insurance Vocabulary. Vocabulaire du Financement et de L'assurance à L'exportation. Vocabulario del Financiamiento y Seguro a la Exportación.** Quebec, Canada Communication Group, 1996. 572p. (Terminology Bulletin, no.230). $36.95pa.(U.S.). ISBN 0-660-59978-3.

This is one of a series of Terminology Bulletins published by the Translation Bureau on various topics. It contains 1,400 entries in English, French, and Spanish concerning export financing and insurance and includes 470 definitions and notes. These entries are filed alphabetically in each of the three languages, with the filing language in the first column and the interpretation into the other two languages listed in the second and third columns. Below these terms (in the English listing only) one finds definitions and notes in the three languages running across the page. Synonyms in the same language are frequently included and are found in both alphabetic places in the same listing. In the English listing, however, *see* references are used from synonyms to the main listing. A bibliography is found at the end of the book.

The printing is clear and easy to read. The terminology is in bold typeface, while the definitions and notes are in regular typeface. The choice of words is satisfactory and the translations and definitions are accurate. The work was prepared by experts in the field and is especially valuable and useful for those involved in export financing and insurance.—**Barbara E. Brown**

207. **World Trade Almanac 1996-1997: Economic, Marketing, Trade, Cultural, Legal, & Travel Surveys....** By Molly E. Thurmond and others. San Rafael, Calif., World Trade Press, 1996. 844p. illus. maps. $87.00. ISBN 1-885073-07-0.

208. **World Trade Almanac and the Dictionary of International Trade.** 1997 ed. [CD-ROM]. San Rafael, Calif., World Trade Press, 1996. Minimum system requirements (Windows version): 386 processor. CD-ROM drive. Windows 3.1. 4MB RAM. 5MB hard disk space. VGA 640 x 480 monitor (SVGA

recommended). Mouse. PostScript or PCL printer and ATM or TrueType font manager (for best printing results). Minimum system requirements (Macintosh version): Macintosh 68020-68040 or Power Macintosh. CD-ROM drive. Apple System Software 7.0. 4MB RAM. 5MB hard disk space. Color monitor. Mouse. PostScript or PCL printer and ATM or TrueType font manager (for best printing results). $149.00.

Aside from providing international businesspeople with a blueprint for success in foreign markets, the *World Trade Almanac* supplies useful data on subjects ranging from economics to legality issues to travel for 100 of the world's leading trade nations. Its logical, easy-to-follow format permits ready comparison of business environments in many different countries. Readers will easily understand overall conditions and requirements of doing business in these countries.

Each country entry, arranged alphabetically, contains sections on economy, foreign trade marketing, business culture, legal aspects, money, travel, contacts, and an "At a Glance" section. This last part gives readers a quick overview of the country: its demographics, infrastructure, politics, and environment. Also furnished for each entry is a map with such features as major highways, railways, waterways, major cities, and more. The introductory matter includes essays on economic trends, basics of importing, basics of exporting, trade agreements (such as the North American Free Trade Agreement), international marketing, business culture, international travel, country legal trends, international banking and foreign exchange, international payments, and a glossary.

The CD-ROM version of the *Almanac* is simple to install, including Adobe Acrobat to speed access to its features. The disc version seems to include a few unique features, but it mainly contains the same information as the book! Considering the price difference, most libraries will probably opt for the book version of the *Almanac*. All business collections serving importers and exporters should add it.—**Susan C. Awe**

Directories

209. **Companies International.** [CD-ROM]. Detroit, Gale, 1996. Minimum system requirements: IBM or compatible 386 (486 recommended). Double-speed ISO 9660 CD-ROM drive with MS CD-ROM Extensions 2.2. DOS 5.0. Windows 3.1. 4MB RAM (8MB recommended). 5MB hard disk space. VGA monitor and graphics card. Windows-compatible mouse. Printer (optional). $2,495.00. ISBN 0-8103-5148-X.

This is a Windows Version 2.0 CD-ROM of *Companies International*, a semiannually updated directory of U.S. and foreign companies derived from databases underlying *Ward's Business Directory* (see ARBA 93, entry 198) and *World Business Directory* (WBD) (see ARBA 93, entry 261). The number of companies has increased since the last review (see ARBA 95, entry 245) to more than 325,000. There are 140,000-plus U.S. companies, with the other 191 countries represented proportionately to their world trade involvement. Companies in WBD were selected "for their interest in international trade" (1996 WBD front matter). There are no stated selection criteria for *Ward's*, other than companies being "culled from more than 4,000 business publications" (1997 *Ward's* introduction). All company sizes and business sectors are present.

There are 28 record fields. A close examination of 368 sample records reveals that—beyond the standard address, telephone number, and industry/product codes/descriptions fields—the following are often present: officers, number of employees, fax number, date founded, revenue, company type, fiscal year ends, and importer/exporter designation. The year of the data is consistently indicated for revenue, less so for number of employees. U.S. companies have revenue, number of employees, and company type data more frequently than foreign ones. A search for companies in the United Kingdom discovered 471 virtually "empty" records, containing, at maximum, the company name, country, and company type. Many of these were for parent or holding companies mentioned in other records. In addition, revenue for some publicly held companies is from 1993—surprising, considering the easy accessibility of more recent data.

The interface accommodates different user needs and experience, offering five search modes. Searching by company name allows browsing of an index and keyword searching of words/phrases in names. A search by industry/product grants browsing of Standard Industrial Classification and Harmonized Commodity codes and descriptions. Searching by location affords browsing of city, state/region, postal code, area code, and country indexes. Extended and expert modes of searching possess Boolean and truncation capabilities. Extended mode allows the combination of 2 or more of 21 fields arranged thematically on a series of 4 cards (contact, industry/product, location, and scope) and free-text searching of words/phrases in any text field. Clicking on the field name in a card produces either a box for entering ranges of values or an index list. Limiting to either *Ward's* or WBD records is also possible. Expert mode involves input of commands and field labels and creation and manipulation of search sets. Two difficulties were encountered: Searching by state resulted in an error message, even when trying the example from the user's manual, and searching for a word/phrase in company names retrieves only those companies having the word/phrase as their entire name, not as part of their name.

To view full records for companies, users must select names from an alphabetic list. Other formats are mailing label, telemarketing card, and customized. Users can sort records in seven ways in addition to company name. Unfortunately, there is no way to print lists, other than short ones. Screens are uncluttered, with typing areas well demarcated and clickable buttons clearly labeled. The Windows Menu Bar has five options: File, Edit, Search (which allows rapid switching to different search modes), Format, and Help. Both online Help and the substantial user's manual provide clear instructions.

Records for 50 U.S. companies were compared to their counterparts on the fourth-quarter 1996 disc of *Dun's Million Dollar Disc* (MDD) (Dun & Bradstreet) a database covering only U.S. companies. Both fairly consistently report data for fields they have in common. However, they significantly disagree on revenue and number of employees for some private companies, even allowing for the slightly greater currentness in MDD.

This reviewer is unaware of a comparable single-disc international directory. Although MDD and *Principal International Businesses* (Dun & Bradstreet), combined would provide international scope, their selection criteria emphasize larger companies. The *Ward's* records are also available in *Gale Business Resources*, as part of a Galenet subscription. Although the unusual records and the two search difficulties mentioned above are cause for concern, business collections would profit from *Companies International*'s global scope and well-designed interface. A network license is also available.

—John Lewis Campbell

210. **Directory of American Firms Operating in Foreign Countries.** 14th ed. New York, Uniworld Business Publications, 1996. 3v. (A World Trade Academy Press Publication). $220.00/set. ISBN 0-8360-0041-2.

For more than four decades, various editions of the *Directory of American Firms Operating in Foreign Countries* have been an indispensable reference guide for businesses, researchers, libraries, students, and others who have found the need for information about foreign subsidiaries of U.S. corporations. The 14th edition of this important resource is much enlarged; more comprehensive and updated; and comes in 3 volumes covering companies, large and small, from 3Comm Corp to Zycard Corp. This edition of the directory lists a total of 2,500 U.S. corporations with 18,500 subsidiaries or affiliates operating in 132 countries.

Volume 1 contains a summary listing of all U.S. corporations with foreign subsidiaries or affiliates in alphabetic order. Each entry in volume 1 includes the name of the corporation, U.S. address, telephone and fax numbers, principal line of business, number of employees, names of key executives, and countries in which it has subsidiaries or affiliates. Volumes 2 and 3 contain detailed listings, in alphabetic order by country, of U.S. firms' foreign subsidiaries or affiliates. Each entry in volumes 2 and 3 gives the name of the U.S. company, its U.S. address, the principal line of business in the foreign country, and the name and address of its subsidiary/affiliate in the foreign country. Because the foreign subsidiary may not have the same name as its U.S. parent company, this arrangement makes it easy for cross-references of the names and addresses of the foreign subsidiary with that of the parent company. The directory is extremely useful for businesses, researchers, and policy-makers alike and should be an indispensable reference in any library, business, university, or other organization.—**Kwabena Gyimah-Brempong**

211. **Directory of Japanese-Affiliated Companies in the EU: 1996-97.** Tokyo, Japan External Trade Organization; distr., Bristol, Pa., Taylor & Francis, 1996. 471p. index. $240.00pa. ISBN 4-8224-0733-0.

Published by the Japan External Trade Organization (JETRO), this directory lists almost 3,000 companies operating in 15 European countries in mid-1995. The countries are Austria, Belgium, Denmark, Finland, France, Germany, Greece, Ireland, Italy, Luxembourg, the Netherlands, Portugal, Spain, Sweden, and the United Kingdom. *Japanese-affiliated* is defined as "any firm owned in whole or in part by a Japanese entity . . . subsidiaries of Japanese affiliated firms, as well as subsidiaries of subsidiaries." Religious organizations and personal service firms are not included. The companies are arranged by country and listed alphabetically. Each entry includes the company name; type of establishment (e.g., subsidiary, branch, representative/liaison office, affiliate); address; telephone and fax numbers; year established; executive officers; annual sales; number of employees; and type of business. Businesses are categorized as manufacturing, distribution/wholesale, import, export, retailing, service provider, and other.

Three indexes provide additional access. In the first index, the companies are arranged by type of product or service (e.g., accounting, construction, industrial machinery and equipment, toys, and transportation services). The second index lists the companies by type of business. The third index lists the companies alphabetically. Two appendixes focus on country information. The first appendix covers Japanese information sources in the European Union (EU) and lists, by country, government offices and trade associations. The second appendix lists EU information sources in Japan and includes embassies, consulates general, and chambers of commerce. The directory is recommended for libraries needing such specialized information.—**Barbara E. Clotfelter**

212. **The Directory of Overseas Catalogs, 1997.** Lakeville, Conn., Grey House Publishing, 1996. 522p. illus. index. $199.00; $165.00pa. ISBN 0-939300-36-2; 0-939300-75-3pa.

This directory lists alphabetically by country 1,327 mail order catalogs from 41 nations other than the United States. The majority are from Canada, the United Kingdom, and Europe, with representation from other parts of the world. Each entry has a short description of the products carried and address information including telephone and fax numbers and e-mail addresses. Key contact names, specific credit cards accepted, cost of the catalog, circulation, frequency of publication, how long the company has been in business, and the number of employees are given, when available. Catalog specifications are provided as to the number of pages, type of stock, and how it is bound. The reader is also told if the company imports, exports, or does business in the United States.

The book is indexed by type of product and also alphabetically by catalog or company name. This easy-to-use reference is also available in an electronic format that can be merged with several database software programs. The publication yields a fascinating potpourri of products. Many of the catalogs are narrowly defined and have long histories. Entries range from industrial products to Bunka With Flair (this Canadian company sells Japanese punch embroidery kits and has been in business for 16 years).

U.S. catalogers looking for international mailing lists or strategic partners for expansion into the global market will be the primary users of this directory. It will be helpful also to the general reader with a passion for a specific product, such as Scottish woolens or South African plants.—**Adrienne Antink Bendel**

213. **The International Directory of Business Information Sources and Services 1996.** 2d ed. London, Europa; distr., Detroit, Gale, 1996. 550p. index. $185.00. ISBN 1-85743-007-7.

This 2d edition (see ARBA 88, entry 173, for a review of the 1st edition) has been revised to include information on 23 additional countries from Latin America, the Middle East, the Far East, the Russian Federation, and central Europe. Forty-six countries are covered, and the directory is divided into that number of chapters, one for each country. Chapters are organized into sections listing chambers of commerce, foreign trade-promoting organizations, government organizations, independent organizations, research organizations, sources of statistical information, and business libraries. Each entry lists the organization's address, telephone and fax numbers, and generally provides a description of varying detail. International organizations are listed in a separate chapter, and an index is included.

While separate directories exist for many of the sections covered by this title, and therefore exceed the amount of information presented here, this is an impressive compilation overall. However, shortcomings can be found; for example, in the chapter on the United States, under the sources of statistical information, only the Bureau of the Census and its regional offices are listed. Nonetheless, the directory is recommended for comprehensive collections. [R: Choice, July/Aug 96, p. 1774]—**Barbara E. Clotfelter**

214. **International Directory of Company Histories. Volume 12.** Tina Grant, ed. Detroit, St. James Press, 1996. 771p. $155.00. ISBN 1-55862-327-2.

215. **International Directory of Company Histories. Volume 13.** Tina Grant, ed. Detroit, St. James Press, 1996. 793p. index. $155.00. ISBN 1-55862-341-8.

216. **International Directory of Company Histories. Volume 14.** Tina Grant, ed. Detroit, St. James Press, 1996. 793p. index. $155.00. ISBN 1-55862-342-6.

With volumes 12, 13, and 14, this continually growing set now covers more than 2,500 major international companies, with the majority still public companies. Criteria include a minimum annual sales intake of $100 million and a presence as a leading influence in the particular industry or geographic location. Also noteworthy is that "companies are selected without reference to their wishes and have in no way endorsed their entries" (p. ix, v. 14). A comprehensive index in each volume helps users locate their company and identify in which volume or volumes the company is listed.

Entries begin with a company's legal name; the address of its headquarters; its telephone and fax numbers; a statement of public, private, state, or parent ownership; the founding or incorporation date; the number of employees; an estimate of the most recent sales figures; exchanges on which a company's stock is traded; the principal Standard Industrial Classification (SIC) codes; and the history of the firm. Information for the histories was gleaned from publicly accessible sources. The signed, two- to four-page histories trace major acquisitions and mergers, with little description about inventions and marketing successes.

These volumes continue the tradition of this unique set, which is without equal in scope, currentness, and price. This set is a must-purchase for academic business collections and is highly recommended for large public libraries.—**Susan C. Awe**

217. **Jane's International ABC Aerospace Directory 1996.** 46th ed. Ian Tandy and others, eds. Alexandria, Va., Jane's Information Group, 1996. 1234p. index. $390.00. ISBN 0-7106-1344-X.

Jane's Information Group's reference for the world aerospace industry covers 24,000 organizations in 200 countries. The major listing is by country, subdivided into 90 major categories of equipment and service providers, such as engine accessories, fixed-wing aircraft manufacturers, and missiles and components. Each of these categories begins with a list of companies fully described elsewhere (under other categories), along with their category assignments, and then followed by the alphabetized full descriptions of companies and organizations. The listing for each organization includes its name and address; telephone (voice, fax, telex) numbers; financial data (capital, turnover, labor force); and roofed area. The summary continues with executives, a short description of the company with cross-references to any other activity group where it may be found, subsidiaries and affiliates, and the year the data were updated. A company may be listed in more than one country or category, but it will only have one full listing. There is an index of the 45,000 executives mentioned and an alphabetic index to all organizations and companies.

Jane's has a well-deserved and long-standing reputation for the accuracy of its information. If a profile has not been updated during the past 18 months prior to publication, it is left out, while each full listing indicates the year of the update. This directory affords the user thorough coverage of all the components of the aerospace industry, from airlines and airports to aircraft and missile manufacturing to avionics and services, including governmental bodies. The organization is logically structured and is direct and accessible, especially with the "quick index" for alphabetic look-up of companies. The directory is highly recommended for special and academic libraries serving aerospace information needs.
—**Gerald L. Gill**

218. **Jane's International Defence Directory 1997.** Alexandria, Va., Jane's Information Group, 1996. 1096p. index. $450.00. ISBN 0-7106-1365-2.

This annual directory, which was published from 1985 to 1993 as *International Defence Directory*, includes some 14,000 companies and organizations from more than 185 countries and contact data for more than 35,000 senior-level decision-makers. The firms and agencies listed—those that responded to Jane's "free listing" questionnaire—are suppliers of defense and military products and services, government armed forces, police, and customs agencies.

The volume is divided into four sections. The first section is an alphabetic index to companies/agencies. The second segment (the largest) is an A to Z list of countries, each of which has information given under activity key numbers. Entries in this section include firm or agency name, address, telephone and fax numbers, e-mail and Internet addresses, product/service provided, number of employees, contact data for key personnel, and a description of activities.

The third section is an index to more than 3,500 products/services, each of which is assigned a code number. By consulting that number in the fourth section, one finds a list of manufacturers' or suppliers' names, country, and the contact reference page/key number in the second section. For example, under 743, "Military band regalia," 5 companies are listed. Defense-related organizations with products or services to sell may find this international directory valuable for its precise information on contact personnel of appropriate procurement agencies. Large academic libraries with defense-related clientele may also find this a useful source.—**Wiley J. Williams**

219. **Major Companies of Africa South of the Sahara 1996.** D. Franklin, ed. London, Graham & Whiteside; distr., Detroit, Gale, 1996. 626p. index. $360.00. ISBN 1-86099-020-7.

One of the major factors inhibiting the development and growth of businesses in African countries has been the lack of information on business organizations on the continent. Franklin's *Major Companies of Africa South of the Sahara 1996*, a directory that lists all the major companies in all Sub-Saharan African countries, will go a long way to solve this problem. It lists 3,700 major companies of the 43 countries in Sub-Saharan Africa, from Angola to Zimbabwe.

Each entry provides company address; telephone and fax numbers; principal activities; names of directors; senior management; company subsidiaries and branch offices; date of establishment; number of employees; and financial information that includes sales volume, profits, and dividends. This information makes it extremely useful to get a better picture of company performance. Three color-coded indexes—alphabetic order index, an alphabetic order of companies in a country index, and a standard industrial classification (SIC) code of business activity index—complete the book. It is very readable and easy to use as a reference resource. The book also includes definitions of all SIC classifications at the beginning of the book.

The reference will make it easy to identify customers, potential partners, candidates for acquisition and mergers, and business contacts generally in addition to helping in strategic planning and the globalization of the economies of Africa. This source is a major piece of work that may be as important and as successful as the other volumes in the Major Companies series (see entries 220, 233, and 247). Every library and business that deals in international trade should have this work on its shelf.

—**Kwabena Gyimah-Brempong**

220. **Major Companies of Central & Eastern Europe and the Commonwealth of Independent States 1996/97.** 6th ed. Diane Butler, ed. High Wycombe, England, Dun & Bradstreet International and London, Graham & Whiteside; distr., Detroit, Gale, 1996. 1081p. index. $765.00. ISBN 1-86099-032-0.

Regularly released business books may be going the way of the dinosaurs. With access to information available for free, or at very low cost, on the Internet and as more libraries provide access to the Internet, demand for published, and therefore dated, information is decreasing. Today's businesses and businesspeople want instant, up-to-the-minute data.

Based on a Graham & Whiteside database, this directory aims to provide details on organizations whose identities are known, for seeking companies of a particular type or in a particular location, and for identifying key business executives. This includes information on 8,000 of the most important business organizations in Eastern and Central Europe and the former Soviet Republics, and 35,000 senior executives in them.

The main section contains the complete record for each of the organizations, which are listed alphabetically within the country. Each entry gives the usual company data: name, address, executives, telephone number, sales figures, employees, and so on, plus occasionally additional marketing, international, and sales activities. Additional access points are provided by company name, geographic location, and activity indexes. The activity index uses U.S. Standard Industrial Classification codes.

Large corporations with business interests in this region of the world may be able to purchase the volume, but the cost of this resource puts it out of the reach of most libraries. As a British publication, CIP is not included, which presents another problem to libraries. Because Graham & Whiteside's databases are available online, on CD-ROM, and on mailing labels and disks, the question remains: Why was this book published?—**Susan C. Awe**

221. **Profiles in Business and Management: An International Directory of Scholars and Their Research.** [CD-ROM]. Boston, Harvard Business School Publishing; distr., New York, McGraw-Hill, 1996. Minimum system requirements (Windows version): IBM or compatible 386 CPU. CD-ROM drive. DOS 5.0. Windows 3.1. 4MB RAM. VGA monitor and graphics card with 125K memory. Mouse. Minimum system requirements (Macintosh version): CD-ROM drive. System 7. 4MB RAM. Color or monochrome monitor. Mouse. $495.00. ISBN 0-87584-681-5.

Profiles in Business and Management provides background, publications, and current research for more than "5,600 international scholars, researchers, and practitioners engaged in business and management research." Operational with Windows, DOS, or Macintosh, the CD-ROM's instructions for installation are straightforward and easily accomplished. The program allows the user to search a single index or perform a customized search by searching up to seven indexes at one time. The options include a name index (scholars alphabetized by last name), institution (current position), main disciplines, current research, address (geographic location), publications, languages (language fluency), professional organizations, education (earned and honorary degrees), and research region. Searching just a single index, the user activates the Index Selection window, chooses "New" from the Search menu, or double-clicks on the Index Selection icon. Next, the user double-clicks on the index name or moves the highlight bar with the cursor keys and then presses Enter. In most indexes, the user can scroll through a Word List or use an Alphabetic Browser. If the user has searched by keyword or phrase, occurrences of that word or phrase are highlighted on the screen. The User Guide provides specific instructions for the Custom Searching option.

Profiles in Business and Management has value to private industry, research organizations, and the academic community, making the CD-ROM a useful purchase for large corporate libraries, research entities, and university libraries supporting graduate business programs at the doctorate level. Students contemplating graduate education in business/management fields would find the information about faculty publications and research interests a useful guide in selecting a particular institution.—**Dene L. Clark**

222. **World Retail Directory and Sourcebook.** 2d ed. London, Euromonitor; distr., Detroit, Gale, 1995. 886p. index. $510.00. ISBN 0-86338-549-4.

In its 2d edition, this directory remains a useful but expensive guide to the global retail sector (see ARBA 93, entry 262, for a review of a previous edition). Tailored for academic, special, and large public libraries, this edition incorporates a fifth section, retail legislation to categories (e.g., a market overview, company profiles, sources) in the earlier edition. The market overview explores trends, such as niche retailing and home shopping, with 30 informative statistical tables.

The directory's core consists of brief geographically arranged profiles for 1,700 retailers in 90 countries. This section has top 10 rankings, basic location, and financial data; however, the personnel listings are limited and new technologies (e.g., listservs, World Wide Web homepages) have been excluded. The in-depth profiles for 70 leading retailers offer excellent evaluations of corporate operations, financial results, strengths, weaknesses, strategies, trading details, and products. A fourth section identifies important associations, publishers, research firms, and a selection of print and nonprint sources, although the appearance of some data (e.g., language, price) is inconsistent.

Three indexes list retailers by name, type of outlet, and country, while the fourth tabulates information sources. A key to outlet types would assist less knowledgeable patrons. While the usefulness of this edition has been enhanced by the new indexes, the format is confusing, creates difficulties in identifying entry headings, and hinders efforts to meet access requirements under the Americans with Disabilities Act. These problems might be eased with a CD-ROM version or a searchable World Wide Web site.—**Sandra E. Belanger**

Handbooks and Yearbooks

223. **China Environmental Report.** By Michael G. Gallagher. Rockville, Md., Government Institutes, 1996. 172p. (International Report Series). $495.00 spiralbound. ISBN 0-86587-514-6.

224. **Mexico Environmental Report.** By Paulette S. Wolfson. Rockville, Md., Government Institutes, 1996. 254p. (International Report Series). $495.00 spiralbound. ISBN 0-86587-516-2.

These highly specialized reference tools are intended primarily for businesspeople and multinational organizations, particularly businesses and corporations that are, or that are considering, doing business in Mexico or China. The greatest use of these resources will be in the business libraries of organizations doing business with Mexico or with China. However, public libraries with patrons who have a need for such resources, or academic libraries supporting international environmental studies, may find that these and others in the series are a useful addition to their collections.

Mexico Environmental Report and *China Environmental Report* are two examples of a series of reports issued by the publisher for the international business community. These highly specialized and relatively expensive reports, which provide a broad overview of the environmental, cultural, and legal infrastructure of reported countries, are important to the success of businesses and individuals who must understand these countries' environmental laws and regulations, as well as the structure of their environmental organizations, in order to be successful.

Each report is written by an expert on the country reported upon. While the layout of the reports follows a generally uniform format, such as each country's history, background, economy, political structure, government, and laws, the actual text and relevant documentation of each country are distinctively different because of the great differences that exist between countries, their cultures, and their respective business environments. For example, the *China Environmental Report* devotes the majority of its discussion to China's environmental crisis, infrastructure, and laws. On the other hand, the *Mexico Environmental Report* devotes most of its outline to appendixes that, among other matters, include the North American Free Trade Agreement's (NAFTA) supplemental agreement on environmental cooperation and standards for various kinds of pollution.—**James M. Murray**

225. **Historical Statistics 1960-1994. Statistiques Rétrospectives.** 1996 ed. Washington, D.C., OECD Publications and Information Center, 1996. 180p. $39.00pa. ISBN 92-64-04850-2.

In 180 pages of tables and graphs, *Historical Statistics 1960-1994* provides an overview of the economic development of the member countries of the Organization for Economic Cooperation and Development (OECD) since 1960. There are two main types of statistics given: percentage rates of change and percentage ratios. For the most part, data have been drawn from other OECD statistical publications, including the annual and quarterly issues of *Labour Force Statistics, National Accounts,* and *Main Economic Indicators,* among others.

The work is organized in three parts. The first provides 1994 benchmark data for national accounts and domestic finance (e.g., gross domestic product), labor force participation rates and age and gender distribution, foreign trade, and exchange rates. The second contains analytic statistics intended to chart the movements of major economic variables or the structure or composition of specific economic aggregates, such as foreign trade by partner country group. The analytic tables in this second section show developments from 1960 to 1994. The last section comprises a series of graphs that illustrate some of the important changes that have been taking place in the economies of the OECD member countries. The work is also available on disk.—**G. Kim Dority**

226. Maturi, Richard J. **The 105 Best Investments for the 21st Century.** New York, McGraw-Hill, 1995. 277p. illus. index. $22.95. ISBN 0-07-040939-0.

Maturi, author of five previous investment books and publisher of three investment newsletters, believes the world is changing so fast one must continually evaluate an investment portfolio. Taking the approach that there are no more blue-chip investments, and one can no longer successfully buy and hold stocks for years at a time in light of changes in the global economy, Maturi has listed the investments he feels will be good performers into the twenty-first century.

The investments are categorized into chapters covering stocks, American Depository Receipts, mutual funds, real estate, precious metals, oil and gas, coins, cars, and other collectibles. Each chapter includes an introductory passage giving an overview of the subject, reasons supporting the investment, and occasionally a few caveats. Most of the entries for the 105 recommended investments have brief sections providing an industry review, company profile, description of management talent, financial status, dividend reinvestment plan details, particular strengths of the company, financial statistics, and a final assessment of the investment.

Each of the investment profiles is easily read and understood by the average investor, making this title a useful addition to circulating collections. The book will also appeal to those unaccustomed to monitoring changes in the international, political, and economic environments, and to those seeking to diversify their investments. A glossary and index are included.—**Barbara E. Clotfelter**

227. **OECD Statistical Compendium 1996/1. Compendium des Données Statistiques de L'OCDE.** [CD-ROM]. Washington, D.C., OECD Publications and Information Center, 1996. Minimum system requirements: IBM or compatible 286. ISO 9660 CD-ROM drive. MS-DOS or PC-DOS. 512KB RAM. 4MB hard disk space. $1,800.00. ISBN 3-929498-18-9. ISSN 0947-4889.

This semiannual compilation of primarily member country data, some since 1960, represents the full scope of the Organization for Economic Cooperation and Development's areas of expertise (economic indicators, economic outlook, national accounts) combined with the International Energy Agency's (IEA) oil and gas statistics. More than 300,000 statistical economic and energy time series (monthly, quarterly, annually) from 31 databases can be searched, combined, and stored for future use.

Easily installed in three languages (English, French, and German), the powerful, DOS-based Maxdata software employs pull-down windows, menu-driven options, full-text, and Boolean operators. Prompts appear at each crucial step with choices to establish the frequency, statistical method, and presentation mode for the search. The resulting display can be changed immediately by altering any of these factors. An unclear table can instantly become a graph. Keyword searching is possible, but does not tolerate word variations (e.g., French, France). Downloading, accomplished through the export function, supports numerous formats and locations. The option of creating a user-defined database for further data manipulation will be attractive to researchers. The basic, downloadable user manual describes the classification plan and 9-digit time series codes required to understand the database structure. This disc is recommended for libraries with patrons seeking comparative data about industrialized countries.—**Sandra E. Belanger**

228. Savitt, William, and Paula Bottorf. **Global Development: A Reference Handbook.** Santa Barbara, Calif., ABC-CLIO, 1995. 369p. index. $39.50. ISBN 0-87436-774-3.

This is a fascinating book. It has definitions, a survey with statistics, and a discussion of approaches, problems, and results; it is as up-to-date as can be for a printed book. Yet, the handbook is too cursory for academicians, too brief for policy-makers, and too expensive for the "just interested" reader. Luckily, it will be available (one hopes) in libraries.

The overview covers development economics, international debt, food production and shortage, the role of women in development, population, refugees, and the environment. Most interesting is the chronology of development since the 1940s. Less interesting are the biographical sketches of a few selected people considered as history makers in development. The judgment is subjective and not very complimentary, as the process of development has not been a great success. The statistical survey, based on World Bank publications, is useful but brief, as is the list of references. The list of institutions and government agencies involved in development serves as a useful reference source.

An innovative contribution is the reference list of nonprofit sources, such as audiovisuals and computer resources, that give the reader Internet homepages and e-mail addresses when available. The glossary and index add to the usefulness of this volume. The identity of the collaborating agencies and individuals reveals the humanistic objectives of the authors. How much more accessible would the message have been had this been published in paperback, with a more attractive title, and at a lower price! [R: Choice, June 96, p. 1623; LJ, Mar 96, pp. 74-76; SLJ, June 96, p. 164]—**Elias H. Tuma**

229. **Trilingual Vocabulary of Road Transport Vehicles. Vocabulaire Trilingue des Vehicules de Transport Routier. Vocabulario Trilingue de Autotransporte de Carga.** Quebec, Canada Communications Group, 1995. 316p. illus. index. $29.95pa.; $38.95pa.(U.S.). ISBN 1-551-16391-9.

Designed for simple access to terminology found in the trucking/land transport industry, this volume updates an earlier edition published exclusively in French. The current edition, published in English, French, and Spanish, will be immediately useful because of the recent North American Free Trade Agreement between Canada, Mexico, and the United States. The volume is arranged by a classification system that combines terminology relating to specific areas of the vehicle together. For example, body understructure, cab, vehicle, superstructure, and braking are grouped together. Within each major category further division is applied: suspension, transmission, engine compartment, clutch, and chassis all appear as subcategories under the heading "body understructure." Individual terms within categories are cross-referenced where appropriate. Each major classification section is completed with illustrations showing the location of the terms defined in the section. References in the illustrations refer the user of the volume to the appropriate entry in the section. The definitions themselves typically run one to two sentences in length and are regularly accompanied by further explanatory notes. These notes often are longer than the definition of the term itself. English, French, and Spanish indexes complete the volume and are useful to a researcher unfamiliar with associations between terms and major components.

The work is a useful resource that has great appeal in this time of ever-expanding cross-border trade and transport. Reasonably priced, this volume will find a spot on any library shelf. Those libraries with an interest in trade issues, transportation, or mechanical engineering will find this work particularly helpful in answering many questions.—**Gregory Curtis**

230. **The Washington Almanac of International Trade & Business, 1995/96.** William O. Scouton, ed. Washington, D.C., Almanac Publishing, 1995. 610p. illus. index. $149.00pa. ISBN 0-886222-01-0.

Originally published in 1994 as *The International Washington Almanac* (see ARBA 95, entry 760), this book provides access to a great deal of information on international business. The first section of the book includes a biography, and usually a photograph, of ambassadors to the United States; the commercial contact person at each embassy; a staff listing at specific embassies; the address of foreign consular officers from other countries who are in the United States; and the identification of the monetary unit, holidays, and timetables for each country.

Section 2 lists general export information, encompassing services provided by the U.S. government; federal export regulations; and a glossary of export terms. It identifies and provides policy contacts in both houses of Congress, including committees. The section also provides contacts in the Office of President, the federal departments, and independent government agencies. In the third section, other groups involved in international affairs are listed. They include multilateral development banks; the International Monetary Fund; private and intergovernmental interest groups; research institutions; a list of foreign agents; the international press in Washington, D.C.; world trade centers in each state; a list of higher education institutions in the Washington, D.C., area that teach international trade and business; foreign chambers of commerce in the United States; U.S. chambers of commerce in foreign countries; and state government offices relating to international trade. The index in the back of the book provides quick access to specific organizations or groups. To save space and maintain costs, the section on country information, from the Central Intelligence Agency's 1994 *World Factbook* (see ARBA 95, entry 8), is provided on a 3.5-inch floppy disk inserted in a pocket on the inside of the front cover.

Some of the information in this book can be found in more current sources, such as the latest edition of *Europa World Year Book* (Europa, 1996) or the U.S. Department of State's *Foreign Consular Offices in the United States*. Few publications, however, are available that contain all of this information. Libraries that have frequent demand for more extensive international business information should find *The Washington Almanac* especially helpful. [R: Choice, Oct 96, p. 259]—**O. Gene Norman**

Africa

231. **Economic and Social Survey of Africa, 1994-1995.** By the Economic Commission for Africa. New York, United Nations, 1995. 224p. $46.00pa. ISBN 92-1-125070-6. S/N E.95.II.K.8.

This volume, published annually by the United Nations Economic Commission for Africa, is a basic source of information and data for recent conditions in Africa. It begins with a review of the continent's economic performance for 1994 and 1995, with some specific data by region and country. Africa's place in the world economy comes next, followed by a discussion of its major challenges in the near future. The next chapter focuses on fiscal and monetary developments and exchange rate policy. The second part of the book emphasizes main economic sectors, agriculture, forestry, and fisheries; mining; energy; manufacturing; transport; and communication. There are data on production over some years and information on privatization efforts. Part 3 discusses external trade, external debt, and regional cooperation and integration. Trade price indexes are given, along with diversification and debt service trends. In parts 2 and 3, there are many tables to supplement the text, which often describes the situation by individual country. The last part is a special study of gender disparities in formal education in Africa. The statistical annexes contain eight tables of economic and social indicators.—**J. E. Weaver**

Arab Countries

232. Khan, Javed Ahmad, comp. **Islamic Economics and Finance: A Bibliography.** New York, Mansell/Cassell, 1995. 157p. index. $80.00. ISBN 0-7201-2219-8.

This bibliography covers sources in English on the disciplines of Islamic economics and finance, which are emerging as an alternative to and critique of Western practices primarily in the Arab and Islamic worlds. As such, the volume will be welcome to researchers in Middle Eastern and Islamic studies, as well as to those interested in alternative economic theories and practices. It is not annotated.

The bibliography itself is arranged into 2 main sections ("Islamic Economic Systems" and "Money, Banking and Finance"), which are in turn divided into 16 subject chapters ranging from Islamic economic alternatives and economic history of the Muslim people in the first part, through Islamic financial institutions and commercial laws in the second. Most of the material is drawn from a wide variety of specialty journals published both in the Islamic countries and in the West. An appendix contains annotations on 12 journals on Islamic economics. In addition to a detailed table of contents, there are author and subject indexes.

The work was based upon research projects undertaken by the author starting in 1990 at the Centre for West Asian Studies, Aligarh Muslim University, Aligarh, India, apparently as part of a doctoral program. This book should be strongly considered for academic research collections covering Middle Eastern and Islamic studies and alternative economics.—**Nigel Tappin**

233. **Major Companies of the Arab World 1996/97.** 20th ed. Giselle C. Bricault, ed. London, Graham & Whiteside; distr., Detroit, Gale, 1996. 1350p. index. $790.00. ISBN 1-86099-036-3.

This is the 20th edition of a directory that was first published in 1975 and has appeared annually since then (see ARBA 92, entry 133, and ARBA 88, entry 175). Data provided on 6,000-plus of the most important companies of the Arab world include address, telephone and telex numbers, directors, senior executives, activities, parent companies and subsidiaries, agencies held, branches, bankers, financial results, principal shareholders, date founded, and number of employees. The entries are set in double columns in clear typeface, with the name of the company boldfaced. References from variants of the company's name to the form used are inserted where necessary and are also in bold typeface.

The basic arrangement in the main text is alphabetic by country, then by company. Then follow three indexes on blue pages: an alphabetic index by company; a second index by country; and a third index by business activity, using the U.S. Standard Industrial Classification (SIC) code, and under that by country and company. Companion volumes to this directory include those covering Europe (see ARBA 96, entry 253; ARBA 92, entry 131; and ARBA 88, entry 174), Eastern and Central Europe (see entry 220), the Far East and Australasia (see ARBA 96, entry 245; ARBA 93, entry 281; and ARBA 88, entry 176), Latin America (see entry 247), and the United States (see ARBA 88, entry 177). This is a thorough and accurate directory and guide to companies in the Arab world, and it is extremely useful for large government and corporate libraries.—**Barbara E. Brown**

Asia

234. **Asian Markets: A Guide to Company and Industry Information Sources.** 4th ed. By Washington Researchers. Washington, D.C., Washington Researchers, 1996. 487p. index. $335.00pa. ISBN 1-56365-043-6. ISSN 1044-8713.

This volume is a guide to company and industry information sources for 13 countries in Asia on such topics as the economic and political situation, business regulations, business practices, potential markets, analyses of the industries, and names of individual companies. The compilers have organized the book into three sections. The first section, which encompasses more than a third of the book, is devoted to identifying U.S. government departments and agencies that work in the area of international commerce, providing names, addresses, and titles of relevant publications. The remaining part of this section has been allocated to noting individual state offices that deal in international trade, a skimpy section listing some of the primary international organizations, and an incomplete section on private sector organizations such as banks or accounting firms that can also provide a potential importer or exporter with information for doing business in Asia.

The 2d section of 65 pages is devoted to highlighting mostly standard directories, indexes, periodicals, databases, and CD-ROM products that could also be used to find information on Asia. This section is not very helpful except for the newest of researchers. No insight is provided into how items were selected. Also, as in the first section, there have been title changes, publications have ceased, and there is no consistency in referring the reader to nonprint sources such as World Wide Web sites and electronic bulletin boards. No references to CD-ROM products are provided.

The 3d section supplies specific information on 13 Asian countries (e.g., India, China, Japan, the Philippines, and Thailand), starting with a 4- to 6-page overview of the economic and business realities of each country. This is followed by a list of sources for acquiring additional information, such as U.S. government offices and experts in that country, business associations, research organizations, financial institutions in that country, relevant publications, and information sources on the Internet. The individual country profiles average 16 pages, although Japan's coverage is 29 pages and China's is 24 pages. The most useful part of this section is the inclusion of Internet resources; much of the other material can be found in other sources, such as government documents and such standard reference tools as *The Europa World Year Book* (see ARBA 94, entry 82, and ARBA 90, entry 91). There are too many omissions and errors to make this a reliable reference resource, especially at the price being charged.—**Judith J. Field**

235. **Directory of Trade and Investment Related Organizations of Developing Countries and Areas in Asia and the Pacific.** 7th ed. By the Economic and Social Commission for Asia and the Pacific. New York, United Nations, 1995. 196p. index. $40.00pa. ISBN 92-1-119716-3. S/N E.96.II.F.8.

This is a networking tool for business and economic associations and institutions in Asia and the Pacific, and those dealing with them. The prefatory materials indicate that approximately 300 organizations are included. There has been a title change since the 6th edition, from *The Directory of Trade Promotion/Development Organizations of Developing Countries and Areas in Asia and the Pacific*. The work is issued about every second year. It will be of interest to larger business collections with client interest in this high-growth region.

The directory is divided into two parts. The first part lists national organizations by country, from Afghanistan to Vanuatu and Vietnam. The second part lists regional organizations. The detailed table of contents lists all the groups by name. In addition, there are name and classified indexes. The entries themselves include sections for directory information (including address, cable, and telephone, telex, and fax numbers); principal function; services/activities; local branches; membership structure; offices abroad; regional offices; publications; and training. Headings are omitted where not relevant or information is not available. Most entries seem to take at least an entire double-columned, 11-by-8½-inch page, with some being longer. The typeface is quite small. The information was assembled largely from questionnaires sent to the groups, as well as through regional organizations and other sources. The classified index groups organizations under 13 headings, from "Chambers of Commerce/Trade Associations" through "Trade Facilitation Bodies" to "Others."

This work seems a competently produced directory on business organizations in a high-interest part of the world. As such, it should be considered by larger business collections with the relevant mandate.
—**Nigel Tappin**

236. **Philippines Business: The Portable Encyclopedia for Doing Business with the Philippines.** Edward G. Hinkelman and others, eds. San Rafael, Calif., World Trade Press, 1996. 342p. illus. maps. index. (World Trade Press Country Business Guides). $24.95pa. ISBN 1-885073-08-9.

Recent years of political and economic stability in the Philippines point to a bright future for this island nation of Southeast Asia. The rapid economic growth within all of Southeast Asia has created a demand for information on the economies and opportunities for foreign investment. *Philippines Business*, part of World Trade Press's Country Business Guides series, seeks to meet the demand for business information crucial to the foreign entrepreneur wishing to establish business connections in the Philippines. As with the other volumes in this series (see entries 237 and 245), the 25 chapters cover the current political economy; establishing a business, including chapters on legal aspects, demographics, and marketing; foreign investment and trade, with individual chapters on trade agreements, trade zones, and import and export policies; labor; finance and financial institutions; taxation; business travel; and transportation and communications. Geared to the individual entrepreneur or small- to medium-sized business, the editors provide a wide range of practical information, from lists of trade shows in the Philippines to data on the current status and business climate of Subic Freeport Zone and other export processing zones to social skills and elementary vocabulary.

The substantial information given by the editors is both accurate and current. Equally important, *Philippines Business* is easy to use with helpful graphics, maps, and contents guides. The extensive lists of addresses expedite the search for additional contacts and sources of information from government agencies, trade organizations, and services within the Philippines. In addition, the editors suggest readings that are important Filipino trade publications. This is a useful addition to library collections attempting to meet the demand for "how-to" business and investment information for the region. As the Philippines's economy continues to attract foreign investors, there will be a need for such guides that provide an initial step for the novice to the region.—**Carol L. Mitchell**

Australia

237. **Australia Business: The Portable Encyclopedia for Doing Business with Australia.** By James L. Nolan and others. San Rafael, Calif., World Trade Press, 1996. 328p. maps. index. (World Trade Press Country Business Guides). $24.95pa. ISBN 1-885073-03-8.

World Trade Press specializes in authoritative but inexpensive country business guides. They have a series of import-export manuals, almanacs, CD-ROMs, and guides, principally to profitable countries around the Pacific Rim, such as Canada, China, Hong Kong, Japan, the Philippines, and Australia. This book on Australian business covers economic and commercial policy, as well as foreign investments and government. For its sources, it relies on the Australian Trade Commission for statistics, reference librarians in California for some "steps and tips," specialized researchers and writers, and some reprints from both the International Monetary Fund and Ernst & Young.

Standard formats for the series ensure that everything is covered. There are 25 broad topics, including labor, marketing, law, demographics, etiquette and culture, foreign exchange, trade fairs, and taxes. There is a 450 word/phrase business dictionary, as well as 1,000 addresses, some small maps, and even some advertisements. Some obvious defects here include nary a word about the wine industry (one of Australia's greatest exports and potential for foreign investments), few e-mail addresses, and only a handful of Websites. The book has a 1996 copyright date, so the editors surely had some time to track down more Internet connections. It is a shame, considering how far away Australia is and how many international businesses have e-mail access; it would seem realistic for this book to include more of these cost-saving devices.—**Dean Tudor**

Europe

General Works

238. **The Book of European Forecasts.** 2d ed. London, Euromonitor; distr., Detroit, Gale, 1996. 441p. $320.00. ISBN 0-86338-557-5.

Today's world economy presents challenges as well as opportunities to investors and traders. Before a firm commits to investing in or trading with entities within a foreign country, however, it first engages in an extensive market research program. Along with other concerns, it studies the economic, social, and demographic profiles of the nation, considering the present situation and projections for the foreseeable future. *The Book of European Forecasts* was created to answer just such market research questions on

Europe. The volume begins with background information on broad topics, such as macroeconomic prospects, employment trends, demographic changes, and policy shifts. This is followed by forecasts for specific sectors and services ranging from automobiles and transport to chemicals and pharmaceuticals, cosmetics, and toiletries.

The forecasts were developed by pan-European and international sources, pan-European trade associations, private consumer research publishers, and national statistical offices. Financial data in tables appear in U.S. dollars, making this source particularly useful for U.S. audiences. The searcher will discover that some tables cover both western and eastern European nations, while other tables understandably give forecasts only for European Union countries. Similar data may be available in *Worldcasts*, published by Predicasts. The Economist Intelligence Unit (EIU) publishes journals and country forecasts, which also provide comparable information. Predicasts and EIU titles are expensive, however, making *The Book of European Forecasts* a bargain by comparison.

The title under review is highly recommended for special libraries where budgetary concerns are not paramount. It would also be valuable in large public libraries and academic libraries with strong international marketing collections.—**Dene L. Clark**

239. **Economic Survey of Europe in 1995-1996.** By the Secretariat of the Economic Commission for Europe. New York, United Nations, 1996. 192p. $60.00pa. ISBN 92-1-116648-9. ISSN 0070-8712. S/N E.96.II.E.1.

Although replete with charts and tables, much of this book appears meant to be read as much as for lookups. It is organized into chapters with scholarly discussions of economic topics. Even though specific countries are mentioned in the essays, and are broken out in the tables, the text is mainly concerned with Europe as a whole. The chief geographic distinction in most discussions is to compare trends in Eastern Europe and the Baltic States with Western Europe. There are a detailed table of contents and a statistical appendix but no index, so one cannot easily find all references to a specific country. European economic conditions are frequently compared to those in the United States and other regions of the world.

The major economic topics covered are output and demand, labor markets, prices, external balances, fiscal policy and monetary conditions, and short-term outlook. There is also some historical background, with emphasis on specific situations such as banking reform or migration. Figures for 1995 are included in most statistical tables, making this admirably current for a title published in 1996.

This work would be essential for European economists and policy-makers, or for those concerned with Europe. It gives a snapshot of how well Europe is performing economically, and has in-depth commentary on problems and needs. The title can be enthusiastically recommended for libraries interested in international economics.—**Susan V. McKimm**

240. **European Drinks Marketing Directory.** 4th ed. London, Euromonitor; distr., Detroit, Gale, 1996. 438p. index. $425.00pa. ISBN 0-86338-626-1.

The *European Drinks Marketing Directory* is the premier beverage marketing directory for Western Europe. It profiles more than 1,600 leading drinks companies in 17 major Western European countries. The directory is divided into three main sections. Section 1, which constitutes the core of the directory, arranges the companies in an alphabetic sequence by country and includes "every type of company involved in the drinks sector, such as manufacturers and product marketing companies, retailers, wholesalers, distributors, importers and exporters."

The drink products run the gamut from milk, fruit juices, mineral water, and soft drinks to beers, wines, and spirits. The directory lists companies dealing with beverages exclusively as well as companies carrying drink products only as incidental items. Section 1 provides standard directory information but, more importantly, it contains in-depth company information regarding manufacturers' products and brands and up-to-date financials. Information in the profiles comes from the companies' annual returns, supplemented by desk research from Euromonitor.

Section 2 profiles key information sources for drinks marketing in Western Europe, including official organizations and publications, trade and business associations, trade and business journals, market research companies, and online databases. Section 3 consists of 5 indexes. *Beverage World Databank* (Keller International, annual) is a competing directory only in a limited sense. *European Drinks*

Marketing Directory is a necessary purchase for corporate libraries that support firms carrying beverage items. It is highly recommended for large public libraries and academic libraries that support international marketing clientele.—**Dene L. Clark**

241. **European Private Label Directory.** London, Euromonitor; distr., Detroit, Gale, 1996. 257p. index. $450.00pa. ISBN 0-86338-519-2.

A private label is a brand owned by a retailer. There are four types, with changing price and advertising spending attached to the four "generations." The retailer owns the brand exclusively all the way through the process of development and sale, from conception through putting it on the shelf. This directory, on European firms, provides information on 500 retailers who sell private label products and 500 manufacturers who make them. The information given includes address; key personnel or chief executive officers; parent company and major subsidiaries; contract details; size of the company (such as number of employees, manufacturing capacity, financial information on profits and turnover); and what is being produced or sold. While most of the book consists of the listing of retailers and manufacturers in 17 major European countries (the member states of the European Union and all major European Free Trade Association countries), the first 2 sections provide an overview of the concept of the private label in Europe and statistics showing relevant trends and data for Europe and individual countries. This book provides specific company information on a small (approximately 12.5 percent of total retail sales), but growing, part of the market.—**J. E. Weaver**

242. **Europe's Medium-Sized Companies Directory.** London, Euromonitor; distr., Detroit, Gale, 1996. 639p. index. $550.00. ISBN 0-86338-548-6.

One of a new series of Euromonitor directories that includes *World's Major Companies Directory* (see ARBA 96, entry 229), this directory is well printed on quality paper in a two-column-per-page format. Entries on 6,500 medium-sized Western European companies from all business sectors are provided. Selection criteria, coverage, compilation methods, and a brief description of a typical entry are given in the introduction. A medium-sized company is defined by turnover, and the definition varies by country, ranging from a turnover between $10 million and $100 million for Greece and Portugal to between $50 million and $299 million for France, Germany, and the United Kingdom.

Entries are arranged in alphabetic order by country and then by company. A typical entry contains standard directory information for each company, including name; address; telephone, fax, and telex numbers; a brief description of the company's activity, products, services, and brands; ownership; key personnel (usually only one or two officers); and the number of employees. Typical entries range from 10 to 20 column lines.

The directory differs from other sources by supplying brief financial statistics (turnover and profit [for a maximum of four years] in the currency of the country). Published in 1996, the text covers figures from 1991 to 1994. There is an alphabetic index by company name, but there is no indexing by industry/service/product or by parent company/subsidiary.

The information is authoritative and up-to-date, and the inclusion of financial statistics makes this a more valuable source for business reference. However, the lack of indexing previously mentioned is a major liability. Without such indexing, it will be difficult for all but the most specialized business collections to justify purchasing such an expensive source.—**Richard H. Swain**

243. Yuill, Douglas, John Bachtler, and Fiona Wishlade. **European Regional Incentives, 1996-97: Directory and Review of Regional Grants and Other Aid Available....** 16th ed. New Providence, N.J., Bowker-Saur/Reed Reference Publishing, 1996. 478p. maps. $130.00pa. ISBN 1-85739-198-5.

This resource contains helpful and specific guidance for businesses wishing to expand or relocate to any of the member countries of the European Union (EU). The work is divided into three parts; the first part covers changes in incentive administration, coverage, and values with trends highlighted since the last edition. Changes are then noted on a country-by-country basis. Two chapters discuss EU regional policy and competition policy.

Part 2 consists of individual country surveys. These are different for each country depending on available incentives. Greece, for instance, has four programs described, while Ireland has two and Portugal only one. The program descriptions are extremely detailed, with about 50 elements for each program area.

The broad categories of elements include basic details, administration, coverage, factors affecting award values, award statistics, and sources for more information. Each element provides specific and comprehensive information. The third and final part of the volume features comparative country tables on regional incentive packages, administration, coverage, values, and expenditures.

The text and tables use a high number of abbreviations (different for each country) that are decoded in the front of the volume along with a table of exchange rates from pounds sterling. There is no index, but the arrangement as such eliminates the need for one. This is a specialized source using specific vocabulary and is clearly intended for firms with a European focus. It is therefore likely to be used in corporate information settings and graduate business libraries that emphasize international business.

—Gerald L. Gill

Eastern Europe

244. **Major Business Organisations of Eastern Europe and the Commonwealth of Independent States 1995/96.** 5th ed. Diane Butler, ed. London, Graham & Whiteside; distr., Detroit, Gale, 1995. 809p. index. $720.00. ISBN 1-86099-000-2. ISSN 0966-0372.

The newest edition of this reference source has grown to list more than 4,200 organizations with a broad territorial coverage of all countries created from the former Soviet Union and the former communist countries of Eastern Europe (with the exception of Yugoslavia, of which only Slovenia is included here). The main part of the book, running almost 700 pages, consists of an alphabetically arranged list of business organizations by country. Each entry includes the address, the telephone number with a separate international telephone number, telex and fax numbers, a list of principal officers, a description of main activities, names of the principal banks, the date of establishment, and the number of employees.

Three indexes add to the accessibility of the basic information: an alphabetic index of all firms; an index of firms by country; and an index of business organizations by their four-digit Standard Industrial Classification (SIC) code, again in each of those classifications divided by country (SIC codes are listed in the introduction). Diplomatic representatives are listed separately. Carefully prepared with a view to encouraging contacts, this source testifies to the impressive growth of commercial links between the former communist countries and the noncommunist, more industrialized countries, and, consequently, to increasing business opportunities in the trade between those areas.—**Bogdan Mieczkowski**

Latin America and the Caribbean

245. **Argentina Business: The Portable Encyclopedia for Doing Business with Argentina.** Edward G. Hinkelman and others, eds. San Rafael, Calif., World Trade Press, 1996. 372p. illus. maps. index. (World Trade Press Country Business Guides). $24.95pa. ISBN 1-885073-04-6.

Argentina Business provides a broad range of information of value to any organization or individual contemplating doing business in this important South American country. The encyclopedia's 25 chapters include survey information (economy, current issues, industry reviews, and the like) plus specific, practical coverage of such high-interest topics as export and import policies and procedures, trade fairs, business law, and international payments. These materials are supplemented by a 450-entry dictionary of terms (and their pronunciations) appropriate for conducting business in Argentina; a directory of 750 business contacts; cross-references; chapter lists for further reading; numerous tables; and occasional listings of electronic resources where appropriate. A thorough index concludes the handbook.

The value of *Argentina Business*, part of this publisher's Country Business Guide series, is its clear focus on practical information for the business reader. For example, one table details the average lease prices for types of commercial real estate in Buenos Aires. In another chapter, one finds three pages of tips for attending trade fairs. Although much of this information will become dated fairly quickly and will need updating on a regular basis, this moderately priced work is nevertheless a solid resource for anyone contemplating business in Argentina.—**G. Kim Dority**

246. **Argentina Company Handbook: Data on Major Listed Companies.** 1995/96 ed. Rio de Janeiro, IMF Editoria; distr., Austin, Tex., Reference Press, 1995. 86p. index. $34.95pa. ISBN 1-57311-006-X.

The handbook gives concise factual coverage on each of 32 major companies in the Balsa de Comercio de Buenos Aires (BCBA, Buenos Aires Stock Exchange). The small-sized format is packed with general information on Argentina: basic information, a computer-produced map, the political background, an economic overview, and an analysis of the Argentine economy from January 1994 to June 1995. The text reviews Argentina's securities market and the stock market performance in 1994.

The data of the stock market are in a table format that lists the 32 companies and what sector each belongs to with market capitalization, net income, EDS and price/book ratios, and index participation. In addition, the Merval Index, Burcap Index, and Value Index are explained. Most comprehensive information and data on public companies come from reports of Standard & Poor's Corporation records, stock reports, stock guide, and market scope. A comprehensive review of the Argentine stock market is provided, which is needed if the user wants to participate in the BCBA.

Each company's data are organized in a large table in alphabetic order by sector: banking, beverages, carports, cement, electric power, food, gas distribution, holding, iron and steel, paper and pulp, petroleum and petrochemical, telecommunications, textiles, and tobacco. A company index follows. The company table gives background, officers, number of shares, affiliations of market and competition, major stockholders, per share data, a balance sheet, income statement data, and ratios for the two years from June 1992 to June 1994.

A handy little guide for the international business investor, the handbook provides analysis for those who do not have *Moody's International Manual*. It is affordable and should be in Latin American business collections.—**Gerald D. Moran**

247. **Major Companies of Latin America 1996.** D. Shave, ed. London, Graham & Whiteside; distr., Detroit, Gale, 1996. 773p. index. $630.00. ISBN 1-86099-019-3.

This book—of monumental proportions, handsomely printed and bound, detailing the 6,000 most important exporters and manufacturers in Latin America—serves as a valuable tool for American and European companies seeking access to Latin American markets. The work is a well-organized directory of the major companies in Argentina, Belize, Bolivia, Chile, Colombia, Costa Rica, El Salvador, French Guiana, Guatemala, Guyana, Honduras, Mexico, Nicaragua, Panama, Paraguay, Peru, Suriname, Uruguay, and Venezuela. Each listing incorporates pertinent information as follows: company name; address; telephone, telex, and fax numbers; names of the chairpeople, board members, executives, and other officers; principal activities and business of the company; brand names and trademarks; branch offices and parent company; subsidiaries; bankers; auditors; financial information; main shareholders; date company was established; and number of employees.

Simplifying the efficient and productive use of this book are three indexes: a list of all the companies arranged in alphabetic order, a list of companies by country, and a list of companies by Standard Industrial Classification (SIC) business category within each country. In sum, the book is well worth its elevated price because of the ample information gathered together between its covers from hundreds of sources usually beyond the reach of company managers seeking trade with Latin America. [R: Choice, July/Aug 96, p. 1775]—**S. D. Markman**

North America

248. Burgess, Philip M., and Michael Kelly. **Profile of Western North America: Indicators of an Emerging Continental Market.** Golden, Colo., North American Press/Fulcrum Publishing, 1995. 419p. maps. index. $39.95pa. ISBN 1-55591-907-3.

While the book is obscurely titled *Profile of Western North America*, more specifically it contains statistical information on 23 states of the United States west of the Mississippi River (omitting Louisiana but including Alaska and Hawaii), all the provinces of Canada along with its 2 territories, and all the states of Mexico plus its Federal District. The division of the United States seems arbitrary but may be appropriate for some purposes. In the 16 chapters, there are data on basic resources, farms and fisheries, population, health, housing, transportation, energy, communication, education, public safety, environment, economics, finance and trade, business and employment, government finance, financial institutions, and international trade. The data include such items as beef production, urbanization, national park acreage, patents issued, labor force participation, and life expectancy. They are most often presented in bar graphs and charts, usually given by state or province. Most of the data are for 1990 or 1991, with some comparisons to the recent past. There is a directory of western states' government and private organizations for business, development, commerce, and trade; Canadian government and private organizations; Mexican government offices; and selected United States, Canadian, and Mexican corporations.

—**J. E. Weaver**

LABOR

Bibliography

249. Ross, John M. **Employment/Unemployment and Earnings Statistics: A Guide to Locating Data in U.S. Documents.** Lanham, Md., Scarecrow, 1996. 244p. index. $45.00. ISBN 0-8108-3099-X.

This bibliographic guide brings together references to publications issued by the U.S. government on the subjects of employment, unemployment, and earnings. It lists only documents that are issued serially or that are revised periodically. All relevant publications from the Census Bureau and the Bureau of Labor Statistics are included, but only representative samples of industry and occupation reports are cited. No single-issue reports are covered.

The three bibliographic sections (one or more chapters each) cover comprehensive reports on employment/unemployment and income/earnings data, other reports on employment or unemployment, and other reports on income/earnings. Each section is organized by frequency of publication, then lists titles alphabetically, concluding with irregularly published documents. A complete citation is given for each publication, and the highly compact annotation details the relevant labor force characteristics. Notations for title changes are given.

A three-page ready-reference guide lists publication titles, with a checklist showing coverage of geographic, ethnic, congressional district, zip code, industry, occupation, and foreign country information for employment, unemployment, and income/earnings. An entry number for each title refers the user to the bibliographic guide. The appendixes include abbreviations, a glossary, a title index, and two subject indexes. Entries in each of the subject indexes encompass occupational, industry, and geographic terms.

This guide is highly recommended for any library providing information on employment and earnings from U.S. government publications. This valuable resource will provide a useful entrée into the extensive data published by the U.S. government, and even those familiar with the structure of government publications will find it to be a time-saver.—**Joan B. Fiscella**

250. Stern, Robert N., and Daniel B. Cornfield, with Theresa I. Liska and Dee Anne Warmath. **The U.S. Labor Movement: References and Resources.** New York, G. K. Hall/Simon & Schuster Macmillan, 1996. 356p. index. (Reference Publications on American Social Movements). $40.00. ISBN 0-8161-7277-3.

The U.S. Labor Movement is a useful annotated bibliography of literature published on the U.S. labor movement since World War II. This reference work reflects the multiple disciplines that have an interest in this subject, including economics, political science, and psychology. There is, however, a distinctly sociological bent to the volume, reflecting the background of its authors.

The book lists more than 1,200 entries in 9 chapters. The first chapter provides an overview of the work, and the remaining eight chapters divide the literature reviewed into topical areas. These areas include social movement theory, the organizational structure of the labor movement, movement mobilization, labor and politics, the impact of the labor movement on social inequality, antilabor countermovements, the labor movement in relation to other social movements, and data sources and reference works. The chapters are divided into subtopics, with each section of a chapter beginning with a brief essay. The entries are arranged alphabetically, and each entry includes a synopsis of the source. Author and subject indexes are included. This work is highly recommended for academic libraries and for scholars interested in the U.S. labor movement.—**Paul F. Clark**

Dictionaries and Encyclopedias

251. Docherty, James C. **Historical Dictionary of Organized Labor.** Lanham, Md., Scarecrow, 1996. 357p. (Historical Dictionaries of Religions, Philosophies, and Movements, no.10). $54.00. ISBN 0-8108-3181-3.

The intent of this volume is to allow readers "to know what has been achieved by organized labor in the advanced countries" (p. vii). It is not meant to be encyclopedic in coverage. The author's objectives are threefold: to make the subject accessible, to show the variety of labor studies, and to encourage a greater international outlook on the topic. His efforts are successful in all three areas.

The book includes the editor's foreword, a preface, a list of acronyms, an introduction to organized labor, 277 entries, a glossary, a chronology, union membership statistics, and a bibliography. The author has somewhat subjectively, and (admittedly) with bias toward his native Australia, selected 277 entries covering countries, labor organizations, major labor unions, leaders, ideas, political parties, and changes in composition of union membership. The scope is international and historic. Entries range from one paragraph to three or four pages in length—succinct but informative. Each entry is supported by the extensive bibliography. Most of the bibliographic entries are annotated.

Docherty has incorporated a vast amount of information into a small volume. This dictionary will be valuable to the beginner and useful to almost anyone, including specialists in the field. It is recommended for academic libraries.—**Joanna M. Burkhardt**

252. Kushner, Michael G., Virginia L. Briggs, and Michael J. Schinabeck. **Employee Benefits Desk Encyclopedia: An Annotated Compendium of Frequently Used Terms.** Washington, D.C., BNA Books, 1996. 245p. $95.00pa. ISBN 0-57018-005-9.

This reference provides in-depth explanations of more than 500 key terms in the area of employee benefits. It includes citations to statutory and regulatory references to both the Employee Retirement Income Security Act (ERISA) and the Internal Revenue code, as well as citations to rulings, case law, and treatises. The entries also use minimal legalese jargon; they are written in layperson's English, easily understood even by the novice. Common acronyms (such as ADA, COLA, FICA, FMLA, HMO, IRA, and RIF) are listed, along with many unfamiliar ones used in this specialized area of the law (such as ADEA, GULP, and ISO). Some of the general topics of employee benefits covered are insurance, securities, compensation, retirement, and health care. All three authors are lawyers who have written or edited books and articles on federal taxation. This reference work would be especially useful as a learning tool to people new to this area of the law, as well as a ready-reference to those who work in this area. It is recommended for large public and academic libraries.—**George A. Meyers**

Directories

253. Gove, Thomas P. **The Best Directory of Recruiters.** 4th ed. Dracut, Mass., Gove Publishing, 1996. 814p. index. $39.99pa. ISBN 0-9636121-2-3.

254. Gove, Thomas P. **The Best Directory of Recruiters On-Line.** Dracut, Mass., Gove Publishing, 1996. 228p. $34.99pa. ISBN 0-9636121-6-6.

Two sections, by industry and by geography, form the major portion of these directories of recruiters. Recruiters pay fees to be listed. Entries include e-mail and homepage addresses, contact and company names, addresses, telephone numbers, and recruitment specialties; however, not all information is provided for each entry. A firm's full listing is available in each of its specialty areas and its geographic section. Directory introductory material contains information about recruiters' roles and how to interact with recruiters, both as a potential candidate and as a recruiting company, as well as a brief guide to using each resource. The concluding eight career resource appendixes are advertisements, four of which are for companies affiliated with Gove.

The Best Directory of Recruiters (BDR), with more than 5,500 recruiting companies listed, is organized alphabetically by company name within each category. *The Best Directory of Recruiters On-Line* (RON), with more than 1,100 recruiters listed, is organized similarly, but each entry begins with an e-mail address; this arrangement does not promote easy lookup. The single index of BDR is a list of recruiter names referring to the state location of the full entry. RON has e-mail and homepage address indexes; the former has no apparent use, as it does not refer to a full listing or even a recruiter name.

BDR is a potentially useful resource for libraries that support job seeking or personnel recruitment activities, the lack of company names and addresses in a small percentage of cases notwithstanding. RON, a subset of BDR, is not recommended as a print work, due to its lack of effectiveness as a reference or a lookup tool. A check of selected homepage addresses indicated numerous missing files or incorrect server addresses, not unexpectedly given the rate of change in electronic communications. This same volatility raises the question of the worth of a directory organized around such information.

Both directories indicate that a computer disk is available, but it was not provided for review. BDR would be more useful on disk, particularly with an interface that allows searching by any of the fields within the individual entry, and with the possibility of changing information as necessary.
—**Joan B. Fiscella**

255. **Hoover's Directory of Human Resources Executives 1996.** Austin, Tex., Reference Press, 1995. 421p. index. $39.95pa. ISBN 1-878753-97-5.

Another in the series of Hoover's business directories, this employment-oriented book includes entries for 5,000-plus public companies with annual sales of more than $500 million or at least 5,000 employees. The directory is organized by state, then by company, in alphabetic order. Each company entry lists the highest-ranking officer of human resources, the number of employees, and the number of jobs added or eliminated the previous year, as well as basic directory information. An icon indicates the availability, by fax, of an in-depth profile of the company; there is a charge for the company profile.

The directory also provides two rankings of companies: the largest companies, by state, and the biggest job creators. Indexes by company name, by industry, by human resource executive names, and by metropolitan area increase the usefulness of the directory. An introduction explains how the information was gathered and suggests how to make effective use of the directory.

The names of human resources executives and the jobs census make this directory particularly valuable for those interested in charting directions for career planning. The numbers of new jobs are suggestive rather than solid, however, because it is not clear whether the numbers indicate new jobs or new hires for open positions. The book is easily readable thanks to significant white space and the judicious use of bold typeface. Reasonably priced, *Hoover's* will be useful in public, academic, and corporate libraries. Its one drawback is that some pages began to tear out during the review; if this is typical, the binding will not stand up to heavy use. [R: Choice, May 96, p. 1450; RBB, 1 April 96, pp. 1388-89]—**Joan B. Fiscella**

256. **Peterson's Internships 1996: Over 35,000 Opportunities....** 16th ed. Princeton, N.J., Peterson's Guides, 1995. 537p. index. $21.95pa. ISBN 1-56079-525-5. ISSN 1082-2577.

This comprehensive directory provides complete information on internships and has been significantly expanded from the 15th edition, up to 537 pages from 423 pages. More than 35,000 paid and volunteer internship opportunities are listed for all 50 states and the District of Columbia, as well as 2 foreign countries. The internships are arranged in 27 career areas. Most fall into five broader fields—business and technology; communications; creative, performing, and fine arts; human services; and research.

Entries are arranged into these informational categories for each company or organization: general information; type and number of internships available; benefits, such as training opportunities, college credit, and housing; eligibility requirements; and contact information. Three indexes (field-of-interest, geographic, and employer) provide the complementary access to finding just the right internship. In addition to the entries themselves, there is a useful and informative introductory section explaining the whole internship experience, with intern profiles and tips on everything from applying with winning résumés and cover letters to the special requirements of international internships.

The professional experience of an internship can provide a real edge for a jobseeker in today's competitive job market, which is why this guide is so useful to students and recent graduates. The guide also includes an invitation to visit Peterson's Education and Career Center on the Internet at http://www.petersons.com. The directory is recommended for all academic and public libraries.—**Edward Erazo**

Handbooks and Yearbooks

257. Buckley, John F. **Multistate Payroll Guide.** New York, Panel, 1996. 1v. (various paging). $145.00pa. ISBN 1-56706-309-8.

Over time, public policy concerning the employment relationship has expanded significantly. This is particularly the case in the payroll and tax area, where state laws have become increasingly complex. The *Multistate Payroll Guide* was compiled to guide practitioners through the tangled web of legislation addressing this issue. Information in this comprehensive volume is organized in a concise and user-friendly format that allows the reader to find how each state treats several different payroll issues. The issues include wages and hours, employee benefit requirements, unemployment compensation, benefits and unemployment compensation taxation, payroll administration, calculation of income, state withholding and reporting requirements, and workers' compensation laws. The guide is a valuable reference work that brings together widely dispersed information. It is recommended for business, law, and professional libraries.—**Paul F. Clark**

258. Krannich, Ronald L., and Caryl Rae Krannich. **The Directory of Federal Jobs and Employers.** Manassas Park, Va., Impact Publications, 1996. 278p. index. $25.95pa. ISBN 1-57023-033-1.

The federal government, with nearly three million employees, is the largest single employer in the United States. It offers the most diverse opportunities of any employer in terms of types of jobs, ranging from such trades as plumbing and carpentry to medicine, science, and law. It also offers diverse opportunities in terms of geographic location, with job sites across the nation and the world. These jobs, however, are difficult to identify and the application process is somewhat complex.

The Directory of Federal Jobs and Employers is a useful resource for those interested in exploring the arcane world of government employment. The book provides a clear and complete guide to federal departments and agencies in all three branches of government. It furnishes a road map for applying for jobs and discusses strategies that can benefit jobseekers. Finally, the directory gives a useful discussion of employment trends in federal government, looking specifically at recent employment trends in various departments and agencies. This is a reference work whose benefits clearly outweigh its reasonable cost.
—**Paul F. Clark**

259. Plunkett, Jack W. **The Almanac of American Employers 1996-97: The Only Guide to America's Hottest, Fastest-Growing Major Corporations.** Galveston, Tex., Plunkett Research, 1996. 682p. index. $125.00pa. ISBN 0-9638268-3-2.

Plunkett has compiled information about 500 companies that attempts to answer such questions for jobseekers as: What are the fastest-growing companies, and which are the best to work for? The first section consists of a series of essays on such topics as tips for jobseekers and the outlook for selected occupations. The second section includes the individual company profiles. Criteria for selection were that the companies be publicly held, nongovernmental, with a minimum of 2,500 employees, and at least a 9 percent growth in sales over the last five years. Standard directory information is provided (with the addition of e-mail and World Wide Web addresses, if available), along with financial data based on 1995 or latest year available (although the user is never told which it is).

One must read the preface to know that the information found in the "apparent salaries and benefits" chart does not indicate if these benefits are given to all workers in the firm, or only to the top executives in the parent company. Footnotes also remind users that financial information, salaries, and benefits may have changed since this book was compiled. The number of "apparent" women and minority officers is also given. The most useful part of the profiles is the brief descriptions of growth plans and special features of the companies. The third section has numerous indexes and tables with various rankings. While the several disclaimers throughout the text may make the user aware that no source will be completely accurate and up-to-date, they also make one particularly uncomfortable in using this title as a major source of information, especially when there are so many other reputable sources to find most of these data.

—Michele Russo

260. **Sources and Methods: Labour Statistics. Volume 2: Employment, Wages, Hours of Work, and Labour Cost (Establishment Surveys). Sources et Méthodes. Fuentes y Metodos.** 2d ed. Washington, D.C., International Labor Office, 1995. 766p. free with Yearbook of Labour Statistics. ISBN 92-2-009992-6. ISSN 1014-9856.

261. **Yearbook of Labour Statistics 1995. Annuaire des Statistiques du Travail. Anuario de Estadisticas del Trabajo.** 54th ed. Washington, D.C., International Labor Office, 1995. 1069p. index. $189.00pa. ISBN 92-2-009993-4. ISSN 0084-3857.

The yearbook is an annual volume published by the International Labor Office. It contains data by country on population, employment, unemployment, hours of work, wages, labor costs, consumer prices, occupational injuries, and strikes and lockouts. There are subcategories in most of these groups, such as paid employment in nonagricultural activities and fuel and light indexes.

The yearbook is now accompanied by a methodological volume, *Sources and Methods: Labour Statistics*, which was formerly called *Statistical Sources and Methods*. This volume provides descriptions of the data published in the yearbook, including information on data collection, coverage, concepts and definitions, classification, historical changes, and technical references for each country. Each *Sources and Methods* volume will cover different subjects (the present being on employment, wages, hours of work, and labor cost [establishment surveys]). Gradually, all the subjects in the *Yearbook of Labour Statistics* will be covered by a volume in this series. These statistical texts are basic sources of the data and, as such, are valuable to many.—**J. E. Weaver**

262. **Specialty Occupational Outlook: Trade & Technical.** Joyce Jakubiak, ed. Detroit, Gale, 1996. 252p. index. $49.95. ISBN 0-8103-9645-9. ISSN 1083-4680.

This is another Gale career reference, a companion volume to *Specialty Occupational Outlook: Professions* (SOOP) (see ARBA 96, entry 274). These resources are creative enhancements of career information found in the U.S. Department of Labor's *Occupational Outlook Handbook* (OOH) (see ARBA 94, entry 281), with 150 additional occupations including ultrasound technicians, bodyguards, gambling dealers, locksmiths, and nuclear reactor operators. Ten occupation areas are covered: technicians and related support; marketing and sales; administrative support; service; agriculture, forest, and related; mechanics, installers, and repairers; construction trades and extractive; production; transportation and material moving; and handlers, equipment cleaners, helpers, and laborers.

These 10 trade and technical areas contrast very much with the 3 areas used in SOOP. Each job description reviews the nature of work, the working conditions, employment, availability, training, other qualifications, advancements, job outlook, earnings, and related occupations. Each occupation has a fact box that gives the *Dictionary of Occupational Titles* reference number; preferred level of completed education; average salary; and useful information about the occupation, such as employment trends, training requirements, and industry outlook.

Although similar to the OOH, *Trade & Technical* is an essential reference for vocational/technical schools, community college libraries, and all school career centers. The price is expensive for the school market, but it is still a reasonable cost for grades 9 and up. The OOH is still the essential first purchase. [R: Choice, May 96, p. 1458]—**Gerald D. Moran**

263. **The World Almanac Job Finder's Guide 1997.** By Les Krantz. Mahwah, N.J., World Almanac Books, 1996. 672p. index. $14.95pa. ISBN 0-88687-806-3.

This book is full of useful information for anyone just entering the workforce, considering changing jobs, or working abroad, as well as those seeking summer employment, relocating, or temping. The book covers such needed information as preparing a résumé, interviewing tips, and networking. Krantz's book lists jobs by career field, then by state. Each entry lists address; telephone number; employees; revenues (when available); key personnel; and a description of the company, including background.

Interestingly, a section on job descriptions is included, in which 250 jobs are profiled. There is also an annual earnings survey, literature that is available from the government, and a listing of professional magazines/journals. An added feature is a section on job opportunities, including jobs in the federal government, job hotlines, internships for students, and summer jobs for students. There is a section on job hunting in cyberspace and a section listing temporary agencies, employment agencies, computer-search agencies, and executive/sales recruiters.

The index typeface is a little small, but the index is quite adequate for this book. All in all, this is an excellent resource for anyone job hunting in the 1990s. The book is highly recommended.

—**Pamela J. Getchell**

264. **Young Person's Occupational Outlook Handbook: Descriptions for America's Top 250 Jobs.** Indianapolis, Ind., JIST Works, 1996. 262p. illus. $19.95pa. ISBN 1-56370-201-0.

With the publication of the 22d edition (1996-97) of the *Occupational Outlook Handbook* (OOH), the U.S. Department of Labor, Bureau of Labor Statistics celebrates the 50th year in print of occupational outlook information. During those 50 years, schools, colleges, veterans' offices, guidance counselors, employment agencies, and community organizations have used this information to educate individuals about the world of work. The demand for such information has been so great that this government publication has been widely reprinted by private publishers. Some have published the identical source under the same title (Bernan Press and VGM Career Horizons, to name a couple). Others have reorganized the information and retitled their editions, such as *The Big Book of Jobs* from VGM Career Horizons (1996) and *America's Top 300 Jobs* from JIST Works (see ARBA 94, entry 276, and ARBA 91, entry 241). More recently, publishers have repackaged the handbook in a variety of formats (a slide series, a video, microcomputer versions, multimedia editions on CD-ROM, and hypertext translations available on the Internet).

Occasionally, the repackaging is designed to target a specific audience. The *Young Person's Occupational Outlook Handbook* is one such republication. While not so stated, its content, format, and length appear to be crafted for young adolescents. Cartoonlike illustrations on the cover and first page of each section will appeal to preteens, but the vocabulary, differing little from the government source, rules out a younger audience. Each one-page entry includes a clarified version of the Department of Labor's job description, working conditions, and list of related occupations, but for only 250 jobs. While the title implies that these are the top jobs, there is no rating of the occupations or substantiation for this claim. Simple black-and-white graphics for the categories of earnings, education and training, and outlook add little to the information. The user must turn to the inside back cover for an explanation of the ratings.

Other attempts to add value are interesting, but not always informative. A large portion of each page is made up of a box labeled "Something Extra," which provides interesting facts, occasionally vaguely related to the job. For instance, a discussion of the discovery of gold is added to the entry for mining engineers. An account of early attempts at flight seems better suited to pilots than flight attendants. The "Subjects to Study" is a nice link from school to work, but inconsistencies in subjects abound. What is listed as "social sciences" on one page, is "social science" on the opposing page. Both "physics" and "physical science" appear in the same list. This lack of attention to detail carries over into the text as well. Several job descriptions lack uniform style, and "complimsents" rather than "accomplishments" appears on page 89. The paper cover and glued binding will not hold up to frequent copying any better than the original OOH.

While young people may appreciate the abbreviated format of the *Young Person's Occupational Outlook Handbook*, it refers readers to OOH for more information. Parents, teachers, and counselors dedicated to helping adolescents explore career possibilities may prefer the original. Middle school libraries may want to offer both to their students. [R: BR, Nov/Dec 96, p. 47]—**Debra S. Van Tassel**

MANAGEMENT

265. Berryman-Fink, Cynthia, and Charles B. Fink. **The Manager's Desk Reference.** 2d ed. New York, AMACOM, 1996. 370p. index. $24.95. ISBN 0-8144-0342-5.

Updating the 1989 edition (see ARBA 90, entry 266), the authors have included new topics such as change management, diversity in organizations, and violence in the workplace among the 45 subjects covered in this alphabetically arranged source. Each chapter attempts to provide "practical, yet substantive, sources of information" for managing people—peers, subordinates, supervisors, customers, the press, and the public. Topics average from five to seven pages in length and chapters begin with a brief introduction and conclude with an unannotated bibliography of three to six current books or journal articles to provide additional sources of information. Depending upon the subject, the discussion may also include legal issues, how to overcome obstacles, and guidelines for influencing desired behaviors.

To its credit, the writing style is clear and concise. Cross-references in the text help to guide the reader to other related topics, and a 13-page index provides detailed access into the body of the work. As a general introduction to the popular management literature, patrons and library managers may find this work useful. Yet, library managers may benefit more from *The Library Manager's Deskbook* (American Library Association, 1995), which is specifically tailored to a library setting (e.g., "how can library professionals be distinguished from paraprofessionals?"), with a "library management tip" section in each chapter. Nonetheless, this modestly priced, quick-reference source provides a current overview of timely issues written in a concise fashion, suitable for both the beginner and the seasoned professional.
—**Ilene F. Rockman**

266. **A Critical Guide to Management Training Videos and Selected Multimedia, 1996.** William Ellet and Laura Winig, eds. Boston, Harvard Business Reference/Harvard Business School Publishing; distr., New York, McGraw-Hill, 1996. 381p. index. $49.95pa. ISBN 0-87584-680-7.

One of the most effective qualities of this guide is its user-friendly format. In a well-written preface, the editors clearly delineate the need for a review of training media and pinpoint the audience: trainers and managers who want objective information about available management training videos. From beginning to end, the format and layout make the content accessible and useful to its designated audience. Each page is divided into two columns: The wider one provides the video title, producer, running time, price, release date, and an in-depth review. The narrower column rates the video in categories such as holding viewer attention, acting or presenting, instructional value, and production quality. Other potentially useful categories are portrayal of women and minorities and value for the money. Reviews also include overall ratings.

Chapters are arranged by content. These cover areas from change management, communication skills, customer service, and diversity to innovation, leadership, and team building. The supervisory and managerial skills topic includes the largest number of training materials. In addition to a comprehensive index, a separate listing of videos that the reviewers rated most highly supplements this format. Another useful index lists the training materials by price range. This book is an invaluable source of information for managers and educators who regularly rent or buy training products. As such, it can help them to avoid expensive mistakes. [R: Choice, Sept 96, p. 94]—**Renee B. Horowitz**

267. Keen, Peter G. W., and Ellen M. Knapp. **Every Manager's Guide to Business Processes: A Glossary of Key Terms & Concepts for Today's Business Leader.** Boston, Mass., Harvard Business School Press; distr., New York, McGraw-Hill, 1996. 219p. index. $24.95; $14.95pa. ISBN 0-87584-627-0; 0-87584-575-4pa.

Concentrating on 100 leading business process concepts, this book is less a glossary and more of a guidebook to an area that has taken on increasing importance. The volume begins with a 36-page introduction to business processes, their history, significance, and development in terms of process movements. The terms covered range from the familiar, such as *total quality management* and *benchmarking*, to the more exotic—*informate* or *penzias axiom*. Entries vary from one paragraph to several pages. Most constitute essay-length articles going well beyond straightforward definitions. Almost every entry gives the historical, conceptual, and business context in language that is uncluttered and free of jargon. Value judgments are sometimes included, such as for the entry for *folklore processes* where the authors advise, "They can and should be abandoned."

Cross-references give links to related terms. Notes in the margin provide anecdotes, reports on major corporations' experiences, extended remarks, and other supplementary information. Tables, charts, and diagrams are supplied in many articles. Bibliographic citations are in the introduction in full form and in the entries as abbreviated references. An index at the end completes the volume.

Much more than a simple glossary, this book is a guide to the conceptual landscape of business processes, giving insight and perspective to ideas that are quickly passing into popular speech and culture. The writing is so interesting and instructive that this book could be used as a supplement to management texts. It is suitable and highly recommended for any academic or public library.—**Gerald L. Gill**

MARKETING AND TRADE

268. **Consumer Canada 1996.** London, Euromonitor; distr., Detroit, Gale, 1996. 197p. $750.00pa. ISBN 0-86338-645-8.

269. **Consumer Mexico 1996.** London, Euromonitor; distr., Detroit, Gale, 1996. 192p. $750.00pa. ISBN 0-86338-650-4.

270. **Consumer South Africa 1995.** London, Euromonitor; distr., Detroit, Gale, 1995. 118p. $750.00pa. ISBN 0-86338-635-0.

271. **Consumer USA 1996.** London, Euromonitor; distr., Detroit, Gale, 1996. 334p. $750.00pa. ISBN 0-86338-660-1.

These four sources are part of Euromonitor's growing array of consumer and marketing statistical guides to the world's major established and emerging consumer markets. Their purpose is to give an analysis of market opportunities and to present a range of statistical market information. The "Consumer" series also includes guides for Asia, Latin America, China, Eastern Europe, Japan, and an international volume (see ARBA 96, entry 242; ARBA 95, entry 287; ARBA 95, entry 268; ARBA 96, entry 251; ARBA 95, entry 269; and ARBA 95, entry 248, respectively). Each of the sources starts with an overview of the region's market and economy, giving context, background, prospects, and an analysis of the consumer. The next section on marketing parameters provides data on such areas as economic and price indicators, marketing and promotional factors, and households, and may include such areas as retailing and tourism. The remainder of each volume examines the consumer market size. This last section details the various markets, such as food; cosmetics; consumer electronics; and personal goods (jewelry, camera film, bicycles, and the like).

The content is primarily statistical with the presentation consisting of bordered tables (up to four per page) in large typeface. Some sections are preceded by a narrative analysis. The commodity tables provide six years' worth of data for sales and six years of forecasts, with growth rates given in many cases. The Mexico volume, for instance, gives the years 1990-1995 for sales and the years 1995-2000 for forecasts. The "Consumer Market Sizes" text analysis preceding the tabular presentations consists largely of short, bulleted paragraphs in no apparent order and not tied in with the tables. They are rather supplemental to and independent from the data that follow.

The narrative material clearly takes a back seat to the data. The Mexico volume has 528 tables, the USA volume includes 250 tables, the volume on South Africa features about 300 tables, and Canada's volume weighs in with 544 tables. Although these sources have a table of contents followed by a list of tables, there is no index to locate specific commodities or products. This makes locating relevant information more time-consuming because not only does one need to find the right table, but also any applicable narrative analysis. Scanning for the table is made more difficult by the lack of any page headings to follow. The only alternative is to use the table of contents or thumb through the pages and then to read or skim the narratives in case one's product is mentioned. For librarians and businesspeople under a deadline, this is not the most efficient way to locate information.

The sources of information for the tables are given for each. These sources are noted in the introduction in terms of which organizations supplied data. However, on many tables, the sources do not correspond to those on the list. Additionally, many other tables indicate the source as "trade interviews," or "Euromonitor." These attributions would be impossible to verify independently for authenticity or accuracy. On the positive side, these sources provide information difficult or impossible to find anywhere else. Data on markets in these and other countries (excepting the United States) represented in this series are nearly nonexistent. These volumes fill a large gap in international business information needs. On the "needs improvement" side, Euromonitor should add an index to narrative as well as tables and provide better documentation of sources. The price per volume is steep, especially for sources such as the Canada book, which is only 118 pages. Nonetheless, the sources in Euromonitor's Consumer series would be valuable to any library serving international business students or clientele, businesses thinking of doing business abroad, or even small business development centers serving those clients.—**Gerald L. Gill**

272. **Economics, Trade, & Development: English-Spanish General Terminology. Terminologia General de Economia Comercio y Desarrollo.** New York, United Nations, 1995. 488p. index. $60.00pa. ISBN 92-1-100694-5. S/N GV.E/S.95.0.6.

This glossary is another title in the occasional publication series generated by the United Nations Terminology and Technical Documentation Section. The editors have provided users with an updated and consolidated version of several glossaries that have been previously published by their unit in various publications. A list of those publications has been included for reference.

This title covers 4,008 English business and commercial terms and phrases with their Spanish counterparts. Only rarely are clarifying definitions provided, normally when a term may have more than one meaning. Each English entry has been assigned a number, which is useful if the reader uses the Spanish index (at the back of the book) that refers the reader to an entry number. The reader will also note that each English entry has a designation as to whether this is a general term or a term used by the European Union or within the General Agreement on Tariffs and Trade (GATT) Uruguay Round accord.

With the increasing interest in doing business in Latin America, most large business and commercial libraries will want to acquire this publication. To gain the full benefit of this work, one should use it in conjunction with a good business dictionary.—**Judith J. Field**

273. **European Marketing Data and Statistics 1996.** 31st ed. London, Euromonitor; distr., Detroit, Gale, 1996. 504p. maps. index. $340.00. ISBN 0-86338-568-0. ISSN 0308-2938.

An overview of the European market, a guide to using the handbook, and an extensive list of source publications and agencies all comprise the introduction to this compilation of European marketing statistics. The body of the work is composed of 24 sections devoted to marketing geography (statistics and narrative on each of the countries) and tables covering demographics; economic and employment indicators; financial, industrial, retail, consumer, and service sectors; and environment and cultural indicators. Every table lists each of the European countries organized into groups ("European Union," "European Free Trade Association," "Eastern Europe," and "Other Europe"), although data are not necessarily available for each country on every subject. Four data periods are covered: an 18-year trend table (1977-1994), a different trend period, latest year available, and a single year. The choice of the data period hinges on availability of data and space.

Two types of maps illustrate the section on marketing geography, standard regions, and marketing regions. One or more statistical graphs illustrate each of the 24 data table sections. An alphabetic index provides access to subject information. The compilation differs from previous editions by taking into account the political changes in Eastern Europe. It remains clear and easy to use, particularly for those needing compiled data. The researcher needing more complete information will need to follow the less-than-specific references to original data.—**Joan B. Fiscella**

274. **Importers Manual USA and the Dictionary of International Trade.** 1996-97 ed. [CD-ROM]. San Rafael, Calif., World Trade Press, 1996. Minimum system requirements (Windows version): IBM or compatible 386. CD-ROM drive. DOS 3.3. Windows 3.1. 8MB RAM. 10-20MB hard disk space. VGA 640 x 480 monitor (SVGA recommended). Windows-compatible mouse. PostScript or PCL printer and

ATM or TrueType font manager (only for printing). Minimum system requirements (Macintosh version): 68020. CD-ROM drive. System software 6.0.7. 5MB RAM. 5MB hard disk space. 13-inch monitor or PowerBook. $149.00.

The electronic version of *Importers Manual USA* consists of a CD-ROM and an 11-page guide. The guide provides instructions for easy installation and an explanation of the nine main sections of the manual. One of these sections, the "Commodity Index," is the main feature of the reference. It is organized according to the 99 chapters of the Harmonized Tariff Schedule of the United States (HTSUS), used by the U.S. Customs Service to classify and assign duties for U.S. imports. The paper version of this title (see ARBA 96, entry 298) includes a product index. This index is not available on the CD-ROM, yet finding the appropriate chapter for a given product in the "Commodity Index" proves to be relatively easy.

The other eight sections of the manual, covering topics ranging from "International Banking" to "Container Packing," may be accessed directly from the main screen by clicking on the appropriate icon or through hot links (blue underlined items) found in tables, indexes, and text throughout the CD-ROM. When the user clicks on a hot link, it becomes highlighted and the screen shifts to that chosen topic. When initially played on a 486DX66 with 8MB RAM and CD-2X, the disc yielded disappointing results—the response time was too slow. However, when the CD-ROM was switched to a Pentium 100 MHz with 16MB RAM and CD-6X, response time evaporated and desired screens appeared in split seconds following appropriate commands. Corporate libraries, libraries that support trade promotion activities, academic libraries with major business collections, and large public libraries will all find this CD-ROM extremely useful, providing the libraries have upgraded equipment as well as the printing capabilities contained in the bibliographic description.—**Dene L. Clark**

275. **Market Information 1995/96.** New Providence, N.J., Headland Business Information/Reed Reference Publishing, 1996. 125p. index. $260.00pa. ISBN 1-85739-152-7.

This expensive directory provides evaluative descriptions of the major sources of market data in the United Kingdom for 1995. Official British statistical publications are briefly described, as well as a short list of guides to official statistics (both British and European). There is an extensive listing of the annual and quarterly reports available in the "UK Markets" series for the manufacturing industry. The most useful section of this publication covers market research reports. All of the series of reports from major publishers and research organizations are listed (e.g., Datamonitor, Frost & Sullivan, MAPS, Mintel, Euromonitor, the Economist Intelligence Unit), while the reports of many other publishers are simply described in one or two paragraphs. Other sections of the book cover the important marketing organizations in the United Kingdom, reference publications, consumer surveys, online and CD-ROM sources, and select business libraries. There is also a guide for conducting market research. This book will be most useful for academic libraries that support a strong international business curriculum.—**Thomas A. Karel**

276. **Markets of the U.S. for Business Planners: Historical and Current Profiles....** Thomas F. Conroy, ed. Detroit, Omnigraphics, 1996. 2v. maps. index. $240.00/set. ISBN 0-7808-0019-2.

This 2d edition updates the 1st edition of 1992 by using the most recent income and population data from the Bureau of Economic Analysis (BEA), part of the U.S. Department of Commerce. Serving the needs of business planners, marketing executives, corporate librarians, market researchers, and students, *Markets of the U.S.* presents ample statistical data, analytic commentary, graphs, charts, and maps for 183 local economies.

Examples of statistics included for rural and urban counties are personal income data, economic data on 77 major industries, population data, economic profiles for every year from 1969 to 1991 in constant 1991 dollars, and precalculated ratios and indexes for analysis and comparison. These data help users gauge the economic vitality of any location in terms of the personal income, and what major industry groups are responsible for that income. Volume 1 presents BEA areas 1 through 91, and volume 2 covers areas 92 through 183.

Personal income data are presented for 11 major economic sectors: farming, nonfarm resource industries, mineral industries, construction, manufacturing, transportation and utilities, wholesale trade, retail trade, financial services, services, and government. The measures presented here identify the significance of an economic activity to the local economy and its relative importance to the U.S. economy. Most business collections will want to add this outstanding resource, especially at its reasonable price. [R: Choice, Mar 96, p. 1100]—**Susan C. Awe**

277. **Trade Data Elements Directory Volume III.** By the Economic Commission for Europe and the Working Party on Facilitation of International Trade Procedures. New York, United Nations, 1996. 333p. (Trade Facilitation Recommendations). $90.00pa. ISBN 92-1-116650-0. S/N E.96.II.E.13.

A three-volume publication, the *Trade Data Elements Directory* is intended to be used as a reference by those individuals and organizations engaged in the process of "simplifying and rationalizing" trade procedures. International trade is currently valued at an astounding $3.3 trillion; however, its continued growth will, according to the editors, depend not only "on its adherence to free trade principles, but on substantially improving the efficiency of the overall trade process." Information transfers comprise a massive part of that process, and it is the administration of these transfers that *Trade Data Elements Directory* seeks to address.

Volume 1 of the directory, *Standard Data Elements* (see ARBA 96, entry 306), constitutes International Standard ISO 7372. Volume 2 covers the User Code Lists. Volume 3 is a compendium of recommendations issued by the Working Party on Facilitation of International Trade Procedures (WP.4) of the United Nations Economic Commission for Europe (UN/ECE). These recommendations deal with such items as the organization, layout, and coding of trade documents; standardization of the two-letter alphabetic country codes; establishment of committees dedicated to facilitation of trade procedures within participating countries; and agreement upon an international standard for abbreviations for widely used and accepted trade terms. There are 26 such recommendations; for each are included the history of the issue, relevant oversight committees, the recommendation and its rationale, and occasional information about implementation. Although not a necessary purchase for most libraries, those serving clients or corporations with major interests in global commerce will want to have all three volumes on hand.
—**G. Kim Dority**

278. Tran, Hoai Huong. **The Official Guide to Household Spending: The Number-One Guide to Who Spends How Much on What.** 3d ed. Ithaca, N.Y., New Strategist, 1995. 492p. index. $89.95. ISBN 1-885070-01-2.

Since 1980, the Bureau of the Census has gathered ongoing, nationwide data on U.S. household expenditures, primarily for use by the Bureau of Labor Statistics (BLS) in updating the Consumer Price Index. *The Official Guide to Household Spending* provides access to an otherwise formidable accumulation of data from the Census Bureau surveys. Because there is a lag time of several years in preparing data, the 3d edition reflects data gathered in 1993.

The guide consists almost entirely of tables, the first of which shows broad spending trends, followed by more detailed information on significant products and services within major categories (e.g., apparel, health care, and so forth). The tables provide average spending, indexed average spending, total spending, and shares of total spending—each by age, income, household type, and region. In some cases, projections are made to the year 2000.

The BLS/Census Bureau surveys represent the most comprehensive source of information on U.S. consumer spending, which makes the guide an essential reference tool, especially for students of economics and marketing as well as for managers who require information on household spending for establishing plans and strategies. This is a book for serious readers, as there are no graphics and little text to illustrate points that can be drawn from the tables. Yet the well-designed tables carry a great deal of useful information for interested readers.—**William C. Struning**

279. **Wholesale and Retail Trade USA: Industry Analyses, Statistics, and Leading Organizations.** Arsen J. Darnay and Gary Alampi, eds. Detroit, Gale, 1995. 993p. maps. index. $195.00. ISBN 0-7876-0865-3. ISSN 1084-8622.

This book provides extensive statistics for 69 wholesale and 64 retail industries, primarily from federal government statistics. Part 1 presents national and state statistics arranged numerically by 4-digit Standard Industrial Classification (SIC) code and covering data from 1982 through 1992, with projections for later years. This section also lists the leading companies in an industry, indexes of change from one year to the next, and specific occupations employed by an industry. Small maps indicate the concentration of an industry in a particular state or region.

Part 2 of the book records tables for 591 cities and metropolitan areas arranged alphabetically. Each table lists industries, which reported the required data, numerically by SIC number. In the back of the book, five indexes provide access to the book by SIC code, subject, name of company, city or metropolitan area, and occupation. An appendix follows the indexes and briefly describes the industry represented by each 4-digit SIC number.

The purpose of this book aims toward providing accurate and current information from authoritative government sources. The book lists 20 used car dealers (SIC 2521) in the Terre Haute, Indiana, area, but the 1995-1996 Terre Haute telephone directory lists 75 used car dealers in the yellow pages, reflecting the increase since 1992. Many of the statistics in this book can be gleaned from such publications as the *1992 Economic Census* on CD-ROM (U.S. Bureau of the Census), but *Wholesale and Retail Trade USA* presents this information in a more convenient, enhanced, and expanded format. Even though the price is high, business, academic, and large public libraries will find this title especially useful for their business clientele. [R: Choice, Dec 96, pp. 596-97]—**O. Gene Norman**

280. Williams, Jane A. **The Authentic Jane Williams' Home School Market Guide.** Placerville, Calif., Bluestocking Press, 1996. 368p. index. $125.00 spiralbound. ISBN 0-942617-25-8. ISSN 1080-4730.

Home schooling is becoming an increasingly popular option for families disenchanted with the perceived problems of the United States' public school system. Consequently, such works as *Home School Market Guide* are springing up to help individuals and companies reach the parents of this country's roughly one million home-schooled children.

The work leads off with roughly 40 pages of how-to and why-to advice, plus current statistics about the home schooling market. This practical, hands-on preliminary material is geared toward helping the reader make the sale. The master directory, an alphabetic listing of some 550 advertising opportunities, associations and networks, card deck mailers, exhibit opportunities and services, consultants, curriculum developers, direct mail sources, freelance opportunities, mail-order catalogs and their publishers, reviewers, retail stores, and Internet Websites, forms the core of the guide. Entries provide contact names, addresses, and telephone/fax/e-mail/Website; a three- or four-sentence description; and conference information, circulation figures, editorial descriptions, and catalog requirements as appropriate to the entry. The directory listings are followed by 28 "specialty indexes" that organize the listing names according to such topics as advertising opportunities, distributors, media, online services, support groups, and so on.

The target audience for this work will be publishers of books, software, audiotapes, and videotapes, as well as product developers and marketers of educational toys and games. *Home School Market Guide* will be a useful, albeit expensive, tool for this group. Most public libraries will probably prefer the standard guides to home schooling resources that are geared toward parents'—rather than marketers'—needs.—**G. Kim Dority**

281. **World Marketing Data and Statistics 1996 on CD-ROM.** 2d ed. [CD-ROM]. Chicago, Euromonitor International, 1996. Minimum system requirements: IBM PC-AT or compatible 386. CD-ROM drive with interface card and Microsoft Extensions 2.2. Windows 3.0. 4MB RAM (6MB recommended). 10MB hard disk space. $1,490.00.

This CD-ROM product is based on the merged contents of Euromonitor's print publications, *European Marketing Data and Statistics* (31st ed.; see entry 273) and *International Marketing Data and Statistics* (18th ed.; see ARBA 95, entry 252). The 1996 CD-ROM edition features useful socioeconomic data for the years 1977 to 1994. Data are accessible by text, by country, and by table of contents searching. Truncation and Boolean logic searching are both available. A browse feature allows the user to search through specific indexes, including geographic location, field, table or chapter names, and original source title. Data retrieved through the text search feature can be displayed in report format. Data retrieved via the table of contents and countries search feature can be displayed in a spreadsheet format that can be sorted, edited into another Windows application, or charted in bar or pie formats. For example, graphs could be easily created, then captured using Windows clipboard commands, and inserted into word processing documents or slide shows. In just a few minutes, the user can easily generate a bar chart illustrating the number of cellular telephone users per 1,000 population for all of the European Union countries in 1994. Users comfortable with Windows commands and spreadsheet applications will find this a welcome and more flexible alternative to Euromonitor's print publications. The price of the product does not seem excessive due to the quality of the data and numerous output options available to the user.

The product is easy to install in a stand-alone configuration, or may be installed on a network (network configuration was not tested for this review), which requires a reasonable amount of computer memory. The minimum requirement of IBM PC-AT or 386 may result in processing speeds too slow for users accustomed to current computer configurations. A 22-page guide includes installation instructions, brief explanations of search functions, an explanation of data coverage and sources, and customer service information. The spreadsheets were easy to manipulate and mark for output of comparative data. Help was context-sensitive and generally simple and directly stated.

This product presents a good example of how CD-ROMs can be used to create a product with value beyond the equivalent print publications. Easy manipulation of data allows the user to create a variety of comparative data in spreadsheet or graphic format that are far superior to the output allowed via print products. Libraries with a heavy demand for data related to international studies, international business development, and entrepreneurship will want to invest in this product.—**Lynne M. Fox**

REAL ESTATE

282. **Directory of Designated Members, 1996.** Chicago, Appraisal Institute, 1996. 322p. index. free.

This directory is designed for both real estate professionals and consumers who need appraisal services. The listings are limited to those real estate appraisers who have earned one or more professional designations from the Appraisal Institute. The directory is organized in a straightforward manner, with designated members listed first geographically, and later alphabetically. An especially helpful adjunct to the listings is a guide to metropolitan areas, which notes the names of suburban communities close enough to major cities to be of interest to anyone seeking appraisal services in a particular metropolitan area. With some of the nation's most active real estate markets now located in suburban "edge cities," a focus at the metropolitan area, rather than city, level is crucial.

As a supplement or alternative to the directory, the Appraisal Institute's Website (http://www.realworks.com/ai) offers the same directory at no charge to Internet searchers. The Website promises a number of value-added features, such as the ability to search for specialized appraisers by type of property or service. Unfortunately, the supplementary listings containing information on appraiser specialties are only active for appraisers willing to pay for these listings. Apparently so few appraisers have purchased supplementary listings that most searches produce no results. A search for retail property specialists in the Boston metropolitan area, for example, yielded zero listings—not because there are no such specialists in the region but, more likely, because none had paid to be listed. Despite these shortcomings, the Website works well for straightforward geographic and alphabetic searches. One small bonus is that the Website will list all appraisers in a metropolitan area together, rather than requiring use of the metropolitan area guide mentioned above to find names of suburban communities.

This directory, in its print edition, is recommended for any large public library or any academic library supporting a curriculum in real estate. The hard copy will be especially valuable in a ready-reference environment, where quick lookups in a book may happen more rapidly than a search can be performed via the Website. For other libraries, where use is more occasional and less likely to occur in a ready-reference environment, reliance on the Website alone may be sufficient and can save shelf space.—**David Bickford**

5 Education

GENERAL WORKS

Bibliography

283. Mitchell, Bruce M., and Robert E. Salsbury. **Multicultural Education: An International Guide to Research, Policies, and Programs.** Westport, Conn., Greenwood Press, 1996. 383p. index. $85.00. ISBN 0-313-28985-9.

This book examines multicultural education in 42 countries, showing how this important educational issue is handled in countries representing a variety of socioeconomic, political, and religious systems and perspectives. Chapters are devoted to individual countries and are arranged alphabetically, starting with Afghanistan and ending with the United States. Each chapter is divided into five parts: the history of the country's educational system, its structure, recent developments specifically in the area of multicultural education, a summary, and a list of references. The book also includes an extensive bibliography and a useful index.

Because the ultimate goal of multicultural education is to prepare students to function effectively in pluralistic societies, this is a timely and important book in its thorough address of an issue of global importance. The authors, both professors of education at Eastern Washington University, are to be commended for providing a reference work that will be a valuable resource for scholars in a number of spheres of education, especially comparatists.—**G. Douglas Meyers**

284. Murphy, Christina, Joe Law, and Steve Sherwood, comps. **Writing Centers: An Annotated Bibliography.** Westport, Conn., Greenwood Press, 1996. 287p. index. (Bibliographies and Indexes in Education, no.17). $69.50. ISBN 0-313-29831-9.

More than 1,400 entries make up this comprehensive bibliography on writing centers, which was compiled by 3 experts in the field. Chapters on anthologies, history, program descriptions, professional concerns, writing center theory, administration, writing across the curriculum, educational technology, tutoring theory, tutor training, tutoring, ethics, and research serve to group related citations, which are listed in alphabetic order by author. The authors have included entries from nearly 100 years of writing center scholarship, although the majority of resources are from the past 20 years. The one- to three-sentence annotations are succinct and informative. Many of the articles cited come from the National Writing Centers Association's *Writing Lab Newsletter* (published since 1976), which is not indexed in ERIC. Author and subject indexes are included. Faculty and professional staff who are involved with writing instruction in a variety of educational settings will benefit from this timesaving bibliography. It is recommended for most reference or circulating collections.—**Deborah V. Rollins**

Dictionaries and Encyclopedias

285. **Encyclopedia of African-American Education.** Faustine C. Jones-Wilson and others, eds. Westport, Conn., Greenwood Press, 1996. 575p. index. $95.00. ISBN 0-313-28931-X.

The struggle for African Americans to achieve educational equality is a significant issue in the history of the United States. This resource provides an overview of pertinent theories, laws, people, places, and events. Each alphabetic entry ends with a bibliography for further reading. Coverage is broad, but there are some omissions. For example, Elizabeth Koontz is not included, even though she was the first African American president of the National Education Association. The editor explains in the preface that the encyclopedia has length restrictions, and subsequently biographical entries were reduced. Instead, Greenwood Press is scheduled to issue a companion volume, *Biographical Dictionary of African-American Educators*. Other omissions are random, in an effort to provide the broadest possible scope, including local and regional information in addition to national data. Strong coverage of legal cases and numerous profiles of colleges and universities proliferate. For the history student, a chronology would have been a welcome addition. As a whole, the encyclopedia is still a useful reference tool.—**Jean Engler**

286. **Historical Encyclopedia of School Psychology.** Thomas K. Fagan and Paul G. Warden, eds. Westport, Conn., Greenwood Press, 1996. 448p. index. $95.00. ISBN 0-313-29015-6.

This volume is the first historical reference book dealing with school psychology. The introduction makes the important distinction between school psychology and educational psychology: Educational psychology studies the general processes of learning and instruction, while school psychology studies the individual learner's adjustment to those processes. While some overlap occurs, the *Historical Encyclopedia* is oriented to the field of school psychology and its historical traditions and development.

More than 100 authorities contributed to the approximately 500 entries, which appear in alphabetic order and provide details of domains that influenced the development of school psychology in the twentieth century. Each entry includes a definition or description, followed by a discussion of the entry's historical context, if applicable, and concludes with a limited number of key bibliographic references for further information. The entry selection process focused on the areas relevant to the field of school psychology, identified as the following: assessment; interventions; consultation; research, evaluation, and accountability; in-service education; administration and supervision; major events; significant persons; training and practice settings; organizations and regulatory agencies; and professional issues.

The index includes each entry with its page number. In addition to the body of entries, the *Historical Encyclopedia* furnishes a list of contributors and an appendix for sources for further study, composed of major organizations in the field, major archival sources of information, journals in the field of school psychology, major books on school psychology, and a list of publications covering historical overviews of the field of school psychology. The encyclopedia is intended for use in undergraduate and graduate training programs for school psychologists. It should also be included in the academic libraries at colleges and universities offering programs in educational, clinical, and counseling psychology and departments of special education. In addition, this volume would be useful to editors of journals in these fields and to individual practitioners as a quick reference to terms that are used frequently and for those seeking both historical and contemporary information. [R: Choice, Sept 96, p. 99]—**Sharon Thomerson**

287. **Philosophy of Education: An Encyclopedia.** J. J. Chambliss, ed. New York, Garland, 1996. 720p. index. (Garland Reference Library of the Humanities, v.1671). $95.00. ISBN 0-8153-1177-X.

Nearly 200 contributors have provided more than 200 essays in this impressive encyclopedia on the philosophy of education. Users can sample a wide variety of philosophers, from Plato to Jean-Jacques Rousseau to Maria Montessori. Topics, which often explore additional philosophies and their proponents, range from the complexities of Marxism to a fascinating essay on work.

The design is economical but functional, with enough marginal space for the occasional note. Each essay and bibliography provides just enough information, two or three pages generally. Internal cross-references provide those in search of more information with useful leads. Although it would have been useful to have a detailed table of contents to see the range of items in the encyclopedia, the index is especially impressive and thoughtfully developed. Researchers, professors of education, librarians, and anyone interested in the history of education will find this a useful and intriguing resource. [R: RBB, 1 Nov 96, pp. 539-40]—**Suzanne I. Barchers**

288. Unger, Harlow G. **Encyclopedia of American Education.** New York, Facts on File, 1996. 3v. illus. index. $175.00/set. ISBN 0-8160-2994-6.

If one reads through this amazing three volume-reference on education in the United States, one can get not only a written and visual history of education in the United States, but also can be brought up-to-date with current controversies and issues. Published by the well-known and esteemed people at Facts on File, Unger and his colleagues have put together a most useful reference tool for students of education. The entries are well written and concise and refer to other topics within the encyclopedia. The three-volume set is sprinkled with superb black-and-white photographs of people, places, and buildings. The author has maintained the historical entries and provided contemporary "facts" as well. For example, the work lists Emma Willard and Robert Owen as well as Theodore Sizer and the Coalition of Essential Schools.

A complete index is provided, along with appendixes covering the chronology of important landmarks in U.S. education, significant federal legislation for U.S. education, significant U.S. Supreme Court cases on education, and a listing of graduate and undergraduate education majors in U.S. universities and colleges. A substantial bibliography of major resources is also given, arranged by subject. This set would be a welcome addition to most basic libraries, and would also be helpful as a quicker and more usable reference in the larger academic library. Individuals may also want to have their own copies. In the age of overinflated reference works, *Encyclopedia of American Education* is a welcome addition to the field. [R: LJ, 15 Sept 96, p. 60; RBB, 15 Nov 96, pp. 609-10]—**Anne F. Roberts**

Quotation Books

289. Noble, Keith Allan. **The International Education Quotations Encyclopaedia.** Buckingham, England, Open University Press; distr., Bristol, Pa., Taylor & Francis, 1995. 382p. index. $59.95. ISBN 0-335-19394-3.

Drawn from an impressive array of academic and general media sources, Noble has assembled nearly 2,700 quotations in English and English translation. The entries themselves are equally diverse, embodying in their tone and intent the pedantic, the quaint, the sardonic, and the comic. Recent espousers of popular education theory are well represented, as are a surprising number of novelists. The bons mots extend from Thomas J. Watson's succinct "THINK!" to the 300-word Hippocratic oath; few quotations, however, exceed 75 words.

Noble has subsumed this treasury's maxims and observations beneath more than 400 alphabetically ordered subject categories, with respective pagination notation, on the 26 pages that introduce each letter section. The nomenclature of these headings ranges from the mundane to the esoteric, testifying to the subjective and broad scope of the enterprise. Mingling with such expected terms as *truancy*, *spelling*, and *critical thinking* are *vivisection*, *full-time*, *stupidity*, and *banking* (the theory that education consists of the depositing of bits of knowledge into one's brain). The cosmopolitan and scholarly dimensions of this volume are evidenced by the inclusion of such headings as *lycée*, *mens sana in corpore sano*, and *école polytechnique*.

Under each category, the quotations are ordered alphabetically, by author surname or printed source citation, such as the *Chronicle of Higher Education* and the *International Herald Tribune*. Multicultural proverbs are sprinkled throughout the text. For instance, a proverb translated from Russian immediately follows a pearl of wisdom dispensed by Bertrand Russell. Regrettably, however, the index scatters proverb entries by language nationality rather than clustering them under the subhead "Proverbs."

Another index defect lies in its inconsistent supplying of initials of authors' first names. Also, the addition of an occupational index, and the breaking out of title entries from the book's sole index, would enhance the volume's usefulness. Finally, although this work cannot feign to be comprehensive, it is nonetheless astounding to find no quotations within it by Eleanor Roosevelt, James B. Conant, Nicholas Murray Butler, or Thomas Jefferson. [R: Choice, Jan 96, p. 758]—**Jeffrey E. Long**

ALTERNATIVE EDUCATION

290. **The Independent Study Catalog.** 6th ed. Princeton, N.J., Peterson's Guides, 1995. 301p. index. $16.95pa. ISBN 1-56079-460-7. ISSN 0733-6020.

Published jointly by Peterson's Guides and the National University Continuing Education Association (NUCEA), the present edition is the most recent update in the catalog's three-year publication cycle. More than 10,000 continuing education courses from 100 institutions are profiled. Course listings span academic levels from elementary to graduate education, with the majority being at the high school and college level. All courses are correspondence in nature and do not include any requirements to attend classes.

A valuable feature of this catalog is the accreditation information provided: All programs and courses are covered by the accreditation of the institution and one of six regional accrediting associations (two exceptions are noted). Most institutions profiled are NUCEA members (a membership list is included). The catalog follows an alphabetic arrangement of institutions, with entries providing information concerning average tuition, the availability of degree or certificate programs, a list of course offerings including their assigned credit units, and contact information. There are geographic indexes for both external degree programs and certificate programs that identify institutions granting degrees or certificates with little or no attendance on campus. In addition, there is an extensive index of subject areas that identifies all the subjects in which correspondence instruction is offered. This guide continues to provide valuable information for those wishing to pursue independent study, particularly those interested in earning academic credit.—**Michael Weinberg**

291. **Peterson's Distance Learning 1997.** 2d ed. Princeton, N.J., Peterson's Guides, 1996. 486p. index. $24.95pa. ISBN 1-56079-664-2.

Distance learning incorporates two components: teaching students who are off-site or at a distance from the teacher; and teaching through media, such as videotape or computer modem. *Peterson's Distance Learning* lists such programs and courses offered at both United States and Canadian institutions of higher education. The directory is arranged alphabetically by the name of the institution. Each entry lists the institution's name, its programs, and then individual courses, with a brief description of each program and the name and address of a contact person or department. Associate, baccalaureate, master's, and doctoral programs are noted, as well as both undergraduate and graduate certificate programs. Additional information includes access methods; costs; application procedures; and other student services, such as financial aid, counseling, career help, and library services.

Although earlier guides to distance learning programs exist, with the growth and change in programs, a new guide is welcome, even for libraries that own the earlier ones. Peterson's Guides last published this guide in 1993, under the title *The Electronic University* (see ARBA 94, entry 376); it listed some 100 institutions offering programs. A similar guide, *The Oryx Guide to Distance Learning* (see ARBA 95, entry 342), was published in 1994, and it listed about 300 schools. The volume under review lists more than 700 such institutions.

Peterson's Distance Learning has several other selling points besides currentness. It includes a discussion of many questions that potential students may have: What is distance learning? How does it differ from traditional methods of education? How does one earn credit? What questions should one ask to locate a suitable program? and, What are some financial considerations? The guide also inserts a series of "Student Profiles," in which students who have participated in distance education write about their own experience. Their comments, combined with the questions addressed, will be useful to people who are considering participating in a distance education program.

Three indexes provide various points of access. Two are subject indexes to programs and courses. The other is a geographic index, arranged by state or Canadian province. As distance learning is a growing industry, used by many segments of the population, this directory will be a standard reference in all types of libraries.—**Terry Ann Mood**

292. Thorson, Marcie Kisner. **Campus-Free College Degrees.** 7th ed. Tulsa, Okla., Thorson Guides, 1996. 255p. index. $19.95pa. ISBN 0-916277-44-5.

The 7th edition of this guide continues to be aimed at adults wishing to earn high school diplomas, college credits, and degrees in a nontraditional manner with programs that offer more flexibility (see ARBA 95, entry 376, for a review of the 6th edition). The first sections of the guide provide information that enables students to evaluate schools and programs before making a final choice, and information on where to go to receive credit for past education or life experience. The information includes lists of accrediting agencies with address, telephone numbers, and regions they accredit; lists of state agencies for higher education that can be contacted to determine whether a school or certificate meets state requirements; examinations that, if passed, allow credit for college-level learning outside the classroom; sources to contact for schools offering correspondence study; addresses of agencies that evaluate education completed in other countries; opportunities for earning a high school diploma through distance learning; and how to obtain credit for knowledge gained through life experience.

The largest portion of the book lists, in alphabetic order, schools that offer distance learning bachelor's, master's, and doctoral degrees with little or no residency required. The entries provide address, telephone number, and degrees offered with complete description of the programs. The indexes of areas of study with schools that offer them, geographic list of schools by state, and alphabetic list of the schools are particularly helpful. This book furnishes the necessary information required to help adults choose off-campus programs that meet their needs in obtaining education or retraining to stay viable in today's job market. It is affordable and should be on the shelves of most libraries.—**Marilyn Strong Noronha**

COMPUTER RESOURCES

293. **ERIC on CD-ROM.** [CD-ROM]. Baltimore, Md., National Information Services Corporation, 1995. 2 discs. Minimum system requirements: IBM or compatible 286 AT-class or greater. CD-ROM drive. 512K RAM. 2MB hard disk space. Color or monochrome monitor. $125.00/yr. ISSN 1069-9279.

The Educational Resources Information Center (ERIC) database covers literature dealing with virtually every aspect of education, from preschool through postgraduate work. *ERIC on CD-ROM* is available from a number of vendors, including EBSCO, ERIC, Knight-Ridder, National Information Services Corporation (NISC), Oryx Press, and SilverPlatter. Pricing varies according to what years are covered on the archival disc and the current disc, and other options, such as LAN/WAN support and package purchase options. The ERIC database is updated monthly by most commercial online systems, but ERIC CD-ROM vendors update quarterly.

Most vendors offer both of the major ERIC files: Resources in Education (RIE), which includes documents such as technical reports, conference papers, reviews, syllabuses, curricula, and theses; and Current Index to Journals in Education (CIJE), which covers selected journal articles. Most vendors also provide the *Thesaurus of ERIC Descriptors* (13th ed.; see ARBA 96, entry 318) and 1,300 full-text ERIC digests of 2-page research syntheses addressing selected major topics in education. When considering a subscription to ERIC or other CD-ROM products, users should be sure to find out if the older discs are not set to expire.

The NISC ERIC discs are the same as sold by the ERIC facility. The current version uses DOS-based search software, but a Windows version is expected soon. The archival disc covers the years 1966 to 1979 and must be used in conjunction with a current disc, which carries the retrieval software and ERIC files from 1980 to the present. The 2 discs contain the more than 850,000 ERIC records, including RIE, CIJE, the thesaurus, and ERIC digests. The NISC discs include a user's manual and come network-ready for no additional charge.

NISC claims that their ERIC product is faster, easier to use, and more powerful than the ones from SilverPlatter or Knight-Ridder. Retrieval software was easy to load and in performing several searches, the NISC product was indeed quite fast. However, this speed was obtained only after loading included, but optional, software that took an additional 3MB of storage, beyond the 2MB recommended as a minimum. Contributing to the ease of use are three search modes: novice, advanced, and expert. Each mode displays the thesaurus, which can help in formulating search strategies, but which can be toggled off. An explode command lets one search narrower and related terms. Major features of the NISC disc are full Boolean and proximity retrieval, truncation, and field-specific indexes. Other features include highlighting of search terms in retrieved documents, record tagging for printing, e-mail ordering of selected documents, alternate screen formats for short and long record display, and user-friendly help functions. In addition to search features, users can control the interface, output, and LAN performance.

While many of these features are also available from other vendors, the NISC product provides a comprehensive set of features and is easy to use. It is flexible enough to meet the needs of end users and experienced searchers.—**Andrew G. Torok**

ELEMENTARY AND SECONDARY EDUCATION

Bibliography

294. **Educators Index of Free Materials 1995.** 104th ed. Mary P. Parent, ed. Randolph, Wis., Educators Progress Service, 1995. 462p. index. $46.95 looseleaf. ISBN 0-87708-274-X.

Titles in this particular guide, part of a series of free and inexpensive instructional materials, are aimed at audiences of upper elementary, secondary, and postsecondary students. Now in its 104th edition, the 1995 listing includes 2,277 items (830 of which are new) offered by 470 sponsoring organizational sources (of which 125 are also new).

All materials described are completely free of cost and can be retained permanently by the requester. Entries are arranged in a category devoted to educational administration as well as seven major curricular categories: fine arts, health and physical education, language arts, science, mathematics, social studies, and vocational education. A ninth category covers special areas such as consumer education, driver education, guidance, special education, and so forth. Print materials (consisting primarily of books and booklets, brochures, and fact sheets) are followed by a separate listing of visual and audiovisual materials (charts, pictures and posters, exhibits, magazines and newsletters, and maps) arranged alphabetically by subject. Prefatory materials describe how to use the index and how to request desired materials.

The publishers claim that currency of information is maintained in each annual edition. For example, in this edition, 267 new items have been added to the health education section, 37 to nutrition education, 33 to general science, 79 to citizenship, 75 to guidance, and 13 to family life education. Although the publishers say item selection is based on currency, copyright dates are not included in the bibliographic descriptions. Annotations vary in length, but 50-word descriptions are typical. There is ample information in this guide, but its physical composition will not withstand hard use because of the nature of the binding. *Educators Index of Free Materials* is particularly useful for maintaining comprehensive and up-to-date vertical file collections and should not be overlooked by teachers, school media specialists, public librarians, and academic librarians in institutions with teacher education programs.—**Lois J. Buttlar**

295. Totten, Samuel, and others. **Middle Level Education: An Annotated Bibliography.** Westport, Conn., Greenwood Press, 1996. 428p. index. (Bibliographies and Indexes in Education, no.16). $79.50. ISBN 0-313-29002-4.

The appearance of this annotated bibliography is timely in view of heightened interest in developing middle-level programs to meet the unique intellectual, social, emotional, and physical needs of young adolescents. Academic and school libraries, especially, should find that this resource can meet the needs of nearly anyone interested in any aspect of the education of this age group. Introductory material briefly describes unique aspects of exemplary middle-level programs, chronicles the increased focus on them during the past decade, and concludes with a plea for more research and commitments by federal and state governments and colleges of education.

Compiled by teacher educators and an expert in nursing care for children, the bibliography addresses a variety of factors influencing adolescents; it offers annotations on resources identified through a variety of print and online sources relating to education as well as to nursing, psychology, and health education. Formats of works listed include articles, books, reports, dissertations, conference papers, and videotapes. A strength of the work is the number of topics and subtopics presented. Administrators and teachers will find resources to answer some of their practical questions about middle-level facilities, interdisciplinary team organization, classroom management, flexible and block scheduling, educational technology, multicultural concerns, assessment, and—of course—achievement. Among the many other topics included are core subjects (language arts, reading, mathematics, science, social studies, physical education, writing); social issues; early adolescent development; family and community; pedagogical issues and strategies; teacher preparation; and professional development.

The only drawback to this comprehensive print resource is the same as any of its nature: timeliness. Published in 1996, the most recent citations are for 1995 works. Readers will want to know what new resources have become available since the compendium was published. [R: Choice, Nov 96, p. 434]—**Jan Bakker**

Dictionaries and Encyclopedias

296. **A First Dictionary of Cultural Literacy: What Children Need to Know.** 2d ed. E. D. Hirsch Jr., William G. Rowland Jr., and Michael Stanford, eds. New York, Houghton Mifflin, 1996. 288p. illus. maps. index. $13.95pa. ISBN 0-395-82352-8.

Many historical, geographic, and scientific changes have taken place since the publication of the 1st edition of this book (see ARBA 90, entry 312). Users may not be aware that this is a revision, as nowhere on the cover does it say so. Designed for children through sixth grade, and based on standards developed by the Core Knowledge Foundation, the guiding premise of the book is that all U.S. children, regardless of their ethnic and cultural backgrounds, need a solid foundation of shared knowledge as the basis for successful schooling and effective citizenship. The opinions of several hundred teachers and parents provided the guidelines for terms included.

Divided into 21 sections on subjects such as fine arts, mathematics, world geography, literature, the Bible, U.S. and world history, earth and life sciences, and medicine and the human body, the two-column presentation is easy to read and handle. The 12-point typeface, appropriate for younger readers, is crisp and well presented. The text is complemented by 200 black-and-white photographs, woodcuts, maps, and line drawings. Cross-references occur frequently and are printed in small capital letters. Pronunciation guides appear in parentheses after main entry terms. The new food pyramid, *AIDS*, and *unsaturated fats* appear, as do *CD-ROM*, *e-mail*, *global village*, and *World Wide Web*. Six pages of books appropriate for ages six through twelve, which appeared previously in *Reference Books for Children's Collections* (New York Public Library, 1988), are arranged by subject to loosely follow the order of the table of contents of the book under review. A combined author/title/subject/illustrator index concludes the volume.

All the terms in this book could be found in general dictionaries and encyclopedias. However, current interest in early literacy as a social issue makes dictionaries such as this one useful reference tools for early learning. It could also be of use in ESL programs for adults.—**Judy Gay Matthews**

Directories

297. Rogg, Carla S., Oskar H. Rogg, and Kiliaen V. R. Townsend. **The Boarding School Guide.** Atlanta, Ga., Care Solutions, 1996. 364p. maps. $19.95pa. ISBN 1-887203-02-8.

Any parent who has considered sending a child to boarding school will want to begin by consulting this useful resource. The introduction alone is worth the price of the book, particularly the sections that discuss the "hidden dollar value" of boarding schools and "what to look for." The majority of the book profiles more than 300 schools, providing the following information: school name, address, telephone number, key personnel, nearest airport, affiliation, student body makeup, tuition, extra costs, total aid awarded, endowments, annual gifts, alumni giving, admissions information, application deadline, class size, student/teacher ratio, special programs, Advanced Placement courses, median SATs, library size, dormitories, student life, sports, colleges attended by the 1995 graduating class, and other information.

Other features that make this a useful guide include regional maps showing the school locations; tables that show boarding schools by state, for boys and girls, by size, by number of states represented, with a high percentage of foreign students, and the oldest schools; and tables that show boarding schools by type, by special programs, with uncommon sports, and with large libraries. Additional tables outline college information, such as boarding schools with high average SAT scores, financial information, and admissions information. The profiles and tables are well organized, easy to access, and interesting to sample, even if one is not in the market for a boarding school.—**Suzanne I. Barchers**

Handbooks and Yearbooks

298. **International Encyclopedia of Teaching and Teacher Education.** 2d ed. Lorin W. Anderson, ed. New York, Pergamon Press/Elsevier Science, 1995. 684p. illus. index. $150.00. ISBN 0-08-042304-3.

This is one of Pergamon Press's single-volume encyclopedias drawing upon articles in the *International Encyclopedia of Education* (2d ed.; see ARBA 95, entry 337), with revisions and additions. It contains 140 articles including 11 section introductions, all signed, grouped into 2 parts—teaching and teacher education. At the end of the text are a list of contributors, a name index, and a subject index.

Part A consists of eight sections. It deals with the nature and characteristics of teachers (17 articles in 3 groups); theories and models of teaching (9 articles); instructional programs and strategies (9 articles); teaching skills and techniques (28 articles in 4 groups); school and classroom factors (16 articles in 3 groups); students and the teaching-learning process (13 articles in 2 groups); teaching for specific objectives (10 articles); and the study of teaching (6 articles). Part B consists of 3 sections: concepts and issues in teacher education (10 articles in 3 groups); generic initial teacher education (6 articles); and continuing teacher education (5 articles). In both part A and part B there is an introduction dealing with the subject and highlighting articles in the section.

All articles are well written, each ending with references. As compared with the 1st edition, according to the editor, the present volume provides new conceptual frameworks. First, the framework is developed for teachers, schools, classrooms, students, teaching, and learning. Second is the framework on the relationship of various areas of teacher education.

In an era of cyberspace, an article on digital information, particularly the Internet, and its use and impact on teaching and teacher education, is noticeably absent. The title implies international coverage, but how international is international? Although some 30 countries and regions are covered in more than 20 subjects, only 2 articles deal with primarily different countries: "Comparative and International Studies of Teaching and Teacher Education" and "Teacher Education Accreditation and Standards." The index needs improvement. By random check, China (p. 565), Finland (p. 311), Hong Kong (pp. 311, 507), Hungary (p. 311), the Philippines (p. 311), Nepal (p. 565), Swaziland (p. 311), and Thailand (pp. 507, 510) are not indexed. Even with its limitations, the book is an outstanding reference.—**Tze-chung Li**

299. Karnes, Frances A., and Tracy L. Riley. **Competitions: Maximizing Your Abilities.** Waco, Tex., Prufrock Press, 1996. 346p. $24.95pa. ISBN 1-882664-28-0.

This work consists of a comprehensive list of more than 275 different competitions covering the areas of business, foreign languages, creative thinking, language arts, mathematics, science, fine and performing arts, social studies, and technology. There are also lists of competitions that test students' leadership abilities and their commitment to serve their communities. All of the competitions have sponsors, ranging from Pizza Hut and *USA Today* to the National Women's Hall of Fame and the U.S. Fish and Wildlife Service, Federal Duck Stamp Office. Awards are as varied as the competitions and their sponsors—from stickers, poster art, full tuition, scholarships, and government bonds for $25 to monetary awards of $25,000. Each entry lists information, such as the name of the competition, sponsor, purpose, area of expertise covered, description of the competitions, eligibility, deadline, and awards. The amount of information given depends upon the amount of information received from the sponsor.

The authors have also included a "competitions journal," which the student is encouraged to photocopy and keep, with information on which contests the student wants to enter; what the student hopes to learn from the experience; a sample letter of inquiry; one of thanks; a sample press release; and other materials useful to the hopeful entrant, such as an evaluation form of the student's strengths and abilities. Also included is a short bibliography of resources for further study on many of the areas appearing in the list. Although there is a table of contents, this handbook, unfortunately, lacks an index—an extremely useful tool for someone looking for information regarding a specific sponsor or competition. This handbook will be helpful for schools, teachers, and individual students who want to compete on many levels, enjoy competing, and are looking for some lucrative and not so lucrative ways to enrich their education.—**Mary Jo Aman**

300. **National Guide to Funding for Elementary and Secondary Education.** 3d ed. James E. Baumgartner and others, eds. New York, Foundation Center, 1995. 663p. index. $135.00pa. ISBN 0-87954-607-7.

With the ongoing fiscal constraints on states and municipalities, public school funding continues to be problematic. For all schools, public or private, grants from philanthropic foundations and corporations may allow the support of programs, facilities, and personnel that might otherwise be lost due to tight economies. This guide provides essential background information on likely sources of funding. It includes descriptive information on more than 2,000 foundations and corporations that are either interested in supporting K-12 education or have recently given $10,000 or more to schools.

The entries are arranged geographically by state and city, then alphabetically by foundation. For each foundation or corporation, there is usually an address and telephone number, the name of a contact person, financial data, the foundation's purpose and activities, its fields of interest, the types of support it provides, limitations (geographic and otherwise) on grants, and application information. For 547 of the foundations, there are lists of recent grants, giving the user specific information on what requests have actually been funded.

There is a substantial amount of supplementary information, including a user's guide, a glossary, a bibliography, a list of other Foundation Center publications and services, and a list of Foundation Center and cooperating reference collections around the country. Various elements of the entries are traced in the guide's six indexes: donors, officers, and trustees; geographic location (state, city); types of support; foundation giving programs by broad subject classification (e.g., reading, school reform); grants by subject; and foundations and corporate giving programs (listed alphabetically).

This is an essential research tool for teachers, curriculum coordinators, school administrators, school board personnel, and education college faculty active in school projects and research. It is highly recommended for school, public, and academic libraries, although its contents somewhat overlap *The Foundation Directory* (15th ed.; see ARBA 94, entries 890-891) and *The Foundation Grants Index* (24th ed.; see ARBA 96, entry 883).—**Stephen H. Aby**

HIGHER EDUCATION

Bibliography

301. **Religious Higher Education in the United States: A Source Book.** Thomas C. Hunt and James C. Carper, eds. New York, Garland, 1996. 635p. index. (Source Books on Education, v.46). $95.00. ISBN 0-8153-1636-4.

If theologians, religious studies students, and academic librarians wish a concise overview of higher education amongst various U.S. religious denominations, they will refer to this source. As part of Garland's Source Books on Education series, this volume is a synthesis of a 1988 book entitled *Religious Colleges and Universities in America* (see ARBA 89, entry 1308) and a 1989 title, *Religious Seminaries in America* (see ARBA 90, entry 1377). As such, it lacks a consistent pattern or criteria for material coverage. Yet, this small discrepancy does not detract from an overall solid presentation of essential information.

Beginning with an introductory chapter that describes government aid to and regulation of religious colleges and universities, 23 chapters follow that individually address higher education involving Mormons, Quakers, Lutherans, American Reformers, Baptists, Methodists, Jews, Catholics, and many others. Each chapter contains information concerning the theological origins for a particular denomination's higher education, the need for the establishment of a specific faith's colleges and seminaries, the citing of all or a representative sample of a denomination's educational institutions, a contemporary discussion of problems involving a denomination's institutions, and an annotated bibliography of appropriate books and articles.

The contributors to this volume are well qualified to write about their respective faiths. Many are prolific publishers about the subject of religious higher education. An author and subject index concludes this worthy addition to the Garland series.—**Kathleen W. Craver**

Directories

302. Bruce-Young, Doris Marie, and William C. Young. **The Higher Education Money Book for Women & Minorities: A Directory of Scholarships....** 1997 ed. Washington, D.C., Young Enterprises International, 1996. 413p. index. $25.00pa. ISBN 0-9639490-1-2.

This reviewer's first reaction to this work was to wonder why anyone would produce yet another financial aid directory for women and minorities when the two Reference Service Press directories are available (*Directory of Financial Aids for Women 1995-1997* [see ARBA 96, entry 879] and *Directory of Financial Aids for Minorities 1995-1997* [see ARBA 96, entry 880]). Yet on closer inspection, this single-volume work has several advantages. First, at least in its new 1997 edition, the information for several entries is more up-to-date than the Reference Service Press directories. Second, the cost of this volume is $25, a price that makes it readily available to most public and secondary schools.

Although a detailed explanation of how the information for the entries was collected is not available, the authors do indicate that the information was prescreened to include only funding agencies that specifically targeted women and minorities, show preferential treatment toward women or minorities, and welcome applications from these groups. This means, of course, that many of the entries are not limited to those funds available to women and minorities—but that could obviate the need for a more general directory. The guide is organized into sections that target readers by educational level and subject areas. The entries are elliptic or synoptic in nature, rather than encyclopedic. In addition, the guide contains alphabetic, geographic, and keyword indexes. The keyword indexing was found to be a little unpredictable but, when used in conjunction with the different named sections of the books, it was relatively effective.

In all, this work is likely to be useful to secondary school and public libraries, as well as a good addition to the funding collections of college or community college libraries. Other institutions specifically interested in assisting the targeted groups (public agencies, churches, and the like) should also seriously consider its purchase. For libraries with substantive budgets, this guide's limited size (approximately 350 pages of entries) suggests that it should be purchased in addition to the Reference Service Press guides listed above.—**Caroline M. Kent**

303. **College Chemistry Faculties 1996.** 10th ed. Washington, D.C., American Chemical Society, 1996. 363p. index. $84.95pa. ISBN 0-8412-3300-4.

This new edition of the *College Chemistry Faculties* directory is a welcome addition. The directory is a valuable source of information on college and university teachers of chemistry and chemistry-related fields in the United States and its territories and Canada. It provides, where available, pertinent information such as departmental addresses, telephone number(s), fax numbers, e-mail addresses, Gopher and World Wide Web addresses, and the undergraduate and graduate degrees awarded by the department.

This directory is arranged by state, with an alphabetic list of institutions followed by faculty in alphabetic order by surname. The rank of the faculty member and some indication of their field of specialization is provided. Moreover, each faculty member entry furnishes an address for e-mail, which has the potential for sending text, lengthy narrative, and scientific materials rapidly. This information makes the directory an important source for finding information quickly on a chemistry faculty member's location and communication access.

While somewhat expensive, this directory is a convenient and useful source of information on college and university chemists. It is recommended for purchase by departmental libraries, special libraries, college and university libraries, and large public libraries.—**Roberto P. Haro**

304. **Directory of College Cooperative Education Programs.** Polly Hutcheson and the National Commission for Cooperative Education, eds. Phoenix, Ariz., American Council on Education and Oryx Press, 1996. 219p. index. (American Council on Education/Oryx Press Series on Higher Education). $49.95pa. ISBN 0-89774-998-7.

This new title in the American Council on Education/Oryx Series on Higher Education was created in conjunction with the National Commission for Cooperative Education (NCCE) and replaces and updates NCCE's *Cooperative Education Undergraduate Program Directory*. It also builds on the *Engineering Cooperative Education Directory* published by the American Society for Engineering Education. Cooperative education is defined in the work under review as "an academic program that integrates classroom studies with a series of paid, productive work experiences in a field related to a student's career or education goals."

Entries for programs from 460 community, technical, undergraduate, and graduate institutions are arranged by state, then alphabetically by institution name. The extensive information given for each program includes number of students placed; number by academic division; program administrative structure; program type (alternating/parallel); co-op degree requirements (whether the program is mandatory or optional); length and number of work periods; percentage of paid placements; number of active employers; representative employers (large, local, and public sector firms); work locations; and more. Institutional addresses are supplemented by names, addresses, telephone numbers, and e-mail addresses for key contacts. World Wide Web site URLs are also provided for some programs.

An index listing programs and degrees allows the student to check for all institutions that offer co-op programs in mechanical engineering or nursing, for instance; each school name is conveniently followed by degree type (e.g., master's, bachelor's, associate). An institution name index is also provided. Because many employers in today's competitive job market place increased emphasis on practical experience, this directory will be essential for most reference collections of college and career guides. [R: BL, 15 Oct 96, p. 450]
—**Deborah V. Rollins**

305. **Funding for United States Study: A Guide for International Students and Professionals.** 2d ed. Marie O'Sullivan and Sara J. Steen, eds. New York, Institute of International Education, 1996. 462p. index. $39.95pa. ISBN 0-87206-219-8. ISSN 1047-2541.

This excellent directory provides valuable information to foreign nationals who want financial assistance to pursue their educational objectives in the United States. The 630 funding sources, which are generally accessible to all, do not require the applicants to be recommended by their government or an international organization. The Institute of International Education surveyed some 10,000 worldwide private and public institutions and organizations between 1995 and 1996 to obtain the information.

The total numbers of funding sources remain approximately the same as the 1st edition (see ARBA 91, entry 343). However, a sampling of the sponsoring agencies beginning with the letter "A" indicates a 40 percent change. Additional information available in the new edition includes a section providing the following information on U.S. colleges and universities: addresses, degrees, application deadlines, costs, and financial aid resources. There is a brief bibliography of additional resources and an expanded list of overseas educational advisory centers.

Aside from the indexes that list sponsoring organizations, countries of origin, and fields of study, there are four new indexes. They include funding resources by amount of support, funding resources with special conditions, destination institutions, and awards indexed by U.S. state or region where the award must be used. This one-volume, reasonably priced title is a necessity for college and universities, as well as large public libraries.—**Karen Y. Stabler**

306. **Peterson's Top Colleges for Science: A Guide to Leading Four-Year Programs....** Princeton, N.J., Peterson's Guides, 1996. 314p. index. $24.95pa. ISBN 1-56079-390-2. ISSN 1086-2226.

Using criteria established by the editor, this reference guide for students seeking distinguished undergraduate science programs, their parents, and their counselors fills a critical need. The first and most important place to begin is to evaluate the selection criteria. Unlike the criteria used by many institutions with established reputations of excellence, the criteria here were based on outcomes. Three outcomes were used: the percentages of graduates who majored in each of the basic sciences and mathematics, the percentages of graduates who went on to earn doctoral degrees, and the percentage of graduates who were awarded National Science Foundation Fellowships for graduate study in the sciences and mathematics. The following fields are included: biological sciences, chemistry, geologic sciences (including marine and atmospheric science), mathematics and statistics, and physics and astronomy.

The information in the guide is conveniently and concisely presented, with information about the institution, fees, tuition and general expenses, undergraduate financial aid, institutional contacts, programs offered, special features, facilities, career paths pursued by graduates, and unique program features. Of particular interest are the practical chapters on careers in science, issues facing women and minority students, and the very real challenges surrounding the financing of a college education. As one may expect, the text is user friendly, the information complete and easily accessed. The guide addresses the concerns of serious students and those who are helping them select the right college. Even more impressive is the honesty expressed in the brief articles designed to help in the selection process, including the fact that colleges "continue to select, reward, and nurture mainly those undergraduates who look like the professors did when they were undergraduates themselves—researchers working at the bench." As always, no reference book can be perfect when it relies on self-reported information, but students will likely pore over this readable volume. [R: Choice, Sept 96, p. 104]—**Karen D. Harvey**

307. **The Princeton Review Hillel Guide to Jewish Life on Campus.** 1996 ed. Ruth Fredman Cernea, ed. New York, Princeton Review/Random House, 1995. 242p. illus. index. $17.00pa. ISBN 0-679-76914-5.

Editor Cernea, as director of research and publications at Hillel: The Foundation for Jewish Campus Life, is certainly qualified to prepare this wonderfully complete and useful guide for Jewish students and their families. As she and Richard Joel, president and international director of Hillel, point out, Jewish students seek differing college experiences and have varying needs related to their Jewish identity and religious practices. With a well-organized directory of more than 500 colleges and universities, such practical tips as how to access further information via e-mail, an extensive directory of opportunities for Jewish students in the United States and overseas, a list of national agencies and institutions offering resources or programs for Jewish students, and a bibliography of books of interest to Jewish young people, the work offers a rich storehouse of information to aid in the selection of a college. Cernea's experience working with Jewish students and their families is evident in the content, organization, and readability of the guide.

Perhaps the most important section of the book leads students and their families in a personal exploration of their own Jewish identity and the reasons why they would seek a Jewish life in their college experience. Such questions as "What do I want as a Jew in college?," "Which interests or causes are important to me, as an American and a Jew?," and "Will I find religious services and rituals just like the ones I'm used to?" are raised. These fundamental, practical, and often complex questions should be explored by students and their families before reviewing the directories and selecting a college. The impetus that this section provides for introspection, exploration of values, and family discussion may well make it the most valuable part of the book.—**Karen D. Harvey**

308. **World Academic Database.** [CD-ROM]. New York, Stockton Press, [1996]. Minimum system requirements: IBM or compatible 486. CD-ROM drive with MS-DOS CD-ROM Extensions. DOS 3.3. Windows 3.1 (Windows only). 4MB RAM (Windows only). 5MB hard disk space. $399.00. ISBN 1-56159-192-0.

The *World Academic Database* provides access to institutions of higher education (with addresses), faculty, degrees conferred, requirements, and detailed information concerning programs and processes for application to more than 12,000 institutions in 175-plus countries. In addition, information can be found that explains the credentials necessary for various fields of study. The CD-ROM contains a database that is compiled from the *International Handbook of Universities* (14th ed., 1996), the *World List of Universities* (20th ed., 1995), and additional information from TRACE (an international higher-education data collection and sharing consortium).

The CD-ROM is relatively easy to load and use, but it does take up a considerable amount of disk space and memory to run. More than 4MB of RAM is required, and at least 5MB of hard disk space is required. Finding information is done through one of four search systems: educational systems, institutions, credentials, or a full-text search. The full-text search requires the user to put in his or her own keywords and, of course, depends on the accuracy of the searcher to produce good results. Using the keyword approach, it is possible to search the same degree information in all institutions at the same time, or limit the search to particular universities by country, state, region, and the like. A search by institution name provides information concerning the size and general strengths of a school, along with additional data on admissions, student information, costs, statistics concerning the college, and information concerning the institution's cooperation with other schools. It is possible to contain searches so that only basic information is provided for many or a few institutions, if that is wanted. Once a search has been completed, it can be further refined using a filter system and proximity searches. Also, users are provided with an index of key terms, which is very useful.

While the search system takes some getting used to, there is a low learning curve, and most users should be able to work with the database with little assistance. The advantage of searching this kind of information on a CD-ROM is immediately apparent (i.e., searches of a number of institutions may be done quickly and accurately). Also, of course, once the information has been found and put through the appropriate filters, it can be printed for future reference. This CD-ROM is highly recommended for high schools, college and university libraries, and larger public libraries. The relatively low cost should put it within reach of most institutions.—**Robert L. Wick**

INTERNATIONAL EXCHANGE PROGRAMS AND OPPORTUNITIES

309. **Financial Resources for International Study: A Guide for US Nationals.** 2d ed. Marie O'Sullivan and Sara J. Steen, eds. New York, Institute of International Education, 1996. 280p. index. $39.95pa. ISBN 0-87206-220-1.

This guide to support for overseas study focuses on programs open to U.S. students at all postsecondary levels, from undergraduate through doctoral and professional. It lists more than 650 grant, fellowship, scholarship, and paid internship programs for teaching, study, research, or other education-related activities. The sponsoring bodies include government agencies, corporations, foundations, associations, and research centers. The list of programs is organized by region or country in which funded activities may be pursued, although more than a third of the programs are classified as "Worldwide." Within each geographic section, entries are further subdivided by city and then alphabetized by name of the administering agency—an arrangement not readily apparent, as there are no headings for these subdivisions.

The entries vary in length and can include, in addition to award title and administering agency, the sponsoring institution, the number, the size and purpose of awards, applicable geographic region(s) and field(s) of study, eligibility requirements, and application and contact information. Efforts to encourage applications from diverse populations are noted. This edition is more heavily indexed than the 1st (see ARBA 91, entry 342), with access provided by administering and sponsoring bodies, level and type of award, field of study, amount of support, special conditions, destination institution, and destination country. As the earlier ARBA review pointed out, *Financial Resources* overlaps with such guides as *Study Abroad* (see ARBA 90, entry 348) and *The Grants Register* (see ARBA 95, entry 367). However, this work's various indexes compensate for the deficiencies of its arrangement, and both its limitation to programs for U.S. nationals and its inclusion of programs for undergraduates, as well as higher levels, may appeal to some users.—**Gregory M. Toth**

310. **An International Student's Guide to Mexican Universities.** Alan Adelman and Sylvia Ortega Salazar, eds. New York, Institute of International Education, 1995. 121p. illus. maps. $19.95pa. ISBN 0-87206-63820.

The Institute of International Education (IIE) was founded in the early part of this century to promote educational and cultural exchanges with overseas institutions of higher education. Through its publications, it disseminates unique and valuable information to students and educators on study abroad programs. The present title was produced and published jointly by the Mexican Association for International Education and IIE/Mexico.

Color photographs and 2-page summaries provide descriptive information for 50 public and private universities. Summaries give a historical overview of each university, descriptions of campus (including libraries) and local environments, curricular offerings, faculty qualifications, and the academic calendar. Separate chapters discuss application procedures, guidelines for transfer credits, and tips for international students in Mexico. Unfortunately, there are no indexes or quick access points for answering the question, "which universities offer specific courses or degree programs in a particular subject?"

This source may prove to be useful to comprehensive collections in international or comparative education. It may also serve to assist students interested in study abroad programs. —**Ilene F. Rockman**

311. **Open Doors 1994/95: Report on International Educational Exchange.** Todd M. Davis, ed. New York, Institute of International Education, 1995. 208p. maps. $39.95pa. (with disk). ISBN 0-87206-230-9. ISSN 0078-5172.

This annual provides extensive information on more than 452,000 international students attending U.S. colleges and universities and 76,800 U.S. students abroad. Data are clustered into 14 chapters, including an overview of topics such as academic level, economics of exchange, and U.S. study abroad. A variety of tables, graphs, and charts succinctly summarize and analyze a large quantity of information.

Statistics profile student demographics as well as enrollments by university, area of study, and academic level. Current survey results and information previously gathered for other editions are consolidated to show trends in international education. The print source is accompanied by a diskette, which the publisher indicates contains data previously published as *Profiles*. This statistical compendium provides inexpensive access to ample information on the state of international education and will be useful to most academic libraries.—**Ahmad Gamaluddin**

NONPRINT MATERIALS AND RESOURCES

312. **Educational Media and Technology Yearbook 1995/1996, Volume 21.** Donald P. Ely and Barbara B. Minor, eds. Englewood, Colo., with ERIC Clearinghouse on Information & Technology and Association for Educational Communications and Technology, Libraries Unlimited, 1996. 409p. index. $60.00. ISBN 1-56308-359-0. ISSN 8755-2094.

The previous editions of this highly respected reference have been devoted almost entirely to educational media and technology in North America. In this edition, the scope has been enlarged to encompass articles by several European specialists who portray current developments from a worldwide perspective. Topics covered in this edition include trends, issues, developments, the profession and professional concerns, and suggested research projects. Most articles provide bibliographies; many are illustrated by charts and tables.

Activities of the six major professional organizations are reviewed, and information is given on their memberships, services, conferences, publications, subdivisions, and affiliated organizations. Current officers and board members are listed. Two biographies of leaders in the profession, Robert Marion Morgan and Paul Saettler, are accompanied by photographs. A comprehensive directory of doctoral, master's, and six-year graduate programs in educational technology is organized by state within each of the three categories of program. There is also a list of scholarships, fellowships, and awards available to students in the field.

Annotated entries for several hundred associations and organizations whose interests are related to educational technology provide additional information. Those in the United States are also classified under 40 categories. The annotated mediagraphy of print and nonprint resources, begun by EMTY's first editor, James Brown, has been continued and now offers a broad overview of new materials in most media formats. An index of names, authors, titles, and subjects and the classified list in the main body of the work provide rapid access to information. The yearbook is essential for all subject collections. [R: EL, May/June 96, p. 42; SLMQ, Summer 96, p. 219]—**Shirley L. Hopkinson**

313. Jordan, Barbara, and Noreen Stackpole, with the Staff of Middle Country Public Library. **Audiovisual Resources for Family Programming.** New York, Neal-Schuman, 1995. 437p. index. $29.95pa. ISBN 1-55570-191-4.

The 1,700 entries in this guide cover a wide spectrum of topics on every aspect of family life, from how to be a well-behaved kid to becoming an outstanding parent or grandparent. Many entries provide help for understanding oneself and others and give guidance for coping with myriad problems, such as disabilities, specific diseases and conditions, adolescent pregnancy and parenting, AIDS, substance abuse, child abuse, and family violence. Other entries are concerned with the roles various members can play in a good, functional family. The information on stress management, substance abuse, anger, and conflict resolution could be of use to others outside a family situation. Most of the items listed are videotapes, but games, kits, audiocassettes, and workshop and program curricula are also listed.

Entries are arranged alphabetically by title and include media category, name and address of the producer or source, running time, information on accompanying materials, and, in some cases, date of production. Each has a concise descriptive annotation detailing contents or possible uses. A subject index groups titles under broad subject headings and gives page references. A series index provides lists of all titles within a specific series. Although this directory began as an access tool for the holdings of the Suffolk Family Education Clearing House in Centereach, New York, the items are recent, and, presumably, most are available in other collections or from the source. The guide should be of interest and of use to concerned parents, educators, social workers, and family counselors. It could also serve as a selection aid for collection development librarians.—**Shirley L. Hopkinson**

314. Wendling, Patricia A. **Adventures in Video: A Guide to the Best Instructional Videos.** Denver, Colo., Arden Press, 1995. 228p. index. $38.00; $24.00pa. ISBN 0-912869-19-4; 0-912869-20-4pa.

The burgeoning home video market has led to the availability of countless "how-to" tapes aimed at the general public. Wendling, a Pennsylvania businesswoman, has compiled a lively, readable subject guide to more than 2,000 "quality" videos from 70 different sources. The book is arranged in 10 chapters that cover most areas of popular interest, including "Around the House" (home improvement, gardening, housework, cooking, party giving); hobbies and crafts; sports; outdoor recreation; academic and vocational skills; fitness and healthy living; and self-help guides. Individual videos are described in an enthusiastic sentence or two, and the source is given with current addresses and telephone numbers (most are toll free). Large print, attractive layout, and the use of bold typeface for headings and titles make the book easy and fun to browse. A useful name and subject index is also provided.

While the videos all sound worthwhile and appealing, there is no indication of how these "best" videos were selected other than to thank sources for "providing the necessary information." One suspects videos were chosen from catalog annotations rather than actual viewing. Videographic information is also minimal, consisting of title, source, and annotation. Detailed credits, running times, production dates, and prices are missing. This is a useful and well-written publication, but librarians and patrons would be wise to use it in conjunction with other such reference tools as *Bowker's Complete Video Directory* (see ARBA 96, entry 986) and *Media Review Digest* (see entry 9). [R: Choice, Oct 96, p. 259; LJ, Mar 96, p. 64]

—**Joseph W. Palmer**

6 Ethnic Studies and Anthropology

ANTHROPOLOGY AND ETHNOLOGY

315. **African Ethnonyms: Index to Art-Producing Peoples of Africa.** By Daniel P. Biebuyck, Susan Kelliher, and Linda McRae. New York, G. K. Hall/Simon & Schuster Macmillan, 1996. 378p. index. $95.00. ISBN 0-7838-1532-8.

Distinguished African art scholar/anthropologist Biebuyck and his colleagues McRae and Kelliher have filled a great gap in the reference literature. Citing hundreds of monographs in art, anthropology, linguistics, history, and so forth, the authors have created an alphabetic-by-ethnonym list of more than 4,500 names representing 2,000-plus African groups. Each full entry includes a preferred ethnonym; countries in which the group resides; variant forms of the ethnonym; subgroup names; the preferred usage from *Art and Architecture Thesaurus* (2d ed.; see ARBA 95, entry 650) and *Library of Congress Subject Headings* (see entries 533-534); and a list of abbreviations from the master list of more than 1,000 sources used to construct the entry, with key source(s) marked by an asterisk. Most full entries also include cross-references, and many give explanatory notes. All variant forms and subgroup names are listed with cross-references in the main index.

The 43-page bibliography is a list of reference works, exhibition catalogs, and other books focusing on sub-Saharan Africa. The user would have been better served if some explanation on how citations were chosen had been included; for example, why use the 5th edition (1975) rather than the 6th edition (1983) of George Peter Murdock's *Outline of World Cultures*, published by Human Relations Area Files Press, or exclude its still-useful predecessor, James Leyburn's *Handbook of Ethnography* (Oxford University Press, 1931)? The introduction is thorough and clear, as is the chapter on language. The work includes a toponym index and a list of all ethnonyms by country. This outstanding reference, intelligently conceived and carefully and laboriously constructed, will be an essential work for Africanist scholars of all disciplines.—**Fred J. Hay**

316. **Encyclopedia of Cultural Anthropology.** David Levinson and Melvin Ember, eds. New York, Henry Holt, 1996. 4v. illus. maps. index. $395.00/set. ISBN 0-8050-2877-3.

The Human Relations Area Files sponsored this work, which in many ways complements the publisher's *Encyclopedia of World Cultures* (see entries 318-320). Any encyclopedia attempting to cover a field as diverse and eclectic as cultural anthropology must set some coverage limits. Nearly 350 articles, written by 310 of the leading scholars in the field, cover 9 major areas: broad subfields, such as medical anthropology and economic anthropology; significant "organizing" concepts, such as cultural evolution and cultural materialism; data collecting methods, such as cross-cultural analysis, ethnography, and network analysis; topics of special interest in the field, such as marriage, sorcery, and witchcraft; major theories, such as alliance, optimal foraging, and decision theory; cultural regions and subregions; important recent controversies, such as Mead-Freeman and the Wild Yam Question; major professional organizations in the field; and topics from the fields of linguistics, biological anthropology, and archaeology that are of interest to cultural anthropologists.

The set does not include biographical information, although one can gain some insights into who the leading scholars were/are from the number of times they are mentioned in an article. There are few illustrations, far fewer than might be desirable in a work intended for laypersons, students, and scholars. Articles are signed and conclude with a selected bibliography. The dictionary arrangement means one must know the theory, controversy, or topic, as there are no index entries for the nine areas covered. No factual errors were found in the sample of articles read in their entirety. Indexing is adequate, except as noted, with a large number of useful cross-references. The one concern is the quality of binding, which seems lightweight for what will be a heavily consulted set in any social science reference collection. All in all, this is an excellent title. [R: Choice, Sept 96, p. 96; LJ, 15 May 96, pp. 53-54; RBB, June 96, pp. 1760-61]—**G. Edward Evans**

317. **Encyclopedia of Social and Cultural Anthropology.** Alan Barnard and Jonathan Spencer, eds. New York, Routledge, 1996. 658p. maps. index. $120.00. ISBN 0-415-09996-X.

The intent of this one-volume encyclopedia is to provide a set of entries for topics in the fields of social and cultural anthropology. The editors hope ". . . to help our readers find their way around a discipline which is far too interesting and important to be left in the hands of academic specialists" (p. x). By including the terms *cultural* (used in North America) and *social* (used in Europe) in the title, the editors indicate an international approach.

Topics are listed in alphabetic order. The 231 signed articles, written by leading authorities in the field, are substantial in length (2-6 pages) and furnish lists for further reading and cross-references. A broad spectrum of key terms from past and present usage is considered. More than 200 short biographies of influential people in the field follow the longer articles. A glossary is provided, giving brief, discipline-based definitions for approximately 500 terms and concepts. Indexes are by names, by people and places, and by subject. Introductory materials include a list of entries, a list of contributors, an analytic table of contents, and an itemization of contributions by author.

General concepts are well covered and well defined, but this encyclopedia is only an introduction to social/cultural anthropology of industrial and nonindustrial peoples. Exhaustive coverage of the discipline in a one-volume work is not possible, but the further reading lists do well in directing readers to sources where they can find more specific or in-depth information. The biographical index and the glossary are concise and useful additions. The editors warn that readers must consult more than one entry on a given topic to gain a balanced understanding of its meaning. This work fills a gap in the reference sources in social and cultural anthropology and is recommended for all academic libraries.—**Joanna M. Burkhardt**

318. **Encyclopedia of World Cultures. Volume VIII: Middle America and the Caribbean.** James W. Dow and Robert Van Kemper, eds. New York, G. K. Hall/Simon & Schuster Macmillan, 1995. 329p. maps. index. $110.00. ISBN 0-8161-1816-7.

319. **Encyclopedia of World Cultures. Volume IX: Africa and the Middle East.** John Middleton and Amal Rassam, eds. New York, G. K. Hall/Simon & Schuster Macmillan, 1995. 447p. maps. index. $110.00. ISBN 0-8161-1815-9.

320. **Encyclopedia of World Cultures. Volume X: Indexes.** David Levinson, ed. New York, G. K. Hall/Simon & Schuster Macmillan, 1996. 322p. $110.00. ISBN 0-8161-1817-5.

After 10 years of effort and the work of 820 contributors and translators, this set on world cultures is complete. With the publication of the index, the encyclopedia's true value can be realized. Volume 8 covers Middle America and the Caribbean. Middle America includes Mexico through Panama, and the Caribbean covers all the islands, including those off the coast of Venezuela (Aruba, Curaçao, and Trinidad and Tobago, for example). Volume 9—Africa and the Middle East—covers all the African continent, Turkey, Syria, Lebanon, Israel, Jordan, Saudi Arabia, Yemen, Oman, United Arab Emirates, Qatar, Kuwait, Iraq, Iran, and Afghanistan.

The format of volumes 8 and 9 follows that of the earlier volumes, and the newer volumes have the same quality of content. What will make this set a valuable tool in academic libraries is the index. The preface to volumes 1-9 describes the "New Diaspora"—the dispersal of cultural groups to new locations around the world. The index volume demonstrates what the concept means. Each of the three sections of the index contains material reflecting a worldwide cultural diversity. The larger countries in the section entitled "List of Cultures by Country" contain entries such as Afro-Bolivians, Creoles of Belize, Vietnamese—France, Italian Mexicans, South Asians in Southeast Asia, and Anglo-Indians—United

Kingdom. In the "Ethnonym Index," one finds further evidence of the spread of cultures; for example, Creole Chinese, Creoles, Creoles—American Isolates, Black Creoles of Louisiana, Creoles—Mauritian, Creoles-Afro-South Americans, Creoles Martiniquais, and Creoles of Nicaragua.

The set was developed from Human Relations Area Files, and one of the major goals of HRAF is to encourage cross-cultural studies. The subject index to this set, the largest section (243 out of 322 pages), provides access to material for cross-cultural projects. Three examples illustrate the point: "Adoption practices" lists 88 cultural groups (whose entry contains material about adoption). In addition, there is a *see also* reference to "fosterage" that lists an additional 20 entries. The second example is "maize growing," which lists 358 cultures. Entries under "marriage" cover seven pages, with many subdivisions such as "abduction," "arranged" (with further subdivisions), "ceremonies," and "marriage within caste." This is a set well worth its price. [R: Choice, Nov 96, p. 428; RBB, June 96, pp. 1760-62]

—G. Edward Evans

321. Olson, James S. **The Peoples of Africa: An Ethnohistorical Dictionary.** Westport, Conn., Greenwood Press, 1996. 681p. index. $99.50. ISBN 0-313-27918-7.

Although this dictionary contains more than 1,800 entries, the author does not claim it is a comprehensive volume on the numerous African ethnic groups. Each entry contains a brief description of the group, including occasional population estimates. Many entries conclude with a brief bibliography listing the title and publication date but no publisher. The final section of the book includes a cursory chronology of African history and a selected bibliography.

Because reference sources on the peoples of Africa are not abundant, it is particularly regrettable that this work is so deficient. Most of the entries are merely a sentence or a paragraph, providing little useful information. Even populous ethnic groups such as the Ibo in Nigeria, the Yoruba in West Africa, and the Zulu in South Africa barely fill a page. The date of the population estimates is usually not cited. No maps appear in this volume, although a significant part of many entries describes the locale of individual groups. Furthermore, this reference work does not provide ethnological charts, an important feature that would show the historical connections among the various groups. The spelling of some ethnic group names is not consistent with Library of Congress authority records. The concluding bibliography does not supply the publisher or place of publication. This work is probably most useful for very cursory reference citations to more substantive sources. [R: Choice, Dec 96, p. 593; RBB, 1 Sept 96, p. 169]

—Donald Altschiller

ETHNIC STUDIES

General Works

322. Bataille, Gretchen M., Miguel A. Carranza, and Laurie Lisa. **Ethnic Studies in the United States: A Guide to Research.** New York, Garland, 1996. 295p. (Garland Reference Library of Social Science, v.923). $45.00. ISBN 0-8153-1476-0.

This is a useful compendium of study programs, associations, journals, institutions, newsletters, and publishers related to ethnic minorities in the United States. It also has a brief bibliography on ethnic studies. As a reference book, this volume will help in the initial steps of researching in ethnic studies. It identifies the where and what of ethnic studies by ethnic group in each of the states, alphabetically. The quality of the entries regarding the actual programs varies according to how much detail the surveyed institution offered. However, even the brief entries are useful because the interested researcher will find a name, an address, and a telephone number to contact for more details.

The most interesting part of the book is the introduction, which surveys the evolution of ethnic studies and raises basic questions regarding the justification for, quality of, and future prospects of ethnic studies. This introductory chapter could have been expanded with great benefit to the reader and to the ongoing debate regarding the purpose and place of ethnic studies in solving problems of discrimination, undereducation, and the relative gap between minorities and the majority. Unfortunately, as with most reference books, this small volume is too expensive for individuals, especially for students. To serve its intended purposes, it would be efficient to republish the book in paperback at the lowest possible price, with an expanded introduction. By that means, freedom of choice for the student and researcher will certainly be enhanced.—**Elias H. Tuma**

323. **DISCovering Multicultural America.** [CD-ROM]. Detroit, Gale, 1996. Minimum system requirements: IBM or compatible 386SX XT, AT, or PS/2 (486 or higher recommended). ISO 9660 CD-ROM drive with Microsoft CD-ROM Extensions 2.2 (double speed or faster recommended). MS-DOS 3.3. Windows 3.1. 4MB RAM (8MB or more recommended). 10MB hard disk space. SVGA 640 x 480, 356-color monitor and graphics card. Windows-compatible mouse. 16-bit (or higher) Sound Blaster-compatible sound card with Windows 3.1 (or higher) compatible drivers (optional). Printer (optional). $500.00/stand-alone version. ISBN 0-8103-9891-5. [Also available for networks.]

As a specialist familiar with only certain portions of U.S. history, this reviewer found the CD-ROM well worthwhile. Although unable to vouch for its accuracy and depth across all the many fields it attempts to cover, this reviewer found its treatment of known areas substantial. Because it juxtaposes an abundance of information concerning the ethnic and cultural histories of Native Americans, African Americans, Asian Americans, and Hispanic Americans, the program can lead students seeking information about one of these areas to discover related or parallel topics in another area. The program thus enables those who use it to overcome one of the principal drawbacks of ethnic studies: that is, a tendency toward parochialism.

In terms of content, then, this seems to be a most practical tool. Especially valuable are the large number of original source documents: treaties, laws, key court decisions, speeches, and the like. The format is user friendly, although it lacks a simple Boolean search mode. One has to scroll in order to locate topics and materials. Searches can, however, be limited by ethnic groups, subjects, places, or via a timeline. A "power search" allows the user to limit or expand searches to combinations of these categories. Downloading to printers and files was simple and straightforward. Dedicated students will make real use of this program, and learn a great deal from it. [R: RBB, 15 May 96, p. 1606; BR, Nov/Dec 96, p. 59]—**Glenn Petersen**

324. Russell, Cheryl. **The Official Guide to Racial and Ethnic Diversity: Asians, Blacks, Hispanics, Native Americans, and Whites.** Ithaca, N.Y., New Strategist, 1996. 634p. index. $89.95. ISBN 0-885070-03-9.

This is a systematic, well-organized, and detailed rearrangement of data on the various ethnic groups in the United States. Each ethnic group (Asians, blacks, Hispanics, Native Americans, and whites) is treated in one chapter. Chapters begin with an overview of the group and cover education, health, household and living arrangements, housing, income, labor force, and a population profile. In addition, a chapter devoted to the total population covers the same topics, presumably for comparison purposes.

A final chapter, which is the most interesting, summarizes a survey of attitudes toward minorities. The survey is based on the General Social Survey taken annually by the National Opinion Research Center of the University of Chicago. It surveys attitudes toward unity versus diversity, black progress, affirmative action, politicians and their function as role models, freedom of expression, group stereotypes, immigration, and bilingualism. The inclusion of this survey is somewhat unusual as it is based on opinions that have to be surveyed many times before they can be used as a basis for analysis. The oddity of this inclusion is reflected in the introduction to the chapter, which begins with, "While in many ways Americans are more tolerant than ever toward people of other races and ethnicities . . . ." (p. 585). Who are these Americans? Do they not include the racial and ethnic groups in the United States?

Another contradiction lies in the title of the volume as the "official" guide to racial and ethnic diversity. What makes it official? The data are taken mostly from the census, which means there is a duplication from another source, and from unpublished material, although that material is not carefully cited. Hence, one may find it difficult to verify the accuracy of the data. A useful feature of the volume is the glossary of relevant concepts and terms. The book is not inexpensive, and it will not replace the census reports or other institutional documents for purposes of research. [R: LJ, Aug 96, p. 65]—**Elias H. Tuma**

325. Weinberg, Meyer, comp. **Racism in Contemporary America.** Westport, Conn., Greenwood Press, 1996. 838p. index. (Bibliographies and Indexes in Ethnic Studies, no.6). $125.00. ISBN 0-313-29659-6.

The 14,671 citations (with only a few duplications) included in this volume, combined with the entries in the compiler's previous bibliographies—*Racism in the United States* (see ARBA 91, entry 384) and *World Racism and Related Inhumanities* (see ARBA 93, entry 618)—produce more than 36,650 entries. Weinberg's is an inclusive view of racism that chooses references on violations including not only racism but sexism, anti-Semitism, and extreme nationalism.

Citations are arranged alphabetically by author in 86 subject chapters (not 87 as Weinberg states). The "Locality" chapter is subdivided into 44 states and the District of Columbia. Numbered citations include brief but consistently accurate bibliographic data and an occasional explanatory word or phrase in brackets. The bibliography provides author and subject indexes. The latter index lists 22 ethnic groups plus "Women," each subdivided by the 86 subject headings (and 45 locations) of the table of contents. This form of indexing makes specific retrieval difficult (e.g., the bibliography gives citations to the Appalachians, the index does not). Other problems include inadequate explanation of subject headings and an incomplete "Bibliography" chapter that also suffers disproportionately by Weinberg's failure to include citations for electronic resources.

This volume contains a significantly greater number of citations to African Americans than other ethnic groups and in spite of the use of the word *contemporary* in the title, Weinberg includes many older or historical citations (e.g., a chapter on "Slavery"). In view of its exhaustive scope, this bibliography, along with its predecessors, has become the standard research bibliography on one of this century's greatest social and economic evils. [R: Choice, Nov 96, p. 438]—**Fred J. Hay**

Asian Americans

326. **Asian American Chronology.** Deborah G. Baron and Susan B. Gall, eds. Detroit, U*X*L/Gale, 1996. 173p. illus. index. $29.00. ISBN 0-8103-9692-0.

Asian American Chronology is another title in the impressive collection of Asian American reference books published by Gale. Other volumes on this subject include *The Asian American Almanac* (see ARBA 96, entry 392) and *Asian American Biography* (see ARBA 96, entry 393). The title under review is published under the U*X*L imprint. It is important to note that books published under this imprint are "devoted to serving the information needs of students in grades five and up" (publisher's press release). The tone and emphasis of this volume definitely indicate that it is designed for middle school students; it does not have the scholarly depth and academic apparatus of the *The Asian American Almanac*, for example.

The book covers Asian Americans from 11,000 B.C.E. to 1995 C.E., and its scope includes peoples from more than 20 Asian nations and regions. Entries are arranged chronologically by year, and sometimes by month and day, and focus on important events and personalities (with appropriate photographs) in Asian American history. The biographical entries are especially informative, but where is the one for Lea Salonga? Ninety well-chosen black-and-white illustrations enhance the text; they include maps, photographs, statistical tables, and drawings.

The bibliography, while brief and not completely annotated, is compatible with the needs of the book's intended audience of young readers. The index is well structured and provides smooth access to the book's copious information. Public and school libraries will find *Asian American Chronology* to be an important addition to their collections.—**Marshall E. Nunn**

327. Nordquist, Joan, comp. **Asian Americans: Social, Economic, and Political Aspects: A Bibliography.** Santa Cruz, Calif., Reference and Research Services, 1996. 80p. (Contemporary Social Issues: A Bibliographic Series, no.42). $15.00pa. ISBN 0-937855-82-0.

This publication is part of a bibliographic series containing current information on important social issues. "Particularly, works from multicultural presses, alternative publishers, the small presses, the feminist presses and activists organizations are included" (p. 7). The bibliography's 824 entries include books, government publications, pamphlets, theses, and dissertations. It lists only printed materials. The entries are organized into 30 sections or chapters. The initial 27 sections are subject areas, such as mental health, substance abuse, discrimination and anti-Asian violence, women, the elderly, and testimonials (biographies and autobiographies). There are separate sections for each major Asian American group, including Asian Indian Americans. The last three sections list resources—statistics, bibliographies, and directories. The selection of bibliographic entries is judicious and includes a representative mixture of several types of authoritative sources.

The entries provide bare-bones bibliographic data and are unannotated. They are listed alphabetically by personal or corporate author in each section. Some sections also have topical and nationalities indexes. There are no author or title indexes and no overall index to ethnic groups. Adding these would greatly enhance the work's reference value. This type of material dates quickly, so users of this bibliography should also consult online databases. This is true even though the publisher offers this title as an alternative source to these databases. However, who could complain about the bibliography's price?—**Marshall E. Nunn**

Blacks

328. **African American Voices.** Deborah Gillan Straub, ed. Detroit, U*X*L/Gale, 1996. 2v. illus. index. $55.00/set. ISBN 0-8103-9497-9.

This work consists of a collection of excerpted speeches delivered by African American civil rights activists, religious leaders, educators, feminists, abolitionists, politicians, writers, and other key figures who have changed the course of history by speaking out on a variety of issues. Here the reader will find the words of Frederick Douglass, Henry Highland Garnet, Mary McLeod Bethune, Rita Dove, Alex Haley, Stokely Carmichael, Eldridge Cleaver, Roy Wilkins, Ben Carson, Fannie Lou Hamer, Marcus Garvey, Martin Luther King Jr., Thurgood Marshall, Adam Clayton Powell Jr., and more. Speech topics include abolition, arts and literature, black nationalism, black power, childhood and family, civil rights, discrimination, education, employment, family history, black history, Jim Crow laws, lynching, militancy, poverty, religion, slavery, violence, voting rights, and more.

Divided into two volumes for easy handling, the entries are arranged in alphabetic order by speaker. Each entry begins with introductory material, including a biographical sketch of the speaker and the historical context of the speech that follows. Sidebars expand on topics mentioned within the entries. A listing of sources provides bibliographic information on books, periodicals, and other sources for additional information related to the speech. Words and phrases that might be unfamiliar to the reader are defined in the lower margin of the page on which they appear. Additional features of the work are more than 90 black-and-white photographs and illustrations, a subject index, a listing of speeches by major topics, and a timeline. Highlighted headings, wide margins, and generous typeface size further enhance the work and its accessibility.—**Dana McDougald**

329. **The African-American Yellow Pages: A Comprehensive Resource Guide and Directory.** Stanton F. Biddle, ed. New York, Henry Holt, 1996. 342p. index. $19.95pa. ISBN 0-8050-4070-6.

This is an interesting compendium for both positive and negative reasons. It has 2,274 entries on 65 subjects from 10 areas relating to African American life. The subjects include art, the humanities, business, education, health, media, politics, religion, science, social services, and sports from cities and states across the nation. Almost by necessity, the coverage cannot be exhaustive on national or local levels. The entries give the name and address of each organization and, in some cases, an annotation. The listings concentrate on African American interests but occasionally relate to other minorities. A peculiar category lists all embassies of African countries.

As a reference, this volume is too brief. It is not clear whether these "yellow pages" are intended as advertising, or whether the entrants have paid for their inclusion. The volume must be of use to some people, but there are also costs. For example, why would a professor use valuable time to supervise the simple listing of entries? Another cost is the misleading impact of listing certain integrated state universities as resources and excluding others, such as the University of California system, which welcomes African Americans with open arms. The third and most serious potential cost is entailed by the mere issuing of a volume of "yellow pages" separately for African Americans. Rather than serve as a "guide . . . to expand . . . knowledge of and access to the wealth of African American resources," this volume runs the risk of promoting separatism rather than integration, discrimination rather than equalization, and deprivation rather than enrichment of the life of African Americans. [R: RBB, 15 Sept 96, p. 280]

—**Elias H. Tuma**

330. Curtis, Nancy C. **Black Heritage Sites: An African American Odyssey and Finder's Guide.** Chicago, American Library Association, 1996. 677p. illus. index. $55.00. ISBN 0-8389-0643-5.

Black Heritage Sites is a welcome resource for travelers and historians who have found that historical sites of multicultural interest are often overlooked and ignored by the mainstream travel press. A brief preface testifies to the author's dedication in bringing this labor of love into existence. It is an enterprise of enormous value to travelers or historians with an interest in visiting African American sites.

The arrangement of the guide is regional. Each section features both listings by state and city and brief historical essays on the role African Americans played in that region's politics and culture. Essays include such topics as southern housing for African Americans before and after the Civil War, southern religious life, northern opposition to slavery, fugitive slave laws, Buffalo soldiers, and African Americans in Alaska and Hawaii. Also included are an essay and listings for Canadian sites and communities associated with escape from slavery. Individual entries provide well-researched and detailed descriptions of the history of the sites, an address, a telephone number, hours, fees, and sources for descriptive information. Three sets of excellent black-and-white photographs illustrate the architectural history of black America. The index is thorough and includes names mentioned in essays and entries, subjects, and site names.

Sites in the South, Northeast, Midwest, and California make up the majority of the work. The mountain west region receives less attention, due in part to the lack of preservation of African American sites and perhaps also to the author's lack of contacts in this region. This source is inconsistent in discussing sites that are not exclusively African American but that provide tours, exhibits, or resources also of interest to readers. For example, the entries for Salt Lake City include the Latter-day Saint Family History Library and other monuments, while the entries for Wichita, Kansas, omit the Old Cowtown Museum's "Black Cowboys Tour." These are minor flaws in a useful source of interest to all libraries where African American history and culture are of interest. [R: Choice, Dec 96, p. 588; RBB, 1 Oct 96, p. 367]—**Lynne M. Fox**

331. **Encyclopedia of African-American Culture and History.** Jack Salzman, David Lionel Smith, and Cornel West, eds. New York, Macmillan Library Reference/Simon & Schuster Macmillan, 1996. 5v. illus. index. $425.00/set. ISBN 0-02-897345-3.

Multiculturalism has prompted a spate of new reference works such as this encyclopedia devoted to African Americans. Focusing on the black American experience, it recounts their history beginning with the arrival in 1619 of the first slaves from Africa up to the present time. Diverse articles reflect the multiple aspects of culture. Examples are Cornel West's discourse on black identity, David Levering Lewis's lengthy history of the Harlem Renaissance, Robyn Spencer's discussion of hair and beauty culture, Walter Friedman's identification of "Forty Acres and a Mule," and John Michael Vlach's essay on cemeteries and burials.

About $2/3$ of the more than 2,200 signed entries are biographies of African Americans both living and deceased, highlighting their place in culture and history. Personalities from every walk of life appear—novelist and filmmaker Oscar Micheaux, basketball great Michael Jordan—as well as other, lesser-known figures. Other entries trace histories of subjects, identify concepts, or provide descriptions. Cross-references to related articles are noted in all capital letters. Most entries conclude with at least one bibliographic reference. Lengthier articles, however, do not necessarily have more extensive bibliographies.

An appendix, almost 160 pages in length, complements the entries with statistical charts and lists on topics ranging from agriculture to sports, with business, health, politics, and religion in between. Also included is a listing of biographical entries by profession. The whole is enhanced by excellent indexing. Interspersed throughout the text are black-and-white photographs and prints culled from various archival sources, identified in the captions. Their quality varies, no doubt because of the quality of the originals.

In general, the language is accessible to a wide range of users. Overall, however, the writing is uneven, and sometimes not without bias or prejudice. Some articles do not go beyond the level of popular opinion, stating opinions as facts with no supporting evidence. Others, in contrast, treat subjects with objectivity, and from a scholarly framework (e.g., the article "Black English Vernacular"). Coverage of topics varies as well; for example, the article on softball begins with a sentence stating that "several black players have excelled in softball, one of the most popular sports in the United States" (p. 2527). Following this statement are three short paragraphs naming three black softball players. The entries on baseball and basketball are decidedly longer and cover many aspects of the respective sport.

Despite some limitations, the encyclopedia is a major work and an important contribution to African American studies. The set should find a place in both public and academic libraries. [R: Choice, Sept 96, p. 95; RBB, 15 Feb 96, p. 1037; SLJ, Aug 96, p. 183]—**Bernice Bergup**

Filipino Americans

332. Crisostomo, Isabelo T. **Filipino Achievers in the USA & Canada: Profiles in Excellence.** Farmington Hills, Mich., Bookhaus, 1996. 369p. illus. index. $65.00. ISBN 0-931613-11-6.

This coffee-table-format book is the first biographical reference work on Filipino Americans and Canadians published in the United States. It is an important source for this fast-growing and increasingly visible Asian American group of more than 2.2. million people. This is not a biographical dictionary. Rather, it consists of 3 parts: Part 1, "The Filipino Odyssey in North America," is a history of Filipino immigration to the United States and Canada, 1763 to date, with demographic data and sociological analysis. This useful and interesting section includes a fascinating article by Lafcadio Hearn entitled "Saint Malo: A Lacustrine Village in Louisiana," which was published in *Harper's Weekly* on March 31, 1883.

Part 2, "Profiles of Filipino Achievers in the USA & Canada," is the most important and longest part of the book. It consists of 8 sections, from "Arts & Culture" to "Science and Technology"; the achievers' profiles are arranged in 69 separate chapters within each of these broad designations. Each biography is generally between three and eight pages in length, with many black-and-white photographs. Many familiar names (Lea Salonga, Irene Natividad, Ninotchka Rosca, and Loida N. Lewis) appear here. Interestingly enough, the coauthor and publisher of this book, Veltisezar B. Bautista, is the subject of chapter 13 in the "Business and Finance" section. Part 3, "Brief Profiles of Other Filipino Achievers," is an addendum to part 2. It provides information on 29 biographees whose profiles for various reasons were not included in part 2. Parts 2 and 3 have a total of more than 100 biographical profiles.

Inclusion in the book was by nomination, "except for a few who were invited by the writer" (p. xii). Bautista made many contributions to the book, writing some profiles and coauthoring other parts with Crisostomo, who is the author of biographies of such well-known Philippine politicians as Ferdinand and Imelda Marcos and Corazon Aquino. The book's bibliography, in two sections, has little value because almost all of its entries lack complete bibliographic data (pagination and publication dates, most notably). There are two indexes (general and achievers'), with many personal names needlessly listed in both. *Filipino Achievers* also has an Internet Website at http://www.bookhaus.com. [R: RBB, June 96, p. 1767]
—**Marshall E. Nunn**

German Americans

333. Pumroy, Eric L., and Katja Rampelmann, comps. **Research Guide to the Turner Movement in the United States.** Westport, Conn., Greenwood Press, 1996. 358p. index. (Bibliographies and Indexes in American History, no.33). $85.00. ISBN 0-313-29763-0.

The German-American Turner movement began in the 1850s with immigrants who fled the failed 1848 revolution in Germany. The cultural, social, and sometimes political societies it established in numerous cities, particularly in the East and Midwest, flourished at the turn of the century and into the 1920s, only to decline with increasing assimilation and the crisis of World War II, until today only the imposing Turner halls still found in many urban areas serve as reminders of the organization's past prominence.

Pumroy and Rampelmann's guide provides unprecedented, valuable documentation of the Turners on both national and regional levels. After a succinct historical overview, three chapters list existing publications and historical records, first for the national organization, then for regional circuits and districts, and finally for local societies by state and city. Two more chapters document the movement's influence on physical education with listings of records relating to the Turner-inspired Normal College of the American Gymnastic Union, one of the nation's first schools for gymnastics instructors, and other Turner-related writings on the topic in general. A final chapter lists books, articles, and theses on the movement from the period before 1920 and from 1920 to the present.

Especially useful are an appendix listing Turner Societies by state, city, and dates of tenure; and another providing addresses of those still in existence. A third appendix explains Repository Codes used in the first three chapters to indicate locations of listed items. A subject/title index refers to both entry and page numbers. The introduction elucidates history, methodology, and scope of the project; throughout the work explanatory annotations abound. This comprehensive, well-organized compilation preserves and makes accessible a significant piece of U.S. ethnic history. All collections with interest in same will do well to purchase this volume.—**Willa Schmidt**

Hispanic Americans

334. **Dictionary of Hispanic Biography.** Joseph C. Tardiff and L. Mpho Mabunda, eds. Detroit, Gale, 1996. 1011p. illus. index. $120.00. ISBN 0-8103-8302-0.

The *Dictionary of Hispanic Biography* (DHB) is a much-needed, single-volume source for information concerning Hispanic individuals from the past and present. With more than 450 entries, this dictionary is among the largest biographical sources available. The only other source that comes to mind that provides a larger list of names is the *National Directory of Latin Americanists* (see ARBA 87, entry 139), which includes not only Hispanics but also individuals who are scholars in Hispanic studies. Other such works as *Champions of Change: Biographies of Famous Hispanic Americans* and *The Hispanic 100* (see ARBA 96, entry 408) provide a much smaller listing and concentrate on Hispanics living in the United States.

DHB profiles Hispanic men and women who lived from the fifteenth century to the present, and covers all endeavors from art, business, education, and entertainment to journalism, politics, religion, science, sports, and activism. Approximately 70 percent of the individuals listed are contemporary. Each entry provides an in-depth biographical sketch (usually from 300 to 700 words), along with lists of the sources used to obtain the information. Many of the entries have black-and-white photographs. Indexes include an occupation index, a nationality/ethnicity index, and a subject index.

DHB appears to be well balanced in that most of the Hispanics who come to mind are listed; the compilation seems very satisfactory. The editors contend that their original list contained more than 700 names, and was carefully cut down to the 450-plus notable Hispanics chosen for inclusion. This work is recommended for all libraries. While it is essential for all larger academic and public libraries, one hopes that smaller public and school libraries will also consider DHB as an important reference tool for students. [R: LJ, Feb 96, p. 142; RBB, 15 Mar 96, p. 1312]—**Robert L. Wick**

335. **Hispanic American Chronology.** Nicholàs Kanellos and Bryan Ryan, eds. Detroit, U*X*L/Gale, 1996. 195p. illus. maps. index. $29.00. ISBN 0-8103-9826-5.

Hispanic American Chronology offers readers a concise narrative of important events concerning Hispanics in the Americas. The chronology is arranged by year and then by month and day. The reference encapsulates the principal social, political, economic, cultural, and educational contributions of Hispanic Americans. The entries are brief and lack the type of detail that would have made this volume truly worthwhile. It seems that the only purpose and use of the chronology is to verify dates of important events, although the information provided can be obtained from any encyclopedia. However, there are many illustrations, maps, and photographs to supplement the entries. This book can only be recommended for public libraries, primary/secondary school libraries, or for classrooms that serve Hispanic students. [R: BR, Sept/Oct 96, p. 54; SLJ, Nov 96, p. 138]—**Dario J. Villa**

336. **Hispanic Resource Directory.** 3d ed. Alan Edward Schorr, ed. Juneau, Alaska, Denali Press, 1996. 493p. index. $60.00pa. ISBN 0-938737-33-3.

This new edition lists more than 3,400 national, state, and local Hispanic organizations and associations (see ARBA 93, entry 429, for a review of an earlier edition). In addition, it identifies research centers; libraries and museums; Hispanic studies programs; postsecondary education institutions with significant Hispanic enrollment; and migrant and bilingual education associations, centers, and programs. The directory's scope is broad, including chapters on the Congressional Hispanic Caucus; state and local Hispanic commissions; foundations; human rights and equal opportunities; migrant health; minority and small businesses; media (including publishers, distributors, and booksellers); and diplomatic offices. However, the directory does not supply information about organizations or agencies dealing with Hispanic refugee and immigrant issues. The information is based mostly on mailed questionnaires. In order to be included in the directory, respondents need to provide services primarily to Hispanics, provide information or data about the Hispanic population, or be an organization whose membership is principally Hispanic.

The directory consists of 18 chapters and 8,042 consecutively numbered entries, organized first by broad topic, then, in most cases, alphabetically by state. There are a user's guide and three indexes that give access by name of organization, state, and contact person. For most of the entries, the information is limited to name, address, telephone number (and sometimes fax number), and contact person. However, there is a brief description of the research centers, libraries and museums, newspapers, periodicals, and reference serials.

The entries are presented in three columns, using bold typeface for names and reference numbers, which simplifies readability. Geographic subdivisions (states) are marked clearly in black, another useful feature. The typeface is dark, clear, and easy to read. The 3d edition has approximately 100 more pages than the previous edition, as well as 4 new chapters. The comprehensive nature of the book and its wide scope make it a convenient, useful, and recommended tool for all types of libraries (particularly public) serving Hispanic users.—**Susan J. Freiband**

337. **The Latino Encyclopedia.** Richard Chabran and Rafael Chabran, eds. North Bellmore, N.Y., Marshall Cavendish, 1996. 6v. illus. maps. index. $459.95/set. ISBN 0-7614-0125-3.

The Latino Encyclopedia consists of six volumes and focuses on the Latino experience in the United States. The editors have attempted to be inclusive and not offend with the term *Latino*, especially as "acceptable and preferred group names are constantly in flux" (publisher's note). For convenience the encyclopedia is alphabetized and indexed on the English, not Spanish, alphabet. The encyclopedia provides essays on Latino terms, people, cultural groups, pertinent legislation, geographic locations, and more. It covers a wide terrain, from Henry Cisneros (Bill Clinton-appointed Secretary of Housing and Urban Development) to Sandra Cisneros (acclaimed author of *The House on Mango Street*), from vaqueros to Vatican II.

The entries fill the first five volumes and much of the sixth, with several useful appendixes completing the final volume. A list of broadcast media whose programming is geared toward a Latino audience (although not necessarily in Spanish) is provided, as are directories of educational institutions and programs, businesses owned by Latinos, and organizations. A timeline furnishes brief chronological information on sports, literature, politics, religion, labor, and so on, beginning at 1000 B.C.E. and ending in 1994. A list of serial publications is also included, as well as extensive bibliographies. A bibliography of literature by Latino writers is divided into several categories: novels and autobiographies, short stories, poetry, drama, essays, anthologies, and criticism and bibliographies (although Gloria Anzaldúa's feminist anthology *Making Face, Making Soul=Haciendo Caras* seems strangely placed under novels and autobiographies). A bibliography of reference works is divided by topic, such as history; religion; and social issues (e.g., gangs, the border between Mexico and the United States, intermarriage). Many of the titles listed are in Spanish; works focusing on Chicanos dominate, but Puerto Ricans and Cubans are also represented. The set is completed by a comprehensive index.

As the focal point of the encyclopedia is Latino culture in the United States, Central and South America are not discussed. While their inclusion would be both useful and interesting, such information would greatly expand an already voluminous set. *The Latino Encyclopedia* thoroughly covers the subject matter it seeks to illuminate, and it can be used in conjunction with such sets as *Encyclopedia of Latin American History and Culture* (see entry 349) for a complete picture of Latin American life and culture.

Works such as the one under review are important for grasping the whole story of the United States, with all its diverse populations and cultures. The set is highly recommended; the appendixes alone make it a worthy acquisition. [R: BR, Sept/Oct 96, p. 58; Choice, Sept 96, p. 100; RBB, 15 April 96, pp. 1461-62; SLJ, Nov 96, p. 137]—**Melissa Rae Root**

Indians of North America
Bibliography

338. Gray, Sharon A. **Health of Native People of North America: A Bibliography and Guide to Resources.** Lanham, Md., Scarecrow, 1996. 393p. index. (Native American Bibliographies Series, no.20). $55.00. ISBN 0-8108-3170-8.

This latest offering in the publisher's series is a combination bibliography and directory, always problematic because of the rapid obsolescence of the latter material. Consisting of more than 1,500 numbered entries, the work provides 9 annotated listings of bibliographies, electronic resources and indexes, books and chapters, conference proceedings, dissertations, audiovisual materials, health organizations and libraries, health facilities, and educational programs. The guide does not attempt to incorporate the vast journal literature, other than special issues. The range of materials covers 1970 to the present and is highly interdisciplinary, including both Western and traditional health care and related issues. Archaeological studies and fiction have been excluded, as have most government publications. Coverage of Canada is excellent, and some French Canadian publications are represented.

The first 1,000 or so entries are bibliographic, with generally well-written, descriptive annotations. The remainder of the numbered entries are in the three directory sections, which are alphabetically organized. Some of the directory entries are also annotated. Locating facilities and organizations by either state/province or subject is difficult, and the subject index does not help much, as it is poorly laid out and sketchy, missing many terms found in the listings. Rounding out the volume and providing a historical perspective is an essay by Edward R. Starr, "Health Care Systems in Indian Country." While it does give the reader an overview of the issues involved, its style is needlessly argumentative. In spite of a number of shortcomings, this bibliography will be useful for health care and Native American studies collections.
—**Jeff Wanser**

Biography

339. **Native North American Biography.** Sharon Malinowski and Simon Glickman, eds. Detroit, U*X*L/Gale, 1996. 2v. illus. index. $55.00/set. ISBN 0-8103-9821-4.

Intended for middle and high school students, this work does not pretend to the coverage of other references such as Duane Champagne's *The Native North American Almanac* (see ARBA 95, entry 439). However, it usefully profiles 112 Native North Americans from the United States and Canada, both living and deceased. The result is enjoyably browseable. Written in a somewhat journalistic style and objective in tone, the work only rarely includes controversial evaluations.

The contents are alphabetically ordered, with portraits accompanying most entries, and a list of sources at the end of each. It must have been difficult to decide what prominent Native Americans should not be included: One might have welcomed such personalities as the anthropologists Francis La Flesche (Osage) and Edward Dozier (Tewa), the painters Fritz Scholder (Luiseño) and Harry Fonseca (Maidu), and the poets Wendy Rose (Hopi/Miwok) and Simon Ortiz (Laguna).

The front of each volume has an index by tribal groups/nations that runs into problems of terminology. Thus, the entry on Charles Alex Eastman identifies him as "Santee Sioux writer," but he is indexed only under "Dakota," while Amos Bad Heart Bull, "Oglala Sioux artist," is indexed only under "Lakota"; there is an index entry "Sioux," but no cross-referencing. Each volume ends with another index by field of endeavor, such as art, dance, or education. A more complete index—including the variant name forms for many of the personalities who are profiled—would have been useful. [R: BR, May/June 96, p. 45; SLJ, Aug 96, p. 182; VOYA, Aug 96, p. 190]—**William Bright**

Dictionaries and Encyclopedias

340. Lyon, William S. **Encyclopedia of Native American Healing.** Santa Barbara, Calif., ABC-CLIO, 1996. 373p. illus. maps. index. $55.00. ISBN 0-87436-852-9.

Emphasizing anthropology over medicine, this is a comprehensive introduction to Native American healers and their world. Ceremonies are described, objects and plants used in healing rituals are identified, and the conceptual underpinning of the healers is defined. In addition, there are biographical data on famous healers, and the tribal origins of concepts and ceremonies are visually mapped to give the reader a geographic sense of this activity. Entries vary in length from one sentence to two or three pages, with a black-and-white photograph, drawing, or marking appearing every couple of pages. An index and a selected bibliography end the book.

Browsing the entries takes one from the obvious term *fasting* to the esoteric term *sbatatdaq* (a specific supernatural power). The people identified include renowned medicine men (e.g., Santiano and John LeClair); scientists (Franz Boas); and supporters of Native American causes (musician Natalie Curtis). A great number of the more than 1,200 terms defined are, naturally, from various Native American languages.

This is a significant contribution to the study of Native American shamanic healing. It benefits from the author's expertise gained through 26 years as a field researcher. This is a purchase suitable for general Native American collections and for comprehensive medical collections.—**Ed Volz**

Handbooks and Yearbooks

341. **The ABC-CLIO Companion to the Native American Rights Movement.** By Mark Grossman. Santa Barbara, Calif., ABC-CLIO, 1996. 498p. illus. index. (ABC-CLIO Companions to Key Issues in American History and Life). $57.00. ISBN 0-87436-822-7.

The contemporary Native American rights movement began in the 1960s, but it has a long history of progress and setbacks, hopes and massacres. This book provides brief descriptions of individuals, laws, movements, terms, trends, and events that have shaped the movement since its earliest days. As the author correctly points out in his preface, "the social movement for American Indian rights has depended on both Indian activists and on whites—reformers, jurists, legislators, and others." These are represented alongside a wide range of Native American leaders, including Russell Means, Dennis Banks, Ada Deer, Susette La Flesche Tibbles, Wassaja (Carlos Montezuma), Wovoka, and Vine Deloria.

Many quotations from primary documents, including government reports on massacres, as well as passages from laws and legal decisions, are given. This is extremely valuable because, first, it brings together an abundance of hard-to-find primary source information, and second, because the quotations impart a chilling realism to what could otherwise be a detached litany of facts. Reading excerpts from the reports about the Sand Creek and Wounded Knee massacres, or the text of the Alcatraz Proclamation, or the 1961 American Indian Chicago Conference brings one face-to-face with what this movement is all about. The only problem with the frequent and long quotations is that the format of the book does not allow one to easily discern where extended quotations (offered without quotation marks) begin and end. This minor snag can be overcome by looking carefully at the text.

One oddity is the absence of a discussion on gaming or gambling. Two brief entries deal with issues related to laws and regulations, but there is no overview for this topic as there are for other important issues, such as alcoholism. Illustrations are few, and all are in black-and-white. Most are "head shots," or posed photographs of individuals. It should be noted that Native Americans in this context excludes, for the most part, Alaskan Natives and Hawaiians.—**Constance Hardesty**

342. **American Indian Reservations and Trust Areas.** Veronica E. Velarde Tiller, comp. and ed. Albuquerque, N.Mex., BowArrow, 1996. 698p. illus. maps. index. $65.95pa. ISBN 1-885931-01-8.

Tiller is Jicarilla Apache and a historian, both of which are critical qualifications that lend credibility to this resource guide. Prepared with the support of an award from the Economic Development Administration of the U.S. Department of Commerce, this extensive volume is intended to help Native Americans determine their economic destiny by attracting outside investment to generate opportunities on reservations.

Since the publication of the 1st edition of this work more than 20 years ago, many changes have taken place in Indian country. Tiller believes that Native American tribes already are or are about to become vibrant participants in the economic life of the United States.

Essentially, the volume provides a rich compilation of information about the economy of 587 Native American tribes. The format includes the name of the reservation (where one exists), the most used name of the tribal group occupying the reservation, the county or counties where the reservation is located, telephone and fax numbers, the landholdings, demographic information regarding the size and educational level of the labor force, the reservation population, tribal enrollment, location and land status, culture and history, government, economy, infrastructure and community facilities, and maps. Tiller has made a significant attempt to present information that was provided by the tribes themselves, giving the book an authenticity and perspective often lacking in reports about Native American tribes.

An extensive bibliography including books, tribal publications and resources, government publications, newspaper articles, journals, magazines and newsletters, and unpublished sources, as well as an extensive index, is provided. To avoid excessive repetition, some sections are prefaced with a general history and cultural overview. The book has been enthusiastically received by the Native American community, which is a tribute to its usefulness and accuracy. This book is published by Tiller's own company—a tribute to Native American entrepreneurship, economic self-sufficiency, and self-determination.—**Karen D. Harvey**

343. Ilko, John "Jake" A., Jr. comp. **Ojibwa Chiefs, 1690-1890: An Annotated Listing.** Troy, N.Y., Whitston Publishing, 1995. 79p. illus. maps. $6.50pa. ISBN 0-87875-462-8.

This resource provides short biographical entries for several hundred leaders of the Ojibwa/Chippewa/Anishinaabe people of the western Great Lakes region for the historical period up to 1890. Organized alphabetically by most popular name (many chiefs were known by more than one), each entry typically includes alternate or translated names; date of birth, if known; group affiliation and places of residence; treaty signings (a major means of identification); prominent relatives; and participation in major events. No entries are longer than a paragraph, and the researcher looking for in-depth treatment of prominent chiefs will need to look elsewhere.

A preface outlines the purpose of the book and the various research problems encountered, while an introductory section discusses the nature of Ojibwa chiefly positions, types of chiefs, their authority, and activities. A center section consists of black-and-white portrait photographs of some prominent chiefs from the late nineteenth century. Four maps of place-names are poorly done and could have used more detail. Also, an index to alternate names and a chronological listing would have added to the value of this work. The resource is most appropriate for regional and Native American studies collections.—**Jeff Wanser**

344. Thompson, William N. **Native American Issues: A Reference Handbook.** Santa Barbara, Calif., ABC-CLIO, 1996. 293p. index. (Contemporary World Issues). $39.50. ISBN 0-87436-828-6.

One wonders how many guides it takes to saturate a market niche. This title should come close to reaching the limit for general guides on native peoples of North America. After a long introductory section (84 pages), which includes a solid section on Canadian native peoples, one encounters the usual general guide categories—chronology, biography, organizations, quotations, legislation/court cases, and selected print and nonprint resources. The most useful section is the introduction, which contains a concise summary of today's major issues confronting Native Americans. However, the linkage of that material to the balance of the book is weak. As with any highly selective list, it is possible to take exception to what is included and excluded. Overall, the problem is trying to cover too much material in too little space. For example, in the section called "Native American Leaders of the Modern Era," there are only 22 entries, ranging from tribal leaders such as Peter MacDonald (but not Dick Wilson), Dennis Banks, and Leonard Peltier to Will Rogers and James Thorpe. The latter two are well known but hardly "leaders in the modern era."

If a library is seeking a relatively short and inexpensive guide, it will get more for the money with *The Native American Almanac* (see ARBA 95, entry 441) or *Native America: Portrait of the Peoples* (see ARBA 95, entry 438). Should one wish for more comprehensive coverage, excellent choices are *The Native North American Almanac* (see ARBA 95, entry 439), *Native America in the Twentieth Century* (see ARBA 95, entry 434), and *Reference Encyclopedia of the American Indian* (7th ed.; see ARBA 96, entry 412).—**G. Edward Evans**

Quotation Books

345. **American Indian Quotations.** Howard J. Langer, comp. and ed. Westport, Conn., Greenwood Press, 1996. 260p. illus. index. $49.95. ISBN 0-313-29121-7.

Divided into three major sections—the introduction, "American Indian Quotations," and "Anonymous Quotations, Prayers, and Proverbs"—the text offers 800 quotations of Native American people of the past and present. Included are quotations of the well known, the lesser known, and the anonymous. One should remain aware that the earliest quotations are rendered from the reports of the discoverers, traders, missionaries, politicians, and other non-Native Americans, as the latter relied on the oral, not written, tradition—a point not mentioned by the editor.

The editor does state that quotations are "the building blocks of popular history" and "the words breathe life into past history, giving it a relevance and dignity we cannot get from names, dates, and places." This statement is hard to argue with; the words of any people reflect who they are, what they believe in, and what they stand for. In contemporary parlance, they are also sound bites, often without appropriate and meaningful context. Therefore the reader, while cherishing many of the words that help form a sense of Native American identity and a knowledge of their values and worldviews, should be reminded to probe beyond the quotations. The citations are presented in chronological order, and the primary source is usually given, making the book convenient to use. Important to the book's usefulness are the 23 illustrations or photographs of well-known Native American people of the past and present, an author index, a subject and keyword index, and the tribe index.

The book is a welcome addition to other books providing useful historical quotations, among them *I Have Spoken* by Virginia I. Armstrong (Swallow, 1971), *Indian Oratory* by W. C. Vanderwerth (University of Oklahoma Press, 1979), and *Native American Testimony* by Peter Nabakov (Viking/Penguin, 1992). It extends these works by including words by contemporary Native Americans. Some of the sayings, particularly the contemporary words, do seem like sound bites, especially when multiple quotations come from one speech or article or are simply one or two words. Obviously, lacking the benefit of hindsight, it is exceptionally difficult to determine the importance or long-term impact of contemporary words. In addition, as a non-Native American, it is also difficult to determine whose words are respected within the Native American community. Nonetheless, the book is a step forward and a useful reference. [R: RBB, 15 Nov 96, pp. 607-08]—**Karen D. Harvey**

Irish Americans

346. Shea, Ann M., and Marion R. Casey. **The Irish Experience in New York City: A Select Bibliography.** New York, New York Irish History Roundtable; distr., Syracuse, N.Y., Syracuse University Press, 1995. 130p. index. $29.95. ISBN 0-8156-8121-6.

This bibliography aims to make accessible materials on the Irish in New York City, and is valuable for including unpublished master's theses and doctoral dissertations. Time constraints have prevented the authors from including most fictional works, family histories, and articles from the *Irish Echo*, the *Irish Voice*, and *Irish America*. However, the authors anticipate a 2d edition where these materials will be added, along with a list of archival holdings, newspaper and photograph collections, and feature films relating to the Irish in NYC.

The introduction discusses previously published bibliographies and describes sources left out of the current volume. Section 2, a methodology, describes libraries in New York holding relevant theses and dissertations and their locations within each library. City College of New York, Hunter College, and Lehman College are not covered. Section 3, "Unpublished Theses and Dissertations," is arranged by institution and gives two- to three-sentence summaries for each work. Section 4 "Published Sources," is arranged by author and gives a short abstract of most, but not all, works. Reference to Dissertation Abstracts International is given for those works based on dissertations. Section 5 on audiovisual materials, is arranged by producer and lists sound recordings and videos. No films are listed, and there are only three listings of music (remasterings of 78 recordings by influential fiddle players Michael Coleman, James

Morrison, and Packy Dolan). There are no recordings of other instrumentalists, bands, or vocalists. Section 6 lists more theses and dissertations—works that have not been examined by the authors, who did not summarize items in section 6 nor include them in the indexes.

There are separate author and subject indexes that cover sections 3, 4, and 5 only. The author index is straightforward and complete, but the subject index is less successful. For example, if one is looking for materials on the Irish from County Mayo in New York City, one must look under "Ireland, Natives, of: Mayo," and there is no cross-reference from "Mayo." This is a highly focused work, which can only be recommended to the most specialized collections. It would be of general interest to historians, genealogists, and devotees of Irish culture if it were complete, but it explicitly omits the things that would make it of greatest interest—novels, feature films, the vast majority of sound recordings, and so forth. It is especially unfortunate that the authors did not see fit to index the materials in section 6. By leaving a large number of unpublished theses and dissertations out of the index, the authors have drastically reduced the value of the bibliography. All but the most specialized libraries should wait for the promised 2d edition. [R: Choice, May 96, p. 1456]—**Richard H. Swain**

Jews

347. **An Index to *American Jewish Historical Quarterly/American Jewish History*: Volumes 51-80 [1961-1991].** By the American Jewish Historical Society. Brooklyn, N.Y., Carlson Publishing, 1995. 2v. $150.00/set. ISBN 0-926019-77-5.

With this latest reference from the American Jewish Historical Society, researchers of American Jewish history are able to look up subjects, titles, and authors in 80 volumes of arguably the most important journal in the field. It has been a lengthy wait, and this index is long overdue. An index to volumes 1 through 20 came out in 1914, and the major index to numbers 21-50 (1913-1961) did not get published until 1994 (see ARBA 95, entry 449). The same publisher that put out the 1994 index has followed 1 year later with this index to volumes 51-80 (1961-1991), divided into 2 parts, A-K and L-Z.

The first part contains a historiographical overview of the significance of the time period covered. It provides a worthy supplement to a survey in the 1994 volume that discussed the role of the journal in the emergence of a disciplined global approach to Jewish studies after World War II from an earlier period of American "apologetics." The introduction notes the significance of the 1960s to the 1990s for the flowering of professional writing and attention to group identity.

The structure of the index is the same as the 1994 volume. It is a combined listing of subjects, titles, and authors. While this format offers consistency from the last volume, it still presents problems evident in the last issued index. Titles are not cross-referenced to authors, and titles continue to be subsumed under author and subject headings. For example, the article "The Question of the Kosher Meat Supply in New York in 1813" is found under the entry for "Kosher Meat" but is not listed under "Question." The author of the article is not given with the listing under the subject, and there is no volume-by-volume listing to separately check for the identity of the author or the other contents of the issue. While the latest indexes covering volumes 21-80 could have been designed to answer more reference questions, they nonetheless will be highly valued as a tool for access to the journal's long record of publishing the essential scholarship in American Jewish history.—**Simon J. Bronner**

Latin Americans

348. **Dictionary of Twentieth Century Culture: Hispanic Culture of Mexico, Central America, and the Caribbean.** Peter Standish and others, eds. Detroit, Gale, 1996. 327p. illus. maps. index. $60.00. ISBN 0-8103-8484-1.

The contributions of Spanish culture to the American social and cultural melting pot are, needless to say, considerable and significant. As a means of communication, Spanish has almost become a "need-to-know" language when traveling to such exotic North American cities as Miami, Los Angeles, and San Antonio. The fourth volume in the Dictionary of Twentieth Century Culture series (see ARBA

96, entries 406 and 545, and ARBA 95, entry 927, for reviews of the previous volumes) will be a welcome addition to most libraries. Students at all levels, from high school to university, will find this well-written resource interesting to read for the scholarly information it provides and for pleasure.

The topics covered in this volume include such literary luminaries as Ruben Dario and Nicolas Guillen, such literary movements as modernismo and indigenism in literature, politics, history, the fine arts, significant events, and the individuals who contributed to the drama of Spanish-speaking countries of the North American continent. All of the essays are signed and run from approximately 50 to 1,000 words. There are many black-and-white photographs of prominent individuals and of representative art.

The volume includes a well-thought-out foreword, a comprehensive timeline covering the years 1898 to 1995, a photograph index, and a general index. This reference source will be highly useful for the secondary education libraries and public libraries and is recommended for both public and academic libraries. [R: LJ, Sept 96, p. 166]—**Dario J. Villa**

349. **Encyclopedia of Latin American History and Culture.** Barbara A. Tenenbaum and others, eds. New York, Scribner's/Simon & Schuster Macmillan, 1996. 5v. illus. maps. index. $449.00/set. ISBN 0-684-19253-5.

Great strides have been made in recent years in the study of Latin American culture, which accounts for the abundance of entries (5,000-plus) in the *Encyclopedia of Latin American History and Culture*. Five years in the making, the encyclopedia covers all aspects of Latin American life and history. Drawing from such predecessors as Helen Delpar's *Encyclopedia of Latin America* (see ARBA 75, entry 316), this encyclopedia shows the benefit of recent research in its thoroughness and currency.

The alphabetically arranged, signed entries cover all the Latin American countries and include biographies of well-known or significant Latin Americans. Essays on individual countries are lengthy, detailing such aspects as politics, religion, history, and movers and shakers. Brazil receives special attention. Biographies are shorter, but no entry has fewer than 100 words. The entries provide *see* and *see also* references where appropriate. Throughout the encyclopedia are black-and-white illustrations and shaded maps that illustrate points made in the entries.

Volume 5 contains a lengthy, comprehensive index and a list of biographies in the encyclopedia, divided by topic (e.g., journalism, exploration and conquest). An impressive list of the nearly 850 contributors to this work also appears in this volume. Although the set is helpful and informative, bibliographies and other informational materials such as appear in *The Latino Encyclopedia* (see entry 337) would increase its usefulness even more. The list of biographies is a nice touch, although the people profiled are also accessible through the index. The division by topic in that list, however, provides access points for the researcher who may not be looking for a specific name but a more general subject.

In the shrinking global village, the study of cultures outside of one's own is important and illuminating. Works such as the *Encyclopedia of Latin American History and Culture* aid in the quest for multicultural knowledge and understanding. By using this set with others such as *The Latino Encyclopedia*, one can ascertain the similarities and differences between Latin American culture in Central and South America and Latino culture in the United States, and also draw comparisons to other cultures around the world. The set under review is a significant feat and should be considered for all large public and academic libraries. [R: Choice, July/Aug 96, p. 1771; C&RL, Sept 96, p. 473; SLJ, Nov 96, p. 139]

—**Melissa Rae Root**

7 Genealogy and Heraldry

GENEALOGY

Bibliography

350. **Genealogical & Local History Books in Print: Family History Volume.** 5th ed. Marian Hoffman, comp. and ed. Baltimore, Md., Genealogical Publishing, 1996. 449p. index. $25.00pa. ISBN 0-8063-1513-X.

The 5th edition of this family history catalog is strong evidence that the torrent of genealogical publications continues unabated (see ARBA 82, entry 459, for a review of an earlier edition). This volume lists 4,634 pedigrees, biographies, and family newsletters currently available from 455 vendors (some also offer reprint-on-demand of noncopyrighted materials). Each entry indicates full title, author, date of publication, price of cloth or paper edition, number of pages, whether indexed or illustrated, and vendor number; some entries include a descriptive annotation supplied by the vendor. Entries are arranged into two sections: family histories and compiled genealogies. The former are listed by surname, the latter by title. For compiled genealogies, a geographic classification may have been more useful. The volume also contains vendors' address lists and surname and advertisers' indexes.

Unfortunately, there are some major limitations to this catalog. First of all, the listing is not complete because vendors must pay to have titles included; it is especially weak on family newsletters. Second, some entries give only the most cryptic information. Without an annotation, the researcher may decide not to purchase the item or request it on interlibrary loan. However, the vendors' address lists provide telephone or fax numbers, and even e-mail addresses for many firms, so one can easily request further details. Third, there is no list of abbreviations used in titles. Finally, the surname index is rather redundant for the family histories, which are already arranged alphabetically by surname, and pointless for any compiled genealogies without annotations listing surnames covered. Nevertheless, this catalog is recommended for genealogical and public collections.—**John D. Blackwell**

351. Gilchrist, J. Brian, and Clifford Duxbury Collier, comps. **Genealogy and Local History to 1900: A Bibliography Selected from the Catalogue of the Canadian Institute for Historical Microreproductions (CIHM). Genealogie et Histoire Locale D'avant 1900.** Ottawa, Canadian Institute for Historical Microreproductions, 1995. 514p. index. (The Early Canadiana Microfiche Series). $40.00 spiralbound. ISBN 0-665-94444-6.

In 1978, the Canadian Institute for Historical Microreproductions (CIHM) was established to microfiche pre-1901 Canadian imprints. CIHM's complete catalog of more than 70,000 books and periodicals is available in microform (*Canada: The Printed Record* [8th ed., CIHM, 1995]) and online (http://www.nlc-bnc.ca/cihm/home.html). Gilchrist's and Collier's select bibliography provides a convenient tool for genealogists and local historians to access relevant material in this invaluable historical collection. The compilers have chosen more than 6,000 titles (arranged by CIHM series number); have prepared an informative introduction; and have compiled indexes of personal names, English and French place-names, and English and French subject headings. The last do not necessarily conform to Library of Congress Subject Headings but are designed to meet users' needs. Although the compilers specify rigorous criteria for inclusion and exclusion, they concede that they have made exceptions and that "this bibliography is . . . [their own] limited selection" (p. viii). They also acknowledge that almost any source may be helpful to the local or family historian.

Users will be somewhat frustrated by this bibliography. First of all, the flimsy card covers and coil binding will not stand up to heavy reference. Moreover, there are no author or title indexes. One can easily find works about, but not by, an individual; some researchers will therefore also have to consult the complete CIHM catalog. Nevertheless, this substantial bibliography will provide yeomanly service by making more researchers aware of this rich historical resource. A list of libraries holding the full CIHM series, as well as information on how to order microfiche or paper copies of individual titles, further enhances accessibility. The bibliography will be an important addition to Canadiana and genealogical collections.—**John D. Blackwell**

Dictionaries and Encyclopedias

352. **The Oxford Companion to Local and Family History.** David Hey, ed. New York, Oxford University Press, 1996. 517p. $49.95. ISBN 0-19-211688-6.

Covering a wide range of topics in the British Isles, 17 contributors combined forces to create this extensive companion in the field of local and family history. Alphabetic arrangement assists the reader to quickly find subjects and terms, enhanced by the use of numerous *see* references on related topics. Obscure and medieval terms are given equal space with more modern topics. Interspersed throughout the text are brief biographical sketches of authors and historians, listing their works. Also included in an appendix are the names and addresses of national, county, and local record offices. The work is highly readable, offering a wide array of subjects, from *gavelkind* to *smoke-penny*, the *Solemn League and Covenant* to *council housing*, and many more. The companion is highly recommended. [R: LJ, Aug 96, p. 64; RBB, 1 Oct 96, p. 372]—**Carol Willsey Bell**

353. Rowlands, John, and Sheila Rowlands. **The Surnames of Wales: For Family Historians and Others.** Baltimore, Md., Genealogical Publishing, 1996. 217p. maps. index. $19.95pa. ISBN 0-8063-1516-4.

Anyone interested in Welsh family history will value this masterful new study—the first comprehensive survey of surnames in Wales. Written by two leading experts, this scholarly and highly readable volume offers essential guidance in a challenging field of genealogical research. The Rowlandses not only provide a glossary of more than 250 Welsh surnames but also discuss the historical development of surnames in Wales. The authors draw their data from marriage records for the period 1813 to 1837; the former date marks the first use of printed parish registers, and the latter the beginning of civil registration in Wales. This time span also saw the marriages of many emigrants and parents of emigrants.

One of the book's most useful features is the abundance of maps showing the distribution of common surnames among the administrative hundreds of Wales. Genealogists have traditionally been frustrated by the small number of common Welsh surnames (the most recurrent include Jones, Williams, Davies, Thomas, Evans, Roberts, Hughes, Lewis, Morgan, and Griffiths). Because of the Rowlandses' extensive research on the distribution of Welsh surnames during the early nineteenth century, genealogists now have a highly reliable method for predicting the geographic origins within Wales of emigrant ancestors, even those with common surnames. As such, this study is an excellent example of how the efforts of family historians are making a significant contribution to wider historical understanding. The only shortcoming of this book is the small typeface. *The Surnames of Wales* is highly recommended for genealogical, onomastic, research, and public collections.—**John D. Blackwell**

Directories

354. Bentley, Elizabeth Petty. **Directory of Family Associations.** 3d ed. Baltimore, Md., Genealogical Publishing, 1996. 355p. $34.95pa. ISBN 0-8063-1523-7.

The purpose of this directory is to provide access to persons or organizations that specialize in genealogical research on a particular family surname. This 3d edition is an update to volumes published in 1991 (see ARBA 92, entry 385) and in 1993 (see ARBA 94, entry 431). Arranged alphabetically by surname, the current edition includes reunions, associations, surname exchanges, databases, periodicals, and (for the first time) publishers of family histories. An entry may be brief or it may give extensive information about the purposes of the association and any costs involved. The numerous *see* references are invaluable in leading the user to related names, for example "CASTLETON (see McCune)." The author states that the present listing consists of 21,131 items, an increase of more than 20 percent since the last edition. The directory is an absolute necessity for any genealogical library worth its salt.—**Carol Willsey Bell**

Handbooks and Yearbooks

355. **Family Archive Viewer.** [CD-ROM]. Baltimore, Md., Genealogical Publishing, 1996. (Family Tree Maker). Minimum system requirements: IBM or compatible 386. CD-ROM drive. Windows 3.1. 4MB RAM (8MB recommended). 9MB hard disk space. VGA 16-color monitor. Microsoft-compatible mouse. free.

Family Archive Viewer is a pared-down version of *Family Tree Maker*, the computer software industry's flagship product for novice and professional genealogists to record information about family members. The viewer's simple installation and intuitive interface allow a novice computer user to immediately sit down and search archive data. When the user opens the viewer, contents of an archive data CD-ROM appear in a large window. Typically, each data CD-ROM includes three parts: an introduction, a name index, and the genealogical records. The viewer's simple search engine allows the user to locate people by last name, first name, such as "Presley, Elvis." A more advanced find feature uses names and birth and death dates from the user's own genealogical data set to identify possible matches on the archive disc.

One recurring issue in ancestor research is tracking immigrants to their homeland. Many times this involves tracing possible spelling variations of family names because the immigration officer recorded a name based on its sound rather than its spelling. The user can turn on a search enhancement feature that matches the name being searched with other names using a Soundex code, a unique code for all names that sound the same, even when they are spelled differently. One example is "Baird" and "Baerd."

Available export and report functions depend on the archive disc used. For example, the two discs for *World Family Tree Volumes 1 & 2, Pre-1600 to Present* contain more than 5,900 family trees created by *Family Tree Maker* owners. Users can see a tremendous amount of information, such as dates, places, children, parents, and spouses. In addition to data export features, four printed reports are available: ancestors, descendants, kinship, and pedigree. In contrast, users of the "Social Security Index" collection can only copy brief information, such as birth and death dates and social security number, from the archive disc and paste into their own family data set. No printed reports are available.

Professional genealogists, serious hobbyists, archivists, and public librarians will find the viewer and the archive data CD-ROMs indispensable. Descriptions of all archive data discs with their costs are on the World Wide Web at http://www.familytreemaker.com.—**Susan D. Baird-Joshi**

356. Platt, Lyman D. **Hispanic Surnames and Family History.** Baltimore, Md., Genealogical Publishing, 1996. 349p. $19.95pa. ISBN 0-8063-1480-X.

At first glance, this appears to be simply an extensive listing of Hispanic names located in various sources and a bibliography of Hispanic family histories. However, it is more than that. While this volume stands alone from others, it is the first of a series to be published by the Institute of Genealogy and History for Latin America (IGHL) that promises to become the most comprehensive source of genealogical information for persons of Hispanic descent. The author's background in this field ensures a work of quality and accuracy.

This volume serves at least partially as an introduction to the series. The 1st section provides basic data on Hispanic surnames: their development, history, heraldry, numerical ranking of the top 1,000 names in terms of commonality, and an alphabetic list of the 1,500 surnames studied by the IGHL. The 2d section identifies some of the sources, by state or country, that provide surname information. The heart of this work is its 100-plus-page bibliography of published Hispanic family histories in the United States and Latin America. Four lengthy appendixes survey the contents and give pertinent data contained in the U.S. census of 1980 and three major works on Hispanic surnames.

The author claims this to be a groundbreaking work in its field, the first analytic work on Hispanic surnames, and the most extensive bibliography of Hispanic family histories ever published. This reviewer sees no reason to disagree with him. *Hispanic Surnames* is recommended for libraries with genealogical collections and an interest in Hispanic studies. [R: Choice, July/Aug 96, p. 1776; LJ, 15 May 96, p. 56]

—**Donald E. Collins**

357. Reid, Judith Prowse. **Genealogical Research in England's Public Record Office: A Guide for North Americans.** Baltimore, Md., Genealogical Publishing, 1996. 148p. maps. index. $22.50. ISBN 0-8063-1504-0.

This useful guide unlocks the secrets of doing family history research in the British Public Record Office (PRO), the counterpart to the United States National Archives. It is intended for people of the United States and Canada who are researching British and Welsh ancestors. The book provides an introduction to PRO record series of particular interest to North Americans: those relating to the Colonial United States, English Canada, and the West Indies. Chapters explain when, and how, to use the PRO. Logistical information includes travel directions and rules and procedures. Records of special interest to genealogists are discussed; for example, emigration (voluntary and transported) and immigration; censuses; vital records; military data; and taxation records. Especially helpful is the recognition that not all will be able to visit the PRO. Sources of PRO records are given that are closer to home, such as the Family History Library, the Library of Congress, and the National Archives of Canada. Published titles containing PRO data are also cited.

Valuable appendixes include the addresses of North American and British Isles research facilities, a "Before You Go" checklist, and a glossary of terms found in PRO records. Illustrations convey the scope of PRO holdings (a 1681 map of Virginia and Maryland) or provide tips for the researcher (closest underground and bus stops). The index provides a number of access points, including type of record. There is a full bibliography of all sources cited, evidence perhaps of the author's profession: Reid is the British Isles Genealogy Reference Specialist at the Library of Congress, and this guide is the result of a Fulbright Research Librarian Fellowship. The work will be indispensable to its intended audience, but also of value to United States and Canadian colonial historians. An added bonus: It is compact and will fit easily into a suitcase. [R: Choice, Nov 96, p. 435; RBB, Aug 96, p. 1925]—**Ruth A. Carr**

358. Schaefer, Christina K. **The Center: A Guide to Genealogical Research in the National Capital Area.** Baltimore, Md., Genealogical Publishing, 1996. 148p. illus. index. $19.95pa. ISBN 0-8063-1515-6.

Washington, D.C., is one of the major sources of genealogical research materials in the world. The city has been the subject of numerous works on family history research. Some of these titles emphasize individual institutions, while others attempt to survey the region's repositories collectively. Schaefer takes the latter approach and does it well. The title of this work comes from her reasoning that the vicinity of the nation's capital is arguably the center of the greatest body of genealogical research materials in the world. Her book is based on and is an update of the author's former work, *Lest We Forget*, which appeared in eight editions beginning in 1965.

The Center is intended for the visitor to the Washington area and provides directions for finding repositories, addresses, telephone numbers, hours of operation, and other pertinent information for each place cited. For the larger and more important institutions, the information is superb, guiding the user through the various departments, services, and research tools, as well as providing helpful hints on various aspects of research. A number of useful illustrations are included in addition to a bibliography of sources, a section of selected National Archives order forms, and a subject index for easy access to the contents.

The only criticism is that lesser institutions are treated too briefly and the information given on some repositories is insufficient to tell what, if any, value the site has for family research. Of the 23 entries in chapter 11, for example, 17 fall into this category. This is not a major fault, however, and may be corrected in a future edition. The book's recency, ease of use, and useful data on the larger institutions make it well worth the price, which is quite reasonable. It is recommended for individuals and libraries of all types and sizes with an interest in genealogy. [R: Choice, Nov 96, pp. 435-36]—**Donald E. Collins**

359. **A Student's Guide to African American Genealogy.** By Anne E. Johnson and Adam Merton Cooper. Phoenix, Ariz., Oryx Press, 1996. 170p. illus. maps. index. (Oryx American Family Tree Series). $24.95. ISBN 0-89774-972-3.

One of twelve in the Oryx American Family Tree Series, this book takes on the challenge of searching for African roots. Unlike European research, tracing African families is severely hampered by the lack of official records due in great part to the effects of slavery. This volume covers some useful genealogical methods including computer resources, census information, the unique aspects of searching for slave ancestors, and steps for adoptees to pursue. A brief discussion on preserving one's family history concludes the text. The strength of this book lies in its overview of history and the African immigration process, as well as the lengthy annotated lists of books, films, and organizations at the end of every chapter. [R: RBB, 15 Mar 96, p. 1318]—**Jean Engler**

360. **A Student's Guide to British American Genealogy.** By Anne E. Johnson. Phoenix, Ariz., Oryx Press, 1996. 168p. illus. maps. index. (Oryx American Family Tree Series). $24.95. ISBN 0-89774-982-0.

Part of the Oryx American Family Tree Series, this book focuses on the heritage of England, Scotland, and Wales. It covers all of the basics from getting started to preserving what is found, and includes an annotated resource list at the end of every chapter. Johnson also provides the student researcher with a brief general history of Great Britain and the immigration process. One chapter covers the unique aspects of British names, clans, and nobility. As a whole, the book is an interesting read, and the recommended resources should prove useful to those who want to pursue their British genealogy. [R: RBB, 15 Mar 96, p. 1318; SLJ, April 96, p. 162]—**Jean Engler**

361. **A Student's Guide to Chinese American Genealogy.** By Colleen She. Phoenix, Ariz., Oryx Press, 1996. 168p. illus. maps. index. (Oryx American Family Tree Series). $24.95. ISBN 0-89774-980-4.

This volume is part of the Oryx American Family Tree Series, designed to instruct beginners in the art of working with Chinese American records. Arranged in a readable fashion, subjects encompass learning the Chinese language, ethnic diversity, family structure, and Chinese clan registers. Other topics instruct the user in where to locate records, including the National Archives, computer databases, and published resources. Chinese history and information about various Chinatowns in the United States provide additional sources to be examined. The guide is recommended for libraries with extensive "how-to" genealogical collections, and those individuals with interest in this very specific topic.—**Carol Willsey Bell**

362. **A Student's Guide to German American Genealogy.** By Gregory Robl. Phoenix, Ariz., Oryx Press, 1996. 168p. illus. maps. index. (Oryx American Family Tree Series). $24.95. ISBN 0-89774-983-9.

363. **A Student's Guide to Italian American Genealogy.** By Terra Castiglia Brockman. Phoenix, Ariz., Oryx Press, 1996. 168p. illus. maps. index. (Oryx American Family Tree Series). $24.95. ISBN 0-89774-973-1.

364. **A Student's Guide to Scandinavian American Genealogy.** By Lisa Olson Paddock and Carl Sokolnicki Rollyson. Phoenix, Ariz., Oryx Press, 1996. 168p. illus. maps. index. (Oryx American Family Tree Series). $24.95. ISBN 0-89774-978-2.

More than a "how-to" manual on tracing one's family roots, this highly recommended genealogical series can easily be used by novices of any age. Most notable are the numerous annotated resource lists. Included are not just ethnic genealogical resources but also music, literature, and history sources; articles; museums to visit; online resources; addresses to archives; genealogical societies and libraries; and famous names to pique the imagination. Each author annotated several of the same general resources but to different degrees. Although some resources are old, they are still pertinent. Clearly the authors are dependent on students to use resource lists to go into more detail.

Each volume provides concise, readable chapters on how and why one should do genealogical research; a concise cultural and historical background of the specific ethnic group; basic pedigree and family group genealogical charts; basics of how to do an oral history; costs that may be involved in doing genealogical research; explicit ways to make the best use of interlibrary loans; the whys and hows of tracing the roots of students who are adopted or come from nontraditional families; a glossary; and an index. Suggestions for further study (e.g., if one were to go to the country of origin) are included. Each book comes extensively illustrated with black-and-white photographs throughout, and full-color photographs and a map in the center leaves.

Minor irritants include the absence of a pronunciation guide to foreign words and phrases, references to difficulty in researching Jewish ancestry in and from Germany without a clear explanation as to why, the lack of a clear ending in some of the volumes, and only once was it even suggested that the researcher keep clear records of *all* useful research to avoid repeating work. Each author in this series was clearly given a template of what was to be discussed in each book and was chosen because he or she was of the ethnic origin to be written about. Certainly each did a genealogical history, to some extent, of his or her own family. Some notable positive differences between the volumes are the in-depth discussion of the position of Italian-American women then and now, and the specificity about what to look for in each resource down to chapter or index in the Scandinavian volume. With the shortage of young adult genealogy books available, this set is a welcome addition to the field. [R: SLJ, Oct 96, p. 152; SLMQ, Fall 96, p. 63]—**Nadine Salmons**

365. **A Student's Guide to Irish American Genealogy.** By Erin McKenna. Phoenix, Ariz., Oryx Press, 1996. 168p. illus. maps. index. (Oryx American Family Tree Series). $24.95. ISBN 0-89774-976-6.

This engaging little book takes the young, novice genealogist on a journey to discover his or her Irish ancestry. The work starts the reader off with a short history of Ireland, followed by annotated lists of books, films, and documentaries for further enrichment. After fully indoctrinating the reader in Irish lore, the author introduces the reader to the genealogical research process. More annotated lists follow that feature: recommended resources and places to look for ancestry information in the United States and Ireland.

This work attempts to cover all the bases and does it well. The author shows the reader, step by step, how to do a comprehensive genealogical search, from conducting interviews to constructing a family tree. Page after page of annotated lists of resources are given, which might be annoying to some, but are nice for those who like to quickly scan for applicable materials. Black-and-white pictures and drawings and a large section of color photographs complement the work.

This book was written for younger readers, "students" according to the book's title. The simplicity of the language used in the work reflects this intended audience. To the older reader, this simplicity makes it a clear, easy, and quick read. Regardless of the age level, the book is useful to anyone interested in learning how to research their Irish roots and get a short lesson in Irish history.—**Kelly M. Jordan**

366. **A Student's Guide to Native American Genealogy.** By E. Barrie Kavasch. Phoenix, Ariz., Oryx Press, 1996. 168p. illus. maps. index. (Oryx American Family Tree Series). $24.95. ISBN 0-89774-975-8.

This volume is one of the Oryx American Family Tree Series, designed to instruct neophytes in the art of working with Native American records. Chapters covering the heritage and diversity of native groups help to explain the types of records that may exist to assist the genealogist. Some of the topics addressed are slavery, adoption, migration, libraries, the Bureau of Indian Affairs, and tribal enrollment. Illustrations, maps, a glossary, and bibliographies all instruct in the use of the unique records needed for this study. The work is nicely done and appears to offer useful advice to the person wishing to explore this interesting aspect in the field of genealogy.—**Carol Willsey Bell**

Indexes

367. Passenger and Immigration Lists Index, 1996 Supplement: A Guide to Published Records.... P. William Filby and Paula K. Byers, eds. Detroit, Gale, 1996. 559p. $195.00. ISBN 0-8103-9329-8. ISSN 0736-8267.

Genealogists and their librarians have long been familiar with the annual supplements to the original 3-volume *Passenger and Immigration Lists Index* of 1981 (see ARBA 82, entry 465). This supplement adds approximately 131,000 new names, drawn from more than 110 previously unknown or unindexed sources. This brings the total number of recorded immigrants between the years 1538 and about 1940 to more than two-and-a-half million persons. The number is not precise because, while the editors can rightly assume that in the early years almost all passengers were immigrants, in later years this is not quite true. A small percentage were surely visitors.

The entries give, as far as the evidence supplies, family name; personal name of head of household; age; port of arrival or location of naturalization (even inland, such as Arizona); date of the event; family members with ages if known; and the source of the information, including the exact page. In practice, most names do not give an age, and in many cases the location given is general, such as Virginia, or "port uncertain." Even so, a surprisingly large number of entries are complete.

This year's supplement will presumably be accumulated with the next four years and republished as a five-year cumulation, 1996-2000, as has occurred for 1982-1985, 1986-1990, and 1991-1995. This rather expensive work is useful primarily for genealogical libraries, where it is indeed almost indispensable. Public libraries with large genealogical collections must determine for themselves whether to invest in one or more of the cumulations or individual incomes; but all librarians who deal with genealogically minded patrons should be acquainted with this valuable set.—**Raymund F. Wood**

PERSONAL NAMES

368. Diamant, Anita. **Bible Baby Names: Spiritual Choices from Judeo-Christian Tradition.** Woodstock, Vt., Jewish Lights Publishing, 1996. 123p. $9.95pa. ISBN 1-879045-62-1.

As Diamant points out, a book of baby names does not require scholarly precision. This book (almost a booklet) does offer a quick guide to an admittedly personal selection of about 500 names each for boys and girls. Scholarly or not, the entry format could be slightly more consistent. The language of origin is sometimes listed, but often it is not. The pronunciation guide is not as described in the introduction. There are usually chapter and verse references to the most famous biblical holders of the name, but not always. Male names are plentiful in the Bible, so the list has been pruned. Some names are too hard, some too odd, and some too freighted with negative implications. (On the other hand, the exclusion of Ahab may have been a mistake: Few moderns would know that Ishmael's captain was named after the evilest man who ever lived.) Female names are much rarer, and therefore the list has been enhanced with feminizations of masculine names, as well as place-names and other terms.—**Robert M. Slade**

369. Dickson, Paul. **What's in a Name? Reflections of an Irrepressible Name Collector.** Springfield, Mass., Merriam-Webster, 1996. 268p. illus. index. $14.95pa. ISBN 0-87779-613-0.

This interesting book poses a question immediately: Is it really a reference book? Should *American Reference Books Annual* be reviewing it? A pedant might argue that it is not; it is merely a browsing book, full of entertaining information, but not likely to give an easily findable answer to a specific question. On the other hand, it is published by the people at Merriam-Webster; its contents are listed in alphabetic order; and it does have a bibliography and an index—all earmarks of a conventional reference book. Let us then accept it, and pass the word on to fellow librarians so that all may enjoy.

The book, one of several others on words and names by the same author, is divided into chapters or categories of names, such as animal names, anagrams or palindrome names, automobile names, commonest names of cities or counties, team names, hurricanes, last names appearing in telephone books, pseudonyms, stage and screen names with their real names revealed, changing fashions in children's names, and so on. As a sample, 1 chapter has 365 names of apples, although strangely omitting braeburn, golden delicious, and pippin (red delicious is listed). An interesting chapter discusses words that originated in people, such as berserk, boycott, guppy, martinet, nicotine, shrapnel, and the like. Many entries are humorous and often ingenious—a suggested name of a self-service gas station, We Fuel You Not; or a slogan for a lunch counter for German diplomats, Delegate-Essen.

The book is recommended for all public libraries, even if it is felt that the work is not serious enough for the reference collection. Patrons will love it, and usage may have to be restricted to short-time loan, as this is the sort of book that someone can find fascinating hour after hour.—**Raymund F. Wood**

370. Lawson, Edwin D., comp. **More Names and Naming: An Annotated Bibliography.** Westport, Conn., Greenwood Press, 1995. 298p. index. (Bibliographies and Indexes in Anthropology, no.9). $69.50. ISBN 0-313-28582-9.

This is a comprehensive, annotated bibliography of books and journal articles on the study of onomastics—the history, content, and practice of names and naming. This edition updates a similar work by Lawson published in 1987 (see ARBA 88, entry 442). The bibliography is designed to supplement *Personal Names*, a bibliography published in 1952 by Elsdon C. Smith and published by the New York Public Library. The compiler has arranged these resources alphabetically by author under 47 subject areas that include ethnic and cultural names, first names, middle names, popular names, women's names, and so forth. Each entry provides complete bibliographic information together with a brief annotation. Many of the entries contain cross-references to other works in the bibliography. Author and subject indexes are also included.

The range and inclusiveness of this work are impressive and should be of interest to historians, genealogists, or anyone interested in the study of names and naming. It is recommended for all libraries. [R: Choice, May 96, p. 1454]—**Jane Jurgens**

8 Geography and Travel Guides

GEOGRAPHY

General Works

Atlases

United States

371. **Kentucky: Atlas of Historical County Boundaries.** John H. Long, ed. Gordon DenBoer, comp. New York, Scribner's/Simon & Schuster Macmillan, 1995. 485p. maps. $55.00. ISBN 0-13-309543-6.

An atlas of historical county boundaries is of particular interest for the commonwealth of Kentucky, which has an inordinately large number of counties for its size (120) and in which there are frequent discussions of possible county consolidations. The title under review describes and illustrates the numerous county boundary changes in Kentucky from the colonial period, when Kentucky was part of Virginia, to 1990. The majority of the volume consists of an alphabetically arranged series of outline maps that show the configurations of each Kentucky county following significant boundary changes. Boundaries appear as heavy black lines superimposed on United States Geological Survey (USGS) maps. The USGS maps show major geographic and political features, including current county lines.

The brief text, in tabular form, references each map and lists the date of each change, the impact of or explanation for the change (e.g., "created from Franklin and Shelby [Counties]"), and the resulting area of the county in square miles. Very minor changes, usually made to accommodate individual property owners, are described but not shown. The atlas also features an alphabetic table showing when each county was created; a chronology of county creations and changes; a series of state maps depicting county boundaries at the times of various censuses; and a bibliography. The source of information for boundary changes is state law.

The maps in this atlas are of outstanding quality and, combined with the tables, present information clearly and succinctly. The atlas will be an important and lasting resource for state and local history and geography. It will be of particular interest to genealogists and may find an audience as a ready-reference for government officials and attorneys. The work is highly recommended.—**Gari-Anne Patzwald**

International

372. **Collins Nations of the World Atlas.** New York, HarperCollins, 1996. 223p. illus. maps. index. $11.00pa. ISBN 0-00-448367-7.

This atlas is a convenient desk compendium of up-to-the-minute data from every country in the world for use in civic centers, libraries, classrooms, homes, or offices. The text opens on a colorful, uncluttered display of nations by continent and a listing and explanation of abbreviations (for example, OPEC, GNP, and ECOWAS). Unfortunately, the tight binding and shrinkage of a small time zone map over the gutter impede a clear understanding of North America's breakdown by zone. The layout of international organizations by continent is clearly delineated by bold colors and stripes. A two-page spread showing population density, life expectancy, energy consumption, and gross national product clarifies many of the differences between nations.

The main body of information follows an appealing, easily understood arrangement marked by a running head and the proper name of each country. Listed alphabetically, entries provide a full-color map; a locator map; a picture of the national flag; and panels of data on size, currency, religion, population, language, and membership in world organizations. The text briefly describes topography, climate, politics, recent history, and economy. Map details indicate key cities, bodies of water, shared borders, major highways, and airports and express distances with a kilometer scale. The breakdown of the United States and Canada by state and province further delineates population, area in square miles and kilometers, and the capital city. A map of Antarctica and a concise index conclude the text. The index features a four-column arrangement of pages, headwords, and cross-references; for instance, referring questions about England to the entry on the United Kingdom.—**Mary Ellen Snodgrass**

373. **The Dorling Kindersley World Reference Atlas.** 2d ed. New York, DK Publishing, 1996. 731p. illus. maps. index. $49.95. ISBN 0-7894-1085-0.

The core of this publication is a country-by-country description of the 192 countries defined by the United Nations, with information for each organized into 18 topics: climate, transportation, tourism, people, politics, world affairs, chronology, aid, defense, economics, resources, environment, media, crime, education, health, wealth, and world rankings. Abundant use of color, bar and pie graphs, colored landscapes, photographs of persons, and country maps summarize much of the information. Use of symbols and icons helps to visually locate information. Less detailed information is presented on 57 overseas territories and dependencies. In addition to three maps under each country, special map sections are devoted to world and continental maps and to global issues. An index-gazetteer of about 20,000 places completes the work.

Strong features include clear organization, graphic summaries of data, and concise relevant textual characterizations. The information is up-to-date and comparable from country to country and is effectively presented for quick location and easy comprehension. An intriguing feature is graphic depiction of world rankings of countries on eight variables, such as life expectancy, infant mortality, gross national product per capita, and literacy. Overall, this is a useful, graphic, colorful, information-packed, pointed basic reference handbook on countries of the world. Although designated as an atlas, its 600 generally small maps, useful in combination with the other information for quick reference within the volume, are not a substitute for a larger, more detailed general reference atlas.—**Chauncy D. Harris**

374. **Hammond Citation World Atlas.** Maplewood, N.J., Hammond, 1996. 328p. illus. maps. $19.95pa. ISBN 0-8437-1295-3.

The regional, national, and state political maps of the United States in this atlas are accompanied by smaller, full-color "Topography" (relief) maps and "Agriculture, Industry and Resources" (economic) maps. Also included are illustrations of flags; global locator maps; and indexes by cities and towns, by other features, and by counties in the United States. Some countries' and regions' entries contain maps of population distribution, vegetation, temperature, rainfall, time zones, and highways. The body of the atlas is preceded by 20 plates of world terrain maps.

The atlas' best features are that the political maps have clearly readable county, state, and provincial boundaries (helpful for family history researchers); that indexes are printed next to the maps, not at the end of the atlas; and that the indexes contain population figures (1990 census figures for the U.S. maps). Its disappointments are that all maps have been reduced so much that many captions for cities require a magnifying glass for reading; that its gutters (the inside margins between facing pages) are too wide for the easy reading of maps printed on two pages; and that a low percentage of the number of named cities and towns appearing on maps are not indexed. A study of its indexing coverage of Rhode Island found that only 62 percent of its cities and towns are indexed.

This atlas is not recommended for libraries, but it could be useful for the home libraries of patrons in need of readable county, state, and provincial boundaries, who would prefer not coming to the library to check the same in the *Rand McNally Commercial Atlas and Marketing Guide* (see ARBA 95, entry 326). It also could be a home aid for those interested in recent population figures not provided in almanacs.

—**J. Carlyle Parker**

375. **Hammond New Century World Atlas.** Maplewood, N.J., Hammond, 1996. 183p. maps. index. $29.95; $19.95pa. ISBN 0-8437-1196-5; 0-8437-1197-3pa.

A feast for the eyes, this data-crammed atlas provides copious information for a small price. Its precision and thoroughness are inviting to the student, researcher, librarian, historian, and general reader. Included are explanations of map reading; a guide to flags and data on each country; global studies of the solar system; topography; the physical world; maps; and indexes covering time zones, world statistics, and a unique arrangement of place-names and page numbers in black and green. No page goes to waste; for example, the end papers guide users to selections on specific areas of each continent (e.g., the São Paulo/Rio de Janeiro area and an overview of the Caribbean and Central America).

Layout and graphics are spectacular. The drawing of the solar system sets a glowing yellow sun among red, pink, and blue planets against a deep purple firmament. Inset deep-space photographs depict each planet as a unique heavenly body. A cut-away diagram of the sun uses reds and golden yellow to represent sunspots, solar flares, the corona, the convection zone, and the radiation zone around a cool, ice-blue core. Diction is precise and scholarly without overburdening the reader with erudite technicalities. World studies reveal the ocean floor as more than just a patch of blue on the map. A useful addition to physical geography includes spreads on world languages and religions, standards of living, energy and resources, agriculture and manufacturing, and such environmental concerns as air and water pollution, ozone depletion, acid rain, deforestation, and threats to animal species. The only additions that would enhance this atlas are a pronouncing gazetteer and a general index. [R: Choice, Mar 96, p. 1096; RBB, 1 Feb 96, p. 956]—**Mary Ellen Snodgrass**

376. **Oxford Atlas of the World.** 4th ed. New York, Oxford University Press, 1996. 288p. maps. index. $70.00. ISBN 0-19-521266-5.

The 4th edition of the *Oxford Atlas of the World* looks similar to the 3d (1995), with some relatively minor changes; for example, colors seem more vivid in the later edition; the "Contents" pages maps are in color; the world gazetteer has some changes (different headings at tops of pages); some colors have been changed in the "Introduction to World Geography" section (e.g., on p. 146, the map of global warming is changed from purple to yellows and oranges); and the globe on the cover does not have continents, just latitude and longitude lines. The atlas is composed of approximately 10 pages of world statistics, 45 pages of an introduction to world geography (small-scale thematic maps), 32 pages of city maps, 160 pages of maps of countries and continents, and nearly 140 pages of gazetteer entries (the city maps have a separate gazetteer).

By the proportion of pages devoted to each continent, the atlas indicates that its audience is primarily Western people. Europe, whose area covers only 7 percent of the Earth and whose population totals 9 percent of the world's peoples, receives 30 percent of the pages in the atlas. North America, with 16 percent of the world's landmass and 5 percent of the population, is granted 17 percent of the atlas' pages. On the contrary, Africa, covering 20 percent of the Earth's area and 15 percent of the population, only merits 12 percent of the pages. (Area and population figures were taken from *The World Almanac and Book of Facts 1996* [see ARBA 96, entry 7].) As in previous editions, the maps are clear, are easy to read, and have pleasant color combinations. This atlas is recommended for reference collections.—**Mary Larsgaard**

377. **Oxford Encyclopedic World Atlas.** 3d ed. New York, Oxford University Press, 1996. 264p. illus. index. $39.95. ISBN 0-19-521264-9.

The *Oxford Encyclopedic World Atlas*, now in its 3d edition, is a comprehensive compilation of profiles of each country's geography, history, economy, and culture. Starting the journey, the table of contents is divided into continents, including Central America and countries in the Atlantic and Indian Oceans. Statistics of population, area, and physical dimensions are found in the beginning of the atlas for quick information. This portion of the work will alleviate students' need of an almanac to find sizes of mountains, ocean depths, islands, and the like. A country index, listed alphabetically, is found on page viii.

The section prior to the world maps contains charts; graphs; and information on such topics as climate, population, wealth, and travel and tourism. These topics are arranged alphabetically for ease of use. At the beginning of the world map section are the symbols used on the maps themselves. That is the only place where they are found, which is a drawback. Students using this atlas will have to refer back to that page many times as they extract information from this book.

Beginning each section is a complete map of all countries on the continent or islands. Additional maps showing topographical features and climatic regions, natural vegetation, annual rainfall, population, and land use are furnished. Each page's layout is attractive and comprehensive. Pictures of flags are supplied, as are a climate chart and a brief overview of the country. A comprehensive index is found on pages 226-64, along with instructions on how to use it. The directions are well written and will help students avoid confusion. Also included are maps of regions in the news, such as Bosnia-Herzegovina, Taiwan, and the Near East, to name a few.

This comprehensive atlas will be a welcome addition to middle school and high school libraries. It will be used extensively by students.—**Barbara B. Goldstein**

378. **The World Afghanistan to Zimbabwe.** Skokie, Ill., Rand McNally, 1996. 208p. maps. index. $49.95. ISBN 0-528-83773-7.

This book is a beautifully designed, 11¼-by-15-inch book with 235 countries and some other political entities arranged in alphabetic order and a 1-page introduction captioned "Gazetteer of the Countries of the World." The United States is allocated 4 pages, with a 2-page physical map 8¾-by-14½-inches in size (the largest map in the book), a pie chart of ethnic groups, and 9 high-quality color photographs of various subjects in an assortment of sizes. Most countries merit only a single page, with smaller countries often sharing a page. Maps are in a multitude of scales and sizes, from the United States, mentioned above, to Niue, only 1½-by-1⅝ inches.

All entries contain a global locator map that shows the country's location in its part of the globe; an illustration of its flag; a short statistical chart of 18 items from population to elevation lows and highs; and a short narrative about the people, the economy, and history and politics. All full-page or larger entries also contain a simple outline map illustrating a country's size compared to the continental United States and the ethnic pie chart. The index (in the back of the book) includes page numbers, latitude, and longitude. Seventeen preliminary pages include worldwide information charts with short related narratives, and seven pages of the same for eleven large world cities.

Library collections will normally have better gazetteers and collections of maps. Any of the five or six leading encyclopedias contain more information and, in many cases, better maps. Nevertheless, this work is recommended for public and academic libraries as an interesting, appealing approach to the world's geography. [R: LJ, Mar 96, p. 76]—**J. Carlyle Parker**

Dictionaries and Encyclopedias

379. **The DK Geography of the World.** New York, DK Publishing, 1996. 304p. illus. maps. index. $39.95. ISBN 0-7894-1004-4.

Each of the six major sections of this work opens with a two-page spread showing the major physical features of a continent, followed by another spread that highlights the people of the region. Following spreads cover a country (or group of countries) with maps showing main physical and political features, and other maps that show the relation of the country to the continent, while photographs and descriptive paragraphs highlight features such as festivals, national foods, major industries, the economy, and other topics related to that nation or region. Fact boxes provide access to key facts. The United States is covered in four spreads, including one spread each on the western, central, and eastern states.

Through the thorough index, one may access, in addition to physical and political places, information on such varied topics as acid rain, cotton growing, debtor countries, and immigrants. The presentation on each spread is rather busy, but the attractive arrangement of photographs, drawings, and text introduces a wide variety of topics suitable for further research. The concise but clear explanation of the crisis in the former Yugoslavia attests to the currency of the coverage.

The work opens with general information about the physical and political world, and concludes with a reference section that highlights political systems, international organizations, world religions, world trade, and similar topics. A glossary, gazetteer, and index are included. Colors and printing are crisp, the binding is sewn, and the paper is of high quality.

This attractive, up-to-date atlas is suitable for elementary students. Another fine atlas that serves this same audience is *The Dillon Press Children's Atlas* (see ARBA 95, entry 476). [R: RBB, 1 Nov 96, pp. 534-36]—**Vandelia L. VanMeter**

380. **Merriam-Webster's Pocket Geographical Dictionary.** Springfield, Mass., Merriam-Webster, 1996. 360p. $3.95pa. ISBN 0-87779-506-1.

This 3½-by-5½-inch pocket reference contains 12,000 entries for place-names around the globe. It also provides essential geographic data such as population and area and location, and offers pronunciation of geographic names. The dictionary includes adjectives and nouns derived from various location designations. The typeface is small but readable, and because one does not read large quantities at a time, is therefore adequate. This book would be extremely useful for an international traveler and even more useful for an office that deals with international correspondence. The dictionary is up-to-date, and the reasonable price makes it an absolute requirement for all libraries and all corporate offices except those dealing in a very provincial environment.—**Herbert W. Ockerman**

PLACE-NAMES

381. **The Cambridge Gazetteer of the United States and Canada: A Dictionary of Places.** Archie Hobson, ed. New York, Cambridge University Press, 1995. 743p. $49.95. ISBN 0-521-41579-9.

The geographic scope of this gazetteer is limited to places affiliated with the United States and Canada and their possessions. The listings are not limited to municipal features, but also include physical geography, national forests and monuments, historic and legendary places, and military sites. For example, Devils Tower (Wyoming), Mall of America (Minnesota), Route 66, and River City, Iowa, stand alongside traditional gazetteer listings. A typical entry includes the population, or size (in acres and hectares), and in many cases the distance and direction from a major city. There is no latitude or longitude given. The emphasis is on description and economic geography, but many entries include historical background or significance. Entries are linked together by highlighting with capital letters to signify additional or related information. There are also entry *see* references that are helpful.

The quality of the entries is uneven. Some entries surprise with their completeness, while others are vague or include some inaccuracies or misinformation. It is unfortunate that the incorporation date/founding date is not noted for every city or municipality, as this is likely a key need for the user. The supplementary maps are suitable for quick reference and encompass several historical periods, and there are general maps of several cities most likely to receive tourists.

In spot checking entries, recently popular Madison County, Iowa is not mentioned, several colleges that have changed names five years ago have not been updated, and a number of entries have misleading statements. Yet there are numerous entries offering greater-than-expected depth and lengthy descriptions of lesser-known locations that may barely be mentioned in other gazetteers or geographic dictionaries.

The gazetteer is suitable and recommended for any site with frequent North American place-name identification questions, whether actual or fictional. Sites with few of these requests may do just as well with a comprehensive world gazetteer and an additional one for regional (e.g., state, province) coverage.
—**Gary R. Cocozzoli**

382. Room, Adrian. **Placenames of Russia and the Former Soviet Union: Origins and Meanings of the Names....** Jefferson, N.C., McFarland, 1996. 282p. index. $58.50. ISBN 0-7864-0042-0.

This work draws an impressive picture of geographic, historical, and political changes on the map of Russia and the former Soviet Union since the nineteenth century up to the present day and the collapse of the USSR. The dictionary contains six sections: an introduction, the list of place-names, appendix 1 (common place-name elements), appendix 2 (regional names), a select bibliography, and a Cyrillic-to-roman index. The introduction helps one understand the arrangement of entries, and also some causes of place-name changes.

The major part of the place-name section presents the origins and meanings of the names for more than 2,000 towns, regions, countries, and natural features in all 15 former republics of the USSR. Each entry contains four "strands" or items of information: the name itself, as the headword; its Cyrillic equivalent, in parentheses; a brief description of the named place, with its country and approximate geographic location in that country; and the meaning of the name. The explanatory text of each entry opens with a locational description. An account of the name's origin and meaning then follows. There may be cross-references to other names (former names and alternate spellings or forms of current names) within the text or at its conclusion and appropriate historical, topographical, and biographical references.

The two appendixes consist of a list of common place-name elements and a list of regional names. The select bibliography includes books, dictionaries, atlases, guides, gazetteers, journals, and individual articles. The Cyrillic-to-roman index lists the Russian originals of all headwords in the book, together with English equivalents. The market for the dictionary is wide, stable, and promising.—**Ludmila N. Ilyina**

TRAVEL GUIDES

General Works

383. Anderson, Sarah. **Anderson's Travel Companion: A Guide to the Best Non-fiction and Fiction for Travelling.** Brookfield, Vt., Scolar Press/Ashgate Publishing, 1995. 552p. index. $65.00. ISBN 1-85928-013-7.

"I travel not to go anywhere, but to go," remarked Robert Louis Stevenson famously. "I travel for travel's sake. The great affair is to move." And indeed, during the past half-century, tourists have become an increasingly familiar part of the landscape in all corners of the world. This phenomenon (tourism revenues continue to expand at an impressive 7 percent annually) relates to the increasing amounts of discretionary time and money in the hands of more and more people, as well as to the continued brutal competition among destination regions for "clean" tourism income. Yet at the same time, tourists are becoming more sophisticated, seeking "in-depth" experiences and demanding more background and context for any potential destination.

Anderson, founder of the famous Travel Bookshop in London, provides here a detailed and comprehensive guide for the discriminating tourist. Based logically on a bookstore arrangement, with the world divided into continents, subcontinents, countries, regions, and cities, the book lists both fictional and nonfictional, modern and classical contributions, all in English, to local understanding. A typical national entry would include annotated listings under anthology, art and architecture, biography, fiction and poetry, food, guidebooks, history, leisure, natural history, photography, and travel literature. Indexes of authors, titles, places, and photographers occupy 110 pages, while standard guidebooks are discussed in a separate section. The handful of maps could be much improved and expanded, and experienced travelers will always be able to spot omissions of their favorite places, but this is nonetheless one of the most comprehensive (and tempting) volumes yet to appear for the prospective or armchair traveler. [R: Choice, July/Aug 96, p. 1767]—**James R. McDonald**

384. Dervaes, Claudine. **The Travel Dictionary.** new ed. Tampa, Fla., Solitaire Publishing, 1996. 326p. maps. $19.95pa. ISBN 0-933143-53-2.

This publication is not a general interest book. The author states that it was devised to help people in the travel industry. More than half of the content is devoted to a dictionary of terms, codes, acronyms, and abbreviations related to the travel industry. An additional 82 pages contain lists of various codes associated with travel, such as for countries, states, and provinces; currencies; cities/airports; airlines; fares; car rentals; hotels; and special meal requests. The handbook also lists travel industry reference books and publications, travel video companies, travel organizations, chains, consortia, franchises, and networks.

Other information provided—capitals of countries, territories, states, and provinces; a metric conversion chart; comparative sizes for clothing in the United States, the United Kingdom, and Europe; time zones; populations; highest and lowest points; largest islands; oceans, lakes, rivers, and so forth—can be found in general reference sources, but these facts are useful here for a quick, superficial answer. The 11 maps are not detailed and will provide only the most general information. The lack of an index is partly redeemed by a comprehensive table of contents.

The physical publication has the look of a work put together in pieces at different times. The various sections vary widely in font style and typeface size, with the smallest typeface requiring good eyesight. Despite these few drawbacks, this is a useful handbook for those for whom it has been written.—**Jean Weihs**

United States

385. Barnes, Rik. **Complete Guide to American Bed and Breakfast.** 4th ed. Gretna, La., Pelican Publishing, 1996. 956p. illus. maps. $19.95pa. ISBN 1-56554-036-0. ISSN 1059-6917.

A popular form of American lodging is attested to by the more than 2,000 listings in this 4th edition of the guide (see ARBA 87, entry 458, for a review of the 1st edition). Directories such as this one can never really be complete because new bed-and-breakfasts are always being established, and others close down. Between 1991 and 1996, approximately 500 inns went out of business. There are two bed-and-breakfasts listed in this reviewer's telephone book that are not included in the guide. Bed-and-breakfast accommodations must be booked well in advance and are not for those travelers who get in their cars, drive 10 to 12 hours, and then hope to find a place to stay for the night.

This guide is logically arranged and formatted. First, it is arranged alphabetically by all 50 states, and then by town or city. An outline map of each state, divided into numbered regions, precedes the state listings. Each listing is keyed to the numbers and includes the name, address, and telephone and fax numbers of the establishment. Following this, the name of the innkeeper; number of rooms; rates; credit card acceptance; and restrictions such as no smoking, no pets, and no children are furnished. Next are notes describing the building, its setting and furnishings, whether it is listed on the National Register of Historic Places, the innkeeper's interests and hobbies, cats or dogs in residence, foreign languages spoken, and the like. Vignette sketches of the buildings illustrate many of the listings. This is a useful guide.

—**Frank J. Anderson**

386. Cantor, George. **Historic Festivals: A Traveler's Guide.** Detroit, Gale, 1996. 392p. illus. maps. index. $39.95. ISBN 0-8103-9150-3.

"It is important to remember the place's past," Cantor writes, and his book, *Historic Festivals*, certainly does an exemplary job of explaining where festivals are, and when, and why. The book is divided into five regions: North East, South East, Great Lakes and Ohio Valley, Great Plains, and the West and Pacific. The 271 festivals are well divided among the regions. Each regional section has its own calendar of dates and places before going into the annotations. Each entry lists the place of the festival, the name of the festival, when the festival occurs, and a short annotation of what people can expect and why the event is being held. Annotations end with location directions, event listings, and a contact address or telephone number.

Some interesting entries include Stonehouses Day in Hurley, New York; the Daniel Boone Festival in Barbourville, Kentucky; the Cereal City Festival in Battle Creek, Michigan; the Garlic Festival in Gilroy, California; and the Pony Express Day in Ely, Nevada. The author does not explain his selection criteria and this reviewer would argue about the inclusion of the Fairplay, Colorado, World's Championship Pack Burro Races while the largest two festivals in Colorado—the Festival of Mountain and Plain and the Capitol Hill People's Fair (the first being celebrated in the state for over a century) are excluded.

The book includes a timeline and indexes by national calendar, event, and subject. All are done well except the timeline, which references specific dates in history that have triggered festivals annotated in the book without referencing which festival is being discussed. This guide is recommended for small libraries. The calendars will help travel agents and families wanting to plan a different sort of trip to see the country and learn about U.S. history. [R: RQ, Summer 96, pp. 560-61]—**Kevin W. Perizzolo**

387. Cantor, George. **Pop Culture Landmarks: A Traveler's Guide.** Detroit, Gale, 1995. 401p. illus. maps. index. $34.95; $17.95pa. ISBN 0-8103-9399-9; 0-8103-9899-0pa.

For those who have traveled to all the usual cities and visited all the usual museums and other places of note, this guide should prove to be a welcome directory to new adventures and little-known sites of interest. Arranged in five major geographic sections—Northeast, Southeast, Great Lakes/Ohio Valley, Great Plains, and West and the Pacific—the work subdivides alphabetically by each state. Unusual landmarks, sometimes accompanied by photographs, are then detailed in terms of their popular culture value. Most entries average 500 words and include a chatty description of the landmark. This is followed by straight directory information—location, hours, admission fees, and telephone number. Examples of these landmarks include Tony Packo's Cafe in Toledo, Ohio; the Helen Keller Shrine in Tuscumbia,

Alabama; the Drive-In Movie Motel in Monte Vista, Colorado; and the National Cowgirl Hall of Fame in Hereford, Texas. Some standard travel sites—other halls of fame, Wrigley Field, the World Trade Center, various theme parks—are also included here, mainly for their popular culture relevance.

This guide has a locator map at the beginning, and each of the five sections opens with its own locator map, a handy feature for those planning regional trips or weekend jaunts. Although some entries can be found in standard travel guides, public libraries might consider adding this to travel collections to round out information on lesser-known sites.—**Edmund F. SantaVicca**

388. **City Profiles USA 1996: A Traveler's Guide to Major US Cities.** Detroit, Omnigraphics, 1996. 443p. maps. $65.00. ISSN 1082-9938.

This data-packed reference work is indispensable to libraries, schools, travel and vacation planners, businesses, and civic managers who seek the best in updates on city facts, metropolitan locations, average temperatures and precipitation, telephone numbers and addresses, data sources, airports, transportation, lodging and food, services, media, education, and attractions and events. In addition to factual listings, the book includes a map showing the position of each city featured in the text plus area codes and projected changes, topographical abbreviations, airports, airlines, car rental agencies, credit card companies, an intercity mileage chart, convention and visitor information, hotel brokers and chains, weather information, and radio format abbreviations.

The work offers balanced coverage of cities across the United States, including those in Hawaii and Alaska. Choice of cities reflects the population density of the East Coast. Entries on cities, arranged alphabetically, include land and water area, topography, significant telephone and fax numbers, colleges and universities, sports teams, banks, shopping malls, television and radio stations, zoos, theaters, museums, and a thin sprinkling of e-mail addresses. Brief introductions note that Fairbanks was named for a U.S. senator and vice president and that a trip to Honolulu may include a ride in an outrigger, a visit to the U.S.S. *Arizona*, or a hike through a rain forest. Clear typefaces and ample white space relieve this compendium of cramped columns and resultant eye fatigue. The editors are surprisingly stingy with Internet data, which might link the book with many useful World Wide Web locations for up-to-date weather and travel information and connections with firms offering reservations, previews of events, routes, and tickets. [R: RBB, Jan 96, p. 870]—**Mary Ellen Snodgrass**

389. **Hostelling USA, 1996: The Official Guide to Hostels in the United States of America.** Washington, D.C., Hostelling International-American Youth Hostels, 1995. 287p. illus. maps. index. $1.50pa.

Hostelling USA gives information on just under 150 hostels and homestay sites in the United States. Prices at these hostels run as low as less than $15 per night (and sometimes are less than $10 per night), so *Hostelling USA* provides a service for a younger, less affluent traveler than the one who might turn to *The All-Suite Hotel Guide* (8th ed., Ten Speed Press, 1995), *World Hotel Directory 1996* (Longman), or one of the many bed-and-breakfast guides on the market. For each hostel listed, the guide supplies telephone numbers, prices, information on making reservations, and detailed directions. In addition, for most hostels there is a black-and-white photograph of the hostel plus a small map. The introduction (which is printed in English, German, French, and Japanese) gives information on hosteling associations, a key to the symbols used in the entries for individual hostels, and an introduction to hostel customs—which in some cases call for guests to help with the cleaning and cooking. This book will be useful to any library that serves young travelers, and at the price, it is a bargain.—**Donald A. Barclay**

390. **The National Trust Guide to Historic Bed & Breakfasts, Inns, and Small Hotels.** 4th ed. By Suzanne G. Dane. Washington, D.C., Preservation Press and New York, John Wiley, 1996. 561p. illus. maps. $18.95pa. ISBN 0-471-14973-X.

This edition of *The National Trust Guide* adds approximately 100 new listings of historic U.S. lodgings, bringing the total to more than 700. To qualify for a listing in this guide, the inn or hotel must be more than 50 years old and retain its architectural integrity. The National Trust hopes to showcase unusual accommodations as well as to emphasize the diversity in U.S. architecture throughout history. Structures range from colonial to pre-World War II. Their original purposes represent everything from taverns to bakeries.

Listings are organized by state. As in earlier editions, each entry includes a description of the structure's architectural style, construction, and unusual features. Many entries have line drawings of the buildings. Brief notes on the historic significance of the sites and their historic owners are given. Following the descriptions are particulars about accommodations, rates, methods of payment accepted, restrictions, handicapped accessibility, and local activities available.

The mission of the National Trust—to increase the awareness and appreciation of the United States' diverse cultural heritage through the preservation of significant historic sites, buildings, and objects—is well served by this guide. The book is well organized and provides an abundance of information about citizens of the United States and their buildings. The guide is recommended for general collections.

—**Joanna M. Burkhardt**

391. Wheeless, Carl. **Landmarks of American Presidents: A Traveler's Guide.** Detroit, Gale, 1996. 809p. illus. maps. index. $49.95. ISBN 0-8103-8301-2.

The two sections of this remarkable reference book are of great value to those interested in presidential history and lore. The first part provides snippets of history (sometimes gossip, sometimes idiosyncrasies) of our presidents, and then details of birthplace, baptism, church attendance/membership, education, marriage/honeymoon, homes, travel, and death or funeral and burial. A "Life in Review" panel offers a capsule version of each president's career and administration (however, one wonders why the eruption of Mount Rainier is included as part of President John Tyler's administration). The material included has been subjected to considerable censorship: There is no mention of extramarital affairs, so the impression one gets is of a series of model husbands and gentlemen.

Although the author certainly deserves great praise for having assembled so much detail, there are several notable shortcomings. For example, no mention is made of John Adams and James Monroe having worshipped at First Presbyterian Church in Trenton, New Jersey, and the memorial to General George Washington is placed on the wrong street in Princeton, New Jersey. (One suspects that there are many other similar omissions and slips.) Some of the photographs (apparently taken by the author) are of poor quality and could have been replaced by stock file photographs. Editing and proofreading are poor: Examples of typographical errors include "Airforce base," "Nurenburg," "Obergammerau," "Guadacanal," French place-names without hyphens and accents, and dropped italics. One also finds such compositional solecisms as "On the way to Paris he visited . . . and Paris." Despite these flaws, the strengths of the book are immense and reflect the dedication of the author. Travelers will find part 2, "Geographic Guide to Presidential Landmarks," helpful when touring throughout the United States. [R: Choice, Sept 96, pp. 107-08]—**Marian B. McLeod**

Australia

392. **Sydney.** By Ken Brass and Kirsty McKenzie. New York, DK Publishing, 1996. 264p. illus. maps. index. (Eyewitness Travel Guides). $22.95 flexibinding. ISBN 0-7894-1069-9.

The Eyewitness Travel Guides place great emphasis on visual information. The philosophy behind the guides is that visitors relate to a new place better using a guidebook with clear, lifelike pictures. This guide to Sydney, Australia, is full of photographs, maps, and drawings. The book is divided into five main sections. "Introducing Sydney" includes maps, history, key events that occur every year, key sporting events, and "Sydney at a Glance." This last section is a quick overview of sights that are discussed in more detail elsewhere. "Sydney Area by Area" breaks the city into six segments and discusses each segment in detail. Also included are four guided walks. "Beyond Sydney" covers places of interest outside of Sydney, but that are easily accessible. "Travelers' Needs" is full of places to stay, eating places, shopping, and entertainment. "Survival Guide" contains much of the same information previously presented, but in an encapsulated format.

This is an excellent guidebook. It is easy to follow, and the index is comprehensive. Each section contains a summary list of the sights described in that section. All sights are numbered and plotted on an area map. Façades of important buildings are reproduced pictorially. Visitor's checklists are included throughout. Practical information is provided, such as how to use ferry ticket machines. The maps are excellent, and the street finder index is useful, as is the "Sydney Transit" map. The only negative feature of the guide is that, in order to accommodate the pictures, the text is sometimes small and hard to read.—**Linda Main**

Canada

393. Pantel, Gerda. **The Canadian Bed & Breakfast Guide.** 12th ed. Toronto, Penguin Books Canada, 1996. 408p. illus. maps. $13.95pa. (U.S.). ISBN 0-14-025751-9. ISSN 0836-5717.

Now in its 12th edition, this informative guide covers bed-and-breakfast accommodations across Canada, including the Queen Charlotte Islands (in British Columbia), the Yukon, and the Northwest Territories. For the uninitiated, the author describes at the outset what a bed-and-breakfast is and details some of the history of the B&B concept in Canada. In addition, she provides tips on how to use the guide and where to obtain additional travel information. Each chapter consists of a separate province or territory, beginning with the most westerly provinces and moving east. Within the chapters, each entry is arranged alphabetically by town or city.

The author provides a handy map at the beginning of each chapter, depicting all the towns and cities having bed-and-breakfast locations described in the text. In addition, useful addresses and toll-free numbers for the local tourist authority are provided. Most entries include a photograph of the bed-and-breakfast; directions and an address; room rates; number of rooms and beds; bathing facilities; restrictions such as children, pets, or smoking; and a short commentary on the host home and locale. Each of these features can easily be found in the text with the use of intuitive symbols (a key to these symbols is provided on the front flap).

This guide is updated on an annual basis, so one can be sure the information is current. Also, the author makes an attempt to visit as many bed-and-breakfasts as possible in her travels. This guide is highly recommended for the travel section of all public libraries.—**Katherine Margaret Thomas**

Europe

Great Britain

394. **English Castles: A Guide by Counties.** By Adrian Pettifer. Rochester, N.Y., Boydell & Brewer, 1995. 344p. illus. maps. index. $45.00. ISBN 0-85115-600-2.

This descriptive gazetteer provides a brief overview and history, organized by county, of 900 English castles. The period covered is from the Norman Conquest to the Tudor era. Almost all the masonry castles still in existence, and many of the larger earthwork castles, are included. The castles are listed alphabetically within each county. Access information, related sites, and references are appended to the entries. Information is also provided as to whether the castle is maintained by English Heritage, National Trust, or the local authorities.

The guide furnishes a short historical introduction to English castles and a glossary. The index contains Ordnance Survey grid references. Plans for many of the castles are included, as are 16 black-and-white plates. This gazetteer is extremely comprehensive. It is useful for the traveler interested in English castles and as a guide for the serious historian who wishes to do in-depth research on English castles. [R: Choice, June 96, p. 1622]—**Linda Main**

Italy

395. **Italy.** New York, DK Publishing, 1996. 672p. illus. maps. index. (Eyewitness Travel Guides). $29.95 flexibinding. ISBN 0-7894-0425-7.

The Eyewitness Travel Guides are visual encyclopedic guidebooks that feature 3-D aerial drawings of districts and historical buildings and much more. In this volume on Italy, there are some 1,400 full-color photographs and many useful maps. There are 15 regional chapters that give detailed information on all aspects of each region. The book offers historical and cultural overviews; describes important sites with helpful maps and illustrations; covers regional food specialties; supplies data on hotels and restaurants; and gives practical information concerning transportation, shopping, etiquette, tours, the police, medical problems, banking, currency, and so on. It is not often that one finds an index in a travel book—this one contains a comprehensive general index that can help one pinpoint a subject in a little amount of time. The illustrations are a delight to the eye and the copious data on the various areas are staggering.

This well-designed publication has a durable binding with a sewn endband that defies splitting. *Italy* is a travel guide built to take the rigors of hard travel, one that will last for many trips and not fall apart after one short visit. The pages are of glossy paper so that the full-color illustrations stand out brilliantly. The editorial staff has put together an excellent volume that contains much more useful data than the average guidebook. Anyone who looks through this book will surely want to take the next flight to Italy. The guide is highly recommended for a trip to Italy, or if a trip is not imminent, for use in preparation for a future visit. It has it all!—**Robert Palmieri**

Spain

396. **Spain.** New York, DK Publishing, 1996. 672p. illus. maps. index. (Eyewitness Travel Guides). $29.95 flexibinding. ISBN 0-7894-1068-0.

A high level of detail, profuse color photographs and illustrations, and a nonlinear layout mark this guide as a DK publication. More than 650 pages, brimming with facts and photographs, introduce readers to the sights and delights of Spain. Arranged by broad geographic region (e.g., northern Spain, central Spain), the book also contains entire sections on the cities of Barcelona and Madrid and on the Spanish islands, some of the country's more popular destinations for tourists. In addition, there are maps; traveler's tips; a guide to hotels and restaurants; a brief phrase book of Spanish terms; and a general overview of the country's history, climate, landscape, architecture, industries, flora and fauna, art and literature, festivals, sports, and people.

This is a well-made book, of a size compact enough to pack along on a trip, and the text is clear and well written. The index is thorough and pages are even color-coded by area for quick reference. Seemingly there is nothing missing from this book, which may be its biggest weakness. While photographs are profuse and text is plentiful, the size of both print and illustrations tends to be small, so the overall effect is a little too busy. Also, some of the photograph captions do not clearly indicate the content of the pictures but rather comment on them. These complaints are, perhaps, minor in such an impressive publication. However, would-be travelers may want to compare this to other similar guides. One impressive alternative is the Insight Guide, *Spain* (2d ed., APA Publications [HK] Ltd., 1994). In fewer pages and at a lower price ($19.95), it covers the same territory. It does not have as many photographs, but there are plenty that are larger and therefore more dramatic. The layout is, if more pedestrian, also more straightforward, and the writing is excellent. The Insight Guide also contains feature articles on flamenco, Spanish painting, bullfighting, and so on. Tourists who desire a more in-depth look at these Spanish traditions may prefer the Insight Guide to the DK one. On the other hand, the book under review is newer, and therefore some of the information is more up-to-date. Both guides are excellent and there are many others available, so if travelers want only one book, they should consider their options.—**Barbara Ittner**

9 History

ARCHAEOLOGY

397. **An Encyclopedia of the History of Classical Archaeology.** Nancy Thomson de Grummond, ed. Westport, Conn., Greenwood Press, 1996. 2v. illus. index. $225.00/set. ISBN 0-313-22066-2.

Classical Archaeology is defined as the study of the visual remains of the ancient classical lands, Greece and Italy, plus the historical or protohistorical cultures of the Bronze Age Aegean and the Etruscans. This compilation is the first comprehensive encyclopedia of the field. Its value is enhanced by the fact that the editor-compiler has included manifestations of the classical cultures outside of Italy and Greece as well as the study of classical antiquity during the Middle Ages, the Renaissance, and the seventeenth and eighteenth centuries. Biographical and interpretive entries for travelers, collectors, artists, and scholars whose studies and works have added to the knowledge of the sites and monuments and to archaeological scholarship have also been included.

The 1,125 entries cover persons, sites, monuments, works of art, and archaeological terms. Many were written by the 170 contributors, others by the editor. Arranged alphabetically by main entry word, the entries give both historical and descriptive information, references to sources where the artifact or monument has been cited, and a short bibliography prepared by the contributor. Supplementary sections contain a chronology of the history of classical archaeology from 480 B.C.E. to 1989 C.E.; a 7-page selected bibliography by Joann McDaniel; a 73-page, detailed index of names and subjects in 1 alphabetic sequence; and a list of contributors with identifications and qualifications.

This much-needed compilation will, of course, be an essential tool for students, teachers, and writers concerned with classical studies. It should also be of great interest and help to art historians and scholars in the subject areas of ancient history, architecture, and the humanities.—**Shirley L. Hopkinson**

398. Peregrine, Peter N. **Archaeology of the Mississippian Culture: A Research Guide.** New York, Garland, 1996. 192p. index. (Research Guides to Ancient Civilizations, v.6; Garland Reference Library of the Humanities, v.1457). $35.00. ISBN 0-8153-0336-X.

This sixth title in the Research Guides to Ancient Civilizations series covers the North American Mississippian civilization that existed from 800 to 1600 C.E. Aiming at the nonspecialist reader, Peregrine, who has published several articles on the subject, has compiled more than 500 annotated entries that meet his criteria of being easily accessible, written by serious scholars, and, except for certain classics, written during the past 15 years.

The arrangement starts with general surveys, goes through cultural history and sociopolitical organization, settlement, subsistence and economic organization, and into those papers that focus on a specific or regional site. All entries have full bibliographic citations and extremely clear and well-written annotations discussing both the scope and conclusions of the work. Access to the entries is provided through author, place-name, and subject indexes.

Peregrine has added to the worth of the book with his introductory essay, which not only discusses theories of Mississippian culture, but also offers copious suggestions for further research, including state archaeological and historical societies and Internet access to online catalogs and databases. This is a thorough and user-friendly work that should be available in academic and larger public libraries throughout the central and southeastern United States.—**Deborah Hammer**

AMERICAN HISTORY

Almanacs

399. Purvis, Thomas L. **Revolutionary America 1763-1800.** New York, Facts on File, 1995. 383p. illus. maps. index. (Almanacs of American Life). $70.00. ISBN 0-8160-2528-2.

Traditionally, librarians have had to consult diverse sources for statistics, facts, and perspectives to illuminate the living conditions that prevailed in the parts of the United States that had been settled by Europeans prior to the nineteenth century. Oft-consulted publications have ranged from such periodicals as *American Heritage* and *Smithsonian* to histories by such writers as J. C. Furnas, Alice Morse Earle, and Daniel J. Boorstin. Lamentably, *Historical Statistics of the United States* devotes less than 3 percent of its purview to the period 1607-1789.

Purvis's aim in this volume is to obviate the need for such research. The extensiveness of the interdisciplinary approach he used in compiling and assimilating the information in his handbook is shown by a sampling of the work's 19 chapter titles: "Native American Life," "Diet and Health," "Arts and Letters," "Science and Technology," "Popular Life and Recreations," and "Crime and Violence." A thematic bibliography, an appendix of tables, and a 43-page index complete this, the second volume of the Almanacs of American Life series.

Within each chapter, an abundance of ancillary data and illustrations appears. Hundreds of boxed statistics and lists accompany a text that is laden in example. In one chapter, for instance, a discussion of factors effecting the movement of state capitals is juxtaposed against tables listing these capitals and tracing the chronologies of their respective congressional sessions and relocations. Dozens of reproductions ably render such subjects as floorplans, portraits, and newspaper advertisements.

Two signal features of this volume highlight the contributions made by certain eighteenth-century individuals. The first consists of the profiles of 23 persons, among whom are such regularly neglected figures as Native American sympathizer Simon Girty, printer/postmaster Mary Katherine Goddard, and sharpshooter Timothy Murphy. The second feature is the series of verbatim accounts of life by a Seneca-kidnapped white woman, a Continental Army veteran, and a Kentucky farm boy.

No errors and few weaknesses are evident in this milestone reference. Among said weaknesses, the work's running heads, inconspicuously situated at the foot of each page's bicolumnar layout, should appear at the top of each sheet. Military data, warranting their own chapter, are buried within the already bloated "Government" chapter. Benjamin Franklin's proposal for daylight saving time is absent from the "Holidays and Calendar" chapter. Finally, there are only three maps throughout the book, encompassing the entire U.S. landmass east of the Mississippi River. These oversights stated, Purvis's achievement is a dazzling one; bejeweled with statistics, this is a reference source that few libraries should do without. [R: BR, Jan/Feb 96, p. 57; SLJ, Feb 96, pp. 126-27; Choice, Feb 96, p. 932]—**Jeffrey E. Long**

400. Shifflett, Crandall. **Victorian America, 1876 to 1913.** New York, Facts on File, 1996. 408p. illus. maps. index. (Almanacs of American Life). $70.00. ISBN 0-8160-2531-2.

This volume provides readers with a broad picture of life in the United States between 1876 and 1913 in all its various aspects, using text, photographs, charts, lists, chronologies, and statistics. The book is attractive in appearance and is well organized for ease of use. Individual chapters are devoted to climate, natural history, Native Americans, the economy, population, religion, government, education, literature, science and technology, sports and popular culture, and crime. Other chapters include selected biographical sketches, relevant documents of the period, and data on each of the 50 states and major cities. A subject index provides access to the contents.

The compilers present the positive and negative sides of life in this country during the time period covered. Song titles of the 1890s reveal the extent of racism, while certain documents illustrate the bigotry of many U.S. citizens toward Catholics, immigrants, and other groups. While the compilers generally accomplish their purpose, this reviewer was less than satisfied with several aspects of the book. Chapter authors are not identified, and the text is not very well written. In an attempt to be concise, narrative sections too often give insufficient information. Abbreviations are occasionally used without identification, and careless errors are a cause for concern. Little space is devoted to the major war of the period (the Spanish-American War), while the capsule histories of North and South Carolina incorrectly refer to the eight proprietors as noblemen and the "Carolina" colony of 1663 as the "Carolinas." Such topics as the Philippine Insurrection and U.S. imperialism are scarcely treated. The work further falls short by the fact that terms and events are frequently referred to without clarification under the apparent assumption that readers will already be familiar with them. The almanac is therefore recommended with reservations for libraries needing material on this period of U.S. history.—**Donald E. Collins**

Archives

401. **The Civil War CD-ROM: The War of the Rebellion. A Compilation of the Official Records of the Union and Confederate Armies.** [CD-ROM]. Indianapolis, Ind., Guild Press, 1996. Minimum system requirements: IBM or compatible 386 (Pentium 100 recommended). CD-ROM drive (4x or higher recommended). Windows 3.1 (Windows 95 recommended). 4MB RAM (16MB RAM recommended). $69.95. ISBN 1-878208-76-4.

This CD-ROM is a major contribution to Civil War research. It includes three of the most important standard works on the subject, as well as two supplemental works to aid researchers in the use of the primary volumes. The keystone title, *The War of the Rebellion: A Compilation of the Official Records of the Union and Confederate Armies*, was originally published in 128 volumes between 1881 and 1900. This series, popularly referred to as simply the *Official Records* or *OR*, is the single most used and valuable source for research on this war. Frederick Dyer's monumental three-volume *A Compendium of the American Civil War (1861-1865)* (1908) complements OR with statistical data and capsule histories of all Union army regiments. William F. Fox's *Regimental Losses in the American Civil War (1861-1865)*, published in 1889, provides almost 600 pages of text and statistics regarding the losses of Union and some Confederate regiments. Alan and Barbara Aimone's *A User's Guide to the Official Records of the American Civil War* (White Mane Publishing, 1993) provides users with an overview of the history and significance of OR.

The fifth title on the CD-ROM is *Military Operations of the Civil War: A Guide Index to the Official Records of the Union and Confederate Armies* (Government Printing Office, 1968-). This work consists of a reindexing effort of OR done at the National Archives in the 1950s and 1960s. The five-volume guide supplies information and references to pages on geographic places as well as military actions arranged by theater of operations, state, county, and date. Cross-references are given to data in the army records, as well as to the *Official Records of the Union and Confederate Navies* (Government Printing Office, 1894-1922) and the *Official Atlas* (T. Yoseloff, 1958), these latter two do not appear on the CD-ROM). Guild Press has greatly added to the usefulness of this title through the provision of tens of thousands of hypertext jumps from the *Guide Index* to the actual documents in the Army Official Records.

As a Civil War historian and former reference librarian, this reviewer is impressed with the ability of the CD-ROM to speed research that until now has been tedious and time-consuming. The review copy of this disc was easily installed and was successfully put to immediate use for an article on North Carolinians in the Union army. Documents were quickly found, retrieved, and printed. This represents a significant timesaving feature over the former method of relying on the cumbersome and inadequate cumulative index to OR that sends users to 1 or more of the 128 individual volume indexes rather than to specific documents and pages.

The search features of this CD-ROM are excellent. Search methods and procedures are clearly explained on-screen via the Help key. Users are given the choice of simple one-word searches that include all but such common words as "the," "and," and so forth, or of carrying out advanced searches using Boolean operators AND, OR, NOT, and NEAR. Proximity searches may be set from as little as two to as many as thousands of words. Field searching allows retrieval of documents by the signer, addressee, and date sent. Users are further given the option to carry out a search in a single multivolume set, a single volume, or in every title on the CD-ROM. Books may also be read page-by-page or by jumps made to specific pages. References to documents found are listed for quick retrieval, and search words are highlighted in the text for easy recognition. Other useful features include the ability to bookmark documents and to save them in subject file folders.

This is an important contribution to small libraries that heretofore could not afford the essential OR, as well as the other works on this disc, and for the many college, university, and public libraries whose sets are missing volumes or are in disrepair with torn pages and broken spines from frequent use. This CD-ROM is highly recommended for all libraries, professional and amateur historians, students, hobbyists, and all with an interest in the Civil War.—**Donald E. Collins**

Atlases

402. Carnes, Mark C., and John A. Garraty, with Patrick Williams. **Mapping America's Past: A Historical Atlas.** New York, Henry Holt, 1996. 288p. illus. maps. index. $50.00. ISBN 0-8050-4927-4.

According to Carnes, a good historical atlas condenses the fog of the past into streams of meaning, revealing not just what happened but what mattered. This filtering of the gritty ambiguities of the past is what makes historical atlases so appealing and the authors' stated reason for producing this product. The authors of this atlas focus on incorporating statistical information in examining public or scholarly debates (e.g., maps of population density to consider the impact of frontier conditions on human fertility). Their perspective has been influenced by the tremendous expansion of social and cultural history during the past 30 years. For example, the authors profess to have devoted more space to gender and sexuality than to the American Revolution. Yet they state that while social and cultural history adds color and depth to the historical landscape, such topics can never overshadow the political and military struggles that carve its contours, illustrated by nearly 200 maps. Nearly 100 maps of other countries are also included in this atlas, as the United States is a nation of immigrants with its history deriving from many societies and cultures.

According to *Books in Print*, this work is the most recent edition of any historical atlas on the United States currently in print. The volume is divided into nine parts: "Pre-Columbian America," "Colonial America," "A New Nation," "Slavery and the Civil War," "America in the Gilded Age," "America in the Early 20th Century," "Post-War America," "America and the World after World War II," and "America, an Evolving Superpower." The work contains extensive bibliographical sources and notes and an adequate index.

The 1993 revision (originally published in 1988) of National Geographic Society's *Historical Atlas of the United States* (see ARBA 95, entry 525) is a far superior product. It excels in captioned graphics that include many era photographs and artifacts in addition to maps and charts. The color and print quality is also much better. The National Geographic atlas contains useful, clear, and concise timelines, which are lacking in the volume at hand. In addition, the National Geographic product more broadly portrays diversity over a longer period of time. *Mapping America's Past* does provide more in-depth narrative; however, National Geographic's product is much more visually appealing and probably covers sufficient information that the typical user would be seeking.

Mapping America's Past would be a suitable complement in the reference collection of high school, public, and undergraduate libraries. However, it would best be offered as a circulating copy of a historical atlas due to its smaller size (12-by-9-inches). Finally, for a volume on the United States' past, information feels more authentic coming from such an established American institution as National Geographic than from the collaborative effort of researchers in the United Kingdom, Canada, and the United States, as is the volume under review.—**Sharon Thomerson**

Bibliography

403. **Benjamin Rush, M.D.: A Bibliographic Guide.** Fox, Claire G., Gordon L. Miller, and Jacquelyn C. Miller, comps. Westport, Conn., Greenwood Press, 1996. 216p. index. (Bibliographies and Indexes in American History, no.31). $79.50. ISBN 0-313-29823-8.

Despite a title that implies that this is simply a medical bibliography, the work under review is in fact a fascinating resource for the thoughts on the formative years of the United States by a man who was a physician, an educator, a social advocate, and a political activist. Benjamin Rush was a member of the Continental Congress, a signer of the Declaration of Independence, the first U.S. professor of chemistry, a pioneer abolitionist, a temperance advocate, and a proponent of prison reform. This bibliography reflects all of these concerns.

Historians of the American Revolution and the early national period will find this a valuable resource for identifying and locating works by and about Rush. Arranged chronologically by year, each entry provides complete bibliographic information, lists all editions of each title, and identifies libraries in which each work may be found. The bibliography is preceded by a vita and a chronology of Rush's life, and a bibliographic essay that categorizes his writings by topic. Indexes provide quick access to authors, titles, and subjects. This work is recommended for libraries with an interest in early U.S. and medical history. [R: Choice, Dec 96, p. 589]—**Donald E. Collins**

404. Bertuca, David J., Donald K. Hartman, and Susan M. Neumeister, comps. **The World's Columbian Exposition: A Centennial Bibliographic Guide.** Westport, Conn., Greenwood Press, 1996. 440p. illus. index. (Bibliographies and Indexes in American History, no.26). $85.00. ISBN 0-313-26644-1.

In commemoration of the 400th anniversary of Christopher Columbus's voyage, the Chicago World's Fair of 1893 was situated on 633 acres and hosted more than 27 million visitors. Modeling itself on the Paris Exhibition, the Chicago planners developed a fiscal plan and international contacts and hired Frederick Law Olmsted as landscape artist and the architectural partners of Daniel Hudson Burnham and John Wellborn Root. The expense and planning were a good investment, as the Columbian Exposition was noted for its elegant and innovative architecture and landscapes. The sculptures, the waterways, transportation, electric lighting, and the amusement area were unique attractions, but the Exposition is also famous for its contributions to arts and sciences. The event witnessed the stock market crash of 1893, the first Ferris wheel, an address by Frederick Douglass on "The Race Problem in America," Aunt Jemima's first pancake, Buffalo Bill's Wild West Show, and the inaugural sessions of many prestigious academic congresses.

In a few short years, many of the buildings had succumbed to neglect or were accidentally destroyed by fire, or deliberately pulled down in the interest of municipal progress. What remains is a legacy of contemporary and current documents describing the numerous aspects of the fair. Unfortunately, these sources are scattered throughout the United States and the world. Meticulously researched, this bibliography covers 26 subject approaches to the literature. Individual entries are accurate, consistent, and frequently annotated. The compilers also describe major archival collections and include in their description useful institutional access policies. The index to the volume is both detailed and straightforward. Aside from providing an excellent and unique bibliography of the Columbian Exposition, this reference book is also a model of the bibliographer's art. [R: Choice, Nov 96, p. 425]—**Mary Hemmings**

405. Hardaway, Roger D. **A Narrative Bibliography of the African American Frontier: Blacks in the Rocky Mountain West, 1535-1912.** Lewiston, N.Y., Edwin Mellen Press, 1995. 242p. index. (Studies in American History, v.9). $89.95. ISBN 0-7734-8879-0.

The uninitiated will be surprised by the range of dates in this bibliography's title, indicating as it does that the first African American to traverse the American West did so more than 450 years ago. Those centuries of abuse and small victories are explicated in chapters on topics such as the buffalo soldiers, discrimination issues, mountain men, farmers and ranchers, the mining industry, and women. Individual bibliographic entries are given thorough narratives that are typically several sentences in length with each of the 15 chapters featuring a separate introductory essay. Entries appropriate for younger readers are identified (a commendable service).

The book concludes with several indexes: by state names, by journal names, and by personal names and subjects. It is unsurprising that most of the journals indexed are regional in scope and rather obscure. This, of course, adds to the value of Hardaway's in-depth annotations. It seems unlikely that most students of the topic could ever see these materials firsthand. Annotated bibliographies often substitute for a textbook, and this one could comfortably fill that role. While this is neither an inexpensive nor a visually appealing volume, its purchase seems natural for collections in Western Americana or African American studies. [R: Choice, May 96, p. 1448; C&RL, Sept 96, pp. 468-69]—**Ed Volz**

406. Merriam, Louise A., and James W. Oberly, comps. **United States History: A Bibliography of the New Writings on American History.** Manchester, England, Manchester University Press; distr., New York, St. Martin's Press, 1996. 227p. index. (History and Related Disciplines Select Bibliographies). $60.00. ISBN 0-7190-3688-7.

This is a bibliography of what the compilers believe to be the most important books and articles in U.S. history written during the 1980s and 1990s. Included also are earlier works considered to be either too significant to be omitted or the most recent, although dated, studies on the topic. The intended audience is broad, ranging from persons with a casual interest in history to the scholar. Selected bibliographies are included to send readers to works not included in this volume. The inclusion of dictionaries, encyclopedias, and atlases enables users to find specific reference information. This book is the work of librarians and historians who joined together to develop an appropriate historical organizational pattern and to select historical studies for inclusion. The contents are arranged in 10 chronological categories, each of which is subdivided by subject. A more specific alphabetic subject and author index provides another avenue of access.

This reviewer, who has had long careers as a U.S. historian and a reference librarian, finds much to criticize in this volume. The 4,000 titles listed are insufficient to do more than touch the surface of most areas of history. Users may come away with a single, several, or no works on the topic of interest. Although the purpose is to select the best books, it fails in this task, and the selection is often poor. Annotations are not included for journal articles, and those annotations for books are only descriptive, leaving no clue to the significance or importance of a work in the particular field. This reviewer was disappointed in the selections for his areas of expertise. Japanese Americans, included under the more general Asian American heading, merit 12 titles. Inexplicably, five of these are about Hawaii, and none of the remaining seven are on the evacuation and internment of World War II, despite the fact that it is one of the most important events in their history. Under the Civil War heading, campaigns are divided between the western and Virginia fronts. There is no section for eastern events outside of Virginia. General William Tecumseh Sherman's march to the sea is misplaced among works on the western front.

One final note of criticism needs to be made. The two primary compilers failed to identify those persons involved in selecting titles for this book other than the provision of a single combined list of authors, editors, and compilers, without distinction. Because the quality of a work depends on knowing who did the work, this is a significant omission. The subject index needs further work to be of real value. Many entries are too broad for easy retrieval of items. The 21 references under Franklin Delano Roosevelt, for example, lack subdivisions, causing the user to look under each entry to find a specific aspect of his life or administration. The compilers should be commended for a worthy effort, but the task needs a work of much greater volume, and the problems cited above need to be eradicated. Meanwhile, the audience group this work aims at should consider outstanding historical bibliographies such as *America: History and Life* (see ARBA 96, entry 512, for a review of the CD-ROM version). The title under review is not recommended.—**Donald E. Collins**

Biography

407. **American First Ladies: Their Lives and Their Legacy.** Lewis L. Gould, ed. New York, Garland, 1996. 686p. illus. index. $95.00. ISBN 0-8153-1479-5.

This is a fascinating account of the first ladies of the United States from Martha Washington to Hillary Rodham Clinton. A separate chapter is devoted to each first lady, and each is written by a different scholar. For all first ladies there are a portrait, a chronological account of her life, an evaluation of her place in developing the role of first lady, selections from her own writings, recollections of family and friends, important newspaper articles and scholarly writings, and the location of her personal papers and other manuscript sources.

The book successfully gives a sense of personality and appeal of each first lady and discusses any precedents she set while occupying the White House. This is a well-rounded account that presents the problems, controversies, and perceptions by her peers that each first lady faced. One can also get a picture of how the role of first lady has changed from the beginning of the country to the present and how it reflects the period in which she lived. A lengthy subject index at the back of the volume, which includes topics such as assassinations, artists who performed at the White House, health of first ladies, and so forth, enables the reader to find specific information quickly. This book will be of value both to the casual reader who simply wishes to read interesting accounts of first ladies and to the scholar who is doing serious research. It belongs on the shelves of all libraries. [R: Choice, Oct 96, p. 247; RBB, Aug 96, p. 1920; SLJ, Aug 96, p. 186; VOYA, Dec 96, p. 297]—**Marilyn Strong Noronha**

408. **American Reform and Reformers: A Biographical Dictionary.** Randall M. Miller and Paul A. Cimbala, eds. Westport, Conn., Greenwood Press, 1996. 559p. index. $115.00. ISBN 0-313-28839-9.

This volume is far more than a biographical dictionary. The introduction includes an expanded definition of reform and an analysis of its role and context in U.S. history. Each of the 38 essays that follow combines biographical data with historical analysis of the specific reform movement for which each individual is known. The strength of the book lies in the in-depth treatment of the reform movements represented in the volume, and the importance of the role each of the biographees played in that movement.

Most of the individuals profiled in this dictionary represent reform movements of the late nineteenth through the twentieth century. Jane Addams, Cesar Chavez, John Dewey, Martin Luther King Jr., Margaret Sanger, and Russell Means are but a few examples of those included in the book. A wide range of topics includes education, unionism and labor reform, consumer rights, religious rights, and much more. Each of the essays is written by a notable expert in the field and provides notes and bibliographic references. A chronological chart of important events for reform movements in U.S. history from the revolutionary period to 1994 is also most helpful in understanding reform and its historical significance. An adequate index lends to its usefulness as a reference tool.

The dictionary is an excellent supplement of readings for the student or researcher of social history, or anyone interested in the historical treatment of reform movements. Its basic drawback is its price. At $115, the work is recommended for academic libraries with strong liberal arts and social history strengths; however, this volume may only receive casual use in public libraries, precluding its purchase from all but larger libraries. [R: Choice, July/Aug 96, p. 1767; RBB, 15 Mar 96, p. 1308]—**Susan Zernial**

409. Ancell, R. Manning, with Christine M. Miller. **The Biographical Dictionary of World War II Generals and Flag Officers: The U.S. Armed Forces.** Westport, Conn., Greenwood Press, 1996. 706p. index. $95.00. ISBN 0-313-29546-8.

Locating information about World War II flag officers and generals would have been an easy task in 1945 or 1946. Unfortunately, it took 50 years for the scholarship to catch up with the participants. Using such diverse sources as records at Carlisle Barracks (Army War College), files at the Naval Historical Center, and biographical materials at Arlington National Cemetery, among others, the authors have completed to the 99 percent-level basic information for each officer. For approximately 1 percent of the officers, information could not be found beyond the basic name-and-rank level.

The volume is arranged by service (Army, Navy, Marine Corps, Coast Guard, Air Force, National Guard). Entries include birth and death dates, service record, decorations, and post-service records for some individuals. As an example of the difficulty in researching this volume, Brigadier General Francis Augustus Woolfley was born in 1893, but no death date could be found. There is of course the possibility that he is still alive, but the authors could find no current pension records, so his death will remain a mystery. The entries are done well but are, of necessity, brief. Two appendixes are provided: a summary count of birthplaces (by state and service) and birthdate (by year and service), and a list of officers who died during World War II. There is also a name index, which is useful considering the volume is arranged by service.

The volume is exhaustively researched, but there are no illustrations. Libraries with patrons interested in military history, World War II, and genealogy will want to collect this book. [R: Choice, Oct 96, p. 247; RBB, 1 May 96, p. 1519]—**Ralph Lee Scott**

410. **Roots of the Republic.** Danbury, Conn., Grolier, 1996. 6v. illus. maps. index. $159.00/set. ISBN 0-7172-7608-2.

This set pulls together, in an attractive, hardbound format, basic information about the founding of and the "movers and shakers" in the U.S. government. The major portion of the material consists of biographical sketches 1.5 to 3 pages in length, with black-and-white photographs or pen-and-ink drawings of most persons profiled. This information is usually available only in scattered sources.

Unfortunately, the set lacks a clear sense of audience. The first two volumes especially need to be read with a book on U.S. history at hand. Plenty of adjectives describe the biographees, but there is often a paucity of hard information. Too many references will be puzzling to young readers. Few are likely to know the meaning of "born to the purple" or "straight-laced" in a day when class and behavior are defined so differently from what they were 200 years ago. Occasionally, someone is described in terms of political outlook without defining phrases; for example, ". . . it was equally difficult to decide whether he was a Federalist or a Democrat." The remainder of the set is stronger, with personalities and achievements of the chief justices of the United States more clearly defined. The sketch of Bill Clinton sounds partisan. All books have useful essays, such as "The Accomplishments of the First Congress" and "The Power of Judicial Review." The set needs a firmer editorial hand.

These volumes could serve as supplementary material for U.S. history classes. The set possesses thorough indexes and scholarly bibliographies. [R: BL, 15 Oct 96, p. 452]—**Edna M. Boardman**

411. Scanlon, Jennifer, and Shaaron Cosner. **American Women Historians, 1700s-1990s: A Biographical Dictionary.** Westport, Conn., Greenwood Press, 1996. 269p. illus. index. $75.00. ISBN 0-313-29664-2.

Scanlon and Cosner, both educators, have compiled the first biographical dictionary of U.S. women historians. Two hundred women of diverse backgrounds were selected for inclusion based on their publications and their participation in defining a certain field of study. Hence, the specific historical fields covered range from architectural history, religious history, and the history of sexuality to world history and local history of various regions and states. Each historian is given a one- to two-page biography with emphasis on her educational background and career, especially her publications; personal information is minimal. Each entry includes a bibliography of the historian's publications as well as a list of where further information about her can be located. There is a general bibliography for the entire volume and an index by name and historical subject specialty.

While many of the names, such as Ariel Durant, Alice Morse Earle, and Barbara Tuchman, are familiar to many, other women are listed here for the first time, such as Sarah Elbert, a cultural historian of the nineteenth-century United States, and Bettye M. Collier-Thomas, who studied African American social history. A collection of photographs adds to the work. This is a unique, valuable reference source that should be available in college, university, and public library reference centers.—**Deborah Hammer**

Chronology

412. **African American History in the Press 1851-1899: From the Coming of the Civil War....** Detroit, Gale, 1996. 2v. illus. index. $150.00/set. ISBN 0-8103-9555-X.

This anthology reprints more than 1,200 articles of editorials and 470 illustrations, mostly from the Richard C. Schneider Collection, that pertain to African America during the period 1851 to 1899. Of the 13 newspapers excerpted, 5 of them are represented by 5 articles/illustrations or less. Of the remaining, the most frequently reprinted is *Harper's Weekly* (more than 13 columns in the newspaper index) and second, *The New York Times* (just less than 2 index columns). This anthology was selected from the newspapers of New York City, with significant supplementary material from Boston, Richmond, Charleston, and Atlanta.

The selections are arranged chronologically by date published. Each year is a chapter and includes a brief but adequate introduction by one of the four scholars listed as "Advisors" (their role in selecting articles, if any, is not made explicit). Each reprint includes title or caption, newspaper, date, and page number. The book is nicely produced and the reproductions of cartoons and engravings are well done (although some readers will need a magnifying glass to read the captions). Volume 1 begins with Schneider's moralizing introduction, an elementary map, and a chronology of African American history for the period. Volume 2 concludes with brief histories of the newspapers and indexes for newspapers, illustrations, and keywords.

Emphasis is given to firsthand accounts of important events (e.g., John Brown's activities, Ku Klux Klan atrocities) but includes some more homely material depicting the everyday life of African Americans. This anthology will be frequently consulted by undergraduates and high school students, and it will be useful to scholars beginning research.—**Fred J. Hay**

Dictionaries and Encyclopedias

413. **Colonial Wars of North America, 1512-1763: An Encyclopedia.** Alan Gallay, ed. New York, Garland, 1996. 856p. illus. maps. index. $95.00. ISBN 0-8240-7208-1.

Defining warfare broadly so as to include both military and diplomatic events, this excellent encyclopedia provides details on battles, wars, treaties, places, forts, weapons, individual colonies, imperial rivalries, and Native American groups, from 1512 (Juan Ponce de León's discovery of Florida) to 1763 (the end of both Pontiac's War and the Seven Years' War). Contributors are historians and experts in their fields from several countries, and have used both primary and secondary source materials in covering their subjects in more detail than *Encyclopedia of the North American Colonies* (see ARBA 95, entry 540).

The 650-plus signed articles, which include approximately 150 biographical profiles, range from a paragraph to several pages in length. There are numerous black-and-white illustrations and maps, a chronology, many cross-references, and an overall subject index. The editor has purposely avoided the customary Anglocentric focus and includes coverage of the Spanish Southwest, Alaska, Canada, African-American soldiers, and the West Indies, as well as the traditional 13 colonies. No doubt some students will be confused by the placement of entries on forts under their proper name; hence, Fort Lawrence is under *L*. Although it lacks an overall historiographical article, this volume more than makes up for it by including subject matter that has long been neglected, and is a welcome addition to the literature on colonial North America.—**John A. Drobnicki**

414. **Dictionary of American History Supplement.** Robert H. Ferrell and Joan Hoff, eds. New York, Scribner's/Simon & Schuster Macmillan, 1996. 2v. index. $200.00/set. ISBN 0-684-19579-8.

This two-volume set is a supplement for the *Dictionary of American History* (DAH) (see ARBA 77, entry 384). All together, the supplement contains 757 entries by 340 authors. Entries are arranged alphabetically, from the American Association of Retired Persons to zoology; each one ends with suggestions for additional reading and a cross-reference to related subjects in the DAH. Readers should be aware that biographies do not appear, in deference to Scribner's companion work, the *Dictionary of American Biography* (see ARBA 96, entry 36, for a review of supplement 10). This work also has a brief essay in the front describing the sweeping changes that have occurred in the United States and the world community in the 20 years since the last revision of the DAH. A directory of contributors, an alphabetic list of entries, and an index round out the set.

Entries often reflect recent trends in the historical profession. Social and cultural topics receive great attention, and a real effort is made to be inclusive. Music Television (MTV), rock and roll, and numerous references to sports reflect the increasing preoccupation of historians and others with popular culture. Concentration on the part minorities and women have played in the past counteracts a lingering bias in the bicentennial revision of the DAH. African Americans, Native Americans, Asian Americans, Hispanics, and females are no longer slighted. Of course, it is possible to find omissions (examples being New Federalism, original intent, and Hootie and the Blowfish), but these amount to picayune criticisms. The supplement is well written, balanced, and comprehensive, and strongly recommended for public libraries, high schools, colleges, and universities. [R: RBB, 1 Nov 96, p. 534]—**Richard E. Holl**

415. **Encyclopedia of the American West.** Charles Phillips and Alan Axelrod, eds. New York, Macmillan Library Reference/Simon & Schuster Macmillan, 1996. 4v. illus. maps. index. $375.00/set. ISBN 0-02-897495-6.

This four-volume work is truly encyclopedic in its coverage of the West's history during the eighteenth and nineteenth centuries. The preface states that all the 23 states west of the Missouri River are covered in the more than 1,700 entries, written by approximately 400 authors. However, it should be noted that of these 1,700 entries, about 290 were written by the editors, and 145 by a single, other person. The time limits of the set are given as from ca.1803 (the Louisiana Purchase, Daniel Boone, the American Fur Company, and so forth) to the end of the nineteenth century, with occasional spillover into the twentieth century (cowboys, Roy Rogers and Dale Evans, Theodore Roosevelt). Following the preface is a list of all contributors and their affiliations.

The text is a judicious mix of subject and biographical articles, about equal in number, although the former are generally longer. Typical biographies run from about three-quarters of a page (e.g., Calamity Jane, Chief Joseph, Peter Ogden), while a few run to a full page or more (e.g., George Armstrong Custer, John C. Frémont, John Muir). More than 1,000 black-and-white photographs and maps illustrate the articles. Topical articles are interestingly written, on such subjects as disease, divorce, the fur trade, intermarriage, and the noble savage theory (although this article makes no mention of either Jean-Jacques Rousseau or François-Auguste-René de Chateaubriand). Also, articles on specific subjects (e.g., Ghost Dance, Penitentes, Virginia City) are done well. Instead of brief articles on the separate Indian tribes or peoples, all are included in a rather top-heavy omnibus article, "Native American Peoples," with nine subdivisions—not quite so useful.

The usage of maps is peculiar and somewhat unsatisfactory. With rare exceptions, there is but one map used throughout. This is a reduction of the map of the United States as a whole, which forms the endpapers. It is a natural-features-only map. For each western state, this map is reused, with the outline of the pertinent state drawn upon it. The only city named on each map is the state capital. Thus, the map of Nevada locates neither Reno nor Las Vegas.

Each article is signed, and most have a bibliography attached. There are *see also* references, and cross-references within the text are printed in "capitol" (sic) letters. In a work of this magnitude, some inconsistency is bound to occur. One article claims that Zane Grey "invented the popular western novel." Elsewhere, the same author says that he "established and refined the genre that Owen Wister had created." Biographical articles repeat information normally found for prominent people in standard encyclopedias, but errors may occur for lesser-known names. The entry for Jedediah Smith contains three of them: the words "Because of [problems with the Mexicans]" should read "Despite [the problems] he was able to rejoin his men." The year 1839 is a misprint for 1830 (Smith died in 1831). Finally, the words "the California" in the bibliography should read "the Californians."

This encyclopedic work, with its excellent index and with a listing of all biographees arranged by occupation or profession, brings together a tremendous amount of condensed information—names, dates, trends, conflicts, heroes and villains, all the wide variety of western lifestyles—and presents it all to the public in a single alphabetic order, easy to use, well illustrated, and well written. The set is recommended for any academic or public library in the United States. [R: LJ, 1 Nov 96, p. 58; RBB, 1 Dec 96, p. 680]
—**Raymund F. Wood**

416. **Encyclopedia of the United States in the Twentieth Century.** Stanley I. Kutler and others, eds. New York, Scribner's/Simon & Schuster Macmillan, 1996. 4v. illus. maps. index. $385.00/set. ISBN 0-13-210535-7.

As the editors of this splendid encyclopedia acknowledge, change is the only absolute in history, a truism easily supported by developments in twentieth-century America. The United States had few automobiles in 1900 and no airplanes, televisions, social security, Internet, women senators, AIDS, or suburban sprawl. The Northeast was the most densely populated section of the country, and white, Protestant, Anglo-Saxon males dominated society everywhere. Today, by contrast, California and Texas are the nation's most populous states, and pluralism and multiculturalism are societal hallmarks. Eighty contributors to this encyclopedia offer explanations for and analyses of such changes.

Organizationally, this work is divided into six major parts: the American people; politics; global America; science, technology, and medicine; the economy; and culture. Subsumed under each of these headings are interpretive essays dealing with everything from gender, class, bureaucracy, and limited wars to evolution, nontraditional religions, mass culture, and industrial research. Aiding access to this information is an exhaustive index. Minor errors and omissions are unavoidable in a work of this magnitude, and this one is no exception. Pat Robertson is a Baptist, not a Pentecostal (p. 1507), and the failure to include a feature on the religious right will puzzle some observers. Such trifles aside, however, this excellent encyclopedia will be of value to scholars and nonscholars alike, and municipal, high school, and college libraries should add it to their reference collections. [R: Choice, April 96, p. 1284; RBB, 1 Mar 96, pp. 1205-06; RQ, Summer, 96, pp. 556-57]—**John W. Storey**

417. **Encyclopedia USA: The Encyclopedia of the United States of America Past & Present. Volume 22: DNA - Dowling, Eddie.** Donald W. Whisenhunt, ed. Gulf Breeze, Fla., Academic International Press, 1995. 249p. $37.50. ISBN 0-87569-076-9.

This work, the 22d and most recent volume in the Encyclopedia USA series, contains 121 entries on various topics considered by the editor to be pertinent to the United States, past and present. Notwithstanding the subtitle of the series, the editor does not provide coverage on living people. Consequently, while the work furnishes information on Charles Fletcher Dole, James Drummond Dole, and Sanford Ballard Dole, it omits an entry for Robert J. Dole. Most (about 3 in 4) of the entries are approximately 2 pages (800-1,500 words) in length. Each entry concludes with a short bibliography. Occasionally, however, as in the cases of the little-known nineteenth-century politicians James Cochran

Dobbin and Andrew Jackson Donelson, the entries are twice the average length. Many of the contributors, who are identified with an author's byline following the bibliography, are academics employed in liberal arts colleges or small public universities.

Volume 22 is economically formatted. Following the title and dedication pages and a 2-page listing of the contributors, the first entry, "DNA," is placed on page 1—without an introduction, a preface, or a table of contents. Similarly, following the concluding entry on page 247, there is only a 2-page alphabetized listing of the entries and contributors. No index is included or mentioned in the volume. Apparently, however, a composite index for volumes 1-22 can be purchased separately from Academic International Press for $51. No graphs, charts, tables, illustrations, or photographs are included in this work. Although the volume contains some interesting information about dog shows, the Donner party, and the donkey of the Democratic Party, it will be of limited value to researchers or to serious students of the American past.—**Terry D. Bilhartz**

418. **Encyclopedia USA: The Encyclopedia of the United States of America Past & Present. Volume 23: Dowling, Richard William "Dick" - Dull Knife Campaign.** Donald W. Whisenhunt, ed. Gulf Breeze, Fla., Academic International Press, 1996. 249p. $37.50. ISBN 0-87569-076-9.

In the preface to volume 1, the editor of *Encyclopedia USA* wrote, "topics selected will be those of most interest and use to a wide readership." The latest installment of this multivolume encyclopedia, volume 23, continues to include entries that appeal to a diverse population. As with earlier volumes, 75 percent of the 128 entries are biographical, including many minor historical figures from a variety of backgrounds and occupations. A handful of entries cover broad themes, such as the draft, drama, and due process of law. This reviewer was surprised to see that the editor had not commissioned an essay on drugs in the United States. Instead, he added a narrower piece on the Drug Enforcement Administration, a subject that would have fit naturally into the broader subject.

The most useful entries are those that are treated briefly in other reference books, but given extended treatment in *Encyclopedia USA*. Examples of these include the Drago Doctrine, drive-in theaters, dry farming, and dugouts. As with its predecessors, volume 23 also has a few popular television and radio programs: *Dragnet* and *Dr. I.Q., the Mental Banker*, for example. Each essay concludes with a descriptive or evaluative bibliography and is signed by the author, who is usually affiliated with a college, university, or think tank. The least desirable aspect of this set is its glacial publication rate. With the publication of volume 23, the encyclopedia is almost through the letter D. At the current rate of one to two volumes a year, this title will not be complete until well into the next century. Nonetheless, it is recommended for summaries on many aspects of U.S. life. (See entry 417 for a review of volume 22.)—**John P. Stierman**

419. Purvis, Thomas L. **A Dictionary of American History.** Cambridge, Mass., Blackwell, 1995. 454p. $34.95. ISBN 1-55786-398-9.

In 1976, Scribner's published a revised edition of James Truslow Adams's classic multivolume *Dictionary of American History* (see ARBA 77, entry 384). The revised edition consists of 8 volumes, with 7,200 entries. A subject as vast as U.S. history requires such lengthy treatment. Anything less will exclude many significant historical events and thereby frustrate the curious user.

The latest entry in the field of inadequate, one-volume dictionaries on U.S. history is Purvis's *A Dictionary of American History*. In less than 500 pages, the author has collected an odd assortment of approximately 3,000 entries, including many well-known people and events, but excluding many others. For example, Purvis discusses some great writers, such as Sidney Lanier and Archibald MacLeish, but not others, such as Oliver Wendell Holmes Sr. and Eudora Welty. On the subject of 1960s activism, he lists the Student Nonviolent Coordinating Committee, but not Students for a Democratic Society. When it comes to sports, he includes the nineteenth-century boxer John Lawrence Sullivan, but excludes all-around great athlete and Native American Jim Thorpe.

The author could have made his intent clearer to the reader by adding an inclusion statement, explaining that the book is stronger in some areas, such as Native Americans or military history. He also could have made space for additional entries if he had excluded all biographical entries, as Adams did in his dictionary, only mentioning significant people within entries. If users want biographical information, they can use a biographical dictionary. Although there are some *see* references, there are not enough; students looking for information on the Bakke decision, for example, will not know to look under *Regents of University of California v. Bakke*.

Librarians who want to buy a solid, one-volume dictionary of U.S. history should order the *Concise Dictionary of American History* (see ARBA 84, entry 353), an abridged version of the eight-volume source mentioned previously, and still in print. Librarians who want more than a one-volume dictionary and already own the 1976 revised edition of the *Dictionary of American History* should consider acquiring the recently published, two-volume supplement to this classic (see entry 414). [R: Choice, May 96, pp. 1455-56]

—John P. Stierman

Handbooks and Yearbooks

420. **The ABC-CLIO Companion to American Reconstruction, 1862-1877.** By William L. Richter. Santa Barbara, Calif., ABC-CLIO, 1996. 505p. index. (ABC-CLIO Companions to Key Issues in American History and Life). $60.00. ISBN 0-87436-851-0.

Another in the publisher's series of encyclopedic guides to major events in U.S. history, what sets this book above the rest is the author's discussions of and observations on the nature and ramifications of Reconstruction. These are well explained in an extensive preface and introduction, as well in the lengthy entries that make up the body of the book.

In the preface, the author defines and describes the effort and era called Reconstruction. The introduction discusses various historians' treatment of the topic. Adding a contemporary interpretation, the author concludes that, since the 1960s civil rights movement, the entire cycle of a "Second Reconstruction" and conservative backlash have been repeated, resulting in "the profoundest irony of all: a viable Republican party in the South dominated by those very whites whose ancestors rode with the . . . Ku Klux Klan, leaving black Americans a dominant force in the Democratic party that had once crushed the hopes of their great-grandparents."

The ensuing 400-plus pages delve into the details of the era: people, places, events, trends, beliefs, laws, and policy issues. More than the bare recitation of facts, each entry offers historical interpretations, insights, and explanations of the relationships among seemingly unrelated important issues of the day. Contemporary interpretations are also offered, as in the entry for "Black Codes," which begins by stating that passing the codes was, "from a modern perspective, one of the greatest follies the South committed." The book is well documented, with extensive references at the end of most entries and a comprehensive bibliography. Cross-references are plentiful and accurate. A chronology is helpful, as is the index.

The author's approach and expertise set this book head and shoulders above others in the series. It will be useful to any library that has need for books about the topic.—**Constance Hardesty**

421. **The American Civil War: A Handbook of Literature and Research.** Steven E. Woodworth, ed. Westport, Conn., Greenwood Press, 1996. 754p. index. $99.50. ISBN 0-313-29019-9.

This is an important bibliography containing 47 essays on published and nonpublished sources. These essays, written by scholars, promote interest and are useful to both other scholars and laypersons. Comments about works cited are evaluative. Coverage centers on works published after the Second World War, serving to complement an older two-volume bibliography with brief annotations, *Civil War Books: A Critical Bibliography* by Allan Nevins, J. I. Robertson, and Bell I. Wiley (Louisiana State University Press, 1967-1969).

A reading of these essays introduces students to major themes and subtitles associated with interpretive history, especially the articles devoted to slavery, constitutional questions, and economic factors. When possible, essays suggest topics for scholarly research without, however, identifying and locating untapped primary research materials available to researchers. The articles devoted to popular media (novels, films, television, musicals, and sound recordings) should prove seminal for many readers. Citations to sources cited in entries are given in complete form in the bibliographies following each entry.

The index is complete, citing titles and including subjects. Without question, this important new bibliography is a necessary purchase for all academic, secondary school, and public libraries. [R: RBB, 15 Nov 96, p. 607]—**Milton H. Crouch**

422. **American Decades 1900-1909.** Vincent Tompkins, ed. Detroit, Gale, 1996. 589p. illus. index. $78.00. ISBN 0-8103-5722-4.

423. **American Decades 1910-1919.** Vincent Tompkins, ed. Detroit, Gale, 1996. 632p. illus. index. $78.00. ISBN 0-8103-5723-2.

424. **American Decades 1920-1929.** Judith S. Baughman, ed. Detroit, Gale, 1996. 554p. illus. index. $75.00. ISBN 0-8103-5724-0.

These three volumes, covering the first three decades of the twentieth century, are the last to be published in the American Decades series, and, until the volume for the 1990s appears some years hence, complete coverage of this century. (Other volumes were reviewed in ARBA: See entry 425, ARBA 96, entries 513-516; and ARBA 95, entry 544.) As with the others in the series, each, after a helpful encapsulating introduction and a chronological list of world events, treats its decade from 12 different topical perspectives: the arts, business and the economy, education, fashion, government and politics, law and justice, lifestyles and social trends, media, medicine and health, religion, science and technology, and sports.

All sections are similarly organized: a chronology of events; an essay overview; discussions of particular aspects of the topic; brief biographies of "Headline Makers"; biographies, 400 to 1,000 words, of "People in the News"; deaths of notables during the decade; and finally, a list of important publications on the topic that appeared in that decade. (The useful "General References" list toward the end of the volumes contains a selective listing of more recently published items on each of the topical areas.) Black-and-white illustrations are scattered throughout the volume, as well as frequent sidebars on more entertaining, although not necessary, information. Each volume concludes with a list of contributors, an index to the photographs, and a detailed general index.

As with the others in the series, these three volumes can be recommended to a wide audience. The information is accurate and well presented; the bibliographies are brief but helpful; and everything is nicely packaged in sturdy, attractive volumes. While the series is especially aimed at high school and public libraries, it should also prove useful in libraries serving undergraduates. [R: LJ, June 96, p. 56]
—**Evan Ira Farber**

425. **American Decades 1980-1989.** Victor Bondi, ed. Detroit, Gale, 1996. 774p. illus. index. $75.00. ISBN 0-8103-8881-2.

Using the same format as the other volumes in the American Decades series (see entries 422-424), this volume chronicles the significant people, events, and issues of the 1980s. It was the decade of the Ronald Reagan administration (and one year of George Bush's) when the federal debt soared to its highest level to date; when the rich were getting richer and their lifestyles were ever present in television shows such as *Dallas* and *Dynasty*; when AIDS deaths multiplied; when gang violence, child abuse, and drug abuse were rampant; and the intergenerational dispute over values was ongoing. The decade, similar to the earlier ones, is surveyed from 13 perspectives (world events, the arts, business and the economy, education, fashion, government and politics, law and justice, lifestyles and social trends, media, medicine and health, religion, science and technology, and sports).

Chapter 1 consists of a chronology of world events, but all other chapters include, in addition to a chronology, an overview, topics in the news, headline makers, people in the news, awards (if applicable), deaths, and publications. The text is interspersed with a variety of photographs (e.g., eruption of Mount St. Helens, Michael Jordan, Prime Minister Margaret Thatcher and Reagan at Camp David) and sidebars and tables ("Vietnam Veterans Memorial"; "Leading Causes of Death in 1981, by Sex and Race"). This work concludes with a general bibliography; a list of contributors; an index of photographs; and a comprehensive subject index of people, books, periodicals, plays, movies, television shows, corporations, government agencies, and the like.

American Decades 1980-1989 is complemented by the chronological/tabular treatment in *Day by Day: The Eighties* (see ARBA 96, entry 503), a rearrangement of material in *Facts on File Yearbooks* and to which set readers need to turn for additional information on a person, event, or place cited in *Day by Day. American Decades* is recommended for public, academic, and high school libraries.—**Wiley J. Williams**

AFRICAN HISTORY

426. Jenkins, Everett, Jr. **Pan-African Chronology: A Comprehensive Reference to the Black Quest for Freedom....** Jefferson, N.C., McFarland, 1996. 440p. index. $49.95. ISBN 0-7864-0139-7.

Each year in this chronology is subdivided by geographic region. The book is useful in that it encompasses wide-ranging topics and regions. Historical events that are less directly related to the primary subject are also noted when warranted. There is ample information found within these covers. However, this work suffers from a major handicap that prevents it from being as valuable a reference tool as it could be: For most entries, the day or even the month when an event occurred is not mentioned. This is surprising when one considers all of the research the author has done and what purpose the chronology serves. (Yet, this criticism is also true of *Black Chronology: From 4000 B.C. to the Abolition of the Slave Trade* [see ARBA 85, entry 350] and *The Timetables of African-American History* [Simon & Schuster Trade, 1995]. *Chronology of African-American History* [see ARBA 92, entry 347], although it only goes back to 1619, does provide the month and day for a majority of its entries.) Thus, the contents are more general in nature than they could be, and the book's usefulness is limited. Also, it would be nice if there were bibliographic notes at the end of the entries to direct readers to other sources of information—the three-page bibliography lists more general works. However, the index appears to be well constructed. This solidly bound title is suitable, despite its flaws, for all public and academic reference collections. [R: C&RL, Sept 96, p. 466; LJ, Feb 96, p. 144]—**Daniel K. Blewett**

427. Nuñez, Benjamin. **Dictionary of Portuguese-African Civilization. Volume 2: From Ancient Kings to Presidents.** New Providence, N.J., Hans Zell/Reed Reference Publishing, 1996. 478p. $110.00. ISBN 1-873836-65-1.

The first volume of this set (see ARBA 96, entry 532) dealt with entities. The more than 1,500 entries in this work deal with people. The biographies range from Portuguese kings to African slaves, with many more of the latter. Some people profiled (e.g., Francis of Assisi) probably do not belong, but their number is insignificant.

The author wrestles with the issue of compound name entry form and a hybrid execution emerges. Contrary to Library of Congress practice, more entries are alphabetized under the first element of the compound than the last. The peroration to look under every possible element, while necessary, might not be sufficient. There are more misspellings than there ought to be, but these affect access less than the name problem, and cross-referencing is adequate.

In a work such as this, few categories are completely covered. Only the kings of Portugal are accorded completeness. It would have been useful, as a means of rounding out the prosopography, to provide tables of governors, *capitães-mores*, and the rulers of the major African states involved. These would have been more helpful than the 4 maps, which appear in volume 1 in any case. The bibliography is surprisingly short (including only one item by René Pelissier) and lists more titles in English than in Portuguese.

This work, in company with the previous volume, provides the single best nonbibliographic reference work—in English, at least—on the Portuguese presence in Africa. One final revision would have enhanced its value even further. On the other hand, in today's budgetary circumstances, many libraries will balk at the price.—**David Henige**

428. **The Penguin Atlas of African History.** new ed. By Colin McEvedy. New York, Penguin Books, 1995. 144p. maps. index. $14.95pa. ISBN 0-14-051321-3.

Employing a rich and unique method of surveying the development of African society from the earliest human settlements to the present, this atlas provides 60 maps of Africa with brief expository text. The base map includes the southern part of Europe and southwestern part of Asia; it does not include

Mauritius, Réunion, or the Seychelles. Because of the way the maps overlap, and the continuing chronological framework on which the narrative is built, the atlas should be regarded as an outline history rather than as a work of reference.

Printed on sturdy white paper, each historical era has brief supporting commentary. Captions on the maps' surfaces are clear, easily understood, and do not unreasonably intersect important information. The text recounts the development of flora and fauna, and some maps have stippled areas to show ranges and habitats. On the maps detailing political strife, heavy black lines lead the eye through areas conquered, shifting boundaries, cities where battles took place, and transportation routes.

After the 1880s, when the French and British began to lay serious claim to the lands of Africa, the maps become increasingly complex and overlain with reservoirs of information. To reflect population growth, shifting borders, and political stratagems over time, the text increases exponentially. By the year 1994, which marked the end of the colonial era in Africa, 705 million people inhabited the area. Population distribution is shown on a separate map, and the associated narrative explores contemporary issues, such as a fall in the per capita gross national product over the last 20 years, attempts to expand the agricultural base, the impact of AIDS, and a reevaluation of the role of government.

The index references the text, not the maps, but for location purposes nearly all entries for places and peoples start with a map reference, printed in bold typeface. Although not the first stop for authoritative information on Africa, students and librarians will appreciate the unique presentation, which will provide hours of casual browsing and may lift this unusual book into a true learning tool.—**Judy Gay Matthews**

ASIAN HISTORY

General Works

429. Pluvier, Jan M. **Historical Atlas of South-East Asia.** Kinderhook, N.Y., E. J. Brill, 1995. 1v. (various paging). maps. index. (Handbook of Oriental Studies). $142.00. ISBN 90-04-10238-8. ISSN 0169-9571.

A difficult book for the mature reader, whether uninformed or knowledgeable, Pluvier's groundbreaking atlas is well written. Because of its foreign and complex data, the atlas needs to be read twice and then kept around as a reference, for it provides 64 ingenious maps complete with details of 2,000 years of seminal history not easily recalled. The compilation of material is amazing even for a lifetime of concerned study. The maps are dense with facts, including the 450-count bibliography of English, Spanish, and Dutch sources.

The author makes short shrift of religion and dismisses art as hierarchical but records thousands of place-names and powerful people chronologically and geographically in 72 period descriptions, most of which end with a listing of the political leaders. In covering modern times, the author accuses colonialism of incremental greed, taps Japan for supporting nationalism, and sees neither capitalism with its complicity in usury nor socialism with its depression of initiative as promising. War dominates the whole story of this atlas and this area; facing that reality alone is essential.—**Elizabeth L. Anderson**

Indic

430. Pandiri, Ananda M., comp. **A Comprehensive, Annotated Bibliography on Mahatma Gandhi. Volume One: Biographies, Works by Gandhi, and Bibliographical Sources.** Westport, Conn., Greenwood Press, 1995. 401p. index. (Bibliographies and Indexes in World History, no.42). $95.00. ISBN 0-313-25337-4.

The first volume in a predicted three-volume set, the *Bibliography* is a lengthy, annotated compilation of resources for the study of Mohandas K. Gandhi. The major part of this resource lists biographies of Gandhi, books written by him, prefaces and forewords by Gandhi appearing in other works, and a selected list of books he read. It also includes bibliographies, general indexes where information can be found, and major periodical sources as well as a short list of repositories and catalogs where substantial collections of Gandhian information can be found.

A researcher unfamiliar with the events in the life of Gandhi would be better served if the work contained a biographical sketch of the subject. The chapter entitled "Books by Gandhi," which includes edited works, translations, collections, correspondence, and speeches, is arranged alphabetically by title. The location of specific works would be simplified if the entries were grouped into such divisions as "Edited Works," "Translations," and the like. It is also redundant to repeat the name Gandhi as author for every entry in this section.

The bibliography contains author, title, and subject indexes. Despite some difficulties, it is a major accomplishment, and is recommended for larger academic libraries. [R: Choice, Mar 96, p. 1102]

—**Jane Jurgens**

Korean

431. **The Korean War: Handbook of the Literature and Research.** Lester H. Brune, ed. Westport, Conn., Greenwood Press, 1996. 460p. index. $79.50. ISBN 0-313-28969-7.

Nearly 50 years after it began, researchers have seen many recent monographs, articles, and reference tools covering the Korean conflict. Brune reveals the vast range of published (and by reference, unpublished) materials, effectively characterizing them by subject focus; historical school of thought; and relationship to the origins, conduct, and results of the war. Emphasis is on English-language sources, although translations of others (e.g., Chinese and Korean) are represented. The basic organization is by background and general, international participation (with particular attention to the Chinese and Soviets), the military struggle, reunification, and domestic influence and impact.

The essays provide helpful overviews of the general situation and identify the many significant issues—some still unresolved—including the firing of Douglas MacArthur, the atomic weapons threat, the McCarthy hearings, the occupation of Japan, participation by Chinese and Soviet forces, and what really led to the North Korean invasion in June 1950. (It is particularly interesting, concerning this last issue, to see how much weight different scholars assign to documents recently released by the Chinese and Russian governments.) The advantages of review essays—specific works placed in context of topics or alternative views—are effectively demonstrated.

The volume can be read as a whole, for a total perspective, or can be used as a more focused resource for topical interest. There is sufficient consistency of style and quality across the essays, possibly because most of them were written or cowritten by the editor. There are two indexes, author and general subject, although had the latter been more detailed, the book would be a much more useful reference resource. The handbook is nonetheless highly recommended for most history, military, and political studies collections. [R: Choice, Dec 96, p. 590; RBB, 1 Mar 96, p. 1212]—**Kenneth W. Berger**

Philippines

432. Netzorg, Morton J. **The Philippines in World War II and to Independence (December 8, 1941-July 4, 1946): An Annotated Bibliography.** 2d ed. Detroit, Cellar Book Shop Press, 1995. 2v. $150.00/set. ISBN 0-9647506-0-0.

The 2d edition of this monumental bibliography includes all of the more than 2,500 works listed in the 1st edition (see ARBA 78, entry 299) plus new materials published from 1975 through November 1994. Autobiographical and personal accounts, novels set in the time period and locale, and commentaries are cited, along with historical, sociological, and economic studies. Books, selections from books, periodical articles, theses and dissertations, published government documents, and newspapers and journals published in the Philippines during the war or by Filipinos in exile are included. Deliberately excluded are manuscripts, microfilms, secret or restricted materials, and short items published in newspapers.

Most of the works cited are in the English language, but works in the Filipino languages, Spanish, French, Russian, Indonesian, and the Malay languages are also represented. Writings in Japanese and Chinese have been excluded. Standard bibliographic form is followed, and many entries are annotated. The annotations are descriptive and critical. Some entries include quotations from the works.

The author gives a caveat in his introduction, warning that his personal biases may be present in his comments and in his choice of quotations. He was born in the Philippines of American parents and was a longtime resident of the islands. His family suffered or became casualties of the occupation and war, a factor that sparked his interest in the subject of this bibliography. This will be an indispensable tool for historians and researchers, and will be an important resource in collections of Philippine history, Pacific area studies, the history of World War II, and the sociology of warfare. [R: Choice, Sept 96, p. 104]

—Shirley L. Hopkinson

Vietnamese

433. **Encyclopedia of the Vietnam War.** Stanley I. Kutler, ed. New York, Scribner's/Simon & Schuster Macmillan, 1996. 711p. illus. maps. index. $90.00. ISBN 0-13-276932-8.

This new volume enters a crowded field of excellent reference works on the Vietnam War that includes two fine almanacs, a dictionary, several outstanding reference handbooks, an order of battle, a battle chronology, a book-length glossary, and several book-length bibliographies. The references are both general and specific, on topics such as films, literature, and many other genres. Another encyclopedia on the war will be out soon.

This volume contains two types of entries. Ten long, interpretive essays, written by leading scholars, provide in-depth coverage of major topics such as the French colonial era, diplomacy, the antiwar movement, and Vietnamese perspectives. Shorter topical entries treat people, events, places, and the like. Most of the latter are by unknown names whose only identification (Madison, Wisconsin) leads one to the conclusion that they are graduate students at the University of Wisconsin, the editor's institution. For the most part, all entries are well written. Each entry has a brief bibliography and the volume concludes with an exhaustive topical bibliography. Augmenting the text are 13 maps and 210 photographs. Appendixes include a chronology, a synoptic outline, tables of abbreviations and acronyms, a list of medal of honor winners, and so forth.

The encyclopedia is closest in nature to James S. Olson's *Dictionary of the Vietnam War* (see ARBA 89, entry 457) and Harry G. Summers Jr.'s *Vietnam War Almanac* (see ARBA 86, entry 519), but it is a much more expansive and authoritative work than either of these. The large-folio volume is a readable, handy, and attractive reference source useful for all libraries. [R: Choice, July/Aug 96, pp. 1771-72; RBB, 1 May 96, p. 1524]—**Joe P. Dunn**

434. Summers, Harry G., Jr. **Historical Atlas of the Vietnam War.** New York, Houghton Mifflin, 1995. 224p. illus. maps. index. $39.95. ISBN 0-395-72223-3.

Two of the foremost authorities on the Vietnam War combine their expertise and experience to give readers this major reference work on that most complex and ambiguous of all U.S. wars. Summers, himself a Vietnam veteran, is the author of two other standard titles on the war: *On Strategy: A Critical Analysis of the Vietnam War* (Presidio Press, 1982) and *The Vietnam War Almanac* (see ARBA 86, entry 519), as well as the founding editor of *Vietnam* magazine. Stanley Karnow, who wrote the introduction and conclusion for this volume, is a distinguished journalist and author whose popular Asian histories (*Vietnam: A History* [Viking, 1991] and *In Our Image: America's Empire in the Philippines* [Random House, 1989]) have gained him widespread praise and recognition. His introduction and epilogue are succinct, shrewd, and valuable.

The atlas' 100, 4-color maps are outstanding and distinctive; they are accompanied by 150 color and black-and-white photographs. The maps are the work of Swanston Publishing Ltd. in Great Britain. These features, particularly the spectacular maps, are what distinguish this book from similar books on the war; it is truly the first major visualization of that conflict.

The book is clearly organized into seven parts. The first three parts set the stage for the U.S. phase of the war, from 1954 to 1975. They discuss and illustrate Vietnam's geography and culture; its historical legacy, 500 B.C.-1945; and the First Indochina War between the French and the Vietnamese Communists under Ho Chi Minh, 1945-1954. Parts 4 through 7 are the heart of the book. They explore chronologically specific aspects of the war through the format of a single full-page text facing a beautifully executed color map (also a single full-page). This is an effective combination.

Summers's book is designed to be a complete military history of the war, but it does neglect certain unresolved issues: Agent Orange, Vietnam veterans' problems such as post-traumatic stress disorder, Vietnamese refugees' exodus and resettlement, and the troublesome POW-MIA question.

Nevertheless, the Historical Atlas of the Vietnam War is a stunning achievement and is indispensable as a reference source and a textbook for use in Vietnam War courses. [R: RBB, 1 May 96, p. 1528]

—Marshall E. Nunn

EUROPEAN HISTORY

General Works

435. Dickinson, W. Calvin, and Eloise R. Hitchcock, comps. **The War of the Spanish Succession, 1702-1713: A Selected Bibliography.** Westport, Conn., Greenwood Press, 1996. 140p. index. (Bibliographies of Battles and Leaders, no.15). $65.00. ISBN 0-313-28302-8.

The dynamics of succession are just as important today as they were in the era of European monarchies. The War of the Spanish Succession was a general European war between England and France aiming to extend their respective influence, power, and control over European events. Each country sought to maintain safety, security, and power. When Charles II of Spain died in 1700, Louis XIV sought to place his grandson, Philip V, on the throne of Spain, thus bringing Spain and the Netherlands under French domination. The published and unpublished material dealing with England's struggle to prevent French hegemony in Western Europe is broken into topical categories ranging from bibliographies and reference works to general histories and administration and diplomatic histories to campaigns in France, Germany, Spain, and Italy. There are two chapters that deal with the Duke of Marlborough and Eugene of Savoy, and one chapter on trade and naval warfare.

This volume is number 15 in a series of handy little volumes on battles and leaders that are aimed at both the general and in-depth researcher. Major libraries holding large collections on the War of the Spanish Succession are also mentioned. The work is not extensively annotated, but it is sufficient to guide the researcher. The bibliography is recommended for public, college, and university reference collections. [R: Choice, Sept 96, p. 94]—**Norman L. Kincaide**

436. Frank, Ben G. **A Travel Guide to Jewish Europe.** 2d ed. Gretna, La., Pelican Publishing, 1996. 600p. illus. maps. index. $18.95. ISBN 1-56554-037-9.

This book is a practical guide to notable Jewish sites throughout Europe, including for the first time much of Eastern Europe, the Czech Republic, Slovakia, Poland, and Hungary (where the largest Jewish community in Eastern Europe is found). In addition to useful information about kosher restaurants, cafés, synagogues, and museums, anecdotal information about the cultural and "heritage sites" is included for more than 50 cities.

The chapter on Ireland notes the Jewish mayors of Dublin, while the chapter on Italy points out that Jews sell cameos in St. Peter's Square. More provocative, the chapter on Spain asks if Christopher Columbus might have been Jewish (the conclusion is "we do not know"). The chapter on France notes that it is the fourth largest Jewish community in the world, whereas the chapter on Germany simply proclaims "Jews do live there." Illustrated with black-and-white photographs, this guide recommends a limited number of hotels, lists local Jewish organizations, covers Jewish neighborhoods, recommends other points of interest, and offers short lists of "suggested readings" at the end of each chapter.

—**Joseph W. Dauben**

437. Higbee, Joan F. **Western Europe Since 1945: A Bibliography.** Lanham, Md., Scarecrow, 1996. 183p. index. (Scarecrow Area Bibliographies, no.9). $29.00. ISBN 0-8108-3112-0.

This rather slender bibliography purports to reflect the changes and interrelationships between the countries of Western Europe, as well as their cultural climate, from the end of World War II until the present day. With few exceptions, the works cited are secondary sources in the humanities and the social sciences, although there is a scattering of organization documents and working papers.

The predominantly English-language works are ordered in four sections: Europe, the European Union, individual countries of Western Europe, and prominent people. Each section has pertinent subdivisions; for example, the broad topic "Europe" has subheadings for agriculture, art, the Council of Europe, industry and state, literature, monetary policy, technological innovations, terrorism, and women, among others. Individual countries have similar subheadings, although these can vary greatly depending on the country. Germany subdivides into Germany, Germany post-1990, East, and West.

Aside from the section/subject arrangement, which is cumbersome to use, there is no subject index. There is an author index, but no cross-references. Undergraduates beginning research in this area may find the work useful for identifying relevant titles on a given topic. Overall, however, this bibliography may be considered marginal.—**Bernice Bergup**

438. Urwin, Derek W. **A Dictionary of European History and Politics, 1945-1995.** White Plains, N.Y., Longman Group/Addison-Wesley, 1996. 423p. $18.95pa. ISBN 0-582-25874-X.

This new dictionary's purpose is to include the most significant features of European history and politics since 1945, the end of World War II. Arrangement of the work is strictly alphabetic and relies heavily on liberal use of cross-references. These cross-references are critical as there is no index, and they are so numerous throughout the book that some people may tend to view the pages as unnecessarily cluttered in design. This feeling of clutter is exacerbated by the fact there are no spaces between any of the entries. There is a self-proclaimed bias toward the larger European states. Coverage extends to most of the former Soviet Republics except those situated more deeply in the Asian continent.

There are four major categories of entries used in this book: events/issues, territories, organizations, and individuals. Those entries pertaining to European organizations and agencies are by far the most valuable and the hardest about which to locate information. Entries for the other categories are already well covered in such standard reference books as *The Columbia Dictionary of European Political History Since 1914* (see ARBA 93, entry 529); *The Oxford Companion to Politics of the World* (see ARBA 94, entry 717); and *The European Political Dictionary* (see ARBA 87, entry 690). The strength of Urwin's work is its relatively recent publication date. It is one of the more concise reference books of its type and carries a reasonable price. Written in an easygoing and nonscholarly style, this book will appeal to the patrons of high school, lower division undergraduate, and public libraries. [R: BL, 1 Oct 96, p. 368; Choice, Nov 96, p. 438]—**Stephen W. Green**

British

439. Cowie, Leonard W. **Sir Robert Peel 1788-1850: A Bibliography.** Westport, Conn., Greenwood Press, 1996. 142p. index. (Bibliographies of British Statesmen, no.13). $65.00. ISBN 0-313-29447-X.

This bibliography is a comprehensive guide to the life and writings of Peel, prominent British statesman of the nineteenth century. The work includes manuscript/archival resources and locations, newspaper and journal articles, published works, parliamentary papers and debates, and critical studies of Peel. Essays on his life and a chronology of significant events are also included. The author provides additional introductory essays to selected chapters, greatly assisting both the beginner and the more advanced student in understanding nineteenth-century British politics and the importance and influence of this major political player. Unique entries in the bibliography include "Caricature of Peel: and "Places Associated with Peel." Author, subject, and artist indexes complete the volume.

This bibliography is number 13 in a series produced by Greenwood Press entitled Bibliographies of British Statesmen. It is recommended for academic libraries with extensive collections in British history. [R: Choice, July/Aug 96, pp. 1770-71]—**Jane Jurgens**

440. Foster, Janet, and Julia Sheppard. **British Archives: A Guide to Archive Resources in the United Kingdom.** 3d ed. New York, Stockton Press, 1995. 627p. index. $160.00. ISBN 0-333-532-554.

Foster and Sheppard have once again succeeded in updating, expanding, and improving their extremely useful *British Archives* (see ARBA 90, entry 507, for a review of the 2d edition). In the 3d edition 155 new entries have been added, bringing the total number of entries to 1,203. The new edition also records that approximately 50 collections listed in the 2d edition have been incorporated into other, larger archives.

As in earlier editions, individual entries are numbered and arranged geographically by the town in which the archive is located, and then alphabetically by the name of the archive. Each entry supplies addresses, telephone numbers, hours of operation, availability of microfilming and photocopying, major collections, and finding aid—all of which have been updated where necessary. The authors encouraged archivists to increase the information in their entries, and many did.

Alphabetic lists of archives and lists of archives by county continue to be provided in this edition for the assistance of readers needing lists of useful addresses and a bibliography of helpful publications about archives. Libraries supporting advanced research on virtually any topic in British studies will need the 3d edition of what has become a standard guide.—**Ronald H. Fritze**

441. Gutzke, David W., comp. **Alcohol in the British Isles from Roman Times to 1996: An Annotated Bibliography.** Westport, Conn., Greenwood Press, 1996. 266p. index. (Bibliographies and Indexes in World History, no.44). $69.50. ISBN 0-313-29420-8.

Alcohol use and production have played a major role in British history for at least 2,000 years and continues their social function today through the ubiquitous pub. This work reflects an increased interest in the study of alcohol since the 1970s as part of a growing social history specialty. Gutzke, a history professor at Southwest Missouri State University, has written extensively about alcohol use and production in Great Britain. Here he pulls together references to 2,200 secondary works on the subject. His main criterion was that they should have historical content. Specialized materials or materials of only localized interest are excluded. The result is a thorough, scholarly bibliography, with well-written and informative annotations. The topics covered are wide-ranging and include different alcoholic beverages, brewing science, inn signs, regulations, temperance, and biographies of individuals. In fact, some topics, such as checks and tokens, are so esoteric that they could use more introduction. There are an author index and an excellent subject index. The highly specialized nature and price of this book will probably limit its purchase, but it should be acquired by any library that collects heavily in British history or has an interest in alcohol studies.—**Christine E. King**

442. **Historical Dictionary of Stuart England, 1603-1689.** Ronald H. Fritze, William B. Robison, and Walter Sutton, eds. Westport, Conn., Greenwood Press, 1996. 611p. index. $95.00. ISBN 0-313-28391-5.

The editors see this as a critical time for the publication of a general reference handbook on English history of the seventeenth century, as revisionist historians have been active on this turbulent period. The readability of the 320 entries is enhanced by the technique of starring words in the entries that are the subjects of entries themselves (i.e., cross-references). Many entries have more than 25 such references. The 80 contributors range from those with posts at Oxford and Cambridge Universities through independent scholars to middle school teachers. The editors themselves are active reviewers and were involved in the earlier companion volume on Tudor England that this publisher issued in 1991 (see ARBA 93, entry 532).

As a sample subject area, the entries relating to religion were skimmed and found fully acceptable. While a general bloodthirsty tone was much in evidence in entries, this does reflect the times covered accurately. The dictionary is highly recommended for libraries serving undergraduates in British history, but also merits consideration by larger public libraries serving general readers. [R: Choice, Sept 96, p. 99]
—**Eugene B. Jackson**

443. Richardson, R. C., and W. H. Chaloner, comps. **British Economic and Social History: A Bibliographical Guide.** 3d ed. Manchester, England, Manchester University Press; distr., New York, St. Martin's Press, 1996. 271p. index. $79.95. ISBN 0-7190-3600-3.

This compilation begins by listing general works, including historiographical studies, then lists books and articles on English, Welsh, Scottish, and Irish history. Each section is organized by country and time (England from 1066 to 1300, for example, and so on). Within each section, entries are arranged thematically (e.g., agriculture and rural society, industry, labor). All together, 7,400 items appear—an increase of 1,600 from the 2d edition (1985). Annotations are provided for some works but not others. An index of authors and editors completes the text.

More extensive coverage of subjects, such as law and order, crime, popular culture, women, the family, and the social history of war, distinguishes this volume from earlier editions. English assizes, mob psychology, pubs, the brewing industry, feminism, gender roles, and the British home front during World

War I and World War II are several topics that receive significant treatment. A largely successful effort has been made to cull mediocre or repetitive sources. Titles have been added for the period from 1971 to 1980. One might wish, however, that the scope of this bibliography had been broadened still further. Some mention of the more prominent works in British history prior to 1000 and after 1980 would have been helpful. A larger number of annotations throughout the volume, accompanied by somewhat greater detail, was merited as well. Even with these limitations, *British Economic and Social History* remains a useful contribution. Specialists, in particular, will benefit from it. The guide is recommended for research-oriented colleges and universities. [R: Choice, Sept 96, p. 106]—**Richard E. Holl**

444. Stewart, John. **The British Empire: An Encyclopedia of the Crown's Holdings, 1493 Through 1995.** Jefferson, N.C., McFarland, 1996. 370p. index. $65.00. ISBN 0-7864-0177-X.

The appearance of this handbook is timely because the British Empire is in the news now. The fact that Oxford University Press has a five-volume *Oxford History of the British Empire* in progress has made both the British literary press and even their newspapers. The inevitable flood of undergraduate term papers on British Empire topics in liberal arts colleges will be aided by the availability of Stewart's handbook. The author lists 15 kinds of relationships an entity may have with the United Kingdom of Great Britain and Northern Ireland (or even the Queen personally). One of the less usual is that of "Condominiums," which was the title held by Sudan, Togoland, and the New Hebrides.

The several hundred entries have sketches for colonies and other protectorates, averaging close to a page each. The entries typically include location, history, and the senior resident British official. Those last named may be accessed through the index. While it will not bother the undergraduates or honors high schoolers attracted to this title, this reviewer missed all indication of sources consulted in its compilation. *The British Empire* should be considered by libraries serving undergraduate history students and medium-sized and larger public libraries. [R: Choice, Oct 96, p. 258; LJ, Aug 96, p. 66]—**Eugene B. Jackson**

445. Usilton, Larry W. **The Kings of Medieval England, c. 560-1485: A Survey and Research Guide.** Pasadena, Calif., Salem Press and Lanham, Md., Scarecrow, 1996. 115p. index. (Magill Bibliographies). $29.50. ISBN 0-8108-3194-5.

This slim volume attempts to succinctly encompass the rulers of England for nearly 1,000 years of medieval history, and it succeeds admirably. The author neatly divides the dynasties of the Anglo-Saxon and Danish, Norman, early Plantagenet, later Plantagenet, and Lancastrian and Yorkist periods into five chapters. Each chapter has a lengthy introduction, followed by an annotated bibliography of approximately 50 works, consisting mainly of monographs but with some periodical articles also. Most of the works cited are secondary sources, and the majority are biographical in nature. A chronology of the kings and an author index are included. The author admits that the bibliography is highly selective, but the references were chosen carefully, and the annotations are informative. This work would be a good starting point for both identifying and reviewing materials on the medieval kings and would be equally useful to scholars, students, and Anglophiles.—**Christine E. King**

Eastern Europe

446. Hupchick, Dennis P., and Harold E. Cox. **A Concise Historical Atlas of Eastern Europe.** New York, St. Martin's Press, 1996. 120p. maps. index. $49.95; $17.95pa. ISBN 0-312-15893-9; 0-312-15895-5pa.

The authors produced this historical atlas to provide students with an affordable visual aid for the study of Eastern Europe. The atlas (encompassing present-day Albania, Austria, Bosnia-Herzegovina, Bulgaria, Croatia, the Czech Republic, eastern Germany, Greece, Hungary, Macedonia, Montenegro, Poland, Romania, Serbia, Slovakia, and Slovenia) is presented in a series of 50, 2-color (white and green), full-page maps. A facing page contains a two-column explanatory text. The atlas is divided into six parts: introductory maps (political, 1996, physical, demographic, cultural); early medieval to the thirteenth century; late medieval (the thirteenth to the fifteenth centuries); early modern (the sixteenth to the eighteenth centuries); the period of nationalism (the nineteenth century to 1918); and the modern and contemporary period (1918-1991). The work also contains a bibliography and an index.

The atlas has a few minor defects, such as inconsistencies in the labeling of bodies of water (on some maps they are labeled, on others not). The shadings of green used to delineate different areas are often difficult to discern. However, although there is another commercially available atlas (*Historical Atlas of East Central Europe* [see ARBA 94, entry 520]) that is superior in terms of layout and detail, Hupchick's and Cox's work will be more than sufficient for the occasional student of the area.—**Robert H. Burger**

French

447. Dwyer, Philip G., comp. **Charles-Maurice de Talleyrand 1754-1838: A Bibliography.** Westport, Conn., Greenwood Press, 1996. 218p. index. (Bibliographies of World Leaders, no.4). $69.50. ISBN 0-313-29354-6.

Talleyrand was an influential figure in French and European politics and diplomacy for the almost 50 years between about 1780 and 1830, particularly at the Congress of Vienna. He has often been vilified as the ultimate cynical politician because of his ability to shift allegiances and serve prominently in almost every government during the period. He was particularly criticized because, although he was a bishop and an aristocrat, he led the nationalization of church property at the onset of the French Revolution. Here, Dwyer has compiled the first major bibliography on Talleyrand, documenting historians' changing critical attitudes toward his subject.

An introduction and chronology provide background on both Talleyrand's life and reputation, and suggest directions for further research. The 844 entries are arranged chronologically within sections by type, and they provide brief, pithy annotations. The most significant titles are starred. The first section describes archival and manuscript sources, in France and abroad, consisting mainly of Talleyrand's diplomatic correspondence. Some descriptions are in French. Other sections include his published works; contemporary publications, including revolutionary pamphlets; and biographical works, including books, essays, articles, and dissertations. A special topics section gives information on places associated with Talleyrand, portraits, and literary works mentioning him. Works in languages other than French or English are listed.

Although Dwyer does not claim this to be a complete bibliography of works by and about Talleyrand, he does say that most of such works are included. This bibliography is highly recommended for academic and large public library collections. [R: Choice, July/Aug 96, p. 1771]—**Marit S. MacArthur**

Greek

448. Feuer, Bryan. **Mycenaean Civilization: A Research Guide.** New York, Garland, 1996. 421p. illus. maps. index. (Research Guides to Ancient Civilizations, v.5; Garland Reference Library of the Humanities, v.1525). $75.00. ISBN 0-8153-0602-4.

This is a comprehensive, annotated bibliography that contains both general and specialized resources covering many aspects of Mycenaean civilization and Bronze Age Greece. The focus of the bibliography is on publications written in the English language, with a selection of publications produced in German, modern Greek, Italian, and French. The arrangement of the bibliography is by broad subject heading and alphabetically by author's last name. Annotations are provided for the majority of citations. A general introduction includes a chronology of the Aegean Bronze Age; a brief history of the origin, growth, decline, and destruction of the Mycenaean civilization; a list of major research centers; and a list of major journals in which recent archaeological updates on specific sites are included. A unique feature of this bibliography is the section "Regional and Site Reports," which lists the major archaeological reports for specific Mycenaean sites.

The historical material listed in this bibliography is often difficult to locate in a single source and will prove invaluable to the beginner. It would have been better served by a more detailed map of Greece showing the location of major centers of Mycenaean civilization. The accompanying illustrations, such as the map of Tiryns, are artistic renderings. Their lack of accuracy can be misleading to beginning students and frustrating to more advanced researchers. The print coverage of the bibliography is extensive and will be a convenient research tool for investigating Mycenaean civilization, but it fails to address electronic resources available to researchers. The amount of such material available on the World Wide Web, for example—such as course syllabuses, core lists of sources, and photographic images of major artworks—is impressive. The guide contains author, place-name, and subject indexes, as well as glossary terms. The work is recommended for large academic libraries. [R: Choice, June 96, p. 1616]

—Jane Jurgens

449. **The Penguin Historical Atlas of Ancient Greece.** By Robert Morkot. New York, Penguin Books, 1996. 144p. illus. maps. index. $16.95pa. ISBN 0-14-051335-3.

Before the beginning of the Christian era, Greece was a great intellectual and artistic center. In this book, a timeline from 7000 B.C.E. to 30 B.C.E. displays various elements of ancient Greek civilization, including Greece's interaction with the Near East and North Africa, Europe and the Mediterranean, and its culture and technology. Five parts cover Crete and the Heroic Age, the Dark Ages to Athenian ascendancy, the meteoric rise of Persia on the political scene, the flowering of classical culture and the Peloponnesian War, and Alexander the Great. Each part begins with a brief statement and quotation to set the tone of the material to follow. Overviews of ancient Greek society cover a broad sweep of peoples through an examination of artifacts, architecture, myths and legends, clothing and personal objects, historical events (frequently military campaigns), and political changes. The typeface has delicate serifs and is not an easy read.

The use of mini-timelines within articles helps the reader keep a perspective on the changing political climate of the area. Sixty maps, printed in clear, sharp colors with adequate keys, abound. The reproductions of artwork, photographs, and timelines are crisp and well registered with surrounding text. Artwork, photography, and text are smoothly interwoven and allow the reader to move from event to event, gaining a sense of time and place. A current bibliography supplements the text, and an index aids access. Secondary school libraries or small public libraries that need an overview of individuals, events, and other miscellaneous aspects of ancient Greece may consider purchase of this volume.—**Judy Gay Matthews**

450. Sacks, David. **Encyclopedia of the Ancient Greek World.** New York, Facts on File, 1995. 306p. illus. maps. index. $40.00. ISBN 0-8160-2323-9.

Similar to Matthew Bunson's *Encyclopedia of the Roman Empire* (see ARBA 95, entry 579), Sacks's *Encyclopedia of the Ancient Greek World* has been promoted by Facts on File as a reference source on the classical world written for the layperson. Intended as an introductory handbook of information, this volume is useful for those who would like to find out about topics in Greek antiquity but do not care to wade through the off-putting academic prose of *The Oxford Classical Dictionary* (2d ed.; see ARBA 71, entry 1427). The quality of the information is quite good, due in some part, no doubt, to the work of editorial consultant Oswyn Murray, a noted British classicist. Readers looking for further reading are at a loss, however, as there is only a woefully inadequate general bibliography at the book's end. The index is thorough, but, as with so many of Facts on File's offerings in this area, the illustrations are next to useless. As a final note, this reviewer put the book on reserve for a college class on Greek civilization taught in the summer of 1996, and many of the students reported that they found it helpful. [R: BR, Mar/April 96, p. 49; Choice, Feb 96, pp. 932-34; LJ, 15 April 96, p. 74; SLJ, April 96, p. 170]

—**Christopher Michael McDonough**

Spanish

451. Kern, Robert W. **The Regions of Spain: A Reference Guide to History and Culture.** Westport, Conn., Greenwood Press, 1995. 411p. illus. maps. index. $55.00. ISBN 0-313-29224-8.

Any student of Spanish history is aware of the tremendous regional variation and diverse cultural development of Spain's 18 traditional regions. In this encyclopedia, Kern (professor of history at the University of New Mexico) provides readers with concise information on Spanish regional and provincial history, literature, art, music, and other facets of civilization. As the author of eight previous monographs and coauthor of *The Historical Dictionary of Modern Spain, 1700-1988* (see ARBA 91, entry 116), this is a subject Kern is uniquely qualified to explore.

Each chapter begins with a section on regional characteristics that provides vital statistics on population, area, physical features, universities, and locations referenced to other regions and provinces. Next, the current economy is explored, followed by sections on history, literature, art, music, customs, historic sites, and cuisine. A typical chapter on Galicia (which encompasses the provinces of La Coruña, Lugo, Orense, and Pontevedra) includes a map and 21 pages of text. Provinces are treated alphabetically. Discussion ranges from Ramón Menéndez Pidal under literature to the cathedral at Santiago de Compostela, and ends with a recipe for oven baked eel (anguila al horno).

A glossary, a chronology, a bibliography, an index, and 20 black-and-white photographs complement the text. This book will be a valuable reference for all students of Spanish civilization. It deserves a place in all high school, public, and academic libraries. [R: Choice, April 96, p. 1288; RQ, Summer 96, pp. 564-65]—**Brian E. Coutts**

452. Smith, Angel. **Historical Dictionary of Spain.** Lanham, Md., Scarecrow, 1996. 435p. maps. (European Historical Dictionaries, no.11). $69.50. ISBN 0-8108-3080-9.

During the past two centuries, Spain, buffered on the north by the Pyrénées, has been transformed from a nation that was able to stand apart from much of the conflict that wracked the rest of Europe. Today it is an open democracy and a full member of the North Atlantic Treaty Organization (NATO). Smith, a British academic who specializes in Spanish history, explains the many institutions, events, people, organizations, places, movements, wars, and other elements that have played a part in those changes. More than 400 articles explain both the facts about these topics and their significance in Spain's history. Embedded *see also* references within the text of articles refer to related articles.

Smith's specific-entry approach complements the greater selectivity of topics and accompanying increased depth of the articles in Robert Kern's and Meredith Dodge's *Historical Dictionary of Modern Spain, 1700-1988* (see ARBA 91, entry 116). Smith's introductory chronology of Spanish history starts a century later than Kern's and Dodge's, but does not have the same depth as the latter. However, Smith's 64-page bibliography dwarfs the other dictionary's bibliography. Because these two historical dictionaries complement each other in approach, contents, and structure, any library that needs one ought to have both.
—**James Rettig**

LATIN AMERICAN AND CARIBBEAN HISTORY

453. Bunson, Margaret R., and Stephen M. Bunson. **Encyclopedia of Ancient Mesoamerica.** New York, Facts on File, 1996. 322p. illus. index. $45.00. ISBN 0-8160-2402-2.

An A to Z, user-friendly guide to Mesoamerican cultures, this work includes attractive charcoal sketches of deities, artifacts, and archaeological pieces, and many factual tables. In a terse and straightforward style, the authors describe topics that range from the general (Aztec civilization, for example) to the specific (individual Maya and Aztec gods). There are many aids for the novice, such as a pronunciation guide to the main Indian languages, Nahuatl and Maya, and a chronology of Mesoamerican cultures. The reference sources are also useful to the more experienced student of this field, as they include such topics as Aztec cosmogony and Mesoamerican flora and fauna.

Obvious omissions include maps (baffling, in view of the regional scope of the work), photographs or sketches of archaeological sites, and examples of such important texts as the *Popol Vuh* and Aztec codices. Although Indian names appear to be accurate, Spanish does not fare well in this text. Words are often incorrectly spelled, with not an accent to be seen on a Spanish word (e.g., "Mueseo de Antropologia"). There are also grammatical mistakes, such as the lack of agreement in "Historia de *la* Mexicanos," a cited source. This demonstrates careless proofreading that detracts from the work's reliability and authority. Nevertheless, this encyclopedia remains a useful starting tool for those teaching and researching pre-Columbian cultures and civilizations.—**Stella T. Clark**

MIDDLE EASTERN HISTORY

454. Grossman, Mark. **Encyclopedia of the Persian Gulf War.** Santa Barbara, Calif., ABC-CLIO, 1995. 522p. illus. maps. index. $65.00. ISBN 0-87436-684-4.

The Persian Gulf War has been subject to many interpretations. It has been defined alternately as a failure of deterrence, a resurrection from the tragedy of the Vietnam War, a glorious success, a flawed and incomplete victory, an unwise and unnecessary bloodletting, the advent of future military engagements, and a unique situation that doubtfully will ever be reprised. For such a brief event, it has spawned a rather considerable body of literature, including such useful reference works as *Operation Desert Shield/Desert Storm* (see ARBA 96, entry 563) and *The 1990-91 Gulf War* (see entry 456). However, this large-folio volume is the first comprehensive encyclopedia.

The encyclopedia contains biographies of key players, weapons designations and capabilities of all contending forces, theaters of operation, and a discussion of crucial diplomatic events. The text is well written, and the whole volume—including a colorful dustjacket and more than 100 beautifully dispersed maps, illustrations, and photographs—is exceptionally well designed, which makes it a most inviting reference tool. Each entry includes bibliographic references, and many are cross-referenced. Appendixes include U.S. casualty lists, a glossary, various statistical tables, 80 documents, and a commendable bibliography. The volume is highly recommended for all libraries. [R: Choice, May 96, p. 1448; RBB, 15 April 96, p. 1458; SLJ, Aug 96, p. 181; VOYA, June 96, p. 132]—**Joe P. Dunn**

455. **An Historical Encyclopedia of the Arab-Israeli Conflict.** Bernard Reich and others, eds. Westport, Conn., Greenwood Press, 1996. 655p. index. $99.50. ISBN 0-313-27374-X.

The continuing saga of the Arab-Israeli crisis is media newsworthy, yet it remains perplexing in the public eye, outside a few special enclaves. An alternative to ignorance is this book-length encyclopedia about the Arab-Israeli conflict, designed for pundits and general readers alike, that traces the account from the adoption of the Palestine partition plan in November 1947 to the consequences of today. Well-crafted and clearly written entries cover the important historical facts; episodes (diplomatic, military, and political); topics; and personalities that have molded the sequence of events both on stage and behind the scenes.

From bio-capsules to moderately sized articles, such as the Six-Day War (1967), USSR policy on the Arab-Israeli conflict, Jerusalem, and so on, most pieces contain a mixture of known and less-understood facts. Combined with nonpoliticized information gathering, extensive cross-references, and a bibliography for further reading and research, the result is an indispensable sourcebook for who is who and what is what in Arab-Israeli history and politics.

There is an occasional snafu. For example, biblical references are presented more popularly than academically. The item on the Nobel peace prize mentions Yasir Arafat, Shimon Peres, and Yitzhak Rabin but omits reference to the 1978 prize awarded to Menachem Begin and Anwar as-Sadat for their role in the Camp David Accords. Also, no examination of Vatican policy on the Israeli-Palestinian dispute is provided. Nonetheless, Reich, a seasoned Middle East expert, and his team of editors and contributors have provided valuable insights on Israel and the Arab world. Their engaging portrait deserves a wide audience. [R: LJ, Jan 96, p. 88]—**Zev Garber**

456. Orgill, Andrew. **The 1990-91 Gulf War: Crisis, Conflict, Aftermath. An Annotated Bibliography.** New York, Mansell/Cassell, 1995. 224p. index. $80.00. ISBN 0-7201-2174-4.

Orgill, compiler of an earlier bibliography on the Falklands War (see ARBA 94, entry 684), provides a valuable service by bringing some degree of order to the incredible volume of publications on the Persian Gulf War. The 1,423 annotated items in this bibliography cite record books, document collections, and journal articles (with a minimum length of 2,000 words) published up to September 1993. Most citations are in English, although a few items in French, German, and Italian are included. The entries are divided into five general categories—reference sources, general studies, the origins of the crisis, the war, and the aftermath—with a number of subcategories under the final three areas. The introductory essay, "The Literature of the War," addresses the various interpretations on many questions concerning the conflict and is an excellent starting point for anyone beginning study of the war. The journal and serial titles and the author/subject indexes are helpful.

This is a useful reference source on the early round of literature on the Persian Gulf War. However, the amount of material on the war has continued unabated since the stopping point of this compilation. For many libraries, the price may be a bit exorbitant for an interim reference source.—**Joe P. Dunn**

457. Peretz, Don. **The Arab-Israeli Dispute.** New York, Facts on File, 1996. 288p. index. (Library in a Book). $24.95. ISBN 0-8160-3186-X.

Arguably, the Arab-Israeli conflict is the most demanding and politically treacherous foreign policy issue in the Middle East today. The why and the how-so are explicitly documented by political scientist Peretz (emeritus, State University of New York at Binghamton) in this volume. In it are essential data: an extensive, 108-page historical, diplomatic, and political overview; a chronology of events; a glossary of terms; a 100-page annotated bibliography; and a selection of important documents on group identity and aspired national goals. What makes the text useful and needed is the author's ability to weigh primary and secondary sources in understanding the peculiar combination of internal and external forces that contribute to flashpoints and the peace process, disappointments and successes alike. The result is a user-friendly reference tool designed for understanding the day-by-day problems between two contentious nationalistic rivals in Israel/Palestine.—**Zev Garber**

WORLD HISTORY

Atlases

458. **The Atlas of Human History.** Renzo Rossi, Martina Veutro, and Andrea Dué, eds. New York, Macmillan Library Reference/Simon & Schuster Macmillan, 1996. 6v. illus. maps. index. $175.00/set. ISBN 0-02-864505-7.

Colorful illustrations and maps, line drawings, photographs, charts, and other graphics are found on every page of this attractive set; the readable text is suitable for students in grades 5 through 9. The 6 volumes (64 pages each) provide coverage of the first peoples, the first settlers, the cradles of civilization, early Europeans (ca. 1400 B.C.E. to 500 B.C.E.), Asian civilization (ca. 200 B.C.E. to 600 C.E.), and life in the Americas (ca. 10,000 B.C.E. to 1500 C.E.). Coverage includes migration, settlement, technological progress, culture and religion, politics, and daily life.

The brief text is respectful of the cultures under discussion and introduces topics that will interest the target audience. Each volume concludes with a glossary and an index; a cumulative index is also available. The set would have been strengthened by a running timeline and a bibliography. Similar titles suitable for the same audience include *The Children's Atlas of Civilizations* (see ARBA 95, entry 572), which provides an overview of the development of civilization from prehistory to the Renaissance in 1 volume, and the Cultural Atlas for Young People series (Facts on File, 1989-1994), an excellent 8-volume set that also offers an interdisciplinary look at ancient civilizations. [R: SLJ, Nov 96, p. 137]

—**Vandelia L. VanMeter**

459. **Hammond Atlas of the 20th Century.** Maplewood, N.J., Hammond, 1996. 239p. illus. maps. index. $39.95. ISBN 0-8437-1148-5.

Hammond, well known for its atlases, has packed a great deal of information into this large-format world atlas dealing with the major events of the twentieth century. The book is divided into five chronological sections: "The End of the Old World Order," "The World Between the Wars," "The World at War," "The Cold War World," and "Towards a New World Order." Not surprisingly, well over half the book is devoted to wars and the events surrounding them. The sixth section treats world themes, reflecting the globalization of life in the twentieth century, such as migration, epidemics, technology, and the environment.

Each event or theme is allotted a two-page spread that includes a general essay, two to four maps of the regions covered, charts of statistical data, and color and black-and-white illustrations. All illustrations are accompanied by lengthy and informative captions. The more than 250 maps are well drafted and color-coded; map keys and captions add many details to supplement the text.

Richard Overy, the general editor of the atlas, is professor of history at King's College in London. Essays are not signed, but the 12 contributors and their credentials are listed in the front matter. All are British, and British spelling has been used throughout the text. A chronology; a glossary of key people, events, and treaties; a bibliography; and an index add to the book's usefulness. The *Hammond Atlas of the 20th Century* is a browser's delight; its length and scope necessarily limit its use as an in-depth reference source but make it an excellent starting point for further reading and research. Thus it is most suited for home, high school, and public libraries. The atlas' solid construction and heavy paper should stand up to heavy use.—**Lori D. Kranz**

Bibliography

460. Baxter, Colin F. **The War in North Africa, 1940-1943: A Selected Bibliography.** Westport, Conn., Greenwood Press, 1996. 119p. index. (Bibliographies of Battles and Leaders, no.16). $49.95. ISBN 0-313-29120-9.

Long before D-Day and the ensuing battle for Europe were under way, British, Commonwealth, and United States troops waged a tenacious campaign against Luftwaffe and Afrika Korps forces commanded by the legendary Erwin Rommel. The struggle for control of North Africa lasted three years and molded such major leaders as Dwight D. Eisenhower, Bernard Montgomery, and George S. Patton, who would later mastermind the liberation of Europe and the destruction of the Hitler regime. Baxter deftly handles the diverse political and military views as to the necessity of the campaign in North Africa. In addition, he gives special attention to the sad state of the U.S. II Corps, composed of newly trained divisions with no significant combat experience. Their trial-by-fire in Tunisia, particularly during the battle for the Kasserine Pass, provided a rude awakening for the U.S. Army command, and a painful glimpse of the awesome might of the German Wehrmacht.

The War in North Africa furnishes the scholar or student with all the necessary material for further research on this phase of World War II. After a narrative and historical survey of the major events, generals, and related literature, it lists more than 500 titles dealing in small or large part with this 3-year war. The bibliography of works related to the North African campaign and the onset of World War II is particularly rich in that it contains a number of titles written by combatants and historians from the former Axis powers (Germany, Italy, and Vichy, France). Baxter's selected bibliography will be extremely useful for military historians, researchers, and students who want to gain further appreciation of an early campaign that in many ways determined the outcome of the war against Adolf Hitler. [R: Choice, Oct 96, p. 248]
—**John B. Romeiser**

461. Jenkins, Fred W. **Classical Studies: A Guide to the Reference Literature.** Englewood, Colo., Libraries Unlimited, 1996. 263p. index. $43.00. ISBN 1-56308-110-5.

This is a well-written, easy-to-use annotated guide to 667 reference materials for classical Greek and Roman studies. Focusing on the best and most current sources for studies covering the Bronze Age through the sixth century C.E., the author has divided the book into three parts: bibliographic resources, information resources, and organizations. All areas of classical Greek and Roman culture and civilization are covered. Although preference is given to English-language printed sources, reference works in French, German, and Italian are included in each of the sections. The table of contents, and the author/title and subject indexes at the end of the book, make it easy to quickly locate a title.

Researchers will find the section entitled "Information Resources" particularly useful in that it lists numerous Internet sources, including electronic discussion groups, and gives their World Wide Web sites. As with the printed materials, each Internet resource is annotated and details such information as the level of discussion of certain discussion groups, the kinds of material that may be found on a given site, and how well the information is gathered and arranged. The section on Internet resources alone would make this a useful book for general readers and others interested in classical studies; classical scholars who are just beginning to take advantage of the Internet will find that this book is indispensable. The guide is highly recommended. [R: Choice, July/Aug 96, p. 1774; RBB, 1 May 96, p. 1520]—**Sandra Adell**

462. Rasor, Eugene L. **The Southwest Pacific Campaign, 1941-1945: Historiography and Annotated Bibliography.** Westport, Conn., Greenwood Press, 1996. 279p. index. (Bibliographies of Battles and Leaders, no.19). $75.00. ISBN 0-313-28874-7.

The Southwest Pacific Campaign, 1941-1945 is an invaluable resource for anyone seeking to gain more knowledge on the Pacific theater just before and during World War II. The book is a treasure trove of arcane and basic information about the Asian/Pacific war and serves as an excellent starting point for the student or military history buff who wants to be pointed in the right direction for his or her research. Rasor legitimately reminds readers that in one sense World War II began as early as 1931 with the movement of the Japanese army into China.

Conceived as both a historiographical survey and annotated bibliography of the Southwest Pacific area, the book brings together all of the pertinent and useful writing about this particular campaign. The historical section that begins the book is quite informative and surveys such topics as general histories, diaries, and oral histories; Allied and Japanese operations; and such colorful, larger-than-life personalities as Douglas MacArthur and Chester Nimitz. The more than 1,500 annotations are succinctly written and provide the reader with adequate information concerning the content and usefulness of a given title.

The Southwest Pacific Campaign is an indispensable reference work for all levels of students, researchers, scholars, and persons interested in both the Pacific campaign and World War II in general. It is a meticulous and painstakingly researched contribution to the field and comes highly recommended.

—John B. Romeiser

Biography

463. Boatner, Mark M., III. **Biographical Dictionary of World War II.** Novato, Calif., Presidio Press, 1996. 733p. $50.00. ISBN 0-89141-548-3.

Boatner, the author of several historical reference works, worked for many years on this biographical dictionary of the Second World War. Using an objective counting method, he selected 1,000 key people to be included. The entries vary in length depending on the importance of the person, and the writing is colorful and entertaining. A glossary of places, events, documents, and other relevant information allows the user to read a biographical entry and refer to the glossary, effectively avoiding repetitive descriptions within each entry.

While considerably greater in scope than earlier biographical dictionaries of World War II, such as those edited by David Mason (Routledge, 1978) and Christopher Tunney (see ARBA 74, entry 303), Boatner's dictionary contains no illustrations. The entries conclude with bibliographic references for further reading. An annotated bibliography of sources and authorities consulted is given at the end of the work. Coverage includes people from all parts of the globe related to World War II, from entertainers to military and political figures. Selected from existing printed reference works as well as firsthand eyewitness accounts, this reference work is particularly useful for the entries on Russian officials and officers. Boatner, a colonel in the U.S. Army (Ret.), served in Europe during World War II and taught military history at West Point from 1959 to 1963.

This otherwise outstanding work is slightly flawed by typographic errors (e.g., "Pasadina," "Reichssicherheitshauptnamt," "Sach[s]enhausen," "subver[si]ve"). Sloppy errors in editing, as in the entry for Joseph Goebbels that refers to him alternately as [Hermann] Göring, are also unfortunate. In addition, some readers may be offended by such language as "the little cripple" and "the strident dwarf" (page 187).

Aficionados of the history of World War II will find this dictionary to be an indispensable browsing tool. Most libraries will want to add it to their reference collections; smaller libraries that already have one of the earlier biographical dictionaries may choose not to add this as price may be a factor.

—Ingrid Schierling Burnett

Chronology

464. **Chronicle of the World.** rev. ed. Derrik Mercer and others, eds. New York, DK Publishing, 1996. 1175p. illus. maps. index. $59.95. ISBN 0-7894-0334-X.

The curious idea of telling the story of humankind through newspaper-type reporting is the concept behind a new book published by DK Publishing and touted on its cover as "the ultimate record of world history." An ultimate record it is not, but the book is in its own way intriguing. It opens with a timeline, mapping the milestones of human history from 3.5 million years B.C.E. to 1995 C.E. The chronicle that follows, which covers the same span of time, is a sequence of stories written as though being told by journalists reporting on the event at the time. Consequently, no information (or reference to information) that comes after the date of the event being discussed is contained in the articles.

Each two-page spread begins with a sidebar chronologically listing the highlights (e.g., births, deaths, declarations of war, treaties, inventions) of the period covered on those pages. In the first part of the book, these spreads may cover hundreds of thousands of years, but by the book's end, the average coverage is two years per spread. A number of well-illustrated articles (i.e., line drawings and photographs—many of them in color) follow. This, along with the bold attention-grabbing headlines and clipped journalistic style of writing, makes for lively reading. However, as a reference tool, this work has serious limitations.

A single volume—even of this size and heft—cannot hope to encompass the entire course of world history in any depth. Therefore, coverage is not thorough, nor is it balanced. This is evidenced in the book's index, which includes a page and a half of listings for the United States, more than 20 listings for Armenia, yet not a single entry for Ukraine. The index is itself inadequate for researchers and serious information-seekers. There is no listing for "Holocaust," although some information on this topic can be found under "Jews," "Auschwitz," and the like. Likewise, the term *kristallnacht* is listed only as a sublisting under "Jews" and is not cross-referenced.

Casual readers and history buffs will no doubt enjoy this work with its unique approach and handsome graphics. For reasons cited above, the book is worth considering as an addition to any library collection. It is heartily recommended as a resource for the history section, but only with hesitation for the reference shelf.—**Barbara Ittner**

465. **Chronicle of the Year 1995.** New York, DK Publishing, 1996. 120p. illus. index. $16.95. ISBN 0-7894-0374-9.

This inexpensive, well-illustrated summary of the year's events will remind some readers of the "Year in Review" issues of *Time* or *Newsweek*. The annual review has a chronological arrangement, with each week's stories occupying two facing pages. More significant stories merit photographs with their short narrative, while a sidebar briefly mentions smaller news events. The stories balance a variety of interests: politics, international affairs, science, sports, and entertainment. A few topics, such as the O. J. Simpson trial and the war in Bosnia, receive special treatment. The book has an index and carries *see also* references in the text for continuing stories. It is important to use them both, because stories such as the nomination and eventual defeat of Henry Foster as surgeon general are linked only in the index.

The contemporary report of the annual gives it a sense of immediacy, but there is little here of research value. While an attractive book, it is more likely to be used for browsing than for reference. One clear advantage it holds over other news digests is the presence of high-quality photographs of people and events. The chronicle could be enhanced with a simplified world atlas and a brief analysis of the top stories of the year. The favorable price and breezy presentation should appeal to high school and public libraries seeking to build their chronology collections. [R: RBB, 15 Mar 96, p. 1312; SLJ, May 96, p. 151]

—**John P. Schmitt**

466. **Pocket Factfile of 20th Century Events.** St. Catharines, Ont., Vanwell Publishing, 1996. 208p. illus. index. (The Pocket Factfile Series). $10.95pa. ISBN 1-55068-081-1.

In this small, chronologically arranged volume, a single two-page spread is devoted to the major political, cultural, and scientific events of each year from 1900 to 1996. One-sentence statements describe selected events, while a heading and subheading highlight significant news items; each spread is illustrated by a picture of one of the year's events described in the text. The index is selective. The pocket size (4 by 6 inches) of this work severely limits coverage, but this type of book has appeal to individuals interested in trivia. Chronologies are, by their nature, subject to nit-picking, but libraries would find Clifton Daniel's *Chronicle of the 20th Century* (see ARBA 96, entry 558) or *Chronology of the Modern World: 1763 to 1992* (see ARBA 96, entry 562) more useful.—**Vandelia L. VanMeter**

Dictionaries and Encyclopedias

467. **The European Powers in the First World War: An Encyclopedia.** Spencer C. Tucker, Laura Matysek Wood, and Justin D. Murphy, eds. New York, Garland, 1996. 783p. index. (Garland Reference Library of the Humanities, v.1483). $95.00. ISBN 0-8153-0399-8.

World War I formed a pivotal moment in world history, although the exact nature and extent of its significance remain the subject of controversy among scholars. Still, it is only fitting that World War I, excluding the participation of the United States, should be the subject of a large encyclopedia consisting of more than 600 entries written by 94 contributors and arranged alphabetically by the subject heading of the entries. The scope of the entries covers all aspects of the war, including its causes (the Balkan Wars, 1912-1913) and immediate aftermath (Stab-in-the-Back Myth). Battles (Caporetto); weapons (zeppelins); strategies (French War Plan XVII); treaties (London, Treaty of, April 26, 1915); and other miscellaneous topics (art, casualties, literature, and medals and decorations) exemplify the wide-ranging subjects of the entries.

The roles of individual countries in the war are surveyed in separate entries. Some 350 of the entries are biographical and cover individuals as diverse as Gavrilo Princip, the assassin of Archduke Ferdinand; the British foreign secretary Edward Grey; the Turkish hero Mustafa Kemal; and the German admiral Maximilian Graf von Spee. Individual entries range from 100 words to several thousand words in length, are signed by their authors, include bibliographies for further reading, and conclude with *see also* references to related entries. Fifteen maps help illuminate the text, while a detailed index will aid readers in finding additional information on various topics. Students, scholars, and the general public will find *The European Powers in the First World War* to be useful and interesting for research, ready-reference, and browsing. [R: Choice, Nov 96, p. 428; SLJ, Nov 96, p. 139; VOYA, Dec 96, p. 299]

—**Ronald H. Fritze**

468. **International Dictionary of Historic Places. Volume 4: Middle East and Africa.** K. A. Berney and Trudy Ring, eds. Chicago, Fitzroy Dearborn, 1996. 766p. illus. maps. index. $125.00. ISBN 1-884964-03-6.

469. **International Dictionary of Historic Places. Volume 5: Asia and Oceania.** Paul E. Schellinger and Robert M. Salkin, eds. Chicago, Fitzroy Dearborn, 1996. 955p. illus. maps. index. $125.00. ISBN 1-884964-04-4.

These two volumes cover the historic places of the Middle East, Africa, Asia, and Oceania. They discuss 377 places in all, arranged in alphabetic order. Each location comes with a short essay on the human events that transpired there. Contributors take care to pinpoint the historical significance of each site. In the process, readers learn why they might want to visit these places. A section labeled "Further Reading" concludes each entry. An index and notes on contributors round out the text.

The essays are generally well written and informative. Some of the facts presented are expected, others surprising. Almost everyone knows, for instance, that Jerusalem is revered by Christians, Jews, and Muslims alike as a holy place; fewer people may be aware that Abeokuta, Nigeria, is home to both ancient Yoruba tribal traditions and 1986 Nobel prize-winner Wole Soyinka. Famous cities (such as Jerusalem, Cairo, Beijing, and Sydney) receive their just due in these volumes, and seemingly obscure places (e.g., Abeokuta, San'a, and so on) take on a life of their own. The black-and-white photographs accompanying most essays are attractive. A few omissions do occur, examples being Abidjan, the Ivory Coast, and Nairobi, but the selections are basically sound. Tourists, in particular, will be able to make good use of these volumes. They are recommended for public libraries. (See ARBA 96, entries 467-469, for reviews of volumes 1-3.)—**Richard E. Holl**

470. Levinson, David, and Karen Christensen. **The Global Village Companion: An A-to-Z Guide to Understanding Current World Affairs.** Santa Barbara, Calif., ABC-CLIO, 1996. 438p. maps. index. $60.00. ISBN 0-87436-829-4.

If one is looking for a cross between a dictionary and an encyclopedia to explain selected terms that recur in news stories from around the globe, this is the book. The authors, a journalist and an anthropologist, have compiled readable explanations of 400 terms they found as they "traveled throughout the United States and Europe, reading many newspapers, magazines, and books, as well as talking to people." The result is an uneven compilation that has many quirks but few serious flaws. Most entries include a definition; background information; cultural and national perspectives; and, where relevant, various points of view or arguments related to the topic. When a certain topic, such as agribusiness, has different effects in various regions of the world, a survey of its effects is given. The book has a Western and, more particularly, a U.S. slant, which is understandable, given the authors' background and the intended audience of U.S. high school students. Thus, absolutism is defined in terms of what it is not, as compared to democracy. The incidence of AIDS is discussed first in terms of developed Western nations, then how it relates to the rest of the world.

Because the authors used an admittedly serendipitous approach to compiling the terms, this reviewer used a similar approach. Clitoridectomy was much in the news a few years ago, when this book was being compiled. It does not appear in the work, but genital mutilation does. This raises a question: If the term itself is used in the media, then would it not make sense to list that term as a cross-reference, or in the index? Likewise, there is no entry devoted to homosexuals, although the index leads one to a number of related topics, such as minority rights, multiculturalism, and Proposition 187. (This last seems in error, because it deals with immigration in California; homosexuals are not mentioned in the article.) It is impossible to tell whether the authors are simply squeamish about discussing terms related to sex in a book for high school students. Nevertheless, the failure to address homosexuality in the AIDS entry is a serious omission. There, the authors explain that "many nations experience resistance to AIDS prevention programs, often led by those who oppose government intervention in sexual behavior and religious leaders who are opposed to any form of birth control." The authors fail to mention homophobia and attitudes toward addicts as exacerbating the AIDS problem in the United States. This exclusion is shocking, first because the topic has been much discussed in the media, so it cannot be an oversight, and second because the authors are careful to portray a wide range of arguments in all of their entries—except this one.

Other checks of the information presented proved more or less what one would expect. Agriculture discusses kinship groups, and yes, there is an entry for kinship. Oustees (people ousted from their homes to make way for development) and Think Globally, Act Locally appear as entries, but NIMBY (not in my backyard) does not. There is an entry on bilateral agreements—but not unilateral actions. New World Order, perestroika, welfare state—all are present and ably explained. Both cross-references and the index are spotty, but the authors do provide a detailed topic finder, grouping entries by general topic, such as children, commerce and trade, and global governance.—**Constance Hardesty**

471. **The Middle Ages: An Encyclopedia for Students.** William Chester Jordan, ed. New York, Scribner's/Simon & Schuster Macmillan, 1996. 4v. illus. maps. index. $350.00/set. ISBN 0-684-19773-1.

Although designed expressly for students, this reference work will serve the needs of anyone interested in knowing more about the Middle Ages, roughly the period from 500 to 1500 C.E. Based on the authoritative *Dictionary of the Middle Ages* in 13 volumes (see ARBA 90, entry 533), this smaller, less expensive version in 4 volumes has been meticulously compiled by academic experts on subjects ranging from Aachen, the Abbasids, Abelard, and Pierre and Héloïse to Ypres and Zanj. The result is a balanced encyclopedia with focused, compact articles on medieval life. These include half-page profiles (e.g., those on *Beowulf*, the Medici family, and relics), along with more extensive articles on broader subjects (e.g., those on agriculture, feudalism, and Islamic art and architecture).

More than 300 illustrations cover medieval art and architecture; illuminated manuscripts; diagrams depicting the construction of castles; fortifications; medieval clothing; and armor, with numerous maps (showing trade routes, migration patterns, changing political boundaries, and so forth). There are a total of 45 full-color plates, but the vast majority of illustrations are either in black-and-white or limited to, at most, 2 colors. There is a bibliography of suggested readings at the end of volume 4, and a detailed, 28-page index for easy reference.

This encyclopedia of the Middle Ages is an informative and reliable but readable work that will bring the most up-to-date, authoritative understanding of this diverse and complex period within the grasp of younger readers and interested adults alike. It should certainly be included in the reference section of any public library, and would serve well any curious reader with an avid interest in the Middle Ages. [R: RBB, 1 Sept 96, p. 168; SLJ, Nov 96, p. 138]—**Joseph W. Dauben**

472. Moss, Joyce, and George Wilson. **Profiles in World History: Significant Events and the People Who Shaped Them.** Detroit, U*X*L/Gale, 1996. 8v. illus. maps. index. $225.00/set; $29.95/v. ISBN 0-7876-0464-X/set; 0-7876-0465-8 (v.1); 0-7876-0466-6 (v.2); 0-7876-0467-4 (v.3); 0-7876-0468-2 (v.4); 0-7876-0469-0 (v.5); 0-7876-0470-4 (v.6); 0-7876-0471-2 (v.7); 0-7876-0472-0 (v.8).

This eight-volume set intended for young readers provides a glimpse into the lives of people who had a great impact upon world events. More than 175 individuals who represent many varied viewpoints or groups, or who affected the outcome of a historic event, or exemplify the role of ordinary persons are featured in a chronological presentation from 3100 B.C.E. to the present day. Each biographical profile (approximately 6-10 pages in length) provides a personal background, the role of the individual in the notable event, and the effect of this occurrence upon society and upon the individual's later life. The readable text is enhanced by many portraits, maps, and other illustrations; pronunciation guides; and sidebars that highlight other people of the time or especially interesting cultural practices. A brief bibliography concludes each profile, and a more extensive bibliography is found at the end of each volume.

The individual volumes are indexed, with many cross-references. At the conclusion of volume 8, a cumulative index provides access to the entire set. Unique in reference sets suitable for libraries serving students grades 5 and up, the accessible text and attractive format will find a wide audience. The 12-volume *McGraw-Hill Encyclopedia of World Biography* (see ARBA 74, entry 106); its 4-volume *20th Century Supplement* (see ARBA 93, entry 39; ARBA 89, entries 21-22; and ARBA 88, entry 30); and Salem Press's 5-volume *Great Lives from History: American Series* (see ARBA 88, entry 513) and its 5-volume *Great Lives from History: Renaissance to 1900 Series* (see ARBA 91, entry 549) serve a similar purpose for grades 8 and up. [R: BR, Sept/Oct 96, p. 54; SLJ, Aug 96, p. 182]—**Vandelia L. VanMeter**

473. Parrish, Thomas. **The Cold War Encyclopedia.** New York, Henry Holt, 1996. 490p. illus. maps. index. (A Henry Holt Reference Book). $60.00. ISBN 0-8050-2778-5.

As the Cold War recedes into the fog of history and new conflicts and challenges in foreign affairs take the place of that state of codependency between the Western powers and the Soviet bloc, the up-and-coming generation may start to ask such questions as: What was détente? What was mutually assured destruction? Where was Check Point Charlie? When was the Cuban Missile Crisis? For some 45 years, the struggle between the Soviet Union and the United States and their respective allies and puppet states ruled the international scene. The seeds of that struggle and its final playing-out can be found in this handy guide to events, places, people, and doctrines that molded and shaped this curious struggle of ideology and military power.

All aspects of life during the Cold War seemed to be driven by a struggle to beat the Soviet Union or to beat the United States. The struggle also seemed to take on the aspects of a comfortable codependency between the Soviets and the Western powers. No real cold warrior could function without the ongoing struggle. The removal of the conflict, the dissolution of the Soviet Union and the Warsaw Pact, and the resultant reduction in military power on the two sides tended to push the world into a new era of uncertainty in foreign affairs. Parrish has provided well-written and concise entries and a timeline that chronicle the events of the Cold War. This work is a must for college, university, public, and private reference collections. [R: RBB, 1 Feb 96, p. 952]—**Norman L. Kincaide**

474. Pope, Stephen, and Elizabeth-Anne Wheal. **The Dictionary of the First World War.** New York, St. Martin's Press, 1995. 561p. maps. $40.00. ISBN 0-312-12931-9.

The Dictionary of the First World War offers the student, scholar, and general public a well-organized and detailed reference work on all aspects of the Great War. Stressing the truly global nature of the conflict that stretched from 1914 to 1918 and involved practically every continent, the authors focus their attention on all theaters of the conflict as well as the participants representing the Allied and the Central Powers.

The excellence of this book resides in its comprehensive, 15-page introduction that is both readable and insightful; its 1,200 carefully cross-referenced entries; a monthly chronology of the major battles and political events; and finally, the 25 clearly drawn and understandable maps. The informative entries touch on weaponry, political and military leaders, and the countless battles and campaigns waged from France to the Pacific. The reader will discover references ranging from such legendary World War I-era figures as Mata Hari (the stage name of Dutch dancer and prostitute Margaretha Geertruida Zelle) and Sergeant Alvin York to the more predictable heads of state and major players, such as Georges Clemenceau and Generals Ferdinand Foch, John Joseph Pershing, and Paul von Hindenburg. Other entries are poignant reminders that such issues as war crimes, ideology, and propaganda, which many people associate with World War II, were not only born but thrived as a result of what has been called "the war to end all wars."

The Dictionary of the First World War will prove to be an essential resource tool for those interested in such a vast and complex topic. It is highly recommended for all libraries. [R: Choice, April 96, p. 1292; RBB, 1 Feb 96, p. 953]—**John B. Romeiser**

475. Reill, Peter Hanns, and Ellen Judy Wilson. **Encyclopedia of the Enlightenment.** New York, Facts on File, 1996. 485p. illus. index. $50.00. ISBN 0-8160-2989-X.

This is a handsome and useful reference work, containing well more than 700 entries in an alphabetic format, with entries on general subject areas (e.g., music, science); terminology (natural law, social contract); important individuals; significant written works; and geographic locations. The encyclopedia is carefully cross-referenced and includes a chronology and a bibliography of major scholarly works on the Enlightenment era. The inside cover blurb is wrong, however, in saying that "never before has [the Enlightenment] been comprehensively surveyed in an A-to-Z format," for in fact this volume was preceded on the market by *The Blackwell Companion to the Enlightenment* (see ARBA 93, entry 555), a work with approximately 50 percent more entries that were written by a long list of scholars.

While Reill and Wilson have fewer biographical entries, these tend to be longer than those in the Blackwell volume. There are some surprising omissions, however. Among monarchs, for example, the authors include Louis XIV, Louis XV, and Louis XVI; the "enlightened despots" Catherine the Great (Russia), Frederick the Great (Prussia), Joseph II (Austria), Charles III (Spain), and Christian VII (Denmark); but otherwise only Maria Theresa of Austria, Peter the Great of Russia, William and Mary of Great Britain, and three of the eighteenth century's eight popes appear. Along with missing kings, one may also reasonably expect an entry on Napoléon I. Where ministers are concerned, Reill and Watson include Wenzel Anton von Kaunitz (Austria), but not André-Hercule de Fleury (France), and for England, Henry St. John Bolingbroke and Robert Walpole are included, but not the two William Pitts. Of course, no reference work can cover everything and everyone, and good reference libraries and Enlightenment scholars will want to own both the Blackwell volume and this one. [R: Choice, Nov 96, p. 428; RBB, 1 May 96, pp. 1521-24; SLJ, July 96, p. 110]—**William B. Robison**

476. **The Supplement to *The Modern Encyclopedia of Russian, Soviet, and Eurasian History*. Volume I: A-Type Rockets - Alma-Ata Agreements.** George N. Rhyne, ed. Gulf Breeze, Fla., Academic International Press, 1995. 250p. $41.50. ISBN 0-87569-142-0.

Collapse of the Soviet Union in 1991 wrought powerful changes in Soviet institutions. This volume is intended to begin updating *The Modern Encyclopedia of Russian, Soviet and Eurasian History* (Academic International Press, 1988) by drawing upon new resources only recently available. In particular, this supplement to the original strives to give greater attention to cultural, social, and economic history, including topics that now can be discussed objectively, in detail, for the first time. It also treats at greater length non-Russian areas and cultures included in the former USSR than was the case in the original *Encyclopedia*.

Forty-three specialists have contributed to this volume (which covers topics from "A-type Rockets" to the Alma-Ata agreements signed by the 11 former republics of the USSR ending the Soviet Union and inaugurating the Commonwealth of Independent States). Among subjects to be found here: abortion, military academies, Dean Acheson, John Q. Adams, advertising, *advokatura* (defense attorneys), Afghan Civil War, aircraft industry, and alcoholism, with substantial articles devoted to agriculture and related topics. Most entries run several pages or more and contain brief bibliographies (most titles are either in

English or Russian). For anyone interested in the contemporary history of Russia and the former Soviet Union, this volume offers interesting reading on a wide variety of topics and should certainly be a part of any reference library.—**Joseph W. Dauben**

477. van Creveld, Martin. **The Encyclopedia of Revolutions and Revolutionaries: From Anarchism to Zhou Enlai.** New York, Facts on File, 1996. 494p. illus. index. $75.00. ISBN 0-8160-3236-X.

It is generally accepted that any government is better than anarchy, the equivalent form of government during a revolution. The romantic, dreamy-eyed view of revolutions can only be vouchsafed if one is removed from the bloody barricades and the stack of dead bodies. *The Encyclopedia of Revolutions and Revolutionaries* brings together in a single volume more than 500 entries that examine the social, economic, and political forces of insurrections and the people associated with them. The book is international in scope and covers seditions from antiquity to the present day.

Both violent and passive mutinies are covered, with articles on, for example, the Russian, American, and French Revolutions; the Civil Rights Movement; and Mao Tse-tung's bloody and deadly Cultural Revolution. Along the way readers will meet not only the well-known Thomas Jefferson, John Adams, Mohandas Gandhi, Che Guevara, and Václav Havel, but also the lesser-known Georges-Jacques Danton, Walther Darre, Janos Kis, Mobutu Sese Seko, and Thomas Sankara. Readers will also find the classified bibliographies helpful, along with the expanded name and subject indexes. While the information in this volume is available elsewhere, having it in one volume is a most useful service to readers. [R: Choice, June 96, p. 1614; RBB, 15 May 96, p. 1620]—**Mark Y. Herring**

Handbooks and Yearbooks

478. **Great Events: The Twentieth Century, Supplement.** By the Editors of Salem Press. Pasadena, Calif., Salem Press, 1996. 3v. illus. maps. index. (A Magill Book). $80.00/set. ISBN 0-89356-425-7.

Providing a welcome update of the original 10-volume *Great Events: The Twentieth Century* (see ARBA 94, entry 539), these 3 supplemental volumes cover 119 events that occurred between the beginning of 1992 and the end of 1995. The original format for the individual entries is continued, and each volume includes five indexes for chronology, keywords, categories, geography, and people. Volume 13 furnishes a detailed timeline covering 1900-1995. Events treated range from the breakup of Yugoslavia in 1992, to the Church of England ordaining women in 1994, to the acquittal of O. J. Simpson in 1995. Libraries owning the original set will definitely want to add these supplemental volumes.

—**Ronald H. Fritze**

479. **History of Humanity. Volume II: From the Third Millennium to the Seventh Century BC.** A. H. Dani, J. -P. Mohen, and others, eds. Paris, United Nations Educational, Scientific, and Cultural Organization and New York, Routledge, 1996. 569p. illus. maps. index. $149.95. ISBN 0-415-09306-6.

The burden of the UNESCO team of historians, who are responsible for the work under review, is whether, to use Arnold Toynbee's phrase, the humanity at large is an intelligible field of study. The kind of history that in the nineteenth century emerged in Western consciousness has been one of hierarchies and value judgments, the drawing of differences between cultures, peoples, and states. History, to the degree it is a story, may require a drama. UNESCO cannot but operate from a multicultural consciousness, in which all peoples and states, large or small, have equal value. The question, however, is whether good history, or history at all, can be written on that basis.

The volume at hand, which is the second in the series (see ARBA 96, entry 568), may not be enough to answer the question, because its subject matter deals narrowly with scientific and technological developments. The work, although it deals with a familiar subject matter, does manage to expand the traditional story by deimperializing it—by pushing the discussion into territories of Africa, South America, Australia, and Asia. However, the question remains whether a multicultural history can persuasively explain the emergence of Isaac Newton and Albert Einstein in the imperialist West. The work may be most useful as a reference work, to supplement an encyclopedia. The reference is well produced, well illustrated, and contains a full index.—**Andrew Ezergailis**

10 Law

GENERAL WORKS

Bibliography

480. Anglim, Christopher. **Annotated Catalog, South Texas College of Law, Special Collections.** Buffalo, N.Y., William S. Hein, 1995. 433p. illus. index. $65.00. ISBN 0-89941-902-X.

This wonderful bibliography was compiled in order to fulfill the publicity mission of its collection's mandate, but it also fulfills twin missions of instruction and delight. Because it serves as a general guide, its 400 or so titles are not the totality of the collection, but the gems. These titles are explicated with fine essays containing historical perspective, wit, and hard fact. Moreover, each includes the rating provided by the Association of American Law Schools's *Law Books Recommended for Libraries* (Fred B. Rothman). The various form subdivisions of the bibliography—for example, "Law Dictionaries," "Contracts," and "Suretyship"—are preceded by an essay defining what is meant by that term. These essays also reflect the author's graceful and learned style.

In addition to "General Legal Materials," the major divisions of the collection are "British Materials," "Scotland and Ireland Legal Materials," "United States Legal Materials," "State Legal Materials," "Texas Legal Materials," and "Houston (Texas) Legal Materials." The preponderance is far and away Great Britain's, occupying 208 pages of text. Houston's legal materials, by way of contrast, require only two pages. The subject arrangement of the work itself is complemented by a complete main entry index.—**Judith M. Brugger**

481. **Law Books & Serials in Print 1996: A Multimedia Sourcebook.** New York, R. R. Bowker/Reed Reference Publishing, 1996. 3v. index. $675.00/set. ISBN 0-8352-3771-0.

Three previous reviews (see ARBA 93, entry 565; ARBA 87, entry 539; and ARBA 86, entry 523) have indicated how this comprehensive, annual, primarily English-language legal bibliography has expanded through the years, having added brief, descriptive annotations to many titles and nonprint media (audio- and videocassettes and software). Social science book entries that are not, strictly speaking, law publications have been eliminated. As in previous editions, titles have been selected from several R. R. Bowker databases (Books in Print, American Book Publishing Record, Ulrich's International Periodicals Directory and Ulrich's Update, Words on Cassette, Bowker's Complete Video Directory, and Software Encyclopedia), from the Library of Congress MARC tapes, and from domestic and foreign legal publishers.

The standard elements of identification R. R. Bowker has used in its various bibliographic works are employed in this set: author(s), title, edition, note for numbered and unnumbered series, pagination, ISBN/ISSN, publisher, and annotation. *See* and *see also* references are liberally used. In a few instances, however, the in-print information appears to be incomplete. In the "Books—Title Index," the *United States Code, 1988* volumes are cited, but none of the 1994 *Code* volumes (published 1995-) are listed. Similarly, only volumes 481-482 of *United States Reports* (the Government Printing Office version of Supreme Court opinions and decisions) are listed; in truth, earlier and later volumes are available. (A case, of course, could be made that both the *U.S. Code* and *U.S. Reports* are serials, but they are not so treated in this set.)

Use of the nonprint media portion of volume 3 should present no problems, nor should the keys to publishers' and distributors' and multimedia publishers' and distributors' abbreviations concluding the volume. The set is kept up-to-date by a mid-year supplement included in the subscription price. Nevertheless, everything considered, *Law Books & Serials in Print 1996* can be recommended for law, academic, and large public libraries as a comprehensive legal bibliographic information source.—**Wiley J. Williams**

482. Matthews, Elizabeth W. **The Law Library Reference Shelf: Annotated Subject Guide.** 3d ed. Buffalo, N.Y., William S. Hein, 1996. 229p. index. $47.50. ISBN 0-89941-991-7.

This bibliography provides a near-comprehensive list of useful legal reference works for law library reference collections. It does so in a well-organized, easy-to-use format. Every entry is annotated with a clear, objective description of the purpose and usefulness of the work.

The guide is perhaps best suited for use by academic law libraries with larger reference collections, but it can be of value to any type of library, including non-law libraries, that have a need to purchase reference materials related to law. For example, many libraries may wish to add legal dictionaries, directories, occupational aids, or dictionaries of legal quotations to their reference collections. This book provides perhaps the only comprehensive listing of titles in these areas and will assist bibliographers in making educated decisions regarding selection of these materials.

The book is divided, by subject, into 14 chapters and numerous subchapters, making referral to particular topical areas of a legal reference collection easier. An author/title index helps the user zero in on particular works, although a subject index would be more helpful to many, particularly non-law librarian bibliographers charged with building or evaluating a legal reference collection. The absence of a subject index is virtually the only shortcoming of this book. Overall, the guide is a work of great value to any library acquisition and reference department, although law libraries, and academic law libraries in particular, will benefit more from its use. [R: Choice, Sept 96, p. 102]—**Richard A. Leiter**

483. **Noble's International Guide to the Law Reports.** 1995 ed. Scott Noble, comp. and ed. Etobicoke, Ont., Nicol Island Publishing, 1995. 367p. $110.00 spiralbound; $90.00 spiralbound (U.S.). ISBN 0-9699467-0-8.

In this unusual book, Noble has examined the court reporters of countries from A to Z (Afghanistan to Zimbabwe, to be precise), and has charted out various characteristics of the reporters from those countries. Has Noble included every country? It is difficult to tell without consulting an encyclopedia. Is he accurate? Again, it is difficult to ascertain, but for the state of Virginia the information he provides seems fine.

So what exactly does Noble tell the reader? Much of his work consists of a matrix that includes the following information for each court reporter: (1) the abbreviation of the court reporter (in Noble's words, the abbreviation he has encountered most often. Presumably this means citations approved by the *Uniform System of Citation*); (2) the full, original title of the reporter; (3) the country (or state) whose cases are published in the reporter; (4) the years in which the published cases were decided; (5) the number of volumes in the reporter series; and (6) occasional comments by Noble, such as alternative citations, cross-references, and references to earlier or later series.

Is the guide useful? One cannot vouch that Noble's work is flawless, but it will help readers figure out the meaning of obscure legal citations and identify the judicial reporters from approximately 130 nations. Is it worth the price? If the user regularly answers questions about foreign court reports, it could be. The *Uniform System of Citation* includes much of this information for about 30 countries. The *World Dictionary of Legal Abbreviations* (see ARBA 93, entry 562) provides 8,400 abbreviations, but not the extras provided by Noble. Should the guide be purchased? For academic and other large law libraries, the answer probably is yes. Smaller law libraries probably can do without.—**James S. Heller**

484. Nordquist, Joan, comp. **Affirmative Action: A Bibliography.** Santa Cruz, Calif., Reference and Research Services, 1996. 68p. (Contemporary Social Issues: A Bibliographic Series, no.41). $15.00pa. ISBN 0-937855-80-4.

Affirmative Action constitutes another bibliographic entry in the outstanding Contemporary Social Issues Series by Reference and Research Services. There is no question but that any research on a topic covered in this series enhances and expedites the research process. This entry is no exception. The bibliography is divided into 13 chapters, including chapters on general works, philosophical works, consequences of affirmative action, 3 chapters on the affirmative action debate, attitudes about affirmative action, affirmative action and employment, women and affirmative action, race and affirmative action, affirmative action and the law, and federal government policy.

Each chapter is divided into two parts, namely, books (including pamphlets, government documents, dissertations, and theses) and articles. A list of sources is provided, enabling researchers to know immediately if their interests are covered. The sources are wide in range and include "social, political, philosophical, legal, feminist and multicultural literature" (p. 7). In addition, alternative publishers, small presses, feminist presses, and activist organizations are well represented in this collection. In general, this series is highly recommended; in particular, this entry is outstanding and appears at a timely moment in the national debate about affirmative action policies, programs, and consequences.—**Michael A. Foley**

Biography

485. **Women in Law: A Bio-bibliographical Sourcebook.** Rebecca Mae Salokar and Mary L. Volcansek, eds. Westport, Conn., Greenwood Press, 1996. 376p. index. $85.00. ISBN 0-313-29410-0.

Women in Law features biographical essays on 43 women from countries in the Western legal tradition who have been prominent in the legal and related fields. Coverage is international, although limited by the editors' "inability to locate and interest specialists from some regions" (e.g., Latin America, Australia, and the Mediterranean). Subjects range from the famous (e.g., Barbara Jordan, Sandra Day O'Connor, Janet Reno) to the more obscure (e.g., Japanese legislator and activist Takako Doi and Rwandan prime minister Agathe Uwilingiyimana).

Articles are from approximately 4 to 10 pages in length and include family background and education, career development, and achievements and contributions, as well as notes and references. They are generally adulatory and written from liberal and feminist perspectives. Depth of treatment varies, and some articles give considerable anecdotal detail. Several authors assume prior knowledge of historical events. Quality of writing ranges from adequate to excellent. The work provides a superficial introductory essay on the history of women and the law, a brief bibliography, and a subject index.

Were it not for its high price, this work might be suitable for public libraries as an inspirational work for aspiring lawyers and activists, especially women. Of limited reference use, it can be recommended as an optional purchase for circulating collections in law libraries and elsewhere where there is interest in law or women. [R: RBB, 1 Nov 96, p. 542]—**Gari-Anne Patzwald**

Dictionaries and Encyclopedias

486. Dahl, Henry Saint. **Dahl's Law Dictionary: An Annotated Legal Dictionary. Spanish-English/ English-Spanish. Diccionario Jurídico Dahl.** 2d ed. Buffalo, N.Y., William S. Hein, 1996. 801p. $79.95. ISBN 1-57588-082-2.

This work is an expansion of the author's 1992 two-volume compilation bearing the same title (see ARBA 94, entry 552). In concept, it combines the functions of a standard Spanish-English legal dictionary with detailed information on "codes, case law, statutes and legal writing" that may vary sharply between Hispanic and English systems of jurisprudence, particularly in the areas of civil and common law. Spanish sources used cover the five basic codes (civil, commercial, civil procedural, criminal, and criminal procedural) as well as the Civil Code of Louisiana, the Standard Penal Code for Latin America, and decisions handed down by the Puerto Rico Supreme Court. One added feature is the table of keywords, structured so as to permit readers unfamiliar with legal terminology to identify related or component concepts under a broader field of law. This dictionary will be most useful for large public libraries serving a Hispanic clientele, university and college libraries supporting programs in law and international business, and corporate and government libraries.—**Robert B. Marks Ridinger**

487. Krohn, Lauren. **Consumer Protection and the Law: A Dictionary.** Santa Barbara, Calif., ABC-CLIO, 1995. 358p. index. (Contemporary Legal Issues). $39.50. ISBN 0-87436-749-2.

This informative, well-written dictionary examines the concepts, laws, organizations, and individuals that comprise consumer protection. An excellent resource for everyone from students to lawyers, the clear explanations of key legislation (e.g., Hazardous Substances Act) and buzzwords (e.g., Delaney clause) reflect the author's knowledge of and experience with the field.

Using the same organizational structure as the series, a general introduction precedes the alphabetically arranged entries, annotated reading list, table of cases, and topical index. The often-lengthy definitions feature examples and highlight historical contexts and other relevant developments. The legal citations and *see also* references promote additional research. An excellent production and a recommended purchase, this dictionary should prove valuable, particularly for libraries with legal and consumer advocate collections. [R: Choice, June 96, p. 1619; RBB, 1 May 96, pp. 1520-21]—**Sandra E. Belanger**

488. **Merriam-Webster's Dictionary of Law.** Springfield, Mass., Merriam-Webster, 1996. 634p. $15.95pa. ISBN 0-87779-604-1.

Merriam Webster's Dictionary of Law provides more than 500 pages of legal definitions, in large and easy-to-read typeface, and appears to be rather standard for a legal dictionary. Obviously, this book is not intended for a practitioner of law, but it will certainly help out any first-year law student attempting to find a definition of a legal term to the satisfaction of the professor. What is impressive in the book, however, are the appendixes. These explain in some detail the judicial system and how it runs; they also include important cases, law, and agencies in U.S. jurisprudence. The book also includes a copy of the United States Constitution.

Also featured are pronunciations of legal terms, so the book appears designed to help laypeople as well as attorneys understand and use legal terminology. As with any dictionary or encyclopedia, however, its use is for relatively pedestrian purposes, not complex technical issues. For those purposes, this dictionary seems comprehensive and well constructed. The definitions are short at times and lengthier at others, but in general this dictionary serves its function as an introduction to the language of the law.—**James E. Root Jr.**

489. **Ready Reference: American Justice.** By the Editors of Salem Press. Pasadena, Calif., Salem Press, 1996. 3v. illus. maps. index. (A Magill Book). $270.00/set. ISBN 0-89356-761-2.

Salem Press's *American Justice* includes more than 800 articles ranging in length from 200 to 3,000 words on a wide variety of topics. Written by college, university, and law school professors from throughout the United States, the articles cover important federal court decisions and legislation, significant individuals, organizations and commissions, historic events, and civil and criminal law issues. Each of the three volumes contains an alphabetic list of the entries in that particular volume and a list for the entire set. The editors also have created 12 broad categories and, in the back of each volume, assign each article to a category. The final volume has several appendixes, the most interesting of which are a listing of famous American trials (from the 1634 conviction of Roger Williams for blasphemy to the 1995 O. J. Simpson acquittal); a timeline of significant events and personages (from the 1215 Magna Carta to the 1995 Supreme Court *Adarand* decision holding unconstitutional a Department of Transportation affirmative action program); and selective Supreme Court cases.

American Justice covers much ground. About 180 different authors contributed to this work, and the articles are, if not uniform in style, at least lucid. This encyclopedia will not win any awards for intellectual rigor, and although it deals with law, it will be of modest use to law students and lawyers. However, the set does offer a starting point for schoolchildren, university students, and the general public researching U.S. law. It is recommended for school and university libraries and for law libraries open to the general public. [R: Choice, Nov 96, p. 425; RBB, 1 Oct 96, p. 366]—**James S. Heller**

490. Strouthes, Daniel P. **Law and Politics: A Cross-Cultural Encyclopedia.** Santa Barbara, Calif., ABC-CLIO, 1995. 301p. illus. index. (Encyclopedias of the Human Experience). $49.50. ISBN 0-87436-777-8.

This concise encyclopedia aspires to define important concepts of law and politics while emphasizing similarities and differences among different legal and political entities. The alphabetically arranged entries, which range in length from 100 to 3,000 words, cover the rather specific ("servitas" and "legal fiction") to the very broad ("natural law" and "jurisprudence"). Strouthes's goal "is to provide a precise and accurate definition for an important concept, as well as some concise background detail and discussion, using data gathered from a variety of legal and political systems around the globe" (p. xi). Many definitions include illustrative examples from U.S. law and contrasting examples from other legal systems. *Law and Politics* concludes with a 250-entry bibliography of articles and books, and a subject index.

This reviewer found it hard to get a handle on what this book is. Strouthes may have intended to create a smaller encyclopedia that grew somewhat unwieldy. But he also may have had in mind a grander work—perhaps an Oxford-like encyclopedia of law and politics—that proved to be a larger bite than one person could reasonably chew. Users end up with a work that struggles to be all things to all people, and which in the end is difficult to classify. It is not easy to find the connection between "Big man," "Black market," and "Canon law"—all of which are defined in the encyclopedia.

It is probably impossible to create a cohesive cross-cultural encyclopedia of law and politics in approximately 300 pages, but Strouthes gave it a shot. *Law and Politics* offers interesting definitions that may benefit some researchers, particularly college students. However, libraries not having this volume on their shelves will not be doing their patrons too much of a disservice. [R: BR, Sept/Oct 96, p. 58; Choice, June 96, p. 1624; SLJ, June 96, p. 160]—**James S. Heller**

491. Taylor, Bonnie B. **Education and the Law: A Dictionary.** Santa Barbara, Calif., ABC-CLIO, 1996. 288p. index. (Contemporary Legal Issues). $39.50. ISBN 0-87436-813-8.

Although the title indicates a dictionary, the author indicates in the preface that this book is an encyclopedia. In truth, it probably falls somewhere in between. A number of broad topics, such as compulsory education, discipline, freedom of speech, and some specific cases, such as *Brown v. Board of Education of Topeka*, are discussed in short articles, arranged alphabetically. Related laws and other court cases are cited throughout the entries. Topics and specific cases are cross-referenced by the use of bold typeface, directing the user to related topics. A table of cases and additional resources are included for the user who wants to pursue the study of educational law further. An excellent index provides good access to topics and issues. The introductory chapter gives a broad overview of the history and sources of education law.

By the author's own assessment, this is not meant to be an in-depth treatment of the topic, and for those looking for specific analysis of legal issues, this book would not be appropriate. However, as a basic introductory volume, this volume does give the user an understanding of the basic principles of educational law and the roots of U.S. education. Written in layperson's terms, this reference book would be of interest to parents, students, teachers, and administrators as a basic tool and resource to school law. It is recommended for public and school libraries.—**Susan Zernial**

Handbooks and Yearbooks

492. Bauman, Richard W. **Critical Legal Studies: A Guide to the Literature.** Boulder, Colo., Westview Press/HarperCollins, 1996. 279p. index. $59.00. ISBN 0-8133-8980-1.

The justice and validity of legal institutions and theories, similar to literary and other cultural traditions, have come under the fire of disillusioned postmodernist critics. A scholarly area involving radical critiques of established legal doctrines and methodologies is necessarily diverse. This useful guide and bibliography is intended to cover a wide range of authors, including some who are not members of the Conference of Critical Legal Studies and may not consider themselves associated with the field, but whose work in some sense critiques established legal doctrine.

Bauman, an associate professor of law at the University of Alberta, has taken the useful approach of organizing his bibliography around a wide range of topics. Some are traditional, such as legal history and theory; the legal profession; and contract, tort, constitutional, criminal, labor, and domestic relations law. Others are less traditional areas, such as feminist jurisprudence, critical race theory, Marxist legal theory, and alternative dispute resolution. For each of the 32 chapters, Bauman provides a 2- to 3-page introduction, giving a summary of the issues raised in this area and discussing the viewpoints and methodologies of a few scholars. The actual bibliographic citations are not annotated or individually evaluated; they most often discuss books and law review articles. The emphasis is on encompassing a range of viewpoints, including conflicting and mutually critical ones, and providing citations for further study in that area. The final chapter provides critiques of critical legal studies as a field.

This is the most comprehensive and up-to-date bibliographic guide available in this field, and it should be useful not only to students of law but also to those interested in current political and other radical thought. The guide is highly recommended for all academic and large public libraries. [R: Choice, Sept 96, p. 93]—**Marit S. MacArthur**

493. Cohen, Morris L., and Sharon Hamby O'Connor. **A Guide to the Early Reports of the Supreme Court of the United States.** Littleton, Colo., Fred B. Rothman, 1995. 237p. illus. $42.50. ISBN 0-8377-0468-5.

This book is a wonderful and concise guide to the early U.S. Supreme Court nominative reports of decisions. The book has several important strengths, the first of which is directly related to its stated scope. Because the book sets out to specifically and exclusively deal with the subject of early Supreme Court bibliography, no faults can be found with lack of scope or coverage of its topic.

The book contains well-written sections on the early process of reporting Supreme Court cases, as well as interesting sections containing biographies of the early reporters themselves. Supreme Court cases, in their early days, were reported in a much less formal way than those of today, to the surprise of many. Novice legal researchers who may not be aware of some of the anomalies, or oddities, in the early volumes of the United States Reports, such as the fact that volume 1 contains no Supreme Court cases at all, will find the book informative in the fact that all such details are exposed and explained. However, even experienced legal researchers can benefit from the level of detail presented in this volume. Many legal research teachers will enjoy reading the guide in order to add to the information that they can draw on in lectures and to answer those annoying questions, such as: Why are there no Supreme Court cases in volume 1 of the *United States Reports*?

However, the majority of the book is filled with a detailed bibliography of the early sources of Supreme Court cases. Virtually every edition and every printing of all nominative volumes of the United States Reports is listed in this bibliography. The authors obviously spent considerable time with the materials that they are writing about, because the minutiae that they have uncovered about different printings and editions of the United States Reports is incredible. For example, in the entry for volume 4 of Dallas's reports, there is a note that "running title on page xv is in error: Title should read 'of the State of Delaware' rather than 'of the State of Pennsylvania.' " Overall, this is an enlightening book, recommended for collections and patrons with research emphases on law and legal history.—**Richard A. Leiter**

494. **Covenants Not to Compete: A State-by-State Survey.** 2d ed. Brian M. Malsberger, Arnold H. Pedowitz, and Robert W. Sikkel, eds. Washington, D.C., BNA Books, 1996. 2v. $195.00pa./set. ISBN 1-57018-030-X (v.1); 1-57018-032-6 (v.2).

Using a question-and-answer format, this work is a treatise on the development in the 50 states and the District of Columbia of postemployment covenants not to compete, which are designed to protect employers' interests in proprietary information, trade secrets, and other confidential data that former employees were trusted with. These covenants prevent ex-employees from entering into competitive employment and otherwise eroding the former employer's business success. Written by members of the American Bar Association Section of Labor and Employment Law, it is a companion to the Section's *Employee Duty of Loyalty: A State-by-State Survey* (see entries 495-496).

The front matter includes, for quick reference, a finding list by each of 14 "general questions" (e.g., Is there a state statute of general application that governs the enforceability of covenants not to compete? What damages may an employer recover and from whom for a breach of such a covenant?). The list is subarranged by state, followed by another finding list of some 100 additional topics (antiadvertising covenants, covenants not to use name, statute of frauds, and the like). This in turn is followed by a section on 1995 developments with respect to the general questions and selected additional topics (age discrimination, antitrust law, statutes of limitation, trade secrets, and so forth). The text sets forth for each state relevant statutes, analyses of leading cases, and discussions of emerging trends vis-à-vis "noncompete" law. The appendixes include a Uniform Trade Secrets Act and State Professional Conduct Rules Barring Restrictive Covenants Among Lawyers.

A paperbound companion volume—the first in a series of annual supplements—begins with a table of cases arranged alphabetically by case name and indicating citation, the occupation or transaction relationship, industry, state, and question numbers; for example, "*Hirsch v. Miller*, 187 So.2d 709 (La. 1966), Exterminator, Pest control, LA, 1." The companion volume concludes with six indexes to the cases: occupation specific, occupation unspecified, industry, sale-of-business, covenants not involving employment or sale of business, and noncovenant cases. *Covenants Not to Compete* will be most useful to corporate lawyers and private practitioners specializing in labor and employment law, law students, and "sophisticated nonlawyers" (foreword).—**Wiley J. Williams**

495. **Employee Duty of Loyalty: A State-by-State Survey.** Stewart S. Manela, Arnold H. Pedowitz, and Brian M. Malsberger, eds. Washington, D.C., BNA Books, 1995. 635p. $135.00. ISBN 0-87179-853-0.

496. **Employee Duty of Loyalty: A State-by-State Survey. 1996 Supplement Covering 1994.** Arnold H. Pedowitz, Robert W. Sikkel, and Brian M. Malsberger, eds. Washington, D.C., BNA Books, c1995, 1996. 187p. $50.00pa. ISBN 0-87179-853-0.

Easily, the most difficult kind of question that a reference librarian in a law library faces is the one that calls for a state-by-state survey on a particular legal issue. These questions arise frequently, and the only realistic way to solve them is to find a library with a collection of all 50 state codes, begin with Alabama, and keep on going. To date, there are very few reference tools that provide this kind of information, and of the ones that do, whether they cover a wide range of topics or a limited number, there still remain tens of thousands of topics that are not covered.

A recent attempt at filling this gap, *Employee Duty of Loyalty* focuses on a narrow slice of labor law and covers the subject with remarkable thoroughness. The level of detail is, perhaps, a function of the apparent level of expertise that the editors themselves possess. The topic of the book, employee duty of loyalty, which translates into plain language as the law of "an employee's obligation to protect trade secrets," is not a topic for which one would expect to find more than 600 pages of text needed to describe it. What is more, only one year after publication, the law in this obviously volatile area of employment law has warranted a 186-page, 1996 supplement.

The book's structure is useful, making for relatively easy state-by-state comparisons of particular issues of law. The introduction, which is approximately 50 pages in length, provides an informative description of the legal issues involved. It is heavily annotated and provides nearly enough detail to stand on its own as a reference tool for state-by-state comparison of these particular laws. The remaining 530-plus pages comprise the state-by-state summaries. The material in this portion of the book is arranged alphabetically by state, and the information in each state's section is arranged according to a standard outline of issues. This makes for easy state-to-state comparisons of particular issues.

The only thing lacking from this book is a chart summarizing and comparing, side by side, the laws of each state. In its present format, it is virtually impossible to do a quick comparison of the laws on any issue. Although the book obviates the necessity of going from state code to state code in a library, it still requires the user to go from state chapter to state chapter, and through the supplement, in the same fashion. Yet the book is a survey of the laws, not a comparison, and in this respect it fulfills its promise extremely well.
—**Richard A. Leiter**

497. Epstein, Lee, Jeffrey A. Segal, Harold J. Spaeth, and Thomas G. Walker. **The Supreme Court Compendium: Data, Decisions, and Developments.** 2d ed. Washington, D.C., Congressional Quarterly, 1996. 744p. index. $62.95. ISBN 1-56802-168-2.

The authors succeed in bringing together a copious amount of data concerning the Supreme Court, its judges and judicial staff, petitions and decisions, political climate, public opinion, and much more, in a well-organized reference work. This 2d edition is strengthened by the elimination of the earlier tables pertaining to the lower federal courts and state courts of last resort, and directing the focus on the Supreme Court. Every table has been updated, and, where possible, backdated, which is particularly useful for longitudinal analysis and research.

There are nine chapters, each with suggested methods of using the information and the rationale for the data collection and inclusion. The data, in tabular format, present a concise, easily accessible presentation. Although the index is not as comprehensive as hoped for, the tables are easy to locate, and specific information can be extracted quickly by browsing. The inclusion of current Internet/Websites in this edition is welcomed by those users pursuing online research.

Those libraries that purchased the 1st edition will want to consider acquiring the 2d edition, because the updating of information and expanded resources to the electronic formats is most valuable. The compendium is highly recommended.—**Susan Zernial**

498. **The Legal Researcher's Desk Reference 1996-97.** Arlene L. Eis, comp. and ed. Teaneck, N.J., Infosources, 1995. 424p. maps. index. $58.00pa. ISBN 0-939486-39-3.

This combination almanac/directory presents a dizzying variety of information (some 122 tables or lists arranged under 13 broad headings) on federal, state, and international government and law; legal education, associations, and publishing; and financial, economic, and miscellaneous information. Representative types of information covered are directories of U.S. Senate committees, federal bankruptcy judges, state notary officials, foreign diplomatic representatives, and state bar associations; lists of past and present U.S. Supreme Court justices, countries of the world, Standard Industrial Classification (SIC) code groups, and proofreaders' marks; and charts showing the court structure of each state. In addition, there are two groups of information directed at law librarians; in these one finds lists of used law book dealers, shelving suppliers, Internet providers, and American Library Association-accredited graduate library education programs (to name just a few). While many of these lists have been compiled by the editor, a number have been reprinted from other sources.

The reference claims that the information is "current and reliable as of October 1995," but this is not always true. The reprinted table "Governors of the States and Territories" lists governors whose terms expired as early as January 1994; a subsequent directory of gubernatorial addresses contains quite a few new names. While a plea is made to bear with changing area codes, the Maryland change from 301 to 410, which occurred several years ago, has been missed in a troubling number of directory listings. Although this sourcebook does contain much that is useful, one of its lists—URLs of leading law-related World Wide Web sites—suggests the likelihood that up-to-date information in an arena where currency is of enormous value will increasingly not be looked for in a print source.—**Jack Ray**

499. Posner, Richard A., and Katharine B. Silbaugh. **A Guide to America's Sex Laws.** Chicago, University of Chicago Press, 1996. 243p. $26.95. ISBN 0-226-67564-5.

This guide is a compendium of state and federal statutes relating to personal sexual activity. It does not cover the laws about entrepreneurial activity, such as the production of pornographic materials as opposed to the purchase of materials for private consumption. Posner is chief judge of the U.S. Court of Appeals, Seventh Circuit. He has written numerous books on a variety of topics, including the subject at hand. His coauthor is a professor at the Boston University School of Law.

Posner and Silbaugh introduce each of the 17 chapters with a brief overview of its topic, followed by an alphabetic listing of every state and its treatment of the issue. (This reviewer's copy was missing all of chapter 2, obviously a production flaw.) Descriptions of federal law conclude each chapter. Subjects include rape, age of consent, marital exemptions from rape, public nudity, bestiality, abuse of authority, obscene communications, and so on. A brief glossary defines common sexual terms as they are generally used in the law.

The authors hasten to point out that laws may change quickly, but they direct this book to professional and general readers as an introduction to individual state and federal treatments of sexual behavior. Libraries should find it useful for quick reference on a sensitive subject. [R: BL, 15 Oct 96, pp. 451-52]
—**Berniece M. Owen**

500. **The Sourcebook of Federal Courts: U.S. District and Bankruptcy.** 2d ed. Tempe, Ariz., BRB, 1996. 410p. maps. (The Public Record Research Library). $33.00pa. ISBN 1-879792-25-7.

Existing court directories include Information Resource Press's *National Directory of Courts of Law* (see ARBA 93, entry 586); *BNA's Directory of State and Federal Courts, Judges, and Clerks* (4th ed.; see ARBA 93, entry 582); *Want's Federal-State Court Directory* (see ARBA 94, entry 564, and ARBA 91, entry 582); and *Judicial Staff Directory* (see ARBA 94, entry 736, and ARBA 91, entry 576). More specialized directories include *Directory of State Court Clerks and County Courthouses* (see ARBA 91, entry 574) and the *County Courthouse Book* (2d ed.; see ARBA 96, entry 588). *The Sourcebook of Federal Courts* offers a different slant from these other directories: It provides detailed information on where and how to locate case records in federal courts. A companion to the publisher's *Sourcebook of County Court Records* (see ARBA 95, entry 609), this new edition provides updated information on some recent technological innovations that affect how one locates court records, including the growth of the PACER system (an online case index and docketing database) and the Voice Case Information System (VCIS).

The first section of the sourcebook provides information on the federal court structure, court record retention, obtaining case records, and using electronic access methods such as PACER. Section 2, which comprises nearly 90 percent of the text, summarizes the federal court structure for each state, provides maps and lists for the judicial district and division in which each county lies, and profiles each district and bankruptcy court. The court profiles, which are arranged by state, then district, then division, provide information on how cases are indexed and stored within each court, how to search by telephone or mail, in-person searches, and PACER access. Addresses, telephone numbers, and fees are included. The third and final part of the directory provides information about retrieving cases from the 14 federal records centers. Also given are names and telephone numbers of selected firms that can retrieve information from the records centers.

Of course, a person no longer has to rely entirely on print. One can find helpful information on the Internet, including the Office of Federal Records Center's Home Page (http://dolley.nara.gov.nara/frc/frchome.html), the Directory of Electronic Public Access Services to Automated Information in the U.S. Federal Courts (http://www.uscourts.gov/PubAccess.html), and PACER (http://www.teleport.com/richh/pacer.html). *The Sourcebook of Federal Courts* is a valuable reference tool for all types of libraries whose patrons inquire about getting federal court records. At only $33, libraries cannot go wrong on this one.—**James S. Heller**

CRIMINOLOGY

Bibliography

501. Prunckun, Henry W., Jr. **Shadow of Death: An Analytic Bibliography on Political Violence, Terrorism, and Low-Intensity Conflict.** Lanham, Md., Scarecrow, 1995. 406p. illus. index. $77.00. ISBN 0-8108-2773-5.

For those researching the many facets of violence, this annotated bibliography is an ample resource listing books, periodicals, and databases. A brief dictionary of pertinent acronyms precedes an introductory segment that examines the definition and history of terrorism. The main body of the work is organized by specific topics such as anti-Semitism, arms dealing, assassinations, bombings, counterintelligence, hijacking, kidnapping and hostage taking, political movements, piracy, racial violence, riots and civil disturbances, and the like, as well as by selective geographic areas.

The bibliography fills a need for breadth of subject rather than depth, including resources through 1993. Plus, the author provides a list of booksellers and dealers specializing in this subject matter. Prunckun is a criminologist who has written numerous textbooks, journal articles, and software packages relating to his field of expertise. [R: Choice, June 96, p. 1622]—**Jean Engler**

502. Stern, Peter A. **Sendero Luminoso: An Annotated Bibliography of the Shining Path Guerrilla Movement, 1980-1993.** Austin, Tex., SALALM Secretariat, University of Texas at Austin, 1995. 363p. index. $56.95pa.. ISBN 0-917617-43-6.

The violent and bloody Peruvian revolutionary movement Shining Path and the Peruvian government's equally violent response to it have spawned a large body of literature that is made accessible through this outstanding bibliography. Stern has used standard library resources (e.g., indexes, online catalogs) and personal contacts to identify, select, and personally review 1,185 monographs and articles on Shining Path in Spanish and English. The bibliography is arranged chronologically, beginning with the first mention of Shining Path that Stern was able to locate in an obscure Peruvian magazine in December 1993. Emphasis is on publications of scholarly interest available in U.S. libraries. The abstracts, which are well written, are in English and average from a quarter to a half page in length; the typeface is very small. An excellent short history of Shining Path, a chronology of the movement, and author and subject indexes are also included. *Sendero Luminoso* is highly recommended for college and university libraries and for larger public libraries where patron interest justifies the expense.—**Gari-Anne Patzwald**

Biography

503. Frasier, David K. **Murder Cases of the Twentieth Century: Biographies and Bibliographies of 280 Convicted or Accused Killers.** Jefferson, N.C., McFarland, 1996. 552p. index. $65.00. ISBN 0-7864-0184-2.

Murder always has and most likely always will inspire a level of interest quite disproportionate to its frequency. In the present era, the enduring historical fascination with murderers—especially those who commit the most heinous or bizarre forms of murder—continues unabated and is reflected in the massive attention in virtually all forms of media. In the realm of books, "true crime" accounts—principally of murder cases—are exceptionally popular, and often make the best-seller lists.

Given the level of attention to murder, it is unsurprising that quite a number of encyclopedias on murderers or murder cases, or closely related topics, have been produced. The author of the present work is a librarian at Indiana University. He has chosen to provide accounts and accompanying bibliographies of 280 convicted or accused murderers. His cases are restricted to the twentieth century. The largest single proportion of entries are of U.S. citizens, although killers from many other countries—especially Great Britain—are also included. The author reports that his selection criteria focused on the historical or legal importance of the cases, their unique and extreme nature, and their reference value. Political killers and gangsters are among those excluded.

The accounts range from a brief sentence (and cross-reference) to several pages. They are typically both reasonably concise and exceptionally readable. Aliases (when applicable) and other essential facts about each offender are provided. Information on the present status of the offender, if alive, is an especially useful feature of these accounts. The narrative is then followed by a scrupulously compiled, detailed listing of major references. The volume includes an appendix classifying the different cases, an author and title index, and a general index.

All together, this is an admirable reference work that strikes a remarkable balance between human interest value and valuable reference source. It should prove exceptionally appealing to both amateur and scholarly students of murder. Accordingly, it can be recommended for both public libraries and university library collections.—**David O. Friedrichs**

Dictionaries and Encyclopedias

504. Axelrod, Alan, and Charles Phillips, with Kurt Kemper. **Cops, Crooks, and Criminologists: An International Biographical Dictionary of Law Enforcement.** New York, Facts on File, 1996. 321p. illus. index. $45.00. ISBN 0-8160-3016-2.

This work contains sketches of more than 600 individuals chosen for their impact on criminal law enforcement and criminology. As the catchy title indicates, this includes criminals, police, and theoretical contributors. It also encompasses philosophers and rulers. This dictionary is both a useful reference and a work to browse.

There is a brief essay by the authors sketching some highlights of the development of Western (and particularly Anglo-American) criminal law enforcement. No indication of sources used to compile the work is provided, nor are criteria used for inclusion or exclusion indicated in any detail. Why, for example, is Ur-Nammu (Sumerian king) included, while the emperor Justinian I (whose code shaped continental European law) is excluded?

Entries average half a double-columned, 8-by-11-inch page. They provide basic biographical information and a few informative paragraphs on the subject's significance for criminology. With subjects running the gamut from judges and philosophers to private detectives and gangsters, the dictionary makes entertaining reading. Entries are well written, and subjects include such contemporary figures as William Bennett and Tom Bradley. The bias is clearly toward profiling U.S. figures. Material appears to be up-to-date (e.g., F. Lee Bailey's entry includes a couple of sentences on O. J. Simpson's defense).

There are cross-references, with names profiled in other entries capitalized. At least some gaps appear in this work—Napoléon I is not capitalized in the entry on his great-nephew Charles Bonaparte. The index seems thorough, with references to main entries in bold typeface. Compared to current reference works, the volume is reasonably priced. It is recommended as an acquisition for large- and medium-sized public libraries. [R: Choice, July/Aug 96, p. 1768; RBB, 15 Mar 96, p. 1312]—**Nigel Tappin**

505. **Encyclopedia of American Prisons.** Marilyn D. McShane and Frank P. Williams III, eds. New York, Garland, 1996. 532p. index. $95.00. ISBN 0-8153-1350-0.

The *Encyclopedia of American Prisons* is a storehouse of information relating to virtually any aspect of U.S. prisons. More than 160 essays cover topics as narrow as the handling of prisoners with AIDS to subjects as broad as the history of prisons. This one-volume encyclopedia is designed for ease of use. First, there is a table of contents listing every major entry found in the next 516 pages. Second, there is a comprehensive index that allows the reader to locate subjects that might not have a separate listing in the table of contents (e.g., numerous court cases are cited here). Furthermore, every major entry concludes with a select bibliography and relevant court cases.

Included in this encyclopedia are biographies of some of the key players in the development and administration of prisons (e.g., Sanford Bates, Dorothea Dix, Benjamin Rush); an overview of some major prisons both past and present (e.g., Alcatraz, Angola, Marion); details of prison operations (e.g., diet and food service, double celling, security and control); and a vast variety of other offerings (e.g., prison argot, architecture, escapes, parole boards). In addition, issues of wider scope are handled with greater detail: children of prisoners, correctional officers, crowding, and legal issues, to mention a few.

If one's research has to do with prisons in the United States, this encyclopedia is the place to begin. The entries are uniformly well written and enjoyable to read. Anyone interested in the history and present status of U.S. prisons will find this volume an essential reference work; it is highly recommended. [R: Choice, Sept 96, p. 95; LJ, 1 June 96, p. 94]—**Michael A. Foley**

506. Williams, Vergil L. **Dictionary of American Penology.** rev. ed. Westport, Conn., Greenwood Press, 1996. 488p. index. $89.50. ISBN 0-313-26689-1.

The rise in the prison population in the United States has been dramatic. At present there are more than one-and-a-half million inmates in U.S. prisons and jails (although this population growth slowed in 1996 for the first time in a decade). Furthermore, prison conditions in some states have been made harsher, with previous amenities now denied to inmates. Whether either of these developments is a factor in reported lower crime rates is a matter of some dispute. What is incontestable, however, is that this *Dictionary of American Penology*, originally compiled in the 1970s (and published in 1979—see ARBA 80, entry 747), was overdue for the current revised and expanded edition.

The first half of this volume includes entries, typically ranging from one to three pages in length, on a broad variety of penological topics. The federal system and the different state systems are described, as are various prison programs (e.g., conjugal visits, literacy, and so forth). Other entries explore such concepts as disparity in sentencing and recidivism. There are also some entries of historical interest (e.g., Eastern Penitentiary, the Attica Uprising). Of course any such listing must be selective. For example, there is an entry on Robert Martinson—whose critical study of rehabilitation programs was widely cited—but many other influential figures are left out. The included entries are generally informative, up-to-date, and usefully end with a list of a few key references.

The second half of this volume is composed of a series of appendixes: for example, a listing of prison reform organizations, statistical tables from the Department of Justice and the Bureau of Prisons, and tables of data drawing upon attitudinal surveys. There are some 25 tables pertaining to the death penalty. Finally, the volume concludes with a selective bibliography and an index. The author/compiler of this volume, a professor of criminal justice at the University of Alabama, is to be commended for producing a work that will be thoroughly useful to any student of contemporary U.S. penology.—**David O. Friedrichs**

Handbooks and Yearbooks

507. Dobrin, Adam, and others. **Statistical Handbook on Violence in America.** Phoenix, Ariz., Oryx Press, 1996. 394p. index. $54.50. ISBN 0-89774-945-6.

Anyone who needs or wants to know something about the reality of violence in the United States should make this reference work the first stop. The book is logically and clearly divided into the following five chapters: "Fatal Violence in America" (homicide); "Other Interpersonal Violence in America" (e.g., rape, robbery, carjackings, aggravated assaults); "Groups and Situations" (groups and situations vulnerable or at high risk, including children, women, and police officers); "Impact of Violence" (e.g., psychological trauma, injuries, economic losses); and "Opinions About Violence" (public opinion surveys about public perceptions on violence).

Each chapter begins with a brief introduction providing background information, where necessary, on definitions, data sources, chapter focus, and chapter organization. In addition to the table of contents, the researcher will find a detailed, 11-page "List of Tables and Figures" that expedites the search process. For example, if someone wants to know something about murders in which the victim and offender were related, one quickly finds Table 1.10, "Murders, by Victim-Offender Relationship and Gender, 1992." There one finds that "Relationship" is divided into the categories of "Family" (e.g., spouse, sibling, stepparent) and "Others Known to Victim" (e.g., neighbor, boy/girlfriend, employer). If a specific table or figure cannot be identified from this list, there is an excellent index that breaks down the information into numerous subject headings. The presentation of the material is outstanding. The handbook is highly recommended. [R: Choice, May 96, p. 1458]—**Michael A. Foley**

508. Durham, Jennifer L. **Crime in America: A Reference Handbook.** Santa Barbara, Calif., ABC-CLIO, 1996. 318p. index. (Contemporary World Issues). $39.50. ISBN 0-87436-841-3.

Crime in America provides users with seven chapters on the product of the seven deadly sins. Various types of crimes are described (white collar, drugs, organized crime), the justice system is limned, a brief history of the volume of criminal laws descried. Additionally, sketches of those who have played key roles in the understanding (or tolerance) of crime are included: Lyndon Johnson, J. Edgar Hoover, Eliot Ness, and James Q. Wilson, to name but a few. To round out this excellent tool, a chapter on criminal statistics is offered, along with one on both federal and private crime organizations. The usual periodicals, books, and other help close out the tome.

This most helpful tool is part of the stellar Contemporary World Issues series from ABC-CLIO. While such tools will never *écrasez l'infâme*, they will aid the understanding of it. Librarians who wish for a one-volume treatment of a multiply complex subject will certainly want to add this one to their collections; it would be criminal not to.—**Mark Y. Herring**

509. Kinnear, Karen L. **Gangs: A Reference Handbook.** Santa Barbara, Calif., ABC-CLIO, 1996. 237p. index. (Contemporary World Issues). $39.50. ISBN 0-87436-821-9.

Anyone who desires to understand more fully the nature of gangs in the United States must turn to this wonderful book. The material presented can be used at both high school and college levels and would be enormously useful to legislators and community leaders concerned about gang activity in their communities or states. Chapter 1 offers various definitions of "gang," provides some general explanations about why people join gangs, and examines briefly the growth of gangs and increasing levels of violence, among other matters. The chapter ends with an excellent set of references. Chapter 2 presents a chronology of gangs from 1791 to 1994, which will certainly help people understand the development of this problem. Chapter 2 ends with a set of references as well.

Chapter 3 offers brief biographical sketches of some of the leading researchers on gangs. Chapter 4 provides a superb collection of facts and statistics, along with numerous excerpts from state law documents and one excerpt from the federal level pertaining to juvenile gangs. The chapter closes with some useful quotations from both experts and gang members on gangs and a set of references. Chapter 5 lists private, state, and local government organizations that work in one way or another with gangs, including research-, prevention-, and service-oriented organizations. Chapter 6 contains an annotated selection of print resources. Chapter 7 provides an annotated selection of nonprint resources, including videos, online searches, and Internet resources. The book concludes with a useful index. The handbook is highly recommended for all collections.—**Michael A. Foley**

510. Kruschke, Earl R. **Gun Control: A Reference Handbook.** Santa Barbara, Calif., ABC-CLIO, 1995. 408p. index. (Contemporary World Issues). $39.50. ISBN 0-87436-695-X.

This truly excellent resource is another noteworthy addition to the Contemporary World Issues series. The volumes in this series are exceptionally user friendly and manage to collect between two covers copious useful information on a certain issue of current concern (see entries 508, 509, and 515 for other examples). Gun control continues to be a hotly contested topic that inspires various legislative initiatives and considerable research or commentary. Kruschke is a professor emeritus of political science whose claim of 35 years of interest in the issue at hand is thoroughly documented by his virtually comprehensive command of the vast literature involved.

The format of this volume corresponds closely to that of other volumes in the series. A long introductory section identifies the basic parameters of the gun control issue, including the contrasting interpretations of the Second Amendment, dimensions and demographics involved on both sides of the issue, and the role or liability of the police and gun manufacturers. A chronology lists important dates, from 380 B.C.E. to 1995, and brief biographical sketches of key figures are provided. Fairly detailed synopses of important legal decisions, constitutional amendments, legislative acts, and statistics (on such matters as gun ownership and dealers) fill one section, with the next section describing (and listing addresses for) a wide range of organizations or associations concerned with the gun control issue. Two final sections of the volume contain annotated listings of print and nonprint resources pertaining to gun control. A glossary and an index are also included.

Altogether, a teacher on any educational level who wishes to address the gun control issue in some depth will find this volume invaluable. Although an interested general public and students on the secondary school level and above are the most likely larger audience for *Gun Control*, one would imagine that even a scholarly researcher will find it a handy reference work. [R: BR, Sept/Oct 96, pp. 60-61; Choice, June 96, p. 1619; SLJ, May 96, p. 140; VOYA, June 96, p. 133]—**David O. Friedrichs**

511. **Statistics on Crime & Punishment: A Selection of Statistical Charts....** Timothy L. Gall and Daniel M. Lucas, eds. Detroit, Gale, 1996. 235p. index. $55.00. ISBN 0-7876-0528-X.

During the 1996 presidential election campaign, President Bill Clinton, repeatedly called attention to FBI crime statistics indicating a decline in the crime rate. As criminologists well know, the meaning of and explanation for such statistics are open to interpretation. The present volume provides readers with a large number of statistical charts, graphs, and tables concerning various aspects of crime and justice, drawn from a range of sources, with some accompanying commentary. The sources drawn upon include not only the well-known FBI Uniform Crime Report, but also juvenile court statistics, the National Crime Victimization Survey, National Prisoner Statistics, and United States Secret Service statistics. An introductory essay by the well-established criminologist Peter C. Kratcoski, in association with Lucile Kratcoski, offers readers some general observations on crime and criminal justice trends, and some specific guidance on making sense of the crime statistics furnished in this volume.

This reference source is divided into two major segments, crime and punishment, with each section further broken down to include as few as 1, or as many as 21, graphs or tables on more specific topics such as historical, demographic, and geographic trends; different types of crime (e.g., violent, property, and hate crimes); arrests; sentencing patterns; and economic costs of crime and justice. Each graph or table is accompanied by a brief comment, an identification of the source of the statistics, and an agency address to be contacted for further information.

Certainly, this volume can serve as a handy reference source, especially for those who need information on crime and criminal justice trends but are not professional researchers with access to primary sources. Although the ordering of graphs and tables appears to be somewhat haphazard in places, the overall format of presentation is user friendly. All together, this volume, which includes a glossary and index, would appear to be an appropriate acquisition for libraries serving the general public, as well as secondary schools or colleges, and is likely to be frequently consulted.—**David O. Friedrichs**

512. **Statistics on Weapons & Violence: A Selection of Statistical Charts, Graphs, and Tables....**
Timothy L. Gall and Daniel M. Lucas, eds. Detroit, Gale, 1996. 226p. index. $55.00. ISBN 0-7876-0527-1.

The editors do a superb job of rendering statistical data intelligible to the nonspecialist in this timely and important aggregation of information on a troubling subject. Each entry is laid out with statistical data in the form of graphs and tables on the verso and brief, generally balanced interpretations on the recto. This system is a bit relentless when the book is read all the way through, but the volume will certainly be more often consulted than perused. The fundamental arrangement, with statistics on weapons before those on general violence, reflects a certain dogmatic perspective on handguns, as do other elements of the book, but the treatment is fairly evenhanded. Most issues indicated by the title can be found here, including much reporting of general violence, types of weapons used by types of individuals in categories of crimes, sources of weapons, the effect of resistance to violence, and the occurrence of preventative measures. An interesting omission that may not have been available in the sources consulted is the role of Asian martial arts in crimes of violence. Even so, this is a useful book that belongs in most larger libraries.—**John Newman**

ENVIRONMENTAL LAW

513. Nordquist, Joan, comp. **Environmental Racism and the Environmental Justice Movement: A Bibliography.** Santa Cruz, Calif., Reference and Research Services, 1995. 72p. (Contemporary Social Issues: A Bibliographic Series, no.39). $15.00pa. ISBN 0-937855-76-6.

This listing of 588 books and articles on environmental racism and the environmental justice movement is divided into 7 main subject areas. Two of the sections ("Environmental Racism: The Problems" and "Activism and Solutions to the Problems of Environmental Racism") contain a useful index of racial groups. The main subject subdivisions are not especially helpful, unless patrons specifically need to narrow their topics. Entries generally cover the period from 1990 to 1995; however, classic citations from earlier years are not excluded. An example is a spring 1983 article by Ward Churchill and Winona La Duke on Native Americans and radiation pollution in *Insurgent Sociologist*.

As with all the bibliographies in the Contemporary Social Issues Series, a broad scope is used. Books, pamphlets, government documents, and dissertations are included from mainline publishers and small, alternative, or specialized presses. The broadness of scope is particularly important with this subject, which was brought to first light by social justice, church, and environmental organizations. It is gratifying to find citations from the American Bar Association alongside those from *Essence*, the United Methodist Church, and *Covert Action Quarterly*.

The list of organizations at the end would be more useful if telephone numbers were included with the addresses. Likewise for the listing of periodicals, which seems rather short with only 12 items. An introductory paragraph for the periodical listing explains why those chosen would be helpful. Overall, this bibliography has good value if it is used in the near future. Its value would be greatly enhanced with even short annotations.—**Georgia Briscoe**

514. Patton-Hulce, Vicki R. **Environment and the Law: A Dictionary.** Santa Barbara, Calif., ABC-CLIO, 1995. 361p. index. (Contemporary Legal Issues). $39.50. ISBN 0-87436-749-2.

The author states, in her preface, that this dictionary "is written for high school, college, and postgraduate students as well as researchers and people interested in environmental studies." Certainly a wide-ranging group of people; one wonders who is not included in that group (and perhaps "middle school" could be added to the list). That said, Patton-Hulce's dictionary provides an adequate introduction to environmental law, but really is not designed for those doing sophisticated environmental law research.

Patton-Hulce begins with a 32-page introduction to environmental law, including a snapshot of the legislative, administrative, and judicial processes. She then proceeds to define approximately 200 terms, from *acid rain* to *wetland*. Those make sense in this kind of dictionary, as do nearly all of the other definitions—which range from 40 words to several pages in length. A bit puzzling are the entries for George Herbert Walker Bush and Ronald Reagan, although one may appreciate the well-deserved criticism of those two presidents' environmental records. The book concludes with a selective bibliography of articles and books, a brief table of federal and state court decisions, a listing of some federal environmental statutes and regulations, and a fairly thorough index.

Because Patton-Hulce's definitions are more thorough than those found in the typical dictionary, her book really is more than a dictionary. (Compare it to Neil Stoloff's more abbreviated *Environmental Law Dictionary* [Oceana, 1993], for example.) Yet it would not be fair to call it encyclopedic, either. For more in-depth treatment of environmental issues, one should look at William Cunningham's *Environmental Encyclopedia* (Gale, 1994), or the more scientific-oriented *McGraw-Hill Encyclopedia of Environmental Science and Engineering* (3d ed.; see ARBA 94, entry 1999). The work under review does fit a niche, however, and it is recommended for school and public libraries, junior college libraries, and university undergraduate libraries. [R: Choice, May 96, p. 1455; LJ, 15 April 96, p. 74; RBB, 1 May 96, pp. 1520-21]

—**James S. Heller**

HUMAN RIGHTS

515. Edmonds, Beverly C., and William R. Fernekes. **Children's Rights: A Reference Handbook.** Santa Barbara, Calif., ABC-CLIO, 1996. 364p. index. (Contemporary World Issues). $39.50. ISBN 0-87436-764-6.

As part of ABC-CLIO's Contemporary World Issues series, this work is an outstanding addition. Using an encyclopedic approach to the subject, parts 1-3 provide an overview of children's rights from their early conceptual stages; information about current issues involving children's rights regarding the law, violence, family, sexual exploitation, and refugee status; and a summary of implications for children's rights in the United States. Chapters 2-9 include: (1) a historical chronology of children's rights; (2) biographical sketches of notable children's rights activists and reformers; (3) international guidelines, proposals, and declarations concerning children's rights; (4) relevant U.S. policy recommendations and Supreme Court rulings; (5) statistics concerning existing conditions of poverty, health, violence, and organizations associated with children's rights; and (6) two separate chapters containing annotated lists of additional print and nonprint resources. A glossary and index conclude the text.

The authors recommend their work as an initial reference tool for high school and college students, scholars, general readers, legislators, businesspeople, activists, and others. They have not exaggerated their target audiences. Thoroughness, accuracy, and consultation with acknowledged children's rights legal experts, social workers, United Nations personnel, and government document librarians have ensured that this publication is an invaluable authoritative resource in a much-needed subject area. Given today's preference for initiating research by accessing online databases, CD-ROMs, and the Internet, the annotated lists of Gopher and World Wide Web sites is nothing short of impressive. Academic, public, school, and subject-related special librarians should consider this work a mandatory purchase. It successfully bridges the gap between a print and an electronic reference work in a reasonably priced, comprehensive format.—**Kathleen W. Craver**

516. Gibson, John S. **Dictionary of International Human Rights Law.** Lanham, Md., Scarecrow, 1996. 225p. $42.00. ISBN 0-8108-3118-X.

Gibson provides an excellent guide to the meanings of terms and concepts found in international human rights law. The book is clearly and coherently organized and written. It divides into two basic parts, namely, an "Issues and Contexts" section, which defines the framework within which the dictionary will develop, and the dictionary, which provides definitions for the specific components of the rights themselves. The five categories of human rights are: civil and political; legal; economic, social, and cultural; collective; and declaratory. For example, terms defined under the category "civil and political rights" include assembly, association, asylum, discrimination, life, nationality, press, property, religion, speech, and women; terms defined under "legal rights" include appeal, arrest, bail, death penalty, due process, equal protection of the law, ex post facto law, habeas corpus, juvenile due process, privacy, punishment, and torture.

Each definition contains several components, namely, the right itself, other sources, an expanded definition, landmark decisions, and cross-references. These are indeed comprehensive definitions. A directory that states the primary resources for entries in the dictionary is provided. Each category of human rights begins with an introduction to the right, followed by the dictionary entries. The book concludes with a substantial bibliography. While the dictionary can be used to seek definitions for specific terms found in specific treaties related to the rights, the book can be read profitably from the beginning, especially the "Issues and Contexts" section. This dictionary will be useful for anyone doing research in international law and is recommended highly for general, college, and university collections. [R: LJ, Aug 96, p. 64]—**Michael A. Foley**

517. Lawson, Edward. **Encyclopedia of Human Rights.** 2d ed. Bristol, Pa., Taylor & Francis, 1996. 1715p. index. $275.00. ISBN 1-56032-362-0.

The act of liberation and the struggle for collective and individual freedoms are constants throughout the world. It is hard to imagine any part of the globe that has not suffered some form of human degradation. The 2d edition of the *Encyclopedia of Human Rights* is an ideal source for those interested in locating information on specific liberation movements, ranging from the Tamil Separatives to a thorough discussion of the issue of race. The 2d edition has incorporated many new documents and reports, while materials found out-of-date have been omitted. The philosophy for inclusion was to rely not on government-produced reports but rather on "Special Rapporteurs." This practice, according to the author, aims at eliminating bias and self-interest from government reporting agencies.

The structure of the encyclopedia is alphabetic and includes much basic material on human rights, international organizations and agencies involved in the protection of human rights, the conditions of human rights in 186 countries and territories around the world, and biographical information on Nobel peace prize winners and their contributions to human rights issues. Many of the entries provide cross-references (in bold typeface) to related sections, a helpful feature for students looking for research paper topics. Many of the reports and documents are reproduced in full or in part. The alphanumeric symbols used on many of the documents provide an efficient way to locate these documents in United Nations (UN) repository libraries or how to order them from Human Rights Internet. The majority of the entries include extensive bibliographies.

There are two appendixes: a chronological list of the documents in the work and a list of statuses (ratifying countries) of major UN human rights treaties and conventions. A subject index allows for simple access to all the materials. This reference work is indispensable for all levels of interest in human rights. It is highly recommended for both academic and public libraries.—**Dario J. Villa**

518. **World Directory of Human Rights Research and Training Institutions. Repertoire Mondial des Institutions de Recherche et de Formation sur les Droits de L'homme. Repertorio Mundial de Instituciones de Investigacion y de Formacion en Materia de Derechos Humanos.** 3d ed. By UNESCO Social and Human Sciences Documentation Centre. Paris, UNESCO Publishing; distr., Lanham, Md., UNIPUB, 1995. 178p. index. $30.00pa. ISBN 92-3-003204-2.

The primary purpose of the 3d edition of the *World Directory of Human Rights Research and Training Institutions*, last reviewed in ARBA 93 (see entry 619), is essentially to promote the dissemination of materials and ongoing research on a variety of issues regarding human rights. There are 368 entries, and the completeness of each entry depends upon the type of organization and in what part of the world the agency is located. Each entry provides basic information, such as address, telephone and fax numbers, head of the organization, relationship to other organizations, type of research/publications, and the type of instructions they provide. The single volume is well organized (alphabetic by country, including a section listing international and regional organizations). This essential reference is recommended for academic and large public libraries, especially for those serving students in international studies programs or social work who may benefit from the educational programs made available through these organizations.

—**Dario J. Villa**

INTELLECTUAL PROPERTY

519. McCarthy, J. Thomas. **McCarthy's Desk Encyclopedia of Intellectual Property.** 2d ed. Washington, D.C., BNA Books, 1995. 505p. $75.00pa. ISBN 0-87179-899-9.

McCarthy is a professor of law at the University of San Francisco and has written extensively in the field of intellectual property. This revision of his desk encyclopedia has 70 new entries to help bring this rapidly changing field up-to-date. New terms include *NAFTA*, *Trademark Law Treaty*, *European Trademark*, *World Trade Organization*, and *harmonization*. Congress incorporated the GATT TRIPS agreement into U.S. law in 1994, and the effects on intellectual property law have been numerous.

A simple list of entries and a table of cases precedes the encyclopedic definitions. Full items begin with an indication of the area of intellectual property (patent, copyright, or trademark) that relates to the term. Following is a brief description of the concept with references to more comprehensive treatises. Items also include citations to governing legislation, treaties, and case law. The appendixes list the superintendents and commissioners of patents and trademarks and the registers of copyrights since the positions were created. There are counts of patent applications and issuances and trademark registrations and renewals through 1994.

The author defines his primary audience as attorneys in the field—both novice and experienced. The book is a practical, quick-reference tool that readers can use profitably as a first step in their research on intellectual property.—**Berniece M. Owen**

520. **Patent, Copyright, & Trademark: A Desk Reference to Intellectual Property Law.** By Stephen Elias. Lisa Goldoftas, ed. Berkeley, Calif., Nolo Press, 1996. 430p. illus. $24.95pa. ISBN 0-87337-236-0.

Anyone who needs easy-to-understand but comprehensive information on patents, copyright procedures, or trademarks will appreciate this book. In the introduction, the author, an intellectual property law expert, discusses how intellectual property laws work, explains how to use this book to find the needed information, and provides a useful chart entitled "Guide to Use of Intellectual Property Protection." He also gives a list of other resources available from the publisher, Nolo Press.

Each of the remaining four chapters highlights a different property law. Elias explains the laws surrounding each legal device and the protection the device offers, defines pertinent terminology, discusses the statutes involved, and gives examples of actual cases. Sample forms and agreements are provided where relevant, as are resource lists.

Written in simple English and extensively cross-referenced, this guide is extremely user friendly; it is hard to imagine a more helpful, quick guide to the intricacies of intellectual property concerns. It would surely be the first book of choice for the layperson needing to understand property law and should make a useful reference guide for anyone else who deals with this facet of the law. [R: LJ, Feb 96, p. 142]

—**Jo Anne H. Ricca**

11 Library and Information Science and Publishing and Bookselling

LIBRARY AND INFORMATION SCIENCE

General Works

Bibliography

521. Slade, Alexander L., and Marie A. Kascus. **Library Services for Off-Campus and Distance Education: The Second Annotated Bibliography.** Englewood, Colo., Libraries Unlimited, 1996. 239p. index. $65.00. ISBN 1-56308-465-1.

In 1991, Sheila Latham, Slade, and Carol Budnick published the first *Library Services for Off-Campus and Distance Education* (see ARBA 92, entry 577). That review noted the usefulness of the book and suggested that the editors plan to update the work. Now comes the update, by Slade and Kascus, as useful and necessary as the first. As with the previous edition, the new volume annotates books, papers, journal articles, and all types of material, from brief news items to major research reports and dissertations. Also similar to the first volume, the second concentrates on material written about postsecondary education, whether formal or informal. However, much of the material will be germane to people involved in secondary learning.

The update has 15 chapter headings. Fourteen are the same as the premier edition: bibliographies, general works, historical studies, the role of libraries in distance education, guidelines and standards, organization and planning, collection management, information and support services, bibliographic instruction document delivery, interlibrary cooperation, library surveys, user studies, and library case studies. One topic is new: a chapter on remote access to electronic resources. The three final sections are arranged geographically so that the user can easily find information written about specific countries. Annotations are detailed. Four indexes provide access by author, geographic location, institution, and subject. The subject index could have benefited by more finely defined subdivisions. Under technology, for example, there are 15 lines of references to entry numbers. It is tedious for the user to look up each reference under such a broad topic.

Although distance education is a growing field garnering increasing attention, study of the library's role in serving the consumers of distance education has been slight. This book, along with its predecessor, should help focus more attention on the demands placed on libraries and library services. It should be part of the collection of any library looking outward from its own campus users to the increasing number of off-site users. [R: JAL, Sept 96, p. 407]—**Terry Ann Mood**

Catalogs and Collections

522. Buttlar, Lois J., and Lubomyr R. Wynar, comps. **Guide to Information Resources in Ethnic Museum, Library, and Archival Collections in the United States.** Westport, Conn., Greenwood Press, 1996. 369p. index. (Bibliographies and Indexes in Ethnic Studies, no.7). $75.00. ISBN 0-313-29846-7.

Resources in the guide represent 70 ethnic groups. They are arranged alphabetically in 68 categories, from Afghanistan American resources and African American resources to Welsh American resources. Cross-references are provided in some categories, such as under "Black American Resources," where the reader is referred to African American resources. Each complete entry includes the name of the cultural institution; the type of institution (museum, library, archives, art gallery); an address; telephone and fax numbers; the sponsoring organization; personnel; the contact person; the date founded; scope; availability; the admission price; publications; and so on. Information contained in each entry is sufficient enough for quick reference.

Data in the guide are based primarily on questionnaires and secondary sources. Omissions are unavoidable. From a random check, one ascertains that Plains Indians and Pioneers Museum Foundation, the San Francisco China Town Library, and the Asian American Studies Library at the University of California at Berkeley are not listed. Many institutions listed here can be found in other reference sources, such as *Encyclopedia of Associations* (see entry 49 for a review of the CD-ROM version), but the guide focuses on museums, libraries, archives, and art galleries. In this respect, the information is unique.

There are two indexes: an institutional index and a geographic index. The usefulness of the guide would be enhanced if an index to publications was also included. It is a quality work, nonetheless, and an invaluable resource to ethnic information sources. [R: Choice, July/Aug 96, p. 1770; RBB, 15 Mar 96, pp. 1314-15]—**Tze-chung Li**

523. **Libraries Unlimited Professional Collection CD 1995.** [CD-ROM]. Englewood, Colo., Libraries Unlimited, 1995. Minimum system requirements: IBM or compatible. CD-ROM drive. Windows 3.1. 4MB hard disk space. Color monitor (recommended). Mouse (recommended). $75.00 (Humanities); $45.00 (Subject Headings for African American Materials); $66.00 (Conversion Tables); $22.00 (Cutter Two-Figure Author Table); $34.00 (Cutter Three-Figure Author Table); $36.00 (Cutter-Sanborn Author Table). ISBN 1-56308-400-7; 1-56308-361-2 (Humanities); 1-56308-391-1 (Subject Headings for African American Materials); 1-56308-399-X (Conversion Tables); 1-56308-384-1 (Cutter Two-Figure Author Table); 1-56308-385-X (Cutter Three-Figure Author Table); 1-56308-386-8 (Cutter-Sanborn Author Table). [Also available for site licenses.]

This CD-ROM presents six tools for librarians for acquisitions, cataloging, and general reference. Titles included are: (1) *The Humanities CD*; (2) *Subject Headings for African American Materials*; (3) *Conversion Tables: LC-Dewey; Dewey-LC*; and (4) 3 versions of the Cutter tables, *C. A. Cutter's Two-Figure Author Table*, *C. A. Cutter's Three-Figure Author Table*, and *Cutter-Sanborn Three-Figure Author Table*. The work also includes a preview selection, which is, in essence, a neat marketing device, but has the advantage of allowing users to try out the specific preview titles before making a commitment to actually order them.

Some CD-ROM versions are enhanced from the print version. For example, *The Humanities CD* contains the complete text of the 4th edition of *The Humanities: A Selective Guide to Information Sources* (see ARBA 95, entry 921) plus 215 additional updated titles. Previews include, besides the sample clip from the total work, an overview of the book's features, tables of contents, and indexes for some. The clip from *The Humanities* illustrates chapter 6, "Principal Information Sources in Religion, Mythology, and Folklore," by featuring 8 citations under "Bibliographic Guides."

The disc uses Folio VIEWS electronic publishing software, which claims to be "an extremely powerful infobase management system." This is the same software used by Library of Congress's *Cataloger's Desktop*, and it provides these features for users: It indexes every word in the infobase; contains hypertext links; provides full Boolean searches with truncations (author, title, publisher); and allows customizing options such as notes, bookmarks, highlighters, or addition of the user's own text.

If the librarian wishes to access the full database of any of the 6 titles on the disc, prices are given on an accompanying sheet and the user may call an 800 telephone number provided, simply order the item for purchase, provide some sort of payment method, receive a password, and the customer already has the full work itself at hand. A disadvantage to the product is it does not include school library and educational titles, which would increase its value to school librarians. Pluses are the powerful search features, hypertext linking, and customizing ability. The preview feature is helpful to get a better feel for the products before actually purchasing them. The product titles are easy to install and use.—**Carol Truett**

Dictionaries and Encyclopedias

524. Encyclopedia of Library and Information Science. Volume 58, Supplement 21. Allen Kent and Carolyn M. Hall, eds. New York, Marcel Dekker, 1996. 352p. $99.75. ISBN 0-8247-2058-X.

This newest volume of the ever ongoing *Encyclopedia of Library and Information Science* includes 16 new essays. These essays, for the most part approximately 20 pages in length, cover such topics as indexing and retrieval of hypermedia information, ethics in library and information service, primary records, the information society, medical informatics, technical services workstations, sublanguages, the household registration system, self-checkout technology, and the universal availability of publications.

The shortest entries cover the contributions of Asa Don Dickinson to Indian librarianship and the Oriental Manuscript Library, whereas the longest essay addresses online public access catalogs. This latter entry, because of its length and currency, deserves to be published separately. As in the past, the essays are thorough, comprehensive surveys of their subjects, and heavily referenced. Marcel Dekker continues to do an excellent job in their production of the work. Two minor concerns about the choice of material can be expressed: the short essay on "Public Interest Ethics" could, and probably should, have been included in the more encompassing essay on ethical aspects of library and information science; and the reprinting of two previously published essays seems questionable for a work such as this.—**Glenn R. Wittig**

525. Keenan, Stella. **Concise Dictionary of Library and Information Science.** New Providence, N.J., Bowker-Saur/Reed Reference Publishing, 1996. 214p. index. $35.00. ISBN 1-85739-022-9.

In her work as an abstractor, the author became aware of the need for a book that would cover current terminology in the areas of information sources (e.g., fugitive material or superfiche), information handling and retrieval, computers and telecommunications, resource management, research methodology in library and information science, and publishing. To avoid duplication with existing dictionaries, such as the *ALA Glossary of Library and Information Science* (see ARBA 84, entry 86), emphasis is on terms that are not conventional. Definitions are generally one or two lines, with numerous cross-references indicated by bold typeface. Organization is by the seven focuses listed above, and an index provides cumulative A to Z access. Although the author makes a good case for dividing terms into multiple categories, this reviewer's preference, particularly for a work in which some sections are only a dozen pages, would be to have a single A to Z sequence, and then an appendix with the terms divided into categories. [R: Choice, Oct 96, p. 253]—**Robert Skinner**

526. Prytherch, Ray, comp. **Harrod's Librarians' Glossary: 9,000 Terms Used in Information Management, Library Science, Publishing, the Book Trades, and Archive Management.** 8th ed. Brookfield, Vt., Gower/Ashgate Publishing, 1995. 692p. $99.95. ISBN 0-566-07533-4.

Slightly longer than the 7th edition (see ARBA 92, entry 565), and with 1,400 new entries, the latest *Harrod's* has been revamped to provide more information on the automated elements of librarianship. Retaining its international scope, and including for the first time the addresses of major libraries, associations, cooperatives, and institutions, the 8th edition of *Harrod's* is as indispensable a resource as its predecessors. Some 9,000 terms are defined, with a new emphasis on the fields of conservation and preservation, records management, and networking. The book trade, publishing business, and archiving process continue to receive superior coverage. The activities of myriad associations are explained; acronyms, words, and phrases are clearly defined.

Entries range from a few words to a few pages in length, with liberal use of cross-referencing. Definitions are occasionally a bit circular: "Reference librarian. A librarian in charge of, or undertaking the work of, a reference library." The use of British spelling seems a bit inconsistent ("reference center" versus "referral centre"). However, no other source has in one volume a list of the NISO Z39 standards, a history of the horn book, a definition of publishers' house corrections, and the address for OCLC.

This glossary remains the preeminent source for demystifying the terminology of librarianship and its related fields. It is recommended for collections of any size.—**Ed Volz**

Handbooks and Yearbooks

527. ARL Statistics 1994-95: A Compilation of Statistics from the One Hundred and Nineteen Members of the Association of Research Libraries. Martha Kyrillidou, Kimberley A. Maxwell, and Kendon Stubbs, comps. and eds. Washington, D.C., Association of Research Libraries, 1996. 118p. $65.00pa./yr. ISSN 0147-2135.

Since its inception as a reporting service in 1961, the *ARL Statistics*, an annual publication issued by the Association of Research Libraries (ARL), has been considered the bible for those interested in the growth and comparative rankings of large research libraries. In the current survey, 108 of the reporting libraries are located at universities, while 11 are in public, government, and private research institutions. The first 50 pages of the survey are devoted to data tables in which the statistical information covers such items as "Volumes in Library," "Volumes Added," "Current Serials Purchased," "Salaries and Wages," and "Total Staff." The next 25 pages use those figures to provide a rank order for all contributing institutions. In the category of "Total Library Expenditures," for example, Harvard is first, followed by Stanford, Yale, and the University of California at Los Angeles.

With an increasing emphasis on service as a measure of success—rather than on the raw number of volumes in the collection—the ARL has started to include questions and resulting statistics on such topics as "Number of Reference Questions" and "Number of Library Presentations to Groups." With its long-standing reputation for accuracy, the annual *ARL Statistics* summary is recognized as a useful and informative tool. An interactive version is available on the World Wide Web, offering researchers access in spreadsheet format with documentation. [R: JAL, Sept 96, p. 404]—**Donald C. Dickinson**

528. The Bowker Annual Library and Book Trade Almanac, 1996. 41st ed. Dave Bogart, ed. New Providence, N.J., R. R. Bowker/Reed Reference Publishing, 1996. 908p. index. $169.75. ISBN 0-8352-3739-7. ISSN 0068-0540.

The preeminent almanac of the book trade and library profession has been reviewed in *American Reference Books Annual* many times, most recently in ARBA 96 (see entry 623). The book's arrangement will be familiar to its many regular users. The "Reports from the Field" section this year includes essays on library funding, the dissemination of government information, library networking activity, and the status of copyright law. Updates follow on library legislation, the library profession, research in publishing and librarianship, book award winners, and a directory of book trade and library organizations. Back matter includes an activities calendar (primarily for library association conferences), a list of book trade and library-related acronyms, and a five-year cumulative index of subjects and organization names.

This is an invaluable accumulation of wide-ranging data. The curious can find a Center for the Book status report, a listing of scholarships available for library studies, the steps in obtaining an International Serial Standard Number, and a chart of *Publishers Weekly*'s bestsellers for 1995. This annual is a necessary ready-reference source for medium-sized and larger libraries; small libraries could get by with purchasing it every few years.—**Ed Volz**

529. Library Literature 1995: An Index to Library and Information Science. Cathy Rentschler, Mary M. Brereton, and Mark A. Gauthier, eds. Bronx, N.Y., H. W. Wilson, 1996. 823p. priced on service basis rate. ISSN 0024-2373.

Along with *Bibliographic Index* (see ARBA 92, entry 4), *Book Review Digest* (see ARBA 93, entry 76, and ARBA 92, entry 54), and *Cumulative Book Index* (see ARBA 93, entries 23-25), *Library Literature* (print subscription only) is available on a service basis, based on a three-year average of a library's annual budget. *Library Literature* has been reviewed in *American Reference Books Annual* on many occasions (see ARBA 94, entry 616; ARBA 92, entry 572; ARBA 91, entry 613; and ARBA 90, entry 594, for example). It was also reviewed in Libraries Unlimited's *Library and Information Science Annual* (LISCA) and discussed in some detail in the article "The History and Current State of Library Publishing in the United States," written by Norman D. Stevens (see LISCA v.1 [1985], pp. 17-28). The structure of this volume is similar to previous issues. It offers complete bibliographic data in alphabetic order, indexing approximately 230 key library journals and some 600 monographs per year. As most users of this important index know, online service is updated twice weekly, the magnetic tape subscription is updated monthly, and the CD-ROM subscription is accumulated and updated quarterly. *Library Literature* is an essential indexing service for all types of librarians who should be interested in the latest publications and essential trends in the library profession.—**Bohdan S. Wynar**

530. Maier, Ernest L., and others. **The Business Library and How to Use It: A Guide to Sources and Research Strategies....** [6th ed.] Detroit, Omnigraphics, 1996. 329p. index. $45.00. ISBN 0-7808-0026-5.

First published in 1951 as *How to Use the Business Library* (4th ed.; see ARBA 73, entry 193), this revised and updated 6th edition of a well-known handbook will be welcomed by the neophyte business major, the specialist, and the business librarian. Divided into 16 chapters in 4 sections, the volume provides a detailed and systematic introduction to business research in the library, offers research strategies using general reference works, pinpoints specific research works, and outlines how to organize and write a business report. Types of works covered include such traditional sources as handbooks, directories, and manuals as well as the nontraditional works (e.g., CD-ROMs, government documents, and online databases). All references are annotated.

An example will illustrate a striking advantage of this volume over *The Basic Business Library* (3d ed.; see ARBA 96, entry 173). A person interested in directories will find an entire chapter devoted to them in Maier's volume, with a succinct introduction followed by listings broken down into more than a dozen subject areas. In *The Basic Business Library*, all titles in the 96-page "Core List" are simply arranged alphabetically; thus, unless users have specific titles in mind, they must scan the entire bibliography. A search under the word *Directories* in the index only aggravates the problem by turning up numerous citation numbers that users must laboriously check. The Maier book is an essential purchase for all business libraries, and is also recommended for academic general reference collections. [R: Choice, Dec 96, pp. 586-87; RBB, 15 May 96, pp. 1616-18]—**Jack Bales**

531. **National Guide to Funding for Libraries and Information Services.** 3d ed. James E. Baumgartner and others, eds. New York, Foundation Center, 1995. 234p. index. $95.00pa. ISBN 0-87954-605-0.

Containing entries for nearly 600 grantmaking foundations and corporate giving programs, this guide is a place to begin when identifying sources of support for library and information service programs. Each source included here has shown a substantial interest in libraries and information services as part of its stated fields of interest or through reported grants of $10,000 or more. Entries have been evaluated by the Foundation Center staff for inclusion in this guide. The Center has used a "Grants Classification System" based on the National Taxonomy of Exempt Entities to provide subject, types of support, and other grant information. Information is provided both online through two DIALOG files, and in print through various publications, four of which (*The Foundation Directory* [see ARBA 94, entry 890, and ARBA 91, entry 866], *The Foundation Directory Part 2* [see ARBA 94, entry 891], *National Directory of Corporate Giving* [3d ed.; see ARBA 95, entry 196], and Foundation Grants Index database) provide all the information included here. There is no claim, however, for inclusion of all possible foundation funding sources for library and information service programs. The editors urge grantseekers to learn about community and local foundations, especially for small grants that might be omitted here.

Entries are arranged alphabetically by state and then by foundation name. References in the indexes are to entry numbers assigned to the descriptive entries. Each entry includes 34 basic data elements for contact information, including assets, expenditures, qualifying factors, purpose and areas of interest, and application procedures. Six indexes are provided to identify entries by donors, officers, geography, type of support, subject of giving programs, grant subject, and foundations and corporate giving programs. Prior to the entries, a glossary and a bibliography supplement orientation material for grantseekers.

This guide joins other publications emerging to meet the market of interest in funding for library programs. Similar data about library money are provided, although by more entries in other directories such as *The Big Book of Library Grant Money* (see ARBA 95, entry 643). Information in the Foundation Center's guide is a by-product of other sources of funding data, but it is concise, focused on the library field, and slightly less expensive than other similar publications. The resource is suggested for library managers, program planners, and fund-raisers with identified needs and continuing interest to investigate possible sources of external funding.—**Danuta A. Nitecki**

532. Wertsman, Vladimir F. **The Librarian's Companion: A Handbook of Thousands of Facts....** 2d ed. Westport, Conn., Greenwood Press, 1996. 225p. index. $65.00. ISBN 0-313-29975-7.

This book is a summary of interesting facts about books, libraries, librarians, publishing, and journalism around the world. This 2d edition includes more than 350 more entries than the original 1987 publication (see ARBA 88, entry 612). Almost half of the text is an alphabetic list of 194 countries with concise data about location, population, type of government, illiteracy rate, library volumes per person, number of libraries with their holdings, publishing and newspaper industry, noted libraries, and primary librarian organization.

The rest of the book includes a chapter with brief (three to four sentences in length) biographies of noted librarians; a chapter of quotations about libraries and books; a bibliography of writings that feature librarians or publishers; a description of postage stamps featuring books, newspapers, or libraries issued by various countries; a glossary of Latin library or bookish expressions; and a list of librarians' job-finding sources. Following the text are several short appendixes that provide a list of American Library Association (ALA) awards and the UNESCO Public Library Manifesto.

Author Wertsman immigrated to the United States from Romania. He received his library degree from Columbia University in 1969. He has written numerous multicultural histories of immigrants in the United States and has been active in ALA and other learned societies. His experiences and research have served him well in compiling this interesting, although expensive, reference book.—**Berniece M. Owen**

Cataloging and Classification

533. **Classification Plus: Library of Congress Classification and Library of Congress Subject Headings.** [CD-ROM]. Washington, D.C., Library of Congress, 1996. Minimum system requirements: IBM or compatible, Intel-compatible 386 (486 or greater recommended). CD-ROM drive with MS CD-ROM Extensions. Windows 3.1 or OS/2 2.1. 4MB RAM (8MB recommended). 2MB hard disk space. EGA, VGA, or compatible monitor and video graphics adapter (256-color graphics driver and 800 x 600 graphics resolution recommended). Microsoft-compatible mouse. $410.00/single user.

534. **Library of Congress Subject Headings.** 19th ed. By the Cataloging Policy and Support Office, Library Services. Washington, D.C., Library of Congress, Cataloging Distribution Service, 1996. 4v. $200.00pa./set. ISSN 1048-9711.

The Library of Congress (LC) began compiling subject headings in 1898, using the American Library Association's 1895 publication *Subject Headings Used in the Dictionary Catalogues of the Library of Congress* as its inspiration and source material. This became necessary when LC adopted a dictionary catalog (names, titles, and subjects interfiled) to complement its newly devised classification scheme to replace Thomas Jefferson's. The *Library of Congress Subject Headings* (LCSH) set has been issued sporadically since the first edition was published between 1909 and 1914. The 1975 release, the 8th edition, was the first known by the current title. This 19th edition contains all of the verified headings from the subject authority file through December 1995. The total of 222,900 headings is an increase of 8,000 over the previous edition, about the average number added annually. Internet access is available for the weekly subject headings updates provided by LC (the URL is gopher://marvel.loc.gov). A variety of informative subject headings publications can be requested via the Internet at any time from the address cdsinfo@mail.loc.gov.

The format of this 4-volume set will be familiar to the users of any edition from the 12th on (see ARBA 90, entry 602). The useful written guides continue, such as BT (broader terms) and NT (narrower terms), as do the "May Subd Geog" and "Not Subd Geog" designations. Bold typefaces, the use of parentheses, and a logical indenting scheme make this a model of readability for a book printed three columns to the page. The purchasing decision one faces is not whether to buy this indispensable cataloging and reference tool at all, but at what point and how often to buy it. Aside from its 8,000 new headings, this edition does not differ substantially from its immediate predecessor except for its binding. The softcover 19th edition will not stand up without substantial side support. The result of LC's economizing gesture is annoying; one hopes it saved them a great deal of money.

The CD-ROM known as *Classification Plus* contains the text of the 4-volume LCSH set, with the Library of Congress classification scheme included as well. The CD failed to boot up on this reviewer's Windows for Workgroups platform, but ran flawlessly on Windows 95. The expected benefits of CD-ROM technology are here, primarily in the ability to save changes, creating a shadow file to personalize the database. There are also functions for highlighting, bookmarking, making links, and doing queries. In short, the disc-based text becomes a flexible and fluid database (that can be networked), greatly simplifying a cataloger's duties. Libraries that welcome CD-ROM technology will prefer this disc to the set of floppy paperback books.—**Ed Volz**

535. **Dewey Decimal Classification and Relative Index.** 21st ed. Joan S. Mitchell, Julianne Beall, Winton E. Matthews Jr., and George R. New, eds. Dublin, OCLC Forest Press, 1996. 4v. index. $325.00/set. ISBN 0-910608-50-4.

536. **Dewey for Windows.** [CD-ROM]. Dublin, Ohio, OCLC Forest Press, 1996. Minimum system requirements: IBM or compatible 486. CD-ROM drive. Windows 3.1. 8MB RAM. 20MB hard disk space. Color VGA monitor and adapter. Mouse. $400.00/yr./single user; $500.00/yr./site license.

One feels great anticipation and excitement, coupled with a degree of anxiety, when a new edition of the *Dewey Decimal Classification and Relative Index* (DDC) is presented to the library profession. Although it involves study, decision making, and the time-consuming process of some reclassification on the part of the librarians, it also reflects the constant growth the library profession experiences as it mirrors the explosion of new information and material that is occurring in the international environment. DDC 21 is a good example of the library community's continual effort to reflect the progress of society by making some important changes and additions to the scheme. It includes 3 major revisions: 350-354 Public Administration, 370 Education, and 560-590 Life Sciences. These revisions have been in progress for quite some time because it was obvious that these areas were experiencing major growth and change. The Editorial Policy Committee focused on these areas and produced entirely new schemes.

DDC 21 continues to stress the importance of user convenience, a major focus of DDC 20 (see ARBA 90, entry 599), by working to simplify schedules and clarify vague headings. DDC 21 is continuing work on the multiedition plan to reduce the Christian bias that was built into the original classification scheme. With this edition, Christianity, formerly 201-209, has been relocated to 230-270, while 296 Judaism and 297 Islam have both been revised and expanded. DDC 21 is also moving toward an international scope and departing from the bias toward the United States as there is greater and greater worldwide usage of DDC. This edition includes a major revision of Table 2-47 for the countries of the former Soviet Union, and new numbers for the administration of Nelson Mandela. Overall, this edition works to update terminology to reflect currency, while being aware of sensitive areas.

The most exciting feature to arrive with DDC 21 is the CD-ROM *Dewey for Windows*. This disc enables the cataloger to access DDC 21 online, working with the classification schemes and the index. Multiple screens can be seen simultaneously so that the hierarchy of a proposed number can be analyzed and subdivisions can be added. There is also a program to compare the number with the Library of Congress's use of it to confirm the choice for accuracy. This software may be purchased for a single workstation for $400, or used in a local network environment for an additional $100. The price for this software may seem high at first, but this is the long-awaited opportunity for the process of cataloging to move to a faster, more streamlined, and efficient format.

The purchase of DDC 21 and the accompanying compact disc *Dewey for Windows* would be a benefit to any librarian working in cataloging. The cost may be prohibitive for some libraries, but the tools should definitely be considered in any long-range planning for the library. [R: JAL, Mar 96, p. 151]—**Bridget Volz**

537. Huber, Jeffrey T., and Mary L. Gillaspy. **HIV/AIDS and HIV/AIDS-Related Terminology: A Means of Organizing the Body of Knowledge.** Binghamton, N.Y., Haworth Press, 1996. 107p. index. $24.95. ISBN 1-56024-970-6.

Library of Congress Subject Headings (LCSH) (see entries 533-534), *Medical Subject Headings* (MeSH) (National Library of Medicine Annual), and the *Sears List of Subject Headings* (14th ed.; see ARBA 92, entry 585) fall short of providing the scope necessary in dealing with the organization and cataloging of the massive quantity of materials related to acquired immunodeficiency syndrome (AIDS) and the human immunodeficiency virus (HIV). *HIV/AIDS and HIV/AIDS-Related Terminology* by Huber and Gillaspy attempts to create subject headings that broadly and specifically cover myriad aspects of this disease.

By using LCSH, MeSH, and *Sears* as a beginning, the authors have created a structured vocabulary hierarchically arranged. MeSH is the main source; terms from there are noted with an asterisk, and minor changes are noted with a "greater than" (>) sign. The arrangement is divided into 10 broad domains, such as "Education and Prevention," "Fine Arts," "Clinical Manifestations," and "Treatments." Each domain is further subdivided into headings and subheadings, such as **FINE ARTS—MUSIC—INSTRUMENTAL MUSIC.** Scope notes are included as needed to help individuals identify where information should be categorized. The scope note for the above example indicates this heading should be used to "include accounts of performances dedicated to persons living with AIDS or persons lost to AIDS; as distinguished from Benefits used for fund raising." Proper names, organizations, and special events were left out of the listings on purpose. A means for adding further headings is provided in the scope notes and in the front matter.

Following the listings is a universal subdivisions list to promote further access to information. The book ends with an alphabetic list of all the headings and references to their placement in the hierarchy, as well as extensive *see also* and *see* references. This resource is recommended for small and private libraries, counseling centers, clinics, and AIDS service and information providers. [R: RBB, 1 Oct 96, p. 370]
—Kevin W. Perizzolo

Information Technology

538. Gay, Martin K. **The New Information Revolution: A Reference Handbook.** Santa Barbara, Calif., ABC-CLIO, 1996. 247p. index. (Contemporary World Issues). $39.50. ISBN 0-87436-847-2.

The introduction to this work is one of the best overviews of the subject around. The author manages to get his arms around a huge, amorphous subject and then organize and explain it—and wide-ranging related issues—in clear, sensible terms. A layperson can easily understand the technical concepts and social issues, as well as their relation to one another. Unfortunately, the body of the work does not hold up to the same standard. Much of the book focuses on the Internet and computer-based networking, which is quite different from the "information revolution" of the title. Important issues related to cable, as well as broadcast, satellite, and other wireless technologies, are mentioned only in passing, although these are key elements of the information revolution.

In short, the book says it will deliver more than it does. This is not due to the author's misunderstanding of the issue but the effort to stuff this broad topic into the confines of the publisher's Contemporary World Issues series. The series takes a cookie-cutter approach to a broad range of social issues. Each book in the series offers, in about 250 pages, an overview of the issue, a chronology, biographical sketches of key figures, statistical data, primary source material, a directory of organizations and agencies, a resource list, and a glossary. These are ample details to pack into 250 pages, and the fact is, it cannot be done. Every section suffers from the effort. The "detailed" chronology covers such tangential topics as railroads and mail delivery, but not cable television or satellite transmission. There is also a Western European bias; for example, the chronology covers the development of movable type and newspapers in Europe, but neglects the earlier developments in Asia.

When working without much room, every choice about inclusion becomes crucial. Thus, it seems odd that the "very first mechanical calculator" by Schickard appears in the chronology, but Leibniz's calculator, which used the repetitive addition algorithm that is still used in today's computers, does not. Given that space constraints allowed only one of the two to be included, Leibniz's seems a more relevant choice. Oddities abound in the biographical sketches as well. Charles Babbage is included, but George Boole is not. Bill Gates is included, but Steven Jobs and Stephen Wozniak are not. Although Gates proved shrewder than Apple's founders, it was Jobs and Wozniak who introduced to the public the graphical user interface that made personal computers for the masses possible.

The book's emphasis on social aspects is obvious in the choice of primary documents included. Almost 30 pages are devoted to the Magna Carta for the Knowledge Age, released by the conservative Progress and Freedom Foundation. Yet only the table of contents is given for what may be the most important public policy document related to the Information Superhighway itself: the Telecommunications Act of 1996. Because this law addresses the very structure of the Information Superhighway (particularly relevant for issues of access), a summary of its most important measures and impacts is called for. At the least, an address to the full-text document online is needed. This is not included, even in the online bibliography.

The oddities continue. The Communications Decency Act, the one part of the Telecommunications Act that is reprinted in full, is erroneously called the Exxon Amendment (its author was Senator J. James Exon of Nebraska). The Telecommunications Act itself is erroneously referred to as the Telecommunications Reform Act. This error persists in the index, so that there are two entries for the act: one under the correct name and one under the incorrect name.

If libraries can afford $39.50 for the introduction, it is well worth having. Otherwise, they should put that $40 toward a more comprehensive or better-targeted work.—**Constance Hardesty**

539. Plunkett, Jack W. **Plunkett's InfoTech Industry Almanac: The Only Complete Guide to the Technology and the Companies.....** Galveston, Tex., Plunkett Research, [1996]. 697p. index. $125.00pa. ISBN 0-9638268-2-4.

Geared toward a nonfinancial business audience, *Plunkett's* defines information technology (IT) as "any technology that moves or manages voice, data or video." Following this definition, the almanac profiles 500 leading companies from telecommunications, network and data linking, digital communications, electronic publishing, consulting and engineering, information management, online and Internet services, and computer systems and software.

The majority of *Plunkett's* is devoted to single-page company profiles. These include the familiar basics—financial performance, research and development investment, products and services, growth plans—as well as unique items, such as a note on the company's perceived competitive advantage, a ranking of the corporate culture for women and minorities, and an overview of salaries and benefits. A glossary of IT terms and chapters describing the domestic IT industry, industry descriptions, potential global opportunities, and an occupation-by-occupation description of IT careers precede the profile section. Numerous indexes—including geographic, name brand, subsidiary name, research and development budget, and advancement opportunities—complete the directory.

Given the abundance of company evaluation tools, such as the products from Hoover's (see entry 166, for example); Standard & Poor's (see entries 171 and 202); and like publishers, one may question the usefulness of a tool such as *Plunkett's*. However, the real value of this work lies in its usefulness for those who would pursue a career in information technology. The industry overviews present a realistic picture of the IT environment, and the company profiles provide prospective employees a good starting point for job-hunting. At the price, *Plunkett's* may be too expensive for smaller- and medium-sized libraries, but it will be a valuable resource for college and larger public libraries. [R: Choice, July/Aug 96, p. 1776; RBB, June 96, pp. 1766-68]—**G. Kim Dority**

540. **The Sourcebook of Online Public Record Experts.** Tempe, Ariz., BRB, 1996. 368p. index. (The Public Record Research Library). $29.00pa. ISBN 1-879792-31-1.

This sourcebook is 12th in a series of reference guides that help the information professional locate vendors providing automatic public record information, search services, and investigative services. The company profiles were provided by 668 firms and associations that collect public records at the source and distribute them in some electronic format or directly use online databases from those distributors or directly from government agencies. Five types of businesses are represented in the publication: firms that conduct searches, distributors, preemployment screening firms, private investigators, and tenant screening firms.

The guide is divided into four sections. Section 1 provides a review of privacy issues, what public records are, what is available through the private sector, how to determine the right public vendor, and a survey of public record searching on the Internet. Section 2 includes 4 indexes: geographic, information category, communication type, and media type, with an introduction that explains how to read the indexes. Section 3 is the central index and contains the company profiles listed in alphabetic order. Section 4 identifies 88 professional organizations and associations that play a large role in the public record industry, 25 of which are profiled in depth.

Section 1 is essential reading, especially for the novice. It begins with a brief but critical explanation of public records, their legal framework, and the typology of 25 categories of public information for classifying the companies included in this sourcebook. The authors then suggest questions that the novice needs to ask prior to requesting a vendor's services, including frequency of usage and complexity and geographic boundaries of the search. Section 1 concludes with an explanation of vendors that use the Internet and an important caveat about searching public information on the World Wide Web.

How useful is this sourcebook? Several questions come immediately to mind, revolving around the notion of an "expert" in today's complex and dynamic information marketplace in which, more than ever before, it has become exceedingly difficult to locate a highly trained vendor. For example, what questions does one ask to determine whether a company has well-trained personnel and performs quality service at an affordable price? What standards have been established to determine the knowledge base and level of training required of an "expert" who provides public information services? To what standards, including integrity, are investigators held? Given the quantity and complexity of public information, highly knowledgeable content people are needed, and searching is a skill that requires extensive experience. Integrity is a quality that must always be carefully evaluated. All these attributes will always be difficult to determine from reading a sourcebook. As such, this reference will only get one started, and its caveats are worth reading carefully.—**Alice Robbin**

Intellectual Freedom and Censorship

541. **Freedom of Speech Decisions of the United States Supreme Court.** Maureen Harrison and Steve Gilbert, eds. San Diego, Calif., Excellent Books, 1996. 220p. index. (First Amendment Decisions Series). $16.95pa. ISBN 1-880780-09-7.

General and lay readers interested in reading some of the leading Supreme Court decisions in first amendment law as it relates to freedom of speech would be well advised to turn to this collection of edited Supreme Court decisions. The 13 majority opinions of the U.S. Supreme Court that comprise this collection constitute many of the leading decisions that try to define freedom of speech rights and limits. Included in this collection are cases involving fighting words, violent speech, hate speech, filthy words, offensive speech, unwanted speech, protest speech, and vulgar speech, to mention just a few.

The book opens with a general and useful, albeit brief, introduction to free speech issues, followed by the Supreme Court decisions. Each case opens with a one-page introduction and a one-page list of Supreme Court justices who heard and decided the case, along with the legal citation from the United States Reports, where the cases can be found in their entirety. Each case is carefully edited to ensure that lay readers will obtain the essence of the majority opinion without being accosted and confused by legalese. Where necessary, brief definitions for legal terms are provided. In addition, only the majority opinion is presented. As an introduction to the case and to the issue before the Supreme Court, general readers not trained in the law will profit immensely from this collection. The book concludes with the complete text of the United States Constitution, a useful bibliography, and an index. The resource is very highly recommended.—**Michael A. Foley**

542. **Intellectual Freedom Manual.** 5th ed. Compiled by the Office for Intellectual Freedom of the American Library Association. Chicago, American Library Association, 1996. 393p. index. $35.00pa. ISBN 0-8389-0677-X.

Issues of censorship and intellectual freedom have always been of prime concern to librarians, but access to R-rated videos, cruising the Internet, materials about AIDS, and sex education have intensified the debate. Along with this change, pressure groups on both the political right and left have become more vocal and taken notice of libraries' role in selecting information. As a result, no library can consider itself immune from a potential censorship challenge. Recognizing this, the American Library Association's Office of Intellectual Freedom has produced this 5th edition of its *Intellectual Freedom Manual*. The Library Bill of Rights is the basic policy on intellectual freedom in libraries, but as issues facing libraries have grown in complexity, this document has needed to be interpreted to encompass a host of new situations. The areas covered in this book include electronic networks, gender orientation, diversity in collections, and economic barriers to information, as well as the more traditional areas, such as selection, evaluation, access for minors, and freedom of expression. With the growth of automated systems, libraries also need to review their policy on confidentiality of records and government pressure.

Part 2 deals with protecting the freedom to read and addresses these areas with statements on guidelines and history. Essays thematically grouped make up the remaining four sections of the volume. Preparation for a challenge, including making policy, handling complaints, and using public relations, offers a solid plan for protecting libraries from censors. This section is particularly valuable, offering breakdowns of policy issues, a sample form for reconsideration, tips on handling the media, and information on talking with reporters. The manual then covers types of libraries, examining the differences between public, academic, school, and others. The next section reviews legal concerns. This includes a discussion of the public forum issue that arose as a part of the Morristown case. The final part covers what librarians can do to support the fight for intellectual freedom, including working with their local associations and educating legislators. This edition of the manual hopes to better prepare librarians to not only deal with challenges to intellectual freedom but to be proactive in terms of policy, advocacy, and history of censorship—and it succeeds. The manual is well organized, readable, and practical, offering a concise guide for libraries on the front lines. [R: EL, Sept/Oct 96, p. 39; SLMQ, Summer 96, pp. 219-20]—**Joshua Cohen**

Research

543. Borne, Barbara Wood. **100 Research Topic Guides for Students.** Westport, Conn., Greenwood Press, 1996. 234p. index. (Greenwood Professional Guides in School Librarianship). $39.95. ISBN 0-313-29552-2.

This book lists topics in alphabetic order and gives a brief, general definition of each, along with a list of resources the student or librarian should check. Sample resources are Dewey decimal call numbers for browsing, the Library of Congress subject headings, reference sources (books and CD-ROMs), online databases, keywords and descriptors that could be useful, videotapes on the topic, a brief bibliography of fiction titles dealing with the subject, periodical indexes, and national organizations involved in the subject. The author includes suggestions for narrowing the topic, as well as suggestions for related topics. The resources suggested are those normally found in many secondary schools, or public or academic libraries. The author includes resources such as DIALOG, America Online, Prodigy, and Wilsonline in her list of databases. Periodical indexes on CD-ROM include *Infotrac*, *NewsBank*, *Readers' Guide*, *SIRS*, and *Wilsondisc*.

Research topics are indexed under "Science and Technology," "Social Issues," "Social Studies," and "Biography." The diverse topics range from Malcolm X to Nostradamus to Dr. Seuss, from the McCarthy hearings to the independent republics of the former Soviet Union, from home schooling to mysterious circles and other ancient curiosities. The appendixes also yield much useful information, such as how to take notes, how to create a bibliography, and how to search databases. Also included are information on developing a search strategy and a "Research Topic Guide Template," which is identical to the guide that the author uses, and which, with permission of the author and publisher, may be photocopied for use with one student or a class. This guide is a useful reference tool for school, public, or academic libraries. [R: EL, Sept/Oct 96, p. 42; SLMQ, Fall 96, p. 63]—**Mary Jo Aman**

School Libraries

544. **The Elementary School Library Collection: A Guide to Books and Other Media.** 20th ed. Linda L. Homa and Ann L. Schreck, eds. Williamsport, Pa., Brodart, 1996. 1157p. index. $139.95. ISBN 0-87272-105-1.

545. **The Elementary School Library Collection: A Guide to Books and Other Media.** 20th ed. [CD-ROM]. Williamsport, Pa., Brodart, 1996. Minimum system requirements: IBM or compatible 286. CD-ROM drive with any MS-DOS Extensions. MS-DOS 3.3. 640K RAM. VGA color monitor. $249.00 (other pricing options available for networks).

A standard collection tool for 30 years, *The Elementary School Library Collection* (ESLC) celebrates its 20th anniversary with continued expansion of entries and material formats. This edition covers more than 10,000 entries in 12 formats, including CD-ROMs, audiovisuals, software, and videodiscs. Also, ESLC is available in both book and CD-ROM formats.

The criterion for inclusion of most materials is that they be valuable for use by or with students in pre-K through sixth grades. Some adult materials are also included; these have been judged as valuable for parent collections or as relevant professional materials for educators. While 8,550 new titles were evaluated for this edition of ESLC, only 29 percent were selected for inclusion. The remainder of this compilation is made up of titles appearing in previous editions that have been reexamined and found to still be effective; there are even a few titles that first appeared in the original edition.

The editors recommend titles based on "phase of acquisition." These are defined as "Phase 1, essential for all libraries regardless of size; Phase 2, for continuing development or for larger collections; Phase 3, of special interest or regional importance." Each annotated entry gives suggestions for curriculum use as well as full citation information and a description. Among other special features of this anniversary edition are brief biographies of the editors; a seven-page list of ESLC classics for the core collection; and the Gold Star/Selectors' Choice list, which is made up of "titles ... recognized in previous editions as outstanding contributions to children's materials." All listed titles are fully described in the first section of this resource, the classified catalog. The second of the three sections is made up of author, title, and subject indexes. The final section contains appendixes that list materials for preschool children, books for independent reading, author's series, and publisher's series. A directory of publishers and producers concludes the volume.

The CD-ROM edition of ESLC provides users with the expected array of search capabilities available in this medium, and is available in both single-user and network versions. The CD-ROM makes all of ESLC's 16 fields completely searchable, with cross-searches easily designed and executed. A genre category could be combined with an author's name, for example, and matched to a specific reading level. Also, the user could quickly create a bibliography of titles on South America written at a seventh-grade reading level. Such a bibliography could be printed in any of three formats or saved to a file. This sort of fast and easy data manipulation is what sells CD-ROMs, and certainly makes ESLC a powerful bibliographic tool. Librarians comfortable with the CD-ROM platform will find much value in this disc.

This 20th edition continues to meet the high standards set so long ago by the editors of the initial volume. ESLC remains an important and valuable tool for all school, public, and academic libraries. [R: EL, Sept/Oct 96, p. 42]—**Jo Anne Ricca and Ed Volz**

Special Libraries and Collections

546. Light, Laura. **Catalogue of Medieval and Renaissance Manuscripts in the Houghton Library, Harvard University. Volume 1: MSS Lat 3-179.** Binghamton, N.Y., Medieval & Renaissance Texts & Studies, State University of New York, 1995. 347p. index. (Medieval & Renaissance Texts & Studies, v.145). $40.00. ISBN 0-86698-185-3.

The first of a projected five-volume catalog of the Houghton's Western manuscripts antedating ca.1525, and the first of two volumes describing the Latin manuscripts so dated (plus a few later ones), this offering provides ample new and updated information on a collection that has been both reorganized and added to since the publication of the de Ricci *Census* in 1935-1940. Great attention has been paid to physical description, to decoration, and to provenance. There is considerable subject and geographic range within the collection, and the opinions of pertinent specialists (most often the paleographer A. C. de la Mare) enrich many individual entries. There are eight special indexes and a general index, all of which invite perusal. A final section of 67 plates has reproductions from all dated manuscripts described and reproduces some undated material as well.

The collection consists chiefly of late medieval and early Renaissance codices, usually liturgical or humanistic in nature. Indeed, its greatest single strength is in Renaissance humanism. Yet persistent small errors (not all of which can be typographical errors) and the occasional use of Latin name forms for persons much better known by vernacular ones suggest that Light is not entirely at home in this particular area. Again, solecisms for which she is responsible (e.g., "Phaonis" for "Phaon" on pp. 31 and 72, *Gaufredus*

Anglici on p. 332) cast doubt upon the origin of some ungrammatical Latin reported in the textual descriptions (e.g., *Noctivm Atticac vii* on p. 80), especially when one is told that "abbreviations are expanded silently" (p. xvii). That caution aside, this is on the whole a learned and valuable book. It is recommended especially for university and major college libraries.—**John B. Dillon**

547. Walsh, James E. **A Catalogue of the Fifteenth-Century Printed Books in the Harvard University Library. Volume IV: Books Printed in France, The Netherlands, the Iberian Peninsula, England, and Montenegro.** Binghamton, N.Y., Medieval & Renaissance Texts & Studies, State University of New York, 1996. 330p. index. (Medieval & Renaissance Texts & Studies, v.150). $45.00. ISBN 0-86698-190-X.

With this volume, Walsh, keeper of printed books at the Houghton Library, concludes the publication of descriptions of incunabula in the various units of the Harvard University Library. The catalog includes books printed in France, the Netherlands, the Iberian Peninsula, England, and Montenegro, as well as Hebraica and supplementary entries. The total number recorded in the Harvard collection as of 1994 comprises 3,517 editions in 4,187 copies. Volume 1 in this series, issued in 1991, described books printed in Germany, German-speaking Switzerland, and Austria-Hungary (see ARBA 92, entry 36); volume 2 described books printed in Rome and Venice (see ARBA 94, entry 31); and volume 3 described books printed in Italy with the exception of Rome and Venice (see ARBA 96, entry 42). A final volume is planned that will contain cumulative indexes and a brief history of the collection.

The books described in this volume are arranged by country, by city, and by printer, then chronologically by date of publication. The elements of description remain as in previous volumes: author, title, date, collation, notes about illustration and rubrication, citations to standard bibliographies, notes on provenance, and the location of the book in Harvard's libraries. The Hebraica, consisting of 35 entries, are arranged in a separate list by city of publication, and the supplement lists books that were omitted from the previous volumes. There are 16 plates illustrating works described in this volume, a list of references additional to those in volumes 1-3, and indexes to author/title, editors and translators and secondary works, printers and places, provenance, those books containing manuscripts, and identified bindings. Also included are concordances to four major catalogs of incunabula.—**Dean H. Keller**

548. **World Directory of Business Information Libraries.** London, Euromonitor; distr., Detroit, Gale, 1996. 357p. index. $550.00. ISBN 0-86338-547-8.

This is the 2d edition of a work first published in 1993, and an outgrowth of the earlier *European Directory of Business Information Libraries* (see ARBA 92, entry 615). Approximately 1,800 libraries are included, grouped in 7 major geographic sections, roughly coinciding with continents (Asia through Oceania). In each section, libraries are listed alphabetically by country. Information for each is supplied by the library itself and supplemented by the editorial staff. Data given are brief: address; telephone number; year established; chief officer; type of library (public, government, academic, company); hours of operation; availability; size of collection and kinds of materials; services offered; and publications issued. The text is in English, and for some Eastern European and Asian libraries, library names are translated. Several indexes conclude the volume: a general index that lists all libraries in one alphabetic sequence, an index by region and country that duplicates the arrangement of the directory, and a subject index with libraries grouped under 39 subjects (accountancy through travel and tourism).

No cross-references or alternate forms of library names are provided to aid the searcher. For example, in the U.S. section, the Bureau of the Census Libraries are listed under B, and the Department of Commerce Libraries are listed under U.S. Other general library directories will include more institutions; for example, *World Guide to Libraries* (11th ed.; see ARBA 94, entry 612). Also, for more developed areas of the world, other directories can probably give more complete data. This guide, however, will be useful for browsing and suggesting resources in developing nations. A simple but legible sans serif typeface is used throughout. Because of the price, the directory will find a home only in very specialized collections, especially those seeking comprehensive coverage of resources throughout the world.—**Richard D. Johnson**

Storytelling

549. **National Storytelling Directory, 1996.** By the National Storytelling Association. Jonesborough, Tenn., National Storytelling Press of the National Storytelling Association; distr., Little Rock, Ark., August House, 1995. 152p. illus. $11.95pa. ISBN 1-879991-19-5. ISSN 1079-3607.

Published by the National Storytelling Association (NSA), this handy sourcebook provides access to a wide variety of useful information about storytellers and storytelling and will be welcomed by anyone interested in the subject. The emphasis is primarily on the United States, but a number of entries from other countries are also included. A brief preface introduces the work, which consists of two main sections: "Directory Listings" and "A Storytelling Guidebook." Directories are provided for storytellers, broadcast programming, educational opportunities, events, organizations and centers, periodicals, and production companies. Each directory supplies an alphabetic listing of entries; the entries themselves are arranged alphabetically by state and country. In all cases, the entries are brief, providing name, address, telephone number, and other pertinent information (including some pictures) about the item being discussed. A list of area code changes concludes this section.

The guidebook portion is essentially a collection of short essays on a variety of topics that provides information on everything from the spiritual side of storytelling to storytelling on the Internet. Preceded by an introduction and an explanation of how to get involved in NSA, the essays are grouped into three categories that deal with using stories for healing and spiritual growth, for fostering values and tolerance, and in school. The quality does vary, and it goes without saying that this book is not a substitute for the classic, more comprehensive works in the field by writers such as Caroline Feller Bauer (*Caroline Feller Bauer's New Handbook for Storytellers* [American Library Association, 1993]); nevertheless, some of these articles are excellent and would provide insight and ideas for those who will take the few minutes necessary to read them.

Concise, comprehensive, and well arranged, this inexpensive handbook will be a useful resource for teachers, librarians, parents, youth directors, and others who need information on storytelling. It should find a place in the reference collections of most large public and school libraries and academic libraries that support programs in education, folklore, and multicultural studies. [R: RBB, Jan 96, p. 888]

—**Kristin Ramsdell**

University and College Libraries

550. Leckie, Gloria J., and Kim G. Kofmel, comps. **Directory of College and University Librarians in Canada. Répertoire des Bibliothécaires des Collèges et Universités du Canada.** 2d ed. Toronto, Ontario College and University Library Association/Ontario Library Association, 1996. 173p. index. $18.95 spiralbound. ISBN 0-9699462-1-X.

Many people need to contact Canadian academic librarians but, until the appearance of this welcome volume, have not had one source where most names and addresses could be found easily. This directory, the 1st edition of which appeared in 1995, provides a listing of approximately 1,740 librarians at 275 colleges and universities in Canada; the roster is fairly complete, but inclusion remains voluntary. Entries are arranged by province or territory, and then by institution. A mailing address is given for each institution, and the entry for each librarian at that school contains the person's name, title, telephone and fax numbers, and e-mail address. Institutional and name indexes greatly ease access to information in the directory.

If it is to provide "a current, comprehensive and accessible listing of college and university librarians from across the country" (p. 2), the directory will have to be updated annually and expanded to include all academic librarians. The name index, which supplies each librarian's institutional affiliation, could also be improved by adding the page number where an individual's entry appears. As it is, one has to go through the intermediary step of turning to the institutional index. These concerns can easily be addressed in the next edition. In the meantime, this handy reference source belongs on the desk of every academic librarian in Canada and in all Canadiana, research, and large public collections.—**John D. Blackwell**

PUBLISHING AND BOOKSELLING

General Works

Bibliography

551. Musiker, Reuben. **South African Bibliography: A Survey of Bibliographies and Bibliographical Work.** 3d ed. New York, Mansell/Cassell, 1996. 142p. index. $70.00. ISBN 0-7201-2225-2.

A scholar once remarked that South Africa is the most thoroughly documented African country south of the Sahara. Originally published as a companion volume to D. H. Borchardt's *Australian Bibliography*, this 3d edition expands and updates bibliographic information published since the 1st edition in 1970 (see ARBA 71, entry 241). Divided into two major parts, this reference work offers a narrative survey of South African bibliographies and includes a list of sources, arranged in alphabetic order, of the works cited. The text covers national and subject bibliographies, periodicals, newspapers, theses, official publications, archives, and manuscripts. Although the work makes no claim for comprehensiveness, it is an essential source. The narrative survey offers concise and useful information. The author also demonstrates diligence for including recent information on bibliographic databases on CD-ROM. The bibliography is highly recommended for students and scholars of South Africa and libraries with a strong African studies collection.—**Donald Altschiller**

552. Zell, Hans M., and Cecile Lomer. **Publishing and Book Development in Sub-Saharan Africa: An Annotated Bibliography.** New Providence, N.J., Hans Zell/Reed Reference Publishing, 1996. 409p. index. $100.00. ISBN 1-873836-46-5.

A revised and updated edition of the 1984 volume, this annotated bibliography includes more than 2,200 citations. This work covers books, reports, journal articles, government publications, some theses and dissertations, and ephemera. The vast majority of the entries cover the period from the early 1960s to October 1995 (a few publications produced from 1940 to 1960 are also included). Each entry provides basic bibliographic information: author or main entry, title, place of publication, publisher and date, and number of pages. The periodicals cited in the bibliography, including ceased journals, are listed in the front of the volume. Most of the entries are annotated; they are descriptive, not critical, and vary in length from a sentence to a paragraph. The volume furnishes an author, subject, and geographic index, and some entries provide cross-references. Organized in clearly defined chapters with an easy-to-read typeface, this work exhibits the diligence and intelligence of highly skilled editors. For students and scholars interested in African publishing, this bibliography is an essential and unique reference source. [R: Choice, Oct 96, p. 260]
—**Donald Altschiller**

Dictionaries and Encyclopedias

553. **The British Literary Book Trade, 1700-1820.** James K. Bracken and Joel Silver, eds. Detroit, Gale, 1995. 366p. illus. index. (Dictionary of Literary Biography, v.154). $128.00. ISBN 0-8103-5715-1.

As noted in the editors' 2,000-word introduction, this volume complements *Dictionary of Literary Biography* (DLB) volumes 106 and 112 (Gale, 1991), which examine British literary publishers who achieved prominence between 1821 and 1965. The book at hand focuses on the transitional period that witnessed the merging of such ancillary trades as printer, bookseller, and stationer into the monolith of the publishing house. Disclaiming any intent toward exhausting their subject, Bracken and Silver have overseen the production of 37 essays (by 28 academics) on such representative individuals and firms as William Blake; Edmund Curll; William Blackwood and Sons, Ltd.; and the Strawberry Hill Press. Most entries run 5-10 pages in length. Where applicable, the evolving variants of businesses' names appear at the head of the article. Anne Dodd is the only featured woman, although Mary Jane Godwin receives her due attention in the piece on the publishing house named after her by William Godwin (her spouse and the company's principal operator).

Black-and-white pictures and facsimiles of title pages and frontispieces are scattered throughout the text. Each essay concludes with a list of references and a list of institutions holding papers about the publisher under review. Back matter includes an appendix on British copyright developments and a bibliography of 32 recent titles. An index to the names of specific major authors or works published by the firms encompassed by this survey would have added to the work's usefulness. A subsequent volume—covering aspects of Britain's seventeenth-century book trade—is scheduled to be published. In summary, this work of composite scholarship makes a solid contribution to an often-neglected period of publishing history. [R: Choice, April 96, p. 1281]—**Jeffrey E. Long**

554. Glaister, Geoffrey Ashall. **Encyclopedia of the Book.** 2d ed. London, the British Library and New Castle, Del., Oak Knoll Press, 1996. 551p. illus. $75.00; $49.95pa. ISBN 1-884718-15-9; 1-884718-14-0pa.

Containing nearly 4,000 entries of defined terms, Glaister's encyclopedia remains the definitive source on the book as an object and on bookmaking as a trade. There are entries for people (bookseller Thomas Gosden); businesses (Pelican Press); places (Little Britain); slang terms (the French *livres cochons* for illustrated erotica); pieces of equipment (joiner's press); the parts of a book (foot); printing processes (ink grinding); book-related organizations (the Poetry Book Society); and even individual reference titles (*Books in Print*). Entries vary in length from a few to more than 3,000 words, with the average being about 80 words. There are four appendixes: a sample of different specimens of typeface, a listing of Latin place-names used in early imprints, British proof-correction symbols, and a bibliography of further readings for the true bibliophile.

For this printing of Glaister's standard work, retired librarian Donald Farren has changed the alphabetizing to a letter-by-letter arrangement, from the previous word-by-word system. Also, about a third of the book has been rewritten—1,144 of this edition's entries are new. As for competing titles, Glaister is focused clearly on books, unlike *Harrod's Librarian's Glossary* (see entry 526), which obviously has a different scope and purpose. *Encyclopedia of the Book* also is more comprehensive than R. R. Bowker's *Bookman's Glossary* (1983), but the latter may be appealing if one is concerned about a British bias in the former. This has been a benchmark source since 1960; its reputation as such is deserved. The field of librarianship has undergone a well-documented erosion of interest in bibliology. Purchase of a resource this erudite and entertaining could be a quick cure.—**Ed Volz**

Directories

555. **Publishers, Distributors, & Wholesalers of the United States 1996-97.** New Providence, N.J., R. R. Bowker/Reed Reference Publishing, 1996. 2v. index. $199.95/set. ISBN 0-8352-3740-0.

As noted when previously reviewed in *American Reference Books Annual* (ARBA) (see ARBA 95, entry 674), this two-volume source is the most inclusive directory of publishers in the United States. Using R. R. Bowker's in-house database as its source, this edition of *Publishers, Distributors, & Wholesalers* (PD&W) lists more than 85,000 corporate entities—those named in the book's title as well as others, such as software and audio vendors, associations, and museums. Most of the set's first volume is taken up by a general company name index. Each entry lists ISBN, telephone/address directory data, and Standard Address Numbers (SANs). Participants in the cataloging-in-process program are noted by a "CIP" designation. When possible, entries also contain the following elements: corporate affiliation, linked imprints, abbreviated company name (used in other R. R. Bowker publications), e-mail/World Wide Web site addresses, sales discount schedule, and returns policy. Three other indexes list entities geographically, by ISBN, and by activity type (e.g., software producers and small presses).

Five other permutations of the R. R. Bowker database create the following additional lists: imprints, subsidiaries, and divisions; company name abbreviations as used in R. R. Bowker publications; toll-free and fax numbers; names of wholesalers and distributors; and inactive/defunct companies. Prospective buyers should compare this title with its competitors, such as *Literary Market Place* (R. R. Bowker, annual). Each resource has its distinct strengths and limitations, and few libraries will want or need to own every directory of this type. PD&W can be recommended for its inclusiveness and variety of listings. R. R. Bowker's typically high standards are once again evident.—**Ed Volz**

12 Military Studies

GENERAL WORKS

Atlases

556. **The Cambridge Illustrated Atlas of Warfare: Renaissance to Revolution, 1492-1792.** By Jeremy Black. New York, Cambridge University Press, 1996. 192p. illus. maps. index. $39.95. ISBN 0-521-47033-1.

This volume is the second in the series of Cambridge Illustrated Atlases of Warfare, and follows an initial volume on the Middle Ages (see entry 557). Readers familiar with other military atlases will likely be unprepared for the novel approach of this particular effort. Less a collection of maps, it is more a military history supported by superb cartography. Forty-one chapters under six broad headings cover the world, including such generally ignored areas as sub-Saharan Africa and the Russian expansion in Asia. Typically, each features one or more Mercator maps, and many include perspective maps of individual battlefields as well. In addition, there are superb period illustrations throughout, a number of which are cartographic. Both, however, are but complements to Black's masterful text. His account of the period's history combines succinct exposition while avoiding the easy explanation or riding the hobbyhorse of a few grand themes. Renaissance warfare has too often fallen into the hands of the technologists, for instance, with their disposition to see the field as a subset of pyrotechnics. Black is more inclined to attribute success to those armies that were able to field balanced forces, flexible to a variety of challenges. He is also generous in crediting the influence of such nonmilitary factors as geography and culture. As he points out, while the Aztecs collapsed quickly under Spanish assault, the Maya were unconquered for nearly two centuries. Broadly, however, he describes a process whereby military forces that were widely dissimilar at the outset came more and more to resemble one another by the conclusion. This is an atlas equally useful for the reader as the student. It is also one that will be welcomed by those searching for quality additions to multicultural collections. [R: SLMQ, Fall 96, p. 62]—**Paul L. Holmer**

557. **The Cambridge Illustrated Atlas of Warfare: The Middle Ages, 768-1487.** By Nicholas Hooper and Matthew Bennett. New York, Cambridge University Press, 1996. 192p. illus. maps. index. $39.95. ISBN 0-521-44049-1.

A reasonably priced reference work, this comprehensive guide to European warfare from the reign of Charlemagne to the end of the Middle Ages is divided into 4 time periods and includes an introduction and 12 essays on such topics as cavalry, infantry, siege techniques, laws of war, and other aspects of military theory and practice. Appended to the text are a glossary; a list for further reading; and an extensive tricolumnar chronology coordinating events in France and Britain, Germany and north and central Europe, the Mediterranean, and routes and sites of the Crusades. The index is coded with boldfaced entries showing map references.

Each entry begins with a clear overview; for example, reasons for the Latin conquest of Constantinople. Sidebars offer peripheral knowledge (e.g., Henry II's seal, helmets, tomb reliefs, a photograph of Caernarvon, an English coin from the tenth century, a detailed study of the Battle of Agincourt, and a print showing an Irish cattle raid). The star of the text is the cartography, generously highlighted with color landmasses, troop movements, military and supply routes, symbols of strongholds, cutlines, and incisive legends. Presentation is colorful, concise, and scholarly, particularly detailed information on weapons, missiles, castle planning, mercenaries, and amphibious warfare. The glossary highlights derivations and complex particulars of medieval power struggles; for instance, *motte and bailey architecture*, *ballista*, *pavise*, and other terms from Scandinavia, Mongolia, Islamic, and Egyptian realms, plus Greek, French, and Latin terms dating to the military style of ancient Rome. [R: BR, Nov/Dec 96, p. 48; RBB, June 96, pp. 1764-64; SLJ, Aug 96, p. 182]—**Mary Ellen Snodgrass**

Bibliography

558. Erickson, John, and Ljubica Erickson, comps. **The Soviet Armed Forces, 1918-1992: A Research Guide to Soviet Sources.** Westport, Conn., Greenwood Press, 1996. 197p. index. (Research Guides in Military Studies, no.8). $75.00. ISBN 0-313-29071-7.

Both compilers of this bibliography are longtime students of the Soviet Union. The reference traces the Soviet military systems from the rise of the Red Army to the collapse of the USSR. Listed are more than 1,400 titles that should appeal to a wide audience as well as to the specialist (although readers with a knowledge of the Russian language would be served best).

The book opens with some 300 general sources: archives guides, biographies, dictionaries, military manuals, and an interesting section on imperial antecedents. The compilers then shift to a chronological treatment covering the Communist revolution and ensuing civil war; the development of the armed forces, 1922-1940; and the Great Patriot War, 1941-1945. The third section deals with the nuclear age and the relationship between the army and the Communist Party. Also provided are an overview and a helpful list of 15 titles of key sources called "breakthrough books." There is both a name and a subject index. [R: Choice, July/Aug 96, p. 1772]—**David Eggenberger**

559. Friedl, Vicki L., comp. **Women in the United States Military, 1901-1995: A Research Guide and Annotated Bibliography.** Westport, Conn., Greenwood Press, 1996. 251p. index. (Research Guides in Military Studies, no.9). $69.50. ISBN 0-313-29657-X.

As the only comprehensive annotated bibliography on women in the U.S. military to date, this book capably fills a gap in library research collections. The compiler is a librarian and history bibliographer at Boston University; she has had active military service as an Army officer from 1980 to 1984. In addition to the extensive annotations, Friedl has given the serious student an outline of steps to follow in conducting research with the first chapter, a guide to the important sources of information on military women. Access points for searches through OCLC and RLIN, as well as other online databases, are described. While Internet access is not addressed in this chapter, one of the appendixes lists a sampling of World Wide Web pages on military women.

The 857 entries are divided into chapters with broad subjects (e.g., Marine Corps, sex issues, women in combat). Each chapter begins with an introduction to the topic. Author, title, and subject indexes provide additional access points to the extensive annotations. Friedl has reviewed books, research reports, student papers for service schools, technical reports, conference papers, theses and dissertations, archival materials, government documents, and articles from scholarly journals. Excluded are articles from popular magazines, such as *Time*, and service magazines, such as *Airman*. Coverage is from the beginning of the Army Nurse Corps in 1901 through August 1995. Valuable appendixes list archival resources, women's military associations, a chronology of women's service, and military World Wide Web pages.

In many instances, a single-volume subject bibliography is not as useful, and certainly not as current, as searching through various print indexes and online databases for relevant citations. This is not so in the case of *Women in the United States Military*. As the compiler points out, even the broader discipline of women's studies has "no one source, print or electronic which provides comprehensive coverage of the subject" (p. 4). By reviewing an extensive corpus of sources, including online catalogs (LOCIS, CARL, MELVYL, and HOLLIS), online databases, journal indexes, bibliographies, and dissertation indexes, she has performed a valuable service with this bibliography, which is an important purchase for any library.—**Ingrid Schierling Burnett**

560. Sexton, Donal J., Jr., comp. **Signals Intelligence in World War II: A Research Guide.** Westport, Conn., Greenwood Press, 1996. 163p. index. (Bibliographies of Battles and Leaders, no.18). $69.50. ISBN 0-313-28304-4.

Signals intelligence, or "Sigint," covers the interception, decryption, and analysis of coded communications. Sigint came into its own in World War II, most prominently in the now widely known Ultra and Magic, the major, successful efforts to read the German and Japanese codes. Sexton's exhaustive coverage of the literature reveals the central importance of Ultra and Magic, but he also reveals other efforts by the Allies and the Axis. While the vast majority of sources are in English, materials in other Western languages (e.g., French, German, Russian, Polish) are included. Virtually all of the entries are annotated, often with evaluative as well as descriptive content. The range of formats is also diverse: journal articles, books, conference proceedings, dissertations, bibliographies, microfilm collections, and so on.

The basic arrangement is under the four major headings: "Reference Works and Research Guides," "General and Introductory Works," "General and Theoretical" (subdivided by country) and "Strategy and Operations" (general, special operations, and by theater of the war). The organization is admittedly awkward at times, as it is often difficult to characterize and sort writings that address such diverse technical, historical, and geographic issues, but the subject index does help. Other supplementary sections include a listing of acronyms and abbreviations, a chronology, and an index. The comprehensive coverage of the topic, including materials ranging from popular to research level, makes this an important purchase for both public and academic libraries with any significant interest in the Second World War and military intelligence.—**Kenneth W. Berger**

561. van Hartesveldt, Fred R., comp. **The Battles of the Somme, 1916: Historiography and Annotated Bibliography.** Westport, Conn., Greenwood Press, 1996. 137p. index. (Bibliographies of Battles and Leaders, no.17). $65.00. ISBN 0-313-29386-4.

The Battle of the Somme conjures up a vision of titanic struggle and enormous slaughter, as does the Battle of Verdun. The opening of the battle and its consequences have engendered considerable controversy. Number 17 of the Bibliographies of Battles and Leaders series sets the tone for historical debate and provides an excellent annotated bibliography of English, British Empire, French, and German sources on the battle.

World War I still engenders considerable intellectual curiosity and research. The crucible of that conflict wrought changes in warfare that are evident today. This work is commendable in providing a discussion of the historical debate and an effective annotation of sources. Yet a more thorough discussion of archival resources needs to be undertaken. There is no mention of why there is a paucity of German documents from the Great War. (The German Military Archives at Potsdam, which produced the official German history of the conflict, was destroyed in a bombing raid toward the end of World War II. The remnants of German military documents from World War I are to be found at archives in Freiburg, Karlsruhe, Munich, and Stuttgart.) As a researcher, this reviewer would have found it extremely useful to know what document collections are still extant in Germany, France, Great Britain, and the former Empire countries.

This volume is fine as far as it goes, but more needs to be done to get the word out to doctoral students and other researchers about existing document collections, public and private. No doubt the Internet may help in this communication. This volume is recommended for public, college, university, and private reference collections. [R: Choice, Nov 96, p. 438]—**Norman L. Kincaide**

Biography

562. **Generals in Muddy Boots: A Concise Encyclopedia of Combat Commanders.** By Dan Cragg. Walter J. Boyne, ed. New York, Berkley, 1996. 196p. illus. $29.95. ISBN 0-425-15136-0.

Concise is an appropriate adjective for this work on combat field commanders. Not intended to be all encompassing, this volume identifies some of the more noteworthy commanders in the history of warfare from ancient times to the Vietnam era. Entries provide a brief biography, describe military education, and discuss combat career. The alphabetic presentation eliminated the need for an index, making this a quick-reference guide. Cragg has written a more popular and anecdotal rather than a strictly scholarly work. Notable omissions from an otherwise star-studded assembly of commanders are Wilhelm Balck, Kurt Student, James Gavin, and Hasso von Manteuffel. Oversights and a lack of a more scholarly treatment aside, this is a solid, competent survey of combat commanders, and is recommended for middle school, high school, public library, and private reference collections. [R: LJ, Feb 96, p. 142; RBB, 1 May 96, p. 1519]—**Norman L. Kincaide**

563. Sherrow, Victoria. **Women and the Military: An Encyclopedia.** Santa Barbara, Calif., ABC-CLIO, 1996. 381p. illus. index. $60.00. ISBN 0-87436-812-X.

Women and the Military explores the significant contributions women have made to the armed services throughout U.S. history. These include the familiar—such as the computer work of Grace Murray Hopper during World War II—as well as the less well known, such as the courageous exploits of widow "Mad Anne" Bailey during the Revolutionary War. The A to Z entries are preceded by an interesting and informative introduction that surveys the history of women's contributions to military undertakings throughout civilization and more recently in the United States.

The nearly 400 entries cover individuals, events, laws, court cases, concepts, organizations, wars, and military branches. The editors have made generous use of cross-references, and bibliographies accompany many of the longer articles. The entries, ranging in length from several sentences to a page, are current and do not shy away from the controversial, as witnessed by the lengthy article on the Tailhook incident. The intended audience for this encyclopedia is students, librarians, journalists, members of the military, and general readers. They will find *Women and the Military* a useful and welcome resource.—**G. Kim Dority**

Dictionaries and Encyclopedias

564. Davis, Paul K. **Encyclopedia of Invasions and Conquests from Ancient Times to the Present.** Santa Barbara, Calif., ABC-CLIO, 1996. 443p. illus. maps. index. $60.00. ISBN 0-87436-782-4.

Engaging writing, sensible organization, nice (but too few) illustrations, interesting and obscure facts, and useful maps make this book a pleasure to read, even if one has no interest in the history of war. The book benefits from the author's narrow definitions of the words *conquest* and *invasion*. *Conquest* is defined as "the long-term domination of one country by another," and it includes colonization as well as occupation (i.e., colonization with military activity). *Invasion* is defined as the violation of national borders. Interestingly, although invasions are always military, conquests may be political or economic.

The book is organized chronologically into sections ("The Ancient World," "The Age of Empires," and so on). Within each section, entries are organized alphabetically by the name of the invading/conquering empire. Each entry is numbered; at the beginning of each section is a world or regional map with the site of each invasion marked by the corresponding number. Some entries are broad-brush summaries, others offer detailed accounts of specific battles. All contain interesting information, quotations from primary source documents, or observations from the author. Cross-references, a reference list for each entry, and a comprehensive bibliography are included, as is an index. Because individual entries are arranged in alphabetic order, a chronology would have been helpful.

The author draws from a wide range of sources, including the Bible, which he uses as the basis for his account of the Israelite invasion of Canaan. It would have been useful to offer some corroborating evidence, or at the least a brief discussion of the historical veracity of this work. For example, is there evidence that the walls of Jericho really did collapse all at once, as the author (drawing on the Bible) says they did? The book's design is quiet and elegant, and the typeface makes reading a pleasure.—**Constance Hardesty**

565. **The Oxford Companion to Australian Military History.** By Peter Dennis and others. New York, Oxford University Press, 1995. 692p. illus. maps. $75.00. ISBN 0-19-553227-9.

From the violence that accompanied European settlement to the 1991 Persian Gulf War, the military has figured prominently in Australian history. This history is well described in this volume, which is really an alphabetically arranged encyclopedia (one of a series of commendable Oxford companions, such as *Ships and the Sea* [see ARBA 78, entry 1549], *World War II* [see entry 571], and *Australian Literature* [2d ed.; see ARBA 96, entry 1248]).

The book has 4 authors, all with appropriate experience and expertise, and 27 distinguished contributors of the 800 entries. It is amply illustrated with 100 photographs and more than 30 maps. Entries include major battles and campaigns (Gallipoli, Kodoka); biographies of military as well as relevant civilian figures (Thomas Blaimey, Charles Bean); weapons; military units; and thematic essays on such topics as conscription, prisoners of war, and war crimes trials. There are six pages on "Anzac Legend" describing the development of the reputation of the Australian fighting man. The term is enshrined in the annual Anzac Day of April 25.

Two criticisms can be made about this book: The articles are not signed, and the attempts at bibliography are woeful. Nevertheless, the work is highly recommended. It is well made and will serve as a valuable reference for students and the general public as well as interested specialists.—**David Eggenberger**

566. Tomajczyk, S. F. **Dictionary of the Modern United States Military: Over 15,000 Weapons, Agencies, Acronyms....** Jefferson, N.C., McFarland, 1996. 785p. index. $125.00. ISBN 0-7864-0127-3.

This dictionary is concerned with the terminology of modern (post-1945) U.S. military forces and, to a lesser degree, of organizations such as the National Aeronautics Space Administration, the Central Intelligence Agency, and the National Security Agency. The work covers weapons and equipment (for naval, air, ground, and covert operations); slang (sometimes pretty strong language); health, medicine, and psychology; bases; administration and personnel management; and more. It does not include battles, people, or purely historical subjects. The definitions are complete and usually provide the origin of the term and background information. Few terms are defined in a mere sentence; some terms have articles up to a half-page in length.

There have been a number of dictionaries on military subjects published in the last few years, and the work under review fits nicely among them. *Dictionary of Military Abbreviations* (see ARBA 95, entry 679) and *Jane's Defence Glossary* (see ARBA 94, entry 676), while comprehensive, simply decipher acronyms and abbreviations. In Tomajczyk's dictionary, however, almost all entries for acronyms and abbreviations have *see* references to the full term, where one finds a brief or extended definition. The *U.S. Department of Defense Dictionary of Military Terms* (rev. ed.; see ARBA 92, entry 649) is concerned only with operational terms and hardware used in joint military activities. Tomajczyk's work is both narrower and broader than the Department of Defense work, leaving out much of the specialized terminology while still including weapons nomenclature and, in addition, the day-to-day language of the soldier or sailor. *The Dictionary of Modern War* (see ARBA 92, entry 647) is perhaps closer to the work under review than any of the above, but it emphasizes weaponry (ships, aircraft, technology) to a much greater extent than Tomajczyk.

Naturally, there is some overlap among these titles, but each is slightly different, and each complements the others. The work at hand provides broad coverage of modern U.S. military terms and subjects, a nice combination of the technical and the social, the mechanical and the organizational. It will be an admirable choice for public and academic libraries that are looking for a wide-ranging, all-around dictionary of the modern U.S. military. [R: Choice, July/Aug 96, p. 1778; LJ, Feb 96, p. 70; RBB, June 96, p. 1768]—**Eric R. Nitschke**

Directories

567. Kerr, Donald. **World Directory of Defence and Security.** New York, Stockton Press, 1995. 527p. $195.00. ISBN 1-56159-145-9.

How important are a nation's defense forces? In this volatile world, that is a question too often requiring an answer. In the Middle East, Central America, and Eastern Europe, there is a need to assess military strength and strategic potential. Nations find themselves brought to the brink of conflict, and peacekeeping missions are all too often called upon to maintain a security balance in regions coping with national instability. Kerr's selection is a no-nonsense guide to world military forces—162 nations in all. Arranged in an alphabetic sequence, each national listing includes information in seven categories: geography; external threats; agreements, alliances, and affiliations; arms control; internal dynamics; defense; and foreign military commitments. The geographic and internal information is provided to set a context for the role of the military, but the main emphasis of the entries is the strength of each nation's armed forces—army, navy, and air force.

A typical entry lists each branch, its strength (in personnel), organization, bases, and equipment. If applicable, nuclear capability is detailed. Foreign military commitments vary from country to country, but are generally brief. Such nations as France, Britain, and the United States have extended listings of troops in foreign countries. The information is generally reliable when compared to such sources as the International Institute for Strategic Studies's *The Military Balance* (see ARBA 89, entry 594). A useful but expensive reference volume, the information is soon out-of-date. If a library already owns *The Military Balance*, it should save its money.—**Boyd Childress**

Handbooks and Yearbooks

568. Arnold, Guy. **Wars in the Third World Since 1945.** 2d ed. New York, Mansell/Cassell, 1995. 670p. maps. index. $95.00. ISBN 0-304-33086-8.

Arnold's work on the wars in the Third World is well organized, informative, and poses questions about intervention by major powers and the United Nations in conflicts in developing countries. The book is divided into five parts according to type of conflict: colonial liberation, big power intervention, border and wars between Third World countries, Israel and its neighbors, and civil wars. Each part is then divided into geographic regions, and then by individual conflict. The conflict is then described by origin, outbreak and response, course of the discord, estimated costs and casualties, and immediate and long-term results.

The problem with this work is that perhaps the term *Third World* has lost its meaning since the end of the Cold War. The term originated as a result of the Cold War and the competition between the Western democracies and the Soviet Union. The demise of the Soviet Union brought about a restructuring of power throughout the world; there is a reorientation of purpose and the use of power by the developed industrial nations and the developing nations of the world. With the substantial change wrought by the end of the Cold War, there has to be considerable reevaluation of how the whole world is classified, historically, economically, ideologically, and politically. The world does not need to be defined by conflict, whether it be military, economic, or ideological. However, until historians and world affairs analysts reorient themselves to a post-Cold War world, in which there may not be a third world at all, this work will fill the needs of reference collections in public, college, and university libraries.—**Norman L. Kincaide**

569. **A Handbook of American Military History: From the Revolutionary War to the Present.** Jerry K. Sweeney, ed. Boulder, Colo., Westview Press, 1996. 319p. $59.00. ISBN 0-8133-8569-5.

This handbook consists of six chronological sections covering U.S. military history from 1775 to 1994, supplemented with a brief glossary at the end. Each section contains five subdivisions: a brief introductory note; a chronology; a summary of military operations; biographical notes; and a selected, annotated reading list.

The introductory notes of two to three pages each are well written and of value although their brevity limits their usefulness. The chronologies average about 400 entries and include a disconcerting selection of events ranging from the significant to the trivial (e.g., on August 25, 1916, the "Liberty aircraft engine . . . completes . . . endurance test"). Some of the entries are unclear. For example, a number of firsts are noted but there is no indication if it is a U.S. or worldwide "first." Also, a number of the events listed are so general or vague as to be almost meaningless.

The summaries of military operations (typically 3 to 10 pages each in length) contain anywhere from 15 to 40 citations. The relatively few number of operations covered, plus the fact that virtually all of the operations cited are available in relatively concise form in a number of common reference sources, makes the value of these military operations subdivisions doubtful. The biographical notes are also of questionable value because, again, most of the individuals cited are also covered in standard biographical reference tools. A potentially confusing aspect of the biographical notes subdivisions is that most of the major figures, such as Dwight D. Eisenhower and Ulysses S. Grant, are given virtually no coverage. Instead, only a sentence or two is provided, and the reader is then referred to a biographical work. The selected readings, while brief, are the only truly useful part of this handbook. Altogether, the readings make up 91 pages, with approximately 900 citations.

The editor does a good job of presenting an overview of historiographic trends; the topical groupings are logical, and the annotations are useful and well focused. Overall, this work is of limited value primarily because most of the material is readily available in common, easy-to-use, and concise reference works, such as encyclopedias, biographical dictionaries, and the numerous single- and multivolume works covering U.S. military history. Therefore, the question remains: Is the really useful part of this work—the 91 pages of annotated readings—worth the price of this book? For most libraries, the answer is no, and the volume is thus not recommended.—**Anthony J. Dedrick**

570. **Jane's NBC Protection Equipment 1996-97.** 9th ed. Terry J. Gander, ed. Alexandria, Va., Jane's Information Group, 1996. 295p. index. $290.00. ISBN 0-7106-1358-X.

The 1995 terrorist nerve gas attack by a Japanese religious cult in Tokyo's subway brought to world attention the increasing dangers of chemical and biological weapons, along with still-existing dangers from nuclear weapons. The relative ease of transporting these armaments and the difficulty of tracking and deterring potential users of such weapons pose an increasingly important problem for national security and law enforcement officials and policy-makers worldwide. The acute vulnerability of the general public to such attacks is also troubling. This annual publication from Jane's Information Group provides detailed information about trends and developments in nuclear, chemical, and biological weaponry and protection equipment. As with other Jane's publications, it opens with an editorial assessment of the current international weapons environment.

Detailed sections of this work feature nuclear, biological, and chemical weapons inventory summaries and national policies for individual countries, along with analysis of the effects of these weapons. Additional sections feature recommended materials to use in protective equipment for personnel dealing with these weapons and international descriptions of protective equipment such as protective masks, decontamination kits, chemical and biological detection equipment, and aircrew respiratory systems. A concluding section features a directory of domestic and foreign manufacturers and suppliers of protection equipment. This work provides excellent coverage and analysis of an increasingly important national security issue for the world community. It measures up to the high editorial and content standards of other Jane's publications, and belongs in libraries with significant national security and scientific collection holdings.—**Bert Chapman**

571. **The Oxford Companion to World War II.** I. C. B. Dear and M. R. D. Foot, eds. New York, Oxford University Press, 1995. 1343p. illus. maps. $60.00. ISBN 0-19-866225-4.

This massive volume is the most comprehensive of several World War II encyclopedias. Prolific British military historians Dear and Foot led a team of 140 international experts who address every aspect of the conduct and experience of the conflict from grand strategy to daily wartime life. The 1,700 alphabetically arranged entries vary from brief identifications to lengthy essays on such topics as the origins of the war and major campaigns. The longer essays have brief bibliographies, and many entries are cross-referenced. The 300 photographs, diagrams, and maps are among the best found in a reference volume. The nine color maps in the appendix are particularly excellent, as is the comparative chronology.

This excellent source should be in all libraries alongside the recent more specialized reference volumes, such as *Who's Who in World War II* (see ARBA 96, entry 681); *The D-Day Encyclopedia* (see ARBA 95, entry 686); and *The D-Day Atlas*, edited by John Man (Facts on File, 1994).—**Joe P. Dunn**

AIR FORCE

572. **Jane's Aircraft Upgrades, 1996-97.** 4th ed. Simon Michell, ed. Alexandria, Va., Jane's Information Group, 1996. 536p. illus. index. $290.00. ISBN 0-7106-1366-0.

Jane's Information Group has long been the world leader in publishing reference books on weapons, equipment, and service branches. Volumes such as *Jane's Fighting Ships* (see entry 573) and *Jane's All the World's Aircraft* (see entry 1440) are only two representatives of the Jane's family. As a general rule, these books are highly detailed, lavishly illustrated, and very expensive.

Aircraft Upgrades is no exception to these generalities, with more than 1,000 illustrations (photographs and scale drawings) and a price of $290. The volume is arranged alphabetically country by country. Each corporation recording upgrades is listed with a brief corporate description, followed by the specific aircraft that has been upgraded through equipment, modifications, or other enhancements. The aircraft included are military and commercial, fixed- and rotary-wing, which are no longer in production or nearing an end to their production cycle, but still in service. Entries are indicated as either new or updated (as this is the 4th edition).

While the aircraft descriptions are detailed and technically specific, the volume does provide unique and specialized corporate information. Although 45 nations are covered, more than 33 percent of the pages cover aircraft manufacturers in the United States and more than 100 pages represent French, British, and Russian corporations. *Aircraft Upgrades* is a supplement to *All the World's Aircraft* and a significant reference work for collections appealing to a technical, aeronautical audience.—**Boyd Childress**

NAVY

573. **Jane's Fighting Ships 1996-97.** 99th ed. Richard Sharpe, ed. Alexandria, Va., Jane's Information Group, 1996. 902p. illus. index. $335.00. ISBN 0-7106-1355-5.

This naval annual's current edition holds the structure and format course established in previous years. From the foreword with its pungent opinions on a variety of naval topics to the more than 40 pages of advertisements (some annoyingly interpolated with the reference text), the editor's inclusive aim is achieved: In addition to naval and coast guard forces, police, customs, and army waterborne craft are also covered, so the "Swiss Navy" is included. Modern typesetting methods now enable addenda to be dispensed with while making regular updates available to those who purchase the subscription edition.

The text sets out the facts with compact precision: Dimensions are given in feet (with metric equivalents following) while weapons ranges/payload weights are stated in metric only. The value of the entries is increased by the fact that their verification/update status is provided. In comparison with its major competitor (*The Naval Institute Guide to Combat Fleets of the World* [see ARBA 94, entry 704, and ARBA 91, entry 695]) *Jane's* coverage of minor navies is superior, with more pictures and more detailed entries. Its coverage of medium navies is also better, with more data overall and larger pictures, but smaller drawings. *Jane's* coverage of major navies is not clearly superior (*Combat Fleets* devotes nearly three times the pages to the U.S. Navy, with much more information on the Ready Reserve Force in particular). For major fleet units, the two competitors provide nearly identical data, although *Jane's* has slightly longer entries for these ship types. It may seem somewhat odd that the Russian Navy gets 10 more pages than the U.S. Navy, but the fleet counts indicate that the former has 1,112 ships while the latter only has 594.

The scaled and keyed drawings are well drawn, and the overall quality of the monochrome photographs and their reproduction is excellent. The color photographic supplement introduced last year returns, with mixed results: Some of the pictures practically sail off the page, whereas others are badly out of register. There is the occasional blurry shot (for some publicity-shy navies); strangely, a few of the photographs in the new edition are not as clear as those in the previous edition. About 40 percent of the pictorial coverage is new, compared to the 1995/96 version, but some navies do better than others in this. A random selection of 406 pictures ranging from the Bulgarian to the Danish navies showed that 174 dated from before 1993 (with the oldest dated 1973!), 58 were from 1993, 67 were from 1994, 101 dated from 1995, and 6 were from 1996. The majority of recent photographs are in the sections devoted to major navies; indeed, the pictorial coverage of auxiliary ships in the minor navies has been pruned considerably from last year's edition.

Perfection nevertheless remains elusive. The text is set in a tiny sans serif typeface, which is rather hard to read, and the occasional typographical error creeps in. More serious are outright errors of fact (for example, that the Russian *Kirov* class was the first surface warship with nuclear propulsion, when it was preceded by many U.S. Navy aircraft carriers and cruisers), but there do not appear to be many of these. The occasional omission was also noted (e.g., the coverage of rank structure/insignia omits the Latvian Navy). Despite these blemishes, the overall accomplishment is impressive and well indexed. A sample of the indexes was checked and proved accurate. Provision of a class index strengthens the ready-reference utility of this book, as some ships are only known by their class name. It also clearly shows how many navies operate a particular ship class (so one quickly sees that the *Asheville* patrol craft is used by Colombia, Greece, the Republic of Korea, Turkey, and the United States). Crisply printed on quality-coated stock with a sturdy, lay-flat binder, this 9-pound ready-reference is such a heavyweight that it can only be used comfortably from a table or stand, something that will doubtless not deter any library patron with naval interests.—**John Howard Oxley**

574. Whitley, M. J. **Cruisers of World War Two: An International Encyclopedia.** Annapolis, Md., Naval Institute Press, 1995. 288p. illus. index. $49.95. ISBN 1-55750-141-6.

Cruisers were combat workhorses in World War II, yet they have not received attention comparable to that given most other major ship types, so this well-illustrated volume by a noted expert on Second World War warships fills a major gap. Coverage is comprehensive and includes the ships of neutral nations; arrangement is alphabetic by country, and generally (although, confusingly, not always) chronological within the country.

This is a compendium from secondary works, rather than a work of original scholarship. Clearly written, it provides statistical data (in both metric and English measurements), design notes, and service histories for each class. Much of the book's attraction comes from the illustrations, with most of the photographs being large and crisp (the French, Italian, and Soviet views in particular not being readily available elsewhere). Unfortunately, a number of the double-page spreads suffer from guttering. The unscaled line drawings (which appear to be close to 1:1,200) provide profile and overhead views; while accurate, they are rather rudimentary, with some over-heavy line work.

In general, little fault can be found with the contents, although some errors were noted, the most serious of these being the captioning errors for the photographs of H.M.S. *Delhi* (p. 77) and H.M.S. *Frobisher* (p. 79); the service history for HIJMS *Naka* in fact being that of her sister ship *Jintsu*; and the reference to the refitted turrets in the *Principe Alfonso* class being in "A" and "B" positions (p. 218) when they were in fact in "A" and "Y" positions. In addition, the index can be faulted for referring to ship names only, thereby excluding many important text items. Clearly printed on high-quality paper in a sturdy, lay-flat binding, this ready-reference book will be useful in any collection serving World War II naval history interests. [R: Choice, Sept 96, p. 108]—**John Howard Oxley**

WEAPONS

575. **Jane's Armour and Artillery 1995-96.** 16th ed. Christopher F. Foss, ed. Alexandria, Va., Jane's Information Group, 1995. 833p. illus. index. $275.00. ISBN 0-7106-1260-5.

This annual covers the following types of armor and artillery: main battle tanks, medium and light tanks, reconnaissance and armored personnel vehicles, armored fighting vehicles and tank destroyers, self-propelled guns and howitzers, towed guns and howitzers, multiple rocket launchers, and coastal artillery guns and missiles. As is common in Jane's Information Group publications, each type of weapon is listed and analyzed by country of manufacture (or, as is becoming increasingly common, by an "international" designation for consortium-built weapons).

All articles provide a design and development history of the item; a description, including technical specifications; and notices of variant models. The foreword gives a global view of significant new weapons, modifications, development contracts, sales, and withdrawn models. There are also summary pages listing items new to this edition and items deleted since the last edition. Photographs, line drawings, or schematics are supplied for almost every weapon described. Photographs are now labeled with a date and articles are categorized by three formulas: verified (presumably unchanged but still accurate), updated, and new entry. The photographs and drawings are clear, and most of them are new for this edition (for reviews of earlier editions, see ARBA 91, entry 704, and ARBA 85, entry 612).

The Jane's series of publications are known for their accuracy and authoritativeness. They are not inexpensive, but they are invaluable for the library supporting research on defense, disarmament, or military strength.—**Eric R. Nitschke**

576. **Jane's Tank & Combat Vehicle Recognition Guide.** By Christopher F. Foss. New York, HarperCollins, 1996. 510p. illus. $19.95pa. ISBN 0-00-470995-0.

One of the foremost writers on the subject provides in this book recognition data and basic information on tanks; tracked armored personnel carriers; wheeled combat vehicles (4x4, 6x6, 8x8); self-propelled guns (wheeled and tracked); and self-propelled antiaircraft guns and missiles. Each of these weapons types is discussed in a separate section with one or more photographs (most also are depicted in a line drawing). Each section is highlighted by a generic identifying silhouette. Within each type, vehicles are arranged alphabetically by operating nation, and then by manufacturer/mark number, resulting in a valuable tool filling a major gap in military publications.

Each vehicle depicted is presented in one or more clear photographs (with the exception of the occasional blurry shot, such as the BTR-40 on page 279); the line drawings provided (a few of which are rather poorly printed) are mostly side views. Along with basic tabular data and employment notes, each entry has a verbal summary of the principal vehicle recognition characteristics from front, side, and rear.

In addition to rather more than the usual number of typographic errors (the most severe being persistent errors in rendering diacritical marks), some general errors were noted. There are occasional inconsistencies in the details specified for recognition (in particular, track return rollers are not always mentioned); too many of the armor thickness data remain classified; cross-references are occasionally confused; and vehicle widths are not always specified. Overall, however, this is a handy guide to its subject, sturdily bound in a volume that readily fits in pocket or purse, and clearly printed on high-quality paper. Its value as a ready-reference source is considerably reduced, however, by the lack of any index, so that many vehicle subtypes mentioned in the text are essentially lost. Because most libraries serving military interests will want to consider this title, such an omission is indeed regrettable. —**John Howard Oxley**

577. **Jane's Warship Recognition Guide.** By Keith Faulkner. New York, HarperCollins, 1996. 541p. illus. $19.95pa. ISBN 0-00-470981-0.

This book provides recognition data and basic information relating to a selected set of combat vessels, each of which is depicted in a photograph and a small silhouette drawing, and most of which are also depicted in a line drawing. Ships are arranged by type, and within this, alphabetically by operating nation, resulting in a handy tool filling a major gap in naval publications.

The introduction includes naval ensigns in color and a set of composite ship/submarine drawings identifying principal external features (oddly enough, while the recognition feature known as a "knuckle"—a discontinuity in the sheer of a ship's side—is shown in the drawings, it is not identified, and "tumblehome" is not shown at all). With one or two exceptions, the photographs are clear and serve well as recognition aids. They are mostly sized to the page, meaning the smaller ships (which only get small pictures in the major naval annuals) receive particularly welcome emphasis. Marginal notes supplement the illustrations by guiding the reader's eyes to key specifics, while the tabulated data and notes provide necessary background.

Apart from some typographic errors (the most severe of which on page 66 completely confuses that presentation), the most annoying error in the book is the persistent use of "mainmast" to refer to the principal mast on a ship (proper use of the term refers to the second mast from the bow of the ship). On pages 58-62, A6-E aircraft are specified as elements of U.S. aircraft carrier air wings, when the last of these was in fact retired in 1996; on page 116, reference is made to the *Yamagumo* class, but this is nowhere illustrated; and there are occasional inconsistencies in the recognition notes (e.g., a depressed forecastle is nearly a hallmark of French surface escort design, yet this is only noted for ships other than French ones).

Overall, however, this is a handy guide to its subject, sturdily bound in a volume that is easily carried in pocket or purse, and clearly printed on high-quality paper. Its value as a ready-reference source is considerably reduced, however, by the lack of any index, so those not knowing the class to which a specific vessel belongs cannot easily locate the relevant entry. This is particularly a pity because those libraries with limited client interest in naval matters, as well as those serving young adults, may find this the only volume they will need.—**John Howard Oxley**

578. **Nuclear Test Ban: Glossary in English, French, and Arabic.** By the Languages Service, Terminology and Technical Documentation Section. New York, United Nations, 1996. 293p. index. $30.00pa. ISBN 92-1-000057-9. S/N GV.E/F/A.96.0.27.

This specialized glossary provides English, French, and Arabic equivalents of a broad spectrum of terminology used in nuclear test ban verification. English words and phrases are arranged alphabetically, with French and Arabic translations listed immediately below. Terminology included ranges from general phrases (e.g., *search area*) to technical jargon (e.g., *radionucide signature*). Appendix 1 is a separate list of abbreviations and acronyms with English, French, and Arabic meanings. Appendix 2 is an "Index

Français," with references from French terms to page numbers of English entries. No Arabic index is provided. This is a thorough, accurate guide to nuclear test ban terminology designed to aid translation rather than to define terms.—**Ahmad Gamaluddin**

579. **The Vital Guide to Combat Guns and Infantry Weapons.** Chris Bishop, ed. Shrewsbury, England, Airlife Publishing; distr., Stillwater, Minn., Voyageur Press, 1996. 123p. illus. index. $14.95. ISBN 1-85310-539-2.

If the heft, price, advertising, and expanse of *Jane's Infantry Weapons* (see ARBA 95, entry 700) are beyond the budget and shelf space of small libraries, then *The Vital Guide to Combat Guns and Infantry Weapons* will definitely fill a niche in the reference guide field. This beautiful little book is packed with information on pistols, submachine guns, assault rifles, machine guns, combat shotguns, grenade launchers, mortars, and antitank and antiaircraft weapons. Entries provide a brief narrative description of the weapon; its use; and a box with a weapon profile and specification: name, type, caliber, weight, dimension, range, rate of fire, and a list of users. Interspersed with halftones and color photographs, this is a well-organized and attractive reference work on combat infantry weapons. Compact size, economical price, and a handsome presentation make this small volume an excellent choice for middle, high school, small public, and branch libraries, and for private collections as well.—**Norman L. Kincaide**

580. **The Vital Guide to Fighting Aircraft of World War II.** Karen Leverington, ed. Shrewsbury, England, Airlife Publishing; distr., Stillwater, Minn., Voyageur Press, 1995. 121p. illus. index. $14.95. ISBN 1-85310-586-4.

Not intended to be a comprehensive treatment of World War II aircraft, this compact volume is efficiently organized, beautifully presented, and economically compact. This enticing little book covers the major combat aircraft of World War II. Each page is devoted to one aircraft type, with at least three visual presentations of the aircraft, a profile drawing, a halftone or color photograph, and a color drawing. Squadron markings are identified, where possible. There is a brief narrative of the development, production, and employment of each type of aircraft and a box with the aircraft specifications. Some photographs are familiar and others, particularly the color photographs, are a pleasant surprise. There are color schemes and clear markings for modelers and the photographs, which at the least are representative of the aircraft type, and at the most, stunning for a reference work. This book would make an excellent addition to middle, high school, small public, large public, and branch library reference collections, not to mention private reference collections of aircraft enthusiasts of all ages.—**Norman L. Kincaide**

13 Political Science

GENERAL WORKS

581. **The Annual Register 1995: A Record of World Events.** Alan J. Day and Verena Hoffman, eds. London, Cartermill Publishing; distr., Detroit, Gale, 1996. 608p. index. $185.00. ISBN 1-86067-053-9.

This perennial British-based classic provides useful, concise summaries and overviews of the events of the previous year. With relatively minor adjustments, the arrangement and coverage remain the same, emphasizing initially regional sections, with chapters for individual countries, then separate sections on international organizations, defense and security, religion, law, arts, sports, international economics, and social affairs. The country-related chapters run from 1 to 31 pages in length; they cover major political, social, military, and economic events and contain brief factual data (e.g., gross national product per capita in U.S. dollars, leadership, political system). The section on intergovernmental organizations (IGOs) has been expanded to include, in addition to major IGOs, chapters on Arab organizations and the Organization of the Islamic Conference. Each chapter in this section summarizes the organization's activities and gives brief reference facts (e.g., objectives, membership, director). The publication also includes a limited set of full-text documents; for example, the Dayton Accord on Bosnia and Herzegovina, lists of the U.K. and U.S. cabinets, 80 brief obituaries, and a chronology of principal events in 1995.

The work is sparsely illustrated and should present more than the five tables and maps it already includes. The contributors are primarily British and European experts in government, international relations, and economics, and the Advisory Board consists of representatives from major British scholarly organizations. Even the 17-page United States chapter is written by a British authority. An excellent name/subject index is furnished. Published since 1758, this source has proven its usefulness over time, and the current edition continues its tradition of excellence. Its scope and arrangement are comparable to *The Statesman's Year-Book* (132d ed.; see ARBA 96, entry 102) and the *Europa World Year Book* (see ARBA 94, entry 82), but the register's focus, unlike theirs, is on the events of the previous year. The book would probably benefit from broadening its authorship to authorities from within the countries covered.
—**Marilyn Domas White**

582. Derbyshire, J. Denis, and Ian Derbyshire. **Political Systems of the World.** New York, St. Martin's Press, 1996. 684p. maps. index. $95.00. ISBN 0-312-16172-2.

This tool gives users a good sense of the triumph of democracy (an increase from 83 to 145 independent, democratic states since this title first appeared six years ago). Available for the first time in the United States, *Political Systems of the World* provides tables, charts, graphs, and demographics on the nine continental regions of the world. The front matter concerns itself with defining terms: What is a political party? How are ideologies governing systems? What is the system of voting, and what are the patterns? The remainder of the text is devoted to defining political systems. A sample entry will provide information on the geography, ethnic composition, religions, political features, heads of state and government, political parties and systems, and the country's political history.

No other tool provides readers with as much information in one place. Libraries with *Political Parties of the Americas* (see ARBA 84, entry 465); *Encyclopedia of Government and Politics* (Routledge, 1991); and Hobday's much smaller *Communist and Marxist Parties of the World* (2d ed.; see ARBA 92, entry 728) will want to add this latest and much-needed volume. [R: Choice, Oct 96, pp. 249-50]
—**Mark Y. Herring**

583. Minahan, James. **Nations Without States: A Historical Dictionary of Contemporary National Movements.** Westport, Conn., Greenwood Press, 1996. 692p. illus. maps. index. $99.50. ISBN 0-313-28354-0.

There are many standard reference books dealing with "states," the various sovereign nations throughout the world. This useful handbook by Minahan, an independent researcher, covers the much more obscure subject of "nations without states," those aspiring states that wish to become sovereign. The author identified 210 of these would-be nations using three criteria: a claim to a recognizable geographic area; the display of the trappings of national consciousness (such as a flag); and the formation of a nationalistic organization that reflects the claim to self-determination.

For each entry (several pages in length), statistical and directory information is provided on population, geography, language, political status, and flag. An overview of historic, political, and ethnic circumstances is also furnished. Each entry begins with black-and-white maps and a flag and concludes with a short bibliography. The appendixes include a list of national organizations.

The daily news on Québec, Palestine, Chechnya, Bosnia, and so forth makes clear the relevance of this handbook. It would be even more useful if the flags were in color, the maps had greater detail, and a clearer appraisal was given on the viability of many of these nationalistic movements. It is not clear in some cases, such as Newfoundland, Cornwall, or Tannu Tuva, if their movements are substantial political activities or means of escapism for small groups of enthusiasts. [R: Choice, June 96, p. 162; RBB, 1 May 96, pp. 1532-34]—**Henry E. York**

POLITICS AND GOVERNMENT

United States

Bibliography

584. Goehlert, Robert U., Fenton S. Martin, and John R. Sayre. **Members of Congress: A Bibliography.** Washington, D.C., Congressional Quarterly, 1996. 507p. index. $175.00. ISBN 0-87187-865-8.

As stated in the introduction, the purpose of this book is to provide "an extensive listing of biographical references of individuals who have served in the U.S. Congress from 1774 through 1995." Individuals are arranged alphabetically by last name, and entries under each name are listed alphabetically by author. Birth and death dates, party affiliation, state represented, and years served in Congress are given for each individual. The bibliography lists more than 9,000 journal articles, books, dissertations, and essays from collected works that cover a member's public and private life. Emphasis is placed on scholarly materials. Government documents, popular magazines, newspaper articles, obituaries, and eulogies are not included.

The citations listed for those individuals who have served as president or as Supreme Court Justice were selected on the basis of representing all aspects of their lives rather than focusing on service in Congress. However, the authors recommend that other sources should be consulted to obtain the broadest coverage of an individual's life and suggest two books from Congressional Quarterly, *The American Presidents* (see ARBA 88, entry 507) and *The U.S. Supreme Court* (see ARBA 91, entry 566), as supplementary sources. Volumes published as part of the Bibliographies of the Presidents of the United States series from Greenwood Press provide additional references.

Citations were gleaned from researching 25 online, print, and CD-ROM indexes. RLIN and OCLC bibliographic databases were used to find books. Overall, this bibliography provides a strong foundation to begin researching a member of the U.S. Congress, especially for those individuals who are not well known. However, if the individual is famous, such as William Jennings Bryan, or has served in a leadership role in another branch of government, such as Andrew Jackson, other bibliographies should be consulted to supplement the content of this work. [R: Choice, July/Aug 96, pp. 1772-73]

—**Robert V. Labaree**

585. Martin, Fenton S., and Robert U. Goehlert. **How to Research Congress.** Washington, D.C., Congressional Quarterly, 1996. 107p. index. $29.95; $19.95pa. ISBN 0-87187-870-4; 0-87187-869-0pa.

586. Martin, Fenton S., and Robert U. Goehlert. **How to Research the Presidency.** Washington, D.C., Congressional Quarterly, 1996. 134p. index. $29.95; $19.95pa. ISBN 1-56802-029-5; 1-56802-028-7pa.

The purpose of these guides is twofold: to provide a foundation for developing a research topic and, to this end, to describe key sources of information relevant to researching the presidency and Congress. Both guides are arranged in a similar fashion with an introductory essay and three main parts. The introductory essay gives an overview of legal resources and a discussion on how to design a research strategy. The first part of each book contains concise descriptions of secondary reference and finding tools. The second part examines primary resource finding tools, including a guide to researching specific characteristics of each institution. For example, the guide to researching the presidency supplies information sources associated with "Presidential Advisory Committees" and television coverage, while the guide to researching Congress provides information sources covering "Congressional Support Groups" and campaign finance. Sources of oral histories, audiovisual materials, Internet sites, archives, and data files are described for both institutions.

The final part of the guides contains a selected bibliography of major books. The bibliography for the congressional guide is arranged by subject, while the presidency guide is arranged by both subject and individual president. Both volumes conclude with an author and title index. In addition, the guide on Congress furnishes a helpful glossary of terms, and the presidency guide has two appendixes that list, in tabular format, all presidents and vice presidents and background data.

The organization of each book is logical and accessible. Entries are concise and well written, with electronic formats of key reference tools and indexes described whenever appropriate. The bibliographies are thorough but, as acknowledged by the authors, only touch upon the vast number of books published about Congress and the Executive Office. Unfortunately, no mention is made as to what criteria were applied in selecting these books. For example, why was Theodore Roosevelt's *An Autobiography* not included as a "major book"? This absence of evaluative information, however, does not detract from the overall usefulness of these guides, and both should be included in any medium- to large-sized library collection. [R: BR, Nov/Dec 96, p. 50; Choice, Dec 96, p. 592; RBB, 1 Oct 96, pp. 370-71]—**Robert V. Labaree**

Biography

587. **Biographical Dictionary of the United States Secretaries of the Treasury, 1789-1995.** Bernard S. Katz and C. Daniel Vencill, eds. Westport, Conn., Greenwood Press, 1996. 403p. index. $115.00. ISBN 0-313-28012-6.

This biographical dictionary is a highly readable collection of 67 biographies covering the secretaries of the Treasury, from Alexander Hamilton in 1789 to Robert E. Rubin in 1995. Written and signed primarily by academic economists, whose credentials are listed in an appendix, each biography covers not only the particulars of the individual's life (e.g., education, family and professional background, personality) but also the problems he faced during his term, and assesses his contributions during his tenure. The biographies vary in length, usually according to the importance of the individual. Albert Gallatin's entry, for example, is 12 pages long. Each entry is documented by a list of about 5 to 15 articles and books, usually secondary sources. The book would be even more valuable if, as in *Notable American Women* (see ARBA 72, entry 221), the authors had identified the major manuscript collections for each individual.

The book begins with a list, by presidential administration, of the names and tenures of the various secretaries; then the individual biographies are arranged alphabetically. This arrangement is supplemented by an extensive subject index. The editors have published a similar publication, *Biographical Dictionary of the Board of Governors of the Federal Reserve* (see ARBA 93, entry 240), with many of the same authors. Katz is professor emeritus of economics at Lafayette College and now a lecturer at San Francisco State University, where Vencill is a professor of economics.

Although the subjects were prominent in their day, not all are covered well in modern reference sources. The authors have done a good job of presenting current thinking on the secretaries' lives and tenure as secretary of the Treasury in short essays that are intelligible, even to those with limited economics backgrounds.—**Marilyn Domas White**

588. Havel, James T. **U.S. Presidential Candidates and the Elections: A Biographical and Historical Guide.** New York, Macmillan Library Reference/Simon & Schuster Macmillan, 1996. 2v. $175.00/set. ISBN 0-02-897134-5.

The emergence of Ross Perot's Reform Party in the last two presidential elections provides a rare glimpse into an electoral process that extends beyond a two-party system. Throughout U.S. history, a great diversity of candidates, political parties, agendas, and ideologies have existed in obscurity, hidden behind the current system. A number of factors, such as financial wherewithal, tradition, organizational resources, and media attention, dilute the electorate's perception that their choices consist of a Democrat, a Republican, and an occasional third-party candidate. Havel's work provides a unique point of discovery from which researchers can explore the hidden diversity within each presidential election from 1789 to 1992.

The first volume, "The Candidates," contains an alphabetically arranged list of individuals who have sought the office of the presidency and vice-presidency, with the spectrum of diversity extending from George Bush to Lawrence Welk (Democratic presidential candidate, 1976). Entries give standard information (birth, death, education, children, organizational membership, and so forth) and a current mailing address when appropriate. As with most biographical reference tools, the length and the amount of detail contained in each entry are determined by how famous the person was. The second volume, "The Elections," provides a summary of each election, highlighting important events, parties, conventions, and platforms. Results from primary, general, and electoral college balloting are also given. The volume begins with an introductory essay outlining the early history of the presidential nominating and election processes and concludes with a comprehensive bibliography. This reference work represents a major contribution to the understanding of both the diverse nature of presidential elections and the process that decides who leads the Executive Office. It is highly recommended for all library collections. [R: LJ, 1 Oct 96, p. 68]—**Robert V. Labaree**

589. **The Presidents: A Reference History.** 2d ed. Henry F. Graff, ed. New York, Scribner's/Simon & Schuster Macmillan, 1996. 811p. illus. index. $105.00. ISBN 0-684-80471-9.

A scholarly, meaty tome, Graff's reference work fills a need for a data-rich summary on each of the presidents of the United States. To the original 1984 edition (see ARBA 85, entry 448), he adds three presidencies and an article discussing the demands on First Ladies, from Martha Washington to Hillary Rodham Clinton. Each major entry provides a biography, a period history, direct citations from important speeches and interviews, an evaluation of each presidency, and a generous annotated bibliography. To the body of this incisive work, Graff appends a general bibliography; tabular data on each president, including a breakdown of Congress by party, appointments, and key events; and an overview of the expanding role of the executive branch of government.

Graff's commentary is anything but dry or predictable. To a description of Lyndon Johnson's Great Society, he quotes the president as he yells into a detractor's face the unfairness of racism; in the entry on Bill Clinton, Graff adds a touching scene in which the president, shortly before moving to Washington, D.C., returns his daughter's frog to Arkansas waters so it can live a normal life. Graff salts his text with valuable information on wars, political initiatives, and errors—for example, Ulysses S. Grant's admission that he required on-the-job training after moving from the military to the White House, and Warren G. Harding's public humiliation after *The President's Daughter* named him as the father of an illegitimate child. In describing the political scene when John Quincy Adams came to power, the text offers a tally of popular and electoral votes. The only failing of this admirable reference work is the puzzling absence of maps to indicate the size of the country in each term, action shots, or reproductions of Washington, D.C., art to show the development of the city and public appearances of presidents while in office. [R: LJ, 1 Sept 96, p. 170; RBB, 1 Sept 96, p. 170]—**Mary Ellen Snodgrass**

590. Waldrup, Carole Chandler. **The Vice Presidents: Biographies of the 45 Men Who Have Held the Second Highest Office in the United States.** Jefferson, N.C., McFarland, 1996. 271p. illus. index. $35.00. ISBN 0-7864-0179-6.

Despite historical and contemporary denigration of its significance and value, the office of vice president of the United States is still an important government position, as the 1996 presidential election and other recent historical events have demonstrated. *The Vice Presidents* presents biographical portraits of the 45 individuals who have theoretically been "a heartbeat from the presidency." These portraits are presented in chronological order of service, from John Adams to Albert Gore Jr. Individuals profiled include vice presidents who later ascended to the presidency, such as Martin Van Buren, John Tyler, Millard Fillmore, Theodore Roosevelt, Harry Truman, and George Bush. Other vice presidents with lesser historical significance, including George Mifflin Dallas, Henry Wilson, Levi Morton, and James Sherman, are also covered.

These portraits average approximately six pages in length, covering the broad outlines of the professional and personal lives of these men. Individual entries include bibliographies, although they omit standard biographical reference sources, such as the *Dictionary of American Biography* (see entry 32). This work is a useful quick introduction to the lives of the United States' vice presidents. Readers desiring more substantive analysis of the lives and careers of these individuals should consult the biographies listed in the bibliographic entries, personal papers, and government documents pertinent to the political careers of these personalities. [R: RBB, 1 Dec 96, p. 686]—**Bert Chapman**

Dictionaries and Encyclopedias

591. Klingaman, William K. **Encyclopedia of the McCarthy Era.** New York, Facts on File, 1996. 502p. illus. index. $50.00. ISBN 0-8160-3097-9.

Facts on File's *Encyclopedia of the McCarthy Era* does an adequate job of providing a general overview of the events and personalities of this period in U.S. history, emphasizing the latter. Arranged alphabetically, a substantial majority of the entries are biographical treatments of the myriad prominent individuals involved in the controversies of the era. Entries range from several brief paragraphs (Morton Kent) to more than half-a-dozen pages (Joseph McCarthy), often supplying a photograph of the subject. Also included are entries for key topics that encompass not only events, organizations, and cases but also titles of artistic works that came under scrutiny. Internal cross-referencing in bold typeface provides ease of access to related articles.

Following the main body of entries are a chronology of significant events of the period 1919-1960, a bibliography (surprisingly short considering the author's stated intent to provide a basis for further research), and 18 appendixes giving the entire or excerpted text of critical documents of the times. Possibly the most valuable contribution of this encyclopedia, these appendixes provide a single source for the chronological documentation of an era that has so profoundly impacted recent U.S. history. [R: LJ, 1 Sept 96, pp. 168-69; RBB, 1 Sept 96, p. 165]—**Virginia S. Fischer**

592. Kurz, Kenneth Franklin. **The Reagan Years A to Z: An Alphabetical History of Ronald Reagan's Presidency.** Los Angeles, Calif., Lowell House, 1996. 288p. illus. index. $30.00. ISBN 1-56565-462-5.

In *The Reagan Years A to Z*, Kurz has compiled a guide to the eight years covered by the presidency of Ronald Reagan. This was accomplished with short essays of several pages, each of which provides a historical overview of the topics selected. These topics deal with important events, such as the air traffic controllers' strike and the assassination attempt; with important persons, such as Robert Bork and Mikhail Gorbachev; or with political matters, such as the Christian Right and press relations. Nancy Reagan and the Reagan family are also extensively covered. The essays provide factual summaries of events without imposing judgments on the various controversial political and personal matters related. The individual entries do not have footnotes or bibliographies.

In addition to the entries, there is a table of contents, an index, and a selected bibliography of the Reagan years. Because all of the topics addressed in this guide were written about extensively in newspapers, magazines, and books at the time and subsequently, the value of this book is in the convenience of having the major facts on important subjects gathered together under one cover.—**Henry E. York**

593. Levy, Peter B. **Encyclopedia of the Reagan-Bush Years.** Westport, Conn., Greenwood Press, 1996. 442p. illus. index. $49.95. ISBN 0-313-29018-0.

Somewhat unusual in its attempt to reference such recent political history, the *Encyclopedia of the Reagan-Bush Years* nevertheless does quite an adequate job of providing a factual summary of the key topics of the era. While the focus is concentrated on the presidential administrations, listings also include a wide range of entries that define the sociocultural milieu for the period 1980-1992. Levy, a history professor, readily acknowledges the difficulties inherent in a lack of historical perspective, choosing instead a balanced summary and overview of the period and deferring judgment to more analytic accounts.

Prefaced by a brief list of pertinent acronyms, the volume is alphabetically arranged, with entries from a paragraph ("just say no") to several pages (Middle East) in length. Entries include suggested readings and, often, related entries with cross-referencing in bold typeface. A substantial index provides additional access points. Illustrative materials consisting of tables, charts, and photographs are generously included and add to the overall appeal of the volume. A timeline and a statistical appendix conclude the work. For content, style, and utility, this one-volume reference is highly recommended. [R: BR, Nov/Dec 96, p. 54; LJ, 15 June 96, p. 58]—**Virginia S. Fischer**

594. Maddex, Robert L. **The Illustrated Dictionary of Constitutional Concepts.** Washington, D.C., Congressional Quarterly, 1996. 335p. illus. maps. index. $79.95. ISBN 1-56802-170-4.

Maddex's dictionary covers a wide-ranging array of concepts and historical figures important to the development of constitutionalism from ancient Greece to the present day. A brief introduction outlining events relating to constitutionalism in a number of historical epochs is followed by the major section of the book, an A to Z listing of entries ranging from a column to a page in length and often accompanied by a photograph or illustration. Many of the entries provide examples from constitutions of nations. The entry for "Natural Law," for instance, briefly charts the development of the concept from the Greek Stoics of the third century B.C.E., through Thomas Aquinas, culminating with the U.S. Declaration of Independence and the French Revolution; it then provides brief quotations from the 1958 French constitution and the 1986 Liberian constitution, which are thought to be derived from this principle. Historical personages found in the source include such thinkers as Plato, Niccolò Machiavelli, John Locke, and Saint Augustine, and such leaders of nations as Abraham Lincoln, Jawaharlal Nehru, and Sun Yat-sen. An index, which separates main dictionary entries in bold typeface and illustrations in italics from terms and persons found within main entries, concludes the work.

One may always quibble with how entries for a work of this kind are chosen—for example, why is Joseph Stalin included as a main entry and not Adolf Hitler? For that matter, neither Hitler nor Nazi Germany is listed in the general index, although that regime's decision not to repeal the Weimar constitution seems an interesting fact. Also, why is William Blackstone mentioned in nearly 30 entries and given a full-page illustration, yet not awarded an entry of his own? The entries are brief and provide no bibliographies, and although the illustrations may make for a more attractive volume, their real value is somewhat questionable. Still, by bringing this material together in one accessible volume, the author has provided a worthwhile service to general readers, high school students, and undergraduates.

—**Lee Weston**

595. Nelson, Richard Alan. **A Chronology and Glossary of Propaganda in the United States.** Westport, Conn., Greenwood Press, 1996. 340p. index. $79.50. ISBN 0-313-29261-2.

Although closely linked to warfare and ruthless international competition, propaganda can also refer to more benign means of persuasion. The preface sounds the warning that the public must be careful when evaluating the sources and intent of the various types of information absorbed every day. A brief outline of some of the main events in the development of propaganda is provided in the introduction. The chronology starts with Christopher Columbus's arrival in the New World in 1492, and stretches to the end of 1995, when a new federal lobbying law that is supposed to make lobbyists' activities more open to public inspection was signed by President Bill Clinton. Somewhat irritating is the practice of having a year entry that lists several events of that year, but does not provide the specific date when it is readily available (e.g., the date of Edward R. Murrow's death).

The majority of the book is the glossary, which provides useful definitions of both well-known and obscure terms (how many people know what *granfalloons* means?). There is sufficient cross-referencing in this section, with relevant terms in all capital letters for easy identification. At the end of the volume, one finds a 28-page selective bibliography of useful references and a name/subject index.

This reviewer, while liking the book, thought that some entries (in both the glossary and the chronology) needed more exposition of their connection with propaganda. Students or general readers may not immediately see this relationship with regard to the Monroe Doctrine or the death of Posse Comitatus leader Gordon Kahl. A further suggestion is that, where possible, future compilers should include a relevant bibliographic citation with a chronological or glossary entry, to save readers from having to search a separate bibliography for an appropriate reference.

Nelson, of the Manship School of Mass Communications at Louisiana State University, is also working on *Propaganda: A Reference Guide*, a bibliographic companion volume from Greenwood Press. The title under consideration here will be of interest to those in the areas of history, political science, sociology, ethics, journalism, and communications, and it is a valuable complement to standard reference dictionaries. The work is recommended for the reference collections of all public and academic libraries.—**Daniel K. Blewett**

596. Vile, John R. **Encyclopedia of Constitutional Amendments, Proposed Amendments, and Amending Issues, 1789-1995.** Santa Barbara, Calif., ABC-CLIO, 1996. 427p. index. $75.00. ISBN 0-87436-783-2.

Vile (professor of political science, Middle Tennessee State University), a prolific writer on the U.S. constitutional amending process, focuses on providing a history and analysis of the 27 amendments that have been proposed and ratified. He does so within the framework of more than 400 alphabetically arranged topics (e.g., affirmative action; aliens; Anthony, Susan B.; *Baker v. Carr*; balanced budget; *Brown v. Topeka Board of Education*; Dirksen, Everett; Jefferson, Thomas; prayer in public schools; right to life; *Roe v. Wade*; Schlafly, Phyllis; Stanton, Elizabeth Cady; victims' rights; Wilson, [Thomas] Woodrow). He discusses the nearly 11,000 proposed amendments grouped by topic rather than treating them individually. For example, the Equal Rights Amendment, the most frequently introduced amendment (nearly 1,000 proposals since 1923 were introduced in Congress), is discussed in one essay.

A few entries are devoted to unresolved issues on the amending process (for instance, the constitutional convention mechanism, time limits on ratification). Many entries end with cross-references and suggestions for further reading. Concluding this scholarly, readable work are four appendixes (the constitution and its 27 amendments; dates of proposal and ratification of the amendments; number of amendments proposed and adopted by decade; and the most popular amending proposals, 1683-1996); an extensive bibliography of books; portions of books and periodicals from the early nineteenth century to 1996; a list of cases; and a comprehensive subject index. The audience for this authoritative volume ranges from high school students, general readers, and college students to advanced researchers. The encyclopedia is highly recommended, especially for academic and larger public libraries. [R: RBB, 1 Dec 96, p. 684]—**Wiley J. Williams**

597. Wilson, William. **Dictionary of the United States Intelligence Services: Over 1500 Terms, Programs, and Agencies.** Jefferson, N.C., McFarland, 1996. 191p. $38.50. ISBN 0-7864-0180-X.

The end of the Cold War has not diminished the field of intelligence, only changed its focus. Now, industrial espionage and antiterrorism activities have become growth industries, according to the author of this dictionary. About 40 American colleges even offer courses in the study of espionage. This dictionary concentrates exclusively on U.S. intelligence terms and concepts used since the Vietnam War. Wilson, a former intelligence officer, has extracted the definitions from various civilian and military documents available to the public. He also provides terms from such related fields as weapons, psychological warfare, mapping, surveillance, and signal intelligence.

Special features include a list of acronyms and abbreviations and a bibliography of books published between 1975 and 1995. Some online sources are also listed. The dictionary goes from *abort* to *Zulu time*, with entries ranging from a sentence to about 30 lines in length. Numerous cross-references are provided. For example, the term *eyes only* has a *see* reference to *distribution codes*. An unintended (?) pun occurs in the description of invisible ink, which notes that ". . . invisible ink has virtually vanished from espionage" (p. 111). Readers of spy novels or college and university students and faculty will find this authoritative dictionary to be a useful resource.—**Gary D. Barber**

Directories

598. Borders, Rebecca, and C. C. Dockery. **Beyond the Hill: A Directory of Congress from 1984 to 1993.** Lanham, Md., Center for Public Integrity and University Press of America, 1995. 215p. index. $46.50; $19.50pa. ISBN 0-8191-9819-6; 0-8191-9820-Xpa.

This biographical directory is a guide to former Capitol Hill lawmakers. Current addresses are provided, along with information on what they are doing now and why they left Congress. Included are 353 representatives and senators who began or finished their congressional service between 1984 and 1993. Of these, 15 currently serve in Congress, 93 are lobbyists, and others have either left politics or are deceased. The data have been compiled via telephone interviews, personal visits, questionnaires, electronic news libraries, and lobbying reports filed with the House and Senate. Even so, information for former New York representative Stan Lundine is outdated. He lost his job as lieutenant governor of New York in 1994 when Governor Mario Cuomo was voted out of office.

Also furnished are six short essays: "Hard Feelings: Roy Dyson," "Starting Over: Peter Smith," "The Revolving Door," "A Place in History: Dick Cheney," "You Can't Go Home Again: Bob Kastenmeir," and "Going Home Again: Lindy Boggs." An epilogue groups members into categories such as retired, defeated, elected to other offices, or ran for other offices and lost. While the book's reference value is marginal, it provides some insight into the motivation of individuals who seek positions of power.—**Gary D. Barber**

599. **Public Interest Profiles 1996-1997.** By the Foundation for Public Affairs. Washington, D.C., Congressional Quarterly, 1996. 890p. index. $190.00. ISBN 1-56802-220-4. ISSN 1058-627X.

Federal policy-making is influenced by a variety of governmental and nongovernmental players. A significant force in federal legislative and regulatory policy formulation, enactment, and legislation is various public interest organizations. Covering a wide variety of subject interests, these entities present their conceptions of sound public policy options to the executive, legislative, and judicial branches of government and to the U.S. public by diverse media mechanisms.

This reference work, updating a previous edition of this title (see ARBA 93, entry 795, for a review of an earlier edition), provides information about a multitude of public interest organizations. Entries feature organizational data such as address, telephone and fax numbers, e-mail address and World Wide Web URLs (if available), tax status, funding sources, budget, political orientation, boards of directors, publications, and conferences. Entry quality and length for individual interest groups vary due to the failure of listed organizations to supply uniform levels of data to the publisher.

Public Interest Profiles is organized into 12 chapters by interest group subject areas. Subjects profiled include business/economic, civil/constitutional rights, consumer/health, environmental, international affairs, political governmental process, religious, and think tanks. Specific interest groups chronicled include U.S. Chamber of Commerce, Children's Defense Fund, Eagle Forum, AIDS Action Council, Center for Business Ethics, Greenpeace USA, TransAfrica, Electronic Frontier Foundation, Common Cause, Washington Legal Foundation, Christian Coalition, and Cato Institute. A total of 233 organizations are discussed.

Whether people like it or not, interest group organizations influence public policy development. This effort is a good introduction to these groups, which will maybe stimulate additional study of these entities by students, scholars, and the general public. One hopes the publishers will keep this work updated at regular intervals, and consider a World Wide Web version of this title for more frequent updating of the continually growing number of organizations desirous of influencing federal policy-making.—**Bert Chapman**

Handbooks and Yearbooks

600. Christianson, Stephen G. **Facts About the Congress.** Bronx, N.Y., H. W. Wilson, 1996. 635p. illus. index. $55.00. ISBN 0-8242-0883-8.

In 1995, the Simon & Schuster Academic Reference Division published an impressive four-volume *Encyclopedia of the United States Congress* (see ARBA 96, entry 720), which provided lengthy essays on the workings of Congress. Now, *Facts About the Congress* has appeared, and it is a perfect complement to the Simon & Schuster set. *Facts* gives a thorough, and convenient, presentation of the accomplishments of each Congress, arranged chronologically from 1789 through the first session of the 104th Congress.

For each session, the following information is given in an easy-to-use format: dates of the Congress, election results, political background, Senate and House leadership (including chairs of committees), organizational issues, major legislation that was passed, a chronology of activities, a table of key votes, failed legislation, relations with the president, appointment, nominations, confirmations, impeachments, constitutional amendments, and a brief list of "further reading" titles. Appended is the text of the U.S. Constitution, congressional leadership charts, pay rates, a list of congressional buildings, and a useful glossary. There is a brief bibliography of general works about Congress and an index. This work belongs in reference collections next to the fine Congressional Quarterly publications on the U.S. Congress (especially the *Guide to Congress* [4th ed.; see ARBA 93, entry 747] and *Vital Statistics on Congress* [see ARBA 93, entry 754]) and is highly recommended for public and academic libraries.—**Thomas A. Karel**

601. Cox, Elizabeth M. **Women State and Territorial Legislators, 1895-1995: A State-by-State Analysis, with Rosters of 6,000 Women.** Jefferson, N.C., McFarland, 1996. 398p. index. $48.50. ISBN 0-7864-0078-1.

This unique compilation fills an information gap that Cox uncovered almost a decade ago. As a political scientist, she was interested to know how women had faired running for state legislative offices. She found that little research had been done on the topic, and that the available raw data had never been organized or collated. Also, while biographical information was easy to find, in-depth political analysis was generally lacking. Her hope is that this book will prove to be a useful tool to other researchers as they examine the dynamics of women in leadership.

The year 1995 marked the 100th anniversary of women serving in state legislatures (Colorado being the first state to elect a woman, in 1895). A 24-page introduction gives an overview of women's suffrage, the difficulties they have faced running for and holding office, and their accomplishments. Graphs are used to show percentages, such as House and Senate membership by gender and party and historical trends by regions. The arrangement is alphabetic by state or territory. Each entry includes information on when women first gained suffrage in that particular state, when they first voted there, and a count of those who have served in the state legislature. Tables list legislators' names, city/county represented, party affiliations, and years in office. Footnotes provide special details where necessary. Six appendixes, a selected bibliography, and a name index complete the volume, which is recommended for all college and university libraries, but especially for those supporting women's studies programs. [R: RBB, 1 May 96, p. 1542]—**Gary D. Barber**

602. Hellebust, Lynn. **State Legislative Sourcebook 1996: A Resource Guide to Legislative Information in the Fifty States.** Topeka, Kans., Government Research Service, 1996. 488p. $150.00pa. ISBN 1-879929-17-1. ISSN 0898-7297.

This 11th edition of the *Sourcebook* is in softcover, which is a plus for libraries, as its former 3-ring binder format was ill-suited for general use (see ARBA 93, entry 750, for a review of an earlier edition). The new format also helps keep costs down and annual updates more readily distributed. All 50 states, the District of Columbia, and Puerto Rico are included in this alphabetically arranged volume.

The information provided in each entry follows a standard format that covers general legislative information (best initial contact, length of session, Internet sites); information sources on legislators, legislative sessions, lobbying, and state governments (with World Wide Web addresses); and lists of newspapers, journals, newsletters, and registers covering state politics. Entries are six to eight pages in length, which allows for full descriptions of the sources cited and for detailed background information on such topics as financial disclosure procedures and costs of public documents and services.

Appendixes provide legislative bill status and bill room telephone numbers for each state and a 25-page annotated bibliography of resources on the state legislative process, how to influence legislators, and state governmental and political systems. Any library needing information on state governments will not regret expending some of its limited reference budget on this uniquely useful source. [R: Choice, Sept 96, p. 99]—**Gary D. Barber**

603. Jost, Kenneth. **The Supreme Court Yearbook 1995-1996.** Washington, D.C., Congressional Quarterly, 1996. 358p. illus. index. $37.95. ISBN 0-87187-897-6. ISSN 1054-2701.

This 7th edition of *The Supreme Court Yearbook* analyzes and chronicles the work of the U.S. Supreme Court during its 1995-1996 term. Jost includes various statistics and the comments of both conservative and liberal court watchers to tell the story of this year in the Court's history. Chapter 1 analyzes the justices' voting records and examines the possibility of an ideological shift on the court after the 1996 presidential election. Chapter 2 gives an overview of the term's decisions and detailed accounts of the most important cases, including *U.S. v. Virginia* (the Virginia Military Institute case) and *Romer v. Evans* (Colorado's anti-gay rights amendment). These accounts include background leading up to the decisions, some discussion of oral arguments and justices' questions, and a brief commentary on the rulings and dissents. Excerpts from these major decisions appear in the appendix. Chapter 3 contains summaries of all the Court's decisions during the term, arranged by subject categories. Chapter 4 previews the 1996-1997 term. Appendixes include a copy of the U.S. Constitution and biographies of each of the justices, and an index assists the reader in finding information on various subjects. The book is an excellent resource for anyone wanting information on the Court's rulings or how this term compares with other Supreme Court sessions.—**Kay Mariea**

604. **The United States Government Manual 1996/1997.** Lanham, Md., Bernan Associates, 1996. 860p. index. $36.00pa. ISBN 0-89059-067-2.

The term "essential reference tool" is a broadly applied statement often used to describe items perceived as important additions to any reference collection, even if that item is essential to only a small spectrum of users. This is not the case with regard to *The United States Government Manual*. Published annually as a supplement to the *Federal Register*, the *Manual* provides lucid and penetrating information about each branch of government and the independent agencies that make up the federal bureaucracy. It is especially useful as a consumer affairs resource tool that links key personnel within the federal government with the citizenry they serve.

As noted in the introduction, each entry includes a list of key personnel; a statement about the agency's mission and role in government; a brief history, including its legislative or executive mandate; a description of programs and activities; and public affairs information with telephone numbers and mailing addresses. Electronic mail and agency homepage addresses are not provided. The manual is arranged by branch, executive agencies, and independent agencies. Agency information is frequently formatted in each entry by office, division, section, or bureau, and is accompanied by an organizational chart. Three appendixes list common acronyms and abbreviations, terminated or transferred agencies, and citations to agencies listed in the *Code of Federal Regulations*. The volume concludes with a name index, agency/subject index, and personnel changes noted just prior to publication. This work should be available in all library collections, regardless of purpose or clientele served.—**Robert V. Labaree**

Europe

General Works

605. Cossolotto, Matthew. **The Almanac of European Politics 1995.** Washington, D.C., Congressional Quarterly, 1995. 321p. index. $51.95; $31.95pa. ISBN 0-87187-914-X; 0-87187-913-3pa.

The title of this book is misleading: The scope of coverage is actually focused on Scandinavia and Western Europe, with Greece and Turkey thrown in for good measure; otherwise, the Balkans and Eastern Europe are ignored. Each of the 19 established democracies has its own chapter containing brief profiles of the country and its politics, some comparative statistical data, descriptions of the political parties, a review of recent elections, statistical results of recent elections, a lexicon of political/election terms, and a chronological synopsis of important political/electoral events. There is a separate chapter for the European Union. One funny feature is that all the flags in the book are in black-and-white (but in color on the front and back covers of the paperback version reviewed here), when what readers need is a color representation of the flag with the country's section (although this would have increased the cost of production). Maps of the region and individual countries would have been helpful, along with brief bibliographies of important reference works or monographs relating to each nation.

Despite these criticisms, this volume is still useful because it collects various types of information in a single volume that one would ordinarily have to look for in several other sources. Definitions and electoral statistics cannot always be found in the standard serial reference sources, such as *The Europa*

World Year Book (see ARBA 94, entry 82), or the *Political Handbook of the World* (see ARBA 91, entry 722), although they can provide some narrative background. Older election statistics can be found in *European Political Facts 1918-90* (see ARBA 94, entry 766). One resource that is similar in structure and content is *The Almanac of Transatlantic Politics* (see ARBA 92, entry 675), but it is outdated now. One hopes the title under review will be periodically revised and updated, and its scope expanded. The information also could be made available online. This reviewer's advice is to purchase the paperback version, as the contents do not warrant the high price of the hardback edition. This almanac is suitable for all reference collections.—**Daniel K. Blewett**

606. **The Directory of EU Information Sources 1995-1996.** 7th ed. Belgium, Euroconfidentiel; distr., Concord, Mass., Paul & Company Publishers, 1995. 1v. (various paging). index. $295.00. ISBN 2-930066-19-9.

This 7th edition of the directory has been compiled on the basis of questionnaires submitted by correspondents and institutions listed here. Since the entry of three new member states into the European Union in the beginning of 1995, a significant number of changes in procedure and personnel in the majority of the European Union's (EU) institutions has occurred. This new edition also includes some new information, such as details of all major EU funding programs, a review of the EU's new agencies, more extensive organization charts for the Economic and Social Committee and the Committee of the Regions, details of universities that have created chairs in European integration, and comprehensive coverage of the new member states' permanent representations.

The directory is divided into 10 basic sections, each identified by a letter. The various sections include information about the European Commission, the European Parliament, other institutions of the EU, foreign representations in Brussels, press agencies and journalists specializing in EU news, consultants, lawyers and legal advisors, trade and professional organizations, postgraduate degrees in European integration, and EU grants and loans. Arrangement within each section is dependent on the type of information provided. Use is simplified by an alphabetic keyword index and a laudable user's guide. This source is indispensable for any library needing information about virtually any aspect of the EU. [R: Choice, Oct 96, p. 250]—**Robert H. Burger**

607. **The European Union Encyclopedia and Directory 1996.** 2d ed. London, Europa; distr., Detroit, Gale, 1996. 478p. $385.00. ISBN 1-85743-009-3. ISSN 0962-1032.

Previously entitled *The European Communities Encyclopedia and Directory* (see ARBA 92, entry 711), this is a useful reference tool for perhaps the most important regional intergovernmental organization in the world. The encyclopedia and directory collects in one publication much disparate information that one would have to look in several separate sources to find. There is an adequate 113-page dictionary of European Union (EU) terms, organizations, people, documents, and events. There are seven essays on the present social, legal, and political aspects of the EU. Also included are a summary of the five most important EU treaties and a statistical survey of the Union, providing country data on health, education, welfare, demographic, and numerous economic topics. The years covered are primarily 1990-1992. There is also a description of EU databases, along with a list of distribution organizations and information centers. The table of contents is detailed, and the components have been rearranged slightly since the previous edition.

The majority of pages consist of the directory, which is the reason that most people would use this book. Names, official titles, addresses, and telephone and fax numbers of the EU executive and parliamentary departments and programs are supplied in generous measure. The section for the member countries includes names of government ministries and ministers. The volume has a map of the Union, organization charts for cooperation and decision-making procedures, a list of abbreviations, and a chronology of important events, but no index.

This sturdily bound directory is of obvious interest to those in history, political science, international affairs, and other related fields. It is recommended for the reference collections of large public and academic libraries and specialized collections. Smaller institutions and those husbanding their limited budgets can probably get by with the annual *Europa World Year Book* (see ARBA 94, entry 82, and ARBA 90, entry 91) for most questions, as it contains similar, up-to-date information.—**Daniel K. Blewett**

British

608. Powell, John. **Art, Truth, and High Politics: A Bibliographic Study of the Official Lives of Queen Victoria's Ministers in Cabinet, 1843-1969.** Pasadena, Calif., Salem Press and Lanham, Md., Scarecrow, 1996. 221p. index. (Magill Bibliographies). $36.00. ISBN 0-8108-3139-2.

The Official Lives of British Cabinet members during the reign of Queen Victoria were a series of 70 biographies written over a period of more than 120 years by many different authors. Although much maligned for their dry style and lack of critical objectivity, they are nevertheless an essential source of information on nineteenth-century politics. They contain documents, illustrations, family pedigrees, and background details, all vital to gaining an understanding of each cabinet minister. Many of the diaries and letters consulted in compiling them are no longer extant.

A long introductory essay critically examines the scholarly value of the Official Lives. The majority of this work is a series of studies on the biography of each Cabinet member, arranged alphabetically by the name of the biographee. They include bibliographic data and a biographical sketch of the author. All editions and the principal primary materials incorporated into each work are listed. To aid in judging the reliability of each biography, archival sources and selected published works on both the biographee and the biographer (if available) are also given. Illustrations, political cartoons, and any other materials, such as maps or lists, included in the biography are listed. Various appendixes with statistics about the publication of the Official Lives and a subject index complete the bibliography.

Powell's work is an impressive accomplishment. With great thoroughness, he demystifies the role of the Official Lives as a significant source of information about Victorian politics and society. This resource belongs in all graduate-level collections on British history.—**Christine E. King**

Latin America and the Caribbean

609. Gross, Liza, with the Council on Hemispheric Affairs. **Handbook of Leftist Guerrilla Groups in Latin America and the Caribbean.** Boulder, Colo., Westview Press, 1995. 165p. illus. $59.95. ISBN 0-8133-8494-X.

Despite their relatively small numbers, leftist guerrillas have played a disruptive role in recent Latin American history. While casualties have been numerous (more than a half-million in Guatemala alone), these groups have made only modest gains, for the most part. However, they succeeded in bringing government to a virtual standstill in Uruguay in the 1970s and more recently in El Salvador and Guatemala, and they continue to disrupt government in Peru.

Gross, a native of Argentina, is a former executive editor of the *Times of the Americas*. With staff assistance from the Council on Hemispheric Affairs, she drew information from prominent Latin American journalists, historians, and even from some of the former guerrillas themselves. Her goal was to provide a factual basis about leftist guerrilla movements in Latin America. Gross views these groups as having the following common characteristics: They are driven by a leftist ideology, they seek subversion of the established order and its replacement with a Marxist state, they are committed to armed struggle, and they operate clandestinely.

The handbook is organized alphabetically by country. For each group, the author describes when it was active, details where it operated, discusses who provided assistance, and identifies principal leaders. There is detailed coverage of groups, ranging from the FMLN in El Salvador to the Tupamaros in Uruguay. The book concludes with a useful bibliography of secondary sources arranged by country. There is a list of abbreviations to help sort out the various groups often known only by their initials and a small sample of photographs of leaders and groups.

With the Tupac Amaru in the news in Peru and the recent accord signed with the guerrillas in Guatemala, this excellent handbook based on "insider information" will be frequently consulted. It is recommended for academic library collections.—**Brian E. Coutts**

Russian Federation

610. **Maximov's Companion to Who Governs the Russian Federation. Summer 96, Volume 2, Number 1.** Andrei Maximov, ed. Sausalito, Calif., Maximov Publications, 1996. 537p. index. $295.00/yr. ISSN 1358-8230.

The gradual democratization of the Russian Federation has prompted an increased number of Western individuals and organizations to invest in Russian economic ventures. These entities must conduct business with a wide array of Russian government officials. This reference work is a directory of Russian governmental and legislative officials and can be regarded as similar to works such as the *Almanac of American Politics* (see ARBA 94, entry 746).

Featuring text in English and Russian, this work opens with a users' guide, a preface, an introduction, and a Russian Federation map broken down by time zones. Subsequent sections list the names of Russian officials from the President's Executive Office, federal government ministers and ministries, the Federation Council, State Duma, Central Election Commission, judiciary, local authorities, and foreign diplomatic representatives in Moscow. Individual entries list official names and telephone numbers, while departmental entries include mailing addresses and fax numbers.

Entries for Duma members include party affiliation, birth date, geographic area represented, committee membership, and the number and percentage of votes received in their most recent election. Prominent figures listed include President Boris Yeltsin, Prime Minister Viktor Chernomyrdin, Vladimir Zhirinovsky, and Grigory Yavlinskiy. All entries are current up to the 1996 Russian presidential elections.

This directory is most successful as a telephone directory or rolodex card listing of Russian government officials. It falls short of being a reference tool similar to the *Almanac of American Politics*. While there is a partial introductory overview of the Russian political scene, there is no substantive analysis of the forces shaping Russian Federation politics. There are no pictures of these officials and no description or analysis of the constituencies represented by Duma members. It appears that the publisher is committed to making this a regular publication, and the preface notes that there will be a postpresidential election supplement delivered to subscribers.

Maximov's Companion is useful as a quick reference guide to Russian government officials and agencies. Enhancements such as those just suggested, along with reasonable pricing policies, can help make this publication a staple of academic and research library reference department collections. [R: Choice, Feb 96, p. 930]—**Bert Chapman**

South Africa

611. Gastrow, Shelagh. **Who's Who in South African Politics, Number 5.** Johannesburg, South Africa, Ravan Press; distr., Athens, Ohio, Ohio University Press, 1995. 319p. illus. $24.95pa. ISBN 0-86975-458-0.

The differences between this title and the 4th edition of *Who's Who in South African Politics* (see ARBA 94, entry 762) reflect the political changes in South Africa under majority government. Many of the leaders listed in the previous edition who had been active in "civil" institutions, such as the antiapartheid movement, voter education, or women's organizations, have now become active in party politics or have moved into the state bureaucracy. The result is that this edition focuses, as one would expect in a political who's who, almost exclusively (with the exception of about 5-10 entries) on those in positions of power in political parties or the government (e.g., ministers, members of parliament). There is also a slight increase in women represented in this edition (from 6 to 12).

Of the 103 people listed, 46 appeared in the previous edition, 69 who were in the last edition were deleted, and 57 names are new. Each entry includes a portrait, the person's current title, a biographical sketch, and the sources used to compile the information. There is also a listing (current as of June 1995) of major national- and regional-level government officials and political party officials.

This is a useful, inexpensive reference source for any library that collects material on the current political situation in South Africa. Although many of the persons listed here (21 out of a sample of 30) are also found in *Who's Who of Southern Africa* (1995/1996 ed., Johannesburg, Jonathan Ball, 1996), the listings are more detailed in the work under review, making it a valuable complement to the larger, more general work or simply useful by itself. [R: RBB, 15 April 96, p. 1460]—**Paul H. Thomas**

IDEOLOGIES

612. **The Encyclopedia of Democracy.** Seymour Martin Lipset, ed. Washington, D.C., Congressional Quarterly, 1995. 5v. illus. maps. index. $395.00/set. ISBN 0-87187-675-2.

During the past decade democracy and democratization have emerged as perhaps the leading issues in international affairs. The recent movement toward democracy in countries around the globe has resulted in a vast new scholarly literature dealing with the various dimensions of democracy. This entirely new and outstanding encyclopedia provides a comprehensive survey of democracy in this era of democratization.

There are more than 400 separate, signed articles by 200 leading scholars whose work has contributed to the study of democracy. Entries include biographies of historical and contemporary political leaders who have worked for democracy; country and regional studies; and topics such as economic issues, democratic processes, nationalism, war, and philosophical approaches. In addition, there are nearly 150 pages of key democratic documents from Pericles's Funeral Oration to the 1993 Czech constitution. Each article includes a bibliography and many entries include maps or photographs. While the articles address key scholarly concerns, they are written at a level accessible to all informed readers. This new encyclopedia is highly recommended for all types of libraries and for other institutions and individuals concerned with the political, social, and economic changes under way at the end of the twentieth century. [R: BR, Sept/Oct 96, p. 57; Choice, April 96, p. 1282; LJ, Feb 96, pp. 142-44; RBB, 1 Mar 96, p. 1205; SLJ, April 96, p. 170]—**Frank L. Wilson**

613. Hamilton, Neil A. **Militias in America: A Reference Handbook.** Santa Barbara, Calif., ABC-CLIO, 1996. 235p. index. (Contemporary World Issues). $39.50. ISBN 0-87436-859-6.

Events at Waco, Ruby Ridge, Oklahoma City, and elsewhere have brought right-wing militias to general public attention. A good, objective handbook on the subject would be welcome. Despite its reputable publisher and experienced author, this title is doubtful. There is much useful, factual information in such sections as historical background, chronology, biographies, a bibliography, and a list of World Wide Web sites. Government documents and publications of antimilitia groups are quoted at great length, often with little introduction or discussion. There may be a bias. To take a statement of official National Rifle Association policy from a publication of the Institute for Alternative Journalism is hardly objective or fair. Moreover, Hamilton, whose credentials are those of a historian, makes free use of such terms as *paranoid* and *obsession*, which have precise meanings to psychologists. Historians are trained to separate assertion from fact, yet Hamilton claims to know, impossibly, the intentions of the FBI sniper who killed Vicky Weaver at Ruby Ridge. Proofreading is weak; "manta" used for "mantra" and phrases punctuated as sentences, for example. The glossary lists some groups mentioned in the text and leaves out others, including the important Posse Comitatus. In the index, some place-names are given and others are not. The apparent selectivity may be the accidental result of haste. This is an important subject. Librarians concerned with questions of objectivity and shortcomings of craftsmanship should look elsewhere for a basic handbook.—**John Newman**

614. **The Left Guide: A Guide to Left-of-Center Organizations.** Derk Arend Wilcox, ed. Ann Arbor, Mich., Economics America, 1996. 516p. index. $74.95. ISBN 0-914169-03-3.

This directory is a companion volume to *The Right Guide*, the 2d edition of which was published by Economics America in 1995. Entries for the 1,100 "liberal, progressive, and left-of-center" organizations profiled in the directory are accessible in a variety of ways: an alphabetic arrangement of the main entry profiles; a profile subject index by categories, such as abortion and reproductive rights, environmental, feminists, civil rights and liberties, foreign policy, socialists, and so on; a geographic listing; and a rotated keyword index. A separate periodicals list is also included, as are addresses for nonrespondents and last known addresses of organizations that are defunct or may have ceased to exist. In all, more than 2,200 organizations are listed.

The profile entries are thorough and contain information not usually provided in such standard sources as *The Encyclopedia of Associations* (see entry 49 for a review of the CD-ROM version). For instance, in addition to the commonly listed address, mission or interest, key personnel, publications, and the like, one may find detailed financial data, funding sources, and recent accomplishments and expenditures. Other information may be provided that obviously was not given by the organization. The entry for the Monthly Review Foundation, for example, indicates that a key figure, Harry Magdoff, once spied for the Soviet Union.

One problem this reviewer found with *The Left Guide* is the somewhat dubious set of criteria for inclusion. It is difficult, for instance, for most to think of the Council on Foreign Relations as anything other than a centrist, establishment organization. While acknowledging this, the editor nonetheless discusses it, presumably because it is a frequent target of the far right. When one remembers that the John Birch Society once accused Dwight Eisenhower of having Communist leanings, it becomes evident that this type of selection can produce occasional bizarre results. Nevertheless, this is a solid, informative work deserving a place in most reference collections. [R: RBB, 1 Dec 96, p. 685]—**Lee Weston**

INTERNATIONAL ORGANIZATIONS

615. Arnold, Guy. **Historical Dictionary of Aid and Development Organizations.** Lanham, Md., Scarecrow, 1996. 196p. (International Organizations Series, no.10). $32.50. ISBN 0-8108-3040-X.

Arnold, a freelance writer and authority on international aid, north-south relations, and the Third World, has provided in this volume comprehensive coverage of aid and development organizations. The introduction traces the beginning of modern aid to the American Marshall Plan, which was designed for the recovery of Western Europe after World War II. From that beginning, the principle grew so that the rich, developed nations had a duty to give economic assistance to the poor, less developed nations. The book proceeds to describe and analyze the principal organizations (such as the World Bank), events (such as the 1955 Bandung Conference), concepts (technical assistance), political and regional organizations (Commonwealth), individuals (Robert McNamara), and the role of the United Nations and its specialized agencies involved with aid. A major focus is the north-south relationship and the development problem of the Third World.

This study of aid is carried out principally through the dictionary section, which contains approximately 170 entries. These vary in length from a paragraph to several pages. In addition to presenting the major relevant facts in summary form, the entries are particularly useful in explaining interrelationships and historical development as a part of international relations. In addition to the introduction and dictionary, this study is supplemented by an extensive bibliography on aid subdivided into regional and subject areas, a list of abbreviations and acronyms, an "Aids and Development Dateline," and a list of countries that belong to the Third World.—**Henry E. York**

616. Mays, Terry M. **Historical Dictionary of Multinational Peacekeeping.** Lanham, Md., Scarecrow, 1996. 340p. (International Organizations Series, no.9). $49.50. ISBN 0-8108-3031-0.

This book is a wide and deep study of peacekeeping operations. The author chose the broad interpretation of *peacekeeping*, that is, a tool to assist a separate negotiation process normally undertaken by the same international organization that mandated the neutral military operation. Peacekeeping includes actions such as refugee assistance, forced separation of belligerents, election supervision, disarmament, and state building. It includes information on operations, organizations, and crises. It also covers the actions of countries and individuals that have significantly contributed to the accomplishment of numerous multinational peacekeeping missions.

The goal of this book is to present enough information on the major multinational operations to allow readers to gain a better understanding of the many military missions fielded by international organizations since 1920. Evidently not enough research efforts have gone toward this topic. Most of the published research studies tend to concentrate on operations fielded by the United Nations and often ignore the many missions carried out by regional international organizations, such as the League of Arab States and the Organization of African Unity.

The book is organized into several categories. First, there is a list of acronyms and abbreviations. The next section is a chronology of peacekeeping operations and related events since 1920. This list is especially useful for those who are interested in understanding the peacekeeping happenings during certain periods in the world. The chronology is followed by the dictionary itself, key military and civilian individuals, political crises, international organizations, and specific events. A 114-page comprehensive bibliography follows the dictionary. The bibliography gives much well-deserved credit to this book. The citations are listed under 17 categories, such as the type of publications, the names of countries, and the organizations. The bibliography is easy for the serious researcher to use in finding out additional resources on peacemaking and its related topics.

The last segment of the book is a set of appendixes. The appendixes include a collection of documents, such as examples of mandates, a status of force agreement, resolutions, financial and organizational arrangements, and a text of President Bill Clinton's report to Congress outlining U.S. military support for the United Nations Protection Force. Very little information is included here about peacekeeping efforts involving countries, organizations, and individuals in Asia. Nevertheless, this book can be a useful guide to studying international relations and military and political history of the recent past decades.—**Eveline L. Yang**

617. Schraepler, Hans-Albrecht. **Directory of International Organizations.** Washington, D.C., Georgetown University Press, 1996. 424p. index. $65.00. ISBN 0-87840-607-7.

Schraepler, a German diplomat and head of information of the Council of Europe, has provided with this handbook a concise source of information on international organizations. Coverage begins with the United Nations and its specialized agencies, followed by the North Atlantic Treaty Organization (NATO), important regional organizations, then the Organization for Economic Cooperation and Development (OECD), the Organization of Petroleum Exporting Countries (OPEC), the Commonwealth, and the Commonwealth of Independent States. The book ends with nonpolitical worldwide organizations such as the Olympic Movement and the Red Cross.

Each organizational profile, which varies in length from about 3 to 10 pages, contains these common elements: legal basis, objectives, membership, and structure. The information is presented in fact-sheet style with many lists and outlines of the principal facts. A complete address for each organization including telephone, telex, and fax numbers is provided at the beginning of each entry. There is no listing of current personnel. Some of the additional features concerning international organizations in this handbook include an extensive list of abbreviations, a chronology of events, and a membership table showing the membership of the world's nations in major international organizations.

For anyone requiring a convenient, one-volume overview of major international organizations, this handbook furnishes a clear résumé. Libraries will want to compare this volume with standard reference sources. The 1996 *Europa World Year Book* (Europa, 1996), for example, has a 296-page section on international organizations that is updated annually. It contains more information on the major organizations and brief directory information on many others across all fields of interest. Schraepler's handbook can also be compared with Giuseppe Schiavone's recent effort, *International Organizations: A Dictionary and Directory* (3d ed.; see ARBA 94, entry 793), which covers more organizations. It supplies more background and historical information, but less detail on factual matters such as structure and membership. [R: Choice, Dec 96, p. 594; LJ, 1 Sept 96, pp. 170-71; RBB, 1 Sept 96, pp. 164-65]

—**Henry E. York**

INTERNATIONAL RELATIONS

618. Cole, Robert. **Propaganda in Twentieth Century War and Politics: An Annotated Bibliography.** Pasadena, Calif., Salem Press and Lanham, Md., Scarecrow, 1996. 402p. index. (Magill Bibliographies). $48.50. ISBN 0-8108-3196-1.

The term *propaganda* originated from the Church's mission to propagate religious doctrine. Cole examines the principle of propaganda for political ideology relating to wars. He separates the book into periods around wars. The first chapter is devoted to concept, which provides an overview of general studies, public opinion, measurement, techniques, and mass communications. Each chapter after that examines resources for each period from World War I to the Cold War, breaking them into three sections: "History and Function," which deals with motivation, planning, and purpose; "Channels and Techniques," which deals with dissemination and tactics; and samples.

Cole notes that this is a select rather than a comprehensive bibliography and offers 10 other bibliographies for further study. He does not clearly state selection criteria other than promising a useful sampling, which he does deliver, providing a wide range of materials and formats. Cole has included citations for primary as well as secondary sources. For each reference, he gives bibliographic information and an annotation. The strength of this volume is in the annotations. They effectively describe the item and, in many cases, offer a comment or suggestion as to their usefulness.

The scheme of the work makes it easy to follow and compare. Unlike other bibliographies on this subject, which focus on a discipline or a specific aspect of propaganda, Cole covers a broad spectrum of materials, making this resource useful for researchers in a variety of areas, including psychology, communications, history, and film. Especially interesting is the indexing of included films. This is a well-organized, well-annotated volume that demonstrates the role of propaganda in directing and motivating national political ideology and interests over an extended time period.—**Joshua Cohen**

619. **International Relations Research Directory.** London, Europa; distr., Detroit, Gale, 1995. 347p. index. $225.00. ISBN 1-85743-013-1.

This new directory collects information on political, economic, and military institutes that engage in international relations activities. More than 1,000 institutes are listed, arranged by country. For most entries, there is a brief description of the institute's activities and names of any publications associated with the institute. Address, telephone and fax numbers, e-mail address, and principal officers are also included. The section on the United States fills 23 pages, while unexpected locations such as Barbados and Guyana are also covered.

The second section of the directory is a separate listing of periodicals that support international relations research. General titles, such as *Foreign Affairs* and *Orbis*, are listed, along with many specialized titles (e.g., *Defence and Peace Economics*, *The Journal of Strategic Studies*, *Russian Nonproliferation Monitor*). There are many non-English titles furnished. While much of this information can be found in other sources (*Ulrich's* [see entry 66], *The International Periodicals Directory* [see ARBA 96, entry 88], *Europa World Year Book* [see ARBA 94, entry 82, and ARBA 90, entry 91]), the convenience and timeliness of this book make it an essential addition for most research libraries. [R: Choice, July/Aug 96, p. 1774]—**Thomas A. Karel**

620. Ziring, Lawrence, Jack C. Plano, and Roy Olton. **International Relations: A Political Dictionary.** 5th ed. Santa Barbara, Calif., ABC-CLIO, 1995. 458p. index. $60.00. ISBN 0-87436-897-9.

International relations and foreign policy have exploded from short, one-page worldwide overviews in most newspapers to front-page headlines, and not only when the U.S. military is involved. The high-profile appointment of Madeline Albright to the post of secretary of state has only increased the prominence of international politics. The increasingly sophisticated vocabulary and knowledge necessary for understanding these headlines require references available to the public, educators, and students that address fundamental issues.

This 5th edition update attempts to revise references and vocabulary toward understanding the 1990s post-Cold War "new world order." The book is divided into subject-oriented sections, such as "The Nature and Role of Foreign Policy" and "International Organization." Within these sections, terms are arranged alphabetically with two explanations—the first a straightforward academic definition, the second describing the term's significance in theory and practice. Each section has a *see also* cross-reference. The book contains an essential index, listing the terms chronologically, rather than by page number.

While the book is a much-welcomed update of essential information, there are several difficulties that limit effectiveness. A scope note at the beginning of the index should have been included explaining that numbers were entry, not page numbers, and bold typeface was used to denote main entry. The use of the term *dictionary* also raises certain expectations—that its primary organization is alphabetic. This is only true within subject areas, and readers unfamiliar with the field (presumably for whom a term dictionary is primarily designed) are left to guess a term's larger context, or use the index. Finally, the dictionary implies that term definitions are clear and settled, something many of the terms are not. *Third World*, for example, does not discuss its coining or the ambiguous use of the term since 1955. The significance section, while helpful, often is quirky, necessarily selective, and debatable. Perhaps this would be better titled *International Relations: An Encyclopedia*. This would alert readers to its broad and introductory nature, its subject-oriented structure, and the terms' short descriptions and ambiguity.

With all these caveats, the book is still recommended for large city libraries, and especially all university and college libraries. The benefits of its material and revisions far outweigh structural problems. Students and teachers of international relations will find it an invaluable reference if its limitations are kept in mind. [R: Choice, June 96, p. 1625; RBB, 1 April 96, p. 1390]—**Curtis D. Holmes**

PUBLIC POLICY AND ADMINISTRATION

621. Miller, E. Willard, and Ruby M. Miller. **United States Immigration: A Reference Handbook.** Santa Barbara, Calif., ABC-CLIO, 1996. 304p. index. (Contemporary World Issues). $39.50. ISBN 0-87436-845-6.

United States Immigration is the newest contribution to the Contemporary World Issues series, which addresses vital issues impacting today's world. The authors note that immigration to the United States has played a major role in the development of the country's population since the first colony was established in 1607. More than 60 million people have immigrated to this nation so far, and millions more seek admission each year. As this reference work points out, immigration can and has had significant effects on demographics, culture, education, welfare, and labor.

This book, as with the other volumes in the series, is well organized and easy to use. It contains an overview of the subject (chapter 1); a detailed chronology in chapter 2 that lists the evolution of laws and regulations government the complex issue of who will be admitted to the United States; facts and data from the U.S. Immigration and Naturalization Service, *Statistical Yearbook, Annual Report*, 1930-1992, and the U.S. Bureau of the Census, *Census of Population*, 1790-1990; a directory of the vast number of organizations and agencies that handle different aspects of immigration; an annotated bibliography of books dealing with a variety of related topics, as well as more than 600 articles from journals and government publications; and an annotated list of print and nonprint resources. This handbook concludes with a glossary and an adequate index.

The books in this series are authoritative, clearly written, up-to-date, and objective. The only comparable volume is part of The Reference Shelf series published by H. W. Wilson. The Reference Shelf series, however, presents the issues in the format of reprints of articles and excerpts from books, addresses, and speeches. As such, it fails to give full coverage, as does the Contemporary World Issues series. This volume is highly recommended as an excellent starting point for research by high school and college students, as well as scholars and others who wish to better understand the social, political, and economic issues facing the world today.—**Sharon Thomerson**

622. **Think Tank Directory: A Guide to Nonprofit Public Policy Research Organizations.** Lynn Hellebust, ed. Topeka, Kans., Government Research Service, 1996. 397p. index. $125.00 spiralbound. ISBN 1-879929-18-X. ISSN 1063-3340.

Since 1945, the number of think tanks in the United States has grown from 2 to more than 1,200. In this directory, the compilers have defined think tanks as nonprofit public policy research organizations that are both independent and university-affiliated. They admit that a precise definition is still elusive. The directory is arranged in alphabetic order by name of the think tank. Each entry (1,212 in all) consists of name, address, telephone and fax numbers, e-mail address, Website, chief administrative officer, board members, year established, purpose, publications, funding source, areas of interest, method of operation, staff size, and budget. The information for most entries has been confirmed by the editor with the organizations themselves.

The work also includes a short (11-item) bibliography of publications concerning think tanks and their importance for contemporary U.S. political life, a geographic index, an alternate name index, a subsidiary index, and an index of policy areas. The shortcomings of this latter index, however, will be immediately evident to any user. It consists of only 13 subject categories (e.g., agriculture, children, youth and families, defense and foreign affairs) with long strings of undifferentiated page references following.

The directory will be of evident use to anyone working in any aspect of policy analysis. The publishers plan to issue the directory annually. One suggestion that may improve future editions is to number each entry and use this reference in the various indexes. This would make searching for relevant information much easier. —**Robert H. Burger**

14 Psychology and Parapsychology

PSYCHOLOGY

Bibliography

623. Lubin, Bernard, C. Dwayne Wilson, Suzanne Petren, and Alicia Polk. **Research on Group Treatment Methods: A Selectively Annotated Bibliography.** Westport, Conn., with NTL Institute for Applied Behavioral Science, Greenwood Press, 1996. 246p. index. (Bibliographies and Indexes in Psychology, no.9). $69.50. ISBN 0-313-28339-7.

The increase in research in group treatment methods during the past several decades mirrors the growing importance of these methods in the mental health field. This bibliography represents a sampling of English-language books and journal articles, from 1970 to 1995, available in university and large public libraries. About 50 percent of the 1,793 items included are annotated. While *group therapy*, *group psychotherapy*, *group counseling*, and *psychodrama* are terms used throughout the entries, emphasis is placed on their common techniques and methods.

Citations are successively numbered and are divided among five age groups—children, adolescents, college students, adults, and the elderly. The majority of these involve group comparisons using a large number of subjects, although a few case studies are included. An index follows, enabling subject access. Categories consist of keywords from the citations and annotations and focus on areas of special interest, such as anxiety and depression.

The type of therapeutic interventions discussed are particularly pertinent in a time when cost-effectiveness and length of treatment are under close scrutiny. Future editions would be welcome, perhaps as annual supplements.—**Anita Zutis**

624. **Psychology: An Introductory Bibliography.** By the Editors of Salem Press. Pasadena, Calif., Salem Press and Lanham, Md., Scarecrow, 1996. 431p. index. (Magill Bibliographies). $55.00. ISBN 0-8108-3119-8.

This annotated bibliography is intended for use by high school students, undergraduates, and general readers, and covers books, chapters in books, and articles for the nonspecialist. There are many textbooks discussed, as well as some classical works (by Sigmund Freud and B. F. Skinner, for instance). The articles are primarily from such periodicals as *Scientific American* and *American Psychologist*. Topics are arranged in the same sequence as the chapters in many psychology textbooks, making it a useful supplement to class work. The topics covered include all of the major subdisciplines in psychology. Subjects of interest to the general public, such as aging, stress, and drug abuse, are well represented.

The primary shortcoming of the bibliography is its time coverage. Most of the references are from the 1970s and 1980s, with only a few from the early 1990s. The most recent references located in a spot check of the volume were from 1994, and most of them were in a single section. Unfortunately, many new developments in such popular fields as aggression and post-traumatic stress syndrome have been missed. Aside from this shortcoming, the bibliography would be a useful purchase for supplementing textbook readings or for readers interested in the more academic, less changeable fields. Despite its 1996 copyright, however, it is not recommended for people wanting information about rapidly changing fields in psychology.—**Diane Schmidt**

625. **PsycLit.** [CD-ROM]. Baltimore, Md., National Information Services Corporation, 1995. 2 discs. Minimum system requirements: IBM or compatible 286 AT-class or greater. CD-ROM drive. 512K RAM. 2MB hard disk space. Color or monochrome monitor. call publisher for pricing (see number below).

A computer program can both enhance and frustrate the work people do. The music librarian at Brigham Young University (BYU) reports that, in the past, updates for the *MusicROM* on ROMWright confused even the BYU technicians. The *PsycLit* program, however, loaded with no problems. Yet, after exiting the program and then restarting it, the program would not permit another search. Some National Information Services Corporation (NISC) discs are designed to expire on a certain date, after which new updates should have been installed and old discs returned to NISC. According to ROMWright's document #101, "Most Frequently Asked Questions," this has been a problem for subscribers in the past (i.e., the expiration date passed before the company was able to ship the update discs). ROMWright claims that this problem has been corrected. Despite these and other frustrations (this reviewer could not, before being locked out, get the citations to print on an HP Laserjet 4 printer), *PsycLit* appears to be a useful reference tool for psychologists, students, teachers, businesspeople, medical personnel, social workers, and others needing psychological information.

Users will like being able to select the search option best suited to their skills: novice, advanced, or expert. The producer states that the database contains more than 700,000 citations and abstracts from 1,300-plus journals. The database covers literature from 1974 to the present. "Present," however, is somewhat of a misnomer as there is a lag time of at least three months between updates. In 1987, books and book chapters were also added to the database. About 53,000 citations and abstracts are added each year. One should note that without 180K of free conventional memory and 1.5MB of extended memory, the program requires 512K of RAM. Pricing information must be obtained by calling (410) 243-0797.—**Nathan M. Smith**

Dictionaries and Encyclopedias

626. **The Blackwell Dictionary of Neuropsychology.** J. Graham Beaumont, Pamela M. Kenealy, and Marcus J. C. Rogers, eds. Cambridge, Mass., Blackwell, 1996. 788p. index. $95.00. ISBN 0-631-17896-1.

This is a hefty, helpful, comprehensive, encyclopedic dictionary about human neuropsychology. Although the book was published in London, it does not discuss neuropsychology according to the British. The contributors (126 of them are listed) were chosen from around the world because of their international reputation on the topic(s) they were assigned. The book will be of value to practicing clinical neuropsychologists, of course, and also to undergraduates, clinical workers and researchers, postgraduates in clinical psychology, speech and musical therapists, neurologists, neurosurgeons, and psychiatrists.

Articles in the dictionary are arranged alphabetically by keyword. Readers have three ways to access information in the book: by keywords, by cross-references and bibliographies found within the article, and by an index at the end of the book referencing topics not worthy of keyword entries. Some entries that are central to the book contain more than 8,000 words. These articles are supported by shorter entries of 500 to 5,000 words. In presenting the information on neuropsychology, the editors strived for a balance between core, enduring principles and current ideas, but contributors were invited to give their personal evaluation of the current concepts and theories. This book is a good value for the price.—**Nathan M. Smith**

627. **Concise Encyclopedia of Psychology.** 2d ed. Raymond J. Corsini and Alan J. Auerbach, eds. New York, John Wiley, 1996. 1035p. illus. index. $175.00. ISBN 0-471-13159-8.

The articles in this volume were abridged from the 4-volume 2d edition of the *Encyclopedia of Psychology* (see ARBA 95, entry 779), a work that has earned high praise. The statistics on this encyclopedia are impressive: 2,000 articles by 500 authors on 1,200 major topics, including all major psychological tests; plus brief biographies of 1,000 psychologists. This abridged single volume contains about 95 percent of the articles in the full encyclopedia, with the savings in space coming from dropping the extensive bibliography of the original, and abridging a number of articles and all of the biographies. The numerous cross-references of the original were kept in this concise version. Subjects were chosen for their long-term importance, so Antabuse (a drug used in treating alcoholism) is included, but Prozac is not. Articles discuss a wide range of topics, both in "pure" and clinical psychology, as well as allied fields. Controversial areas such as parapsychology or some of the odder forms of psychotherapy are also considered.

Concise Encyclopedia of Psychology is an impressive achievement. As with the original, it covers almost every topic or term that may be of interest to psychologists or students, but in far less space. The abridgment has been skillfully done, so that an article that was cut in half still reads well and contains all of the important information of the original. The editors have done an excellent job, even including at least one update (in the article on sadistic ritualistic abuse) that notes new problems with the data used in the original article.

The concise encyclopedia is as worthy as its parent set, and will be particularly valuable where budgetary restraints do not permit purchasing the full 4-volume set. The primary shortcoming of the concise encyclopedia is its lack of a bibliography, but it still covers an incredible breadth of subjects in a clear, authoritative manner suitable for all levels—from high school students to practicing psychologists, both academic and clinical. Buy the full set where the need exists for in-depth articles and bibliographies; the concise volume is more than satisfactory for other uses. [R: Choice, Oct 96, p. 249; LJ, 15 May 96, p. 53]—**Diane Schmidt**

628. **The Gale Encyclopedia of Psychology.** Susan Gall, ed. Detroit, Gale, 1996. 435p. illus. index. $99.00. ISBN 0-7876-0372-4.

This is an encyclopedia for high school and undergraduate students. Entries are usually short and are arranged alphabetically by psychological term. Many entries end with a list of two or three books for further reading, and some end with a *see also* reference to related terms. Enough pictures are included to keep a young person's interest, but pictures for psychologists/psychiatrists are inconsistent. The encyclopedia has a glossary; a bibliography; a selected list of organizations; and a subject index, indexed by subfield. Listing of an author under "Further Reading" does not ensure his or her inclusion in the bibliography (e.g., an Aaron Beck book is listed under the entry for "Cognitive Behavior Therapy," but he is not listed in the bibliography). In the subject index under the term *psychologist(s)*, inclusion of psychologists' names seems to be inconsistent (e.g., Alfred Adler is listed, but prominent psychologists, such as William James, B. F. Skinner, and others, are not). Despite its minor shortcomings, this is a Gale publication, and Gale reference books are a mainstay in many libraries. School, public, and academic libraries will want to seriously consider this one for their reference collection.—**Nathan M. Smith**

629. Stuart-Hamilton, Ian. **Dictionary of Developmental Psychology.** London, Jessica Kingsley Publishers; distr., Bristol, Pa., Taylor & Francis, 1995. 163p. $49.95. ISBN 1-85302-200-4.

Developmental psychology spans the life cycle from infancy to old age. Child psychology, adolescent psychology, and gerontology are all specialties within this field, and all are given their share of coverage within this brief dictionary. Some 2,500 American and British terms are defined. Systems, psychometric and other tests of psychological development, and general terms are among those included. On the whole, the definitions seem clear, lucid, and thorough. Entries chosen for selection are, necessarily, subjective, and the author does not claim comprehensiveness or complete coverage of current jargon. The definitions, no matter how lengthy, are intended solely as guides, and are not a substitute for consulting a textbook or journal article.

Cross-references are used frequently to refer to acronyms and related terms. Bold italic typeface indicates that the term is fully defined within the entry; synonyms are indicated by light italic typeface. The two-column format provides wide margins and much white space to avoid eyestrain. While one will derive no clear understanding of developmental psychology as a discipline from this work, students, mental health professionals, and medical transcribers may find it useful.—**Judy Gay Matthews**

630. Sutherland, Stuart. **The International Dictionary of Psychology.** 2d ed. New York, Crossroad Publishing, 1996. 515p. illus. $29.95pa. ISBN 0-8245-2509-4.

This 2d edition has added a substantial number of new definitions to the previous 1987 publication. The author states that the entries come mainly from psychology, but are reinforced with material from the allied fields of biology, physics, neurology, computer science, and the like. He also insists that his work is a dictionary, not an encyclopedia. Therefore, there are no extended entries. All definitions are terse and rarely extend beyond three sentences (unfortunately, some definitions are too terse for adequate usage). In addition, the author assumes some level of sophistication on the part of the reader, which makes this volume inappropriate for the novice. The dictionary is best suited for psychologists who need a refined definition for a term or area of which they have some rough acquaintance.

The volume is a comfortable size, not a monstrous tome, which indicates that the book is limited in scope. No author can include everything, and therefore some selection is necessary. Sutherland has emphasized experimental and physiological terms to the detriment of personality and social terms. This is exemplified by the inclusion of five appendixes, each of which is a different map of the brain. While there are non-hard science terms defined, the social- and personality-oriented psychologist would do well to seek information from other dictionaries on psychology. Also, why this tome has the word "international" in its title is a mystery, as all the defined terms are English. [R: Choice, Sept 96, p. 107; RBB, 1 April 96, pp. 1389-90]—**Charles Neuringer**

631. Turner, Jeffrey S. **Encyclopedia of Relationships Across the Lifespan.** Westport, Conn., Greenwood Press, 1996. 495p. index. $99.50. ISBN 0-313-29576-X.

Attempting to cover the full span of human interaction, this work provides more than 500 entries to current and historical theories, concepts, persons, and perspectives. Each brief entry includes a list of further readings for those seeking more in-depth analysis, and ample cross-references are provided to other entries in this encyclopedia. An appendix lists selected relevant professional journals and organizations, and a selected bibliography supplements the readings furnished in the body of the text. An author-title and limited subject index also is supplied. No information is given regarding the selection process for inclusion in this work, but it is clear that considerable effort has been made to provide a multicultural focus and make use of a copious cross-disciplinary terminology.

The complexity of headings used for entries and the limited nature of the subject index sometimes make this a difficult volume to use. Neither vernacular terms nor recognized subject headings such as those used by *Psychological Abstracts* (American Psychological Association) or *Sociological Abstracts* (Sociological Abstracts, Inc.) are used. Rather, a sometimes convoluted and complex heading is chosen. Therapeutic Relationship, For Survivors of Violence and Abuse, is used in place of the standard term Survivor. The entry describing midlife crisis is subsumed under the larger heading Middle Adulthood, and the Midlife Transition, although no index listing for midlife crisis (referred to repeatedly in the entry) is provided. Users are often left to guess under which entry their particular topic may fall. In comparison to other resources in this field, such as Robert Kastenbaum's excellent and quite accessible *Encyclopedia of Adult Development* (see ARBA 95, entry 781), this work all too often falls short of the mark. [R: Choice, Sept 96, p. 107]—**Elizabeth Patterson**

PARAPSYCHOLOGY

632. Clark, Jerome. **High Strangeness: UFOs from 1960 Through 1979.** Detroit, Omnigraphics, 1996. 777p. illus. index. (The UFO Encyclopedia, v.3). $95.00/v.; $228.00/set. ISBN 1-55888-742-3 (v.3).

The 100 detailed entries in this, the final volume of The UFO Encyclopedia, cover the important events of the 1960s and 1970s. As with its two predecessor volumes (see ARBA 93, entry 807, and ARBA 91, entry 797), it is largely based on the serious research that has been done at the Center for UFO Studies. As such, the encyclopedia presents a balanced and objective view of the field.

While a few of the entries are relatively brief, many of them are lengthy discussions of particular events, encounters, or incidents that describe the happening in detail and examine its likely validity. The set is a good companion to David Ritchie's *UFO: The Definitive Guide to Unidentified Flying Objects and Related Phenomena* (see ARBA 96, entry 789), which provides somewhat briefer coverage of many of the same topics. Each entry (e.g., Moody Abduction Case) in the volume under review brings together a wide range of information and commentary on the topic, supplemented by a good listing of sources. Unfortunately in many cases, the sources cited would not be readily available in most academic or public libraries, so Clark's summaries are apt to serve as the primary source of information.

An overall table of contents for the series, a cumulative bibliography, and a cumulative index bring unity to the set. Taken as a whole, this set is by far the most detailed, comprehensive, and valuable source on UFOs available.—**Norman D. Stevens**

633. **Encyclopedia of Occultism & Parapsychology: A Compendium of Information on the Occult Sciences....** 4th ed. J. Gordon Melton, ed. Detroit, Gale, 1996. 2v. index. $315.00/set. ISBN 0-8103-5487-X.

The compilation of the 4th edition of this 2-volume encyclopedia of the occult sciences, magic, demonology, superstitions, spiritualism, mysticism, metaphysics, psychical science, and parapsychology has spanned most of the twentieth century. Leslie Shepard, the editor of the first 3 editions (see ARBA 92, entry 762, for a review of the 3d ed.), published over the last 17 years, originally combined 2 previous works: Lewis Spences's *Encyclopedia of Occultism*, first published in London in 1920, and Nandor Fodor's *Encyclopedia of Psychic Science*, first published in 1934 (also in London), were updated and supplemented in 1978 after the heightened wave of interest in the 1970s.

This 4th edition of *Encyclopedia of Occultism & Parapsychology* has received harsh editing of the original materials in light of current scientific research. The earlier references have been culled and updated by recent scholarly works. Three hundred new entries have been added to address recent developments. These two volumes offer a substantial reference work from a scholarly perspective. The updated source list after each entry is of particular value to the researcher and curious student.

—Linda L. Lam-Easton

634. **The Encyclopedia of the Paranormal.** Gordon Stein, ed. Buffalo, N.Y., Prometheus Books, 1996. 859p. illus. index. $149.95. ISBN 1-57392-021-5.

This encyclopedia proposes to be a comprehensive work on the paranormal from a scientific perspective. By scientific, the editor means to include materials from "quantifiable evidence," and in his foreword, the late Carl Sagan praises the "skeptical backbone" found in the work. Materials compiled by 50 scientists, theologians, philosophers, magicians, historians, and other noted scholars are presented in more than 90 articles. While not exhaustive, the entries are thorough and include the "strictly paranormal," such as psychokinesis, channeling, levitation, phrenology, and palmistry; the historical, such as Harry Houdini, mediums, psychic research, and alchemy; and the philosophical, such as miracles, reincarnation, and death survival; as well as work on the Bermuda triangle, statistics, the media, and photography.

The contributors are individually pro-paranormal, neutral, and antiparanormal, and state their bias accordingly. They conclude with decisions such as "unproven," "unlikely," "disproved," or "quite likely." This combination of data and belief is complicated to assess because much is said to be scientific and yet hard to substantiate. Readers will learn from the data and can draw their own conclusions. [R: Choice, Oct 96, pp. 250-52; RBB, June 96, p. 1772]—**Linda L. Lam-Easton**

635. Hauck, Dennis William. **Haunted Places: The National Directory: Ghostly Abodes, Sacred Sites, UFO Landings, and Other Supernatural Locations.** rev. ed. New York, Penguin Books, 1996. 485p. illus. index. $15.95pa. ISBN 0-14-025734-9.

Both a travel guide and a guide for researchers, this interesting book describes some 2,000 sites of paranormal activity in the United States. Entries are listed alphabetically by state and then by city/area within the state. All 50 states are represented. Entries discuss the otherworldly occurrence, give detailed directions, and provide boldfaced references to a bibliography at the back of the work, leading researchers to more in-depth discussions of the hauntings. From I-15 coming out of Barstow, California, supposed home to a secret underground alien base; to Cheesman Park in Denver, *Poltergeist*-style site of a former cemetery where all the bodies were not removed; to El Santurario de Chimayo, New Mexico, with its miraculous cross and healing dirt; to Devil's Tower National Monument in Wyoming, Native American sacred site and spot of close encounters; to the White House, where the ghosts of William Henry Harrison, Abigail Adams, Abraham Lincoln, Andrew Jackson, Dolley Madison, and others are said to reside—all are covered here.

Some omissions were noted. There is no mention of the Stanley Hotel in Estes Park, Colorado, reputed to be haunted and the basis for *The Shining* (although Stephen King and his famous work of horror are mentioned in another entry under Estes Park). More tales of ghostly occurrences on college campuses might certainly have been included, although an entire book could be written on that subject: Nearly every college has its own ghost stories. Also, despite the fact that the directions supplied in each entry are thorough, maps of the individual states with the featured locations marked would increase the work's value as a travel guide. The bibliography is fruitful, while the index is merely adequate.

Whether the reader is searching for an interesting vacation destination or is writing a paper on paranormal phenomena, this book will serve the purpose. Libraries can afford to have a copy in both the reference section and the circulating collection. Individuals would also benefit from purchasing the volume; the entries are addictively readable, and as a coffee-table book, it could spark some interesting conversations.—**Melissa Rae Root**

636. Julien, Nadia. **The Mammoth Dictionary of Symbols.** English-language ed. New York, Carroll & Graf, 1996. 524p. illus. $9.95pa. ISBN 0-7867-0301-6.

This dictionary is an excellent guide to the various signs and symbols found in the majority of works about parapsychology and the occult. Elfreda Powell's English-language translation has remained true to the original work in ease of use and clarity of explanation. Although not intended for the true scholar of the supernatural, this dictionary will serve the curious researcher and the layperson well.

There is no guide to the usage of the dictionary because one is not needed. The arrangement is in dictionary order with brief paragraphs on the meaning of the symbol in the various religious and ethnic groups that employ the symbol. Many of the paragraphs are footnoted to the items in the bibliography and, when appropriate, cross-referenced to an associated symbol found in the dictionary. Illustrations are in black-and-white, which can sometimes make it slightly difficult to fully distinguish subtleties of image, but still meets the needs of the general reader.

There is enough information to be found in this small paperback to recommend it to most general and public library collections. The larger research libraries will find this one of only secondary interest for a collection of materials on occultism and parapsychology. However, because the price is certainly not prohibitive for most libraries, this work is well worth investigating.—**Christine E. Thompson**

637. Randi, James. **An Encyclopedia of Claims, Frauds, and Hoaxes of the Occult and Supernatural: James Randi's Decidedly Skeptical Definitions of Alternate Realities.** New York, St. Martin's Press, 1995. 284p. illus. maps. index. $24.95. ISBN 0-312-10974-1.

This informative and entertaining reference demystifies and debunks the fascinating world of the occult and supernatural. The work contains hundreds of entries that define and describe people, events, theories, and history. The book is not so much written as "exposed" by Randi (a.k.a., the "Amazing Randi"), who is a professional magician/conjurer, author, and lecturer, as well as an internationally recognized authority and outspoken skeptic of the world of magic and psychic phenomena. Randi spent 10 years working on this, his 10th, book. Randi is also the winner of the MacArthur "Genius" Fellowship for his investigations of paranormal and occult claims, and he is often featured on television.

Subjects are drawn primarily from the eighteenth and nineteenth centuries, but topics from the twentieth century are also included, such as crop circles, Uri Geller, L. Ron Hubbard, channeling, and UFOs. Entries are from 10 to more than 500 words in length. Of particular note are the two fine appendixes: "Curse of the Pharaoh Personnel" and "Forty-Nine End-of-the-World Prophecies that Failed (992 to 1999 A.D.)." Ample cross-references and an index make the book easy to use. Dozens of drawings and black-and-white photographs enhance the easy-to-read, two-column format text. The bibliography contains more than 40 references.

As the end of both the century and the millennium approaches, there will surely be an increase in the number of end-of-the-world prophecies as well as hoaxes and fraudulent claims. At the price, this authoritative work belongs in all libraries.—**Edward Erazo**

638. **Strange & Unexplained Happenings: When Nature Breaks the Rules of Science.** Jerome Clark and Nancy Pear, eds. Detroit, U*X*L/Gale, 1995. 3v. illus. maps. index. $57.00/set. ISBN 0-8103-9780-3.

Clark, coeditor of the volumes at hand, has a 30-year reputation as a competent and even-handed writer on paranormal subjects. Focusing on bizarre physical (rather than spiritual or psychic) phenomena, the work presents hard and soft documentation on the possible existence of (and explanations for) spontaneous human combustions, lake monsters, fairies, Fortean rains, teleportation, the 1908 Siberian explosion, werewolves, extraterrestrials, and so forth. A repackaging of the one-volume *Unexplained!* (Visible Ink Press, 1993), this set principally targets middle and high school readers. Many passages have been removed, condensed, or truncated, especially those that include detailed accounts or lengthy affidavit testimony. Illustrations have been added, such as cartoons of flying saucers and photographs of hairy bipeds. Boxed biographical profiles and "Reel Life" insets that connect subjects to their appearances in science fiction films are scattered throughout the text. The work's 85 entries are arranged thematically and are preceded by a helpful glossary of 75 terms (cryptozoology, porphyria, Lemuria). Each volume concludes with a comprehensive subject index.

The set is generally balanced in its examination of the bizarre. It disparages and discredits the supernatural and extraterrestrial hypotheses that some had advanced to account for activities regarding the Bermuda Triangle, crop circles, and the Ummite cult, among others. Because UFOlogy has long been Clark's forte, 3 of these volumes' 19 chapters relate directly to that subject, and some others do so tangentially. Each chapter concludes with a brief bibliography, supplemented at the back of each book with an annotated reading list of recent books and periodicals, as well as a section that supplies thumbnail histories, missions, and addresses of 11 pertinent organizations. In summary, this is a publication that, with a healthy dose of skepticism by the user, will go far in providing information not readily available elsewhere. [R: SLJ, May 96, p. 145]—**Jeffrey E. Long**

15 Recreation and Sports

GENERAL WORKS

Almanacs

639. **Chase's Sports Calendar of Events 1997.** Chicago, Contemporary Books, 1996. 348p. illus. index. $29.95pa. ISBN 0-8092-3133-6. ISSN 1091-2959.

Who knows that August 15 is the birth anniversary of Charles Comiskey . . . or that he was born in 1859 and died in 1931? Who knows that August 15 is also the anniversary of the first woman in pro football, the anniversary of major league baseball's "Forfeit by Ground Crew," and the anniversary of "Three Men on Third"? *Chase's Sports Calendar of Events* supplies this information and much, much more. The listing for August 15 includes six events scheduled to take place in 1997 as well. Also listed for each day of the year are the birthdays of living athletes, emphasizing baseball, basketball, football, and hockey players, but additionally treating sportscasters, actors noted for sports films, and other sports-related figures.

This book comes in an easy-to-read, 8½-by-11-inch format with readily recognizable boldfaced headings. The useful index not only lists each name and event alphabetically, but organizes the entries by sport as well. These features make *Chase's* easy to use. The day-by-day calendar listings are supplemented by separate listings of league and team addresses, halls of fame, annual sports award winners, U.S. national champions, and a directory of sports organizations. While much of this information is available in other volumes, having it all included in one volume with the events upcoming for 1997 makes *Chase's* a valuable source.—**David A. Doman**

Biography

640. Brownstone, David, and Irene Franck. **Sports People in the News 1996.** New York, Macmillan Library Reference/Simon & Schuster Macmillan, 1996. 358p. illus. index. $85.00. ISBN 0-02-864525-1. ISSN 1090-6681.

This new series is scheduled to be an annual, as is *People in the News* (see ARBA 95, entry 24), from which it is modeled. The volume contains biographies of more than 400 sports figures, such as coaches, broadcasters, journalists, and stars, both professional and amateur, drawn from baseball, basketball, boxing and wrestling, figure skating, football, golf, gymnastics, hockey, racing, swimming and diving, tennis, and track and field. Recently deceased sports-related figures are also included. Of the 400 biographees, 100 are women, and 50 are also found in the companion work. These 50 are updated twice a year because the 2 titles are published approximately 6 months apart.

Selection is based on current activities and importance, not on past achievements or celebrity status alone. Entries include the person's role in sports from spring 1995 through May 1996, a brief career summary, and a short descriptive summary, and conclude with a further reading list. More than 300 of the 400 profiles include black-and-white photographs.

Although the volume is arranged alphabetically, there are two indexes, by name and by sport, which will cumulate in future volumes, making it valuable for reference. The 2 authors have written more than 70 books, mainly reference, on a variety of topics. This book is easy reading, making it useful for high school libraries. Public libraries will find its reference use to be quick and handy.—**Kathleen J. Voigt**

641. **Sports Stars: Series 2.** Michael A. Pare, ed. Detroit, U*X*L/Gale, 1996. 2v. illus. index. $44.95/set. ISBN 0-7876-0867-X.

Sports Stars: Series 2 presents biographies of 60 amateur and professional athletes, including 2 sports teams—the women's baseball team the Colorado Silver Bullets and the yachting team Mighty Mary. According to the reader's guide (the first section of the book), the athletes meet one or more of the following criteria: They are currently active in amateur or professional sports, are considered top performers in their field, and are role models who have overcome physical obstacles or societal constraints to reach the top of their professions. Other critical selection criteria, which this reviewer tested with the neighbor kids (two middle school boys who do not like to read), are the popular appeal of the athletes chosen and the readability and ease of use as perceived by this kind of reader. Some of the interesting and convenient features consist of the listing of the athletes by sports; a wide range of sports covered, including the less popular (bicycle racing, golf, horse racing, speed skating, yachting); a "Scoreboard Box" listing the athlete's top awards; a "Growing Up" section presenting the early life and motivations of the person or team; a "Superstar" section highlighting the athlete's career; a "Where to Write" section with an address to contact the athlete; and a list of sources for further reading.

As one would expect, fewer women are listed than men, for sports are male-dominated, but the editor has taken care to profile many women. Their struggles to be successful in these male bastions have been accurately portrayed. The athletes presented, because of the very nature of the field, encompass a realistic range of ethnicity. The reading level is appropriate for middle school students, and the text is down-to-earth, describing what actually happened in these athletes' lives—divorce, illness, failure, disappointment, personal problems, racial conflict—making it more interesting to the age group targeted. Interesting sidebars and many photographs are provided. Finally, each profile is just eight pages in length, which is attractive to many less-skilled readers.

Teachers and parents struggle to get young people, particularly active boys, to read. They also strive to find suitable role models for kids, particularly girl athletes, and to locate engaging reference materials for budding writers and researchers. This series answers many needs of students and their teachers and builds a bridge from the typical interests of young people to books.—**Karen D. Harvey**

Chronology

642. **Sports in North America: A Documentary History. Volume 5: Sports Organized 1880-1900.** Gerald R. Gems, ed. Gulf Breeze, Fla., Academic International Press, 1996. 514p. index. $96.00/single volume; $76.00/volume with subscription. ISBN 0-87569-148-X.

There is hardly a thing that can better evoke the ambience of the past, in all its former glory, than the reading of contemporaneous news accounts and other documents. In dredging up the documents that detail the coalescing of sports in Canada and the United States from a loose agglomeration of athletes and promoters into the advent of sporting leagues and tournaments, the editor of this, the fifth volume of a proposed set, has chosen wisely. Indeed, certain of the accounts show remarkable foresight; for example, in *The Nation* in 1890, an anonymous commentator on the future of football predicts the founding of what today is the National Football League (NFL) in only 10 years' time. (It took about two-and-a-half decades.) There was already a professional team in Canton, Ohio, at that time, as shown by a clip from *The Scrapbook History of Pro Football*, as well as a short-lived American League of Professionals.

Gems addresses such issues as the growth of technology even at this early date: Transport networks, motoring, electricity for lighting, photography, and equipment all played a part in the new organization and formality of sports. He begins with a chapter on the organization and rationalization of sport, including how the top universities, such as Yale, were studying the human body as if it were another one of the machines of the day. Most of the sports of the day are covered: baseball; basketball (which was just getting started, although women were already participating in it at Smith College and in Chicago, as documented here); bicycling (at its zenith, it would seem); football; golf; gymnastics; and track and field. Also here are more minor sports, such as lacrosse, boxing, bowling, equestrianism, racket sports, and winter sports.

The documents presented are of two kinds: the organizational and the reportorial. In baseball, it is interesting to read the accounts of new grounds being built in Chicago. Of course, these preceded by a good many years the founding of even so venerable an institution as Wrigley Field. On boxing, there is a nine-page "Story of the Fight by Rounds" of a heavyweight title match between James J. Corbett and Bob Fitzsimmons (nobody would read such a long story today). The football chapter features the intercollegiate rules as amended by Walter Camp, clearly showing the evolution of the game.

This book is part of a long series that will document the rise of sports in the United States and Canada, from its lowly status when the puritans frowned on it to its godlike presence in life today. To judge solely by the titles of the first six books in the series, sport's rise has been as steady as it has been spectacular. This collection of old newspaper articles and other, more official, documents goes a little way in putting into perspective for modern observers the societal and cultural phenomenon known as sports. It will earn its place in the academic library by saving the researcher valuable time. The volume includes a geographic and place-names index, an institutions index, a subject and name index, and a select bibliography of primary and secondary sources.—**Randall Rafferty**

Dictionaries and Encyclopedias

643. Coppell, Bill. **Sportspeak: An Encyclopedia of Sport.** Port Melbourne, Australia, D. W. Thorpe/Reed Reference Australia; distr., New Providence, N.J., Reed Reference Publishing, 1995. 594p. $24.95pa. ISBN 1-875589-73-2.

Sportspeak is a conflated sports rule book and dictionary of sporting slang. Some 250 sports and games are practiced in Australia—and here the lexicographer's primary aim is to include all these plus others from the world over. He has been quite successful. The whole of the sporting experience is represented in this handy book. Games, too, are included, although they are not set apart as such. The introduction asserts that "dance and chess and orienteering are just as much sports as tennis and hockey and football." The inclusion of *dancesport*, a neologistic term for competitive ballroom dancing, demonstrates the broad scope of the terms.

On the face of it, this book would seem to approach completeness. A lifetime spent observing ESPN or reading the sports pages would not have familiarized one with even half of the terms in *Sportspeak*. Sports in the United States are included; American football and baseball are being played in Australia, although with "limited success," the author notes. A typical word bandied about in American football is *seam*. Here is how it is defined in the book at hand: "American football: when the ball is snapped . . . for the extra point, the holder lines up the seam. . . ." That is fine, as far as it goes, but there is no mention of the term's use in the zone defense: finding the *seam* as a "wide receiver." Also treated are words used to deal with sports medicine (hematoma, rotator cuff tear), injuries (syncope, syndrome) and equipment (sticks, clubs).

The subtitle asserts that the book is an encyclopedia. By sheer number of terms listed, this is true. To be able to fill 587 pages with sporting terms would seem to indicate that people living today are obsessed with sports, a concept noted in the introduction. Many of the words and phrases are defined briefly, in just a line or two: They deserve such a short length because they are rather trivial. Many other terms are treated more fully, such as those that have multiple meanings or that are common to more than one game or sport. Tae kwon do and other martial arts have not been slighted. As noted earlier, an interesting slant is lent to many of the terms and indeed to the definitions because the author is Australian and the book was published there. His book is littered with terms and descriptions only an insider could know, and it is characterized by loving observation of athletes and their games.

Although *Sportspeak* can easily double as a reference book in the most complete U.S. library or as a good browse for the curious, a librarian will not find anything in here about the Dallas Cowboys or the New York Yankees or any well-known U.S. sports personalities. This might be a drawback for some.

Also, there are no drawings, diagrams, or illustrations. For comparison with a well-known title in the library world, the *Oxford Companion to World Sports and Games* (see ARBA 76, entry 701) comes to mind. There, the entries are much fuller, and personalities and their records are included.—**Randall Rafferty**

644. Sherrow, Victoria. **Encyclopedia of Women and Sports.** Santa Barbara, Calif., ABC-CLIO, 1996. 382p. illus. index. $60.00. ISBN 0-87436-826-X.

Laws and societal pressure have discouraged women from participating in sports around the world for centuries. Chronicling the history of women athletes and the barriers that they have faced and overcome is the focus of the *Encyclopedia of Women and Sports*.

The introduction guides readers through a fascinating overview of the history of women and sports, beginning with the first Olympic Games in Ancient Greece, where not only were women banned from competition, but were also banned from watching the games at all. This is a readable, enlightening introduction that describes societal beliefs of the "weaker sex," the negative attitudes of "unfeminine" women, sexism, and the "experts" who deemed that sports would be detrimental to a woman's health. The first acceptable sports for women—golf, croquet, and archery—helped to make athletic pursuits more permissible for women, and the arrival of the bicycle had a great impact on society. It provided an important form of transportation as well as a popular pastime, but the bicycle also presented a problem with women's attire: How were women to ride with long skirts without getting them tangled in the spokes? Amelia Bloomer and her supporters suggested a freer style of dress consisting of wide pants beneath a loose-fitting dress. Thus, the arrival of the Bloomer in 1851. "Both cycling and bloomers came to symbolize a new spirit in America and were linked to the broader social efforts of the suffragist movement as women struggled for the right to vote" (p. xii). The introduction also chronicles minority women and the struggles they overcame, women athletes who defied society and helped to change common thinking, the fight for Olympic participation, athletic scholarships, and the media role models who encouraged the message that sports could be "feminine."

More than 600 alphabetically organized entries highlight key individuals who have participated in or advanced the cause of women in sports and include related topics, such as sexual and racial discrimination, tournaments, organizations, leagues, awards, health issues, segregation, sport history, scholarships, and officiating. The volume not only records athletic achievements but chronicles other accomplishments as well. Tenley Albright, for example, overcame polio to become a gold-medal figure skater in the 1936 Olympics, graduated from Harvard Medical School, became a surgeon, and served as the first woman on the U.S. Olympic committee.

Encyclopedia of Women and Sports underscores the progress women have made not only as athletes but as coaches, officials, teachers, administrators, sportscasters, sportswriters, and women's rights advocates. Current as of the 1996 Summer Olympic Games, entries are concise, interesting, and readable with *see also* and bibliographical references. A timeline of events from 776 B.C.E. to 1996 gives a clear overview of progress. A bibliography and an index complete the work. The encyclopedia is highly recommended.

—**Deborah A. Taylor**

BASEBALL

645. **Inside Sports World Series Factbook.** By George Cantor. Detroit, Visible Ink Press/Gale, 1996. 617p. illus. index. $18.95pa. ISBN 0-7876-0821-1.

This book by *Inside Sports* magazine is a work on the history and statistics of the World Series. The events of the World Series from 1903 to 1995 are described. It is a highly readable book of more than 600 pages, which offers 6 or 7 pages on each Series. It should appeal to the casual observer as an introductory glimpse into our national pastime or to the seasoned fan as a comfortable reliance on which to review facts already known or to check statistics for accuracy.

The book lays out the dynamics of each World Series, giving a preview of the matchup, a turning point to the Series, and information on the respective managers, heroes, "zeroes," and aftermath of the Series. An especially good element of the book is the hundreds of black-and-white photographs, and the "facts" included in sidebar graphics are entertaining as well.

Written by Cantor of the *Detroit News*, this book should be recognized not as an in-depth serious study of baseball or its numerous personalities, but rather as an overview or encyclopedic analysis of the game. As a baseball fan, this reviewer hesitates to focus on a single World Series, but the description of the 1919 Series involving the famous Black Sox scandal and the tale of Shoeless Joe Jackson seems timeless. However, that is what this book is: a comfortable synopsis for baseball fans to have in their library when arguing about stats or when one just wants to take a few minutes to reminisce about history.—**James E. Root Jr.**

646. Jones, Donald D. **Former Major League Teams: An Encyclopedia.** Jefferson, N.C., McFarland, 1995. 233p. index. $35.00. ISBN 0-7864-0035-8.

This encyclopedia appears to be the first publication wholly devoted to providing information on former major league clubs. Aside from profiles of erstwhile organizations of the National and American Leagues (the Kansas City Cowboys, the Worcester Ruby Legs, the Seattle Pilots), overviews are supplied for all teams that played at least one game in the other leagues (Players' and Federal) and associations (National, American, and Union). Each team entry discloses its years of operation; names of affiliated ballparks, team presidents, and managers; statistics on the club's best hitter and pitcher; an all-time player roster (with players' respective positions and years of service), with Hall of Famers printed in bold typeface; and a year-by-year breakdown of wins, losses, and season standings. When archivally available, Jones has supplied team history highlights, such as Guy Hecker (of the Louisville Colonels) becoming the first major-leaguer to score seven runs in a game.

The text is complemented by two brief chapters tracing the origins and subsequent name changes of today's major league teams. For example, the Chicago Cubs have competed through the decades as the White Stockings, the Babes, the Colts, the Broncos, the Cowboys, the Rainmakers, and the Orphans, becoming the Cubs in 1901. Franchise movements are also chronicled: The Athletics have called Philadelphia, Kansas City, and Oakland their home. No errors were noted in this volume. The durability and value of the encyclopedia seem to ensure use in libraries for decades to come. Future editions would, however, be improved by the inclusion of team or player nicknames, as well as by descriptions or sketches of team uniforms. Finally, a case could be made for incorporating the contributions made to professional baseball by such participants of the Negro Leagues as Buck Leonard and Josh Gibson. Otherwise, this book makes solid contact with its subject.—**Jeffrey E. Long**

647. Snelling, Dennis. **The Pacific Coast League: Statistical History, 1903-1957.** Jefferson, N.C., McFarland, 1995. 392p. $29.50pa. ISBN 0-7864-0045-5.

The Pacific Coast League is the dry if accurate title of a much livelier book. Snelling originally began compiling it as an appendix for a history of the Pacific Coast League (PCL). Much love and care were put into the book, especially in attempts to re-create lost statistics (including those destroyed in the 1906 San Francisco earthquake) and to correct errors listed in official guides.

Snelling's table of contents and introductions to each section are straightforward about what each covers, be it team rosters, team standings, or individual statistics. Those interested in specific players may wish to look them up in Snelling's "Player Register—Hitting" and "Player Register—Pitching" chapters (both of which are not complete, but do cover the highlights). These chapters hint at the stories behind the statistics: not just the famous, such as Ted Williams or Joe DiMaggio (who had a 61-game PCL hitting streak) but also, for example, Jimmie Reese, a fine second baseman, later a coach for the California Angels, and for whom Nolan Ryan's son Reese is named; or "Prince Hal" Chase, maybe the most corrupt man ever to play the game. Several "Black Sox" players played in the PCL, which had a gambling scandal about the time the "Black Sox" were throwing their World Series.

The latter date in the subtitle coincides with the relocation of the Dodgers and Giants to the West Coast, finishing any aspirations the PCL had of being a third major league. I hope Snelling writes his history of the PCL. For anyone not statistics-oriented, this book will not be of much interest, but it is worthwhile for the greater stories it hints at, and therefore cautiously recommended.—**R. S. Lehmann**

648. *The Sporting News* **Baseball Guide.** 1996 ed. Craig Carter and Dave Sloan, eds. St. Louis, Mo., Sporting News Publishing, 1996. 608p. index. $13.95pa. ISBN 0-89204-544-2.

With a minimum of the hype common in such handbooks, editors Carter and Sloan have teamed up here for the fourth consecutive year. As an almanac with a primary focus on the performance of today's players and teams, this volume closely resembles earlier editions in the series (see ARBA 92, entry 776, for a review of the 1991 edition). Current information on each National and American League organization includes season schedules, ballpark diagrams (the seating section numerals are often too fine to read), lists of club officials and minor league affiliate teams, and spring training rosters. Historical data—now expanded to provide annual attendance figures—appear in the guide's history section, rather than in the section on individual teams.

Reporting on the 1st year of division playoffs, this edition offers 20 pages of highlights, box scores, and other statistics that echo this title's perennial coverage of championship and World Series competition. Following the day-by-day chart that reprises each team's 1995 successes and failures on the diamond, related summary information has been gathered on a separate page for the first time. Scrupulously updated, this year's guide adjusts the capacity of Montreal's Olympic Stadium by 100 occupants and supplies spring training information on the Cincinnati Reds absent from the 1995 edition.

The general layout is less cluttered than previously. The substitution in some tables of dagger and double-dagger reference notations with the more easily discriminated solid geometric symbols is gratifying. On the other hand, the editors should be charged with an error for their removal of each organization's local television and radio broadcast names. The addition of more graphics, as well as information on team mascots and triple plays, and international baseball league news would improve this work also. Yet, at a convenient size, this is a book that should be taken out to the ball game; libraries may wish to purchase duplicate circulating copies of this reference toward that end.—**Jeffrey E. Long**

649. *The Sporting News* **Official Baseball Register.** 1996 ed. Sean Stewart, Kyle Veltrop, and John Duxbury, eds. St. Louis, Mo., Sporting News Publishing, 1996. 599p. $13.95pa. ISBN 0-89204-545-0.

This is the volume to find statistics on everyone who appeared in at least one major league game in 1995 and on other players who did not appear in a game in the last year but were listed on a 40-man major league roster as of December 28, 1995. That makes the *Register* an exhaustive listing of the names in the game today. Each entry provides minor league as well as major league records; personal information (including any high school, junior college, and college the player attended); transactions the player was involved in; records and honors; and any other item of statistical or miscellaneous interest (e.g., "tied for A.L. lead with three balks in 1995" or "led A.L. with 32 sacrifice hits in 1989").

The *Register* has all players listed in a single alphabetic volume, and pitchers and other players are listed together, which makes it easier to use. However, the National League pitchers' entries do not furnish hitting statistics. Some additional interest is provided by the football records for those few individuals who have played both games (Brian Jordan of the St. Louis Cardinals and Deion Sanders, who is a free agent in major league baseball, for example). The section on major league managers supplies each individual's minor and major league playing statistics, as well as their minor and major league managing records. The *Register* is an essential book for reference collections and serious baseball fans.

—**David A. Doman**

650. Stang, Mark, and Linda Harkness. **Baseball by the Numbers: A Guide to the Uniform Numbers of Major League Teams.** Lanham, Md., Scarecrow, 1996. 2v. (American Sports History Series, no.4). $85.00 spiralbound/set. ISBN 0-8108-3054-X.

Until seeing this 2-volume, 1,125-page work, this reviewer believed that all conceivable major league data had been collected and published. Stang and Harkness, however, have discovered a gap—the numbers worn by all players since their adoption on a permanent basis by most teams in the early 1930s, one exception being the New York Yankees, who first wore numbers in 1929. One volume of the reference lists National League teams, the other American League teams. The numbers are presented in three ways for each team: a year-by-year listing, an alphabetic listing by player, and a numerical listing. Most of the numbers were gathered from scorecard collections held by individuals or by the Baseball Hall of Fame.

Baseball fanatics will surely glean interesting nuggets from this work (e.g., Hank Aaron inherited number 5 from Sam Jethroe when he arrived for his first season with the Atlanta Braves in 1954; the following season he switched to his familiar 44, a number subsequently retired by two teams—Atlanta after his last season there in 1974, and the Milwaukee Brewers with whom he concluded his career in 1976). Still, it remains doubtful whether sufficient interest exists in most settings to justify a high expenditure for this exhaustively researched, narrowly focused resource.—**Lee Weston**

651. Wright, Marshall D. **Nineteenth Century Baseball: Year-by-Year Statistics for the Major League Teams, 1871 Through 1900.** Jefferson, N.C., McFarland, 1996. 350p. index. $37.50. ISBN 0-7864-0181-8.

One of the distinctive features of *The Baseball Encyclopedia* (9th ed.; see ARBA 94, entry 830) has been its year-by-year team rosters, including a typical lineup composed of the players who played the most games at each position in a given year. As Wright notes, however, these rosters have not been provided for years prior to 1901, the year in which the American League began play, and the beginning of what is generally considered to be the modern era of major league baseball.

To fill this gap, Wright has used available data for individual players to construct team rosters back to 1871 for leagues considered "major" in the nineteenth century (the National Association, the National League, the American Association, the Union Association, and the Players' League). Number of games played at each position and offensive statistics for the year are provided for each player. Hence, a researcher may see at a glance that a typical lineup for the 1886 Detroit Wolverines in the National League would include Dan Brouthers at first base, Fred Dunlap at second base, Jack Rowe at shortstop, and so forth. That same researcher can also see that those 1886 Wolverines, managed by Bill Watkins, were 87-36 on the season (an eye-popping .707 percentage), but still finished second, 2.5 games behind the Chicago White Stockings.

The statistical data for each league's year are preceded by a one- to two-page overview of that season. In reading these, one cannot help but be struck by the relative instability and imbalance that plagued major league baseball in its formative years. A bibliography and an index of player names rounds out this compendium, which is a signal achievement and should take its place as a fundamental baseball reference source.

—**Jack Ray**

BASKETBALL

652. **NCAA Basketball: The Official 1997 Men's College Basketball Records Book.** Overland Park, Kans., National Collegiate Athletic Association and Chicago, Triumph Books, 1996. 368p. illus. $15.95pa. ISBN 1-57243-137-7. ISSN 1089-5280.

NCAA Basketball has been available to National Collegiate Athletic Association (NCAA) members for many years, according to a representative from the NCAA, but it has only been available for sale and general distribution through Triumph Books for three years. NCAA began the record section in 1981, and in this edition, the men's and women's records are in separate volumes.

This volume of almost 400 pages includes Division I, II, and III records—individual, team, all-time individual leaders, annual individual champions, all-time team leaders, annual team champions, statistical trends, all-time most winning teams, winning streaks, and national polls. Following in order are individual collegiate records; award winners (consensus and academic award winners and NCAA postgraduate scholarship winners); coaching records (all-time leaders and top active coaches); championships (year-by-year winners by division and individual records); statistical leaders (individual, game highs, team); conferences; attendance records; playing rules history; 1997 schedules; and 1996 results (all teams in every division).

NCAA Basketball is a must for the reference collection of all public and academic libraries. It is useful to have every possible basketball statistic available in one rather inexpensive source.

—**Kathleen J. Voigt**

653. **NCAA Final Four: The Official 1997 Final Four Records Book.** Overland Park, Kans., National Collegiate Athletic Association and Chicago, Triumph Books, 1996. 203p. illus. $13.95pa. ISBN 1-57243-139-3. ISSN 0267-1017.

The annual National Collegiate Athletic Association (NCAA) basketball tournament, commonly hyped by the media as "March Madness," features 64 teams competing for the collegiate championship. The three-week event continues to grow in popularity and attendance every year. Although only one team can win six games and be crowned champion, this ideal book is yet another winner. Similar to its football counterpart (see ARBA 96, entry 819), the basketball volume is literally full of records and statistics, both on teams and individuals.

From the 1939 tournament featuring 8 teams to the 64-team field of 1996, the coverage includes all kinds of unique information. An example is a year-by-year listing of each participating team, its conference, records in regular season and conference play, its NCAA tournament record, its tournament seed, and how the team qualified for the "big dance" (as many call the championship bracket). Individual and team tournament records are presented, as are coaching records. The entire bracket for each year is a highlight of the book, indicating where the games were played and the result of every game. Here is an example of some of the interesting information supplied in the book: The University of California at Los Angeles, an 11-time tournament winner, including 7 in a row (1967-1973), won 3 tournaments (1965, 1968, 1972) without ever leaving the far west region.

There are few record books with which to compare this excellent volume. *The Encyclopedia of the NCAA Basketball Tournament* by Jim Savage (Dell Publishing, 1990) is comparable—it includes box scores from all tournament games but does not indicate where the games were played. Even if a library owns this earlier volume, the official guide under review is still reasonably priced. But if not, the book is a must for the sports reference collection.—**Boyd Childress**

FOOTBALL

654. **Official 1996 National Football League Record & Fact Book.** New York, Workman Publishing, 1996. 464p. $15.95pa. ISBN 0-7611-0482-8.

Ever wonder where professional football announcers and commentators find some of the detailed statistical information seen and heard on television and radio? For example, where did a player go to college, where was he drafted, how has he done against other teams in the league, or how have some teams fared versus others? This book is one of many that media personnel use to locate numbers and records, and a good one at that. The 1992 edition was well reviewed (see ARBA 94, entry 846), as was the 1988 volume (see ARBA 89, entry 734), and, for 1996, there are slight enhancements. The arrangement includes 1996 schedules; a detailed team-by-team section (4 pages per team including franchise information, 1995 player and team statistics, rosters, 1996 draft choices, and profiles of coaches); a review of the 1995 season; and a history section, with numbers and yet more numbers.

Strengths include a listing of team front office personnel, small stadium diagrams, a brief "by the numbers" section, and a complete player draft summary dating back to 1936. A concise 14-page conclusion details officials and rules. An introductory index replaces a table of contents and concluding index—a minor weakness. A better index would have only added to an already attractive and useful reference work. Several typographic errors were noted, but the Workman Publishing book is superior to similar books published by Sporting News Publishing (see entries 655-656) and St. Martin's Press (see ARBA 95, entry 820).—**Boyd Childress**

655. *The Sporting News* **Pro Football Guide.** 1996 ed. Craig Carter and Dave Sloan, eds. St. Louis, Mo., Sporting News Publishing, 1996. 389p. illus. $14.95pa. ISBN 0-89204-553-1.

This is just the book for football fanatics and trivia nuts! Or, as the book jacket describes, "a pro football fan's best friend." The volume certainly contains just about everything one would want to know about the 1995 season, with weekly highlights and game-by-game summaries (including team and individual statistics) from week one through the Pro Bowl. Also provided are player participation lists, trades, and complete National Football League (NFL) statistics.

Other sections of the book include a preview of the 1996 season with team-by-team schedules, rosters, directories, and the college draft; and a variety of historical statistics, some going back as far as 1920, such as year-by-year final standings, statistics leaders, a Hall of Fame list, NFL records, and a variety of team-by-team information. The book will appeal to a limited audience, but will serve as a useful reference tool, its datedness notwithstanding.—**Andrew G. Torok**

656. *The Sporting News* **Pro Football Register.** 1996 ed. Mark Bonavita and Sean Stewart, eds. St. Louis, Mo., Sporting News Publishing, 1996. 500p. $14.95pa. ISBN 0-89204-554-X.

This book promises to discuss "the NFL from A to Z" and delivers on the promise in terms of statistical information. With only the briefest of explanations (one page) of how it works, the book jumps right into the list of players, arranged alphabetically by last name. The first, larger section is "Veteran Players," in other words, those players already in the league who were expected to return for the 1996 season. The middle section is "1996 Draft Picks," which gives the college records of those players selected by National Football League teams this past year. Finally, the last section has a list of NFL head coaches and their records, capped with a two-page tribute to Don Shula, the all-time most winning coach in the NFL who retired at the end of 1995. A list of 1995 league leaders (one page) is thrown in for good measure.

While not as comprehensive in scope as some works, the information is presented clearly and sensibly. Interestingly, some players' team affiliation is not listed next to their name, which reflects their uncertain state (e.g., they have been released by their team, but there is a chance they will be picked up by someone else). One cannot help but wonder when this information will be replaced by electronic versions on the Internet. Currently, sites such as www.nfl.com have only the current year's statistical information, which a book such as this cannot hope to reproduce (newspapers do that). Still, its format and compactness make this work easily used by those less-wired among us. The book is recommended for public, and other sports-minded, libraries.—**Bob Craigmile**

HOCKEY

657. *The Sporting News* **Hockey Guide.** 1996-97 ed. Craig Carter, ed. St. Louis, Mo., Sporting News Publishing, 1996. 348p. index. $14.95pa. ISBN 0-89204-557-4.

658. *The Sporting News* **Hockey Register.** 1996-97 ed. Mark Bonavita and Sean Stewart, eds. St. Louis, Mo., Sporting News Publishing, 1996. 416p. $14.95pa. ISBN 0-89204-567-1.

The bibliographic information given above can almost serve by itself as a review of these books. Sporting News Publishing is probably the oldest and largest publisher of sports data books and has a solid reputation for accuracy and objectivity. These annuals have now been running for a number of years; their contents and format have thus been well tested—and approved—by the audience they seek. Also, given the number of pages, their price is right. One may then, quite rightfully, call these two compendiums standards in their field. They are indeed, to quote their own claim, "accurate, detailed, convenient." Whether they are also, to quote a further claim, "absolutely essential for anyone who loves hockey" is more doubtful. The sheer mass of information presented will certainly be manna for the zealous fans, but probably daunting for others.

One may guess that the library or person who wants one publication will want the other, too. If not, here is the difference between them. The *Register* is a record for each player now on the roster of a National Hockey League team: age, weight, birthplace, statistics, awards, trades, injuries, plus—a most useful item—the pronunciation of his name. The *Guide* is a team-by-team account covering rosters; schedules for the 1996-1997 season; a review of the 1995-1996 season; and a "memory lane" section giving main features, such as final standings and play-off results, for each year of each team's history. Remembering those millions of kids who collect hockey cards religiously and their millions of parents who pack the arenas and watch the broadcasts, it would seem to be a good bet for most larger public libraries to acquire these two books; many school libraries will want to as well.—**Samuel Rothstein**

MARTIAL ARTS

659. Tuttle Dictionary of the Martial Arts of Korea, China, & Japan. Sun-Jin Kim and others, comps. Boston, Charles E. Tuttle, 1995. 318p. $12.95pa. ISBN 0-8048-2016-3.

U.S. martial artists who were active in the 1950s respect Charles E. Tuttle as the publisher of such seminal and elegant texts as Hidetaka Nishiyama's and Richard C. Brown's *Karate* (1959). The present work does not rise to that level. There is no substantial, scholarly introduction to document what pertinent academic qualifications the authors may have or to reveal anything of their methodology. It is difficult to know who might want this book, certainly not the "traditional purists and eclectic practitioners" mentioned on the back cover. Most martial artists practice a particular style, and most style manuals include a glossary of approved terms. This dictionary, in a single alphabet with very brief definitions, lacks the essential authority of any major martial arts organization.

While much is included in the *Tuttle Dictionary*, much is also missed. Neither Bruce Lee (Lee Jun-Fan) nor his style, Jeet Kune-Do, is listed, although he began and ended his martial arts career in China. The well-known style Wing Chun and its paramount practitioner, Yip Man, are listed as Wihng Chuen and Yihp Mahn respectively, rather than in the forms more familiar to Westerners. This awkward practice is continued throughout. Birth and death dates are not given for individuals. The entry for Shotokan is partly wrong: It is a style, not an organization. Comprehensive collections of martial arts literature will need this dictionary, but it is not recommended for any other library.—**John Newman**

OLYMPICS

660. Chronicle of the Olympics 1896-1996. New York, DK Publishing, 1996. 312p. illus. index. $29.95. ISBN 0-7894-0608-X.

This fine pictorial history is the English edition of a German work published in 1995. The most attractive feature of the work is the 875 (until 1972, largely black-and-white) photographs, secured mostly from German sources. The 22 Summer Games actually held from Athens in 1896 to Barcelona in 1992 and the 17 Winter Games held from Chamonix in 1924 to Lillehammer in 1994 are each given approximately equal coverage on 4 pages, except the most recent Games merit 8-10 pages, with nearly 50 pictures each. The chapters, together with a six-page introductory chapter and a six-page preview to Atlanta in 1996, constitute a brief history of the modern Olympic Games. This initial part of the volume is thoroughly indexed on the last three pages of the volume.

Sports records cover 97 pages, arranged by year and then sport/event with three columns for gold, silver, and bronze medal winners. The individual's name and country are given; for team events only the country is provided, which makes it impossible to compile a list of major medal winners over a period of years. At the beginning of each year, the top five countries and top five individual winners are listed.

The Complete Book of the Olympics (see ARBA 93, entry 841) has been the standard work in this subject area, but it is harder to use as it is arranged event-by-event. In *Chronicle of the Olympics*, one can piece together profiles of Olympic greats. Household names given good coverage for the Summer Games include Johnny Weissmuller, Jesse Owens, Wilma Rudolph, Mark Spitz, Nadia Comaneci, Carl Lewis, Florence Griffith-Joyner, Matt Biondi, and Vitali Sherbo. For the Winter Games, favorites include Sonja Henie, Dick Button, Eric Heiden, Jayne Torville and Christopher Dean, and Katarina Witt. This reference book—with coffee-table appeal—is highly recommended. [R: Choice, July/Aug 96, p. 1770; RBB, June 96, pp. 1765-66; SLJ, Aug 96, p. 185]—**William G. Wilson**

661. Historical Dictionary of the Modern Olympic Movement. John E. Findling and Kimberly D. Pelle, eds. Westport, Conn., Greenwood Press, 1996. 460p. illus. index. $79.50. ISBN 0-313-28477-6.

Findling and Pelle have edited another fine reference book, similar in arrangement and format to their *Historical Dictionary of World's Fairs and Expositions, 1851-1988* (see ARBA 91, entry 1336). The bulk of the text consists of capsule histories of 28 Summer Games (including the Intercalated Games in Athens in 1906) through Sydney in the year 2000; 20 Winter Games from 1924 to 1998 in Nagano, Japan (including those for 1940 and 1944, not held because of World War II); and short biographical sketches (each with a portrait photograph) of the 7 presidents of the International Olympic Committee (IOC). Among these, perhaps of greatest interest to a United States audience are Pierre de Coubertin, the French aristocrat who was the moving force behind modern Olympianism, and Avery Brundage from Illinois, who reigned from 1952 to 1972. The Olympic ideal was that the "Games should bring nations together, overcome national disputes, and serve as a symbol for peace" (p. 353).

Emphasized are the site selection process and the internal politics of the IOC. Themes that reappear and that can be traced through a detailed 16-page index are international politics; countries divided by war and the ensuing effect on forming Olympic teams; terrorism; racism; the shift from amateurism to professionalism; commercialism; excessive growth; the importance of television in building an audience of more than 2 billion people and in raising money to sustain what is an enormous enterprise; and the use of drugs. The chapters are by more than 50 scholars or journalists. Each entry ends with a bibliographic essay, which together total about 48 pages, plus a 14-page general bibliography, including CD-ROMs and online databases. There is frequent reference to archival collections. An interesting chapter discusses approximately 100 Olympic films, of which nearly $2/3$ are documentaries. Besides the portraits, there are 15 photographs.

This excellent reference book should be in most comprehensive collections, but in the circulating collection if funds are insufficient for two copies. For Olympic sport records, the definitive work is *The Complete Book of the Olympics* (see ARBA 93, entry 841). For a smoother narrative, see Allen Guttmann's *The Olympics: A History of the Modern Games* (University of Illinois Press, 1992). The dictionary is highly recommended. [R: RBB, 15 April 96, pp. 1460-61]—**William G. Wilson**

SKIING

662. **The Good Skiing Guide 1997: The Essential Guide to What's What and Where's Where in 500 Ski Resorts Across Five Continents.** Peter Hardy and Felice Eyston, eds. Woodstock, N.Y., Overlook Press, 1996. 591p. maps. index. $24.95pa. ISBN 0-87951-683-6.

More than 500 resorts are given in-depth treatment in this edition of the annual publication. New to this edition is the best information available on snowboarding. The guide covers North America, Europe, and, also new this year, Australia, New Zealand, South America, and Japan. There is a reference section in the back, providing such information as a snowboarding guide, safety tips, details of ski travel companies, and a resort index, among other things. An interesting introduction starts the guide with a discussion of the state of the ski industry internationally. Here also is a request for readers to write in about their ski vacation experiences at resorts not covered this year. Those submitting the most comprehensive reports will receive a complimentary copy of the next edition of *The Good Skiing Guide*. A "Resort Verdict" segment furnishes informational tables on the resorts covered, giving a good (check mark), bad ("X"), or satisfactory (blank) rating for various criteria.

The in-depth profiles come next, listed alphabetically by country or region, then alphabetically by resort. Austria is covered first, followed by France, Italy, Switzerland, North America, best of Europe, and best of the world. The individual entries give accounts of lift ticket prices; the quality of ski schools; accommodation locations and quality; details of runs (if they are suitable for children, beginners, experts, or anyone else); après-ski options; restaurants (both on and off the mountain); other activities aside from skiing; and much more. Each entry has a full-color map of the mountain(s), and tourist contact information is also given. "Round-up" sections complete each broad area segment, giving brief data on those resorts not covered in the larger entries.

While this is an informative and entertaining guide, there are a few caveats. This is a useful resource for people planning a ski vacation, but not necessarily for those who are merely looking for a day of skiing. The use of "lift queues," "fitness centre," and "acclimatisation" reflects the European slant of the guide. No eastern North American resorts are given larger profiles; resorts in Vermont receive only brief mention in the round-up section on North America. A mistake appears in the entry on Ski the Summit: Contrary to what the entry states, snowboarding is now allowed at Keystone. Also, the entry on Vail lists the lack of activities for nonskiers as a drawback, when in fact many nonskiers make Vail a vacation destination. Aside from these problems, *The Good Skiing Guide* is a good investment for most public libraries.—**Melissa Rae Root**

TRACK-ATHLETICS

663. Baldwin, David. **Track and Field Record Holders: Profiles of the Men and Women Who Set World, Olympic, and American Marks, 1946 Through 1995.** Jefferson, N.C., McFarland, 1996. 338p. index. $48.50. ISBN 0-7864-0249-0.

Because biographical information is not readily available on many track and field stars, especially international figures, even the rather sketchy information provided here concerning the nearly 700 men and women who have set records is invaluable. The focus is, of course, primarily on the person's track or field career and, in particular, on the record(s) he or she set. Equally valuable is the detailed step-by-step information that the text provides on the changing world, Olympic, and U.S. records since 1946 in 16 women's and 20 men's events. This includes, incidentally, information on the record prior to 1946.

The text is arranged by sport (e.g., 1500 meters), then by world, Olympic, and U.S. records, and, in each of those categories, chronologically. This format enables the reader to track progress in record changes and, at the same time, to learn about the individual who set the record. Biographical information about each individual is provided the first time that person is mentioned, with access via cross-references from later records and through a detailed index. Even though the data are already outdated (e.g., they do not include new records set in the 1996 Olympics), this is by far the best source of ready-reference information about the records in these popular sports. It is also the only source of information about many of the people who set the records.—**Norman D. Stevens**

664. Tricard, Louise Mead. **American Women's Track and Field: A History, 1895 Through 1980.** Jefferson, N.C., McFarland, 1996. 746p. illus. index. $75.00. ISBN 0-7864-0219-9.

What a perfect time for this title to be published—the year of the Olympic Games in Atlanta, Georgia, where U.S. women competed in track and field. Tricard presents 100 years of the history of women's track and field based on her meticulous research into primary source documents, newspapers, magazines, books, and scrapbooks of the women who made the history, in addition to personal interviews.

It all began in 1895 when the Vassar College Athletic Association held its first field day for U.S. women, which provided intense competition in five track and field events. They ignored all the athletic constraints placed upon females, and the event led other colleges across the country to offer women the opportunity to compete. In 1922, the United States selected 22 women to compete in the World's World Games in Paris, and when the team was triumphant, the organizer was criticized by women physical educators who sought to protect girls from the "evils" of competition. Because of this, women's track and field suffered. Women competed and won many gold medals, but had little encouragement or recognition. In 1962, when Wilma Rudolph triumphed in the Rome Olympics, a renewed support for women in U.S. track and field was sparked.

This history follows the significant setbacks and victories until 1980, when Title IX gave some rewards for athletic achievement in the sport shared with women. After 1980, there was an explosion of opportunity. The book presents a compendium of records and personality profiles by a woman who was a member of the 1959 Pan-American team. The five appendixes include halls of fame; Olympic gold medalists, 1928-1980; marathon winners; and chronologies of women's events. An excellent lengthy bibliography for each chapter and a detailed index conclude the volume. The work is authentic and a must for public and university libraries.—**Kathleen J. Voigt**

16 Sociology

ABORTION

665. Abortion Policies: A Global Review. Volume III: Oman to Zimbabwe. By the Department for Economic and Social Information and Policy Analysis, Population Division. New York, United Nations, 1995. 236p. $25.00pa. ISBN 92-1-151296-4. S/N E.95.XIII.24.

This volume completes the set of abortion policies in all member and nonmember states of the United Nations. In addition to covering the countries listed in the title, volume 3 covers 3 countries that gained independence following the publication of earlier volumes (Andorra, the Czech Republic, and Eritrea). As in the earlier volumes, there are three introductory chapters that provide background and definitions of terms used in the country profiles. The user would be well advised to spend the time reading these important chapters prior to examining the individual profiles. To illustrate: The profiles of some countries state that while abortion is allowed in order to preserve the physical health of the mother, it is not permitted in order to preserve the mother's mental health. However, in reading the introductory chapters, readers learn that some countries define physical health broadly enough to include mental health, and this is not always noted in the profiles. The user must keep this in mind while examining the tables.

Country profiles begin with background notes that give a brief history of abortion laws, the importance of religion in the formulation of abortion laws, and the current governmental concerns regarding abortion. In addition to covering in some specificity the grounds on which abortion is permitted, the profiles include additional legal requirements that must be observed to qualify for a lawful abortion; tables listing the fertility and mortality context (the government's policies on fertility control, the use of contraception, maternal mortality rate, and so forth); and statistics for induced abortion.

On the whole, the compilers have done an admirable job in organizing complex policies from each country in a succinct and consistent format. There are a few minor flaws, such as listing "The former Yugoslav Republic of Macedonia" in alphabetic order under "the"; however, these kinds of errors can be overlooked when considering the overall usefulness of the information provided. The appendixes include technical notes citing the sources for the statistics appearing in the volume and an extensive bibliography.
—**Michele Russo**

666. Costa, Marie. **Abortion: A Reference Handbook.** 2d ed. Santa Barbara, Calif., ABC-CLIO, 1996. 339p. index. (Contemporary World Issues). $39.50. ISBN 0-87436-827-8.

Abortion: A Reference Handbook begins with an introduction, an overview, and a chronology. It goes on to give biographical sketches of key people; court cases and their outcomes; annotated bibliographies of print and nonprint sources; and names, addresses, and telephone and fax numbers of organizations. Most listings are up-to-date, although some statistics and videos cluster a bit too heavily in the 1980s. There is a section called "Resources on the Internet," a glossary, and an index.

Costa, an author with a special understanding of the issue, strives to reflect all viewpoints. The book contains both basic information and specific sources for further study. Informative sections include the problem of violence and harassment at clinics, trends, access, techniques, complications and long-term impact, and a description of the pre-birth development of the fetus.

A comparison with the 1st edition (see ARBA 93, entry 851) shows the author has given careful thought to the revision of all aspects of the book, with material rearranged or retitled for clarity and the addition of 81 pages. Introductory material is much the same, but there are major changes and additions to the sections on statistics and court cases, the directory of organizations, the biographical sketches, and the bibliographies. This book will be useful to students, writers, leaders and program planners of organizations, and public officials. Despite the Contemporary World Issues series title, all information except a brief world overview pertains to the United States. Libraries should get the 2d edition even if they have the original.—**Edna M. Boardman**

AGING

667. **Encyclopedia of Gerontology: Age, Aging, and the Aged.** James E. Birren, ed. San Diego, Calif., Academic Press, 1996. 2v. illus. index. $300.00/set. ISBN 0-12-226860-1.

Today, persons over 65 years of age are emerging as the largest segment of developed societies. This massive age shift occurring in the population is affecting all institutions, from universities to corporations to hospitals. In addition, the growth of information about the processes of aging has been exponential in recent years. The study of gerontology, or the study of the aging process from the biological, mental, and social perspectives, helps to answer the multitude of questions being raised about the aging of individuals and societies. This encyclopedia was developed to assemble the expanding knowledge and make it easily accessible.

This work has been edited by the distinguished gerontologist Birren, associate director of the Center on Aging at the University of California, Los Angeles, and the former president of the Gerontological Society of America. An international editorial group of five distinguished scholars on gerontology decided the content and identified prospective writers for the input on the emerging topics within the scope of gerontology. Contributions by an impressive group of approximately 200 scholars from academia, medicine, and health-related agencies have been compiled for this encyclopedia. Articles cover broad discipline-related titles, such as "Demography" and "Pharmacology"; research topics, such as "Dementia" and "Creativity"; and areas of public interest and concern, such as "Abuse and Neglect of Elders" and "Ethics and Euthanasia."

Articles in the encyclopedia are arranged alphabetically by subject. Each article contains an outline, a glossary, cross-references, and a bibliography. A comprehensive index, a few appropriate illustrations, and many tables add to the overall excellence and usefulness of the work. This encyclopedia will prove an authoritative reference source for all libraries serving students or professionals in the many disciplines that bear upon gerontology. [R: RBB, 1 Dec 96, p. 682]—**Vera Gao**

668. Kausler, Donald H., and Barry C. Kausler. **The Graying of America: An Encyclopedia of Aging, Health, Mind, and Behavior.** Champaign, Ill., University of Illinois Press, 1996. 356p. index. $39.95. ISBN 0-252-02159-2.

The objective of the Kauslers' book is to present "the results of research on aging and health, mental and social functioning" in language that can be understood by the nonprofessional. The authors have done just that, effectively, accurately, and concisely summarizing research studies dealing with more than 300 topical areas in geriatrics and gerontology. Unfortunately, the topics represented are not always the ones that would be most relevant or most important to the lay reader. For example, "discourse memory," "constancies of perception," and "sequential method" would seem to be of little interest to the average reader who desires more information on aging. Topics such as home care, polypharmacy, and adult day care are absent. Rare diseases, such as Creutzfeldt-Jakob disease, Huntington's chorea, and Korsakoff syndrome are included, but the common disease osteoporosis is not. Almost 50 percent of the entries relate to psychology; 33 entries address various aspects of memory. The emphasis on psychology obviously speaks to the primary author's area of expertise. A comprehensive encyclopedia of aging for the general public would be a valuable resource. This book, unfortunately, is not it.—**Mary Ann Thompson**

669. **365 Ways...Retirees' Resource Guide for Productive Lifestyles.** Helen K. Kerschner and John E. Hansan, eds. Westport, Conn., Greenwood Press, 1996. 215p. index. $35.00. ISBN 0-313-30196-4.

The editors of this book have collected 365 ways retirees (or about-to-be retirees) can make their lifestyle more satisfying and rewarding through a variety of activities. In the introductory section, the editors state that "productive aging" is supported by thousands of retired persons through a 25-year study conducted by the National Institute of Mental Health. They feel that the older population in the United States is an opportunity, a solution, an asset, and a resource to be drawn upon in the future. The background section gives some excellent statistics on the aging population, including role models for productive involvement.

The book is divided into seven categories: education—teaching and learning, employment, fitness, leisure, political action and advocacy, travel and alternative tourism, and volunteering and service. There are two indexes, one of which is a resource index, an alphabetic list of organizations and programs. The second index is an A to Z keyword index that provides the reader with a list of entries related to a specific topic or activity (e.g., consumer education, environment, and so on). Each entry has the contact agency at the bottom. The title under review is not as comprehensive as books such as *The Second 50 Years* (Paragon House, 1992). However, it is an excellent addition to public libraries for circulating collections.—**Theresa Maggio**

DISABLED

670. **Encyclopedia of Disability and Rehabilitation.** Arthur E. Dell Orto and Robert P. Marinelli, eds. New York, Macmillan Library Reference/Simon & Schuster Macmillan, 1995. 820p. illus. index. $105.00. ISBN 0-02-897297-X.

Currently, estimates suggest that there are approximately 43 million Americans affected by some form of disability or undergoing some type of rehabilitation. This extremely impressive reference tool has been created to meet many of their diverse information needs, as well as the needs of their caregivers and families. Written in nontechnical language, this encyclopedia is the best available resource to assist the disabled in finding resources that enable them to regain some, if not all, of their former independent lifestyle.

The 159 essays in the volume are written by a wide variety of experts and vary from a couple of pages to more than 10 pages in length. The range of alphabetically arranged topics is striking. While the essays do examine a few narrow subjects, such as Alzheimer's disease, schizophrenia, and the Americans with Disabilities Act (1990), most of the essays address broad subjects of interest to the disabled. Readers will find worthwhile information on such diverse areas as civil rights, dance therapy, housing, and vocational evaluation. These essays, often including useful illustrations, provide easy-to-understand information; helpful bibliographic guidance to more specific literature in each field addressed; and, when available, addresses of organizations the disabled can turn to for further assistance with their particular concerns. *See* and *see also* references, along with a comprehensive index, make this large volume easy to use. A separate list of resources is provided, although telephone numbers for these organizations/societies are omitted.

This reference book is the standard for anyone looking for information concerning the rights of and treatments for the disabled. It will provide an invaluable starting point for readers searching for material on rehabilitation equipment and techniques, the disabled person's rights as a consumer and in the workplace, and the psychosocial adjustments the disabled encounter in U.S. society. [R: Choice, Sept 96, p. 96; RBB, June 96, pp. 1769-70]—**Jonathon Erlen**

671. **Living with Low Vision: A Resource Guide for People with Sight Loss.** Lexington, Mass., Resources for Rehabilitation, 1996. 288p. index. $43.95pa. ISBN 0-929718-14-3.

One of the fundamental needs of individuals with handicapping conditions is to identify the resources, organizations, and services that may help ensure their independence and quality of life. This guide identifies such resources for those living with low vision. It is arranged into 12 chapters: experiencing vision loss, laws, self-help groups, reading, working, high-tech aids, everyday living, services for elders, services for children and adolescents, services for veterans, services for people with vision loss, and special services and products (arranged by eye condition).

Each chapter begins with a concise overview of the topic and a discussion of some important issues, followed by briefly annotated directories of organizations and publications. Directory entries include addresses, telephone and fax numbers, and the cost of publications. The introductory chapter, "Experiencing Vision Loss," provides a short and useful capsule of vision loss, definitions of key terms, and descriptions of types of services and service providers. In addition, there are two appendixes. The first is a directory of state agencies serving visually impaired or blind individuals, while a second lists division offices of the Canadian National Institute for the Blind. An index to organizations is also provided. For the ease of use of low-vision readers, the entire book is done in large, 18-point, bold typeface.

Guides such as this one are invaluable to individuals and families trying to negotiate disabilities for the first time. Because of its multitude of resources and readable layout, this guide is recommended for both public and academic libraries.—**Stephen H. Aby**

672. **Resources for Elders with Disabilities.** 3d ed. Lexington, Mass., Resources for Rehabilitation, 1996. 336p. index. $48.95pa. ISBN 0-929718-16-X.

673. **Resources for People with Disabilities and Chronic Conditions.** 3d ed. Lexington, Mass., Resources for Rehabilitation, 1996. 288p. index. $49.95pa. ISBN 0-929718-17-8.

The 1990s has witnessed an explosion in publications, services, and devices intended to help both the elderly populace and those suffering from chronic health problems and major disabilities live as independent a lifestyle as possible. How to find these resources is a serious challenge for the interested public and reference librarians assisting those patrons. The two above volumes, compiled by the nonprofit organization Resources for Rehabilitation, are excellent reference tools to guide these individuals, their families, and health providers to useful resources. Both volumes are organized similarly and written at the appropriate level for the general public and the health professional.

The chapters contain the following types of information on the specific topic being covered: an overview, appropriate types of professional service providers, assistive devices, organizations in this specific area, bibliographic references for further reading, and tapes and publications. When available, addresses and telephone numbers are provided. The volume on resources for the elderly examines such diverse health concerns as vision and hearing loss, stroke, arthritis, diabetes, and osteoporosis. The guide for chronic conditions and disabilities presents services and products for low back pain, speech and hearing disorders, multiple sclerosis, epilepsy, sight loss, and spinal cord injuries.

Resources for Rehabilitation has made a significant contribution through these reference works. The volumes will be a major reference guide for both public and academic/health science libraries.

—**Jonathon Erlen**

FAMILY, MARRIAGE, AND DIVORCE

674. **Family Studies Database: 1970-December 1995.** [CD-ROM]. Baltimore, Md., National Information Services Corporation, 1995. Minimum system requirements: IBM or compatible 286 AT-class or greater. CD-ROM drive. 512K RAM. 2MB hard disk space. Color or monochrome monitor. $595.00/yr.

This unique English-language database is a valuable resource containing a variety of nonevaluative research literature on the family and family-related subjects. At present, more than 135,000 bibliographic records and abstracts are included, with approximately 6,000 records added per year. Since 1990, citations have been gathered from books, journals, and magazines, but for the years 1970 through 1990, the database also includes an "idea bank" of works in progress, a human resource directory of family specialists, and a directory of family life research agencies. It is a shame that these features cannot be updated, because the information now on the product will not be very useful.

Family Studies Database (formerly *Family Resources*) can be searched in either English or Spanish. Other languages for the software are in development. This product has three different search levels, with a wide assortment of search operators. Users should read the screens carefully using the novice, advanced, or expert modes. There are many options available to refine searches, so instructions must be followed carefully to perform an effective search, no matter which interface is used. The search interfaces are not as easy to use as those found on SilverPlatter or H. W. Wilson products, but one can get excellent results using the detailed directions. The database thesaurus is helpful to inexperienced and experienced searchers alike. This easy-to-load product provides an excellent user's guide covering the many features, such as search levels and languages, that can be turned off or left on at the discretion of the librarian.

Although information on families and related topics can be found in a variety of databases, such as Expanded Academic Index and PsycLit, this CD-ROM provides comprehensive information in family social sciences on one compact disc. It is recommended for large public and academic libraries.

—**Diane J. Turner**

675. McCue, Margi Laird. **Domestic Violence: A Reference Handbook.** Santa Barbara, Calif., ABC-CLIO, 1995. 273p. (Contemporary World Issues). $39.50. ISBN 0-87436-762-X.

McCue, a consultant in services to victims of domestic violence, presents a starter reference for teachers, students, writers, and social service professionals. The book begins with a careful definition of the types of behavior commonly described as "domestic violence," most often but not exclusively effectuated by men against women. There is a succinct historical rundown—how women have endeavored to handle the problem themselves and what the responses have been. McCue looks at the role of the media in shaping public understanding and at efforts to deal with it through shelters and the law enforcement and legal systems.

There are historical and contemporary biographical sketches of persons who have affected the course of this issue and influenced its emergence as a mainstream topic. A solid bibliography of print and nonprint sources is provided, and each item has a paragraph-length annotation. A chronology of the issue from ca. 753 B.C.E. to 1995 C.E. and an index are also furnished.

As is the case with other volumes in the series, *Domestic Violence* was developed by a professional with broad knowledge and sensitivity, not by a researcher/packager who moves from topic to topic. However, despite the series' claim to cover world issues, almost all books in the series address their subject only as it exists in the United States. [R: BR, Sept/Oct 96, pp. 60-61; Choice, May 96, p. 1454; SLJ, May 96, pp. 140-42]—**Edna M. Boardman**

GAY AND LESBIAN STUDIES

676. Dawson, Jeff. **Gay & Lesbian Online.** Berkeley, Calif., Peachpit Press, 1996. 310p. illus. index. $15.95pa. ISBN 0-201-88453-4.

Amidst the plethora of printed subject-specific directories of the World Wide Web appears the first title oriented toward gays and lesbians. The author's stated intention to review only the most stable of sites addresses the print-publishers' difficulties in dealing with the ephemeral nature of the Internet. He appears to have succeeded, despite the inclusion of more volatile sites, such as personal homepages. In addition to the Web, discussion of the commercial online services as well as bulletin board systems is included (although the emphasis is clearly the Web).

The 75 chapters begin with a brief, well-written description of the most important sites pertinent to the topic at hand, followed by a more extensive, unannotated listing of Web pages and their URLs. The first chapter, "Search and Reference Tools," is unfortunately the weakest. Clearer explanations might have been provided to explain the differences among searchable Internet catalogs such as Yahoo!, robot-constructed Internet indexes such as Lycos (many of the currently popular search engines are not mentioned), and popular personal homepages in terms of their value as reference tools.

The goal here, however, is clearly entertainment as much as it is reference: Topics range from "AIDS and HIV" and "Law and Legal Issues" to "Cooking" and "Leather, S&M." With the aid of a detailed subject index, the author admirably covers a broad spectrum of gay interests to be found online.

—**Michael Weinberg**

677. **The Gay Almanac.** Compiled by the National Museum & Archive of Lesbian and Gay History. New York, Berkley, 1996. 525p. illus. index. $16.95pa. ISBN 0-425-15300-2.

As with most almanacs, one would expect to find here a combination of current and retrospective information. In this case, however, the information pertains to specific groups, and is tailored to a specific audience. The work is arranged into nine sections, covering such topics as history, biographies of notable individuals, quotations, a glossary, statistics, an overview of AIDS, a directory of lesbian and gay community centers, and a directory of lesbian and gay organizations and resources. The largest of these nine sections is devoted to overviews of lesbian and gay achievement in the areas of activism, art and design, business and industry, culture, education, film, television, video, health, homes and families, legal issues, literature, media, military, performing arts, politics, religion and spirituality, sex and sexuality, sport, and travel. Black-and-white photographs, as well as a topic index, complement the main text.

Comprehensive as it is, the work appears to be uneven only in one area: consistency of date coverage. Some information takes the reader through 1995, while other information—especially in awards sections—has a cutoff date of 1993 or 1994. In spite of this shortcoming, the almanac is recommended for all libraries as a viable source of information regarding the significance and contributions of the lesbian and gay cultures and individuals of the United States. [R: Choice, Dec 96, p. 589; LJ, 1 Sept 96, p. 168]

—**Edmund F. SantaVicca**

678. Gillon, Margaret. **Lesbians in Print: A Bibliography of 1,500 Books with Synopses.** Irvine, Calif., Bluestocking Books, 1995. 478p. index. $19.50pa. ISBN 1-887237-13-5.

Despite its subtitle, *Lesbians in Print* has 1,727 (not 1,500) numbered entries for books on lesbian-related themes and issues. Most have annotations, ranging from a brief paragraph to half a page, designed to help select books of interest. All types of books are included—fiction, poetry, drama, biography, autobiography, collections, reference and nonfiction books on a wide range of topics, and books for children and young adults. In the typical library, these books will be scattered throughout the collection and entered under many different subject headings, so this bibliography will be especially helpful in libraries without special gay or lesbian sections. The main listing is by title, supplemented by indexes for authors, broad subject and genre categories, and publishers, plus a list of bookstores.

There are quirks and flaws. The brief bibliographic citations include author, title, publisher, ISBN, and price, but omit date of publication. Initial articles are treated inconsistently. Titles beginning with the indefinite articles "A" and "An" are placed under these words, but the initial definite article "The" is moved to the ends of titles, and is therefore ignored in the arrangement. Titles are listed under broad headings in the subject/genre index. Under the headings "Autobiography" and "Biography," there is no indication of "subject" persons unless they are mentioned in the title, often not the case. When these problems are resolved in a new edition, *Lesbians in Print* will be even more useful. [R: Choice, Feb 96, p. 930]

—**James D. Anderson**

679. **The Lesbian Almanac.** Compiled by the National Museum & Archive of Lesbian and Gay History. New York, Berkley, 1996. 534p. illus. index. $16.95pa. ISBN 0-425-15301-0.

In the tradition of all good almanacs, this one is as fun to read as it is a useful reference source. While it is possible to object that the focus of the text is not purely lesbian—gay men are occasionally referenced—multiple focuses can be adduced. This comprehensive work uses statistics, linguistics, photography, business, humanities, arts, education, sports, medicine, and geography (among other lenses) to get at its subject. Some of the photographs—for example, those on pages 166 and 382—share the intensity and Americanism of National Archives materials or the Works Progress Administration's projects.

The first section is a timeline, and that is where most (but not all) of the gay man information is contained. Another section ("Don't I Know You From Somewhere?") is a delightful suite of one-page biographies of notable lesbians and "women who have, at some time in their lives, loved other women" (p. 37). This section ensures the scope is not focused entirely on women who would score a 6 ("one whose sexual experience and identification is exclusively homosexual" [p. 85]) on the Kinsey scale. Although there are addresses for lesbian organizations in business, health, community, and parenting, there were none listed in the states of Delaware, Kentucky, New Mexico, and Rhode Island, which made this reviewer wonder if there were indeed no lesbian organizations in those states or whether the local level might be more greatly focused on in a subsequent edition of this excellent almanac. Witty quotations are also included; for example, "Extreme heterosexuality is a perversion," spoken by Margaret Mead (p. 64). [R: Choice, Dec 96, p. 592; LJ, 1 Sept 96, p. 168]—**Judith M. Brugger**

680. McLeod, Donald W. **Lesbian and Gay Liberation in Canada: A Selected Annotated Chronology, 1964-1975.** Toronto, Homewood Books and ECW Press, 1996. 302p. illus. index. $30.00pa.(U.S.). ISBN 1-55022-273-2.

This informative and well-organized book is a year-by-year annotated chronology of the first 12 years of the organized Canadian gay liberation movement (1964-1975). The years of artistic, informational, legal, political, and social developments of, by, and relating to the Canadian homophile movement are amply documented in 12 different chapters, each of which is devoted to a single year and each of which is itself organized chronologically.

The annotations, generally one to five sentences, are models of conciseness and communicate considerable information about the significance of important dates. Information is made all the more accessible through excellent cross-referencing and a superior index. Texture and detail are augmented by the inclusion of a variety of illustrations and three appendixes—lists of gay and lesbian organizations, periodicals, and clubs/bars of the period. The author, an archivist for the Canadian Lesbian and Gay Archives, has created a uniquely important reference tool that will serve readers in every public or academic library.—**G. Douglas Meyers**

681. Ridinger, Robert B. Marks. **The Gay and Lesbian Movement: References and Resources.** New York, G. K. Hall/Simon & Schuster Macmillan, [1996]. 487p. index. (Reference Publications on American Social Movements). $40.00. ISBN 0-8161-7373-7.

This excellent annotated bibliography of research and critical sources on the history and development of the gay and lesbian movement belongs in every public and academic library. Its thoroughness in the field is unequaled, for it contains more than 1,900 individual entries, each clearly written and highly informative. The book is divided into three main sections, each of which opens with an essay summarizing the highlights of the period. Section 1, "Foundations and Philosophies, 1864-1939," contains 13 entries, emphasizing the German homosexual rights movement, particularly the work of Karl Ulrichs and Magnus Hirschfeld. Section 2, with 178 entries, traces the movement in the United States from its roots up to Stonewall (1924-1968), emphasizing the material on ONE, the Mattachine Society, and the Homophile Movement.

Section 3 accounts for the vast majority of the book, containing more than 1,600 entries on the period from 1969 to 1993, a time in which Gay Liberation, marches on Washington, AIDS, and the NAMES Project quilt all figure prominently. Most of part 3 is dedicated to annotations about gay and lesbian communities throughout the United States (e.g., New York City, Chicago, Los Angeles), and these are organized by region. A unique feature of this work is, indeed, its extensive use of both local and national gay presses to document the gay and lesbian movement.

A massive index keyed to the individual numbers given each annotation makes it easy to locate information. This is an exemplary reference work in the social sciences.—**G. Douglas Meyers**

PHILANTHROPY

Bibliography

682. McKenty, Elizabeth J., and Jean E. Johnson. **The Literature of the Nonprofit Sector: A Bibliography with Abstracts. Volume 7.** New York, Foundation Center, 1995. 140p. index. $45.00pa. ISBN 0-87954-649-2.

This work lists 1,005 bibliographic entries, 808 of which have abstracts. These are materials, both print and audiovisual, that have been collected by the foundation's five libraries, as well as selected literature from other sources. This is not a definitive bibliography of works on philanthropy. Inclusion in the directory is not an endorsement by the Foundation Center. There are 34 periodicals that are completely indexed, and another 37 are scanned for selected articles to be indexed and abstracted. The bibliography covers materials published mostly in 1994 and 1995, with a few items published in 1993.

The work is divided into five parts: philanthropy and the foundation world; the nonprofit sector; related and reference works; indexes, which include three separate indexes—by subject, by author, and by title; and foundation center services and publications. The first three parts are further subdivided into chapters discussing such things as philanthropy and philanthropists, foundations, corporate philanthropy, international philanthropy, nonprofit organizations, fund-raising, proposal development, tax and legal implications, voluntarism, and government funding. *The Literature of the Nonprofit Sector* will be useful for libraries that have a strong philanthropy collection.—**Robert L. Turner Jr.**

Directories

683. **AIDS Funding: A Guide to Giving by Foundations & Charitable Organizations.** 4th ed. C. Edward Murphy and James Baumgartner, eds. New York, Foundation Center, 1995. 206p. index. $75.00pa. ISBN 0-87954-647-6.

This useful guide provides copious information for agencies concerned with securing funds to support initiatives related to AIDS. An introductory section includes a brief overview of foundation and corporate support for AIDS/HIV funding, an essay describing the steps one should follow to pursue funding, a guide to researching foundations and grants from corporations, a guide to using *AIDS Funding*, and a glossary of terms useful in understanding the information contained in the major part of this guide. Also included in the introductory material is a bibliography of funding for AIDS/HIV, a list of publications and services of the Foundation Center, and a directory of networked libraries and collections that support information-seeking queries about grants and foundations.

The major body of the work is given over to profiling the many foundations and other sources for AIDS/HIV funding. The section is arranged alphabetically by state, then by foundation name or organization name. A typical entry includes: name, address, telephone and fax numbers, date of incorporation, donors, type of foundation, financial data, purpose and activities, fields of interest, types of support, limitations, publications, application information, officers and directors, number of staff, Employer Identification Number, and a list of recent grants awarded by that foundation. Multiple indexes—by donors, officers, and trustees; by geographic location; by types of support; by subject; and by grantmaking organization—provide access to needed information. *AIDS Funding* is recommended for collections of educational institutions and agencies providing health care and other AIDS support services as a comprehensive and easy-to-use guide to funding.—**Edmund F. SantaVicca**

684. Bauer, David G. **The Complete Grants Sourcebook for Higher Education.** 3d ed. Phoenix, Ariz., American Council on Education and Oryx Press, 1995. 340p. index. $85.00. ISBN 0-89774-821-2.

Higher education grantseekers often must search through several volumes and computer indexes in an attempt to find funding sources. Information is needed on foundation, corporate, and federal funding sources as well as on how to write a grant proposal. Bauer's 3d edition contains all this information in an easy-to use volume (see ARBA 87, entry 346, for a review of the 2d edition).

The first section of the sourcebook is entitled "How to Increase Your Grants Success." It provides practical insights into the grantseeking process and provides sample letters, forms, and worksheets that can be used by the grantseeker. However, much of this section is a summary of information presented in another of Bauer's works, *The How-to Grants Manual* (3d ed., Oryx Press, 1995).

The subsequent sections consist of three directories of funding sources: foundation, corporate, and federal. Foundation and corporate entries are listed alphabetically, while federal entries are listed by Catalog of Federal Domestic Assistance (CFDA) number. There are a total of 258 entries, which include address and in-depth information on the organization's program description, assistance types, eligibility, contact persons, financial profile, and sample grants. Indexes by subject, state, and name are provided to use with these sections.

Appendixes new to this edition are a list of Foundation Center Cooperative Collection locations and a list of additional resources for grantseekers. New indexes include federal listings by title and by CFDA number. Although information found in this work can be accessed by accumulating data from other sources such as *Catalog of Federal Domestic Assistance* (Government Printing Office, 1995) and *The Foundation Directory* (see ARBA 94, entries 890-891, and ARBA 91, entry 866), Bauer's work will be appreciated by faculty and higher education administrators because of the ease of finding all this information in one place. [R: Choice, June 96, p. 1608]—**Laura K. Blessing**

685. **Corporate 500: Directory of Corporate Philanthropy.** 13th ed. San Francisco, Calif., Datarex Corporation; distr., Detroit, Gale, 1995. 1511p. maps. index. $375.00pa. ISBN 0-916664-58-0. ISSN 0197-937X.

This edition covers 573 corporations with each entry including a graphic, Grants-at-a-Glance. Included in this graphic is a pie chart giving proportions of grants made to various areas, a generosity index, and a rating given for the probability of getting a grant in relation to the number of proposals received. The generosity index is a standardized scale of how generous companies are in relation to each other. Each entry includes the corporation name; address; contact person; business profile; eligibility; analysis (of how grants were made); the funding areas; various officers and boards; a contributions profile; the application process; and for many corporations, sample grants.

The introduction stresses that efforts have been made to provide correct and current material. It notes that for the third year, subscriptions to *Corporate 500* include access to the Datarex exclusive online service, Corporate Philanthropy Online. This reviewer thinks that this service is no longer available because Datarex went out of business, and Gale furnished the money for this last edition. This information was obtained by not locating Datarex in San Francisco at the number listed, and by contacting Gale in Detroit. This reviewer was unable to find out how the corporations were chosen. Earlier reviews of the directory had this information (see ARBA 92, entry 823, and ARBA 88, entry 841).

There are 9 indexes: 1) activities eligible—such as building funds, capital campaigns, conferences/ seminars, employee matching gifts, endowments, general support, matching/challenge grants, scholarships, renovations, and research; 2) corporate headquarters; 3) funding areas (e.g., arts and culture, civic affairs, community development); 4) geographic areas of giving—regions; 5) geographic areas of giving—states and cities; 6) grant recipients (sample grants); 7) grant recipients by state; 8) main subsidiaries (of the corporations); and 9) who's who in corporate philanthropy (an alphabetic listing of corporate officers, boards of directors, and foundation boards of directors).

The information is valuable and useful for development offices and community fund-raisers. Prospective purchasers should also investigate the *Annual Register of Grant Support* (see ARBA 94, entry 888, and ARBA 90, entry 802) and the *Corporate Giving Yellow Pages* (see ARBA 94, entry 162, and ARBA 86, entry 804).—**Lorna A. Wiggins**

686. **The Directory of Corporate and Foundation Givers 1996: A National Listing....** Katherine E. Jankowski, ed. Detroit, Taft Group/Gale, 1996. 2v. index. $235.00pa./set. ISBN 1-56995-008-3. ISSN 1054-108X.

This large two-volume set is intended for anyone in the business of grantseeking for nonprofit organizations. The 8,050 entries are arranged in alphabetic order. Each entry has the address and telephone number, name of contact person, corporate or giving officers, a financial summary of gifts, and a brief summary of contribution categories and recent grants awarded. Some entries include extensive application procedure descriptions and other things to know, but most entries do not have this extra information. Although the Standard Industrial Classification (SIC) major group label is given for an organization, the SIC code is not provided in the entry. This can be a frustrating omission, as many people conduct searches by SIC code.

Most people will need to use an index to search these volumes, and there are several from which to choose. There are indexes for the headquarters state, operation location, grant type, nonmonetary support type, recipient type, major products/industry, officers and directors, and recipients by state, followed by a master funder index. Within the recipient type index, there are five pages of givers' names (in small typeface) under the library heading, which is within the "Arts and Humanities" division, so it may be beneficial for librarians to take a look at this title. Each volume includes a preface, a user's guide, a nonprofit recipient categories list, a recipient organization types list, an abbreviations list, a glossary, and a list of the major products and industries categories.

The Taft Group has published two other companion works, which comprehensive collections will want to consider: *Corporate and Foundation Grants* (see ARBA 95, entry 861), and *Federal Support for Nonprofits* (see ARBA 95, entry 866). *Directory of Operating Grants* (see ARBA 94, entry 889) does not contain nearly as much information. Libraries watching their pennies may be happy with the standard *Foundation Directory* (15th ed.; see ARBA 94, entry 890) or cheaper print or Internet alternatives. The title under review is suitable for reference collections of academic and public libraries, as well as other organizations.—**Daniel K. Blewett**

687. **Directory of Research Grants 1996.** Phoenix, Ariz., Oryx Press, 1996. 1174p. index. $135.00pa. ISBN 0-89774-877-8.

This substantial and well-established guide to funding sources for research and research-related activities is now in its 21st annual edition. While the number of funding programs listed has not increased since it was last reviewed here (see ARBA 93, entry 873), the directory's organization and scope have remained the same, and it should continue to appeal especially to academic grantseekers with interests in the arts and humanities, the physical and social sciences, and medicine. The sponsoring organizations included, primarily in the United States and Canada, are federal and state government bodies, professional and other associations, private foundations, corporations, and universities.

The main directory section is an alphabetic listing of grant programs by their titles. Each entry describes the program's aims, restrictions, requirements, and deadlines; indicates its funding level; and provides the name and telephone number of a specific contact person or officer and the name and address of the sponsoring organization. Arrangement by grant title rather than sponsor means this latter information is repeated when a number of grant programs are offered by the same organization.

The introduction urges users of the directory to consult the publisher's GRANTS database, updated monthly, for any additional listings or changes. The introductory matter also includes a helpful guide to planning and writing a grant proposal, and the volume provides indexes to the sponsoring organizations and to those programs with specific geographic restrictions. A subject index groups the programs by discipline or area of study, using GRANTS database subject terms, and a grants by program type index groups them by purpose or type of activity funded. ("Basic Research" and "Fellowships" are the largest categories.) While there is some overlap in this work with other grants directories, especially the *Annual Register of Grant Support* (26th ed.; see ARBA 94, entry 888), which is both broader in scope and more expensive, the directory's particular value lies in its concentration on research-related programs available from academic, public, and private sources.—**Gregory M. Toth**

688. **Directory of Social Service Grants: A Reference Directory Listing Social Service....** Loxahatchee, Fla., Research Grant Guides, 1995. 164p. index. $58.50pa. ISBN 0-945078-11-0.

This directory, in its 1st edition, is designed to assist fund-raisers seeking grants for social service and related areas. It lists 903 foundations that award grants to nonprofit organizations in the areas of child welfare, disabled persons, the elderly, family services, food banks, homeless services, minorities, religious welfare, shelters, substance abuse, and women services. The directory provides traditional information, but its uniqueness is that it offers some information not available in the *Foundation Directory* (see ARBA 94, entry 890, and ARBA 91, entry 866); for example, the name and address of the organization, what agencies it services, what grants it awards, and the typical grant range. The *Directory of Social Service Grants*, instead, is a specialized directory that has three lengthy articles on social service funding, proposal writing, and tips on how to write competitive grant proposals.

The appendixes list detailed information on the Foundation Center and the Grantsmanship Center. Fund-raising library foundation reference collections located in various states and cities throughout the country are listed in an index with telephone numbers and addresses, giving users quick access to the closest foundation information center in their area. The subject index lists not only the title of the foundations in alphabetic order, but also an entry number for each of the categories listed above. The substance of the book is in the foundations directory, which is arranged geographically as most funding is restricted to the specific geographic area of the foundation itself. This is a handy guide, the price is right, and it provides a quick introduction to fund-raising through foundations in the social services. The directory would be useful in every public, academic, and special social services library.—**Gerald D. Moran**

689. Dumouchel, J. Robert. **Government Assistance Almanac 1996-97: The Guide to Federal Domestic Financial and Other Programs.** 10th ed. Detroit, Omnigraphics, 1996. 875p. index. $145.00. ISBN 0-7808-0051-6. ISSN 0883-8690.

This title was last reviewed in ARBA 93 (see entry 874). The new edition covers 1,392 federal domestic programs, 22 more than were in the *Government Assistance Almanac 1995-96*. During the last year, 86 programs were added and 64 deleted. Descriptions of the new programs are incorporated into the 10th edition, along with changes in programs that existed previously.

Based upon the December 1995 update of the General Services Administration's *Catalog of Federal Domestic Assistance*, this work lists all programs of federal agencies offering either financial or nonfinancial aid in the form of grants, loans, insurance, personal payments and benefits, subsidies, fellowships, scholarships, traineeships, technical information, advisory services, investigation of complaints, and sales and donation of property. Each entry indicates the type of assistance, its purposes, those eligible to apply, the level of funding, and the program headquarters.

Also included in this volume are a helpful introduction, funding summaries by agency, listings of field office contacts with more than 3,000 addresses and telephone numbers, an agency index, and a comprehensive master index. Anyone seeking federal domestic assistance will find this title practically as informative and reliable as the government catalog, but hardly as cumbersome and difficult to use. Only its higher price may deter libraries from purchasing this user-friendly work.—**Leonard Grundt**

690. **Environmental Grantmaking Foundations 1996.** 4th ed. Rochester, N.Y., Environmental Data Research Institute, 1996. 952p. index. $84.00pa. ISBN 0-9631943-3-X.

This directory is indeed, as it set out to be, an excellent guide to grantseekers, as well as a useful reference tool for grantmakers in environmental fields. At the price, it is a good buy for any organization or library whose clientele includes those considering environmental grant options. The directory includes 703 corporate, community, and individual foundations, the majority of which reside in the United States. Only 30 are found outside the United States, and of those, only 3 are located outside of North America. These foundations contribute around $425 million annually for environmental purposes.

Profiles of these foundations are arranged in alphabetic order, and all entries are selected from the Environmental Data Research Institute (EDRI). Detailed contact information is supplied with each entry, along with up to 12 added elements, such as financial data, issues and activities funded, funding analyses, sample grants, application processes, emphases, and limitations. This should provide users with all the necessary information they require for choosing the most appropriate agency. There are eight in-depth indexes that take up almost a third of the text, which makes for extensive cross-reference. There are also nine useful appendixes, one in particular that lists grant application deadlines. The only impediment to the directory's usefulness is that the indexes do not refer to page numbers, but only the profile heading, which leads to prolonged perusal.—**John T. Lloyd**

691. **Fund Raiser's Guide to Religious Philanthropy 1996.** 9th ed. Bernard Jankowski, ed. Detroit, Taft Group/Gale, 1995. 1208p. index. $155.00pa. ISBN 1-56995-021-0. ISSN 1042-0053.

This compilation of the 9th edition of the fundraiser's guide is clear, concise, and inclusive. More than half of the volume contains foundation profiles, and each of the more than 1,000 profiles is updated. This represents a 50 percent increase in the number of profiles from previous editions. Data such as this include the information on $58.9 billion, which represents 45 percent of the total charitable donations in the United States for 1994. Nearly all (97 percent) of the foundations profiled give more than 1 million dollars in each reporting period. The 10 top donors are featured. This new edition lists up to 20 grant recipients in each profile and up to 10 historical grants.

The indexes and appendix are what make this guide workable. Arranged by headquarters site, denominational preference, geographic preference, type of grant, type of recipient, officers or directors, recipients by location, master index to corporations, and a list of an additional 2,000 foundations, the volume provides significant data and thereby advice on grantseeking. Of particular value is the glossary, which will help the novice to become acquainted with terminology used in this type of fund-raising.

—**Linda L. Lam-Easton**

692. **Funding Sources for Community and Economic Development 1996: A Guide to Current Sources for Local Programs and Projects.** Phoenix, Ariz., Oryx Press, 1996. 854p. index. $55.00pa. ISBN 0-89774-952-9. ISSN 1080-6318.

Oryx Press has found yet another group to assist with a specialized funding guide. Approaching community development as projects to enrich or improve the lives of community residents, the compilers explain 1,922 supportive sources for "bricks and mortar" programs, social services, and selected research grants. Entries supplement and enlarge the listings for community development funding sources in the GRANTS database.

Grant program entries consume nearly 600 pages of the guide and define the program, title, grant purpose, restrictions, requirements, funding amount, application/renewal date, and sponsor information. The 160-page subject index, arranged alphabetically, uses as its source *The GRANTS Subject Authority Guide* (see ARBA 93, entry 637). Common sense, however, dictates that looking first under specific interests and then moving to general subjects will prove effective in locating appropriate information. Additional indexes provide entry by the program title under the sponsoring organization and by 26 program types under categories such as cultural outreach, materials/equipment acquisitions, scholarships, or training grants. The final index, by geographic location, lists sources by title and entry number under the United States and Canada. The United States is divided by individual states, but Canadian entries are merged into one list. In the main section a diamond next to the title indicates a grant program with geographic restrictions.

This title will prove useful in general reference as well as subject-specific collections. It will aid grantseekers and others interested in charitable programs geared to community development as defined by the compilers.—**Eleanor Ferrall**

693. **Grant Seekers Guide: Foundations That Support Social & Economic Justice.** 4th ed. James McGrath Morris and Laura Adler, eds. Wakefield, R.I., Moyer Bell, 1996. 611p. index. $39.95pa. ISBN 1-55921-138-5.

To focus on the grantmakers in the front of this book would leave untapped an exceedingly valuable resource: the appendixes. Appendix 1 gives "An Overview of the Nonprofit Sector," followed by "Planning for Fundraising," "Responsive Philanthropy," "The Foundation Center," and "Funding Exchange Member Funds." These appendixes lay groundwork that both experienced and inexperienced fundraisers can use in finding the correct sources and the most successful methods of approach. The editors are to be commended for including this valuable information.

This publication was originally conceived by members of the National Network of Grantmakers, whose interests lay in the areas of economic and social justice. The present editors have sought to continue this tradition and have produced a publication geared to the smaller, nonprofit organizations that may lack professional fundraisers. Some 70 new grantmaker listings appear in this 4th revised edition (see ARBA 90, entry 810, for a review of the 3d edition). Items listed for each grantmaker include name, address, and telephone and fax numbers; contact person; area of interest; financial data; application procedures; grant limitations; meeting times of the board of directors; and publications.

The selected bibliography lists recommendations by various grantseekers that are particularly useful for community-based social and economic justice initiatives. Much of this material can be found at the Foundation Center depository libraries listed in appendix 5. The volume concludes with an index of grantmakers by field of interest, by geographic preference, by size of grants, and by number of grants awarded. The final index is an alphabetic list of contact people.

Public and university libraries should hold this title. Its modest price also makes it available to individual agencies.—**Lorna A. Wiggins**

694. **Grants and Awards Available to American Writers 1996-97.** 19th ed. New York, PEN American Center, 1996. 230p. index. $13.00pa./individuals; $18.00pa./libraries and institutions. ISBN 0-934638-14-4.

Since 1969, the PEN American Center has attempted to gather together a comprehensive listing of domestic and foreign grants and awards that are available to United States and Canadian writers into a low-cost, single reference volume. The 19th biannual edition features 192 new listings, bringing the total number of grants and awards to more than 900. To be included, a grant or award must offer a cash stipend of $500 or more, publication of a manuscript, or production of a performance work. A few prizes with lesser cash prizes are discussed when the prize itself carries a special distinction or honor.

Entries are usually listed in alphabetic order by the name of the sponsoring organization; however, foreign entries are grouped under either "International" or their country rather than the award name. A typical listing offers a brief description of the award and its requirements. Full contact information is provided, as well as the entry deadline and any availability restrictions. Symbols representing broad categories are used to categorize the individual entries: fiction, poetry, drama, journalism, nonfiction, children's literature, multiple listings, writer's residences, and internal nominations. Indexes in the back of the volume group entries by category, sponsoring organization, and award name. A list of state arts councils is furnished in the appendix.—**Steven J. Schmidt**

695. **Grants on Disc.** [CD-ROM]. Detroit, Gale, 1995. Minimum system requirements: IBM or compatible 386SX. ISO 9660 CD-ROM player. DOS 3.3. Windows 3.1. 4MB RAM (8MB recommended). 2MB hard disk space. VGA monitor. Mouse. $695.00/single user; $895.00/2-8 users. ISBN 1-56995-182-9.

This service offers information on 30,000 recently awarded cash grants plus 90,000 other grants offered in the last year. It provides quick access via menu, hot key, or mouse to detailed information on grant recipients, including name and location, dollar amount of recent grants, recipient type, granters contact information—all of which can be viewed simultaneously in different windows. Searches can be done by keyword or Boolean searches combining terms, grant amount, recipient location (city or state), zip code, and recipient type. There are 9 major types with 215 subcategories, including funder location, funder zip code, and funder area code. Data can be selected for downloading to disk, exporting to any spreadsheet application, or printing out. Various reporting results can be designed by the user. Although the publisher says that a 386 PC is sufficient, this reviewer found that a Pentium provides the best service.

Grants on Disc provides users with various quick access points to information in this fast-paced world of funding support; however, there is not any advantage to using the disc as opposed to using a print version outside of the fact that there is keyword searching, which does expand the index capability of the source. The price is significant, but Gale provides the information world with access to major directories of people of wealth, corporations, and foundations. *Grants on Disc* is not an excellent value for libraries, but it is a good value for specialists.—**Gerald D. Moran**

696. **The International Foundation Directory 1996.** 7th ed. London, Europa; distr., Detroit, Gale, 1996. 817p. index. $190.00. ISBN 1-85743-017-4.

Revised and enlarged, this 7th edition provides information on more than 1,450 foundations, trusts, and similar nonprofit organizations in 104 countries. The introduction defines the term *foundation*, adding criteria for inclusion that examine charitable purposes; substantial, continuing capital assets; discretion in allocation of its funds; and international operation or impact. The threshold of size and assets may vary among countries. Europa chose to place emphasis on the significance of a foundation's international activities within the context of its total organized charitable picture.

Each entry is arranged under its country, and both title and country are in alphabetic order. Titles have English translations. The amount of information in each entry may vary, but listings generally include a brief description, activities, publications, finance, officials, an address, telex and fax numbers, and e-mail addresses. Introductory material lists the required international telephone code for each country and currencies and exchange rates, which would need verification at the time of usage. The select bibliography, dominated by titles in English, notes 50 sources for further study. The first of 2 indexes is to foundation name, both indigenous and in English translation; the second is by 11 main activity areas, including 1 devoted to foundation centers and coordinating bodies.

Following a tradition set in previous editions, Henry Vincent Hodson, former provost of the British Ditchley Foundation, again provides the scholarly introduction, tracing the history of foundations throughout the world. His overview of foundations in the 1990s covers international activities and cooperation, the emergence of the global community with attendant attention to disasters, environmental concerns, and political involvement. Containing the most current information on international foundations available, this title will be sought by students in international studies, by libraries, by social historians, by governmental units, and by grantseekers. Hodson's point is well taken when he emphasizes the importance of authoritative philanthropic information in a world that ever-increasingly moves toward a global community. This reference tool provides such material.—**Eleanor Ferrall**

697. **National Directory of Grantmaking Public Charities.** James E. Baumgartner, ed. New York, Foundation Center, 1995. 301p. index. $95.00pa. ISBN 0-87954-651-4.

Three years in compilation, this newest addition to the Foundation Center's (FC) grant directories explores a heretofore elusive field of funding. Its editor concentrates on nongovernmental public charities. By definition, he identifies a grantmaking public charity as a publicly supported nonprofit organization that has been classified as not a private foundation and not required to file a 990-PF tax return. Included in the coverage are medical research institutes. Public charities differ from other donors by their more restricted fields of interest, by their often narrowly defined geographic limitations, by their emphasis upon charitable activities in addition to grantmaking, and by their status as potential grantseekers as well as grantmakers.

The volume is organized alphabetically by organization name in a descriptive directory and 5 indexes: officers and trustees (in alphabetic order by name); geographic (by state); types of support (33 with *see* and *see also* listings); giving interest (almost 300 topics from the FC Grants Classification System); and the public charity name, including former names. Numbers used in the indexes refer to the fund's entry number. In addition to these multiple indexes, a well-defined glossary and how-to-do-it section leads the user to more effective exploration of the information.

The 801 entries in the descriptive directory list 456 community foundations, nearly half of which appear in no other FC publication. Entry completeness varies due to the availability of information, but entries may list up to 32 basic data elements, from fields of interest to limitations. The listing in each entry of selected grants affords the user an insight to the organization's actual grant practices. This well-begun exploration of public charities will expand with future editions. Its entries will prove useful to scholars, journalists, and researchers in the field of giving by nonprofits. The directory opens up a new field of possibilities for grantgivers and grantseekers.—**Eleanor Ferrall**

698. **National Guide to Funding for Children, Youth, & Families.** 3d ed. James E. Baumgartner and others, eds. New York, Foundation Center, 1995. 1095p. index. $145.00pa. ISBN 0-87954-603-4.

Grants reported in this 3d edition rose to 13,224, representing more than $900 million in awards. Listed are 3,272 grantmaking foundations and 137 direct corporate giving programs. New to this and all current Foundation Center directories is the use of a Grants Classification System (GCS) with its unified code of classification, expanded scope of terminology, and identification of international interests. Study of the introductory material is always recommended; this guide is no exception. Of special interest should be the analysis and evaluation of the grantees' needs, the grantors' interests, the glossary, and the bibliography of grant publications.

Grantees, covering 890 pages, are arranged by state, then alphabetically by name. A sequence number, used for indexing, is assigned to each entry. Thirty-four units comprise an entry, including directory information on the grant organization and its personnel, financial information, purpose and activities, interests, types of support, limitations, publications, and recent grants. The entry sections most affected and enhanced by the GCS are "Fields of Interest," which include all indexed subject terms rather than just primary areas of giving, and the general statement of funding priorities in the "Purpose and Activities" section. Indexes are to donors, officers, and trustees; geographic, which includes locations plus states of activity; to types of support with entry names in bold typeface that support national, international, or regional activity; to giving programs by subject (a list of subject headings used precedes this section); alphabetically to grants by subject; and to foundations and corporate giving programs.

Enhancements are always welcome, and the GCS is a valuable one. It is based on the National Taxonomy of Exempt Entities, a comprehensive coding scheme developed by the National Center for Charitable Statistics and adopted by the Internal Revenue Service. Public libraries, university libraries, and social workers and their organizations will find this edition highly useful.—**Eleanor Ferrall**

699. **National Guide to Funding for Community Development.** Elizabeth H. Rich and others, eds. New York, Foundation Center, 1996. 808p. index. $95.00pa. ISBN 0-87954-659-X.

Grantseekers looking for foundation, corporate, and other charitable support for community development will be grateful for this compilation, which can serve as a starting point in their research. This national guide includes 1,895 grantmaking foundations, 351 direct corporate giving programs, and 273 public charities that in 1994 awarded more than $11 billion in grants to nonprofit organizations. In its preparation, the editors drew information from the following Foundation Center collections to identify those grantmakers with a specific interest in community development: *The Foundation Directory* (see ARBA 94, entry 890, and ARBA 91, entry 866); *The Foundation Directory. Part 2* (see ARBA 94, entry 891); *The National Directory of Corporate Giving* (3d ed.; see ARBA 95, entry 196); *The Foundation Grants Index* (24th ed.; see ARBA 96, entry 883); and the *National Directory of Grantmaking Public Charities* (see entry 697).

The guide under review is arranged alphabetically by state and, within states, by foundation name. Each entry is numbered, and references in the various indexes are to this entry number. For each entry, complete information is given: name, address, telephone number, and name of contact person. This is followed by grantmaker type, financial information, purpose and activities, fields of interest, and types of support sections. An entry continues with an indication of limitations, publications, application information, Employer Identification Number (EIN), and recent grants that were awarded in 1994. Several indexes that help the user pinpoint specific data are the index to donors, officers, and trustees; the geographic index; the types of support index; the index to grantmaker by subject; the index to grants by subject; and the grantmaker name index. For those persons interested in any number of community development projects, such as annual campaigns, capital campaigns, building and renovation, conferences, consulting services, endowment funds, equipment, general/operating support, and scholarships, this useful directory provides an entryway to billions of dollars available in the form of grants.—**Sara R. Mack**

700. **Search for Security: Foundations in International Affairs.** Mary E. Lord and Bruce Seymore II, eds. Washington, D.C., ACCESS, 1996. 183p. index. $75.00pa. ISBN 1-878597-14-0.

Global economies, the global issues of the environment, peace, security—all of these impinge upon the internationalization of people's thinking. This 3d edition of *Search for Security* has identified 388 founders who are trying to deal with the great global transformations at the end of the twentieth century. Information on international affairs includes private foundations, government agencies, and corporate international giving grantmakers. ACCESS, a leader in information in the field of international affairs, is funded by the Fund for Peace, a nonprofit organization founded in 1966 and dedicated to international engagement.

Fundings for international development, the environment, and population that were not in previous editions of *Search for Security* are listed now (see ARBA 91, entry 772, for a review of a previous edition). The foundation entries supply information on active programs with guidelines and recent grant activity, including corporate and community grantmakers that only support the local community where the company operates. Even small grantmakers are noted with shortened entries. Information from the research of the Foundation Center is given and would be helpful to the grantseeker. Each foundation has a detailed listing of the name, the year of founding, the address, telephone and fax numbers, e-mail addresses, contact people, mailing addresses for grant applications, guidelines, types of grants that they support, assets, giving, the grant range, and a sample of grant awards. Also provided are details on application procedure. However, some entries are sparse.

An invaluable information tool in international peace issues and global transformational issues, the issues of peace, security, and international relations give this edition more stature. This is an excellent resource for all academic librarians whose institutions are interested in international affairs and sending faculty/students to world areas in need. *Search for Security* is a must-have resource for international nonprofit human services agencies.—**Gerald D. Moran**

Handbooks and Yearbooks

701. **The Awards Almanac 1996: An International Guide to Career, Research, and Education Funds.** Miranda H. Ferrara and Sandra Jaszczak, eds. Detroit, St. James Press, 1996. 899p. index. $105.00. ISBN 1-55862-331-0. ISSN 0084-2699.

This 3d edition directory for individuals covers scholarships and grants awarded in English-speaking countries in business industries, social services, arts and humanities, and graduate and postgraduate programs from nongovernmental sources. It profiles 2,500 awards offered by 1,500 organizations. The awards can be used for academic and scientific research, the purchase of equipment for research, project development, publication subvention, submission, residencies, creative artistic projects, training, fieldwork, career advancement courses and seminars, continuing or vocational education, postdoctoral scholarly work, graduate course work, master's thesis and doctoral dissertation research, travel, and exchange plans.

The awards are listed in alphabetic order by administering organization, and then by a single numbered sequence. Each entry furnishes the study level, the award type, the purpose of the award, and what topics or disciplines are covered. Indexes include the award index, the grant organizations index, the place of study index, and the special recipients awards index. Awards in particular categories are identified (e.g., African American awards, Asian American awards, association awards, disabled persons awards, employer awards, ethnic awards, female awards, fraternal awards, Hispanic awards, military awards) with the discipline.

This is a fine scholarship guide for the postbaccalaureate researcher who is looking for support for study, research, or pursuing licensure. It is similar to *Foundation Grants to Individuals* (see ARBA 96, entry 872) and Dan Cassidy's *Worldwide Graduate Scholarship Directory* (see ARBA 96, entry 334). *Peterson's Grants for Graduate Study* and *Peterson's Grants for Postdoctoral Study* (see ARBA 93, entries 374-375) are more comprehensive for graduates. The real advantage of this particular grants guide is that it provides a one-volume resource for scholars and professionals who would like to do research and are seeking assistance. The price tag is a little expensive; therefore, it would only be available in large public libraries and large career and academic libraries.—**Gerald D. Moran**

SEX STUDIES

702. Jones, Constance. **Sexual Harassment.** New York, Facts on File, 1996. 280p. index. (Library in a Book). $24.95. ISBN 0-8160-3273-4.

This latest volume in a series noted for comprehensive treatment of current topics focuses on sexual harassment in its many forms and environments. Included are a historical survey of the topic, a chronology of significant events, and concise biographies of noteworthy individuals.

An annotated bibliography of more than 100 pages comprises the major portion of this work. Formats and topics include bibliographies; handbooks and manuals; collections of essays; fiction; general information; legal information; sexual harassment in the workplace, book reviews, news articles; government incidents and perspectives; professional instances; military, scholarly, and professional journal articles; psychology; education; government documents; and audiovisual materials. The sum of these sources provides a more than sound introduction and adequate coverage of the topic.

Additional features of this volume include a directory of agencies and organizations, appendixes of primary source documents, and a full subject index. On the basis of scope of treatment, currency, and cost, this work is highly recommended for all libraries, with due consideration given to purchasing a second copy for staff and administrative use. [R: BR, Nov/Dec 96, p. 56]—**Edmund F. SantaVicca**

703. **Strength in Numbers: A Lesbian, Gay, and Bisexual Resource.** Christa Brelin, ed. Detroit, Visible Ink Press/Gale, 1996. 311p. index. $16.95pa. ISBN 0-7876-0881-5.

Information directories covering the wide variety of organizations within the homosexual and bisexual communities have most often taken the form of listings within local gay and lesbian newspapers or, at best, citywide publications such as Chicago's *Lesbian and Gay Pink Pages* or the District of Columbia's *The Other Pages*. While nationwide coverage has been available since the appearance of the first annual volume of *Gayellow Pages* (Gayellow Pages) in 1979 and its 1995 successor *The Gay & Lesbian Address Book* (see ARBA 96, entry 53), neither source received much critical evaluation as a reference tool. *Strength in Numbers* is the most comprehensive resource publication of this type aimed at the existing mass market, containing data on 1,000 distinctive people and groups of various purposes.

The volume opens with an essay by the director of the Bridge Project of the American Friends Service Committee, discussing the need for the creation and awareness of gay and lesbian community resources. Subject areas included are the arts and literature, community, family, health and HIV/AIDS, legal and political action, media action and archives, spirituality and religion, sports and recreation, workplace issues, and youth. Groups at the city, state, national, and international levels are reviewed, with each entry providing complete contact information (including fax numbers and e-mail addresses if available). The final part of each section covers electronic resources related to the topic, most often those organizations that have established homepages on the World Wide Web or discussion forums on Usenet.

Indexes provide access by country, state or province, and city. The basic listing is augmented by 22 sidebars interspersed throughout the text, covering a diverse sample of groups, individuals, and projects ranging from the Gay Games to veteran lesbian publisher Barbara Grier and the NAMES Quilt. One flaw is that the section of the geographic index on "Online Resources" (covering the World Wide Web, Usenet, bulletin boards, and such general services as PlanetOut) is not separately indicated in the table of contents and may be missed by many users without librarian assistance. The resource is recommended for reference collections in all libraries.—**Robert B. Marks Ridinger**

SOCIAL WELFARE AND SOCIAL WORK

704. **International Handbook on Social Work Education.** Thomas D. Watts, Doreen Elliott, and Nazneen S. Mayadas, eds. Westport, Conn., Greenwood Press, 1995. 453p. index. $99.50. ISBN 0-313-27915-2.

This volume's primary purpose is "to provide an overview of social work education around the world" (p. 1). While not covering every country, the essays in this collection do provide broad enough coverage of industrialized and developing countries to allow for useful comparative study of social work education. The editors hope that this may lead both to the inclusion of more international content in social work education and to a more global view of social problems.

The 24 chapters are arranged in 5 categories by geographic region: North and South America, Europe, Africa, the Middle East, and Asia and the Pacific. Most chapters focus on specific countries, although some focus on whole continents or regions. The essays typically cover the historical development of social work education in that country, as well as more recent practices in undergraduate education, graduate education, and accreditation. There is also some discussion of current issues and future trends. Each essay is supplemented by references for further reading. The final chapter, a comparative and international overview of social work education, defines what is meant by internationalism, reviews its history, discusses some model curricula, surveys the current content and scope of internationalized curricula, and makes recommendations for the future. There is a combined name/title/subject index for additional access to the essays.

The book's foreword, introduction, and concluding chapter argue convincingly for internationalizing social work education and for addressing social issues across national boundaries. However, the country chapters mostly review how social work education has developed in that particular country or region and how it is practiced. There is little attention to or systematic discussion of how this practice relates to the broader themes identified elsewhere. While all of the themes are important and usefully addressed, they are not well integrated across the chapters. Yet, the editors have identified important and timely issues in social work education and professional practice, and this volume should help advance that curricular agenda. The handbook is recommended for collections servicing undergraduate and graduate programs in social work. [R: Choice, May 96, p. 1450]—**Stephen H. Aby**

705. **International Thesaurus of Refugee Terminology.** 2d ed. Compiled by Jean Aitchison and the United Nations High Commissioner for Refugees. New York, United Nations, 1996. 560p. index. $80.00pa. ISBN 92-1-000052-8. S/N GV.E.96.0.3.

Intended for organizations and individuals involved in information indexing and retrieval in the field of refugee work, this new edition provides detailed coverage of the technical terms used by international agencies, administrators, and researchers. An introductory section outlines the purpose and history of the thesaurus and describes its structure and layout, including facet analysis, the technique chosen to determine the organization of subjects and subfields. A series of indexes follow, beginning with the "Systematic Display," which systematizes the nearly 2,300 preferred and 1,150 nonpreferred terms into a sequenced conceptual framework, encompassing refugee-specific concepts, associated subject fields, and geographic areas.

Entries contain scope notes and lists of nonpreferred and related terms. The "Alphabetical Display" provides the same information as the above listing but in a more easily accessible order. Notation codes refer back to the appropriate parts of the "Systematic Display." A key-word-in-context index provides another alphabetic listing of words making up the preferred terms of the thesaurus. Finally, French and Spanish indexes give equivalent terms and links to the earlier displays. Overall, this thesaurus is logically organized and easy to use once the reader becomes familiar with the notation scheme. It is recommended for university and research collections in law, international relations, political science, and social services.—**Jeff Wanser**

706. **The Jane Addams Papers: A Comprehensive Guide.** Mary Lynn McCree Bryan, Nancy Slote, and Maree de Angury, eds. Bloomington, Ind., Indiana University Press, 1996. 674p. index. $59.95pa. ISBN 0-253-21036-4.

Jane Addams was a notable turn-of-the-century social reformer involved in the settlement house movement, women's suffrage, and the peace movement. Because of her historical importance, an 82-reel microfilm collection of her papers (the JAPP Microfilm) was released by the Jane Addams Papers Project (JAPP) in 1985. The guide under review provides detailed indexing of her writings and correspondence, which comprise two parts of that collection.

Included here are six chapters of information and finding aids. Chapter 1 provides the table of contents from the microfilm edition of *The Jane Addams Papers*. This includes the detailed guide to Addams's documents, her clippings file, and Hull House Association Records. Chapter 2 is a genealogy of Addams's family. Chapter 3 discusses the sources of *The Jane Addams Papers*, including an alphabetic listing of various collections. Chapter 4, the "Writing Index," is an index to titles, sources, personal/proper names, and subjects found in the 1,000 texts comprising part of the microfilm set. Also furnished are two bibliographies of Addams's writings, one arranged chronologically and the other textually, with different versions of the same text grouped together. The extensive index to Addams's correspondence makes up chapter 5 and is accompanied by lists of relevant organizations, classmates, secretaries, and Hull House residents and workers. The final chapter is a chronological index to correspondence, although there are no accompanying indications of to whom the correspondence was sent or from whom it was received.

Collecting and microfilming Addams's papers was a monumental and important project, and this guide is indispensable in effectively using that set of materials. Libraries need not own the microfilm set for researchers to benefit by this guide. It is a valuable stand-alone resource for scholars researching Addams, Progressivism, women's suffrage, the peace movement, and the settlement house movement.—**Stephen H. Aby**

SUBSTANCE ABUSE

707. **Encyclopedia of Drugs and Alcohol.** Jerome H. Jaffe, ed. New York, Macmillan Library Reference/Simon & Schuster Macmillan, 1995. 4v. illus. index. $340.00/set. ISBN 0-02-897185-X.

Drug use and abuse continues to be a topic of major interest. Objective, current material on this subject is always in demand. This new encyclopedia offers comprehensive coverage of this broad field. Editor in chief and doctor Jaffe, an authority on addiction, has assembled a group of editors and contributors who are acknowledged scholars in their respective fields. Among them are Edward Sellers, Chris-Ellyn Johanson, Daniel X. Freedman, David E. Smith, and Andrew Weil.

The four-volume set is arranged alphabetically by subject. Entries vary in length from several paragraphs to several pages. Cross-references ease access to related material. All articles are signed, and most contain bibliographies. Black-and-white illustrations augment the articles. Subjects covered include specific drugs and drug classes (e.g., analgesic, cocaine); effects on the body (e.g., complications, cognition, diagnosis of drug abuse); legal and ethical issues (e.g., legal regulation of drugs and alcohol, policy alternatives); social and political issues (e.g., international drug supply systems; industry and workplace, drug use in); and articles on the history of drug and alcohol use, drug use in various countries, and addicted babies. Volume 4 of the set contains appendixes listing certified poison control centers, federal and state government drug resources, a state-by-state directory of treatment and prevention programs, information from the Bureau of Justice Statistics, a schedule of controlled substances, and a comprehensive index.

The depth and breadth of information in this encyclopedia make it an excellent starting point for research on drug-related topics. This source is easy to use and accessible to secondary school students and adults. The *Encyclopedia of Drugs and Alcohol* is an outstanding addition to academic, public, and health sciences collections. [R: RQ, Spring 96, pp. 408-09]—**Barbara M. Bibel**

YOUTH AND CHILD DEVELOPMENT

708. Broude, Gwen J. **Growing Up: A Cross-Cultural Encyclopedia.** Santa Barbara, Calif., ABC-CLIO, 1995. 376p. illus. index. (Encyclopedias of the Human Experience). $49.50. ISBN 0-87436-767-0.

Useful, well-written, multicultural reference works are necessary and overdue. The need for such works, however, has created a snazzy marketing niche too many publishers have rushed to exploit and too many librarians, anxious to fill the demand, have encouraged. This volume is an example of the rush to jump onto the multicultural bandwagon, and fails to live up to expectations.

This book is one volume in ABC-CLIO's Encyclopedias of the Human Experience series. The other titles thus far include *Marriage, Family, and Relationships* (see ARBA 96, entry 862); *Law and Politics* (see entry 490); *Human Environments* (see ARBA 96, entry 1797); *Ethnic Relations* (see ARBA 96, entry 389); and *Aggression and Conflict* (see ARBA 96, entry 835). Each is subtitled *A Cross-Cultural Encyclopedia*.

Growing Up has the frame but not the substance of an encyclopedia. It is more properly a collection of essays on selected sociological and anthropological topics ranging from "Abortion" to "Infants, carrying devices for," to "Parent's preferences for a boy or girl" and "Sex taboo, postpartum." The encyclopedic arrangement by subject, rather than by culture, requires constant flipping among maps and the culture group index and subject index to obtain information about a particular culture. *Growing Up* takes into account 98 cultures, not all of which are discussed in every entry. No explanation is given for the choice of these particular cultures, which include the Cubeo, Tarahumara, Ingalik, Pomo, Ainu, and Gusii. Each subject essay contains a short bibliography that users may find useful, and a few black-and-white photographs break up the print throughout the book.

Collections in child development, education, psychology, and social works will not find this a useful work. It is both too limited in its selection of subjects and cultures and too broad in treatment, evidence of which includes the continuously repeated phrases "across-cultures" and "in many cultures." If a user needs to compare play among North American Indian children with play behaviors of Australian aboriginal children, this work simply will not do.

These are interesting essays on various topics having to do with the human experience generally; collectively, they are not an encyclopedia, and not suitable for ready-reference. Given its subtitle, the book may already be owned by collections needing good cross-cultural materials, but they would have done better to wait until a publisher comes along with the patience and vision to create a truly useful reference work. This work is not recommended. [R: BR, Sept/Oct 96, pp. 57-58; Choice, May 96, p. 1446; SLJ, Aug 96, p. 167]—**Glynys R. Thomas**

709. Wagner, Hilory. **The New Parents Sourcebook: Information, Products, and Services for You and Your Baby.** New York, Citadel Press/Carol Publishing Group, 1996. 240p. $12.95pa. ISBN 0-8065-1794-8.

This sourcebook identifies products, services, organizations, and publications of interest to parents of infants. The 42 subjects include such things as adoption, clothing, midwives, baby shower ideas, and health. Product sections are composed of a list of appropriate catalogs. Each entry gives a description of the catalog. The content of the sections varies. Some subjects, such as health and hygiene, are comprehensive and cover publications, special products, and support and referral organizations. Other sections are less inclusive. For example, there are seven entries under adoption resources, and none of them are print sources. Single parenting and grandparents have a single entry each, and there are no entries for gay and lesbian parents. Short informational essays reprinted from other sources discuss such things as child development issues, safety information, and consumer recommendations.

The book is identical in format to *The Parents' Resource Almanac* (see ARBA 96, entry 901), but that title's scope is broader in that it includes information of interest not only to parents of newborns but also to those who have toddlers and preschool-age children. In addition, many more resources are covered. While the review title has some unique information, such as sources for unusual birth announcements, it cannot compare with the breadth of information in the almanac. [R: RBB, 1 Oct 96, p. 371]

—**Marlene M. Kuhl**

710. Walker, Bonnie L., comp. **Injury Prevention for Young Children: A Research Guide.** Westport, Conn., Greenwood Press, 1996. 182p. index. (Bibliographies and Indexes in Medical Studies, no.12). $69.50. ISBN 0-313-29686-3.

This book, a volume in Greenwood Press's Bibliographies and Indexes in Medical Studies series, reads like a catalog of parents' nightmares. The compiler of this title has also compiled *Injury Prevention for the Elderly* (see ARBA 96, entry 844). *Injury Prevention for Young Children* is a literature review for curriculum designers and others who train child caretakers. It lists books, magazine articles, curricula, and handbooks for use in developing child safety programs.

Primarily journal articles, materials compiled here are from familiar indexes such as Articles1st, Expanded Academic Index, Educational Resources Information Center (ERIC), and MEDLINE and are grouped in chapters defined by the most common causes of injury to children—including child abuse and firearms and motor vehicle, pedestrian, and riding toy accidents. The first chapter covers general injury prevention. Despite what its title may suggest, this is not a source for children's books and articles, such as *What to Do When Your Mom or Dad Says: Be Prepared* (Sebastopol Living Skills Press, 1982) or *Play It Safe* (Play It Safe, 1995).

The standard bibliography format includes 370 abstracts of materials published between approximately 1975 and 1995, numbered and cross-referenced in author and subject indexes. Entries are selective rather than exhaustive. A title index is sorely missed. Comprehensive education collections, especially those with an early childhood education and child care focus, should consider purchasing this book. [R: Choice, July/Aug, p. 1778]—**Glynys R. Thomas**

17 Statistics, Demography, and Urban Studies

DEMOGRAPHY

711. Cook, Kevin L. **Dubester's U.S. Census Bibliography with SuDocs Class Numbers and Indexes.** Englewood, Colo., Libraries Unlimited, 1996. 357p. index. $85.00. ISBN 1-56308-295-0.

In this volume, Cook has provided a value-added service to users of the original *Catalog of United States Census Publications 1790-1945* (Government Printing Office, 1950) by Henry J. Dubester. The original volume was prepared for the Library of Congress as an attempt to list comprehensively all materials issued by the Bureau of the Census and its predecessor organizations. Part 1 of Dubester's work contains numbered entries for the 1st through the 16th decennial censuses listed in separate sections that may include final reports, statistical atlases, abstracts, general reports, special or miscellaneous reports, and bulletins. Part 2 contains numbered entries for census publications that are other than decennial. Listings in both parts include the agency, full title, collation, annotation, and Library of Congress call number. An index provides subject access. The year 1945 was chosen as the cutoff date because the Census Bureau began to publish its annual *Catalog & Guide* in 1946. The Census Bureau has also published a cumulative *Catalog of Publications: 1946-1972.*

Cook's work reprints the text of Dubester's original catalog, and then adds useful supplemental entries and indexes. In his introduction, Cook states that his major objective is to make Dubester's work more usable. The scope of Cook's work is the same as the original work, to list U.S. census publications issued from 1790 through 1945, and it is based on Dubester's bibliography, not on the publications themselves. Whereas the original work is targeted to general users of census data and reference librarians, Cook's work is specifically targeted to librarians and users of census data in federal documents collections.

The most obvious omission in the original volume—the lack of Superintendent of Documents (SuDocs) classification numbers—is treated in Cook's section of supplemental entries. The entries, in order by Dubester's entry numbers, include the SuDocs number, the publication title, and notes. Cook omitted a few entries for which SuDocs numbers could not be found, and conversely, integrated a few entries for publications not covered separately in Dubester. Cook also added a title index, a series index, and an index by SuDocs number, all of which refer back to Dubester's entry numbers. Cook's thorough additions to the original Dubester catalog make it a much more useful tool for librarians and users of census data in federal documents collections for reference work and historical collection management purposes, and is therefore recommended. [R: Choice, Nov 96, p. 426]—**Jeanette C. Smith**

712. **County and City Extra, 1995: Annual Metro, City, and County Data Book.** 4th ed. Courtenay M. Slater and George E. Hall, eds. Lanham, Md., Bernan Press, 1995. 1027p. maps. $89.95. ISBN 0-89059-038-9. ISSN 1059-9096.

County and City Extra is an annually updated volume of useful statistical information arranged along state, county, and city boundaries as well as metropolitan areas and U.S. congressional districts. It is a detailed and well-organized collection of practical and relevant data, arranged mostly in logical tables. The volume also contains a number of maps that will help users identify regions and draw effective comparisons. As a reference work, this substantial and thorough volume will be of great value to economists, sociologists, political scientists, and demographers.

Among the many subjects covered in this valuable reference work are land areas and populations; various health and vital statistics; crime; education, income, and poverty data; the types and distribution of housing units; employment, manufacturing, agricultural, and trade statistics; the provision of public services and government finance; and election results. Because these data are provided not only for every state and county but also for every U.S. city with a population above 25,000, this reference work not only contains plentiful information but significantly enhances one's ability to compare and contrast regions and areas. The population tables even include population projections that could be used to infer future constraints or developments. These tables were created from newly released data, for the most part derived from the Census Bureau and other federal government sources, but including some data from other established sources. This is a reference work that will appeal to and serve many users.—**Timothy E. Sullivan**

713. Lavin, Michael R. **Understanding the Census: A Guide for Marketers, Planners, Grant Writers, and Other Data Users.** library ed. Kenmore, N.Y., Epoch Books; distr., Phoenix, Ariz., Oryx Press, 1996. 545p. maps. index. $59.95. ISBN 0-89774-995-2.

Any researcher familiar with Lavin's *Business Information: How to Find It, How to Use It* (2d ed.; see ARBA 93, entry 209) would come to this new work with high expectations, for the author is that felicitous combination, a librarian who can translate information into words and phrases easily understood and acted upon by the average human being. *Understanding the Census* does not disappoint. Once again, Lavin has taken a complex, daunting topic and rendered it approachable, understandable, and navigable.

The handbook is based on the premise that the decennial census of population and housing, the most extensive demographic survey in the United States, should be a vital source of information for decision-makers and researchers in business, government, the media, academia, and the nonprofit sector. (This is, as well, the target audience for the guide.) In order to help users approach "this massive storehouse of information," the book explains census concepts, methods, terminology and data sources; provides guidance for locating specific census data; and examines how easily figures are used and interpreted inappropriately or incorrectly.

The material is organized into five sections. Part 1 provides an overview of the 1990 census, how it is used, how it was conducted, and how its data are being processed. Part 2, "Understanding the Census," explains census terminology and includes an item-by-item discussion of the 1990 questionnaire. Part 3 describes all of the 1990 census publications (print and electronic) and how to most effectively use them, while part 4 addresses special topics, such as "Rules Affecting Metropolitan and Urbanized Areas." The concluding section of appendixes includes a 10-page list of subject-arranged titles for further reading. Supplementing the text are 160 figures and more than 350 sidebars of boxed tips, frequently asked questions and answers, and highlighted changes in the 1990 census. Although the index is generally sufficient, there are occasional lapses; for instance, there are separate entries for Native Americans and American Indians, with no cross-references and with different page listings. Well written and enhanced by the generous use of effective graphic elements, *Understanding the Census* is a bargain for those individuals and organizations seeking to master the intricacies of the 1990 census. [R: Choice, Nov 96, p. 432; RBB, 1 Sept 96, p. 172]—**G. Kim Dority**

STATISTICS

714. **An Atlas of U.S. Economy, Technology, and Growth: Recent History and Prospects.** Washington, D.C., NPA Data Services, 1996. 484p. maps. $225.00 spiralbound. ISBN 0-936555-26-2.

An Atlas of U.S. Economy, Technology, and Growth is a comprehensive atlas showing in some detail how the U.S. economy is structured. The emphasis is on local economic geography, and some 400 state and county maps show employment, households, and income structures within their geographic space. The maps also show the changing technology base of regional economies in terms of science and engineering education, research and development activities, and the geographic origins of patents in different product fields. In addition to a brief preface, there is a rather detailed introduction and user's guide that will assist the user in finding needed information. In general, the atlas covers the years 1970-1994, and there are several projections for the years up to 2005 and 2005-2015. All in all, this is a well-executed project that will be of essential assistance to all business schools and departments of economics, political science, urban development, and similar disciplines. All major public libraries also should have this volume.—**Bohdan S. Wynar**

715. **Compendium of Human Settlements Statistics 1995.** 5th ed. By the Department for Economic and Social Information and Policy Analysis, Statistics Division, and the United Nations Centre for Human Settlements (Habitat). New York, United Nations, 1995. 519p. $65.00pa. ISBN 92-1-161378-7. S/N E.95.XVII.11.

The United Nations is responsible for many compilations and publications. It has the advantage of worldwide contact and the intent to press for uniformity. This example is an attempt to provide uniform data for all nations and for all large urban areas. Most of the book consists of tabular data, explained in detail in the introduction. The tables are ordered by continent and within each continent, alphabetically by country. The population of each of the countries is divided by age, sex, trade and occupation, and other categories. Most of the material is also grouped by communities within each country. The concluding tables give estimates and projections for each five years from 1980 through 2015 for percentage of urban population, number of urban areas by size, and the population of each urban area more than 750,000.

The number of countries is 243; thus, many among them are not independent member nations but other areas, such as Hong Kong, Bermuda, and the Virgin Islands. Among the present metropolitan populations are some surprises; for example, Istanbul and Lima appear larger than London and Chicago. Partly this reflects the greater growth rate in underdeveloped countries, but it also reveals the many difficulties that always arise when comparing one urban area to another. The compendium is useful as a reference in any event, and should be of use to demographers for many purposes.—**Arthur R. Upgren**

716. Fleming, Michael C., and Joseph G. Nellis. **Instat: International Statistics Sources. Subject Guide to Sources of International Comparative Statistics.** New York, Routledge, 1995. 2v. index. $250.00/set. ISBN 0-415-08634-5.

This two-volume reference is known as *Instat*, an abbreviation for international statistics sources. Its primary purpose is to provide a comprehensive guide to sources of statistical data, with emphasis on the internationality of those sources, whether of public or private origin. Sources that are national in character, that is, those that are constrained to data for a single country, are not included here. After a few pages of introduction and explanations for many abbreviations and acronyms, the remainder of both volumes covers detailed information grouped by subject in alphabetic order. Thus, in volume 1, data sources for the subjects of "Accidents," "Agriculture," "Civil Aviation," and so on through "Income and Wealth" are listed, with "Industries" through "Welfare" treated similarly in the second volume. As an example, "Climate" forms one of the shorter entries. Its subjects include atmospheric pressure, humidity, precipitation, sunshine, and temperature, among others, with the units, territorial coverage, and source given for each subheading. Users will then be led to detailed information on the subjects of their choice. This set appears to be a useful addition to any reference collection that is international in its coverage.—**Arthur R. Upgren**

717. Mitchell, Susan. **The Official Guide to American Attitudes: Who Thinks What About the Issues That Shape Our Lives.** Ithaca, N.Y., New Strategist, 1996. 415p. index. $89.95. ISBN 0-885070-02-0.

Since 1972, the National Opinion Research Center at the University of Chicago has been conducting the General Social Survey (GSS) nearly every spring, asking a representative sample of noninstitutionalized, English-speaking persons ages 18 or older and living in the United States hundreds of questions. For many years, the data collected were only available in machine-readable form for use by social scientists and other academic researchers.

Written for market researchers and other nonspecialists, this book by a contributing editor at *American Demographics* magazine analyzes the responses to about 125 questions in the 1994 GSS that reflect attitudes toward the environment, race and immigration, religion, work and money, marriage and family, women's roles, personal outlook, sex and morality, and such public arena issues as gun control and sex education. In cases where the same questions have been asked repeatedly since as far back as 1974, changes in attitude are noted. Mitchell's brief essays are accompanied by nearly 200 tables (1 to a page) that present the questions asked and report the percentage responding in various categories broken down by sex, race (only black or white), age, and education, but do not show the actual number of respondents. Data for no more than three different years are supplied for each question.

The GSS is now being conducted every two years. Selected data from the 1996 survey will be analyzed in the next edition of this book, tentatively scheduled for 1998. This volume, with its large typeface and abundant white space, is attractive in addition to being useful and informative, but the price seems a bit too high given its limited content. An older work that contains complete data on more than 300 GSS questions but lacks any analyses is *An American Portrait—Opinions and Behavior, 1972-1989* (see ARBA 92, entry 79). [R: BL, July 96, p. 1846]—**Leonard Grundt**

718. **Statistical Handbook on Adolescents in America.** Bruce A. Chadwick and Tim B. Heaton, eds. Phoenix, Ariz., Oryx Press, 1996. 323p. index. $54.50. ISBN 0-89774-922-7.

This text offers a comprehensive presentation of U.S. adolescents from 12 to 21 years of age. Numerous tables and charts identify findings from several resources covering such topics as adolescents' family contexts, sexual behavioral patterns, health, education, recreation, deviance, and parent-child relationships. The challenges, opportunities, and problems facing adolescents today are highlighted also. The authors describe today's adolescents as both "showing promise" and as "a generation out of control." The future for adolescents is described as both bright and foreboding. Although findings are summarized in narrative form in each section, no conclusions or recommendations are offered. True to its title, the book is a thorough compilation of statistics regarding U.S. adolescents. It serves as an updated source of information and is highly recommended for students and others studying or working with youth.—**Maria O'Neil McMahon**

719. **Trends in Europe and North America 1995: The Statistical Yearbook of the Economic Commission for Europe.** By the Economic Commission for Europe. New York, United Nations, 1995. 137p. maps. $35.00pa. ISBN 92-1-116626-8. S/N E.95.II.E.13.

This slender volume serves as a statistical overview of the 53 countries of Europe plus the United States and Canada. Europe is broadly defined here and includes such far-flung states as Israel, Kyrgyzstan, Cyprus, and Russia. Included also are newer countries such as Bosnia-Herzegovina and the Czech and Slovak Republics. This is the first work produced by one of the United Nations's regional commissions and is the 1st edition of this particular source.

The information is divided into two parts. The first half of the book is a country-by-country statistical profile. Each profile includes such basic data as population; per capital gross national product (GNP); land area; life expectancy, infant mortality; main trading partners; and a six-year perspective on gross domestic product (GDP), change in GDP, exports, imports, exchange rates, and unemployment rates. Charts depict infant mortality, the consumer price index, and the real GDP.

The second half of the book consists of a subject breakdown with country comparisons. The 11 chapters in this section focus on such areas as population, education, health, housing, transportation, crime, and the environment. Each chapter begins with a one-page summary and highlights feature, which is followed by one page of basic comparative data. Specialized tables follow, concentrating on various issue areas (e.g., trends in births outside marriage, long-term unemployment, or percentage of the labor force that is unionized).

The information is well presented in a variety of formats (tables, graphs, charts), is uncluttered, and is easy to read. The country profiles provide data that can be found more up-to-date in a number of other sources, including *The World Factbook* (see entry 80); *The World Almanac and Book of Facts* (see ARBA 96, entry 7; ARBA 95, entries 6-7; and ARBA 90, entry 3); and the more expensive *The Europa World Year Book* (see ARBA 94, entry 82, and ARBA 90, entry 91). Libraries already owning *The World Factbook* and *The Europa World Year Book* will not need to acquire this publication although it supplements them well.—**Gerald L. Gill**

720. **Women and Men in Europe and North America 1995.** New York, United Nations, 1995. 86p. $28.00pa. ISBN 92-1-100698-8. S/N GV.E.95.0.12.

Women and Men in Europe and North America is a collection of statistics on the relative situations of women and men. Its purpose is to shed light on gender inequality. The work is a coproduction of the United Nations (UN) Economic Commission for Europe (ECE) and Statistics Sweden. Information on population, households, health, paid and unpaid work, income, education, crime, and decision-making is provided. ECE countries are covered (the ECE consists of Europe, the Europe/Asia fringe, Canada, and the United States). Of 55 ECE countries, 43 are profiled (all the countries that returned questionnaires). Missing ECE countries include Israel, Albania, and Bosnia-Herzegovina.

As is expected from a UN publication, the statistics and methodology are well documented and authoritative. Information is presented in easy-to-read bar graphs and source statistics appear in an appendix. The focus is more European than North American: Mexico is absent, and smaller nations such as Kyrgyzstan seem almost as well covered as the United States. Significant statistics such as age distribution are often missing for specific countries. This is partly a result of unavailable data, but the editors sometimes chose to limit coverage.

The book has no index. Subject categories in the table of contents are useful, but it can be difficult to locate information. For example, abortion statistics appear under "population and households" rather than "health and lifestyle." This book adds value to basic statistics by arranging them around a particular subject. Because of this, the book is accessible even to those unfamiliar with statistics. At the same time, it is authoritative and handy to more demanding researchers. The reference would be useful for almost any library—school, public, or academic—that covers the subject area of women's issues.—**Ken Feser**

721. **World Statistics Pocketbook.** By the Department for Economic and Social Information and Policy Analysis, Statistical Division. New York, United Nations, 1995. 221p. (World Statistics in Brief Series V, no.16). $10.00pa. ISBN 92-1-161376-0. S/N E.95.XVII.7.

Except for its awkward size ($3\frac{7}{8}$-by-$8\frac{3}{8}$-inch), lightweight paper binding, and variation in what is available for any given country, this compact volume is a source of considerable value to anyone who wishes "key statistical series for countries and regions of the world" (preface). By this statement, the editors mean that for United Nations (UN) member countries, economic and social indicators; environment data; and general descriptive information (geographic location, currency, population, surface area, population density, sex ratio, largest city, date of membership in the UN, major language) are listed from Afghanistan to Zimbabwe (a total of 205 single-page entries). Due to variations in availability of statistics, the listed items range from as few as 7 (the former Yugoslav republic of Macedonia) to more than 50 for major countries.

The economic entries (e.g., exchange rate, consumer price index, gross domestic product, labor forces in industry and agriculture, motor vehicles) have two dates, 1985 and 1994; entries under "Environment" (e.g., number of threatened species, forested area, energy consumption, precipitation) are for 1990-1991; and the section of "Social Indicators" (e.g., growth rate of population, age groups, educational enrollments, urban population, refugees, television receivers) covers 1990-1995. Other time frames vary, but the 1990s period covers most data.

The data in this reference are abstracted from a number of well-known publications produced by the UN, such as their *Statistical Yearbook* (see ARBA 95, entry 898); yearbooks on demographics, industry, national accounts, international trade, energy, world population, finance, labor, tourism, food and agriculture; and reports on refugees, threatened species, and climate. The 21 titles are cited in a bibliography at the end of the text. Also included is a brief but useful set of "Technical Notes" defining entries and identifying the source of the data. For example, the *exchange rate* is "the amount of one currency required to purchase a fixed amount of another currency, as compiled by the International Monetary Fund," and the rate in the *Pocketbook* is taken from the *Monthly Bulletin of Statistics* (p. 208).

Searchers familiar with the breadth of information in UN publications may find this small volume a shortcut to answers on numerous statistical questions, from health to education and culture to finance, trade, and additional topics. Other users will never think to look at the *Pocketbook*—assuming that its size has not doomed it to being lost behind standard reference texts. On the other hand, the physical size is offset by its minimal cost and comprehensive coverage of basic statistical data on most countries of the world.

—**Laurel Grotzinger**

URBAN STUDIES

722. **The Challenge of Urbanization: The World's Large Cities.** By the Department for Economic and Social Information and Policy Analysis, Population Division. New York, United Nations, 1995. 290p. maps. $29.00pa. ISBN 92-1-151301-4. S/N E.96.XIII.4.

For 100 of the world's largest cities (or significant midsized urban areas in smaller countries), city problems and special city planning issues are discussed in this text. In a two- to four-page profile, a short history of each city is provided, followed by an overview—covering the last few decades—of the city's demographic characteristics; economic structure; and available social services and infrastructure (health, housing, water supply, sanitation, transportation). Each profile concludes with a discussion of planning issues, including the degree of success achieved by efforts to develop and modernize each urban area. This concluding two- to four-paragraph section of the profile is what distinguishes this source from other sources of general information on cities; yet, for some cities, this information is sparse or nonexistent.

Coverage ranges from modern cities, such as New York and Tokyo, to those that are in early stages of modern development, such as Maputo in Mozambique and Dar es Salaam in Tanzania. This book is strong in its comprehensive yet concise portrayal of the developmental status of cities throughout the world's hemispheres. The descriptions, which depict the interplay of historical and political factors and the social and economic status of each urban area, should be very instructional to researchers needing baseline information on any of the cities. The weakness of this 1995 volume is its lack of currency. For more than 20 percent of the city profiles, the most recent source cited has a publication date of 1991 or even earlier.—**Jan Bakker**

723. Moffat, Riley. **Population History of Western U.S. Cities and Towns, 1850-1990.** Lanham, Md., Scarecrow, 1996. 344p. $45.00. ISBN 0-8108-3033-7.

The title of this work tells it all. For the 19 states west of North Dakota and south to Texas, populations are listed for each community in each decennial census since 1850 or the particular year that the place came under U.S. control. The populations are also shown or a few intermediate and earlier years. As an example, the population of Tucson, Arizona, is given as 400 from the census of 1850, and as 405,390 from that of 1990. The author has compiled similar lists of topographic and population data for other places, although no direct or equivalent volume for the eastern, central, or southern United States is listed among his works. It appears that this is a convenient compilation of data taken from the U.S. Bureau of the Census, the Rand McNally Commercial Atlases and Marketing Guides, published annually, and a few other similar sources. Convenience of listing appears to be the primary, if not the only, attribute of the book.

—**Arthur R. Upgren**

724. **MSA Profile, 1996.** Washington, D.C., Woods & Poole Economics, 1995. 907p. index. $295.00pa.; $395.00pa. (with disk). ISSN 1043-8629.

Metropolitan Statistical Areas (MSA) are geographic units defined by the Office of Management and Budget as integrated economic and social areas consisting of recognized large population centers and adjoining townships or counties with a population of at least 50,000. Those with populations of 1 million or more are identified as Primary Metropolitan Statistical Areas. The advantage of using these units for research purposes is that they are measured by the federal government using consistent standards that are continually updated as shifts in population and social conditions occur over time.

Published annually, the *MSA Profile, 1996* is an essential reference tool that takes full advantage of the current statistical data gleaned from MSAs and uses these units as the basis for producing projected regional economic outcomes to the year 2020 for all established MSAs in the United States. Chapter 1 provides a broad but detailed descriptive overview of 1996 projections and emerging trends in regional demographics, immigration, employment, economic growth, and related subjects. The second chapter describes the methodologies used in gathering and formulating the projected regional economic data. This is followed by a series of appendixes listing the MSAs and related geographic units. The statistical tables begin with state and MSA rankings of residential population, employment, demographic, and comparative data tables.

The remainder of the volume consists of statistical tables providing historical, current, and projected data on total population, employment, earnings, personal and household income, and retail sales for all MSAs. The statistics are consistently presented from one table to the next for easy comparison among metropolitan areas. Data prior to 1995 are obtained from Bureau of the Census records. Data from 1995 to 2020 are given in five-year increments and are formulated by the staff at Woods & Poole Economics using complex statistical methodologies.

The density of data contained in this work is enormous, and it is difficult to conduct detailed comparative analysis using the print volume. However, the product is available on CD-ROM or disk files without the text of the introductory chapters. Statistics can be downloaded into spreadsheet software programs such as Lotus 1-2-3 or Microsoft Excel. The disk files are available in both PC and Macintosh formats. Although this is a very specialized reference tool, it contains an abundance of information. Researchers in urban planning, marketing, and economics, as well as spatial, human, and economic geography, will find that the depth of presentation and the well-formulated regional economic projections make this an indispensable tool for helping to understand regional economic growth and future trends in population growth, income distribution, and employment patterns.—**Robert V. Labaree**

18 Women's Studies

BIBLIOGRAPHY

725. Azikiwe, Uche, comp. **Women in Nigeria: An Annotated Bibliography.** Westport, Conn., Greenwood Press, 1996. 144p. index. (African Special Bibliographic Series, no.20). $59.95. ISBN 0-313-29960-9.

In the 20 years since the beginning of the United Nations (UN) Decade for Women, women's studies has become a respected academic discipline, and reference books on women's studies have become common. However, much of the research to date has focused on Western women. Azikiwe's annotated bibliography—only the second ever done on women in Nigeria—is a needed addition to the available resources.

Women in Nigeria includes 521 entries, about 90 percent of which have brief informative annotations. The types of publications covered are diverse: books; articles; theses and dissertations; published and unpublished conference papers; and institutional, governmental, and UN reports. As Azikiwe explains in the preface, materials were gathered from leading universities in Nigeria and surrounding countries. Perhaps because of this, many items that one might expect to find are not listed. For example, a quick comparison between this book and searches on "women and Nigeria" in Expanded Academic Index and Educational Resources Information Center (ERIC) showed less than a 5 percent overlap.

The high proportion of unpublished and limited-availability items makes this a particularly valuable resource for the advanced (or very serious) researcher, but also means that this bibliography cannot stand alone as a tool for the less committed scholar or student. In addition, it suffers from occasional typographic errors and a few incomplete citations. Therefore, this book is primarily suitable for purchase by large research libraries and serious scholars in the field. [R: Choice, Dec 96, p. 585]—**Susan Davis Herring**

726. Hannam, June, Ann Hughes, and Pauline Stafford, comps. **British Women's History: A Bibliographical Guide.** Manchester, England, Manchester University Press; distr., New York, St. Martin's Press, 1996. 150p. index. $79.95. ISBN 0-7190-4652-1.

British Women's History is a guide to selected English-language sources on the history of women in Great Britain and Ireland from 500 C.E. to the present time. The arrangement of the bibliography is under three broad time periods—"Medieval: circa 500-1500"; "Early Modern: circa 1500-1800"; and "Modern: 1800 to present"; with additional chapters entitled "General Surveys" and "Methodology." The entries are highly selective, often annotated, and include both books and journal literature. They are arranged alphabetically by author under the subtopics. An index to authors is provided, as well as a list of journal abbreviations.

This is not an easy bibliography to use. The method of selecting the sources to be included under a particular category is unclear and makes searching troublesome. The lack of a subject index increases the complexity of locating specific information on a topic. An excess of notations and the method of cross-referencing give the work a cluttered appearance and make reading difficult. Despite the fact that complete bibliographic information is provided for the journals, the same information is inconsistent for most of the books cited.

Although the compilers have stated that the bibliography is suitable for students and amateurs with an interest in women's history, only those researchers familiar with the work of selected authors in the field will find this resource less than frustrating. Despite its flaws, the bibliography does contain material that is valuable and often hard to locate. The title is pricey and is therefore recommended, with reservations, to academic libraries with large collections supporting programs in women's studies. [R: Choice, July/Aug 96, pp. 1773-74]—**Jane Jurgens**

727. Nordquist, Joan, comp. **Feminism and Postmodern Theory: A Bibliography.** Santa Cruz, Calif., Reference and Research Services, 1996. 60p. (Social Theory: A Bibliographic Series, no.41). $15.00pa. ISBN 0-937855-81-2.

Reference and Research Services, through its Social Theory: A Bibliographic Series, strives to provide information-seekers with alternatives to traditional fare for such topics as those discussed in the volume at hand. All works listed are in English and come from books, articles in books, and journal articles. Many of the publishers and journals are alternative, leftist, feminist, or small presses. This is in keeping with Reference and Research Services's pledge "to offer bibliographies that expand the range of perspectives for library users" (press release). It is only fitting that a volume on feminist theory and postmodern theory should provide access to the alternative press, as they have been much written-on in the past 20 or so years, but not always covered by the mainstream press.

A list of bibliographic sources and an introduction to feminism and postmodernism begin the work. The bibliography itself is divided into five sections: feminism and postmodernism in general; feminism and poststructuralism; feminism and deconstruction; feminism and postmodernism in specific disciplines (law, education, anthropology, geography, and literature); and feminism and Michel Foucault. Each section is further divided into lists of books and articles.

The one fault of this volume, and the series in general, is the flimsy paperback cover. With the abundance of ready-references available in this small volume (much of which is not available elsewhere), users will be sure to consult it frequently. The cover will scarcely last through such use. However, one of the aspects of the alternative press is its lack of corporate backing and sufficient funding. The importance of disseminating this information outweighs the drawback of its cover, and the subscription rate ($55 per year for 4 bibliographies) is certainly affordable.—**Melissa Rae Root**

728. Nordquist, Joan, comp. **Latinas in the United States: Social, Economic, and Political Aspects. A Bibliography.** Santa Cruz, Calif., Reference and Research Services, 1995. 80p. (Contemporary Social Issues: A Bibliographic Series, no.40). $15.00pa. ISBN 0-937855-78-2.

This title is number 40 in the Contemporary Social Issues bibliographic series compiled by Nordquist and shares features with previous titles. It includes books, pamphlets, dissertations, book chapters, government documents, and periodical articles culled from more than 35 standard, alternative, and subject-specific sources. It also focuses on English-language materials published for the most part within the past five years. Finally, it does not provide annotations or an index, but the title is broken down into numerous categories, subdivided by books and articles.

In this case, Nordquist arranges more than 950 citations into 20 categories, such as economics, health and medical care, sex roles, violence, lesbians, feminism, and religion. The first section lists general materials, materials pertaining to specific countries, and materials relating to immigrant and undocumented Latinas. The last category lists bibliographies and directories.

This title is generally useful for recent materials, despite a few omissions. For example, it includes the 1990 edition of *Unequal Sisters: A Multicultural Reader in U.S. Women's History* (Routledge) edited by Ellen DuBois and Vicki Ruiz, but not the 2d edition published in 1994. Also missing is Lillian Castillo-Speed's *The Chicana Studies Index* (see ARBA 94, entry 971), although some of her bibliographic articles are cited.

Another source that provides a significant number of entries on Latinas is Women of Color and Southern Women: A Bibliography of Social Science Research, a database maintained by the Center for Research on Women at the University of Memphis. The Center issues print supplements (see ARBA 94, entry 955) from the database, and the CD-ROM, *Women's Resources International*, includes it as well. Nordquist's title is reasonably priced and contributes to the Latina studies literature. It is recommended for Latin American, women's studies, or reference collections in academic and large public libraries.

—**Linda A. Krikos**

729. Nordquist, Joan, comp. **Women of Color: Feminist Theory. A Bibliography.** Santa Cruz, Calif., Reference and Research Services, 1995. 76p. (Social Theory: A Bibliographic Series, no.40). $15.00pa. ISBN 0-937855-79-0.

This bibliography, from the publishers of *The Left Index* (see entry 61), covers publications on feminist theory from the perspective of women of color, complementing a similar title also published this year: *Feminism and Postmodern Theory* (see entry 727). Part of the Social Theory: A Bibliographic Series collection, the volume remains consistent in format and content to its companion volumes. The series covers both important theorists, such as Jean-Paul Sartre and Julia Kristeva, and important theoretical movements, such as the title at hand. The publisher relies heavily on reviewing sources to make these publications known to the library world.

Identifying not only periodical sources but also edited books of essays, the stress lies on small presses and alternative viewpoints, providing a different route to tackle complex topics. Even a cursory examination yields an exciting assortment of titles. The structure of the bibliography is broken down into 16 parts, covering women of color feminist theory in general, women of color feminist literary theory, and women of color anthologies, and then these broad divisions by specific ethnic groups. Entries are alphabetic by author or main editor last name and are not annotated.

Although the number of entries equals 874, some titles are duplicated. For example, *Making Face, Making Soul=Haciendo Caras*, edited by Gloria Anzaldùa, is listed three separate times; in the "Women of Color—Feminist Theory," the "Women of Color and Feminist Literary Criticism," and the "Women of Color Anthologies" sections. A title index would be a helpful addition, not only to pinpoint such duplications as this but also to track down titles where authors are not known. However, this need seems to indicate a familiarity with the topic, and the true value of this bibliographic series is in its quick access to hundreds of titles for those who may know little or nothing of the topic the bibliography addresses. A must for academic libraries, public libraries should also provide this valuable service to their patrons, thereby giving them new or unique perspectives. One may not always agree with the political slant of some of the titles listed, but it is an important—if not necessary—service to provide the viewpoint to the public.
—**Melissa Rae Root**

730. Ogilvie, Marilyn Bailey, with Kerry Lynne Meek. **Women and Science: An Annotated Bibliography.** New York, Garland, 1996. 556p. index. (Garland Reference Library of Social Science, v.859). $95.00. ISBN 0-8153-0929-5.

Ogilvie's new bibliography is a significant contribution to a rapidly expanding field. Almost 2,700 entries are listed alphabetically by author. Each includes a bibliographic citation and any reprint information; most include a brief annotation; and each lists relevant categories (nationality, general time period covered, named individuals, scientific fields, type of reference, and general theme) that correspond to the six indexes.

As with any bibliography, this one is not comprehensive. Although Ogilvie states, "Both monographic and journal sources are included, covering all time periods, geographic locations, and languages" (p. x), the entries are primarily from English-language works, and the majority deal with either British or United States individuals. There are also notable gaps; for example, there is nothing on Grace Hopper, and Cynthia Gay Bindocci's 1993 *Women and Technology: An Annotated Bibliography* (see ARBA 94, entry 948) is not listed.

The six indexes are well intended, but the lack of any fine categorization makes their use difficult. The "Fields" index, for example, lists more than 500 entries under the broad category of medicine, and the finest breakdown under "Periods" is by century. Still, this is a significant reference for anyone interested in women in science, and it would be a valuable resource for any academic or larger public library.
—**Susan Davis Herring**

731. **Women in Christian History: A Bibliography.** Carolyn DeArmond Blevins, comp. and ed. Macon, Ga., Mercer University Press, 1995. 114p. index. $30.00. ISBN 0-86554-493-X.

"One of the distinctive features of Jesus' ministry was the involvement of women. Yet the traditional story of developing Christianity curiously omitted the roles and contributions of women"; this according to Blevins's preface. She states that her bibliography on Christian women will assist teachers in rectifying this problem. The work is contained in 114 pages, so researchers will find this volume easy to use.

Citations are divided by subject, then in alphabetic order by author. Subjects include historical periods, denominations, ethnic groups, and general reference, with most entries containing a sentence or two identifying the material. A name index is provided. Unfortunately, this index does not include all cited authors, which would have been helpful. Availability of materials is stated as the overriding criterion for inclusion; this curtails the addition of historical materials difficult to obtain. The majority of entries were written in this century, and thus historical perspective is limited.

A subtle bias seems to occur in Blevins's work. The material splits between historical works regarding Christian women and materials promoting the feminist agenda. Titles reviewed include *Jesus as Mother: Studies in the Spirituality of the High Middle Ages*, *The World of Witches*, and *Birth and Rebirth of Feminism: Responses of Church Women*. Similar titles are prevalent, yet one searches in vain to find a solid work identified as supporting the traditional role of women. Blevins's annotations range from the practical, such as "Good Documentation," to such comments as "Chronicles the significant ways women were involved in Christian ministry before Fundamentalism stifled their opportunities." Although this volume will have its uses, the researcher will need to look elsewhere to round out religious discussion on the role of women in the church.—**Brad R. Leach**

732. **Women Workers: An Annotated Bibliography, 1983-94.** Washington, D.C., International Labor Office, 1995. 290p. index. (International Labour Bibliography, no.14). $31.50pa. ISBN 92-2-109201-1.

Despite the fact that women are approximately 40 percent of the world's labor force, conventional models have been slow to recognize and appreciate the relative impact that women workers have had on economic and social developments. Consequently, a good deal of the scholarly analysis of the employment of women in paid labor has occurred only during the last decade or so. This useful reference book, which was published on the occasion of the Fourth World Conference on Women held in Beijing in September 1995, brings together a variety of diverse and useful articles on the labor force participation of women around the world. Moreover, because it lists works that have placed women within the appropriate cultural and economic context, users will be able to examine the lives of a variety of women in a variety of settings.

As a reference guide to women workers, this book outlines some 955 English-language articles, technical reports, working papers, and other documents published by the International Labour Office (ILO) between the years of 1983 and 1994. Entries are arranged by subject categories, including social and economic development, law and human rights, the humanities and the arts, education and training, rural development, trade, management, labor and employment, population, race relations, health and safety, environmental issues, and libraries and research methods. Users should be able to locate practical information by subject as well as by country and area. Another nice feature is that titles are listed in chronological order from the LABORDOC database of the ILO, and entries are cross-referenced with other entries. An author index, subject index, and title index are also included.—**Timothy E. Sullivan**

BIOGRAPHY

733. Baldwin, Louis. **Women of Strength: Biographies of 106....** Jefferson, N.C., McFarland, 1996. 242p. index. $28.50pa. ISBN 0-7864-0250-4.

Short, lively portraits of 106 women who have excelled in traditionally male fields comprise this book. Arranged chronologically by birth date, the work profiles such popular heroes as Amelia Earhart, Mother Teresa, Rosa Parks, Jane Goodall, and Wilma Mankiller. In addition, the author describes some less familiar figures, such as Rosalyn Yalow (the developer of radioimmunoassay), Violeta Chamorro (president of Nicaragua), Felice Schwartz (C.E.O. of Catalyst), and Sharon Matola (a zoologist). The concise, sometimes quirky, portraits provide background information on each character and describe their achievements. An index will help readers find information in specific subject areas or about particular persons.

This slim volume would have benefited from an occasional photograph or illustration, but its real problem is one of balance. The book spans recorded history around the world, but the bias is definitely toward contemporary women from the United States. Furthermore, the author focuses on the field of journalism and the media, while such fields as sports and the arts are only thinly represented. One may also question how the position of first lady fits into a traditionally male field or why blue-collar laborers and leaders were virtually excluded. These gaps detract from what might have been an enlightening collection. Because there are numerous alternatives for women of achievement biographies, many with only slightly different focuses (e.g., *Prominent Women of the 20th Century*, a four-volume set published by U*X*L/Gale [see entry 26], and *Amazing American Women*, a softcover book published by Libraries Unlimited in 1995), those with limited resources are advised to check carefully before making a purchase.—**Barbara Ittner**

734. **Contemporary Australian Women 1996/97.** Port Melbourne, Australia, Reed Reference Australia; distr., New Providence, N.J., Reed Reference Publishing, 1996. 306p. index. $39.95pa. ISBN 1-875589-92-9. ISSN 1326-1649.

By focusing on more than 2,000 Australian women from all walks of life, this compact volume tries to remedy the pathetically low number of women in its brother companion, *Contemporary Australians 1995/96* (Reed Reference). In a traditionally chauvinistic society, it is encouraging to find a work whose stated purpose is to make the business and academic communities, the public, and journalists aware of who the leading women are Down Under. The publishers succeeded in creating a solid reference book that is entertaining and informative and offers insight into human nature. The publishers started with a list of women and brief contact information, and gave them three chances to respond to the questionnaire. Nonrespondents received cursory treatment and have an asterisk by their names. Exciting to see is that Ann McGrath, one of this reviewer's former women's studies and aboriginal history professors at the University of New South Wales, Kensington, had responded and included her e-mail address.

Acutely aware that biographical reference works can be "too dry or reader-unfriendly," the publishers created a questionnaire soliciting personal as well as professional information. In addition to containing the standard contact information, career history, and honors, most listings describe the person's "most formative influences," "other public figures in the family," or "recreations/interests/passions." These categories enliven many listings. For example, an administrative assistant during the workweek, Nicole Boegman is the Australian record holder in the long jump and triple jump. Like many of her countrywomen, Boegman sees herself as a citizen of the world; her most formative influences include the German long jumper and Olympic world champion Heike Dreschler. It is no surprise that sports is a passion, but Boegman rounds out her interests with art, music, and fashion.

One of the most useful features in this work is an index by broad general categories. An improvement would be to add a notation for more specific subcategories: Christian, Jew, and Muslim for women in religion; swimming, hockey, and track and field for women in sports. While the publishers did an adequate job of representing current leaders, they should also include women to watch in these fields. This volume is an excellent choice for university and public libraries and special collections focusing on women, Australia, or the Pacific Rim.—**Susan D. Baird-Joshi**

DICTIONARIES AND ENCYCLOPEDIAS

735. Boles, Janet K., Diane Long Hoeveler, with Rebecca Bardwell. **Historical Dictionary of Feminism.** Lanham, Md., Scarecrow, 1996. 429p. (Historical Dictionaries of Religions, Philosophies, and Movements, no.6). $49.50. ISBN 0-8108-3042-6.

Boles and Hoeveler are coeditors of what they claim to be the "first dictionary of feminism written as a collaborative effort by faculty of one university" (p. ix). This dictionary, as with most of the productions of Scarecrow, includes much more than mere dictionary entries. The publication also contains a 21-page introduction that sketches a history of the various movements commonly grouped under the generic title "feminism," a 15-page chronology of major events ranging from the 1405 publication of Christine de Pizan's *The Book of the City of Women* to the 1995 United Nations's Fourth World Conference on Women; and an extensive 119-page bibliography that lists more than 1,000 sources grouped into some 27 content categories. Unfortunately, the 429-page volume does not include an index.

In the center of the volume are some 800 alphabetically arranged dictionary entries. The typical length of each entry is about 125 words. The entries provide an abundance of basic information on individuals, organizations, campaigns, court cases, and so on, that have had an impact on the history of feminism. The majority of the entries cover topics in American and British feminism, although no section of the world is neglected. High school and college students interested in the history of feminism will find this volume to be a useful addition to their libraries.—**Terry D. Bilhartz**

736. Cullen-DuPont, Kathryn. **The Encyclopedia of Women's History in America.** New York, Facts on File, 1996. 339p. index. $45.00. ISBN 0-8160-2625-4.

Cullen-DuPont (author of *Elizabeth Cady Stanton and Women's Liberty* [Facts on File, 1992]) has compiled this encyclopedia of women's history in the United States from Colonial times to the present. Apart from biographical entries, the encyclopedia includes synopses, explanations, and definitions of acts, court cases, organizations, movements, and places that have had, in the author's view, significant impact on U.S. women's lives. About 70 percent of the book is made up of entries (approximately 500 total). The last third of the volume consists of the full text of documents (such as the U.S. Constitution, *Roe v. Wade*, and passages from *Blackstone's Commentaries*); a bibliography; and a useful index.

Similar titles to the one under review include Handbook of American Women's History, edited by Angela Howard Zophy (see ARBA 91, entry 929), and Doris Weatherford's *American Women's History* (Prentice Hall General Reference, 1994). Cullen-DuPont's volume is most similar to Weatherford's but without the photographs. The full text of key documents alone increases its reference value, so if a library can buy only one volume on U.S. women's history, the Cullen-DuPont volume should be considered over that of Weatherford. The Zophy book, which was compiled by women's studies professionals, is a more comprehensive treatment of the subject and a better purchase than either the Cullen-DuPont or Weatherford volumes. Although the Cullen-DuPont encyclopedia is newer, it does not add significant information to the Zophy book. The encyclopedia would be beneficial for high school and college-level collections or general readers not owning the Zophy work. [R: Choice, Sept 96, p. 94; RBB, 15 Mar 96, p. 1313; SLJ, Aug 96, p. 180]—**Glynys R. Thomas**

DIRECTORIES

737. **U.S. Women's Interest Groups: Institutional Profiles.** Sarah Slavin, ed. Westport, Conn., Greenwood Press, 1995. 645p. index. (Greenwood Reference Volumes on American Public Policy Formation). $99.50. ISBN 0-313-25073-1.

This compilation of 180-plus women's organizations was a combined effort of the editor and more than 106 contributors. The contents were culled from a variety of sources: a questionnaire, publications of the organizations, interviews within and outside the organization, reviews, and others. The groups represent many types: Some are political or social in nature, some focus on research and others on service, some are professional affiliations, and others are oriented around a social cause. Individual group profiles contain information on the group's scope and influence, the organization's origin and development, organizational structures and funding, policy concerns and tactics, electoral activities, and more.

The introduction gives an estimable overview of the major focus and concerns of women's organizations, starting with 1961 and the President's (John F. Kennedy) Commission on the Status of Women. Topics cover agenda setting, mobilization, social capital formation, and exchange relations. Appendixes include profiles of six government agencies, the complete questionnaire sent to the organizations, a combined index, and a list of contributors to the volume.

This volume provides a good overview of the strong political forces operating on women's behalf in modern times. The following list shows the range of women's organizations that are profiled: Association of Black Nursing Faculty in Higher Education, Catholics for a Free Choice, Federally Employed Women, the Institute for Women's Policy Research, and the National Association for Girls and Women in Sport. The work will be an invaluable resource for libraries, and especially essential for university libraries that have a women's studies program. [R: Choice, July/Aug 96, p. 1778]—**Barbara J. O'Hara**

HANDBOOKS AND YEARBOOKS

738. Davis, Cynthia J., and Kathryn West. **Women Writers in the United States: A Timeline of Literary, Cultural, and Social History.** New York, Oxford University Press, 1996. 488p. index. $45.00. ISBN 0-19-509053-5.

This lengthy timeline is a continuation of the timeline that appeared in *The Oxford Companion to Women's Writing in the United States* (see ARBA 96, entry 1200). Davis and West were research assistants on the *Companion* and the conceptualizers and compilers of the timeline published in that volume. In addition to being much extended, *Women Writers* benefits from a more user-friendly format. The timeline lists both "Texts" (women's writings) and "Contexts" (social, political, and other developments in the arts) in two columns on the same page. If one column's length exceeds that of the other column for the same year, nothing is printed in the shorter column until the new year begins. This makes for easier comparison within years than in the *Companion*, which has a separate-page format in which the years do not necessarily line up.

The "Texts" column covers such disparate genres as fiction, poetry, biography, political manifestos, essays, advice columns, songs, travel writing, medical treatises, Native American oral storytelling, and cookbooks. The "Contexts" column provides a look at social and cultural history deemed to be pertinent to women's lives, although some seem somewhat irrelevant in light of more significant events (e.g., "Side-laced boots first become fashionable as women's footwear" for 1828 and "Pimps make their first appearance in New York City" for 1835). The timeline begins at the year 1 C.E. and goes through 1994 and the publication of Oxford's Companion. Only writers from the United States are covered in the "Texts" column, although important writings by women from different countries are sometimes included in "Contexts."

In comparing *Women Writers* with *Timelines of the Arts and Literature* (see ARBA 95, entry 925), some interesting things come to light. Obviously, *Women Writers* is much more in-depth in covering U.S. women's literary achievements, especially in the earlier years covered (there is more overlap as the decades go on). The benefit of *Timelines* over the book under review is that it makes note of birth and death dates for authors in addition to the years of publication for their works. Also, there are some entries in *Timelines* that are not found in *Women Writers*. For instance, there is no mention of Olympede de Gouges's 1790 *Declaration of the Rights of Women*; Noah Webster's *American Dictionary of the English Language* (1828) is not found in the "Contexts" column, even though similar items are listed elsewhere; and there is no entry for Maya Angelou's *Gather Together in My Name* (1974).

Although it is important to document women's active role in the literary arts, one must question the purpose of such a reference work. The volume in question is fun to browse and presents interesting dichotomies between developments in women's writing and developments in the world at large. Students would be able to confirm dates with such a source, and the common criticism of chronologies—that such information can be found in any good encyclopedia—may not hold true in this case, as women writers are traditionally underrepresented in standard reference works. The index is both extensive and helpful, providing cross-terms and references to both page number and column. Reference librarians could use this to answer pesky reference questions, and professors could tailor the information into their own timelines for specific courses. Therefore, the reference value of this particular chronology seems to outweigh the price; academic and large public libraries would benefit from having it in their collections. [R: Choice, Nov 96, p. 427; RBB, 1 Sept 96, p. 173]—**Melissa Rae Root**

739. Holland, Francis Schmid. **Feminist Jurisprudence: Emerging from Plato's Cave—A Research Guide.** Lanham, Md., Scarecrow, 1996. 193p. index. $28.50. ISBN 0-8108-3141-4.

The purpose of this annotated bibliography is to provide the researcher with a list of available sources on feminist jurisprudence and a starting point for developing a research collection on this subject. Covering the works of more than 200 writers in publication from 1976 through 1993, the author has created a comprehensive bibliography on feminist jurisprudence. This book is of interest to everyone concerned with the effect of the legal system on women. In comparison to prior works, this book is valuable because it appears to be the first bibliography. Prior titles, such as *Feminist Jurisprudence: The*

Difference Debate, edited by Leslie Friedman Goldstein (Rowman & Littlefield Publishers, 1992), and *Feminist Legal Theory*, edited by Frances E. Olsen (New York University Press, 1995), are compilations of various theories.

Chapter 1, "Research Strategies," gives a quick list of keywords, leading authors on the topic, databases, and sources useful for beginning research. The second chapter, "Defining Feminist Jurisprudence," includes brief views of the principal feminist theories. These first two chapters are particularly useful to the reader in that they give background on the issues and theories of feminist jurisprudence and the research process. Beyond the first two chapters, arrangement of the entries is by main topic, then alphabetically by author or editor. Although it is a short book, the author has covered a broad range of topics, from educational sources to workplace policy. The annotations give short descriptions of content, depth of coverage, date of material, and scope. While focusing primarily on the U.S. legal system, the author did include a section on international sources for a comparative analysis. The cross-referencing and author and topic indexes add to the ease of use. The quotations and brief discussions at the beginning of each chapter add to the readability and enjoyment of the book.

This book is an excellent resource for researchers within the communities of law and women's studies who need a source to begin their research. Libraries starting to build a feminist jurisprudence collection should also consider the guide.—**Judith A. Valdez**

740. **Statistical Handbook on Women in America.** 2d ed. Cynthia M. Taeuber, comp. and ed. Phoenix, Ariz., Oryx Press, 1996. 354p. index. $54.50. ISBN 1-57356-005-7.

This welcome 2d edition of Taeuber's handbook serves more as a companion to the 1st edition (see ARBA 92, entry 867) rather than a chart-by-chart revision, providing 353 charts and tables compared to the 437 in the earlier edition. The handbook still reproduces data from federal sources, most notably the Bureau of the Census, the Bureau of Labor Statistics, the National Center for Health Statistics, and the National Center for Education Statistics, but includes more nongovernmental sources—for instance, the Alan Guttmacher Institute and the Institute for Women's Policy Research.

The handbook also retains the same 4 main sections as the 1st edition: demographics, employment and economic status, health, and social characteristics. Each section begins with a useful, brief introduction presenting clear interpretations and summaries of the data. Subsections provide anywhere from 3 to 36 tables and charts accompanied by complete citation information. Coverage basically ranges from 1988 to early 1994. However, many tables provide historical statistics, most often beginning in the 1960s or 1970s, with a few going back as far as the 1890s or early 1900s. The majority of the tables and graphs furnish comparisons by gender, and many show comparisons by race, ethnicity, and country of origin. The index gives excellent access to these comparisons by including entries for each group and country as well as a general "race and ethnicity" entry.

This edition gives more attention to younger women and girls than the previous edition and reflects this by increasing the number of entries under "adolescence," "children," and "age/age distribution" in the index. It adds a welcome subsection on reproductive health and lists three tables on sports. Unfortunately, one of these is mislabeled, leaving only two. Also supplied are telephone and fax numbers, e-mail addresses, and Internet addresses for the four main federal sources. This edition omits some useful features, such as international comparisons and one-sentence summaries for each table. Future editions would benefit by greatly expanding the number of nongovernmental sources.

Once again, Taeuber performs a great service for researchers, students, and librarians by gathering a huge amount of important statistical data into one convenient source. Other titles, such as the biennial *American Women* status reports (W. W. Norton, 1987/88-) and *Women's Changing Role* (rev. ed., Information Plus, 1994), are updated more frequently but do not contain the depth or range of information provided in this handbook. *Statistical Handbook on Women in America* is recommended for all academic and most public libraries. [R: Choice, Nov 96, p. 438]—**Linda A. Krikos**

INDEXES

741. Phenix, Katharine Joan. **Subject Guide to Women of the World.** Lanham, Md., Scarecrow, 1996. 516p. index. $79.00. ISBN 0-8108-3190-2.

This volume is intended to be used in conjunction with two indexes by Norma Olin Ireland: *Index to Women of the World from Ancient to Modern Times* (see ARBA 72, entry 215) and its 1988 supplement (see ARBA 90, entry 878). Ireland's indexes lead users to published biographies in collected works of women whose names are known; the volume under review provides access by occupation or subject area to women's names in Ireland's volumes. Phenix's index is broken down into an alphabetic index by subject and a geographic index. Subject headings follow the model of H. W. Wilson's *Biography Index* (see ARBA 93, entries 33-34). Phenix alphabetizes by ASCII value, differing from Ireland's alphabetization scheme.

Such an effort reflects Phenix's library science background. However, stronger editorial control would have made this volume better. Two typographical errors were found in the introduction: Elaine Showalter is referred to as Elaine *Showalder*; and a sentence on page xi appears to be missing a word—"A woman listed under the same occupation with two or more of [ ] may also turn out to be the same person." Also, a mistake was found in the running heads on pages 70 and 71. Page 70 has the head "Bishops," page 71 has the head "Agriculturists"; page 72 returns to the alphabetic sequence. The term "Agriculturists" is mentioned in a *see also* reference under "Botanists," the last subject heading found on page 71. On another note, boldfaced, all capital letter subject headings—such as those found in the *Library of Congress Subject Headings* (see entries 533-534)—would have eased searching and relaxed eyestrain. It is a shame that such a useful work, with an author so well known in the library science field, should suffer from editorial glitches. Nonetheless, this volume will serve its purpose when used with the Ireland indexes. Those libraries that do not have the Ireland titles need not acquire this volume, as it would be of little use without the companion volumes.—**Melissa Rae Root**

742. **Women's Studies on Disc.** [CD-ROM]. New York, G. K. Hall/Simon & Schuster Macmillan, 1995. Minimum system requirements: IBM or compatible. CD-ROM drive with MS-DOS CD-ROM Extensions 2.0. 640K RAM. $495.00. ISBN 0-7838-2139-5.

G. K. Hall's *Women's Studies on Disc* is a product with appeal to research libraries that feel they must provide indexing for specialized journals not indexed elsewhere, or feel they must provide a one-stop women's studies index as a convenience to researchers. Most general libraries will find that the *Women's Studies Abstracts*, *Readers' Guide*, *Expanded Academic Index*, and similar indexes will provide adequate coverage of the subject without unduly inconveniencing most patrons. However, 20 of the 100 journals indexed in this product are not indexed in other indexes. Coverage includes lesbian feminist journals as well as popular women's periodicals and research journals. *Women's Studies on Disc* does not provide abstracts, which would have improved the product's usefulness.

The index places few demands on hardware, and any older DOS computer with a CD-ROM drive can be used. The disc can run from the CD-ROM drive or from the hard drive, depending on the user's needs, and is quick and easy to install. It has function key commands, and allows nested Boolean searching, right-hand truncation and internal wildcard options, index searching, and limiters for searching specific fields. Output via printer and download is available, although the download option does not allow appending to a prior file. An annoying truncated line display prohibits easy review of keywords used in prior search statements. Bibliographic citation style is inconsistent. For example, *Lear's* for 1989, 1992, and 1993 included volume and issue information, while 1990 and 1991 entries did not. The product runs sufficiently well and occupies a niche as a helpful tool in the field of women's studies, despite its shortcomings. [R: BR, Nov/Dec 96, p. 59; Choice, Dec 96, p. 597]—**Lynne M. Fox**

PERIODICALS AND SERIALS

743. **Women's Periodicals in the United States: Social and Political Issues.** Kathleen L. Endres and Therese L. Lueck, eds. Westport, Conn., Greenwood Press, 1996. 529p. index. (Historical Guides to the World's Periodicals and Newspapers). $110.00. ISBN 0-313-28632-9.

This book profiles 76 periodicals from the nineteenth and twentieth centuries created by women to address various issues, such as abolition, dress reform, suffrage, temperance, birth control, working women, pacifism, sexuality, and feminism. Endres and Lueck do not claim to be comprehensive, but see this as a beginning point in the field of women's publishing. They selected titles based on listings in standard reference sources, histories, and textbooks; the reputation of the editor; the editorial approach; the size of circulation; and the availability of a sufficient run of the periodical. The editors state that the last criterion eliminated many periodicals edited by African American and Hispanic American women. The volume covers periodicals from most geographic areas of the United States, and editorial approaches run the gamut from reactionary to radical. The introduction by Endres succinctly examines the difficulties faced by women publishers and serves as a brief overview of women's publishing.

Arranged alphabetically by periodical title, each signed entry provides a 3- to 12-page profile of the periodical that places it within its social context. Profiles also include reference notes; information sources (bibliography, index sources, and location sources); and publication history (title changes, volume and issue information, publisher and place of publication, editors, and circulation figures, if available). Researchers will find the information sources and publication histories particularly helpful. For example, location sources mention a periodical's availability on microfilm, and title changes bring many people close to tears. An appendix lists the periodicals in chronological order, a useful feature. The book also contains a substantial bibliography and a subject, title, and name index.

Endres and Lueck also edited another title in this series, *Women's Periodicals in the United States: Consumer Magazines* (see ARBA 96, entry 950). Nancy K. Humphreys's *American Women's Magazines* (see ARBA 90, entry 880) lists articles from mostly feminist and alternative sources that examine women's periodicals generally or that discuss specific magazines and journals. Mary Ellen Zuckerman's *Sources on the History of Women's Magazines, 1792-1960* (see ARBA 92, entry 861) focuses on more popular, mainstream titles, but also covers such topics as the portrayal of women, studies of magazine content, advertising, critiques, and women publishers.

Despite the small number of periodicals edited by women of color, this title makes an important contribution to the literature on women's publishing. The work is recommended for academic libraries. [R: RQ, Spring 96, pp. 425-26]—**Linda A. Krikos**

Part III
HUMANITIES

19 Humanities in General

HUMANITIES IN GENERAL

744. **The American Humanities Index for 1995: Volume XXI.** Troy, N.Y., Whitston Publishing, 1995. 2v. $275.00/set. ISBN 0-87875-477-6. ISSN 0361-0144.

This is the 21st edition of *The American Humanities Index* (AHI). The goal of the publication is to provide "an index to creative, critical, and scholarly journals in the arts and humanities," as stated in the preface. The 277 titles of journals (400 issues) indexed in the 1995 issue of AHI represent the category of "little magazines"; some of them are indexed nowhere else.

AHI is a 2-volume work with a total of 1,837 pages. The index has two main access points: the author's name and the most relevant subject heading of the article. Sometimes the main subject heading is very detailed. It can go up to three levels of subheadings (e.g., **HISTORY—CANADA—POLITICS AND GOVERNMENT—19TH CENTURY**; **ART—GERMANY—WOODCUTS—16TH CENTURY**). The main subject "Poems" covers 259 pages and lists thousands of titles, followed by the author, and then by the references to the publication source. The main heading "Poetry" has geographic and time subheadings (e.g., **POETRY—UNITED STATES—20TH CENTURY**) that are cross-referenced with the authors' names in the index.

The review articles offer three access points: the reviewer's name (as author), the author's name, and the main subject of the work. AHI also includes authors with all of their literary productions, such as poems, individually listed by title. For instance, the entry for "Lifshin, Lyn" lists 59 poems published in 15 journals during the period 1991-1994. AHI is a great reference source that enables the researcher to trace poems or short stories either by title or by author. The work is recommended for reference departments in public and academic libraries.—**Hermina G. B. Anghelescu**

745. Bowler, Gail Hellund. **Artists and Writers Colonies: Retreats, Residencies, and Respites for the Creative Mind.** Hillsboro, Oreg., Blue Heron Publishing, 1995. 285p. illus. index. $15.95pa. ISBN 0-936085-34-7.

For those who are inspired to communicate via the printed page and need a "quiet, but clean and well lighted place" to weave mental/verbal ideas into various plots, there is now a guide that will (and can, if one reads it carefully) lead to just that place. *Artists and Writers Colonies* is a wonderful guide that runs the gamut from the dreamy-sounding (for women) Hedgebrook (located on Whidbey Island in Puget Sound near Langely, Washington) to Jacob's Pillow, a residence for performance and nonperformance artists who teach in public and private schools.

Most colonies are given full descriptions of what they will offer in terms of a place to read, write, and create; and facility amenities (some have hot/cold running water, and some, well . . .). All programs have specific deadlines, so one should read the descriptions carefully because each has its own set of rules and deadlines concerning applications. The book also contains a section on "Foreign Artists and Writers Centers," and several appendixes that include facilities listed by state and facilities for writers only, artists only, and multiple disciplines. This book is a work of art for assisting in making an artist's dream come true. [R: Choice, April 96, p. 1281]—**Lillian Jane Steele**

746. **A Dictionary of Cultural and Critical Theory.** Michael Payne, Meenakshi Ponnuswami, and Jennifer Payne, eds. Cambridge, Mass., Blackwell, 1996. 644p. index. $74.95. ISBN 0-631-17197-5.

More than 100 contributors aided in the writing of this dictionary, a comprehensive look at cultural and critical studies. Its interdisciplinary focus covers both the humanities and the social sciences. The content mainly reflects the path of twentieth-century thought, but earlier work is treated that helps to supply the context for later ideas.

Readers are encouraged to contact the publisher if any errors are found, so that they may be eradicated for a possible 2d edition. Such letters will scarcely be necessary. This dictionary discusses difficult topics in a clear manner, without lessening the complexity of the ideas. All the subjects and people one would expect to find in a dictionary covering cultural and critical theory are here. Terms such as *affective fallacy*, *binary opposition*, *name of the father*, and *ontological relativity* are treated, as are such broad topics as the black aesthetic, discourse, femininity, literary criticism, socialist realism, and women's studies. The dictionary also covers such people as Louis Althusser, T. S. Eliot, Frantz Fanon, Shoshona Felman, Julia Kristeva, Claude Lévi-Strauss, Jean-Jacques Rousseau, and Mary Wollstonecraft, as well as important publications or journals—*Critical Inquiry*, *New Left Review*, *October*, and *Scrutiny*, for example.

The format of the dictionary is useful, if typical. An introduction, which details the historical background of cultural and critical studies, starts the volume. The entries themselves, in alphabetic order, vary in length according to the depth of analysis available on a particular topic or the relative difficulty of its concepts. The articles contain cross-references to other entries within the dictionary (in all capital letters) and are often followed by a suggested reading list, which includes an individual's own writings for biographical entries. All are signed by the contributor who wrote the article. *See* references lead the user to the appropriate entry. A comprehensive bibliography and an index, unusual in a dictionary, round out the volume.

One aspect of the dictionary that may annoy users is the occasional bias in controversial articles. However, as stated in the preface, contributors were encouraged to take a stand on issues if it benefited the explanation of the topic. Also, occasional Briticisms sneak in (e.g., "swingeing"), reflecting the mostly British production of the work, but the coverage of the subject matter embodies the universality of cultural and critical theory. This dictionary is especially recommended for undergraduate and postgraduate institutions. [R: Choice, July/Aug 96, p. 1771]—**Melissa Rae Root**

20 Communication and Mass Media

GENERAL WORKS

747. Greenberg, Gerald S. **Tabloid Journalism: An Annotated Bibliography of English-Language Sources.** Westport, Conn., Greenwood Press, 1996. 187p. index. (Bibliographies and Indexes in Mass Media and Communications, no.10). $65.00. ISBN 0-313-29544-1.

While it places greater emphasis on materials pertaining to the increasingly pervasive sensationalism of news during the past two decades, this timely bibliography also covers the historical aspects of tabloid journalism, the roots of which extend back to the penny press of the nineteenth century and even beyond that to early English broadsides. Greenberg, a librarian at Ohio State University, has identified a wide variety of English-language sources relating to this phenomenon, including books; chapters within books; articles in scholarly and trade journals, law reviews, and popular magazines; theses and dissertations; and court cases. Descriptive annotations accompany all of the 819 entries.

Following a one-page primary bibliography that briefly describes the holdings of three major research libraries that collect supermarket tabloids, secondary sources appear within four major categories. The first three are devoted to print journalism, television, and legal issues in the United States, while the fourth covers tabloid journalism in other countries. When appropriate, publications within these categories are divided into those that give a historical perspective and those that pertain to modern practice. Separate author and subject indexes conclude the volume, but, unfortunately, numerous omissions, errors, and inconsistencies in the subject index diminish its effectiveness as a key to the bibliography. For example, the index contains no entry for Cher although item 619 discusses *Cher v. Forum International*; only a small number of the publications relating to yellow journalism are reflected under the index entry for "yellow press"; and the item number provided for "Wyeth, Andrew" is incorrect.

Because a search of several indexes revealed a number of pertinent sources that are omitted from this bibliography, it cannot be relied on for comprehensiveness. However, it can serve as a starting point for students and scholars who are interested not only in the effects of tabloid journalism and the viewpoints of its defenders and detractors, but also in the broader issues of journalistic ethics, censorship, and first amendment rights. Despite its flaws, it should be considered by academic libraries that support programs in journalism and mass media or popular culture.—**Marie Ellis**

748. Newton, David E. **Violence and the Media: A Reference Handbook.** Santa Barbara, Calif., ABC-CLIO, 1996. 254p. index. (Contemporary World Issues). $39.50. ISBN 0-87436-843-X.

The unnumbered series, Contemporary World Issues, began in 1988 with the publication of Marie Costa's *Adult Literary/Illiteracy in the United States* (see ARBA 89, entry 324). Since then, the series has addressed such issues as abortion, homelessness in the United States, childhood sexual abuse, gangs, gun control, legalized gambling, sports ethics, and violent children. In the title under review, Newton (author of approximately 50 books, including *Gay and Lesbian Rights* [see ARBA 95, entry 859] and *The Ozone Dilemma* [see ARBA 96, entry 1874] in this series) informs readers at the outset that the question of how violence in the mass media affects viewers is an issue "about which humans have disagreed from the very first appearance of mass media itself, more than 2,000 years ago."

The handbook is divided into seven chapters. Chapter 1 is an overview of the issue, its historical background, and major questions involved in the debate over violence and the mass media (discussed under such subtopics as violent themes in history; violence in motion pictures, cartoons, television, popular music, and video games; and efforts by governmental agencies and industry executives to contain violence). The second chapter is a chronology on the development of the major forms of mass media (newspapers, magazines, literature, radio, television, comics, and so on) in the United States from the early eighteenth century to 1996. Chapter 3 contains biographical sketches of approximately 20 important figures in the controversy over mass media violence; for example, Peggy Charren, founder of Action for Children's Television; ex-senators John Pastore and Paul Simon, watchdogs on violence in the media; Jack Valenti, president and CEO of the Motion Picture Association of America; and Donald Wildmon, founder of the American Family Association, which seeks to influence the content of mass media by boycotts and letter-writing campaigns to influence advertisers that pay for mass media presentation. Chapter 4 consists of significant documents (laws, regulations, court decisions, industry standards, and policy statements) relating to mass media violence.

The fifth chapter is a directory of organizations (American Civil Liberties Union, Comics Magazine Association of America, National Coalition on Television Violence, the National PTA, and the like) interested in mass media violence, followed by a directory of organizations responsible for the production of broadcast and cable television programming. Chapters 6 and 7 are annotated lists of print (bibliographies, books, congressional hearings, and 1 periodical) and nonprint (mostly video) resources. An extensive glossary and index conclude this book. A useful reference title for high school, public, and academic libraries, both for its ample information and as a starting point for further investigation. [R: SLJ, Dec 96, p. 148]—**Wiley J. Williams**

AUTHORSHIP

General Works

749. **A Directory of American Poets and Fiction Writers.** 1995-1996 ed. New York, Poets & Writers; distr., Pushcart Press/W. W. Norton, 1995. 318p. index. $25.95pa; $30.95pa (institutions). ISBN 0-913724-47-0. ISSN 0734-0605.

This work contains the names and addresses of approximately 7,000 poets and fiction writers whose work has been published in the United States and who have applied to be included in the directory. The purpose of the work is to list contemporary writers, many of whom give readings or performances based on their work. The 1995-1996 edition has information about 4,000-plus poets, nearly 2,000 fiction writers, and more than 1,000 individuals who produce both poetry and fiction. Playwrights, nonfiction writers, translators, critics, biographers, journalists, and authors of children's books are not included.

The entries are arranged alphabetically by the state of the writers' home address. Each listing provides the writer's name (with pseudonyms cross-indexed), address, telephone number, type(s) of writing, and a representative sample of the publications in which the writer's work has been published. According to the publishers, the information was correct as of June 1, 1994; readers are given a telephone number to call for updated information.

Poets & Writers is a nonprofit service organization that supports writers' professional efforts. With the aid of grants from the Literature Program of the National Endowment for the Arts and other sources, it publishes a bimonthly magazine and other reference books in addition to the title under review. Inclusion in the directory does not constitute any sort of endorsement. Those wishing to contact contemporary writers personally will find this unique book valuable; however, most others will continue to rely on other, more inclusive, reference books.—**Kay O. Cornelius**

750. **Writer's Encyclopedia.** 3d ed. By the Editors of Writer's Digest. Cincinnati, Ohio, Writer's Digest Books/F & W Publications, 1996. 499p. illus. maps. $22.99. ISBN 0-89879-749-7.

This compact volume has more than 1,300 entries relating to writing in general; publishing; and writing for the broadcast media, films, the theater, music, advertising, and public relations. This is an increase of more than 100 entries from the previous edition, published in 1990 as *Writing A to Z* (see ARBA 91, entry 952). Arranged in alphabetic order with many cross-references, the concise entries clearly define terms, identify awards and organizations, explain techniques and procedures, and offer guidance on such diverse topics as how to read the masthead of a magazine and which items might be tax deductible for a writer. Many of the entries refer the user to sources of additional information. Also provided is a bibliography of the works most often consulted by the editors of the volume. More than 60 charts and tables enhance the work by giving a variety of publishing industry figures, examples of writing, samples of forms (such as résumés), an application for copyright, and submission of a gag (joke).

This is a handy reference book designed to answer basic questions arising from the occupation and process of writing. It will be especially helpful to the neophyte or casual researcher interested in professional writing rather than writing as literature. As such, it would be a popular addition to most reference collections, including personal libraries.—**Barbara E. Kemp**

Handbooks and Yearbooks

751. Henderson, Kathy. **The Market Guide for Young Writers: Where and How to Sell What You Write.** 5th ed. Cincinnati, Ohio, Writer's Digest Books/F & W Publications, 1996. 309p. illus. index. $16.99pa. ISBN 0-89879-721-7.

When a young patron requests material about writing for publication, often libraries can produce only guides for adult writers. In this well-balanced work, Henderson makes the adaptation to youth needs. The book contains pieces of published writing by people as young as nine, and a sample of very early writing by Stephen King. It answers typical questions: How do I copyright my work? (Often the first question asked about even the most halting efforts.) Who publishes work by teens? How do I get started? Where do I get ideas? What format and style guidelines should I use? What if the editor suggests changes? There is an annotated contest list and a list of publications that welcome young people's writing. Henderson speaks of the need for study, practice, and growth in professionalism; youth writing from the editor's point of view; and the inevitable rejection slips. She provides some nuts and bolts, some inspiration, and some caveat.

As evidence of updating in this 5th edition, the author assumes that students have access to computers and the Internet. *Market Guide* is an excellent source for teachers who assign authentic achievement projects. The table of contents and the index make the book easy to use as a reference. The guide is a good purchase, although its billing states "for writers 8-18," and the very young student on the cover may sit uneasily with the 18-year-olds.—**Edna M. Boardman**

752. Metter, Ellen. **The Writer's Ultimate Research Guide.** Cincinnati, Ohio, Writer's Digest Books/F & W Publications, 1995. 332p. index. $19.99. ISBN 0-89879-668-7.

Here is a guide to books and databases designed to assist writers in constructing factually accurate fiction or nonfiction. The first two chapters (part 1) offer "Research Tips for Writers." Chapter 1 covers such basics as types of libraries, classification schemes, catalogs, and Boolean logic for online searching, and the 2d chapter differentiates types of periodicals (journals, magazines, newsletters) and indexes. In the remaining 15 chapters (parts 2 through 5), annotated listings of hundreds of sources usually found in larger public or academic libraries are cited in chapters with such titles as "Climate and Local Customs," "Architecture and Decor," "Modes of Travel," "Legal Details," "How to Kill Your Character," "Diseases and Mental Illness," and "Science and Invention." (The part headings, however, are mere cosmetic additions; divisional markers and textual support are lacking in the body of the work.) One appendix offers a subject guide to periodical indexes, and another discusses types of online vendors. The 3-column-per-page subject/title index at the end extends 14 pages.

The book's title overstates its case; the book is not an "ultimate" source, even though it is well written in a "lively and upbeat tone" and exceptionally well produced. Metter has done an outstanding job in writing and organizing this guide for an educated reader. The book should be a priority purchase item for any serious writer. Public libraries also may want to make multiple copies available for circulation while keeping one in reference. All libraries could use it profitably as a selection checklist. [R: Choice, June 96, pp. 1620-21]—**Glenn R. Wittig**

753. **Novel & Short Story Writer's Market, 1996.** Robin Gee and Barbara Kuroff, eds. Cincinnati, Ohio, Writer's Digest Books/F & W Publications, 1996. 631p. index. $22.99. ISBN 0-89879-713-6. ISSN 0897-9812.

Divided into three parts, this volume contains sections on writing technique (articles on the craft of writing, the business of publishing, and interviews) and resources (conferences, workshops, organizations, and retreats). The largest section is "The Markets," including literary markets, the small press, commercial periodicals, and book publishers. The volume also contains a section on contests and awards. The market entries offer much valuable information: address, publication frequency, pay scales, rejection rates, and annotated descriptions. These data are mostly quoted from information provided by the editors and publishers. (The entries also note comments written by the editors of *Novel & Short Story Writer's Market*.) An especially useful feature is notations indicating subsidy publishers and book packagers. As noted in an earlier review (see ARBA 93, entry 966), the listings are not comprehensive and the paragraph-style index is awkward to consult. Nevertheless, this volume is an important reference source, frequently requested by public library patrons.—**Donald Altschiller**

754. **Romance Writer's Sourcebook: Where to Sell Your Manuscripts.** David H. Borcherding, ed. Cincinnati, Ohio, Writer's Digest Books/F & W Publications, 1996. 378p. illus. index. $19.99. ISBN 0-89879-726-8. ISSN 1081-6739.

This is the 1st edition of a planned biennial publication that should attract a wide audience. Most likely it is no longer news that romance novels make up nearly 50 percent of U.S. paperback sales, and many of the novels' readers are struggling to become romance writers. It follows that advice on how to produce and sell manuscripts will be in demand.

This publisher of *Writer's Market* (see ARBA 95, entry 670) has an excellent track record with this type of book, and editor Borcherding presents a well-rounded package. Best-selling author Nora Roberts wrote the opening "Trends" section, a piece produced with Roberts's usual grace and humor. Following are essays on romance writing skills by other experts in the field. There is a lengthy section on who the publishers are, with information on addresses, telephone numbers, whom to contact, and details of which type of story is likely to sell.

Also provided is a list of romance agents, along with some author success stories and excerpts from published works. The book concludes with a useful unit on resources that directs readers to online services, organizations, conferences, contests, and magazines. The book ends with a seven-page glossary of terms and several useful indexes. Barring a couple of editorial niggles (e.g., Jayne Ann Krentz has no "e" on "Ann," and Janet Dailey does have an "e" before the "y"), which may be indicators of other slips in accuracy, this is a useful tool for most public libraries.—**Berniece M. Owen**

Style Manuals

755. **A Manual for Writers of Term Papers, Theses, and Dissertations.** 6th ed. By Kate L. Turabian. Revised by John Grossman and Alice Bennett. Chicago, University of Chicago Press, 1996. 308p. index. (Chicago Guides to Writing, Editing, and Publishing). $27.50; $12.95pa. ISBN 0-226-81626-5; 0-226-81627-3pa.

Buy this book. Most librarians will know that they should, and many students will learn that they must. All will be well served by this excellent, classic guide to the details of putting words on paper. The authors of this new edition discuss other media as well. They provide cogent guidance for those who use computers in academic work without ever descending to the depths of technical specificity that will become instantly obsolete.

Continuing traditional and useful practice, the current work is related to the most recent edition of *The Chicago Manual of Style* (14th ed.; see ARBA 94, entry 1001). The smaller manual can be used with that larger work, but more often it will stand alone to show those who write academic papers how to deal with punctuation, quotations, tables, illustrations, notes, bibliographic citations, and much more. The arrangement is familiar and logical, the text is coherent, the examples are clear and pertinent, and the index is superb. Turabian lives on in this essential guide to academic writing that, as always, serves as the best possible example of how to make specialized, complicated text agreeable to view and possible to understand.—**John Newman**

756. **The New Fowler's Modern English Usage.** 3d ed. H. W. Fowler, ed. Revised by R. W. Burchfield. New York, Clarendon Press/Oxford University Press, 1996. 864p. $25.00. ISBN 0-19-869126-2.

H. W. Fowler's original book on English usage, published in 1926, has long been considered one of the foremost authorities on the British use of the English language. This 3d edition of that classic has been undertaken by Burchfield, formerly chief editor of the Oxford English dictionaries. This 864-page book contains more than 3,500 entries on word usage and grammatical constructions. While Burchfield's addition of information on American English adds an important dimension to this work, users will find this a completely different book from the 1st and 2d editions of Fowler's work.

Burchfield, who created a database to help him examine various usages, has not just updated previous editions; he has largely rewritten them. Those people who referred to Fowler's book for his concise, opinionated, authoritative discussions on proper usage and for his dry wit will be disappointed with this edition. Burchfield reveals his background in dictionary work with his tendency to describe present use of various words and phrases rather than to dictate one use over another. While his writing style is clear and straightforward, his discussion may not satisfy someone looking for clear direction on proper usage. Burchfield seems to frown on efforts to eliminate gender bias, but in many entries he appears to be more accepting of new words and constructions than many editors. For example, he seems to accept the application of the word "input" and other computer terminology to noncomputer uses, while most editors are still resisting these new constructions. *Modern English Usage* should be considered Burchfield's book, not Fowler's, but it is still an important and useful reference work for anyone needing guidance on word selection and acceptable grammatical construction.—**Kay Mariea**

757. **Sports Style Guide & Reference Manual: The Complete Reference for Sports Editors, Writers, and Broadcasters.** Jennifer Swan, ed. Chicago, Triumph Books, 1996. 375p. $24.95. ISBN 1-57243-101-6.

Although (as the subtitle indicates) ostensibly written for sports editors, writers, and broadcasters, this style guide and reference manual for a wide variety of sports played or followed in the United States will appeal to a somewhat broader audience. Certainly few libraries will purchase it for the intended audience as almost all of those potential users are apt either to purchase it or to have access to it at their place of work. While much of the main section of the text, which deals with style and usage, covers arcane issues of the use of abbreviations, capitalization, hyphens, and similar items that are truly of use only to professional sports media people, in almost all cases the stylistic advice is accompanied by a succinct definition (e.g., "*enveloppement*: Note the spelling of this fencing movement when an opponent's blade is carried for at least one full circle"). It is those definitions, the identification of abbreviations, and other added features that give this guide broader appeal, especially because, in a number of cases, that information is not readily available in standard dictionaries or encyclopedias.

The second part of this guide, which covers individual and team sports, also provides useful information not readily found elsewhere on the basic terms of a sport, the addresses of its governing bodies, scoring, listings of leagues and teams, and the like. While perhaps particularly useful as a beginning reference point for a sport with which a library user may not be familiar, this guide—as with so many sports reference books—will appeal to a range of sports fans and may be helpful in answering some odd reference questions. [R: RBB, 15 Sept 96, p. 285; BR, Nov/Dec 96, p. 59]—**Norman D. Stevens**

758. **Wired Style: Principles of English Usage in the Digital Age.** Constance Hale, ed. San Francisco, Calif., HardWired; distr., Emeryville, Calif., Publishers Group West, 1996. 158p. index. $15.95 spiralbound. ISBN 1-888869-01-1.

What do people think when they open *Wired* magazine? "Cool!" or "I must be getting old." That is probably how people will react to *Wired Style*, a style book for "the Digital Age." As with the magazine, the style guide has an in-your-face format guaranteed to set it apart from competitors. The neon yellow pages definitely take some getting used to, but it is possible. This style guide has some strong points and some weak ones. There are few cross-references, and the chapter format makes it hard to use for easy reference, but makes it a more interesting read. Some terms show up in two places, like *bandwidth* in chapter 2 and chapter 3. Unless the user is familiar with its layout when looking for particular terms, he or she must rely on the index. Overall, however, the work is informative, includes pronunciations, and lays down some much-needed rules about editorial style for Internet terms. Also, there is enough self-effacing humor here that readers know the writers did not take themselves too seriously.

The subtitle, "Principles of English Usage in the Digital Age," is slightly overstated. (*Wired* is not the first publisher guilty of this.) It is either cutting-edge hip or slightly immature. It has a "Screw the Rules" (title of one chapter) attitude and approach, forgetting, however, that a style manual is a rule book, no matter how hip.

If users do not need to know about such terms as *grok* ("A verb meaning to scan all available information regarding a situation, digest it, and form a distilled opinion") and *wankware* (X-rated software) or that *microsofties* are Microsoft's "incorrigible fans (people with the uncanny ability to see all the company's bugs as 'features')," they can get by without this book. If library patrons need guidance on breaking URLs at ends of lines and styling Internet-related terms or help getting through all the cyberjargon, libraries will want this book. Those wanting a more modest, but still reliable, alternative may want to consider *The High-Technology Editorial Guide and Stylebook* (see ARBA 93, entry 969), which unfortunately does not have the same extensive Internet coverage. [R: LJ, 1 Oct 96, p. 70]—**Stephen Haenel**

759. **The Writer's Digest Dictionary of Concise Writing.** By Robert Hartwell Fiske. Cincinnati, Ohio, Writer's Digest Books/F & W Publications, 1996. 336p. $19.99pa. ISBN 0-89879-755-1.

According to Fiske, "wordiness is a flaw of style—in how we express our language. Today, the style is prevailingly shoddy." First published in 1990 as the *Guide to Concise Writing*, this updated edition is described as having "thousands of alternatives to wordy phrases." This anti-thesaurus also is a primer of plainspeak, offering simpler terms for thousand-dollar words. For example, readers are urged to use "name" or "title" instead of "appellation"; "mention" instead of "make mention of."

Part 1 contains two chapters on the use and importance of words, along with Fiske's "clues to concision." Also included are brief, frequently smug, and occasionally wordy essays on the jargon of business, law, politics, journalism, and academia (described as being "unusually afflicted with wordiness"). Part 2 is the dictionary, arranged alphabetically, which contains suggested alternatives to wordy phrases. This has the potential to be a handy tool for long-winded writers, provided they recognize their verbosity and seek to cure it.—**Jo A. Cates**

NEWSPAPERS AND MAGAZINES

760. **Bacon's International Media Directory 1996: Directory of Magazines and Newspapers in Western Europe.** Chicago, Bacon's Information, 1995. 363p. maps. index. $275.00pa. ISSN 0161-4363.

Covering 15 West European countries, the directory lists 25,478 magazines and 1,214 newspapers. The listings are organized under country, then subdivided by market classification. For each publication, information provided includes address; telephone, fax, and telex numbers; editor's name; publication frequency and circulation; and finally, a profile that is very brief (rarely more than seven or eight words, and usually less), but supplemented by numbers that refer to a listing of types of material considered for inclusion in the publication (e.g., new products, personnel news, book reviews, case studies). There is an alphabetic index of publications for each country, but not for the entire volume.

Libraries will obviously want to compare this with *Ulrich's International Periodicals Directory* (see entry 66). *Bacon's* is somewhat more comprehensive for these 15 countries (a random sample showed about a third more titles, most of them of very specialized interest), but it contains no price information, either for individual issues or subscriptions. Given its cost, the rapid changes in the data provided, and the availability of *Ulrich's*, *Bacon's* is needed only for highly specialized collections.—**Evan Ira Farber**

761. **Freedom of the Press Decisions of the United States Supreme Court.** Maureen Harrison and Steve Gilbert, eds. San Diego, Calif., Excellent Books, 1996. 239p. index. (First Amendment Decisions Series). $16.95pa. ISBN 1-880780-10-0.

Fourteen historic Supreme Court decisions affecting the rights and responsibilities of a free press society are presented here. The paragraphs selected for inclusion are, for the most part, jargon-free. In words most adult English-speaking people can understand, the editors have compiled rulings regarding malicious and scandalous newspapers, libel of public officials, protecting confidential news sources, "gagging" the press, search and seizure in newsrooms, and X-rated cable broadcasting, among others. A disclaimer is presented to remind novice users that no legal or professional service is being rendered by the purchase and use of the book. While works of the federal government are in the public domain when published, those same works when gathered together and republished are copyrighted, so users beware before making multiple copies from this book for distribution.

The cases reprinted are part of the majority opinion as expressed by the justice chosen to speak. Each entry is preceded by a list of justices who heard the case, with a source note of where the unedited text of the case can be found in the *United States Reports*.

Entries in the bibliography are from the mid-1970s to the mid-1980s; one source has a 1996 date. The index is essential, and users will enjoy accessing such entries as "fighting words" and "My country 'tis of thee" (*New York Times v. Sullivan*, March 9, 1964), to see how these phrases are connected to the legal opinions of the Supreme Court. Large typeface and wide margins ensure no eyestrain during use. This would be a good investment for literate adult readers.—**Judy Gay Matthews**

RADIO, TELEVISION, AUDIO, AND VIDEO

Biography

762. DeLong, Thomas A. **Radio Stars: An Illustrated Biographical Dictionary of 953 Performers, 1920 through 1960.** Jefferson, N.C., McFarland, 1996. 306p. illus. index. $59.50. ISBN 0-7864-0149-0.

As radio became more familiar to thousands of U.S. homes in the 1920s, the people behind the voices became almost members of the family. This work provides biographies of some 950 radio performers from the period 1920 through 1960. Many of these people are household names, while others have disappeared into the time warp of the past. Reading this volume brings back many memories and opens vistas into an age that will never return. Aside from providing the standard biographical information on personalities of the period, insight can be obtained into the life and times of the period covered.

Historians will find this work appealing because of the scenes into the past the entries provide. Each person's story is told as completely as possible, given the obvious space constraints of a volume such as this. In addition, an emphasis is placed on why the individual was memorable in the field of radio broadcasting. For example, Wendell Hall's entry states, "Ukulele-playing vocalist, he popularized that stringed instrument among flappers and sheiks in the 1920s." DeLong's style of writing makes this work all the more important and memorable to the reader. The work is extensively illustrated.

This volume is bound in a sturdy library binding. Most reference collections will find it invaluable.
—**Ralph Lee Scott**

763. Lieberman, Philip A. **Radio's Morning Show Personalities: Early Hour Broadcasters and Deejays from the 1920s to the 1990s.** Jefferson, N.C., McFarland, 1996. 204p. illus. index. $29.95. ISBN 0-7864-0037-4.

The title of this volume pretty much tells it all. The volume contains 33 biographies of major morning radio talk show personalities as well as brief listings of several hundred other prominent morning personalities. From *Rambling with Grambling* to Howard Stern, the author covers the important a.m. radio jocks who shaped this uniquely American form of morning entertainment. The biographies roughly parallel the development of this radio genre staring "morning men" who at first talked to their listeners, then graduated to playing recorded music, and finally ending with the current target audience "shock jock" type of show characterized by Stern. (While in the classic era, there were no major women morning radio show personalities, several women radio personalities are listed in the "other prominent" section.) Covered are such deejays as Gene Rayburn, Bob Elliott, Ray Goulding, Arthur Godfrey, Buffalo Bob Smith, Don Russell, Wolfman Jack, John Leslie, Joe Roberts, and Don Imus.

The volume is well constructed and interesting to read. The entries give a lively and accurate picture of each personality. A number of the entries contain show dialogues, thereby giving the real flavor and humor of each deejay. The author spent four years doing research and conducting live interviews with a number of personalities. Libraries with patrons interested in early and current radio will find this volume both a quick reference and a useful history.—**Ralph Lee Scott**

Catalogs and Collections

764. **Catalogue of Forbidden German Feature and Short Film Productions Held in Zonal Film Archives....** English language ed. By John F. Kelson. K. R. M. Short, ed. Westport, Conn., Greenwood Press, 1996. 198p. index. $75.00. ISBN 0-313-30106-9.

This is a catalog of selected feature, feature-length documentary, and short films released in Germany between January 30, 1933, and May 8, 1945. These films were seized at the end of World War II and were denied exhibition in the British Zone of Occupation because of their Nazi propaganda content. Originally, there were 700 titles (1,200 prints) of feature films and 2,500 titles (5,000 prints) of short films. These were viewed, and those that were deemed harmless were returned to their owners. The remaining 141 titles of feature films and 254 titles of short films are annotated in this catalog. Most of the films are 35mm positive black-and-white sound prints. Each has a brief annotation of the film, which includes the name of the production studio, the director, the cast, and a brief synopsis of the film that gives some reason why the film was considered objectionable. There are indexes, one for feature films and one for the short films. Following this is an index of English translations of the German titles. In order to find a film, starting from the English list, one then has to search both of the indexes in order to find the correct page. This is awkward.

This volume is, strictly speaking, neither a facsimile nor a new edition of the work. The original was published in 1951; it was computer scanned and a typeface was chosen that faithfully reproduced the original. All the mistakes of the 1st edition are duplicated in this edition. The page numbers have been modified to reflect the pages of this edition and not the original. A different typeface has been used for "new" materials in this edition, including the introduction, the index, and one appendix. The catalog is for specialized film collections and for those interested in post-World War II censorship.

—**Robert L. Turner Jr.**

Dictionaries and Encyclopedias

765. Lackmann, Ron. **Same Time ... Same Station: An A-Z Guide to Radio from Jack Benny to Howard Stern.** New York, Facts on File, 1996. 370p. illus. index. $45.00. ISBN 0-8160-2862-1.

Americans gathered in their homes during the period 1920-1950 every night to listen to their favorite radio shows and major news events. This so-called "Golden Period of American Radio" is chronicled in this excellent compendium. In this volume one will find descriptions of dramatic, comedy, quiz, and news shows, such as *Kay Kyser's Kollege of Musical Knowledge, Information Please, Truth or Consequences, Abbott and Costello, Arthur Godfrey Time, Blondie, Coast to Coast on a Bus, Eddie Cantor Show*, and *The Hartz Mountain Canaries Show* (the last featuring a live orchestra and a studio full of active singing birds). *Same Time ... Same Station* also includes biographies of directors, writers, comedians, and scores of other radio personalities. Brief histories are given for the major networks (NBC, CBS, NPR). More than 100 vintage photographs, many of which have never been published before, illustrate the volume.

Appendixes include a U.S. radio event chronology; a Canadian radio chronology; a sponsor index (e.g., Blatz Beer, Cocomalt, and Fatima Cigarettes); a supplemental index of additional radio personalities (that space did not permit fuller entries); a list of vintage radio show clubs, conventions, museums, newsletters, and organizations; a list of current stations featuring vintage radio shows (as of May 1995); a section entitled "Logs of Long-Running Dramatic Anthology Shows" that provides program notes listed by year. There is also a one-page bibliography and a detailed index.

This is a well-produced volume. The entries are easy to read and convey copious information. One minor complaint is that the index is set in very small typeface; however, it is still clear and easy to read despite its size. Lackmann is an actor and has taught at Central High School in Valley Stream, New York for 30-plus years. He has produced a book that is a delight to any old-time radio enthusiasts. The entries will bring back many memories. The guide is recommended for purchase by libraries with clients interested in this period in American history and in the history of radio. [R: Choice, April 96, p. 1288; RBB, 15 Feb 96, p. 1044; RQ, Summer 96, p. 565; SLJ, April 96, p. 170]—**Ralph Lee Scott**

Directories

766. **Film Producers, Studios, Agents and Casting Directors Guide.** 5th ed. David M. Kipen, comp. and ed. Los Angeles, Calif., Lone Eagle, 1996. 484p. index. $55.00pa. ISBN 0-943728-82-7. ISSN 0894-8666.

This is another volume in Lone Eagle's exemplary series of reference books for the motion picture community. Unlike some of their other volumes, it does not have much appeal for anyone not involved in film production.

The main body of the book deals with the work of film producers. "Not listed," the preface states, "are most foreign films; short films; films made for television; films produced by people who are deceased (unless co-produced with people who are not); grade-Z exploitation films (unless the producer later graduated to at least grade-B); and films released directly on videocassette." Associate and executive producer credits are likewise not considered. The movies covered are followed by their dates and distributors. The other sections take up less space, but are no less useful—studios (all executives listed), agents and managers (individuals enumerated by company), and casting directors and their films.

As with the *Film Writers Guide* (see entry 767), the contact information supplied is admirable but not ideally complete. The producer and casting director portions are cross-indexed by film titles and individuals and the studios and agents by both individuals and the firms they represent. A listing of the Best Picture nominees throughout Academy Award history rounds off the proceedings. This volume stands as a highly regarded and indispensable resource for those in "the business."—**Walt Mundkowsky**

767. **Film Writers Guide.** 6th ed. Susan Avallone, comp. and ed. Los Angeles, Calif., Lone Eagle, 1996. 660p. index. $60.00pa. ISBN 0-943728-83-5. ISSN 0894-864X.

The Lone Eagle line of reference books (10 titles in all) is designed to meet the needs of the motion picture industry. This volume may have wider application than others in the series, given the substantial market for how-to screenwriting manuals.

An opening interview with veteran screenwriter William Goldman examines the current landscape in bleak terms. The book's main business is to list the output of active Hollywood scriptwriters, also indicating the date and production company (not director, alas) for each movie. (Fascinatingly, a list of the writer's unproduced scripts is also provided.) Major Canadian writer-directors appear, as does a selection of international types. Some of them merit inclusion by working over here, while others are apparently just too important to leave out. French writers Jean Gruault and Jean-Claude Carrière turn up, also avant-garde filmmakers Nina Menkes and Sara Driver. Information on how to contact individual writers is not always available, especially for the less prominent (and often most intriguing); and some of the entries are more representative than complete.

A section on notable writers of the past chronicles figures from this book's previous editions who are now deceased, and both film titles and writers are fully indexed. A helpful register of writers' agents and managers completes this fine effort, along with an entertaining look at the Academy Award screenplay nominations since 1960. Who recalls that distinctive work as unique as *The Wild Bunch* and *Mon Oncle d'Amérique* were honored?—**Walt Mundkowsky**

768. Pickard, James D. **North American Shortwave Frequency Guide. Volume 3.** Burbank, Calif., Artsci; distr., Chicago, Independent Publishers Group, 1995. 205p. maps. $19.95pa. ISBN 0-917963-09-1.

The *North American Shortwave Frequency Guide* (NASFG) contains an introduction; a note on "Universal Time Coordinated"—that is, UTC, usually referred to in English as Coordinated Universal Time—with explanatory charts and maps to aid in local time conversion; notes on shortwave antennas and propagation; and seven shortwave station maps showing the location of well-known shortwave broadcasters in North America, Western Europe, Eastern Europe, the Middle East, the Far East, East Asia, Africa, and South America. There is also a programming schedule for the British Broadcasting Service (that is, the British Broadcasting Corporation, or BBC). This introductory matter is followed by more than 200 pages of shortwave frequencies in ascending order from .1225MHz to 29890MHz. Each entry gives the mode of transmission, call letter (if any), the name of the broadcaster or the type of service provided, and air times in UTC.

Volume 3 of the NASFG reviewed here was already a year out of date when it was received. Although not thoroughly proofed, the guide's errors and oversights will probably not create serious difficulties for the user. When first opening the guide, the time was 20:45 UTC (2:45pm CST). Checking to see what was available at that hour on the shortwave bands, this reviewer was disappointed to find no listing in the guide by time, only by frequency. Picking out a frequency at random (7465MHz) it was ascertained to be The Voice of Israel, as indicated. However, the guide gives the schedule for the English Service only (broadcast times between 00:00 and 05:15 UTC). When tuned in at 20:55 UTC, Voice of Israel's Spanish Service, not mentioned at all in the guide, was playing.

With a good shortwave receiver, listeners can tune across the frequencies listed in the guide, and they will find abundant shortwave programming. However, the programs one hears may or may not correspond to NASFG's listings. Hence, the usefulness of this guide is at best limited. It will probably be most beneficial for newcomers to the hobby of DXing.—**Warren L. Meinhardt**

769. **Television Writers Guide.** 4th ed. Lynne Naylor, comp. and ed. Los Angeles, Calif., Lone Eagle, 1996. 534p. index. $50.00pa. ISBN 0-943728-75-4. ISSN 0894-8658.

Intended primarily as a reference resource for television industry types—producers, directors, and agents—*Television Writers Guide* is a no-frills alphabetic directory of more than 5,000 writers. Each name listing in the main section of the directory includes the writer's credits, agent, guild affiliation, and Emmy nominations or wins. Authorial territory runs the gamut from comedy and drama pilots and series to specials, miniseries, and movies-of-the-week.

Coverage in this 4th edition is from 1974 to the 1994/1995 season—and therein lies a major rub for library ready-reference collections. Do not go looking for *Your Show of Shows* under Mel Brooks's name, or for any mention of Rod Serling or Paddy Chayefsky at all; only shows actually produced within the last (arid) 20 years of network television make the cut. While some cable programming is covered, there is nary a trace of a single program aired on PBS.

A group of useful cross-indexes is provided at the end of the directory, including listings by genre and program title. A small annoyance is the decision to list each writer for a program on a separate line in the title index, rather than under a single entry (probably the result of machine-generated indexing). Frighteningly, Roseanne alone gets 72 single-line entries in this index. A roster of Emmy Awards (again from the period 1974-1994) and directories of guilds, agents, and managers is also provided. *Television Writers Guide* is perhaps the most up-to-date and comprehensive list of industry writers currently available, a fact that, despite its limited chronological coverage, commends its purchase by larger public libraries or academic libraries serving programs in film, television, or popular culture.—**Gary Handman**

Handbooks and Yearbooks

770. **International Motion Picture Almanac, 1996.** 67th ed. Barry Monush and James D. Moser, eds. New York, Quigley Publishing, 1996. 765p. $109.00. ISBN 0-900610-55-7. ISSN 0074-7084.

A great deal of information regarding the entertainment industry, and the personalities in it, is provided by the 67th edition of the *International Motion Picture Almanac*. Although much of this guide is a who's who, containing thousands of brief biographies of people currently active in films and television, other chapters are involved with the behind-the-scenes workings of the industry.

An index of subjects promotes access to the text and precedes a summary of last year's activities and its releases from major film companies. The biographical listing includes the person's work in theater, film, and television, and is followed by the year's obituaries and chapters on awards, services, major studios, corporations, and organizations enabling the entertainment industry to flourish. "Feature Pictures of 1980-1994" includes production company, year, and cast. Also available is information about the industry in select foreign countries.

Such an almanac is a helpful reference tool, containing up-to-date information regarding a major national and international industry. Future annual editions will ensure the volume's continued usefulness.—**Anita Zutis**

771. **International Television & Video Almanac, 1996.** 41st ed. Barry Monush and others, eds. New York, Quigley Publishing, 1996. 701p. $80.00. ISBN 0-900610-56-5. ISSN 0539-0761.

The 1996 edition of the *International Television & Video Almanac* remains a staple for any good reference collection. The almanac serves as a helpful first resource for finding a variety of facts and information about the U.S. television industry. Useful sections include "The Year in Review," which details major events in broadcasting for the year; statistics about the viewing habits of households and persons; and corporate histories of ABC, CBS, and NBC. Also provided is an extensive "who's who of the entertainment field," which includes the birth date and place and the television, theater, and "picture" credits of producers, directors, writers, and actors. In addition to listings for television companies, producers, and stations, the section on home video supplies information on video companies, retailers, and equipment manufacturers in addition to providing profiles of international television and video enterprises. Although the almanac offers an excellent collation of various kinds of information about the entertainment field, it would be strengthened if the corporate histories included newer broadcasting entities such as Fox, Turner Broadcasting, and Warner Brothers.—**Elizabeth A. Ginno**

772. Mackenzie, Harry, comp. **Command Performance, USA! A Discography.** Westport, Conn., Greenwood Press, 1996. 252p. illus. index. (Armed Forces Radio Service Discographies; Discographies, no.64). $75.00. ISBN 0-313-29828-9.

Difficult to use partly because it is divided into four separate performance chronologies for the years 1942-1949, *Command Performance, USA!* is a treasure trove of obscure Armed Forces Radio Service (AFRS) facts greatly diminished by what is left out. Mackenzie could have provided a sample entry to help the reader understand the murky typography of this compilation of more than 800 radio shows, but he did not. The four chronologies (two of which are indexed) offer listings of only the musical performances from four different AFRS variety shows (*Command Performance*, *Mail Call*, *GI Journal*, and *Special Programmes*) that were transmitted to Allied troops during and shortly after World War II. According to Mackenzie, "Comedy spots, playlets, sketches, etc., have not been logged although the performers have been noted in the cast list" (p. 2).

Although *Command Performance, USA!* is a tremendous compilation of useful data, it is flawed by its structure and presentation. A more forceful editor may have saved this work. At the price, *Command Performance, USA!* is no bargain and can only be recommended to libraries with the most comprehensive collections in radio history and the performing arts.—**Clay Housholder**

773. **World Radio TV Handbook.** 1996 ed. Andrew G. Sennitt and others, eds. New York, Billboard Books/Watson-Guptill, 1996. 608p. illus. maps. index. $24.95pa. ISBN 0-8230-5927-8.

This is the 50th edition of the *World Radio TV Handbook* (WRTH). Started by a Danish journalist, O. Lund Johanssen, during World War II as a column in a local newspaper listing various shortwave stations, the WRTH has become the bible to shortwave listeners around the world. This volume is particularly memorable because of a number of special 50th anniversary articles relating to the history of shortwave radio broadcasting. This reviewer found the section on "Pardon My Blooper" especially memorable. The volume begins with a series of general articles regarding current tips in the shortwave world. Sections are devoted to music, English-language programming, the Internet, and new technology in international broadcasting. Each year, the WRTH has a highly regarded "Equipment Test Bench" that gives rather honest appraisals of current shortwave receivers. This is followed by a scientific analysis of the propagation conditions for the coming year.

The main portion of the WRTH is a country-by-country list of shortwave broadcasting stations, along with their frequencies, times of operation, brief transmission schedules, and contact information (this year features e-mail or Internet addresses for the major stations). Next follows a list of stations by frequency, where the reader can check for likely suspects on the radio dial. This is a handy feature to have when one is not sure to which station one is listening. The WRTH concludes with a section entitled "Essential Information," which is a compendium of DX clubs, religious broadcasters, abbreviations, a world timetable, standard frequency and time signals, and last-minute changes to radio frequencies. The 1996 edition came out in the fall of 1995, so current buyers may want to look toward the purchase of the 1997 or 1998 edition. Most libraries with patrons interested in shortwave radio listening will not want to be without this essential and unique handbook.—**Ralph Lee Scott**

774. Yoder, Andrew. **Shortwave Listening on the Road: The World Traveler's Guide.** New York, TAB Books/McGraw-Hill, 1996. 183p. illus. maps. index. $17.95pa. ISBN 0-07-076509-X.

Shortwave listening has always been an exciting hobby. Now it is portable, too. This guide for mobile shortwave listening includes an introduction to shortwave basics and is divided into five chapters, four appendixes, and an index.

In the first four chapters, the author offers tips on choosing receivers and accessories, where to buy them, and how to get the most out of using them on the road. Chapter 5 ("International Shortwave Broadcasts in English") is an alphabetic listing by country of more than 100 broadcasters from Albania to Zimbabwe. The appendixes include a Coordinated Universal Time (UTC) chart, calling codes for the countries included in chapter 5 (and for some cities), guides to other shortwave services, data on worldwide power voltages and line frequencies, and information on using radio Bulletin Board Services (BBSes). The inclusion in the topical index of the countries listed alphabetically in chapter 5 seems superfluous.

The listing of countries in chapter 5 is highly selective. The user will find Bhutan, Botswana, and Bulgaria, but not Bolivia; China, the Clandestines, and Cuba, but not Chile; Malta, Moldova, and Mongolia, but not Mexico. For those countries listed, information includes frequencies, times, addresses, telephone and fax numbers, and station features in random instances. Map icons show at a glance what areas of the world are targeted by each broadcaster.

Yoder's guide is suitably small and easy to carry, but of limited usefulness. It will be most helpful for the novice setting out on the road with his or her shortwave equipment for the first time.

—**Warren L. Meinhardt**

21 Decorative Arts

COLLECTING

Autographs

775. Baker, Mark Allen. **Collector's Guide to Celebrity Autographs.** Iola, Wis., Krause Publications, 1996. 416p. illus. $19.95pa. ISBN 0-87341-464-0.

From the introduction, to the celebrity address directory, this book takes readers through the many aspects of autograph collection. Starting with the who's who of the celebrity status section, readers will find the most sought-after celebrities of today and why these particular autographs are so popular. This can be helpful to both the beginning and the advanced autograph collector.

The tools and terms of the trade section set the stage for the type of collection a person may wish to acquire. A signed photograph may not be the best way to obtain a marketable celebrity autograph. Considering this in advance will arm collectors with both the tools and the knowledge to get a more valuable addition to their collection (e.g., sports heroes signing sports equipment, rock musicians signing instruments).

The book also offers helpful hints on what may be the best way to acquire celebrity autographs (searching records, finding addresses, writing agents, or purchasing at auctions). A short list of some of the more popular autographs and their current value will give a reference to what types hold value better and to when an autograph is most marketable. The celebrity autographs and addresses section is a complete guide to the mailing addresses of popular celebrities from all genres and includes a chart rating response time and response quality. Illustrations of a wide variety of famous autographs accompany the directory.

A "College and Professional Sports Directory" and a "Soap Opera Directory" offer more specific avenues to these prospective areas of interest. A directory of "Celebrity Hotspots" in the United States and Europe lends ideas to the collector willing to go into the trenches to create a more personal collection.

This directory as a whole is a useful guide to both the novice and the advanced autograph collector. Those who simply enjoy collecting memorabilia for a hobby will find the directory an exciting look into the big business and big profits of celebrity autograph collection.—**Michael Florman**

Books

776. **Huxford's Old Book Value Guide.** 8th ed. Paducah, Ky., Collector Books, 1996. 414p. $19.95. ISBN 0-89145-700-3.

This book supplies the current market value of some 25,000 collectible books arranged alphabetically by author. The guide is based on the catalogs of 195 U.S. book dealers listed by code number in the back. The majority of the books listed have current market values of under $40, although there are many entries for much more expensive books. *Huxford's* is one of three annually published reference works based on dealer catalogs. It contains about as many entries as its two more expensive competitors (*Bookman's Price Index* and *Book Prices: Used and Rare* [see ARBA 96, entries 1004 and 1003, respectively]), and even though its focus is on moderately priced collectible books, it is these books that most book dealers and book collectors are most likely to encounter. Given its very modest price, *Huxford's* should be the priority acquisition of book dealers, book collectors, and librarians interested in the current market value of collectible books. Future editions should eliminate books costing less than $20 and should include more catalogs of dealers associated with the American Antiquarian Booksellers Association.—**Joseph Cataio**

Clocks

777. **The Charlton Price Guide to Canadian Clocks.** By James E. Connell. Toronto, Charlton Press; distr., Chicago, Independent Publishers Group, 1995. 117p. illus. $19.95pa.; $17.50pa. (U.S.). ISBN 0-88968-170-8. ISSN 1198-984X.

Collectors always need resources to help identify and appraise interesting and unusual finds. This is no less true in the world of clock collecting. The present volume fills an important niche in the literature. Mechanically, Canadian clocks are much like their United States counterparts, but their Canadian manufacture and in some cases, their rarity make a catalog of Canadian clocks a necessity for the serious collector.

Connell's work has much to recommend it. Entries are presented alphabetically by the name of the manufacturer. Each entry identifies the clock's type, movement, dial type, strike mechanism, height, width, and rarity. In addition, there is a description of the case and prices listed for each clock in fair, good, and mint condition. A concise description of what constitutes fair, good, and mint is found in the introduction. The prices listed were determined after consulting a number of expert collectors and taking the median price. The author could lend credibility to the work if he identified his panel of experts. Brief background information on the manufacturer or retailer of the clocks also accompanies each entry. Entries include a clear black-and-white photograph of the clock discussed.

This work does not attempt to present a history of the Canadian clock industry but is strictly a price guide. While its brevity may leave some collectors wishing for more detail, many will find the slim volume a handy and convenient reference. It is recommended for serious collectors and dealers in antiques and clocks.
—**Gregg S. Geary**

Coins (and Paper Money)

778. **Handbook of Ancient Greek and Roman Coins.** By Zander H. Klawans. K. E. Bressett, ed. Racine, Wis., Western Publishing, 1995. 288p. illus. index. $10.95pa. ISBN 0-307-09362-X.

The *Handbook of Ancient Greek and Roman Coins* is the updated, revised, and combined version of two 1959 works: *An Outline of Ancient Greek Coins* and *Reading and Dating Roman Imperial Coins*, both published by Whitman. This book will be useful for collectors just entering the ancient coin arena. Maps displaying the ancient names of cities and countries, an alphabetic guide to cities and symbols, detailed description of notable rulers and other people depicted on ancient coins, and detailed treatment of inscriptions give the novice a rich reference source. The photographs of hundreds of coins are of high quality, showing adequate detail; however, a handful of examples are of poor quality.

Any collector of ancient Greek or Roman coins will appreciate the many lists and tables, such as the alphabetic list of the names of the emperors as they frequently appear on coins, mint marks, an alphabetic list of typical reverse inscriptions, and examples of dating inscriptions. To have all of this information in such a convenient package is a delight. Research has been extensive on ancient coinage, and it is customary to attribute an identification of a coin to the original scholarly work. Although major references and standard works are offered in the bibliography, the lack of attributions to individual coins is a serious omission. Surprisingly, there is no identification of coin type to its metallic composition. Nonetheless, this work is highly recommended for the private collector and the reference collections of public and academic libraries.—**Margaret F. Dominy**

779. Herbert, Kevin. **The John Max Wulfing Collection in Washington University, Volume III: Roman Imperial Coins....** Wauconda, Ill., Bolchazy-Carducci, 1996. 92p. $80.00; $50.00pa. ISBN 0-86516-322-7; 0-86516-332-4pa.

This is the third in a series of volumes cataloging the John Max Wulfing Collection at Washington University (St. Louis). The first two catalogs, published in 1979 and 1987, cataloged the ancient Greek and Roman Republican sections of the 13,000-coin Wulfing Collection. The present volume covers Roman Imperial coins in the collection issued from 31 B.C.E. to 180 C.E. (roughly from Augustus to Hadrian). Herbert lists the coins according to the Crawford standard of description. The author has discovered 18 coins not previously listed in Crawford's catalog.

The volume begins with an extensive and excellent essay on the coins and policies of the Imperial Roman government. The publisher claims that this is a "non-technical introduction to the history of coinage." The definition of the term *nontechnical* may hinge in this case on statements like "a later denarius has a fuller titulature." This reviewer would argue that to most readers this is technical language, and to argue that this is a nontechnical introduction is to mislead the general reader.

Nevertheless, this is an excellent catalog of an important university coin collection. Extensive photographs and complete descriptions are given for each coin in this period. There is an index preceding the photographs (i.e., not at the end of the book) by name, coin legend, and coin type. This volume is recommended for libraries specializing in classical studies and numismatics.—**Ralph Lee Scott**

780. Krause, Chester L., and Clifford Mischler. **Standard Catalog of World Coins 1601-1700.** Iola, Wis., Krause Publications, 1996. 1152p. illus. $65.00pa. ISBN 0-87341-271-0.

The newest volume in the series of World Coins and Paper Money by the publisher, this current work covers coins minted between the years 1601 and 1700. Extensive coverage of coins struck by countries, principalities, states, and provinces is included. For example, Germany and Austria are arranged alphabetically by state. Each political division begins with a brief paragraph description, locating it geographically and historically. Sufficient coverage of non-Western coins for this time period is also included; Chinese empires and Vietnam are but two such listed entries.

Each entry has at least one black-and-white photograph for visual comparison with the coin in hand. Distinguishing marks or features are listed. Pricing information is as current as possible, although with any work of this nature, it must be used as a guide and not as an exact guideline. An extensive introduction discusses unique points to consider when collecting and trading coins of this time period. Dating, identification, and privy marks are three examples of the items in the introduction. A legend abbreviations table with numerical item references rounds out the volume.

This work will find use in any collection supporting interests in numismatics, general collecting, or the history of the seventeenth century. As noted earlier, currency of the pricing information is always a concern in any collector's catalog, and so it is with this volume. This can easily be solved by further revisions of the present volume.—**Gregory Curtis**

Dolls

781. Smith, Patricia. **Patricia Smith's Doll Values: Antique to Modern.** 12th ed. Paducah, Ky., Collector Books, 1996. 320p. illus. index. $12.95pa. ISBN 0-89145-694-5.

The most recent edition of a long-standing work in the collecting field, this volume provides updated information and pricing. The work is divided into two sections, antique and modern, for easier reference. Each section is arranged alphabetically by company, or in the case of famous dolls, by name of the doll. A brief background, typically 50 to 100 words in length, on the doll and the company are given in each entry with distinguishing marks or features noted. Pricing information for variants is also included. With popular dolls, such as the Barbie series, accessories information is provided as well. At least one and, many times, multiple color photographs for each entry visually reference notes in the text. A doll and maker index, a mold/model number index, and a letter/symbol index complete the volume.

With the increased interest in collectibles, the new information and pricing of the current edition make this a valuable source for any public library or specialized library supporting research in antiques or cultural research. As with any pricing guide, currentness of the information in the volume is vital to its usefulness. Further editions of the work will continue that currentness.—**Gregory Curtis**

Firearms

782. The Illustrated Encyclopedia of Handguns: Pistols and Revolvers of the World, 1870 to the Present. By A. B. Zhuk. John Walter, ed. London, Greenhill Books; distr., Harrisburg, Pa., Stackpole Books, 1995. 304p. illus. $49.95. ISBN 1-85367-187-8.

Zhuk's drawings of handguns reflect masterful draftsmanship and great artistic talent. He had access to an apparently unrivaled collection of weapons in the former Soviet Union and, except for some guns produced in the last few years, he covers virtually every pistol made by anyone, anywhere, since 1870. For this review, 22 different handguns were compared to his drawings, and each representation was found to be complete, detailed, and accurate.

Unfortunately, the text does not match these superb illustrations. In general, it is skimpy and incomplete. Moreover, the major market for this book must be in the United States, where readers will find the European division of handguns into categories of pistols and revolvers unusual and awkward. The use of British English is also occasionally jarring, especially the imprecise use of "effectual" when "effective" is meant. A future edition, tailored to the U.S. market, could marry these superb illustrations with any of the several detailed, extensive, and accurate texts already on hand in U.S. publications. As it stands, this book will be best appreciated by readers who already know something of handguns, and it should be considered by libraries serving such patrons.—**John Newman**

Folk Art

783. Rosenak, Chuck, and Jan Rosenak. **Contemporary American Folk Art: A Collector's Guide.** New York, Abbeville Press, 1996. 320p. illus. index. $29.95pa. ISBN 1-55859-897-9.

Literature on folk art has become popular since the early 1990s. The authors of this title, collectors of folk art for 20 years, also published *Museum of American Folk Art Encyclopedia of Twentieth-Century American Folk Art and Artists* (see ARBA 92, entry 982). The focus of the book at hand is new artists, and therefore does not include artists from the first half of the century. The book is divided geographically into six regions of the United States. Each regional chapter begins with an introductory essay highlighting folk art, followed by an alphabetic directory of artists. Each entry includes brief biographical information, collecting tips, and where one can see and buy the art. The entries are supplemented by color and black-and-white illustrations of the artists' work. Brief introductory essays are also provided, covering the topics of evaluating, buying and selling folk art, and folk art at auctions. The appendixes contain conservation advice, a glossary of terms, a price guide, and a brief bibliography. This source is a helpful guide for collectors in addition to an introduction to contemporary folk art. It is recommended for libraries with general art collections. [R: Choice, Oct 96, p. 258]—**Monica Fusich**

Glass

784. Edwards, Bill. **The Standard Carnival Glass Price Guide.** Paducah, Ky., Collector Books, 1996. 63p. illus. $9.95pa. ISBN 0-89145-690-2.

785. Edwards, Bill. **Standard Encyclopedia of Carnival Glass.** 5th ed. Paducah, Ky., Collector Books, 1996. 350p. illus. $24.95. ISBN 0-89145-689-9.

The most recent edition of this standard work in the field, the current encyclopedia volume brings up-to-date the items and prices in the collectible world of carnival glass produced between 1905 and 1930. As with the earlier editions (see ARBA 89, entry 873, for a review of the 2d ed.), this edition provides a descriptive catalog of the most well-known pieces, arranged alphabetically with cross-references to other entries. The entries provide a color photograph of each piece discussed and a brief text description. A brief historical note on the major companies—Dugan, Fenton, Imperial, Millersburg, and Northwood—as well as lesser-known companies, including English and Australian, producing carnival glass from the 1890s to the 1930s introduces the volume.

A price guide, including color variations for more than 33,000 pieces, appears at the end of the volume, as well as in the separate companion volume. Illustrations of many of the glass pieces listed in the price guide are helpful in matching the piece in hand to the entries in the guide. As with any price guide, currentness of information is vital to the usefulness of the work; maintaining pricing information is the key to success of the volume. This separate pricing guide will find use with those who do not want to manage the larger volume when visiting antique dealers or auctions, for it is easy to use and carry and filled with information of interest to collectors and dealers. Its reasonable price recommends it as a companion to the larger encyclopedia.

The encyclopedia itself is a worthwhile addition to library collections supporting research in the arts, collecting, glassmaking, or antique trades. The value in any volume such as this is the continual addition of newly discovered items and the updating of pricing information (as previously mentioned) to the general public who may not have access to the trade magazines. One anticipates that further editions of this work will continue that trend.—**Gregory Curtis**

Marbles

786. **Greenberg's Guide to Marbles.** 2d ed. By Dennis Webb. Waukesha, Wis., Greenberg Books/Kalmbach Publishing, 1995. 160p. illus. index. $45.95. ISBN 0-89778-330-1.

This book is for students of U.S. toys, games, and industries; archaeologists, linguists, promotion designers, artists, and meditators on roundness; and, perhaps most of all, antique collectors. "In the 1990s . . . a marble become[s] a collectible the minute it is produced" (p. 134). Webb is conscientious, committed, well versed and thorough in his subject, without being complex or obtuse. His history of U.S. production of spheres made of stone, ceramic, metal, and glass is a gathering of printed information of varying primary sources, personal contacts, and visits to sites.

The author mentions uses of the little balls other than as toys; he also includes some import and export history. Webb enjoys marbles as color studies, which he facilitates by supplying many lovely color photographs and descriptions. Particularly interesting is the depiction of marbles made in the 1970s to look like the Earth from a space satellite. According to the book, prices have been pretty stable since the early 1970s; the current price lists makes them rather expensive.

Webb leaves it to other writers to tell how to play the many games using these items; some games (e.g., Chinese Checkers) he mentions because he finds the packaging of these games collectible. He does not systematically cover regional variations in naming of this popular plaything, but some local names are mentioned. The transparent glass marbles this reviewer called "puries" in 1930s Connecticut, Webb identifies as "clearies." The thought of the sacrifice and thrill of working with molten glass, the nature of marble-making machines, their arduous copyright history, and the competition and vagaries of the market also make this an inspiring and educational book.—**Elizabeth L. Anderson**

CRAFTS

787. Bray, Charles. **Dictionary of Glass: Materials and Techniques.** Philadelphia, University of Pennsylvania Press, 1995. 240p. illus. $47.95. ISBN 0-8122-3357-3.

Dictionary of Glass is a quick reference source of fundamental words and phrases that relate to glassmaking, with a focus on small-scale rather than industrial production. Entries describe materials, equipment, and technical processes in as little as a paragraph or up to several pages of text. The language used is highly understandable, and many entries are accompanied by illustrations or photographs, mostly in black-and-white. The author, who has an extensive background in glass art and technology, does not cover the history of the subject in his book. Biographical information is also limited, with just a paragraph or two about prominent people in the field. Appendixes include lists of suppliers, professional organizations and societies, museums and galleries with significant glass collections, and schools offering glass courses. The book is intended to be a companion to *The Potter's Dictionary of Materials and Techniques* by Frank and Janet Hamer (rev. ed.; see ARBA 88, entry 998). [R: Choice, May 96, p. 1446]—**Jean Engler**

DESIGN

788. Tambini, Michael. **The Look of the Century.** New York, DK Publishing, 1996. 288p. illus. index. $39.95. ISBN 0-7894-0950-X.

Packed with hundreds of color illustrations that are bolstered by concise captions and carefully edited survey articles written by design specialists, this is a lively and authoritative summary of design in the twentieth century. During the past 96 years, the work of designers has virtually taken over the objects, machines, fashions, and look of the world around us. This compilation presents brilliant coverage of the efforts and accomplishments of designers in many fields since the turn of the century. Each of the major areas of design has been covered separately, and all run the gamut chronologically. This adds greatly to the overall usefulness of the book and results in logical reading while controlling the masses of material that could so easily get out of hand if not based on time frames.

The selection and high quality of the reproductions of the massive treasure trove of illustrations deserve special mention. Picture researchers have done a great service to the design community in gathering together so many key pieces that focus on a decade or an important style. The book has been decidedly enriched by using the collections and staff expertise of the National Design Museum, the Cooper-Hewitt in New York City. The author has had varied experience as a professional in British museums, and this results in ample coverage of British and Continental contributions to the world of design. Packaging, posters, photocopiers, and automobiles are all here, as well as the classic Coca Cola bottle, the Mickey Mouse watch, Steiff teddy bears, the rolodex, the Cadillac Eldorado, and Kewpie dolls. Brief biographies of more than 300 significant designers are a welcome bonus in this exemplary survey, which will benefit collectors, antique dealers, designers in all fields, social historians, and the academic community.

—**William J. Dane**

PHOTOGRAPHY

789. **Index to American Photographic Collections.** 3d ed. Andrew H. Eskind and others, eds. New York, G. K. Hall/Simon & Schuster Macmillan, 1995. 1058p. $165.00. ISBN 0-7838-2149-2.

This is the 3d edition of a title that began as part of *Photography: Source & Resource* (see ARBA 74, entry 1037). Since that time, both the number of institutions and the number of photographs have increased enormously: There are now some 582 collections reporting 66,830 items. This last number is twice that reported in the 2d edition (1990). In part, this reflects the growing acceptance of photography as art, but it is also the result of increasingly sophisticated reporting efforts. As with previous editions, the current index is divided into two sections: a "Collections Listing," describing the holdings of individual collections, and a "Photographers Index," listing all institutions holding works by individual photographers. The first is organized alphabetically by geographic place-name, the second alphabetically by the photographer's last name. In addition, the photographers index contains the names of many more photographers whose work is not included in the collections, but who have appeared in one or more of the several thousand exhibition catalogs collated by the editors. They suggest that these photographers may be "opportunities" for new collectors. Although not for every library, the index is essential for any institution supporting research in or collections of photography. [R: Choice, Nov 96, pp. 431-32]

—**Paul L. Holmer**

22 Fine Arts

GENERAL WORKS

Bibliography

790. **BHA: Bibliography of the History of Art: Subject Headings/English. Bibliographie D'histoire de L'art: Mots-Matière/Français.** Vandœuvre Cedex, France, Institut de L'information Scientifique et Technique and Santa Monica, Calif., J. Paul Getty Museum Book Distribution Center, 1996. 389p. free with CD-ROM. ISSN 1150-1588.

791. **BHA: Bibliography of the History of Art 1996. Bibliographie D'histoire de L'art.** [CD-ROM]. Vandœuvre Cedex, France, Institut de L'information Scientifique et Technique and Santa Monica, Calif., J. Paul Getty Museum Book Distribution Center, 1996. Minimum system requirements: IBM or compatible 386. CD-ROM drive. Windows 3.0. 4MB RAM. VGA monitor. Mouse. $700.00. ISSN 1085-5114.

The *Bibliography of the History of Art* (BHA), produced in three CD-ROMs, covers the history of postclassical Western art and is published in both English and French. The CD-ROM version is published jointly by the Art History Information Program of the J. Paul Getty Trust, and the Institut National de L'information Scientifique et Technique (INIST) of the Centre National de la Recherch Scientifique. The publications (previously printed in paper version) that have been used to provide the basic database are the *International Repertory of the Literature of Art* (RILA) and *Le Répertoire d'Archéologie* (RAA). RILA began in 1975 (some earlier versions of the bibliography were published irregularly) and merged with RAA in 1989 with volume 16. RAA began in 1910 and was produced as an automated database for the first time in 1973. This CD-ROM version of RAA contains all records from 1973 and 1989, and all records included after the merger. The RILA CD-ROM contains all records beginning with 1975.

The BHA surveys current writing on Western art, beginning in the fourth century C.E. and continuing to the present. In the area of contemporary art, only what the compilers of BHA consider "critical and theoretical publications" are included, but this restriction appears to be taken quite liberally in that the bibliography includes most standard sources concerning fine arts. In all, the complete production of art of the European and New World successors to the Greco-Roman world and those people and cultures studied in relation to them are detailed in the database. The types of art covered are extremely broad and encompass architecture, sculpture, painting, drawing, prints, popular and folk art, photography, and new media. Also covered are decorative and applied arts, industrial design and architectural theory, and material culture of interest to art historians.

The CD-ROMs are relatively easy to install and use. At the beginning of each search, it is necessary to select either French or English, and if a user has a system that will load all three CD-ROMs at the same time, he or she must select the desired database to search. (Otherwise, the discs must be switched when prompted by the software.) Search techniques used are complete, including Boolean and relational operators, searching with indexes, and searching with wildcards. Of course, all standard search techniques are possible (i.e., title of artistic work, artist, art schools, historical periods, and the like). Once a search has been completed, it is possible to custom display the results using a variety of selections, including full records, titles only, and so forth. Also, before displaying, it is possible to mark records so that only desired items are printed or saved to disk. In addition, a sophisticated sort system allows the user to prepare custom lists.

The CD-ROMs come with two books: an instruction manual for loading and using the discs, and a 389-page manual entitled *BHA: Bibliography of the History of Art: Subject Headings*. The CD-ROMs are extremely inclusive and relatively convenient to use. It should be remembered that there is a certain amount of training needed to use the databases, so they should be made available where assistance is provided. They are strongly recommended for all public and academic libraries that have large fine arts collections.
—Robert L. Wick

792. Ford, Simon. **The Realization and Suppression of the Situationist International: An Annotated Bibliography 1972-1992.** San Francisco, Calif., AK Press, 1995. 149p. index. $10.95pa. ISBN 1-873176-82-1.

The International Situationist Movement was founded in 1957 by artists Asger Jorn, Guy Debord, Heimrad Prem, René Viénet, and others, and is generally considered another in a long list of avant-garde art movements in the twentieth century. The major thrust of the movement was the attempt to renew the Surrealist liaison between political and aesthetic thought and practice. The Situationists's ideas were laid down in the magazine *Internationale Situationniste*, published in 1958 and 1959. From the beginning, the movement had contradictory political and artistic factions that led to a split in 1962, when the Debordist followers parted ways with Prem and the other German and Scandinavian members. To some extent, the movement produced more theory than actual artworks, and in practice resembled the methods employed by the classic Leninists of establishing a journal and then issuing manifestos and leaflets to further the cause. Many of the articles in *Internationale Situationniste* were more concerned with the organization of the movement than the art it espoused. Ford points out in his introduction that the "bibliography has been produced to assist inquirers in discovering the existence and determining the identity of books and other documentary material which may be of interest [to researchers of the movement, and] to illustrate how historical processes and critical reception acted upon the S. I. and to chart the spread of this discourse."

In all, there are more than 350 works listed with brief annotations. Most of the works are in English or are English translations. The organization of the materials is based on the history of the movement: general works; related movements; works on or by ex-Situationists; "American Pro-Situs and Milieu"; "British Pro-Situs and Milieu"; book reviews; 1989 exhibition and catalog reviews; selected addresses (of organizations, publishers, and bookstores that have materials concerning the movement), and a well-developed index. In addition, the prefatory material contains a list of abbreviations, a chronology of key publications, and notes concerning the work.

There are few existing sources of information on the International Situationist Movement, and even the new *Grove Dictionary of Art* (1996) does not devote much space to it. The only other bibliography of any size is in Sadie Plant's *Most Radical Gesture* (Routledge, 1992). The bibliography will be of interest to all researchers and students of the movement and its aftermath. The work is recommended for larger academic and public libraries with extensive art collections, and for individuals who are students or scholars of the avant-garde movement in the twentieth century.—**Robert L. Wick**

793. Puerto, Cecilia. **Latin American Women Artists, Kahlo and Look Who Else: A Selective, Annotated Bibliography.** Westport, Conn., Greenwood Press, 1996. 237p. illus. index. (Art Reference Collection, no.21). $69.50. ISBN 0-313-28934-4.

Multiculturalism has taken on great significance in the U.S. society of the past decade. This interest in related cultures has especially manifested itself in the arts with increased numbers of exhibitions and publications; one of these areas is in the documentation of Latin American women artists. Puerto's compilation consists of 15,000 citations on 800 women of Mexico, Central and South America, the Caribbean, and the West Indies. Artists included are those born in the 1900s or late 1800s who work(ed) in the varied media of painting, drawing, printmaking, sculpture, photography, mixed media, installation, and performance art; excluded are those who fall under the rubric of folk art.

The volume encompasses selectively annotated citations to books, periodicals, exhibition catalogs, dissertations, theses, videorecordings, and substantial newspaper articles. These are arranged by country, and then by artist in part 1. Part 2 consists of general works also arranged by country. Because there is no index to the general works (books and periodical articles), the researcher must consult the general name index at the back of the volume to ensure that all information on a given artist has been located.

As a reference librarian and bibliographer of Latin American studies, Puerto realizes the importance of good annotations and makes note of such useful information as artist's statements and reproductions of works. Many of the artists listed have only one or two citations referring to their work; one can therefore imagine the long hours of searching that went into the compilation of this bibliography. The reference will become a vital source for scholars working in the area of Latin American studies, women's studies, art, and women artists.—**Lamia Doumato**

794. Silverman, Helaine. **Ancient Peruvian Art: An Annotated Bibliography.** New York, G. K. Hall/Simon & Schuster Macmillan, 1996. 275p. index. (A Reference Publication in Art History). $95.00. ISBN 0-8161-9060-7.

The phenomenon of several thousand years of extraordinarily fine and fascinating craft-producing cultures in the Americas is now impressing North America's academies and art collectors. What indigenous Spanish-trained and German scholars have collected, cataloged, and interpreted is in the late twentieth century being published in English and further pursued. At a time when leisure, that is, unemployment, is a challenge, and the natural environment is often being hurt by present employments, these mastercraft-oriented societies have relevant advice: A myth, a ritual, and a craft make survivors of subsistence-level economies.

Silverman, in a seminal introduction, tells the history of the scholarship, which she lists by author with annotations in the body of the book. Only a set of catalogs interrupts this organization; it should be integrated into the author list in the next edition. All the work of each researcher is organized chronologically and described for content, illustrations, quality, and place in the history of the study. Silverman's perspective as a trained and able researcher in Peruvian arts is beneficial to the organization of these publications. By thoroughly organizing an index by subject (e.g., animal imagery, sites, cultures), she gives even the novice researcher a useful starting place. This tome should be available to all who touch on Peruvian studies for any reason.—**Elizabeth L. Anderson**

Biography

795. **Contemporary Artists.** 4th ed. Joann Cerrito and others, eds. Detroit, St. James Press, 1996. 1340p. illus. index. $160.00. ISBN 1-55862-183-0.

The 4th edition of this biographical dictionary is a welcome update to the 3d edition, published in 1989 (see ARBA 90, entry 948). Profiles of more than 800 individuals representing all areas of the fine arts are arranged alphabetically. The editor notes that for this edition a special effort was made to include artists working in the fields of video and computer art. Selection criteria continue to be a record of exhibitions in major galleries or museums that have attracted significant critical attention. Entries for deceased artists are included only when they are perceived to be a continuing influence on current practice, although no artist who died before 1965 has been included (as opposed to 1960 for the 3d edition).

Entries include biographical data, a list of individual exhibitions and selected group exhibitions, collections, sites of permanent public installations (a new feature), an artist's statement when supplied, bibliographies of publications by and about the artist, and a signed critical essay. Black-and-white photographs of representative works accompany many of the entries. As a source of in-depth information on the most prominent of contemporary artists, this title remains an essential acquisition for all art libraries.—**Michael Weinberg**

Catalogs and Collections

796. Baker, Christopher, and Tom Henry, comps. **The National Gallery Complete Illustrated Catalogue.** London, National Gallery Publications; distr., New Haven, Conn., Yale University Press, 1995. 790p. illus. index. $60.00. ISBN 1-85709-050-0.

Having spent an entire day in the National Gallery in London, England, this reviewer was pleased to see the release of *The National Gallery Complete Illustrated Catalogue*, compiled by Baker and Henry. Quickly turning the pages showed many of the famous paintings that had been contemplated for hours. Happily, this reviewer's (somewhat obscure) favorite painting—Savaldo's *Saint Mary Magdalene Approaching the Sepulchre*—was included, thus proving that the catalog was indeed complete.

The 2,200-plus paintings are presented in full color, 3 to a page, arranged alphabetically by artist and listed by year of creation if more than 1 work by the same artist is in the collection. Each painting is annotated by artist name, title of work, date, inventory number, medium and size, explanation of subject matter, origin of the work, commentary on the work, means of acquisition, bibliography for further reference, and an artist's biography. The actual catalog is preceded by a short history of the gallery from its 1824 inception to the present day. A glossary explains terms used in the annotations, which is of benefit for nonartists. The painting catalog is followed by a list of the few sculptures in the collection, new acquisitions (mostly those of Georges Seurat), and the large reproductions of pieces that could not have shown much detail in the three-column format.

The only shortcomings in this beautiful work would be the bibliography, arranged alphabetically by author of the article or book. A breakdown by artist and subject area would have helped it greatly. The bibliography is followed by an index of the entire collection arranged by inventory number and seems to serve no further purpose, as there are no page references included. Instead, a title index of the paintings would have been more useful for people who know the name of a painting but not the artist. An extensive subject index finishes the book, including artists and titles of works listed under the artists. Subjects of works are listed extensively.

This catalog is recommended for libraries, art schools, and teachers. The book will be a valuable tool for those doing research. The references in each annotation will help guide students to more information. The CD-ROM version of the catalog (not reviewed) would be of even more benefit to teachers and students for classroom use.—**Kevin W. Perizzolo**

Dictionaries and Encyclopedias

797. Apostolos-Cappadona, Diane. **Encyclopedia of Women in Religious Art.** New York, Continuum Publishing, 1996. 442p. illus. index. $44.50. ISBN 0-8264-0915-6.

This detailed encyclopedia is thoughtfully presented and, because of this, serves a far wider purpose than describing women only in religious art. The concise but thorough descriptions will enable a reader in any subject about women in religious studies to have a quick and accurate source of reference. Designed to give information in simple style concerning the 2,000 entries from all the major religious traditions of the world, this 1-volume source depicts female figures as goddesses, celestial beings, demons, metaphorical beings, and legendary women as well as historical women, religious leaders, artists, and writers. Themes and motifs associated with women are also presented. The author is sensitive to a feminist perspective, and the book engages cultural and gender issues.

Of special value are the rich appendixes that guide users to variant names of figures and provide topical guides to the various types of women represented. The one regret is that the 101 illustrations are not enough for the curious reader. One would have wanted a larger and more copious treatment of the images. On the whole, this is a serviceable desk reference to female figures in the history of world religions. [R: LJ, 15 Nov 96, p. 54]—**Linda L. Lam-Easton**

798. Earls, Irene. **Baroque Art: A Topical Dictionary.** Westport, Conn., Greenwood Press, 1996. 332p. index. $95.00. ISBN 0-313-29406-2.

This topical dictionary, an expanded version of the author's earlier work, *Renaissance Art: A Topical Dictionary* (see ARBA 89, entry 899), covers terminology used in relation to artworks during the seventeenth century, the historical period known as the baroque. The dictionary covers popular subjects of painting, sculpture, and decorative arts of Italy and northern Europe (i.e., German-, French-, Dutch-, Flemish-, and Spanish-speaking countries), during the 1600s up through the first part of the eighteenth century. The selective entries cover characteristic schools, media, techniques, and other terms for the baroque period.

Baroque Art is valuable for a basic art history vocabulary and an understanding and clarification of baroque topics, iconographic inclusions, and mythological gods and goddesses. Entries in the major section are in one alphabetic sequence, covering topics of artists illustrating Bible stories, the lives and deaths of Christian saints, mythological subjects, certain historical events, and the importance of influential individuals. The dictionary is centered on mainstream works of art. The entries are brief. At the end of each entry, an example of a work depicting the topic is provided, including the name of the artist, the title of the work; the location of the work; and the book in which a picture of the illustration appears, along with an illustration or page number. There are full references to the illustrated sources named in the bibliography at the end of the volume.

This work often notes that major topics used in paintings and sculpture come from primary sources, such as *The Golden Legend* and the Bible. Topics range from entries on *alla prima*, bacchanal, and camera obscura to those on Cleopatra, the Eucharist, foreshortening, iconography, night painters, the *Rape of Lucretia*, and wash. The volume includes two appendixes, one on a list of popes of the baroque age, and a second with a list of artists covered, from Francesco Abani and Pieter Lastman to Peter Paul Rubens and Diego Rodríguez de Silva y Velázquez. A brief bibliography is provided for further study, along with an index to terms and page numbers.

For the beginning art history student, a museum and gallery visitor, and anyone interested in gaining some knowledge of the meaning of works of art during the baroque period, this work will be of interest. Prefatory and introductory pages, although brief, present a helpful synopsis of this time period in artistic expression. [R: LJ, 15 Sept 96, p. 54]—**Maureen Pastine**

799. Ross, Leslie. **Medieval Art: A Topical Dictionary.** Westport, Conn., Greenwood Press, 1996. 292p. index. $75.00. ISBN 0-313-29329-5.

Well-chosen and clear entries elucidate the familiar or the obtuse subjects of medieval art, answering the questions: What is that? and, Why is it there? Included is the relevant history from polytheism, Judaism, early Christianity, and Byzantium, giving precedents for the art of Europe from ca.600 to 1450. Typological story connections from Judaism to Christian incidents is constant, a positive relationship to balance the concurrent anti-Semitism: Moses crossing the Red Sea prefigures Jesus's baptism, the latter probably growing out of Hellenistic and Judaic rites.

Following a general description of when in medieval times an image was used and in what medium, and the literary sources (the Bible, the Apocrypha, early Christian and medieval writings), an example with date and present site is noted from a current medieval art history book. Revered sources for the literature, such as the fourteenth-century Golden Legend, have recently been newly published. The author is admirably aware of manuscripts, but other media are sufficiently included. Both devotion and academic scholarship inform these definitions. The choices for the bibliography could start deeper research. Unfortunately, the issue of art styles is only mentioned in dense paragraphs in the introduction, which could better be a timeline. [R: LJ, 15 Sept 96, p. 54]—**Elizabeth L. Anderson**

Directories

800. Shipp, Steve. **American Art Colonies, 1850-1930: A Historical Guide to America's Original Art Colonies and Their Artists.** Westport, Conn., Greenwood Press, 1996. 159p. illus. index. $69.50. ISBN 0-313-29619-7.

Art colonies are not a modern concept. For generations, artists have gathered together for support, inspiration, and a sense of community. This book examines the American interpretation of the late-nineteenth-century European idea of shared aesthetic experiences and does so in terms of the settings and the actors involved. The lists of names are long; some are familiar, some less so, and some are of interest only to art historians of the period.

Each chapter deals with a specific colony, from East Hampton to Santa Fe, Old Lyme to Laguna. It describes the colony, its development along philosophical and aesthetic lines, and the importance of its geographic location: For some artists the colony was a temporary escape from a city; for others, a departure to "unspoiled" areas. This section is followed by short biographical sketches of the major figures. The information supplied is particularly useful for the lesser-known artists and is based on multiple sources.

The use of an asterisk to mark those artists whose biographies follow is less than felicitous to the reader's eye, and a change in typeface may have been a better tool for this indication. The bibliography is excellent, including periodicals, and the index seems errorless. This is a useful work, both for its own content and for its sources for further study.—**Paula Frosch**

ARCHITECTURE

801. **Dictionary of Building Preservation.** Ward Bucher, ed. New York, John Wiley, 1996. 560p. illus. $39.95. ISBN 0-471-14413-4.

Perhaps the lack of availability in the English language of a similar lexicon—OCLC lists only one other like lexicon in German—encouraged John Wiley to publish a building preservation dictionary of limited usefulness. The editor of this tome gives two main purposes for putting it together: clarification of specialized terms used in the preservation field in the United States and Canada, and allowance of a recorder to fully describe a historic resource. Unfortunately, he falls short of his goals. Before reviewing the terminology the user must read the introduction. Bucher's prologue to his seemingly endless list of limitations (e.g., "Due to the constraints of time and the limits of my expertise, this dictionary is more focused on buildings than structures, sites, or objects") immediately sent up a red flag. With so many limitations, his "comprehensive coverage" should read "limited coverage."

Sadly, this dictionary offers definitions that are frequently unclear to the average citizen who has little or no background in building preservation or its allied fields. There is an attempt at frequent cross-referencing within the dictionary to clarify terms, and the contributors are authoritative—building and design professionals, preservationists, attorneys—which gives credibility to the definitions. However, because these reviewers are well-versed in this complex terminology, some words are defined using other words that are not explained in the dictionary (e.g., *fanlight* gives a description using a term not listed, *mutins*). This lexicon is illustrated with more than 400 measured drawings from the Historic American Building Survey and the 1st edition of *Architectural Graphics Standards*, but they are of limited usefulness because of their minute size. [R: RBB, 1 Dec 96, p. 684]—**Nadine Salmons**

802. Langmead, Donald. **Dutch Modernism: Architectural Resources in the English Language.** Westport, Conn., Greenwood Press, 1996. 243p. illus. index. (Art Reference Collection, no.22). $85.00. ISBN 0-313-29618-9.

Aside from being useful, this bibliography raises some interesting notions regarding the Netherlands's role in the formation of twentieth-century European architecture. In his opening essay, "More Than Cheese and Windmills," Langmead, associate professor of architecture at the University of South Australia and head of the Louis Laybourne Smith School of Architecture, provides an overview of the Netherlands's past and sketches a history of Dutch architecture from 1900 through 1940—a history that he maintains was unfairly overshadowed by the work of German architects who relocated to the United States during the war years. Citing the influence of the De Stijl art movement and Frank Lloyd Wright (whose work was strongly promoted in Europe, through the writings of Dutch architect and theorist Hendrik Petrus Berlage in the early years of this century), the author convincingly (although at times somewhat obliquely) portrays the Netherlands as the catalyst of the European Modernist Movement.

Although it has been claimed that few monographs of Dutch architecture have been published, more than a thousand books and journal articles are cited in the text. They are arranged chronologically (from 1895 through 1995), and most are in English (a few Dutch publications are included, especially those of historical importance). A chronology of key or significant buildings (with cross-references to the bibliography) and indexes to both the authors and the architects provide additional access. Unfortunately, an undifferentiated clot of reference numbers following some entries is frustrating and almost impossible to plow through. Nonetheless, the book fulfills its aim of providing a guide to an esoteric subject.

—**Margarete Gross**

803. Petersen, Andrew. **Dictionary of Islamic Architecture.** New York, Routledge, 1996. 342p. illus. maps. index. $89.95. ISBN 0-415-06084-2.

There is a noticeably rising contemporary interest in Islamic culture and civilization all across the globe. This first major reference book devoted to the broad sweep of Islamic architecture is most welcome, for it is organized with great care to provide concise and highly readable definitions and descriptions for experts as well as for neophytes. The author is director of the Ottoman Survey of the British School of Archaeology in Jerusalem, and he has personally visited many of the diverse sites and multiple locations that are described.

The text is substantially augmented by scores of photographs, architectural drawings and diagrams, and maps, which are essential for geographic accuracy of the diverse locations. There are summary accounts of Mecca, Mamluks, Timurids, Ottomans, and Mughals, along with descriptions of many cities, such as Cairo, Jerusalem, Damascus, and Istanbul, and in-depth coverage of extensive regions and nations, including West and East Africa, Iran, Jordan, Arabic Spain, and the United Arab Emirates. Architectural sites with vast and historic popular appeal are amply covered, such as Agra's Taj Mahal, Granada's Alhambra, and the Great Mosque in Cordova.

Clear definitions of words that have moved over from Islamic culture into international terminology (e.g., *caravanserai*, *hajj*, *harem*, *kiosk*, *minaret*, and *yurt*) are clarified, along with 14 Islamic words starting with the letter "q" and not followed by the letter "u." Crossword puzzle enthusiasts will find this particular listing to be of value and tangential interest. The total coverage is indeed worldwide to include Bengal, China, Java, Pakistan, the Philippines, and the United States, where more information on Islamic building in the Northeast over the past decades would be helpful. It is also disappointing to read the entry for Bosnia, where there is no mention of the 1,200 mosques that have been destroyed in recent times, according to a report from Harvard University. These are, however, minuscule omissions from what is in reality an outstanding addition to current production of notable reference information on Islamic societies past and present, and also a key to the understanding of a more rounded history of architecture. [R: Choice, Dec 96, p. 593]—**William J. Dane**

PAINTING

804. Baetjer, Katherine. **European Paintings in the Metropolitan Museum of Art by Artists Born Before 1865: A Summary Catalogue.** New York, Metropolitan Museum of Art; distr., Bergenfield, N.J., Harry N. Abrams, 1995. 527p. illus. index. $100.00. ISBN 0-87099-734-3.

The Metropolitan Museum of Art in New York City has enjoyed an illustrious history since opening in the 1870s. This summary catalog updates the three-volume set by the same author and title issued by the museum in 1980 and represents holdings as of March 1995. Included are approximately 2,500 paintings, oil sketches, and finished pastels. Arrangement for this edition is by nationality and regional school, then chronologically. The strength is in French and Italian art, representing more than 1,500 works. These have a particularly high quantity of paintings with Judaic and Christian themes. The remainder consists of Spanish, British, German, Netherlandish, Flemish, Dutch, and Belgian artists.

For this edition, detailed data about the painting are usually on the same or adjacent page as the artwork itself, including dimensions, inscriptions, the date of the work (if known), and source of acquisition. There are two indexes, one by artist, the other by accession number from the collection. The paper is of high quality, and there is generally fine resolution of the images. The only disappointment is that, with the exception of the jacket and four illustrations on preliminary pages, all of the paintings are in black-and-white. Such similar artists as Henri-Julien-Félix Rousseau (1844-1910) and Vincent van Gogh (1853-1890) made markedly different use of color. The museum has issued other books in color. In *The Metropolitan Museum of Art Guide* (1983), Paul Gauguin's signature on his *Ia Orana Maria* is clearly more visible than in the present volume. Nevertheless, this volume would serve well the needs of researchers and academic and art libraries. [R: Choice, June 96, p. 1620]—**Ralph Hartsock**

805. Bock-Weiss, Catherine C. **Henri Matisse: A Guide to Research.** New York, Garland, 1996. 690p. index. (Artist Resource Manuals, v.1; Garland Reference Library of the Humanities, v.1424). $95.00. ISBN 0-8153-0086-7.

In addition to the important critical works of Jack D. Flam (*Matisse, the Man and His Art, 1869-1918* [Cornell University Press, 1986]), Russell T. Clement (*Henri Matisse: A Bio-bibliography* [see ARBA 95, entry 997]), and Robert Benjamin (*Henri Matisse* [Rizzoli, 1992]), this guide to research on Matisse and his paintings, sculpture, and graphic works by Bock-Weiss (the School of the Art Institute of Chicago) is an excellent reference work for identifying the critical reception of and tracing the literary evidence of how the work of a major French artist has been perceived. Following a brief foreword, the introduction supplies a superb historical essay on Matisse. Following the introductory pages is a chronology from the artist's birth in 1869, through his studies and work in the legal profession, to his art studies and life as an artist, chronicling his exhibitions and artworks through 1954.

The major portion of this guide is made up of 10 selective, critical, annotated bibliographic sections, including primary documentation, archives, writings, and interviews; general studies, catalogs, and collections of essays; specific media; fauvism; collections and collectors; and books on Matisse for children, to name a few. The sections focus on the primary sources and the most critical secondary literature of monographs, oeuvre catalogs, exhibition and auction catalogs, articles in newspapers, Festschriften, museum bulletins and yearbooks, and primary sources of the artist's own writings. The major literature is documented through exhibition catalogs included from France, the United States, Germany, and the Scandinavian countries where the majority of his works are located. The author notes that although many important Matisse works are held in the former Soviet Union, little research literature has yet come from that part of the world.

The guide ends with three indexes, the first an index of authors; the second an index of subjects and themes from abstraction and cubism to dance, decorative arts, drawing, film, photography, related named artists' influences, and the impact of the First World War; and the third an index of artworks, separated by titles in French and followed by those in English. Each name and topic index term is referenced with appropriate page numbers. As one of the major reference sources on Matisse, this volume will prove to be one of the most valuable for scholars and graduate art history students and faculty because of its narrow focus on the most crucial Western and non-Western interpretations and criticism of the artist and his life and work.—**Maureen Pastine**

806. Clement, Russell T. **Four French Symbolists: A Sourcebook on Pierre Puvis de Chavannes, Gustave Moreau, Odilon Redon, and Maurice Denis.** Westport, Conn., Greenwood Press, 1996. 583p. index. (Art Reference Collection, no.20). $99.50. ISBN 0-313-29752-5.

Clement, professional humanities librarian and Francophile, gives users indispensable research on the late nineteenth-century beginnings of modern art. This thorough survey of exhibits and literature on four of the artistic stars is a good read as well as a source on this prelude to twentieth-century millennialist reactions. "Symbolism" is an uneasy title for what was called Romanesque in 1000 C.E., mannerism in the sixteenth century, and an as-yet-unnamed movement in the twentieth century. Its components include abstract form; search in alternative lifestyles; esoteric aspects of world religions; "indies" (art exhibitions then, films now); and a general malaise and hypersensitivity. The nature of the art of de Chavannes (1824-1898), Moreau (1826-1898), Redon (1840-1916), and Denis (1870-1943) and how they carried on the influence of the impressionists, as well as Édouard Manet, Paul Cézanne, Vincent van Gogh and Paul Gauguin, is well displayed. Concentrating on writing and therefore without pictures, one would need other books to recall the actual works. Some material repeated in Clement's biography, chronologies, primary and secondary book and article bibliography, and exhibition lists was never boring for its redundancy. All his annotations are worthwhile reading. This book is a fat, fruitful friend to all who would understand the history of art and its repetitions.—**Elizabeth L. Anderson**

807. Lester, Patrick D. **The Biographical Directory of Native American Painters.** Tulsa, Okla., SIR Publications; distr., Norman, Okla., University of Oklahoma Press, 1995. 701p. index. $49.95. ISBN 0-8061-9936-9.

Biographical information on Native American painters is always difficult to find. One of the only other attempts at such a listing was Jeanne Snodgrass's *American Indian Painters: A Biographical Directory*, published in 1968 (Museum of the American Indian, Heye Foundation). While Snodgrass's compilation was, and still is, a useful directory, many of the younger Native American painters are not listed. The directory under review begins with the Snodgrass directory and brings it up-to-date with a number of format changes (e.g., references to private collections have been deleted, as have all references to specific biographical publications). In addition, the format of the entries has been changed somewhat in the update. Artists' spouses and children are no longer listed, and some of the abbreviations have been made clearer.

Each entry contains the artist's name; the name of his or her tribe (both the prior European name and the current official tribe name); birth and death dates; area of residence; education; occupation; media; a list of published works; illustrations appearing in books; commissions; works in public collections; exhibits (which are coded and must be looked up in another list); awards; and honors. While there is no biographical narrative as such, the traditions established by Snodgrass of providing a narrative in the margins of the work has been continued. These narratives vary in content, but are generally biographical in nature. They are direct quotes from individuals familiar with the artist and are signed.

One question that always surfaces in such a compilation (by ethnic background) is what the author calls "the question of 'Indian-ness'." Lester points out that it is not his "responsibility to define 'Indian,' nor [does he] intend to become embroiled in the Indian Arts and Crafts Act of 1990 definition of 'Indian-ness'." He goes on to point out that he has accepted each artist's "attestation as to his or her Indian heritage, whether or not he or she is on a particular tribal roll" (preface).

The Biographical Directory of Native American Painters is an important reference source. It will, no doubt, be welcomed by researchers, collectors, museum personnel, and admirers of the many important American Indian artists who provide such wonderful art. The directory is recommended for all library collections, especially larger academic and public libraries. Also, because of its relatively low price, it should be considered for smaller public and school libraries. In addition, readers interested in Native American painters will find it a useful addition to their private collections. [R: Choice, Jan 96, p. 760]
—**Robert L. Wick**

808. Puniello, Françoise S., and Halina R. Rusak. **Abstract Expressionist Women Painters: An Annotated Bibliography.** Lanham, Md., Scarecrow, 1996. 361p. illus. $55.00. ISBN 0-8108-2998-3.

This needed compilation with short summaries of some lives and the art style that brought the art world's attention to the United States will promote research on, looking at, and making art. Six heroines and their publishers emerge. The movement began in New York in the 1950s. Each artist sought isolation to do her mostly large, remarkably nonrepresentational, rhythmic, brashly or subtly colored, feeling-oriented, enigmatic oils, acrylics, or prints. Elaine de Kooning (1920-1989) was an art critic, series painter, and teacher. Helen Frankenthaler (b. 1928) is famous for the style-initiating *Mountains and Seas* (1952) and stain-soaked canvas. Grace Hartigan (b. 1922), without formal education, started a graduate program in painting in Maryland. Lee Krasner (b. 1908) worked small and large paintings and cut up her paintings to make collages. Joan Mitchell (1926-1992) maintained she deliberately composed her masterpieces. Ethel Schwabacher (1903-1984) was inspired by Greek artists and biblical imagery and wrote about Arshile Gorky. What to call the style orients Rutgers University librarians Puniello and Rusak: action painting, gestural, linear, post-painterly, and landscapes are among the names. On the attitude toward women artists, these librarians usually witness suppression; the artists and critics vacillate between empathy for the persecuted and confidence that good work is acknowledged.—**Elizabeth L. Anderson**

23 Language and Linguistics

GENERAL WORKS

Bibliography

809. Gneuss, Helmut. **English Language Scholarship: A Survey and Bibliography from the Beginnings to the End of the Nineteenth Century.** Binghamton, N.Y., Medieval & Renaissance Texts & Studies, State University of New York, 1996. 152p. index. (Medieval & Renaissance Texts & Studies, v.125). $24.00. ISBN 0-86698-130-6.

The title needs to be read carefully: This monograph-cum-bibliography deals with the historical development of English-language study as a field of scholarship, not with English-language studies per se. The book consists of two distinct parts. Part 1 is an account of how the study of the English language began, grew, and matured from the occasional, almost offhand observations made in the ninth century to the full-blown science it had become by 1900. The narrative flows smoothly, and the points are well taken. (The sections on the development of dictionaries will be of special interest to librarians.)

Part 2, the bibliography, is essentially a listing of the works cited in part 1; hence it is limited in scope, although therefore also claiming the advantage of selectivity. Unfortunately, the bibliographic and other information supplied is also limited—unduly so. The listings do not indicate pagination, publisher, or series; there are no annotations; and foreign-language titles are not translated. There is an author index, but no subject index. Despite the 1996 copyright date, no references are dated after 1995 and there are, in fact, rather few dated after 1988. (The original publication of this monograph, in German, appeared in 1989.)

These deficiencies severely detract from the book's value for reference work. One suspects that the author thinks the specialists who are the most likely users of his monograph do not need more than the sparse bibliographic information he has given here. Perhaps he is right, but the interests of nonspecialists are certainly not served well enough by what is otherwise a worthy and welcome publication. [R: Choice, July/Aug 96, p. 1772]—**Samuel Rothstein**

810. Singerman, Robert. **Indigenous Languages of the Americas: A Bibliography of Dissertations and Theses.** Lanham, Md., Scarecrow, 1996. 311p. index. (Native American Bibliography Series, no.19). $57.50. ISBN 0-8108-3032-9.

A valuable bibliographic tool for research in Native American languages, of both North and South America, is provided by the present volume, which lists not only doctoral dissertations, but also hard-to-find master's theses. Titles are listed from United States, Canadian, and British institutions, for the century 1892-1992. Apart from an introductory section on general sources, the book is organized by language family. In an impressive number of entries, Singerman has been able to provide information about the subsequent publication of material contained in dissertations and theses—whether in books, monograph series, or journals. An index provides access to the names of authors, and another index gives access to the names of languages, dialects, and tribes. The preface by Mary Ritchie Key points to the value of Singerman's work as a guide to the history of American Indian linguistics. Indeed, many famous names in the field—such as Edward Sapir, Harry Hoijer, Mary Haas, and Charles Hockett—are among the scholars whose careers were launched in the dissertations listed here.

One criticism may be made. In arranging his book by linguistic families, Singerman has evaded a serious challenge: the lack of scholarly agreement about the appropriate classifications of Native American languages. His use of putative families such as "Hokan" and "Penutian" is thus problematic: It has the virtue of consistency with many other existing reference works, but many scholars believe that no validity has been demonstrated for such families. Singerman thus perpetuates what some would consider a serious error. Nevertheless, the indexes will give readers access to information on the languages of their interest, regardless of controversial classifications.—**William Bright**

Dictionaries and Encyclopedias

811. **The Blackwell Encyclopedia of Writing Systems.** By Florian Coulmas. Cambridge, Mass., Blackwell, 1996. 603p. illus. $74.95. ISBN 0-631-19446-0.

There are several good books on alphabets and writing systems but, unlike the present volume, none are alphabetically arranged as reference works. Sociolinguist Coulmas, the author of *Writing Systems of the World* (Blackwell, 1991) and other major studies, provides a concisely composed, authoritative survey of this vast field. More than 400 writing systems are described and lavishly illustrated in this handsome, durable volume. In addition to specific systems and their histories, Coulmas presents short essays on such general topics as literacy, the origin of writing, calligraphy, and typography, as well as briefer entries on such specific matters as writing tools, word processing, incunabula, and diacritics. The author takes a broad view of his subject, ranging into the psychological and sociological aspects of the writing process, in addition to purely linguistic considerations. Each article is followed by a reference that directs the reader to the volume's 600-item bibliography.

The encyclopedia shows an immense range of erudition, but specialists in particular areas may find an occasional lapse. One such fault is in the "Cyrillic" entry, where it is asserted that the letter representing the sound *yu* is a "combined letter" composed of *F* plus *O*. The correct constituents are *jod* plus *O*. The volume will be of greatest value to those who are professionally involved with diverse, mostly "exotic" languages—linguists, literary scholars, and historians. The book is not without its delights for the casual browser, however. Where else can one find an illustration of a single-handed finger alphabet for Chinese, a Hebrew crossword puzzle, or a picture of a Babylonian cylinder seal, ca. 2050 B.C.E.? [R: LJ, Feb 96, p. 68]
—**D. Barton Johnson**

812. **Routledge Dictionary of Language and Linguistics.** By Hadumod Bussmann. Gregory Trauth and Kerstin Kazzazi, eds. New York, Routledge, 1996. 530p. $99.00. ISBN 0-415-02225-8.

Originally published in German in 1983 (revised edition, 1990), this work has now been translated, adapted, and brought up-to-date in English. The dictionary, almost 25 years in development, was designed to provide users both an introduction to the concepts of linguistics and a considerable amount of source material for conducting their own linguistic research. Arrangement is alphabetic, providing a mix of ethnolinguistic groups, domain terminology, and individual language entries. For each language, there is a classification note, the approximate number of native speakers, principal dialects, and the countries or areas in which it is used or spoken. Little space is devoted to a language's past, but each entry is provided with a bibliography of sources for history, grammar, etymology, and recommended dictionaries.

Other entries include parts of speech, usage notes, and morphological terms, each with at least one bibliographic reference to turn to for fuller treatment. The tone is scholarly—the material is written by linguistic specialists for other specialists, and dilettantes may find some entries beyond their depth and comfort level. Some references cited are to older, German sources, and thus unlikely to be easily found in American libraries, but there are also plenty of modern ones (e.g., to "Franglais," a comparatively recent French/English blend epitomized by coinages like *le weekend*). As with most reference books, this one is designed not to be read sequentially but to be consulted for specific terms. The untutored reader with only a passing interest in linguistics may be amazed at the endless combinations of terms that have evolved from the study of language (e.g., the distinctions among pragmalinguistics, sociolinguistics, and psycholinguistics).

Every modern language is in a state of continuous evolution, so while this is the first English-language edition of this work, it will almost certainly not be the last—such a work is never actually finished. The dictionary is recommended for scholarly collections for its clear entries and for pointing the way to other works that delve deeper. Popular reference libraries, however, can probably pass on this expensive volume. [R: Choice, Dec 96, p. 587]—**Bruce A. Shuman**

Handbooks and Yearbooks

813. Campbell, George L. **Concise Compendium of the World's Languages.** New York, Routledge, 1995. 670p. $75.00. ISBN 0-415-11392-X.

Campbell's *Concise Compendium of the World's Languages* (CCWL) is a one-volume edition of his *Compendium of the World's Languages*, published in two volumes in 1991 (see ARBA 92, entry 1012). *Concise* refers to the reduced number of languages covered (100-plus) and not to the content of the articles, which in some instances have been amplified. The purpose of the new edition remains the same: "To provide brief descriptions . . . in non-technical language of a fairly wide cross-section of contemporary natural-language systems" (p. vii).

The articles are arranged alphabetically by language from Afrikaans to Zulu and cover dialects, script, phonology, morphology, and syntax. As in the 1991 edition, each article in CCWL closes with verses 1-8 of the initial chapter of the Gospel of St. John translated into the language and printed in the native script—a useful and interesting example of the language at work.

There is also an "Appendix of Scripts" that includes transliterations and diacritics for vowels; consonants; numerals; capital and lowercase letters; characters and strokes for Chinese; and syllabaries for Amharic, Tamil, and Japanese. The bibliography that accompanies CCWL has been reduced but is still extensive. It is divided into "Collective Works" (9 titles) and "Individual Languages," which includes from 1 to 10 entries for each of the languages covered. This compact edition of the *Compendium* will be a useful tool for linguists in the field and as a desk reference for students, teachers, and other language professionals.—**Warren L. Meinhardt**

814. Katzner, Kenneth. **The Languages of the World.** new ed. New York, Routledge, 1995. 378p. index. $15.95pa. ISBN 0-415-11809-3.

Six thousand years after the Tower of Babel, there are perhaps three thousand languages still spoken today, although less than two hundred of them are of international importance. If trends continue, English has the best chance of becoming the universal tongue. These are some of the hundreds of facts that users will find within the pages of the latest edition of Katzner's universal linguistic guide first published in 1975 (see ARBA 76, entry 1110).

This new edition of *The Languages of the World* (TLW) is divided into three parts. Part 1, "Language Families of the World," begins with a chart of the major language groupings, followed by a brief discussion of each grouping. Part 2, "Individual Languages," comprises the bulk of TLW and contains descriptions of the more important languages of the world. Here each section begins with a sample text in the language, followed by an English translation. Part 3, "Country-by-Country Survey," is a review of the languages spoken (with the number of speakers) in each country from Afghanistan to Zimbabwe. TLW concludes with a list of sources of literary passages and an index of languages.

This is a handbook that will appeal to many tastes. It is, of course, an essential tool for linguists. Literature buffs will also appreciate the passages (with translations) included here in the original language and in the native script if the language uses a nonroman alphabet. Additionally, anyone with an interest in other languages and cultures will find TLW an indispensable *livre de chevet*.—**Warren L. Meinhardt**

815. Pullum, Geoffrey K., and William A. Ladusaw. **Phonetic Symbol Guide.** 2d ed. Chicago, University of Chicago Press, 1996. 320p. index. $75.00; $19.95pa. ISBN 0-226-68535-7; 0-226-68536-5pa.

This guide is a revision of the 1986 reference work (see ARBA 88, entry 1057) and contains descriptions of hundreds of phonetic symbols used by linguists in phonetic transcriptions of the world's languages and dialects. This edition adds 61 symbols to the 1986 edition; it also incorporates both the

1989 and 1993 revisions to the International Phonetic Alphabet. The guide has a language index to more than 200 languages. It has been made easy to use by including subject and symbol name indexes as well as symbol charts of vowels, consonants, and diacritics. A glossary and extensive references are also furnished in the guide.

This reference covers the complexity of phonetic symbols in great detail. The work would serve linguists, philologists, and phoneticians as well as students of linguistics, languages, and anthropology. It is recommended for all libraries.—**Edward Erazo**

816. **The World's Writing Systems.** Peter T. Daniels and William Bright, eds. New York, Oxford University Press, 1996. 920p. illus. index. $150.00. ISBN 0-19-507993-0.

This comprehensive reference covers every major writing system from the earliest known scripts to those used in the present time. It contains more than 80 articles, written by a similar number of contributors, and provides in-depth explanations of the scripts themselves, emphasizing how the writing systems work by analyzing their elements, characters, features, and symbols.

The work is arranged in 13 parts divided into 74 sections covering various aspects of the world's writing systems. Sections include a sample passage of a script, a transliteration (a romanized version), a phonetic transcription (in most cases), a gloss (an English translation), and in some cases, a discussion of the social and cultural contexts. Both parts and sections are signed and provide extensive bibliographies. Dozens of tables and charts of scripts, syllabaries, calligraphy, numerals, petroglyphs, and cartoons enhance the text. Also furnished in the work is a chart of the international phonetic alphabet (revised in 1989), which fills two facing pages and includes consonants, diacritics, vowels, and other symbols. The colophon lists more than 100 fonts used in the text.

This major work is a fine addition for any reference collection and could be used by both student and scholar. Complex writing systems such as Arabic writing, Chinese characters, cuneiform, Egyptian hieroglyphics, Maya and other Mesoamerican scripts, and Tibetan (Mongolian) stylography are especially well presented and easy to understand. This excellent reference is recommended for all libraries.

—**Edward Erazo**

817. Zeno, Susan M., Stephen H. Ivens, Robert T. Millard, and Raj Duvvuri. **The Educator's Word Frequency Guide.** Brewster, N.Y., TASA, 1995. 1375p. $79.95. ISBN 1-56497-021-3.

This highly specialized resource is of most value to educators, researchers, and scientists, as it can enable them, for example, to design instructional materials tailored to the age and educational level of students as well as to study the structure of language. As such, it is of most value to specialized and academic libraries, although a number of public libraries, as well as public school administrative libraries, may find there is a need or demand to have this work in their reference collections. Current technology has enabled the authors to assemble a text that includes more than 17 million tokens and 154,000 word types. This far exceeds the 5 million entries of the classic work, *The American Heritage Word Frequency Book* (see ARBA 73, entry 1178), which is more than 20 years old.

The text is preceded by a useful introduction that outlines such matters as how the corpus was created, the kinds of sampling procedures, and the organization of the guide. The body of the work is broken down into 4 statistical sections, of which the 1st part is an alphabetic list of 19,468 word types with a U value greater than or equal to 1 in the total corpus. The second section consists of an alphabetic list of word types with a U value less than one in the total corpus. The third section contains an alphabetic list of word types that include apostrophes, single quotation marks, and dashes, and the final section is a rank-order list of all word types displayed in the first two sections and that are based upon unrounded U values.

—**James M. Murray**

ENGLISH-LANGUAGE DICTIONARIES

General Usage

818. **The Oxford Large Print Dictionary.** 2d ed. Elaine Pollard, ed. New York, Oxford University Press, 1995. 938p. $39.95. ISBN 0-19-861322-9.

This 2d edition of *The Oxford Large Print Dictionary* claims to be the most up-to-date volume of its kind. It contains more than 60,000 entries, 5,000 of which have been added to this edition, including a number of new words. Many biographical and geographic entries are also included in the listings. The two guide words on each page are placed together at the outside margin, assisting their use. The dark print and the use of white space tend to make the print appear larger than it actually is, and the pages open easily and almost lay flat.

Each main entry includes the word in bold typeface, followed by its part of speech label and definition(s). Syllabication and etymologies are not included, and there are very few phonetic respellings. "Correct English" usage notes are included for many entries. For example, the word *different* contains this information: "*Different from* is the preferred phrase; *different to* is acceptable when it feels natural in a particular context, e.g., when *similar* occurs near by; *different than* is common in American use." Entries use British spelling, with such words as *color* being defined as "the American spelling of *colour*."

People who require a large-print dictionary primarily for spelling and word meanings and who have no need for information on hyphenation or etymology will probably find *The Oxford Large Print Dictionary* to be adequate for their needs. However, its size and the considerable weight of its 938 pages could make this volume difficult for some people to handle. [R: RBB, 15 Feb 96, p. 1040]

—**Kay O. Cornelius**

819. Trask, R. L. **A Dictionary of Phonetics and Phonology.** New York, Routledge, 1996. 424p. $59.95; $18.95pa. ISBN 0-415-11260-5; 0-415-11261-3pa.

Trask, a lecturer in linguistics in the School of Cognitive and Computing Sciences at the University of Sussex, England, previously wrote *A Dictionary of Grammatical Terms in Linguistics* (see ARBA 95, entry 1040); *Language Change* (1994); and *Language: The Basics* (1995), all published by Routledge. This work, written for students of applied linguistics and speech therapy, includes definitions for more than 2,000 terms in phonetics and phonology, a field in which many entries have multiple, and even conflicting, definitions and uses. Trask's aim is to be both comprehensive and concise at the same time. Overall usefulness of the work is enhanced via range and breadth of terms selected, *see* and *see also* references, explanation of the most important theoretical approaches to phonology, and help with pronunciation. On this last point, Trask uses pronunciation common in the south of England as his standard, which accounts for all the Briticisms in the term list. There are brief etymologies of numerous terms and, often, commonsense advice on usage. Some examples are provided, many entries have suggestions for further reading, and the work concludes with 29 pages of references.

It should be noted that this is *not* a dictionary of general linguistics. It focuses, rather, on just one major subset of the field—phonetics/phonology—and tries to provide detailed coverage of that area. While the 2,000-plus terms defined may be considered a smallish subset of the entire field, they include, in the author's opinion, "virtually every term you are likely to encounter outside the most specialized monographs." It does seem a good assortment, listing terms specific to other languages, which are added for their prominence in English phonology.

There is much to admire in this work. Even the most casual browser is sure to come across numerous intriguing and colorful phrases used in phonetics, such as *Bill Peters effect*, *McGurk effect*, *crazy rule*, *creaky voice*, *cut-glass accent*, and *lah-di-dah*. Also, users will want to read what Trask has to say about pig Latin and (Cockney) rhyming slang. The dictionary is recommended for its useful definitions and fascinating reading, even if one might wish for more examples used in context. [R: Choice, May 96, p. 1458]

—**Bruce A. Shuman**

Abridged

820. **The Merriam-Webster Dictionary.** home and office ed. Springfield, Mass., Merriam-Webster, 1995. 704p. illus. $9.95pa. ISBN 0-87779-606-8.

Dictionaries intended for the mass market should be cheap (1. "of a relatively low price") but not cheap (3. "of little account; of small value"). The Merriam-Webster name on the above dictionary means that it can be safely presumed to be of good intrinsic quality, and the price is agreeably modest. Are there other reasons to buy this abridgment of the *Merriam-Webster Collegiate Dictionary* (10th ed.; see ARBA 94, entry 1076)? Yes, many. The comparatively large, highly legible typeface makes this dictionary easy to read—in fact, easier than many larger counterparts. The definitions are crisp, clear, and comfortably brief. The perfect binding is sturdy and looks likely to last. The encyclopedic features—personal and geographic names, a handbook of style, most popular first names—will be useful for those people (probably a great majority) who do not own other reference books.

There are some criticisms to be made, of course. The illustrations (approximately 150) are arbitrarily chosen and, because of their size and layout, are obtrusive. The number of newer words is disappointingly small (e.g., how can a 1995 dictionary not include "Internet"?). Also, do not look here for help with word origins or usage. Oh well, not even Merriam-Webster is perfect. But at the low price, this dictionary is still worth buying for every worker in the office and for every school-age kid at home.

—**Samuel Rothstein**

821. **The Oxford Dictionary of Current English.** 2d ed. Della Thompson, ed. New York, Oxford University Press, 1996. 1080p. $7.95pa. ISBN 0-19-860075-5.

Formerly known as the *Pocket Oxford Dictionary of Current English*, this paperback dictionary comes from the substantial Oxford Dictionary family with its heritage of careful scholarship. It purports to provide some 140,000 definitions, giving the pronunciation; definitions from current to historical with apparently no period given; and a brief, undated word origin note. The pronunciation guide is given only at the front of the book and does not follow typical U.S. guides.

The dictionary compares favorably with the *The New Merriam-Webster Dictionary* (Merriam Webster, 1989), advertised as the United States' "#1 Paperback Dictionary," in number of words and length of definition. The Oxford title is less complete than the major collegiate dictionaries, such as the *Merriam Webster's Collegiate Dictionary* (10th ed.; see ARBA 94, entry 1076), which has more, and frequently longer, definitions.

This Oxford dictionary attempts to recognize American English when pronunciation or definition differs. It appears to do a better job than the small dictionaries originating in the United States do of recognizing British English. However, if the user wishes for a good overall desk dictionary, one of the collegiate dictionaries, such as the Merriam Webster dictionary mentioned above, the *Webster's New World Dictionary* (see ARBA 92, entry 1018), or the *American Heritage College Dictionary* (3d ed.; see ARBA 94, entry 1075), is recommended. If a small dictionary with a British flavor is needed, and the paperback format is adequate for the projected usage, *The Oxford Dictionary of Current English* can be a practical and inexpensive choice.—**Betty Jo Buckingham**

822. **Webster's New American Dictionary.** By the Editors of Merriam-Webster. New York, Smithmark, 1995. 687p. illus. $9.98. ISBN 0-8317-9165-9.

The editors claim that "*Webster's New American Dictionary* is a dictionary designed to meet the needs of dictionary users in the home, office, and classroom." Does it stand up to this claim? The dictionary boasts 63,000 entries. An old 1966 Merriam-Webster's college dictionary has 142,000 entries (the average college graduate possesses a vocabulary of 40,000 words). Definitely not a "heavy-hitter," the work does well in offering simple definitions; pronunciations; parts of speech; and, inconsistently, etymologies. Also helpful to a young student or perhaps a nighttime family discussion are the many appendixes: "Common English Given Names"; "Foreign Words and Phrases"; "Biographical, Biblical, and Mythological Names"; "U.S. Presidents"; "Canadian Prime Ministers"; various population tables; "Signs and Symbols"; and a comprehensive "Handbook of Style and Documentation of Sources." This leaves 615 pages for the actual dictionary.

What is missing? The editors claim to include "all the latest terms from business, technology, science, and general use." This is untrue. Among the terms not listed are *Pentium*, *CPU*, *ebola*, *ablation*, and a listing of Roman numerals. The dictionary omits all vulgar and many slang expressions. The latter reinforced a supposition that this dictionary is really intended for a grade school to middle school audience, and certainly a less-than-college-educated one. It may even be insufficient for an enterprising high school student.

With that caveat, what the dictionary does, it does acceptably. The definitions are succinct and to the point, the graphics clear, the addenda helpful. All in all, it reminds one of a phrase omitted from the dictionary's listing, *dolce far niente*—in this case, the joy of cutting and pasting for profit.—**Kenneth I. Saichek**

Eponyms

823. Muschell, David. **What in the Word? Origins of Words Dealing with People and Places.** Bradenton, Fla., McGuinn & McGuire Publishing, 1996. 216p. illus. index. $14.95pa. ISBN 1-881117-14-6.

Muschell must be doubtful of reviewers' ability to accurately describe his book's contents, so he has given his own summary on the front cover: "Discover the origin of 274 words derived from the names of people and places, the meaning of 1,065 common first names and the origin of 554 names of places." Each of these 1,893 entries is given a paragraph or so (about 10 to 20 lines in all) covering not only etymology and meaning but also "lore"; in other words, material calculated to arouse in the reader the kind of "wonder, amusement or surprise" that led Muschell to select these words for inclusion in his book.

Almost all the factual material in *What in the Word?* is readily available elsewhere (most obviously in the unabridged dictionaries), so the book is of little reference value. What the more compendious and scholarly sources will not offer, however, is Muschell's storytelling approach. For some years he conducted a radio program on "the fascinating stories behind our everyday words," and to judge from its humorous tone and colloquial style, his present book may well derive from his radio material.

There is nothing wrong with a "word book" meant for popular taste, and Muschell offers a good buy for the many people who want such material. It is reasonably priced, well laid-out, and, aside from some occasional strained jocularity, quite engaging in style. The book is recommend for personal use and for the circulating stock of public and school libraries. [R: Choice, May 96, p. 1455]—**Samuel Rothstein**

824. Room, Adrian. **An Alphabetical Guide to the Language of Name Studies.** Lanham, Md., Scarecrow, 1996. 123p. $34.00. ISBN 0-8108-3169-4.

Anyone who loves words should try to define the following (an example of each is included in brackets): *colponym* [Great Australian Bight], *deanthroponymization* [diesel], *syssitionym* [Tavern on the Green], *gyneconin* [Anin], and *marsionym* [Juvenata Chasma]. Hmmmm. Give up? Okay, here are some easier ones: *dickensonym* [Emily Peggotty], *necronym* [Forest Lawn], *pluralia tantum* [the Sex Pistols], and *zoonym* [Bugs Bunny]. These terms are all used in the field of onomastics, or, the study of names and naming. The prolific Room has produced a small, easy-to-use dictionary defining many terms used in this field of study. It is not an exhaustive list (where are *ouronym* and *mesonym*?), but this book will be an excellent addition to appropriate collections. Unlike other published onomastic glossaries, Room nicely includes copious examples (including some modern ones) in many of the definitions.

There is a "Glossary of Greek and Latin Elements," and also a select bibliography containing not only those works that are referred to in the body of the dictionary, but also to some titles that contain more detailed information (but the bibliography is far from complete). Better bibliographies can be found in such works as Frank Neussels's *The Study of Names: A Guide to the Principles and Topics* (Greenwood Press, 1992).

The study of names is a somewhat obscure field, but one that has value for linguists and historians alike. University research libraries should consider the purchase of this book. Other possible purchasers would be academic, large public, and special libraries that specifically address geographic or genealogical research. Also, if individuals are personally in the habit of buying books of weird and interesting words and terms, this volume is one to consider.—**Caroline M. Kent**

Etymology

825. **The Barnhart Concise Dictionary of Etymology.** Robert K. Barnhart, ed. New York, HarperCollins, 1995. 916p. $50.00. ISBN 0-06-270084-7.

This book is a condensed version of *The Barnhart Dictionary of Etymology* (see ARBA 89, entry 941). The word "concise" in the title refers to the fact that most of the entries are briefer versions of the original: The actual number of entries (25,000) is only 5,000 fewer than the parent volume. Most of the entries are American English and much of the scholarship was developed by Americans. A brief but informative history of the English language precedes the dictionary proper. Each main entry is given the year of the word's first appearance, as far as that can be determined. Many other dictionaries, including *The Oxford English Dictionary* (2d ed.; see ARBA 90, entry 1006), were consulted for information. Careful distinctions are made in the entries between words borrowed from other languages and words that have undergone internal changes in meaning. Separate entries discuss all currently active suffixes and prefixes. Numerous cross-references point to otherwise remote connections between words. One of the most welcome features is that the only abbreviations used are for parts of speech.

This dictionary is helpful primarily for users interested in just what the title suggests—the source of currently used English words, whether that source is an earlier English root or another language. Some word histories are complicated, and many are speculative. The work under review is not a good source for entertaining stories about word origins, such as *Morris Dictionary of Word and Phrase Origins* (2d ed.; see ARBA 89, entry 944) or *The Facts on File Encyclopedia of Word and Phrase Origins* (see ARBA 88, entry 1066). Readers needing a more British approach to etymologies will want to consult *The Oxford English Dictionary* or the now somewhat dated *Oxford Dictionary of English Etymology* (1966), edited by C. T. Onions.

The *Barnhart Concise* covers many words a general reader would be interested in, although it does exclude vulgarisms and is selective with slang. Included, for instance, are *nerd*, *yuppie*, and *Afro*, but excluded are *bro*, *dweeb*, and *wimp* (except in the rare sense of "whimper"). There are at least three reasons why it makes better sense to buy *The Barnhart Dictionary of Etymology* rather than this concise edition: 5,000 more words are listed (including, for example, the sense of *wimp* as "a weakling"); more information is usually found in an entry; and the original volume only costs a few dollars more. Both volumes conclude with a glossary of language terms and a select bibliography.—**David Isaacson**

826. Flavell, Linda, and Roger Flavell. **Dictionary of Word Origins.** London, Kyle Cathie; distr., North Pomfret, Vt., Trafalgar Square, 1995. 277p. index. $13.95pa. ISBN 1-85626-214-6.

This entertaining dictionary has been compiled by a British couple and contains almost 300 English-language words "that have a story to tell." Each entry contains one or more definitions of the word, followed by several quotations that show the word in use, with dates. The majority of the listing is a thorough etymology that often gives insight, not only into the entry word, but into related words as well. For example, under *cartoon*, other words discussed include *papyrus, card, carton, cartridge, chart*, and *charter*.

Scattered throughout the book are 30 essays on word origins with such titles as "Words from Arabic," "Months of the Year," "Fabrics," and "Viking Conquests." In addition, many pages feature sidebars on topics such as "Acronyms," "Homonyms," and lists of quirky words, such as those that accept the suffix *-less* but not its contrary, *-ful*, and words that have a bias toward being negative, such as *uncouth* and *inept*.

Dictionary of Word Origins contains an introduction that addresses the development of the English language, an index, and a short list of books for, according to the authors, "the word lover." While the material in this volume is accurate enough to satisfy the scholar, it is not extensive. However, this book should be welcomed by anyone who loves to explore interesting word origins.—**Kay O. Cornelius**

Euphemisms

827. Holder, R. W. **A Dictionary of Euphemisms.** New York, Oxford University Press, 1995. 470p. index. $25.00. ISBN 0-19-869275-7.

Euphemisms exist and apparently have always existed in every language. English has not only created many of its own, but has borrowed richly from other languages as well. Even today, when it appears that almost anything can be printed in magazines and newspapers, or said on television and the movies, euphemisms still abound. Indeed, political correctness is creating a growing number of euphemistic terms to ensure that no one is offended by a word. Euphemisms enable people to avoid the unpleasantness often associated with body parts, bodily functions, sexuality, taboos, fears, death, and even God. They also enable people to enhance, inflate, and make things appear grander and more important (e.g., "associate" for "salesclerk," "personal assistant" for "maid").

Holder's new edition of the 1987 *A Dictionary of American and British Euphemisms* (Bath University Press) and its revised edition, *The Faber Dictionary of Euphemisms* (see ARBA 91, entry 1057), includes some of the newer terms as well as many older ones. Except for those terms that "struck [him] as interesting," all of Holder's entries are found in common or literary use. The usage in Great Britain predominates, although many American and Commonwealth examples are included and so labeled. The dictionary is easy to use. Its alphabetized, boldfaced entry terms are amplified by a brief explanation or definition and illustrated by examples identified by author and date. For a quick guide to the most common areas of euphemisms, the "Thematic Index" arranges the terms under 67 categories, such as abortion and miscarriage, brothels, bribery, espionage, funerals, female genitalia and breasts, male genitalia, masturbation, obesity, politics, sexual pursuit, sweat, and warfare. The bibliography lists the published sources of the examples identified in the text.

This dictionary is recommended for all libraries as a supplement to standard dictionaries that often do not label euphemisms. Because no complete euphemism dictionary exists, libraries will also want to include *Rawson's Dictionary of Euphemisms and Other Doubletalk* (rev. ed.; see entry 828), which is more scholarly and more fully reflects American usage. [R: Choice, Nov 96, p. 430; LJ, Mar 96, pp. 72-74]
—**Blaine H. Hall**

828. Rawson, Hugh. **Rawson's Dictionary of Euphemisms and Other Doubletalk.** rev. ed. New York, Crown, 1995. 463p. $25.00. ISBN 0-517-70201-0.

People and cultures have always wanted to have ways to refer to subjects that (for whatever reason) are best not mentioned in as many words, and although he does not number his entries, Rawson's revision of his 1981 *Dictionary of Euphemisms and Other Doubletalk* (see ARBA 82, entry 1202) lists and defines approximately 2,000 of these terms. They range from the hilariously dated (*unmentionables* rather than trousers and associated garments) to the politically correct (*vertically challenged* rather than short), and include the politically evasive (*revenue enhancement* rather than tax increase), the pompous (*enciente* rather than pregnant), the meretricious (*the Final Solution* rather than the extermination of Europe's Jews), and the deliberately mendacious (*terminological inexactitude* rather than falsehood). As one would anticipate, a substantial number of definitions involve bodily parts and functions and sexual activities, and these definitions have been completely revised and expanded; the entry for *bosom*, for example, is more than twice as long as it was in the earlier edition. As in the 1981 edition, Rawson documents his citations.

Easy to browse and enjoyable though it is, this volume has flaws. Rawson's etymologies are occasionally debatable, as when he states that *hooker* derives from the Arabic word *houri*. Equally serious, citations frequently include references to other terms, but few of these are given as entries in the volume itself: A researcher looking to learn about *Connecticut River pork* or find a definition of *kate* must know in advance to look under "Cape Cod turkey" and "prostitute" respectively, for these terms (and hundreds of others) are not cross-referenced in the body of the book. Nor is the text indexed.

Researchers interested in euphemisms and doubletalk will find that *The Faber Dictionary of Euphemisms* (see ARBA 91, entry 1057) contains more terms but has briefer definitions. Also, when it is completed, the *Random House Historical Dictionary of American Slang* (see ARBA 95, entry 1061) will render much of Rawson unnecessary. Larger academic and public libraries may nevertheless find a use for this volume.—**Richard Bleiler**

Foreign Words and Phrases

829. Wilkes, G. A. **A Dictionary of Australian Colloquialisms.** 4th ed. New York, Oxford University Press, 1996. 426p. $35.00pa. ISBN 0-19-553798-X.

Although the compiler indicates that colloquialisms cover a wider area than slang, "essentially deriving from the spoken rather than the written language," the vast majority of the entries are illustrated by examples culled from Australian books and periodicals. A brief introduction sets the parameters for inclusion: expressions that have a distinctly Australian (rather than, say, a British or American) meaning; obsolete British words and phrases that have gained new currency or denotations; and neologisms that are of restricted use. After almost 30 years, Wilkes is clearly established as *the* authority on Australianisms; however, there are some terms that could have been included, as they occur frequently in colloquial speech: *do* (a formal event, a sex partner), *milkers, buds* (breasts); *pork sword* (penis); *screw* (sex act/partner); *knock up* (impregnate); *flogging it* (masturbating/promoting something such as a book). Other terms that occur in literary works—although they may well have been considered and rejected—are *heeler* and *blue* (cattle dog); *Balts* (Baltic immigrants); *wogs* and *wops* (Pacific Islanders, Italians); *baldies* and *ballies* (white-headed cattle); *back of beyond* (beyond settlements); and *Our Joanie* (Joan Sutherland, after the fashion of *Our Glad*, referring to Gladys Moncrieff, a popular singer of an earlier generation). Nevertheless, this is an excellent reference work that should be held by libraries and all those interested in Australian culture.—**Marian B. McLeod**

Historical

830. **A Dictionary of South African English on Historical Principles.** Penny Silva and others, eds. New York, Oxford University Press, 1996. 825p. $150.00. ISBN 0-19-863153-7.

As one expects from publications based on the format of the *Oxford English Dictionary* (2d ed.; see ARBA 90, entry 1006), this lexicon is an incredible repository of information (25 years in the making) about the vagaries of the English language in South Africa. Although tribute is paid to the pioneering efforts of its predecessors, especially *A Dictionary of English Usage in Southern Africa* (see ARBA 77, entry 1083) and *A Dictionary of South African English* (4th ed., Oxford University Press, 1991), those works constitute little more than samplers of a work in progress completed with the volume under review.

The dictionary has recorded the specialized vocabulary of English as developed in South Africa from the late sixteenth century to the end of 1994. Included are not only the words used by the educated elite, but those used by ordinary South Africans as well. As South African English "belongs" not only to those whose first language is English, but also to the majority of South Africans for whom English is a second or third language, words from both groups are represented in the dictionary, so that the provenance of regional or "group" vocabulary is provided whenever a word is not widely familiar to all South Africans (let alone non-South Africans).

A few words and phrases not of South African origin, but that have a particular significance for South Africans (e.g., *constructive engagement*), have been included. In general, however, the entries show how English in South Africa borrowed words from European languages, especially Dutch/Afrikaans, and from other South African languages. It also shows where a word or phrase has acquired a particular sense, or when it has been coined for local phenomena. One interesting example is the entry "Mary Decker" (p. 445): "n. phr. slang. [The name of a U.S. middle distance athlete of the 1980s. considered a rival of S. Afr. athlete Zola Budd.] In urban (esp. township) Eng.: a. A police vehicle, the hippo, esp. a fast one; b. A small bus . . . used for taxi shuttle service." This fascinating volume will be indispensable to anyone studying the regional or historical development of English, linguistics, or, most importantly, anyone studying South Africa.—**Paul H. Thomas**

831. Wright, Laura. **Sources of London English: Medieval Thames Vocabulary.** New York, Oxford University Press, 1996. 245p. index. $55.00. ISBN 0-19-823909-2.

The language people use can reveal a great deal about their lives and culture, especially when it is intended for mundane rather than literary use. Wright's study of the language used on the River Thames from the year 1220 to 1500 is drawn not from writers such as Geoffrey Chaucer and John Gower but from records preserved at the Corporation of London Records Office: business texts, accounts, inventories, proclamations, letters, and so forth. Most of these documents were written in a mixture of English and either Latin or Anglo-Norman. Wright explains that these macaronic texts have been hitherto ignored because they were not monolingual, but that they contain an abundance of information. Whereas earlier researchers regarded them as "debased" and therefore worthless, Wright approaches them from the contemporary linguistic understanding that their language fulfills important needs and has a consistent structure of its own.

Wright's study is limited to technical terms having to do with life on and in the river—parts of London Bridge, species of fish, traps, water conditions, ships, and trades and the people who pursue them. Headwords are organized by semantic category (there is also an alphabetic index). Each entry contains a definition; a list of manuscript occurrences; selected quotations illustrating the meaning; variant spellings; and earlier references, usually to *The Oxford English Dictionary* and *The Middle English Dictionary* (if they include the word). Wright has found a number of terms not in these basic sources, although still in use by people in the modern English fishing industry. This list is followed by an analysis of spellings and what they indicate about pronunciation and language changes, morphology and grammar, and a listing of place-names. There is also a substantial bibliography and index.

The technical character of this work makes it too specialized for general libraries. The quality of its scholarship makes it a required purchase for research libraries with holdings in linguistics and medieval literature.—**Lynn F. Williams**

Idioms, Colloquialisms, and Special Usage

832. **Cassell Cluefinder: A Dictionary of Crossword Clues.** By J. A. Coleman. London, Cassell; distr., New York, Sterling Publishing, 1995. 249p. $14.95. ISBN 0-304-34587-3.

This is no ordinary crossword puzzle dictionary, although the book's dust jacket may lead one to expect such a volume. It is, instead, a help in finding answers to those maddening clues that bedevil a particular brand of crossword puzzle. In recent years, the "British" type of puzzle has started appearing in the United States with increasing frequency, mainly in *New York* magazine (*Guardian* reprints) and *The New York Times Magazine* (the so-called cryptic puzzle). Armed with this volume, a puzzle solver may have a chance of getting acquainted with the way these clues are concocted. Here is an example: The answer to "little boy" might be *weened*, as in *wee Ned*. "Little for each" might be *weeper*. "Little the German" comes out as *weeder*, *der* being the German equivalent of *the*. "Money belt" comes out as *brass band*; and so on.

At the beginning of each letter in the book, which is arranged in the typical dictionary A to Z format, is a list of what a particular letter alone might mean. The letter *G* could mean acceleration, agent, clef, conductance, four hundred, string, suit, guinea, Germany, George, and so forth. Anagrams are included, as are wordplays and hidden words. Because the book originated in the United Kingdom, a number of entries are relevant to the British Isles and Europe, particularly the plethora of abbreviations that are largely unknown on this side of the Atlantic. This "cluefinder" will be a great help to the beginner, but even the expert crossword puzzle solver may benefit from a lengthy session with it, during which some devious clue origins will be revealed.—**Koraljka Lockhart**

833. **Dictionary of American Regional English. Volume III: I-O.** Frederic G. Cassidy and Joan Houston Hall, eds. Cambridge, Mass., Belknap Press/Harvard University Press, 1996. 927p. maps. $75.00. ISBN 0-674-20519-7.

If readers are feeling kinky (lively, high-spirited) rather than meeching (skulking, cringing), they should pick up this lalapalooza (exceptionally fine, remarkable) of a book and find out what it is the rest of the country has been saying for years. This third volume of an amazing linguistic study offers a scholarly trip across the nation, across the centuries, and across the cultural divides. In a time of homogenicity spurred on by television and technology, it is quite wonderful to be reminded of the unique quality of regional speech still alive and well: a communication both historic and picturesque, the result of a variety of linguistic backgrounds and a shared new experience.

As in the earlier volumes, the terms examined are in use only in a part or parts of the country or by a particular social group, as well as those words that are handed down through family and friends rather than formally taught. The aim has been to trace particular usage from its first appearance in the language to the present time, with sources covering close to 400 years of U.S. speech and writing. The form of entry is complicated, and the computer-generated maps, conforming to population rather than topography, seem strangely distorted, but after a few excursions into some of the 900-plus pages, it becomes a fascinating combination of information and amusement, scholarship and whimsy. This is a most welcome volume that continues a singular achievement. One hopes that the final volumes will not be far behind.—**Paula Frosch**

834. **Dictionary of Caribbean English Usage.** Richard Allsopp, ed. New York, Oxford University Press, 1996. 697p. $75.00. ISBN 0-19-866152-5.

Even though Francis Drake introduced the English language to the Caribbean more than 400 years ago, this volume is the first comprehensive inventory of that region's distinctive language. Earlier dictionaries focused on Jamaican and Bahamian English, but Allsopp's work covers all the anglophone islands as well as the mainland countries of Belize and Guyana. He acknowledges the need for a regional dictionary on historical principles, but declares that this book is instead a record of current usage. With a geographic range that includes 5 geopolitical territories and 12 independent nations—each entitled to its own national standard of linguistic correctness—Allsopp's task as a lexicographer is formidable. To accurately describe such linguistic diversity, many of his 20,000 entries include territorial labels as well as status labels (from *formal* to *erroneous* and *vulgar*). Guides to pronunciation offer international phonetic transcriptions along with digits to indicate gradations in pitch. Allsopp documents numerous loanwords (from various African languages, from Mayan dialects in Belize, and more recently from Hindu and Islamic cultures) and offers abundant citations from both print and oral usage.

A useful supplement to the dictionary provides Caribbean French and Spanish equivalents for selected terms describing regional flora and fauna. Among francophone territories, this supplement focuses mainly on Martinique and Guadeloupe; among Spanish-speaking territories, it focuses on Puerto Rico and Santa Domingo. The book's only illustrations, showing the construction of steel drums and the layout of a steel band, are in an appendix. Endpapers offer maps of the Caribbean and of Africa (to indicate distribution of sub-Saharan languages that have influenced Caribbean English). This scholarly dictionary observes rigorous principles of lexicography but remains easily accessible to all users.—**Albert Wilhelm**

835. Hendrickson, Robert. **Yankee Talk: A Dictionary of New England Expressions.** New York, Facts on File, 1996. 255p. (Facts on File Dictionary of American Regional Expressions, v.3). $24.95; $14.95pa. ISBN 0-8160-2111-2; 0-8160-3507-5pa.

The compiler of this series' earlier volumes on southern and western U.S. expressions (see ARBA 94, entry 1089, and ARBA 95, entry 1043, respectively) now focuses on more than 3,500 past and present regionalisms, many of them associated with whalers, farmers, Native Americans, and cracker-barrel philosophers. Sadly, once one has navigated beyond the harbor of reliable scholarship that is Hendrickson's 13-page introduction, one feels a bit out to sea. The author certainly merits praise for his solid entries on *bundling*, *gerrymander*, *monkey wrench*, *scrimshaw*, and *Yankee peddler*. Moreover, he has rescued from obscurity many undeservedly forgotten terms—such as *cat-ice*, *diddledees*, *inheaven*, *intervale*, *netop*, and *tortience*—which are absent from both Charles F. Haywood's *Yankee Dictionary* (Jackson & Phillips, 1963) and John Gould's *Maine Lingo* (Down East Magazine, 1975).

Nevertheless, weaknesses abound. With no keyword arrangement of phrasal entries, and no subject index, one must look under *home* for John Collins Bossidy's toast to Boston (where "the Cabots talk only to God"). Also, entry cross-referencing is spotty: None exists either from *Salem Gibraltar* to *black jacks* or from *bulkhead* to *hatchway doors*. Many entry terms are followed by only a pronunciation key and cursory geographic data: *Leominster* is identified not as the home of Johnny Appleseed, but as just "a Massachusetts town." Most entries contain no etymology, and definitions are vague: "*I'll be jiggered!*/An old-fashioned exclamation not heard much anymore." Also, such entries as *mebbe/mehbe* and *belly-bump/belly bumping* could have been merged.

Several errors of commission also mar this dictionary. Patriots' Day is said to be observed April 16 (not 19), *Worcester* appears for *Worcester, chocorua plague* is far out of alphabetic sequence, and Mary Sawyer and her lamb are stated to have lived some 40 miles east of their true hometown of Sterling, Massachusetts. Obviously, institutions with sufficient budget and patron need should instead opt to acquire the emergent *Dictionary of American Regional English* (see entry 833). If purchased, Hendrickson's book must be used with decided caution. In surveying the seemingly unbridgeable chasm that falls between these two works, one is reminded of what folks say Downeast (if not in *Yankee Talk*): "You can't get theyuh from heah."—**Jeffrey E. Long**

836. **Merriam-Webster's Crossword Puzzle Dictionary.** 2d ed. Springfield, Mass., Merriam-Webster, 1996. 775p. $17.95. ISBN 0-87779-121-X.

This 775-page revised crossword puzzle dictionary has been expanded to meet the specific needs of crossword puzzle solvers, with updated and enlarged entries to provide the latest coverage of the words puzzle makers use most often. The dictionary is structured in accordance with the way crossword puzzles are constructed and solved. Main entries are in alphabetic order letter-by-letter. If the main entry is a large category, the list of answer words is broken down into alphabetically arranged subcategories. When more than one answer is possible to a clue representing a main entry, the answer words are grouped together according to the number of letters they contain, with the specific number appearing in bold typeface before each numerical grouping. Answer words usually range from 2 to 13 letters.

This dictionary has a broad range of the most current words used in crossword puzzles. The format is easy to use. It is a welcome addition to an existing library or an excellent initial dictionary for the new puzzler solver.—**Tommie Brett Geer**

837. **NTC's Dictionary of Folksy, Regional, and Rural Sayings.** By Anne Bertram. Richard A. Spears, ed. Lincolnwood, Ill., National Textbook, 1996. 383p. index. $16.95pa. ISBN 0-8442-5834-2.

Containing more than 2,800 expressions from the rural United States, this dictionary lists sayings in alphabetic order (by the first word of the expression) from all over the country and spanning 3 centuries. Entry heads are in bold typeface; cross-references, which are abundant, are in italics; and the definitions are in roman typeface. Also in italics are the example sentences, of which there are generally at least two for every saying. Multiple definitions are given for expressions that may have more than one meaning, and each definition has its own example sentences. The volume is completed by a phrase-finder index (70 pages in length) that lists keywords, with expressions using the word (but no page number) appearing beneath it.

Aside from its user-friendly format, the dictionary has little to recommend it. Many of the idioms are so common it seems almost unnecessary to include them. For example, the dictionary lists " 'gator" for alligator; "coke" for Coca Cola (or other soft drinks); "sweet tooth" for liking sweets; and "spittoon" for, well, a spittoon (how many people actually say "cuspidor"?). A major flaw is that there is no mention in the entries of the first known usage of a saying or of the people who use it or of the place where it is commonly used (or was used). To document such information would give users insight into a constantly evolving language. These may well be folksy, regional, or rural sayings, but based on this dictionary, one cannot determine what folks are saying them, what region they are saying them in, and how rural that region may be.

Any true linguistic reference value is undermined by the dictionary's lack of documentation concerning origins and geographic areas of the utterances. The book is fun to browse, but its acquisition necessity is questionable at best. Writers of fiction may find the work useful, but many of the phrases are too clichéd to be used in more formal writing. Its purchase is therefore recommended for individuals rather than libraries.—**Melissa Rae Root**

Obsolete Words

838. **Medieval Wordbook.** Cosman, Madeleine Pelner. New York, Facts on File, 1996. 294p. illus. index. $35.00. ISBN 0-8160-3021-9.

The strength of Cosman's dictionary lies in its rare and happy blend of scholarship and clear, straightforward writing. Covering the period from 500 to 1500 C.E., the wordbook selects and identifies some 4,000 words for their relevance to the medieval world of Western Europe. The purpose of the work is to provide glimpses into this world that are both pleasurable and informed. Although it is not an etymological dictionary, it does provide origins for words from Latin, French, Italian, Spanish, German, Hebrew, and Arabic, and it translates phrases in their medieval context.

Entries range from brief identifications to longer explanations of phrases; for example, "to bring home the bacon," the symbolism of the pear, or the multiple meanings for "speculum." The selection covers many fields, among them the church, architecture, clothing, warfare, agriculture, literature, medicine, music, trade, and everyday life. Black-and-white photographs, line drawings, and engravings enhance the text and are especially well chosen. Cross-references, appearing in capital letters, enable the reader to maneuver easily through the text. Cosman's work both informs and delights, and it should find a welcome place in most libraries. [R: Choice, June 96, p. 1612]—**Bernice Bergup**

Other English-Speaking Countries

839. Upton, Clive, and J. D. A. Widdowson. **An Atlas of English Dialects.** New York, Oxford University Press, 1996. 193p. maps. index. $15.95pa. ISBN 0-19-869274-9.

For anyone who wants to know why Dick Van Dyke sang of "chimbleys" in *Mary Poppins*, this is the book in which to look. It is entertaining, easy to use, and educational; it is not, however, a traditional reference book. The subtitle is somewhat misleading, as the book is too short and too selective to be more than anecdotal. The authors, members of the Centre for English Cultural Tradition and Language at the University of Sheffield, based this volume on the findings of the Survey of English Dialects, which was conducted between 1948 and 1961 and concerned rural dialects primarily. It is important to note, then, that the information in this atlas is several years old.

The 90 words and phrases profiled in this book are organized into 3 general groups: pronunciation, grammar, and vocabulary, with the vocabulary section being divided into sections describing people, the body, states and conditions, animals, nature, objects, seasons and times, and actions. Each of the entries has a page-length linguistic commentary with an accompanying map that shows how the word, phrase, or sound differs in various parts of England (dialects from Scotland and Wales are not represented). The maps reflect the county boundary changes of 1974. Fortunately for nonspecialists, the authors did not use a phonetic alphabet but spelled words and sounds as they are pronounced.

An excellent introduction gives a short history of the development of the English language in Great Britain and offers an explanation for the development of distinct dialects. A bibliography, an index of maps, an index of linguistic terms, and a general index complete the volume.—**Hope Yelich**

Rhetoric

840. **Encyclopedia of Rhetoric and Composition: Communication from Ancient Times to the Information Age.** Theresa Enos, ed. New York, Garland, 1996. 803p. index. (Garland Reference Library of the Humanities, v.1389). $95.00. ISBN 0-8240-7200-6.

Although compiled by a single editor, the material in this 1-volume, 803-page encyclopedia has been contributed by 288 specialists. The 467 entries, alphabetically organized, range in time from Aristotle to the New Rhetoricians and computer applications and cover the history of rhetoric; its tools; and practitioners including Arabic, Chinese, African American, Native American, and Indian (Sanskrit). It goes beyond the usual applications of composition and language arts into other contexts, such as anthropology, linguistics, philosophy, psychology, and pedagogy.

Entries consist of four types: brief identification of terms from *accumulation* to *zeugma* and individuals from Alcuin of York to Zoeliner; longer notes for subjects such as hermeneutics or men such as Friedrich Nietzsche and Jacques Derrida; essays discussing topics in depth (e.g., feminist rhetoric, ethos); and full articles explaining methodology (e.g., argument, invention). Each entry is followed by the name of the contributor and the associated academic institution. Most have a bibliography of key texts and recommended readings.

A comprehensive index makes it easy to locate material buried within the text. Words that appear in the alphabetic listing are cross-referenced with a *quod vide*. Such a broadly based volume has required selectivity; such terms as *oxymoron* and such critics as Cyril Connolly have been omitted. Many of the longer articles presume familiarity with specialized terminology, but both students and teachers of rhetoric will find this reference book a useful guide. [R: Choice, June 96, p. 1614]—**Charlotte Lindgren**

Slang

841. Clark, Thomas L. **Western Lore and Language: A Dictionary for Enthusiasts of the American West.** Salt Lake City, Utah, University of Utah Press, 1996. 266p. illus. maps. $24.95. ISBN 0-87480-510-4.

This title may evoke images of cowboys and gold prospectors, but the book's scope is much more expansive. With a geographic range from Alaska to El Paso, Texas, and a chronological span from the eighteenth century to the present, this volume includes approximately 2,000 words and phrases that originated in the West or are associated with the region. Along with the expected entries describing local geography, topography, flora, and fauna, one also finds the jargon of Mormons and moviemakers, gamblers and gaffers, surfers and Silicon Valley computer wizards. Words borrowed from Spanish and Native American languages are numerous, but Clark chooses to exclude Hawaiian talk with its Polynesian and Asian influences. Clark's inclusion of commonplace terms (such as *Idaho* and *Arizona*) may seem unnecessary, but even these entries provide useful etymologies (factual as well as fanciful folk derivations), historical background, and information about variant names.

In compiling a lexicon notable for its comprehensiveness and currency, Clark has drawn from oral collections, newspapers, and specialized works on the language of a particular locality, vocation, or avocation (e.g., *Surfin'ary: A Dictionary of Surfing Terms and Surfspeak* [see ARBA 92, entry 802]). His synthesis of these highly diverse materials is scholarly but frequently witty. For example, his entry for *mi casa es su casa* offers a well-phrased comment on hypocrisy reminiscent of Dr. Johnson's humorous contributions to lexicography. Some entries offer help with pronunciation (in a nonphonetic newspaper style), but this information is lacking for several unfamiliar words. Illustrations include both line drawings and black-and-white photographs, but the latter are often fuzzy. [R: BL, 15 Oct 96, p. 453; LJ, 1 Nov 96, p. 58]—**Albert Wilhelm**

842. Dalzell, Tom. **Flappers 2 Rappers: American Youth Slang.** Springfield, Mass., Merriam-Webster, 1996. 256p. illus. index. $14.95pa. ISBN 0-87779-612-2.

Dalzell has written a comprehensive and thoroughly absorbing study of U.S. youth slang. More than a reference dictionary of slang terms, this highly affordable book covers the etymology of youth slang from the flapper era through the current rapper slang of the 1990s. He begins with a brief look at the time before the flapper, that is, back to the 1850s, and then proceeds chronologically in decades to the present. Each chapter includes numerous word lists and definitions, as well as innumerable essays on the development and occurrence of particular slang terms.

An academic study, yet highly entertaining, this book is part of a new popular language line from Merriam-Webster. Illustrated with eye-catching, full-color drawings from nationally recognized artists, this is a reference book with browsing appeal. The author, a lawyer and labor rights advocate, spent 10 years researching slang for a novel that was never completed. Instead, his collection of 1,000 books and 2,000 articles and pamphlets on slang became the basis for his research for this book. Bibliographies follow each chapter, and a list of major slang sources is given at the end. Thoroughly documented and cross-referenced with an index, this book will make an outstanding addition to any high school, public, or academic library collection.—**Ingrid Schierling Burnett**

Unabridged

843. **Oxford English Dictionary on Compact Disc.** 2d ed. [CD-ROM]. New York, Oxford University Press, 1992. Minimum system requirements: IBM or compatible 386. CD-ROM drive with MS CD-ROM Extensions 2.0. DOS 3.0. Windows 3.1. 4MB RAM. 2MB hard disk space. VGA monitor. $395.00/single user.

The *Oxford English Dictionary* (OED) is more than just a dictionary, it is a history of the English language as well. The OED was written, revised, and revised again over the past century. The CD-ROM version makes access to this historical record even easier. Although a copyright of 1992 appears in the software manual, the interface software was revised in January 1995, and a price reduction in 1996 allows it to be accessible to more people.

After an easy installation, and once running, two windows appear on the screen: Word Look-up and Word List. Under Word Look-up, the choices for searching (wildcards are allowed) are by word, phrases, and the like; variant forms; phonetics; Greek; date filter; and part of speech filter. Word is obvious in its use: Type a word and press the List or Find button. The Word List shows the choices, and once a word has been selected, a third screen appears on the right, which gives the entry for the word. Display settings can be changed to show only items the user is interested in reading. The rest of the functions operate in a similar fashion. The date filter allows searching of the history of a word by choosing a time frame in which the word appeared. Search capabilities other than by word are available from the pull-down menus. These include text searches, etymological searches, definition searches, and quotation searches. Boolean searches are also supported.

Entries are arranged in a dictionary fashion. The headword is listed, followed by pronunciation, part of speech, homographs, variant forms, etymology (not the short abbreviated descriptions found in most dictionaries), definitions, subordinate headwords, phrases, and quotations. Quotations is where OED deviates from most dictionaries, and is where it becomes most interesting and often most valuable. The list is chronological from earliest to latest use. For instance, *editor* appeared in English, deriving from French, in the year 1649.

OED claims to be a descriptive dictionary, not a prescriptive one, meaning that it is a record of English usage, not a standard thereof. Americans can breathe a sigh of relief in that British English is not used as a pronunciation guide. Those in the United Kingdom can also be relieved to find that American English pronunciation is not the standard in this version of the OED. Instead, the dictionary has chosen to use the International Phonetic Alphabet (IPA), used by most broadcasters in the United States and in the United Kingdom. A list of sorts of the IPA is shown in the manual's appendix under "Character Sets," and in the online help menu under "Phonetics." Pronunciation under IPA tends to be neutral, clearer, and avoids common accents found in both countries. A full description of IPA would have been valuable, but probably would have been inappropriate in this venue.

This incredibly valuable tool is recommended for libraries, schools, educators, and anyone in the field of language, writing, or history. However, the price, even if reduced, will place it out of reach for many.—**Kevin W. Perizzolo**

NON-ENGLISH-LANGUAGE DICTIONARIES

Armenian

844. Baghdasarian, Louisa, and R. David Zorc, comps. **Armenian (Eastern)-English Dictionary.** Kensington, Md., Dunwoody Press, 1995. 824p. $89.00. ISBN 1-881265-07-2.

The choice and description of the vocabulary are the best features of this dictionary. Because this is basically a dictionary of the Eastern Armenian dialect, it is important to note that sources originating in Armenia itself, particularly the four-volume dictionary of the Acharian Institute of Language of the Armenian Academy in Yerevan, have been widely used. As a preparatory step, the two authors compiled an Eastern Armenian newspaper reader and grammar in 1995 (also published by Dunwoody Press); this represents an important task, because in this way they were able to select many culture-bound lexical items of Soviet character and some Eastern neologisms, useful not only to the anglophone user, but also to the speaker of Western Armenian (spoken mostly in Turkey).

Because the dictionary is intended for the Anglophone user, there is not much discrimination of the near-synonyms indicated as equivalents: When reading an entry such as *gtsagrut'yun* [drawing, design, sketch; lineament], the semicolon will help the user make the right choice, and the abbreviation [*ext*] (extended meaning) will give notice that the following equivalents [shapes, features, lines] belong to other contexts. The user is offered well-marked synonyms and antonyms and variants in spelling. For a dictionary of this character, it is unusual to indicate the source of loanwords, a useful feature. Equally unusual and even more useful is the indication that the entry word is a compound, because it brings the anglophone user to an understanding of the structure of Armenian words.

Every entry word is transliterated, but not the synonyms and antonyms nor the Armenian expressions in the front matter. Future editions should broaden the scope of the transliterated passages.—**L. Zgusta**

Delaware

845. O'Meara, John. **Delaware-English/English-Delaware Dictionary.** Toronto and Buffalo, N.Y., University of Toronto Press, 1996. 660p. $75.00. ISBN 0-8020-0670-1.

The Delaware Indians (also called Lenâpé), of the Algonquian linguistic family, play an important role in U.S. history through the fact that they originally occupied the valleys of the lower Hudson and Delaware Rivers, around what were to become the cities of New York and Philadelphia. Their descendants became widely dispersed, and their language is currently spoken by only a few surviving members of two subgroups—the Unami in Oklahoma, and the Munsee in Ontario, Canada. The present dictionary provides information on the vocabulary used by recent speakers of Munsee in the community of Moraviantown, Ontario.

Each of the 7,100 entries in the Delaware-English section (379 pages) includes information on grammatical categories and sample inflected forms. The somewhat shorter English-Delaware section (275 pages) will serve users as an index to the fuller information in the Delaware-English entries. The orthography is a practical one, with a minimum of diacritical symbols. The dictionary marks loanwords borrowed from early Dutch settlers and from English; and although the English source words are specified, the Dutch source words are not, for unexplained reasons.

An introductory "Guide to Using the Dictionary" provides information on grammatical categorization, presented in technical language. In general, the dictionary will be most valuable to users with considerable sophistication in the Delaware language or in Algonquian linguistics. [R: Choice, Dec 96, pp. 592-93]—**William Bright**

French

846. Denoeu, François, David Sices, and Jacqueline B. Sices. **2001 French and English Idioms. 2001 Idiotismes Français et Anglais.** 2d ed. Hauppauge, N.Y., Barron's Educational Series, 1996. 837p. illus. index. $13.95pa. ISBN 0-8120-9024-1.

For students seeking just the right equivalent phrase for an idiomatic expression, this volume will fit the bill. It is divided into two parts, French-English and English-French. Entries are brief, consisting of a phrase, its equivalent(s) in the second language, and an illustrative sentence. There are no pronunciation guides or word-for-word translations. Entries are arranged alphabetically by the first keyword in the phrase. Indexes in each section are limited to additional keywords and, to their detriment, include no general subjects or cross-references.

While their stated aim is to give "as many idioms as possible with their natural, exact equivalents," the compilers were in fact selective. Slang and vulgar expressions are excluded, as are idioms that are exactly the same in both languages. "Not to have a clue" is here, but "to have no idea" is not, as the latter has a literal translation. This rule is understandable, as many such straight translations for idioms can be found in any good French-English dictionary, but it renders the book incomplete. *Au septième ciel* is translated as "on cloud nine, walking on air," but its literal translation—"in seventh heaven"—is not given. Some omissions seem arbitrary; another common French expression for being extremely happy, *aux anges*, is not given in any appropriate English entry but is present in the French section.

Large bilingual dictionaries provide much of the same information. Still, despite a few flaws, this volume is much handier for its intended purpose and will serve as a useful supplement.—**Emily L. Werrell**

847. Grieve, James. **Dictionary of Contemporary French Connectors.** New York, Routledge, 1996. 525p. $65.00. ISBN 0-415-13538-9.

Connectors are words or phrases, such as "also," "in fact," "but," and "however," that function as links or transitions between different ideas. They are useful for persuasive or expository prose. French connecting phrases are much more precise than their English counterparts, and many are impossible to translate into English with the full undertone of meaning and usage. This dictionary is the first French-English reference source to focus on connecting words and phrases. It is intended for English speakers, both for translation purposes and for grammatical instruction in the nuances of the French language.

A chapter on common functions starts the dictionary, outlining the differences between reinforcers, recapitulators, restricters, and the like. A list of English structures with French counterparts comes next, complete with the warning that the words do not necessarily have straightforward French equivalents. The dictionary proper follows, in a letter-by-letter alphabetic sequence. An asterisk by the headword indicates that the expression is also discussed in the first chapter. Cross-references to other main entries in the dictionary are in bold typeface. Entries consist of a brief explanation of the term, followed by its separate functions in written language, examples, variant terms that could be used, and possible English equivalents. The examples come from authentic sources of contemporary prose, including newspapers, magazines, advertisements, essays, books (mostly of the nonfiction variety), and so forth. Quotations illustrating the examples are documented; bibliographic information on these sources is listed in the back of the volume.

This dictionary would be helpful for advanced students of French, whether at the college level or in accelerated high school classes. Translators would also benefit from it. The focus on primarily written rather than spoken language limits its usefulness as a cultural study, but otherwise, the dictionary is highly recommended to libraries for its stated purpose.—**Melissa Rae Root**

848. **Larousse Mini French-English, English-French Dictionary. Larousse Mini Dictionnaire Français-Anglais, Anglais-Français.** new ed. New York, Larousse Kingfisher Chambers, 1995. 314p. $4.95pa. ISBN 2-03-420903-6.

This minidictionary is designed largely for travelers and those beginning to study either French or English, but who do not require extensive technical or sophisticated vocabularies, full grammatical details, or the examples of typical or useful phrases and sentences supplied by more comprehensive dictionaries. Nevertheless, this compact volume includes more than 40,000 translations, with special attention paid to words likely to be found on street signs or menus. Remarkably, in addition to its pocket-sized convenience, the typeface is clear and easy to read.

In addition to direct translation (and phonetic pronunciation guides) of individual words, the French section offers short paragraph descriptions of such ubiquitous abbreviations in France as RER (a Parisian rail network) or the TGV (French high-speed trains); brief histories of the Louvre museum and of Versailles; the significance of the Christmas holiday, *Noël*; and what to expect of *frommage* (cheese) or when buying *pain* (bread). For French readers, the English portion of the dictionary distinguishes between English and American spellings and usage; includes guides for pronunciation; and offers brief descriptions of such diverse subjects as Buckingham Palace and Guy Fawkes Night, as well as bingo, Halloween, and what is meant by Cajun cooking.—**Joseph W. Dauben**

German

849. Bridgham, Fred. **The Friendly German-English Dictionary: A Guide to German Language, Culture, and Society....** Concord, Mass., Libris/Paul & Company Publishers, 1996. 318p. index. $67.50; $26.95pa. ISBN 1-870352-65-3; 1-870352-67-Xpa.

This is a fascinating dictionary, but it comes with a few caveats. First of all, one has to have a fairly adequate knowledge of the German language in order to use it. The basic premise behind this publication was in trying to explain the meaning and etymology of words that straddle both languages but may have a different meaning from the one that sounds likely. For example, *walzen* has nothing to do with waltzing, but with rolling, as in a *Walzwerk*, which is a metal-rolling mill. A *Rathaus* is a town hall, and has nothing to do with rats, not even in Hameln. *Rattengift*, however, is rat poison (*gift* being another word that has nothing to do with presents). *Rat* (one "t") derives from the word for "advice," while a *Ratte* (two "t"s) has four legs and a long shiny tail.

Each entry is meticulously explained, with literary allusions and often with a touch of humor. People obsessed with word meanings will have a field day browsing through this book, and translators will find it a most important tool. The entries have been arranged into 10 categories ("Administration, Law, and the Armed Forces" is one; "History and Politics" is another, and so on), with a word index in the back of the book, a setup that is only good for browsing through sections of one's interest. When searching for a specific word, however, this grouping is mostly a waste of time. Several entries deal with words that came into being in the former East Germany, a fact that makes this volume an important etymological resource. [R: Choice, Nov 96, p. 426]—**Koraljka Lockhart**

850. **Larousse Mini German-English, English-German Dictionary. Larousse Miniwörterbuch Deutsch-Englisch, Englisch-Deutsch.** new ed. New York, Larousse Kingfisher Chambers, 1995. 327p. $5.50pa. ISBN 2-03-420902-8.

This minidictionary is designed largely for travelers and those beginning to study either German or English, but who do not require extensive technical or sophisticated vocabularies, full grammatical details, or the examples of typical or useful phrases and sentences supplied by more comprehensive dictionaries. Nevertheless, this compact volume includes more than 40,000 translations, with special attention paid to words likely to be found on street signs or menus. Remarkably, in addition to its pocket-sized convenience, the typeface is clear and easy to read.

In addition to direct translation of individual words, the German section offers short paragraph descriptions of more difficult concepts, such as the German *Abitur* examinations, a brief history of the *Oktoberfest*, and what to expect to find in a *Weihnachtsmarkt* or when buying *Wurst*. Similarly, for German readers, the English portion of the dictionary distinguishes between English and American spellings and usage; includes guides for pronunciation; and includes brief descriptions of such diverse subjects as Buckingham Palace and Guy Fawkes Night, as well as bingo, Halloween, and what is meant by Cajun cooking.—**Joseph W. Dauben**

851. **Routledge German Technical Dictionary. Universal-Wörterbuch der Technik Englisch.** New York, Routledge, 1996. 2v. $275.00/set. ISBN 0-415-09392-9.

Much time was spent, in vain, with this astounding dictionary, trying to find some item that is not represented. Perhaps the only missing items are stagecraft and stage machinery. What is represented is a list of 64 categories, ranging from acoustics to wave physics, with choice items in between: artificial intelligence, computer technology and data processing, ergonomics, marine pollution, nuclear technology, particle physics, radiation physics, television, waste management, and so on. This two-volume set follows a highly successful previous edition of the same in the French language (see ARBA 96, entry 1499). The enormous database compiled for the earlier publication was used as a basis for the German edition.

These volumes are intended for scientists, students, and specialists in their respective fields, and one would almost have to be highly proficient in one's field *and* be bilingual in order to use the dictionary properly. For example, the term *exhaust* has so many meanings in so many technical categories, it takes up one-and-a-quarter hefty columns of miscellaneous definitions. A scientist or a student specializing in a particular branch of science will not have too many problems, but one has to feel for the poor translator of scientific texts when faced with this many options. The dictionary also includes a postcard, by means of which one may order a CD-ROM version of the same dictionary, which is probably the easier way to use this publication as one would define an area of expertise before looking up a term. North American technical terms are included, and German- and English-speaking experts in their respective categories were consulted throughout. In short, this dictionary was meticulously put together, cleanly laid out, and there are absolutely no typographic errors whatsoever.—**Koraljka Lockhart**

852. Schemann, Hans, and Paul Knight. **German-English Dictionary of Idioms. Idiomatik Deutsch-Englisch.** New York, Routledge, 1995. 1253p. $99.95. ISBN 0-415-14199-0.

This German-English dictionary of idioms is one of a planned series of bilingual dictionaries of idioms; it follows a similar recent German-French dictionary. Its 33,000 expressions are drawn from widely distributed German newspapers and magazines, the spoken language, contemporary German dictionaries, and literary texts of the times. The concept of *idiom* is a broad one: It is essentially a group of words restricted to a specific context (e.g., *in den Kochtopf gucken*, to poke one's nose into someone else's business).

Other than observing in the introduction that there is an enormous difference in idiomatic usage between older people (55 and older) and younger people (younger than 25), the authors do not indicate such areas of difference. Acknowledging also that levels of usage have become blurred and that vulgarisms are more easily accepted, the authors rarely indicate levels of English usage and steer a wide berth around vulgarisms other than the common *Arsch* and *Scheisse*, both of which are milder in their American usage than in British.

The dictionary is much more useful for English-language readers of German than for German-language readers of English. The usage is notably more British than American. Many of the English-language renderings offered are not used in the United States, and some would not be understood here (such as "to take the mickey out of someone"). Common, obvious American renderings, such as "to brown nose someone" for *jm. in den Arsch kriechen*, are at times omitted.

The dictionary is a useful supplement to the standard German-English dictionaries. However, U.S. readers finding "drunk as a lord" for *voll wie ein Fass* may well feel removed from their country and their time.—**John B. Beston**

Greek

853. **A Greek-English Lexicon.** 9th ed. Henry George Liddell and Robert Scott, comps. Revised by Henry Stuart Jones. New York, Oxford University Press, c. 1940, 1996. 1v. (various paging). $125.00. ISBN 0-19-864226-1.

For decades, *A Greek-English Lexicon* has been the standard dictionary for preclassical, classical, and Hellenistic Greek. Early editions were based upon the work of German lexicographer Franz Passow (*Handbuch der Grieschen Sprache*), but since the 4th edition (1855), it has stood on its own reputation. The last major revision of the lexicon itself resulted in the publication of the 9th edition in 1940. In 1968, a supplement was published to take account of new material (primarily from inscriptions and papyri) and to make necessary corrections to the lexicon. The release under review includes a revised supplement, nearly twice the size of the previous one. In addition to more material from inscriptions and papyri, it contains—for the first time—Linear B forms (a syllabic script found on clay tablets discovered at Knossos, Mycenae, and Pylos). This moves the coverage of the lexicon back to approximately 1200 B.C.E. Symbols (a cross and an upright cross) are used in the supplement to indicate new words and entries that have been rewritten.

The supplement is also available separately for $65 (Oxford University Press, 1996). Libraries owning an earlier edition of the lexicon that is still in usable condition should be able to get by with purchasing the supplement by itself. In one form or the other, all academic collections that support classical and biblical studies should have this work on their shelves.—**Craig W. Beard**

Hebrew

854. Bolozky, Shmuel. **501 Hebrew Verbs: Fully Conjugated in All the Tenses....** Hauppauge, N.Y., Barron's Educational Series, 1996. 910p. index. $12.95pa. ISBN 0-8120-9468-9.

This book is a great inflation fighter, giving verbs for 3¢ apiece rather than the 6¢ charged by its predecessor, Barron's *201 Hebrew Verbs* (1970). Bolozky, professor of Hebrew at the University of Massachusetts at Amherst, conjugates and translates each verb in its seven *binyanim* (*kal*, *hitpa'el*, and so on), and then gives helpful illustrations of its use in several sentences, provides idioms, and although the book seems primarily concerned with modern Hebrew, throws in occasional examples of the verb's use in Biblical, Medieval, and Mishnaic Hebrew. The typeface is quite readable, the arrangement of the text useful, and the index accurate. While Israelis and serious Bible scholars read and write Hebrew sans vowels, the rest of us are grateful for Bolozky's almost universal inclusion of them. The brief grammar lessons are helpful, but would be more user friendly with fewer esoteric Hebrew and English grammatical terms.

This reviewer's first use of the book came at a synagogue, where women have recently begun coming to morning *minyan* (prayers) for the first time. After one has performed an honored ritual during prayers, such as blessing the Torah reading, he, up till now, was welcomed back to his seat with a hearty handshake and the greeting *yasher koach* ("more strength to you"), to which he replied, *baruch tiyeh* ("and may you be blessed"). Now how does one reply to *yasher koach* from a woman? At providing a quick answer, Bolozky bats 500. Page 149 made clear that the correct form of the verb "to be" is *tiyee*, but page 85 is unclear about the correct Hebrew for *blessed* in this situation, requiring the user to turn to a grammar. This reviewer now says *baruchah tiyee*, which one hopes will work.—**Anthony Gottlieb**

855. **The Oxford English-Hebrew Dictionary.** N. S. Doniach and A. Kahane, eds. New York, Oxford University Press, 1996. 1091p. $65.00. ISBN 0-19-864322-5.

This dictionary, containing more than 50,000 entries, was edited by Doniach (now deceased) and Kahane (assistant professor of classics at Northwestern University) in collaboration with the Oxford Centre for Hebrew and Jewish Studies. The goal of the editors was to describe the language as it is actually used, and thus they list only words currently attested to in usage, including non-Semitic loan words. The editors did not intend the work to be fully comprehensive, but rather sought to furnish the most common words that would be most likely needed by an average user—slang, idioms and phrases, and specialized terminology. A detailed and helpful guide to the dictionary is incorporated into the preface.

Among the many useful features of the dictionary are the use of numbers to distinguish different headwords with identical spelling and the inclusion of labels indicating parts of speech, levels of usage, national-dialect, and semantic-field. Hints on construction, content, and usage are provided by means of example sentences. Phonetic transcriptions follow the standard British pronunciation, although there may be many other ways of pronouncing the word. The Hebrew text is pointed according to the traditional rules, but modern pronunciations are given precedence when they are different from those deriving from the traditional pointing. The editors have provided a major tool for students of modern Hebrew, and this volume will be a most welcome addition to any reference collection with an interest in the Hebrew language.—**Harold O. Forshey**

856. Zilberman, Shimon, comp. **The Compact Up-to-Date English-Hebrew Dictionary: With Rules of Pronunciation of the English Language.** Jerusalem, Zilberman; distr., New York, Hippocrene Books, 1995. 1v. (various paging). $16.95pa. ISBN 0-7818-0431-0.

This work is an abridgment of *The Up-to-Date English-Hebrew Dictionary*. It contains 28,000 entries that consist of a single English word and its Hebrew equivalent, and a Hebrew word with a single English equivalent. The approach is concise and simple; no lengthy definitions are included. In the case of the English word, the part of speech is given. The dictionary aims to meet the needs of students, home and business users, and others who want "a smaller lexicon" (preface).

Preceding the English/Hebrew section, there is a 29-page guide to English-language pronunciation. Rules of pronunciation, including prefixes and suffixes, are presented. Although the short preface is bilingual, the introduction and explanatory material in both the Hebrew/English and English/Hebrew sections is only in Hebrew. The dictionary therefore is more useful for Hebrew speakers learning English, than for English speakers learning Hebrew.

The book is smaller than average size, with narrow margins and thin paper, where the type can be seen from both sides of the page. Although the English words are in darker bold typeface and easier to read, the Hebrew type is thinner, smaller, and more difficult to read. For libraries in the United States already possessing a hardcover, complete English/Hebrew, Hebrew/English dictionary, this smaller one could be a useful supplement, especially if there are Israeli users needing a convenient, up-to-date, quick reference.

—**Susan J. Freiband**

Hungarian

857. **Hippocrene Concise Hungarian-English, English-Hungarian Dictionary.** By Géza Takács. New York, Hippocrene Books, 1996. 281p. $14.95pa. ISBN 0-7818-0317-9.

The Hungarian language does not belong to the Indo-European language family, thus most tourists to Hungary will have greater difficulty interpreting the written or spoken language than on visits to many other European countries. Although English-speaking natives are encountered frequently in all major Hungarian cities, one can never find an interpreter when needed. To make an English or American tourist's visit more enriching, this pocket book provides 7,000 vocabulary words and expressions most likely to be encountered on a visit to Hungary. Both American and British spellings and meanings of a word are indicated when necessary. The author does an excellent job of explaining the syntax of the Hungarian language, as well as differences in vocabulary, pronunciation, and common Hungarian abbreviations. Brief but useful indexes are also provided for original Hungarian personal and geographic names, typical food dishes, holidays, and a conversion guide for weights and measures.

The book is decidedly geared for the tourist. For example, there are no entries for such terms as *computer* and *technology*, but there are entries for *customs control* and *beer*. The entries include many geographic and other proper names, as well as months, days of the week, and numbers. Some of these concepts (e.g., numbers for counting or days of the week) may have been better presented in a separate index. Overall, the shortcomings of this book are few. The pronunciations are clearly presented, the basic conversational vocabulary is comprehensive, and the volume is portable in pocket or purse. Whether used for translating letters from relatives overseas, or struggling with directions while visiting, the user will be glad to have access to the volume.—**Andrew G. Torok**

Italian

858. **Larousse Mini Italian-English, English-Italian Dictionary. Larousse Mini Dizionario Italiano-Inglese, Inglese-Italiano.** new ed. New York, Larousse Kingfisher Chambers, 1995. 320p. $5.50pa. ISBN 2-03-420901-X.

This minidictionary is designed largely for travelers and those beginning to study either Italian or English, but who do not require extensive technical or sophisticated vocabularies, full grammatical details, or the examples of typical or useful sentences supplied by more comprehensive dictionaries. Nevertheless, this compact volume includes more than 40,000 translations, with special attention paid to words likely to be found on street signs or menus. Remarkably, in addition to its pocket-sized convenience, the typeface is clear and easy to read.

In addition to direct translation of individual words, the Italian section offers short paragraph descriptions of such Italian customs as the *Paseggiata*; significant places such as the Vatican and the *Uffizi* museum; the major holidays including *Natale, ferragosto*, and the *Palio di Siena*; as well as the many varieties of pasta, what to expect of *pane* (bread), or when buying *formaggio* (cheese), *gelato* (ice cream), *caffè*, or *vino*. For Italian readers, the English portion of the dictionary distinguishes between English and American spellings and usage; includes guides for pronunciation; and offers brief descriptions of such diverse subjects as Buckingham Palace and Guy Fawkes Night, as well as bingo, Halloween, and what is meant by Cajun cooking.—**Joseph W. Dauben**

Japanese

859. Akiyama, Nobuo, and Carol Akiyama. **2001 Japanese and English Idioms.** Hauppauge, N.Y., Barron's Educational Series, 1996. 700p. index. $13.95pa. ISBN 0-8120-9433-6.

This volume has been prepared for English and Japanese speakers interested in getting acquainted with commonly used idioms of both languages. The book consists of 2 parts, 1 for Japanese idioms and another for English idioms, and each part contains more than 2,000 idioms. The Japanese idioms are entered by key Japanese words, most of which are nouns, such as *abura* in roman script, followed by writing in Japanese, and by the English translation of—in this case—"oil." Each keyword is followed by one or several idioms. As with the keyword, each idiom is entered in the same order (i.e., in roman script, Japanese writing, and the English translation). The entry idiom is provided with the literal English translation and a sample Japanese sentence in Japanese writing, roman script, and the English translation. As for the English idioms, they are also entered by keywords, many of which are nouns, such as *account*, followed by the Japanese translation written in Japanese writing and roman script. Each English idiom is provided with the Japanese translation, roman script, and a sample sentence with the Japanese translation and roman script. No Japanese literal translations or explanations are provided with English idioms.

As a matter of curiosity, it is said that the Japanese people are shy to use gestures, sign languages, or body language. The reader may notice, however, that, except for "nose," there are more Japanese idioms than the English ones that refer to various parts of the body. Do these idioms offset the lack of the visual language? (The numbers of the Japanese idioms are shown below first, and the English second: head [20, 12]; face [27, 5]; eye [73, 8]; nose [14, 21]; mouth [51, 8]; neck/throat [18, 3]; and so on.) *Hara* (belly/abdomen/stomach), from which the expression of *hara kiri* (ritual suicide by disembowelment practiced by Japanese warriors) is derived, has 50 entries, while English has only 2 under "stomach." Idioms with the keywords "shoes" and "bucket," on the other hand, are not found among Japanese ones.

This book will be particularly useful to readers who have studied the Japanese language for at least two years, because of the relatively small number of words listed in the index. It is recommended for college and university libraries, and possibly for larger public libraries.—**Seiko Mieczkowski**

860. Spahn, Mark, and Wolfgang Hadamitzky, with Kumiko Fujie-Winter. **The Kanji Dictionary.** Boston, Charles E. Tuttle, 1996. 1748p. index. $59.95. ISBN 0-8048-2058-9.

The Japanese title of this dictionary is *Kan(ji)-Ei(go) Jyukugo Jiten* (*Chinese Character-English Compound Dictionary*). A *jyukugo* is "a compound word consisting of two or more *kanji*; for example, *hana mi* [flower viewing] is a two *kanji jyukugo*. *The Kanji Dictionary* contains more than 48,000 *jyukugo*, and this number may indicate that the dictionary lists almost all the *jyukugo* of Japanese general use. Each *jyukugo* is followed by its pronunciation, written in roman letters, and then by the English translation. The first *kanji* of each *jyukugo* is termed "the head *kanji*" or "the component *kanji*," and the dictionary contains 5,910 of them, with *on* and *kun* readings and their English equivalents. These component *kanji* are listed not in their alphabetic order but according to a radical-based reference system, as in most Japanese dictionaries. There are overview lists that present in a condensed form all component *kanji* listed under given radicals.

After World War II the Japanese government simplified *kanji* writing during the reform, and many *kanji* became obsolete. The work includes these obsolete *kanji* as well, which may create confusion. The dictionary provides, in addition to an index of all component *kanji*, 36 appendixes of historical periods, counters, national holidays and annual events, and the like, which are helpful for users. One of them contains a list of 1,006 *kanji* taught in elementary school, and this number plus 939 *kanji* of general use, which are not listed in the appendixes, are called "the *joo yoo kanji*." It would have been helpful for the user if the stroke order was given to the *joo yoo kanji* as users should learn the stroke order on their own.

This dictionary is convenient and useful for those who want quick reference to a particular *jyukugo* or who want to increase the number of *jyukugo* for their knowledge. *Kodansha's Pocket Kanji Guide* (see ARBA 96, entry 1112) is prepared in the same way as the work under review but also contains the stroke order. *NTC's New Japanese-English Character Dictionary* (see ARBA 94, entry 1121) is also comprehensive and includes—in addition to the compounds—the stroke order, synonyms, example sentences, homophones, compound formation, and notes. [R: Choice, Sept 96, p. 106]—**Seiko Mieczkowski**

Lao

861. **Lao-English Dictionary.** William L. Patterson, ed. Kensington, Md., Dunwoody Press, [1995]. 826p. $89.00. ISBN 1-881265-17-X.

This dictionary is a translation of a Lao-Russian dictionary published in 1982, a wise decision instead of compiling an original one. In the 1970s, the Russians had far wider possibilities for compiling a dictionary than are at hand now for anyone, because for political reasons there was ready money for these projects. For a U.S. publisher, undertaking a new dictionary of the language from scratch would probably have been prohibitively costly, and a compilation based on older French and English sources would undoubtedly contain a lower ratio of the modern spoken language to the classical one than is the case now.

The translations of the equivalents are commendable and clear, with plenty of explanatory glosses and restrictions of application. Every entry word is transliterated. There is one editorial decision that may be open to debate according to different opinions: Compounds are listed under what is called "root words" even if the alphabetic order gets disrupted. Thus, the entry *phzeuhng* [to be due; to deserve; to be worth] contains the subentry *bophzeuhngpatthawhna* [persona non grata], and the entry *hlay* [to flow; to drift] contains the subentries *khajhlay* [to sell for a trifle] and *hlayszyhm* [to leak]. Such an organization of the entry accords with the cultural traditions of the East and Southeast Asian area, but still, the English-speaking user will frequently be at a loss as to where to seek such a compound.

In some cases, one can doubt whether the subentry really contains a genuine lexical unit. For example, the entry *phzya* [in order; for the sake] contains such subentries as *szayzphzahawnawtangtangphzya-hayzphzeumphzumphawlihtphoohn* [to use all means to increase production], or *phzyapawhnhootkee-sahntihphzap* [in the name of the cause of peace]. These are clearly contextual examples that the Russian lexicographer in the 1980s felt compelled to include. These are, however, minor points, more entertaining than irritating; the dictionary will no doubt provide beneficial service.—**L. Zgusta**

Lithuanian

862. Piesarskas, Bronius, and Bronius Svecevičius. **Lithuanian Dictionary: English-Lithuanian, Lithuanian-English.** New York, Routledge, 1995. 799p. $74.95; $29.95pa. ISBN 0-415-12856-0; 0-415-12857-9pa.

The two authors of this dictionary have considerable experience in the field, as they have already published, both jointly and separately, several Lithuanian-English and English-Lithuanian dictionaries. Indeed, the present dictionary is basically a reprint of a dictionary published by the two lexicographers in 1994 in Vilnius, Lithuania. From this fact it follows that the Lithuanian speaker is here the intended user of this reference work; hence, while the Lithuanian pronunciation is not given (it is fully predictable anyhow from the spelling), assistance with English pronunciation is provided in both parts of the dictionary: full International Phonetic Alphabet indications in the English-Lithuanian part, and minimal aid, in terms of stress position, in the Lithuanian-English part. Also, all explanatory glosses, grammatical information, and so forth are in Lithuanian in both parts of the dictionary.

A. S. Hornby's *Oxford Advanced Learner's Dictionary of Current English* (Oxford University Press, 1989) and the *Longman Dictionary of Contemporary English* (see ARBA 80, entry 1111) are listed among the references. This kind of lexicographical background guarantees that the selection of the vocabulary is excellent; nevertheless, the grammatical indications given in both these dictionaries are severely limited. Readers do not get the syntactic patterns associated with verbs, but only the usual indication of prepositions that collocate with verbs. There is an important appendix containing Lithuanian geographic names. Although Lithuanian is written in the roman script, many geographic names have the form they acquired in Russian, which transcribes everything into Cyrillic.

The dictionary also contains (sandwiched between the two major parts of the dictionary) a section called "Supplement: Notes on the Alphabet, Pronunciation and Grammar of Lithuanian." This is a short and therefore not exhaustive—yet excellent—survey of Lithuanian grammar. It will not be sufficient for purposes of writing, let alone speaking, in Lithuanian, but it will provide much help for the anglophone user in disentangling the intricacies of a Lithuanian text. [R: Choice, May 96, p. 1455]—**L. Zgusta**

Māori

863. **Te Matatiki: Contemporary Māori Words.** By the Māori Language Commission (Te Taura Whiri i te Reo Māori). New York, Oxford University Press, 1996. 289p. $19.95pa. ISBN 0-19-558341-8.

New Zealand's 1987 Māori Language Act established the Māori Language Commission as the central organ charged, among other things, with providing the neologisms necessary for the introduction into Māori of language registers connected with modern life. The Commission published the first list of such neologisms (under the same title) in 1992; this book is a second list, which amplifies and, regrettably but unavoidably, alters or rectifies some points of the first one. Hence, this is not a dictionary, in the sense that it includes no common words already in general use, such as *man*, *woman*, *eat*, *sleep*, or even *car* or *automobile*, but only the suggested neologisms. Of these, there are two identical lists, organized as an English-Māori glossary and a Māori-English one. What is highly laudable is that the derivation of each neologism is explained by reference to the meaning of its individual morphemes, or by reference to the language from which they are borrowed. The latter possibility prevails generally with the older borrowings. The Commission in its coinages obviously prefers metaphorical or descriptive expressions consisting of native morphemes; even loan translations seem not to be fully welcome. The background source supplying the pre-acculturated meanings of the morphemes is always cited as *A Dictionary of the Māori Language* by H. W. Williams (Government Print, 1985).

To give a few examples: for *malnutrition*, the Commission suggests [pohokore], listed in Williams with the meaning of "starved, emaciated"; for *mammal* [whakangote], listed in Williams as "suckle, cause to suck." In the case of both of these neologisms, the acculturated meaning is added to the original one. The same principle of acculturation is operative in [tāwakawaka], "striped, banded, a cloak of dressed flax made in black and white stripes," suitably endowed with the accultured meaning of "*keyboard* (in music)." Although there are some older foreign-language borrowings in the language, the present policy prefers neologisms even for internationalisms: for *kleptomania*, the list prescribes or suggests [mate ringarau], from nonacculturated [mate] "sickness, disease"; [ringa] "hand"; [rau] "hundred"; [rarau] "lay hold of, grasp."

One of the difficulties associated with the coining of neologisms is the element of arbitrariness even in the best motivated instances of them. For example, [waengero] from [wae] "leg" and [ngero] "very many," suggested for *myriapod*, is good; however, the moment someone needs to coin a term for a millipede or some other multilegged animal, the clarity of the motivation will decrease. Sometimes the docility of the writing public will be sorely tested; loan translations would perhaps be less ambitious, but prospectively more transparent. Beyond the purpose for which this list has been published, it will be useful in courses on language planning; given that Māori has few morphophonological or phonotactic complications, classes will be able to study easily the motivations behind the coinages.—**L. Zgusta**

Polish

864. Gutt-Mostowy, Jan. **Highlander Polish-English/English-Highlander Polish Dictionary.** New York, Hippocrene Books, 1995. 111p. $9.95pa. ISBN 0-7818-0303-9.

The region of Podhale, isolated from Poland by its location in the mountains of southern Poland, preserves the Polish language from becoming "tainted" by foreign influences. This handy, pocket-sized dictionary includes about 1,000 Highlander words with Polish and English equivalents. There is also a listing of English words with Highlander equivalents. In addition, a compilation of Highlander sayings with English translations is provided. Usage would be limited to English-speaking visitors to this area of Poland. The dictionary is recommended for libraries with Slavic collections or extensive travel materials.
—**George S. Bobinski**

Romanian

865. **NTC's Romanian and English Dictionary.** By Andrei Bantas. Lincolnwood, Ill., National Textbook, 1995. 374p. $29.95. ISBN 0-8442-4976-9.

This is a two-way bilingual dictionary with approximately 15,000 entries in each section—English/Romanian and Romanian/English. Each heading indicates its part of speech and, when necessary, is followed by the domain to which the term belongs (e.g., "mil.," for military, "entom.," for entomology, "anat.," for anatomy). The English/Romanian section provides the pronunciation of the word by using the phonetic symbols of the International Phonetic Association. This part of the dictionary is preceded by six pages of examples of pronunciation of English sounds (mostly in British English) aimed at helping the Romanian user to become familiar with the pronunciation of the words included here. The user has no hint to the American pronunciation or the American phonetic transcription.

The preface presents the dictionary as "up-to-date, and of the highest level of precision." The terms selected to be included in this work offer accurate translations from the source language into the target language, and therefore can serve the needs of the intended audience: "students of the Romanian language" and tourists. The recency of the terms, however, has not been considered. This is a dictionary that would have appropriately served the needs of an audience of the 1970s and 1980s. The total of 30,000 words along with their definitions do not cover recent terminology or new connotations the above-mentioned users encounter in books and articles published in the 1990s. Words pertaining to the computer science field (not to mention the Internet) have been omitted, while terms used in everyday speech, such as *browse, mall, freeway,* and *stuff,* have not found their place in the dictionary.

Another weakness of the work comes from the adoption of the spelling in the Romanian language in use during the 1950-1990 period. (Romanian spelling changed in 1991.) The English-speaking tourist will be confused if (s)he sees in Romania the sign "pâine" (*bread*) and (s)he tries to locate this word in the dictionary. The user of the dictionary will need to look for the pre-1991 spelling of the word, "pîine," in order to find the English equivalent. If the searcher is not familiar with both spellings, the dictionary proves to be difficult to consult. Therefore, the English-speaking reader of an article published in a Romanian newspaper (which, of course, will use the latest spelling) will not find this dictionary too helpful if (s)he needs to consult one of the words that have changed their spelling. The work is printed on recyclable paper and abounds in unclear print; a considerable amount of letters are not leveled (some seem to be in superscript). If users have an earlier version of an English/Romanian, Romanian/English dictionary, they should stick with it and wait until a better edition comes out. This is not "the most practical and convenient Romanian and English dictionary," as the cover advertises it.—**Hermina G. B. Anghelescu**

Russian

866. **The Concise Oxford Russian Dictionary.** Colin Howlett, ed. New York, Oxford University Press, 1996. 1007p. $35.00. ISBN 0-19-864338-1.

This practical edition is an abridgment of the *Oxford Russian Dictionary* (1994), and it contains approximately 120,000 words and phrases in contemporary use. Although it is intended primarily for English-speaking users, all headwords in the English-Russian section are transcribed into the International Phonetic Alphabet to make it more useful to non-English-speakers. The 11-page "Guide to the Use of the Dictionary" is professionally done and includes information on grammatical forms provided by the dictionary, phonetic symbols, and abbreviations.

Impressive is the inclusion of technical and institutional abbreviations in the dictionary (such as of the National Health Service), its comprehensive character, the precise indications of the usage of words, and indication of irregular forms of verbs and nouns. Unlike in some dictionaries, special terms, such as *think-tank,* are not simply transliterated but are here meaningfully translated, in that case as "brain center." The dictionary will be convenient and adequate for any general user of the Russian language, and it contains many specialized terms, such as several connected with financial matters. Some commonly used foreign phrases, such as *ex libris* and *en passant,* are given. The inclusion of country names, with their adjectives, seems unnecessary, but is perhaps a matter of taste.—**Bogdan Mieczkowski**

867. **A Russian-English Collocational Dictionary of the Human Body.** By Lidija Iordanskaja and Slava Paperno. Richard L. Leed, ed. Columbus, Ohio, Slavica, 1996. 418p. $29.95. ISBN 0-89357-265-9.

Learning another language well requires more than mastering grammar and vocabulary. Native speakers use slang and idioms that are not often taught in the classroom. This is especially true when dealing with body parts. A Russian-English dictionary that specializes in the rich and colorful expressions relating to the human body is a useful source.

A lengthy introduction explains the structure and function of the dictionary well despite the authors' heavy use of specialized linguistic jargon. The reference is arranged by body part in Russian alphabetic order. Each entry begins with the Russian word and its English translation. These are followed by notes on semantics and morphology; syntax (common sentence structures using the term); lexical relationships (synonyms, diminutives, parts, size and shape, movements, and so on); and sample texts using the term. Entries include technical anatomic and medical terms, literary usage, common speech, and vulgarisms. The differences between Russian and English are pointed out. Russian uses one word, *ruka*, for both "arm" and "hand," and one word, *noga*, for "foot" and "leg," but it has no separate word for the back of the neck ("nape"). English speakers wash their hair. Although Russian has a word, *volos*, for hair, Russian speakers wash their heads, *golova*.

This dictionary describes 63 body parts; 2 organs (heart, stomach); a few body fluids (blood, sweat, tears); 2 physical manifestations of emotion (laughter, smile); and the voice. These physical attributes and the adjectives, adverbs, verbs, and expressions that describe them provide a deeper understanding of the Russian language and culture. This unique source is a valuable addition to Slavic language and linguistics collections.—**Barbara M. Bibel**

Sanskrit

868. **Hippocrene Concise Sanskrit-English Dictionary.** By Vasudeo Govind Apte. New York, Hippocrene Books, 1996. 366p. $14.95pa. ISBN 0-7818-0203-2.

Sanskrit is one of the oldest languages of India. Its origin goes back to the Vedic age in ancient India. At present, this difficult language is not spoken widely in the country, but it is trying to make a comeback. Sanskrit is taught and used in a few other countries of the world also, and Germany, like India, has produced a few excellent scholars in this language.

The author of the *Hippocrene Concise Sanskrit-English Dictionary* has done an excellent job in preparing the text. It is arranged in alphabetic order in Sanskrit alphabets, and simple meanings of every word included in the dictionary have been given in the English language. If a word has more than one meaning, these additional meanings have also been provided. All definitions are written in simple English language and are easy to understand. A list of abbreviations used in the book has been furnished to help users in understanding those abbreviations without any difficulty. According to the author, "a new word formed by the mere addition of a letter or two is indicated by means of a dash before such addition." Thus, the author has certainly made it easier for all users of this well-prepared dictionary. This concise dictionary would be helpful for beginners who are interested in learning one of the oldest languages of the world. It is certainly a good addition to the literature and is recommended for all reference collections and for libraries interested in developing collections on India.—**Ravindra Nath Sharma**

Shan

869. Moeng, Sao Tern. **Shan-English Dictionary.** Kensington, Md., Dunwoody Press, 1995. 367p. $79.00. ISBN 0-93-1745-92-6.

The particular value of this dictionary consists in its being an instrument of careful language planning. When Burma gained its independence after World War II, a plan arose to make Shan, a language closely related to Burmese and the language of one of the federal states (also called Shan), the language routinely used in the institutions of that state. While the project of revising the orthography (and script) had started already in 1940, the real effort was launched in 1958. Between 1960 and 1964, six Shan readers were published; however, the establishment of a socialist system based on a centralization of control in Burma in 1962 put a stop to all efforts at language planning not concerned with Burmese. In any case, the present dictionary is one of the late fruits of the efforts described.

One of the greatest changes wrought by the language-planning efforts is a change in orthography. While Shan uses the Burmese script, the new orthography makes the pronunciation more predictable (on the basis of the new spellings and the new letters introduced) than was the case before the reform. The dictionary also indicates for every word any tones (six possible in all).

The basis of this dictionary is J. N. Cushing's *Shan-English Dictionary* (Rangoon, 1881) and its 2d edition, published in 1914. Naturally, much modern vocabulary has been added in this new work, such as *military affairs, social service, revolutionary movement, business enterprise*, and so on. While the script has the structure of the Indian syllabaries, the Shan lexical items have a structure more typologically similar to that of Chinese; hence, most entries have many listed subentries of lexical compounds formed with the morpheme indicated in the main entry, combined with other morphemes. The respective word class is given in each entry and subentry, but no syntactic or collocational patterns are indicated; only occasionally, a standing expression or idiom is given as a subentry. While this lack of grammatical information is the most noticeable lacuna of the dictionary, it may also be regretted that there are no pronunciation indications, not even in those cases where there remains some uncertainty as to pronunciation even after the spelling reform. Nor is there any indication of pronunciation in the English part.

The front matter also contains an essay on Shan names and name giving. The essay is, indeed, so thorough that consideration should be given to expanding and publishing it in an onomatological journal. This is not a dictionary for the beginner, but it will provide excellent service to the advanced student of this language or this family of languages.—**L. Zgusta**

Sign Language

870. **NTC's Multilingual Dictionary of American Sign Language.** By Claude O. Proctor. Lincolnwood, Ill., National Textbook, 1995. 767p. illus. index. $49.95. ISBN 0-8442-0731-4.

This unique dictionary is self-evident in its design and functionalism. There are 2,446 entries arranged alphabetically by the English word, followed by an abbreviation denoting the part of speech and a small line drawing showing the American Sign Language (ASL) gesture with arrow(s) indicating direction of motion of the hand(s). There are four entries per page. Following the ASL illustration are equivalents in 12 languages, Arabic through Swedish, including 3 Asian and 8 European languages. For Russian and Asian words, a romanized spelling is given before the native script itself.

The names of the months and the days of the week are included, but not the names of cities and only a few countries (e.g., Zambia). Personal names are not given, except for Jesus and God. There is a cross-index on 151 pages, which is really a glossary (4 columns to the page) of the words in each language, keyed to the numbered entries for visual comparison.

This tool will be useful where deaf persons from different language cultures want to communicate, but will be of limited usefulness to most persons wanting to communicate in ASL. This excellent work should be bought by all comprehensive collections on ASL, deaf culture, and dictionaries in general.

—**William G. Wilson**

871. Sternberg, Martin L. A. **Essential ASL: The Fun, Fast, and Simple Way to Learn American Sign Language.** New York, HarperPerennial/HarperCollins, 1996. 322p. illus. $7.95pa. ISBN 0-06-273428-8.

This is a condensed version of Sternberg's *American Sign Language Concise Dictionary* (rev. ed.; see ARBA 96, entry 1132), with one new feature of more than 50 common phrases depicted on pages 267-322. These are modern, interesting sentences (e.g., "Those kids have already become snobs") that demonstrate typical ASL word order, facial expression, number, and tense. Sternberg, deafened as a boy, is an educator of the deaf who has been working on ASL dictionaries for more than 30 years. This 1996 effort has 700 terms, compared to 2,500 terms in the 1994 edition. The 1994 edition had 500 new terms over its 1981 parent, *American Sign Language: A Comprehensive Dictionary* (see ARBA 82, entry 1196). A proportionate number of these new terms (e.g., *disco, lesbian, McDonald's*, and *tape recorder*) appear in the 1996 condensation, but no newer terms.

There are 14 pages of front matter in this edition, compared to 23 pages in the earlier one, but an internal reference on page xi to page xxiii is not changed, which at first confuses the reader. "Explanatory Notes" include sign rationale ("an attempt to offer a mnemonic cue to the sign as described verbally"), verbal description, and sign synonyms, which are references in about 20 percent of the entries (e.g., *lead* refers to *guide*). There are also eight points on understanding the illustrations.

A typical entry gives the word in English; the pronunciation; the part of speech; the sign rationale; a verbal description of how to make the sign; and then one to three good line drawings showing how to make the sign, always from the perspective of the signer. This inexpensive, paperback edition is particularly appropriate for a personal library—or for a small institution with few or no deaf patrons.

—**William G. Wilson**

Siksika

872. Frantz, Donald G., and Norma Jean Russell. **Blackfoot Dictionary of Stems, Roots, and Affixes.** 2d ed. Toronto and Cheektowaga, N.Y., University of Toronto Press, 1995. 442p. index. $65.00; $24.95pa. ISBN 0-8020-0767-8; 0-8020-7136-8pa.

Among American Indian linguistic groups, the Algonquian family includes not only many languages of northeastern and subarctic North America, but also three of the Great Plains: Cheyenne, Arapaho, and what is here called Blackfoot—spoken in local varieties on the Blackfoot, Blood, and Piegan Reserves in the Canadian province of Alberta, and on the Blackfeet Reservation in Montana. The 1st edition of the dictionary by Frantz and Russell (the latter a native speaker of Blackfoot) first appeared in 1989 (see ARBA 92, entry 1064); the present revised edition has more than 300 new entries and amplified information on many others. Special attention is given to botanical terminology.

The main body of this book is a Blackfoot-English dictionary; words are given with both their conventional and etymological senses, as when *ksisísttsomo'ki* [a German] is explained as meaning "having a pointed hat." The second part of the volume is an English index; although this does not constitute a full-fledged English-Blackfoot dictionary, it is of great use in permitting the user to identify words starting from either Blackfoot or English. All entries use a practical Blackfoot alphabet, official on the Canadian reserves since 1975, and explained in an appendix. The system is both systematic and practical, requiring only letters familiar from the English writing system (including the apostrophe).

This authoritative work will be of maximum usefulness not only to scholars, but also to speakers and learners of Blackfoot. The volume is clearly one of the more successful among the recent crop of dictionaries of American Indian languages, inspired by the current swell of interest in the cultures and languages of Native America.—**William Bright**

Spanish

873. **Larousse English-Spanish, Spanish-English Dictionary.** new ed. New York, Larousse Kingfisher Chambers, 1995. 1v. (various paging). $29.95. ISBN 2-03-420280-5.

Aimed at students, teachers, and anyone who uses Spanish or English as a foreign language in the workplace or for leisure activities, this thumb-indexed bilingual dictionary provides ready access to copious information about the two languages. The volume, containing in excess of 160,000 references and 260,000 translations, devotes extensive coverage to geographic terms and proper nouns (*la Plaza de Tiananmen*), abbreviations and acronyms (*RENFE* and *RNE*), and business and computing terminology (*glitch, RAM,* and *mouse*). Emphasis is on contemporary usage, with particular attention paid to vulgar expressions, technical vocabulary, and words and phrases in the news (e.g., *insider trading, sexual harassment,* and so forth). The compilers claim that Latin American Spanish is given generous coverage, but a close inspection reveals more of a focus on Spain. This is perhaps best illustrated by the preponderance of acronyms denoting a wide array of Spanish political parties and the corresponding omission of any reference to the dominant Mexican party, the Partido Revolucionario Institucional (PRI).

Most entries are thorough and comprehensive; for example, included among the various meanings of the word *run* are equivalent expressions in Spanish for "to run a bath" and "her mascara had run," as well as "to run for [political office]." The term *run off* appears in reference to printing, losing weight, and flight, and as the hyphenated *run-off* in the electoral sense. This type of broad coverage sometimes fall short, as in the explanation of the commercial term *futures*. This word appears separately from *future*, but the entry fails to discuss related items that would place the expression in a meaningful context, such as *cattle futures*. Interspersed within the alphabetic arrangement one will find an assortment of thematic groupings of practical words and phrases typical of everyday speech. This unique feature lists illustrative sentences suitable for dealing with complaints, congratulations, good-byes, letter writing, using the telephone, and dozens of other commonplace situations.

In general, the Larousse dictionary's format, content, and number of entries compare favorably with the *Oxford Spanish Dictionary New International Edition* (Oxford University Press, 1996). Of the two, however, the Oxford volume has better coverage of Latin American Spanish, clearer explanations of words with multiple meanings, lengthier and more useful appendixes, and darker typeface—the latter an important feature in a work filled with small print. The Larousse work is, nonetheless, an excellent reference work that should compete well in the bilingual dictionary market.—**Melvin S. Arrington Jr.**

874. **Larousse Mini Spanish-English, English-Spanish Dictionary. Larousse Mini Diccionario Español-Inglés, Inglés-Español.** new ed. New York, Larousse Kingfisher Chambers, 1995. 331p. $4.95pa. ISBN 2-03-420900-1.

This minidictionary is designed largely for travelers and those beginning to study either Spanish or English, but who do not require extensive technical or sophisticated vocabularies, full grammatical details, or the examples of typical or useful phrases and sentences supplied by more comprehensive dictionaries. Nevertheless, this compact volume includes more than 40,000 translations, with special attention paid to words likely to be found on street signs or menus. Remarkably, in addition to its pocket-sized convenience, the typeface is clear and easy to read.

In addition to direct translation of individual words, the Spanish section offers short paragraph descriptions of major holidays, such as the *Sanferines* in Pamplona or *Feria de abril* in Seville, and what to expect to find in a *Prador Nacional* or when enjoying *tapas* or eating in a *taquería*. A useful glossary of signs and menu items in Catalan is also provided. Similarly, for Spanish readers, the English portion of the dictionary distinguishes between English and American spellings and usage; includes guides for pronunciation; and offers brief descriptions of such diverse subjects as Buckingham Palace and Guy Fawkes Night, as well as bingo, Halloween, and what is meant by Cajun cooking. —**Joseph W. Dauben**

875. Navarro, José María, and Axel J. Navarro Ramil. **Mastering Spanish Vocabulary: A Thematic Approach.** Hauppauge, N.Y., Barron's Educational Series, 1995. 400p. illus. index. $8.95pa. ISBN 0-8120-9110-8.

Mastering Spanish Vocabulary is designed to help increase the vocabulary of learners who have some mastery of Spanish. In fact, a basic understanding of Spanish grammar is a prerequisite for using this book to its best advantage. Spanish words are divided into 41 categories ranging from "The Human Body" to "Social Relations" to "Tourism." Entries are clearly laid out, with Spanish terms printed in bold typeface and their English translations printed in roman typeface. Illustrative sentences (in Spanish and English) accompany most terms and help to expand a learner's vocabulary well beyond the 5,245 keywords that comprise the heart of the book. Although not as profusely illustrated as *The Oxford-Duden Pictorial Spanish and English Dictionary* (2d ed., Oxford University Press, 1995), occasional illustrations help to define concepts. A pronunciation guide and an index are provided as well.

The focus of *Mastering Spanish Vocabulary* is the Spanish of Spain, and its small appendix of "Americanisms" insufficiently addresses the differences between Iberian and Western Hemisphere Spanish. Still, this is a useful book for intermediate Spanish speakers—most of whom will want to take it home or carry it on trips. Thin paper covers and narrow gutters mean that a reference copy will be quickly devoured by the copy machine. Still, it can be a useful, inexpensive supplement to standard Spanish-English dictionaries.—**Donald A. Barclay**

Turkish

876. Öztopcu, Kurtuluş, Zhoumagaly Abuov, Nasir Kambarov, and Youssef Azemoun. **Dictionary of the Turkic Languages. English: Azerbaijani, Kazakh, Kyrgyz, Tatar, Turkish, Turkmen, Uighur, Uzbek.** New York, Routledge, 1996. 361p. index. $74.95. ISBN 0-415-14198-2.

The individual members of the family of Turkic languages are so similar to one another that they are to a great degree mutually intelligible. Indeed, one of the first comprehensive dictionaries treated all of them as if they were dialects of a single language: *Opyt slovarja tjurkskikh narechij V. V. Radlova / Versuch eines Wörterbuches der Türk-Dialecte von Dr. W. Radloff* (reprinted with an important preface by Mouton, 1960). With the exception of Turkish and Uighur, the majority of speakers of these languages lived in the former Soviet Union; during that period of time, the regime tried to diversify the individual languages, which meant chiefly making them as different as possible from Turkish (as spoken in the Turkish republic). One of the most obvious features of this campaign was the imposition on all of them of the Cyrillic script, which in itself set a gulf between them and Turkish, which adopted the roman alphabet in 1928; Uighur, however, continued to be written in Arabic script. For identical or very similar phonemes in the various individual languages, different Cyrillic letters were even chosen; whether this move was motivated by the diversification campaign or by natural necessities of the orthographies of those languages remains a moot question.

The important point here is that when the former Soviet republics, where Turkic languages are spoken by the majority of the local population, gained their independence, the scripts of these languages were romanized; on the other hand, the diverging graphic signs (letters) for identical phonemes were not uniform. However, these differences are minimal; for instance, the high, back, unrounded vowel is written as *i* (without the dot) in Azerbaijani, Kazakh, Kyrgyz, Tatar, and Turkish, but as *y* in Turkmen.

The main purpose of this dictionary is to treat the eight languages (the six just mentioned, plus Uighur and Uzbek) in unified entries. Collocations, idioms, syntactic patterns—all of this goes unmentioned. Using frequency-of-occurrence lists, the authors selected some 800 English words. Each entry consists of the English entry word followed by the eight equivalents, one for each of the numbered and alphabetically ordered languages. Polysemy makes its appearance in the dictionary only in a few cases in which the entry word's sense is disambiguated (e.g., **play** (*agame) v. 1., 2. *oyna*-, 3. *oyno*-, 4. *uyna*-; **play** (*an instrument) v. 1. *çal*-, 2. *oyna*-, 3. *chert*-, 4. *uyna*-). A so-to-say "normal" entry in the dictionary looks like this: **divide,** v[erb], 1. [Azerb.] *böl*-, 2. [Kazakh] *böl*-, 3. [Kyrgyz] *böl*-, 4. [Tatar] *bül*-, 5. [Turkish] *böl*-, 6. [Turkmen] *böl*-, 7. [Uighur] *böl*-, 8. [Uzbek] *bo'l*-; numbers 1, 2, 3, 4, 6, and 8 are also given in Cyrillic, while number 7 is in Arabic script. In the indexes, the order is reversed: There are sections for Azerbaijani-English, Kazakh-English, Kyrgyz-English, Tatar-English, and so forth; in short, one for each of the eight languages. Each of these indexes is organized by the alphabet of the Turkic words.

This solid dictionary will be useful not only for the usual practical purposes, but also for introductory comparative studies of the Turkic languages. Above all, it will, in the area of language planning, provide considerable aid to the likely attempts to put a stop to the diversification of these languages.—**L. Zgusta**

Vietnamese

877. **NTC's Vietnamese-English Dictionary.** By Dinh-hoa Nguyen. Lincolnwood, Ill., National Textbook, 1995. 728p. $17.95pa. ISBN 0-8442-8357-6.

This dictionary was first published in 1955 under the title *Vietnamese-English Vocabulary* with some 9,000 Vietnamese words. It was designed as a study aid for U.S. students of the Vietnamese language. By the mid-1960s, in response to the escalation of the United States' involvement in Vietnam, this dictionary was greatly expanded. The work under review is the updated version of this latter edition.

By far, this is the most comprehensive and perhaps the best Vietnamese-English dictionary available. It contains approximately 50,000 Vietnamese words, morphemes, compound words, and phrases. Also, unlike previous editions, this volume includes more sociopolitical, economic, literary, and Vietnamization of English and French terms (e.g., *ga-lo-ri* [gallery]). Entries are accompanied by their English equivalents and, where appropriate, synonyms, antonyms, and usage are provided. Also included are a guide to pronunciation and a 50-page supplement of new Vietnamese words. Native Vietnamese speakers who have been living abroad for some time should find the supplement useful.

The paper, printing, and binding of the dictionary are good, and the price is reasonable. Overall, this is an excellent resource. It should prove useful not only for students of the Vietnamese language, travelers, and businesspeople, but also for Vietnamese users.—**Binh P. Le**

Yiddish

878. **Hippocrene Practical English-Yiddish, Yiddish-English Dictionary: Romanized.** expanded ed. By David C. Gross. New York, Hippocrene Books, 1995. 146p. $9.95pa. ISBN 0-7818-0439-6.

This volume is the 3d edition in 4 years of a romanized English-Yiddish/Yiddish-English dictionary. The 2d edition of this pocket-sized digest (see ARBA 93, entry 1105) was identified as the "revised edition," while this one is the "expanded edition." Unfortunately, it is not an improved edition. Many of the inadequacies reviewed previously remain. It still is overly simplified and incomplete. The few selected idioms introduced in the last edition are still randomly arranged. The new material in this edition is "A Selection of Yiddish Words That Have Become Part of English," covering 14 pages of material. The definitions in the selection are minimal. They lack any explanation or historical and linguistic annotation. Much more is offered in Leo Rosten's three popular volumes: *The Joys of Yiddish* (Simon & Schuster Trade, 1991), *Hooray for Yiddish* (Simon & Schuster Trade, 1984), and *The Joys of Yinglish* (NAL-Dutton, 1990). Other dictionaries using romanized Yiddish, such as *The Yiddish Dictionary Sourcebook* (see ARBA 87, entry 1057) or *Transliterated English-Yiddish, Yiddish-English Dictionary* by D. M. Harduf (Harduf Books, 1991), will probably be more satisfying for most users.—**Simon J. Bronner**

Yoruba

879. **Hippocrene Concise Yoruba-English, English-Yoruba Dictionary.** By Ọlabiyi Babalọla Yai. New York, Hippocrene Books, 1996. 257p. $14.95pa. ISBN 0-7818-0263-6.

This is a truly subminimal dictionary, or rather a glossary. No one would expect a book as thin as this to contain much information, because the pages are small, and the lines are short and not very compact. Moreover, the selection of vocabulary for inclusion is most uneven. If one takes as an example the human body and its parts in the English-Yoruba part, one finds the following: *face, nose, mouth, neck, finger, leg,* and *toe.* One does not find *head* (although *headline, headmaster,* and *headquarters* are included); *hair; eye; arm; elbow; hand* (although there is *handball); knee; ankle* (although there is *anklet);* or *heel.* The same unevenness or haphazardness of selection can be observed in other areas of the vocabulary.

Pronunciation is given both for the Yoruba headwords (although unnecessarily, the spelling being regular) and for the English items. There are numerous misprints in the latter. For example, the pronunciation of *patch* is given as [pastọ], with a diacritic dot under the "o," indicating reduction; in reality, it should be [patṣ], with a diacritic dot under the "s." Inconsistencies are also to be found: *palm* is given as [paam], but *palm tree* and *palm wine* are given as [palm tri] and [palm wain]. The position of the stress, so important in English, is not indicated at all. The tones in Yoruba are given in both parts of the vocabulary.

Grammatical indications are restricted to the identification of the traditional parts of speech both in Yoruba and in English. There is no front matter containing grammatical indications. One hopes a 2d edition will improve on this one.—**L. Zgusta**

24 Literature

GENERAL WORKS

Bibliography

880. Baker, William, and Kenneth Womack, comps. **Recent Work in Critical Theory, 1989-1995: An Annotated Bibliography.** Westport, Conn., Greenwood Press, 1996. 585p. index. (Bibliographies and Indexes in World Literature, no.51). $99.50. ISBN 0-313-29434-8.

Part of Greenwood Press's Bibliographies and Indexes in World Literature series, this volume highlights recent work in literary theory and criticism, with an "emphasis upon the multiculturalism and interdisciplinarity [sic] that mark contemporary literary study" (as stated on the press release). The bibliography annotates nearly 2,000 titles in 7 broad chapter areas: general criticism; semiotics, narratology, rhetoric, and language systems; postmodernism and deconstruction; reader-response and phenomenological criticism; feminist criticism and gender studies; psychoanalytic criticism; and historical criticism. Relatively uniform in length, annotations are concise and to the point, but illuminating. Unfortunately, the volume suffers from some major flaws that cannot be overlooked.

The general criticism section annotates critical works written or edited by such well-established critics as Harold Bloom, Terry Eagleton, Susan Gubar, Richard Kostelanatz, and Octavio Paz. Women authors and editors are surprisingly underrepresented in this section, as they are in other segments, except in the area of feminist criticism and gender studies. The limitation of entries to books and not to journal articles, essays in books, or theses and dissertations severely cramps the field of literary criticism. Some surprising entries also appear; for example, inclusion of volumes in the Greenwood Press Bio-bibliographies series seems questionable at best. Even more disturbing are the enormous gaps of coverage. *The Critical Tradition: Classic Texts and Contemporary Trends*, edited by David H. Richter (St. Martin's Press, 1989), is not included; nor are several recent titles published by Garland: *Rereading Modernism: New Directions in Feminist Criticism* by Lisa Rado (1994); *Ntozake Shange: A Critical Study of the Plays* by Neal A. Lester (1995); or *Chaucer's Humor: Critical Essays*, edited by Jean A. Jost (1994), for example. In a genre that has received much critical study and interpretation of late, the Gothic, Kari J. Winter's *Subjects of Slavery, Agents of Change* (University of Georgia Press, 1992) is included, but Kate Ferguson Ellis's *The Contested Castle* (University of Illinois Press, 1989) and Eugenia C. DeLamotte's *Perils of the Night* (Oxford University Press, 1990) are not. While no real selection criteria are given, and it is nearly impossible to provide an absolutely comprehensive source on such a broad topic as literary criticism, for this reviewer's cursory examination to uncover so many gaps speaks to the inadequacy of this particular source.

Further problems abound with the format of the bibliography. An "Organization of the Bibliography" section details the format breakdown of the volume, although it rather states the obvious, and the breakdown is again discussed in the introduction. The entries themselves do not contain complete bibliographic information, limiting their usefulness. The volume is completed by an author index (by author or editor of the title under discussion, not the author discussed) and a subject index, but no title index, which again limits the bibliography's utility. Some titles are difficult to locate without a title index; for example, Jean Wyatt's *Reconstructing Desire* (University of North Carolina Press, 1990) is placed in the psychoanalytic section, which is fitting, but it could have also found a home under feminist criticism or reader-response criticism. Without knowing Wyatt wrote the book, searching for it without a title index could be time consuming.

Aside from such problems as those stated previously, the bibliography suffers from one overwhelming flaw. With such sources as the *Essay and General Literature Index* (see ARBA 96, entry 81), other periodical indexes, and online searches providing much greater access to literary criticism, will anyone really find this book useful enough to justify its purchase?—**Melissa Rae Root**

881. Kiell, Norman. **Food and Drink in Literature: A Selectively Annotated Bibliography.** Lanham, Md., Scarecrow, 1995. 361p. index. $62.50. ISBN 0-8108-3030-2.

Kiell is a professor emeritus of psychological services at Brooklyn College of the City University of New York. He combed libraries in the New York area and surfed the Internet in search of titles for this stunning bibliography. In 300-plus pages, Kiell lists more than 1,500 titles—1,110 of them annotated. Those not annotated are ones he could not access. The titles profiled are mostly English-language publications, but the occasional Spanish, German, and especially French publication also appears. Coverage only goes through 1993 copyright dates, with an occasional 1994.

The bibliography consists of two separate sections, one for food and one for drink, with the titles appearing alphabetically by author. There are nearly twice as many entries for food as for drink, here defined as alcoholic beverages, not drugs or other such "intoxicating" beverages as coffee or tea. Most of the titles in this section concern alcoholism and how it relates to literature. A few titles about alcohol and television or film also appear, but on a very selective basis. A single author index completes the volume.

The fact that an entire bibliography was compiled on the topic of food and drink in literature symbolizes the interesting turns literary studies are taking. The relative datedness of the bibliography is a disappointment, as this is a topic little written about prior to the 1980s that is now coming into its own. However, the lack of currency also leaves open the hope for another, more current, edition. [R: Choice, Nov 96, p. 432]—**Melissa Rae Root**

882. **The New York Public Library's Books of the Century.** Elizabeth Diefendorf, ed. New York, Oxford University Press, 1996. 229p. $14.95. ISBN 0-19-510897-3.

The staff of the New York Public Library has performed a delightful and informative service for researchers, historians, writers, teachers, librarians, students, and bibliophiles in selecting the 150 pivotal works of the twentieth century. For good or ill, choices express the issues of the era, such as *And the Band Played On* by Randy Shilts (AIDS), *The Bonfire of the Vanities* by Tom Wolfe (greed), *The Politics of Ecstasy* by Timothy Leary (recreational and personal drug use), and *Night* by Elie Wiesel (the Holocaust). Organized into 11 categories, the range of fiction, plays, treatises, children's literature, and other nonfiction works covers colonialism, protest, economics, utopia, war, optimism, feminism, and childhood. A brief introduction of the work provides translation of non-English titles; publication date; author; author's life span; and commentary on the purpose and effect of the book, including quoted lines, public adulation, honors, lawsuits, television and film versions, sequels, and a sprinkling of tasteful ink illustrations. An example of a controversial entry is *Lolita*, a best-seller labeled both masterpiece and filth. The editor concludes with 1st editions compiled alphabetically by author, followed by sources of citations, a note on the artist, and a list of project team members.

Although the century list is dominated by U.S. writers, it abounds in work from varied nations, religions, cultures, points of view, and backgrounds; for example, Chinua Achebe's *Things Fall Apart*; Simone de Beauvoir's *The Second Sex*; Federico García Lorca's *Gypsy Ballads*; Kahlil Gibran's *The Prophet*; Rigoberta Menchú's *I, Rigoberta Menchú*; Tayyim al-Salih's *Season of Migration to the North*; Mahatma Gandhi's *Non-Violent Resistance*; Buchi Emecheta's *The Bride Price*; and the United Nations charter. Players of the inevitable parlor game of "what they left out" will cry false on the diminution of works by Asians, Africans, Native Americans, and Caribbeans, but the 150 are undeniably solid choices. A major fault—especially for a librarian—is Diefendorf's omission of an index, which would have enabled users to locate specific interests (e.g., pollution, the Bible, existentialism, drama, verse, publishers, and commentary by notable critics). Another useful adjunct would be a list of also-rans. [R: LJ, 1 April 96, p. 76]—**Mary Ellen Snodgrass**

883. **Recommended Reading: 500 Classics Reviewed.** By the Editors of Salem Press. Pasadena, Calif., Salem Press, 1995. 300p. index. $35.00. ISBN 0-89356-911-9.

The volume at hand is for the shelf already bowed beneath the likes of *The Reader's Adviser* (see entry 11 for a review of the CD-ROM edition), *Good Reading* (see ARBA 91, entry 3), and Clifton Fadiman's *The Lifetime Reading Plan* (rev. ed., Crowell, 1978). In 300-word précis that are unsigned, the editors of this guide provide basic outlines with commentary on works of fiction and nonfiction commonly assigned in high schools and colleges. The compilation contains novels, short stories, poems, essays, plays, and philosophical and historical works.

The title may mislead, as only about 270 authors are represented (works by William Shakespeare, Charles Dickens, and Edgar Allan Poe alone account for 40 of the 500 synopses). Modern selections abound, with 100 of the titles having appeared since World War II; on the other hand, about 125 works written before 1800 are discussed. Only a few juvenile titles are found here, such as some by Lewis Carroll, James Barrie, and Kenneth Grahame. (The entry on J. R. R. Tolkien's *Lord of the Rings* unaccountably fails to mention its famous prequel, *The Hobbit*.)

Although the naming of best books is mired in subjectivity, certain omissions from this volume must be noted: Frank Norris, Graham Greene, Sir Walter Scott, Alexandre Dumas (*père* and *fils*), Herodotus, Robert Frost, Sean O'Casey, Petronius, and Francis Bacon. Having profiled such contemporary talents as Toni Morrison and Yasunari Kawabata, it is a bit surprising to find that such giants of the twentieth century as Anthony Burgess and William Trevor are not. While the book covers a handful of Eastern works, conspicuous absences include Tsao Hsueh Chih's *Dream of the Red Chamber* and Shikibu Murasaki's *The Tale of Genji*.

The plot summaries with thematic discussion are competently written. Because of their succinctness, these abstracts say little of biographical influences from the writers' lives in their respective works. Also, the pieces on John Fowles's *The Magus* and Theodore Dreiser's *Sister Carrie* make no mention of these novels' variant editions. Otherwise, as a ready-reference source, *Recommended Reading* may be just so adjudged: recommended.—**Jeffrey E. Long**

884. **The Romantic Movement: A Selective and Critical Bibliography for 1995.** David V. Erdman and others, eds. West Cornwall, Conn., Locust Hill Press, 1996. 489p. index. $60.00. ISBN 0-933951-72-8. ISSN 0557-2738.

The Romantic Movement is the latest annual volume in this series published by the Modern Language Association. Drawn from a search through more than 900 journals, it lists critical books and articles published in 1995, but goes back as far as 1991 for material overlooked earlier. Reviews of books cataloged in earlier volumes also receive mention. The bibliography covers a narrow body of European literature (e.g., English, French, German, Italian, and Spanish); the romanticism of other places, such as Portugal, Russia, and the Americas, is not included. Most entries are annotated, sometimes by a brief "not seen" or a list of reviews; sometimes, for major works like Carl Woodring's *The Columbia History of British Poetry*, the annotations run to several pages. For scholars with a serious interest in nineteenth-century literature, these volumes are essential. Large research libraries will undoubtedly need the entire series.

—**Lynn F. Williams**

885. Wortman, William A. **A Guide to Serial Bibliographies for Modern Literatures.** 2d ed. New York, Modern Language Association of America, 1995. 333p. index. $37.50; $19.75pa. ISBN 0-87352-965-0; 0-87352-966-9pa.

While the electronic age has rendered the print versions of many library reference materials obsolete, such is not the case with regard to the 2d edition of this work. It should be considered a core reference tool for librarians, students, and faculty pursuing the study of modern literatures and related subjects at the undergraduate and graduate levels. The author has improved upon the 1st edition, published in 1982 (see ARBA 83, entry 1123), by adding 273 serial bibliographies, increasing the number of cross-references significantly, and creating an Internet site called "Serial Bibliographies" (http://lib.muohio.edu/serial-bibliographies). The Internet site will contain regular changes and corrections to the guide and will serve as an electronic supplement.

A total of 777 serial bibliographies in the area of general humanities and periodical indexes, national literatures, literacy periods, genres, themes and subjects, and literary authors are cited. Standard reference tools, such as the *Vertical File Index* (see ARBA 92, entry 575), *Essay and General Literature Index* (see ARBA 96, entry 81), subject-related electronic databases, and bibliographies contained in journals and newsletters are also included. The contents are well organized and accessible. Chapters 1 and 2 describe the guide's scope and list all-inclusive bibliographies. Chapters 3 and 4 are devoted to British, American, and foreign literatures. Chapter 5 provides serial bibliographies ranging from African American and alternative press to women's studies literatures. The final chapter covers selected notable authors, such as Samuel Beckett, the Brontës, James Joyce, and William Butler Yeats. An "Electronic Bibliographies and Indexes" section is appended, and a separate bibliography and index conclude the text.

All large public and academic libraries should consider this well-priced book a recommended purchase for their humanities reference collections. [R: RBB, 15 Nov 96, pp. 610-11]

—Kathleen W. Craver

Biography

886. **Feminist Writers.** Pamela Kester-Shelton, ed. Detroit, St. James Press, 1996. 641p. index. $130.00. ISBN 1-55862-217-9.

Bio-bibliographic encyclopedias of women writers are today in fortunate abundance. Kester-Shelton's compilation strives for uniqueness by focusing on female (and a few male) writers of fiction, poetry, nonfiction, and journalism who espouse a "feminist viewpoint." Although most of its 290 entrants have written in the twentieth century, pertinent figures from all periods (e.g., Aphra Behn, Mary Wollstonecraft, Susan B. Anthony) are included, as are non-English-language writers if their works are available in English. Entries contain biographical facts, a list of publications by genre, a selection of critical studies, and a critical essay signed by one of a lengthy list of mostly academic scholars. Helpful are indexes by nationality of author, by subject/genre, and by titles mentioned in entries; lists of additional print and other resources, including electronic ones, are also useful. Hortense Spillers's foreword, "Feminist Writings: At Century's End," is aimed at aficionadas/os rather than the students and general public the editor claims as the book's intended audience.

A related work, *The Feminist Companion to Literature in English* (see ARBA 92, entry 1095), contains more than 2,700 entries, including many of the names found in the present volume. Disadvantages of the earlier title are briefer coverage and emphasis on British and Commonwealth women. Also, *Feminist Writers* includes writers of very current interest—such as Barbara Ehrenreich, Susan Faludi, or Camille Paglia—not found in the *Companion*. At less than one-half the cost, however, the earlier work may suffice for many libraries; those that can pay this volume's hefty price will find it a useful supplement.

—Willa Schmidt

887. **World Authors 1900-1950.** Martin Seymour-Smith and Andrew C. Kimmens, eds. Bronx, N.Y., H. W. Wilson, 1996. 4v. illus. (The Wilson Authors Series). $395.00. ISBN 0-8242-0899-4.

The World Authors series is well known to librarians for its concise but informative biographical and critical essays on important writers. This four-volume work comprises a comprehensive rewriting of two of its most popular titles, *Twentieth Century Authors*, first published in 1942, and *Twentieth Century Authors First Supplement*, published in 1955. This edition includes nearly all of the 2,500 writers from the original work plus others added to reflect significant authors who came into prominence post-1955.

Entries retain the first-person sketches written in the authors' own words found in the previous editions. All entries have been updated to reflect recent scholarship and current critical thinking about each author's works. In all, *World Authors 1900-1950* lives up to the literary biography standards set by this series for critical evaluation; lively anecdotal narratives; and extensive, authoritative biographical information.—**G. Kim Dority**

Dictionaries and Encyclopedias

888. **The Gay and Lesbian Literary Heritage: A Reader's Companion to the Writers and Their Works, from Antiquity to the Present.** Claude J. Summers, ed. New York, Henry Holt, 1995. 786p. index. $45.00. ISBN 0-8050-2716-5.

A confluence of scholarship by more than 150 credentialed writers, *The Gay and Lesbian Literary Heritage* (GLLH) consists of signed articles that are arranged in a single alphabetic sequence, a sequence that dovetails essays bearing 265 author name headings with those bearing some 100 topical headings. The articles on individual authors seamlessly blend biographical detail with critical evaluation, and typically extend from 600 to 1,200 words in length. Entries that comment upon and assess literary subgenres and philosophical cross-currents germane to the study of homoeroticism in literature often run for several thousand words; these display a commensurate level of academic refinement in their composition.

As with Sharon Malinowski's accomplished *Gay & Lesbian Literature* (see ARBA 95, entry 1111), this text betrays a bias toward United States and British writers born after 1850. Although GLLH offers approximately 60 more author entries than its counterpart, it omits such contemporaries gathered by Malinowski as Terrence McNally, Marion Zimmer Bradley, and Quentin Crisp. Also, the book in hand fails to showcase such deserving nonfiction writers as Havelock Ellis and Magnus Hirschfeld (the latter of whom founded the world's first homosexual rights organization). Summers's compendium falls down, too, in the paucity of primary works appearing in its bibliographic citations following author entries.

In its defense, GLLH puts its rival to shame in its depth of historical research. Besides its abundance of pre-nineteenth-century authors accorded entries (e.g., Monk Lewis, Marquis de Sade, Sappho), GLLH rewards its users with a 27-page overview of homosexual literary history in the United States, as well as other extended historical disquisitions. Also, Summers presents entries of some modern authors who are unaccountably absent from Malinowski's volume (e.g., Reinaldo Arenas, Manuel Azana, and Hélène Cixous). Although GLLH captures the most prominent writers of the genre back to Plato, it is impressive in its garnering of information and analysis on the life and literature of such contemporary figures as Cherrie Moraga (born 1952) and Lisa Alther (born 1949), the latter of whom has no entry in Malinowski. Noteworthy as well are the 1995 death dates for Patricia Highsmith and Paul Monette in the pages of GLLH.

With blindspots for such twentieth-century giants as Noël Coward, Elizabeth Bishop, and Roland Barthes, Malinowski is an ultimately inadequate, if serviceable, resource. The two works complement each other superbly, but if one's budget cannot withstand expenditures for both titles, Summers's volume is the preferred choice for gay and lesbian literary reference collections.—**Jeffrey E. Long**

889. Jackson, Guida M. **Encyclopedia of Literary Epics.** Santa Barbara, Calif., ABC-CLIO, 1996. 660p. illus. maps. index. (ABC-CLIO Literary Companion). $65.00. ISBN 0-87436-773-5.

Similar in format and scope to its companion volume, *Encyclopedia of Traditional Epics* (see ARBA 95, entry 1322), this literary encyclopedia focuses on written works rather than the traditional epics that emerged from an oral culture. Thus the *Iliad* and the *Odyssey* are both here, but only with *see* references to the earlier volume. In its nearly 600 entries, details on epic poems, the poets who wrote them, characters, and literary traditions or styles are presented in clear and simplistic prose. Mock-epics and epic romances are also featured, but epic drama, because of space issues, is not. The basic criterion to be judged "epic" is scope, or "the height, depth, and breadth of a work, and the lengths to which it reaches into the common human psyche" (p. xv).

The entries on characters, poets, and traditions are relatively brief. Those on the poems themselves are longer. The analyses are sometimes subjective; Virgil is called "the greatest poet Rome ever produced" (p. 7) and *Gawain and the Green Knight* is "the greatest of the Arthurian legends" (p. 194). The length of the epic entries is sometimes a mystery; the entry on the *Aeneid*, "the greatest book of the Western world for 2,000 years" (suddenly ending in the 1980s?), is shorter than those of *The Bruce*, *John Brown's Body*, and *Tristrant und Isalde*. Nonetheless, these brief articles are informative, giving a plot synopsis, a breakdown of characters, the type of verse in which it was written, and other relevant historical details. The more well-known epics have plot synopses broken down into the individual cantos or books that make up the whole work, and many have sample lines from the original text. A bibliography at the end of the text helps lead users to titles related to epic. Left out of this volume are the three appendixes found in the companion volume.

The greatest use of this encyclopedia would come from high school and beginning college students. Those libraries that already have the earlier work should consider adding this volume to their collection; others should weigh their options concerning patron interest and necessity for such a work.—**Melissa Rae Root**

890. Leeming, David Adams, and Kathleen Morgan Drowne. **Encyclopedia of Allegorical Literature.** Santa Barbara, Calif., ABC-CLIO, 1996. 326p. illus. index. (ABC-CLIO Literary Companion). $65.00. ISBN 0-87436-781-6.

Each book in the series of ABC-CLIO Literary Companions is intended to provide a one-step guide to a particular subject area. Here the subject is the entire literary history of allegory, an immense subject and a difficult one. Part of the difficulty lies in defining the subject and wresting a precise limitation on the term, which is related to parable, fable, myth, and symbolism. Leeming and Drowne attempt to deal with some of the difficulties of the subject in their introduction, in which they discuss the differences among the various terms and define the scope of their book.

The book itself is arranged as a basic encyclopedia: brief (one-half to one page in length) entries on a variety of topics, such as authors, concepts, and characters. Some of the longer entries treat a major allegorical work, such as *The Faerie Queen* and *Pilgrim's Progress*. As might be expected, many entries concern standard allegorical works—*Gulliver's Travels*, *The Pearl*, and *Beowulf*. Others, however, treat more modern authors and works—William Faulkner, Allen Ginsberg, *The Wind in the Willows*, and *The Wonderful World of Oz*. Copious cross-references lead the user to related entries; from an author, for example, to a specific work. Illustrations of authors and manuscript pages make this an attractive book.

Supplementary information includes two appendixes, a bibliography, and an index. Appendix A alphabetically lists all titles of works that appear as entries. Appendix B lists these titles in chronological order. The bibliography is extensive, including books and chapters of books of criticism on particular authors of allegorical works. The index differentiates between terms or names that are actual entries in the encyclopedia and terms or names that are merely mentioned in an entry. The index, too, lists titles of books that are mentioned in an entry but are not entries themselves.

There is little reference material of a simple nature available on allegory. This encyclopedia will be useful for beginning students of the genre, who can glean from the entries enough introductory information to satisfy themselves. More enthusiastic or advanced students who want to pursue the subject will find the bibliography useful. The work is recommended for many types of libraries: high school, academic, and public.—**Terry Ann Mood**

891. Room, Adrian. **Literally Entitled: A Dictionary of the Origins of the Titles of Over 1300 Major Literary Works....** Jefferson, N.C., McFarland, 1996. 249p. index. $48.50. ISBN 0-7864-0110-9.

Room has compiled an interesting list of title explanations that will prove useful to serious scholars and also satisfy the curiosity of many persons who like delving into American and British fictional works. Both types of readers will just enjoy browsing over the alphabetized and numbered titles of nineteenth- and twentieth-century writers as they play a game of both serious and trivial pursuit.

Although Room's introduction to his dictionary states the obvious and thus adds little to the book, the title commentaries express a great deal of painstaking research. Each entry gives the author's nationality (sometimes race) and the publication order of the book's appearance in the writer's career. The significant relationship of the title to the theme or plot of the literary work is usually attempted, and at times helpful references are made and frequently quoted that reveal the source of the book's name. When Room is uncertain about the particular derivation of a title, he states possible interpretations of what may have inspired its author's choice.

Many little-known or forgotten books are resurrected for discussion in this dictionary, but all the recognized major works up to the early 1990s are included. Most of the titles are of books of fiction; however, there are a few poetry and drama collections mentioned. A puzzling aspect has to do with how Walt Whitman is treated. The title of his great poetry collection *Leaves of Grass* is explained, but then there are a few separate entries for individual poems from that work, such as "I Sing the Body Electric" and "Pioneers! O Pioneers!" Why those particular poems are discussed while many other major ones are ignored is a mystery. However, most of Room's dictionary is a useful scholarly project that will be helpful and enjoyable to both general and specialized readers of literature. [R: Choice, June 96, p. 1623; LJ, Mar 96, p. 74; RBB, 1 May 96, p. 1530]—**Angelo Costanzo**

892. Snodgrass, Mary Ellen. **Encyclopedia of Satirical Literature.** Santa Barbara, Calif., ABC-CLIO, 1996. 559p. illus. index. (ABC-CLIO Literary Companion). $65.00. ISBN 0-87436-856-1.

Encyclopedia of Satirical Literature, a volume in the ABC-CLIO Literary Companion series, seeks to define and discuss that slippery literary genre, satire. Not irony and not allegory, satire encompasses a genre all its own. As with other volumes in the series, this encyclopedia covers authors, works, characters, and literary devices and styles prevalent in the field of interest. This particular volume covers a variety of works, from Jonathan Swift's *Gulliver's Travels* to Margaret Atwood's *The Handmaid's Tale*.

The entries describe the author, work, character, or style in question, giving examples from the primary text, references to the bibliography at the end of the volume, and cross-references to other entries. The tone of the entries in this encyclopedia is more scholarly than that in other volumes of the series. The main body of the encyclopedia is followed by a chronology of satirical literature, beginning in the eighteenth century B.C.E. and ending in 1995. A bibliography of primary sources; a bibliography of secondary sources; and an index to authors, works, and terms finish the encyclopedia.

This literary reference is interesting and informative. Only a couple of concerns mar its overall usefulness. The inconsistent use of "timeline" ("time line") in the introduction and the inconsistent use of diacritical marks within the main text call into question the editorial authority of the work as a whole. Also of concern is the possible overlap between this volume and others in the ABC-CLIO series; however, even if the same title or author is treated in more than one encyclopedia, the approach will, by nature of the series, be different. *Encyclopedia of Satirical Literature* is therefore recommended for high school and academic libraries.—**Melissa Rae Root**

893. Zimbaro, Valerie P. **Encyclopedia of Apocalyptic Literature.** Santa Barbara, Calif., ABC-CLIO, 1996. 400p. index. (ABC-CLIO Literary Companion). $65.00. ISBN 0-87436-823-5.

This volume is another in a series of ABC-CLIO Literary Companions, a series that attempts to treat single and often difficult concepts in one easy-to-use volume. *Encyclopedia of Apocalyptic Literature* contains more than 300 entries on works of literature, authors, characters, and themes that revolve around the end of the world. The encyclopedia discusses such works as William Golding's *Lord of the Flies*, William Shakespeare's *The Tempest*, and Leslie Marmon Silko's *Almanac of the Dead*. The inclusion of multicultural entries was strived for in producing this encyclopedia, but compared to others in the series, it has very few—but for a good reason. As stated in the introduction, many Eastern philosophies do not espouse an Armageddon-type ending to the world, thereby limiting the amount of apocalyptic literature to be found in those cultures.

Entries range from a brief paragraph to a few pages in length and are followed by cross-references to other entries. Missing are the references to the bibliographies that close out the main text as in other ABC-CLIO Literary Companions. Appendixes include lists of authors; titles; titles in chronological order; and apocalyptic literature from world scriptures, myths, and legends not featured in the encyclopedia proper. A bibliography of primary sources, a bibliography of secondary sources cited in the text, supplementary references, illustration credits, and an index complete the volume.

As is the case with any single-volume encyclopedia of this kind, omissions do occur (e.g., where is Jorge Luis Borges?). Also, overlap with other volumes in the series makes one question the validity of this encyclopedia. However, even with overlap, the items treated are approached from a different angle in the different volumes, and none in the series claims comprehensiveness. *Encyclopedia of Apocalyptic Literature* is a useful place to start in the study of end-of-the world literature and should serve this need well in high school and academic libraries. —**Melissa Rae Root**

Handbooks and Yearbooks

894. **Cambridge Paperback Guide to Literature in English.** By Ian Ousby. New York, Cambridge University Press, 1996. 436p. $19.95pa. ISBN 0-521-43627-3.

This paperback guide is an abbreviated version of the original hardbound volume published in 1988 (see ARBA 89, entry 991) and revised in 1993 (see ARBA 95, entry 1103). The number of the entries in this guide, compared to the original, are fewer, but not by much as the author abbreviated the original text more than he reduced entries. Ousby did update many of the entries for those authors still living and writing. For example, added to Anne Tyler's entry is her novel *Ladder of Years*, published in 1995.

Entries include information on writers and major works, movements, groups or schools in literature and criticism, literary magazines, theaters, genres and subgenres, and critical concepts and rhetorical terms. The entries are arranged in alphabetic order in bold typeface with headings for titles of books and magazines in italics. As in the original edition, all literatures in English throughout the world are represented (e.g., the United States, Canada, the Caribbean, Africa, India, Australia, and New Zealand). Drawings and photographs in the original edition are excluded.

The greatest value of this guide is its inexpensiveness compared to the original edition, its portability, and its use to undergraduate and graduate students, particularly in American and English literature. Although many recent novelists and poets of note are not included, it does have many of those most frequently taught in institutions of higher education, from Chinua Achebe, Matthew Arnold, and William Blake to Henry Wadsworth Longfellow, Elizabeth Inchbald, William Inge, Ken Kesey, Mary McCarthy, Carson McCullers, Kath Walker Oodgeroo, Marge Piercy, May Sarton, William Shakespeare, Mary Wollstonecraft Shelley, Gary Snyder, William Carlos Williams, and hundreds of others.

Many children's authors and illustrators are also treated, from Judy Blume and Joel Chandler Harris to Maurice Sendak and Laura Ingalls Wilder. Key ethnic authors are also discussed, such as Paul Laurence Dunbar, Countee Cullen, Gwendolyn Brooks, and N. Scott Momaday. In addition, there are playwrights, screenwriters, and film actors of importance scattered throughout. Other entries cover such items as the Abbey Theatre, the Beats, the Theater of the Absurd, detective fiction, euphuism, the gothic novel, onomatopoeia, satire, and the Scottish renaissance.

Unfortunately, at least one error mentioned in the review of the 1993 edition has not been corrected in the entry in this paperback volume. In revised future editions, it would be useful to include, at least for the major writers, a few of those key people primarily responsible for biographical, bibliographical, and critical commentary. [R: BR, Nov/Dec 96, pp. 53-54]—**Maureen Pastine**

895. **Contemporary Literary Criticism. Yearbook 1994: The Year in Fiction, Poetry, Drama, and World Literature....Volume 86.** Christopher Giroux and others, eds. Detroit, Gale, 1995. 560p. illus. index. $129.00. ISBN 0-8103-4996-5.

Part of the ongoing Contemporary Literary Criticism (CLC) series, this yearbook volume highlights the literary events of 1994. The series as a whole strives to give critical background on contemporary creative writers, with *contemporary* meaning currently living artists or those who passed away after December 31, 1959. The emphasis is on authors popular on syllabuses in high school or college courses. The entries provide a biographical introduction, a portrait of the artist, an excerpt from the writer's work where available, a list of principal writings, excerpts of criticism (with complete bibliographic data), and cross-references to other CLC volumes or other resources published by Gale that have featured the writer in question.

The yearbook begins with essays (written specially for this volume) on the year in fiction, poetry, drama, and world literature. The essays discuss the various works and events of the year; titles are in bold italics, easing scanning. The next section introduces new authors who made an appearance on the literary scene; they include Douglas Cooper (*Amnesia*), Nathan McCall (*Makes Me Wanna Holler: A Young Black Man in America*), and Anchee Min (*Red Azalea*). Another section details prizewinners for the year. The section starts with a list of the major awards and honors announced in 1994, then profiles 11 winners/winning works. Such prizes as the Pulitzer Prize for Drama (awarded to Edward Albee for *Three Tall Women*); the National Book Critics Circle Award (presented to Ernest Gaines for *A Lesson Before Dying*); and the OBIE Award for Best New American Play (given to Anna Deavere Smith for *Twilight: Los Angeles, 1992*) are included. An "In Memoriam" segment gives obituaries for some of the many talents lost in 1994; six in-depth profiles give further discussion of such lost literary giants as Alice Childress, Ralph Ellison, and Eugène Ionesco. The volume is completed by four indexes: a cumulative author index for all volumes in the Literary Criticism series, a topic index also covering all Literary Criticism volumes, a nationality index for the more specific CLC series volumes, and a title index for this volume only.

In between the memorial portion and the indexes lies the most interesting feature of this yearbook: three topic studies detailing pertinent, controversial subjects that inspired much debate or discussion in 1994. The first topic, "Electronic 'Books': Hypertext and Hyperfiction," discusses one of the most controversy-laden subjects in the field: hypertext, the aid or detriment to traditional literary studies, and hyperfiction, this decade's electronic equivalent of the Choose Your Own Adventure children's books popular in the early 1980s. The second topic discusses graphic narratives and expounds on whether they expose new readers to classic works of literature or provide them with further excuses not to read in a decreasingly literate society. The final theme study, "Sylvia Plath and the Nature of Biography," discusses Janet Malcolm's biography *The Silent Woman* (Alfred A. Knopf, 1994). Malcolm brings up issues in writing a biography, such as how writing the biography affects the biographer's life; the "penchant for deviant details" (p. 433) of the biographee's life; and the right to privacy of friends and family of the biographee (especially relevant in Plath's case, as Ted Hughes has adamantly protected the privacy of his years with Plath).

The topics alone that are studied in this volume make it a worthy acquisition. Libraries already possessing the set to date should definitely purchase this volume, and academic libraries with strong literature departments not already having the set may wish to purchase the yearbook as well.—**Melissa Rae Root**

896. **Contemporary Literary Criticism: Excerpts from Criticism of the Works of Today's Novelists.... Volume 87.** Christopher Giroux and others, eds. Detroit, Gale, 1995. 535p. illus. index. $129.00. ISBN 0-8103-4997-3.

Part of the ongoing Contemporary Literary Criticism (CLC) series, this volume profiles 13 prominent contemporary writers, although not all are generally considered "authors" in the conventional sense. The series as a whole strives to give critical background on contemporary literary figures, with *contemporary* meaning currently living artists or those who passed away after December 31, 1959. The emphasis is on writers popular on syllabuses of high school or college courses. The genres encompass anything from traditional novels, plays, short stories, and poems to philosophy, memoirs, essays, diaries, and screenplays.

The writers discussed in this volume are James Clavell, Robert Coover, Jacques Derrida, M. F. K. Fisher, John Fowles, Che Guevara, Shirley Jackson, Maurice Kenny, Toni Morrison (the entry is devoted to *Beloved*), Ben Okri, Delmore Schwartz, Robert Towne, and Marguerite Yourcenar. Each entry provides a biographical introduction, a portrait of the writer, an excerpt from the author's work (where available), a list of principal writings, excerpts of criticism (with complete bibliographic data), a list for further reading, and cross-references to other CLC volumes or other resources published by Gale that have featured the writer in question. Completing this volume are a cumulative author index (for the entire Literary Criticism series), a cumulative topic index (also for the larger series), a cumulative nationality index (for the CLC series only), and a title index for volume 87.

The variety of writers covered in this series is part of what makes it valuable. Libraries already owning the set should definitely purchase this volume. Those libraries not already subscribing should consider this volume on a need basis.—**Melissa Rae Root**

897. **Contemporary Literary Criticism: Excerpts from Criticism of the Works of Today's Novelists.... Volume 88.** Christopher Giroux and others, eds. Detroit, Gale, 1995. 476p. illus. index. $129.00. ISBN 0-8103-9264-X.

898. **Contemporary Literary Criticism: Excerpts from Criticism of the Works of Today's Novelists.... Volume 89.** Christopher Giroux and others, eds. Detroit, Gale, 1996. 493p. illus. index. $129.00. ISBN 0-8103-9265-8.

Despite its relatively high cost, this series is indispensable for any library serving either a population studying literature or a community of serious readers. The breadth of creative writers covered by the series—poets, short story authors, essayists, novelists, playwrights, screenwriters, and so on—is admirable.

Clearly, given the purchasing audience, the greatest amount of coverage is devoted to English-language authors, but there are several entries in each volume covering non-English-language authors as well. An editorial policy states that the series gives serious attention to critically acclaimed but nonmainstream authors about whom critical work is difficult to locate.

The entry for each author contains brief biographical information, a list of major works, a section on the author's critical reception, a bibliography of principal works, further critical readings, interesting excerpts from interviews, a portrait if available, and actual excerpts from reviews and critical material. For the more well-known authors, the entry may only cover the background and reception of that individual work. Each volume also contains cumulative author, nationality, and topic indexes, covering not only the volume in hand but also the other Gale literary publications, such as *Black Literature Criticism* (see ARBA 93, entry 1115), *Poetry Criticism* (see ARBA 96, entry 1265; ARBA 94, entry 1303; and ARBA 92, entry 1247), and the like. Most volumes in the series also contain a title index to the works mentioned; in every fifth volume, this is absent (as in volume 89). Instead, Gale produces a separate volume that cumulates the last five indexes.

The authors included in volume 88 are as follows: Toni Cade Bambara, Adolfo Bioy Casares, Annie Ernaux, Kaye Gibbons, Günter Grass, W. S. Merwin, Erin Mouré, Sean O'Casey, Graham Swift, and Frank Waters. Those profiled in volume 89 are John Barth, Emmanuel Carrère, Thomas King, Valerie Martin, Peter Mayle, D'Arcy Mcnickle, Anna Maria Ortese, Adam Clayton Powell Jr., Martin Scorsese, William T. Vollmann, Sherley Anne Williams, and Bernice Zamora.

Clearly, the serious research needs of a literary community are not addressed by a digested work such as this. However, any college, university, or large public library would have a large number of patrons needing the level of information presented here. Many of the entries make fascinating casual reading.—**Caroline M. Kent**

899. **Dictionary of Literary Biography Yearbook: 1995.** James W. Hipp, ed. Detroit, Gale, 1996. 380p. illus. index. (Dictionary of Literary Biography). $135.00. ISBN 0-8103-9367-0.

This is the 16th yearbook of the Dictionary of Literary Biography (DLB) series. Each yearbook reviews the events of the literary year in poetry, fiction, literary biography, drama, and children's books. The 1995 annual has 20 articles by contributors from academia and publishing, varying in length from 5 to 55 pages. Some of the longer articles deal with such matters as the World War II Writers' Symposium, book reviewing in the United States, primary bibliography, and Nobel prize-winner Seamus Heaney. Lists of literary awards announced in 1995, a necrology, and a two-page checklist of contributions to literary history and biography round out the volume.

The articles in the *DLB Yearbook* are generally well written and interesting, especially for literary scholars and followers of publishing trends. However, the yearbook has slight reference value, considering its cost, especially for libraries that already subscribe to the *Bowker Annual* (see entry 528). Larger libraries may purchase the *DLB Yearbook* for their circulating collections.—**Jonathan F. Husband**

900. **DISCovering Authors Modules.** [CD-ROM]. Detroit, Gale, 1996. Minimum system requirements: IBM or compatible 286 (386 or higher recommended). ISO 9660-compatible CD-ROM drive with cables, interface card, and MS-DOS CD-ROM Extensions 2.1 (double-speed or faster drive recommended). MS-DOS 3.3. 640K RAM. 10MB hard disk space. VGA monitor and graphics card. Mouse (optional). $600 (first module); $300 (each additional module). ISBN 0-8103-5104-8.

This revised and expanded CD-ROM offers much of the same kind of information found in many of Gale's printed literary criticism sources. Each entry gives an overview of the author's work, biographical and bibliographical information, excerpts from one or more critical sources, sources of additional information, and suggested paper topics. Some entries also include a portrait of the author. Purchasers can choose to install any combination of six modules provided: Most-Studied Authors, Multicultural Authors, Dramatists, Novelists, Poets, and Popular and Genre Authors. The entire set covers more than 1,200 authors, with many authors appearing in more than 1 module. In comparison, version 1.0 covered only 302 of the most-studied authors (see ARBA 94, entry 1146). As noted in that review, the disc is easily installed and features attractive screen designs and easy-to-use navigation through a series of on-screen menus and clearly labeled buttons on the screen. An inexperienced user should be able to find information easily, although some of the more sophisticated features, such as the use of Boolean operators, will probably require instruction.

It is unfortunate, however, that such an attractive product has several serious flaws. As with any such tool, one might question the criteria for inclusion or exclusion, but the absence of such classic authors as James Fenimore Cooper and Jules Verne stands out. There are more serious problems, however, some of which might be attributable to the search software and some to editorial control. In many cases, the user is led to marginal or totally irrelevant material. For example, clicking on either "Afghanistan" or "Khyber Pass" as a subject leads the user to Jay McInerney's *Bright Lights, Big City*, a novel about New York City. If one reads the entire entry for McInerney, Afghanistan is briefly mentioned in a discussion of another of his books, *Ransom*. A search for "Jondalar," a character in the novels of Jean Auel, yields four titles under her name, none of which were actually written by her. However, clicking on any one of those titles does take the user to Auel's entry. A search on "pilot" in the career category yields, among other names, that of Thomas Tryon, the actor turned author. Examination of his entry shows that he once appeared in "Moon Pilot." While perhaps technically correct, this sort of result is misleading and would be confusing to someone who may be legitimately expecting to find references to authors who also had the occupation of pilot. Use of the character list is made more difficult by the apparent editorial choice not to standardize entries. Therefore, a character search for "Dracula" does not retrieve the classic Bram Stoker novel. To find that, one must enter "Count Dracula." Similarly, there are two formats for most personal titles: "Dr." and "Doctor," "Sgt." and "Sergeant," "Rev." and "Reverend." Editorial control seems to have been lax in general. Misspellings and typographic errors can be found throughout, including errors such as stating that Alexandre Dumas *père* (1802-1870) worked as a librarian for the Duc d'Orleans from 1923 to 1930.

Such sloppiness is unacceptable and unexpected from such a company as Gale. It is a shame that such a promising, potentially useful product is so flawed. Libraries contemplating purchase should take full advantage of the 45-day trial period in order to assess these problems in light of their specific situations and user communities. [R: RBB, 15 May 96, p. 1606; VOYA, Dec 96, p. 296]—**Barbara E. Kemp**

901. **Literature Criticism from 1400 to 1800: Excerpts from Criticism of the Works of Fifteenth-, Sixteenth-, Seventeenth-, and Eighteenth-Century Novelists....Volume 28.** James E. Person Jr., Jennifer Brostrom, and Michael Magoulias, eds. Detroit, Gale, 1995. 540p. illus. index. $129.00. ISBN 0-8103-8944-4.

With major publishers downsizing in the 1990s, it is refreshing to see *Literature Criticism from 1400 to 1800* still being published. Part of the Gale Literary Criticism Series, this work contains excerpts of prominent French writers such as Pierre Corneille, Claude Prosper Jolyot de Crébillon, Alaine-René Lesage, Molière, and Jean Racine, with an essay on French drama in the age of Louis XIV. Drama was preeminent in this time period, and the essay was a popular form for literary studies. The novel was just beginning to gain popularity for its structure, so this period is filled with interesting literary forms and their authors.

In addition to giving an introduction to the author, this volume highlights the most lauded interpretations of their works, thus making it a dual-purpose reference work as well as a work of criticism. Illustrations of the authors are also presented in the biographical sections of the book. The arrangement consists of the author section, the biographical and critical section, a thematic section, a listing of principal works, a chronological criticism section, annotations, and a bibliography section. This solid reference will be wanted by all reference departments of academic libraries as well as scholars of the periods covered in many fields (e.g., history, literature, philosophy). This work is a solid source for an extremely important period.—**Anne F. Roberts**

902. **Literature Criticism from 1400 to 1800: Criticism of the Works of Fifteenth, Sixteenth, Seventeenth, and Eighteenth-Century Novelists....Volume 29.** Jennifer Allison Brostrom and others, eds. Detroit, Gale, 1996. 612p. illus. index. $129.00. ISBN 0-8103-8945-2.

The 29th volume of this standard reference series successfully fills a void in readily accessible literary criticism. Focusing on eighteenth-century Scottish poets and poetry, this work covers Robert Burns, Robert Fergusson, James Macpherson, Allan Ramsay, and James Thomson. Each entry begins with a brief biographical essay, followed by extensive, substantive excerpts from the criticism that present both the important aspects of the poet's work and the critical reception. A lengthy section entitled "Eighteenth-Century Scottish Poetry" covers comparative criticism, focusing on the major vernacular poetry but touching on the ballads and the lesser poets.

The selection of criticism is inclusive, offering leading critics such as David Daiches and Allan MacLaine, as well as lesser-known scholars. However, emphasis tends to be on fairly recent work, with only the section on Ramsay extending more than a few years before the twentieth century. This is a weakness for anyone trying to follow the historical reception of a poet's work, and is most detrimental in the case of Macpherson, where none of the early responses to the Ossian poems are included. Yet, this lack will probably be of little concern for the average high school or undergraduate user.

The very existence of this volume indicates the growing scholarly interest in Scottish vernacular poetry. It will be a welcome addition to any collection serving a high school- or college-level community.

—**Susan Davis Herring**

903. **Literature Criticism from 1400 to 1800: Criticism of the Works of Fifteenth, Sixteenth, Seventeenth, and Eighteenth-Century Novelists....Volume 30.** Jennifer Allison Brostrom and others, eds. Detroit, Gale, 1996. 559p. illus. index. $129.00. ISBN 0-8103-9275-5.

904. **Literature Criticism from 1400 to 1800: Criticism of the Works of Fifteenth- Through Eighteenth-Century Novelists....Volume 31.** Jennifer Allison Brostrom and others, eds. Detroit, Gale, 1996. 558p. illus. index. $129.00. ISBN 0-8103-9276-3.

With volumes 30 and 31, "Seventeenth-Century Women Writers" and "The New World in Renaissance Literature," respectively, the view that the Literature Criticism from 1400 to 1800 (LC) series constitutes "an innocuous finding aid" (see this reviewer's assessment in ARBA 88, entry 1121) must be reconsidered and perhaps even retracted. Both volumes seriously compromise the governing principles that initially inspired the series and were manifested in the earliest volumes. Neither LC 30 nor 31 really surveys the full range of critical responses to the included writers. What is dangerous about this is that there is little that tells the intended users otherwise.

A more revealing title for LC 30 would be "Recent Feminist Criticism of Seventeenth-Century Women Writers." The majority of the volume covers seven writers: Aphra Behn, Anne Bradstreet, Aemilia Lanyer (who were all included in previous volumes), Elizabeth Cary Falkland, Margaret Cavendish, Katherine Philips, and Mary Wroth, the latter four presented in the LC series for the first time, and therefore deserving full historical critical surveys. As in other LC volumes, each author section consists of a bio-critical introduction, a primary bibliography of principal works, a selection of excerpts, and a list of further readings.

The trend in recent LC volumes seems to be to excerpt fewer works more extensively and cite fewer readings. Selections in LC 30 include about 8-10 extensive excerpts and 10-12 readings. Some "excerpts" consist of the entire texts of articles, minus the footnotes, from readily available scholarly journals. By comparison, the section for Behn in LC volume 1 included 24 shorter excerpts and listed 24 further readings. While LC 30's earliest critical excerpt dates from 1881 (for Philips), and the selections for Behn and Cavendish commence with excerpts from Virginia Woolf in the 1920s, most of the excerpts date from the 1980s and 1990s and substantially reflect recent feminist and gender-role responses to the writers. The individual introductions note earlier critical receptions—that, for example, Samuel Pepys, Charles Lamb, and Isaac Disraeli commented on Cavendish (p. 180); and that Philips was "hailed by her contemporaries as a 'model' woman poet" (p. 269). However, substantive documentation of early criticism is lacking for Cary, Cavendish, Philips, and Wroth.

LC 30's general introduction provides an overview consisting of 2 sections on "Women and Education," "Women Autobiographies," and "Women's Diaries," each with 1 excerpt, and "Seventeenth-Century Feminists," with 3 excerpts. That six of these excerpts date from the 1980s affords little historical balance, and that many of the seven writers (the volume claims) have "only recently received significant scholarly attention" (p. 1) all depends on definition. In that LC 30 largely seems to equate significance with currency, the volume essentially presents feminist responses to the writers in a critical vacuum.

LC 31, "The New World in Renaissance Literature," shares LC 30's problematic emphasis on recent criticism. The volume covers the Spaniards Hernán Cortés, Bernal Díaz del Castillo, and Bartolomé de Las Casas and the Englishmen Richard Hakluyt, Walter Raleigh, and John Winthrop. As none of them have been covered in previous LC volumes, full historical surveys of critical receptions are to be expected. In fact, however, the selection for Raleigh consists of only seven excerpts dating from 1951 to 1991, and the introduction does not specifically identify any earlier critical responses. Critical excerpts for Winthrop and Hakluyt date back to 1702 and 1925, respectively.

For the Spanish writers, LC 31's emphasis on recency is all the more troublesome because of the series' most serious limitation—LC only does English-language criticism of non-English-language writers. Nothing in the introduction for Cortés suggests that his critical reception through the twentieth century consists of more than an anonymous essay in *The North American Review* in 1843. Likewise, while the introduction for Diaz notes an early critical reception that included translations into English, excerpts for Diaz date from an anonymous essay in *The Living Age* in 1844. The introduction for Las Casas fails to identify by author or by title any of the contemporary Spanish commentaries that branded him as "a traitor and a fanatic" (p. 171). The earliest excerpt for Las Casas dates from 1867; and for all six writers featured in this volume, the majority of the excerpts date from after 1970. LC 31's general introduction, which includes the articles "Utopia vs. Terror in the New World" and "New World Explorers and Native Americans," shows the same emphasis on current criticism: 5 of the 6 excerpts date from after 1970. A more appropriate title for LC 31 may have been "Recent English-Language Historical Re-visioning of the New World in Three English and Three Spanish Writers."

The presentation in thematic LC volumes of critical responses to important writers, such as the 7 women in LC 30 and the 6 men in LC 31, does not entitle the LC series to abridge and skew their full and true historical critical receptions. Intended users must consult these volumes with more than the usual caution.—**James K. Bracken**

905. **Magill's Survey of World Literature.** Frank N. Magill, ed. North Bellmore, N.Y., Marshall Cavendish, 1995. 2v. illus. index. $134.95/set. ISBN 0-7614-0104-0.

It is wonderful to meet an old friend in the reference book world, and this two-volume supplement to the six-volume 1993 set of *Magill's Survey of World Literature* (see ARBA 94, entry 1158) is indeed such a friend. How one remembers discovering the treasures hidden in these works when trying to write school research papers or critical papers—*Magill's* always reaffirmed one's assessments. In the 6-volume set, some 215 of the world's writers were initially written about; this 2-volume supplement updates and extends that original by some "seventy-nine contemporary or hitherto neglected writers who have had a substantial effect on the evolution of world literature." All varieties of literature are included: fiction, nonfiction, poetry, drama, and short stories. Many postcolonial writers are treated as well.

Biographical sketches are presented, followed by an analysis of the author's themes, styles, and other characteristics. A bibliography is attached to each entry as well, providing lists of further reading for the serious researcher. Full-page photographs are given, and this set, as the others, is designated for middle school and high school libraries, although college and university undergraduates will find the information both current and useful for their own research.

Each work is "boxed" and set off, so that researchers can easily locate the work they are searching for under each author's listing. Not all of the entries are contemporary: One finds Sappho with David Storey, and Hans Christian Andersen with Kobo Abe, or Aphra Behn with Brendan Behan, and Anita Desai with Isak Dinesen. This is a solid general reference work to major world literature authors, and one that will be welcomed.—**Anne F. Roberts**

906. **Masterplots: 1,801 Plot Stories and Critical Evaluations of the World's Finest Literature.** 2d ed. Frank N. Magill, Dayton Kohler, and Laurence W. Mazzeno, eds. Pasadena, Calif., Salem Press, 1996. 12v. index. $600.00/set. ISBN 0-89356-084-7.

Magill has produced a useful reference tool with the revised 2d edition of *Masterplots*. This standard reference work contains 1,801 articles, a comprehensive selection of world literature available in English. All articles from the 1976 edition were reviewed, with titles that no longer reflect high school or college curricular use being deleted; 425 new titles were added; and a significant number of entries were rewritten. A new feature of this edition, which makes it even more beneficial to the user, is an annotated bibliography following each article.

The format remains constant from the earlier edition. Entries are arranged alphabetically by title, with the type of work, author, type and time of plot, locale, first publication date, and principal characters listed. A plot synopsis is followed by a critical essay and a brief bibliography. Each entry is three to four pages in length. The four indexes included are by chronological date, by geographic locale, by title, and by author. The title *Masterplots* does not convey the depth of information contained in the 12 volumes.

The titles treated range chronologically from antiquity to the early 1990s, with the major emphasis on literature of the nineteenth and twentieth centuries. While the majority of the entries are British, European, and United States fiction, the work also encompasses drama, works or collections of poetry, and nonfiction. The other geographic areas range from a number of Latin American countries to Iceland, China, South Africa, and Poland. The works covered are inclusive and eclectic, with 16 titles by Charles Dickens; 39 works of William Shakespeare; and titles by current authors, such as Amy Tan, Margaret Atwood, Isabel Allende, Sandra Cisneros, Reynolds Price, Václav Havel, and Salman Rushdie. Ease of use, attractive format, concise entries, and breadth of coverage make this set extremely useful for high school and college libraries, but it would be a valuable purchase for public libraries as well.

—**Lynda Welborn**

907. **Modern Women Writers.** Lillian S. Robinson, comp. and ed. New York, Continuum Publishing, 1996. 4v. index. (A Library of Literary Criticism). $95.00/v; $285.00/set. ISBN 0-8264-0813-3 (v.1); 0-8264-0814-1 (v.2); 0-8264-0815-X (v.3); 0-8264-0920-2 (v.4); 0-8264-0823-0 (set).

Eight years in the making, and a part of Continuum Publishing's Library of Literary Criticism series, *Modern Women Writers* (MWW) provides excerpts of criticism on writers of the twentieth century. The writers profiled are all women, although the slant of their work need not be feminist; the author must have attracted some critical attention to be discussed. For those women who have been included in previous volumes or sets of the series, the same critical excerpts may be employed, with new criticism as available.

Entries consist of anywhere from 2 to 10 excerpts of criticism concerning the author under discussion. Criticism can be either positive or negative as long as it reflects an important aspect of the individual writer's oeuvre. No biographical information is supplied, as that is not the intent of this work, but such data can be found in other sources (e.g., certain volumes of the Dictionary of Literary Biography series). Each excerpt lists an author; the source of the critical assessment (whether book or journal); and other bibliographic information, such as publisher, issue, and page number, where pertinent. A few typographical errors turn up, but one must wonder if these are present in the original critical essay or a result of the current editing. The particular strength of MWW is its value for students, who may need a starting point for researching critical responses to certain writers.

A list of authors covered in the set (complete with country/ethnic designations) precedes the main text. Volume 1 expands this list to cover all 4 volumes; the other volumes only list those writers appearing in that particular text. An acknowledgments document (in place of a bibliography) appears at the end of volume 4, as does an index to critics. The critics index furnishes information on which author(s) the critic wrote about, the volume number, and the page number. Many critics are famous writers in their own right (and many are profiled in this set): Margaret Atwood, Louis Auchincloss, James Baldwin, Willa Cather, W. E. B. Du Bois, T. S. Eliot, Langston Hughes, Bobbie Ann Mason, V. S. Naipaul, Joyce Carol Oates, Philip Roth, Susan Sontag, Amy Tan, Gore Vidal, and Eudora Welty are but a few examples. Despite the usefulness of the lists of authors covered and the critics index, one misses the "authors as critics" index present in *Modern Black Writers* (see ARBA 96, entry 1157).

In comparing MWW with two other works on women writers—*Masterplots II: Women's Literature Series* (see ARBA 96, entry 949) and *Third World Women's Literatures* (see ARBA 96, entry 946)—some interesting points emerge. More than 15 percent of the entries in MWW are found in *Third World*, indicating the editor's effort to encompass postcolonial writers. MWW covers women from Leila Abouzeid to Nikki Giovanni, Oba Minako to Mayy Ziyadah. Approximately 25 percent of the writers are also profiled in *Masterplots*, which has a much greater scope time-wise. However, those twentieth-century authors appearing in *Masterplots* but not in MWW are easily justified omissions in most cases. Sandra Gilbert, Susan Gubar, Juliet Mitchell, Elaine Showalter—all stray from the primarily fiction focus of the work under review. For Laura Esquivel, Susan Howe, Barbara Kingsolver, Terry McMillan, Ayn Rand, and Jade Snow Wong, one could say that there is not a strong enough critical base from which to pull excerpts (although this seems somewhat suspect in a few instances).

In conclusion, even those libraries already possessing the *Masterplots* volumes should purchase MWW. Its focus on contemporary writers, its accessible format, and its truly global approach make the set a valuable acquisition for public and academic libraries alike. [R: LJ, 15 May 96, p. 54; RBB, 1 Nov 96, pp. 538-39]—**Melissa Rae Root**

908. **Nineteenth-Century Literature Criticism: Excerpts from Criticism of the Works of Novelists.... Volume 47.** Joann Cerrito and Marie Lazzari, eds. Detroit, Gale, 1995. 461p. illus. index. $129.00. ISBN 0-8103-8938-X.

909. **Nineteenth-Century Literature Criticism: Criticism of the Works of Novelists....Volume 48.** Marie Lazzari, Catherine C. Dominic, and Jelena O. Krstović, eds. Detroit, Gale, 1995. 439p. illus. index. $129.00. ISBN 0-8103-8939-8.

910. **Nineteenth-Century Literature Criticism: Criticism of the Works of Novelists....Volume 49.** Marie Lazzari and Catherine C. Dominic, eds. Detroit, Gale, 1995. 519p. illus. index. $129.00. ISBN 0-8103-8940-1.

Volumes 47 and 49 of these 3 related volumes follow the standard format of other volumes in the Nineteenth-Century Literature Criticism series. Each contains lengthy excerpts of criticism on a variety of authors. A key point is the age of the criticism. According to the subtitle, the criticism includes that "from the First Published Critical Appraisal to Current Evaluations," and indeed this is true, with criticism of Richard Jefferies (1848-1887), for example. This back-reaching method provides a useful overview of the critical reception of these authors.

The choice of authors discussed is somewhat curious. Again referring to the subtitle, these volumes examine the life and work of "Novelists, Poets, Playwrights, Short Story Writers, Philosophers, and Other Creative Writers." The ones highlighted in these volumes include naturalist John James Audubon, travel writer Laurence Oliphant, the Comte de Sade, William Cobbett, and Alexander Hamilton. The common thread is clearly not genre or nationality but rather time period, all authors accomplishing their work during the nineteenth century.

Volume 48 in this trio is somewhat different. Instead of examining particular authors, it offers a series of essays on various genres. Again, it is an eclectic mix: "The Connecticut Wits," "The Essay," "Nineteenth-Century Historical Fiction," and "Women's Diaries." While the quality of the work is not at issue—this series has earned its long tradition of respect—the somewhat mixed bag of material provided makes it doubtful that libraries that do not subscribe to the series would wish to purchase these as individual titles.—**Terry Ann Mood**

911. **Nineteenth-Century Literature Criticism: Criticism of the Works of Novelists....Volume 50.** James E. Person Jr., Catherine C. Dominic, Marie Lazzari, eds. Detroit, Gale, 1996. 497p. illus. index. $129.00. ISBN 0-8103-9291-7.

912. **Nineteenth-Century Literature Criticism: Criticism of the Works of Novelists....Volume 51.** Marie Lazzari, ed. Detroit, Gale, 1996. 479p. illus. index. $129.00. ISBN 0-8103-9297-6.

913. **Nineteenth-Century Literature Criticism Topics Volume: Excerpts from Criticism of Various Topics in Nineteenth-Century Literature....Volume 52.** James E. Person Jr. and others, eds. Detroit, Gale, 1996. 459p. illus. index. $129.00. ISBN 0-8103-9298-4.

914. **Nineteenth-Century Literature Criticism Annual Cumulative Title Index for 1996.** Detroit, Gale, 1996. 135p. free w/purchase of NCLC. ISBN 0-8103-9296-8.

Volumes 50 and 51 of *Nineteenth-Century Literature Criticism* (NCLC) cover the writers Anna Letitia Barbauld (English poet, essayist, and children's writer); Orestes Brownson (American essayist); Lorenzo Da Ponte (Italian librettist); Charles Dickens (the entry is devoted to *Hard Times*); Margaret Fuller (American essayist); Christina Rossetti (English poet); Harriet Beecher Stowe (the entry is devoted to *Uncle Tom's Cabin*); Jane Austen (concerning only *Northanger Abbey*); Maria Edgeworth (British novelist); Charles Fourier (French utopian social philosopher); John William Polidori (English novelist, dramatist, poet, and diarist); Arthur Schopenhauer (German philosopher); and Paul Verlaine (French poet). As in previous volumes of the series, there is a brief biographical sketch, a list of principal writings, and then substantial excerpts from critical essays arranged chronologically, followed by a list for further reading. The annual, cumulative title index lists entries for all volumes of this series published to date.

Every fourth volume of NCLC is devoted to specific literary topics rather than to individual authors. Volume 52 is one of said topics volumes and deals with the following subjects: American humor writing, children's literature, French Realism, the Lake Poets, and Polish Romanticism. Each entry includes an introduction and list of representative works, which is followed by lengthy excerpts from published criticism, and concludes with suggestions for further reading. Thus, each topic entry achieves the same goal as an author entry—to provide the reader with a quick, convenient, and surprisingly thorough overview drawn chiefly from professional critics.—**Jeffrey R. Luttrell**

915. **Reader's Guide to Literature in English.** Mark Hawkins-Dady, ed. Chicago, Fitzroy Dearborn, 1996. 970p. index. $125.00. ISBN 1-884964-20-6.

This fat volume, beyond what the title suggests, provides a comprehensive overview of English literature criticism, encompassing literature from the United States, Great Britain, Canada, Australia, and more. Entries are given for those figures with a substantial body of criticism and who elicit strong interest in today's multiethnic, multigenre approach. More general entries (on national traditions, periods, genres, literary theories, cultural contexts, movements, and so forth) may cover writers not given their own entries elsewhere. Coverage includes discussion of Old English and Medieval literary figures and trends, on through the present day. Large topics (e.g., "Drama: Medieval") are subsectioned for further specificity and clarity.

Entries appear alphabetically; a list of them is also available in the front matter, following the list of advisers and contributors (notes on affiliations and other publications fall after the indexes). Also improving accessibility is a thematic index (also before the main text); a booklist index (listing books or articles discussed in the entries by author or editor name); and a general index (the latter two at the end of the volume). Entries begin with a list of books or articles selected by the contributor. Details of the thematic or critical background appear next, in essay form. All essays are signed. Cross-references appear in bold typeface at the end of the articles. Paragraphs addressing specific theories championed by individual theorists contain that theorist's name in capital letters, aiding the ease of skimming for desired information. British spelling is evident throughout, reflecting the work's dual publication in the United States and Great Britain.

The volume is quite scholarly in tone, and public libraries may therefore wish to weigh patron interest before purchasing. Academic libraries will want to acquire the guide; undergraduate and graduate students of literature or literary theory may want to consider purchasing the work as a supplement to their class texts, as personal funds allow. A crucial research guide, *Reader's Guide to Literature in English* provides one-stop shopping for inquiry into English-language literature. [R: Choice, Dec 96, p. 594; RBB, 15 Sept 96, p. 284]—**Melissa Rae Root**

916. **A Reader's Guide to Twentieth-Century Writers.** Peter Parker and Frank Kermode, eds. New York, Oxford University Press, 1996. 825p. $35.00. ISBN 0-19-521215-0.

Poignant, intriguing snippets fill this volume on twentieth-century writers, a companion text to *A Reader's Guide to the Twentieth-Century Novel*, published in 1995 and produced by the same editorial team. Those profiled are all English-language writers, predominantly from the United States and Great Britain; but some authors from Australia, India, the Caribbean, and other locales are also treated. Novelists, poets, playwrights (less fully covered because of the nature of their genre), and short story writers are all discussed in this educational and entertaining book. Select crime and mystery writers have earned a place in the text; solely nonfiction writers are not included at all.

The writers are listed alphabetically by the name under which they wrote. The entries provide biographical details as well as a critical assessment. Following an entry, which is usually a column and a half in length, is a bibliography of works by that writer, broken down by genre. A biographical work about that author is commonly provided as well. The entries consist of minutiae not always found in a scholarly work. Biographical details range from the mundane to the oftentimes bizarre. Much of the information is interesting, but some is questionable (e.g., do readers really want to know about Joseph Conrad developing an anal abscess?). The writing is sometimes a bit convoluted; for example, the entry for Ernest Hemingway states, "While in war hospital, he conceived the passion . . . ," and later, "He contrived to become involved . . ." (p. 324).

Despite these criticisms, the work is recommended for most libraries. The entries entice the user to want to learn more, and the bibliographies and biographies help with that goal. A bibliography of works about the authors in question would have served the public even better, but for ascertaining quick biographical and critical data, this volume serves its audience well. [R: RBB, 1 Sept 96, pp. 170-71; SLJ, Aug 96, p. 183]—**Melissa Rae Root**

917. **Reference Guide to World Literature.** 2d ed. Lesley Henderson and Sarah M. Hall, eds. Detroit, St. James Press, 1995. 2v. index. $260.00/set. ISBN 1-55862-332-9.

First published as *Great Foreign Language Writers* (see ARBA 86, entry 1088), this 2d edition increases coverage from 253 to 490 writers. The historical range covers ancient Greece through the present day, although living authors are few and far between, as 350 living writers are discussed in a similar publication, *Contemporary World Writers* (see ARBA 94, entry 1144). This reference begins with an editors' note, followed by a lengthy contributor's list, and lists of writers and works treated in the two-volume set—in both alphabetic and chronological order. Entries on authors include biographical information, primary works, awards and honors, a critical overview, and bibliographies. The works discussed run the gamut from novels, short stories, poems, and plays to television and radio scripts, essays, travel writing, memoirs, letters, and theoretical works. Anonymous writings, such as the epic of Gilgamesh, and collaborations, such as the Bible, are also given entries. No American or British writers are profiled here.

As stated in the review of the initial edition, the critical overviews consist of only one or two pages and only serve as introductory assessments (indeed, as much information can be found in any Norton anthology). Differing slightly in content from the previous edition, occasional references to foreign-language critical studies are found in the bibliographies, but often in English translation. Coverage of women writers is surprisingly inadequate.

The set is completed by a couple of indexes. New to this edition is the language index, which lists writers under their primary language. A title index follows (no author index is necessary due to the alphabetic format of the main text). A list of advisers and contributors, complete with affiliations and publications, concludes the second volume. While it is refreshing to see a set concerned solely with world literature, and having said information at hand in two volumes is useful, much of the data can be found elsewhere. The bibliographies and lists of critical studies are still woefully remiss—more fulfilling lists can be found online. The benefits of this set do not live up to its price.—**Melissa Rae Root**

918. **The Schomberg Center Guide to Black Literature from the Eighteenth Century to the Present.** Roger M. Valade III with Denise Kasinec, eds. Detroit, Gale, 1996. 545p. illus. index. $75.00. ISBN 0-7876-0289-2.

This volume on black literature is an ideal guide for people seeking quick access to key information on black fiction and nonfiction writers. Most of the authors are from the United States, but the alphabetically arranged reference tool also includes data on international black artists whose works are available in English. Other entries deal with plot summaries of 460 major literary pieces; cross-references of characters to the works in which they appear; and concise information on topics, terms, genres, and literary movements relating to black writing during the past 3 centuries.

The guide is handsomely done and is designed to attract high school and university students who are beginning to delve into black literary studies. There are photographs of nearly 100 authors and reproductions of about half as many dust jackets, title pages, book covers, and manuscript pages. The information is useful, brief, and adequate. Those desiring more comprehensive and in-depth information are given references to other works for further study, especially to volumes in the Gale family.

The book is introduced by a short, interesting essay concerning the history of the Schomberg Center for Research in Black Culture. The introduction also provides a chronological list of the major biographical and historical events relevant to black literature. A significant feature of this reference is the addition of numerous minor or little-known (but still worthy) creative artists, such as Chester Himes, Ida B. Wells, and Eric Walrond. Also, the book ably shows the worldwide connections of black writing by including coverage of authors outside the United States. *The Schomberg Center Guide* is excellent for finding key information on black literary subjects, but it should be used as a starting point for more serious study or as a fascinating place to browse for facts about a rich field of creative work. [R: Choice, May 96, p. 1459; RBB, 15 Feb 96, pp. 1045-47]—**Angelo Costanzo**

919. **Twentieth-Century Literary Criticism Topics Volume: Excerpts from Criticism of Various Topics in Twentieth-Century Literature....Volume 58.** Jennifer Gariepy and others, eds. Detroit, Gale, 1995. 443p. illus. index. $129.00. ISBN 0-8103-2440-7.

Every fourth volume of the Twentieth-Century Literary Criticism (TCLC) series is devoted to "Topics," a catchall that provides for treatment of more general subjects than individual authors. The contents of the present volume are disparate indeed: "Holocaust Denial Literature," "Latin American Literature," "The Modern Essay," and *"The New Yorker."* Each topic is divided into subheadings, under which relevant, reprinted essays are incorporated in whole or part. The subheadings provide a roughly uniform format: an introductory paragraph, "Representative Works," an essay providing an overview, a half-dozen thematic categories appropriate to the particular topic, and "Further Reading."

The first section, "Holocaust Denial Literature," is almost unique as a category type in the series for it does not deal with literature at all, but rather with political science, history, and sociology. The remaining topics are more appropriate. The essays making up "Latin American Literature" afford a panoramic survey of Latin American novels, short stories, drama, and poetry. Pieces on the writer and society and on Native Americans round off the section that, on the whole, is slanted toward the historical and slights the post-1960s prose. The reprinted articles in "The Modern Essay," admittedly a much easier topic to survey, represent better chronological coverage. The volume's final section surveys the evolution of *The New Yorker*, the United States' most illustrious wide-circulation literary periodical, from the days of its founding editor, Harold Ross, to Tina Brown's makeover of the 1990s. Oddly missing from its bibliography is Brendan Gill's *Here at The New Yorker* (Random House, 1975), although it is discussed in more than one of the essays. As in all of the Gale Literary Criticism volumes, cumulative author and topic indexes for the entire series are appended.—**D. Barton Johnson**

920. **Twentieth-Century Literary Criticism: Excerpts from Criticism of the Works of Novelists.... Volume 59.** Jennifer Gariepy and others, eds. Detroit, Gale, 1995. 437p. illus. index. $129.00. ISBN 0-8103-9303-4.

921. **Twentieth-Century Literary Criticism: Excerpts from Criticism of the Works of Novelists.... Volume 60.** Jennifer Gariepy and others, eds. Detroit, Gale, 1995. 465p. illus. index. $129.00. ISBN 0-8103-9305-0.

A companion to Contemporary Literary Criticism for authors born or deceased after 1960, Twentieth-Century Literary Criticism covers authors from 1900 to 1960. To date, the series has treated more than 500 authors of 58 nationalities and more than 25,000 titles. (For earlier reviews, see ARBA 96, entries 1159-1160; ARBA 92, entry 1110; ARBA 89, entries 994-995; and ARBA 85, entries 1005-1006.) As more volumes appear, the number of writers discussed has declined, although the degree of coverage has remained relatively stable. The first eight volumes included novelists, poets, playwrights, and short story writers. With volume 9, essayists and journalists were added. In 1988, with volume 26, Gale designated every 4th volume an archive volume devoted to literary topics, movements, themes, responses to political and historical events, and the literatures of non-English-speaking cultures—subjects not easily treated by an author approach.

Volumes 59 and 60 illustrate other developments in the series: a broadening of the term *writer* to include a philosopher, Ludwig Wittgenstein (v. 59), and an anthropologist, Ruth Benedict (v. 60). These volumes also include entries for authors treated in previous volumes. This time, however, the entries focus on the critical reception of single works; for example, *The Adventures of Tom Sawyer* and *Tonio Krueger*, by Mark Twain and Thomas Mann, respectively. Entries follow the pattern established for the series. Each begins with a sketch of the writer's life and career, noting major critical issues. A bibliography lists works chronologically by publication date. Plays are entered under the date of first performance. The remainder of the entry is composed of excerpts of criticism, again in chronological order with full citation. This arrangement conveys a sense of the critical response to an author's work over time. In instances where permission to reprint was not available, works are cited in a list for further reading. Each volume in the series is cumulatively indexed by author, topic, and nationality. Both public and academic libraries will continue to find this an important and valuable resource for the study of twentieth-century literature.

—Bernice Bergup

922. **Twentieth-Century Literary Criticism: Excerpts from Criticism of the Works of Novelists.... Volume 61.** Jennifer Gariepy and others, eds. Detroit, Gale, 1996. 410p. illus. index. $129.00. ISBN 0-8103-9306-9.

923. **Twentieth-Century Literary Criticism Annual Cumulative Title Index for 1996.** Detroit, Gale, 1996. 221p. free w/purchase of TCLC. ISBN 0-8103-9304-2.

Since its beginning more than 15 years ago, Gale's Twentieth-Century Literary Criticism (TCLC) series has gradually expanded its coverage, and it now includes criticism of notables whose achievements involved neither literature nor creative writing. The primary criterion for inclusion in the series has, however, remained constant: The subject must have died between 1900 and 1960. The 61st volume of TCLC surveys and criticizes the work of 6 people, only 3 of whom were noted as writers. Four of these six—Australian psychologist Alfred Adler, German philosopher Ernst Cassirer, English novelist E. M. Delafield, and American linguist Alfred Korzybski—have not been previously profiled in TCLC, although Delafield has been profiled in volume 34 of Gale's Dictionary of Literary Biography series. The final two writers—D. H. Lawrence and Thomas Wolfe—have been profiled several times each by TCLC and many times by other Gale series, but the criticism in the present volume focuses on Lawrence's 1915 novel *The Rainbow* and Wolfe's 1935 novel *Of Time and the River*, novels that TCLC has hitherto accorded only cursory attention.

As in all of Gale's literary criticism series, the criticism is arranged chronologically, allowing researchers to trace the subject's rise (or decline) in academic reputation. Each biographical entry begins with a bibliography listing the author's principal works and concludes with a briefly annotated list of secondary and tertiary sources. A title index specific to this volume and cumulative indexes to author, nationality, and the TCLC topic volumes conclude the book. A separate annual cumulative title index for 1996 is complimentary with the purchase of TCLC, and covers all volumes of the series. TCLC would not be a first stop in looking for information on Adler, Cassirer, and Korzybski, but the series nevertheless belongs in all academic libraries.—**Richard Bleiler**

924. **A Writer's Companion.** Louis D. Rubin Jr. and Jerry Leath Mills, eds. Baton Rouge, La., Louisiana State University Press, 1995. 1041p. $39.95. ISBN 0-8071-1992-X.

At last, a balm to soothe every aggravated writer, editor, or student who has ever tried to verify an obscure fact or fiction: Rubin's *A Writer's Companion*. Definitions of various terms, details on philosophic and artistic movements, discographies of popular songs and ballads, capsule biographies of biblical characters, descriptions of bird habitats for numerous species, and much more are found in this remarkable volume. The text is divided into 19 sections, including "Travel and Transportation," "Literature and Language," "Religion, Folklore, and Legend," "Business and Finance," "Science and the Natural World," "Law and Laws," "Gastronomy," and "Sports." The focus is slanted toward the humanities, in keeping with its status as companion to writers. A final section, titled "Some Reference Books That Writers Use," neatly lists such helpful works as *Who's Who in America* (see ARBA 96, entry 37); Samuel Johnson's *A Dictionary of the English Language* (London, 1755); the *Oxford Dictionary of Quotations* (4th ed.; see ARBA 93, entry 92); William Benét's *The Reader's Encyclopedia* (2d ed., T. Y. Crowell, 1955); and *Dr. Spock's Baby and Child Care* (NAL-Dutton, 1985).

This volume makes for fascinating browsing. A writer or editor searching for specific information may very well get sidetracked in the cornucopia of miscellanea. Readers can learn about the erotogenic zone; Bottom the Weaver; the timpani; the Norton Simon Museum in Pasadena, California; the Battle of

Britain; Constantin Brancusi; the Gabrielino tribe of Native Americans; common law; subjectivism; and the law of conservation of mass, all through this single volume. The entries are not detailed but merely offer the basic facts; nonetheless, the information appears to be accurate. This is the source to turn to if data sought cannot be found in the common dictionary or encyclopedia.

Part biographical dictionary, part biblical companion, part folklore compendium, part sports almanac, part artistic and literary dictionary, *A Writer's Companion* serves a unique function and fills an important niche. As important for individual bookshelves as for public and academic libraries, the affordable price makes its purchase feasible. People searching for more detailed discussions of a variety of factual topics would make good use of such works as *The Larousse Desk Reference* (see entry 46). Those seeking the information left out of that volume will be well served by the *Companion*. [R: Choice, Feb 96, p. 936; RBB, Jan 96, p. 893; RQ, Spring 96, pp. 426-27]—**Melissa Rae Root**

CHILDREN'S AND YOUNG ADULT LITERATURE

General Works

Bibliography

925. **Your Reading: An Annotated Booklist for Middle School and Junior High.** 1995-96 ed. Barbara G. Samuels, G. Kylene Beers, and the Committee on the Middle School and Junior High Booklist of the National Council of Teachers of English, eds. Urbana, Ill., National Council of Teachers of English, 1996. 381p. index. $21.95pa. ISBN 0-8141-5943-5. ISSN 1051-4740.

This resource is one of five in a series of book lists published and periodically updated by the National Council of Teachers of English (NCTE). The other four works are *Adventuring with Books* (pre-K through grade 6 [see ARBA 94, entry 1173, and ARBA 90, entry 1075]); *Kaleidoscope* (multicultural literature, grades K through 8 [see ARBA 96, entry 1182]); *Books for You* (senior high [see ARBA 94, entry 1165]); and *High Interest Easy Reading* (middle school, junior/senior high reluctant readers [see ARBA 91, entry 366]). The specialized audience for this work, and others in the series, makes it particularly useful in public school libraries or school administrative offices. However, because of the relatively inexpensive cost, public libraries may also want to consider the entire series for their reference collections in light of the home schooling trend that is taking place around the United States today. The only caveats here, on the other hand, are for librarians to keep in mind the ongoing cost of updating this material and whether to make an investment in acquiring earlier publications in order to have a complete set.

The listing of books is not exhaustive, but books that a committee of professionals in the field thought would be useful, interesting, and meaningful have been included. The work lists books published in 1993 and 1994. Earlier editions of cited books are covered in previous editions of *Your Reading*. The text is divided into seven sections: books concerning growing up (e.g., such topics as family, friendship, romance, and playing sports); books about imagined lands, myths, folklore, and science fiction; books involving mysteries, unexplained phenomena, and adventure and survival; books about people, customs, problems, and places from today and yesterday; books interested in science (e.g., animals, nature, ecology, and physical and mental health); volumes of poetry and short stories; and books containing facts, figures, and fun events such as crafts, music, and the arts. The 7 sections consist of 24 chapters.

The real value of this work lies in the detailed annotations for every listed book, as teachers and parents home schooling their children will likely appreciate how much more quickly they will be able to decide upon which book(s) to suggest for reading. All annotations are arranged alphabetically by the author's last name. The main text is followed by a useful appendix selectively listing the top 100 young adult literature books from 1967 to 1992. A second appendix lists award-winning books. Following the appendixes are a directory of publishers; an author, title, and subject index; names of the editors; and the backgrounds of the 24 committee members who selected the materials for inclusion in this book list. [R: EL, May/June 96, p. 42]—**James M. Murray**

Biography

926. **Something About the Author: Facts and Pictures About Authors and Illustrators of Books for Young People. Volume 81.** Kevin S. Hile, ed. Detroit, Gale, 1995. 319p. illus. index. $92.00. ISBN 0-8103-2291-9.

927. **Something About the Author: Facts and Pictures About Authors and Illustrators of Books for Young People. Volume 82.** Kevin S. Hile, ed. Detroit, Gale, 1995. 263p. illus. $92.00. ISBN 0-8103-2292-7.

928. **Something About the Author: Facts and Pictures About Authors and Illustrators of Books for Young People. Volume 83.** Kevin S. Hile, ed. Detroit, Gale, 1996. 328p. illus. index. $92.00. ISBN 0-8103-2293-5.

929. **Something About the Author: Facts and Pictures About Authors and Illustrators of Books for Young People. Volume 84.** Kevin S. Hile, ed. Detroit, Gale, 1996. 262p. illus. $92.00. ISBN 0-8103-9370-0.

930. **Something About the Author: Facts and Pictures About Authors and Illustrators of Books for Young People. Volume 85.** Kevin S. Hile, ed. Detroit, Gale, 1996. 316p. illus. index. $92.00. ISBN 0-8103-9371-9.

These five volumes continue the excellent series by Gale that focuses on authors and illustrators of works for young people and has been cited as an "Outstanding Reference Source" by the Reference and Adult Services Division of the American Library Association. Biographies range from less than one page to six pages in length and follow a fairly standard format. Most, but not all, include a portrait of the individual and also such details as personal data, address, brief career highlights, awards and honors received, a bibliography of writings or works illustrated, work in progress, sidelights of the person's life, and sources for the biography. The extensive references attest to the meticulous research done for each person, and where the biographees themselves could not review the listing, the entry is marked with an asterisk.

Strengths of this series include the excellent format, large readable typeface, ease of use, and sample book illustrations found in many of the biographies. Also helpful is that there is both an illustration and an author index at the end of alternate, odd-numbered volumes, which include references to previous volumes in this series, plus three other Gale titles—*Yesterday's Authors of Books for Children*, Children's Literature Review series, and Something About the Author Autobiography Series. Obituaries are also included, and the series attempts to include emerging and lesser-known authors and illustrators.

The only disadvantage of this work would be cost, because with two volumes in 1995 and three in 1996, many libraries and media centers (unfortunately) probably cannot afford the series. Yet for those public, school, and academic libraries that can, this work is highly recommended for its well-researched and interesting insights into the world of young people's literature.—**Carol Truett**

931. **Who's Who of Australian Children's Writers.** 2d ed. Port Melbourne, Australia, D. W. Thorpe/Reed Reference Australia; distr., New Providence, N.J., Reed Reference Publishing, 1996. 205p. $35.00pa. ISBN 1-875589-77-5.

This biographical dictionary of living Australian children's authors is based on a national database created by sending questionnaires to published authors. Those writers who have written at least one work for children were selected from the larger database. This 2d edition makes corrections on the 1st and adds new names, but there is no change in format.

The information contained in the entries is factual and basic. Each entry gives the author's birth date, pseudonyms, education, employment history, books, types of writing, re-creations, memberships, awards, availability for appearances or work, and well-known relatives. Publications in which the author's articles appear are given, but no specific bibliographic details are included.

Space considerations, say the editors, have obliged them to abbreviate almost every entry except titles. This book would not be suitable for children or their parents who wanted to know a little about the author because of the time required to check these excessive abbreviations. For librarians or serious researchers inquiring about Australian children's authors, the information is detailed and useful. Purchase is recommended only for academic libraries, or libraries that have a special children's literature research collection. For other libraries, the Something About the Author series (see entries 926-930) is much more detailed and readable, and a number of Australian children's authors are described.—**Joann H. Lee**

Handbooks and Yearbooks

932. **Children's Books: Awards & Prizes.** 1996 ed. Compiled and edited by the Children's Book Council. New York, Children's Book Council, 1996. 497p. index. $75.00. ISBN 0-933633-03-3. ISSN 0069-3472.

This tool has become a standard reference work for the compilation of regional, national, and international awards for children and young adult literature since its 1st edition in 1969 (see ARBA 70, v. 2, p. 68). The new 10th edition follows the format of the previous edition, published in 1992 (see ARBA 94, entry 1191). The work is divided into four main sections: "United States Awards Selected by Adults"; "United States Awards Selected by Young Readers"; "Australian, Canadian, New Zealand, and United Kingdom Awards"; and "Selected International and Multinational Awards," with a total of 213 awards and prizes. Each section is arranged alphabetically by the name of the award. Descriptions and criteria for each award precede the list. Most helpful new awards included in this edition are for nonfiction, poetry, folklore, fantasy, and the gay and lesbian experience. A fifth section lists the publications and organizations that evaluate books for young readers. A helpful addition would have been telephone numbers, e-mail addresses, or Websites for the various publications (only an address is listed).

While access to these awards may be found in a number of sources, this handy one-volume guide provides quick and easy reference. The table of contents gives an alphabetic listing of all awards in the volume, and both a title and a person index are included. The cost of $75 may seem prohibitive, but when amortized over the years between editions, the usefulness of the publication outweighs the cost. All except the very smallest libraries dealing with children's literature would benefit from purchasing this reference tool.
—**Lynda Welborn**

Children's Literature

Bibliography

933. Lind, Beth Beutler. **Multicultural Children's Literature: An Annotated Bibliography, Grades K-8.** Jefferson, N.C., McFarland, 1996. 270p. index. $34.50. ISBN 0-7864-0038-2.

More than 1,100 fiction and nonfiction works published in the last 15 years are featured in this work compiled by a Wisconsin middle school teacher. Annotations are evaluative and cover plot and character synopses, with emphasis on K-8 titles about African Americans, Asian Americans, Hispanic (not Latino) Americans, and Native Americans. Works include novels, realistic fiction, biographies, historical fiction, folktales, myths, legends, and short stories. Within each ethnic group, arrangement is by level (grades K-3, or grades 4-8), then alphabetic by author. Rounding out the work are lists of children's literature publishers, curricular resources for teachers, reading and research sources, and an integrated author/title index.

Unfortunately, there is no quick way into the work to find books on specific groups within the larger populations, such as Filipino Americans, Cherokee people, or Puerto Ricans. Also, unlike an earlier McFarland publication, *Developing Multicultural Awareness Through Children's Literature* (1993), there are no suggestions for integrating the literature into language activity units or writing assignments. Yes, guides such as this one do assist teachers in the identification of literature that can help students to gain cultural pride in their own heritage, modify beliefs/stereotypes about others, and transmit positive role models about various cultures. [R: RBB, 15 Nov 96, p. 612]—**Ilene F. Rockman**

Biography

934. **British Children's Writers, 1800-1880.** Meena Khorana, ed. Detroit, Gale, 1996. 428p. illus. index. (Dictionary of Literary Biography, v.163). $135.00. ISBN 0-8103-9358-1.

Hooray, hooray! Children's writers are making it into standard reference works, and one no longer has to rely on the Something About the Author series (see entries 926-930) or *The Oxford Companion to Children's Literature* (see ARBA 85, entry 1034) for biographical information on authors across the water. Gale is to be commended for adding this contribution to its series of the Dictionary of Literary Biography (DLB). The focus is on the "golden age" of children's literature, which flowered in the nineteenth century.

Khorana, editor of this volume and well known in the field of children's literature, has done a masterly job of putting together crucial information on these nineteenth-century writers of books for children. Khorana posits that the theories of education, coupled with the theories of raising children, were in part responsible for this incredible outpouring of talent. Some 41 writers are included, with essays following the biographical information on the authors that are authoritative, well written, and provide thoughtful insights into the reasons for the extraordinary works that were written between 1800 and 1880 for children. Superb facsimiles of photographs or tintypes and other types of prints are also included in this 428-page volume, providing realistic images from the time period.

British Children's Writers, 1800-1880 is an excellent addition to the ever-growing body of reference material that is becoming available for serious scholars of children's literature. This volume of the DLB gives information and resources for teaching courses in the field and is an excellent source. [R: Choice, Dec 96, p. 586]—**Anne F. Roberts**

935. **British Children's Writers, 1914-1960.** Donald R. Hettinga and Gary D. Schmidt, eds. Detroit, Gale, 1996. 422p. illus. index. (Dictionary of Literary Biography, v.160). $128.00. ISBN 0-8103-9355-7.

British Children's Writers, 1914-1960 follows the general format of the Dictionary of Literary Biography (DLB) series: lengthy critical articles on particular authors with a bibliography of the author's works and a list of further reading. What makes this particular volume of interest beyond the series is the choice of genre, one that has received less critical attention than have others. All of the approximately 40 authors profiled were popular and influential during their time. Most have retained that popularity, either with their primary market of children (A. A. Milne, P. L. Travers, Mary Norton) or with the secondhand and rare book collector market (Elfrida Vipont, many of the school story series).

As is usual with the DLB series, the essays are thoughtful and well researched, discussing the author's development and the changing critical reception of the works. Most essays make the point that even the most formulaic of these authors, those who wrote books in series or books with repetitive plots and reappearing characters, provided a world of stability for children growing up in a time of turmoil—a time of two world wars, economic insecurity, and deep and disorienting societal changes.

Bibliographies for further reading are uneven in length, but this is no doubt a reflection of how much is available on a given author. The bibliography on J. R. R. Tolkien, for example, is extensive, while only a few items are mentioned for the lesser-known Alison Uttley. Two appended essays treat two particular subgenres: the school series and the pony story, that specifically British story of a country world of riding clubs, horse shows, and children's contests. Libraries with a clientele interested in children's literature will want this volume, even if they are not subscribers to the DLB series. [R: Choice, June 96, p. 1608]
—**Terry Ann Mood**

936. **British Children's Writers Since 1960. First Series.** Caroline C. Hunt, ed. Detroit, Gale, 1996. 394p. illus. index. (Dictionary of Literary Biography, v.161). $128.00. ISBN 0-8103-9356-5.

Thirty children's authors are profiled in *British Children's Writers Since 1960*, an addition to the Dictionary of Literary Biography (DLB) series. Most of the authors included were born well before World War II but produced the bulk of their work during the 1960s, 1970s, and 1980s. The format is similar to other works in the series: Each profile begins with a list of the author's works, followed by a biographical/critical essay, and ending with a list for further reading. Most of the essays give fairly complete descriptions and plot summaries of many of the author's works. The articles are heavily illustrated, not only with a portrait of the author, but with pictures of title pages and dust jackets of the authors' books, pictures of the authors' homes, or photographs of the settings used in the stories. In this way, this particular volume of the DLB continues its tradition of setting an author in a world context.

An introductory essay discusses the development of children's literature in general during the time period covered. For the most part, the authors profiled in this volume follow predictable patterns from the past: They wrote books in series, including an immensely popular series with two generic characters, Peter and Jane; family stories; animal stories; updated versions of the school story; and fantasy stories. The immense social changes of the 1960s wrought a great change in publishing for children. Later in their careers, these authors continued with the same patterns, but in an updated form. Historical fiction became more realistic; family stories incorporated different configurations of family; the problem novel became more popular. *British Children's Writers Since 1960* is a valuable addition to the bibliography of children's literature. [R: Choice, July/Aug 96, p. 1768]—**Terry Ann Mood**

937. **Seventh Book of Junior Authors & Illustrators.** Sally Holmes Holtze, ed. Bronx, N.Y., H. W. Wilson, 1996. 371p. illus. index. $50.00. ISBN 0-8242-0873-0.

Some 235 entries for authors and illustrators of children's and young adult books each give the name, the birth date, a brief autobiographical or biographical sketch, a list of selected works, and often a photograph and reproduction of the person's signature. An initial list of about 1,000 candidates was compiled based on the recommendations of reviewers and critics. Winners of awards and honors voted on by professionals in the area of children's and young adult literature were included as well. In addition, popularity of the author or illustrator was considered. An advisory committee of seven "prominent professionals" in the area of youth literature voted on the initial list and made additional selections, which resulted in the names included in this volume. A cumulative index contains all names and pen names for people in any of the seven volumes of this series.

In general, this is a broad, balanced collection of biographical sketches that continues the work of the *Sixth Book of Junior Authors & Illustrators*, published in 1989 (see ARBA 90, entry 30). It treats both people who have established their careers and those just getting started during the intervening years. More importantly, each sketch tends to have only a few references to sources of additional information about these people. The Contemporary Authors (see ARBA 96, entry 1150) and Something About the Author series (see entries 926-930) are the most frequently cited sources; however, some entries are more limited. For example, an article in *People Weekly* is the only reference given for Reeve Lindbergh. This is one indication that the editors have succeeded in identifying authors and illustrators who are not already included in other sources.

Two editorial concerns are not explained adequately in the book. First, there is a discrepancy of 100 names between the number chosen by the advisory committee (135) and the total number of entries (235) included in the book. This discrepancy may be a typographic error, or it may be a real difference; it is not explained in the preface. Second, the preface states that the author or illustrator wrote a brief autobiographical entry whenever possible. In some cases where entries have been made posthumously, it is evident why the entry is biographical instead. For other entries, readers can only wonder.

Overall, this volume is a competent addition to the series of *Junior Authors & Illustrators* titles, and it will be useful to all library collections having the previous volumes. Moreover, it provides information that will be helpful in academic and public libraries and in school library media centers.—**Carol A. Doll**

Dictionaries and Encyclopedias

938. Helbig, Alethea K., and Agnes Regan Perkins. **Dictionary of American Children's Fiction, 1990-1994: Books of Recognized Merit.** Westport, Conn., Greenwood Press, 1996. 473p. index. $79.50. ISBN 0-313-28763-5.

Librarians, teachers, and children's literature specialists will find this companion volume to the two-volume set *The Dictionary of American Children's Fiction 1859-1984* (see ARBA 87, entries 1094-1095) and the one-volume work *The Dictionary of American Children's Fiction 1985-1989* (see

ARBA 94, entry 1171) a useful addition for collection development, bibliography preparation, and book talk options. The authors' selection criteria include all children's books that evaluators have given awards to or have placed on literary citation lists.

Integrated entries consist of author, title, character, and miscellaneous, respectively. The title entry classifies the plot according to subgenre, provides significant episodes, and briefly discusses important themes. A few sentences are dedicated to a literary critical evaluation; references to sequels, if any; and the book's awards and citations on various literary lists. Author entries provide birth and death dates, educational background, pertinent facts that apply to an author's literary career, titles of significant publications, and the author's main contribution to the genre. Character entries furnish the physical and personal qualities for critical, memorable, or unusual characters who are not sufficiently mentioned in the title entry plot summaries. Miscellaneous entries include information about specific settings and episodes that require further treatment than that supplied in the title entry.

The authors have generated 567 entries for 189 award-winning or citation-listed books. Selection based upon these criteria ensures that all fictional genres, such as contemporary problem novels, historical fiction, fantasy, humor, mystery, science fiction, and thrillers, are evenly represented. There is also a variety in literary presentation and style. Some works cited are, for example, epistolary in format or consist primarily of documents, newspaper reports, and memorandums. Others employ slang, stream of consciousness, flashbacks, and other compositional techniques for literary effect. More than half of the 189 listed works have female protagonists and nearly half use first person narrators.

Although the contents include a key to awards and citations, a list of books by awards, and an index, separate alphabetized indexes of authors and titles would have further complemented this valuable work. School, large public, and academic libraries should consider this book a recommended purchase.—Kathleen W. Craver

Handbooks and Yearbooks

939. **Children's Books and Their Creators.** Anita Silvey, ed. New York, Houghton Mifflin, 1995. 800p. illus. index. $40.00. ISBN 0-395-65380-0.

The editor, with the help of several hundred contributors, has compiled an encyclopedic overview of authors and illustrators (creators) working in the field of children's and young adult literature in the United States over the past hundred years. Silvey's compilation is devoted almost entirely to creators working in the twentieth century, but it also includes some creators from the nineteenth century, due to their continued relevance and popularity in this century (e.g., Mark Twain and Louisa May Alcott). The stated intent for the collection is fourfold. First of all, it is to present the creators working in the twentieth century. Second is to treat the subjects broadly by offering biographical information on the creators; evaluations of the entries; and historical information about the trends, themes, and genres being used at the time. Next, the reference is to be entertaining in its presentation, offering some of the creativity and spontaneity that are evident throughout children's literature. Finally, it is to present a different perspective by featuring various creators speaking for themselves.

Silvey has more than accomplished her desired goal by presenting information that is not only accurate when compared to the Something About the Author series (see entries 926-930) but also with the added perspective of comments supplied by the creator. Although there are only 75 such interviews, interspersed throughout the text and encased in a black border for easy identification, they offer a new dimension to the text beyond the usual biographical and critical evaluations. There are also mostly black-and-white illustrations throughout the book (with 15 pages of color plates), reprinted from the books being discussed, which further add to the understanding of children's literature.

This wide-ranging, although purposely not comprehensive, presentation of children's literature creators during the past century is an excellent addition to any size public or school library. The text, consisting of 800 pages, gives interesting and accurate information, presented in an entertaining fashion. It will be useful for teachers, librarians, parents, and students either studying children's literature or looking for information on a favorite author. [R: BR, Mar/April 96, p. 47]—**Bridget Volz**

Indexes

940. Karp, Rashelle, June H. Schlessinger, and Bernard S. Schlessinger. **Plays for Children and Young Adults: An Evaluative Index and Guide. Supplement 1, 1989-1994.** New York, Garland, 1996. 369p. index. $65.00. ISBN 0-8153-1493-0.

This supplement to *Plays for Children and Young Adults* (see ARBA 92, entry 1129) continues the excellent presentation of the earlier volume. The index lists 2,158 plays in anthologies and separately published plays, including those in *Play* magazine. Evaluative reviews of appropriate plays included in the journal *Play Index* form the core of this work.

Entries are alphabetic by title, and each entry includes grade level and if the play can be produced by students at that grade level; authors; the full title; cast analysis; playing time; a description of settings; the number of acts; the plot summary; an evaluation (which includes controversial aspects and potential difficulties in production); royalty notes; a bibliographic citation for the play's sources; a subject list of main themes; the type of play; and the source if it is an adaptation. There are 7 indexes to the body of the text: The main one is the title index, followed by author, cast, grade level, subject/type, playing time, and publishers indexes. (The last index is a new one added in this supplement.)

This source should be useful in school and public libraries. It would be worth the rather steep price where dramatics is an important element in schools or an active interest of the public. [R: VOYA, Dec 96, p. 300]—**Joann H. Lee**

Young Adult Literature

941. Drew, Bernard A. **The 100 Most Popular Young Adult Authors: Biographical Sketches and Bibliographies.** Englewood, Colo., Libraries Unlimited, 1996. 547p. $55.00. ISBN 1-56308-319-1.

Drew's compilation of *Young Adult Authors* will be helpful for librarians and educators who work with teens. One suspects, however, that it will not be used for its stated primary purpose, aiding teens in research. The profiled authors, most of whom are writing in the 1990s, write for the 12- to 18-year-old crowd. There are a few that appeal to both younger and older readers—authors such as Ann Martin and Betsy Byars for the younger, and V. C. Andrews and Stephen King for the older. The authors are varied in ethnic, geographic, and thematic concerns.

Each entry includes a brief biography of the author, critical commentary, and comments from the writer about the writing process. The bibliographies list all young adult fiction with a short plot encapsulation. This is especially useful for the librarian looking for a book about a particular subject. There is also a list (without a plot summary) of all other written works by the author and a suggested further reading list.

Although the layout and typesetting of the book make it appealing visually, and the table of contents is thus easy to plow through, additional indexes would be useful, especially for thematic, geographic, and ethnic categories. The editor's comment that the new "trend" in young adult writing is toward horror-suspense, as opposed to the family and social dramas of the 1970s, would become apparent with a thematic index. *Young Adult Authors* should make its way onto every librarian's and every high school teacher's bookshelf. [R: BR, Nov/Dec 96, pp. 51-52; RBB, 1 Oct 96, pp. 371-72; SLMQ, Fall 96, p. 63]

—**Barbara J. O'Hara**

942. **Writers of Multicultural Fiction for Young Adults: A Bio-Critical Sourcebook.** M. Daphne Kutzer, ed. Westport, Conn., Greenwood Press, 1996. 487p. index. $75.00. ISBN 0-313-29331-7.

Here is a reference book that all librarians and teachers of children's literature will embrace; 51 authors, many relatively unknown and many who write about ethnic groups not their own, are given prominence in this most solid and sane reference work. The editor is to be highly commended for both her selection of authors and her choice of good writers to profile the authors. Labeled as a "bio-critical sourcebook," *Writers of Multicultural Fiction for Young Adults* contains many of today's multicultural authors—Gary Soto, Laurence Yep, Walter Dean Myers, Nicholasa Mohr, Julius Lester, Alice Childress,

Rosa Guy, Jamake Highwater, and James Berry—but it also includes lesser-known contemporary authors, such as Andrew Salkey and Cynthia Kadohata, and several "forgotten" older writers, such as Florence Crannell Means, Ann Nolan Clark, Laura Adams Armer, and Evelyn Sibley Lampman.

Each entry presents a brief biographical sketch, followed by a section on major works and themes, one on critical reception, and a complete bibliographic listing of the writer's works and some selected secondary sources on the author. Significantly, Kutzer includes authors who write about ethnic groups that are not from that ethnic group; she stresses that she wants to "ensure a historical context for the issues raised by multiculturalism, and the sections on the critical reception of each author addresses [sic] such important issues as the authority and authenticity of the writer to comment on a different culture." Kutzer also defines "young adult" as those people ages 12 or above, although occasionally they may be as young as 10. Kutzer maintains that "multicultural literature *is* American literature, not merely a category." This is an excellent addition to the field. [R: BR, Sept/Oct 96, p. 57; Choice, July/Aug 96, p. 1780]—**Anne F. Roberts**

DRAMA

943. Beach, Cecilia, comp. **French Women Playwrights of the Twentieth Century: A Checklist.** Westport, Conn., Greenwood Press, 1996. 515p. index. (Bibliographies and Indexes in Women's Studies, no.24). $79.50. ISBN 0-313-29175-6.

This checklist extends the work of Beach's preceding volume, *French Women Playwrights Before the Twentieth Century*, published by Greenwood Press in 1994 (see ARBA 95, entry 1405). Its scope is limited to plays written by French women and published or performed in France between 1900 and 1990. Excluded are plays written by women in other francophone countries; translations or adaptations; and puppet theater, music hall, and cabaret works. Very few other restrictions apply, so that playwrights are included regardless of their critical reception or their relative fame or obscurity.

Each entry indicates the location of at least one copy of the play, in either published or manuscript form, at a Parisian library or archive. Entries are brief, arranged by playwright's name or pseudonym, with variant names and a list of plays with places and dates of publication and first performance. Biographical information is unevenly provided, consisting of a few words indicating an author's origin, affiliations, other occupations, or other genres.

A selected bibliography cites general works on French theater/French women writers, catalogs of collections, bibliographies, and periodicals. A play title index is included. One desirable but missing feature is an index of the many varying names—maiden names, married names, patronyms, titles, and pseudonyms—that complicate the researcher's task. Users may wish for more critical and biographical information about the lesser-known playwrights here, but the compiler has succeeded admirably in her stated goal of creating a comprehensive list of twentieth-century plays written by French women. [R: Choice, Nov 96, p. 425]—**Emily L. Werrell**

FICTION

General Works

944. Albert, Richard N., comp. **An Annotated Bibliography of Jazz Fiction and Jazz Fiction Criticism.** Westport, Conn., Greenwood Press, 1996. 114p. index. (Bibliographies and Indexes in World Literature, no.52). $55.00. ISBN 0-313-28998-0.

Albert, associate professor emeritus of English at Illinois State University, who has previously written extensively on the relationship between jazz and fiction, edited *From Blues to Bop*, published in 1990. In the work under review, he examines at greater length the strong impact jazz (including the blues—related, but different in nature, origins, and treatment) has had on contemporary fiction. His work lists more than 400 novels and short stories, either thematically built around jazz and jazz musicians, or dealing with the lives of jazz practitioners.

Some extremely famous writers have written at least one piece of jazz fiction. Consider this list of novels that all deal—at least in part—with jazz themes: *Steppenwolf* by Hermann Hesse; *On the Road* by Jack Kerouac; *Jazz* by Toni Morrison; *Young Man with a Horn* by Dorothy Baker; *Jazz Country* by Nat Hentoff; and *Wynner* by Mel Tormé. Is that an all-star lineup or what? The chapter on jazz themes in short stories includes fiction by such literary luminaries as Maya Angelou, James Baldwin, Julio Cortázar, Peter DeVries, Shelby Foote, LeRoi Jones, John O'Hara, J. D. Salinger, William Saroyan, and Eudora Welty.

This book may be used as a guide to research in the general area of jazz music and jazz-related literature or may be read for interest by any jazz aficionado. For librarians, it may serve an additional purpose as a recommendation list for jazz devotees looking for something to read with a jazz or blues motif. Arrangement is by genre, with separate chapters devoted to anthologies of shorter fiction, novels, drama, individual short stories, and selected criticism. There is one index of novels, plays, and short stories and a general index of everything else.

Each entry is furnished with standard bibliographic information, a short abstract of the work's contents, and, in many cases, Albert's trenchant commentary. All in all, this book makes a useful addition to collections of literature about American music, although the price may scare away smaller libraries.—**Bruce A. Shuman**

945. **Fiction Catalog.** 13th ed. Juliette Yaakov and John Greenfieldt, eds. Bronx, N.Y., H. W. Wilson, 1996. 973p. index. (Standard Catalog Series). $115.00. ISBN 0-8242-0894-3.

This standard bibliography of adult fiction continues, in this latest edition, to provide guidance to both classic and popular novels and short stories. As with the 12th edition (see ARBA 92, entry 1137), this edition includes older writers, such as Edgar Allan Poe, as well as contemporary writers, such as David Plante. Genres include serious literary fiction by such authors as John Updike and Joyce Carol Oates, as well as lighter fiction by writers like Ralph McInerny and Carol Higgins Clark. Some foreign fiction translated into English is featured. This edition indexes 5,461 titles (302 more titles than the 12th edition) as well as 1,820 analytic entries for novelettes and composite works. Purchasers of this edition will receive annual supplements for the years 1996-1999.

Most of the books listed are in-print hardcover editions published in the United States, although some out-of-print titles are also itemized. The first and largest of the three parts of the catalog lists works alphabetically by author. After the bibliographic citation, entries give descriptive summaries for novels, contents notes for short story collections, and, usually, an evaluative comment excerpted from a review. The second part, the subject and title index, continues to make this catalog a useful bibliographic guide, especially for public libraries. A generous number of both broad and narrow subject headings makes this a standard reader's advisory tool. Headings are as broad as "Philosophical Novels" and "Love Stories," or as narrow as "Persian Gulf War, 1991," and "Air Mail Service."

Titles were selected with the assistance of librarians from public libraries in different geographic areas and therefore reflect a broad consensus about the perceived reading interests of the general public. Although academic libraries have many more specialized and scholarly sources providing bibliographic guidance to fiction, this catalog is somewhat useful for an undergraduate audience.—**David Isaacson**

946. Jacob, Merle, and Hope Apple. **To Be Continued: An Annotated Guide to Sequels.** Phoenix, Ariz., Oryx Press, 1995. 364p. index. $43.50. ISBN 0-89774-842-5.

Oryx Press has thrown a counterpunch against Janet and Jonathan Husband's well-received *Sequels* (see ARBA 92, entry 1138). An outgrowth of the readers' advisory file of an Illinois public library, *To Be Continued* is an annotated list of 1,257 series by approximately 1,000 novelists and short story writers. Titles accessible at most U.S. public libraries predominate; science, fantasy, and historical fiction are particularly well represented. This work's coverage of family sagas and Westerns is markedly better than the rival *Sequels*. Sequences composed by various hands are excluded, except in instances of genuine collaboration on a volume. But for a few token classic offerings, juvenile series are excluded.

Main entries are arranged alphabetically by author, with pseudonyms appearing both here and in cross-referenced entries. Bibliographic information supplied for each series includes its respective volumes' titles, publishers, and publication dates. In many cases, a series title is also provided. Works appear to be listed in preferred reading order, regardless of publication date. The annotations are tightly constructed plot synopses; only each series' most significant characters are discussed therein. Genre and subject descriptors, consistent with those in the indexes, complete each entry.

In contrast to *Sequels*, Jacob and Apple have omitted mystery fiction series. Although "espionage" and "technothriller" series are found in *To Be Continued*, Ian Fleming's James Bond novels are curiously absent. This reference work's several indexes are more exhaustive than those in *Sequels*, but some oversights are evident. No cross-referencing appears between the genre index's headings "Adventure" and "Naval Adventure," nor between "Romance" and "Historical Romance." Also, "War" is presented as a genre category, rather than as a subject category.

Although the authors profess to have incorporated fiction united by region, there are no entries for the Wessex works of Thomas Hardy, John O'Hara's Gibbsville stories, or Charlotte Brontë's two novels set in Brussels, (*Villette* and *The Professor*). Lacking as well are sequences containing recurring characters, such as Eric Hodgins's *Blandings* dyad; Robert Louis Stevenson's *Kidnapped* and *David Balfour*; and Madeleine L'Engle's *The Small Rain* and *A Severed Wasp*. Despite these shortcomings, libraries lacking the most recent edition of *Sequels* would do well to invest in this affordable alternative.—**Jeffrey E. Long**

Crime and Mystery

947. Heising, Willetta L. **Detecting Women 2: A Reader's Guide and Checklist for Mystery Series Written by Women.** 1996-97 ed. Dearborn, Mich., Purple Moon, 1996. 384p. index. $24.95pa. ISBN 0-9644593-1-0.

Past, present, and future, women mystery writers are a force in the genre. More than 500 are profiled in this unique publication. A continuation of the author's *Detecting Women* (1994), this volume contains more than 600 series reflecting some 3,400 titles. The strength of this reference is its excellent organization and presentation. The numerous lists provide access to the writers and series in various categories. The "Master List" is the basis for the remainder of the book—here are the brief author profiles, featured sleuths, and series books. Following are lists of series characters, mystery types, settings, pseudonyms, short stories, resources, awards, and more.

The author has attempted to make this volume as comprehensive, useful, and easy to use as possible with helpful explanations, a glossary of terms, an alphabetic list of writers, and a thorough master index. A large amount of material has been gathered and presented in an effective format. Fun reading and chock-full of information, this reference will appeal to everyone researching women's crime fiction, discovering new authors, or reacquainting oneself with old friends. The price is right, the scene is set—a must for mystery collections or where there is demand.—**Joy Hastings**

Science Fiction, Fantasy, and Horror

948. **Magill's Guide to Science Fiction and Fantasy Literature.** T. A. Shippey and A. J. Sobczak, eds. Pasadena, Calif., Salem Press, 1996. 4v. index. (A Magill Book). $300.00/set. ISBN 0-89356-906-2.

Containing plot summaries and story analyses for some 791 fantasy and science fiction books, 238 of which were published during the 1980s and 1990s, the contents of the 4 volumes of the *Magill's Guide to Science Fiction and Fantasy Literature* overlap only slightly with Magill's *Survey of Science Fiction Literature* (see ARBA 80, entry 1211) and *Survey of Modern Fantasy Literature* (see ARBA 84, entry 1136). In many respects, the guide is well made. Arranged alphabetically by title or series title, the entries begin with a statement of the work's themes and provide the author's name and dates; a statement as to whether the work is fantasy or science fiction that links the work to one of 37 genre categories; a description of the work's length (short story, novella, novel, series); and its setting, time, and original publication data. The plot summaries will benefit those unwilling or unable to read the work, and the analyses are generally levelheaded and helpful (exceptions exist). The volume concludes with an annotated bibliography of secondary sources; lists of the winners of the major science fiction and fantasy awards; and indexes by genre category, by title, and by author/title.

Because much of the guide is capably done, its problems are more evident. Prefatory matter is occasionally flawed, as in the attribution that states the authors of *Varney the Vampyre* were James Malcolm Rymer *and* Thomas Peckett Prest: A choice should be offered, and Rymer is definitely the preferred author. Worse, the contents are often of dubious value: Why were the trivial *Upsidonia*, the forgettable fantasies of artist Hannes Bok, the unimportant novelizations of *Star Trek* and *Star Wars*, and a number of nonfantastic works accorded entries, when significant fantastic work by authors as diverse as Ramsey Campbell, Orson Scott Card, Walter de la Mare, Harlan Ellison, Michael Ende, Mark Helprin, Arthur Machen, and George R. R. Martin—to name but a few—has been neglected? Worst of all are omissions of data and significant factual errors: The entry for William Beckford's *Vathek* fails to mention *The Episodes of Vathek*, the entry for H. Rider Haggard's *She* and *Ayesha* docs not discuss either of Haggard's two prequels, and Julian West of Edward Bellamy's *Looking Backward, 2000-1887* does not "eventually [awake] in his bed, back in the nineteenth century"; he remains a resident of the twenty-first century.

The guide would have benefited substantially from stronger editing and a greater historical perspective. Despite its shortcomings, it belongs in academic and public libraries in which there is a significant interest in the literature of fantasy and science fiction.—**Richard Bleiler**

949. Pringle, David. **The Ultimate Guide to Science Fiction: An A-Z of Science-Fiction Books by Title.** 2d ed. Brookfield, Vt., Scolar Press/Ashgate Publishing, 1995. 481p. index. $59.50. ISBN 1-85928-071-4.

This attractively designed and formatted guide continues the coverage of the 1st edition (which listed titles to the end of the 1980s [see ARBA 92, entry 1144]) through 1993 (with a few 1994 titles included). Much of the older material has been revised, and some 40,000 words' worth of new entries have been added. The 3,500 entries are arranged alphabetically by title, with each title followed by the date of publication; a star rating (on a scale of 0 [very bad] to 4 [excellent]); the classification (novel, collection, or anthology); the author's name and nationality; and the body of the entry, usually 2 or 3 sentences of description and evaluation. Frequently, the entry will supply a reviewer's critical comment. Following the entry, there may be information about a television or film "novelization," a revision, or a sequel. Among the categories excluded are works of fantasy (even though the boundaries between science fiction [sf] and fantasy often may be difficult to distinguish), children's fiction, non-English-language sf, and the lesser works of little-known sf writers.

The reader who may forget an author's name but remember a title will find the title arrangement particularly helpful and, through the author index, can find all the author's listed titles. This sturdily bound, comprehensive volume belongs in most public and academic sf collections, if the price is not a deterrent.—**Charles R. Andrews**

950. **St. James Guide to Fantasy Writers.** David Pringle, ed. Detroit, St. James Press, 1996. 711p. index. $95.00. ISBN 1-55862-205-5.

St. James Guide to Fantasy Writers is the first of a planned two-volume set. The second volume will cover horror, ghost, and gothic writers and is scheduled to be published in late 1997. The work under review lists more than 400 fantasy authors who wrote between the late seventeenth century and the present. While the majority of the authors listed wrote in English, a few foreign-language authors are also included, such as Hans Christian Andersen, Anatole France, Charles Perrault, and Jacob and Wilhelm Grimm.

The volume is arranged alphabetically by author with each entry including the nationality of the author, the date and place of birth, a current address, the address of an agent if available, a list of works with the dates of publication, a brief biography, and a signed critical essay about the author. The biographies range from approximately 300 to more than 1,500 words (for well-known authors). Many of the authors listed are known for works generally not considered fantasy, but have been profiled based on one or two works in the genre. The editor points out that "there is no such a thing as 'purity' in the matter of literary genres, least of all in a field as protean as fantasy . . . nevertheless, fantasy as a perceived type of modern fiction, [as] regarded by most readers is quite distinct from horror and science fiction" (editor's note).

The book has some interesting appendixes in addition to the alphabetic list of biographies: a list of works on the genre of fantasy, a nationality index listing each author by nationality, a title index, and notes on advisers and contributors to the volume. While the work is somewhat uneven in its coverage of the various authors, it is generally well written and provides a much-needed source of information on writers in the fantasy genre. The guide is recommended for all academic and larger public libraries. [R: Choice, July/Aug 96, p. 1777; LJ, 15 April 96, pp. 72-74; RBB, 1 May 96, pp. 1538-40]—**Robert L. Wick**

951. **St. James Guide to Science Fiction Writers.** 4th ed. Jay P. Pederson and others, eds. Detroit, St. James Press, 1996. 1175p. index. $135.00. ISBN 1-55862-179-2.

Since its 1st edition (see ARBA 83, entry 1164) through its 3d edition (see ARBA 93, entry 1159), this superlative bio-bibliography (formerly titled *Twentieth-Century Science-Fiction Writers*) has been a staple in most medium- to large-size academic and public libraries with modest science fiction collections. Alphabetically arranged by author, this new edition lists 649 writers of science fiction—from the early nineteenth to the late twentieth centuries—as well as writers of fantasy, horror, and other forms of speculative fiction that have had an impact on the SF field.

Each entry consists of a brief biography, including pseudonyms, nationality, birth and death dates, education, family, career, agent, and address; a complete list of published works; and a signed, critical essay. These essays, varying in length, are helpful and interesting introductions to the writers. For example, one may not remember that Arthur Conan Doyle, Marge Piercy, and Edward D. Hoch—better known for other genres—have also been SF contributors. This heavy, attractively formatted volume also includes H. Bruce Franklin's preface on the history of SF, nationality and title indexes, and a useful six-page reading list.

Larger libraries will most likely want to purchase this 4th edition with its updatings and additions. In spite of its steep price, it nicely complements the various SF handbooks and guides and is a trove of information for even the beginning SF reader.—**Charles R. Andrews**

952. Taves, Brian, and Stephen Michaluk Jr., with others. **The Jules Verne Encyclopedia.** Lanham, Md., Scarecrow, 1996. 257p. illus. index. $54.50. ISBN 0-8108-2961-4.

Despite its title, *The Jules Verne Encyclopedia* is not a single-author encyclopedia in the manner of such works as William B. Hunter's *The Milton Encyclopedia* (see ARBA 79, entry 1250) or A. C. Hamilton's *The Shakespeare Encyclopedia* (University of Toronto Press, 1990). Except incidentally, it neither summarizes Verne's works nor provides lists of Verne's characters and their relationships, and it does not offer explications of Verne's recurrent themes and obsessions. Instead, it consists of nine disparate chapters, two of which contain primary material and consist of, respectively, a "collage" of Verne interviews intended to form an autobiography and the first English translation of *The Humbug*, Verne's mildly satiric account of a trip to the United States. The remaining seven chapters deal with such secondary subjects as "The American Jules Verne Society," "A Day in Amiens," "The Tribulations of a Translator of Jules Verne," "Philatelic Tributes to Jules Verne," and "Hollywood's Jules Verne." The level of this material ranges from adulatory to mildly critical and is of generally dubious value: The autobiographical "collage," for example, seamlessly merges 20 different sources, revealing only in endnotes the sources from which the autobiographical statements were derived.

By far the longest chapter is by Stephen Michaluk Jr., "Jules Verne: A Bibliographic and Collecting Guide." It consists of a chronological list of Verne's monographic works, and beneath each title is a chronological list of every separate English and American edition of that work and (occasionally) commentary. The citations are not given in any standard bibliographic form, however, and are inconsistent in their content; some citations include pagination, some mention the names of illustrators and translators, and some include the month in addition to the year of publication. Furthermore, the diacritical marks used in the original French are nowhere given, and French titles are occasionally misspelled. Michaluk has the latter half of Verne's *Une Ville Flottante Suive des Forceurs des Blocus* as *Suivi de les Forceurs de Blocus*. Thus, although the bibliographic data are substantially lengthier than those to be found in *Jules Verne: A Primary and Secondary Bibliography* (see ARBA 82, entry 1387), they must be used cautiously by bibliographers, even though they may be of some assistance to collectors.

Verne was enormously important as a writer and an influence, and he has been poorly served in English translation. This volume does not document the secondary material surrounding Verne and is not a particularly worthy addition to the canon of Verne studies, but scholars may find something in it to interest them.—**Richard Bleiler**

Short Stories

953. Masterplots II: Short Story Series Supplement. Frank N. Magill, ed. Pasadena, Calif., Salem Press, 1996. 4v. index. $325.00/set. ISBN 0-89356-769-8.

These four volumes pick up where *Masterplots II: Short Story Series* left off a decade ago (see ARBA 88, entry 1141), continuing the pagination (2,765-4,338) and the volume-number sequence (7-10) of the earlier series. This set includes summary and commentary on 511 short stories by 173 authors, ranging from the early nineteenth century to the late twentieth century, arranged in alphabetic order by story title. Together, the two series comprise the broadest critical coverage on the international short story available today, with more than 1.7 million words of text, but not without a price that will place it beyond the reach of many small- and medium-sized public libraries.

Even so, this series reflects favorably on the robustness of short fiction today as reflected in the growing number of short stories being published and their place in the college and university curriculum. These four volumes include "traditional" short story writers, such as Honoré de Balzac, Truman Capote, Joseph Conrad, Ernest Hemingway, James Joyce, Katherine Anne Porter, John Steinbeck, Mark Twain, and Virginia Woolf (just to name a few), that are abundantly complemented by essays on 65 Latino, African American, Asian American, and Native American writers. One-third of the essays deal with writers from outside the United States, continuing the strong international flavor of this series. Each essay, as in the previous volumes, is divided into three sections—the story, themes and meanings, and style and technique—and includes the name and date(s) of the author, type of plot, time of plot, locale, date of first publication, and principal characters in the story.

Internal finding aids, found in volume 10, include a chronological list of all stories; a most helpful keyword list (locating, for example, Arthur Conan Doyle's "The Adventure of the Dancing Men" under "Adventure," "Dance," and "Men"); a geographic index by country; a title index; and an author index. The volume numbers and page numbering appear on the spine of each volume, but not the alphabetic breaks in the short story titles—a minor inconvenience. All in all, this is a rich source on an important literary genre.—**Edwin S. Gleaves**

954. Short Story Criticism: Excerpts from Criticism of the Works of Short Fiction Writers. Volume 18. Drew Kalasky and others, eds. Detroit, Gale, 1995. 573p. illus. index. $95.00. ISBN 0-8103-9282-8.

955. Short Story Criticism: Excerpts from Criticism of the Works of Short Fiction Writers. Volume 19. Drew Kalasky and others, eds. Detroit, Gale, 1995. 543p. illus. index. $95.00. ISBN 0-8103-9283-6.

People like short stories because they are vignettes of their own lives. Whether a humorous story such as that of Walter Mitty, or something far more poignant, such as Hazel Motes, short stories capture the real in people and serve it up as modern civilization loves it best: fast food-like. That is why the continuation of Gale's Short Story Criticism set is so good to see, like an old friend in new threads. Reference librarians will be squealing (quietly, of course) over the new entries. Volume 18 adds Charles Baudelaire, Mikhail Bulgakov, Daphne du Maurier, Hamlin Garland, Henry Lawson, Gordon Lish, Robert von Musil, Gérard de Nerval, and Ruth Suckow. Seeing Musil in such a volume is amusing. His unfinished, billion-word *Man Without Qualities* would seem to disqualify him from anything short. Volume 19 adds such names as Erskine Caldwell, Joel Chandler Harris, D. H. Lawrence, and Cesare Pavese.

To list these names should give readers some idea of the wide—very wide—brush with which Gale is stroking this series. Yet even though the net, to mix metaphors, is wide so that all the fish are caught, the quality is never lacking. The entries are fulsome, detailed, and entertaining. The brief sketches about the authors' works are as enlightening as anything else available, and the snatches of criticism are well wrought. Photographs and sketches adorn the text in enlightening and helpful ways. Sidebars, usually set off in boxes, give users some idea of the writer's craft. It is refreshing to see so excellent a paper work as this. Only the smallest of libraries, and here one thinks of personal libraries alone, can afford to be without this truly remarkable series.—**Mark Y. Herring**

956. **Short Story Criticism: Excerpts from Criticism of the Works of Short Fiction Writers. Volume 20.** Drew Kalasky and others, eds. Detroit, Gale, 1995. 521p. illus. index. $95.00. ISBN 0-8103-9284-4.

957. **Short Story Criticism: Excerpts from Criticism of the Works of Short Fiction Writers. Volume 21.** Drew Kalasky and others, eds. Detroit, Gale, 1996. 526p. illus. index. $95.00. ISBN 0-7876-0753-3.

From its 1st volume in 1988 (listing 11 American and 2 British authors—among them John Cheever, William Faulkner, Ernest Hemingway, and G. K. Chesterton—this handsomely designed series has brought together selective, critical analysis of the short fiction of 218 authors (thus far) from all eras and nationalities. Eight to ten authors are usually included in each volume, and each entry presents a historical survey of the critical response to the author's work.

Each author entry consists of the author heading, listing the name under which the author usually wrote and the birth/death dates; a biographical and critical introduction to the author and the critical debates surrounding his or her work; a portrait of the author and, occasionally, other illustrative material; a list of principal works arranged by date of first publication (short story collections, novellas, and novella collections followed by the author's other major works); criticism, consisting of excerpted, chronologically arranged essays with full bibliographic citations; and a further reading list of additional materials about the author. The critical essays—prefaced with editorial comment relating to the author or the content of the essay—are, of course, the heart of the entries and provide the reader with excellent evaluations of the selected stories.

Authors profiled in volume 20 are Théophile Gautier, Alfred Jarry, Jules Laforgue, Lu Hsün, Arthur Machen, Kenzaburō Ōe, Hubert Selby Jr., Audrey Thomas, and Robert Walser. Volume 21 includes A. E. Coppard, Jean Rhys, William Sansom, William Saroyan, Jun-ichirō Tanizaki, William Trevor, Giovanni Verga, and Angus Wilson. Each volume concludes with three useful cumulative indexes by author, nationality, and title. For academic and larger public libraries not owning these and previous volumes of *Short Story Criticism*, they are a wise investment that should pay handsome dividends.

—Charles R. Andrews

NATIONAL LITERATURE

American Literature

General Works

Bibliography

958. Beam, Joan, and Barbara Branstad. **The Native American in Long Fiction: An Annotated Bibliography.** Lanham, Md., Scarecrow, 1996. 359p. index. (Native American Bibliography Series, no.18). $56.00. ISBN 0-8108-3016-7.

This recent addition to the Native American Bibliography Series by two Colorado State University librarians will be a helpful tool for academic, school, and public libraries with an interest in pointing readers toward novel-length fiction by and about Native Americans written in the past 100 years or in building such library collections. Here they will find such popular writers as Louise Erdrich, N. Scott Momaday, Terry C. Johnston, and Tony Hillerman, along with many others. In their helpful and informative introduction, the authors speak of their work as one that helps to provide a comprehensive bibliography of fictional works that have as their central themes Native American history, culture, realistic fictional characters, historical figures, and contemporary problems.

Each of the approximately 400 novels is alphabetically arranged by author and identifies the period covered (e.g., pre-1500, 1860-1896, contemporary) the tribe involved, and the locale(s) where the action occurs. Following this information is an annotation, usually half a page in length, that summarizes the story and adds critical commentary where necessary. If the author is a Native American, his/her tribe is noted. For many annotations, one or more review sources are cited. The work concludes with six indexes—title, dates (of the action), tribe, historical persons, historical events, literary genre—and two appendixes: novels not included (e.g., outside the geographic scope, written for juveniles or children, not written from a Native American perspective, poorly written, copies not available for examination) and selected book and periodical sources for Native American fiction. Reasonably priced, this bibliography is attractively formatted, well bound, and is an excellent choice for most collections.—**Charles R. Andrews**

959. **A Bibliographical Guide to the Study of Western American Literature.** 2d ed. Richard W. Etulain and N. Jill Howard, eds. Albuquerque, N.Mex., University of New Mexico Press, 1995. 471p. index. $39.95. ISBN 0-8263-1644-1.

The 2d edition of *A Bibliographical Guide to the Study of Western American Literature* brings this landmark 1982 bibliography (see ARBA 83, entry 1166) up-to-date by adding to it "the most important essays and books in the field published from 1981 through 1994." Most of what was in the 1st edition is retained in the 2d, although master's theses, shorter works, and some older monographs have been eliminated. The majority of the 2d edition is composed of bibliographies of critical works devoted to the study of individual authors. More than 500 authors are represented, ranging from James Fenimore Cooper, the founding father of western American fiction, to such relative newcomers as Joan Didion and James Welch.

Other sections of the work provide bibliographies of sources devoted to general topics such as "Western Film," "The Environment and Western Literature," and "Canadian Western Literature." Both the author bibliographies and topical bibliographies are valuable to scholars because they include a number of citations that cannot be found in standard literary reference works, including the *MLA International Bibliography* (see ARBA 93, entry 1107). This bibliographic guide is recommended for all academic libraries supporting programs in American literature.—**Donald A. Barclay**

960. **The Literary Index to American Magazines, 1850-1900.** Daniel A. Wells, comp. Westport, Conn., Greenwood Press, 1996. 441p. (Bibliographies and Indexes in American Literature, no.22). $85.00. ISBN 0-313-29840-8.

The Literary Index to American Magazines is a narrow but exhaustive work that indexes references to major and minor writers in specific U.S. literary magazines. Eleven magazines are indexed in this work: *The Atlantic Monthly*, *Scribner's Monthly/The Century Illustrated*, *The Critic*, *The Galaxy*, *Harper's Monthly*, *Lippincott's Magazine*, *The Literary World*, *The North American Review*, *The Overland Monthly*, *Scribner's Magazine*, and *The Southern Review*. Many magazines and newspapers are obviously not included, but it is hard to fault the compiler for this because he does incredibly detailed and labor-intensive indexing. Wells does not just reproduce the contents of the magazines' original indexes; he has actually gone through every page of every issue of the 11 titles from 1850-1900 and notes every reference to hundreds of writers. Furthermore, all sections of the magazines, including letters, reviews, gossip columns, and so forth, are included.

If the laboriousness of such indexing has limited the number of magazines covered, it has not limited the number of included authors; 700 authors are indexed. Coverage is not limited to contemporary writers of the United States; authors from Geoffrey Chaucer onward can be found. When authors are missing, one suspects that the fault is with the original magazines' coverage and not with the indexing. The index is alphabetically organized by author name. References are also listed by subject, but such coverage is spotty. For example, there is no subject heading for slavery, an important issue that authors of the time would surely have discussed.

The Literary Index to American Magazines covers only a small specific subject, but it does so superlatively well. Any library that could use a detailed literary index to major U.S. magazines of the period will not find a better book on the subject than this one. [R: RBB, 15 Nov 96, p. 612]—**Ken Feser**

Biography

961. **American Writers: A Collection of Literary Biographies. Supplement IV.** A. Walton Litz and Molly Weigel, eds. New York, Scribner's/Simon & Schuster Macmillan, 1996. 2v. index. $199.00/set. ISBN 0-684-19785-5.

The *American Writers* set has spanned two decades. First published in 1974 in 4 volumes (see ARBA 75, entry 1350), the set has had 3 previous supplements (see ARBA 80, entry 1241; ARBA 82, entry 1322; and ARBA 92, entry 1151). It now encompasses 219 signed essays from the seventeenth century through the twentieth century. There are 35 new essays in this 2-volume supplement that reflect the diversity of

American writers and their genres; new profiles include Maya Angelou, Leslie Marmon Silko, Simon Ortiz, Robert Bly, Raymond Chandler, Lorraine Hansberry, Susan Howe (in the first detailed analysis of her life and work), Ayn Rand, and Neil Simon.

The essays found here combine criticism with biography (albeit mostly literary biography, as the subtitle suggests) and strive to comprehensively cover the life and work of each author. The articles are interesting, well written, and thorough, covering important aspects of the writer and placing the individuals within the context of their respective traditions and similar works and authors. The entries are completed by a selected bibliography of works both by and about the writer in question and major interviews (a nice feature). A cumulative index to the entire set completes volume 2 of this supplement.

Although these volumes are interesting to read and are well laid out, some problems do occur. While it is refreshing to see Native American authors receive so much attention in this supplement, there is a noticeable absence of Asian American writers. Analyses of, for example, Amy Tan and Maxine Hong Kingston would have complemented the set nicely. The essays themselves sometimes suffer from slight continuity problems. No portraits of the writers are provided. Quotations within the articles are not always identified internally, and there is no documentation (such as endnotes) for them. Biographical details are sometimes scanty; more is written on a writer's personal philosophies, with biographical information usually included only if it relates to an author's career.

These caveats aside, the supplement is recommended to public libraries, particularly those already possessing the original set and earlier supplements. Although the Dictionary of Literary Biography series (Gale) covers some of the same ground, it furnishes more biographical detail and less in-depth analysis of individual works than the set at hand, thereby not duplicating the material overly much. However, as stated in the review of the second supplement, it would be difficult to recommend the *American Writers* set to university libraries. Students of American literature require more analytic and critical assessments of the writers treated. The set might be more appropriate for high school students and casual readers.—**Melissa Rae Root**

962. **Biographical Dictionary of Transcendentalism.** Wesley T. Mott, ed. Westport, Conn., Greenwood Press, 1996. 315p. index. $79.50. ISBN 0-313-28836-4.

This biographical dictionary complements the *Encyclopedia of Transcendentalism* (see entry 964) in which such terms as *transcendentalism* are defined, and the history of the movement prior to 1830 is given. Cross-references are to both volumes: a single asterisk for other entries in the dictionary and a double asterisk for the encyclopedia.

Following a "Guide to Abbreviations and References" of sources, 204 short biographies are alphabetically arranged in a single-column format with clear typeface and wide margins. Many of the names, such as the Quaker poet John Greenleaf Whittier, are only peripheral to transcendentalism. Most entries are a page or less in length, although there are lengthier essays for such major figures as the Alcotts, Ralph Waldo Emerson, Margaret Fuller, Henry David Thoreau, and Walt Whitman. Entries on William Wordsworth and Samuel Taylor Coleridge bear witness to the importance of English romanticism to the movement. French and German influences are seen by the inclusion of names such as Charles Fourier, Johann Wolfgang von Goethe, Friedrich Schelling, and even Johann Gaspar Spurzheim, whose views on phrenology interested Emerson.

Readers wishing to know more about transcendentalism will be aided by a bibliographic essay as well as by the list of references at the end of each entry. The dictionary concludes with an index and pertinent information about each of the 90 contributors. The biographical dictionary is certainly a useful resource for those familiar with transcendentalism and those wishing to know more about the people associated with it. For people with a more limited knowledge, it will be necessary to also consult the companion encyclopedia.—**Charlotte Lindgren**

963. **Dictionary of Literary Biography Documentary Series: An Illustrated Chronicle. Volume Thirteen: The House of Scribner 1846-1904.** John Delaney, ed. Detroit, Gale, 1995. 442p. illus. index. $128.00. ISBN 0-8103-5706-2.

The House of Scribner is part of the respected Dictionary of Literary Biography Documentary Series. However, it can also stand alone outside the set. The Documentary Series uses such documents as letters, photographs, contracts, interviews, and newspaper articles to bring a particular author or subject into focus and to place that person or subject in a larger context. In this case, the subject is the publishing house of Charles Scribner's Sons.

The volume covers the years 1846-1904; a second volume is planned that will cover 1905 through 1984, when Scribner's merged with the Macmillan company. The first section of the volume consists of a lengthy history of the company, written by Charles Scribner III, the fifth Charles Scribner, in 1978. Scribner details the beginnings of the company and the various changes wrought not only by the strong personalities of the succeeding Charles Scribners, but by the exigencies of the times. This history is followed by a chronology of major events in the company's history.

Delaney adds chronicles of a dozen major authors associated with Scribner's. He includes particular authors because of their importance to the publishing house at the time; indeed, he states in his preface that these authors "were major reasons for its [Scribner's] success." In addition to the chronicles of specific authors, Delaney details the history of the various magazines that Scribner's published, including *Scribner's Magazine* and *St. Nicholas*, their children's magazine. All sections are copiously illustrated and documented. Most of this archival material came from the archives of Charles Scribner's Sons, housed at Princeton University.

This book is many things: the history of a particular publishing house, a detailed look at the careers of various authors, a history of some magazines important in U.S. publishing history, and a look at the publishing industry in general during the latter half of the nineteenth century. Libraries with an interest in the history of books and publishing will want to purchase this, even if they are not subscribers to the series.
—**Terry Ann Mood**

Dictionaries and Encyclopedias

964. **Encyclopedia of Transcendentalism.** Wesley T. Mott, ed. Westport, Conn., Greenwood Press, 1996. 280p. index. $75.00. ISBN 0-313-29924-2.

Seventy contributors have written one hundred forty-five alphabetically arranged entries covering the major philosophical concepts, themes, genres, periodicals, organizations, and places associated with transcendentalism, especially the New England Renaissance between 1830 and the Civil War. European and Asian influences are also included, from classical names (e.g., Plutarch, Plato, and Virgil) and the Hindu Bhagavadgitā to Emanuel Swedenborg, Benedict de Spinoza, Jean-Jacques Rousseau, and even such remote connections as William Shakespeare and John Milton. There is an extremely useful 15-page chronology from the birth of Ralph Waldo Emerson in 1803 up to 1917.

The volume is a companion to the *Biographical Dictionary of Transcendentalism* (see entry 962), which gives brief biographies of major figures associated with the movement. References to these are marked by a double asterisk; cross-references within the volume at hand are indicated by a single asterisk. The encyclopedia discusses the major movements of the times from abolitionism to unitarianism, places from Brook Farm to Walden Woods, and journals from the *Atlantic Monthly* to the *Western Messenger*. It gives a coherent definition of transcendentalism, an elusive concept.

Each entry is followed by a list of references. In addition, the volume has a five-page, up-to-date bibliography of important book-length studies of the transcendental movement organized by areas of interest, such as literature, theology, nature, reform, and transcendental periodicals. An index and a list of contributors complete this volume, which is an essential reference for anyone interested in nineteenth-century American thought.—**Charlotte Lindgren**

Handbooks and Yearbooks

965. **American Nature Writers.** John Elder, ed. New York, Scribner's/Simon & Schuster Macmillan, 1996. 2v. illus. index. $220.00/set. ISBN 0-684-19692-1.

Nature writing has only recently come into its own as a distinct literary genre. The genre is, of course, writing about nature, but it has a strong, reflective, personal element absent in scientific discourse. The writing is a blend of science and an appreciation of the beauty and value of physical creation and humankind's place in it. The genre's maturity has been marked by an increase in the number of popular books, anthologies, magazines, and articles reflecting a heightened environmental awareness.

Although American nature writing has been around since Henry David Thoreau, there has been no single source of information about its leading practitioners. Much of that void is now filled by this elegant set with its 70 alphabetically ordered, bio-bibliographic essays on prominent American nature writers, past and present. The essays, each with a picture of its subject, run from 10 to 20 pages in length, including bibliographies by and about its subject. Chronological coverage is from William Bartram (1739-1823) to Rick Bass (1958-). Nearly two-thirds of the entries are historical, and by reading the essays in chronological order, a reader would, in effect, have a history of the subject from Thoreau and Ralph Waldo Emerson through John Burroughs and John Muir to Peter Matthiessen and Barry Lopez. Women nature writers from Susan Fenimore Cooper to Diane Ackerman also receive their due.

The bio-bibliographic essays are supplemented by a dozen "general topic" articles, in such subjects as Afro-Americans and nature writing, nature in Native American writing, contemporary ecofiction, literary theory and nature writing, modern birdwatching literature, nature poetry, and so on. Although nature writing has now become mainstream and includes some of the best American writers, the field still suffers from critical neglect. This sumptuously produced reference set is a unique and valuable resource.
—**D. Barton Johnson**

966. **The Oxford Companion to American Literature.** 6th ed. By James D. Hart. Revised by Phillip W. Leininger. New York, Oxford University Press, 1995. 779p. index. $49.95. ISBN 0-19-506548-4.

Recently an editor of the rival *Benet's Reader's Encyclopedia of American Literature* (see ARBA 92, entry 1155), Leininger has revised the late Hart's work to produce the first revision of this well-known title in a dozen years (see ARBA 84, entry 1159, for a review of the 5th ed.). Nearly 200 new entries are incorporated in this edition; fewer than half of these were derived from notes left by Hart in 1990. The chronological index has been enlarged as well, appending the major literary and social events from 1983 to 1994.

Notable newcomers debuting in this volume include contemporary writers Amy Tan, Jim Harrison, Gloria Steinem, Larry McMurtry, and Amy Clampitt. Redressing previous editions' oversights, Leininger has written entries for Charlotte Perkins Gilman and Henry Roth. An unspecified number of 5th edition entries have been condensed, truncated, or dropped. Many deleted items are on obscure subjects (e.g., Hiram Chittenden, Moses Coit Tyler). Some writers' statures, however, would seem to warrant longer entries than they are accorded. A few omissions are questionable, such as those of entries treating the literary associations of certain U.S. cities and presidents.

Significant twentieth-century writers remain underrepresented in *The Oxford Companion*. For example, only 4 percent of personal entries for names beginning with *A* through *D* are of women born since 1900. Modern male authors who are missing include Harlan Ellison, Andre Dubus, and Lowell Thomas. Coverage is generally superior, however, in terms of the updated entries carried forward from the 5th edition. The revised article on William Gaddis has been tripled in length, and the Philip Levine entry lists no fewer than five works that appeared since *Oxford*'s previous edition.

Several comparisons with *Benet's* yield telling results. The entry in *Benet's* for each of the following literary icons is more than twice the length of its *Oxford* counterpart: Herman Melville, Edgar Allan Poe, Mark Twain, James Fenimore Cooper, and William Faulkner. Yet, the breadth of the work under review is creditable in terms of embracing expatriates, explorers, colonists, and foreign discoursers on American matters (e.g., Kay Boyle, Richard Hakluyt, Samuel Sewell, and Charles Dickens).

However, more could be written on Latin American and Canadian literature. Besides offering substantive overview essays on these literatures, *Benet's* offers entries on internationally acclaimed writers whose works are readily available in English translation, such as Jorge Luis Borges, Pablo Neruda, and Octavio Paz. Also, unlike *Oxford*, *Benet's* treats such Canadian luminaries as Margaret Atwood, Robertson Davies, and Michael Ondaatje. For such giants as these, it is unfortunate that the researcher using *Oxford* has to consult a supplementary source, whether it be *Benet's* or the Canadian (see ARBA 85, entry 1138) or Spanish (see ARBA 80, entry 1310) volumes in the Oxford Companion series.

Finally, the reduction of typeface size since the 5th edition may prove irritating to librarians using this book on a regular basis. While the praises to be sung for *The Oxford Companion to American Literature* are considerable, one would be better served by employing *Benet's*, except involving more obscure areas of U.S. literature. [R: Choice, Mar 96, p. 1096]—**Jeffrey E. Long**

967. **Voices of Multicultural America: Notable Speeches Delivered by African, Asian, Hispanic, and Native Americans, 1790-1995.** Deborah Gillan Straub, ed. Detroit, Gale, 1996. 1372p. illus. index. $95.00. ISBN 0-8103-9378-6.

The publication of a volume of significant and interesting public speeches delivered over the last 200 years by major American minority ethnic figures has been long overdue. Editor Straub introduces the multicultural compilation with four brief, enlightening essays on the guiding principles that compose each of the traditions of African, Hispanic, Asian, and Native American oral discourses.

There are more than 130 entries included in this volume, and each speaker's selection is prefaced by a biographical sketch and an account of the historical context and the occasion surrounding the public delivery. Most of the speeches are published in their entirety, and at times an entry contains more than one selection. A concluding paragraph provides follow-up information that deals with the speechmaker's remarks and frequently gives additional biographical details. A list of sources is included for looking up more data on the speaker's life and work.

The collection contains a variety of notable discourses presented at important U.S. events, such as civil rights gatherings, antislavery meetings, gay rights demonstrations, women's rights conventions, political rallies, debates on the floor of the U.S. Congress, funerals, and Nobel prize awards ceremonies. The speakers encompass writers, educators, politicians, activists for various interests, Indian tribal chiefs, government officials, military officers, religious leaders, and businesspeople. Many of the deliveries by these influential personages had a profound impact on U.S. cultural and political life, and a number of the speeches produced controversial public debates that continue to this day.

The reader will find that the voices of Henry G. Cisneros, S. I. Hayakawa, Arthur Ashe, David Henry Hwang, Frederick Douglass, Martin Luther King Jr., Anita Hill, Chief Joseph, Geronimo, and Black Hawk are only a few of the many powerful speakers whose memorable words are recorded in this useful and much-needed research work. Students, speechmakers, and casual readers interested in history or current events will find this multicultural reference book a valuable collection. [R: LJ, Feb 96, p. 146; RBB, 15 Feb 96, p. 1048]—**Angelo Costanzo**

Individual Authors

Isaac Asimov

968. Green, Scott E. **Isaac Asimov: An Annotated Bibliography of the Asimov Collection at Boston University.** Westport, Conn., Greenwood Press, 1995. 146p. index. (Bibliographies and Indexes in Science Fiction, Fantasy, and Horror, no.6). $55.00. ISBN 0-313-28896-8.

This bibliography lists books from the personal library of Asimov, now part of the special collections of the Mulgar Library at Boston University. Although it purports to aid "scholars who are doing research on the work of Dr. Asimov," this bibliography does little more than list titles of books, arranged alphabetically, divided into 11 chapters, including sections devoted specifically to novels, short story collections, anthologies, nonfiction, and poetry. Entries identify the earliest editions in the collection and cover artists for illustrated works. For easy reference, both title and general indexes are included. Works not by Asimov are often books for which he wrote the introductions.

Most of the information provided in this volume could be found easily in any public library. More useful to scholars would have been a catalog of unpublished manuscripts and correspondence in the Asimov collection, information not readily available elsewhere. [R: Choice, Mar 96, p. 1094]—**Joseph W. Dauben**

Edgar Rice Burroughs

969. Brady, Clark A. **The Burroughs Cyclopaedia: Characters, Places, Fauna....** Jefferson, N.C., McFarland, 1996. 402p. index. $55.00. ISBN 0-89950-896-0.

Prefigured by British explorers' accounts of African civilizations and Percival Lowell's hypothesis of the synthetic nature of Mars' canals, Burroughs parlayed the public's thirst for escapist reading into a multimillion-dollar empire before his death in 1950. Derivative of themes found in Rudyard Kipling's jungle tales and H. G. Wells's science fiction, Burroughs's adventure fiction is set in exotic locales that range from the Earth's interior to points beyond the solar system. His creation of the character Tarzan has been said to be one of the most recognized figures ever to stride from the pages of fiction.

This A to Z list comprises entries of some 6,000 common and proper nouns, with their respective definitions, of persons, creatures, things, and concepts that appear in or are alluded to in Burroughs's fiction. Some of these items also exist outside of his imaginative prose, but (as Brady admits in his preface) the entries make no such distinction. Thus, unless one investigates beyond the context of such entries as those that define *Mrs. George Burke*, *Giles*, or *Rancho del Ganado*, one is unsure as to whether said terms ever possessed an objective reality apart from Burroughs's brain.

That caveat noted, Brady's selection and explication of entries are most impressive, supplementing the scholarship of George T. McWhorter's *Burroughs Dictionary* (University Press of America, 1987), which omits such fundamental terms as *weapons* and *tribes*. Concluding each entry (and within longer entries) in Brady's work are abbreviated codes that refer to the pertinent Burroughs works and chapters. Cross-referenced entries are plentiful, and boldfaced terms within entries refer to entries elsewhere as well. Entries average 100-200 words apiece in length, but many are longer, with the essay on Tarzan weighing in at more than 5,000 words, and that on John Carter at more than 1,000 words.

Besides a subject index and bibliography, back matter includes a chronology of principal events from Burroughs's fiction; a glossary of some 500 words (from actual and synthetic languages) from the fiction; and a cladogram depicting the relationships between the works of fiction. All in all, this encyclopedia is a valuable contribution to the study of Burroughs.—**Jeffrey E. Long**

T. S. Eliot

970. Blalock, Susan E. **Guide to the Secular Poetry of T. S. Eliot.** New York, G. K. Hall/Simon & Schuster Macmillan, 1996. 228p. index. (A Reference Publication in Literature). $50.00. ISBN 0-8161-7341-9.

This excellent volume supplements and extends the T. S. Eliot research available in Kuntz's *Poetry Explication: A Checklist* (G. K. Hall, 1980). Eliot's secular oeuvre was chosen as a focus because of its frequent excerption into anthologies and, thereby, classrooms; and yet very early and lesser-known pieces are also represented. The author's excellent preface, in which she details her working definitions, her scope, and her method, is a model for all future writers of reference texts.

The body of the text is composed of abstracts of approximately 1,000 articles, essays, and book snippets on 60 or so alphabetically arranged poems. The work on which the annotations are based dates from 1945 to 1993. Poems with the largest numbers of annotations are "Gerontion," (18 pages) "The Hollow Men," (8 pages) "The Love Song of J. Alfred Prufrock," (31 pages) and "The Waste Land" (74 pages). The annotations are arranged alphabetically by critics' surname. Subject access is available only through the back-of-the-book author/subject index: Eliot's subjects are not an organizing principle of the text itself.

The deftness of the abstracts is to be applauded, although critics so summarily recapitulated may be given pause. For example, John Soldo's 13-page article in *American Literature*, "T. S. Eliot and Jules LaForgue," reduces to 3 sentences in Blalock's note on Eliot's poem "Spleen": "While Eliot uses Laforgue's [sic] tone, he takes two important technical steps. He moves toward occasional rhyme and feminine truncation. He also introduces philosophical diction" (p. 109). This same article reduces to one sentence in Blalock's note on Eliot's poem "Circe's Palace": "The repressed homosexual orientation and distaste for women takes the form of Laforgian [sic] irony" (p. 7). This work will lead more than one reader back to the poems again.—**Judith M. Brugger**

971. **A Concordance to the Complete Poems and Plays of T. S. Eliot.** J. L. Dawson, P. D. Holland, and D. J. McKitterick, eds. Ithaca, N.Y., Cornell University Press, 1995. 1240p. index. $85.00. ISBN 0-8014-1561-6.

Thomas Stearns Eliot (1888-1965) was not only one of the most influential English-language poets of the twentieth century, but was also a renowned critic, playwright, publisher, and editor. This exhaustive concordance is based on *The Complete Poems and Plays of T. S. Eliot*, published in England by Faber and Faber in 1969.

Scholars of Eliot textual studies will welcome and value this volume, particularly the preface and introduction, which carefully detail the editors' purpose, methodology, and format. For example, the preparers of any concordance must decide, after a word-frequency list is prepared, at what point they have to remove words whose frequent usage would render the work unwieldy. Dawson and the other editors explain how they made this decision and include a list of omitted words.

The concordance's format is keyword in context. Each word is centered in a line with its preceding and following context. Four indexes follow the concordance: "Reverse Index of Word Forms," "Statistical Ranking List of Word Forms," "Lines Containing Numbers," and "Index of Words Containing Hyphen or Apostrophe." The work is for research and university library collections. [R: Choice, June 96, p. 1612]

—**Jack Bales**

Allen Ginsberg

972. Morgan, Bill. **The Response to Allen Ginsberg 1926-1994: A Bibliography of Secondary Sources.** Westport, Conn., Greenwood Press, 1996. 505p. index. (Bibliographies and Indexes in American Literature, no.23). $79.50. ISBN 0-313-29536-0.

There has not been a bibliography on Allen Ginsberg published since Michelle P. Kraus's 1980 volume, which covered the years 1969-1977 (see ARBA 81, entry 1280); George Dowden's earlier volume (1971) covered 1943-1967 (see ARBA 72, entry 1366). This new bibliography totally overshadows these existing works. Covering the years 1926-1994, it is comprehensive and based on Ginsberg's own compulsively collected personal archives, recently sold to Stanford University. The work has Ginsberg's imprimatur, and deserves it.

The author had complete access to the Stanford archives, and spent more than 15 years compiling this work, which is the companion piece to his 1995 volume, *The Works of Allen Ginsberg 1941-1994* (see ARBA 96, entry 1210). What that volume did for the primary works, this one does for the secondary material. Part 1 of the volume is an extensive descriptive list of the translations of Ginsberg's work into 32 other languages; this first part (89 pages in length) thus is really an extension of the previous volume, covering as it does the primary work. It is fascinating to see which of his poems have been translated into which languages; "Howl," for instance, was rarely translated and published in Asian, African, and Communist countries, while less overtly assertive or offensive poems, such as "Sunflower Sutra," were politically acceptable everywhere. In some nations, translations of Ginsberg have been available since the 1950s, while in the former Soviet Union, serious translation did not begin until the late 1980s.

Part 2 of the work includes bibliographic entries and annotations of 5,835 biographical and critical items, from Ginsberg's birth announcement in the *Newark Star Ledger* through books published in 1994 that contain any significant mention of him. The organization of the material is by year, and by month or day within the year. Most entries are two to three lines in length and contain a brief note that clarifies the content and occasionally also reveals Morgan's deep knowledge of his subject. Item J1742, which concerns a photograph in the *Village Voice* for January 12-18, 1973, notes that "This is the first publication of the often reproduced photograph of AG wearing a stars and stripes hat." Most of the notes, however, are more mundane, stating such things as "AG mentioned throughout" or "AG quoted in Spanish only."

The indexing in this volume is superb. There is a title and first line index, followed by a 68-page general index of personal and publication names, in a 2-column format. Browsing this general index will quickly reveal how many articles Pete Hamill has written about Ginsberg, or how many items have appeared about him over the years in any given publication (56 items in the *Washington Post*), with easy reference back to the bibliographic entries themselves.

In a work of this breadth, many of the items are commercially available, but many are almost unique to the Stanford archive. Simply reading through the annotations in chronological order can teach one much about Ginsberg's life and critical reception; one can almost follow the lecture tours by seeing the articles in the local newspapers following each other in close order. This bibliography is of the highest quality, and is essential to any collection supporting the study of modern U.S. literature. [R: Choice, Sept 96, p. 102]—**Bill Miller**

James Michener

973. Groseclose, David A. **James A. Michener: A Bibliography.** Austin, Tex., State House Press, 1996. 315p. illus. index. $45.00. ISBN 1-880510-23-5.

This bibliography provides a detailed list of all the writings of James Michener, fiction and nonfiction, including books, magazine and newspaper articles, and contributions to anthologies, as well as writings and critics' reviews about Michener and his work. Groseclose, a practicing lawyer, is an avid bibliophile and has obviously taken on this project as a labor of love. Although not working from an academic or literary background in literature, his careful research in compiling, verifying, and indexing all the information is apparent. A foreword by Michener himself also lends credibility to Groseclose's work.

This volume is divided into eight sections: works authored by Michener; contributions to anthologies, collections, and other books; forewords, introductions, and miscellaneous commentary; magazine articles by Michener; newspaper articles by Michener; books about or related to Michener; video materials; and audio materials. Appendixes list books and articles about the writer and critics' reviews. In addition to topical and title indexes, Groseclose has included separate indexes for names, periodicals, and publishers, adding to the usefulness of this volume for research.

The largest portion of this volume, works authored by Michener, is arranged chronologically and provides information relevant to identifying first editions of each publication. Detailed descriptions of the title page, copyright information, contents, collation, binding, and dust jacket follow, along with the price. Each entry is followed by a "Notes" section, which includes a brief annotation of the work, along with other pertinent information concerning the first edition, book club releases, location of original manuscripts, subsequent printings, and the like. This section is followed by a list of first printings and subsequent publications for each title. Michener's contributions to other books, commentaries, magazine and newspaper articles, and any other works about or related to the writer make up the balance of this volume. Foreign editions and publications were omitted, but will be included in a future volume.

This extensive bibliography of materials by, for, and about Michener gives the user a true appreciation for the accomplishment of this most prolific U.S. writer. Collectors of first editions, and those researching the literary accomplishments of the author, will find this a valuable sourcebook. Academic libraries with strong modern literature studies departments will want to add this to their bibliographic collections. [R: Choice, Oct 96, p. 252]—**Susan Zernial**

Marjorie Kinnan Rawlings

974. Tarr, Rodger L. **Marjorie Kinnan Rawlings: A Descriptive Bibliography.** Pittsburgh, Pa., University of Pittsburgh Press; distr., Ithaca, N.Y., CUP Services, 1996. 283p. illus. index. (Pittsburgh Series in Bibliography). $100.00. ISBN 0-8229-3920-7.

The Pittsburgh Series in Bibliography is well known for its detailed primary bibliographies of significant writers. Although Marjorie Kinnan Rawlings is principally known for *The Yearling*, Tarr's impressive book illustrates the diversity of her work, much of which has previously been undocumented: novels; pamphlets; a cookbook; collections of letters and stories; translations; dust jacket blurbs; and numerous contributions to books, pamphlets, journals, magazines, and newspapers.

The intent of the volumes in the Pittsburgh Series is to identify the first publication of each of an author's works and note all subsequent printings and editions. Tarr seems to have painstakingly fulfilled this purpose, and his acknowledgments list the dozens of institutions and persons that have aided him. He lists hundreds of Rawlings's contributions to such unindexed publications as the *Rochester Times-Union* newspaper and the University of Wisconsin's *Wisconsin Literary Magazine*. Tarr includes complete descriptive bibliographic information, such as collation, pagination, binding descriptions, and printing histories, and he reproduces title pages, copyright pages, and dust jackets. All terms are carefully defined and explained. Although this obvious labor of love does not include writings about Rawlings and thus will have limited use to students researching the author's life and works, it is still recommended for academic collections.—**Jack Bales**

John Steinbeck

975. Harmon, Robert B. **John Steinbeck: An Annotated Guide to Biographical Sources.** Lanham, Md., Scarecrow, 1996. 288p. illus. index. $55.00. ISBN 0-8108-3174-0.

It has often been said that the literary works of William Faulkner and Ernest Hemingway, John Steinbeck's contemporaries, have generated a greater amount of scholarship, but it is without doubt that Steinbeck's novels continue to be read and enjoyed by an appreciative audience. The success of *Of Mice and Men*, both on the screen and onstage, attests to the wide appeal that this simple yet moving account of two drifters with an unfulfilled dream has had on the American psyche. Rural areas and the dispossessed were Steinbeck's primary subjects, and he wrote of them with great passion and understanding.

John Steinbeck: An Annotated Guide to Biographical Sources is an excellent and comprehensive compilation that covers both a variety of print and film materials available to the casual reader and scholar alike. The work is divided into 10 sections, the last being a chronology of Steinbeck's life, including commentary. There is a total of 583 entries, and each annotation varies from paragraph length to one full page given to Edward Ricketts, a major influence on Steinbeck's California years and the model for many of Steinbeck's most memorable characters. There are also numerous photographs of Steinbeck and his family. This work is highly recommended for all academic and large public libraries.—**Dario J. Villa**

Thomas Wolfe

976. Bassett, John E. **Thomas Wolfe: An Annotated Critical Bibliography.** Lanham, Md., Scarecrow, 1996. 432p. index. (Scarecrow Author Bibliographies, no.96). $54.50. ISBN 0-8108-3146-5.

Bassett's reasonably comprehensive listing of English-language criticism and scholarship and selected non-English-language works on Thomas Wolfe is not intended to replace John S. Phillipson's *Thomas Wolfe: A Reference Guide* (see ARBA 78, entry 1153) (p. xi). In fact, with 2,876 selectively annotated entries for works about Wolfe published from 1929 to 1994, Bassett's guide substantially supplements Phillipson's coverage of earlier criticism while pulling together Wolfe scholarship since 1976. Bassett's foremost contribution is coverage of a substantial number of previously unrecorded contemporary reviews of Wolfe, particularly reviews in local newspapers. Bassett characterizes early reviews as favorable, unfavorable, or mixed. Typically brief annotations critically assess scholarly contributions, describing them as "balanced," "fully researched," "sensitive," and so forth; in other instances, Bassett helpfully identifies works as indispensable or superseded. Although not a comprehensive survey, the introduction amounts to more than what Bassett modestly calls a "brief preface" (p. xii), neatly summarizing critical responses to Wolfe from earliest reviews to the present.

The guide's weaknesses are awkward organization and limited indexing. Unlike Phillipson's earlier chronologically arranged bibliography, Bassett offers sections for books (hardbound publications of more than 100 pages); reviews and critical articles separately sublisted for each of the four novels; reviews sublisted for each of the collections of short stories, plays, and other writings published before and after 1970; critical studies of short stories, plays, and other writings; general critical, biographical, and bibliographical studies; and other materials, including reviews of books about Wolfe, dissertations, non-English-language criticisms, and additional items. A simple chronological arrangement would have been more generally informative about trends in Wolfe scholarship. Indexing is limited to critics' names. Although Bassett equips each section with cross-references, the lack of thorough subject indexing makes it difficult to locate all comments related to any particular work; moreover, this deficiency makes it impossible to identify studies on particular characters, images, or themes in Wolfe.—**James K. Bracken**

British Literature

General Works

Biography

977. **British Reform Writers, 1789-1832.** Gary Kelly and Edd Applegate, eds. Detroit, Gale, 1996. 465p. illus. index. (Dictionary of Literary Biography, v.158). $128.00. ISBN 0-8103-9353-0.

British reform writers of the late eighteenth and early nineteenth centuries defy neat categorization because their writing took so many forms, including journalism; essays; poetry; fiction; and political, religious, and pedagogical tracts. The common thread connecting their works—some widely published, but many ephemeral—is the broad themes of political, economic, religious, and social reform. The introduction establishes the historical setting and summarizes issues of concern to reform writers.

Most of the 47 writers included here are not well-known literary figures, although Thomas Paine, Percy Bysshe Shelley, and Mary Wollstonecraft will be familiar to most undergraduate readers. The writers were selected not just for their contributions to the various reform movements, but also each writer "should have been remarkable or representative in some way as a writer and not just as a voice for one reform cause or another" (p. xii).

For those writers also covered in other Dictionary of Literary Biography (DLB) volumes, cross-references are provided. The standard components one expects to find in DLB volumes are present here: For each writer, a primary bibliography, a portrait and other illustrations, a biographical essay, bibliographies of published letters and secondary material, and location of papers are furnished. A general bibliography of recommended reading follows the entries, as does a cumulative index of the entire series. Because the subject of this volume is so specialized, despite its accessibility for the general reader, it will be most useful in those libraries serving advanced literature or history students. [R: Choice, May 96, p. 1446]
—**Emily L. Werrell**

978. **British Short-Fiction Writers, 1800-1880.** John R. Greenfield, ed. Detroit, Gale, 1996. 402p. illus. index. (Dictionary of Literary Biography, v.159). $128.00. ISBN 0-8103-9354-9.

British Short-Fiction Writers, 1800-1880 examines 31 writers of the specified time period. The work is a recent volume of the long-standing and respected series Dictionary of Literary Biography (DLB) and similar in format to earlier volumes. Material on an author begins with a list of the author's works, followed by a critical essay on the author's life, works, and influence. A list of further sources completes the profile. All essays are illustrated by portraits of the authors at various stages of their lives, illustrations from their works, and pictures of their homes and families. This is in keeping with the DLB Advisory Board's belief that authors should be studied in context rather than in isolation.

Many of the authors are well known and have been examined in previous volumes of the DLB series (e.g., Anthony Trollope, Mary Wollstonecraft Shelley, Wilkie Collins). This is also in keeping with the DLB tradition: Writers fit into more than one category, and their accomplishments and influence can be examined from more than one perspective. Other authors are perhaps less well known, but all contributed greatly to the expansion of the short fiction genre during the time period in question.

An added bonus to most volumes in the series, and certainly to this one, is the introductory essay. This one discusses the various changes in society that led to the flowering of this particular literary form, and mentions many of the periodicals and literary annuals that flourished at the time and that provided an outlet for short fiction. Libraries with the entire, ongoing set will of course purchase this volume. Others will find this a helpful addition to criticism of short story authors. [R: Choice, June 96, p. 1608]—**Terry Ann Mood**

979. **British Short-Fiction Writers, 1880-1914: The Romantic Tradition.** William F. Naufftus, ed. Detroit, Gale, 1996. 499p. illus. index. (Dictionary of Literary Biography, v.156). $128.00. ISBN 0-8103-5717-8.

The latest volume of the Dictionary of Literary Biography (DLB) acts as a companion volume to volume 135, which covers the realistic short fiction of the same period (see ARBA 95, entry 1209). Profiled are the late Victorian and Edwardian writers who established a tradition of tales of fantasy, high adventure, and romantic love that to this day give British popular fiction a quite different tone from American fantasy and science fiction primarily derived from pulp literature. The authors include the well known, such as Arthur Conan Doyle and H. G. Wells, such writers as Olive Schreiner and Rudyard Kipling who are now returning to critical attention, and those (e.g., Ouida and Frank Harris) better known for their interesting lives than for their artistic achievements. A regrettable omission in both volumes is that of Katherine Mansfield, who was born in New Zealand but did most of her work in England. The DLB solves the problem of such multigenre writers as William Butler Yeats or Kipling by duplicating much of the bio-bibliographical material in other DLB volumes.

The arrangement of this volume follows that of earlier DLB volumes: an introduction surveying the literary, political, and social trends of the period; alphabetic entries on each author; and a useful cumulative index. Each entry contains a bibliography of the author's work; a brief biography; a discussion of the author's short fiction; a critical assessment of his or her achievements and literary reputation; and finally a bibliography of letters, biographies, collections, and other secondary material. The entries, written by different authors, are generally accurate, readable, and well researched.

The DLB is an invaluable resource that belongs in any well-equipped library. Smaller community and school libraries that cannot afford its considerable expense may prefer to purchase the eight-volume *Dictionary of Literary Biography—Concise British*. [R: Choice, April 96, pp. 1281-82]—**Lynn F. Williams**

980. **British Short-Fiction Writers, 1915-1945.** John H. Rogers, ed. Detroit, Gale, 1996. 444p. illus. index. (Dictionary of Literary Biography, v.162). $135.00. ISBN 0-8103-9357-3.

This monumental Gale series has split into so many subcategories that it now resembles less a biographical dictionary than an encyclopedia of literary forms and time periods. This is the fifth volume dealing with British short fiction writers, and many of the subjects covered here are far better known for their contributions to the novel. The biographical information is sometimes brief, as a full account of the writer's life appears in one or more of the other *Dictionary of Literary Biography* volumes. James Joyce, for instance, now appears in four volumes; D. H. Lawrence is in five.

There is no denying that the short story occupies a place of distinction in the literature of the twentieth century, but what may be debatable is the editor's assertion that the British short story began in 1877, specifically with Robert Louis Stevenson. This would seem to negate Gale's *British Short Fiction Writers, 1800-1880* (see entry 978), which includes, among others, Charles Dickens. Nonetheless, this period of literary modernism, postwar disillusionment, declining empire, and ascendant Irish nationalism is amply reflected in the short story genre.

The 30 authors selected for this volume are a diverse group. They include Irish writers, such as Joyce, James Stephens, and Seán O'Faoláin; traditionalists, such as Evelyn Waugh, John Galsworthy, and E. M. Forster; experimental writers, such as Virginia Woolf and Katherine Mansfield; and writers who were born or traveled extensively in the old British colonies. Some, such as P. G. Wodehouse, were prolific but slight writers. Others were like Joyce, who published only one short story collection but was tremendously influential. One common thread for many of these writers is that they turned to the short story to lift themselves out of poverty between novels.

Each essay describes the author's life and principal influences, both personal and literary. In most cases, there is a synopsis and some analysis of individual short stories, with occasional excerpts from literary critics. Each entry contains a primary bibliography, indicates the location of the author's papers, and provides a select list of criticism, bibliographies, and biographies. Exceptional photographs and reproductions of manuscripts enhance the book. The contributors lend a particularly valuable service by giving a good sense of each writer's initial reception and contemporary reputation. The work concludes with a running index of names for the earlier volumes of the series. [R: Choice, Nov 96, p. 426]—**John P. Schmitt**

981. **British Travel Writers, 1837-1875.** Barbara Brothers and Julia Gergits, eds. Detroit, Gale, 1996. 437p. illus. index. (Dictionary of Literary Biography, v.166). $135.00. ISBN 0-8103-9361-1.

How many people have sat as children with large, old, often disintegrating books of engravings of far-off places in their laps, books that came to their parents from their parents? How many have watched movies on weekend afternoons, the scripts for which were fed by accounts of Victorian travelers? Many people have complex, albeit often inaccurate, preconceptions of foreign nations and cultures based on the original works of nineteenth-century travel writers.

This current volume of the *Dictionary of Literary Biography* (DLB) does an admirable job of presenting a cross section of 38 authors from this once popular genre. Included are names that will be recognized as "legendary" in travel writing (David Livingstone, Sir Richard Burton, Lucie Duff-Gordon), several major literary and scientific figures (Charles Darwin, Francis Galton, Edward Lear, Charles Dickens), and several authors that still stand as popular culture icons of travel and work abroad (Florence Nightingale, and Anna Leonowens of *Anna and the King of Siam* fame). Each of the 38 entries includes a bibliography of the author's works; a signed critical essay; a list of biographical sources; and, where possible, a section locating the author's papers. The entries are followed by two bibliographies: The first, entitled "Travel Writing, 1837-1875," is a list of works by authors not included in the body of the volume; the second, a "Checklist of Further Readings," is a bibliography of secondary sources on travelers and travel writing. Each entry is also accompanied by clearly identified black-and-white illustrations, including maps, portraits of the authors, book illustrations, pages from authors' sketchbooks, and photographs ranging from gravesites to the authors in native dress. The volume concludes with an index cumulating the contents of all of the DLB volumes, the 1980-1995 volumes of the DLB yearbooks, and the 13 volumes of the DLB Documentary Series.

Any academic library serving an undergraduate or graduate population studying nineteenth-century history should have this volume. Any large public library that has a historical collection of works of nineteenth-century travelers should also consider purchasing it.—**Caroline M. Kent**

982. **British Writers. Supplement III: James M. Barrie to Mary Wollstonecraft.** George Stade and Carol Howard, eds. New York, Scribner's/Simon & Schuster Macmillan, 1996. 576p. index. $110.00. ISBN 0-684-19714-6.

The third supplement to the essential *British Writers* set continues to fill in major gaps in coverage (see ARBA 93, entry 1191, and ARBA 88, entry 1199, for reviews of the first two supplements). Indeed, this volume concentrates more on older, previously neglected writers than it does on contemporary figures. Of the 25 writers covered in *Supplement III*, only 2 were still alive at the time of publication—the playwright Christopher Fry and the eminent man of letters V. S. Pritchett. The others selected cover a wide span of years, from Aphra Behn (1640-1689) to Angela Carter (1940-1992), with writers from the nineteenth and twentieth centuries most prevalent. The philosopher David Hume is included, as is the humorist P. G. Wodehouse. The creators of Dracula (Bram Stoker) and Frankenstein (Mary Shelley) are profiled, as well as Shelley's influential mother, Mary Wollstonecraft. On a gentler note, Peter Pan (James M. Barrie) and Peter Rabbit (Beatrix Potter) creators are also found within this volume.

The major writings of the authors are highlighted within each 17- to 20-page entry, and many titles are discussed in specific subsections of the text. In addition to basic biographical and critical information, a substantial bibliography of primary and secondary sources is provided for each writer. The book includes a "Complete British Writers Chronology," which lists historical events, publications, and births and deaths of prominent writers from 1325 to 1995 (a shorter "Chronological Table," covering 1835 to 1991, appeared in *Supplement II*). Also, there is a master index of the entire *British Writers* set that lists names and writings. The series remains a useful reference source for academic and large public libraries and, because many important British writers are still not included (e.g., Alan Sillitoe, Anita Brookner, Salman Rushdie, Julian Barnes, David Lodge), a fourth supplement is eagerly awaited. [R: RBB, 15 April 96, p. 1460]
—**Thomas A. Karel**

983. **Sixteenth-Century British Nondramatic Writers, Third Series.** David A. Richardson, ed. Detroit, Gale, 1996. 385p. illus. index. (Dictionary of Literary Biography, v.167). $140.00. ISBN 0-8103-9362-X.

This third volume in Gale's treatment of sixteenth-century British nondramatic writers treats twenty-four authors, a collection, and author-printers of the period with the quality one has come to expect from the *Dictionary of Literary Biography* (DLB). (See ARBA 95, entry 1201, for a review of the first series of British nondramatic writers.) Most of the writers are lesser known, although surprisingly, this is the first DLB volume to cover Philip Sidney, Mary Sidney Herbert, or Edmund Spenser. Gale's ongoing coverage of this period is particularly valuable as it gains popularity among critics and scholars (more than 3,500 citations are given in the 1981-1996 MLA Bibliography for sixteenth-century British authors, excluding Shakespeare).

Arranged similar to other DLB volumes, each entry gives a list of the author's works; a fairly extensive, easy-to-read biographical/critical essay; and a brief list of secondary references. Major biographies and information on the location of original papers or manuscripts are also listed if available; this last item is quite useful for the serious researcher. Essays are written by established experts on their topics, such as Margaret Hannay on Herbert. The introduction gives a concise, interesting overview of the period, the authors, and their work. An appendix of contemporary documents on sixteenth-century literature, including discussions by Richard Tottel, Spenser, and Sidney, provides excellent primary background information. The bibliography is an outstanding resource; more than 150 sources are listed, many from the last 15 years. Along with DLB volumes 132 and 136, this volume is indispensable for any college or university library supporting British literature research, and for any large public library.

—**Susan Davis Herring**

Dictionaries and Encyclopedias

984. **Encyclopedia of British Humorists: Geoffrey Chaucer to John Cleese.** Steven H. Gale, ed. New York, Garland, 1996. 2v. index. (Garland Reference Library of the Humanities, v.906). $150.00/set. ISBN 0-8240-5990-5.

This two-volume set spans the entire history of British literature, from *Beowulf* to John Cleese (of Monty Python fame) and will assist anyone interested in humor. Almost any person of significance born or writing among the nations of the British Isles—England, Ireland, Scotland, and Wales—is included. It should be noted that stand-up comedians, comic actors, and joke writers have been excluded, thus individuals such as Benny Hill will not be found in these volumes.

The set contains 203 entries listed alphabetically by author, covering 206 humorists (there are 3 pairs of duo-authors), written by 118 scholars from 7 different countries. There are indexes of authors, titles, and subjects. A chronological index and a list of pseudonyms are provided at the start, as some authors are listed by given name and some by pseudonym, depending on which is more popularly recognized. Most entries contain a brief biography, a bibliography of sources, a literary analysis, and summary remarks. Entries average about six full pages and provide rich detail and examples. Most major humorists are featured in addition to several minor authors. Also, some authors who are not primarily known for humor are included because they wrote some humorous materials; for example, Winston Churchill and C. S. Lewis. In such cases, only the humorous material is considered.

These volumes, six years in the making, were written to assist both the scholar and the interested layperson. Analysis is insightful and focuses on the humorist's technique and contribution to the field of humor, yet avoids the academe penchant for dry minutiae. Some knowledge of literary history is helpful when using these volumes. Still, providing generous samples of humor, from the ironic to the absurd, the encyclopedia is simply fun to look through. [R: Choice, Oct 96, p. 250; RBB, Aug 96, pp. 1922-24]—**Brad R. Leach**

Drama

985. **British Playwrights, 1880-1956: A Research and Production Sourcebook.** William W. Demastes and Katherine E. Kelly, eds. Westport, Conn., Greenwood Press, 1996. 457p. index. $95.00. ISBN 0-313-28758-9.

This comprehensive sourcebook will be useful for teachers, directors, scholars, and general readers who wish to enhance their knowledge of British drama in one of the most restless and volatile periods in the history of modern literature. Among the 40 authors covered are such major figures as Max Beerbohm, Noël Coward, and T. S. Eliot, and also minor authors such as Cicely Hamilton, Allan Monkhouse, and St. John Hankin.

Each entry provides a concise biographical overview, a list of important plays, and a list of critical receptions of the plays. Also included for each figure is substantial bibliographic material (e.g., lists of scholarly and critical works on the author), as well as listings of locations housing unpublished material.

There is also information on adaptations and productions of the plays and on previously published bibliographies on the playwright. Each section contains a brief but thorough assessment of the playwright's career. Also furnished are a thorough index and a detailed list of contributors.

The editors of *British Playwrights, 1880-1956* are well qualified for their task. Professor of English at Louisiana State University, Demastes is series editor of Greenwood Press's Research and Production Sourcebooks. Among his own books are *Beyond Naturalism: A New Realism in American Theatre* (1988) and the forthcoming *Theatre of Chaos*. Kelly is associate professor of English at Texas A&M University. She is the author of *Tom Stoppard and the Craft of Comedy* (1991) and the general editor of *Modern Drama by Women, 1880s-1930s: An International Anthology* (1996).

British Playwrights is an indispensable tool for the researcher or the professional. Even for the layperson, it is useful as an introduction and a guide to a fascinating period of British drama.—**Peter Thorpe**

986. **British Playwrights, 1956-1995: A Research and Production Sourcebook.** William W. Demastes, ed. Westport, Conn., Greenwood Press, 1996. 502p. index. $95.00. ISBN 0-313-28759-7.

The mid-1950s marked the beginning of a new energy and realism on the British stage, according to the editor of *British Playwrights, 1956-1995*; such plays as Samuel Beckett's *Waiting for Godot* and John Osborne's *Look Back in Anger* turned British theater on its head, replacing the upper-class "genteel comedy of manners" with a "radical social consciousness" (p. ix). Editor Demastes, professor of English at Louisiana State University, and 31 others (mostly professors of English or theater) have contributed chapters on 36 British playwrights active between 1956 and 1995. All but five are still alive, and many have produced work as recently as the 1990s. Included along with Beckett and Osborne are Harold Pinter (considered by some critics to be the greatest English-language playwright of the twentieth century), Pam Gems (the first woman playwright produced by the Royal Shakespeare Company), Peter Shaffer (of *Amadeus* fame), Louise Page (the youngest playwright in the book), and Tom Stoppard (whose *Arcadia* is still touring the United States).

This book presupposes some familiarity with the playwrights' original works. Its purpose is to present the history of each writer's career and critical reception and provide references for further research. Each chapter has a brief summation and assessment of the playwright's career, a production history, a primary bibliography (the playwright's published works and interviews), and a secondary bibliography (reviews and other criticism). Although the focus is on the major plays, mention is also made of their other work, such as motion picture adaptations, translations, television productions, and other prose writing. A selected bibliography of sources on British theater and drama, an index of names, and an index of titles are useful for quick reference.

A few misspellings and typographic errors were noted. The chapter on Gems at first indicates her adaptation of *The Blue Angel* is based on Thomas Mann's novel and, three pages later, on Heinrich Mann's novel (the latter is correct). These quibbles aside, *British Playwrights* will serve well in literary criticism and theater collections of academic libraries.—**Lori D. Kranz**

987. Douglas, Krystan V. **Guide to British Drama Explication. Volume 1: Beginnings to 1640.** New York, G. K. Hall/Simon & Schuster Macmillan, 1996. 552p. (A Reference Publication in Literature). $60.00. ISBN 0-8161-7372-9.

This volume continues the publisher's explication series and is the first of two volumes focusing on English-language explication of British drama. This current volume deals primarily with drama written from the beginning until 1640, the date of the closing of the theaters. Contrary to the timeline and because of the stylistic qualities of their works, John Milton is included in this volume and William Davenant will appear in the second volume. The works listed in this explication adhere to the general ruling that they must involve "a close reading of the drama." A full explanation of this criterion is explained in the preface. There is a guide to the periodicals, journals, and abbreviations. The organization of the volume consists of a list of the dramatists alphabetically by last name, and then the plays alphabetically by title. Anonymous works are listed also. Criticism is itemized by the author's name following each play.

This is a major explication of extreme length, well-defined scope, and presumed depth. It does not include any analytic or critical evaluation of the entries. The guide is an invaluable source for a scholar generating a preliminary bibliography for a study of any English dramatist or dramatic work during the time period. Unquestionably, this volume should be added to research libraries.—**Jackson Kesler**

Individual Authors

Jane Austen

988. Roth, Barry. **An Annotated Bibliography of Jane Austen Studies 1984-94.** Athens, Ohio, Ohio University Press, 1996. 438p. index. $49.95. ISBN 0-8214-1167-5.

Morris Zapp, a character in David Lodge's *Changing Places* (1975), was working on a series of definitive criticisms of Jane Austen's novels that would leave future critics nothing to say about them. Apparently the fictional Dr. Zapp failed in his aim, as the Jane Austen industry is more productive than ever. Ohio University professor Roth's annotated bibliography describes 1,326 items written in a 10-year period (1984-1994), which represents a 25 percent increase over the number of items included in Roth's previous 10-year compilation—*An Annotated Bibliography of Jane Austen Studies, 1973-1983* (University Press of Virginia, 1985).

Roth's bibliography is arranged alphabetically by author in three main sections: books, essays, and articles devoted entirely or in good part to Austen, including reviews of all book-length studies; doctoral dissertations wholly or in part about Austen; "significant mentions . . . when they entail an unusual, perceptive, or otherwise striking idea" (preface). Annotations are brief (75 words or less in length) and are descriptive rather than critical. An author index; a subject index, with rather broad subject headings such as "Egoism" and "Family"; and an index of references to individual Austen titles complete the work.

While eventually (perhaps) all reference materials will be available on the Internet, specialized monographs such as *An Annotated Bibliography of Jane Austen Studies* are still needed by scholars and students. Roth does an excellent job of bringing together material from diverse sources, arranging it, and describing it. David Gilson's *A Bibliography of Jane Austen* (see ARBA 83, entry 1216) covers material published up to 1978, but there has been nothing comparable to Gilson's work covering the years since 1978 except for Roth's two bibliographies. (Roth also published *An Annotated Bibliography of Jane Austen Studies, 1952-72* [University Press of Virginia, 1973].) This bibliography is essential for academic libraries supporting a graduate-level English literature program; it would be useful for other academic libraries and large public libraries.—**Jonathan F. Husband**

Geoffrey Chaucer

989. **Chaucer's Pilgrims: An Historical Guide to the Pilgrims in** *The Canterbury Tales*. Laura C. Lambdin and Robert T. Lambdin, eds. Westport, Conn., Greenwood Press, 1996. 398p. index. $79.50. ISBN 0-313-29334-1.

Some 30 contributors from U.S. universities worked on this informative guide to the pilgrims in Geoffrey Chaucer's *The Canterbury Tales*. The resource consists of a collection of essays that provide in-depth discussion of the pilgrims' vocations and functions within fourteenth-century society, placing them in a context often difficult for modern readers to grasp. The editors claim that this volume fills in a 600-year gap in the study of Chaucer's most well-known work, and the volume does little to dispute that claim.

The preface introduces readers to the main text, reminding them of the history behind the pilgrimage, the likely route taken to the Cathedral at Canterbury, and the basic premise behind Chaucer's literary achievement. The main entries follow and are generally about 10 pages in length, with some longer and some shorter depending on the level of scholarship available and the amount Chaucer wrote in connection with the figure. All the pilgrims outlined in the General Prologue are treated; those who actually tell their tales in the unfinished manuscript receive fuller coverage, drawing comparisons between their vocations and the stories they tell. Each entry is followed by a bibliography of recent critical work on that pilgrim. A selected bibliography and an index round out the text.

A couple of additions could have made this work even stronger. Contributions from Canadian and British literary experts would have furnished a perspective unique from the viewpoint given by the present contributors. Also, a reprint of the entire General Prologue, in both Middle and modern English, would have been beneficial for students. Otherwise, this is a solid guide to the pilgrims of Chaucer's *The Canterbury Tales*. Its particular focus makes it especially valuable for high school and college students; therefore, those school libraries should definitely consider acquiring the title. Public libraries can probably get by without it.—**Melissa Rae Root**

Samuel Taylor Coleridge

990. Crawford, Walter B., with Ann M. Crawford. **Samuel Taylor Coleridge: An Annotated Bibliography of Criticism and Scholarship. Volume III.** New York, G. K. Hall/Simon & Schuster Macmillan, 1996. 946p. index. $90.00. ISBN 0-8161-8727-4.

The Crawfords have finally completed the Samuel Taylor Coleridge bibliography project started by Richard Haven and others in 1967. Previous volumes in the three-volume set appeared in 1976 (see ARBA 77, entry 1230) and 1983 (both published by G. K. Hall). Volume 3 is divided into 2 major parts. Part 1 includes 3 major elements arranged in one chronology: material published from 1793 to 1939 that had not been included in volumes 1 and 2, a comprehensive bibliography of materials written by and about Coleridge from 1940 to 1965, and a selective bibliography of materials published from 1966 to 1994.

Part 2 is composed of several chronological listings, from 1791 to 1965, of Coleridgeana, material that makes use of Coleridgean elements or can be related in some way to Coleridge, such as fiction and drama, cartoons and comic strips, musical settings of Coleridge, and so forth. Many of these items do not refer explicitly to Coleridge, but contain allusions to such matters as albatross and Xanadu. The more than 5,000 items, all annotated, some critically, include many items published in foreign languages, such as translations of Coleridge into Serbian or Japanese. The lengths of the annotations do not reflect the relative importance of the items to Coleridge studies. Volume 3 is supplied with 7 subdivided indexes, by authors, titles, periodicals, book reviews, subject proper names, subject titles, and subjects and categories.

Taken together, the three volumes of this bibliography cover Coleridge exhaustively (not to say exhaustingly) through 1965. Coleridge scholars and writers of dissertations on any aspect of English romantic literature will find it indispensable. The undergraduate or high school student writing a 500-word explication of "The Rime of the Ancient Mariner" or "Kublai Khan" will find this bibliography extremely daunting. The selective bibliography for 1966-1994 covers years left untouched by *Samuel Taylor Coleridge: A Selective Bibliography of Criticism* (see ARBA 79, entry 1235). The Modern Language Association bibliographies for 1965 on cover much of the same ground. This bibliography is indispensable for graduate-level libraries, but a discretionary item elsewhere.—**Jonathan F. Husband**

William Congreve

991. Bartlett, Laurence. **William Congreve: An Annotated Bibliography, 1978-1994.** Lanham, Md., Scarecrow, 1996. 109p. index. (Scarecrow Author Bibliographies, no.97). $29.00. ISBN 0-8108-3166-X.

This bibliography is a selective, annotated guide to resources on William Congreve. The guide, which is part of the series of author bibliographies published by Scarecrow, complements a previous work compiled by the author entitled *William Congreve: A Reference Guide* (G. K. Hall, 1979). The preface clearly outlines the scope, purpose, and arrangement of this new bibliography. A critical essay that follows further illuminates the scope of the resource as well as outlines recent trends of new criticism on Congreve that has surfaced since 1978.

The work is arranged chronologically. As stated in the preface, the bibliography contains books (section A), which includes editions of Congreve plays, monographs, and dissertations. Shorter works/shorter writings (section B) lists critical essays, reviews, chapters in books, and other writing on the work of Congreve. The guide also includes an index for easy referral to specific citations. The bibliography is highly recommended for academic libraries with strong collections in English literature.—**Jane Jurgens**

Charles Dickens

992. **Every Thing in Dickens: Ideas and Subjects Discussed by Charles Dickens in His Complete Works: A Topicon.** George Newlin, comp. and ed. Westport, Conn., Greenwood Press, 1996. 1102p. illus. index. $145.00. ISBN 0-313-29874-2.

This topical concordance of ideas and subjects from Charles Dickens's canon deserves orchids for its comprehensive coverage of the classic author's broad-based commentary. Opening on a three-part table of contents offering separate listings for extended extracts and illustrations, the front matter includes a foreword; a preface; an editor's foreword; a word about the computer; acknowledgments; and a lengthy introduction featuring comments on illustrations, extended excerpts, the text, spelling and punctuation, and indexes. A section on how to use the volume defines the organizing principle and necessary abbreviations. The remaining front matter includes an index of subtopics (e.g., "The Poor"; "The Poor, Abject"; "The Poor, Working") and their locations; abbreviations and dates of Dickens's novels, stories, speeches, feature articles, collaborations, plays, reprints, and sketches; an alphabetized title list; and bibliographic references.

Textual entries appearing under each subtopic list citations and their sources. For example, under "Manners" appears a comment on bashfulness, 2 notes on bowing, 1 on curtseying, and on through the alphabetized list of 13 subtopics. The final entry on this subject appears in tandem with a drawing from *Nicholas Nickleby*. Concluding the main body of the work is a two-part index of words and phrases, an eight-part index of localities, and a brief introduction to the man who put all this together.

A dauntingly arcane arrangement of Dickens's themes and subjects, Newlin's concordance is a scholar's godsend. The endpapers alone—a reproduction of Luke Fildes's *The Empty Chair*—will delight lovers of Victoriana. However, the compiler's deft shuffling of myriad abbreviations—even to the rather chummy use of CD for Charles Dickens in the foreword—is wearying and unnecessarily concise. Newlin might have alleviated user anxiety and welcomed hesitant browsers by providing a few models explaining how to break the code of "¶OCS 44" or "HM1 *See* S:Feelings—*suppression relieved*." Overall, the thorough and tedious methodology and hefty price probably limit the book's use to large research-oriented institutions rather than the average hometown library.—**Mary Ellen Snodgrass**

993. **Everyone in Dickens: Plots, People, and Publishing Particulars in the Complete Works.** George Newlin, comp. and ed. Westport, Conn., Greenwood Press, 1995. 3v. illus. index. $275.00/set. ISBN 0-313-29580-8.

These three volumes locate, discuss, and analyze a gargantuan list of 13,143 names, including whole names; first names only; nicknames; parodied names; allegorical names; historical figures; and allusions to myth, the Bible, and classic literature. In volume 1, the text is preceded by a table of contents of works from the period 1833-1849, including *Oliver Twist* and *A Christmas Carol*. The front matter offers a foreword, a preface, an editor's foreword, and an introduction. A tutorial on how to use the volume defines the organizing principle; it precedes a comprehensive list of abbreviations and dates, which are crucial to the user's understanding of Newlin's working method. The last two segments of front matter are a list of alphabetized titles and bibliographic references and their abbreviations.

Textual entries begin with a précis of the work and a listing of illustrations and characters. Newlin allies each character by name or designation (Boy, Churchwardens, Charwoman, Want, Old Scratch) with Dickens's verbatim exposition of each. The first volume concludes with an index of characters and an index of subjects. Volume 2 follows the same pattern and covers the canon from the period 1849-1869. This segment deals with three of Dickens's most read titles—*A Tale of Two Cities*, *Great Expectations*, and *David Copperfield*.

Volume 3, a taxonomy, presents 12 indexes that survey surnames, given names, nicknames, occupations, kinship, and miscellaneous categories plus genetic, historical, biblical, literary, musical, and mythological references. The final index lists names of ships, schools, prisons, newspapers, boroughs, associations, companies, houses, and hostelries. Appended to this volume is a 34-page timeline of Dickens's life, career, and milieu; a glossary; and a final collection of loose ends.

Newlin's work reaches out to the reader and researcher in numerous ways. His touching respect for Dickens the man, Dickens the artist, and Dickens the social critic reverberates through this massive research effort. As a literary, social, or historical tool, the volumes are demanding: They require some study for full appreciation and access of protagonists, supporting characters, and minute figures. Newlin's candor about difficulties in research method and consistency of source material strips the work of pomposity and reminds researchers and scholars that reference work has its human limitations. The three-volume set makes fascinating reading for the bibliophile and the student of Victoriana. For the serious scholar and the comprehensive library, these three volumes are essentials.—**Mary Ellen Snodgrass**

Samuel Johnson

994. Rogers, Pat. **The Samuel Johnson Encyclopedia.** Westport, Conn., Greenwood Press, 1996. 483p. index. $85.00. ISBN 0-313-29411-9.

Attempting to gather, so far as is possible, in a single volume all the essential facts relating to Samuel Johnson, Rogers's *The Samuel Johnson Encyclopedia* deals with both Johnson's works and his life. Taking into account Johnson's remark to Boswell, "There is nothing, Sir, too little for so little a creature as man," entries include essays commenting on such diverse topics as the Bodleian Library; Johnson's celebration of charity; Quakers and their progressive treatment of women; Omai, the Tahitian who was presented in England as a living specimen of the "noble savage"; and William Hogarth, who when he first met Johnson, thought he had come upon an idiot. Here one will discover Johnson's soft spot for *projectors* ("people with big ideas, whose grandiose ambitions often outran their capacities") as well as his hostile observations about the Scottish ("needy adventurers," many of whom have been advanced beyond their merits).

Not at all a guide through trivia about Johnson, this encyclopedia makes a praiseworthy attempt at including "all salient persons and subjects with a Johnsonian connection, as well as those of less intrinsic importance yet possessing some personal or cultural relevance." Entries may be broadly categorized as dealing with Johnson's works, biographical data, topical subjects, and named locations.

The Samuel Johnson Encyclopedia is designed for general reader and literary scholar alike. The former will find "great things and small" to nourish the mind by stimulating thinking; the latter will find enough references and allusions to Hanoverian England and the key figures of the age to answer questions, absorb attention, and provide opportunities for significant research. [R: Choice, Dec 96, p. 594]

—**Colby H. Kullman**

D. H. Lawrence

995. Poplawski, Paul. **D. H. Lawrence: A Reference Companion.** Westport, Conn., Greenwood Press, 1996. 714p. index. $99.50. ISBN 0-313-28637-X.

This volume is both a tribute to the author's dedication as a scholar and to D. H. Lawrence's literary reputation as one of England's most renowned novelists, short story writers, poets, and essayists. The main section of the book, part 2, contains entries on nearly every work Lawrence produced (the exceptions are individual poems and paintings), including summaries of each and comprehensive bibliographies of criticism. Other sections provide chronologies; bibliographies of general criticism and commentary on Lawrence; specialized bibliographies (such as one devoted to feminist criticism); a discussion of Lawrence and film; maps; and a detailed, 90-page biographical essay by John Worthen, one of the foremost authorities on the author. In short, virtually every facet of Lawrence's life, works, and reputation is covered by this remarkable volume, obviously a labor of love by Poplawski.

Although the author states that his book is both comprehensive for the advanced researcher but still easy to use for beginning students of Lawrence, the latter will likely ignore some of the material presented. For example, Lawrence's father was a coal miner and his son grew up in a working-class environment. Thus, Poplawski includes a chronology that charts key developments in the history of coal mining and the labor movement. Another chronology covers the development of state education in Great Britain. Poplawski has included a variety of indexes to the work, as well as an excellent preface that explains his purpose. Also, he is to be congratulated for providing complete bibliographic information for all of his references, something that this reviewer often finds lacking in many such works. This reference companion is for academic and research libraries. [R: Choice, Dec 96, pp. 593-94]—**Jack Bales**

W. Somerset Maugham

996. Rogal, Samuel J. **A Companion to the Characters in the Fiction and Drama of W. Somerset Maugham.** Westport, Conn., Greenwood Press, 1996. 468p. index. $75.00. ISBN 0-313-29917-X.

As the author points out in his introduction to this guide, characters and their portrayal are a major artistic strength of W. Somerset Maugham's novels, plays, and stories. Keeping track of all the characters—major and minor, named and anonymous, those who appear in more than one work, or appear only in the conversation of other characters—can be a challenge for the serious student as well as the casual reader of Maugham.

The largest section of the companion is an alphabetic list of Maugham's characters, identified as they are in his writings: by name, generic description, relationship, or function. Thus, along with the named characters are listings such as "brother," "Chinese man," "duchess," "jury," "musicians," "neighbor," and "narrator." These entries, ranging from two lines for minor characters to up to half a page for important ones, include the name or other terms by which the character is identified, the work or works in which the character appears, his or her physical features or description, and major actions and relationships.

A brief bibliography lists the editions of Maugham's works and the secondary sources used in compiling this guide. An index of titles indicates for each Maugham work the pages in this guide on which its characters are listed. There is, however, no index to the first appearance of each character in the original works, as found in some other literary character dictionaries. Nonetheless, no other such guide exists for Maugham's writings; therefore, this volume will surely be useful for both scholars and general readers. [R: Choice, Nov 96, p. 435]—**Gregory M. Toth**

John Milton

997. Klemp, P. J. **Paradise Lost: An Annotated Bibliography.** Pasadena, Calif., Salem Press and Lanham, Md., Scarecrow, 1996. 251p. index. (Magill Bibliographies). $39.50. ISBN 0-8108-3152-X.

Commentaries on John Milton and his writings began to appear toward the end of the seventeenth century and have been increasing geometrically ever since. Currently Milton scholarship is prodigious, diverse, and vital. *Paradise Lost* merits approximately 100 books and articles every year. This selective bibliography focuses on those considered the most significant of scholarly works written about Milton's epic during the past 30 years. While not ignoring new approaches undertaken by historicist, feminist, and Marxist critics, it does not include dissertations or highly specialized and esoteric studies.

Among the 450 listings are a few that are introductory in nature, some advanced, but most of those cited are meant to be of value to undergraduate and graduate students, of concern to specialists and researchers. More than one-third of the present entries do not appear in Klemp's previous work, *The Essential Milton: An Annotated Bibliography of Major Modern Studies* (see ARBA 90, entry 1182); not only did he add to this volume, but he has made amends for some oversights and questionable judgments prematurely rendered. The annotations average about 175 words in length and clearly summarize the entries. Two detailed indexes, one of scholars and one of subjects, enhance the usefulness of this critically wrought bibliography.—**G. A. Cevasco**

Ann Radcliffe

998. Rogers, Deborah D. **Ann Radcliffe: A Bio-bibliography.** Westport, Conn., Greenwood Press, 1996. 209p. index. (Bio-bibliographies in World Literature, no.4). $55.00. ISBN 0-313-28379-6.

This bio-bibliography of English gothic novelist Ann Radcliffe (1764-1823) chronicles her life in 22 pages. The primary bibliography fills 12 pages, while the preponderance of the volume is devoted to a secondary bibliography divided into sections: reviews, notices, and critical articles; full-length works; dissertations; and bibliographies. Each section of the secondary bibliography is arranged chronologically by year (1789 to early 1995), and each individual item receives a descriptive annotation ranging from a few words to a short paragraph. Appendixes noting adaptations, abridgments, parodies, imitations, and spurious attributions and an index to authors complete the work. A subject index may be found under the "Radcliffe" listing in the index.

Rogers (of the University of Maine), who edited *The Critical Response to Ann Radcliffe* (Greenwood Press, 1993), has compiled the most complete bibliography on Radcliffe available anywhere. The biography adds little to what is known about Radcliffe's uneventful life, although Rogers did examine her *Commonplace Book* in the Boston Public Library. Radcliffe has received more critical attention in recent years due to increased interest in women writers and gothic fiction, but interest is confined primarily to academia. The work would be useful for academic libraries with graduate-level courses in nineteenth-century fiction. [R: Choice, Sept 96, p. 106]—**Jonathan F. Husband**

William Shakespeare

999. Shewmaker, Eugene F. **Shakespeare's Language: A Glossary of Unfamiliar Words in Shakespeare's Plays and Poems.** New York, Facts on File, 1996. 515p. $50.00. ISBN 0-8160-3276-9.

Users will find this glossary an accessible resource, providing clear and succinct definitions of Shakespearean terms for the modern reader. Although it contains fewer entries than C. T. Onions's *A Shakespeare Glossary* (rev. ed.; see ARBA 88, entry 1223), Shewmaker's definitions are less arcane and more readable, rendering this glossary suitable for a general audience. Also, some entries do not appear in the earlier work, and Shewmaker includes more geographic and mythological entries than does Onions.

The 15,000-plus words in the dictionary are "unfamiliar" in that they are either obsolete or archaic or their meanings have shifted in modern-day usage. Each entry provides the word, part of speech, and definition or definitions. Following each definition is a quotation showing the word's use within one specific Shakespearean work. Text quotations from plays are cited with short title, act, scene, and line numbers, as found in the *Arden Shakespeare* (Methuen, 1976ff). Words found in the sonnets, and some from *Two Noble Kinsmen* are also included, although the latter may have questionable utility among the Shakespearean neophytes most likely to use this source. No pronunciation is provided, an omission common to similar reference tools, but that would be of great use in such a source, although challenging to compile.

Shewmaker has an M.F.A. from the Yale School of Drama and is a retired editor of dictionaries and other reference books. His editorial background is apparent in the accuracy and clarity of the dictionary's entries. Overall, this source would be a welcome acquisition for any collection supporting general Shakespearean research. [R: LJ, 1 June 96, p. 98]—**Marie F. Jones**

Poetry

1000. Mazzeno, Laurence W. **Victorian Poetry: An Annotated Bibliography.** Pasadena, Calif., Salem Press and Metuchen, N.J., Scarecrow, 1995. 247p. index. (Magill Bibliographies). $32.50. ISBN 0-8108-3008-6.

Mazzeno aims his bibliography at high school and college students, stating in his introduction that it is not inclusive or complete enough for the specialist on Victorian poets. His limits are fourfold: He included certain poets only; he attempted to collect and annotate the best criticism; he limited his sources to criticism published after 1970, with the exception of some earlier works that he considers "seminal"; and he included only books and monographs, not articles in scholarly journals. He comments in his introduction that the student may consult the *MLA International Bibliography* (see ARBA 93, entry 1107, and ARBA 86, entries 1077-1078) for listings of such articles.

He of course includes criticism of what Cecil Y. Lang called the "Victorian Trinity"—Matthew Arnold, Robert Browning, and Alfred, Lord Tennyson. To these he adds criticism of poets whose reputation dwindled with the early post-Victorian critics, but who have since regained respect: Elizabeth Barrett Browning (who during her life was a more respected poet than her husband Robert), Arthur Hugh Clough, Gerard Manley Hopkins, George Meredith, William Morris, Coventry Patmore, Christina and Dante Gabriel Rossetti, Algernon Charles Swinburne, James Thomson, and Oscar Wilde.

Mazzeno's decisions on limitations have enabled him to compile a useful bibliography. He has culled useful sources and arranged them in an easy-to-use format, with the critical sources for each poet listed in separate sections. Annotations are brief but cogent, attempting to state the major critical focus of the work and perhaps draw some comparisons with others. This is a useful work that should be helpful to the beginning student.—**Terry Ann Mood**

African Literature

1001. Limb, Peter, and Jean-Marie Volet. **Bibliography of African Literatures.** Lanham, Md., Scarecrow, 1996. 433p. index. (Scarecrow Area Bibliographies, no.10). $55.00. ISBN 0-8108-3144-9.

This is the most comprehensive bibliographic survey of twentieth-century continental African literatures presently available. An important feature of this 5-part bibliography is the number of African-language literatures represented: There are 15, each listed alphabetically, with the names of the countries in which they are spoken included in parentheses. Literature written in Arabic, English, French, and Portuguese, and other literatures—Afrikaans, German, and Spanish—are subdivided and alphabetized according to region and country. Each section includes a general overview of bibliographies, anthologies, and general studies, followed by the authors' works, with critical studies about the authors listed just after the primary works. Secondary sources appearing in journals and periodicals are not listed, although special issues devoted to African literature are included.

The book also provides three indexes: an authors index, a much-needed female literary authors index, and a countries index. Many of the names listed in the indexes are not familiar, which is one of the strengths of this bibliography. The editors have uncovered many young writers who have yet to make their mark in literature but who show great promise. They have also provided a brief historical overview of continental African literature that stretches back to the rich Arabic traditions of the eleventh and twelfth centuries and the seventh-century classical liturgical tradition of Ethiopia. This book will be useful for both general readers and serious scholars and researchers of African literature and is highly recommended.
—Sandra Adell

Australian Literature

1002. Lever, Richard, James Wieland, and Scott Findlay. **Post-Colonial Literatures in English: Australia, 1970-1992.** New York, G. K. Hall/Simon & Schuster Macmillan, 1996. 361p. index. (A Reference Publication in Literature). $65.00. ISBN 0-8161-7375-3.

The postcolonial (to use the catchphrase) writing of Australia stresses Australian rather than Anglocentric cultural values. Although exact definitions of the postcolonial tradition in Australia are hard to pin down, it can be seen interacting or overlapping with other literary movements, such as feminist, postmodern, new critical, and Marxist literatures, also flourishing in Australia. This volume, one of a new series of bibliographies on postcolonial literatures in English, provides annotations to reference works and critical assessments of Australian writers and Australian critical theory in general.

The bibliography starts with an interesting and well-written introduction by the authors. A "Selection and Organization" page immediately following the introduction explains the criteria for titles discussed and the organization of the text. The main text is divided into seven sections: reference aids, survey and overview, nonfiction, drama, fiction, poetry, and individual authors. The first six sections annotate general reference works and articles, theses, and dissertations that cover the broad topic. The final segment lists critical assessments and biographies of individual authors, including such writers as Barbara Hanrahan, Thomas Keneally, and interestingly enough, D. H. Lawrence (definitely not an Australian writer, but he did spend some time there). Surprisingly, Aboriginal writers are scarcer than one would expect in such a volume. Subject and author indexes provide access to the entries by entry number.

As with the Southeast Asian, New Zealand, and Pacific literatures volume (see entry 1013), this bibliography is a useful tool for students and researchers of literature. Scheduled upcoming volumes of the literatures of India, Pakistan, and South Asia will further promote the study of non-Western literary traditions, an important part of today's curriculum.—**Melissa Rae Root**

Canadian Literature

1003. **Canadian Writers and Their Works: Fiction Series. Volume Twelve.** Robert Lecker, Jack David, and Ellen Quigley, eds. Toronto, ECW Press, 1995. 265p. illus. index. $50.00 (U.S.). ISBN 1-55022-215-5.

1004. **Canadian Writers and Their Works: Poetry Series. Volume Eleven.** Robert Lecker, Jack David, and Ellen Quigley, eds. Toronto, ECW Press, 1995. 382p. illus. index. $50.00 (U.S.). ISBN 1-55022-217-1.

This excellent, long-standing series about Canadian fiction and poetry is drawing to a close. Approximately 120 original essays were prepared by experts and spread over 24 volumes. Each volume has an index (Will there be one for the whole set? That is unclear), and there are line drawings of each author. The late George Woodcock, world-renowned Canadian literature scholar, furnishes a short introductory essay unique to each book. The typeface is large, the binding is durable, and the contents are superior for both students and teachers.

The five poets profiled in volume 11 are Roo Borson, Lorna Crozier, Mary di Michele, Erin Moure, and Sharon Thesen. All specialize in producing slim volumes in small editions (except for one of Crozier's works, which managed to top 5,000 in sales). One more volume is scheduled for the poetry series. The creators of fiction discussed in volume 12 are Sandra Birdsell, Timothy Findley, W. P. Kinsella, and David Adams Richards. Both the poetry and fiction series have been roughly in chronological order by birth dates, which means (normally) that the authors are still alive and writing. Therefore, no commentary is provided on their latest works, as the deadlines for these critiques were set for 1994. Thus, there is nothing on Findley's impressive *The Piano Man's Daughter*.

The treatments all follow the same guidelines: For each author there is a sketch drawing and 50 to 60 pages of commentary. A biography section is first, followed by a societal placement ("tradition and milieu"), a critical overview and context, and a discussion of major works. Primary and secondary sources are noted at the end of each commentary. The critiques are written at a fair level, one that is easy to understand and enjoyable for learning. The volumes are very much recommended for the Canadian literature collection—but $50 per volume seems pricey. Will there be a special price if all volumes are purchased at once?—**Dean Tudor**

1005. **The John Metcalf Papers: An Inventory of the Archive at the University of Calgary Library.** Jean M. Moore and Marlys Chevrefils, comps. Apollonia Steele, ed. Calgary, Alta., University of Calgary Press, 1996. 245p. illus. index. (Canadian Archival Inventory Series: Literary Papers, no.16). $27.95pa. (U.S.). ISBN 1-895176-71-9.

The most recent addition to the University of Calgary's archival inventory series describes the initial three accessions documenting John Metcalf's work form the early 1960s to 1988. Two further accessions have since been acquired but are not included in this volume. Further accruals are expected.

Following the format established with previous inventories in the series (see ARBA 96, entry 1249, for another example), the book is prefaced with a substantial bio-critical essay on Metcalf. An archival introduction follows, detailing the methodology for arrangement and description of the fonds with a standardized format for each form/medium series noted in the contents. Reflecting Metcalf's multifaceted involvement in the Canadian literary milieu, materials also relate to anthologies edited by the author, critical works both by and about him, and creative works by other authors as well as a nonfiction prose series and promotional materials. His many and various involvements and interests (e.g., the Writers' Union of Canada and Montreal Story Tellers) provide a wide window on the arts of Canada for the years encompassed. A comprehensive general index and a separate title index, both with extensive cross-references, conclude the publication. A number of photographs and illustrative publicity materials are interspersed throughout the volume.

As with previous contributions to the archival series, the inventories are designed as control tools for literary content of acquisitions. In addition to his emergence as one of Canada's most influential contemporary writers, Metcalf's continuing involvement with and impact on the critical and literary history of his country make this reference a premier addition to the series. It will be an invaluable resource to students, researchers, and many others with an interdisciplinary approach to the development of Canadian arts and culture.—**Virginia S. Fischer**

German Literature

1006. **German Baroque Writers, 1580-1660.** James Hardin, ed. Detroit, Gale, 1996. 459p. illus. index. (Dictionary of Literary Biography, v.164). $135.00. ISBN 0-8103-9359-X.

This excellent addition to the Gale Dictionary of Literary Biography (DLB) series covers 45 major or notable writers of the German baroque period. As the period is usually considered to extend into the eighteenth century (Hardin, the volume's editor, dates it from roughly 1580 to roughly 1720), the terminus of 1660 announced in the title is significant. Although a few figures whose productivity at least largely postdates 1660 have been treated (Daniel Georg Morhof, Philipp Jakob Spencr, Caspar Stieler, Paul Winckler), most of the later baroque writers of note, including Hans Grimmelshausen, are absent. All of the really important literary authors of the earlier part of the period are featured, while the selection of others to go with them is balanced and fair.

The volume follows the standard DLB format of primary bibliography, illustrated bio-bibliographic essay, and secondary bibliography (including location of personal papers when known). The bibliographies, exhibiting varying degrees of thoroughness, cease as a rule in or before 1992. As with other German literature volumes in this series, the contributors are competent and often distinguished specialists, the selection of authors covered reflects an intelligently broad view of what constitutes "literature," and the standard of editing is high. Despite its cost (about the same as that of similar books published in Germany), this volume is highly recommended for college and university libraries supporting strong programs in German literature, comparative literature, or German history. Major public libraries in German settlement areas of North America may also find it useful.—**John B. Dillon**

Irish Literature

1007. **Dictionary of Irish Literature.** rev. ed. Robert Hogan and others, eds. Westport, Conn., Greenwood Press, 1996. 2v. index. $135.00/set. ISBN 0-313-29172-1.

This dictionary could have been more appropriately called *Dictionary of Irish Authors*. Containing more than double the entries of the premier edition (see ARBA 80, entry 1300), it continues the process of discussing important Irish writers and their works both biographically and critically. The structure of the dictionary remains basically the same. An introductory essay, "Gaelic Literature" by Seamus O'Neill, is reprinted from the 1st edition. This is followed by a new essay written especially for this set, "Contemporary Literature in the Irish Language" by Alan Titley. These articles attempt to fill a gap, as much of the great Irish literature (and much of the subject matter in the dictionary) has been written in English as the Irish language slowly dies. The main dictionary segment is followed by a chronology of Irish history and literature; a bibliography focusing on general discussions of Irish literature or certain aspects of it; and a comprehensive index (a rarity in a work in dictionary format) keyed to the dictionary proper as well as to the introductory articles.

As previously mentioned, the entries are mainly on authors. A few general articles appear, but on a highly selective basis. Individual works of literature are only given their own entry if the author is unknown; otherwise they are found under the author's name, making the index very important for finding a title quickly. If one knows the title of the work but not the author, a quick check in the index will lead to the correct place. The length of the entries ranges from a short paragraph to several pages. Some other-than-Irish writers are included if they have made significant contributions to the promotion of Irish literature. Most of the original entries have been revised and expanded, often by the original contributor. A great attempt has been made to include recent writers who have cropped up in the 15 years since the publication of the premier edition. The sexist language used in the introduction (e.g., "The qualities that have formed the Irish writer are the qualities that have formed the Irish man") is not mirrored in the main text in terms of content—many women writers are herein profiled. Entries end with (in many cases extensive) bibliographies that in and of themselves would make the dictionary a worthy acquisition.

All in all, this two-volume set is a worthwhile addition to any library collection. Libraries that own the original dictionary will benefit from the updated entries and new additions; those without that 1st edition will benefit from the well-written, scholarly, and interesting entries on some of the best-known writers in the world.—**Melissa Rae Root**

1008. Durkan, Michael J., and Rand Brandes. **Seamus Heaney: A Reference Guide.** New York, G. K. Hall/Simon & Schuster Macmillan, 1996. 225p. index. (Reference Guide to Literature). $45.00. ISBN 0-8161-7389-3.

Seamus Heaney, the contemporary Irish poet who won the 1995 Nobel prize, has been the subject of more than 20 full-length studies; 50-plus dissertations; hundreds of articles; and myriad reviews, profiles, and interviews. *Seamus Heaney: A Reference Guide*, compiled by the late Durkan, college librarian at Swarthmore College from 1976 to 1996, and Brandes, of Lenoir-Rhyne College, is part of G. K. Hall's Reference Guide to Literature series.

This guide contains approximately 2,000 entries of both scholarly criticism and popular notice written in English since 1965. A brief introductory essay places the writer and his work in context and suggests reasons for his wide popularity. All items are listed chronologically by year of publication and alphabetically by author or title. An index offers accessibility to individual titles and subjects as well as to authors of the included material. Also included is a chronology that lists important events in Heaney's life and career, beginning with his birth in 1939 in Northern Ireland, through his being awarded the Nobel prize.

The summary annotations for each entry are clear, concise, and well written, containing brief quotations where appropriate. This guide is an important reference for any reader of Heaney's work who is interested in a thorough understanding of the poet's work and the culture that produced it. It should save scholars many hours of research while offering those with less interest in the subject some inkling of why Heaney was chosen to receive the Nobel prize.—**Kay O. Cornelius**

1009. Fargnoli, A. Nicholas, and Michael Patrick Gillespie. **James Joyce A to Z: The Essential Reference to the Life and Work.** New York, Facts on File, 1995. 304p. illus. index. $45.00. ISBN 0-8160-2904-0.

This encyclopedia is addressed primarily to a general audience interested in James Joyce's life and work. More than 800 entries focus on 5 major categories: ideas directly introduced in the works; fictional events in the works or historical events forming a background to the fiction; real and fictional geographic places; major fictional characters; and real people used in the fiction or important in Joyce's life and thought. Articles provide explanations and contexts but are not intended to be exhaustive.

Although each of Joyce's major works is explicated in some detail, first-time readers needing more assistance in interpreting a particular work will probably be better served by two earlier books: William York Tindall's *A Reader's Guide to James Joyce* (Noonday Press, 1959) or Matthew Hodgart's *James Joyce: A Student's Guide* (London: Routledge and Kegan Paul, 1978). Neither of these books, however, has the reference value of *James Joyce A to Z*. Many of the 800 entries include cross-references to other articles. Abbreviations are kept to a minimum.

Appendixes include a chronology of Joyce's writings and publications; a list of musical, theatrical, and cinematic adaptations; a chart reproducing Hugh Kenner's schema for *Ulysses*; the text of Judge Woolsey's decision to lift the ban on *Ulysses*; an outline of *Finnegans Wake*; family trees of not only Joyce but also his major literary characters; bibliographies (unannotated) listing selected biographical and critical sources; and a dateline listing important historical events side by side with important events in Joyce's life. A detailed index supplements the A to Z entries, but does not replicate the cross-references. While primarily useful to general readers and students encountering Joyce for the first time, this encyclopedia will also be helpful to scholars for fact-checking. [R: Choice, Feb 96, pp. 927-28]

—**David Isaacson**

Italian Literature

1010. **Dictionary of Italian Literature.** rev. ed. Peter Bondanella, Julia Conaway Bondanella, and Jody Robin Shiffman, eds. Westport, Conn., Greenwood Press, 1996. 716p. index. $99.50. ISBN 0-313-27745-1.

The 1st edition of this work (see ARBA 80, entry 1302) was strongly endorsed by the *American Reference Books Annual* reviewer, and this new edition will surely continue to be a basic information source in all libraries where there is any interest in Italian literature. More than 80 new entries have been added, and many of the original articles have been updated. The timeline in the appendix has been extended through 1995.

Roughly two-thirds of the alphabetically arranged entries deal with individual authors, with the rest treating more general topics, such as time periods, literary movements, genres, and aspects of criticism (worth noting are extended new articles on feminism, literature and art, and literature and film). All entries include bibliographies. The contributors are scholars at North American universities; the articles are signed (except those written by the editors), and if an entry from the 1st edition has been revised by someone other than the original author, both writers are identified. A brief bibliography of reference aids, a good index, and an annotated list of the contributors are included. The one factual error noted by the reviewer of the 1st edition has been corrected, but his recommendation to add an entry for Gaetano Moroni has not been followed.—**Paul B. Cors**

1011. Stych, F. S. **Boccaccio in English: A Bibliography of Editions, Adaptations, and Criticism.** Westport, Conn., Greenwood Press, 1995. 254p. index. (Bibliographies and Indexes in World Literature, no.48). $79.50. ISBN 0-313-28967-0.

This ambiguously titled but technically well-organized bibliography covers with some thoroughness several different aspects of the critical and literary reception of the fourteenth-century Italian writer Giovanni Boccaccio. Devoid of any statement describing its subject scope, the book appears to deal with the following phenomena: English-language translations and adaptations of Boccaccio; non-English-language editions, translations, and adaptations when published in an English-speaking country; discussions of Boccaccio manuscripts housed in an English-speaking country; English-language scholarship on Boccaccio; and non-English-language scholarship on Boccaccio written by inhabitants of an English-speaking country or dealing with some facet of Boccaccio's fortune in the English-speaking world. There are 2,242 numbered entries, concisely and intelligently annotated, plus 7 highly valuable indexes.

Because of their very different approaches, there is not much overlap between this book and Joseph P. Consoli's 1992 *Giovanni Boccaccio: An Annotated Bibliography* (see ARBA 93, entry 1224), whose starting date is 1939. Stych's coverage begins in the sixteenth century and ends in 1993; within each of the three major sections ("Editions," "Adaptations and Parallels," "Criticism") the arrangement is basically chronological with appropriate local modifications. Special attention has been given to book reviews, not all of which are reposited in the most common library indexes. One wishes, however, that Stych had also included the reviews' authors in his index of critics, as it is somewhat incomplete without them. The surprising omission of H. J. Leon's important translation of *Bucolicum Carmen* (in *The Pastoral Elegy: An Anthology* [Austin, 1939]) suggests that anthologies as a class might have been investigated more diligently. More attention could also have been devoted to identifying the subsequent publication (often with revisions) of scholarly articles as chapters in books of broader scope. But these are minor flaws in a useful book, one that certainly deserves to be in most college and university libraries.—**John B. Dillon**

Latin American and Caribbean Literature

1012. **Twentieth-Century Caribbean and Black African Writers, Third Series.** Bernth Lindfors and Reinhard Sander, eds. Detroit, Gale, 1996. 461p. illus. index. (Dictionary of Literary Biography, v.157). $128.00. ISBN 0-8103-9352-2.

The 157th volume of the Dictionary of Literary Biography (DLB) contains essays on 33 writers from Africa and the Caribbean and adds to the 65 writers found in the 2 previous volumes: DLB volume 117 (see ARBA 93, entry 1110) and volume 125 (see ARBA 94, entry 1148). Entries contain photographs of authors and selected dust jackets as well as other illustrations. As with other volumes in the acclaimed DLB series, the biographical information and critical examination of the authors' works are thorough. Researchers will appreciate that entries also include complete lists of the authors' works, bibliographic references, and references of interviews.

The authors represent a younger generation primarily from the same top three countries represented in the first two volumes: Nigeria, South Africa, and Jamaica. In the introduction, the editors explain that the selection of authors was based on influence and reputation: Most of the authors selected have only recently made their reputations in the broader area of postcolonial literature. Unlike their predecessors in the previous volumes, who explored the colonial experience and the past, writers of the Baby Boom generation have tended to look into postcolonial life at home.

As anglophone literature by these fine writers becomes increasingly well known and read within the larger, English-speaking community, more of their work will be studied and enjoyed. This reference is highly recommended for academic and public libraries. [R: Choice, May 96, p. 1458]—**Edward Erazo**

Oceanian Literature

1013. Williams, Mark. **Post-Colonial Literatures in English: Southeast Asia, New Zealand, and the Pacific, 1970-1992.** New York, G. K. Hall/Simon & Schuster Macmillan, 1996. 370p. index. (A Reference Publication in Literature). $60.00. ISBN 0-8161-7353-2.

The indigenous peoples of Southeast Asia, New Zealand, and the Pacific are following in the footsteps of decolonized African countries in inventing a literature of their own. Drawing from a rich oral tradition and often reacting to their colonization by the British, these emerging writers emanate a style very different from more Western writers. Postcolonial or postnationalist literature, as indigenous literatures are often called, are gaining renown worldwide and are inspiring a school of theoretical criticism as well. This volume "helps fill in details of a very large area of topographical and intellectual space" (p. ix).

Following an enlightening and well-written introductory survey by the author, the main text is divided into four broad headings: general, New Zealand, Pacific, and Southeast Asia (in this case meaning primarily Singapore and Malaysia). Missing is an explanation of selection and organization. The general section first lists reference aids, including bibliographies and other finding aids, and then itemizes surveys and overviews. Classics such as *Modern Commonwealth Literature* (see ARBA 79, entry 1184) make the list, along with newer titles—up to 1992 copyright dates—and annuals and regularly updated electronic sources.

Each area section begins with a general selection of titles that annotates scholarly books, collections of criticism, and journal articles. The annotations are concise but useful and vary in length depending on the relative importance or depth of the work discussed. Following the general section is a segment on individual authors, detailing critical assessments and biographies about the writer in question. The individual authors encompass the genres of drama, general fiction, nonfiction, and poetry. The number of entries for any given writer differs according to the amount written by or about the person; Katherine Mansfield, for example, merits more than 150 annotations, while Fleur Adcock receives 6. Each annotation is preceded by an entry number, and the indexes are keyed to these numbers.

One of the first of a scheduled series on postcolonial literatures in English, the volume under review provides a useful service for the researcher. Students of literature would do well to consult the annotations when launching into the study of Southeast Asian, New Zealand, or Pacific-area writers. A volume on Australian writers is already published (see entry 1002); future volumes in the series will cover the literatures of India, Pakistan, and South Asia.—**Melissa Rae Root**

Spanish Literature

1014. Amell, Samuel. **The Contemporary Spanish Novel: An Annotated, Critical Bibliography, 1936-1994.** Westport, Conn., Greenwood Press, 1996. 273p. index. (Bibliographies and Indexes in World Literature, no.50). $75.00. ISBN 0-313-24784-6.

Amell divides his bibliography into two parts: books and articles written about the postwar novel (a term that refers to the Spanish Civil War of 1936-1939). Each section contains an alphabetic arrangement by author of general studies (themes, groups of writers or novels, and so forth) rather than ones dealing with individual novelists or single works. The books portion lists 211 volumes, while the articles section has 667 entries. The vast majority of these items are English- or Spanish-language publications, with the remainder devoted to studies written in Catalan, French, Galician, or Italian. All entries provide detailed descriptive annotations, and in most cases the compiler offers critical evaluations, some of which are highly opinionated.

In a brief (one-page) preface Amell discusses the need for a comprehensive, annotated, English-language bibliography of the subject matter, stating that this volume will attempt to fill the gap. He then goes on to describe the arrangement and content of entries, but his failure to discuss methodology leaves users uncertain with regard to sources consulted and therefore unable to judge the accuracy of the term *comprehensive*. The absence of dissertations, apparently intentional, suggests that Amell's goal was to compile a guide to published sources only.

Two lengthy indexes, one for novelists and the other for titles of novels mentioned in the entries, complete the volume. These indexes greatly simplify the task of locating material on specific authors and works, thereby maximizing the volume's worth as a reference tool. Well organized and easy to use, this bibliography has been designed with the researcher in mind. Scholars specializing in the Spanish postwar novel will find it indispensable. [R: Choice, June 96, p. 1607]—**Melvin S. Arrington Jr.**

POETRY

1015. Alexander, Harriet Semmes, comp. **American and British Poetry: A Guide to the Criticism 1979-1990.** Athens, Ohio, Swallow Press/Ohio University Press, 1996. 465p. $65.00. ISBN 0-8040-0988-0.

This reference work is a supplement to an earlier volume by Alexander listing articles and books written between 1925 and 1978 discussing British and American poets. In the 12 years covered here, 1979-1990, the volume of literary criticism has increased exponentially—most notably on Emily Dickinson.

A prefatory note by the author has a certain defensive quality to it, maintaining that the work is useful even in the day of CD-ROM and online bibliographies and indexes, for other sources do not index the articles as fully as this volume does. However, the indexing here is frequently repetitious. There is a separate entry for every poem that is discussed in an article so that, for instance, there are 14 entries for the 1 article by Henry Hart on Seamus Heaney. At this stage, scholarship can seem as much plodding as thorough. Annotations of selected articles, a much more ambitious undertaking, would have been more useful and made the volume easier to justify.

The list of poets is comprehensive, going back to the Old English poets Caedmon and Cynewulf. Yet Old English and Middle English studies require a special linguistic training, and the inclusion of them here seems again to point to a need to justify a kind of scholarship that is fast becoming out-of-date. [R: Choice, Dec 96, p. 585]—**John B. Beston**

1016. **The Columbia Granger's Index to Poetry in Collected and Selected Works.** Nicholas Frankovich, ed. New York, Columbia University Press, 1996. 1913p. $225.00. ISBN 0-231-10762-5.

Since its first publication in 1904, *The Columbia Granger's Index to Poetry* has remained the authoritative guide to poetry in anthologies (see ARBA 95, entry 1245, for a review of the 10th edition). With the publication of this new volume, Columbia Granger's has ventured into new territory. Joined by James Shapiro, professor of English and Comparative Literature at Columbia University, the editorial staff has focused on the collected and selected works of poetry most likely to be found on library shelves. While the list of collected works numbers 53, only 22 selected titles are included, and both are outnumbered by anthologies, which still make up the majority of references.

As with the previous anthology indexes, this volume is divided into three sections, each arranged alphabetically. The title and first line index is the largest portion of the volume, with more than 1,000 pages and 50,000 poems. As with its predecessors, each title is followed by the author's name and a code linking the poem to its collective work. The author index includes 251 poets, from Catullus and Geoffrey Chaucer to Pablo Neruda, Shel Silverstein, and Louis Zukofsky. An alphabetic list of titles follows each poet's name. Yet it is the cross-referenced subject index, with its numerous related references, that provides greater access to the poems. As stated in the preface, this subject indexing surpasses that found in the collective works themselves. Even electronic catalogs with contents notes do not provide such in-depth indexing.

Scholars will find this work particularly useful, and research libraries will acknowledge this volume to be an excellent companion to their anthology indexes. Smaller libraries, however, may find the price a significant obstacle.—**Debra S. Van Tassel**

1017. **The Columbia Granger's World of Poetry.** [CD-ROM]. New York, Columbia University Press, 1995. Minimum system requirements (Windows version): IBM or compatible 386. CD-ROM drive with MS CD-ROM Extensions 2.0. MS-DOS 5.0. Windows 3.1. 8MB RAM. Minimum system requirements (Macintosh version): Macintosh 68030. CD-ROM drive. 8MB RAM. $495.00. ISBN 0-231-10158-9.

More comprehensive than *Poem Finder 95* (see entry 1018), this resource contains the full text of 10,000 noncopyrighted works, quotations from 7,500 copyrighted poems, and indexing information to 700 anthologies, giving access to 135,000 poems by 20,000 poets. The disc can be searched by author, title, subject, first line, last line, keyword, or category. Complex searches can be done with the Boolean operators AND, OR, and NOT. After the screen records the number of hits for each term or name, the user can display the matches. Users can also search for anthologies by editor, title, or category. Operating on a Pentium processor, search results are displayed quickly. Under the Window menu term, a record of previous searches is kept; these are also minimized at the bottom of the screen. Installation of the disc is easy, and the interface is user friendly.

After completing a search, a list of poems appears from which the user can choose. When pulling up an entry for a poem, the result gives the work's author, title, first line, last line, whether the full text or a quotation of the poem is available on the disc, and the anthologies in which the poem is printed. The anthologies have hypertext links to their full record, including a recommendation from Granger's editorial board (highly recommended, recommended, or no recommendation); date; publisher; editor(s); number of pages; category; and a short review.

This poem-finding tool will be ideal for the reference desk of public, academic, and school libraries. It will be particularly useful for finding full information about poems of which the title and poet are not known. The single-user price is more than *Poem Finder 95*, but *Columbia Granger's* coverage is more extensive, justifying the additional money spent.—**Melissa Rae Root**

1018. **Poem Finder 95: The Ultimate Poetry Reference on CD-ROM.** [CD-ROM]. Great Neck, N.Y., Roth Publishing, 1995. Minimum system requirements: IBM or compatible 286. CD-ROM drive. MS-DOS or PC-DOS 3.3. Hard disk. 525KB conventional memory. $300.00/single user; $475.00/2-8 users.

This fascinating CD-ROM will allow almost any user access to ample information about thousands of poems and hundreds of authors, both well known and obscure. One can search via many options, including author name, profession, nationality, and religion; any word in a poem title, first line, and last line; keyword; poem date; and subject (4,400-plus headings). Moving from the search menu to the browse menu, one can search by already-created lists of authors and by the titles of their poems, which include further information, such as the first and last lines of the poems, a subject entry, and the collections in which the poems have appeared. A glossary of poetic terms is a useful aid that can also be accessed from the browse menu; among them are *terza rima*, *transcendentalism*, *couplet*, *limerick*, *ode*, and *myth*. The keyword search and Boolean options will prove helpful, particularly when one remembers one or two words from a poem and needs to know the title and the poet.

There are shortcomings in occasional references and indexing. For example, "Claus of Innsbruck" in Robert Browning's "My Last Duchess" appears here as "Claus of Innbruuck." Randall Jarrell's World War II poem "An Officers' Prison Camp Seen from a Troop Train" is listed also as "An Officers' Prison Camp." There is a similar error with listings of Winfield Townley Scott's "The U.S. Sailor with the

Japanese Skull." Each entry, unfortunately, does not list the same sources where the poem may be found. These are not, however, major problems for the careful researcher and should not detract from the value of this comprehensive resource.

Intended primarily for the humanities reference desk, *Poem Finder 95* will also appeal to the English professor and his or her graduate students as well as to the poet. Most academic libraries will want to add this disc to their CD-ROM budgets or wish lists. [R: Choice, April 96, pp. 1294-95]

—**Charles R. Andrews**

1019. **The Princeton Handbook of Multicultural Poetries.** T. V. F. Brogan, ed. Princeton, N.J., Princeton University Press, 1996. 366p. $17.95pa. ISBN 0-691-00168-5.

This handbook is essentially a small encyclopedia, with articles selected from the 1993 *New Princeton Encyclopedia of Poetry and Poetics* (see ARBA 94, entry 1302), without further editing. The selection, according to the editor, has sought balance above all, but has not altogether achieved it. The 106 articles on Eastern and Western poetries, ancient and modern, are highly diverse, but are weighted in favor of English-speaking countries and western Europe. The selection also reflects deference to prevailing political correctness and political clout: There are entries on Inuit, Native American, and Chicano and Puerto Rican poetry on the one hand, but none on the poetries of such countries as Samoa or Papua New Guinea on the other. The preface to the volume, which seems at first to be merely an entertaining account of English-department politics in the present-day United States, turns out on further consideration to tell a great deal about the pressures acting upon the selection process.

Entries by so many scholars vary, of course, in quality, but the standard is normally high. Entries on the English-language poetries are outstanding, with the notable exception of the glib entry on Australian poetry (which does not even mention aboriginal poetry in English). The European entries are adequate, but those on German poetry are pedestrian and dull. Spanish American poetries and African poetries in French and Portuguese tend to get lumped together rather cursorily. The book nevertheless does impress by its extraordinary diversity. [R: Choice, June 96, p. 1622]—**John B. Beston**

25 Music

GENERAL WORKS

Bibliography

1020. Ericson, Margaret D. **Women and Music: A Selective Annotated Bibliography on Women and Gender Issues in Music, 1987-1992.** New York, G. K. Hall/Simon & Schuster Macmillan, 1996. 400p. index. $95.00. ISBN 0-8161-0580-4.

Music librarian Ericson has granted a great boon to anyone interested in the subject of women and music by creating this finely organized and annotated bibliography. An outgrowth of her work within the Music Library Association, the book deals with materials as far separated from one another as general reference works and newspaper articles, embracing along the way books, journal articles, theses, conference papers, score anthologies, recordings and videos, and online information sources. First classified in one of several categories (e.g., "Women in the Music Professions," "Women and Gender Issues in Music Education," "Gender and Audience Perception"), then placed under an appropriate subheading, each title receives a full bibliographic entry including, where appropriate, an ISBN and a list of reviews of the item in scholarly or professional journals. The author largely confines her annotations to description rather than evaluation of content. Although this is undoubtedly the proper path given the numbers and range of her sources, it does allow such a notoriously faulty reference tool as Rose Marie Johnson's *Violin Music by Women Composers* to escape with only mild censure of its "somewhat awkward arrangement" (p. 6).

Some flaws in Ericson's plan may also serve as virtues. She excludes from consideration sources that deal with a single individual, thus omitting all recent biographies at the same time that she ensures her book's broad appeal. Her five-year time span seems unduly restricted and less timely than one might wish, yet this limitation allows her to pay thorough attention to the material she has collected and to make sure it is presented in the most convenient and usable form. In fact, the book is both formidable and appealing: formidable in the amount of material it contains, and appealing in the manner in which this material is presented. Students, scholars, performers, and even interested bystanders will find this book a valuable resource. [R: Choice, July/Aug 96, p. 1772]—**Karin Pendle**

1021. Marco, Guy A. **Literature of American Music III, 1983-1992.** Lanham, Md., Scarecrow, 1996. 451p. index. $140.00. ISBN 0-8108-3132-5.

This book is a continuation of David Horn's two inventories of significant works on music by Americans and about American musical life, *Literature of American Music in Books and Folk Music Collections* (see ARBA 78, entry 893) and, with Richard Jackson, *The Literature of American Music in Books and Folk Music Collections, Supplement I* (see ARBA 89, entry 1169). To Horn's 3,862 monographs Marco adds another 1,248 that fit within his selection criteria: monographs in English that appeared in respected, selected source lists, and monographs in other languages that appeared in the same source lists if those monographs contained significant reference material (such as discographies) or other original text Marco deemed important. Some categories of material were excluded outright, such as master's theses, doctoral dissertations, and juvenile books; other categories, such as price guides, music career guides, and books of fewer than 80 pages, were included selectively based on reference value.

In a change from the structure of its predecessors, this bibliography is arranged by Library of Congress (LC) classification, leading off with "BR-BX: Church Music" and ending with "PS3552-3562: Writers." Entries include the *Literature of American Music* identification number, LC classification number, and complete bibliographic data, plus a several-sentence evaluative annotation that places special emphasis on any reference features offered by the work at hand. Although brief, Marco's descriptions are refreshingly candid, as in his description of Joan Baez's life story as "a totally boring anecdotal autobiography by the singer." Each entry concludes with citations to book reviews when available.

The bibliography concludes with a title index, a subject index, and an index of joint authors (individuals who have coauthored listed works). Surprisingly, the subject index is not nearly as detailed as one would expect based on Marco's own comments in the preface regarding "expansive" (subdivisions under main headings) versus "nonexpansive" (all page citations under one heading) indexes. This consideration aside, however, Marco has done an excellent job of bringing Horn's original work into the 1990s. [R: LJ, 1 Nov 96, p. 62]—**G. Kim Dority**

1022. Mixter, Keith E. **General Bibliography for Music Research.** 3d ed. Warren, Mich., Harmonie Park Press, 1996. 200p. index. $40.00. ISBN 0-89990-103-4.

The *General Bibliography for Music Research* was first published in 1964, and again in 1975 (see ARBA 76, entry 991), and now, more than 20 years later, it has been updated to reflect the new and many different kinds of reference works in music. The emphasis of the work is on publications from North America and Europe. The work is extremely inclusive, with listings for basic research, bibliographies, national and trade bibliographies, dictionaries of musical terms, encyclopedias, biography and autobiography sources, bibliographies, indexes, and union lists and library catalogs. All types of materials are included (e.g., books, CD-ROMs, online sources, microforms, and so forth).

The major strength of this bibliography is its inclusion of resources that are not generally thought of for music research, in addition to all of the standard music reference tools. Also, the inclusion of both CD-ROMs and online services provides valuable information for music students and scholars that is often hard to find. For instance, information on how to access the OCLC FirstSearch and EPIC online catalogs is included, along with both the print and CD-ROM versions of major bibliographies. Mixter does not provide much information concerning music resources on the Internet as such. Music students and scholars should refer to the material compiled by Leslie Troutman in "An Internet Primer for Music Librarians: Tools, Sources, Current Awareness," *Notes* 51 (1984-85), and sources such as *The Whole Internet: User's Guide & Catalog* (2d ed., O'Reilly and Associates, 1994).

The chapter introductions provide much information concerning the sources listed, but the individual items are not annotated. Also, title and name indexes are included, but not subject or genre indexes. Because of this, it is not possible to locate online or CD-ROM sources by type; they are buried in the other lists, and are not always easy to identify. Yet taken as a whole, this is an important reference for locating research materials in music. It should be considered a must-purchase for all public and academic libraries with larger music collections, and will be a valuable desk reference for anyone interested in music scholarship.—**Robert L. Wick**

1023. Perone, James E., comp. **Musical Anthologies for Analytical Study: A Bibliography.** Westport, Conn., Greenwood Press, 1995. 182p. index. (Music Reference Collection, no.48). $59.95. ISBN 0-313-29595-6.

Musical Anthologies for Analytical Study is a useful bibliography that provides music theory teachers with a single source for locating musical examples from 14 generally available anthologies. Unlike *Anthologies of Music: An Annotated Index* (ARBA 88, entry 1292), which focuses mainly on historical anthologies, Perone's bibliography includes anthologies compiled specifically for musical analysis. There is minor overlap, but the aims of the volumes and the information covered are completely different.

The scope of each anthology in Perone's guide is described and the contents listed in detail. In addition, the type of score (full, piano reduction, and so on) and the measures included for each example are given. If the anthology is arranged by theoretical topic, the contents of the anthology are also listed that way, and an index by theoretical topics is provided as well. The volume is also indexed by composers and sources, and complete movements and compositions. This book should prove to be of significant value to music theory teachers who can now avoid leafing through various anthologies for appropriate musical examples. It is recommended for academic libraries.—**Allie Wise Goudy**

Biography

1024. The Harvard Biographical Dictionary of Music. Don Michael Randel, ed. Cambridge, Mass., Belknap Press/Harvard University Press, 1996. 1013p. illus. $39.95. ISBN 0-674-37299-9.

Based on *The New Harvard Dictionary of Music* (see ARBA 87, entry 1231), *The Harvard Biographical Dictionary of Music* provides authoritative biographical information on more than 5,500 figures in the world of music, including performers, composers, instrument makers, and music theorists. Randel points out in the preface that the *Harvard Biographical Dictionary* "concerns primarily the history of concert music in the Western tradition. That is, the musicians whose biographies it includes are first and foremost composers of Western concert or art music from the earliest times to the present . . . [and] includes jazz musicians and at least some of the more prominent exponents of popular music." The individual entries follow the standard form used in the other Harvard dictionaries (i.e., name, birth and death dates and places, and a brief biography covering the major events in the individual's life). Each entry also contains a list of works by the individual and a brief bibliography of major books and articles about the individual. In a few cases, there are black-and-white photographs of more prominent individuals, but they are rare and appear to be used in a random manner.

As in the case of *The New Harvard Dictionary of Music*, the scholarship in this biography spin-off is meticulous, and the information provided is to the point and covers the major elements of the individuals' lives. The biographies are written by more than 70 of the most prominent musicologists today. Also, in most cases, the prose of the biographies is lively and easily read.

The major competition for this work is, of course, *Baker's Biographical Dictionary of Musicians* (8th ed.; see ARBA 93, entry 1244), which has been the standard source for brief biographies for at least 30 years. The 8th edition of *Baker's* provides slightly more than 2,500 biographies, far fewer than the Harvard title. In addition, the entries in *Baker's* tend to be shorter than those found in *Harvard*, and *Baker's* does not furnish photographs. Of course, *The New Grove Dictionary of Music and Musicians* (see ARBA 81, entry 1016) supplies a large number of individual biographies of musicians and composers that are usually very detailed, but it does not replace the ease of use of the smaller dictionaries of biography.

The Harvard Biographical Dictionary of Music is highly recommended for all library collections. Its large number of biographies of individuals in non-Western classical music is especially welcome.

—**Robert L. Wick**

Chronology

1025. Hall, Charles J. **A Chronicle of American Music, 1700-1995.** New York, Schirmer Books/Simon & Schuster Macmillan, 1996. 825p. index. $75.00. ISBN 0-02-860296-X.

This comprehensive work is arranged chronologically, with an entry for each year. Oriented toward the field of art music, which the author classifies as the "Cultivated/Art Music Scene," there is also lesser, but significant, inclusion of the "Vernacular/Commercial Music Scene," or popular music. For each year's entry, the music scene is preceded by "Historical Highlights," "World Cultural Highlights," and "American Art and Literature Highlights." Music entries begin with the births and deaths of notables in the music world for each year. Those included are not only composers and musicians but also those in allied fields, such as instrument makers, singers, conductors, writers, and musicologists.

Additional categories are found for debuts, including those at the Metropolitan Opera; honors; new positions, as in the fields of conducting and in education; noteworthy biographical events; and "musical beginnings." This latter category encompasses festivals, companies, performing groups, and others. There are still more entries covering music publications and compositions. Here the breakdowns are specific: for chamber music, concertos, choral/vocal, orchestra/band, piano/organ, symphonies, and others. This well-organized volume should prove valuable for all libraries and fulfill multiple uses, especially with its timeline coverage of news-related U.S. and world events, along with the art, literature, and music highlights that accompany the main music entries for publications and compositions.—**Louis G. Zelenka**

Dictionaries and Encyclopedias

1026. Bliss, Marilyn, comp. **The Compact Music Dictionary: Over 2200 Clear, Concise Definitions of Musical Terms.** New York, Amsco Publications/Music Sales Corporation, 1995. 125p. $5.95pa. ISBN 0-8256-1430-9.

It is difficult to tell just what niche this dictionary is intended to fill. Its format (4½-by-12 inches) seems to indicate that it belongs in an instrument case, as a handy source for musicians wishing to interpret those pesky directions in Italian or German in their scores. However, the entries in the dictionary go beyond the definition of such terms, attempting to define broader terms such as musical forms and instrument families. Thus, the reader who is looking for the meaning of the direction *Affannoso* (given as "anxious, restless") will quickly be able to read a bit about aeolian harps and accordions without turning the page. The definitions are clear, concise, and brief, and only occasionally did the compiler deem it necessary to provide illustration via notation. This stripped-down reference book seems aptly priced for the working-musician market, but libraries can pass if they have any dictionary of musical terms at all.—**David Dodd**

1027. **The Concise Oxford Dictionary of Music.** 4th ed. By Michael Kennedy. New York, Oxford University Press, 1996. 815p. $15.95pa. ISBN 0-19-280037-X.

This work is based on the 2d edition of *The Oxford Dictionary of Music* (see ARBA 96, entry 1270). Users should note the existence of a similarly titled publication, *The Oxford Companion to Music* (10th ed.; see ARBA 71, entry 1236), which was succeeded in 1983 by the 2-volume *The New Oxford Companion to Music* (see ARBA 84, entry 889). The "concise" work is actually quite substantial compared with the original. The author states that some entries have been completed or compressed, and work lists of lesser-known composers abbreviated, leaving entries for major composers unchanged. He is desirous that his readership know how he has resolved the problems presented by translated and transliterated names and titles, particularly Russian ones, but he makes no statement describing the scope of the work.

As with its parent title, the concise version contains a medley of information on composers, individual works, musical theory and terminology, instruments, forms and genres, performers, orchestras, and ensembles. The articles on major composers are of particular value, providing a biography of manageable size, along with a comprehensive list of works, in many cases enumerating each one individually. Within articles, asterisks note references to other entries. The article on the clarinet provides historical and technical information about the instrument in its various manifestations and notes that the term *clarionet* is obsolete. The author's stated preference for American nomenclature has not been consistently applied in the entries for the terms *whole-note* and *minim*.

What stands out most in this work, and its parent, is that both appear to have grown on a free-flowering basis, in the absence of any clearly stated guiding principles for incorporation. The preface to the parent work states that Kennedy has "added nearly 1,000 entries," and whereas some have been deleted for the concise version, no rationale is given in either case. Furthermore, the preface to the 1st edition is not reprinted in the 2d, so one cannot evaluate the relationship between the 2. "Music" is primarily conceived as that of the Western art-music tradition, but not exclusively so; however, entries for popular and traditional music are comparatively few. The Beatles have an entry, but users searching for John Lennon will find neither an entry nor a cross-reference; the article on the Rolling Stones is much briefer, and neither the Beach Boys nor the Sex Pistols have an entry (although the one-paragraph article on rock mentions punk rock). A brief paragraph describes *gamelan*, but no entry for *gagaku* is found. On the other hand, innumerable entries for minor composers and performers, many of them deceased, are to be found; for example, the U.S. pianist William Capell (d.1953), of whom it is noted, "Never played in Eng[land]." Some terms, for example *choragus* and *kantele*, are particularly obscure; it is difficult to conceive that the same readership who needs a pedestrian biography of Wolfgang Amadeus Mozart is also likely to look here for an explanation of such terms as these.

Consequently, it is hard to tell what place, if any, this work should have in a library collection. The readership is entirely unstated. The Oxford imprimatur lends authority to publications bearing its name, and many will find this tool handy for a quick lookup of instantly needed information, such as dates and places of birth and death, middle names, and so forth, rather than consulting more rigorous tools. Perhaps the best virtue of *The Concise Oxford Dictionary of Music* is its price, which is evidently aimed at the mass market.—**Ian Fairclough**

1028. **The Penguin Dictionary of Music.** 6th ed. By Arthur Jacobs. New York, Penguin Books, 1996. 493p. $13.95pa. ISBN 0-14-051290-X.

With the ever-changing and growing topic of classical music, this new edition of *The Penguin Dictionary of Music* is updated for 1996 with more than 500 new entries. Recent compositions, new composers, and rising names of the opera and concert world are included. In easy-to-read, alphabetized entries, readers find details of musical instruments, terms, and genres. Each entry is specific and informative. For example, each composition of music gives information on past and present performers, composers, and even authors whose work inspired them. This book not only explains the difference between *adagio* and *adagietto* in easy-to-understand terms, but provides both English- and foreign-language titles of operas, ballets, and musical theater. Pursuing cross-references of topics is easy because of legible symbols that guide the reader to related topics. This comprehensive edition, intended for musicians, students, concertgoers, or anyone with a love of music, is educational and entertaining.—**Natalie Brower-Kirton**

Directories

1029. Clynes, Tom. **Music Festivals from Bach to Blues: A Traveler's Guide.** Detroit, Visible Ink Press/Gale, 1996. 582p. illus. index. $18.95pa. ISBN 0-7876-0823-8.

There are music festivals in every state and province of Canada and the United States, and not only in the summertime. Perhaps Clynes covers them all in this most useful and stimulating handbook. The entries are first geographically organized, and then listed by month. Pithy descriptions provide all of the initial information one may need, including how to reach the site by car and telephone numbers for tickets and for information on lodging (even more details are provided for the supplemental educational workshops, such as Gunther Schuller's Idaho institute or the various dulcimer camps). The thematic focus of each entry is clearly indicated, usually with sample offerings, and extends beyond the Bach and blues promises—picture a gathering of those variously interested in swamp pop, opera, polka, reggae, Choctaw music, baroque bassoon playing, yodeling, Duke Ellington, klezmer or medieval music, and rap, not to mention features of Chicago's Queercore (which missed the topical index).

It would take a person of rather eclectic tastes to sample all the festivities, which is all the more to the author's evenhanded credit. Side issues include whiskey tasting and beer drinking, religious services, potentials for hiking, and ethnic cuisine explorations. Many photographs illustrate the festivals in utilitarian quality. In addition to two topical indexes (which might have been allied), dates and festival names are traced. Patrons of any public library will be delighted, and music students of any age or inclination would be well stimulated by this guide.—**Dominique-René de Lerma**

Discography

1030. Lynch, Richard Chigley, comp. **Broadway, Movie, TV, and Studio Cast Musicals on Record: A Discography of Recordings, 1985-1995.** Westport, Conn., Greenwood Press, 1996. 254p. index. (Discographies, no.68). $65.00. ISBN 0-313-29855-6.

This is the fourth in a series of discographies, compiled by the retired assistant curator of the Billy Rose Theatre Collection at the New York Public Library. The earlier volumes, all published by Greenwood Press, addressed Broadway musicals (see ARBA 89, entry 1296), movie musicals (see ARBA 90, entry 1234), and TV and studio cast musicals (see ARBA 91, entry 1320). This manual covers issues released between 1985 and 1995 in all three areas, plus 1996's *Forbidden Hollywood*. Entries are alphabetic by title, parenthetically identified by year and media, followed by the discographic data, including duration of the CDs. The cast is specified, but not by role. Credit is given the composer, lyricist, and conductor. Unless there is a need for a special note, the format concludes with a list of songs or other contents in order of presentation.

The terse introduction indicates some recordings were issued before the show opened, at times with a cast variance, and observes that the film musical seems defunct. The indexes are to the names of performers (with a separate index for composers, lyricists, and musical directors) and offer a chronology by premieres that accordingly reach back to 1905. There is no index of the thousands of songs cited (three sources for such reference are offered). Although alphabetic ranges are not cited in the individual page headers, this is a source whose contents are readily located. Particularly when used as one of the four-volume set, the bibliography will prove useful for those working in musical theater research.—**Dominique-René de Lerma**

1031. Ruppli, Michel, comp. **The Decca Labels: A Discography.** Westport, Conn., Greenwood Press, 1996. 6v. index. (Discographies, no.63). $595.00/set. ISBN 0-313-27370-7.

These volumes comprise a definitive indexing of all Decca recordings from the years 1934 to 1973, at which time reissues were henceforth on the MCA label. Subsidiary labels such as Brunswick, Champion, Coral, and Vocalion are also included. While the majority of Decca recordings were of popular music, classical music is also indexed. Listings are in numerical master number order in chronological order by recording location. Entries are by artist(s). Thus, a sample entry is "Judy Garland, Gene Kelly, vocal, with David Rose and his Orchestra, recorded in Los Angeles, July 26, 1942." Also listed are a number of "The Kraft Music Hall" recordings featuring Al Jolson from the 1940s. Each volume is separately indexed by artist.

Volume 1 contains all recordings made in California and Hawaii. Volumes 2, 3, and 4 comprise the eastern U.S. recordings plus (in vol. 4) annual country field recordings made in the South and Caribbean recordings. Volume 5 contains the later country recordings plus all of the classical listings. The final volume contains a complete index by composer and also a general artist index. Reissues on CD up to the present time are also included in the volume 6 listings.

Decca was a preeminent label for nearly 40 years, with a wide variety of music and artists, featuring everything from Hawaiian trios of the 1930s, Dixieland jazz, swing, big band, and top vocalists through the 1960s. These volumes should be a part of any major music library collection.—**Louis G. Zelenka**

Indexes

1032. Snyder, Lawrence D. **German Poetry in Song: An Index of Lieder.** Berkeley, Calif., Fallen Leaf Press, 1995. 730p. index. (Fallen Leaf Reference Books in Music, no.30). $75.00 (with supplement). ISBN 0-914913-32-8.

This work consists of one hardback volume plus a paperback supplement, both of substantial size. Its origins are in the author's need to identify various settings of the same song by different composers. In the absence of a tool listing song texts by their poets, Snyder compiled data from readily available sources, including only titles he actually saw (thereby excluding many that were listed, for example, on the covers of such works). These sources are listed in the fourth section of the main volume.

The first section, "Index of Lieder by Poet, First Line, and Composer," constitutes the body of the work. Cases where the poet is unknown are variously treated in sections headed "Anonymous" and "Not Yet Identified"; 10 pages are devoted to the collection "Des Knaben Wunderhorn," and 20 to "Other Volkslieder." The second section, "Index of First Lines," refers to the poet. The third, "Index by Composer, Poet, and First Line," is likely to receive much usage and may surprise users at first consultation in that, despite the explicit section title, some will approach the composer index with a song's title rather than its first line. (To accommodate this fact, the supplement was prepared—sadly too late for inclusion in the main volume.) The fourth section, "Bibliographies," includes indexes of settings of individual poets, biographical sources, and musical sources. The last will be invaluable to bibliographical researchers for insight into the author's compilation strategy.

Some considerations should be addressed in the next edition. In both the poet and composer indexes, titles and first lines (using typefaces to differentiate them) could be included in one alphabetic sequence. The anonymous and not-yet-identified works would be better in one sequence, which could furthermore include the Volkslieder. Published sets of poems, such as Wilhelm Müller's *Winterreise*, might be identified as a set—in the poet index, they can be so identified only if a composer treated them as a cycle. Abbreviations would be better listed in the "Key to Index Entries" rather than in the section on "Arrangement of Data."

This tool provides an excellent approach to two questions: Which works of a poet's output have been set to music, and by whom? and, Which poets has a composer chosen for texts for his/her songs? A couple of points to note are the filing of the umlaut as a letter "e," and the entry of titles by their articles. The tool is remarkably easy to use and is commendably produced. Users should bear in mind Snyder's caution that the work is by no means exhaustive, and should consult both the introduction, in which the scope is clearly stated, and the section on musical sources for a fuller understanding of what has been indexed. It is to be hoped that the next edition, for which Snyder solicits contributions, will approximate exhaustivity (although sadly the basic one-volume format would probably not then suffice), and that this work will inspire similar volumes for other languages. [R: RQ, Spring 96, p. 411-12]—**Ian Fairclough**

CHILDREN'S

1033. **Children's Song Index, 1978-1993.** Kay Laughlin, Pollyanne Frantz, and Ann Branton, comps. Englewood, Colo., Libraries Unlimited, 1996. 153p. $37.50. ISBN 1-56308-332-9.

The latest contribution to indexing collections of children's songs is precise and readable. This book uses the same format as its predecessor, *Index to Children's Songs* (see ARBA 80, entry 966). Laughlin, Frantz, and Branton's *Children's Song Index* adds 75 new collections containing both lyrics and scores to the body of songbooks indexed.

Besides its title and first-line indexes, this list is thoroughly indexed by plentiful subject headings. The subject index is enhanced by a subject guide that gives cross-references and lists the more specific subjects under more general headings or by type of song (e.g., "FINGER AND HAND PLAY"). The entries are simple, referring to the number assigned to the collection, then the page number in the collection.

A check of titles in a small library system revealed that one-third were already owned, and the children's librarian planned to use the list for book selection for her library. The index is strongly recommended for school and public libraries, and academic libraries with education departments. [R: RBB, 15 Mar 96, pp. 1310-12]—**Joann H. Lee**

COMPOSERS

1034. Charteris, Richard. **Giovanni Gabrieli (ca.1555-1612): A Thematic Catalogue of His Music....** Stuyvesant, N.Y., Pendragon Press, 1996. 597p. index. (Thematic Catalogue Series, no.20). $64.00. ISBN 0-945193-66-1.

An important addition to music library reference collections, this new thematic catalog updates and greatly expands the thematic listings in Egon Kenton's *Life and Works of Giovanni Gabrieli* (American Institute of Musicology [AIM], 1967). It contributes previously unpublished information and brings together extensive information on Gabrieli's works and editions of those works. Charteris brings a high level of scholarship to this work, as he has published extensively on Gabrieli and is the editor of a new 12-volume edition of Gabrieli's complete works published by AIM and Hanssler Verlag.

As in most thematic catalogs, details on early editions, manuscript sources, modern editions, sources of texts, and a commentary, as well as an incipit, are provided for each work. In addition, appendixes offer a description of early prints and manuscript sources, a chronological listing of modern editions, a concordance to Kenton's thematic listing, a discography, and a bibliography. This book is a must-have for academic music collections. It offers extensive information on Gabrieli in a single volume; and at $64, it is a bargain.—**Allie Wise Goudy**

1035. Claghorn, Gene. **Women Composers and Songwriters: A Concise Biographical Dictionary.** Lanham, Md., Scarecrow, 1996. 247p. $68.00. ISBN 0-8108-3130-9.

This book, an enlarged version of Claghorn's 1984 *Women Composers and Hymnists* (see ARBA 85, entry 1162), contains brief biographies of some 950 composers and songwriters, with emphasis on American and British women. Were it not that it may be the only readily available source of information on certain obscure composers of hymns, one would be tempted simply to throw it away. Even for this select group of composers, Claghorn can hardly be considered an authority, given his numerous inaccuracies on every level, starting with the most obvious essential: spelling the women's names correctly. Carla Bley becomes Clara, Ethyl Smyth acquires a terminal "e," Cyndi Lauper appears as Cindi, Lili Boulanger as Lily, and on it goes. Sloppy work is also evident in citations of dates. Although Esther Williamson Ballou, Jeanne Behrend, Imogen Holst, Eva Jessye, U. S. Moore, Kay Swift, and Elinor Remick Warren died before 1993, the years of their deaths are not given. A related problem is that of timeliness: The biographies of several living composers cite nothing they have done within the past 15-20 years, yet that of newcomer Alanis Morissette includes references to work done in 1995.

The lack of cross-references makes for difficulty in locating some prominent composers: There is no Ruth Crawford Seeger, only Ruth Crawford, no Fanny Hensel, only Fanny Mendelssohn-Bartholdy; Pozzi Escot appears under P, as does Anna Amalia, Princess of Prussia. Claghorn's prose is pedestrian at best, nearly incomprehensible at worst, and annoys with its lack of consistency in technical matters.

Claghorn seemingly has no standards, no priorities, no sense of proportion, and—not infrequently—no real appreciation of the women and their work. The entry on Amy Beach illustrates nearly everything that is wrong with this book. Beach, a major composer by any standard, is described as "composer, hymnist, pianist, and songwriter" (a curious overlapping of terms); married to a singer (Dr. Beach was a physician); composer of a *Mass with Orchestra Mass in E* (she wrote only one mass, in E-flat), a symphony, "various orchestral works" (five, four of which involve a soloist), and "several sacred songs" (no mention of her dozens of secular songs, numerous piano pieces, choral works, or chamber music), all in one short paragraph. Hymnists Lesbia Scott and Abigail Patton, along with Hawaiian Queen Liliuokalani, receive more thorough (and, one hopes, more accurate) treatment. In these days of tight library budgets, Claghorn's volume is one book that need not be considered for purchase.—**Karin Pendle**

1036. Dodd, Mary Ann, and Jayson Rod Engquist. **Gardner Read: A Bio-bibliography.** Westport, Conn., Greenwood Press, 1996. 270p. index. (Bio-bibliographies in Music, no.60). $75.00. ISBN 0-313-29384-8.

This is one of the most recent additions to Greenwood Press's Bio-bibliographies in Music series. The format, similar to other books in the series, includes a detailed biography of Gardner Read. This is followed by sections that list his compositions and performances of those compositions; literary writings; a discography; and two bibliographies listing articles about and reviews of Read's significant body of work. Whenever appropriate, citations have been annotated and cross-referenced. There is a system to master in order to use the cross-references correctly, but the authors have included a user's guide that identifies letter codes and other devices peculiar to a musical bibliography, including instrumentation and opus numbers.

Research for this bio-bibliography made use in large part of Read's personal archives. Read has had a strong enough sense of his contributions as both a composer and writer that he has collected nearly everything that has been written about him back to his high school years. Knowing this fact and after having read through numerous annotations, one can sense a highly personal quality to this bibliography.

One concern must be raised about the Bio-bibliographies in Music series in general: the typeface used for the bibliographies. There is no apparent uniformity in the typefaces used from one volume to the next. The volume on Read, following a perusal of several randomly selected bio-bibliographies published by Greenwood, uses a combination of typefaces that are both aesthetically pleasing and easy to read. This reviewer hopes a similar style will be employed for future volumes.

This is a useful bibliography about a U.S. composer whose name and accomplishments are not particularly well known outside musical circles. It would be an excellent addition to any larger fine arts or music collections. Actually, almost any of the bio-bibliographies in the Greenwood series would merit consideration for a library that is looking to increase its holdings about lesser-known twentieth-century composers.—**Phillip P. Powell**

1037. **Film Composers Guide.** 3d ed. Vincent Jacquet-Francillon, comp. and ed. Los Angeles, Calif., Lone Eagle, 1996. 386p. index. $50.00pa. ISBN 0-943728-78-9. ISSN 1055-081X.

Lone Eagle Publishing produces a series of reference books (10 volumes in all) designed to meet the special needs of the motion picture industry. Several of these titles also merit the attention of the serious movie buff, and this one belongs to that group.

Film Composers Guide attempts to list every creator of film music currently working (episodic television is not included). Each film entry also includes the year of release and distributor (but not the director's name, unfortunately). In addition, many international figures turn up, such big names as Ennio Morricone and Philippe Sarde, as well as those musicians strongly identified with a single director (Jürgen Knieper with Wim Wenders; Zbigniew Preisner, with Krzyszlof Kieslowski). Rock groups with important film credits are also here—Goblin, Popol Vuh, and Tangerine Dream. Contact information is available for all but the most shadowy operatives, and a complete index of film titles references the composer entries. One can occasionally think of musicians and titles that go unmentioned (particularly at the low-budget end), but this is a large and impressive achievement—quite beyond the scope of any other attempt to cover the same ground.

There is also a section on "notable composers of the past," and a ledger of Academy Award nominations in the field since 1955. The final indexes are industry-oriented: agents and managers, music publishers, studio and licensing contacts, album and clearance companies, performing rights societies, and music supervisors and orchestrators. All told, this is a uniquely valuable tool for anyone interested in film music.—**Walt Mundkowsky**

1038. Green, Alan. **Allen Sapp: A Bio-bibliography.** Westport, Conn., Greenwood Press, 1996. 239p. index. (Bio-bibliographies in Music, no.62). $69.50. ISBN 0-313-28983-2.

The newest addition to the Greenwood Press Bio-bibliographies in Music series is on U.S. composer Allen Sapp (b.1922). Green offers an in-depth view of the composer. The biographical unit is especially detailed, and in addition to focusing on the prime subject, Green observes the musical climate during Sapp's career and examines the many close contacts the composer had with great musical personalities.

Sapp studied composition mainly with Walter Hamor Piston, Lili Boulanger, and Aaron Copland. Sapp's career is multifaceted; he is a prolific composer; was a music educator and administrator (teaching at Harvard, Wellesley College, University of Buffalo, Florida State University, and the University of Cincinnati); and during World War II, he held the positions of chief of code research and chief cryptanalyst. In 1943, Sapp married pianist Norma Bertolami, who often performed his piano compositions. Sapp continues to compose new music; currently, he is working on two more piano sonatas and two operas.

As mentioned, Green's volume contains a detailed biography of Sapp; it also furnishes a list of works and performances (with pertinent data), a discography (arranged alphabetically by work), writings by Sapp (annotated), writings about Sapp (annotated), endnotes, academic and nonacademic positions held by Sapp, a chronological index of compositions (from 1940 to December 1993), an alphabetic index of compositions, and a name index. This comprehensive study of Sapp is highly recommended; it should prove useful in college/university music libraries and to the many university composition teachers who are active composers. Sapp certainly is a role model of the successful and fruitful teacher-composer.—**Robert Palmieri**

1039. Hitchens, Susan Hayes. **Ross Lee Finney: A Bio-bibliography.** Westport, Conn., Greenwood Press, 1996. 191p. index. (Bio-bibliographies in Music, no.63). $65.00. ISBN 0-313-28671-X.

The 63d addition to Greenwood Press's Bio-bibliographies in Music follows the same format as previous contributions to the series. A biography, dotted with quotations from an interview with Finney, summarizes his career as a musician and composer. This brief section is followed by a thoroughly documented list of works, which includes references to relevant articles in the bibliography and the discography. Addenda include an alphabetic list of works, a chronological list of works, and an index.

Finney has been the partial subject of a book by Edith Borroff—*Three American Composers* (University Presses of America, 1986)—and has written his own autobiography, *Profile of a Lifetime* (Peters, 1992). This resource, compiled with the assistance of Finney, complements those. The volume is a welcome addition to Greenwood's series. It is recommended for academic library collections.—**Allie Wise Goudy**

1040. Hodgson, Peter J. **Benjamin Britten: A Guide to Research.** New York, Garland, 1996. 245p. index. (Composer Resource Manuals, v.39; Garland Reference Library of the Humanities, v.1867). $45.00. ISBN 0-8153-1795-6.

Benjamin Britten: A Guide to Research is the 39th volume in Garland's admirable resource series on composers, notably directed and edited by Guy Marco. The first volume came out in 1981 (*Heinrich Schütz: A Research Guide* [see ARBA 82, entry 1047]), and since then, the series has proved to be an excellent tool for research. This volume concisely covers the life and music of the great British composer Britten (1913-1976).

The volume is divided into three major parts. Part 1 briefly describes the life of the composer; influences in his life; a chronological life synopsis; and a helpful, detailed description of the Britten-Pears Library/Archive located in Aldeburgh, England. Part 2 is concerned with Britten's music and is divided into two sections: "Short Titles," which contains a brief alphabetic and chronological conspectus of the music of the composer, and "Full Titles," which features more detailed information about each work, as well as including youthful works, incidental works, stage music, and so forth. Part 3 is a selective, annotated bibliography that serves as an introduction to the many works written about the composer. The annotations are exemplary and help one quickly understand the content of the cited work.

Hodgson has done an excellent job of working with the many existing resources on Britten and making his volume a concise, clear, and reliable starting point for those studying or researching the composer. This volume should be in the reference divisions of college/university libraries and should be listed as an important bibliographic source. It is highly recommended.—**Robert Palmieri**

1041. Horne, Aaron, comp. **Brass Music of Black Composers: A Bibliography.** Westport, Conn., Greenwood Press, 1996. 521p. index. (Music Reference Collection, no.51). $89.50. ISBN 0-313-29826-2.

This fourth bibliography of music by black composers compiled by Horne follows the format of his earlier works, with the main section containing bio-bibliographies, followed by numerous indexes, a discography, and the bibliography of sources used. The bio-bibliography section groups composers as African, African American, African-European, and African-Latino. Information for each work includes (if known) the publisher, the date of publication, the instrumentation, and the duration. The "Brass Music Index" lists works divided by the number of instruments, the medium, and ensembles.

Horne notes in his discussion of the methodology used that a "comprehensive and inclusive" format was used. This is both a strength and a weakness of the work. In addition to information about well-known black composers (William Grant Still, John Coltrane, and so on), users will be able to find information on composers and their compositions that is not readily available elsewhere. Some of the information was obtained through personal correspondence with composers in Africa, Europe, and the United States. However, by attempting to be inclusive, Horne has included works that would not be considered "brass" music in other standard works (ensemble music for full orchestra or concert band and jazz compositions). Conductors or performers looking for large-ensemble music by black composers would not normally look in a brass bibliography. Another problem is that Horne has included "some arrangements," but has given no criteria for how these were selected or why others were excluded. Horne's attempt to provide a comprehensive list of music by black composers is admirable, and in spite of the weaknesses, this work should be added to all music and black studies collections.—**Michele Russo**

1042. **Latin American Classical Composers: A Biographical Dictionary.** Miguel Ficher, Martha Furman Schleifer, and John M. Furman, comps. and eds. Lanham, Md., Scarecrow, 1996. 407p. $56.00. ISBN 0-8108-3185-6.

Latin American Classical Composers is an important contribution to the recognition and understanding of these composers. The volume focuses attention on a subject that has largely been ignored. It lists approximately 1,200 composers, with Argentina having the largest number of names (370) and Nicaragua having only 2. The book lists the composers alphabetically, including birth date and origin data on each composer, a short career synopsis, a selected list of compositions, and a list of sources. There is also a list of the composers by country and two general bibliographies on the subject. The authors should be commended for revealing how vital serious music is in the Latin American countries, and for their investigation of the many composers who demonstrated or are presently sustaining this vitality.

Although the information contained in the volume fills a void, one wishes the book were twice the size and had much more data on the composers (e.g., extended biographical detail, description of musical style, and a better listing of compositions with most important works noted). Perhaps Scarecrow will urge the authors to expand their fine work in a future edition. Regardless, *Latin American Classical Composers* is an important volume and is a must for library reference divisions. It should be used as a source for university music history/ethnomusicology courses. This work is highly recommended.—**Robert Palmieri**

1043. Pedigo, Alan. **International Encyclopedia of Violin-Keyboard Sonatas and Composer Biographies.** 2d ed. Booneville, Ark., Arriaga, 1995. 341p. illus. $85.00. ISBN 0-9606356-2-9.

This collection of material relating to the violin-keyboard sonata contains much that is useful—and much, alas, that is not. The author has attempted to compile a brief biography of every composer who has produced a work for this instrumental combination; therefore, he presents an abundance of otherwise unavailable information. Unfortunately, these entries are an arid trek of dates, places, and affiliations. No attempt has been made to characterize the musical works in any way; Johann Heinrich Schmelzer and Alfred Schnittke might as well be the same, not to mention Gerhard Schjelderup. Also, several sections—on dance forms, modal scales, history of the violin, and so forth—are sketchy and rudimentary.

On the other hand, the discussion of Wolfgang Amadeus Mozart's violin-piano sonatas (the only such example in the book) is most welcome. The photographic portraits of composers and players strike a fine balance between the prominent and the obscure. The data on music schools and competitions will interest many. However, the discography is keyed to the vinyl era, and not necessarily recent vinyl production at that. Also, it lists only works and album numbers, not performers. The work is an enjoyable volume for browsing (this reviewer learned that famed Czech violinist Petr Messiereur has the same birthday!), but the value is questionable for wider applications. [R: Choice, June 96, pp. 1621-22]

—**Walt Mundkowsky**

1044. Schmidt, Carl B. **The Music of Francis Poulenc (1899-1963): A Catalogue.** New York, Clarendon Press/Oxford University Press, 1995. 608p. index. $105.00. ISBN 0-19-816336-3.

The publication of a comprehensive catalog of the works of the important twentieth-century French composer Francis Poulenc is a welcomed contribution to the literature. Following on the heels of George Keck's fine *Francis Poulenc: A Bio-bibliography* (see ARBA 91, entry 1278), this new resource offers information on every piece of music composed by Poulenc that the author was able to identify, whether or not the piece was complete or published.

Arranged chronologically, each entry provides extensive information on the composition, including its date, dedication, instrumentation, manuscript location, printed editions, performance history, commentary, and literature about the piece and recordings of the piece. The commentary is often lengthy and detailed. References to Keck's bio-bibliography; Keith W. Daniel's *Francis Poulenc: His Artistic Development and Musical Style* (UMI Research Press, 1982); and a 1993 Editions Salabert catalog are frequently cited in the literature and discography portions of the catalog, along with selected relevant secondary literature. A bibliography listing sources cited in the catalog and a general index are included, as well as indexes to titles and first lines of vocal works.

This book is a distinguished addition to Poulenc research. It is highly recommended for academic music libraries. [R: Choice, May 96, p. 1456]—**Allie Wise Goudy**

1045. Simms, Bryan R. **Alban Berg: A Guide to Research.** New York, Garland, 1996. 293p. index. (Composer Resource Manuals, v.38; Garland Reference Library of the Humanities, v.1905). $50.00. ISBN 0-8153-2032-9.

A more thorough understanding of the life and works of Alban Berg has been a slowly evolving process, due to a relatively small body of compositions, historical comparisons with his teachers, and his wife controlling important materials for four decades after his death. This guide, without pretense at completeness, attempts to organize the major research and writings concerning this still-growing giant of twentieth-century music.

Part of the useful Garland research guide series on Western composers, the book begins with a brief but detailed essay on Berg's life, music, and reputation. Subsequent chapters cover such specific topics as writings on his songs, chamber music, and, in more detail, his operas. Most of the 1,064 entries are annotated by the author in concise, jargon-free descriptions that will prove indispensable to the researcher. The index is extensive, but it could have been more graphic in its breakdown of subject areas. The author has eschewed the esoteric and has attempted to include only readily accessible materials, covering 1911 to 1994.

Berg's reputation is still on the rise, and the influence of his personal life on his music is a rich and fascinating field yet to be fully explored. Such timely, carefully prepared research surveys as this will both aid the scholar and assist in updating the literature on this enigmatic man. —**James Moffet**

1046. Still, Judith Anne, Michael J. Dabrishus, and Carolyn L. Quin. **William Grant Still: A Bio-bibliography.** Westport, Conn., Greenwood Press, 1996. 331p. index. (Bio-bibliographies in Music, no.61). $79.50. ISBN 0-313-25255-6.

William Grant Still was a gentle, persevering composer, quietly devout and determined to succeed in the field of serious music despite discrimination and disappointments. He achieved many firsts for a black composer and was championed by influential supporters, but his music has never been as well known as it deserves to be. This volume is a welcome addition to the unjustifiably scant literature and research materials available on Still. It begins with an intimate personal reminiscence by his daughter that gives glimpses into his diaries, compositional techniques, and daily life. This account is followed by a lengthier, more formal biographical sketch, including excerpts from correspondence with such admirers as Leopold Stokowski. The body of the book consists of annotated entries citing writings by and about Still, reviews of performances of his works, and evaluations of his place in U.S. musical history. A discography, particularly important in tracing the sporadic recording history of Still's music, is an essential inclusion. The index is thorough and exhaustive. The centennial year of Still's birth was 1995, and one hopes that that event, along with this timely research guide, will spur others to investigate his music. —**James Moffet**

1047. **Women Composers: Music Through the Ages. Volume 1: Composers Born Before 1599.** Martha Furman Schleifer and Sylvia Glickman, eds. New York, G. K. Hall/Simon & Schuster Macmillan, 1996. 365p. illus. index. $100.00. ISBN 0-8161-0926-5.

After several years of preparation readers finally have the first of a projected 12-volume set, *Women Composers: Music Through the Ages*. It was worth the wait. Ably organized by the general editors, this initial volume contains representative music by women born before 1599. As one may expect, the works are almost exclusively vocal and come from the pens of nuns and noblewomen, the only groups to have access both to musical training and to the means by which music was preserved and propagated. The collection is restricted almost exclusively to white, Western European women, with the exception of Kassia, a ninth-century poet/composer whose home was probably Constantinople. Within these temporal and geographic boundaries one finds music both sacred and secular, intended for the performing skills of the noble amateur as well as the trained professional.

Each woman's music has been edited by a recognized scholar who has also contributed an informative essay on the composer's life and the conditions under which her works were created. These prefaces also include lists of primary sources, statements of editorial policy, text translations, and selective bibliographies. To represent eras in which no written music by women has been found, the editors commissioned essays dealing with the ways in which women were probably involved in the music-making of their times. As for the music itself, it is presented according to standard scholarly practices, yet it is easily accessible to performers who are not also scholars. Indeed, there are some remarkable pieces here, many by composers whose music is not available elsewhere. Particularly noteworthy are the works of Sulpitia Cesis, Francesca Caccini, Lucretia Vizzana, and Claudia Sessa.

As one may expect in a collection with so many editorial cooks, the resulting musical soup is of uneven quality. Among the best offerings are those on Hildegard of Bingen and the Aleottis. Among the worst is the vague, rambling essay on Saint Birgitta, which fails to even cite the saint's birth and death dates. There are inconsistencies in spelling (Lucretia/Lucrezia Vizzana, for example, or Madalena/Maddalena Casulana); bits of organizational confusion (e.g., chapters are numbered in the table of contents but not at the beginnings of the chapters themselves); and slip-ups in proofreading. One wonders as well what criteria were used to decide how many numbers by any given composer would be included. Casulana, the first woman professional composer, is represented by only one madrigal, while Cesis, Caccini, and Vizzana have six to eight pieces each. One would wish not for fewer numbers by the latter composers, of course, but rather for more from Casulana, especially because previous editions of her music are unusable for modern performers. One would also wish that these few problems would not deter anyone from buying this book. It is worth every penny. [R: Choice, Nov 96, pp. 438-40; LJ, 15 April 96, p. 82]—**Karin Pendle**

1048. **Women Composers: Music Through the Ages. Volume 2: Composers Born 1600-1699.** Sylvia Glickman and Martha Furman Schleifer, eds. New York, G. K. Hall/Simon & Schuster Macmillan, 1996. 390p. index. $100.00. ISBN 0-8161-0563-4.

Hard on the heels of volume 1 (see entry 1047) comes volume 2 of *Women Composers: Music Through the Ages*, as exciting a volume as its predecessor. Concentrating on women born between 1600 and 1699, it contains music by some who are already "big names" (Isabella Leonarda, Elizabeth La Guerre) and others whose names, although often cited, seldom appear at the head of any available music. Still others emerge from the shadows but briefly, leaving behind a small number of works written in their youth. There is music by nuns, noblewomen, and persons of unknown status, and the selections include sacred and secular pieces for solo voice(s); excerpts from cantatas and oratorios; and sonatas, sinfonias, and keyboard works to entice instrumentalists. As before, each selection of music has been prepared by a qualified scholar according to the best standards of modern editorial practice, to suit it for use by both scholars and performers.

As with the 1st volume, volume 2 also includes essays about the composers and their music, and again, the quality of this material is uneven. Among the poorest essays is that of Randall Wong, who accepts uncritically the sexist barbs aimed at Strozzi during her life and whose writing is marred by technical errors. Sally Park's material on *alfabeto* tablature is murky; Claire Fontijn provides an extremely limited context for Bembo's work; and Diane Guthrie's essay on La Guerre presents a number of contradictions. One wishes that the general editors would take more care to root out such obvious flaws, along with the grammatical errors, inconsistent punctuation and documentation, and other technical lapses. To establish a standard of quality they need only look to Jane Bowers's essay on Peruchona. Its content and proportions are ideal, its suggestions to performers are clear and helpful, and its critical stance is both feminist and musical.

Nevertheless, the various editors have brought readers some outstanding music. Anyone who expects a nun to write humble music need only look at Meda's *Cari Musici* or Badalla's *Pane Angelico* to be disabused of this error. From the improvised performance of folk poetry to the high art of the baroque oratorio, from Cozzolani's dramatic dialogue between two voluble tenors and three calmer sopranos to Duchess Sophie Elisabeth's *Song of the War Horrors*, in which Death, Hunger, Poverty, and Injustice present a miniature morality play, there is much about this music that seems strikingly modern. The recommendation remains: Buy this book!—**Karin Pendle**

CONDUCTORS

1049. Kiefer, Peter T., comp. **The Fred Waring Discography.** Westport, Conn., Greenwood Press, 1996. 223p. illus. (Discographies, no.65). $65.00. ISBN 0-313-29910-2.

Fred Waring is one of the best-known figures in U.S. popular music, having appeared in stage shows, on radio, on television, in movies, and in concerts for nearly seven decades. He—along with his Pennsylvanians—pioneered the polished choral rendition of popular songs, and much of their work was documented on more than 1,000 records between 1923 and 1974. This latest volume in Greenwood Press's excellent series of discographies provides details on all the group's commercial recordings, as well as on transcriptions from other sources.

The book is divided into sections containing, in order, an alphabetic list of song titles, a chronology of recording sessions, a list of albums, a list of arrangers, and listings of transcriptions. The composite information also includes record labels and numbers, dates of recording sessions and of their issues, and names of composers and soloists. The Greenwood Press volume is the only comprehensive Waring discography in existence. The compiler is the coordinator of Fred Waring's America, a special collection at the Pennsylvania State University library. He also worked closely with Waring over a number of years.

Although some biographical material would have been welcome, this work provides thorough documentation of the recorded output of a musical organization that exerted a great deal of influence on U.S. popular culture. The discography merits a place on music reference shelves.—**A. David Franklin**

INSTRUMENTS

1050. Clinkscale, Martha Novak. **Makers of the Piano, 1700-1820.** New York, Oxford University Press, 1993; repr., 1995. 404p. $85.00. ISBN 0-19-816323-1.

The term *fortepiano* separates pianos made during the first century after their invention ca.1700 from modern pianos. The revival of interest in these rudimentary but charming keyboard instruments as being worthy of study, restoration, and use in actual performances has led to the need for a reference such as this one, and the author expresses the hope that the information presented will further stimulate interest in the preservation and use of antique pianos. The book takes much of its material from a computer database, Early Pianos, 1720-1860, but ratchets the scope backward somewhat to catalog all known surviving pianos made between 1700 and 1820.

Nearly 900 piano makers are listed, with biographical information varying from builders whose name and date only are known but of whom no instruments they made survive, to firms such as Broadwood of England, still producing pianos today, with more than 200 of their extant early instruments enumerated. Approximately 2,000 surviving early pianos are documented. A chart for each piano provides, when known, its date of manufacture, style, compass, case measurements, stringing scale, action, stops, pedals, present and former owners, and bibliographic references. Appendixes include an exhaustive bibliography, a list of collections and museums throughout the world where many of the cataloged pianos reside, and a glossary of piano terminology.

The author's claim of modeling her book on Donald H. Boalch's classic *Makers of the Harpsichord & Clavichord 1440-1840* (see ARBA 76, entry 1012), and her desire that it become the standard reference for early pianos as Boalch is for harpsichords, invites comparison—especially as much information in the two overlaps. While the piano book is of course more current, it is also more detailed in descriptions of the instruments. Boalch excels by including photographs of some instruments. Although Clinkscale decries the need for these in her introduction, this reviewer disagrees, and craves at least a few views (even black-and-white photographs, as in Boalch) to aid both novice and expert in picturing the subject matter. The glossary would also benefit from diagrams to help locate and visualize the complex mechanisms described. Nevertheless, this volume is a vital resource for those who collect, restore, perform on, or have an interest in fortepianos.—**Larry Lobel**

1051. Collver, Michael, and Bruce Dickey. **A Catalog of Music for the Cornett.** Bloomington, Ind., Indiana University Press, 1996. 212p. index. (Publications of the Early Music Institute). $18.95pa. ISBN 0-253-20974-9.

The cornett, an early wind instrument of great popularity from about 1550 to 1650, is not to be confused with the cornet of brass and marching bands of the present time. The instrument, once described by the well-known eighteenth-century writer on music Roger North as sounding "eunuch-like," has new life thanks to the ever-growing number of musical organizations devoted to performing ancient music on original instruments. Both coauthors of this catalog are performers of the instrument who have done an extraordinary amount of research in the United States and abroad in producing this scholarly work. The lengthy introduction provides a detailed history of the instrument and its use during its golden age more than 300 years ago.

The entries in the catalog itself are divided into instrumental and vocal music (the cornett often being used to support the human voice). The publications are old and rare and mostly date from the time of the instrument's popularity. Copies are scattered throughout major European and United States libraries. The compilers have done the detective work necessary to identify and locate the works calling for this instrument themselves. An appendix lists "works with unknown location or source." The bibliography is made up of titles rightly called "secondary sources."

Continuing work on this subject may augment the material found here, but this is a groundbreaking study of the subject. This is certainly a subject as well as a catalog for specialists in early music and ancient instruments, but the title is likely to remain the only major study of the instrument and the music composed for it.—**George Louis Mayer**

1052. **The Illustrated Encyclopedia of Musical Instruments.** Robert Dearling, ed. New York, Schirmer Books/Simon & Schuster Macmillan, 1996. 240p. illus. index. $75.00. ISBN 0-02-864667-3.

The history, manufacture, and playing of musical instruments has been a dry, academic subject in the hands of most writers. Dearling, an experienced and gifted writer, and his five fine contributors have created one of the best and most delightful books on any phases of music ever encountered. It is a gem and certainly should be the title of choice for anyone wanting or needing a book on this subject. The encyclopedia provides a broad survey of the subject, and it makes a great browsing book for those in search of entertaining musical trivia.

The historical chapters cover the making of instruments, instruments of antiquity, instruments and society, and dissemination and experimentation. The major sections of the book naturally cover the instruments by family (strings, brass, wind, percussion, keyboard, and electronic). Other sections cover musical ensembles of various size and makeup; the orchestra old and new; various aspects of authenticity in the performance of early music; non-Western music; obsolete instruments; and scales, pitches, and notation.

This is a serious work that discusses its complicated subject thoroughly and accurately, but the joy of the book is that it does this with flair, wit, and style. It is also a book of uncommon beauty, being oversized and crammed full of fascinating illustrations old, new, and rare, most of which are beautifully reproduced in color. The picture of a fashionably dressed lady playing the sousaphone with what seems to be a singing dog entranced by the sight is typical of the visual delights to be found here. Brief, boxed entries tinted to keep them separate from the running text are scattered throughout the book and offer glimpses of related topics as far-ranging as the spelling variations of ethnic instruments and the reasons for this, the spectacular use of the side drum by the composer Carl Nielsen, and the materials used in the making of harps.

Few subjects have found writers and book designers as exemplary as this. The encyclopedia is recommended without reservation and with enthusiasm to all with an interest in musical instruments.
—George Louis Mayer

MUSICAL FORMS

Choral

1053. Laster, James. **Catalogue of Choral Music Arranged in Biblical Order.** 2d ed. Lanham, Md., Scarecrow, 1996. 711p. index. $75.00. ISBN 0-8108-3071-X.

Laster's dual professions (as reference librarian at Shenandoah University and organist/choirmaster of Trinity Episcopal Church in Upperville, Virginia) qualify him as the perfect compiler of this useful reference work. He knows what a church musician needs and how a first-rate reference tool should be compiled. Musical settings of specific biblical texts are of great importance to those who must plan weekly church services. The music is usually published individually or in collections by specialty publishers, and the number of really good music stores—even in large cities—carrying a full range of such publications is limited. It is difficult, therefore, to know what exists and how to obtain it. Those who need this information will, rightly, consider this book a blessing.

The range and format of the book remain as they were in the 1st edition of 1983 (see ARBA 84, entry 887). A planned supplement was abandoned in favor of a new edition because the number of entries available for inclusion had doubled from that of a little more than a decade earlier. The entries are arranged from Genesis to Revelation, including the Apocrypha, by chapter and verse. Additional, paraphrased, or translated texts are noted. The voicing, solos (if any), and accompaniments are cited. Publisher information, with date, is given in each entry. Titles included in published collections are noted as such. A list of these collections is supplied at the end of the book. No reason is given for entries that lead the user to such collections as *We Praise Thee* and *Music for the Contemporary Choir* (both in multiple-volume sets) that are not listed among the collections but which seem to have been included in individual citations. The important information seems to be here, and these collections should be easy enough to locate. Elaborate indexes are given both by composers and by titles.

The book is beautifully and spaciously printed on large pages, which makes it a pleasure to use. Boldfaced page headings indicating the book of the Bible represented on the page appear throughout, except for a large section of Psalms where they disappear from pages 186 to 295 in the review copy. Church musicians and those who serve them, including libraries and music stores, will find this catalog of great value.—**George Louis Mayer**

1054. White, Evelyn Davidson, comp. **Choral Music by African American Composers: A Selected, Annotated Bibliography.** 2d ed. Lanham, Md., Scarecrow, 1996. 226p. index. $39.50. ISBN 0-8108-3037-X.

First published in 1981 as *Choral Music by Afro-American Composers* (see ARBA 82, entry 1050) and now substantially expanded in a new edition, this is a guide to more than 1,000 compositions by 102 composers, past and present. The basic bibliography, presented in tabular form and arranged alphabetically by composer and title, gives copyright date; pagination; voicing (including solo parts, when applicable); vocal range; an assessment of performing difficulty (necessarily subjective, but the criteria employed are carefully explained); accompanied or a cappella; publisher; and catalog number (if available). Most of the music listed is sacred, and much of it derives from African American tradition (especially the spiritual), but all aspects of choral music are covered.

The work also provides a title index, contents listings for 29 anthologies of spirituals, a selective discography, brief composer biographies, a useful bibliography, and a directory of publishers and other sources. The compiler, who was for many years on the music faculty of Howard University and is also a distinguished choral conductor, knows this repertoire well; her coverage is thorough, and the work will be a valuable resource for any choral musician. All libraries with an interest in vocal music or African American studies should consider this work.—**Paul B. Cors**

Classical

1055. **BBC Music Magazine Top 1000 CDs Guide.** Erik Levi and Calum MacDonald, eds. London, BBC Books and Portland, Oreg., Amadeus Press/Timber Press, 1996. 367p. $12.95pa. ISBN 0-563-38709-2.

If the magazines that cover classical music recordings could be compared to newspapers, the ones like *BBC Music Magazine* would be *USA Today*. The single-column reviews and numerical ratings seem designed for the casual reader, and the number of discs appraised does not compete with the long-established *Gramophone*—or with *Fanfare*, the U.S. equivalent that grants its contributors much freedom. The guide under review takes the same once-over-lightly approach as its parent publication, which compromises its value as a serious reference tool.

The *BBC Guide* bills itself as "the most user-friendly survey on the market," which is another way of saying that it covers substantially less ground than its rivals, *The Penguin Guide to Compact Discs and Cassettes* (Penguin Books, 1996) and *The Gramophone Classical Good CD Guide* (Music Sales Corporation, 1995). The thousand-CD limit is crippling, and the notion that this constitutes a "best of the best" is easily punctured. Clearly intended for the home market, the buy-British parochialism is stunning: as many Benjamin Britten operas as Wolfgang Amadeus Mozart or Giacomo Puccini, about as many orchestral entries for Vaughan Williams as for Ludwig van Beethoven, more Edward Elgar in both choral/song and orchestral than Franz Schubert! This CD count also confines the majority of the choices to the classical main drag—the baroque through Richard Wagner/Gustav Mahler.

Within its narrow angle of vision, the book does pretty well. The reviewers are seasoned observers of the U.K. music scene, and their notices bespeak deep familiarity and affection. (The prose unfortunately tends to a gray sameness.) The classical buff will enjoy a friendly debate with the contents; at different points this reviewer found himself in rabid agreement and head-shaking disbelief. All these survey volumes share insuperable defects: They are planned by a committee and are obsolete before delivery to the printer. This one is breezy and fun, but leaves much unexamined. [R: LJ, Sept 96, p. 166]

—**Walt Mundkowsky**

1056. Fradkin, Robert A. **The Well-Tempered Announcer: A Pronunciation Guide to Classical Music.** Bloomington, Ind., Indiana University Press, 1996. 255p. index. $24.95pa. ISBN 0-253-21064-X.

Designed for classical radio announcers, this guide provides phonetic spellings and other linguistic tools to aid in pronunciation of musicians' names, musical terms, and place-names in approximately 30 European and Asian languages. Fradkin, a linguist and amateur musician, aims to provide enough linguistic background for announcers and others to learn to pronounce most names and terms without the intermediary step of phonetic spelling.

The guide is divided into numerous sections. The first explains Fradkin's transcription techniques and symbols. The second is an alphabetic listing of more than 1,800 names, titles, places, and terms. Given for each are a language designation and phonetic spelling variants and other pronunciation aids. Fradkin's guidance and options for native or anglicized pronunciations are especially helpful. The third section repeats in a language arrangement the phonetic spellings for many of the entries in the second section. Another section provides a detailed discussion of sound production and speech. It covers voicing, consonants, vowels, diphthongs, and accented syllables. The correspondence between specific written languages and their conventions of pronunciation is provided in another section. The final section is an evaluative, annotated bibliography identifying sources giving phonetic spellings or background information useful to announcers.

Classical announcers and musicians will welcome this guide. It is easy to use, with adequate access through the index and the table of contents. If future editions are planned, more careful proofreading needs to be done. In addition, giving pronunciations with first name followed by last name would make quick lookups faster for on-air announcers. Obviously, a guide such as this one cannot cover all terms or names, but Fradkin provides ample linguistic assistance for those who take the time to study it.—**Carol Wheeler**

1057. Perone, James E., comp. **Orchestration Theory: A Bibliography.** Westport, Conn., Greenwood Press, 1996. 183p. index. (Music Reference Collection, no.52). $65.00. ISBN 0-313-29596-4.

In his new book, Perone has compiled an extensive list of books, journal articles, and theses and dissertations on orchestration, instrumentation, and arranging. He has included 327 book-length treatises (books, dissertations, master's theses) written between 1772 and 1994 and provided information on the original language of the treatise, the availability of an English translation, a brief description of the entry's scope, and a bibliography of related sources, most of which are reviews of the item. A second "General Bibliography" profiles more than 550 periodical articles and books of less relevance. These are listed only with bibliographic information and an occasional short annotation. Cross-references to related items are included.

Although there is no subject index, the author offers additional access to the book-length treatises through a chronological list of orchestration treatises, a list of jazz arranging/orchestration treatises, a list of band-related treatises, and a list of treatises dealing with specific instruments. There is, unfortunately, no access to the contents of the "General Bibliography" other than by author in the general index. This lack excludes a significant portion of the book from any meaningful indexing. Despite this caveat, *Orchestration Theory* should be a useful addition to academic library collections. [R: Choice, Nov 96, p. 435]—**Allie Wise Goudy**

1058. Secrist-Schmedes, Barbera. **Wind Chamber Music: Winds with Piano and Woodwind Quintets: An Annotated Guide.** Lanham, Md., Scarecrow, 1996. 186p. index. $27.50. ISBN 0-8108-3111-2.

This bibliography lists chamber music for two to five woodwind instruments with piano and woodwind quintets. Most were available in print at the time of publication. Within each category, works are listed by composer. Additional data consist of nationality, birth dates, and death dates. Information concerning the composition includes title, medium, publisher, and available recordings. Brief annotations vary in length from anecdotal information on the composer's style to characteristics of the specific title. The author also makes suggestions for usage (e.g., Chedeville's *Scherzo* is "good as an encore piece" [p. 5]). These details can assist performers in planning special programs, such as "A Night of American Music," or "New Music from England." There is fine coverage of twentieth-century composers. Appendixes include directories of music publishers and record companies, each preceded by a key to abbreviations used. Occasionally, a record label abbreviation is used that is not in the directory; for example, Elliott Carter's *Woodwind Quintet* is available as a recording, CAN 31016, from the Candide label (p. 68). An index by composer concludes the book. In spite of a few shortcomings, Secrist-Schmedes, an oboist, has compiled a useful source to woodwind performers. —**Ralph Hartsock**

1059. Struble, John Warthen. **The History of American Classical Music: MacDowell Through Minimalism.** New York, Facts on File, 1995. 444p. illus. index. $29.95. ISBN 0-8160-2927-X.

In his foreword to Struble's book, Philip Glass states that there has been a sea change in the way people of the United States view their culture. This change had created an environment for new thinking about U.S. music and, according to Glass, Struble's book is an excellent example of this change. The content of the book that follows bears out the truth of Glass's comments, and a pleasant change this is. Struble has gotten past the well-trod ground of most texts on the art music tradition in the United States. He penetrates deep into the fabric of U.S. culture and discovers an art music tradition that is exciting, vibrant, diverse, and richly rewarding.

Scholarship in U.S. music has grown rapidly in the past 20 years, and this book reflects the maturity that scholarship has attained. While major figures such as Charles Ives, George Gershwin, and Aaron Copland understandably loom large in the discussion, one finds ample examination of a host of other significant contributors to the musical heritage of the United States. Of particular merit is the author's inclusion of some of the most recent scholarship in the field of U.S. musicology. For instance, the generous essay on Charles Tomlinson Griffes draws upon the work of Donna K. Anderson, whose research was published only shortly before the book went to press. The essay sheds new light on the significance of Griffes's music and illustrates his influence on other prominent composers.

The format of the volume is not truly that of a reference work, but rather more like a textbook. The writing is excellent, however, and its combination of readability and accuracy set it above the average textbook. The arrangement of material is basically chronological, and coverage begins with the hymns and psalms of the first European settlers and ends with a fascinating discussion of the elements that compose the present U.S. art music scene.

One major point of criticism about the work is the complete lack of any musical analysis. In fact, there is not one note of music found anywhere in the text. While this may contribute to the book's readability, there should be some accommodation for appropriate musical examples to illustrate the discussion. Special features include 3 appendixes providing a timeline of U.S. music history from 1562 to 1993 (with references to other historical events), a list of 245 significant U.S. composers by place of origin, and a fundamental repertoire of classical music of the United States. Adding to the volume's merits are an outstanding selected bibliography and a detailed index. This would make an excellent text for a course in U.S. art music or a starting point for research in the field. It is highly recommended for any library.—**Gregg S. Geary**

Popular

General Works

1060. **The Billboard Book of Number One Albums: The Inside Story Behind Pop Music's Blockbuster Records.** By Craig Rosen. New York, Billboard Books/Watson-Guptill, 1996. 434p. illus. index. $21.95pa. ISBN 0-8230-7586-9.

Writing on the premise that a great story lurks behind the accolade of "number one hit album," Rosen (*Billboard*'s West Coast bureau chief) has produced a decades-spanning compendium of chart-topping music history. Selecting 423 representative hits, beginning with 1956's *Elvis Presley* and winding down to the present, he delves into the background and circumstances surrounding the hit albums, with 1 page devoted to each. Information tends to run along the lines of career data; recording specifics (little-known facts about who wrote, sang, or played on what); and chart activity. The words "pop music" in the subtitle are apt, as a good 30 percent of the LPs covered (nearly everything through the late 1960s) are indeed pop and not rock or the eclectic sounds that now dominate the charts.

As a register of the quantifiable, this is an excellent book, full of focused insights, beautifully laid out, and featuring many rarely seen photographs (one per artist or group). However, as a chronicle of an era, its impact is less significant, as commercial success (and record chart position) do not necessarily reflect artistic achievement, and indeed tends to follow trends, not to highlight or presage them. A fuller picture of the era may be gained by using Dave Marsh's entertaining and opinionated *The Heart of Rock & Soul: The 1001 Greatest Singles Ever Made* (Plume, 1989) as a companion volume.—**Megan S. Farrell**

1061. **The Billboard Book of Top 40 Albums.** 3d ed. By Joel Whitburn. New York, Billboard Books/Watson-Guptill, 1995. 400p. illus. $21.95pa. ISBN 0-8230-7631-8.

This book is interesting for what it claims to be: a complete chart guide to every album on Billboard's pop album charts between 1955 and 1994. The book has two main sections—artists and record holders. Soundtrack and compilation albums of various kinds are listed separately from artists. Each entry in the artists section indicates the album's debut date; highest charted position; total weeks in the charts; the original album label and number; the Recording Industry Association of America's sales certification (i.e., gold or platinum); and an annotation indicating an album's type if it is not a traditional record release (e.g., comedy, novelty, foreign language, and the like).

Historically, such a compilation is interesting and useful. This book excels at being interesting. For example, each artist entry contains at least a few words of trivia or fact. Included too are occasional pronunciation guides for the pop-culturally enfeebled, and there are spotlight features on the most popular artists. If commercial sales are taken to be the measure of a successful artist, then this book, it could be said, captures the important artists as well. The volume's author seems to think so, but is careful not to make it his point of departure. The inability to move away from album sales to a better measure of success keeps this volume from being a major assessment of popular music. One is left to draw one's own conclusions regarding the relative importance of an artist or an album. The present volume will be useful to reference patrons of the public library.—**David V. Waller**

1062. **The Billboard Book of Top 40 Hits.** 6th ed. By Joel Whitburn. New York, Billboard Books/Watson-Guptill, 1996. 831p. illus. $21.95pa. ISBN 0-8230-7632-6.

This 6th edition follows a familiar format begun in 1983 (see ARBA 84, entry 905). At a glance, the user can glean a variety of information concerning every Top 40 hit from 1983 to the end of 1995: the date of the *Billboard* issue when the single first made the Top 40, its highest position, the number of weeks charted in the Top 40, the label and a catalog number, and whether it went gold or platinum. The data are taken from the Hot 100 chart (and its predecessors) that appears in the weekly issues of *Billboard*. The first section lists the artists in alphabetic order with their charted hits, then in chronological order. Almost all entries include brief notes about the artist. Some titles have also noted items of special interest. Special categories of recordings, such as instrumentals, novelty, and Christmas recordings, are indicated. The second section is an alphabetic list of all the titles that appear in the artists' section. Each entry gives the artist's name, the highest chart position reached, and the year of peak popularity. The final section provides lists of Artist and Record Achievements: "Top 100 Singles, 1955-1995"; "Top 100 Artists, 1955-1995"; "Top Artists and Top Singles by Decade"; "Top 40 Artist Achievements" (most charted singles, most Top 10 singles, most #1 singles, and the like); and the #1 singles listed chronologically, 1955-1995.

Whitburn has proven to be extremely prolific and a reliable source for data on popular music. With so many of his publications available, it seems inevitable that there can be overlap in coverage. For example, the content and format of *Joel Whitburn's Top Pop Singles, 1955-1993* (see ARBA 96, entry 1314) are similar to *The Billboard Book of Top 40 Hits*, but each has unique features. There is no denying, however, both the appeal and usefulness of the work under review. Most libraries will find it helpful for ready-reference or as a resource for research on popular music and popular culture. It will also be a popular addition to many personal libraries. Focusing as it does on the Top 40 hits, it is a gold mine of trivia and will undoubtedly bring on bouts of nostalgia for anyone who grew up listening to the Top 40 radio format.—**Barbara E. Kemp**

1063. **International Who's Who in Music. Volume 2: Popular Music.** Sean Tyler, ed. Cambridge, England, Melrose Press; distr., Bristol, Pa., Taylor & Francis, 1996. 735p. $175.00. ISBN 0-9488-75-07-0.

As one may guess, this work has short (paragraph-length) biographies of popular musicians worldwide. This much seems to be competently done, and fairly inclusive, although inevitable omissions occur (Jewel, for instance). The biographies include interesting tidbits about the musicians' education, whether they were self-taught, hit songs, major concerts/tours and awards, real name and birth date, and the like. Artists are listed by their popular name (e.g., "Sting," not Gordon Sumner).

What is surprising is that the volume lists the individual artist's management representatives and has appendixes covering record companies, management companies, agents and promoters, music publishers, festivals and events, and music organizations, all arranged by country. What this means is that the resource is actually meant to be used by music people, as opposed to serving as an academic reference. This is the kind of source that hard-core music fans will use, but it will be more useful to those in the business of music. The volume is appropriate for entertainment and music collections.—**Bob Craigmile**

1064. Laird, Ross, comp. **Moanin' Low: A Discography of Female Popular Vocal Recordings, 1920-1933.** Westport, Conn., Greenwood Press, 1996. 738p. index. (Discographies, no.67). $99.50. ISBN 0-313-29241-8.

At 700-plus pages, this book consists of information on the recordings of female jazz singers; vaudeville blues singers; dance band vocalists; and music hall, radio, film, and stage performers. All recordings performed in English are listed, regardless of where they originated, so one finds recordings made in 26 U.S. cities. There are also recordings made in other parts of the world, including Montreal, Berlin, Paris, and a number of cities in England and Australia. Laird also includes sound-on-disc recordings, such as those produced by Vitaphone. These contain music made for early motion pictures. In other words, much of this book lives up to Laird's aim of completeness.

The book is organized alphabetically by artist. Each entry provides the name of the artist; an artist description (e.g., soprano, vocal duet, comedienne); accompaniment as shown on the record label; the city where it was recorded; the date of the recording; the matrix number; the take number; the title of each selection; and the original record issues. A useful index of titles is found in the back. It includes composer credits and, when appropriate, the film, show, or play in which a song was featured. Laird's claim that popular music must be urban leads to a few surprising omissions, including country and country blues. Granted there was not much recording of hillbilly music by women before 1933, but surely some mention of those that did record (such as members of the Carter family) is in order.

This book provides a wealth of information. Some of it appears in print for the first time here. This is partly because of its focus on women and partly due to Laird's extensive research. It is an important addition to popular music studies.—**Howard Spring**

1065. Lissauer, Robert. **Lissauer's Encyclopedia of Popular Music in America, 1888 to the Present.** New York, Facts on File, 1996. 3v. $150.00/set. ISBN 0-8160-3238-6.

These three volumes are a revision and update of the 1991 edition (see ARBA 92, entry 1296). The new publisher has used a larger-size typeface and an easy-reading font, which hopefully may set a new trend in reference books. The time frame beginning in 1888 is arbitrary, but does reflect the then-new dominance of New York music publishers (the so-called Tin Pan Alley writers and publishers) over the regional publishing houses. Also, "to the present" in the title means, for now, 1994.

The songs are arranged alphabetically by title in volumes 1 and 2. The entries include the songwriters, the date of the song's introduction and by whom, and the major recordings of the song. When appropriate, the stage or theater musical, or the movie or television production is given. Volume 2 also contains a second section with a chronological listing of these same songs. Volume 3 lists all of the writers alphabetically, followed by a bibliography.

While somewhere near 20,000 popular songs are listed in this encyclopedia, users should realize that this is a selective list of the major popular songs, especially those songs that through the years have proven themselves to be standards, and also those songs that achieved high chart positions. Thus, while not every single song copyrighted since 1888 is listed, the work fulfills the reference needs of most users. [R: RBB, 15 April 96, p. 1462]—**Louis G. Zelenka**

1066. McAleer, Dave, comp. **The All Music Book of Hit Albums.** San Francisco, Calif., Miller Freeman, 1995. 352p. illus. $22.95pa. ISBN 0-87930-393-X.

1067. McAleer, Dave. **The All Music Book of Hit Singles.** San Francisco, Calif., Miller Freeman Books; distr., Emeryville, Calif., Publishers Group West, 1996. 432p. illus. $22.95pa. ISBN 0-87930-425-1.

Popular music fans at last have a tool (although an imperfect one) that lists United States and Great Britain album charts side by side, month by month. Covering the period 1960-1994, three monthly charts are displayed on each page—British listings on the even-numbered pages, American on the odd-numbered pages. *Billboard* magazine is used as the source for American chart information; *Music Week* (formerly *Record Retailer*) for Great Britain's sales charts. News and trivia items border the pages containing monthly charts; decade sections are prefaced by brief overviews. Postage stamp-sized, black-and-white photographs break up the text throughout. Albums are indexed by title and artist; entries for the latter also contain brief biographies and a summation of chart activity. The charts themselves are compiled from the aforementioned sources in a way that is necessarily arbitrary, and that favors sales longevity rather than rapid rises to popularity.

Music sales chart devotees (e.g., the readers of Joel Whitburn's books [see ARBA 96, entries 1313, 1314, 1316, 1319]) will enjoy this new title in what has become a burgeoning area of interest to publishers. However, this tool's usefulness is limited in a few ways: by the availability elsewhere of its news and trivia data; by the unavoidable capriciousness inherent in the compiling of music charts; and most dramatically by choosing to restrict its charts to a "Top 10" format, giving the reader just a fraction of the information that is obtainable on this topic. The format of the *Hit Singles* book is a bit more generous; it lists the top 20 singles of each month. It also covers a longer time period, from January 1954 to April 1996.

A quick survey of the albums book netted two errors: The English band Procol Harum is named Procul Harum in the artist index, and Iron Butterfly's third album (*Ball*) is mistakenly identified as their second. Aside from such trifling lapses, factual content overall seems accurate. No errors were found during a quick check of the singles volume. Both works are recommended for large collections only.—**Ed Volz**

1068. Rimler, Walter. **A Cole Porter Discography.** San Francisco, Calif., N. Charles Sylvan, 1995. 381p. index. $55.00. ISBN 1-886385-25-4.

Cole Porter (1891-1964) was one of the most prolific and is one of the most often-performed of popular composers, writing at a period when most of the jazz standards and pop classics were created. Among Porter's contributions to this corpus are "Love for Sale," "Night and Day," "I Get a Kick Out of You," "Begin the Beguine," "Just One of Those Things," "I've Got You Under My Skin," "It's De-Lovely," and "You'd Be So Nice to Come Home To." The discography is chronologically arranged from 1902 to 1958, with titles and recording artists alphabetically ordered. The discographic citations do not always make clear the performance role of the individual artist, nor are the issue dates consistently provided (and one is not always certain if second entries indicate a variant performance or a reissue), but coverage offers 78rpm discs, LPs, CDs, and cassettes. Two recordings by Charlie Mingus of "What Is This Thing Called Love?" may include his remarkable version with Eric Dolphy (under the title "What Love?"), but this has been subject to several LP reissues, seemingly not included here.

Indexes are to titles of the works, to album titles and musicals, and especially to the recording artists. A few problems are revealed in the latter index (the Adderleys are consistently entered as Adderly, and McCoy Tyner's name is reversed), but it does exhibit the enormous range of those engaged in Porter recordings: Elly Ameling, John Coltrane, the King's Singers, the Empire Brass, and Aretha Franklin, as samples. Bobby Short, long associated with Porter, is of course well represented, but not Josephine Baker. The volume is somewhat a counterpart of the bio-bibliographic series by Greenwood Press, but the format falls short. There are, for example, no biographical data (even though they are easily secured from many sources), no bibliography, and no critique of Porter's work. The serious shortcomings of this handsomely produced volume are relatively few, however, and it will serve many discographic needs adequately. [R: Choice, Feb 96, p. 932]—**Dominique-René de Lerma**

1069. Stubblebine, Donald J. **Broadway Sheet Music: A Comprehensive Listing of Published Music from Broadway and Other Stage Shows, 1918-1993.** Jefferson, N.C., McFarland, 1996. 449p. index. $75.00. ISBN 0-7864-0047-1.

Containing more than 2,500 entries, this compilation covers 75 years of Broadway shows and is the first reference to attempt to include all published sheet music not only from Broadway, but also from off-Broadway shows; productions closed before reaching Broadway; major nightclub revues; and selected ethnic, regional, and military musicals. Arranged alphabetically by show title, listings include the production title as listed on the sheet music cover; the year of the opening; the names of two of the leading performers; and the names of the composers, lyricists, and publishers. Brief comments for each entry convey the theme of the play and the length of the run, with note of its success or failure. The author is not afraid to evaluate productions with his appraisals, using such expressions as "dull," "poor music," "great performance," and other similar descriptions. Interesting notations inform of title changes for productions (e.g., *Oklahoma* opened in New Haven as *Away We Go*).

This reference is a complete source for sheet music collectors, musicians, historians, and the general public. As an aid for sheet music collectors, each entry also includes a description of the cover, including artwork, special lettering, designs, pictures of the stars, authors, and so forth. This description is a tough task to accomplish in two or three words as, for example, "beautiful girl" hardly describes the glamour and color of sheet music from some of the runs of the *Ziegfeld Follies*; nevertheless, such choice words are valuable for identification. The author states in the preface that he personally owns approximately 90 percent of the sheet music listed. His apparent enthusiasm and labor of love have resulted in a thoroughly researched and highly accurate comprehensive reference. [R: Choice, Sept 96, pp. 106-07; LJ, 15 May 96, p. 56]—**Louis G. Zelenka**

1070. Whitburn, Joel, comp. **Joel Whitburn's Top Pop Albums 1955-1996.** Menomonee Falls, Wis., Record Research, 1996. 1053p. illus. $89.95. ISBN 0-89820-117-9.

The companion title to *Joel Whitburn's Top Pop Singles* (see ARBA 96, entry 1314), *Billboard* magazine's largest and costliest title summarizes album sales charts from their genesis in 1955 through September 14, 1996. Billboard has used 24 different album sales chart formats preceding the current list of the top 200 albums. They were all synopsized as objectively as possible into the single ranking used here. Albums are listed alphabetically by artist; by category (e.g., soundtracks, aerobics, Christmas music); and by rank (all-time and decade-by-decade). Artists have separate listings by both sales rankings (the top 500, the top 20 by decade) and into assorted arbitrary achievement categories ("most #1 albums," "one hit wonders"). There is a final chronological listing of every album to reach the top of the charts.

Billboard has become exemplary in its ability to convey copious information in a limited space. They have refined their presentation of data through the inventive use of text coding, indenting, boldfacing, and (less creatively) really small typefaces. The components of each artist entry are: artist name with a cross-reference to other musical entities, when appropriate; brief biographical information; year of greatest chart success; chart debut date and longevity for each album; designation for sales plateaus attained (500,000 unit minimum); song titles and their position on the singles sales chart, if applicable; label name and catalog number; category of album, if not generic (e.g., live recording or greatest hits compilation); approximate dollar value on the used-album market; and other data of a nature both picayune and easier to visualize than to explain. The only useful piece of information lacking is the length (running time) of each album's tracks.

This is one of those resources that is used as much to settle bar bets as to assist in name verification for students and other researchers. Libraries of even modest size should seriously consider its purchase. Interest in *Billboard*'s publications continues to ride the wave of engagement in mass entertainment and all things collectible. This is the flagship publication of the most trusted brand name for popular music statistics. It has no serious competing title.—**Ed Volz**

Big Band

1071. Connor, D. Russell. **Benny Goodman: Wrappin' It Up.** Lanham, Md., Scarecrow, 1996. 179p. illus. index. (Studies in Jazz, no.23). $39.50. ISBN 0-8108-3102-3.

This work, the 23d volume of the Rutgers University Institute of Jazz Studies, is an indexing and annotation of Benny Goodman releases and discoveries that have become available since the author's 1988 publication of *Benny Goodman: Listen to His Legacy* (see ARBA 89, entry 1230). Included is a chronological and annotated discography, supplemented by many previously unpublished photographs. Background information accompanies the listing of Goodman's arrangements that are now in the collections of the New York Public Library and Yale University. Of interest to jazz scholars and swing fans is a list of newly discovered broadcast recordings (air checks) on acetate and tape. The author has also compiled a record of films and videotapes featuring Goodman that are held in various collections worldwide. Narrated in the 12-page prologue are the reminiscences of Connor's many years of friendship with Goodman. Interesting and highly readable anecdotes and additional recollections are scattered throughout the text. For Goodman enthusiasts who are collectors of memorabilia, there is a guide of prices paid, or bids made, during the past decade. A necrology of Goodman's associates completes this unique bio-discography.—**Louis G. Zelenka**

Blues

1072. **All Music Guide to the Blues: The Experts' Guide to the Best Blues Recordings.** Michael Erlewine, Vladimir Bogdanov, Chris Woodstra, and Cub Koda, eds. San Francisco, Calif., Miller Freeman Books; distr., Emeryville, Calif., Publishers Group West, 1996. 424p. index. $17.95pa. ISBN 0-87930-424-3.

The blues? Hard to define with any precision, but whoever once called them "just a good man, feelin' bad" was right on the money. This musical genre may once have been the province of downcast rural slaves with homemade guitars and harmonicas, but today's blues are a popular growth industry, showing up in movies, television shows, and even commercials. This book is intended to help the blues aficionado who, while not knowledgeable in the genre, seeks informed advice in sorting through the thousands of recordings available to collectors.

The handy paperback contains reviews and ratings of more than 2,600 CDs, tapes, and recordings and profiles of the work and lives of 500-plus blues musicians, both currently active and long gone. Proponents of all the major blues styles are included (e.g., the Mississippi Delta, New Orleans, Memphis, Chicago); in fact, it may astonish the neophyte blues-lover to learn just how many blues musicians of the past or present hail from Mississippi.

The aim of this guide is to aid the selector in assembling a good collection of blues recordings, from classic to modern (electric) blues. Reviewed and rated by expert music critics, the recordings presented here are arranged alphabetically by last name, although there are anomalies (e.g., Muddy Waters is found under "W," while Howlin' Wolf is found under "H," without explanation). Many performers' nicknames, in fact, are fascinating. They call (or called) themselves: Barbecue Bob, Cow Cow, Big Chief, Sugar Cane, Juke Boy, and T-Bone. Who is and is not a blues artist is a matter of debate, so some of the artists included may surprise readers—such as Elvis Presley, the Bee Gees, George Winston, and even Patti Page! Artists whose oeuvre is presented are furnished with personal profiles of their lives and work. Summing up, we have a winner here! Handsomely printed and attractively priced, this convenient resource is a must-purchase for everybody's reference collection. [R: LJ, 15 Nov 96, p. 54]—**Bruce A. Shuman**

Folk

1073. Bohlman, Philip V. **Central European Folk Music: An Annotated Bibliography of Sources in German.** New York, Garland, 1996. 316p. index. (Garland Library of Music Ethnology, v.3; Garland Reference Library of the Humanities, v.1448). $50.00. ISBN 0-8153-0304-1.

Bohlman, a noted folk music scholar, provides a meticulously researched and copiously annotated bibliography of sources in the German language dealing with Central European folk music. As an American examining German folk music tradition, he draws on sources from the major German-speaking countries: Austria, Germany, and Switzerland. He turned to German-language scholarship because, as he notes in the preface, "... in my own work I was confronted with problems of ethnicity and nationalism, the politics of identity and religion, the histories of mass migration and modernity." Although his chapter on what Americans call "ethnic minorities" is brief, he offers a discussion on the meaning of the term for German-speakers that provides a perspective for readers.

The work is divided into four broad topics: "Approaching the Subject," "Fields of Folk-Music Scholarship," "Social Contexts of Folk Music," and "*Wozu Volksmusik?*—Past, Present, and Future." Each chapter begins with an introductory essay providing an overview of the topic at hand. Entries include author, title (in German and translated into English), and source. It is the annotations that make this book an important addition to academic library collections. Detailed, although at times subjective, they achieve the author's objective of providing a rich source for information on a general topic sometimes neglected by English-speaking scholars.

Central European Folk Music is a unique work that fills a significant gap in folk music research. It is recommended for academic libraries supporting curricula in folk music.—**Sue Kamm**

1074. Fuss, Charles J. **Joan Baez: A Bio-bibliography.** Westport, Conn., Greenwood Press, 1996. 252p. index. (Bio-bibliographies in the Performing Arts, no.70). $55.00. ISBN 0-313-28463-6.

An excellent bio-bibliography, this volume will serve as a good starting point for anyone beginning to research the career of one of the preeminent members of the folk song revival in the United States. Fuss begins with a succinct and well-written biography of Baez, which places her in the folk tradition carved out by Woody Guthrie, noting that she was the first woman to achieve international fame as a U.S. folk singer. This is followed by a brief chronology of Baez's life, outlining significant life events, concerts, and recordings. Perhaps the highlight of the book is a discography that should serve as a model for such work, in which Fuss gives useful notes on sidemen/women, authorship of songs, session details, and select reviews. The filmography, which follows, is equally well crafted, as is the selective, annotated bibliography.

The only quarrel with the bibliography is its nonchronological organization, which makes one rely overly much on the indexing to find one's way to the citations. The index is in two parts: The first covers people and subjects in general; the second, song titles. Fuss's work on formatting the volume is good—the sans serif typeface is somewhat unfortunate, but overall this is a cleanly presented work (Greenwood Press prints camera-ready copy as supplied by its authors). The book will be of interest to libraries with clients interested in popular culture in general, given Baez's longevity in the field, and to students of folk music, social movements, and popular music. It is recommended.—**David Dodd**

1075. Vernon, Paul. **Ethnic and Vernacular Music, 1898-1960: A Resource and Guide to Recordings.** Westport, Conn., Greenwood Press, 1995. 344p. (Discographies, no.62). $75.00. ISBN 0-313-29553-0.

This book claims to present as much information as possible about ethnic and vernacular music on 78 rpm records. Vernon, a music consultant, intended the guide to promote public awareness about vernacular music and to assist discographical research. The guide includes a list by country, region, or ethnic group of company names, prefixes, and numerical blocks of issued 78 rpm records. The same list contains information on reissues on compact discs, cassettes, and vinyl. It also attempts to provide references to books that elucidate the music. Also supplied are a lexicon of terms used for music in the book, a listing of Gramophone Company engineers and their overseas recording sessions, and additional appendixes for commercial recordings in African languages and national anthems.

The work has a bare-bones introduction that gives a quick guide to the entries and contents of the book. It indicates a limitation of the guide as a worldwide resource: It omits the extensive and diverse heritage of North America. The author refers the reader to other references for this portion of the globe. Special attention seems to be given to African-language recordings, and collectors and ethnomusicologists will appreciate the detail of discographical data given here. However, it is probably too ambitious a task to cover the world with anything approaching comprehensiveness, and several sections seem incomplete. The three reissues listed under "Yiddish," for example, are a small sample of what is a much larger record shelf.

Another point to be considered is access to these resources once researchers become aware of them through the guide. The author provides a list of record companies, commercial outlets, and vernacular music specialists, but neglects libraries and archives that provide access to sound recordings. One might conclude that the guide is aimed primarily at discographers and collectors, who will likely want to add many notes on gaps in the information. It may entice and frustrate ethnomusicologists, anthropologists, and folklorists looking for scholarly sources and sound archives for the heritage of world music.

—**Simon J. Bronner**

Jazz

1076. Carr, Ian, Digby Fairweather, and Brian Priestly. **Jazz: The Rough Guide.** London, Rough Guides; distr., New York, Penguin Books, 1995. 754p. illus. $24.95pa. ISBN 1-85828-137-7.

Jazz: The Rough Guide provides entries for more than 1,600 musicians, arranged alphabetically, that include instrument(s) (and other related categories such as composer, arranger, educator); dates of birth and death (when appropriate); place of birth; a critical musical biography; and, for most, an annotated list of selected LP and CD recordings that the compilers feel are the musicians' most significant. Entries vary from a paragraph to several pages in length and are signed by one of the compilers or one of five additional contributors. The biographies and discographies are informed, scholarly, and accurate. *Jazz* is, in fact, an essential reference book, nicely illustrated with almost 300 black-and-white photographs and supplied with a useful glossary of terms, trends, and music companies. Unfortunately, it does not include an index or bibliography.

The compilers, all from the United Kingdom, are themselves jazz musicians and well-known jazz scholars/educators. They have discussed more non-American musicians in this guide than has any other jazz reference, and have suggested a greater significance for the early white jazz musicians than most other scholars. Although jazz has truly become international and multiethnic, the inclusion of so large a proportion of foreign and non-African musicians (e.g., over one-third of the photographs are of non-Africans) is, in a historical sense, misleading. The positive side to this openness—and an antidote to recent attempts to narrowly canonize jazz—is that it includes many of the classic blues singers, prominent Latino musicians, soul/R&B performers (but not James Brown!), and even rock's Frank Zappa. [R: SLJ, Aug 96, p. 185]
—**Fred J. Hay**

Musicals

1077. Bloom, Ken. **American Song: The Complete Musical Theatre Companion.** 2d ed. New York, Schirmer Books/Simon & Schuster Macmillan, 1996. 2v. index. $175.00/set. ISBN 0-02-870484-3.

The first paragraph of the introduction to the set explains exactly what this compilation is all about. "*American Song* includes data on over 4,800 American musicals. All Broadway, off-Broadway, and off-off Broadway productions from 1877 to the fall of 1995 are included, together with all resident theatre productions of shows by major artists (and some minor), shows that closed out of town prior to Broadway, shows that toured and never intended to come to New York, selected nightclub shows, straight plays with original songs, vaudeville and burlesque shows, and English and French productions of shows by major American songwriters." Updated from its 1st edition (see ARBA 86, entry 1359), this edition contains 5,000 additions and corrections and features original television musicals and many recently discovered musicals. Three indexes accompany the factual entries: a complete list of all the songs of U.S. musicals (totaling 42,000-plus entries); 58,000 entries of the people connected with all aspects of U.S. musical theater; and a list of the show titles by year.

The author and publisher deserve applause for getting this remarkable reference out in less than a year's time from the cutoff date. This in itself deserves great kudos—but there is more! Often the title surpasses a book's content, but all involved with this two-volume source can boast proudly of this indeed being *The Complete Musical Theatre Companion*, as the subtitle states. Whether researching the familiar or obscure, one will find it here. In browsing its pages, the odd is discovered along with the expected. For instance, *Sec Champagne*, produced in 1933 at the Morosco Theatre on Broadway, was directed by Monty Woolley. The same Monty Woolley from *The Man Who Came to Dinner*?

Admittedly, as this is a listing of factual data, it is rather dry. However, the insertion of critique and commentary was not the author's purpose and surely not necessary. The intent here is to provide a complete reference of U.S. musical theater and it is done exceptionally well. Any library with a respectable theater section must have *American Song* on its shelf. By the same token, any library trying to build a good theater collection will profit greatly by offering this reference to its patrons. [R: Choice, Dec 96, p. 586; RBB, 1 Oct 96, p. 367]—**Joan Garner**

1078. Leiby, Bruce R. **Howard Keel: A Bio-bibliography.** Westport, Conn., Greenwood Press, 1995. 309p. illus. index. (Bio-bibliographies in the Performing Arts, no.67). $65.00. ISBN 0-313-28456-3.

Keel was one of the dominant figures in musicals for more than a decade, starring in stage and film performances of *Annie Get Your Gun*, *Show Boat*, *Calamity Jane*, *Kiss Me, Kate*, and *Seven Brides for Seven Brothers*. His voice and acting often were described as "natural," "vigorous," and "dynamic." Keel had equally stellar performances in real life—his poverty-ridden childhood; his 1934 drive with his mother from Illinois to California in search of other opportunities after his father's apparent suicide; his push into a musical career by his friends' landlady; his 3 marriages, currently to a woman 30 years his junior; and his starring alongside some of the acting and singing legends of the mid-twentieth century.

Unfortunately, Leiby fails to accentuate and enliven the dramatic aspects of Keel's life and career. He mixes inconsequential minutiae (who missed a touchdown on the one yard line during a USC-UCLA football game Keel attended) with momentous events, overloads paragraphs with numerous different thoughts, misplaces emphasis, and throws in teaser statements that are left frustratingly unexplained (e.g., Doris Day's tragedy-filled life). The shifts to events in Keel's life are so abrupt that the biography reads like a chronology thrown together in paragraph form, certainly unnecessary as a separate chronology is provided. The writing is choppy, disconnected, strewn with grammatical and spelling errors, and generally not very readable. It is a shame Leiby and the in-house editors did not concentrate on writing a readable and interesting biography, because the other sections on Keel's accomplishments—stage, filmography, broadcasts, discography, sheet music, videolog, night club and concert appearances—are rather full. An annotated bibliography, which includes some sources of dubious relevance, and illustrations are provided. The work is useful purely for a beginning reference, not for reading.—**John A. Lent**

Rhythm and Blues

1079. Whitburn, Joel. **Joel Whitburn's Top R&B Singles 1942-1995.** Menomonee Falls, Wis., Record Research, 1996. 681p. illus. $64.95. ISBN 0-89820-115-2.

This updated and expanded discography contains every song listed on *Billboard*'s various rhythm and blues-oriented top 100 charts from 1942 to 1995. The alphabetic performer list includes every charted single, plus its date; peak position; number of weeks at peak position and on chart; whether gold or platinum; peak positions on subsidiary R&B charts (sales, airplay, jukebox); peak position/duration on pop charts; current value; whether issued with picture sleeve/box; and the record label and number. Each entry indicates format: 45 or 78 rpm, 12-inch vinyl single, or cassette.

Whitburn has done much else to make this work user friendly and comprehensive; he has highlighted all singles achieving the number 1 position; underlined artists' top hits; and included photographs of the top 100 artists, rankings for the top 500, year of artists' peak popularity, and for most, a biographical summary. Excellent cross-references with artists' names—which appear elsewhere in the list—boldfaced and the inclusion in the performers list of alternate versions of proper names also highlight the text.

The introduction is clearly written and gives important information on the history of R&B recording and *Billboard*'s R&B charts. This amazing compilation provides 30 additional lists, including an A to Z list of all chart song titles. This book has an integrity that few reference books of this scope have attained; errors are few and minor (e.g., Junior Parker was not born in Arkansas, Ma Rainey did not compose the folksong "See See Rider"). In short, this is an essential reference book.—**Fred J. Hay**

Rock

1080. **Billboard's Hottest Hot 100 Hits.** rev. ed. By Fred Bronson. New York, Billboard Books/Watson-Guptill, 1995. 497p. illus. index. $21.95pa. ISBN 0-8230-7646-6.

The seemingly endless mining of *Billboard* charts for every possible permutation continues with this reference work. The author, who "became fascinated with record charts just after turning 14," has devised a method of determining which songs, according to *Billboard* chart performance, rank highest against all other songs ever appearing on the *Billboard* charts. This is not an easy or straightforward task and involves a complex method of assigning points (100 points for each week at number 1, 99 for each week at number 2, and so on) for every song tracked while in the top 30 between July 9, 1955, and October 29, 1994. This allows for a cumulation of points resulting in a ranking of the top 5,000 songs for this era.

The book is divided into sections listing the top songs by certain artists (e.g., The Beatles, Elvis Presley); by certain writers (e.g., Carole King, Bob Dylan); by certain producers (e.g., Quincy Jones, Phil Spector); by certain labels; by type of chart appearance (e.g., debut songs, one-hit wonders); by type of performer (e.g., male solo, duets, Canadian artists); by year (top 100 songs of each year and of each decade); by subject (about animals, colors, and so on); and, finally, a ranked order listing of the top 5,000 hits. Songs are identified only by performer; composers are not listed. The index is by song title: There is no access by performer, composer, or any of the other imaginative categories listed above. This book, while in some senses meticulously put together, attractively illustrated, and basically well written, makes extracting information difficult. It is hard to imagine how it would be used and by whom, with the possible exception of radio station music directors.—**David Dodd**

1081. **DK Encyclopedia of Rock Stars.** By Dafydd Rees and Luke Crampton. New York, DK Publishing, 1996. 951p. illus. $29.95pa. ISBN 0-7894-1263-2.

This hefty compilation and rewrite of text from news clippings and press releases could more appropriately be titled *Chronologies of Pop Music Artists*. It lacks the analytic tone of an encyclopedia, is not limited in scope to the famed, and covers folk, pop, and world music artists as well as those in rock. In articles that vary in length to reflect career longevity, yearly summations for solo artists and groups list events such as album and single releases, selected concert appearances, drug arrests, musician and management changes, and all manner of personal data bordering on (and venturing into) gossip. A warhorse outfit such as Jefferson Airplane and its permutations is granted nearly 3 pages of coverage for a 30-year career, while relative newcomers such as Candlebox earn a single column.

Entries are sectioned by year and month, with dates of specific events given in brackets. Information is current through early 1996. The book is neither indexed nor illustrated throughout, an anomaly and disappointment for a publisher so respected for its visual presentation of information. The evaluation of artistic output in a medium this popular and pervasive tends to sound either conformist or capricious as readers of these books come to them with strong opinions. The authors, veterans of music industry writing and research, avoid the issue by doing no overt judging or even categorizing of the musical acts included in their book. Factual mistakes are impressively rare, although the common misspelling of the R.E.M. *Lifes Rich Pageant* album as *Life's Rich Pageant* is made.

The listed criteria for inclusion of artists are rather generic, but in execution display a preference for British over American acts, and the 1960s versus other decades, although very current personalities are featured. It is the odder inclusions that are most valued, as they are entities not represented in other rock reference sources. The British jazz-rock group Caravan is here, for example, but not the stylistically similar and better-documented Soft Machine. There is value, too, in the atypical depth of detail to the chronologies—one reader's minutia being another's revelatory fact. Students and music collectors will have their browsing rewarded. Popular music collections should have this title, priced reasonably given its girth.—**Ed Volz**

1082. Gatten, Jeffrey N. **Rock Music Scholarship: An Interdisclipinary Bibliography.** Westport, Conn., Greenwood Press, 1995. 294p. index. (Music Reference Collection, no.50). $69.50. ISBN 0-313-29455-0.

This bibliography will be a classic work for anyone doing research on rock music. It contains approximately 1,000 citations of monographs, periodical articles, and dissertations, complete with annotations, each one of which is seldom less than 60 words and often more. The annotations summarize the content of the item cited. The bibliography does not include interviews, popular or juvenile fiction, or, as a general rule, news publications that are reporting occurrences rather than analyzing rock music. The reference also does not include rock criticism, but it does list a limited number of citations to films and videos.

The author defines rock music as any popular music, from the mid-1950s to the present. The citations are divided into the following sections: communication, education, ethnomusicality, history, literature and the arts, music, politics, psychology, religion, and sociology. Author and subject (including performers' names) indexes are included. The introduction seems unnecessary; outside of that criticism, there are no cavils. The bibliography is appropriate for reference collections in public libraries and academic libraries. [R: Choice, April 96, p. 1286]—**Mary Larsgaard**

1083. Helander, Brock. **The Rock Who's Who.** 2d ed. New York, Schirmer Books/Simon & Schuster Macmillan, 1996. 849p. illus. index. $75.00. ISBN 0-02-871031-2.

This new edition of the 1982 work of the same title (see ARBA 84, entry 925) has an additional 150 pages (for example, the bibliography has doubled, from 14 to 25 pages). The majority of the work is an annotated list plus a discography for nearly 300 rock and soul artists. Specifically excluded are white cover artists of the 1950s; most "bubblegum" groups of the 1960s; and in the discographies that accompany each artist's entry, any foreign releases or bootleg albums. Each entry is composed of the name of the group or artist, birth and death dates, where born (when known), musical instrument played, annotation, and discography—amounting to approximately two pages per artist, although landmark groups such as the Beatles, the Rolling Stones, and the Who receive about three times that length.

Although the author states on page ix that "all conclusions herein are my own," the annotations are balanced, as is the selection of groups for inclusion. It would help to know what the numeric difference is between levels of hit singles (top, smash, major, moderate, or minor), or whether this is a subjective judgment on the part of the author. There are approximately 50 black-and-white photographs, inserted, one suspects, mainly to give the reading eye some relief from all the text. The list of groups is followed by a selective bibliography; basis for selection is not given, but it seems to be major book-level works for major artists. Following the bibliography is an index of groups, individuals, albums, and specific singles/songs. This is an important reference work for any library whose patrons are interested in rock and soul music.—**Mary Larsgaard**

1084. **MusicHound Rock: The Essential Album Guide.** Gary Graff, ed. Detroit, Visible Ink Press/Gale, 1996. 911p. index. $24.95pa. ISBN 0-7876-1037-2.

1085. Strong, M. C. **The Great Rock Discography.** New York, Omnibus Press; distr., Music Sales Corporation, 1996. 936p. illus. $34.95pa. ISBN 0-86241-541-1.

Rock music reference books tend to be of a standard type. Artists are listed in alphabetic entries, a partial (or purportedly "complete") discography is given, important dates in the artist's musical history are listed in varying degrees of comprehensiveness, and purchase recommendations are made. Some of the books on rock music provide an additional service by linking artists to others they have emulated and influenced. The books under review are useful because each emphasizes a different single component in the repertoire of books of this genre.

As its title implies, *The Great Rock Discography* concentrates on verifying the documented recorded output of rock (and pop) musical artists. Dramatically increasing its effectiveness by limiting its scope, this British paperback features the most complete artist discographies extant. There are, however, limitations: This is a British book about British records, tapes, and CDs ("imports" to the American music collector). While more than 1,000 artists are included, many hundreds are left out. The bias toward singers and recording groups from the United Kingdom is both noticeable and justified. Biographical information is given—recording group members are identified and personnel changes are documented—but such facts are available in other sources. The unique information here is the verification of otherwise fugitive material, such as recordings issued in limited numbers or in an out-of-favor medium (7-inch singles in the 1990s). Mistakes are infrequent but do occur: Arthur Lee's *Vindicator* album is called *Vindictive*, and the popular misnomer for R.E.M.'s *Lifes Rich Pageant* album (*Life's Rich Pageant*) is duplicated. Nonetheless, this is truly a reference book suitable for name, date, and title verification. It will be indispensable for its admittedly select audience. Serious music collectors will probably purchase their own copies.

MusicHound Rock will appeal to readers of a different sort. While the usual biographical and historical data are here, the underpinning of this guide is the act of referral. Each artist's recorded output is categorized with the consumer in mind. Recommendations are made for an initial purchase in each artist's oeuvre, secondary and unnecessary purchases are identified, and readers are led to obscure recordings worthy of a search. Entries end with a listing of several artists (and occasionally a writer) having a style similar to the musical entity being profiled. Links are thus made among the influential and the derivative, the old and the new, the creators and the imitators. Arbitrary judgments of this sort make for a consumer guide worth grazing, but not a reference book. The entries were written by several dozen contributors, including industry publicists, students, music collectors, band members, and music critics from daily newspapers. Their opinions are both capricious and insightful, motivating the reader to argue with every aspect of the book, starting with the selection of the 2,500 artists it includes.

While *The Great Rock Discography* offers a valuable reference service to a narrow audience, *MusicHound Rock* is an exemplary buyers' guide for a broader range of consumers. The former title is appropriate for libraries with large music collections; the latter is a suitable end-user purchase.—**Ed Volz**

Sacred

1086. Rogal, Samuel J., comp. **Sing Glory and Hallelujah! Historical and Biographical Guide to *Gospel Hymns Nos. 1 to 6 Complete*.** Westport, Conn., Greenwood Press, 1996. 229p. index. (Music Reference Collection, no.49). $79.50. ISBN 0-313-29690-1.

At first glance, readers may be somewhat confused as to what Rogal is covering in this guide, but he makes everything clear in the introduction. He points out that his analysis is of a series of hymnbooks published in the late nineteenth century that culminated in a work entitled *Gospel Hymns Nos. 1 to 6 Complete*, published by the Biglow and Main Company and the John Church Company in 1895. This work incorporated two earlier works entitled *Gospel Hymns and Sacred Songs* (1875), and *Gospel Hymns* (published serially in six volumes from 1876 through 1891). The combined work contained 739 hymns and "more than 125 standard hymns and tunes of the church" (introduction).

Sing Glory and Hallelujah! provides an analysis of the hymns and their composers and authors. Section 1 alphabetically lists all writers of the hymns. Each entry contains the name of the writer, birth and death dates, a brief biography, and the writer's hymn(s) by the original number used in the *Gospel Hymns* volumes. (Each hymn listing includes title, date, Bible verse, and first line, along with the name of the composer of the music.) The 2d section is an alphabetic listing of the composers and contains similar information with the exception of the detail on the hymn found in the author section. Additional sections include a list of works cited and consulted and an index to titles and opening lines.

Sing Glory and Hallelujah! is the only research tool in print that provides complete information concerning these standard hymns. It is an important research source for information concerning the hymns and, at the same time, provides valuable information for the study of popular culture in the United States during the last half of the nineteenth century. Additional indexing would be useful (e.g., a list of the hymns by the original numbers for easy cross-referencing and a list of the hymns by original date of publication) and would provide a more historical view. The work is recommended for all larger academic and public libraries and for music collections that emphasize hymnology. It could also provide useful information for clergy who wish to research older hymns still used for services.—**Robert L. Wick**

1087. Rust, E. Gardner. **The Music and Dance of the World's Religions: A Comprehensive, Annotated Bibliography of Materials in the English Language.** Westport, Conn., Greenwood Press, 1996. 476p. index. (Music Reference Collection, no.54). $89.50. ISBN 0-313-29561-1.

Slightly fewer than 3,900 entries, most of which are carefully annotated, appear in this splendid publication. It is an accomplishment of award-worthy informational virtuosity, even if one considers only the structure of the classifications. International geographic areas and denominations are subdivided as prompted by the literature (books, articles, and graduate papers), so that one may find sections on theological aspects of the music of J. S. Bach (14 entries); Asian-American religious music (11 entries); Confucian ceremonial music (8 entries for Korea); and chant, modes, and transmission (47 entries as the topic applies to Jewish music).

The gathering of literature obligated an acute multidisciplinary and multicultural alertness, involving recourse to the most scholarly publications in musicology, ethnic and religious studies, dance, theology, anthropology, and those of small regional presses. The provision of annotations on these speaks well for acquisitional and budgetary latitudes. The front material justifies the alliance of music and dance, both with respect to time and space, while indicating the decision to include reference to publications of only the past two decades (some of which were not yet a year old at the time of this review). The author and subject indexes are meticulously prepared. This handsomely produced volume will be a valuable aid to those even of more parochial orientations, but it should invigorate existing curricula and provide stimulus for future research.—**Dominique-René de Lerma**

26 Mythology, Folklore, and Popular Culture

FOLKLORE

1088. **American Folklore: An Encyclopedia.** Jan Harold Brunvand, ed. New York, Garland, 1996. 794p. illus. index. (Garland Reference Library of the Humanities, v.1551). $95.00. ISBN 0-8153-0751-9.

Packed with entries on folklorists, multiracial performers, crafts, music, and academic discussion, this comprehensive folklore encyclopedia is useful, accessible to most readers, and informative. The layout offers wide columns, pleasant typefaces, guide words, and simple pagination. The editor excels at inclusion of customs from many racial and ethnic backgrounds. Coverage is thorough—from maritime folklore and zydeco to verse, quilts, baskets, proverbs, odori, riddles, and folkways; from Mormon and Jewish lore to Burl Ives, John Lomax, Johnny Appleseed, Austin Fife, and Leadbelly (Huddie Ledbetter).

Above all, the encyclopedia is scholarly. Based on the work of 263 experts from mostly U.S. communities, independent scholars and lecturers, colleges, universities, the Smithsonian Institution, and the Library of Congress, signed entries consist of topic, discussion, and references. Photographs—although grainy and blurred in the case of antique sources—are broad-based, ranging from powwows, roughnecks, and cross-dressers to a Russian Sunday school, xeroxlore, the jitterbug, checkers, street preaching, and Elliot Wigginton's Foxfire writers rebuilding a mountain cabin. Most entries are succinct, lively, and substantiated with anecdotes, lyrics, jokes, advertisements, models, and dialogue.

However, a modest entry on Mark Twain is surprisingly poor; information on Joel Chandler Harris fails to mention the Walt Disney film *Song of the South*, which uses a beloved beast fable in the first cinema blend of acting and animation. The absence of Calamity Jane, Jackie Torrance, and Datsolali is puzzling; also wanting is commentary on Paul Green and Kermit Hunter, founders of outdoor historical pageants. The editor could further strengthen this work with clearer illustrations, a few maps, pronunciation guides, and cross-referencing, but overall, the encyclopedia reads well in its current form. [R: Choice, Oct 96, p. 247; RBB, Aug 96, pp. 1920-21; VOYA, Dec 96, p. 298]—**Mary Ellen Snodgrass**

1089. Mertvago, Peter. **Dictionary of 1000 Spanish Proverbs with English Equivalents.** New York, Hippocrene Books, 1996. 147p. index. $11.95pa. ISBN 0-7818-0412-4.

The Spanish language, like English, contains many brief, colorful, pithy sayings that, be they derived from folklore or learned sources, encapsulate age-old practical wisdom firmly rooted in daily life. Proverbs offer a glimpse at the mind-set of a people, their values, customs, and ways of thinking, as well as obvious insights into their language. Collectively, proverbs represent a compendium of the philosophy of a people.

Mertvago's handy, well-organized collection consists of 1,000 numbered items arranged in alphabetic order according to the first significant Spanish word (usually the first key noun) in the proverb. Most of the best-loved sayings appear here, along with a large number of obscure ones. The focus is on "the 1000 most important and commonly used and understood proverbs of Castillian Spanish as it is spoken and written today" (p. 9). For each saying, the editor aims to provide an English rendition or, when available, an equivalent proverbial expression. In numerous cases, however, the English version fails to convey the same thought as the original. For example, instead of pairing the familiar "Antes que te cases, mira lo que haces" with the English "Look before you leap," he opts for the more literal "Before you marry, 'tis well to tarry." Likewise, for "A lo hecho, pecho" he gives "What's done cannot be undone" rather than "Don't cry over spilt milk." These apparent oversights suggest either a lack of familiarity with North American proverbs or a target audience of English speakers beyond the borders of the United States.

Following an excellent bibliography that refers readers to additional collections and noteworthy scholarly studies, the volume concludes with an English keyword index, which nicely complements the Spanish keyword arrangement in the main body of the collection. Given the user-friendly format, readers should have no difficulty locating specific sayings. This addition to the already voluminous literature devoted to proverbs has appeal on two fronts: as entertaining recreational reading and as a resource for classroom instruction.—**Melvin S. Arrington Jr.**

1090. Rose, Carol. **Spirits, Fairies, Gnomes, and Goblins: An Encyclopedia of the Little People.** Santa Barbara, Calif., ABC-CLIO, 1996. 369p. illus. $49.50. ISBN 0-87436-811-1.

"Between the gods and heroes and mere mortals, there is another group of beings that holds a very special place in the cultural development and expression of human society," writes Rose. She is referring to the *little people*: the spirits, fairies, gnomes, and goblins in her book by the same name. Drawing from materials as diverse as encyclopedias, classical and nonclassical mythology, major religions, folktales, folklore, anthropological surveys, nursery rhymes, and children's fables, Rose has created an encyclopedia that spans the entire world and most of its history. Ancient Babylon to modern Cambodia and Brazil to the North American Inuit are included.

Her main criterion for inclusion was that the *supernatural*, as she calls them generically, must have exerted or exert an active, willful influence on humans or their creatures without being divine themselves. The book is richly illustrated with black-and-white drawings, and the annotations are filled with imagery, history, and lore. Historical supernaturals and literary figures are covered, even J. R. R. Tolkien's Hobbits.

Entries are arranged alphabetically with the most common name being given first and alternative spellings after. Annotations include a description, powers, character, and activities of the spirit. At the end of each are numbered references that refer the reader to the bibliography in the back of the book (although this is not explained, it was easy to figure out). Finally, extensive *see also* references direct the reader to other entries or appendixes. Twenty-seven very short to very long appendixes contain additional names not listed in the encyclopedia. The appendixes add geographic locations and what the spirit or supernatural is associated with doing or with having done.

A subject index would have improved the book for those who do not know a name but know what a spirit did, or want to find all listings about *guardian angels*, for instance. The encyclopedia is recommended for small libraries, writers, students, storytellers, folklorists, and those interested in culture and history.—**Kevin W. Perizzolo**

MYTHOLOGY

1091. McLeish, Kenneth. **Myth: Myths and Legends of the World Explored.** New York, Facts on File, 1996. 736p. illus. index. $50.00. ISBN 0-8160-3237-8.

This alphabetic listing of more than 2,500 characters, cultures, and mythical phenomena, their basic stories and brief commentaries, is generally well written and reflects current scholarship. An exception to that valuation would be the handful of biblical stories (Satan—rather questionably identified with the serpent, Adam and Eve, Cain, Noah, Samson, and Yahweh—why not Daniel, Jonah, and Job?) that are treated as Mesopotamian myths "destroyed and vilified" by the "dogmatic belief systems" (p. 388) of the major Western faiths.

There is an excellent 3-page introduction to myth and 24 pages listing myths by their cultures, for example, African, Greek, Japanese, and Slavic. The largest number of entries are for Native American (including Central and South America), Greek, and Asian Indian stories. Inclusion of many Celtic, Finnish, and Oceanic entries indicates the breadth of the work. A random check of rather obscure myths did not turn up any oversights. There is a helpful and extensive cross-listing of entries. Lack of dating and identification of either the origin or circulation of the stories is a notably deficiency. There is no index, bibliography, or notation of references and few variant tellings of the stories. Research would require a more detailed work, but this listing provides a quick reference to preliterate classical and non-Western myths for teenagers and adults.—**Robert T. Anderson**

1092. Sienkewicz, Thomas J. **World Mythology: An Annotated Guide to Collections and Anthologies.** Pasadena, Calif., Salem Press and Lanham, Md., Scarecrow, 1996. 469p. index. (The Magill Bibliographies). $49.50. ISBN 0-8108-3154-6.

World Mythology is intended for the general reader. While some scholarly works are included, the emphasis is on material that offers significant retellings, translations, and summaries of myths rather than erudite analysis and interpretation. Consequently, the volume emphasizes the myths themselves as opposed to theories of myth. Books on folklore are not the focus here.

Because of the difficulties inherent in any attempt to distinguish definitively between myth and history, this bibliography includes references to material that may be considered semihistorical and religious rather than purely mythical. Ranging wide in its coverage, the volume is intentionally inclusive while not exhaustive. In terms of organization, priority has been given to listing the widest possible cultural range of anthologies, collections, and translations of myths. Thus, the chapters are organized geographically, except for chapter 1, which deals with comparative studies and collections of myths from more than one part of the world. The remaining chapters move from east to west around the world, starting in chapter 2 with the myths of ancient Egypt and sub-Saharan Africa. The oral traditions of the Americas in chapter 3 are followed by Oceanic legends and myths of the Pacific and Australia in chapter 4. In chapter 5, the many different mythologies of Asian peoples, such as the Babylonians, Hebrews, Indians, Chinese, and Japanese, are grouped together. Special attention has been given to present a broad survey of mythological materials from Africa, the Americas, Oceania, and Asia because of their unfamiliarity to the average English-language reader.

Because myths can be presented in a variety of ways, the bibliography includes myths told and illustrated for young children or juvenile readers as well as myths presented in more scholarly formats. The problem of nomenclature has been approached with the aim of consistency, and while spelling is not changed in titles, citations aim toward standardization. The more familiar latinized forms of Greek names are used in Greek contexts, Latin names are used in Roman contexts, and the word "Indian" is replaced with "Native American."

The introduction to this useful volume offers the general reader a good overview of the idea of mythology as discussed and debated by scholars. If there is one shortcoming within the text, it is the lack of distinction between citations for Joseph Campbell, for instance, and scholars of much more substance, such as Patrick K. Ford or Jaan Puhvel. Finally, while no bibliography can ever be 100 percent complete, *World Mythology* does offer its readers a rich catalog of sources of materials from which to draw in the study of mythology. In this respect, the volume should be a welcome addition to libraries of all levels of sophistication.—**Arthur Gribben**

POPULAR CULTURE

1093. Oliver, Valerie Burnham. **Fashion and Costume in American Popular Culture: A Reference Guide.** Westport, Conn., Greenwood Press, 1996. 279p. index. (American Popular Culture). $69.50. ISBN 0-313-29412-7.

With the publication of this title, researchers in fashion and costume history now have a well-researched reference work in which to locate monographic and reference literature on fashion, as well as information on periodicals, research centers, and costume museums and collections. This source reviews and discusses available fashion and costume reference literature, such as dictionaries and encyclopedias, guides to the literature, bibliographies, and histories of fashion and costume. One of the most useful chapters is devoted to specific clothing and accessories. It is divided into sections on wedding dresses, T-shirts, buttons, and shoes, and gives an overview of the research done on each topic, in addition to including a useful bibliography of books and articles.

This source also lists 123 research centers, arranged geographically by state; 176 costume museums and collections of costumes; and 278 periodicals that cover fashion, costume, and clothing. In addition, a list of clothing and accessory subject headings from the Worldcat database is analyzed to reveal the most popular fashion and costume topics. Author, title, and subject indexes are provided in this work. The author, a reference librarian, is a member of the Costume Society of America. This excellent, much-needed reference work fills the void in the area of fashion and costume reference resources. It is highly recommended for both academic and public libraries.—**Monica Fusich**

1094. **Popular American Housing: A Reference Guide.** Ruth Brent and Benyamin Schwarz, eds. Westport, Conn., Greenwood Press, 1995. 248p. illus. index. (American Popular Culture). $75.00. ISBN 0-313-28032-0.

This anthology of eight bibliographic essays explores the methodology of and resources for researching facets of popular housing. *Popular* here is defined as vernacular architecture—the kind of housing everyday people live in, not the signature or innovative houses famous architects may design for wealthy clients. Resources covered include key books and articles, journals, and specialized (e.g., video) and electronic sources.

The essays encompass such varied topics as the history of housing, relationships with the social environment, representation in art and the media, public housing, the financial aspects of real estate, and environmental design and construction technology. Because each section is written by a different author, the style of presentation varies. Typically, each chapter describes and evaluates sources and wraps up with a single or classified bibliography and a recommendation of which periodical titles cover the topic.

The text is generally well written, but two major weaknesses are apparent. Despite the current copyright date, the information from some contributors on technological aspects seems to be at least five years behind. For example, *Infotrac*—which is a search system and not specifically a database—is described as a laser disc, but has been replaced by CD-ROM since the 1980s. Another author announces the GEAC GLIS online catalog system as a good source of housing information. This is disturbing, as it suggests a lack of understanding that it is the *contents* of the specific GLIS used, not the now-discontinued online system software itself, that showcases the information. Fortunately, the book's general chapter devoted to electronic resources, although basic, does not mislead. The secondary weakness is a minimal index that is nothing more than a general guide to broad subjects and greatly limits access to the work.

With the evaluative recommendations throughout, the prime use of this work will be for collection building and for upper-division and graduate-level research. Despite the above caveats, the evaluative aspects make it a worthwhile consideration for most architecture and urban planning collections, and also for comprehensive collections of popular culture, history, and social science. [R: Choice, May 96, p. 1455]
—**Gary R. Cocozzoli**

1095. **Syndicated Comic Strips and Artists, 1924-1995: The Complete Index.** Dave Strickler, comp. Cambria, Calif., Comics Access, 1995. 218p. $16.95pa.

Frustrated in his attempt to answer a query about a comic strip character, librarian Strickler decided the comic strips needed a substantive index. This self-published work is the first stage in that direction and in what could become his lifetime project. Compiled from *Editor & Publisher's Syndication Directory*, 1924-1995, as well as Strickler's scanning of all issues of the weekly *Editor & Publisher* from 1922 to 1995, the index is an alphabetic listing of 4,550 strips and panels (with dates of syndication, all individuals associated with the strips, and dates of association) and 3,250 artists, writers, and creators (linked to all the strips they worked on and the dates of their work).

In an introduction, Strickler points out that his heavy dependence upon *Editor & Publisher* sources resulted in inconsistencies, misspellings, and a shortened time span that dropped all strips that ceased before the first directory appeared in 1924. Strickler readily admits that, at times, it is virtually impossible to determine authorship; the 16 listings under Walt Disney are a case in point, and one must wonder about the comic strip roles played by aviator Eddie Rickenbacker; pitcher Tug McGraw; authors Zane Grey, Ring Lardner, and Victor Hugo; or disc jockey Dick Clark, all included in the artist index. Strickler also lists the types of cartoons he purposely omitted, among which were strips not published in the United States; yet he includes works by Goscinny, Low, Russell, Smythe, and other foreign artists living abroad.

A warehouse of data, this index will obviously be used as a major reference tool, but it can be much more. For one thing, it can be a place to find interesting ideas for "funnies" research, for it includes all artists from the famous Stan Lee to the unknown Lee Stanley, as well as husband-wife and father-son (in the case of Mort Walker, sons, five of them) creative teams, and strips with nearly any title imaginable (*An Altar Boy Named Speck, Bugwine, Pants That Sag*). Strickler is to be commended for advancing the academic nature of comic strips with this index, and he should be encouraged and supported in the next steps of this work in progress. [R: Choice, Feb 96, p. 934; RBB, 1 Mar 96, p. 1206]—**John A. Lent**

27 Performing Arts

GENERAL WORKS
Bio-bibliography

1096. Radovich, Don. **Tony Richardson: A Bio-bibliography.** Westport, Conn., Greenwood Press, 1995. 279p. index. (Bio-bibliographies in the Performing Arts, no.69). $59.95. ISBN 0-313-28981-6.

This work is the 69th publication in the Greenwood Press series Bio-bibliographies in the Performing Arts and covers the life and career of British film director Richardson. Similar in format to other works in the series, this book gives a brief biographical sketch of Richardson's life followed by annotated entries covering his work in theater, film, and television, as well as an annotated discography of all recordings pertaining to his films. Also provided is a 285-item bibliography of English-language books and periodicals touching upon Richardson's life or work. Access to this publication is through a table of contents, name and title index, and occasional cross-references within the body of the work.

Best known today for his 1963 film *Tom Jones*, Richardson was in fact one of the primary leaders in Great Britain to bring social realism into the theater and onto the screen in the late 1950s. Among his early works in the latter realm were *Look Back in Anger*, *The Entertainer*, *A Taste of Honey*, and *The Loneliness of the Long Distance Runner*. However, following the success of *Tom Jones*, Richardson was never able to achieve the artistic or commercial success of his earlier work. Nevertheless, he continued to work extensively in the theater, film, and television and produced a substantial body of work prior to his untimely death in 1991.

Too long neglected by the public and critics alike, one hopes that this well-written and researched work, along with Richardson's own posthumously published autobiography *A Long Distance Runner* (Morrow, 1993), will help revive interest in this creative and courageous filmmaker. The work under review is recommended for libraries with large film collections. [R: Choice, Mar 96, p. 1102]—**Robert Logsdon**

Biography

1097. Lentz, Harris M., III. **Obituaries in the Performing Arts, 1994: Film, Television, Radio, Theatre, Dance, Music, Cartoons, and Pop Culture.** Jefferson, N.C., McFarland, 1996. 197p. illus. $25.00pa. ISBN 0-7864-0254-7.

1098. Lentz, Harris M., III. **Obituaries in the Performing Arts, 1995: Film, Television, Radio, Theatre, Dance, Music, Cartoons, and Pop Culture.** Jefferson, N.C., McFarland, 1996. 208p. illus. $25.00pa. ISBN 0-7864-0253-9.

These reference works combined contain nearly 1,100 obituaries of people from both show business and the performing arts, including film, television, sports, radio, theater, music, and dance. Entries begin with date, place of death, and cause of death, followed by career highlights and other biographical information. Entries range in length from under 50 to several hundred words. Most entries also include periodical references to the reports of the death, from newspapers such as *The New York Times*, *Variety*, the *Los Angeles Times*, *The Washington Post*, and the *Times* (of London), and from such magazines as

People, *Newsweek*, and *Time*. More than half of the entries also supply black-and-white photographs of the deceased. Filmographies are provided with the entries of television and motion picture performers. A brief introduction and a 26-book reference bibliography are also included in each volume.

This work is part of a series of reference works from McFarland. The 1995 edition comes on the heels of the 1994 edition; both were published in 1996. The author has written obituaries of film personalities for more than 20 years, in addition to several significant reference works. These useful additions to the biography reference shelf are recommended. [R: RBB, 1 Nov 96, p. 539]—**Edward Erazo**

Handbooks and Yearbooks

1099. Franks, Don. **Entertainment Awards: A Music, Cinema, Theatre, and Broadcasting Reference, 1928 Through 1993.** Jefferson, N.C., McFarland, 1996. 536p. index. $75.00. ISBN 0-7864-0031-5.

This volume is a compendium of entertainment industry award winners from 1928 through 1933. The prizes consists of acknowledgments in the fields of broadcasting (Emmy Awards, George Foster Peabody Awards, Golden Globe Awards); music (Grammy Awards, CMA Awards, Pulitzer Prize for Music); cinema (Academy Awards, Golden Globe Awards, New York Film Critics' Circle Awards); and theater (Antoinette Perry [Tony] Awards, Pulitzer Prize for Drama, Off Broadway Drama Award [Obies], New York Drama Critics' Circle Awards).

The listings of award winners for each prize within each major category start with the first year that those particular awards were presented. Each award and recipient are listed by year. The author provides a short, descriptive history of each award that precedes the actual listings. Every entry receives it own identification number, starting with the first entry in the book (1) and sequentially extending to the last entry (10,985). These identification numbers are used in the indexes (rather than page numbers) as reference pointers to particular entries. Two exhaustive indexes (by names and organizations and by titles) are provided.

This reference work is limited by space constraints to the major entertainment industry awards. There are many lesser-known—but still worthy—awards that are absent from this work. Yet even so, this reference work is voluminous. It will be welcome to the curious and to those who need information about "who won what when?" The reference also has a potential utility to those wishing to study award trends and fashions by analyzing the entries and the indexes. [R: Choice, Nov 96, p. 430; RBB, 15 Sept 96, pp. 283-84]
—**Charles Neuringer**

DANCE

1100. Getz, Leslie. **Dancers and Choreographers: A Selected Bibliography.** Wakefield, R.I., Asphodel Press/Moyer Bell; distr., Emeryville, Calif., Publishers Group West, 1995. 305p. illus. index. $34.95; $18.95pa. ISBN 1-55921-108-3; 1-55921-109-1pa.

The term *selected bibliography* inevitably makes a user of such tools wary because the success of any such guide is totally dependent upon the skills, sense, and outlook of its compiler. Getz is to be commended for clearly defining and limiting her work's coverage. Ballet's long history is represented from its beginnings until the present, as is twentieth-century modern dance. The sources are limited to works in English, and most are of this century.

The entries, alphabetically arranged, are by the names of the performers and choreographers, with a few additional entries for important teachers, schools, and performing groups with names such as Pilobolus. The bibliographic sources given in each entry are for full-length books about the person, appropriate parts of a carefully selected group of 79 major books and 17 scholarly periodicals keyed by abbreviations, and parts of other books and special articles from more general magazines. By limiting the source materials to the best and most substantial, this bibliographer allows users of her guide to have the rare confidence that they will be directed to worthwhile writings by specialists. This is especially important for a subject as difficult to describe in words as movement.

An excellent subject bibliography, subdivided into categories such as dictionaries, chronologies, ballet guides, criticism, and histories (by time and place), many of which are annotated, will lead the user to additional information. Illustrations are small and are of book dust jackets and periodicals, thus giving the user a glimpse of the sort of thing being searched. Also a nice touch is the big, bold-framed statement on the page before the introduction advising the user to read the introduction if the book is to be used with profit. Fortunately, the users of this book only need simple directions in using the guide with understanding: It has nothing but beneficial effects. [R: Choice, May 96, p. 1448; C&RL, Sept 96, p. 466; LJ, Jan 96, pp. 86-88]—**George Louis Mayer**

1101. Gunzenhauser, Margot. **The Square Dance and Contra Dance Handbook: Calls, Dance Movements, Music Glossary, Bibliography, Discography, and Directories.** Jefferson, N.C., McFarland, 1996. 304p. illus. index. $30.00pa. ISBN 0-89950-855-3.

The Square Dance and Contra Dance Handbook was first published in Danish in 1981 and was updated and translated into English with this 1996 edition. The work describes a number of American folk dances that are basic enough for a person having little or no experience with square or contra dancing to follow. In addition, it provides an overview of square and contra dancing, lists of dances, a glossary of dance terminology, a directory of organizations and institutions that provide materials for dancing, a list of materials for callers and dancers, an annotated discography (163 items), and an annotated bibliography (103 items).

The work is a comprehensive guide to both the traditional-style square dancing and contra dancing, covering both the music and dance styles. Also, there are diagrams and directions for performing more than 90 dances. Probably the most important part of the work (and the part that makes it a reference source) is the supplemental material, including the directory, materials lists, and annotated bibliographies. These lists are inclusive, and the annotations are detailed. The work is recommended for public libraries of all sizes and for private collections. [R: BL, 15 Mar 96, p. 1234]—**Robert L. Wick**

1102. Preston-Dunlop, Valerie. **Dance Words.** Newark, N.J., Harwood Academic/Gordon & Breach, 1995. 718p. index. (Choreography & Dance Studies, v.8). $28.00pa. ISBN 3-7186-5605-1.

The title of this work evokes the expectation of a traditional dance dictionary covering terminology and language to describe the art of dance. A quick initial glance through the pages of this book will immediately cast out that expectation. Instead, the aim of this resource is to unify practitioners, choreographers, researchers, and critics involved in the different dance genres with a common language defined from a choreographic perspective. Without much argument, it succeeds in giving that perspective. Whether or not it will break down the divisions between the different dance genres will be dependent on its acceptance as a major resource work by all those who create, study, and research dance.

This work is organized according to seven central concepts of choreographic studies: the dance domain, the performer, movement, choreography, the dance sound and the dance space, the dance event, and dance research. Each concept is covered in sections and subsections within a range of one to four chapters, and entries are not alphabetically ordered but rather grouped by areas of interest. Additionally, entries are not strictly definitions but include a substantial mix of quotations from interviews with individuals involved in dance who are primarily from Great Britain. The use of the index is essential for anyone doing specific research, as browsing under the major concepts or subsections may prove frustrating. This work is not organized in a traditional way; does not include standard definitions or descriptions found elsewhere in traditional technical dance dictionaries; and is not for the casual spectator, novice dancer, or nondance studies student who chooses to write a term paper on dance. In addition to the index of terms, the lexicon includes an index of names, a bibliography, and a list of oral contributors.

There are no other current works of this kind. It is not comprehensive in coverage and indeed, the compiler clearly states that it is a beginning work of this type and hopes that others will follow suit. This is a highly specialized work for dance libraries or institutions offering choreographic studies or extensive dance courses.—**Elizabeth D'Antonio-Gan**

1103. **Twentieth-Century American Music for the Dance: A Bibliography.** Isabelle Emerson, comp. and ed. Westport, Conn., Greenwood Press, 1996. 198p. index. (Music Reference Collection, no.53). $69.50. ISBN 0-313-29350-3.

While no claim is made by the compiler that this list of U.S. music for the dance covers all of the standard repertory, it provides a much-needed list of compositions, composers, and choreographers. In addition, information is provided concerning first performances, publishers, and location of scores. The bibliography is limited to works created specifically for concert dance by U.S. composers, but if composers were not American-born but worked extensively in the United States, they are included (e.g., Igor Stravinsky's *Rite of Spring* is not included because he was not working in the United States at the time it was composed, but his later *Agon* is included). It appears that there is some logic to these selection criteria, but one would wish that if a composer is selected, all of the works would be listed simply for the sake of continuity.

Entries are arranged alphabetically by composer. Each entry gives the name of the composer; the birth and death dates; an address for the place of employment or publisher; a list of publishers; and a list of compositions providing information on each, including type, first performance, and recordings. There is no additional information provided concerning the composition's length, instrumentation, keys, and so forth. Also, no critical comments are made concerning the compositions. In addition to the major alphabetic list of composers, there are some valuable appendixes, including a list of the composers with the choreographers they worked with listed next to their names, a list of the publishers with addresses, a bibliography of works consulted for compiling the book (more than 200), an index of choreographers with the names of the composers they worked with following, and an index of titles.

Twentieth-Century American Music for the Dance is a valuable addition to the limited reference material on U.S. dance composition. It is recommended for both public and academic libraries of all sizes, and will be an important source of information for anyone interested in the subject.—**Robert L. Wick**

FILM, TELEVISION, AND VIDEO

Bibliography

1104. Baskin, Ellen. **Serials on British Television 1950-1994.** Brookfield, Vt., Scolar Press/Ashgate Publishing, 1996. 332p. index. $69.95. ISBN 1-85928-015-3.

Baskin's comprehensive bibliography identifies more than 900 British serials, defined by the author as "drama broadcast in a number of episodes telling one connected story," or as a multipart, self-contained drama (think *Brideshead Revisited*, *The Jewel in the Crown*, *Pride and Prejudice*, and the recent *Prime Suspect*). The coverage is complete through 1994, but includes some early 1995 productions as well.

The titles are arranged by decade, with each serial listed chronologically by its first episode. Entries note title; date and timing; television production company; availability on video; number of episodes; genre (e.g., science fiction, mystery, thriller); place and era of plot; producer; director; writer; book title and author on which book was based (if applicable); cast members; plot synopsis; and any interesting points about the series. Baskin rounds out the title with a multitude of indexes, including ones for title, type, location and era, producer, director, and cast members. [R: Choice, Oct 96, p. 248]—**G. Kim Dority**

1105. Liebman, Roy. **Silent Film Performers: An Annotated Bibliography of Published, Unpublished, and Archival Sources for Over 350 Actors and Actresses.** Jefferson, N.C., McFarland, 1996. 383p. index. $75.00. ISBN 0-7864-0100-1.

While recent years have seen a revival of interest in performers of the silent era, film research has been hindered by the scarcity of reference tools that provide access to information in a vast and growing body of book and periodical literature. Locating archival materials has been even more challenging. The present volume therefore fills a great need. Liebman has prepared a guide that lists books and periodical articles containing information concerning more than 350 silent-era stars and featured performers and describing relevant clipping and archival resources found in 70 United States, Canadian, and British repositories.

Unfortunately, citations are highly abridged. For periodical articles, all that is given are magazine and date (e.g., *Motion Picture World* June 8 1915). There is no indication of article title, pagination, or content. The issue could contain anything from a mere mention of the performer to a lengthy biographical article. The researcher is told where to look, not what will be found. Book citations are equally brief, but they are arranged by category: biographies, books the individual wrote, sources that list his or her credits, and film reference tools that contain entries for the individual. Descriptions of archival collections are more detailed. Certainly, fuller citations would be wonderful, but given the need to publish a compact and affordable volume, the severe abridgment is understandable.

The guide still makes the researcher's task vastly easier. There are short biographies of each performer, a 48-page annotated bibliography that lists the books cited in the text, and a directory of repositories that lists their personnel and policies. Two small criticisms: The bibliography is arranged by title; an author index would have been a welcome addition. Similarly, a list of the periodicals indexed would have been useful and easy to provide. [R: Choice, May 96, p. 1454]—**Joseph W. Palmer**

Biography

1106. Quinlan, David. **Quinlan's Illustrated Directory of Film Character Actors.** new ed. London, B. T. Batsford; distr., North Pomfret, Vt., Trafalgar Square, 1995. 384p. illus. $35.00. ISBN 0-7134-7040-2.

The author, a British film critic of long standing, has done a great service to the lesser-known actors whose "... names remained a secret between them and their friends, their agents and those producers and directors wise enough to hire these ever-reliables when their image became familiar" (p. 5). The book is composed of entries for 1,110 actors and actresses whose faces are known but whose names elude all but the most obsessive readers of movie credits. It updates and expands a 1985 edition (see ARBA 87, entry 1286). Each entry contains a black-and-white photograph, a brief career assessment, and a filmography. The last is the most comprehensive this reviewer has seen; it includes not only the standard feature film appearances and television movies, but also short subjects and even narrations done. Directorial stints (rare for this group) are noted. Birth and death dates are complete to April 1, 1995. The roster of subjects appears to have an unsurprising partiality for British actors over Americans of equal regard.

Browsers will appreciate the droll and incisive descriptions Quinlan makes of his subjects: Dudley Foster is described as "cadaverous"; Richard Masur is "tall, shambling, [and] benign"; Brenda Fricker is "dumpling-homely." Reading such descriptions while looking at the adjacent photographs makes one appreciate Quinlan's wit and insight. As with most books of this kind, a solid familiarity with the subject matter exponentially increases one's appreciation of the text.

Access is challenging in a directory whose subjects are known by their faces and not their names. The photographs, taken at the approximate time of an actor's greatest success (to ease recognition), are crucial to the use and value of this resource. Nonetheless, without a film title index to narrow the searching process, using this book to identify individual actors will be time-consuming. As it stands, this directory's usefulness is in its impressive filmographies and as browsing material for film fans with a dry sense of humor. It is advisable for film collections with a breadth extending beyond titles on superstars. [R: Choice, April 96, p. 1292]—**Ed Volz**

1107. Slide, Anthony. **Some Joe You Don't Know: An American Biographical Guide to 100 British Television Personalities.** Westport, Conn., Greenwood Press, 1996. 271p. illus. index. $59.95. ISBN 0-313-29550-6.

Contained in this guide are short biographical profiles of approximately 100 British performers who have turned up on television in the United States, principally on PBS stations or Arts & Entertainment cable. Indeed, many British shows have also been recycled on other cable networks, thus exposing these artists even more. Both drama and comedy are covered, from the 1950s up to the modern times (although the entry for Inspector Morse's John Thaw does not mention his role in *A Year in Provence*, seen on A&E two years before the entry's publication date). Also provided is a short history of British programming on American television, which really began in 1969 with the *Forsyte Saga* on PBS, followed by *Masterpiece Theatre* and *Upstairs Downstairs*.

Each biography has a listing of credits, along with dates and a bibliography for further reading. There are 24 not-very-well-reproduced, black-and-white photographs (only one in four can be visualized). Prominent names include Stephen Fry and Hugh Laurie (both of whom played Jeeves), Jennifer Saunders of *Ab Fab* (but not her partner Dawn French of *French and Saunders*), Rowan Atkinson, Jeremy Brett,

Dame Edna Everage, David Frost, David Suchet, and Joan Hickson from Agatha Christie shows. The price seems a little steep for 248 pages of entries, but there is a plus in that there is an index to names of shows and other actors who do not have a separate entry. [R: Choice, June 96, p. 1623]—**Dean Tudor**

1108. Waldman, Harry. **Hollywood and the Foreign Touch: A Dictionary of Foreign Filmmakers and Their Films from America, 1910-1995.** Lanham, Md., Scarecrow, 1996. 316p. $49.50. ISBN 0-8108-3192-9.

This title is described by the author as a "catalog, a listing, and a discussion of significant foreign filmmakers who worked in Hollywood and America between 1910 and 1995." Although the selection criteria are somewhat vague, the work apparently focuses on foreign filmmakers, especially lesser-knowns, who came to the United States, made a film (or several), and then went back to their homelands rather than staying on in the States. Additionally, there are separate entries for significant (if little-known) films made by these foreign filmmakers.

Written in a popular rather than academic or scholarly style, the 527 entries range in length from several sentences to 1½ pages. The entries are strictly biographical and include no evaluation of the films or the filmmakers' careers. There are no supplementary materials that would support further research, such as lists of recommended reading. However, this is not really meant as a scholarly resource. It is instead the work of an amateur film enthusiast who has done a substantial amount of research in a neglected area of film history. Waldman's work will be a welcome supplement to the literature of film history.

—**G. Kim Dority**

Catalogs and Collections

1109. **The British Cinema Source Book: BFI Archive Viewing Copies and Library Materials.** Elaine Burrows and others, eds. London, British Film Institute; distr., Bloomington, Ind., Indiana University Press, 1995. 216p. illus. index. $59.95. ISBN 0-85170-474-3.

This authoritative, easy-to-use sourcebook is divided into two parts. The 1st part contains viewing copies of more than 8,300 British films housed in the prestigious British Film Institute's (BFI) National Film and Television Archives (NFTVA) or films for which the BFI Library and Information Services contains an unpublished script or press book. The materials are organized into five broad date categories (up to 1914, 1915-1928, 1929-1945, 1946-1964, 1965 and later). Within each category, the entries are listed alphabetically by film title. There is also an index to the entries by director's name. The entries for this section have all been extracted from the BFI's Summary of Information on Film & Television (SIFT) database.

The 2d part contains 1,800-plus entries for books, pamphlets, and other printed materials on British film that are housed in the BFI's library. This section's entries are arranged by film title, personality (directory or actor), and subject. There is an author index to the section. *The British Cinema Source Book* also contains 20 color leaves and black-and-white illustrations, including stills, publicity materials, press book covers, programs, and the like. Although these illustrations are well captioned, an actual list of the illustrations should have been included.

The sourcebook is not intended to be a film encyclopedia. It contains little descriptive information and no qualitative judgments. Rather, the book is a compendium of information on materials housed in the BFI's library and its NFTVA. The editors indicate that the source should be used as a new catalog of the archive's viewing copies: In Great Britain, it will be used by researchers in need of viewing copies of films, unpublished materials, and information on some of the library's materials. However, because of the size and prestige of the collections this list represents, the work would be an excellent addition to any reference collection serving as a resource to film historians and students. Large academic and public libraries, particularly ones addressing populations doing film research, will find this a welcome, simple-to-use addition to film reference sections.

There can be the usual critique that the book does not include information on absolutely every British film made, and in the later years, as the editors indicate, there is the inevitable confusion between film, made-for-television film, and television show. However, given the stated scope of the book, these are not flaws. The editors have done an admirable job in presenting the contents of their substantial collection. For a more encyclopedic approach to British film, libraries should consider purchasing Denis Gifford's *The British Film Catalogue 1895-1985* (see ARBA 88, entry 1344).—**Caroline M. Kent**

Dictionaries and Encyclopedias

1110. Bianculli, David. **Dictionary of Teleliteracy: Television's 500 Biggest Hits, Misses, and Events.** New York, Continuum Publishing, 1996. 416p. illus. index. $29.95. ISBN 0-8264-0577-0.

Defining teleliteracy as "an awareness and appreciation of the medium's most popular or meaningful offerings" (p. 15), television critic Bianculli identifies what he considers to be the 500 most memorable television programs or televised events during the 50 years from 1945 to 1995. He offers his compilation as a complement to *The Dictionary of Cultural Literacy* (2d ed.; see ARBA 94, entry 305), which he contends slighted television.

Arranged alphabetically from *ABC World News Tonight* to *Zorro* and spanning the decades from *Arthur Godfrey's Talent Scouts* to the O. J. Simpson trial, Bianculli's selections encompass the best and the worst of television history. Among the programs featured are such stellar dramatic and comedy series as *I'll Fly Away*, *Playhouse 90*, *Taxi*, and *Frasier* and coverage of significant events, such as the moon landing and the Watergate hearings. Reminding readers that memorable television is not necessarily quality television are such entries as *Green Acres* and *Baywatch*. Also represented are documentaries; game, variety, and talk shows; soap operas; and children's programs.

Ranging in length from 50 to 1,500 words, Bianculli's lively, opinionated, and pun-laden annotations provide historical background and critical commentary on each entry. Complementing the text are approximately 100 well-chosen black-and-white photographs. Although individual entries do not provide bibliographic references, a 7-page bibliography follows the dictionary portion of the work. Two excellent indexes cover personal names and program titles.

Other compilations, such as Tim Brooks and Earle Marsh's *The Complete Directory to Prime Time Network and Cable TV Shows: 1946-Present* (6th ed., Ballantine Books, 1995) and Alex McNeil's *Total Television: A Comprehensive Guide to Programming from 1948 to the Present* (3d ed., Penguin Books, 1991), provide more extensive coverage of television programs. However, this work offers a unique perspective that will be especially useful in public and academic libraries. [R: Choice, Dec 96, p. 585]
—**Marie Ellis**

1111. **Encyclopedia of European Cinema.** Ginette Vincendeau, ed. New York, Facts on File, 1995. 524p. illus. index. $55.00. ISBN 0-8160-3394-3.

Published to coincide with the medium's 100th anniversary, this encyclopedia was created to recognize and summarize the accomplishments of Europe's film industry since 1895. The entries were written by 90 contributors representing different countries, most filmmaking specialties, and various academic disciplines. Entries are of four kinds: national essays (surveying the breadth and history of a country's cinema); personnel (mainly directors and actors); critical (to explore topics such as *New German Cinema* or *animation*; and institutional (film schools, festivals, and companies). The entries range in length from a few sentences to half a page or more, with articles on individuals predictably being briefer than the critical and national essays. Cross-references are used when necessary, and an index to names and terms is provided. Four pages of graphs list annual film production figures and annual audience figures, by country, for the period 1945-1993. An introductory essay explains how the expansion of the U.S. film industry (the country's second-biggest exported product) has caused the decline of European cinema.

The popularity of videocassette recorders has created an abundance of printed film guides that limit their reviews to feature films available on videocassette. The purpose of this book is to survey all of Europe's cinema, to discuss films as art and as cultural history. It is an admirable effort, unique in focus and scope, but with some slight failings. Filmographies are lengthy but only occasionally comprehensive. There are no entries for two of Europe's finest (and in the latter case, most prolific) actresses: Falconetti and Bulle Ogier. Respected director Alain Jessua is ignored. Despite the lapses, Vincendeau has filled a gap with this publication. It is more comprehensive than either *Halliwell's Film Guide 1995* (see ARBA

96, entry 1385) or such video guides as *Roger Ebert's Video Companion* (see ARBA 95, entry 1362). This is an indispensable source for students of Europe's sizable film history. [R: Choice, July/Aug 96, p. 1771; RBB, 1 May 96, pp. 1519-20]—**Ed Volz**

1112. Quigley, Martin S, and others. **First Century of Film.** New York, Quigley Publishing, 1995. 319p. illus. $39.50. ISBN 0-900610-54-9.

Essentially a "who was who" of U.S. film during its first 100 years, this compilation provides brief biographical sketches of approximately 1,300 figures associated with the U.S. motion picture industry who died before August 31, 1994. Most of the entries are updated versions of profiles that originally appeared in the 1929 to 1994 volumes of another Quigley Publishing publication, the *International Motion Picture Almanac* (annual).

The biographies represent a broad spectrum of individuals involved in film, including actors, directors, producers, writers, cinematographers, lyricists, composers, company executives, and exhibitors. Consisting of concise biographical information and lists of motion picture credits, the entries note spouses, children, and other relatives only when they are also connected with the film industry. This rather unorthodox practice frequently gives the misleading impression that many stars, such as Gary Cooper and Spencer Tracy, never married; that others, such as Ingrid Bergman and Audrey Hepburn, were married only once; and that most of them were childless! Page headers note whether the filmographies that accompany many of the entries are complete or partial, and a picture number adjacent to an entry indicates when an individual is represented in the section of 147 black-and-white photographs. A 25-page introduction provides an overview of major events in the first century of motion picture production.

A comparison of all entries beginning with "H" in this compilation with the 2d edition of Ephraim Katz's *The Film Encyclopedia* (see ARBA 95, entry 1371) revealed that Katz covers more deceased performers and directors and also provides fuller biographical information. On the other hand, Quigley's coverage of behind-the-scenes figures related to the business aspects of film (e.g., lawyers, executives) is much more comprehensive.

Despite its title, this volume provides an incomplete picture of the first century of film because it excludes Katharine Hepburn, Gregory Peck, and other giants of the era who are still living. It will be of interest mainly to libraries that need more retrospective coverage of film personalities and to those building major research collections pertaining to film.—**Marie Ellis**

1113. Schwartz, David, Steve Ryan, and Fred Wostbrock. **The Encyclopedia of TV Game Shows.** 2d ed. New York, Facts on File, 1995. 341p. illus. index. $45.00. ISBN 0-8160-3093-6.

Rare it is that a book's 2d edition should occupy less shelf space than its predecessor. Yet, in updating this work that was first issued in 1987 by New York Zoetrope (see ARBA 89, entry 860), Facts on File has done just this. A diminution in the amount and size of black-and-white photographs (of show sets, hosts, and other celebrities), as well as a reduction in typeface size, contributes much to the shrinkage. Also, this revision lacks the large white spaces that engulfed the text in the 1st edition.

Schwartz, Ryan, and Wostbrock have added entries on more than 100 programs that debuted after 1987, such as *American Gladiators*, *Grandstand*, and *Yahtzee*. The writing throughout remains highly readable, a delightful mix of frivolity and trivia. Many entries carried forward from the 1st edition have been appreciably expanded with more contest rules and other relevant data. For example, the article on *The Krypton Factor* is eight times longer than its 1987 counterpart. New to this edition, also, are a superb 8,000-word introduction; 3 indexes (show name, personal name, profession); and several appendixes that, among other information, list programs that began on the radio or that have received awards.

The only significant weakness of this edition is its jettisoning of dozens of photographs that enhanced the value of its 1987 predecessor. In the section of shows whose names start with "s," for instance, only 17 illustrations appear, as compared to the 42 of the 1st edition. This abridgment is especially galling when one realizes that the new edition profiles 15 recent shows in this section not covered by the previous edition. Despite this defect, however, libraries featuring popular culture materials will do well to purchase this indexed update, even if they already own the 1st edition. [R: RBB, 15 Feb 96, p. 1044; RQ, Summer 96, pp. 555-56]—**Jeffrey E. Long**

1114. Stephens, Michael L. **Gangster Films: A Comprehensive, Illustrated Reference to People, Films, and Terms.** Jefferson, N.C., McFarland, 1996. 377p. illus. index. $49.95. ISBN 0-7864-0046-3.

Who has not enjoyed a motion picture from the genre known as the gangster/mobster film? Whether they are recent productions such as *The Cotton Club* and *Prizzi's Honor* (the film that established Anjelica Huston as a major star), or classics such as *G-Men* (with Lloyd Nolan and James Cagney) and *The Petrified Forest* (with the eternally but brutally frank Bette Davis), these films capture the attention of audiences and in some cases allow them to see inside the mind of a lawless person or a fascinating or troubling recent era of American history.

The book is filled with thumbnail sketches of familiar stars, along with excellent descriptions of major studios and their bosses. There is also a surprising but welcome number of word descriptions of underworld terms that one would normally find in a textbook of basic criminal justice procedures. The gangster film has been around for many years, and for those who wish to know of its historical origins (as well as a wonderful description of the major gangs and criminals in U.S. history), the introduction to this book should be carefully read.—**Lillian Jane Steele**

Filmography

1115. Biggs, Melissa E. **French Films, 1945-1993: A Critical Filmography of the 400 Most Important Releases.** Jefferson, N.C., McFarland, 1996. 357p. illus. index. $48.50. ISBN 0-7864-0024-2.

Considered by many to be not only the finest works in the history of any national cinema, but the apex of the medium itself, France's postwar films have been the worthy recipients of extensive analysis. In this compact, alphabetic guide, 400 features and short subjects (just a handful of the latter) are described in sequentially numbered entries, each 300-450 words in length. Full production credits are given for each film, all actors with speaking parts are listed, a cogent plot synopsis is provided, brief background information is given, and international award wins and nominations are mentioned. Critical film journal reviews are also excerpted—a welcome element that is lacking in many other filmographies. Each film's original French title is followed by its English translation, with the book's index referring to both. In a nod to serious cinema scholarship, not only are the names of directors, actors, and screenwriters indexed, but cinematographers, set designers, and sound engineers as well. For quick access, the index points to the numbered film entries, not page numbers. Black-and-white photographs of varying size break up the somewhat cramped text.

This is a valuable source for name verification and is also enjoyable as an appreciative survey of a great body of work. *French Films* is comprehensive enough to include the familiar (François Truffaut, Jean and Pierre Renoir), the relatively obscure (Jean-Pierre Melville), and the willfully obscure (Marguerite Duras, Alain Robbe-Grillet). While many filmographies inspire casual browsing with their lavish illustrations, the quality of this title's text and indexing will attract serious use by students of film. It is an appropriate purchase for larger cinema collections. [R: Choice, Nov 96, p. 425; RBB, 1 Sept 96, p. 166]
—**Ed Volz**

1116. Bradley, Edwin M. **The First Hollywood Musicals: A Critical Filmography of 171 Features, 1927 Through 1932.** Jefferson, N.C., McFarland, 1996. 386p. illus. index. $65.00. ISBN 0-89950-945-2.

This work can be used as two references in one, because in addition to being a study and overview of the early years of movie musicals, it is a history of the beginnings of talking pictures. With his extensive research and knowledge of the social life of the era, coupled with the fact that he personally viewed every film available, the author is able to convey to the reader some of the excitement that accompanied the introduction of the "talkies." The early talking pictures were sometimes talking films with musical numbers interspersed—not truly musicals. This work covers in chronological order each film that can qualify as a musical. Picture credits include producers, directors, writers, photographers, studios, and running times. Cast listings cover acting and singing roles, and songs are listed complete with composers, lyricists, and performers. Discography entries include 78 recordings, LPs, CDs, and soundtracks. This basic information is followed by a summary of the plot. These summaries may range from a few paragraphs up to approximately three pages in length. The more successful films receive more detailed coverage.

A frequently repeated statement by the author is that no known copies of a movie exist. This is sad news, although he notes that from time to time viewable copies of films surface, having been lost in vaults or obtained from private collections. Particularly helpful for a time frame of reference is the inclusion of birth and death dates the first time a person's name is mentioned in the text. The addition of movie still photographs enlivens many of the entries. Also adding insight is the author's research into the varied reasons for the success or failure of many of the films.

More than adequate coverage of the plots and casting makes this an outstanding reference. Without boring the reader and managing to keep the text to a minimum, the basic story, nevertheless, is there. The author is not afraid to throw in adjectives and adverbs at times to make a more readable text. It was not easy to reduce the background history and jumbled story of *The Cocoanuts* to slightly more than two pages of writing. When appropriate, there is a tie-in mention of prior stage versions of movies, and even of the silent-era movie musicals—there was available, after all, the pit orchestra or piano player. *Show Boat*, in its various stage and movie versions, is a good example.

All in all, this work is a splendid reference, and it also makes for great reading. This is a thorough work that likely will remain the standard for years to come. It is recommended for all academic libraries and sizable public libraries, and for individuals and film buffs who have a fascination with these old films. [R: Choice, Dec 96, p. 586]—**Louis G. Zelenka**

1117. Galbraith, Stuart, IV. **The Japanese Filmography: A Complete Reference to 209 Filmmakers and the Over 1250 Films....** Jefferson, N.C., McFarland, 1996. 509p. illus. index. $75.00. ISBN 0-7864-0032-3.

Galbraith, whose 1994 book *Japanese Science Fiction, Fantasy and Horror Films* (see ARBA 95, entry 1382) examined in minute detail this popular but critically snubbed genre, here expands his meticulous research to include mainstream Japanese cinema. While much in English has been written about the theory underlying these films, scant attention has been paid to basic reference works that provide information on key personnel (actors, directors, camerapeople, screenwriters, composers) or even a sizable filmography.

In this handy reference tool, Galbraith provides capsule biographies and accompanying filmographies for slightly more than 200 industry personnel and brief entries on the six major Japanese studios (Daiei, Toho, and so on). The concluding filmography of some 1,250-plus films has been carefully chosen from features that have appeared in U.S. theaters, are available on home video, or feature important actors or directors. The films are alphabetically arranged by their original U.S. release titles, and entries include technical and acting credits, alternate titles, studio, sound format, and both United States and Japanese running times and release dates.

Appendixes contain a chronology of important dates in Japanese cinema, industry statistics in Japan, cinema awards, and a chronological list of Japanese animated features. An index of titles and alternate titles is provided that, unfortunately, serves to amplify the omission of a general name index that, although a monumental undertaking, would have proven useful. This guide is recommended for large academic and public libraries supporting a strong interest in film. [R: Choice, Sept 96, p. 98; LJ, 15 May 96, p. 54]
—**David K. Frasier**

1118. Heyman, Neil M. **Western Civilization: A Critical Guide to Documentary Films.** Westport, Conn., Greenwood Press, 1996. 244p. index. $59.95. ISBN 0-313-28438-5.

New historical documentaries appear frequently on the educational channels and even on the major television networks. The educational quality of these films varies greatly, making the first-time use of a film something of a gamble. It is Heyman's achievement to provide critical reviews for 170 documentary films with potential for use in Western civilization courses. The guide is divided into 18 chronologically arranged chapters, starting with prehistory and ending in the post-World War II era. Reviews of individual titles give the films' running time, year of production, the production company, whether it is in black-and-white or in color, if the film is part of a series, a brief summary, a grade for quality, and a 500- to 600-word essay providing a descriptive and critical commentary on the film.

Three indexes help readers to locate films by subject, series, or title. Segments from such well-known series as *The Age of Uncertainty*, *The Renaissance*, and *The World at War* are discussed. Reviews of individual films are thorough, thoughtful, and, if anything, a bit overly critical. Unfortunately, the amount of new films will cause this guide to date quickly. Multiperiod films are also neglected, so there are no entries from such series as *Greek Fire* or *Connections*, nor are any segments included from the popular *Biography* series. [R: Choice, May 96, p. 1450; RBB, 1 May 96, p. 1542; RQ, Summer 96, pp. 566-67]—**Ronald H. Fritze**

1119. Johnson, Tom, and Deborah Del Vecchio. **Hammer Films: An Exhaustive Filmography.** Jefferson, N.C., McFarland, 1996. 410p. illus. index. $65.00. ISBN 0-7864-0034-X.

This book provides a fascinating glimpse of the British movie studio best known for its horror films in the late 1950s and 1960s. As the authors note in their preface and then ably document in the text, Hammer was actually a broad-based company that produced numerous types of films during its existence, ranging from comedies to musicals. However, most readers will probably be drawn to the book for information about Hammer's horror films.

Altogether, 163 films are profiled, beginning with the company's first production in 1935 of *The Public Life of Henry the Ninth* and going through to their last, the 1978 remake of *The Lady Vanishes*. The book is arranged in chronological order by the year of the film's production and gives credit information, release date, running time, and where it was filmed. Also given are a brief synopsis of the plot, facts about the production, and excerpts from reviews. Access to this work is through a table of contents, the chronological arrangement of the films, and a name/title index. The name index is limited primarily to performers, directors, producers, and writers. The book also lists short subjects produced by the company as well as television projects with which it was involved.

Overall, the book is well written and provides an interesting history not only about the films themselves but also about the studio as a whole and the various stars it made famous, particularly Peter Cushing, Christopher Lee, and Oliver Reed. Numerous photographs are provided throughout the text. *Hammer Films* is recommended for libraries with collections pertaining to film.—**Robert Logsdon**

1120. Klepper, Robert K. **Silent Films on Video: A Filmography of Over 700 Silent Features....** Jefferson, N.C., McFarland, 1996. 188p. index. $45.00. ISBN 0-7864-0157-5.

The number of silent films available on video increases every year. In quality, these videos range from dark or faded abridgments of the original motion pictures to superb restorations such as are currently being issued by Kino Video. As interest in the silent era grows, a guide to titles available on video and a directory of sources have been much needed. While the present volume is not up-to-date and it rarely mentions print quality, it is a useful aid that will be welcomed by film students and video collectors.

The filmography lists, describes, and identifies sources for more than 700 silent features, as well as a small number of significant short films. The 1994 cutoff date means many important new releases from Kino, the Library of Congress, and other sources are not listed. Distributors are continuously adding and deleting titles and replacing listings with better-quality prints. Some distributors' catalogs candidly describe print quality and offer warranties of satisfaction. The 1996 catalog of Foothills Video, a source of public domain titles at bargain prices, no longer lists several titles Klepper identifies as being available only from Foothills, while it does list dozens of other titles that Klepper fails to credit as being available from this source.

Klepper's volume will be most useful when used in conjunction with distributors' current catalogs. This is why the final section of the book is particularly valuable. It identifies and describes the policies of all the major silent film video distributors. Despite its shortcomings, *Silent Films on Video* is a valuable addition to the film and video reference shelf.—**Joseph W. Palmer**

1121. Pointer, Michael. **Charles Dickens on the Screen: The Film, Television, and Video Adaptations.** Lanham, Md., Scarecrow, 1996. 207p. illus. index. $42.50. ISBN 0-8108-2960-6.

The works of Charles Dickens remain enormously popular 127 years after his death. They are known and loved by millions, many of whom have never read a word the author wrote. This is because so many adaptations have graced motion picture and television screens. There have been, in the past century, silent shorts and features, classic motion pictures of the sound era, musicals, television specials and series, cartoon versions including one with Mickey Mouse, direct-to-video productions, episodes of television situation comedies, foreign films, and even a pornographic film.

The book under review is an excellent history and guide to Dickens on the movie and television screens. Divided into two parts, the first traces Dickens on American and British screens starting with American Mutoscope's 1897 *Death of Nancy Sykes*. The second lists, in chronological order with credits and casts, more than 400 productions concluding with the 1994 BBC presentations of *Hard Times* and *Martin Chuzzlewit*.

This is no dull chronology. Pointer, author of *Who's Who in Dickens* (Grange Books, 1995) and several books on incarnations of Sherlock Holmes in the popular media, is a writer of verve and vitality who is both a Dickens scholar and a film historian. His narrative, enriched by numerous quotations from contemporary sources and the memoirs of persons involved in productions, is full of interesting historical detail and astute critical commentary. *Charles Dickens on the Screen* is a fine reference book and, for those interested in film history, an interesting read.—**Joseph W. Palmer**

1122. Senn, Bryan. **Golden Horrors: An Illustrated Critical Filmography of Terror Cinema, 1931-1939.** Jefferson, N.C., McFarland, 1996. 518p. illus. index. $55.00. ISBN 0-7864-0175-3.

Senn provides a welcome addition to the literature of fantastic films with *Golden Horrors*. The introduction gives an informative yet brief history of the genre, as well as the author's definition of what is meant by "horror" film. While each of the 46 main film entries contains the usual information (cast, synopsis, reviews), Senn enhances each with sections describing assets and liabilities to the film's artistic and commercial success. Another section details a memorable moment of the film that the author found to be significant. While these moments may not all seem especially memorable, they add a personal and insightful look at the details that made each film important to the genre.

With each entry, Senn shows the reader "strange things about the mind of man" that influenced each film and its impact on future cinematic efforts. Another personal touch is found in appendix B, which lists the "Top 10" horror films of luminaries such as Ray Bradbury, Robert Bloch, John Landis, William K. Everson, and Senn himself. While the index is fairly detailed, it would be more helpful if subheadings had been provided for the lengthy listings of the oft-cited Boris Karloff and Bela Lugosi, and the films *Frankenstein* and *Dracula*. A pleasure to read and an invaluable resource to film researchers and enthusiasts, this work is recommended for most libraries.—**Elizabeth A. Ginno**

1123. Shull, Michael S., and David Edward Wilt. **Hollywood War Films, 1937-1945: An Exhaustive Filmography....** Jefferson, N.C., McFarland, 1996. 482p. illus. index. $125.00. ISBN 0-7864-0145-1.

An ongoing debate concerning U.S. feature films questions whether the film industry creates social attitudes or reflects them, and whether films educate people or merely entertain them. Authors Shull and Wilt here undertake a massive study of 1,282 U.S. feature-length films from 1937 to 1945 to uncover movie portrayals that may have influenced viewer attitudes on world events, the drift toward war, and support for the war effort. The authors regard films as sociopolitical documents reflecting attitudes on subjects ranging from Adolf Hitler and appeasement to war bonds and improved race relations for a more cohesive war effort. Their film-by-film examination has counterparts in the efforts of the Office of War Information, which scrutinized films for their patriotic fervor, and in those of U.S. Senator Gerald Nye's subcommittee, which acted on an isolationist agenda. This is a long-overdue filmography comprehensively documenting the relationship of the movies to U.S. attitudes on the state of the world.

The book is divided into two main sections, one covering the period from 1937 to 1941 and the other scanning the period beginning with the attack on Pearl Harbor. The first part takes a chronological look at 449 films for portrayals of U.S. icons, the military, pacifism, Jews, Germans, immigrants, blacks, isolationism, interventionism, appeasement, collaborators, the Resistance, indigenous fascist organizations, and such events as the Spanish Civil War. The 1942-1945 section, covering 832 releases, has some of these topics, but includes many others: Japanese American relocation, POWs, female labor, the home front, shortages, veterans, and atrocities. The complete list of themes is quite long, and each theme is coded for easy annotation. A single film may carry as many as 20 subject codes.

Each film entry includes the director, studio, release date, genre, locations, and the subject code. The authors provide a 100- to 300-word annotation indicating the war-related scenes and how they fit into the movie's plot. Shull and Wilt add references to remakes, rereleases, sequels, and look-alike films. Occasionally, they reach outside the film itself to sources, such as studio memos, for information on a feature's propaganda value. The authors add to the filmography with lengthy essays examining the context and issues of the time frame and how they played out in the movies. Their chapter on attitudes toward blacks, Latinos, and the Chinese is particularly good. The authors add a valuable 350-item bibliography, statistical tables detailing the growth of films with discernible political or social biases, and a thorough index.

Many of these films will never be seen again on any screen. Some contain overtly propagandistic messages or appear accommodating to fascist expansionism. Most are simply not profitable in today's marketplace. Yet half a century ago, 80 million news-starved people were going to the movies each week for this window on the world. *Hollywood War Films* performs a remarkable service in enabling readers to comprehend the age and its influences. [R: Choice, Dec 96, p. 596]—**John P. Schmitt**

1124. **South American Cinema: A Critical Filmography, 1915-1994.** Timothy Barnard and Peter Rist, eds. New York, Garland, 1996. 405p. index. (Garland Reference Library of the Humanities, v.1077). $64.00. ISBN 0-8240-4574-2.

Abundantly clear in a number of essays in this filmography is how tenuous the distribution and preservation of South American film have been. National governments, the U.S. State Department, and other censors destroyed or made old films otherwise disappear, while other prints disintegrated from lack of care. In at least one case, a processing lab threw out a film when the government producer failed to pay its bill, and the impoverished producer of the world's first animation feature, *El Apóstol* (Argentina), sold many of his early films to a comb company that wanted their celluloid content.

Based on these deplorable conditions, it is a wonder that enough has been preserved to fill a book. Barnard and Rist, and their contributors, searched many archives in North and South America to uncover these 140 most important and representative films. Every South American country is included, except for Suriname, Guyana, and French Guiana, which will form part of a second volume on Mexico, Central America, and the Caribbean. Every genre and era are covered, including the silent period (1915-1931) previously missing from English-language scholarship.

Brazil and Argentina dominate with a total of 82 film essays, most written by Barnard, Rist, or Ana López. Venezuela has 13 entries, and all other countries, 11 or fewer. Only two films each from Ecuador and Paraguay were selected. The essays are arranged alphabetically within country categories and contain technical information, genesis of the films, their themes, credits, and social/political context. A huge appendix includes eight indexes, two glossaries, and a reference list.

The editors have taken some time to explain their operational procedure, even though they failed to provide adequate selection criteria. The book is a fountain of valuable and fascinating, although often sad, information, useful to the scholar and the fan alike. It is a must for research libraries, especially those at institutions with Latin American specialties or programs.—**John A. Lent**

1125. **TLA Film & Video Guide 1996-1997.** David Bleiler, ed. Philadelphia, TLA Publications, 1996. 688p. illus. index. $14.95pa. ISBN 1-880707-02-2.

This latest entry into the overcrowded field of film and video guides focuses primarily on international and independent cinema, while excluding most made-for-television and direct-to-video movies. TLA Video, established in 1985 as a subsidiary of the Theatre of the Living Arts repertory cinema, is a nationwide outlet that, even though offering mainstream titles, specializes in cult and art films and has proven its commitment to such programming. This combination video guide and TLA sales catalog (their toll-free telephone order number appears at the bottom of almost every page) includes more than 8,500 titles.

Unlike the field's standard reference source, *Leonard Maltin's Movie and Video Guide* (see ARBA 95, entry 1361), the TLA guide does not provide much cast information. While each entry does give the film's date, running time, country of origin, director, and purchase price (when applicable), the emphasis is on critical analysis rather than a brief plot synopsis. In addition to film, the guide lists some television shows, such as *Star Trek* and *The Outer Limits*, where 40 individual episodes are discussed.

Five separate indexes group titles by country of origin, genres, directors, stars, and a handy thematic index with such diverse headings as "The Devil," "Homicidal Children," and "Serial Killers." Appendixes include "TLA Bests" and "Awards" (1970-1994), including the Oscar, the Los Angeles and New York Film Critics' Awards, and the National Board of Review. The text is well illustrated with more than 450 photographs. Although not an essential purchase for most libraries, this inexpensive paperback would be useful in public libraries and in those universities supporting a strong media collection.—**David K. Frasier**

1126. **The Ultimate Guide to Lesbian & Gay Film and Video.** Jenni Olson, ed. New York, Serpent's Tail; distr., St. Paul, Minn., Consortium, 1996. 389p. index. $25.00pa. ISBN 1-85242-339-0.

This encyclopedic tome (at 2,000-plus entries, the largest single reference work on gay and lesbian film and video yet compiled) is an expansion of the editor's filmography thesis project at the University of Minnesota. Based upon films both shown at the San Francisco International Gay and Lesbian Film Festival (where Olson served as codirector from 1992 to 1994) since its inception in 1977 and selected older additional material (including silent films), the guide's stated purpose is to supply critical and descriptive commentary on this specific category of cinema. Entries are classified as documentaries, experimental, narrative, and a generic "other" for multitype creations. Information is provided on directors, year and country of production, and running times. Annotations are clearly written and address the significant aspects of plot lines and subject presentation.

While the volume breaks new ground by including numerous titles produced outside the United States and in such marginal genres as clip shows, its contents inevitably overlap with other similar recent reference sources in this field, such as *Gay Hollywood Film & Video Guide* (see ARBA 94, entry 1460), *Gays and Lesbians in Mainstream Cinema* (see ARBA 94, entry 1446), and *Images in the Dark* (see ARBA 95, entry 1374). *The Ultimate Guide*'s primary value lies in combining coverage of alternative and independent filmmaking with the output of major studios in a compact and well-organized format.

The list of distributors and the checklist for programming offer practical assistance to anyone wishing to screen a specific film, while the history of the San Francisco festival and the directory of other gay and lesbian film festivals provide valuable background information. The 56 items in the bibliography have been carefully selected to answer beginning questions and stimulate further research. The guide is recommended for any large public, college, or university library with significant holdings in film history or gay and lesbian studies. [R: LJ, 15 April 96, p. 80-82; RBB, 1 Sept 96, pp. 171-72]—**Robert B. Marks Ridinger**

Handbooks and Yearbooks

1127. Deane, Bill. **Following *The Fugitive*: An Episode Guide and Handbook to the 1960s Television Series.** Jefferson, N.C., McFarland, 1996. 240p. illus. index. $34.50. ISBN 0-7864-0148-6.

Written in a readable and almost chatty narrative style, this volume functions as an exhaustive handbook to all 120 episodes of a television series that remains a hallmark of U.S. popular culture. Arbitrarily divided into 5 sections that provide coverage for all 4 years of the series, entries for each episode include the following: episode number, title, original air date, writer, director, cast/character list, and a 500- to 750-word summary of the show. These summaries are thorough enough to provide their own flowing narrative. The work is supplemented by nine distinct appendixes: list of writers, directors, guest stars, and support players; places visited or lived in (by the fugitive); aliases used; occupations held; romances engaged in; injuries sustained; and other interesting facts.

Considering the revival of interest in this television series, and the amount of information generated on the topic, this volume should be a worthwhile addition to the reference collections of most medium and large public libraries. The guide is recommended for its exhaustive scope and perspective.—**Edmund F. SantaVicca**

1128. *The Hollywood Reporter* **Book of Box Office Hits.** rev. ed. By Susan Sackett. New York, Billboard Books/Watson-Guptill, 1996. 416p. illus. index. $21.95pa. ISBN 0-8230-7549-4.

A well-organized overview of the best in Hollywood filmdom, this reference work avoids the dull reportage of standard filmographies and the cynicism of *Halliwell's Film Guide* (see ARBA 96, entry 1385), a perennial reference classic. Organized by years from 1939 to 1995, each chapter names the five top-grossing titles and describes facets of the filming process, such as the use of animals in *Dances with Wolves*, the life of Annie Oakley for the blurb on *Annie Get Your Gun*, and Elizabeth Taylor's conversion to Judaism after her role as a Jew in *Ivanhoe*. Layout is clear and inviting. Each entry opens with title, date, company, and box office take and features an action shot in black-and-white. Set apart from the text is a list of vital statistics—author, screenwriter, producer, director, composer, cast, and Oscar nominations and wins. Appendixes include films listed by year, title, and studio/distributor; also-rans; a bibliography; photograph credits; and an index.

Sackett's chatty explanation of her selection method and criteria carries over to her evenhanded dealings with a wide range of screen favorites, from *Dumbo*, which has just earned a place among standard hit films, to the latest titles, including *Apollo 13*, *Pocahontas*, and *Ace Ventura: When Nature Calls*. Her commentary on *Spartacus* recounts Dalton Trumbo's emergence from the ignominy of the "Hollywood Ten" and a stretch in jail for challenging McCarthyism. Useful data include Disney's artists' study of a dissected deer for *Bambi* and Bobby Driscoll's failed career after success in *Song of the South*. In her review of *Rocky II*, Sackett cites commentary from *The New York Times*; she accounts for the hiring of Michael J. Fox five weeks into the filming of *Back to the Future*. The author is knowledgeable and the book valuable to students, reviewers, librarians, teachers, reporters, historians, and lovers of film.—**Mary Ellen Snodgrass**

1129. Lance, Steven. **Written Out of Television: A TV Lover's Guide to Cast Changes 1945-1994.** Lanham, Md., Madison Books/University Press of America; distr., National Book Network, 1996. 507p. illus. index. $24.95pa. ISBN 1-56833-071-5.

This encyclopedia purports to provide readers with "the most accurate and detailed information ever available, on one source, about the programs where actors have been written out." Here the dedicated television buff may learn exactly how many different dogs played Lassie, as well as which ones had behavioral problems on the set; the details of the debilitating spinal injury that forced Dick York to leave the cast of *Bewitched*; and the names of the two actors who played Chris on *The Partridge Family*. Despite the author's obsessive attention to detail, there are alarming gaps; for instance, while this book provides an exhaustive list of minor crewpeople who have trooped across the bridge of the Starship *Enterprise*, the reader will search in vain for an account of Edith Bunker's death on *All in the Family*.

Written Out of Television is a labor of love, not scholarship, and the quality of entries varies widely, ranging from complex, well-researched accounts of the dynamics of cast changes to badly written plot summaries of shows. Outside of settling the barroom bets of inveterate couch potatoes, the guide has limited use as a reference tool.—**Kelly Malone**

1130. Lentz, Harris M., III, comp. **Western and Frontier Film and Television Credits 1903-1995.** Jefferson, N.C., McFarland, 1996. 2v. index. $175.00/set. ISBN 0-7864-0158-3.

Lentz, best known for his similar 1983 work, *Science Fiction, Horror & Fantasy Film and Television Credits* (see ARBA 84, entry 967), and its two supplements (see ARBA 90, entry 1350, and ARBA 95, entry 1395), here documents the perennially popular Western/frontier genre from 1903 through June 1995. This ambitious two-volume compendium is a comprehensive attempt to list both film credits for a genre that continuously dates from the inception of motion pictures, as well as television credits for all Western television series.

Volume 1 is devoted to the creative talent (actors, actresses, directors, producers, writers) involved in the production of these films and television series. Entries are alphabetically arranged by the individual's name; provide birth and death dates; and give a chronological listing of film credits, including title, date, and in the case of actors, their characters' names. Volume 2 is divided into film and television indexes and represents the most comprehensive list of this genre material ever collected. Data on each film include year and country of release (if other than the United States), production credits, and cast and character information. Serials are also listed, along with their individual chapter titles. The television index itemizes every Western television series ever aired, accompanied by its regular cast and followed by an episode index containing the individual show's title, original air date, cast, and their characters' names.

This is an excellent resource destined to become a standard in the area of Western film and television reference. It is unreservedly recommended for large public and academic libraries supporting a film studies or popular culture curriculum. [R: RBB, 1 Nov 96, p. 542]—**David K. Frasier**

1131. **Magill's Cinema Annual 1995: A Survey of the Films of 1994.** 14th ed. Shawn Brennan and others, eds. Detroit, Gale, 1996. 828p. illus. index. (A VideoHound Reference). $75.00. ISBN 0-7876-0732-0. ISSN 0739-2141.

With this new edition, *Magill's Cinema Annual* has undergone a complete makeover. Gone is the old familiar Salem Press format made famous by *Masterplots* and its many clones, the godsend of procrastinating undergraduates. Now published by Gale, the transformed *Annual* is considerably more entertaining, with fancier graphics, liberal use of sidebars (which feature background facts and key quotations from the film being discussed), and numerous black-and-white photographs. Each entry starts with a few ultrashort excerpts from film reviews, which kindle interest and add pizzazz. Compared to the old approach (for example, see ARBA 95, entry 1396), for which films were afforded the same rather scholarly, text-only analyses as were literary works in *Masterplots*, the new strategy seems geared to those film buffs who rent videos and who like to get excited about which one to pick up for home viewing. Indeed, the *Annual* is now a member of the VideoHound series of Gale entertainment industry reference books, and there is a new subject index that lets video renters who are in the mood for a film about alcoholism, a Western, or a film set in New York City choose from lists of current movies on those themes and others, many of which are likely to be available on video.

There is a 50 percent increase in film coverage from the previous volume, more essay-length reviews of significant films, more complete awards and nominations lists (including the Cannes Film Festival and the British Academy of Film and Television Arts), information on box office grosses, and a retrospective film title index that covers all 14 volumes of the *Annual*. Continued features include the obituaries section and the annotated bibliography of film books published during the year.

Regardless of exceptional packaging and extensive listings, the backbone of a collection of reviews is the quality of the reviews themselves. They are disappointingly uneven. The large roster of 38 contributing reviewers may partly account for this, as may the reviewers' inexperience, a possibility about which one can only speculate as nearly 75 percent of them are identified only as "Freelance Reviewer," and the rest by the name of the university with which they are affiliated, but no position titles are given.

—**Richard W. Grefrath**

1132. McNeil, Alex. **Total Television: The Comprehensive Guide to Programming from 1948 to the Present.** 4th ed. New York, Penguin Books, 1996. 1251p. index. $22.95pa. ISBN 0-14-024916-8.

This enormous book lists television series, special programming, and movies that have aired on commercial and cable television (network and syndication) for the past 27 years. The 5 parts of the book consist of detailed information on 5,400 series (this composes the major portion of the guide), a chronological list of some special programs and broadcasts, a set of charts showing prime-time fall schedules for the major commercial networks, a list of Emmy and Peabody Award winners, and a list of the top-rated series for each season.

This is probably one of very few books about television that has as much as can be humanly incorporated into a one-volume reference. Naturally, this reviewer's mission, should she decide to accept it, was to find what was not there. Well, there were some. For instance, the special programming included was subjectively selected (most award shows were left out). Also, several separate volumes would have to be compiled to list all the movies that have been made for television, so these two omissions are minor in scope and acceptable. The value of the book lies in what *is* there. Several vague series were looked up that were not expected to be in this source, but were.

This reference piece on television can be considered nothing more than remarkably complete for research use, and deliciously entertaining to just browse through. Also, considering its size and the material within, the book is reasonably priced—low enough that it should entice many people to make it a part of their library (public and private).—**Joan Garner**

1133. *The New York Times* **Film Reviews.** Volume 19: 1993-1994. New York, Times Books and Garland, 1996. 515p. illus. index. $165.00. ISBN 0-8240-7593-5. ISSN 0362-3688.

This book is part of an ongoing series that reproduces every film review that has appeared in *The New York Times* (NYT) since 1913. A new volume is issued every other year; volume 19 covers 1993-1994. The reviews are high-quality, photo-facsimile reproductions of what appeared in the newspaper under the bylines of critics and reviewers, such as Vincent Canby, Bosley Crowther, Stephen Holden, Janet Maslin, and Frank S. Nugent. They provide essential credits; plot synopses; and commentary on and evaluation of performances, production techniques, and audience appeal.

Access to the reviews is made easy by the inclusion of three indexes: alphabetic lists of each film; all personal names to whom the main text refers; and production, distribution, and exhibition companies mentioned in the reviews. The researcher is guided by other professional touches, such as listing foreign films under both English- and other-language titles and adding individual's functions after their names, thus simplifying the search for actors, directors, producers, and so forth.

Separate NYT sections cover the paper's "10 Best," award ceremony rundowns, year-end overviews, and filmmakers' profiles. These are useful but do not fill the void left by the absence of an introduction to the book. Overall, the reprinting of these reviews is a valuable service, allowing the researcher to find them all in one place, presented in their original format.—**John A. Lent**

1134. Robinson, Dale, and David Fernandes. **The Definitive Andy Griffith Show Reference: Episode-by-Episode....** Jefferson, N.C., McFarland, 1996. 328p. illus. index. $45.00. ISBN 0-7864-0136-2.

Here are descriptions of 249 episodes of the *Andy Griffith Show*. For each one, there is its number; its air date (the series was not always shown in episode number order); the writing and directing credits; a plot summary; a "memorable scene" from each show; some cast notes; and some general episode notes (e.g., "Goober states that he is 33 years old"). These notes are not indexed anywhere—indeed, there is no subject index at all, just an index to names. In these modern times, the book cries out for a searchable database. There is also no real indication of videotape availability (most fans have probably just taped off-the-air). Some obscure notes suggest writing to a collectibles store for obtaining the tapes, which is unusual because Viacom owns the series.

For resource competition, one should note that there are many "Mayberry" Websites on the Internet. A casual use of search engines brought forth some five dozen locations and mailing lists, with all kinds of information on them. This is the biggest area of usage by Internet people: resources for the cult or fan. So, just about everything (memorabilia and collecting notes, trivia books, biographies, and other items) found in this book and in similar books for other television shows can be found on the Internet for free. Yet this book does not mention any, and does not even suggest using the Internet to find more details. With many libraries hooked up, the material is easily available (and searchable), and to many people at once.
—**Dean Tudor**

1135. *Sight and Sound* **Film Review Volume: January 1994 to December 1994.** London, British Film Institute; distr., Bloomington, Ind., Indiana University Press, 1995. 274p. illus. $60.00. ISBN 0-85170-529-4.

Interested in identifying the songwriters of the more than 50 musical extracts found in *Forrest Gump*? How about a plot summary of Disney's *The Lion King* to see if it is a suitable movie for a five-year old? Does Amy Tan's novel *The Joy Luck Club* translate well onto the big screen in Wayne Wang's 1993 movie? The answer to such questions as these, and thousands more, are easily found in the British Film Institute's (BFI) annual *Sight and Sound Film Review Volume*, a compilation of reviews from *Sight and Sound*, the BFI's authoritative film magazine.

Containing month-by-month listings, this reference tool provides full credits, a plot summary, a signed critical review, and sometimes a photograph for all films released in Great Britain during 1994. Both English and original titles of foreign-language films are cited with the original title given in parentheses (for example, Germany's *Faraway, So Close [In weiter Ferne, so nah!]*, Hong Kong's *Days of Being Wild [A-fei Zheng Chuan]*, and Spain's *The Red Squirrel [La ardilla roja]*). Published by the BFI and distributed by Indiana University Press, this volume is an invaluable guide for film scholars, cinema enthusiasts, and the general moviegoing public as it is an excellent first stop in researching any recent film worthy of distribution at home and abroad.—**Colby H. Kullman**

1136. *Time Out* **Film Guide.** 5th ed. John Pym, ed. New York, Penguin Books, 1996. 1096p. index. $21.95pa. ISBN 0-14-026132-X.

Many of the titles in the increasing proliferation of film guides have a theme. The emphasis can be on a film genre, such as the cult films in *The Psychotronic Video Guide* (see entry 1140); the collected reviews of one person, as in *Roger Ebert's Video Companion* (see ARBA 95, entry 1362); or the collected reviews of a publication—such as *Variety's Film Reviews* (see ARBA 96, entry 1387). Other such handbooks simply attempt to be as comprehensive as possible, as in *Bowker's Complete Video Directory 1995* (see ARBA 96, entry 986). The *Time Out Film Guide* anthologizes the reviews published since 1970 in the British weekly magazine of the same name. Nearly 11,000 films are reviewed, with international coverage being a specialty. Foreign film buffs will find more foreign films included in this guide than any other, and they are reviewed with insight and familiarity.

This edition contains 900 more reviews than its predecessor, and provides the standard listings for director, cast, running time, plot synopsis, and release date. Alternate titles are given—variations from country to country, or from theatrical to video release—something not all film guides provide. Award winners are listed as well, but with the Berlin, Cannes, and Venice film festival winners featured alongside the expected roster of Oscar recipients. Entries are indexed by film genre; country of origin; director; actors; and subjects (e.g., Korea, martial arts, religion). Libraries whose patrons have access to (thus interest in) international films should consider this title for purchase. Although conceived as a consumer guide, this fairly inexpensive paperback could be used as a survey of world cinema.—**Ed Volz**

1137. **VideoHound's Complete Guide to Cult Flicks and Trash Pics.** Detroit, Visible Ink Press/Gale, 1996. 439p. illus. index. $16.95pa. ISBN 0-7876-0616-2.

Trash, cult, horror, 3-D, camp, alternative, blaxploitation films, they are all here in what the producers call "mongrel videos." This guide covers 1,100 movies and "mongrel" seems the right word for this mix. Of course, one can expect *Assault of the Killer Bimbos*, Billy Jack movies, and Amy Fisher stories. It also includes such mainstream movies as *Saturday Night Fever* and even the Michael Moore documentary *Roger and Me*. Despite the title, there is a rich mixture of art films (such as *Koyaanisqatsi*) as well as movies that do not quite add up as either trash or cult favorites (such as Marx Brothers movies, *The Manchurian Candidate*, and *The King of Hearts*).

Each entry includes a surprisingly complete yet concise synopsis, and often comparative notes about similar films and a discussion of the filming, the stars, and the directors. Each listing also provides any or all of the following: song titles, alternative titles, the year the film was made, its MPAA rating (when available), length in minutes, black-and-white or color, a list of credits, awards, format, price, and distributor. The films are all rated with dog bones. (Somehow, *The Brady Bunch Movie* rates three out of four bones.) There are many still photographs and memorable quotations from movies and sidebars saluting actors, directors, television horror hosts, and genres.

The resources section ("Cult Connection") lists World Wide Web pages, newsgroups, magazines/ newsletters, fan clubs, and books. There are several good indexes, by alternative title, by cast, by director, and by category, as well as a distributor guide. This book is well written, often hilarious, and a lot of fun to read. If one is looking for a film guide to offbeat, horror, cult, or classics, this guide fills the bill superbly.—**Stephen Haenel**

1138. Warren, Alan. **This Is a *Thriller*: An Episode Guide, History, and Analysis of the Classic 1960s Television Series.** Jefferson, N.C., McFarland, 1996. 207p. illus. index. $45.00. ISBN 0-7864-0256-3.

Warren has well researched and well documented this volume on *Thriller*, one of the horror television series of the 1960s. It fills a hole in the category of the genre by giving readers an overview of the origins of and the difficult history of the show, including behind-the-scenes stories and rumors. *Thriller* lived up to its title. A black-and-white mystery/suspense anthology hosted by the legendary Boris Karloff (who starred in about six shows in the series), *Thriller* told of people suddenly trapped in unexpected, sometimes frightening situations fostered through emotion, greed, or the threat of crime. This show developed into a class act based on the pedigrees of the series' behind-the-camera talents. It was packed with familiar names, such as Elizabeth Montgomery, Richard Chamberlain, William Shatner, Leslie Nielsen, and Robert Vaughn. Karloff himself joined Patricia Medina and Sidney Blackmer in a version of Edgar Allan Poe's "The Premature Burial," one of the most frightening episodes in the series.

Biographies of such key figures as producer William Frye; executive producer Hubbell Robinson; and writers Robert Block, Donald S. Sanford, and Karloff are listed, among others. The episode guide covers all 67 installments, providing air date, cast, plot synopsis, and critical evaluations for both seasons. Listed in the appendixes are "Ancestors of Thriller," "Descendants of Thriller," and "The Top 25 Thriller Episodes" (based on requests sent to the Thriller Fan Club in San Francisco, California).

As a reference, one can be fascinated by this volume, along with its appendixes, the bibliography, and the substantial index. The guide is an informative and responsible piece of work. It would be appropriate for academic, public, and special libraries with entertainment collections, specifically television program series and film including video.—**Lisé Rasmussen**

1139. Warren, Patricia. **British Film Studios: An Illustrated History.** London, B. T. Batsford; distr., North Pomfret, Vt., Trafalgar Square, 1995. 192p. illus. maps. index. $27.50pa. ISBN 0-7134-7559-5.

This is an interesting work that profiles more than 90 film studios located throughout England, Scotland, Northern Ireland, and Wales, with primary emphasis upon the English studios. What particularly sets this book apart is its arrangement, which is in alphabetic order by geographic location rather than by name of studio. For the British reading public this may be a particular benefit, but for readers unfamiliar with the particular locations, it greatly limits the value of this type of arrangement.

Warren notes in her introduction that her intention is to give the reader "... a feel of each studio, its major personalities and protagonists, landmark films, stars, anecdotes, takeovers, development and era, with some thumb nail sketches en route...." She succeeds only partially. Because of the large number of studios profiled, she varies greatly in her coverage, ranging from a paragraph or two for some studios to several pages for others. Unfortunately, for the studios with the broadest coverage, much of the information seems to be a listing of films produced with the names of their stars. Readers seeking anything other than film listings or anecdotes will come away disappointed.

Access is through a table of contents, arranged alphabetically by geographic location, and through a name index. The index is by people and studios. Films mentioned in the text are not listed in the index, which greatly reduces its effectiveness. One strong point of the work, however, is its large number of photographs, more than 200 in all, which, although primarily of movie scenes, do provide a visual history of the British film industry. The work is recommended only for the largest film collections. [R: Choice, April 96, p. 1292]—**Robert Logsdon**

1140. Weldon, Michael J. **The Psychotronic Video Guide.** New York, St. Martin's Press, 1996. 646p. illus. index. $29.95pa. ISBN 0-312-13149-6.

Weldon underestimates himself when stating that his book contains reviews of more than 3,000 "horror, science fiction, fantasy, and exploitation" features (p. vii). While focusing on the films that other video guides shun, due to squeamishness or a restricted aesthetic, this guide does include every variety of Hollywood and foreign feature as well. Distinctive here is a refreshingly cockeyed perspective, in both the selection of films and in descriptions of them. Former porn star turned legitimate actress Michelle Bauer earns 42 index entries, while Meg Ryan has 6 (Meryl Streep has none). As for director entries, soft-core pioneer Russ Meyer has 41, François Truffaut has none. Whereas *psychotronic* is not defined by Weldon, a quick check of the index explains the term. This is a parade of honor for genre films of all kinds—martial arts, slasher, biker, "blaxploitation," pseudo-snuff documentaries, and much more. Even big-budget films, if sufficiently distasteful or idiosyncratic, are included.

Individual film entries are brief, consistently containing only the video distributor's name; the year of initial release; and the names of the director, screenwriter, and producer. The concise and quirky narrative descriptions typically mention actors, sometimes music, and always the film's plot. The plot synopses are often just a few words long, but probably do justice to the material. Films are not rated for quality, and what little evaluation there is is done indirectly and inconsistently, a real deficiency when the subject matter is not taken seriously in other sources. A half-page bibliography lists books and (primarily) film journals; a sole index lists just actors and directors. Black-and-white illustrations, film stills, and promotional one-shots ("movie posters") sporadically supplement the text. Occasional charts list the author's favorite films of an era or his personal ruminations on such peripheral topics as New York City's Times Square theaters.

The book's flaws—a lack of focus and scope, an avoidance of content evaluation, incomplete technical-credit listings, and a skimpy index—give it an unschooled feel. The inevitable minor errors are rare, although present (e.g., Neil Young's *Trans* album is listed as *Trains*). A less common frustration for this kind of book is the lack of access, due to weak indexing, to the book's staggering number of obscure factual tidbits. Weldon's enthusiasm has motivated him to gather and share cinematic minutiae that, given the esoteric nature of the films included here, are unlikely to appear in any other source. Yet the details are unindexed and will be found only by browsers. The guide is recommended as a circulating item for libraries with adventurous patrons who may recognize *Psychotronic* as a brand name, and as a reference purchase in larger collections.—**Ed Volz**

1141. Zaniello, Tom. **Working Stiffs, Union Maids, Reds, and Riffraff: An Organized Guide to Films About Labor.** Ithaca, N.Y., ILR Press/Cornell University Press, 1996. 295p. illus. index. $39.95; $18.95pa. ISBN 0-87546-352-5; 0-87546-353-3pa.

This is a guide to films that deal with working people, labor activism or history, and related economic and sociological issues. In order for a film to be included it had to satisfy one or more of the following criteria: 1) be about unions or labor organizations; 2) be about labor history; 3) be about working-class life in which an economic consideration is important; 4) be about a political movement tied closely to the interests of organized labor; or 5) be about the production or the struggle between labor and capital from a top-down, either entrepreneurial or managerial perspective. The author has taught film for 20 years and has developed a course on images of labor in film. He selected films based on the recommendations of trade unionists and labor educators. One hundred and fifty titles were chosen. He has tried to include films that are relatively accessible; most are available on video. A little more than 20 percent are documentaries. Most of those discussed had major theatrical releases.

Each film entry gives the essential information concerning the production, the cast list, and the film rating. The author has tried to expand on the film ratings to give more guidance on the R-rated films. He has also included a brief list of related print sources and films that pertain to each entry. For nearly every entry there is a plot summary, the historical and cultural context surrounding the subject of the film, some critical commentary, and the author's personal judgment. This guide will be useful for those interested in labor as portrayed in mainly U.S. films.—**Robert L. Turner Jr.**

Indexes

1142. **American Film Personnel and Company Credits, 1908-1920: Filmographies Reordered....** By Paul C. Spehr, with Gunnar Lundquist. Jefferson, N.C., McFarland, 1996. 696p. $110.00. ISBN 0-7864-0255-5.

The period between 1908 and 1920 was the U.S. film industry's most prolific. Before feature-length films gained dominance around 1915, production companies churned out short films by the thousands to meet the demands of a burgeoning number of nickelodeons and movie theaters, most of which changed their programs daily. When Einar Lauritzen and Gunnar Lundquist published their *American Film Index, 1908-1915* and *American Film Index, 1916-1920* (University of Stockholm, 1976-1984), they listed more than 33,000 theatrical motion pictures released during the 13-year period. Lauritzen and Lundquist provided an alphabetic list of the films with production details and creative credits, but with no annotations and no indexes.

The catalogs of the American Film Institute (*American Film Institute Catalog: Film Beginnings, 1893-1910* [1995], and *American Film Institute Catalog: Feature Films, 1911-1920* [1988]) cover the same period and provide far more detailed information and excellent indexes. Unfortunately, they exclude non-feature-length films released after 1910. Although the Institute plans to prepare a volume covering short films from 1911-1920 sometime in the future, this means, for instance, that currently hundreds of short films made by D. W. Griffith and more than 80 films in which the actor Robert Harron appeared will not be found in the American Film Institute catalogs, although all are listed in the Lauritzen/Lundquist volumes.

Spehr agreed to undertake the herculean task of preparing an index to personal and corporate names in the *American Film Index*. He has done this diligently and incorporated excellent authority control so that a single form of name is established for each entity. Variant names are listed underneath the selected name, and cross-references are provided. The result is a compilation of filmographies for individuals and companies that were active in the U.S. film industry during its formative years that is of unrivaled comprehensiveness.—**Joseph W. Palmer**

1143. **Film Actors Guide, 1997.** 3d ed. Steve A. LuKanic, comp. and ed. Los Angeles, Calif., Lone Eagle, 1996. 802p. index. $70.00pa. ISBN 0-943728-84-3. ISSN 1055-0836.

The 1997 edition of the *Film Actors Guide* is a staple for any good film reference collection. Useful features include separate indexes for male and female actors, as well as a film title index for those times when the researcher can only remember the movie the actor was in and not his or her name. An advantage of this resource is that it offers access to any actor who is listed in the credits of a production, not just to the stars. Information provided under each full entry includes a list of feature production work, both in film and television and, when known, the actor's birth date and place, agent, and telephone number.

The guide is most useful for those libraries whose clientele need current contact information for working actors of the last 10 years. For most public and academic libraries, a more comprehensive source, such as *The Motion Picture Guide* (see ARBA 94, entry 1457, and ARBA 90, entry 1352), would be more practical. For those researchers and libraries who need current information on working actors, perhaps a better investment would be to join Lone Eagle Publishing's *eagle i* World Wide Web site (http://www.loneeagle.com/eaglei). For $199 a year, one can gain access to not only the *Film Actors Guide*, but also to Lone Eagle's other noteworthy entertainment reference sources (such as their guides to cinematographers, costume designers, producers [see entry 766], and so on).—**Elizabeth A. Ginno**

1144. **Television Program Master Index: Access to Critical and Historical Information on 1002 Shows in 341 Books.** By Charles V. Dintrone. Jefferson, N.C., McFarland, 1996. 133p. index. $36.50. ISBN 0-7864-0150-8.

Some time in the not-too-distant future, when critical studies become fully computer searchable, a reference book such as this one will be produced effortlessly and instantly, if it is produced at all. Until that time arrives, however, this is the kind of book that could only be produced by a dedicated scholar, over many years, with a great deal of trouble. Dintrone, a reference librarian and scholar of television, spent years laboriously combing through hundreds of books about television and indexing the comments found in these books regarding particular television shows. He indexes as little as one sentence about a show, if that sentence is meaningful enough to be useful in a research paper.

The result is an index of comments concerning more than 1,000 television shows that appeared from 1947 to 1995. In order to be indexed, the show had to have appeared on NBC, CBS, ABC, or Fox, and it must have been a series. Also included are the PBS shows *Sesame Street* and *Mister Rogers' Neighborhood*. The 341 books indexed, which are listed in an annotated bibliography at the back of the volume, were published between 1956 and 1995; most academic and public libraries will have a substantial number of these books.

Dintrone's book also contains an appendix indexing comments in the 341 books about particular professions or classes of people (e.g., blue-collar workers, doctors, Hispanics) and another appendix that groups show titles by genre (adventure, comedy, drama, game show, and so forth). This book, therefore, would be absolutely invaluable to anyone writing about a particular television show it indexes, and useful also for anyone doing research on television in general. There is no comparable index. While it would be hard to imagine the average undergraduate using the book as intended, any serious researcher will want to have access to it, and every library supporting serious inquiry into television broadcasting will want to own a copy. [R: Choice, Nov 96, p. 427; RBB, 1 Sept 96, p. 171]—**Bill Miller**

Videography

1145. Lems-Dworkin, Carol. **Videos of African and African-Related Performance: An Annotated Bibliography.** Evanston, Ill., Carol Lems-Dworkin Publishers, 1996. 331p. $57.00pa. ISBN 0-9637048-0-X.

Lems-Dworkin, obviously a talented music educator, writer, and musician (whose interest in the cinema is apparent from the abundance of videos reviewed in the book) has published a well-written guide for anyone who is interested in music from around the world produced by people of Africa and African descent. The book reviews such important videos such as *African and African American Folk Tales* (an animated video that has two African folktales and one African American folktale); *The Caribbean* (an excellent video that covers music culture from 14 different countries of the region); *Didn't We Ramble On: The Black Marching Band* (a short but exemplary account of the origins of African and African American Marching Bands); *Selbe: One Among Many* (a story of daily life in West Africa among women in African society); and many more covering musical, social, and historical arenas.

The book also has an excellent names index; a subject index; an invaluable distributors index complete with addresses and telephone numbers (some of them toll-free); and a key to symbols that describes which videos are in color, optical sound, black-and-white film, and so forth. There is also an appendix that covers videotape formats in current use. The introduction to the book is most helpful in directing the reader/researcher to background information on how the volume was produced and what it includes. Also of use are a users' guide, reference sources, and notes that one can further pursue to read about musical performance concerning people of African descent. This reviewer highly recommends this source because she has personally seen several videos that are reviewed in the book.—**Lillian Jane Steele**

THEATER

Bibliography

1146. Daniel, LaNelle, comp. **American Drama Criticism: Supplement IV to the Second Edition.** North Haven, Conn., Archon Books/Shoe String Press, 1996. 239p. index. $45.00. ISBN 0-208-02393-3.

This is a handy and easy-to-use book for researchers interested in writing about American drama in the 1990s. The names of many relatively new and as yet unknown playwrights are included along with those of Eugene O'Neill, Edward Albee, Ossie Davis and Ruby Dee, and other veterans of American theater. Users should be aware that this bibliography lists the works of the playwrights, along with book-length studies, articles, and reviews, all without critical commentary. The work's purpose is to simplify the search for primary and secondary material. The book and audiovisual materials indexes at the end of the bibliography will be of particular interest to literature and drama scholars and critics. They are thorough and up-to-date. The journal index is valuable insofar as it lists most of the journals and periodicals that publish articles on American drama. This book's one shortcoming has to do with the way it lists book-length studies in the entries: The date of publication should be included.—**Sandra Adell**

1147. Engle, Ron. **Maxwell Anderson on the European Stage 1929-1992: A Production History and Annotated Bibliography....** Monroe, N.Y., Library Research Associates, 1996. 430p. index. $35.00. ISBN 0-912526-67-X.

This highly specialized reference source focuses on the plays of Maxwell Anderson in foreign translation, providing both history and appropriate documentation for more than 195 productions of 29 Anderson plays in 23 European countries. Materials have been gathered from 75 collections in Europe and the United States and range from the scholarly to the ephemeral.

Preceded by a table of contents, a list of illustrations, a preface, acknowledgments, an introduction, and a list of Anderson's plays in translation, the majority of the material is organized alphabetically by country. Country chapters usually include a brief introductory paragraph followed by a bibliography of any relevant general translations, promptbooks, and scripts (arranged by play) and related materials. The production section forms the largest part of each chapter and is arranged by play and subdivided by city. Sections on radio and television productions are also included, when necessary. Each entry gives specific available production information (e.g., date, theater, company, translator, design, cast); an annotated bibliography of relevant scripts, promptbooks, programs, and so on; and a list of reviews and other sources. The entire work is concluded by a 50-page index. (Note: Although the information itself seems well organized, the book's physical layout within the chapters—especially the headings—is occasionally unclear and can be confusing.)

Generally well indexed and filled with information not otherwise available in a single source, this reference work would be of potential interest to any large academic library. However, its specialized nature makes it most appropriate to academic libraries supporting graduate-level programs in theater, popular culture, and American studies.—**Kristin Ramsdell**

1148. **International Bibliography of Theatre: 1992-1993.** Benito Ortolani and others, eds. Brooklyn, N.Y., Theatre Research Data Center, 1995. 1026p. index. $270.00. ISBN 0-945419-05-8.

This impressive and lengthy reference volume continues the series published by the Theatre Research Data Center and provides a listing of theater books, book articles, dissertations, journal articles, and miscellaneous other theater documents published during the years 1992 and 1993. Entries deal with aspects of theater significant to research and are taken from such sources as histories, essays, surveys, papers, catalogs, portfolios, handbooks and other reference sources, records, and production documents. There is no restriction on language, but English is the primary vehicle for compiling and abstracting the materials.

The section of "Classed Entries" contains 1 entry for each of the 6,470 documents analyzed and provides the user with complete bibliographic information, plus such elements as content geography/dates, document treatment, and content abstraction. Classed entries are equivalent to library shelf arrangements. The use of the taxonomy simplifies the process of locating items from the classed entries section in the subject, geographic-chronological, and document authors indexes. The indexes are equivalent to a library shelf card. There is also a list of periodicals, with a guide to their acronyms. This unique volume is vital to current theatrical research and should prove indispensable to any library in this field.—**Jackson Kesler**

Biography

1149. **International Dictionary of Theatre-3: Actors, Directors, and Designers.** David Pickering, ed. Detroit, St. James Press, 1996. 829p. illus. $130.00. ISBN 1-55862-097-4.

This, the 3d and final volume in the *International Dictionary of Theatre*, joins its predecessors, volume 1, on plays (see ARBA 93, entry 1391), and volume 2, on playwrights (see ARBA 95, entry 1421), and nicely completes the series by focusing on actors, directors, and designers. While the earlier volumes are well done and contain much useful information, this latest addition, with its inclusion of less-often covered directors and designers, makes the entire set just that much more helpful and appealing. International and historical in scope, this source covers theater from classical Greece to the present and includes plays written in 20 languages and theater personnel of various cultures and nationalities.

Following a brief introductory editor's note and a list of advisers and contributors, the work continues with an integrated alphabetic listing of generally notable actors, directors, and designers. Each entry will vary with the individual being discussed and may include a brief biography; a chronological list of selected productions or roles; sections on achievements in films, television, and radio; relevant publications authored by the entrant; a bibliography; and a critical essay written by the appropriate contributor. The volume is concluded by two sections—"Notes on Advisers and Contributors" and "Picture Acknowledgments."

Clearly written and organized, nicely formatted, and filled with much useful information, this resource is accessible to a wide range of readers. It will be a welcome addition to most academic and public library reference collections. [R: Choice, May 96, p. 1450; RBB, 15 Mar 96, p. 1315]—**Kristin Ramsdell**

Chronology

1150. Bordman, Gerald. **American Theatre: A Chronicle of Comedy and Drama, 1914-1930.** New York, Oxford University Press, 1995. 446p. index. $49.95. ISBN 0-19-509078-0.

Bordman possesses a remarkable writing skill in which he subtly enables the reader to develop a feeling for the era as this chronicle of comedies and dramas progresses. In barely more than one page of text, the author captures the essence of the era that ended for Western civilization with the start of World War I. Immediately thereafter, he launches into the 1914-15 New York theatrical season. The next 15 years would see an unparalleled period in Broadway history with the presentation of more than 200 new plays. As each new season opens, a brief overview informs the reader of developments in world and national events. The time period of this text was an epoch that witnessed new authors and performers achieving success on Broadway. Yet, at the end of this period, the Great Depression and "talkies" and radio would change the character of public entertainment. Many would make the move to Hollywood.

Without a wince, Bordman usually offers a hint of why a play was an immediate hit or a failure. Throughout, it becomes apparent that good reviews alone did not guarantee a play's success. Yet, whether a play had a short run or a long run, carefully chosen adverbs and adjectives keep this work flowing and readable. Strategically interspersed throughout are short biographies of playwrights and actors. By dividing the index into two sections, entries may be found for the plays or by means of the people. Along with Bordman's other works featuring U.S. theater and Broadway musicals, this work should become an essential part of the collection of academic and major public libraries. [R: Choice, Mar 96, p. 1087]—**Louis G. Zelenka**

Dictionaries and Encyclopedias

1151. **Cambridge Guide to American Theatre.** updated ed. By Don B. Wilmeth, with Tice L. Miller. New York, Cambridge University Press, 1996. 463p. index. $49.95; $24.95pa. ISBN 0-521-40134-8; 0-521-56444-1pa.

First published in 1993 (see ARBA 94, entry 1479), this updated edition provides an encyclopedic history of U.S. theater that is essential to any library from secondary schools upward. It contains more than 2,300 cross-referenced entries that are noteworthy for accuracy, succinct presentation, and suggestions for further reading on the respective topic. The entries are drawn from historical as well as the latest contemporary artists, theaters, plays, and topics. Particularly noteworthy in this edition are the expansions of entries dealing with the theater of diversity and social issues. The topics are drawn from popular areas, such as burlesque and puppetry, as well as the more scholarly areas of criticism and theory and everything in between. There is a biographical index of more than 3,000 names in addition to an extensive bibliography of 1,000-plus sources. This guide represents an essential source for students and scholars of U.S. theater.—**Jackson Kesler**

Directories

1152. **Regional Theatre Directory 1996-97: A National Guide to Employment in Regional & Dinner Theatres....** Jill Charles and others, comps. and eds. Dorset, Vt., Theatre Directories, 1996. 172p. index. $16.95pa. ISBN 0-933919-34-4. ISSN 1041-9411.

A valuable aid to theater directors, producers, performers, designers, technicians, and staff, this newest edition of the *Regional Theatre Directory* offers specific information on hiring and casting procedures at 440 theaters across the country running September through May. Covering equity, non-equity, and dinner theaters, each listing includes a brief description of the company, contact names and addresses, the 1996-1997 season (where possible), the recommended procedure for obtaining an interview or audition, projected hiring and casting needs for the upcoming season, salary ranges, and information on internship opportunities for students and young professionals. This is a perfect companion volume to be used with the *Summer Theatre Directory* (see entry 1153), which profiles more than 450 summer theaters and summer training courses, and the *Directory of Theatre Training Programs* (5th ed.; see ARBA 96, entry 1419), which profiles 420 college and conservatory training programs.

Charles's directory is a treasure chest of significant information for anyone interested in the theater. For example, Montgomery's Alabama Shakespeare Festival, one of the country's finest professional theaters, offers an MFA program in acting, stage managing, administration, and design; accepts new scripts with southern or African American themes through its Southern Writers' Project; and hires a resident company cast for the whole season (all salaries "negotiated"). Los Angeles's Mark Taper Forum, in operation since 1967, has given world or U.S. premieres to more than 200 plays (including Mark Medoff's *Children of a Lesser God*, Luis Valdez's *Zoot Suit*, and Tony Kushner's *Angels in America*). It brings in performers for each show and negotiates each contract individually. With "a mission to create a home for leading theatre artists from around the world to develop their work," Houston's Alley Theatre only accepts new scripts when submitted by an agent, offers various internships (some with a $200/week stipend), and presents the possibility of college credit. Edward Albee joins the Alley Theatre annually. This guide is a must for the theater professional.—**Colby H. Kullman**

1153. **Summer Theatre Directory 1996: A National Guide to Summer Employment for Professionals and Students....** Jill Charles, Debra J. Bromley, and Gene Sirotof, comps. and eds. Dorset, Vt., Theatre Directories, 1996. 148p. index. $15.95pa. ISBN 0-933919-32-8. ISSN 0884-5840.

An attractive, helpful listing of opportunities in summer stock, this 1996 directory offers an abundance of information for performers, musicians, directors, designers, technicians, administrators, civic planners, employment agencies, parents, tour guides, and vacationers. Opening with an upbeat list of 10 reasons to apply to summer theater companies, the volume intersperses a batch of advertisements between front matter and the table of contents and in the end matter. A key explains the format for each entry, including name and address, union and company names, season length, facilities, hiring practices, transportation and housing, application requirements, apprenticeships and internships, and a narrative description. Arranged by state, as indicated by a running head labeled with the two-letter postal codes, the text includes specific shows and spectacles, such as *Horn in the West*, *Hersheypark Entertainment*, *Boston Children's Theater*, and *Six Flags over Texas*.

The editors of this guide to summer stock expand opportunities in the continental United States with a short list of cruise lines, nonequity tours, and combined auditions. Appendixes offer information on finding the right summer experience and tips on auditioning, callbacks, and agencies. A meager index lists theaters only. For what it aims to provide, the compendium is an appropriate purchase for public and school libraries, especially in areas rich with talented young people looking for summer outlets. The editors clearly label each entry with fees, catalog sources, and the desired age and experience of applicants. Editors could enhance entries with more fax and e-mail listings.—**Mary Ellen Snodgrass**

Handbooks and Yearbooks

1154. *The New York Times* **Theater Reviews. Volume 28: 1993-1994.** New York, Times Books and Garland, 1996. 553p. illus. index. $165.00. ISBN 0-8153-0644-X.

Volume 28 of a series, this compilation contains high-quality photo-facsimile reproductions of every theater review that appeared in *The New York Times* during 1993 and 1994. A puzzling aspect of the series is why it takes so long for the compilation to come out in book form. The two-year lapse makes it a little disappointing to peruse a new book and read a review about the opening on Broadway of *Sunset Boulevard* long after the fact.

Therefore, in regarding this volume strictly as a reference source, it is appropriate to look for the required tools necessary in making it effective as such. The work is fairly complete with three alphabetic indexes: the play title index (productions reviewed more than once receive multiple listings and foreign plays are listed under both English- and foreign-language titles); the personal names index, listing every name appearing in the credits (e.g., playwrights, directors, producers, choreographers, composers, and actors); and the corporate name index, providing access to groups and corporate bodies mentioned in reviews or involved in productions. Another section lists awards and prizes given during 1993 and 1994. In going through this in-depth source, one is reminded of just how many theater productions are offered each year. The volume also reaffirms how vulnerable and short-lived the majority of these productions are—a sad commentary on the state of the play in today's culture.

The strongest asset of this volume is that it is part of a series. Although looked upon as an orphan by itself, it serves as an extension to an enormous and invaluable source of theater history (the series began in 1870). The series and this particular volume will best serve university and college libraries as well as large public libraries with an extensive theater section. Naturally, if a library already possesses the series, this latest volume is a must acquisition. If not, volume 28 would be a good place to start.

—**Joan Garner**

Indexes

1155. **Theatrical Design in the Twentieth Century: An Index to Photographic Reproductions of Scenic Designs.** W. Patrick Atkinson, comp. Westport, Conn., Greenwood Press, 1996. 475p. (Bibliographies and Indexes in the Performing Arts, no.21). $95.00. ISBN 0-313-29701-0.

Many scenic designers, directors, theater historians, and avid theater buffs have often wondered what a particular historical or no-longer-available production looked like. The invention of photography and the development of graphic printing techniques have now made it possible to view scenic representations of these long-gone presentations. This reference allows such information-seekers to consult resources that will provide them with graphic answers to their questions. The author has compiled a set of references (to more than 7,000 productions) that provide a combination of photographs, drawings, or model renderings of past productions. The citations are restricted to twentieth-century theater and opera presentations. The references were culled from 114 books and journals likely to be held in a research library. The emphasis is on English-language productions, but a fair amount of foreign designers and their works are included.

This reference work commences with a reference notation code that provides a code name for each of the available sources of information (e.g., TCI stands for *Theatre Crafts International*). The next section is an alphabetic list of productions, giving the name of the designer; the production company; the production site and dates; the type of graphic material (e.g., black-and-white photographs); and detailed reference bibliographic information (i.e., where to find the materials including reference source, date of publication, pages, and the like). The last portion of the book is a stage designer index. Each designer's production and bibliographic information is presented. This reference work is unique and a boon to all theater personnel. It will save people many hours of work and will repay its usage handsomely. [R: Choice, Dec 96, p. 585]—**Charles Neuringer**

28 Philosophy and Religion

PHILOSOPHY

Bibliography

1156. Nordquist, Joan, comp. **Martin Heidegger (II): A Bibliography.** Santa Cruz, Calif., Reference and Research Services, 1996. 80p. index. (Social Theory: A Bibliographic Series, no.42). $15.00pa. ISBN 0-937855-83-9.

This work supplements Nordquist's previous bibliography on Heidegger (*Martin Heidegger: A Bibliography* [see ARBA 91, entry 1402]). It is a selective bibliography of the critical literature on Heidegger in English since 1989. The first section enumerates critical articles and reviews of, respectively, books written by or about Heidegger in English and in German, as well as critical articles on essays written by Heidegger. The second section lists books written about Heidegger in English since 1989. It also provides a list of bibliographies compiled since that time. The third and final section lists articles in books about Heidegger. It should be made clear that this bibliography does not include a list of journal articles on Heidegger. Its use is entirely to be found in the admirable job it does in analyzing books written about Heidegger and in providing access to the reviews and critical articles composed about those specific works. One must go elsewhere for a comprehensive bibliography (i.e., one that includes a list of citations to the bulk of the journal literature). The work could greatly benefit from a more sophisticated desktop publishing system; the typography leaves much to be desired. Nonetheless, the bibliography is recommended for graduate collections in philosophy and continental social theory.—**Mark Cyzyk**

1157. Schaberg, William H. **The Nietzsche Canon: A Publication History and Bibliography.** Chicago, University of Chicago Press, 1995. 281p. index. $36.50. ISBN 0-226-73575-3.

Scholars delving into *The Nietzsche Canon* may want to begin with the short epilogue in which Schaberg refers to it as a "bibliobiography," a designation befitting his intention of examining the relationship between Nietzsche and his publications. *The Nietzsche Canon* is developed in two parts. In the first part, Schaberg recounts in chronological order and in meticulous detail the history of Nietzsche's publications. The text is laced with numerous references, cited in the endnotes. In addition, other references elucidating the text or identifying a person appear in footnotes.

The annotated bibliography comprises the second, and much shorter, part—only 36 pages. This is preceded by a discussion of previous scholarship on Nietzsche's publications; in particular, the bibliographic studies done by Richard Krummel, Karl Jacoby, and Rolf Zimmerman, all of whose work is, in Schaberg's judgment, less detailed and less complete than his own. Schaberg notes omissions of the most minute detail, especially in the bibliographies by Krummel and Zimmerman. Now, scholars may well debate how successfully Schaberg interprets the biographical relationship between Nietzsche and his publications. This contribution to Nietzsche studies belongs in research collections and in libraries with extensive holdings on this important nineteenth-century writer and philosopher. [R: Choice, June 96, p. 1623]
—**Bernice Bergup**

Biography

1158. **Biographical Dictionary of Twentieth-Century Philosophers.** Stuart Brown, Diane Collinson, and Robert Wilkinson, eds. New York, Routledge, 1996. 947p. index. $150.00. ISBN 0-415-06043-5.

With this volume, Routledge has published another well-organized, useful reference work in philosophy. The work is arranged alphabetically by name and contains more than 1,000 signed entries. The term *philosopher*, as the preface states, is construed broadly and is not limited to the Anglo-American world—"[A] dominant principle used in compiling the list of entries has been to consider for inclusion those thinkers regarded as philosophers in the communities and cultures to which they belong." The result is a comprehensive and interesting collection of brief biographical entries for philosophers the world over.

Entries are short (rarely more than two pages and often just a paragraph or two in length) and are composed of birth and death dates, a brief indication of philosophical interests, education, philosophical influences, professional appointments, primary publications, secondary publications, and a list of sources used in compiling the entry. In addition to main biographical entries, there is a concise "Guide to Schools and Movements," as well as indexes for nationality, philosophical categories, philosophical interests, influences, names, and subjects. The dictionary is recommended for both academic and public libraries as a good general source of biographical information in philosophy. [R: Choice, Dec 96, p. 586; LJ, Sept 96, p. 166]

—Mark Cyzyk

Dictionaries and Encyclopedias

1159. **The Cambridge Dictionary of Philosophy.** Robert Audi, ed. New York, Cambridge University Press, 1995. 882p. index. $89.95; $27.95pa. ISBN 0-521-40224-7; 0-521-48328-Xpa.

Put simply, after the venerable *Encyclopedia of Philosophy* (see ARBA 75, entry 1237), the next reference work in philosophy that every library should own is *The Cambridge Dictionary of Philosophy*. International in scope, the dictionary contains more than 4,000 signed entries from "Abderites" to "Zoroastrianism." The entries are well written, concise, understandable, and eminently authoritative; the list of editorial advisors and 381 contributors to the dictionary reads like a "who's who" in late twentieth-century philosophy.

Most entries are in the 500- to 1,000-word range, but several longer discussions (up to 5,000 words in length) are included as well. These longer entries mainly survey large subfields of philosophy, such as ethics, logic, or aesthetics, and cover developments in those disciplines up to the present. The relative inexpensiveness of the paperback version of this dictionary makes it an attractive purchase. As the editor notes in his preface, the hope was to compile a comprehensive and authoritative dictionary of philosophical concepts, terms, schools, and thinkers—one that would supersede all others. The work accomplishes that goal, and is therefore highly recommended for all libraries. [R: Choice, Feb 96, p. 924; RBB, 1 Feb 96, pp. 950-51]—**Mark Cyzyk**

1160. **The Encyclopedia of Philosophy Supplement.** Donald M. Borchert, ed. New York, Macmillan Library Reference/Simon & Schuster Macmillan, 1996. 775p. index. $125.00. ISBN 0-02-864629-0.

For the past 30 years, *The Encyclopedia of Philosophy*, first published in 1967 and reprinted in 1973 (see ARBA 75, entry 1237), has been the cornerstone of the philosophy reference section in most public and academic libraries. Although still a valuable tool, the encyclopedia does not reflect the last three decades of scholarship in philosophy. For example, such influential minds as Noam Chomsky and Thomas Kuhn did not appear in the original publication. Furthermore, new subfields of philosophical inquiry, such as feminist philosophy, originated after 1967.

Rather than completely revise the original multivolume set, Macmillan Library Reference elected to publish a one-volume supplement to the 1967 original. To achieve systematic updating, the editors have included summary articles on all of the major subfields in philosophy, such as aesthetics and logic. Each summary discusses significant contributions made since the 1950s. For students who want to go beyond summaries of subfields, the editors wisely include break-out articles that discuss in greater detail specific topics within a subfield. A useful outline at the front of the book lists the subfields and their respective break-out articles. In addition to the summary and break-out entries are articles on special topics, such as African philosophy and naturalism and biographies of influential philosophers.

Patterned after the original set, the supplement contains articles by scholars from around the world. Each piece is signed and concludes with a bibliography and *see also* references, when appropriate. The supplement's cumulative index supersedes the original index. Libraries that own the original set will want to buy this reasonably priced supplement. [R: Choice, Dec 96, p. 589; RBB, 1 Oct 96, p. 368]

—**John P. Stierman**

1161. **An Encyclopedia of War and Ethics.** Donald A. Wells, ed. Westport, Conn., Greenwood Press, 1996. 539p. index. $95.00. ISBN 0-313-29116-0.

War and ethics, some maintain, have no connection. Interestingly, that extreme position is scarcely discussed in this encyclopedia, although it is mentioned in the article on just war and represented by a half-page on Niccolò Machiavelli. At the opposite extreme, absolute pacifism—the position that engagement in war is always immoral—receives rather more attention, along with weaker versions of pacifism and organized efforts to promote peace. Mainly, however, this reference work focuses on principles and practices on both sides of the traditional distinction between *jus ad bellum* (justifications for going to war) and *jus in bello* (moral constraints governing the conduct of warfare).

Topics include important concepts and terms (e.g., attempts to define aggression, the combatant-noncombatant distinction, intentionality and double effect); key documents and cases (the 1949 Geneva Conventions, the Red Cross Draft Rules for Civilian Protection, the Nuremberg Trials); major thinkers on war and morality (Jane Addams, Carl von Clausewitz, Meng-tzu); the perspectives of major religious, philosophical, and ideological traditions (Christianity, Hinduism, Maoism); specific techniques, methods, and instruments of warfare that raise special issues (fragmentation bombs, guerrilla warfare, incendiaries, nuclear war); notorious breaches or alleged breaches of moral conduct in war (the Holocaust, the My Lai incident, war crimes in former Yugoslavia); and collateral phenomena of warfare and their ethical dimensions (collateral damage, conscription, environmental effects, prisoners of war).

An additional category worth special mention is that of specific wars or quasi-wars, for example, the Arab-Israeli Wars of 1948-1972 or the invasion of Grenada. Entries in this category are confined to post-World War II events, mostly involving the United States. Although the (presumed) intention to relate theoretical and historical material to recent events is admirable, the results often display a loss of thematic focus. For instance, an article on the Korean War discusses in some depth the questions of who started it and motives for U.S. involvement, but the specific ethical issues at stake are never made explicit. Similar comments apply to articles on the Bay of Pigs incident and on Haiti. Treatment of the U.S. military occupation of Okinawa is rich in detail on its historical circumstances and the occupation's effects, but thin on explicit examination of the ethical issues. This example also calls attention to the lack of a general article on occupation: What issues it raises and what principles might justify or circumscribe it. This is one of several regrettable omissions. Other missing entries include revolution and civil war, each of which surely raises special questions. On the whole, however, this is a solid and helpful resource, as the list of contributors and their credentials—nearly four dozen scholars with several hundred relevant publications to their collective credit—should lead one to expect. [R: Choice, Sept 96, pp. 96-98; RBB, 15 Sept 96, p. 283]—**Hans E. Bynagle**

1162. Glock, Hans-Johann. **A Wittgenstein Dictionary.** Cambridge, Mass., Blackwell, 1996. 405p. index. (The Blackwell Philosopher Dictionaries). $54.95; $21.95pa. ISBN 0-631-18112-1; 0-631-18537-2pa.

To do justice to this review, the wary reviewer would write it in something akin to mathematical symbols, *à la* one of Ludwig Wittgenstein's most famous works, *Tractatus Logico-Philosophicus*. Yet to be true to the zeitgeist would be to make this review unreadable. While Wittgenstein is the philosopher extraordinaire when it comes to meaning, the upshot of his work borders on the inscrutable.

Glock has fashioned something of an intellectual map for navigating the strange oceans of thought in Wittgenstein. The work is less a dictionary (it contains fewer than 80 terms) than it is an explication of terms. Following an engaging bit of intellectual biography, the reader is faced with the dictionary, wherein terms are measured in the number of pages instead of words. While most entries do not exceed six pages, it places something of a burden on the cataloger to determine if this is really a reference or more a companion reader to Wittgenstein's work.

Glock has managed a tool that is more apt to be used by scholars in philosophy, and especially by those engaged in research on language and meaning. It is likely to seem limited to use by others. At times Glock wades into interpretative waters on controversial terms, but the dictionary is so generously filled with cross-references to Wittgenstein's works, contrarians will be able to see it for themselves. The work is suitable for comprehensive libraries and libraries specializing in philosophy. [R: Choice, July/Aug 96, p. 1772]—**Mark Y. Herring**

1163. Hester, Joseph P. **Encyclopedia of Values and Ethics.** Santa Barbara, Calif., ABC-CLIO, 1996. 376p. index. $60.00. ISBN 0-87436-857-X.

Hester claims to have written this book "to illuminate the belief systems of the American people." The book does indeed discuss some 400 topics, covering terms, movements, leaders, controversies, events, and organizations in the United States today. Each topic has a short list of books for anyone who wants further information on the subject, and entries are cross-referenced. In addition, the book contains a glossary, a bibliography, and a subject index to assist readers in locating information. Hester's writing style is clear and understandable, but this book hardly represents the beliefs of the American people any more than the Christian Right represents all Christians. The book illuminates Hester's position on many issues and controversies, but its title does not really explain what is in the book. For example, such subjects as charity, tolerance, trustworthiness, generosity, violence, and nonviolence are not discussed in the book. Alcoholism and Alcoholics Anonymous, on the other hand, are discussed, and it is difficult to discern what ethical concerns back their inclusion. Subjects such as divorce are included, not to discuss some ethical concern, but to explain Hester's belief that no-fault divorce has added to the breakdown of the family. While this is an interesting discussion of various topics, it is not a useful reference book on ethical subjects.—**Kay Mariea**

1164. Lacey, A. R. **A Dictionary of Philosophy.** 3d ed. New York, Routledge, 1996. 386p. $15.95pa. ISBN 0-415-13332-7.

This pocket encyclopedia of philosophy is designed "with a bias towards explaining terminology" for nonspecialists. It offers 66 new entries, with many others substantially rewritten or revised and updated from the two earlier editions. Bibliographies have been updated as well. Most of this book is devoted to explaining common terms and ideas as philosophers use them, along with giving descriptions of the major schools of philosophy and the most important open questions and problems associated with them. Thus, readers interested in understanding what philosophers mean when using such ordinary words as *confirmation*, *entailment*, *truth*, and so forth will find this a useful resource. Less attention is devoted to individual philosophers and their works, although approximately 80 of the most important or best-known philosophers are included. Emphasis is given more to metaphysics, epistemology, and philosophical logic than to ethics, politics, or aesthetics.

Anyone wanting a concise description of what philosophers mean by such terms as *propositional calculus*, *hermeneutics*, *entelechy* (as used in particular by Aristotle and Gottfried Leibniz), *Godel's theorem pragmatics*, *a priori knowledge*, *Zeno's paradoxes*, and *the Vienna circle*, for example, will find brief descriptions and a useful bibliography here. From Pierre Abelard to zombies, in nearly 400 pages, this dictionary is any reader's best handbook for a quick understanding of unfamiliar, complicated, or ambiguous philosophical terminology.—**Joseph W. Dauben**

1165. Martinich, A. P. **A Hobbes Dictionary.** Cambridge, Mass., Blackwell, 1995. 336p. index. (The Blackwell Philosopher Dictionaries). $59.95; $22.95pa. ISBN 0-631-19261-1; 0-631-19262-Xpa.

Another in the series Blackwell Philosopher Dictionaries, this tool follows the same format of expansive clarifications, éclaircissements, elucidations, and expanded commentary. Martinich's work is anything but solitary, poor, nasty, brutish, or short. If no other reason can come to mind to buy this tool, the 18-page introduction, "Thomas Hobbes in Stuart England," should provide incentive enough. Provocatively written in clear and concise prose, the essay sets the intellectual and sociological tone for Hobbes's work. While people are not made by their environments, they are ineluctably shaped by them, and such pieces as this one provide a marvelous curative for the forgetful.

The entry portion of the dictionary of fewer than 150 terms provides lengthy discussions of Hobbes's often complex meanings. Martinich sought to answer three questions about each term: How, where, and why did Hobbes use the term in question? The dictionary will be useful to scholars who may need some memory goad, and to students who, whether they realize it or not, are in desperate need of clarification, regardless of how often they have seen *Bill and Ted's Excellent Adventure*. Filled with learning and panache, the volume, with its accessibility and its expansive index, should be found in most libraries. [R: Choice, May 96, p. 1454]—**Mark Y. Herring**

1166.   **The Oxford Companion to Philosophy.** Ted Honderich, ed. New York, Oxford University Press, 1995. 1009p. illus. index. $49.95. ISBN 0-19-866132-0.

The field of general philosophical dictionaries has become crowded of late. Within the past seven years, at least seven new English-language entrants have appeared, and at least four new editions of older works. Honderich's recent addition to the distinguished Oxford Companion series stands out in this crowd as the leading contender for the title "best and most broadly useful single-volume dictionary of philosophy in English," although it faces a tough competitor in the virtually contemporaneous *Cambridge Dictionary of Philosophy*, edited by Robert Audi (see entry 1159).

No similar work since Jonathan Ree and J. O. Urmson's *Concise Encyclopedia of Western Philosophy and Philosophers* (3d ed., Chapman & Hall, 1990) has elicited the involvement of quite so many eminent figures in contemporary philosophy, including Isaiah Berlin, Ronald Dworkin, Paul Feyerabend, Alasdair MacIntyre, W. V. Quine, Anthony Quinton, Nicholas Rescher, John Searle, and Peter Singer, to pick out just a few of many prominent names among the more than 200 contributors. Collectively, these contributors do represent an overwhelming orientation toward Anglo-American philosophy—not surprising in a work coming from Oxford University Press—which is also manifested in the relatively generous representation of entries on living English-speaking philosophers and in the tone and substance of some of the articles on non-Anglo-American topics.

Nonetheless, the *Companion* ranges at some level over all of the world's major philosophical systems and traditions, Eastern and Western, historical and contemporary. It includes, for example, a survey article on continental philosophy as well as separate entries for various recent and contemporary continental figures (e.g., Jacques Derrida, Luce Irigaray); schools (Frankfurt School, poststructuralism); and concepts (*différance*, hermeneutic circle); along with those representing the older continental strains of phenomenology and existentialism. As for Eastern thought, the combined index and list of entries at the back of the volume (highly useful for cross-referencing) reveals a total of 58 entries relating to Chinese, Indian, Japanese, and Islamic philosophies. (Coverage of non-Western philosophy is somewhat more detailed in the *Cambridge Dictionary*, but Audi offsets this small advantage over the *Companion* by his exclusion of living philosophers in any tradition.)

There are also, of course, the predictable entries for major branches, figures, concepts, terms, and controversies of Western philosophy, and a few unpredictable ones as well, such as "brain in a vat," "deaths of philosophers," and "nothing so absurd" (from a remark of Cicero's). Other noteworthy features of this companion include brief bibliographies accompanying most entries; portraits of major philosophers; a chronological table; 15 diagrams of philosophical domains, positions, or theories (e.g., philosophy of mind, rationalism); and a table of logical symbols. [R: Choice, Jan 96, p. 764]

—**Hans E. Bynagle**

RELIGION

General Works

Atlases

1167. Colin, Wilson. **The Atlas of Holy Places and Sacred Sites.** New York, DK Publishing, 1996. 192p. illus. maps. index. $29.95. ISBN 0-7894-1051-6.

Beautifully presented and lavishly illustrated, this atlas of 100 of the world's sacred sites is an interesting introductory volume. The 20 maps in the gazetteer that locate an additional 1,000 sites are more comprehensive and useful, but are treated with less consideration. The question of audience is crucial to this book. For the young student or general reader, this volume would be a colorful and enticing entrance into further study. For the serious scholar, the work lacks depth and rigor.

In the first section, which is the largest, "paranormal" and "traditional" sites are given equal attention. The explanatory captions are often speculation presented as fact. For example, the hypothesis, considered controversial by scholars, that the pyramids are replicating the constellation Orion here is simply stated as actuality. All of the descriptive sites are weighed equally and lack principles of selection.

Of far more value to the serious student is the smaller section entitled the gazetteer. In it each of the 1,000 sites are located, placed in a brief historical context, described in religious terms, and cross-referenced to other sections of the gazetteer and to the front section of the volume. The perspective gained by these maps gives a valuable angle on the development and interactions of religions in specific areas.—**Linda L. Lam-Easton**

Bibliography

1168. Feuerhahn, Ronald R. **Hermann Sasse: A Bibliography.** Lanham, Md., Scarecrow, 1995. 243p. index. (ATLA Bibliography Series, no.37). $40.00. ISBN 0-8108-2969-X.

Hermann Sasse was a German theologian and Lutheran pastor who, like Karl Barth, came of age theologically during World War I. The liberal Protestant theology of his teachers fell apart because of the war, and he was able to find God's presence by meditating on Luther and his "theology of the cross." Later, Sasse joined with Barth and other theologians in creating the Barmen Declaration in opposition to National Socialism in Germany, but did not sign the final document. He was forbidden to travel from Germany and was persecuted heavily during his career. He later emigrated to Australia, where he retired in 1965. As this (200-plus-page) bibliography shows, the fact that Sasse did not achieve the notoriety of Barth or Paul Johannes Tillich was not due to a lack of work on his part. Feuerhahn's present work, and a biography by him due out soon, may well change Sasse's historical fortunes.

This bibliography is well constructed and thought out. It is arranged chronologically and cuts off with 1994 publications. The bibliography distinguishes between published and unpublished works, and tracks various editions and reprints. The work could use more of an explanation of its numbering system and how that integrates with the short-title index, but intrepid researchers will puzzle it out on their own. This work is suitable for theological collections and research collections in religion.—**Bob Craigmile**

1169. Fischer, Clare B. **Of Spirituality: A Feminist Perspective.** Lanham, Md., American Theological Library Association and Scarecrow, 1995. 279p. index. (ATLA Bibliography Series, no.35). $49.50. ISBN 0-8108-3006-X.

Fischer's bibliography is a compilation of materials focusing on feminist spirituality. The more than 1,800 entries are divided into 12 subject chapters, each containing 2 or more subdivisions. The subjects range from women's ministry and spiritual practice to global community.

The subject chapters begin with a one-half- to two-page introduction followed by the unannotated list of books. A cross-check with *Books in Print* and WorldCat revealed several errors in the entries, generally in the copyright date or number of pages. Fischer does not use *see* references or a subject index to help readers locate materials that cover more than one subject area. An author index, however, is included. The final chapter of the book lists journals, publishers, and centers dealing with feminist or spirituality issues.

In the introduction, Fischer mentions Anne Carson's two bibliographies in this same subject area, *Feminist Spirituality and the Feminine Divine* (see ARBA 87, entry 848) and *Goddesses & Wise Women: The Literature of Feminist Spirituality* (see ARBA 93, entry 923). What Fischer fails to mention is what differentiates the scope of her work from Carson's works. In general, Carson's books contain more titles in the areas of fiction/fantasy literature and witchcraft. Fischer includes more titles on cultural politics. She also concentrates on book titles, whereas Carson includes many periodical articles and audiovisual materials.

The less than thorough editing, while distracting, does not subtract from the usefulness of Fischer's work. Including annotated titles and subject indexes, however, would have helped this bibliography become an even more useful title. [R: Choice, Sept. 96, p. 98]—**Laura K. Blessing**

1170. Johnson, Dale A. **Women and Religion in Britain and Ireland: An Annotated Bibliography from the Reformation to 1993.** Lanham, Md., Scarecrow, 1995. 288p. index. (ATLA Bibliography Series, no.39). $37.50. ISBN 0-8108-3063-9.

This annotated bibliography contains more than 1,000 entries of secondary information sources on women and religion in Great Britain and Ireland over a span of nearly 500 years. The author has chosen a wide scope for the purpose of displaying a "broader and more synthetic view of women in religion," which could provide greater context. This bibliography supports and expands his earlier work, *Women in English Religion, 1700-1925* (Edwin Mellen Press, 1984), which contains selections from primary source material. Among sources included in the bibliography under review are monographs, journal articles, denominational reports, and essays in multivolume works and anthologies. The annotations for most entries are up to eight lines in length and primarily consist of brief descriptions of a source's scope or arrangement. A few entries evaluate treatment. Many entries are actually citation listings without annotation. This seems to be done when the subject is narrow, such as a list given for autobiographical narratives by deaconesses.

The table of contents is the best guide to the book and contains chronological division and subject organization. For the best results, users will need to scan all the subtopics within a chapter before attempting to locate information in the book. A good tactic in many searches, scanning is necessary here because there is not any obvious order to the subtopics within the broader chronological division. Additionally, there are a number of catchall groups within chapters that create problems in finding information. For example, a user looking for an entry on Christina Rossetti would need to determine the right chronological period. Next, the user may assume that he or she could find the entry under the "Literary Studies" heading. When no entry is found here, the user will have to flip through a few sections to locate the lengthy article on Rossetti in "Individuals." Sometimes "Others" is used as a topic heading, and "Individuals" is omitted. Readers are advised to take a little extra time scanning the entire work. Searching for a specific person may require some guessing, but there are aids in other forms. Johnson's bibliography provides an index by author and editor, as well as an index of collections with multiple entries. The citations appear in clear, consistent form.

In the introduction, Johnson acknowledges the difficulty of choosing sources for a broad project. Indeed, it would be difficult not to omit or underrepresent topics in a single-volume work covering 500 years. Despite the selection difficulties facing Johnson, and the aforementioned access problems, he has produced a valuable and informative resource for academic libraries supporting humanities and social science collections and programs in religious and women's studies. Browsing this bibliography is a good way for students to make connections between religious, social, political, and cultural topics. Libraries supporting theological schools may use the bibliography more extensively.—**Sandra E. Fuentes**

1171. Lippy, Charles H. **Modern American Popular Religion: A Critical Assessment and Annotated Bibliography.** Westport, Conn., Greenwood Press, 1996. 250p. index. (Bibliographies and Indexes in Religious Studies, no.37). $69.50. ISBN 0-313-27786-9.

Popular religion is an elusive term, somewhat like *civil religion*, which scholars have difficulty pinpointing. While generally agreeing that it is something apart from established religious institutions and formal theology, something that enables ordinary people to make sense of their daily lives, they disagree on almost everything else. Is it "folk religion," resting upon magic and superstition and appealing to society's economically disadvantaged? Is it "common religion," consisting of widely held beliefs and practices that lie outside formal religious channels? Or is it "invisible religion," something not easily identified at all? Lippy, a scholar thoroughly familiar with all the nuances, appreciates the complexity of the subject, as is evidence by this excellent bibliography.

Containing 559 annotated entries of articles, essays, books, theses, and dissertations, this work spans U.S. history from ca.1870 to the present. Nine of its eleven chapters treat different facets of *popular religiosity* (the term Lippy prefers to popular religion)—such as evangelicalism and fundamentalism, radio and television ministries, self-help and inspirational literature, biographical works, and the ethnic dimension. An alphabetic list of studies is subsumed under each major heading, and all this material is made readily accessible by the inclusion of thorough author, title, and subject indexes. This is not an exhaustive bibliography. The literature is vast, and Lippy is highly selective. He chooses for the most part secondary materials, and then primarily those of an interpretive nature. This study will be useful to students and scholars, and college and university libraries should add it to their reference collections. [R: Choice, Sept 96, p. 102]—**John W. Storey**

1172. McKim, Mark G. **Emil Brunner: A Bibliography.** Lanham, Md., Scarecrow, 1996. 98p. index. (ATLA Bibliographies, no.40). $35.00. ISBN 0-8108-3167-8.

Emil Brunner (1889-1966) was a Swiss contemporary of German theologian Karl Barth (1886-1968). While they differed on particular theological points, they cofounded the school of thought known as "neoorthodox" or "Barthian." The nature of truth formed the central question of Brunner's theology. A powerful and lucid writer, Brunner wanted Christians and skeptics alike to better understand the meaning of the gospel. His writings, therefore, are more accessible than Barth's for the general reader.

McKim's introduction summarizes Brunner's life and thought and discusses his views on truth, faith, revelation and reason, and Christ. The bibliography lists more than 600 works by Brunner that show his keen interest in social, economic, and political issues. Included among the 198 secondary sources are books, dissertations, and journal articles. Most sources are in English, but some German-language publications are listed. A helpful subject index to Brunner's major works is provided.

Brunner's writings are in no way outdated. He clearly explicates the unchanging message of Christ and shows its relevance to the "enlightened" scientific age. This bibliography is recommended for all theological and most academic libraries.—**Gary D. Barber**

1173. Wardin, Albert W., Jr. **Evangelical Sectarianism in the Russian Empire and the USSR: A Bibliographic Guide.** Lanham, Md., American Theological Library Association and Scarecrow, 1995. 867p. index. (ATLA Bibliography Series, no.36). $90.00. ISBN 0-8108-2926-6.

Since 1974, the American Theological Library Association (ATLA), in conjunction with Scarecrow, has been doing its best to corner the bibliographies-to-religion-book market, admittedly a small corner of the religious studies world. Adding to the intriguing variety of volumes already published is *Evangelical Sectarianism in the Russian Empire and the USSR*, edited by Wardin, a former professor of history at Belmont University (Nashville, Tennessee). In this bibliography, he delineates *evangelical sectarianism* to mean fundamentalist Protestant individuals and movements that adhere to American-style evangelical norms (believers baptism, revivalism, disciplined Christian lifestyle, and the like). This excludes mainline territorial churches (Orthodox, Catholic, Protestant) and groups, such as Jehovah's Witnesses and Seventh-Day Adventists.

The bibliographic guide covers nearly everything, from the earliest impact of Western Pietism/ evangelicalism on Russian history (1693-1695), to a plethora of missionary doctrine/ideology/worship to such projects as outreach to border territories adjoining the Soviet Union or bringing the USSR to Christ and Marxist critique thereto. The book is divided into three epochal sections, each containing a bird's-eye view of the period. Annotated entries from 17 languages (although mainly in Russian, English, and German) are arranged topically, and the helpful cross-references allow the user to skip, detour, and revisit earlier or later material. This guide is an indispensable source for a little-known chapter in Russian Church history.—**Zev Garber**

Biography

1174. **The Penguin Dictionary of Saints.** 3d ed. By Donald Attwater, with Catherine Rachel John. New York, Penguin Books, 1995. 381p. $13.95pa. ISBN 0-14-051312-4.

This dictionary lists known religious saints. Information includes classification of saints (martyr, confessor, and so on); date of existence; their circumstances in becoming a saint; and their feast day. It also provides a glossary and lists of further reading, some patron saints, some emblems that identify specific saints, and feast days in the order that they arrive within the calendar year.

The 1st edition of this dictionary was published in 1965. The cover is much nicer on this new edition, and some of the text in the front matter (although questionable in necessity and contribution) has been revised. More recently recognized saints have been included in the 3d edition. Also, most significant, a section has been added listing patron saints. This is a nice addition that enhances the overall value of the source.

As in most dictionaries, the data are presented in a straightforward, dry format. Color and character of these intriguing individuals will need to be provided by the interpreter. Yet this dictionary of saints is complete and easy-to-use for quick reference and research. It is also reasonably priced for all reference libraries on a budget.—**Joan Garner**

1175. **Who's Who in Theology and Science: An International Biographical and Bibliographical Guide....** 1996 ed. Compiled by the John Templeton Foundation. New York, Continuum Publishing, 1996. 713p. index. $59.50. ISBN 0-8264-0874-5.

This guide contains four directories and five indexes, all designed to direct users to individuals, organizations, and publications "active in the dialogue between religion and science, or between religion, spirituality, and faith on the one hand, and science and technology . . . on the other." Directory A, consisting of 465 pages, lists individuals publishing in the field, about 30 percent of whom reside in the United States. Each entry provides a basic résumé, listing current addresses, educational history, positions held, and areas of interest, along with selected publications. Directory B is limited to individuals actively interested in the field and runs slightly less than 100 pages. Additional directories are devoted to organizations, journals, and newsletters. The book ends with a brief description of John Marks Templeton, founder and trustee of the John Templeton Foundation, which underwrote publication of this book. His statement, "The Theology of Humility," is also reprinted. The John Templeton Foundation is devoted primarily to furthering research and publication by scientists "related to the creative and purposive activities of God."

The major shortcoming of this directory is that it includes only individuals who responded to a questionnaire circulated by the foundation. Thus, the only information provided is that solicited from individuals who wished to be included in this "who's who." Consequently, many scholars who have actively studied and contributed to the field of science and religion are noticeably absent. Still, as a reference work for anyone interested in this subject in general, but with no other resources at hand, this guide is a helpful starting-place from which to begin a search for more detailed information concerning individuals and organizations interested in the subject of science and theology, broadly conceived.—**Joseph W. Dauben**

Dictionaries and Encyclopedias

1176. **Angels A to Z.** By James R. Lewis and Evelyn Dorothy Oliver. Kelle S. Sisung, ed. Detroit, Gale, 1996. 485p. illus. index. $49.95. ISBN 0-7876-0489-5.

Angels A to Z is a bibliography that packs in fewer pages more information than could be found elsewhere on the subject. Beginning with a detailed introduction about angels, the authors tell readers what angels are and what they are not. Specifically, they are not reincarnated humans, but a separate order of creation. They are messengers of God, errand runners of God, and they interfere in human life for good or evil (remember Satan is an angel, too). The authors write briefly on the history of angels; they first showed up in Persia ca.1000 B.C.E. in the Zoroastrian religion. They migrated to Judaism, and on to Christianity and finally Islam. Primarily members of monotheistic religions, their counterparts can be found in polytheism as demigods, such as "devas." Fairies also fall into this class, but Christianity rejected fairies because they were usually seen as neutral. Angels in the New Age movement are also discussed.

Entries are arranged alphabetically with boldfaced words to indicate related entries. Each entry is well annotated with sources. Sidebars include trivia on famous people, ideas, concepts, and sightings. Black-and-white illustrations, some of famous paintings, are liberally spread throughout the book, usually close to the subject entry. Subjects range from angels' names and what they are known for to television and movie angels. Angels in the arts (architecture and painting) and the meaning of words (*demon* comes from the Greek word *daemon*, meaning soul) are also covered. Mark Twain, Joan of Arc, Billy Graham, Michelangelo, and others are discussed in detail.

A substantial bibliography, filmography, and resources (including World Wide Web addresses) are included. An accurate index, which should have explained that boldfaced numbers were main entries and italics were photographs, is also provided. Writers looking for themes and metaphors, students looking for new topics for papers, and general reference libraries will find *Angels A to Z* a useful starting place for further research, as well as a pleasant read. [R: Choice, Oct 96, p. 249; RQ, Summer 96, pp. 545-46]

—**Kevin W. Perizzolo**

1177. **Dictionary of Feminist Theologies.** Letty M. Russell and J. Shannon Clarkson, eds. Louisville, Ky., Westminster/John Knox Press, 1996. 351p. $39.00. ISBN 0-664-22058-4.

Led by an advisory panel from Yale University and throughout the world, more than 175 distinguished scholars contributed signed articles to this dictionary. Reading selectively, users can get an overview of theological concepts from a feminist perspective, and an appreciation of their interdisciplinary nature. A spate of articles focusing on geographic region or ethnic background reflects the diversity of feminist influence and serves as an excellent introduction to the field. Thus, entries survey Asian, European, Jewish, North American, Pacific Island, South Asian, African, and Latin American feminist theologies. Complementing these are articles on various types of theology: contemporary, liberation, evangelical, historical, mujerista, queer, and womanist.

Because entries focus on concepts, there are no biographical entries, although key persons and scholars may be identified in articles as diverse as "ecofeminism," "heterosexism in biblical interpretation," and the "hermeneutics of suspicion," as well as more traditional topics such as "God," "resurrection," "sacraments," and "justice and social change." Because coverage is worldwide and inclusive, there are articles on "yin-yang," "Buddhism," and "African rituals." Entries vary in length depending on content. The language is accessible to the educated layperson, and cross-references to related articles are identified with an asterisk. Short bibliographic references conclude entries, with complete publishing information detailed in the "Bibliography of Works Cited."

This dictionary has much to recommend it to the educated layperson and to the religious professional. Academic librarians may use the bibliography to analyze their holdings in this important interdisciplinary area. [R: RBB, Aug 96, p. 1922]—**Bernice Bergup**

1178. Levinson, David. **Religion: A Cross-Cultural Encyclopedia.** Santa Barbara, Calif., ABC-CLIO, 1996. 288p. illus. maps. index. (Encyclopedias of the Human Experience). $49.50. ISBN 0-87436-865-0.

Religious beliefs are part of all cultures, and some knowledge of those beliefs can help everyone understand each other better. This book, the seventh in the Encyclopedias of the Human Experience series, provides information on 16 of the world's major religions as well as several lesser-known religions. Written in clear, objective, nonjudgmental language, this book discusses doctrines, rituals, superstitions, and beliefs that connect various peoples to their supernatural beings and to each other. Information is organized into 57 entries, some discussing an individual religion, such as Christianity, Islam, Hinduism, and Judaism; other entries are focused on features of beliefs typical of many or most religions, such as the soul, supernatural beings, prayer, and festivals. These more generalized entries include statistical and comparative information and specific examples. All entries have cross-references and short bibliographies for further reading. Front and back matter in the book feature a chronology of world religions, maps showing the locations of various cultures, an extensive bibliography, and a detailed index. This book is an excellent resource for all libraries and for anyone wanting objective information on religion and how religious beliefs affect and express various cultures.—**Kay Mariea**

1179. **A New Dictionary of Religions.** rev. ed. John R. Hinnells, ed. Cambridge, Mass., Blackwell, 1995. 760p. index. $74.95. ISBN 0-631-18139-3.

Just over 10 years after the publication of *The Facts on File Dictionary of Religions* (see ARBA 85, entry 1284), Blackwell has released a revised, expanded edition of that well-received work. The new edition is about 200 pages longer, due in part (thankfully) to a larger typeface. Primarily, however, the increase in size is due to the addition of more than 125 articles, most of which are part of 7 new subject areas: Afro-Caribbean religions, American religions, cross-cultural studies, Gnostics, Iranian religion, Latin American religion, and new religious movements in Japan. Of the remaining articles, many were revised and others were rewritten. Also, the bibliography has been updated significantly. The "Synoptic Index" (which listed the articles under their appropriate subject areas) has been merged with the "List of Contents by Subject Area and Author" and appears at the front of the volume. Finally, the only thing that did not survive from the 1st edition was the section of maps showing the important places mentioned in the text.

Since the publication of the 1st edition of Hinnells's dictionary, several good dictionaries of religion have been published, especially in the past couple of years: *The Continuum Dictionary of Religion* (see ARBA 95, entry 1440), *Larousse Dictionary of Beliefs and Religions* (see ARBA 95, entry 1443), and *The HarperCollins Dictionary of Religion* (1995). As with the 1st edition, *A New Dictionary of Religions* has fewer articles than the other dictionaries (1,400, compared to around 3,000 for each of the others), but they tend to be fuller. Even with its index, which points the reader to names and terms that appear in the articles, this is not the place to dip in for a definition; the other titles serve that purpose better. Therein lies the primary weakness of this work; an example will serve to illustrate. The article "Rajneeshism" uses the term *ashram* without definition, and it is not defined elsewhere in the dictionary. This is certainly a reference work worth having in the collection, but it would be most useful in addition to one or more of the dictionaries rather than in place of them. [R: Choice, May 96, p. 1455]—**Craig W. Beard**

1180. Queen, Edward L., II, Stephen R. Prothero, and Gardiner H. Shattuck Jr. **The Encyclopedia of American Religious History.** New York, Facts on File, 1996. 2v. illus. index. $99.00/set. ISBN 0-8160-2406-5.

This handsomely bound and printed 2-volume encyclopedia includes more than 700 brief articles on people, denominations, organizations, issues, and movements related to religion in the United States. There is a synoptic index that lists articles under 42 broad headings, and a more detailed general index. The articles are well written and accompanied by short bibliographies, as well as occasional black-and-white illustrations.

Three aspects of the work merit special comment. First, while the three principal authors and eight contributors have appropriate academic credentials, the work attempts to cover such a broad range of topics that one wonders why a larger number of contributors was not enlisted. Surely this would have complicated the logistics, but it would also have allowed considerably more expertise to have been brought to bear on the various topics, and for the treatments to have been a bit more analytic than is the case. Second, the broad range of the work and relatively limited size have resulted in a curious selection and arrangement of topics. For example, all Baptist denominations are treated in a single article, while a moderately long article with illustration is devoted to Walt Whitman. It is especially striking that there is no article devoted to religious music or hymnody, especially in light of the critical importance that music and hymnody have played in the development of U.S. religious thought and practice.

Finally, there is the most basic question of all: What does this work contribute to the literature currently available? It is clear that its breadth and currency are among its strongest points, and this may argue for its inclusion in school or public libraries with few other resources devoted to religion in the United States. However, it may be more difficult to argue for its inclusion in seminary, college, and university library collections that have the reference tools listed in its foreword and introduction (e.g., Daniel G. Reid's *Dictionary of Christianity in America* [see ARBA 91, entry 1444]). [R: Choice, July/Aug 96, p. 1776; LJ, Jan 96, p. 90; RBB, 1 Mar 96, p. 108; SLJ, July 96, p. 110]—**M. Patrick Graham**

Directories

1181. **Directory of African American Religious Bodies: A Compendium by the Howard University School of Divinity.** 2d ed. Wardell J. Payne, ed. Washington, D.C., Howard University Press, 1995. 382p. index. $49.95; $29.95pa. ISBN 0-88258-184-8; 0-88258-185-6pa.

The church has exercised considerable influence within the black community. From slavery to civil rights, from Richard Allen to Martin Luther King Jr., it has addressed issues affecting not only blacks but Americans at large. Carried out under the aegis of the Howard University School of Divinity, this excellent compendium covers the growth of organized religion among African Americans from the colonial era to the present. An introductory overview is followed by separate essays on Baptists, Methodists, Pentecostals, and Catholics. Of these, Baptists are by far the most numerous. Of course, this directory runs the gamut of the black religious experience and so in addition to Protestants and Catholics, it includes Jews, Muslims, spiritualists, and practitioners of vodun.

The most extensive segment of the resource is an alphabetic listing of African American religious bodies, beginning with Black Primitive Baptists and concluding with the Yoruba Village of Oyotunji. A historical sketch of the group accompanies each entry. Other sections are considerably briefer, but just as useful, such as the part on religious educational institutions. This section treats not only seminaries and Bible colleges, such as Shaw Divinity School in Raleigh, North Carolina, and Simmons Bible College in Louisville, Kentucky, but also research projects and professional organizations, such as the African American Congregations Project and the Society for the Study of Black Religion. Fortunately, this volume is exhaustively indexed, thereby affording access to an abundance of information. Every college and university library should have this work, for it will be an invaluable asset to students and scholars interested in African American religion.—**John W. Storey**

1182. **World Guide to Religious and Spiritual Organizations 1996.** Edited by the Union of International Associations. New Providence, N.J., K. G. Saur/Reed Reference Publishing, 1996. 471p. index. $375.00. ISBN 3-598-11296-3.

This comprehensive guide details 3,495 associations, orders, fraternities, institutes, networks, and programs whose goal is tied to religious or spiritual concerns. All major world faiths are covered. The editors of this work are to be commended for assiduously ensuring that it be as useful as possible.

There are several innovative indexes that make it nearly impossible not to find the body one is seeking: If the country of the group's headquarters is known, consult the geographic index; if the field of activity is known, consult the subject index, where the organizations have been assigned keywords such as *cybernetics, health care,* and *societal problems*; if the year of foundation is known, the foundation date index lists bodies by the year in which they were founded; or if one has the name of another organization with a formal relationship with the organization wanted, turn to the description of the known organization, where a reference to the organization sought should be found. A typical description includes the body's name (usually in English, but often with foreign names also noted), an address, the date of founding, a description of the body's aims, the structure, financing data, activities, language(s), staff, and membership.

There is an appendix with statistics on membership in religious organizations by type and by country, a list of related reference works, and several other useful tables. This highly organized, detailed, and up-to-date reference source deserves inclusion in most mid- to large-sized reference collections.

—**Jeffrey R. Luttrell**

Handbooks and Yearbooks

1183. **Freedom of Religion Decisions of the United States Supreme Court.** Maureen Harrison and Steve Gilbert, eds. San Diego, Calif., Excellent Books, 1996. 223p. index. (First Amendment Decisions Series). $16.95pa. ISBN 1-880780-11-9.

General and lay readers interested in reading some of the leading Supreme Court decisions in the first amendment's two religion clauses (Congress shall make no law respecting an establishment of religion [the Establishment Clause], or prohibiting the free exercise thereof [the Free Exercise Clause]) should turn to this collection for their introduction to legal thinking in these areas. General readers will find here 18 major cases in Supreme Court history that have had some of the greatest impact on the understanding and interpretation of the constitutional separation of church and state. There is a brief but excellent introduction to these two religion clauses, followed by the majority opinion in each case.

Each case itself opens with a one-page introduction and a one-page list of the Supreme Court Justices who served on the Court at the time the decision was made. In addition, the specific citation for the complete decision found in the *United States Reports* is provided. Each case is carefully edited to ensure that lay readers will obtain the essence of the majority opinion without being accosted and confused by legalese. Where necessary, brief definitions for legal terms are provided. The cases cover a wide spectrum of first amendment issues on religion, including polygamy, religious liberty, school prayer, tax exemptions for church property, prayers at graduation, and ritual animal sacrifice, among many others. Only an edited version of the majority opinion is provided. The book concludes with the complete text of the United States Constitution, a useful bibliography, and an index. This work is highly recommended.
—**Michael A. Foley**

1184. **National Guide to Funding in Religion.** 3d ed. James E. Baumgartner and others, eds. New York, Foundation Center, 1995. 865p. index. $135.00pa. ISBN 0-87954-606-9.

This directory of endowments and charities in the United States is intended as a starting point for grantseekers looking for funding support for programs related to religion. The guide is published every two years (see ARBA 93, entry 1411) by the Foundation Center, which publishes the well-respected *Foundation Directory* (15th ed.; see ARBA 94, entry 890).

The guide contains entries for 4,212 grantmaking foundations (which is a considerable increase from the 2,824 foundations listed in the 1st edition). The arrangement is alphabetic, first by state, then by name of the foundation or corporate giving program. An excellent general introduction to support in religion is provided. The work also includes a glossary of dozens of terms and several useful indexes: by geographic location; by type of support; to grants by subject; and to names of donors, officers, and trustees.

The entries, which make up 730 of the 865 pages, were carefully selected to ensure that the grantmaker had shown sufficient interest in religious activities to merit inclusion in this directory. The guide is highly recommended for both large libraries with religious collections and especially for libraries in religious communities.—**Edward Erazo**

Bible Studies

Bibliography

1185. **An Exegetical Bibliography of the New Testament. Volume 4.** Wagner Günter, ed. Macon, Ga., Mercer University Press, 1996. 379p. $40.00. ISBN 0-86554-468-9.

This is the fourth volume in a series of New Testament bibliographies, all originally printed as file cards produced by the editor and his students in Switzerland. The previous three volumes published in 1983 (see ARBA 84, entry 984), 1985, and 1987 dealt with the four gospels and the Johannine letters. The present volume focuses on Romans and Galatians. The bibliography for Romans is found on pages 3-274, while the rest of the volume covers the bibliography of Galatians. There is no index.

Wagner begins with a bibliography for large units of each of the two biblical books, for example Romans 1-16, then increasingly smaller units until he is citing bibliography verse by verse. Entries are listed in chronological order beginning with the earliest, citing author, title, place, date, and page numbers for books and the standard format for articles. Publishers of books are not cited. Many German and a few French, Italian, and other languages works are cited. A random check of verses suggests that the inclusions are quite extensive and appropriate. The citations for long sections, particularly the complete books, are puzzling. For example, H. Gamble's *The Textual History of the Letter to the Romans* is the only work cited for Romans in its entirety, and nothing at all is cited for the complete book of Galatians.

Given that some works are cited in full dozens and possibly hundreds of times throughout the work, the author/date system of citation would have been more economical. The work should be useful to advanced New Testament scholars.—**Robert T. Anderson**

1186. Gruber, Mayer I. **Women in the Biblical World: A Study Guide. [Volume 1]: Women in the World of Hebrew Scripture.** Lanham, Md., American Theological Library Association and Scarecrow, 1995. 271p. index. (ATLA Bibliography Series, no.38). $42.50. ISBN 0-8108-3069-8.

This is the 1st of 2 projected volumes on women in the world of the Hebrew Bible (volume 1) and the Apocrypha and the New Testament (volume 2). The work includes references to books, articles from periodicals and collective volumes, and theses and dissertations. The author is to be commended on the breadth of his sources, bringing in such disparate periodicals as *Ms.*, *Iowa Review*, and *Zeitschrift fuer Sexualwissenschaft* in addition to the religious journals one would expect. Even though there is an obvious interest in female biblical characters, both named and unnamed, the scope of the work is much broader than that. Gruber lists resources on women in Ancient Near Eastern culture (Israel, Egypt, Elephantine, Mesopotamia, Mari, Ugarit, Elam, Persia, and among the Hittites, the Hurrians, and the Phoenicians), especially social institutions (such as marriage, family, and royalty) and sexuality. He also focuses on feminine imagery in the literatures of those cultures, particularly the Hebrew scriptures. A large portion of the references deals with biblical books and passages that feature women as main or supporting characters. The bibliography is international in coverage, including materials in major Western European languages as well as modern Hebrew, Arabic, and Greek. The entries are arranged in broad categories and are complemented by author, subject, and scripture indexes.

That this volume represents great effort and is a valuable guide to the literature is beyond question. Unfortunately, it is not an annotated bibliography (although there are some brief notes scattered throughout). Certainly not a requirement for books in this ATLA series, annotations would have been a useful addition. In some cases, it is difficult to know (unless one is already familiar with a certain book, article, or thesis) why an item was included in this bibliography, or at least included where it was. This is not to question whether these items should be there or to be seen as a negative evaluation of the work as a whole. This volume and its forthcoming companion volume deserve a place in collections that support research in religious, historical, and feminist studies. [R: Choice, Nov 96, p. 430]—**Craig W. Beard**

1187. Hostetter, Edwin C. **Old Testament Introduction.** Grand Rapids, Mich., Baker Book House, 1995. 106p. index. (IBR Bibliographies, no.11). $7.99pa. ISBN 0-8010-2017-4.

So far, three volumes have appeared in this series: *Luke-Acts and New Testament Historiography* (Baker Book House, 1994), *New Testament Introduction* (see entry 1192), and the present volume. This is the briefest of the 3, containing 500 entries, compared to 17 and 848 respectively in the other 2. These items (monographs, reference works, and a few dissertations) are presented in a classified arrangement under five broad headings ("Criticism," "Ancient Texts and Versions," "Language," "Cognate Literature," and "The Environment"), each of which is further divided by two or three subheadings. The works are listed, under each subheading, in reverse chronological order and briefly annotated. Hostetter has gathered a good selection of older and newer works for this bibliography, some of them being as current as 1994. His choices generally reflect the breadth of Old Testament scholarship, representing the spectrum from (for lack of better terms) liberal to conservative.

All in all, this is a helpful volume, although in comparison to the previous two, it is at times a bit disappointing. First, this is obviously a selective bibliography (the series limit for a volume is approximately 500 titles), but it would benefit from including more titles in some areas—for example, recent introductory studies on the Dead Sea Scrolls. Also, there are no commentaries listed. Second, the notes introducing the sections of the bibliography could be fuller and more descriptive of the subject, and the annotations more evaluative. Finally, the classification scheme needs to be more detailed. The series editor says in his preface to each volume that Baker Book House plans to publish updates about every five years. One hopes that in five years *Old Testament Introduction* realizes its potential.—**Craig W. Beard**

1188. Klein, William W. **The Book of Ephesians: An Annotated Bibliography.** New York, Garland, 1996. 312p. (Books of the Bible, v.8; Garland Reference Library of the Humanities, v.1466). $50.00. ISBN 0-8153-0364-5.

In the latest volume in this bibliography series, Klein (Denver Seminary) includes monographs, commentaries, journal articles, essays, and dissertations, most of which were published in the past 50 years. Some important older items also found a place here. Most of the entries are annotated, although some that are not would have benefited from an indication of their value for the study of Ephesians.

Chapter 1 lists introductory studies: standard introductions and books and articles on Paul, his writings, and Ephesians. The last 3 chapters treat specific introductory issues: structure, genre, style, and vocabulary (chapter 8); authorship and pseudonymity, historical setting, slavery, and household codes (chapter 9); and thought and theology (chapter 10). Chapter 2 lists commentaries (including 2 dozen premodern ones), even some that are less well known. Chapters 3 through 7 list sources dealing with specific verses and passages in Ephesians. Most of the annotations indicate the particular text under consideration if it does not appear in the title.

Klein did a thorough job of gathering his material, but a few titles still fell through the cracks, among them *Dictionary of Paul and His Letters* (see ARBA 95, entry 1450). The work under review is recommended for libraries supporting biblical and theological studies. [R: Choice, Sept 96, p. 100]—**Craig W. Beard**

1189. Longman, Tremper, III. **Old Testament Commentary Survey.** 2d ed. Grand Rapids, Mich., Baker Book House, 1995. 184p. index. $10.99pa. ISBN 0-8010-2024-7.

In the review of the 1st edition of Longman's survey (see ARBA 92, entry 1407), appreciation was expressed for the work, and it was recommended for biblical studies collections. The 2d edition has been expanded by 24 pages and 55 entries (some of which are parts of commentaries on more than one book of the Hebrew Bible). A few of the previous entries have been updated to reflect new editions of earlier works or additional volumes of previously begun multivolume sets. Longman's comments on the new entries are, as in the 1st edition, objective and helpful. Also, on a minor note, a number of items that were out of alphabetic order in the previous edition have been properly placed. A useful reference work has been improved.

The value of this book is what makes its weaknesses all the more disappointing. There are four major shortcomings, judged primarily upon this being an update. First, several new editions, published since the first survey, were not included; rather, the same entry was carried over (for example, *The New Encyclopedia of Archaeological Excavations in the Holy Land* [Simon & Schuster]). Second, some sets (such as *The Expositor's Bible Commentary* [Zondervan Publishing]) that have been completed are still shown as being in progress. Third, several new titles that one would expect to find in this edition are not there (for example, the *New Interpreter's Bible* [Abingdon Press]). Fourth, quite a few entries do not include a price, and the user is left to wonder if that was an oversight or if the book is out of print. Still, this is a useful addition to biblical studies reference collections, and the survey has the potential to be even better in its 3d edition, if the shortcomings are attended to.—**Craig W. Beard**

1190. Minor, Mark. **Literary-Critical Approaches to the Bible: A Bibliographical Supplement.** West Cornwall, Conn., Locust Hill Press, 1996. 310p. index. $40.00. ISBN 0-933951-69-8.

The supplement volume to Minor's *Literary-Critical Approaches to the Bible* (see ARBA 93, entry 1430) identifies and examines more than 1,100 items (post-1991) of literary criticism on both the Hebrew Bible and the Second Testament. Contrary to the older Enlightenment-inspired historical school of biblical criticism (source, form, redaction, and so on), the more current literary model views biblical passages as a finished whole and inseparable of form and content. The annotated bibliography allows the reader to skip, detour, and revisit earlier sections, aided by frequent and helpful cross-references throughout the text.

Although the compiler provides a compelling survey of what literary criticism says about the Bible, it is unlikely that this reference work will win over experienced scholars. Why so? The cited articles (in the main, although a few books are listed) are confined to English-only writing, and many are succinctly noted rather than more fully explained. Adversely, this provides a useful guide to nonspecialists who are interested in the Bible as religious literature (i.e., theological significance, "inspired" text, role in faith community, and so forth). The supplement is recommended for library holdings in literary criticism and biblical interpretation.—**Zev Garber**

1191. Muse, Robert L. **The Book of Revelation: An Annotated Bibliography.** New York, Garland, 1996. 352p. index. (Books of the Bible, v.2; Garland Reference Library of the Humanities, v.1387). $58.00. ISBN 0-8240-7394-0.

Because of its strange symbolism and frightening imagery, the Book of Revelation has always been controversial, so much so that Martin Luther questioned the wisdom of including it in the New Testament. Luther's reservation is understandable, for the book is as baffling today as it was centuries ago. What does it mean? Is it apocalyptic, foretelling the end of time and beyond? Or is it prophetic in nature, describing in a cryptic way events of the time and suggesting their likely consequences? It is not the purpose of this fine bibliography to resolve these questions, but rather to point scholars and informed laity to the rich body of literature dealing with such issues.

This study is not exhaustive. Drawn almost entirely from the years 1940 to 1990, its 1,407 entries are primarily in English, although there is a sampling of German, French, Italian, Spanish, Dutch, and Greek works. Sensibly organized, each chapter represents a specific approach to the subject. Hence, chapter 2 contains studies on the historical and cultural context of Revelation, while chapter 5 surveys literature of a theological and thematic nature. The books, essays, and selected doctoral dissertations within each chapter are grouped under appropriate subheadings, such as general works, archaeology, and eschatology. Except for the dissertation listed at the end of each chapter, all entries are annotated, albeit the annotations range from only a sentence or two to a third of a page in length. This would be a useful addition to the reference collections of seminary and many university and public libraries. [R: Choice, Sept 96, p. 103]—**John W. Storey**

1192. Porter, Stanley E., and Lee M. McDonald. **New Testament Introduction.** Grand Rapids, Mich., Baker Book House, 1995. 234p. index. (IBR Bibliographies, no.12). $14.95pa. ISBN 0-8010-2060-3.

Porter and McDonald have compiled a useful guide to the literature of New Testament introduction. They have selected 843 current and older items (primarily monographs and reference works, but also some important articles and essays) published in or translated into English. Unlike its Old Testament counterpart in this series (see entry 1187), this volume contains a brief selection of commentaries. The entries are arranged alphabetically within a detailed classification scheme, and most are annotated.

This work is more than just a bibliography, due primarily to the contributions of Porter and McDonald beyond that of being mere compilers. They provide an entrée into the field through the introductory comments they have written for the chapters and sections. By reading these, the novice will know, albeit briefly, what the issues are in the areas of textual and literary criticism, chronology, Jewish and Greco-Roman social and historical context, and so on. In addition, the annotations are, for the most part, descriptive and evaluative, and they are often engaging; for example, the comment on McKnight's *Post-Modern Use of the Bible*: "What is postmodernism? After reading this text, you will still ask the same question but it is an interesting read" (p. 72). Porter and McDonald should be read as well as consulted.

Although there are some typographic errors (very few), and a few titles are out in new editions (notably Vermes's *The Dead Sea Scrolls in English* and *The New Encyclopedia of Archaeological Excavations in the Holy Land*), this bibliography should be in all biblical studies collections.—**Craig W. Beard**

1193. Schandorff, Esther Dech. **The Doctrine of the Holy Spirit: A Bibliography Showing Its Chronological Development.** Lanham, Md., Scarecrow, 1995. 2v. index. (ATLA Bibliography Series, no.28). $110.00/set. ISBN 0-8108-2523-6.

Schandorff has amassed a collection of more than 7,000 citations to literature on the Holy Spirit from the holdings of 126 libraries and various in-print sources. Among these items are both scholarly materials (theses and dissertations, monographs, and collections of essays) and popular materials (such as devotional works) in English and other languages (including translations of English-language works). In addition to the expected print sources, she includes videocassettes, audio tapes, phonograph records, film strips, and software. Volume 1 contains the bibliography itself, a numbered list of citations arranged alphabetically by author (or, in some cases, main entry). Each one includes a two-letter code indicating what type of source it is ("mo" for a monograph, "ut" for an unpublished thesis, and so forth), and some have a symbol for library location. Volume 2 contains "Schandorff's Subject Analysis" and additional indexes, one of them an index to the subject analysis.

The rationale for the subtitle of this work is not obvious until one looks at the second volume. Chapter 2, "Chronology of Literature," lists works written from the Apostolic Fathers down to Catholic and Protestant writers of the late twentieth century, along with critical studies of each author. In addition, many of the topical sections include period subdivisions. Although not comprehensive (and what bibliography is?), this exhaustive guide is the place to start for those interested in a thorough study of the Holy Spirit. It is recommended for all theological library collections. [R: Choice, Sept 96, p. 106]—**Craig W. Beard**

1194. Thompson, Henry O. **The Book of Jeremiah: An Annotated Bibliography.** Lanham, Md., Scarecrow, 1996. 745p. index. (ATLA Bibliography Series, no.41). $92.00. ISBN 0-8108-3178-3.

This is the first volume in the ATLA Bibliography Series devoted to a book of the Bible. It is hoped that it will not be the last. Thompson's work displays the quality characteristics of previous ATLA bibliographies. It includes journal articles, monographs, theses and dissertations, encyclopedia articles, essays in Festschriften and other collective works, book chapters, and commentaries. There is a separate list of dissertations for the benefit of those doing doctoral work on Jeremiah. Some of the dissertations listed in this section duplicate entries in the main text of the bibliography. Occasionally, annotations are duplicated as well (usually, the reader is referred to the main entry). It would have been just as well to have listed the dissertations all in one place or the other. The majority of the items are from the past 50 years, although earlier works are included if they are significant.

Following a brief introduction to Jeremiah (the man and the book), the entries—primarily English-language, with some non-English (mostly European) items—are arranged alphabetically by author and then numbered. Additional access to the entries is provided by three indexes: by author, by subject, and by scripture. The author index is actually an index to editors and secondary authors. The annotations are usually descriptive, although some of them are evaluative.

Even though this is not an exhaustive bibliography (a fact admitted by Thompson), it is a comprehensive guide to the literature on Jeremiah. Annotations are usually well written and complete enough to give the reader an idea of the content of the entries. If Scarecrow and ATLA publish more volumes on the books of the Bible, and they meet the standard set by this one, they should prove to be stiff competition for the Edwin Mellen Press Bibliographies for Biblical Research series. This particular volume is recommended. —**Craig W. Beard**

Dictionaries and Encyclopedias

1195. Browning, W. R. F. **A Dictionary of the Bible.** New York, Oxford University Press, 1996. 412p. $25.00. ISBN 0-19-211691-6.

A Dictionary of the Bible has a wonderful layout and design; however, this volume has a few flaws that are hard to ignore. Although the information in each entry is concise, it lacks thoroughness. For instance, the entry on Abednego states that the name is a corrupted form of "Nebo," but does not elaborate what is meant by that. In *Harper's Bible Dictionary* (see ARBA 86, entry 1382), the entry under Abednego explains that "Nebo" was a Babylonian god of wisdom.

Another minor irritation is that there are no *see also* references, which would have been helpful. A pronunciation guide is also noticeably absent and would have been useful. The section of maps is a nice addition; however, color maps and an index to the maps would have enhanced their usefulness. While *A Dictionary of the Bible* is lacking in several key areas, it is not without value; it is adequate for those just beginning biblical studies.—**Pamela J. Getchell**

1196. **The Collegeville Pastoral Dictionary of Biblical Theology.** Carroll Stuhlmueller and others, eds. Collegeville, Minn., Liturgical Press, 1996. 1120p. $74.95. ISBN 0-8146-1996-7.

"This is a 'pastoral' Dictionary, intended not primarily for the scholar or academician . . . but for priests, religious, teachers at all levels, and educated laity who . . . want to deepen their understanding of the Bible"—so the introduction states. One should note the reference to "priest" is not unintentional; this is a Catholic dictionary designed primarily for Catholic leaders, although others may find it useful.

The book consists of more than 1,100 pages, containing 500-plus entries placed alphabetically by subject. Because of this, no index is needed. Materials are presented so as not to overwhelm either students or laity, while still adequately covering the subject. A series of short articles leads off, discussing the founding and context of the Bible in general. The entries comprise the vast bulk of material, with attention given to biblical themes and persons. Church theological issues, such as the Euchrist and papal authority, are usually not included. Many entries are divided into Old Testament, New Testament, and pastoral-liturgical tradition. The latter category focuses as often on how the priest may apply the subject as on how the church has treated it historically.

One should be aware that two general schools of thought exist in Christendom when such biblical assistance is rendered. Traditionalists accept Holy Writ as prophetic and without error, holding to customary dates and authors. The more liberal tradition, from which this dictionary arises, holds that many books were authored by multiple, unknown parties, usually much later in time than originally thought. Miraculous accounts are denied or downplayed, with emphasis directed on the derived spiritual metaphor. With such awareness, this dictionary can provide valuable assistance and insight to the struggling layperson or priest.—**Brad R. Leach**

1197. **Evangelical Dictionary of Biblical Theology.** Walter A. Elwell, ed. Carlisle, England, Paternoster Press and Grand Rapids, Mich., Baker Book House, 1996. 933p. index. $44.99. ISBN 0-8010-2049-2.

There are few current dictionaries of biblical theology and, until now, none written from an evangelical perspective. As one would expect from Baker Book House, the editor and the other 127 contributors operate from a high view of the Bible and its authority. That, however, does not mean that there is a single perspective reflected in the articles (especially not a "fundamentalist" perspective). For example, the writer of the article "Create, Creation" approaches the subject as essentially theological rather than scientific. Thus, the reader finds not creation-science apologetic but explication of the theological significance of creation and God as the creator. As a matter of fact, the creation week is viewed as a literary device rather than a literal chronology. In addition, the articles "Sexuality, Human" and "Women" present a fairly balanced view of gender issues, although they arrive at moderate conclusions regarding women's roles within the Christian community.

The articles are generally well written and thorough, even though the author of "Servant of the Lord" does not show the progression from the concept in the Hebrew Bible to the attribution of the role of Jesus in the New Testament. Sometimes a writer moves from explanation to exhortation (for example, "Astrology" and "Immorality, Sexual"), but that is the exception rather than the rule. This volume joins Baker's growing list of "evangelical" reference tools that includes their *Evangelical Dictionary of Theology* (see ARBA 85, entry 1313) and *Evangelical Commentary on the Bible* (1989), and the work under review should join them on the shelves in theological reference collections. [R: Choice, Dec 96, p. 589]
—**Craig W. Beard**

1198. **The Hebrew and Aramaic Lexicon of the Old Testament. [Volume] II.** By Ludwig Koehler and Walter Baumgartner. Revised by Walter Baumgartner and Johann Jakob Stamm. Kinderhook, N.Y., E. J. Brill, 1995. 906p. $146.50. ISBN 90-04-09697-3.

The appearance of volume 2 of the Koehler-Baumgartner lexicon comes one year after the first volume appeared (see ARBA 96, entry 1455) and marks the halfway point in the publication of the whole. The work is an English translation of the 3d edition of the German original. In addition, the editor for this translation, M. E. J. Richardson, has introduced corrections to the German original as these were found and several kinds of modifications for the sake of clarity and ease of use for English readers (especially in cases where the works cited by the original have been translated into English). These will significantly enhance the value of the work for English readers.

Entries are arranged in strictly alphabetic order (rather than under Hebrew roots) and supply for each term the cognates in other Semitic languages, the forms in which the word appears, the various meanings of the term, where it occurs in the Bible, and citations of relevant secondary literature. The editors, translators, and publisher are to be commended for undertaking this monumental task that will make a truly excellent philological and exegetical tool more widely available to researchers, students, and pastors. Such publications in the fields of theology and religion are what one has learned to expect from E. J. Brill. No library that supports the study of the Bible in the original languages should be without this lexicon.
—**M. Patrick Graham**

1199. Kohlenberger, John R., III, Edward W. Goodrick, and James A. Swanson. **The Exhaustive Concordance to the Greek New Testament.** Grand Rapids, Mich., Zondervan Publishing/HarperCollins, 1995. 5516p. index. $49.99. ISBN 0-310-41030-4.

Among other things, Hellenization meant that Greek became the common language of trade and correspondence in the ancient Mediterranean world. As with other peoples, Jews living outside Palestine increasingly used this language instead of their native tongue, so much so that Jews in Alexandria found it necessary to translate the Bible from Hebrew to Greek. Completed about 270 B.C.E., the resulting Septuagint was widely read not only by Jews, but also by Christians of the 1st century. Hence, it was this translation that promoted the spread of Christianity into the Gentile world. As seen in his numerous letters, Paul of Tarsus was schooled in the Septuagint. This all indicates that any serious student of the Bible must know Greek, and therein lies the value of such works as *The Exhaustive Concordance to the Greek New Testament*.

A concordance is an alphabetized index of each word in a book. If it is a good concordance, it also provides some context for each word. The work under review is excellent. It is not only exhaustive in its treatment of the Greek New Testament, but also calls attention to differences between it and the New International Version. This study contains 6,068 entries, and subsumed under each are the biblical passage in which the word appears. A reference for scholars, every seminary and Bible-school library should have this volume.—**John W. Storey**

1200. **Theological Dictionary of the Old Testament: Volume VII.** G. Johannes Botterweck, Helmer Ringgren, and Heinz-Josef Fabry, eds. Grand Rapids, Mich., Willam B. Eerdmans, 1995. 552p. $42.00. ISBN 0-8028-2331-9.

The appearance of the 7th volume of the *Theological Dictionary of the Old Testament* (TDOT) marks the steady progress of the translators of the *Theologisches Wörterbuch zum Alten Testament*. The 75 articles in this volume extend from the Hebrew k^e ("like") to *lys ("act arrogantly") and cover such Hebrew terms as those for *atonement*, *cherub*, *Levite*, and *priest*. The editors are internationally recognized authorities in Hebrew Bible studies from Europe, Israel, and the United States, and the translator, David E. Green, is among the most highly regarded and experienced of those who translate German theological works into English.

Each article follows the Hebrew term with its English transliteration, an extensive bibliography, a discussion of the term's occurrence in the Hebrew Bible, rendering in the Greek Bible (Septuagint), etymology, meaning, and theological significance. Appropriate attention is given to matters of philology and semantics, but the articles typically push toward the discovery of the theological significance of the words and word groups. The articles are generally well written and clear, and the generous margins and typeface size (i.e., not too small) ease the reader's task.

Although the TDOT generally is written for the specialist—whether scholar or student—with competence in biblical Hebrew, the determined novice with minimal Hebrew knowledge can benefit from the work. This dictionary is without peer among theological resources and is absolutely essential for university, seminary, and other libraries that support programs in biblical studies. The commitment of William B. Eerdmans to such a massive and long-range project has placed all students of the Hebrew Bible in its debt.—**M. Patrick Graham**

Handbooks and Yearbooks

1201. **Hellenistic Commentary to the New Testament.** M. Eugene Boring, Klaus Berger, and Carsten Colpe, eds. Nashville, Tenn., Abingdon Press, 1995. 633p. index. $69.95. ISBN 0-687-00916-2.

This is not a commentary in the sense that that term is usually understood. The work is not the comments of Hellenistic authors on the New Testament writings. It is, rather, a sourcebook of texts from the Hellenistic world (defined essentially as the Mediterranean basin, influenced by Greek language and culture, between 330 B.C.E. and 300 C.E.) intended to guide interpreters in understanding the historical context of the New Testament. The editors have brought together under the Hellenistic umbrella Greco-Roman (Epictetus, Plutarch, the Corpus Hermeticum); Jewish (Josephus, Philo Judaeus, rabbinic literature, the Dead Sea Scrolls); and Christian (New Testament apocrypha and the patristic writings) sources. They have arranged the passages from these texts canonically according to the order of the New Testament books and verses they illuminate. Following each text is an annotation suggesting how the Hellenistic text may contribute to the understanding of the New Testament text. Users are referred to primary and secondary sources (for which complete citations are listed in the book's bibliography) where they can find and read the Hellenistic passages in their context.

Hellenistic Commentary is a translation and expansion by Boring of *Religionsgeschichtliches Textbuch zum Neuen Testament*, edited by Berger and Colpe. Boring added 350 primary texts and an unspecified number more in the annotations. On occasion, he has also included a longer passage that appeared in the Berger and Colpe volume. Thus, even those libraries that hold the German work would benefit from the addition of the English version. The title is recommended primarily for seminary and university biblical studies collections.—**Craig W. Beard**

Buddhism

1202. **A Páda Index and Reverse Páda Index to Early Jain Canons: Áyáraṅga, Súyagáḍa, Uttarajjháyá, Dasaveyáliya, and Isibhásiyáim.** By Moriichi Yamazaki and Yumi Ousaka. Tokyo, Kosei Publishing; distr., Boston, Charles E. Tuttle, 1995. 537p. $30.00pa. ISBN 4-333-01763-7.

Materials at the confluence of Jain and Buddhist interests have largely gone unexplored by scholars, in part because of the difficulties of the language. The problem is partially remedied by the indexes to the early Jain canons presented in this volume. These Páda and Reverse Páda indexes to the *Áyáraṅga, Súyagáḍa, Uttarajjháyá, Dasaveyáliya*, and *Isibhasiyaim* were originally published in five volumes. This single, more convenient, and more accessible volume was compiled by computer. The additional advantage to scholars of a single volume is the ability to find parallels to specific portions of the text in other texts.

This index of Jain texts is compatible with this publishers' index to the *Suttanipati* and *Dhammapada*, two important early Buddhist works that are much better known. The indexes are based on the roman transliterations of the Devanagari texts and were done on a Macintosh computer. These are highly specialized indexes and as such have use to those scholars deeply immersed in the comparison of early Buddhist and Jain materials. To that select group of experts, this index will be beneficial.

—**Linda L. Lam-Easton**

Christianity

Almanacs

1203. **Our Sunday Visitor's 1997 Catholic Almanac: The Most Complete One-Volume Source of Facts....** Felician A. Foy and Rose M. Avato, comps. and eds. Huntington, Ind., Our Sunday Visitor, 1996. 600p. index. $26.95; $21.95pa. ISBN 0-87973-278-4; 0-87973-277-6pa.

This almanac is the 90th edition in a series of books containing facts and information about the Roman Catholic Church, with special emphasis on the church in the United States. This fact-filled book can be especially useful for anyone looking for information on recent pronouncements from the Holy See, from various church committees, or from U.S. bishops. This year's edition contains information on the Congregation for the Doctrine of Faith's statement on no ordination for women; the Church's statement at the Fourth World Conference of Women in Beijing; letters from various U.S. bishops on partial birth abortions, assisted suicide, euthanasia, and same sex unions; and information on the We Are Church request for a dialogue and the reaction of bishops to that organization. The volume also contains information on Church history, organization, and doctrine. Biographies are included for Pope John Paul II, all of the present cardinals, and all U.S. bishops, providing an easy reference on the church's hierarchy. Other sections include information on church-run facilities, organizations, religious institutes, and shrines. The book's extensive index makes it easy to locate the concisely worded information on various subjects. This almanac should be included in any library needing easy-to-locate, condensed information on the Church.—**Kay Mariea**

Bibliography

1204. Blom, F., J. Blom, F. Korsten, and G. Scott, comps. **English Catholic Books, 1701-1800: A Bibliography.** Brookfield, Vt., Scolar Press/Ashgate Publishing, 1996. 356p. index. $94.95. ISBN 1-85928-148-6.

Continuing the time sequence begun in the bibliography by A. F. Allison and D. M. Roger—*A Catalogue of Catholic Books in English Printed Abroad or Secretly in England 1558-1640* (Boger Regis, 1956)—and extended by T. H. Clancy—*English Catholic Books, 1641-1700: A Bibliography* (rev. ed., Scolar Press/Ashgate Publishing, 1996), this compilation concentrates on eighteenth-century publications. It begins with background information on eighteenth-century Catholic publishers and publishing activities, devotional works, the mission at home and abroad, and emancipation and emigration. Credit is given to the *Eighteenth Century Short Title Catalogue* (ESTC) as the major bibliographic work at the compilers' disposal, but it is claimed that 1,000 new items have been included in the work under review.

Supplements include a reference abbreviations list and a key to library symbols, which are essential to the explanation of each of the 2,960 entries. An entry includes author, title, number of volumes, place and year of publication, format, printer, publisher, bookseller, ESTC number, library locations where a copy may be found, and a general note. Three indexes, by titles; by printers, publishers, and booksellers; and by proper names in titles and notes, complete the volume. This work is an important bibliographic tool for academic and general collections for the study of English literature, history, religion and culture, and the colonial United States. [R: Choice, July/Aug 96, p. 1772]—**Sara R. Mack**

1205. Jones, Charles Edwin. **The Charismatic Movement: A Guide to the Study of Neo-Pentecostalism.... Parts I-IV.** Lanham, Md., American Theological Library Association and Scarecrow, 1995. 2v. index. (ATLA Bibliography Series, no.30). $120.00/set. ISBN 0-8108-2565-1.

The Pentecostal and charismatic movements are the fastest-growing Christian forces having origins in the United States. They have extended among groups as diverse as Roman Catholics and Fundamentalists Anonymous. From lowly beginnings in 1901 in Topeka, Kansas, the movements have spread as "a stream that goes everywhere." Few individuals know as much about the movements as the author of this bibliography. Jones began his own spiritual pilgrimage in the Holiness (Church of God) movement and thereby gained a unique and profound understanding of the entire tradition. Later he obtained degrees in history and undertook additional study at the Episcopal Divinity School in Cambridge, Massachusetts. Today he is acknowledged as the major bibliographer of the Holiness-Pentecostal tradition.

In addition to other books and articles he has written, Jones has already contributed other titles to the American Theological Library Association (ATLA) Bibliography Series, the most significant being *A Guide to the Study of the Holiness Movement* (1974) and *A Guide to the Study of the Pentecostal Movement* (see ARBA 85, entry 1309). This latest volume does for neopentecostalism in the mainline churches what his earlier works did for the parent movements. His indefatigable effort has resulted in 10,910 entries, all carefully organized within 4 distinct parts, with denominations listed alphabetically. A 121-page index enhances the usefulness of this valuable reference tool.—**G. A. Cevasco**

1206. Kari, Daven Michael. **Bibliography of Sources in Christianity and the Arts.** Lewiston, N.Y., Edwin Mellen Press, 1995. 764p. index. (Studies in Art and Religious Interpretation, v.16). $139.95. ISBN 0-7734-9094-9.

As the introduction states, the purpose of this 5,200-entry, selective bibliography is to assist "English speaking westerners ... conducting research in the [fine] arts, especially as they are related to western Christianity." The fine arts are distinguished from arts and crafts and how-to books, most of which are omitted. Rather, the bibliography focuses on references dealing with art movements and groups of individuals. Categories of the fine arts range from aesthetics, architecture, literature, and music to drama, mime, radio, television, and wit and humor. Two chapters on the visual arts include calligraphy, graffiti, lithographs, mosaics, and sculpture.

The layout of the work is a bit complex, so the researcher should invest the time to read the main introduction. Following the bibliographies of general bibliographies chapter, subsequent chapters include an introduction to the bibliographies of the art form. Then, key works are listed for that art form. Cross-references are rare, as a work is listed only in the category that best fits it. Entries are not annotated and are in the *Chicago Manual of Style* format rather than that of the Modern Language Association.

Due to the quantity of works available, resources date back to 1960 and, in some cases, only to the 1970s. However, some older works considered classics by the specialists are included in the bibliography sections of the chapters. The author gives bibliographies and works of more than 40 pages with bibliographies preference over smaller works, such as those put out by the Library of Congress. Also, only a few major journals and articles are listed.—**Patricia M. Leach**

1207. Severson, Richard. **The Confessions of Saint Augustine: An Annotated Bibliography of Modern Criticism, 1888-1995.** Westport, Conn., Greenwood Press, 1996. 149p. index. (Bibliographies and Indexes in Religious Studies, no.40). $65.00. ISBN 0-313-29995-1.

Saint Augustine's *Confessions* has been an extremely important book in Western history, not just among theologians and church historians, but also more recently among psychologists, literary critics, and students of autobiography. Thus, a considerable amount of scholarship has grown up around the book. Severson, a librarian with a doctorate on Augustine, has compiled a list of approximately 500 sources written on the *Confessions* during the last century. Virtually all the sources are written in English, and most are from scholarly monographs and articles; a few Ph.D. dissertations and more popular sources are also included.

This reference volume begins with a bibliographic essay on the history of modern criticism on the *Confessions*, which admirably sets the subsequently listed sources into context. The main section consists of the citations arranged under one of eight different chapter themes, such as autobiography or theological interpretations. The entries themselves consist of citations plus succinct annotations that are universally descriptive, not evaluative or partisan. Cross-references to related sources in the bibliography are provided in many of the annotations and at the end of each chapter. Three indexes—by author/editor, by title, and by subject—are appended; the subject index is particularly well constructed and supplements the thematic division of the main work.

Although this volume is somewhat expensive for its size, the bibliography's topic is one of importance, and its execution is excellent. A spot check of sources on the same subject in major library periodical indexes found no surprising gaps in Severson's coverage. This work is similar to, but may have wider application than, Dorothy Donnelly's *Augustine's De Civitate Dei* (see ARBA 93, entry 1416), which covers another of Augustine's influential works.—**Christopher W. Nolan**

Biography

1208. **The Blackwell Dictionary of Evangelical Biography, 1730-1860.** Donald M. Lewis, ed. Cambridge, Mass., Blackwell, 1995. 2v. index. $195.00/set. ISBN 0-631-17384-6.

Evangelicalism is a term that has a wide range of meanings. This dictionary has defined its topic as a far-flung, Protestant religious movement that emphasizes the conversion experience, personal responsibility, and the central place of the Bible. These volumes provide biographical information on approximately 3,500 persons of religious, historical, or literary significance who flourished between 1730 and 1860, the heyday of the early Evangelical movement, primarily in the English-speaking world (although a few major figures from the European continent are also included).

Evangelicalism appealed to a wide audience during this period. Thus, this dictionary includes a large number of adherents who were not clergy or missionaries. Many women are profiled in an attempt to rectify their lack of coverage in traditional church history reference sources. The editor's goal throughout the work is to emphasize evangelicals' effect on social and political arenas as much as on the theological world.

Individual entries are usually brief, although occasional articles run more than a page in length. Preference has been given to the adequate treatment of neglected or minor figures over the exhaustive treatment of the famous. Articles are signed by the authors, who are mostly academic and clerical scholars in the United Kingdom and the United States. The entries' content is usually brief, useful, and academically objective. Each entry provides at least one bibliographic source for further information, and a bibliography of selected writings is included for those figures who published. An index by country of origin is appended to the work.

The dictionary supplies a useful tool for those supporting church history and English history collections, offering many additional entries over such standards as *The Oxford Dictionary of the Christian Church* (see ARBA 75, entry 1220). It partially overlaps, but does not supersede, *The Australian Dictionary of Evangelical Biography* (Sydney, Australia: Evangelical History Association, 1994), which focuses only on that region.—**Christopher W. Nolan**

Dictionaries and Encyclopedias

1209. Atkinson, David J., and David H. Field, eds. **New Dictionary of Christian Ethics & Pastoral Theology.** Downers Grove, Ill., InterVarsity Press, 1995. 918p. index. $39.99. ISBN 0-8308-1408-6.

Behind this cross-disciplinary work is the conviction that those who are involved in pastoral ministry and other helping professions within a Christian context need to be grounded in Christian moral theology. This conviction is evident in the content of the articles: Those dealing with "ethical" topics contain reflections on the pastoral aspects, and those on "pastoral" issues present ethical foundations and ramifications. The 250-plus contributors are specialists in their fields; in addition to theologians and ethicists, the ranks include physicians, economists, politicians, historians, philosophers, psychologists, sociologists, and lawyers. Most of them teach or practice in Great Britain or the United States, with the scales tipping toward the former. Although a British slant is evident in some articles, it does not detract from the overall usefulness of the volume. Some may feel that there should be a greater awareness of and emphasis on global issues, particularly the Third World, even though this is not altogether absent. Among the pertinent topics are human rights, world hunger, colonialism, genocide, and aid to the Third World. The articles are written from an evangelical perspective and exhibit both a commitment to traditional tenets (God's revelation of his will through Jesus, the Bible, and the Holy Spirit) and a sensitivity to controversial and emotional issues.

The dictionary is arranged in two parts. Part 1 is composed of 18 major articles on fundamental themes, which form the foundation for the rest of the volume. These articles are arranged in "theological order" (p. vii), beginning with God and concluding with "Christian Moral Reasoning." Part 2 has the look of a traditional dictionary: shorter, alphabetically arranged articles on more specific topics. All articles in part 1 and most of those in part 2 include bibliographies, and a thorough job of cross-referencing ties both parts together. Because of its integration of ethics and pastoral theology, this volume should be added to public, academic, and theological collections already having dictionaries that treat the disciplines separately, such as *The Westminster Dictionary of Christian Ethics* (see ARBA 87, entry 1350) and *Dictionary of Pastoral Care and Counseling* (see ARBA 91, entry 1443).—**Craig W. Beard**

1210. **Dictionary of Christianity.** J. C. Cooper, ed. Chicago, Fitzroy Dearborn, 1996. 296p. $45.00. ISBN 1-884964-49-4.

Cooper's work consists of more than 2,000 alphabetically arranged entries relating to all the main branches of Christianity. In the preface, the editor acknowledges that this dictionary is based on the Christian references found in Ebenezer Brewer's *Dictionary of Phrase & Fable* (8th ed., Harper & Row, 1963) and is thus mainly a tribute to Brewer's life and works. Indeed, many of Cooper's entries begin with Brewer's definition verbatim.

Some interesting and useful entries that Cooper has carried over from Brewer's work include a listing of specially named editions of the Bible, details on giants in the Bible, and sketches of the different types of crosses. Cooper's work is not, however, just a partial copying of the *Dictionary of Phrase & Fable*. Cooper has added some 1,000 new definitions, most notably an expansion in the list of saints. Other additions, such as an itemization of the members of the World Council of Churches and a selected list of patron saints, further improve the usefulness of this volume.

The work under review is similar in scope and length to J. C. J. Metford's *Dictionary of Christian Lore and Legend* (see ARBA 85, entry 1314). Cooper's work has better coverage of saints and current theological movements, while Metford's has in-depth coverage of Old and New Testament characters and Christian terms relating to literature and the arts. *Dictionary of Christianity* would be useful for any academic library supporting religious studies programs, but libraries may wish to consider its similarity to Metford's dictionary before purchasing it. [R: Choice, June 96, p. 1613; RBB, 1 April 96, p. 1387]

—**Laura K. Blessing**

1211. **The Oxford Encyclopedia of the Reformation.** Hans J. Hillerbrand, ed. New York, Oxford University Press, 1996. 4v. maps. index. $450.00/set. ISBN 0-19-506493-3.

The sixteenth-century Reformation is widely considered to be one of the pivotal areas in Western, and even world, civilization. Therefore, the appearance of a comprehensive, scholarly, four-volume encyclopedia on the subject is an important event in reference publishing. As defined by Hillerbrand, a renowned scholar, "the Reformation consisted of the broad phenomenon of religion and all its societal ramifications in the sixteenth century" (p. xi). That definition forms the scope of these volumes and is reflected in the more than 1,200 entries by 450-plus international scholars.

Chronologically, the scope of the encyclopedia goes well beyond the sixteenth century to include relevant topics from the late Middle Ages (Brothers and Sisters of the Common Life, conciliarism, and Girolamo Savonarola) and the seventeenth century (Synod of Dordrecht and Jansenism). Geographically, the entries deal with all of Europe, not just the western part. Many individual countries, regions, and cities are the subject of entries (Hungary, Russia, Silesia, Magdeburg, and Constance). Topics concerning Protestantism, Roman Catholicism, and popular religion are all included.

Biographical articles form a major component of the encyclopedia and cover far more people than just the expected, major figures. The editors followed the principle of "resurrection" in that they sought to include many unjustly neglected or forgotten minor figures of the Reformation. *The Oxford Dictionary of the Christian Church* (see ARBA 75, entry 1220) includes an entry for Dirck Volckertszoon Coornhert (1522-1590), although the same entry in *The Oxford Encyclopedia of the Reformation* is considerably longer. Furthermore, immediately before and after the Coornhert entry are substantial profiles on Caspar Coolhaes (1534-1615), Cornelis Cooltuyn (d. 1567), and Nicholas Cop (ca. 1501-1540), people who do not appear in *The Oxford Dictionary of the Christian Church*. The subjects of the entries are by no means confined to religious topics: Entries on such diverse topics as art, discoveries in the New World, magic, population, and travel show the vast range of the encyclopedia.

Individual entries are signed by their author, range from 300 to 7,500 words in length, and include annotated bibliographies. Particularly complex topics are divided into composite articles with two or more separate sections written by different scholars. Cross-references at the end of individual entries direct the reader to related topics, while blind entries guide the reader from alternate forms of a name to the form preferred by the editors. A detailed index in volume 4 allows readers to readily locate desired information throughout the entire encyclopedia. Also included in a separate section of volume 4 are 8 maps.

The Oxford Encyclopedia of the Reformation will immediately take its place among the great historical reference works and will keep that place for years to come. It forms an excellent complement to the *Handbook of European History, 1400-1600*, edited by Thomas A. Brady Jr., Heiko Oberman, and James D. Tracy (E. J. Brill, 1994), which consists of topical and chronological essays somewhat similar to those found in the *New Cambridge Modern History* (14 vols.; Cambridge University Press, 1968-1990). The editors' decision to exclude all illustrations was well taken and practical. In terms of maps, however, they were a little stingy. A political map of Europe in the reign of Charles V or Philip II and a map of the Holy Roman Empire would have been helpful. Otherwise, all university and seminary libraries will want to add this fine reference work to their collections. [R: Choice, July/Aug 96, p. 1776; LJ, 15 May 96, p. 54; RBB, 1 Mar 96, pp. 1206-07]—**Ronald H. Fritze**

1212. Prokurat, Michael, Alexander Golitzin, and Michael D. Peterson. **Historical Dictionary of the Orthodox Church.** Lanham, Md., Scarecrow, 1996. 439p. illus. (Religions, Philosophies, and Movements, no.9). $89.00. ISBN 0-8108-3081-7.

The emphasis in this dictionary coverage of nearly 2,000 years of Orthodoxy is on history. There are almost no entries for titular or liturgical words. For terms such as *hegumen* or *archimandrite*, one should refer to the *Liturgical Dictionary of Eastern Christianity* (see ARBA 95, entry 1467). Among the entries in the work under review are biographies of martyrs, theologians, saints, and famous Orthodox bishops or priests, mostly in the early centuries, but not excluding such recent names as that of Archbishop John Shahovsky of San Francisco (1902-1989). Longer articles deal with topics such as baptism, Christology, the Coptic Church, Logos, synod, and the like. There are entries for each of the 15 affiliated Orthodox Churches, as well as one for the Roman Catholic Church, which is conciliatory and ecumenical in tone. The well-written articles vary in length from approximately one-third of a page to four pages or more, and there are a few line-drawing illustrations.

A few omissions were noted, perhaps from a desire to play down doctrinal differences between Rome and the East. There is no entry for chrismation (confirmation), although the word is included in the article on baptism. Neither is there one for celibacy nor for married clergy, these being delicate points of discussion between the major churches. There is, of course, a slant toward Orthodoxy in most entries. The work ends with a 90-page bibliography. The dictionary is recommended for all religious libraries, both Catholic and Orthodox.—**Raymund F. Wood**

1213. Rousseau, John J., and Rami Arav. **Jesus and His World: An Archaeological and Cultural Dictionary.** Minneapolis, Minn., Fortress Press/Augsburg Fortress, 1995. 392p. illus. maps. index. $48.00; $25.00pa. ISBN 0-8006-2903-0; 0-8006-2805-3pa.

The goal of the authors is to present a clearer picture of the world of Jesus, free from the influence of theology, Christology, and Western culture. Customs, places, and artifacts are among the aspects of the times that are included. Against this background—or more appropriately, within these boundaries—readers are in a better position to appreciate and evaluate the words and deeds of Jesus.

The work is more of an encyclopedia than a dictionary in that the 105 articles are longer and more comprehensive than one would expect in a traditional dictionary, and readers must consult an index to find information on topics treated within the main entries. Each article is composed of five sections—importance, scripture references, general information, archaeological data, and implications for Jesus research—and concludes with a bibliography. A general bibliography is also included at the end of the book, along with a glossary of specialized terms (indicated in the main text by asterisks); 4 indexes (scriptures, early Jewish writings, ancient writers, and names/places/subjects); and a section of 11 tables on archaeological periods, orders and tractates of the Mishnah and the Talmud, weights and measures, and so forth.

Students of the gospels and of the historical Jesus will find this dictionary to be a helpful tool in their research. The articles are up-to-date, informative, and generally well written. The work's weakest point is its subject index. For example, although the article on ritual baths mentions the importance of purity and ritual bathing in understanding baptism in the ministry of Jesus, baptism is not listed in the index. Perhaps the authors will give more attention to this in a 2d edition.—**Craig W. Beard**

1214. Yrigoyen, Charles, Jr., and Susan E. Warrick. **Historical Dictionary of Methodism.** Lanham, Md., Scarecrow, 1996. 299p. (Historical Dictionaries of Religion, Philosophies, and Movements, no.8). $47.00. ISBN 0-8108-3140-6.

This is an excellent resource on the history of Methodism. It features a chronology outlining the history of the major players and events in Methodist history, from the birth of John Wesley to the 1996 World Methodist Conference in Brazil. Also useful is Frank Baker's essay "A Brief History of Methodism," which acts as a preface to the body of the text. The article chronicles the founding and expansion of Methodism from Wesley to its current global scope of nearly 10 million members.

The dictionary covers not only the people and places of Methodism but also its controlling concepts, as evidenced in the articles on "sanctification" and "free will." Interestingly, some notable non-Methodists are covered as well, such as Jacobus Arminius, who had an indirect influence on Wesley. The articles (all signed) tend to be brief, except when more explanation is warranted. An extensive bibliography finishes this book, which is a must for theological collections of all sizes.—**Bob Craigmile**

Directories

1215. Humling, Virginia, comp. **U.S. Catholic Sources: A Diocesan Research Guide.** Salt Lake City, Utah, Ancestry, 1995. 105p. index. $14.95pa. ISBN 0-916489-60-4.

Genealogists have long valued church records of births, deaths, and marriages as great sources for tracing ancestral roots. This Roman Catholic diocesan research directory lists 32 archdioceses and 143 dioceses plus dozens of additional resources from 49 states (only Mississippi is missing) and the District of Columbia. Two sources are of special note: the Archdiocese for Military Services—founded in 1917—because it keeps records of sacraments performed on U.S. military bases worldwide, and the Genealogical Society of Utah because it has microfilmed 19 diocesan records and makes them available through its family history centers located throughout North America.

Each entry in the guide provides the area included in the diocese; fees (if any); and other information as available, such as the name of the archivist, the local Catholic newspaper, and the cemetery. The entries are listed by state, archdiocese, and diocese. The author's introduction provides an overview and tips on using Roman Catholic records, and the index simplifies finding both archdioceses and dioceses by city names. This guide will make a fine source for genealogy research in public libraries.—**Edward Erazo**

1216. **NCEA/Ganley's Catholic Schools in America 1995.** 23d ed. Mary Mahar, ed. Washington, D.C., National Catholic Education Association; distr., Montrose, Colo., Fisher Publishing, 1995. 329p. $40.00pa. ISBN 1-55833-159-X.

This directory's 23d edition was compiled by the National Catholic Education Association (NCEA) and is based on 1994-1995 data on 8,293 elementary, middle, and secondary Catholic schools submitted by 174 archdiocesan and diocesan offices in the United States (a 100 percent response rate), including Puerto Rico, Guam, and the Virgin Islands. The majority of the work lists schools by archdiocese and diocese. Each entry includes name, address, telephone number, grades taught, enrollment figures, and the name of the principal for the school. A list of the superintendents by state and city is also included. The presentation of most of the data is simply reproduced from clear computer data sheets. The horizontal, all-capital-letter, text format is easy to read.

More than a directory, this reference work also presents ample statistical and demographic information in 25 charts, such as enrollment data of the 2,618,567 students and statistics on staffing, as well as future projections through the year 2005. The distribution of the data in most of the charts follows the division by the NCEA into six regions: New England, Mideast, Great Lakes, Great Plains, Southeast, and West/Far West.

This directory makes a fine addition to education collections. It is recommended for all libraries.
—**Edward Erazo**

Handbooks and Yearbooks

1217. **The Encyclicals of John Paul II on CD-ROM.** [CD-ROM]. J. Michael Miller, ed. Huntington, Ind., Our Sunday Visitor, 1996. Minimum system requirements (Windows version): IBM or compatible. CD-ROM drive. Windows 3.0. Mouse. Minimum system requirements (Macintosh version): Macintosh LC. system 7.0. $49.95. ISBN 0-87973-767-0.

Between 1979 and 1995, Pope John Paul II issued 12 major encyclicals that confront the challenges facing humanity on the threshold of the 3d Christian millennium. Because no single compilation of the texts of these formal letters to the Church has hitherto been available, this CD-ROM fills such a need. The collection is intended primarily for preachers, theologians, educators, and students of sacred science. Especially valuable is the comparative study that can be made of such more popular encyclicals as *Centesimus Annus* (1991), *Veritas Spendor* (1993), and *Ut Unuum Sint* (1995).

Searching by word and phrases allows instant access to key thoughts and themes, making them ideal for homily preparations. This disc should also serve as an inspiration for anyone who wishes to investigate the major writings that embody the mind and heart of the present pontiff. For each of the encyclicals, there is an overview and commentary on the contributions to doctrine made by John Paul. Selected bibliographies are provided where proper and helpful. The encyclicals, on the whole, are filled with hope and the confidence that "God is preparing a great springtime for Christianity."—**G. A. Cevasco**

1218. Utter, Glenn H., and John W. Storey. **The Religious Right: A Reference Handbook.** Santa Barbara, Calif., ABC-CLIO, 1995. 298p. index. (Contemporary World Issues). $39.50. ISBN 0-87436-778-6.

At work in a field where there are strong feelings about fine distinctions, the authors choose their words carefully. Even so, this basic reference book contains a useful and discriminating amount of information. Emphasis is on conservative religious organizations and individuals that have been politically active since World War II, but some sections, especially the historical introduction, chronology, and biographical sketches, contain earlier material.

The most interesting chapter reports the results of a survey conducted for the authors in 1994 that details the beliefs of members, rather than leaders, of religious right organizations. A subsequent semichapter of quotations is awkward, as is much of the book. A list of organizations is useful, although it does not list Advocates for Life Ministries or its publication, *Life Advocate*, listed later. Bibliographies, including sources for electronic media, cover the final 136 pages. The index is accurate, but not comprehensive.

Timeliness is important in this field where organizations and publications are dynamic. A library in need of a basic reference book would not be wrong to buy this one, but a wiser choice may be to wait for the next edition, which should be more rigorously edited and better indexed. [R: Choice, May 96, p. 1459; RBB, 15 Mar 96, pp. 1316-18; SLJ, Aug 96, p. 183]—**John Newman**

Islam

1219. **The Muslim Almanac: A Reference Work on the History, Faith, Culture, and Peoples of Islam.** Azim A. Nanji, ed. Detroit, Gale, 1996. 581p. illus. index. $95.00. ISBN 0-8103-8924-X.

The Muslim Almanac introduces readers to Islam, its roots, and how it affects cultures today. The almanac is divided into 12 subject parts, which range from "The Beginnings and Foundations of Islam" and "The History and Extension of Islam" to "Literary Expressions in Islam" and "Women and Their Contributions to Islam." "The History and Extension of Islam" contains chapters on each country or area in which Islam is a major religion. These chapters explain how each culture affects and is affected by Islam. "Literary Expressions in Islam" contains chapters on Muslim literature in differing cultures, as well as Muslim folklore and folklife in general. Subject parts are divided into 2 or more chapters, each written by a scholar specializing in that area, making for a total of 39 chapters.

The Muslim Almanac differs from other reference works in this area in that it is not just a list of terms with essay definitions, as is *The Oxford Encyclopedia of the Modern Islamic World* (see ARBA 96, entry 1477) or *The Concise Encyclopedia of Islam* (see ARBA 91, entry 1448). Its arrangement is similar to a textbook, in which each chapter covers a different major area of Islam. Chapters are basic enough for beginning students of Islam, yet have in-depth coverage appropriate for a graduate-level understanding. Each chapter is signed and includes a bibliography.

This work includes a chronology of major events, a list of the distribution of Muslim populations by nation-state, a brief explanation of the Islamic calendar, a glossary, a general bibliography, and an extensive index, all of which add to its use as a valuable information source. The almanac is a quality reference work from cover to cover, and it is highly recommended for academic libraries with religious studies programs. [R: Choice, June 96, p. 1621; LJ, Feb 96, p. 144; RBB, 15 April 96, p. 1462; RQ, Summer 96, p. 561]—**Laura K. Blessing**

Judaism

1220. **American Jewish Year Book 1996. Volume 96.** David Singer and Ruth R. Seldin, eds. New York, American Jewish Committee, 1996. 644p. index. $35.00. ISBN 0-87495-110-0.

The *American Jewish Year Book* is published yearly by the American Jewish Committee. Its subtitle is accurate: It attempts to be a "record of events and trends in American world Jewish life." As such, most sections appear on a yearly basis with updated information (e.g., sections on Jewish life in the United States and various other countries, obituaries, periodical and population listings). Along with this information, there are generally two lengthy essays highlighting some part of the American Jewish experience. This year they are the "Jewish Experience on Film—An American Overview," by Joel Rosenberg, a Tufts professor of Judaic studies, and "Israelis in the United States," by sociologists Steven J. God and Bruce A. Phillips. Most academic and large public libraries will have many, if not all, of the previous 95 volumes. Volume 96 is a worthwhile addition to the series.—**Deborah Hammer**

1221. **The American Synagogue: A Historical Dictionary and Sourcebook.** By Kerry M. Olitzky. Marc Lee Raphael, ed. Westport, Conn., Greenwood Press, 1996. 409p. index. $99.50. ISBN 0-313-28856-9.

Although admittedly not comprehensive, this history of Jewish congregations in the United States and Canada claims its uniqueness by describing synagogues from the four major movements; namely, Orthodox, Conservative, Reconstructionist, and Reform Judaism. The two most important criteria used for inclusion in the work were historical impact and the age, especially pioneer status, of the synagogues. Other determining factors were contemporary and local impacts and important historical events associated with the temple. A well-documented introduction by Frances Weinman Schwartz presents an overview of the foundation of Judaism in North America and the evolution of the four movements up to the present time. The role of the rabbi and American influences on synagogue architecture are also discussed.

The approximately 350 individual histories give enough detail to make interesting reading and relate dates, geographic sites, and reasons for establishing the synagogues; names of successive rabbis; educational and other activities; conflicts and changes throughout the years (including the 1990s); and current membership numbers. Each entry gives the source(s) drawn from, which may include books, manuscripts, and personal interviews. Synagogues are listed by state/province and city, and range in number from 1 in Alaska to 44 in New York. Only two provinces of Canada are covered. Indexing is by names of synagogues (with locations) and rabbis. This resource will appeal to a specialized audience, but speaks in an intimate, personal voice. [R: Choice, Dec 96, p. 593; LJ, 1 Oct 96, pp. 68-70]—**Janet J. Kosky**

1222. Cohn-Sherbok, Lavinia, and Dan Cohn-Sherbok. **A Popular Dictionary of Judaism.** Richmond, England, Curzon Press; distr., Atlantic Highlands, N.J., Humanities Press, 1995. 199p. $49.95; $18.50pa. ISBN 0-7007-0366-7; 0-7007-0357-8pa.

This work consists of a listing of basic terms from English, Yiddish, and Hebrew that are important in understanding Judaism. The list includes biographical information, key historical figures, places, and events. Cross-references are provided. The definitions are brief, from one or two lines to a short paragraph. There is no bibliographic information. Use of capital letters and bold typeface for the terms defined promotes easy reading. Additional terms within the entries are marked with an asterisk and can be looked up to provide more information. There is a seven-page introduction providing a brief historical glimpse of Judaism.

The book is a handy tool for the nonspecialist, the student, or members of the general public needing clear, brief, nontechnical information about Judaism. In this regard, it is a useful addition to public or school library reference collections. [R: Choice, April 96, p. 1282]—**Susan J. Freiband**

1223. **Dictionary of Judaism in the Biblical Period: 450 B.C.E. to 600 C.E.** Jacob Neusner and William Scott, eds. New York, Macmillan Library Reference/Simon & Schuster Macmillan, 1996. 2v. maps. $175.00/set. ISBN 0-02-897292-9.

This religious dictionary differs from standard works in that while components of Jewish history and culture are discussed from the standpoints of several different authorities, Christian concepts and doctrines originating in Jewish writings are also examined in historical context. The purpose of the work is to define terms and ideas found in various sacred and classical writings from 450 B.C.E. to 600 C.E., which is considered the formative period of both Judaism and Christianity. Among the works referred to are the Old and New Testaments of the Bible, the Dead Sea Scrolls, and rabbinical writings, all "bodies of writings that represented communities of Judaism" (p. viii). Classical Jewish writings drawn upon are the Mishnah, Tosefta, the two Talmuds, and numerous Midrash collections. Appropriately, contributors of the articles are Jewish, Protestant, and Catholic professionals from the United States, Canada, Europe, and Israel.

More than 3,300 entries in 2 volumes cover meanings of transliterated Hebrew and Greek works and idioms; broader theological topics; geographic place-names with recent archaeological discoveries noted; and biographical information. Definitions range from a few lines in length to several columns and are meant to serve a ready-reference purpose rather than be a source of extensive information. Articles are not signed, although responsibility for certain specialty areas has been designated to various editors in the preface.

Most curious is the omission of credentials and areas of expertise in the list of contributors. Political maps of several eras and abbreviations used in the text complete the introduction. The typeface size and format are appealing, and the writing is clear and direct, intended to inform both the layperson and scholar. Given the unique approach of commentaries from both Jewish and Christian sources, this work would be most useful to students of religious history or comparative religion. [R: Choice, Sept 96, pp. 94-95]

—Janet J. Kosky

1224. Sherman, Moshe D. **Orthodox Judaism in America: A Biographical Dictionary and Sourcebook.** Westport, Conn., Greenwood Press, 1996. 291p. index. (Jewish Denominations in America). $79.50. ISBN 0-313-24316-6.

Sherman's look at Orthodox Judaism, written for Marc Lee Raphael's three-volume Jewish Denominations in America series, begins with a fascinating introduction that clearly delineates the fluctuation of both the content and the mission of the Orthodox movement in the United States. He describes how each wave of Jewish immigration brought new personalities, traditions, and outlooks to the United States that were either assimilated by Orthodoxy or rejected by it, thus creating another subgroup of coreligionists.

The body of the book consists of one- to two-page biographies of a "representative sample" of leaders (all men) of the Orthodox movement, none of whom were alive when the book was compiled. Included are rabbis, scholars, founders of yeshivas, cantors, authors, community leaders, philanthropists, and so on. Along with birth and death dates, Sherman concentrates on the education of the subject, and most importantly, the portion of his life that was spent in the United States, and how each individual influenced the Orthodox Judaism of his day. Bibliographies of original writings as well as secondary sources append each entry.

Additional sections briefly discuss several American Orthodox Rabbinic organizations and offer an annotated list of American Orthodox Rabbinic periodicals. There is also a full bibliography and a glossary of Yiddish terms. The dictionary will prove valuable as a reference tool for large public and academic libraries or any collection serving an Orthodox Jewish community. [R: Choice, Nov 96, p. 436]

—Deborah Hammer

Sikhism

1225. Dogra, Ramesh Chander, and Gobind Singh Mansukhani. **Encyclopaedia of Sikh Religion and Culture.** New Delhi, Vikas Publishing House; distr., Columbia, Mo., South Asia Books, 1995. 556p. index. $44.00. ISBN 0-7069-9499-X.

After more than a decade of preparation, this encyclopedia of the religion and culture of the Sikhs in India comes as a welcome reference for those who in reading about the Sikhs find they need further clarifying information. This work lists the materials of a large number of scholarly works that have been selected and edited for this project. The scope of the entries encompasses information on aspects of religion, culture, history, tribes, castes, folklore, customs, fairs, and festivals. Much of what is obscure in the Sikh holy book *Guru Granth Sahib* is defined here, and for that reason alone this encyclopedia is valuable.

The authors' stated reason for the inception of Sikhism is the attempt to reconcile the Muslims and Hindus in northern India, and the introduction provides a condensed history of the religion. The entries compare Sikh terms to Hindu or Muslim concepts and provide a comparative history. The index is simple and could have been subdivided to provide more help to the general reader. The work as a whole is well done, but small. More detailed work or references in the entries would benefit the scholars using it.

—**Linda L. Lam-Easton**

Taoism

1226. **The Shambhala Dictionary of Taoism.** By Ingrid Fischer-Schreiber. Boston, Shambhala, 1996. 235p. illus. $13.00pa. ISBN 1-57062-203-5.

The dictionary is based on *The Encyclopedia of Eastern Philosophy and Religion* (see ARBA 96, entry 1483), which is itself a translation of *Lexikon der Ostüchen Weisheitsleheren* (Otto-Wilhelm-Barth Verlag, 1986). The work is composed of a brief introduction, the dictionary itself (about 225 pages), and a short bibliography. Primary texts are only cited in translation, and all citations in the bibliography are to translations and commentaries in Western languages.

Entries are arranged alphabetically, letter-by-letter according to the Wade-Giles romanization of the Chinese. The introduction includes some simple rules for pronunciation of Chinese and a table showing the modern pinyin equivalent of the Wade-Giles romanization. No Chinese characters appear in the dictionary, even though this means that the same entry title can appear twice with entirely different meanings (e.g., *ming*="luminosity" or "enlightenment" and *ming*="fate").

Although the dictionary is aimed at general readers, it requires English-language-only readers to work from the Chinese romanization. In order to be truly useful to general readers, the work should include an English-to-romanized-Chinese index so that users could look up concepts under widely known English-language terms without knowing the romanization. For example, the entry on trigrams (the basic eight symbols of the *I Ching*) can only be found if one knows to look under the Wade-Giles romanization *pa-kua*. The dictionary is of almost no use to readers who know Chinese, as they must rely solely on romanization without being able to check an entry against the actual Chinese characters.

This work is meant to explain the basic terminology of Taoism to the general reader. The editor describes Taoism as a "wisdom teaching" and states that Taoist technical vocabulary is concerned with the intuitive grasp of the world (and its eschatology), and thus they must ultimately be understood in light of immediate personal experience. Unfortunately, the editing (some errors were found) and organization of the dictionary preclude its use as a general reference work and make it a rather oddly organized treatise. The content of the entries is reliable, but the lack of an English index and an index from Chinese character to romanization makes it unusable for most reference inquiries. The dictionary is really only suitable for enthusiasts who are willing to read it from cover to cover or who know the technical and historical vocabulary of Taoism in Wade-Giles romanization. [R: LJ, 15 April 96, p. 72]—**Richard H. Swain**

Part IV
SCIENCE AND TECHNOLOGY

29 Science and Technology in General

BIBLIOGRAPHY

1227. Jayawardene, S. A. **The Scientific Revolution: An Annotated Bibliography.** West Cornwall, Conn., Locust Hill Press, 1996. 383p. index. $60.00. ISBN 0-933951-71-X.

One of the most fascinating chapters in the history of science is undoubtedly the period that spans the Scientific Revolution: from the Renaissance to the beginnings of the Enlightenment. Considerable scholarly work has been published on this fertile and far-reaching phase of human history in the form of bibliographies, encyclopedias, library catalogs, monographs, source books, articles in periodicals, exhibition catalogs, proceedings in symposia, and essay reviews. There is thus an enormously vast corpus of printed material on the germination, evolution, and establishment of every branch and aspect of the sciences that played a role in the Scientific Revolution. That body of work is not easy to search and locate from the standard reference sources, items that may be of interest to a particular worker in the field. This beautifully bound volume covering a little less than 400 pages does this for the investigator. With its aid, any serious reader can track down sources from which one can get ample scholarly information and analysis on any matter of interest pertaining to the Scientific Revolution. The book is also spiced with a sprinkling of illustrations and reproductions. *The Scientific Revolution* is indeed a valuable book for any library.
—**Varadaraja V. Raman**

1228. **SciTech Reference PLUS 1995-1996.** [CD-ROM]. New Providence, N.J., R. R. Bowker/Reed Reference Electronic Publishing, 1995. Minimum system requirements: IBM or compatible 286. ISO 9660-compatible CD-ROM drive with MS-DOS CD-ROM Extensions. Hard disk. 535K conventional memory. Monochrome or color monitor. $995.00/yr.

This edition of *SciTech Reference PLUS* includes nearly 423,000 bibliographic records of medical, scientific, and technical books from *Books in Print* (BIP) and *Books Out-of-Print* (see ARBA 96, entries 15 and 18); approximately 65,000 records from *Ulrich's International Periodicals Directory* (see ARBA 96, entry 88); some 123,000 biographical records from *American Men and Women of Science* (19th ed.; see ARBA 96, entry 1485); and more than 38,000 company and organization profiles from *Directory of American Research and Technology* (29th ed.; see ARBA 96, entry 182), *Directory of Corporate Affiliations* (see ARBA 91, entry 142, and ARBA 90, entry 175), and *Standard Directory of Advertisers* (see ARBA 94, entry 296, and ARBA 90, entry 280). As expensive as the product under review is, it certainly costs less than buying the print components separately. Users can search any of more than 30 indexed data categories, including author, title, subject, and keyword, as well as research activity type, Standard Industrial Classification (SIC) code, and product description. Search sets can also be combined. Because *database* is one of the searchable categories, searches can be restricted to any one (or more) of the constituent sources. Searching options include the use of Boolean operators and truncation. Eighteen of the indexes can also be browsed as lists (series title, institution, publisher, and the like). There is a variety of formats in which the retrieved records may be viewed; one of them is an order form for items in BIP and *Ulrich's* that can be printed.

There was a minor difficulty in installing the program, but a call to R. R. Bowker's technical support line was all that was required to solve the problem. Also, the user's guide was apparently written for the previous edition of this product. Thus, there was some incorrect information (database coverage and searchable categories and browseable indexes). Additionally, it was not mentioned that the program can be used with a mouse. Some corrections were provided on an update sheet. The disc is recommended for science and technology collections that can afford it.—**Craig W. Beard**

1229. **Walford's Guide to Reference Material. Volume I: Science and Technology.** 7th ed. Marilyn Mullay and Priscilla Schlicke, eds. London, Library Association Publishing; distr., Lanham, Md., UNIPUB, 1996. 967p. index. $249.00. ISBN 1-85604-165-4.

The newest edition of this standard reference tool features more than 7,400 entries, each with full bibliographic information and an annotation; some entries also include prices. The compilers worked with a cutoff date of early 1996, making it extremely up-to-date for this type of publication. The expanding nature of reference is reflected in the inclusion of electronic sources under the subheadings of "Databases," "CD-ROM," and "Software." As always, *Walford's* is international in scope and much more comprehensive than comparable works, such as the 11th edition of *Guide to Reference Books* (see entry 8). Although the price may be somewhat daunting, this is an outstanding resource for any academic or large public library, or any special library that serves a scientific or technical clientele.—**Susan Davis Herring**

BIOGRAPHY

1230. Kessler, James H., and others. **Distinguished African American Scientists of the 20th Century.** Phoenix, Ariz., Oryx Press, 1996. 382p. illus. index. $49.95. ISBN 0-89774-955-3.

While most people can list without difficulty the names of eminent black Americans in politics, sports, music, movies, law, and literature, they cannot with equal ease list the names of famous African Americans in physics, mathematics, chemistry, or medicine. Yet, numerous black Americans have worked actively and successfully in the various sciences, many achieving recognition and eminence in their fields. Given unfortunate racial stereotypes and misperceptions, it is important that black children and adults, as well as other Americans, learn about them.

The book under review serves this important purpose. It presents to the reader the lives and achievements of 100 African Americans who have reached the highest academic levels in such diverse fields as anthropology, physics, mathematics, and endocrinology. The brief biographies are based on information gathered from a variety of sources, in many cases including material provided by the subjects themselves. This is most valuable as readers are able to see reflections of some of the personal struggles these outstanding individuals went through in order to accomplish what they did.

One fine example of the people profiled is young scientist Mae C. Jemison, who became the first African American woman astronaut. Among the others who are listed are George Carruthers, who developed a far UV camera/spectrograph that was used in the Apollo missions to the moon; J. Ernest Wilkins, who received his Ph.D. in mathematics from the University of Chicago when he was barely 19 years old; and Meredith Gourdine, the Olympic medalist and engineering physicist who invented many things and established his own company. Many women scientists are discussed as well. Important to note is the fact that between 1870 and 1900 black inventors had more than 400 patents to their names. Because the book limits itself to the twentieth century, such men as Benjamin Banneker, the self-taught black mathematician of the eighteenth century who studied astronomy and wrote an almanac based on his calculations, and Edward A. Bouchet, the first black Ph.D. in physics who graduated from Yale University in the late nineteenth century, are not mentioned. Fortunately, George Washington Carver, who became one of the most eminent agricultural chemists of his time, has found a place here.

Children should remember that many of the people mentioned in this book grew up under difficult economic constraints, social injustices, and racial prejudices, with little encouragement from the outside. However, they were individuals with enormous determination and a sense of self-worth who struggled against obstacles. Black students have countless role models to draw inspiration from, and this book offers insight into the lives of many such heroes. [R: LJ, 1 April 96, p. 74-76; RBB, 15 Feb 96, p. 1042; SLJ, May 96, p. 146; VOYA, Aug 96, p. 190]—**Varadaraja V. Raman**

1231. **Notable Women in the Life Sciences: A Biographical Dictionary.** Benjamin F. Shearer and Barbara S. Shearer, eds. Westport, Conn., Greenwood Press, 1996. 440p. illus. index. $49.95. ISBN 0-313-29302-3.

The 97 distinguished women scientists listed in this biographical work were selected according to certain criteria: Their names were starred in the 1st editions of *American Men of Science* (R. R. Bowker, 1906), and they won awards such as the Nobel prize and the Lasker prize. The emphasis is on the twentieth century, although the time period covered is from antiquity to the present. Living and deceased scientists are included. All major areas of biology and medicine are covered.

Each biographical entry supplies a brief chronology covering dates of birth and death, education, employment, and awards. The text describes important events in the life of each biographee; how each advanced in her career, including her teaching and interactions with students; major scientific achievements; and how mentors aided her advancement. Portraits of some of the scientists are furnished.

An excellent book such as this one, covering women scientists, is most welcome, as there are not many comparable titles. This dictionary is extremely readable, and the personal lives of the scientists come through in each biography. It should be in the reference collections of academic, school, and public libraries. [R: RBB, 1 Sept 96, p. 168; SLJ, Nov 96, pp. 138-39]—**John Laurence Kelland**

1232. **Who's Who in Science and Engineering 1996-1997.** 3d ed. New Providence, N.J., Marquis Who's Who/Reed Reference Publishing, 1996. 1386p. index. $259.95. ISBN 0-8379-5754-0. ISSN 1063-5599.

After all of these years, the Marquis Who's Who series has settled into a fairly standardized entry for those people who are included. This format requires no new evaluation. The variation, however, is in the collection of new groups of individuals by different subjects or interests, and the compilation of various indexes to the work.

This compilation, which is composed of biographies of living scientists and engineers throughout the world, is one of their newer products. To round out this volume, the publishers have included persons not only in the physical and life sciences and medical technologies, but also in selective "soft" sciences, such as sociology, economics, and psychology.

Altogether, this collection includes more than 26,000 individuals in 110 distinct specialties. Its three primary indexes are a geographic index, professional area index listings, and the major honors and awards organized by fields and by professional organizations within the fields. One of the major benefits of this work will be its assistance to universities and corporations in recruiting new faculty and staff.

—**Robert J. Havlik**

1233. **Who's Who in Science in Europe: A Biographical Guide to Science, Technology, Agriculture, and Medicine.** 9th ed. London, Cartermill International and New York, Stockton Press, 1995. 2v. index. $950.00/set. ISBN 1-56159-132-7.

As a subset of the World Research Database, *Who's Who in Science in Europe* provides biographical references to more than 60,000 individuals at 30,000-plus institutions in 36 European countries, including Turkey but excluding the former Soviet Republic. This work has become a standard over the years and its 9th edition has more than 2,000 new entries. The scientists selected come from the areas of education, government, agriculture, industry, and technology.

The entries furnish the individual's name, year of birth, present job, employer and year appointed, main professional and research interests, higher education and degrees (including the degree-granting institutions), previous professional experience with length of service, current telephone and fax numbers, address, and a list of professional organizations and societies to which the person belongs. In addition, major publications are listed, but full bibliographies of works are not included. While narrative biographies are not supplied, the facts listed provide a high level of information concerning the individuals. The scientists profiled are self-selected in that the editors send forms to various institutions and societies requesting the information (the forms are not sent directly to the individual scientists). Entries that are derived from printed sources or from third parties and not verified by the individual are marked with an asterisk.

In addition to the alphabetic listing, there is a detailed subject index by country that provides access to the individuals by name, area of expertise, and the like. In all, there are 62 categories of scientific endeavor used. The individuals are self-categorized in these areas whenever possible.

As a companion volume to *European Research Centres* (see ARBA 94, entry 1574, and ARBA 90, entry 1431), *Who's Who in Science in Europe* is the most comprehensive listing of biographical profiles of European scientists. Both works are also available on CD-ROM. While the subject index is detailed, the directory would benefit from additional appendixes listing scientific areas, scientists by research center or laboratory, or even major research grants obtained. It would appear that because the information is in machine-readable form, generating these additional appendixes would be relatively simple. *Who's Who in Science in Europe* is an important selection for all larger public and academic libraries and could be considered essential for important scientific collections. The price of the volumes probably makes the work an unlikely purchase for individual scientists. [R: Choice, July/Aug 96, p. 1778]—**Robert L. Wick**

CATALOGS AND COLLECTIONS

1234. **Science & Technology: A Purchase Guide for Libraries 1995.** Pittsburgh, Pa., Carnegie Library of Pittsburgh, 1996. 82p. index. $12.00pa.

The 1996 volume of this purchase guide (see ARBA 91, entry 1458, for a review of the 1989 volume) contains annotated entries for more than 500 recent (most published in 1995) books recommended for general science collections. Only books costing $50 or less are included. Books are arranged by Library of Congress classification. As one may expect, there is some overlap with entries listed in the 1995 supplement to the 10th edition of *Public Library Catalog: Guide to Reference Books and Adult Nonfiction* (10th ed.; see ARBA 95, entry 660), but fewer than one-third of the entries in this guide also appear in *Public Library Catalog*.

However, the quality of this work is not up to the standard set by *Public Library Catalog*. Citations are not as complete (coauthors are not even listed) and the annotations are less authoritative. Also, an arrangement by Dewey Decimal classification would be preferable considering that such works seem to be aimed primarily at small- and medium-sized libraries. This said, the publication under review remains an inexpensive guide to science and technology titles appropriate for lay audiences; it would be best considered as a supplement to *Public Library Catalog* and other standard works.—**Joseph Hannibal**

CHRONOLOGY

1235. Elliott, Clark A. **History of Science in the United States: A Chronology and Research Guide.** New York, Garland, 1996. 543p. index. $83.00. ISBN 0-8153-1309-8.

Modern science in North America began shortly after the arrival of Europeans on the continent, with exploration of exotic plants and grains. No one could have suspected that someday it would all lead to the launching of rockets from this continent to survey the surface of Mars for life. Many things of significance to science have happened in this region of the world, although the floodgates were not opened until the twentieth century. This book succinctly presents the advances in science and scientific institutions that have occurred in the United States during the past five centuries. It is a factual, year-by-year recording of discoveries, events, and organizations in the major branches of science. The guide lists nearly 1,000 names of scientists who may be called "American" one way or another. There are also substantial reference lists and a long research guide that takes the reader through bibliographies, reference works, electronic access, primary sources, and so on. The work will be enormously useful to researchers in any aspect of science history in the United States. It is the sort of work that becomes useful in this age of information explosion. [R: Choice, Nov 96, pp. 427-28]—**Varadaraja V. Raman**

DICTIONARIES AND ENCYCLOPEDIAS

1236. **Biographical Dictionary of the History of Technology.** Lance Day and Ian McNeil, eds. New York, Routledge, 1996. 844p. index. $125.00. ISBN 0-415-06042-7.

This concise, well-organized compendium offers schools, libraries, museums, and businesses a handy source of facts about inventions. Arranged alphabetically by inventor, this upgrade of the 1990 volume opens with a preface expressing the editors' aim, selection criteria, and method of presentation, including a claim to fairer representation for the accomplishments of African Americans. The acknowledgments page lists 23 contributors who covered female, Asian, and Islamic technologists. The body of the text concludes with an index arranged by subject areas (for example, agriculture and food, mining and extraction, ports and shipping, recording, steam and internal combustion engines, and synthetic materials). Additional indexes compile names of particular inventors and topics, such as bridges, printing, pumps, railways, weapons, and shipbuilding.

Biographical entries follow a simple arrangement of name; dates and places of birth and death; and a brief summary of contributions, as in "Scottish cotton spinner and textile machine maker." The text of each brief entry precedes principal honors and distinctions, a bibliography, a list for further reading, and the initials of the contributor. Where appropriate, *see also* notations direct the user to additional data (e.g., from Samuel Thomas von Soemmerring to Samuel Finley Breese Morse).

Overall, coverage is disappointing. For example, the list of entries on electronics mentions Benjamin Franklin and Nikola Tesla, but omits the massive number of patents General Electric derived from the work of Charles Proteus Steinmetz, especially his contributions to electric streetcars. Of the many women who have contributed to the Industrial Revolution, the volume omits Sarah Mather's submarine light and telescope; Katherine Burr Blodgett's invisible glass and plane-wing deicer; Hedy Lamarr's coding system and remote-control torpedo; Grace Hopper's computer language; Bessie Cary Evinrude's motor designs; Mary Engle Pennington's frozen food containers; and Rosalyn S. Yalow's radioimmunoassay. [R: Choice, Nov 96, p. 456; RBB, 1 April 96, p. 1387]—**Mary Ellen Snodgrass**

1237. Callaham, Ludmilla Ignatiev, Patricia E. Newman, and John R. Callaham. **Callaham's Russian-English Dictionary of Science and Technology.** 4th ed. New York, John Wiley, 1996. 814p. $125.00. ISBN 0-471-61139-5.

Forty-odd years ago, *Callaham's* was the standard. That first 1947 edition has now evolved into its 4th instar and has grown from a compact handbook into a 120,000-word tome. Although there has been a great increase in the number of specialized Russian-English technical dictionaries, *Callaham's* remains the standard all-around technical dictionary for native speakers of English. Unlike the many special-purpose dictionaries produced in Russia, this dictionary is physically durable and has remained consistently available. Although designed for English users, its lexicographic virtues were recognized by the Russians themselves, who republished the 3d edition nearly 20 years after it appeared here.

This new edition (completed by technical translator and former electrical engineer Newman and technical editor John Callaham after Ludmilla Callaham's death) has significantly broadened its coverage from the former "chemical and polytechnical" to "science and technology," so that it now includes the biosciences, computer technology, nuclear power, and so on. Special features are the inclusion into the regular alphabetic sequence of abbreviations, adjectives derived from place-names, a useful table of "Technical Word Endings," and a list of declensional endings.

Bilingual automated dictionaries and machine translation of technical texts are now a reality, but such texts require checking and "postediting," while this dictionary is at the ready. Also, there are always those who want to do it on their own. Scientific and technical discourse changes rapidly, and the new *Callaham's*, although not inexpensive, should be on every library reference shelf and on the desk of every translator. [R: Choice, July/Aug 96, p. 1770]—**D. Barton Johnson**

1238. **The Gale Encyclopedia of Science.** Bridget Travers, ed. Detroit, Gale, 1996. 6v. illus. maps. index. $399.00/set. ISBN 0-8103-9892-3.

The six-volume *Gale Encyclopedia of Science* contains 2,000 entries covering biologic and physical science, engineering, and technology, as well as mathematics, health, and medical sciences. The intended audience is presumably high school students and adults. Entries are alphabetically arranged by subject, with length varying from short definitions of a paragraph or two to detailed entries on complex subjects. Many articles include a key terms box. *See* references at the end of articles direct the user to related topics. A general index in volume 6 lists topics, names of people, and many *see* references.

The articles provide a complete and understandable overview of all topics. For example, on a topic such as grasses, ample information on the biology of grasses; native grasses of North America; and grasses in agriculture, horticulture, and as weeds is provided. In chemistry, the user will find a clear description of Fraunhofer lines that includes historical background. Information on recently discovered conditions, such as hantavirus and hepatitis C and E, is given. The encyclopedia has approximately 800 photographs, drawings, tables, charts, and maps, but while the cover of the encyclopedia is very colorful, all graphics are in black-and-white, and thus their effectiveness is greatly diminished. For example, a scanning electron micrograph of a green peach aphid would be stunning in color, but is much less impressive in black-and-white.

The name of the contributor is given at the end of each article, and a complete list of contributors with their affiliation is included in each volume. Articles furnish a brief bibliography, but often the materials have a copyright date between 1989 and 1993. With the abundance of current scientific information available electronically, in periodicals, and on the Internet, information in a print encyclopedia format becomes quickly dated, and it is difficult to justify its purchase. [R: LJ, 15 Sept 96, p. 54; RBB, 1 Oct 96, pp. 368-70]—**Lynda Welborn**

1239. **The Grolier Student Encyclopedia of Science, Technology, and the Environment.** Danbury, Conn., Grolier, 1996. 11v. illus. maps. index. $219.00/set. ISBN 0-7172-7517-5.

This 11-volume set provides an introduction to many aspects of science and technology for children at a 3d- or 4th-grade reading level. The books are colorful, lightweight, and accessible. The entries are in alphabetic order, and an index in the last volume directs the reader to topics that are not necessarily the titles of specific entries. Each entry is short and clear, and explanations are simple and understandable. Inevitably, the entries are superficial, but the reader is referred to other sections that have more information on a particular aspect. The entries stimulate curiosity and interest without being overwhelming.

The entries cover a broad variety of subjects. Science, in general, is defined in an operational way rather than as a collection of facts; the aspect of answering questions and explaining things is emphasized. The many branches of biology are described, chemistry and mathematics are covered, and technology is considered broadly. Generous photography, much from public domain sources, illustrates the entries. Diagrams are clear and uncluttered, and the writing is crisp and engaging.

Despite the fact of being published in Danbury, Connecticut, an Australian influence is felt. Many photographs originate in Australia, such as the Southern Cross in the entry on constellations and the Australian opera in the entry on voice. This is not a negative influence, however. One error was found: The diagram in the entry on Genetics is mislabeled; brown hair and blond hair are reversed. Nonetheless, these volumes are captivating and should grab the interest of any child. [R: RBB, 1 April 96, p. 1388; SLJ, Aug 96, p. 181]—**Margretta Reed Seashore**

1240. **Larousse Dictionary of Science and Technology.** Peter M. B. Walker, ed. New York, Larousse Kingfisher Chambers, 1995. 1236p. illus. $45.00. ISBN 0-7523-0010-5.

Not only has there been an explosion of research and new knowledge in all areas of science and technology, causing some fields to be increasingly isolated, but there has been an increasing overlap of information exchange between fields that has generated a terminology crisis. For the everyday reader, a single-volume dictionary of science and technology is imperative. For more than 50 years, various editions of the *Chamber's Technical Dictionary* and *Cambridge Dictionary of Science and Technology* have tried to meet this need. Now under the imprimatur of Larousse Kingfisher Chambers, a new edition of these standards has appeared.

This edition contains more than 4,900 entries identified by 46 subject categories, as well as 500-plus illustrations that explain many of the concepts. Completely new to this edition are food science entries. The short entries are in strictly alphabetic order and are identified by a single subject category. There are cross-references when alternative words can be used, but only the most common term is defined. More than 25 appendixes appear, mostly presenting physical, chemical, and mathematical symbols and measurements. Also provided is a chronology of discoveries and inventions. This volume is easier to handle than the larger-sized *McGraw-Hill Dictionary of Scientific and Technical Terms* (5th ed.; see ARBA 95, entry 1493), and for this reason will find more places on working bookshelves. [R: Choice, Jan 96, pp. 760-62]—**Robert J. Havlik**

DIRECTORIES

1241. **World Databases in Biosciences & Pharmacology.** C. J. Armstrong and R. R. Fenton, eds. New Providence, N.J., Bowker-Saur/Reed Reference Publishing, 1996. 1325p. index. (World Databases Series). $200.00. ISBN 1-85739-0687.

There is more than one way to crash on the information superhighway. Perhaps one of the greatest and most overlooked hazards is through the blind acceptance of electronic material. This is a difficult concept for trusting travelers, who, in their zeal to explore the digital world, fail to recognize that any hacker with a modem and an opinion can transmit information alongside international authorities. Recognizing the need for consumer assistance, the World Databases Series details various databases into reference directories that can be used with great confidence.

This directory is divided into 11 sections. Topics include a panoramic view of the biosciences; miscellaneous biosciences (bioengineering, evolution, taxonomics, history, ethics, and health and safety); biochemistry topics; pharmacology; ecology/biologic communities defined by habitat; bacteriology/microbiology; botany; zoology (including human biology and anatomy); the biologically relevant aspects of laboratory techniques and equipment; industry news (also reports and investments); and patents. Databases are grouped logically and include contents, size, access, pricing, and detailed third-party reviews. In addition, database linkage provides an avenue for comparisons and contrasts.

Although this volume does not provide comprehensive Internet coverage, if used correctly, it parallels the effect of a car's antilock breaking system—available at the outset, sensitive to environmental changes, and designed to prevent Internet users from skidding out-of-control.—**Sue Lyon Mertl**

HANDBOOKS AND YEARBOOKS

1242. Bunch, Bryan. **Handbook of Current Science & Technology.** [2d ed.] Detroit, Gale, 1996. 834p. index. $50.00. ISBN 0-8103-9552-5.

This hybrid "designed to provide easy access to major developments in science and technology ... during the mid-1990s" is only partly a reference book—as the author indicates, it can be read through or browsed like a magazine. The major sections (on "hard" sciences, anthropology and archaeology, and technology) begin with overviews of the state of the field; these contain timetables of the field's history. Major sections conclude with lists and tables, including lists of Nobel prizes where appropriate, and in some cases other reference information—on subatomic particles for physics, for example. However, much of the reference matter is available elsewhere (Nobel prizes in many places, and more complete timetables in the author's own *Timetables of Science* [see ARBA 90, entry 1422] and *Timetables of Technology* [Simon & Schuster, 1993], among other sources). The volume is often entertaining and informative, but its value as a reference source is hindered by the sketchy index. In seeking information on research into the possible role of RNA in the origin of life, one finds the single index heading "RNA," with 13 entries. Subsections conclude with periodical references and lists of additional reading—citations of articles in *The New York Times, Science, Physics Today, Scientific American*, and so forth. However, these citations do not list the articles' titles, and many subsections include discussion of several related topics. Finding which article is on the topic of specific interest may be frustrating.

Topics treated are partially a matter of the author's judgment. This work is a revision of the *Henry Holt Handbook of Current Science and Technology* (see ARBA 93, entry 1455), which may give information on topics not discussed in the present edition.—**Robert Michaelson**

1243. **McGraw-Hill Yearbook of Science & Technology 1996: Comprehensive Coverage of Recent Events and Research....** Compiled by the Staff of the McGraw-Hill Encyclopedia of Science & Technology. New York, McGraw-Hill, 1995. 415p. illus. maps. index. $125.00. ISBN 0-07-051772-X. ISSN 0076-2016.

At the end of a mammoth rock concert, everyone returns home, and then a crew comes and cleans up the grandiose mess. The rock remnants are mere waste to be discarded and forgotten forever. In a somewhat like manner, scientists and technologists keep working away, amassing vast amounts of knowledge debris, as it were, except that this is useful and of long-range value. Yet it is also complex and incomprehensible to those who are left outside, who need a band of dedicated people to distill out of the vast amount of articles, papers, and other publications the essence of what has been happening in the field of human knowledge as a result of the expansion of science and the explosion of technology.

That is what yearbooks and encyclopedias accomplish. In this solid volume, the staff of the *McGraw-Hill Encyclopedia of Science & Technology* have done precisely that: They have presented to the average educated reader the sum and substance of what has been happening in various fields, from atmospheric aerosols to wavelets, during the past year. The well-written explanations are enriched by a number of clarifying diagrams, compact tables, and interesting pictures.

One of the ironies of civilization is that even with such fine aids and expositions of science and technology, there is appalling scientific illiteracy. This is the kind of news update that few individuals can afford price-wise, but it will find a place in every reference library, and eventually serve future science historians who look back into what the people of this particular year accomplished.—**Varadaraja V. Raman**

INDEXES

1244. **Science Experiments Index for Young People.** 2d ed. By Mary Anne Pilger. Englewood, Colo., Libraries Unlimited, 1996. 504p. $60.00. ISBN 1-56308-341-8.

Children, with their inquisitive natures, and science, with its limitless possibilities, are a wonderful match. Guides such as this one and the *Science Experiments and Projects Index* (see ARBA 95, entry 1506) are excellent resources for parents and teachers who want to help children explore and observe scientific phenomena.

The 2d edition of this resource is a cumulation of *Science Experiments Index for Young People* (see ARBA 89, entry 1360) and *Science Experiments for Young People Update 91* (see ARBA 93, entry 1461) and provides additional information to make it current to 1994. This guide gives access to 1,527 entries with an abundance of scientific experiments and projects that will help answer children's questions and pique their curiosity.

Three sections—subject headings, an alphabetic index of entries, and books indexed by number—cover models, math books, social science experiments, and food and nutrition resources. This index is a great place to start for students, teachers, librarians, or parents trying to find a book that includes the perfect experiment to clarify a point or spark interest in a topic. The reasonable price, ease of use, and information for children of all ages will make this source useful to public and academic libraries. [R: RBB, 1 Nov 96, p. 540]—**Diane J. Turner**

30 Agricultural Sciences

GENERAL WORKS

1245. Maman, Marie, and Thelma H. Tate. **Women in Agriculture: A Guide to Research.** New York, Garland, 1996. 298p. index. (Women's History and Culture, v.11; Garland Reference Library of Social Science, v.908). $46.00. ISBN 0-8153-1354-3.

Future Farmers of America (FFA) first admitted women as official members in 1969. FFA transformed women from prospective farm wife to potential farmer, even though women had always farmed alongside men. During this century's two world wars, the autonomous role of women in U.S. agriculture earned the female farmers the title "Women's Land Army." Such tantalizing tidbits emerge as the reader skips the globe with the reference librarian authors, who culled publications dated between approximately 1985 and 1995, which they deemed easily located through research libraries. They point the reader toward what is available, essentially in English.

Major topical categories (e.g., economic development, sexual division of labor) provide structure. Spanish-language reference works are omitted, except for the citation of a 1985 guide to South American literature by Jacqueline A. Ashby and Stella Gomez. Separate sections list French-language books and articles; bibliographies of women in agriculture; and journals that frequently publish articles on women in agriculture (including addresses, telephone numbers, and publication cycle). The index is thorough.

Some problems, such as typographic errors (e.g., dairies for diaries) and varying depth of synopses, distract. Largely useful, however, the volume also invites reflection: The women of Burkina Faso lose financially even as European cosmetic markets readily snatch up the shea nuts they produce. [R: Choice, July/Aug 96, p. 1775]—**Diane M. Calabrese**

1246. Pillsbury, Richard, and John Florin. **Atlas of American Agriculture: The American Cornucopia.** New York, Macmillan Library Reference/Simon & Schuster Macmillan, 1996. 278p. illus. maps. index. $100.00. ISBN 0-02-897333-X.

This atlas provides a descriptive and statistical overview of U.S. agriculture with historical and current coverage. It is a fairly large book, wider than it is high. Each of its three main sections is replete with maps showing the distributions of various crops, as well as other data, for the United States as a whole, or for each of the major agricultural regions within it.

The first section, "The American Agricultural Scene," charts the history of U.S. agriculture and describes agriculture today. Also covered are farm ownership patterns, conservation, agricultural economics, and marketing, among other topics. "Cornucopia's Regions" paints a portrait of each region, covering geography, economic, and social aspects in addition to many crop statistics maps by region. "Cornucopia's Abundance" covers a large number of crops, farm animals, and aquacultural products. There is a country-wide map for each. The historical, cultural, and economic aspect of each crop is discussed. A brief section entitled "The State of the American Cornucopia: An Afterword" details current developments in agriculture. A bibliography is furnished. There are both a general index and a geographic index.

This major atlas has broad and thorough coverage of its topic. Its quality and interdisciplinary scope make it an important reference in all academic libraries.—**John Laurence Kelland**

1247. **World Databases in Agriculture.** C. J. Armstrong, ed. New Providence, N.J., Bowker-Saur/Reed Reference Publishing, 1996. 1130p. index. (World Databases Series). $165.00. ISBN 1-85739-043-1.

This massive work is a compilation of descriptive information on agricultural databases, including those databases available online through the major vendors (such as KR Dialog), or on CD-ROM, diskette, tape, and so on. This does not include, except for a few, the many databases available on the Internet. Its primary value, therefore, is as an aid for finding appropriate databases to purchase, or to choose the best for-fee database to search from an online vendor.

The work is worldwide in scope and covers the United Kingdom, Europe, Scandinavia, Australasia, and the Far East as well as North America. The subject coverage is broad, treating forestry, fisheries, food science, and veterinary medicine. Database descriptions are arranged under nine headings: "Agriculture," "Agriculture General," "Aquatic Science/Fisheries," "Food Science/Processing," "Soil Science/Irrigation/Fertilizers," "Animal Production/Veterinary Medicine," "Forestry/Forest Products," "Crop Production," and "Pesticides/Agricultural Chemicals."

A beneficial feature is the detail provided for each database description; some are more than two pages in length. The descriptions begin with factual information, such as database type (bibliographic, statistical, factual); year the database begins; languages; coverage; number of records; update period (monthly, yearly); sources (journal, reports, monographs); and if abstracts are available. Keywords are listed that summarize the sort of information found in the database, followed by a paragraph description of what the database contains. This is succeeded by the various forms the database comes in—such as online, CD-ROM, diskette, tape—who the producer of the database is, and pricing information. Another useful feature is citation(s) to published reviews of the database. Comparative information is also valuable when more than one vendor produces the database.

A subject index and a database name index are found at the end of the volume to aid in finding information in the text. The subject index is a huge 375 pages, and ordinarily that would mean good access to the textual material; however, this index is overburdened with many subject headings outside the scope of the subject area. For example, there are headings for mechanical engineering, nuclear physics, paleontology, remote sensing, space medicine, sound recordings, and terrorism, to name a few.

There is no other source that is as comprehensive in listing, describing, and comparing agriculturally related, worldwide electronic database products, and it should prove useful in finding and purchasing an appropriate agriculture database for a library, home, or organization. For those who want information on the many free agriculture databases now available on the Internet, try *Key Guide to Electronic Resources: Agriculture* (see ARBA 96, entry 1518). The work under review is recommended for university, college, and agriculture libraries. [R: Choice, April 96, p. 1294; LJ, Feb 96, p. 70]—**Diane B. Rhodes**

FOOD SCIENCES AND TECHNOLOGY

1248. Bartlett, Johnathan. **The Cook's Dictionary and Culinary Reference: A Comprehensive, Definitive Guide to Cooking and Food.** Chicago, Contemporary Books, 1996. 488p. $35.00. ISBN 0-8092-3120-4.

The title aptly describes this volume with its more than 3,000 entries. It covers fruits, vegetables, meats, breads, dairy products, and almost anything edible, plus measuring terms, spices, wines and spirits, nonalcoholic beverages, utensils, cookware, and appliances as related to cooking or food. The entries vary in length from one word to several words to two or three pages when describing all the varieties of a fruit, vegetable, fish, and so forth.

The addition of syllabication and pronunciation for the entries would enhance the volume. Some of the entries describing ethnic foods are lacking in correctness, such as "Chile rellenos ... They are often served with tomato sauce"—never, unless the author thinks green or red chile sauce is the same as tomato sauce, which it is not, even by his definition. The constant reference to "beef critter" when referring to beef is annoying.

This is a useful dictionary for the price, particularly if a library is lacking such a reference volume. It is recommended for public libraries, school libraries, and vocational schools where baking and cooking curricula are offered.—**Betsy J. Kraus**

1249. **Food and Beverage Market Place, 1996: Companies, Brand Name Products....** Richard Gottlieb and Amy Lignor, eds. Lakeville, Conn., Grey House Publishing, 1996. 1089p. index. $225.00pa. ISBN 0-939300-65-6.

This is the premier edition of a new business directory, to be published annually. It is intended as a marketing tool for companies, as well as a reference for corporate, public, and university libraries needing this type of data. More than 7,200 U.S. food and beverage companies of all sizes are listed alphabetically by name in the main section. Information provided includes company address, telephone and fax numbers, product category, company officers, number of employees, brands marketed, company divisions if applicable, and various additional data for some entries. Not all of the above is listed for every company, however. Additional sections follow the company listing in the main section for 700-plus mail-order food catalogs and also food media (associations, specialized directories, databases, periodicals, marketing studies, and trade shows). Seven separate indexes, including brand name, executive name, geographic location, and product category (there are 28 broad food categories) make this large volume's contents readily accessible.

While most of the information within these pages could be found using a variety of other sources, *Food and Beverage Market Place* has done a creditable job of putting it all together in a single directory. It should serve as a valuable reference for those in the industry and others who often need basic information regarding food and beverage companies, associations, and publications. [R: Choice, May 96, p. 1448]
—**William H. Wiese**

1250. Gay, Kathlyn, and Martin K. Gay. **Encyclopedia of North American Eating & Drinking Traditions, Customs, & Rituals.** Santa Barbara, Calif., ABC-CLIO, 1996. 289p. illus. index. $65.00. ISBN 0-87436-756-5.

If this book had been organized by subject category (perhaps as presented in the index), it would have been a more cohesive work and an interesting and useful reference tool. As it stands, the book is more of an amusement, an exercise in trivial pursuits for general readers with an interest in food customs and traditions or North American popular culture. Arranged alphabetically from "After-Dinner Drinks" to "Zucchini Bread," entries describe a variety of practices associated with eating and drinking in North America. The entries focus on foods and beverages (e.g., bubble gum, spoon bread); eating and drinking establishments (e.g., coffee houses, lemonade stands); and eating and drinking events (e.g., family reunions, Oktoberfest). Many entries are cross-referenced and the authors have also listed references for further information, which are repeated en masse in an extensive bibliography. Generously proportioned black-and-white photographs illustrate the book.

Although priced as a reference book, this work does not pretend to be comprehensive, and it is not. For example, there is no entry for or mention of "cidering," the midwestern custom of touring local cider mills in the autumn to sample cider and donuts, although there is an entry for "cider." Instead, what the encyclopedia offers is "a sampling of the numerous types of eating and drinking patterns in North America." Cross-references are helpful, but not thorough. In the description of eggnog, readers are told that this is a traditional drink of the Christmas season and a cross-reference is made to "Christmas Eve/Day Dinner." However, under that listing, no mention is made of eggnog, nor is it listed as a cross-reference. Unfortunately, the index is not detailed enough to make up for these shortcomings.

There is a great deal of information in this book, and obviously a great deal of research has gone into it. It is a pity that poor organization hampers access to the content. Enjoyable to browse, it is only an optional purchase for the reference shelf.—**Barbara Ittner**

1251. **North American Brewers Resource Directory 1996-1997.** 13th ed. Compiled by the Institute for Brewing Studies. Boulder, Colo., Brewers Publications; distr., Johnson Books, 1996. 429p. maps. index. $100.00pa. ISBN 0-937381-48-9.

This resource directory is a guide to the microbrewery, brewpub, and craft-brewing industry. It begins with a 1995 year in review of the United States and Canadian industries and extensive industry statistics. The directory also lists: United States, Canadian, Mexican, and Caribbean breweries and North American contract brewers; manufacturers and suppliers of brewing equipment and materials; state excise taxes and control agencies (such as the Bureau of Alcohol, Tobacco, and Firearms); and worldwide brewing associations, libraries, and schools. Of more general interest are the bibliography of books and journals and the beer style guides (which list various beer types [e.g., English-style brown ale and German-style bock beer] and the exact specifications that determine the style). The work includes an equipment index and a general index.

This book truly is an industry guide, and considering the high price, there really is little here of interest to all but the most dedicated home brewer. Anyone involved in the industry will consider this item a must-buy. Only larger libraries wanting a complete collection on this topic will want to spend the money to acquire this resource.—**Stephen Haenel**

1252. Robertson, James D. **The Beer-Taster's Log: A World Guide to More Than 6000 Beers.** Pownal, Vt., Storey Communications, 1996. 599p. illus. index. $24.95pa. ISBN 0-88266-939-7.

If anyone doubts that beer has achieved the status once accorded only fine wines, they need only look in this truly comprehensive reference work. "Deep dark brown, almost opaque, toffee-coffee nose, big smoky coffee flavor, medium body, long pleasant coffee-malt aftertaste" reads the description for Sheaf Stout. Well, perhaps not the status of wine, but at least the attention.

Robertson has put together an exhaustive work providing detailed analysis of more than 6,000 beers the world over. Each brew is described in what can only be called loving detail and is assigned a style designation (ales, lagers, stouts, and so on) and a numeric rating. The ratings, based on a 100-point scale, were derived from panel tastings of 90 percent of the beers listed. (A dirty job, but somebody had to do it.) Sometimes other points of interest, such as history and pedigree, are included. Other details, such as malt types and hop varieties, are listed, as are original gravity and alcohol by weight or volume, but only when provided by brewers. Technical data of interest to only the most serious devotee include degrees Plato, degrees Lovibund, IBUs, and SRMs, again as provided by brewers. Unfortunately for the homebrewer trying to replicate that favorite microbrew, these details are generally only provided by the largest brewers.

The book is arranged by region of the world and has an appendix listing U.S. brewers by state, a beer index (with beers listed by brand name), and an index of brewers. The indexes make accessing the contents easy. The book is illustrated with black-and-white pictures of labels every second or third page, and every right-hand page has a notes column. The foreword by Fred Eckhardt is elucidating, providing background on the history of beer and the finer points of zymurgy for the layperson.

As is to be expected in a work of this size, a few problems show through. For instance, Boulder Creek Brewing Co. of California is listed under Colorado (mistaken, no doubt, for the former Boulder Brewing Co.). Also, Buffalo Gold Premium Ale, originated at a brewpub and licensed for commercial production to a microbrewery, is inexplicably listed twice with slightly different descriptions under the brewer's listing and again under the brewpub's listing with a designation as a beer, not an ale. Pilsner Urquell, the venerable patriarch of the pilsner clan (and progenitor of U.S. lagers), is described as excellent, but only receives a rating of 79—very good. There is always room to disagree with many of the ratings, of course: Disagreeing with ratings is part of the fun of books such as this one. However, there is one rating few beer aficionados would disagree with: Zima rates a 13.

Beers from extremely small brewpubs and microbreweries receive the same attention as those from the largest producers. Seasonal beers, which the author admits might not be available, are included. Even nonalcoholic beers are listed. If individuals are looking for the low-down on a local brewpub or microbeer, it is here. Librarians looking for one source on the beers of the world will find all they need in this book.
—**Stephen Haenel**

1253. Vassilian, Hamo B. **Ethnic Cuisines: A Comprehensive Bibliography in the English Language.** Glendale, Calif., Armenian Reference Books, 1996. 200p. illus. $75.00. ISBN 0-931539-13-7.

This is a reference book that covers cookbook bibliography in the English language from more than 50 nations and cultures including Armenia, Georgia, the Middle East, India, Central Asia, Greece, Israel, North Africa, and other Islamic nations. The bibliography is arranged in author, title, and subject matter in alphabetic order and contains full bibliographic information. The book should be useful for those who are interested in finding recipe sources related to a particular ethnic group and those who are interested in studying ethnic foods. The manuscript lists 1,309 titles and provides photographs of 300 cookbooks. The printing, paper, black-and-white photographs, and binding are of average quality. The work has a table of contents but no index. It is strictly a bibliography and contains no recipes. The bibliography would be useful for ethnic food lovers, reference librarians, and cookbook collectors.—**Herbert W. Ockerman**

1254. Wertsman, Vladimir F. **What's Cooking in Multicultural America: An Annotated Bibliographic Guide to Over Four Hundred Ethnic Cuisines.** Lanham, Md., Scarecrow, 1996. 163p. index. $37.50. ISBN 0-8108-3127-9.

Those searching for ethnic cookbooks and books about ethnic cuisines may find some guidance in this slim volume. With the cuisines of more than 400 ethnic groups represented, this work places titles under an alphabetic list of ethnic groups, from "A-Z Ethnic (Worldwide Coverage)" and Afghanistan to Zimbabwe and Zuni. Bibliographic citations are accompanied by descriptive annotations. The author briefly reviews the contents of the book, listing specific cuisines (in multiethnic volumes) and recipe categories (e.g., beverages, vegetables). Appendixes include "Ethnic Ingredients and Food Market Sources," "New York City Ethnic Food Market Sources," "Other Reference Sources of Interest," and "*Bon Appétit* and Similar Expressions in Various Languages." An author index concludes the work.

Although the scope of this book is not explicitly defined, the author states in his preface that emphasis is on English-language books, mostly published in the United States. Coverage is selective rather than exhaustive, but the criteria of selection are not clarified. Seemingly, the author has attempted to represent as many cuisines as possible, rather than covering all publications of a certain era. Publication dates go back to the mid-1960s, and many newer books are not included (e.g., Diane Kennedy's *Recipes from the Regional Cooks of Mexico*).

If it had focused on more current titles, this would be a fine collection development tool. If coverage had been more comprehensive, it would be an excellent research tool. A recipe index would also enhance the book's usefulness. As it stands, Wertsman's work can function in a limited way in either of these capacities, but those interested in ethnic cuisines and cooking will no doubt find many items of interest.
—**Barbara Ittner**

HORTICULTURE

1255. Elliott, Jack. **Bulbs for the Rock Garden.** Portland, Oreg., Timber Press, 1996. 160p. illus. index. $29.95. ISBN 0-88192-346-X.

With an emphasis on cultivation rather than on botanical detail, Elliott, a leading authority on bulbs, has gathered information in this book on easily attainable dwarf bulbs, and some corms and tubers. Although the title refers to bulbs in rock gardens, the collected information is pertinent for anyone interested in this group of bulbs, as they do not have to be grown in this particular environment.

After an overview of dwarf bulbs, including climate, habitat, and pertinent pests and diseases to which they may fall prey, Elliott deals with placement, requirements, and propagation. The remainder of the book, excluding two appendixes—"Bulbs with the Award of Garden Merit" and "Societies and Further Reading"—and an index, is divided into four chapters that group bulbs by season. Concentrating on those that are hardy in the author's native Great Britain, each chapter deals with the various genera that flower within its designated season. Under each genus, in thoroughly enjoyable running text, Elliott describes the various species and, in some cases, subspecies, and discusses their cultivation. Along with relevant and detailed information, he includes wonderful anecdotal material, which makes this book a good read as well as an informative text for the gardener. Color photographs and line drawings of many of the bulbs are scattered throughout the narrative, as are several descriptive charts.

While the book is based on dwarf bulbs that do well in Great Britain, most enthusiasts can pick out the plants that will do well in their particular climate and conditions. Perhaps the only disappointments with the book are the lack of common names for the majority of the flowers and a frustrating, but not uncommon type of index for books of this kind. All species and common names are listed under the genus, making it virtually useless for anyone trying to find information on a particular plant without knowing the genus.

Although there are myriad books written about bulbs, a fact that almost deterred the author from putting pen to paper, this book certainly fills a niche. It should be welcomed by any bulb fancier for its comprehensive treatment of the cultivation of this group of bulbs. [R: RBB, 15 Mar 96, pp. 1231-32]
—**Jo Anne H. Ricca**

1256. Lewis, Colin. **Bonsai Survival Manual: Tree-by-Tree Guide to Buying, Maintaining, and Problem Solving.** Pownal, Vt., Storey Communications, 1996. 157p. illus. maps. index. $21.95pa. ISBN 0-88266-853-6.

The introduction to this attractive and useful volume tells readers that "a bonsai is a microcosm containing within it, unchanged in everything but size, the mystery of the universe." For those who would like to grow bonsai but perhaps have thought that its culture is also a mystery, this introductory but authoritative volume will provide enough clues to the home gardener to get started with some confidence. It covers buying, caring for, and shaping bonsai, as well as pests and diseases, in general chapters. Following are 2-page species profiles of approximately 50 of the most commonly available miniature trees for this type of horticulture.

The manual is generously illustrated with detailed color drawings and photographs well chosen and placed to illuminate important points made in the text. Charts outline species-specific growing information, which follows an interesting narrative. Suppliers and other useful addresses are appended. This volume is a wonderful guide for the novice and may suggest new species for those already growing bonsai to add to their collections. [R: BL, 1 Sept 96, p. 52]—**JoAnn V. Rogers**

1257. Lowe, Duncan. **Cushion Plants for the Rock Garden.** Portland, Oreg., Timber Press, 1996. 160p. illus. index. $29.95. ISBN 0-88192-345-1.

Horticultural proponents of "little is beautiful" have long recognized that the low-growing plants of mountains and other harsh environments often are eminently suited to cultivation in small spaces, and frequently are tolerant of adverse horticultural conditions (although like any plant, they like it best when conditions are good). To this end, there is a long tradition of horticultural interest in low-growing "cushion plants." The present volume is a personal addition to this literature. After a brief introduction to the general nature and biology of cushion plants, the author reviews 87 species in 26 genera from around the world.

There is no particular systematic organization to the presentation, and the descriptions of individual species are scant in details about characters and morphology. However, the descriptions are highly readable, are quite informative about the biology and cultivation of the plants, and are generally accompanied by excellent color photographs that clearly convey the attraction of these plants. The last third of the book is given to a well-written and wide-ranging discussion of the methods of cultivation of cushion plants, of their propagation, and of the control of pests. Appendixes provide an alphabetic list of the species described, sources of seeds and plants, reference to cushion plant clubs and texts, and a quick guide to what to look for in buying specimens. In sum, the book is less a reference than a good introduction to cushion plants, attractively written and well illustrated, and full of anecdotal information. [R: RBB, 15 Mar 96, pp. 1231-32]—**Bruce H. Tiffney**

1258. Simon, Ronald G. **A Reference Guide for Botany and Horticulture.** Phoenix, Ariz., Instructional Media Institute, 1996. 501p. $39.95pa. ISBN 0-9653962-0-7.

This bibliography is designed to help instructors locate media materials to include in presentations designed for garden clubs, 4-H clubs, and groups of schoolchildren. The work is divided into 2 sections: an adult section that includes grades 9-12, and a section listing media developed for children in grade's K-8. Media selected include activity books, CD-ROMs, charts, computer software, fiction and nonfiction books, videotapes, videodiscs or laserdiscs, slides, and transparencies. The adult computer software section is subdivided into botany, horticulture, landscaping, miscellaneous software, and test generating software.

The bibliography also describes materials more suitable for hands-on use in classrooms: learning kits, filmstrips, and mounts. A list of 16mm film rentals is something of an anachronism. The author's annotations help users evaluate products and give full title, copyright date, length, number of slides or frames, and distributors (addresses and telephone and fax numbers are listed in a separate section).

The author fails to stress the importance of copyright concerns for those instructors who may be putting together interactive multimedia presentations for sale or use via the Internet or to incorporate into a Webpage. This guide would be a useful subject bibliography to include in state or regional libraries serving school systems, but it is not a necessary purchase for academic or public libraries.

—**Milton H. Crouch**

1259. **Taylor's Guide to Fruits and Berries.** Roger Holmes, ed. New York, Houghton Mifflin, 1996. 451p. illus. maps. index. (Taylor's Guides to Gardening). $19.95pa. ISBN 0-395-71086-3.

This book is a great overview of fruits and berries, including some that may be considered but are not available commercially. Each fruit has a section on requirements and cultivation. Sections on specific varieties are informative, including the fruiting season, a description, the region of adaptation, and comments about related varieties and production. Specific varieties that are discussed in this book seem to be the primarily used or underused varieties. The sections on planting and pruning are extensive and nicely illustrated.

The book is well edited, easy to read, and maintains a consistent reading quality throughout, which must have been a challenge because there are several contributing authors. Excellent photographs are strategically placed throughout the book. The information on control of insects and diseases is rather simplistic, and the reader should follow the suggestion (given in the book) to seek local advice from the extension service. Specific chemical recommendations will eventually be outdated.

Overall, this book is a well-rounded information source that makes it a good resource for home owners and hobbyists. It may serve the weekend gardener as the primary information source about fruit and berry production.—**John A. Jackman**

1260. **Taylor's Guide to Heirloom Vegetables.** By Benjamin Watson. New York, Houghton Mifflin, 1996. 343p. illus. maps. index. (Taylor's Guides to Gardening). $19.95pa. ISBN 0-395-70818-4.

Many old varieties of vegetables are covered in this book. Paring the list covered down to 500 varieties must have been a challenge, but the author seems to have made wise selections. The short stories about the heritage of varieties make interesting reading. When this information is combined, a history lesson about the seed business emerges. Information about the individual varieties is useful and informative. The many topics covered include unusual and almost forgotten crops, not a trip to the supermarket of today.

The section on seed saving is unexpected but useful. Seed sources are extensive and annotated, allowing the reader to find access to the many varieties discussed. Pest control information is too simplistic, with a decidedly organic theme. Some suggestions are not practical and may not work well. Chemical control alternatives should at least be mentioned, at least as a method to preserve the varieties that make this book a reality.

The book is nicely laid out and well edited. Pictures are in one section, which makes it easy to browse them quickly. The citations to footnotes could be more complete. Anyone who enjoys vegetable gardening and browsing seed catalogs will like this book.—**John A. Jackman**

VETERINARY SCIENCE

1261. Bamberger, Michelle. **Help! The Quick Guide to First Aid for Your Cat.** New York, Howell Book House/Simon & Schuster Macmillan, 1995. 149p. illus. index. $9.95pa. ISBN 0-87605-794-6.

The need for reliable information on cat care has increased as cats continue to enjoy unprecedented popularity as companion animals, and as their owners show more interest in their welfare. Veterinarian Bamberger seeks to fill part of this void with an unusual work devoted to emergency first aid. Her intention is to help people assess and handle emergency situations until a veterinarian can be reached. The book, which covers basic life-saving techniques and general aid techniques, is clearly written and well illustrated. Of particular interest is the chapter that outlines several typical emergencies, and then allows the reader to attempt to diagnose the problem.

However, most, if not all, of this information may be found in comprehensive works on cat care such as *The Cornell Book of Cats*, edited by Mordecai Siegal (Random House, 1989), and *The Well Cat Book* by Terri McGinnis (rev. ed., Random House, 1993). Further, both of these books contain topics missing from the book under review. Bamberger's omissions include any information on the "high-rise syndrome," falls, and first aid for cats suffering from porcupine quills. More significantly, her discussions on CPR and artificial breathing fail to note that these techniques can injure an animal that is breathing normally and has a heartbeat. This book will have most value when it is used as a complement to other works on cat care.—**January Adams**

1262. Murphy, Michael J. **A Field Guide to Common Animal Poisons.** Ames, Iowa, Iowa State University Press, 1996. 330p. index. $29.95 spiralbound. ISBN 0-8138-2934-8.

Poisoning, either accidental or deliberate, is a major health problem of animals, and potential harmful effects or even death cannot be treated or averted without up-to-date information and lengthy diagnoses based on known factors for various poisons. Organized as a quick reference for veterinary practitioners and students, the book covers six major areas of animal interactions with toxins: prevalence of exposure (common and uncommon, subdivided by species exposed and the physiological system affected); treatment regimens (general, supportive, and specific); one- to two-page synopses of facts applicable to the recognition, diagnosis, and treatment of each toxin; books and journals tied to the references listed on the page for each toxin; United States and Canadian colleges of veterinary medicine, diagnostic laboratories, and poison control centers (by state and province); and an index of toxins (clinical signs, diagnostic test results, and toxin names). The data are presented in chart form and are very concise.

Although most poisons affect many parts of an animal's body, injury or death is usually the result of damage to a single organ or system. The heart of the book is the toxin summaries, subdivided by systems affected (neurological, gastrointestinal, dermal, respiratory, cardiovascular, and so on) and the poison responsible for the toxicity. Among the toxic substances referenced are plants (Bermuda grass, locoweed, marijuana, and so forth); pesticides; household and farm products; and inorganic toxins, such as lead. Individual toxin summaries include distribution, toxicity, condition of poisoning, clinical signs, species affected, recommended diagnosis, and treatment. Approximately one-third of the book is a detailed index of clinical signs, diagnostic test results, and toxin names.

A comb binding and tabbed section markers allow one to access the information easily and quickly. For the mobile unit, examination room, or classroom, this field guide is invaluable.—**Judy Gay Matthews**

1263. Plumb, Donald C. **Veterinary Drug Handbook.** 2d ed. White Bear Lake, Minn., PharmVet Publishing; distr., Ames, Iowa, Iowa State University Press, 1995. 722p. index. $47.95pa. ISBN 0-8138-2443-5.

What is the essential advice a veterinarian should give a client about colchicine (given to dogs for treatment of gout)? The answer is: Watch for changes in appetite or gastrointestinal problems. The utilitarian nature of this volume does not end there. Aside from client information, each entry (for more than 350 drugs) includes indications, contraindications, pharmacology, doses, monitoring, and warnings of adverse effects.

The utility just begins with the monographs. The appendix contains a section on topical ophthalmic agents and much more. Consult it to check the estrus and gestation periods for dogs and cats, solubility definitions, abbreviations used in prescription writing, and all sorts of information in between. The index covers all drug names. Appendix topics are outlined in the table of contents. In all, this is a robust volume at a modest price. Professionals take note.—**Diane M. Calabrese**

31 Biological Sciences

GENERAL WORKS

1264. Davis, Elisabeth B., and Diane Schmidt. **Using the Biological Literature: A Practical Guide.** 2d ed. New York, Marcel Dekker, 1995. 421p. (Books in Library and Information Science, no.57). $85.00. ISBN 0-8247-9477-X.

For anyone who wants a thorough, contemporary review of the literature in the life sciences field, this is the book. In its 2d edition, this work keeps pace with the explosive changes in scientific information technology, with new sections on Internet resources and electronic databases. The guide is well organized, beginning with a general section on biological resources, and followed by broad subject chapters covering resources in biochemistry and biophysics, molecular and cellular biology, genetics, microbiology and immunology, ecology, evolution and animal behavior, plant biology, anatomy and physiology, entomology, and zoology. Within each subject chapter, the information is subdivided by form of material (e.g., abstracts and indexes, directories, handbooks, periodicals, databases, societies, and textbooks, to name a few).

A comparison to the 1st edition (see ARBA 83, entry 1295) reveals several major changes. The typeface and the layout of the information in the 2d edition are much clearer and distinct, making it easier to find the desired section and read the entries. The text itself is 70 percent longer than the 1st edition, reflecting the huge increase in both print and electronic biological resources since 1981. As mentioned above, an attempt was made to include recent information about electronic resources, such as GenBank, LiMB, and listservs in the various biological subject areas. Because of its broad scope and currency, this work is recommended for the reference collection of both academic and public libraries. [R: Choice, June 96, p. 1613]—**Elaine F. Jurries**

1265. Navarra, Tova, and Myron A. Lipkowitz. **Encyclopedia of Vitamins, Minerals, and Supplements.** New York, Facts on File, 1996. 281p. index. $35.00. ISBN 0-8160-3183-5.

This book is not unique. There are at least seven records on OCLC for "encyclopedias" of vitamins, minerals, and other supplements that have been published since 1990. One book scheduled for release in 1996 (*The Encyclopedia of Nutritional Supplements* by Michael T. Murray [Prima Publishing]) competes with the work under review for newest publication. However, the two authors of *Encyclopedia of Vitamins, Minerals, and Supplements* are medical professionals rather than full-time nutritionists. Navarra is an RN who has authored other books, and Lipkowitz is a family practitioner and allergist as well as a former pharmacologist with a background in nutrition. Their backgrounds give this book some authenticity absent in other such books, as herbs and supplements are such a popular field for writers of all kinds.

In the introduction, Navarra is careful to support a neutral stance in presenting the information in this book. Contradictions of nutritional studies are cited, and the need for extensive research and clinically controlled studies in this field is discussed. Consequently, the contents are for informational purposes only and should not be construed as endorsements of any kind.

The book is arranged in an A to Z listing of vitamins; minerals; herbs; food technology terms (e.g., additives); food compounds; nutritionally related medical conditions; some drugs; and a variety of other nutritional topics (such as the recommended dietary allowance [RDA]). There are cross-references and nine appendixes of valuable information on dietary matters, such as the food pyramid and drug and nutrient interactions. At the end of the volume is an index that mines the content of the entries and leads the user to all sorts of topics not in the main alphabetic listing. A substantial bibliography is also provided.

The entries vary greatly, from brief ones on herbs to extensive ones on vitamins and minerals. Most entries on herbs give some botanical information, common uses (if known), and contraindications to use. The herbal list seems comprehensive even though the authors claim that only the most commonly known herbs are discussed. The coverage of vitamins, minerals, food substances, and the like also seems complete.

The encyclopedia is well written for the layperson, and should prove useful for personal ownership as well as for basic reference collections. It would also be beneficial for educational institutions supporting basic work in the dietary and nutritional fields. However, *Encyclopedia of Vitamins, Minerals, and Supplements* would not add much to a graduate or professional-level reference collection. [R: Choice, Sept 96, pp. 103-04; LJ, 15 June 96, p. 58; RBB, 1 May 96, pp. 1524-26; SLJ, Nov 96, pp. 141-42]
—Lillian R. Mesner

BIOLOGY

1266. **Concise Encyclopedia Biology.** Friedrich W. Stöcker and Gerhard Dietrich, eds. Revised by Thomas A. Scott. New York, Walter de Gruyter, 1996. 1287p. illus. maps. $99.95. ISBN 3-11-010661-2.

As the title page states, this encyclopedia is a translation from the German original. The translator explains, however, that in doing the translation form the 1986 publication, he has taken the liberty to do some updating and revising of material as well as adding some newly discovered animal species. Coverage of the field of biology is comprehensive. There are 7,000 entries and 12,000 figures, formulas, and tables. The areas of biology covered are biochemistry, botany, ecology, ethology, genetics, molecular biology, paleontology, physiology, and zoology.

Many of the entries in the book are comprehensive as well. For example, the coverage on blood circulation includes many line drawings of circulatory mechanisms and descriptions of the systems in various levels of animals. There is both basic information, such as the general structures of a circulatory system, and precise information on systems of differing vertebrates.

The entries are beautifully written and easy to understand, but they contain some scientific language that would rule out use by students under the high school level. The line drawings are high quality and do not take up inordinate amounts of space in the dense text. Any subject that is able to be portrayed visually is supported by these graphics. The end of the book has plates as well.

This is an important source of biological information for anyone in the teaching/learning environment. Teachers, professionals in other fields, and students will get significant amounts of information from the book. It should be in any library collection that serves general education or above. It also would be a good addition to a public library collection. [R: Choice, Oct 96, p. 249; LJ, 15 May 96, p.; RBB, Aug 96, p. 1921]
—Lillian R. Mesner

1267. **Elsevier's Dictionary of Fundamental and Applied Biology: Russian-English and English-Russian.** N. N. Smirnov and A. N. Smirnov, comps. New York, Elsevier Science, 1996. 400p. $187.50. ISBN 0-444-82397-2.

Scientific research is international, so polyglot dictionaries are essential for understanding the literature. This new Russian-English dictionary of biological terms covers both fundamental and applied biology. Approximately 20,000 terms related to basic biology, medicine, veterinary science, agriculture, forestry, hunting, fish culture, biotechnology, food technology, conservation, and environmental science are included. Words related to machines or mechanisms are excluded, while two-part words with personal names (e.g., Henle's Loop—*petlya' Ge'nle*) are emphasized. The senior author has 40 years of experience as a biologist and translator.

The dictionary has two sections. The Russian-English section is more complete. The English-Russian section is not identical, but it contains most of the terms and serves as an index to the Russian-English section. For example, the entry [analysis] in English provides the Russian terms *analiz* and *issledovanie*. In the Russian section, *analiz* has 31 subentries and *issledovanie* has 7. [Agar] has 20 subentries in Russian and one in English. *Duga'* [arch] has nine subentries in Russian, while [arch] in English has three translations: *duga'*, *du'zhka*, and *svod*.

The entries are arranged alphabetically in their respective alphabets, with an alphabetic list of subentries under the key entries. The definitions are brief, often only one word. Phonetic stress is indicated for Russian words. There is a list of English abbreviations used to indicate scientific fields and grammatical parts at the beginning of the text. Although small, this is a useful dictionary with a fairly broad scope. *The English-Russian Biological Dictionary* (5th ed., Firebird, 1993) is larger, with 70,000 terms, but it is only English-Russian. *Elsevier's Dictionary of Fundamental and Applied Biology* is a good addition to science reference collections in academic and special libraries.—**Barbara M. Bibel**

1268. **Encyclopedia of Life Sciences.** Anne O'Daly and others, eds. North Bellmore, N.Y., Marshall Cavendish, 1996. 11v. illus. maps. index. $449.95/set. ISBN 0-7614-0254-3.

This 10-volume set (plus an index) will be an excellent addition to any middle school, high school, and public library. It is colorful, lavishly illustrated, and well indexed. The material is easily accessible because, as with most encyclopedias, the entries are ordered alphabetically. However, the entry in the alphabetic location provides suggestions for other locations to read. Sidebars, called "connection boxes," appear liberally and provide links to other areas that may not be obvious. Each entry also has a box entitled "Core Facts" that summarizes succinctly half-a-dozen or so key pieces of information to take away from the discussion.

As an example, the entry on DNA offers information on structure, informatively illustrated in color; biochemistry; and molecular biology of DNA. Connections are suggested to energy, classification, and forensic science. The control of protein synthesis is well illustrated. Every few paragraphs there are suggestions to other entries. Two nicely laid-out boxes provide a discussion of DNA fingerprinting and the history of J. D. Watson and F. H. C. Crick's discovery of the double helix. The entry directs the reader to see "Genetics," which sends the reader on to "Chromosomes," and so on.

The writing is accessible and snappy and engages the reader. There is a large variety of photographs. These include many lovely portraits of animals, birds, flowers, and insects, as well as outdoor shots of geographic features, such as heaths and moors, bogs and swamps. There are a number of historical notes and pictures that provide perspective and add value.

There is a substantial amount of biochemistry, anatomy, and physiology. This material is at an appropriate level for high school students, and may inspire them to go further, as there are suggestions for further reading in books. Many references are as recent as 1993 and 1994 (except for historical ones, of course). It is difficult to know how accessible some of these references are, but the listings may serve as a guide for a library wishing to upgrade its holdings. All of the life sciences are represented in this set. Plants, animals, the biosphere, and human beings are all covered. The entries are diverse; for example, memory, metabolism, chromosomes, crustaceans, courtship, endangered species, perching birds, and so on.

There are two ways to use the encyclopedia. The reader can follow a trail from the first entry read in the area of interest along to many other entries that expand the information. It is possible to learn a great deal about a particular subject this way, although perhaps not as efficiently as a textbook. On the other hand, the reader may, as this reviewer and a few biologist friends did, spend an afternoon just perusing the volumes, picking up new information and enjoying the exposition of it.

One wishes the authors of the entries were identified, but only the editors of the sections are. A few things suffer in the effort at simplification (one of the inherited disorders of the urea cycle, arginase deficiency, was omitted, for example). Computer-based encyclopedias are on the rise, and they offer many advantages. Nevertheless, the print encyclopedia will still have a role. Overall, this encyclopedia is attractive, engaging, well illustrated, and diverse. [R: SLJ, Aug 96, p. 181]—**Margretta Reed Seashore**

1269. **Encyclopedia of Molecular Biology and Molecular Medicine. Volume 1: Achilles' Cleavage to Cytoskeleton-Plasma Membrane Interactions.** Robert A. Meyers, ed. New York, VCH, 1996. 462p. illus. $330.00. ISBN 3-527-28471-0.

This six-volume encyclopedia is advertised as the most comprehensive treatment of molecular biology and molecular medicine to date, and admittedly there are few comparable titles. Presently only the first three volumes have been published (see entries 1270 and 1271 for reviews of volumes 2 and 3). Signed articles are arranged alphabetically and are accompanied by a list of contributors' institutional affiliations and addresses at the beginning of the volume. Each entry is intended as a self-contained treatment complete with its own table of contents followed by a brief overview of the topic, a list of keywords and definitions, and an article ranging generally from 2 to 10 pages in length. The articles are concluded with *see also* references and a bibliography. Cross-referencing appears to be somewhat limited; this may become less important with the publication of the sixth volume, which promises a detailed, cumulative subject index. Until that time, subject access is restricted by the lack of an index.

The distinguishing feature of this encyclopedia is the fact that more than 90 percent of the articles relate to human genetics or molecular medicine (including a comprehensive treatment of the Human Genome Project). The molecular biology is geared toward an understanding of disease diagnosis, etiology, and therapy. Although a broader academic audience is implied by the title, this encyclopedia will be most useful to those involved in clinical or pharmaceutical research. It is extremely well written and well illustrated with many diagrams, tables, molecular structures, and photographs, and will no doubt fill an important niche. However, given the cost, the encyclopedia is recommended primarily for collections with a biomedical focus.—**Michael Weinberg**

1270. **Encyclopedia of Molecular Biology and Molecular Medicine. Volume 2: Denaturation of DNA to Growth Factors.** Robert A. Meyers, ed. New York, VCH, 1996. 474p. illus. $330.00. ISBN 3-527-28472-9.

1271. **Encyclopedia of Molecular Biology and Molecular Medicine. Volume 3: Heart Failure, Genetic Basis of to the Mammalian Genome.** Robert A. Meyers, ed. New York, VCH, 1996. 522p. illus. $330.00. ISBN 3-527-28473-7.

This new reference tool is an encyclopedia of molecular genetics and the molecular basis of life, with a focus on molecular medicine, structural biology, and the technology and findings of the Human Genome Project. The first volume, released earlier in the year (see entry 1269), covered Achilles' cleavage to cytoskeleton-plasma membrane interactions. Six volumes total are planned. This encyclopedia is intended to provide a single source for coverage of the molecular basis of life, discase diagnosis, and therapy.

The contents include the following subject areas: nucleic acids; structure determination techniques; purification and processing of DNA, RNA, and proteins; the Human Genome Project; proteins, polypeptides, and amino acids; lipids; immunology and biomolecular interactions; molecular biology of specific organisms and specific diseases; biochemistry and pharmacology; and biotechnology. The encyclopedia contains more than 1,900 keywords. In addition to the keyword definitions, the glossary of basic terms found at the back of each volume defines the most commonly used terms in molecular biology. There is a detailed subject index. Entries give some historical background, descriptions of the characteristics, physical maps, colored tables and illustrations, experimentations, theoretical discussions, and diagnoses. At the end of each entry, there are bibliographies of additional readings. The encyclopedia contains approximately 300 articles written by Nobel laureates and authorities in their fields.

Volume 2: Denaturation of DNA to Growth Factors includes information on genetics and genetic diseases, such as fragile X linked mental retardation, DNA replication and duplication, and genetic mapping. *Volume 3: Heart Failure, Genetic Basis of to the Mammalian Genome* includes such subjects as human chromosome mapping, genetic basis for heart failure and other diseases, and the microbiology of lung and liver cancer. These two volumes are a treasure trove of information. Each article begins with a keyword section, including definitions, to assist the reader who is unfamiliar with the specific subject area, followed by an outline of the article and definitions of abbreviations and acronyms.

The *Encyclopedia of Molecular Biology and Molecular Medicine* is an authoritative reference source of the highest quality. The set is recommended for molecular biologists, biochemists, pharmacists, physicians, and all life scientists.—**Marilynn Green**

BOTANY

General Works

1272. Davis, Elisabeth B., and Diane Schmidt. **Guide to Information Sources in the Botanical Sciences.** 2d ed. Englewood, Colo., Libraries Unlimited, 1996. 275p. index. $49.50. ISBN 1-56308-075-3.

University of Illinois science librarian Davis, with coauthor Schmidt, has competently updated her 1987 volume of the same name (see ARBA 88, entry 1512). Although a comparison of the table of contents pages at first suggests a major reorganization, a more detailed examination shows that Davis has merely eliminated her 3-part framework (bibliographic control, ready-reference sources, and additional sources of information) and turned her 10 subsections of the 3 parts into 11 chapters that, with some minor rearranging, contain the same bibliographic classifications. Certain criteria continue: The citations are largely to English-language works, out-of-print materials are noted where significant, and little attention is given to audiovisual resources.

The 2d edition includes an expanded "Introduction to the Botanical Literature" (pp. ix-xxi) that gives particular attention to computers and the future of botany. The 11 chapters describe bibliographic sources (guides, catalogs); abstracts, indexes, and databases; current awareness sources (journals, book reviews, patents, literature reviews); dictionaries and encyclopedias; handbooks and methods; directories and groups (biographical sources, noteworthy collections, associations and societies); identification sources (atlases, field guides, floras, keys, endangered plants); taxonomy (indexes, nomenclature, electronic resources); biographical and historical materials; textbooks and treatises; and key publishers, institutions, services, and important series. Four of the divisions include references. The book concludes with an author/title/electronic resource index and a subject index. (The latter item is new to the 2d edition and enhances its value through subdivisions and cross-references.)

One of the special strengths of the work is the narrative that begins many of the sections. These introductory essays are useful for both the informed layperson as well as the specialists for whom the work is intended. As the preface to the 2d edition states, "The purpose of this guide is to provide a useful survey of information sources for students, librarians, and avocational and professional botanists." To this end, all the references to materials are recommended, include full bibliographic citations, and provide a precise annotation of relevant contents. If a user or librarian ever consults a guide to the literature in this field, this one is highly recommended for any collection that contains current (as of 1994) print and electronic botanical resources. [R: Choice, May 96, pp. 1446-48; RBB, 1 April 96, p. 1388]

—Laurel Grotzinger

1273. **Elsevier's Dictionary of Plant Names in Latin, English, French, German, and Italian.** Murray Wrobel and Geoffrey Creber, comps. New York, Elsevier Science, 1996. 925p. index. $250.00. ISBN 0-444-82182-1.

This polyglot dictionary comes from the United Kingdom, but is nonetheless perfectly serviceable for the American user, clearly distinguishing between British and North American usage when it differs (as in the case of Queen Anne's Lace). A list of 12,512 Latin plant names forms the basic table, the major part of the book. Genus, species, and family are given (e.g., *Allium sativum*, Liliaceae), followed by the English, German, French, and Italian common names for the plant. Not all entries give common names in all four modern languages, however. If one was working from a common name (e.g., English "garlic"), one would consult the thumb index at the back of the volume, which is in four parts (the English index, the German index, the French index, and the Italian index), and be referred to the appropriate numbered entry in the basic table.

Are 12,512 plant names a lot? There have been more than 250,000 species of vascular plants named so far, so one wonders what the compilers' criteria for inclusion were; all the preface says is that only plants mentioned in the books of their bibliography are included. The book also fails to say who the compilers are and what institution, if any, they are affiliated with.

If people buy this book, they should know that it does not offer much beyond what the title promises—plant names. If some description of plants beyond their names is desired, and if the German, French, and Italian names of this dictionary are not required, one may go with *Plants and Their Names: A Concise Dictionary* (see ARBA 96, entry 1563), cheaper at $29.95.—**Penny Papangelis**

1274. **Perennials.** Helen Parker, ed. New York, DK Publishing, 1996. 352p. illus. index. (Eyewitness Garden Handbooks). $19.95 flexibinding. ISBN 0-7894-0430-3.

A compact catalog of perennials, this handbook provides color photographs and basic information on more than 1,000 of the more common species of these plants. Entries are first divided into groups according to size, then by season within the size range, and then by color. Each entry briefly describes the habit, flowers, leaves, habitat, cultivation, and propagation of a plant, along with the genus, species, variety, subspecies, and common name.

The book begins with an overview of perennials that includes how to choose them for specific areas and for their different characteristics. Propagation and care of perennials are discussed in the final chapter. A concise and clear glossary of terms and an expanded index conclude the book.

Part of DK Publishing's Eyewitness series, the book's size, composition, and information deliver a pleasing handbook that should prove of great interest to amateur gardeners and make a great reference tool for clients, if not the proprietors, of garden shops and landscape companies. For more extensive listings of plants, readers have a variety of books to choose from, including *Random House Book of Perennials* (1991), a two-volume set covering early perennials (vol. 1) and late perennials (vol. 2).

—**Jo Anne H. Ricca**

Flowering Plants

1275. **Ball Perennial Manual: Propagation and Production.** By Jim Nau. Batavia, Ill., Ball Publishing, 1996. 487p. illus. maps. index. $65.00. ISBN 1-883052-10-6.

This manual describes 149 genera and 300 species of herbaceous perennial plants. Well organized, the text begins with a "How to Use This Book" chapter that outlines the template and headings used for each species description. A separate chapter outlines various propagation techniques, such as by division, by cuttings, and by seed. This chapter concludes with a short reference list.

The species descriptions are arranged alphabetically by scientific name. Each description is comprehensive and includes a description of each species; hardiness type; season of bloom; propagation; germination; growing requirements; varieties; plant uses; and suitability for the home garden. The text of the descriptions is easy to read and does not become bogged down in scientific jargon. Longer entries can be found for those species, such as *Hosta* and *Clematis*, that are popular with the commercial trade.

The manual concludes with four appendixes: an extensive reference list and three separate indexes to subject and scientific and common names. The first appendix is a hardiness zone map of the United States. It is unfortunate that only the United States is depicted; it would have been useful to include a similar map for readers in Canada. Commercial growers will find useful the table of perennials common to the commercial trade. Handy as well is the list of seed-propagated perennials and their expected response the first summer after sowing. A perennial source list to the names and addresses of perennial companies in the United States and Canada is included.

Readers should note that this manual is specifically written for professional growers. Amateurs may find it provides too much detail for their home garden needs. The manual is recommended for specialized collections in academic and botanical libraries. [R: RBB, 15 Mar 96, pp. 1308-10]

—**Katherine Margaret Thomas**

1276. **Manual of Bulbs.** John Bryan, ed. Portland, Oreg., Timber Press, 1995. 383p. illus. (The New Royal Horticultural Society Dictionary of Gardening). $49.95. ISBN 0-88192-339-7.

The library at the University of Kentucky has a good horticultural collection, and the only monograph on bulbs this reviewer could find similar to this book was a two-volume set (*Bulbs*) that Bryan produced in 1989 (see ARBA 91, entry 1498). An OCLC search helped to confirm that there is nothing as comprehensive as the present book. The book under review is a derivative of the *New Royal Horticultural Society Directory of Gardening*. Bryan is an authority in this field. He trained at the Royal Botanic Gardens in Edinburgh and the Royal Horticultural Society's garden at Wisley, England. He has also worked in the Netherlands and has traveled widely studying bulbs.

The definition of bulbs is often not clear. Bryan states that "bulbs have a common attribute, a common denominator—namely, they possess the ability to overcome periods where conditions are hostile and to select an opportune time for growth." He also states that the storage organs grow beneath the ground or protruding from the ground. Roots, tubers, and rhizomes, among others, are included in the definition. Consequently, the definition of bulbs in this book is broad. The front matter of the book gives an overview of bulbs including biology, general culture, propagation, pests and diseases, forcing, and early flowering. Then, there are lists of bulbs by families and geographic regions. An excellent glossary completes the section.

The arrangement of the body of the book is alphabetic by genus (but each entry also includes family name). For each genus there is a physical description of the plant and the geographic range of its growth. These descriptions are often extensive, and the book is international in scope. Under each genus is a list of species with specific descriptions of the plants. The book does not have photographs in it, but rather has exquisite line drawings that undoubtedly have more information in them than photographs would. One of the most helpful features of the book is the index of common names at the end.

The book would be good for the amateur gardener, although the person would need to be a little sophisticated as a hobbyist. It should be the bulb bible for the professional horticulturist, and a necessary addition for any gardening or horticultural collection.—**Lillian R. Mesner**

1277. **Roses.** New York, DK Publishing, 1996. 160p. illus. index. (Eyewitness Garden Handbooks). $17.95 flexibinding. ISBN 0-7894-0607-1.

A first glance through *Roses* immediately gives readers a sense that they have found a useful handbook for picking out and growing the perfect rose for their garden. It is one in a series of Eyewitness Garden Handbooks. On closer examination, this book indeed fulfills its promise of being a practical photographic guide. The main body of this text includes full color photographs of more than 300 varieties of roses arranged by type, use, and color. Each entry includes information on the plants' growing habits; a description of the flowers by size, petal formation, scent, and blooming period; and tips on usage, plant hardiness, and care. Also detailed are the sun, soil, and temperature requirements, along with the geographic zone each variety thrives in the best. Avid rose growers will also be interested in the information provided on each plant's parentage, origin, and other identifying names.

The introduction gives helpful advice on plant selection for different locations and purposes, whether it be for a formal border or in a container for a patio garden. This is followed by the catalog of roses, and the handbook finishes with a guide to rose care, a glossary of terms, and an index of every rose by cultivar. This book is visually appealing. The photographs have so much depth that readers can almost feel the texture of the blooms and imagine their perfume. It is also easy to use, and is comparable to the popular *Taylor's Guide to Roses* (rev. ed., Houghton Mifflin, 1995). *Roses* is highly recommended for any library with a gardening collection.—**Elizabeth D'Antonio-Gan**

Fungi

1278. Bessette, Alan E., Orson K. Miller Jr., Arleen R. Bessette, and Hope H. Miller. **Mushrooms of North America in Color: A Field Guide Companion to Seldom-Illustrated Fungi.** Syracuse, N.Y., Syracuse University Press, [1995]. 172p. illus. index. $39.95; $17.95pa. ISBN 0-8156-2666-5; 0-8156-0323-1pa.

There is no lack of good mushroom guides in bookstores today. Many outstanding ones have been published during the last decade, some by these same authors, including *Mushrooms in Color* by the Millers (ARBA 82, entry 1465) and *Mushrooms: A Quick Reference Guide to Mushrooms of North America* by Alan Bessette and Walter J. Sundberg (ARBA 89, entry 1429). However, all these guides tend to illustrate the same small subset of the approximately 5,000 species of mushrooms that occur in North America. This field guide deliberately leaves out the oft-pictured mushrooms, and concentrates on the rest. It is meant to act as a supplement to any of the popular mushroom books on the market.

Just because a mushroom species is not often found in most mushroom field guides does not mean it is rare or unlikely to be encountered by the amateur naturalist. The 70-plus species included in this book range in occurrence from infrequent to common. Some are newly described species. Many are closely related to well-known species and can give mushroom hunters trouble in resembling, but not quite matching, descriptions in their field guide. Here, these neglected species are given full star treatment—gorgeous color pictures and two pages of descriptions and comments by this team of mushroom experts. Descriptions are readable, but technical when they need to be for accuracy.

The book does not include a key. The guide is arranged alphabetically, by order and by family. Because it is meant to be used in conjunction with other field guides, the best strategy is to identify a specimen as far as possible using the key in another book, then turn to the appropriate section in this new source when necessary. The authors of this guide have performed a real service to avid mushroom collectors, who may have several field guides, but generally do not have access to the technical journals and monographs that up until now were the only sources on many of these species.—**Carol L. Noll**

1279. Farr, David F., H. Bartolome Esteban, and Mary E. Palm. **Fungi on Rhododendron: A World Reference.** Boone, N.C., Parkway, 1996. 192p. index. $45.00. ISBN 1-887905-00-6.

This unique source provides comprehensive lists and information on the fungi found on *Rhododendron* worldwide. This genus includes azaleas and rhododendrons. The reference's purpose is to aid in pest risk assessments for importation of *Rhododendron* plants from foreign countries. By knowing the fungi and their hosts, as well as the geographic range and biology of each fungi, risk of importing potentially harmful fungi on *Rhododendron* may be avoided.

The book is arranged first by a host-fungus list, with the hundreds of species of *Rhododendron* listed alphabetically, followed by a list of fungi found on the living or dead plant. A host-fungus list by locality is next, listed by country and, in the United States, by state. The fungus-host list arranges the fungi in alphabetic order by genus, from *Acanthophysium* to *Zygosporium*, with the host plant listed beneath it. The largest section is the fungus list, which again arranges the fungi in alphabetic order by genus and species, with information on the fungus' distribution worldwide; notes on the biology, taxonomy, and pathogenicity of the fungus; and a list of *Rhododendron* species on which the fungus has been reported, plus the geographic location. A fungus index and an extensive list of references used in compiling the host-fungus section information complete the text.

Written by three recognized experts in mycology, this source is authoritative and comprehensive in its coverage. The only other similar source, and one that may be purchased instead of this source for broader coverage of plants, is *Fungi on Plants and Plant Products in the United States* (see ARBA 90, entry 1501). The title under review is recommended for academic, agricultural, and botanical libraries.
—**Diane B. Rhodes**

1280. Læssøe, Thomas, Gary Lincoff, and Anna Del Conte. **The Mushroom Book.** New York, DK Publishing, 1996. 256p. illus. index. $29.95. ISBN 0-7894-1073-7.

Although the title of this book indicates it is a field guide, it is too large and cumbersome to fulfill that role. It is, however, a helpful reference tool. Filled with visual and written information, the book will certainly be helpful to those involved in collecting and identifying mushrooms. Beginning with an identification key and instructions on how to distinguish characteristics of fungi, the work shows users how to measure a specimen, how to take a spore print, and how to look for special features of the mushroom. This is followed by descriptive listings for more than 450 mushroom species. Entries list scientific and common species names; note special features; and describe size, color of spore deposit, habitat, range, fruiting season, and other characteristics. Most entries also indicate whether the mushroom is edible, sometimes edible, poisonous, or deadly, but some mushrooms are not rated. More than 2,000 color photographs and drawings illustrate the book—showing fruit in its entirety and often also show a cross-section, a view of the cap's underside, and the mushroom as it occurs in its environment. The book concludes with guidelines for mushroom hunting, directions for cleaning and preserving mushrooms (freezing, drying, and preserving in oil), preparing and cooking mushrooms, and 16 recipes for specific mushroom types.

The book has several shortcomings, perhaps the greatest of which is its organization. In a brief statement in the section "How This Chapter Works," the author explains that the entries are arranged in a sequence reflecting "how mycologists believe they are interrelated." Furthermore, the table of contents simply divides the species into two categories—ascomycota and basidiomicota—then lists mushrooms by their scientific names. With this approach, amateurs may have difficulty locating particular mushrooms or types of mushrooms. The detailed index is also sometimes inadequate, because the book's perspective encompasses all of Western Europe and North America. Some names that are commonly used in the States are not included either in the index or the text (e.g., pink bottom). Another problem associated with the work's focus occurs in statements about range, which tend to be vague (e.g., "widespread in North temperate zones"). The text does not indicate which mushrooms are safest for beginners, and it does not include a separate glossary. Finally, on some pages, the lush illustrations and photographs actually distract the reader from the page's organization. Pages are not arranged in a consistent fashion, and this can lead to confusion about which information goes with which entry. Another way of saying this is that while a great deal of information is present, readers may find themselves searching carefully to find it.

In spite of its flaws, this book offers a great deal to users, and mushroom hunters will find it a wonderful addition to their libraries. Those seeking an actual field guide would probably be better served by *The Audubon Society Field Guide to North American Mushrooms* (Alfred A. Knopf, 1981) or by *Mushroom Hunter's Field Guide* (see ARBA 82, entry 1466). Another option, which is not a field guide but has a more practical organization for beginners, is *Mushrooms of North America* (see ARBA 78, entry 1302). [R: BL, 1 Sept 96, p. 48]—**Barbara Ittner**

Herbs

1281. Ody, Penelope. **Home Herbal.** New York, Dorling Kindersley, 1995. 144p. illus. index. $19.95. ISBN 1-56458-863-7.

This is an exceptional book that will be of particular interest to beginning herbalists. As a guide to remedies, it is rather ordinary, with one chapter that describes 60 herbs having medicinal properties, and another chapter that identifies herbal remedies for a variety of physical conditions. What sets this book apart from others of its kind is a chapter on growing herbs and preparing herbal remedies. The chapter identifies common garden plants that have healing properties, recommends plants for the beginning gardener, and describes the process of growing herbs from the purchase of plants to the harvesting of various plant parts. Further, it clearly describes the preparation of the various forms of herbal remedies, such as teas, decoctions, tinctures, suppositories, and poultices. The processes are illustrated with color photographs of outstanding clarity. A chapter recommending tonics and remedies for particular age and gender groups will also be of some interest. The guide also includes lists of relevant organizations and herbal suppliers. This is highly recommended wherever there is interest in herbal remedies.—**Gari-Anne Patzwald**

Trees and Shrubs

1282. **Garden Trees.** New York, DK Publishing, 1996. 200p. illus. index. (Eyewitness Garden Handbooks). $17.95 flexibinding. ISBN 0-7894-0428-1.

This handbook is a valuable addition to the limited number of titles available on garden trees. More than 450 varieties are described, each accompanied by a color photograph. Entries contain the tree's family, common, and botanical names; a description of the tree's growing habit, flowers, fruits, and leaves; and information regarding the native habitat, cultivation, and propagation. In addition, there are symbols that reflect each tree's preferences for sunlight, soil conditions, and degree of hardiness. Average height and spread are also indicated. The entries are grouped by size and season of interest and by the color of their main feature, although this grouping is less clear.

A concluding chapter on tree care is a concise and helpful addition. The index is particularly well made. Genus names are followed by a description; names for species, varieties, subspecies, and cultivars are all indexed, along with common names, which are followed by *see* references. In spite of some photographs that sacrifice an image of a full-grown tree for a depiction of its flower or leaf, this guide will prove a useful aid to the selection of garden trees.—**Michael Weinberg**

1283. Jacobson, Arthur Lee. **North American Landscape Trees.** Berkeley, Calif., Ten Speed Press, 1996. 722p. illus. maps. index. $39.95pa. ISBN 0-89815-813-3.

This work's strength is in the list of more than 5,000 tree varieties, arranged in alphabetic order by genus name, and the historical information it provides for each one. For each tree listed, the book provides brief information on who named the tree and why, where it was first cultivated and where it came from, how common it is, a brief description (including maximum size), common names and synonyms, and other notable information. Forty-six color plates are included with photographs, taken by the author, of trees described in the text. An index of vernacular names, found at the end of the text, makes it easy to find trees listed under their genus name in the text.

Although this work has value as a list of tree types with historical information, there are some concerns. First, the title of the book is misleading. It covers primarily cold-hardy trees of the United States and Canada, but not of Mexico; and native trees of USDA zones 9-11 are not included. Therefore, readers living in the southwestern and Gulf Coast states would not find many trees included for their areas. It also does not cover fruit tree varieties, except for a general entry. The handbook also has little useful information on how these trees may be used in a landscape, and so is more a listing of ornamental trees. A better title would be *Cold-Hardy Ornamental Trees of the United States and Canada*.

Another concern is the use of outdated nomenclature. The author uses Leguminosae, the old family name for Fabaceae, and capitalizes the species name (*Acacia Baileyana*) where it should be in lowercase, even when it is a proper name. The author does not state his nomenclature authority, and implies it is simply his own. However, the present authority is *International Code of Nomenclature for Cultivated Plants* (Balogh Scientific Books, 1996), adopted by the International Commission for the Nomenclature of Cultivated Plants, and a reference work should follow that authority.

The author, with a degree in history, has published books on trees of the Washington state area, especially Seattle, and has continued his interest in compiling this book. He does not include a bibliography of sources he used in compiling the historical and other information on each tree, but rather gives a brief list in a section on suggested reading. This guide does not include identification keys, planting or cultivation information, an idea of how a tree would fit in a landscape other than size, or a detailed description of the tree. For this information, a better choice is *Trees for American Gardens* (see ARBA 92, entry 1508).

Aside from the concerns listed above, this may be a useful work for the historical information it contains and the lengthy listing of tree types. It is recommended for public libraries. [R: BL, July 96, p. 1846]
—**Diane B. Rhodes**

1284. Jones, David L. **Palms Throughout the World.** Blue Ridge Summit, Pa., Smithsonian Institution Press, 1995. 410p. illus. index. $49.00. ISBN 1-56098-616-6.

Study botany or plant taxonomy and one moves quickly over the family Arecaceae (Palmae), the palms ... too quickly. Here is an opportunity to savor an acquaintance. Palms are second only to grasses in economic importance, yielding varied food, fuel, furniture, and shelter. Coconut palm cultivars produce as many as 350 nuts per year; the double coconut palm of the Seychelles Islands produces the biggest seed among plants (more than 20 kilograms). Chop off sago palms in Indonesia and the Amazon; then, collect and eat protein-rich butterfly and beetle larvae that collect to feed on the decaying stems. However, avoid "palm heart" or palm cabbage, the apical bud of the palm; harvest the bud and kill the plant. Palms must fend off insect, arachnid, and fungal attacks. Those menaces, as well as nutritional needs and morphology of palms, are deftly detailed.

Approximately 800 species (of the roughly 2,800 extant species) are described, a majority from the area between Malaysia and New Guinea; a good number are pictured. The volume includes many useful features: derivations of Latin names and some full-page reproductions of palm herbarium sheets from *Botanical Magazine*, a substantive glossary, a comprehensive index, and a modest price. Carolus Linnaeus referred to palms as *Principes*, for "princes among plants." That apt name is reinforced here for all sorts of palm enthusiasts: admirers, growers, users, and everyone who missed palms in a plant class—or the class itself.—**Diane M. Calabrese**

1285. **Plants That Merit Attention. Volume II: Shrubs.** Janet Meakin Poor and Nancy Peterson Brewster, eds. Portland, Oreg., Timber Press, 1996. 363p. illus. index. $59.95. ISBN 0-88192-347-8.

The volume of *Plants That Merit Attention* on shrubs is the long-awaited second volume to the successful first volume, *Trees*, published in 1984. Its mission is to illustrate and describe the more unusual shrubs that are not readily found in local nurseries, but that merit attention for their beauty and hardiness, as possibilities for new plants for the garden. Striking photographs and readable text will entice gardeners to do just that.

The work is arranged by genus name from *Abelia* to *Zenobia*. Each shrub is described in 1 or 2 columns with information on the USDA zone (2-10) where it grows best; a history of where the plant came from and when it was first introduced; a botanical description of leaves, flowers, and fruit; culture information, such as disease and insect problems, transplanting, and propagation; landscape use; and a list of abbreviations for gardens where the plant may be seen growing. Beautiful full-color photographs of the plant, and sometimes its flower and fruit, are found on the page opposite the description.

This well-thought-out book includes four useful appendixes that aid in selecting and buying the plants described in the text. The first appendix provides a directory of botanical gardens, arboretums, and parks where the shrubs can be seen growing. The second appendix is a list of the 900 shrubs described in the text and the names, addresses, and telephone numbers of the nurseries where the shrubs may be purchased. The third appendix groups the shrubs by landscape characteristics, such as "Evergreen Shrubs," "Fragrant Shrubs," "Shrubs Listed by USDA Hardiness Zones," and more. The final appendix provides a list of authorities for the plant names. An index of scientific names and a separate index of common names complete the volume.

Sponsored by the Garden Club of America, this work is the compilation of almost 7 years of work by more than 200 gardeners from arboretums, nurseries, botanical gardens, and universities into a highly useful and authoritative work. There is no other work with the purpose of presenting the lesser-known but meritorious plants that would shine in the garden. This volume is highly recommended for all libraries and for any gardener who enjoys a wonderful new plant book. [R: BL, 15 Sept 96, p. 195]—**Diane B. Rhodes**

1286. **Shrubs & Climbers.** New York, DK Publishing, 1996. 336p. illus. index. (Eyewitness Garden Handbooks). $19.95 flexibinding. ISBN 0-7894-0429-X.

From the endpapers map of the hardiness zones of North America to a detailed index including genera, species, cultivars, and common names, this flexibound Eyewitness Garden Handbook will assist amateur gardeners planning a new garden or seeking new features for an established one. Color photographs of more than 1,000 shrubs and climbers are grouped by plant size, seasonal interest, and finally, color. The catalog is further divided into nine feature boxes about lilacs, camellias, rhododendrons, hydrangeas, hollies, fuchsias, heathers, clematis, and ivies. For each plant, the family; common and botanical names; habit(s) (including flowers, fruits, and leaves); native habitat(s); cultivation; propagation; plant portrait; symbols including sun, soil, and temperature requirements; hardiness zone(s); height; spread; and silhouette are given.

Although no general editor is indicated, contributors for families or groups are identified as either horticulturists or botanists; a former curator of the Hillier Gardens and Arboretum near Ampfield, Hampshire, England, is also among the contributors. A helpful introductory essay includes selection, site exposure considerations, and successional interest throughout the seasons while the closing guide to care covers the essentials of soil preparation, planting, routine care, and lucid explanations and illustrations for pruning and training.

Two minor annoyances occur: The biological identification of the catalog consultants is printed only on the inner dustjacket flap, which a library processing this book for circulation will probably permanently remove. Also, the beautiful frontispiece of *Kalmia latifolia*, enlarged from page 110, and *Senecio macroglossus 'Variegatus'*, from page 279 bottom left, were identified only after a careful search of the text. However, this vade mecum will be useful in public libraries, garden stores, and undergraduate biology collections. [R: BL, July 96, p. 1]—**Helen M. Barber**

NATURAL HISTORY

1287. **Eyewitness Encyclopedia of Nature.** [CD-ROM]. New York, Dorling Kindersley, 1995. Minimum system requirements: IBM or compatible 386DX/33MHz. CD-ROM drive. Windows 3.1. 4MB RAM. SVGA 256-color monitor. Mouse. Sound card. Loudspeakers or headphones. $79.95. ISBN 0-7894-0041-3 (Windows); 0-7894-0095-2 (Macintosh). [Also available in Macintosh version.]

Eyewitness Encyclopedia of Nature is a multimedia reference guide to the natural world. The program reflects the visual format found in the Dorling Kindersley Eyewitness books. Attractive high-resolution graphics present basic information on animals and plants, habitats, climate, and ecological topics. The main menu is a "Naturalist's Console" where one can click on the book icons "Web of Life" or "The Green Book" to explore environmental topics; a spinning globe to explore 10 habitats; or click on 1 of the labeled drawers or posters to reach submenus. Throughout the program a pleasant voice will read the text, stop with a click, or repeat with a click. Words, arrows, or icons in red are buttons that lead to more detail or allow the user to navigate.

Coverage is thorough. The bird menu, for example, offers choices of 12 bird groups or a well-organized overview, "What Is a Bird?" where users can click on "Courtship," "Eggs," "Flight" (an animated sequence), "Anatomy" (a slide show), or 4 other topics. Many menus have animation, slide show images, and QuickTime movies with narration. The video sequences are well edited and narrated, with excellent color tone and movement, although enlarged they experience pauses during playback (even with a Pentium processor and 20MB of RAM).

The index has excellent coverage, accepts keyword searches, and shows the researcher the path to the requested topic. In other words, a request for *octopus, blue-ringed* from the index visibly tracks through windows "Animals," "Invertebrates," and "Mollusks" before stopping on "Octopus & Squid." The "Habitats" feature in the main menu can be reached from any animal card. This feature is unique, with brilliant scrolling murals of each ecosystem, and a great tool—a magnifying glass to be dragged over the mural for close-up views of animals in their environments. Another fun feature students will enjoy is "Quizmaster," for a game-like approach to learning. Text can be printed or copied to the clipboard. The only weakness is a somewhat cluttered main menu, and the tab for getting back to it, which is hard to find for lack of a label. Otherwise, this is an excellent product all around. [R: BR, Jan/Feb 96, p. 62; VOYA, Feb 96, p. 404]—**JoAnn Balingit**

ZOOLOGY

Birds

1288. Byers, Clive, Jon Curson, and Urban Olsson. **Sparrows and Buntings: A Guide to the Sparrows and Buntings of North America and the World.** New York, Houghton Mifflin, 1995. 334p. illus. maps. index. $40.00. ISBN 0-395-73873-3.

This is the eighth title in the highly acclaimed Helm (after its British publisher) Identification Guide series. It lives up to the high standards of *Warblers of the Americas* (see ARBA 96, entry 1613) and other predecessors. The authors fully describe and portray 110 species of buntings (all Old World species) and sparrows, longspurs, and towhees (all New World). So-called American buntings such as the Indigo, Painted, and Lazuli do not conform to this book's scope and are not in these pages. As with other Helm guides, this volume has extensive species accounts with sections on identification, hybridization, description, molting and aging, measurements, geographic variation, voice, habits, status and habitat, distribution and movements, references, a range map, and excellent color paintings with 2 to 11 figures of each species. The range maps, some of vast areas of Asia or North America, would be much more useful if they included political boundaries.

Readers are bound to be confused, unavoidably, by the respective scope of this book and the earlier Helm guide, *Finches & Sparrows* (Princeton University Press, 1993) by Peter Clement. Most of the birds in the latter work are Old World types, and no New World sparrows are included. The fault is less with the books than with the redundancy in bird nomenclature. A minor failing of both titles is the lack of inverted index entries. Thus "sparrow" is not an entry in either one. To locate "song sparrow," one must look under "song" for this species. Byers's book includes few Southern Hemisphere birds in spite of its subtitle. Regardless of these criticisms, both books are excellent references if one keeps in mind their respective scopes, which are mutually exclusive. The title under review is highly recommended.—**Henry T. Armistead**

1289. DeGraaf, Richard M., and John H. Rappole. **Neotropical Migratory Birds: Natural History, Distribution, and Population Change**. Ithaca, N.Y., Comstock Publishing/Cornell University Press, 1995. 676p. maps. index. $27.50pa. ISBN 0-8014-8265-8.

This hefty paperbound handbook is a useful source of basic information on 361 species of Neotropical migrants, "species that for the most part breed in the United States and Canada and migrate to wintering grounds in the Caribbean, Mexico and southward" (p. 1). For the past 15 years or so, such birds have received much publicity as the destruction of rain forests, tropical slash-and-burn agriculture, and massive deforestation have finally received some of the notice and concern they deserve.

Introductory chapters provide basic information, such as "What Is a Neotropical Migratory Bird?" and a look at the principles of studying population change. The heart of the book, 488 pages, consists of the 361 species accounts. These contain a range map plus a written summary of each bird's distribution; its status (abundance, rarity, and so forth); its habitat usage; special habitat requirements; and references for further reading. The habitat sections emphasize the breeding range, probably because less is known about winter ranges in the tropics. In some cases, the maps do not show Canada's arctic islands, important for many shorebirds covered by this book, a minor sore point. Spanish and French bird names are also given, but not Portuguese.

Two excellent appendixes detail breeding and wintering habitat use and population changes (in North America) by physiographic region. The 39-page bibliography is impressive. DeGraaf and Rappole, both professional biologist/naturalists, have done an excellent service. This resource is highly recommended.
—**Henry T. Armistead**

1290. **National Audubon Society Interactive CD-ROM Guide to North American Birds.** [CD-ROM]. New York, Alfred A. Knopf/Random House, 1996. Minimum system requirements (Windows version): IBM or compatible multimedia 386/25MHz (486dx recommended). MPC-compatible CD-ROM drive with at least 150KB transfer rate (300KB recommended). DOS 5.0. Windows 3.1 or 95. 8MB RAM. 15MB hard disk. VGA/SVGA, 640 x 480 pixel screen, 256-color monitor. SoundBlaster Pro or compatible sound cards. Mouse. Minimum system requirements (Macintosh version): Powerbook 180c Macintosh II, Quadra, or Performa Series Motorola 68030 processor (68040 or Power PC recommended). CD-ROM drive (double-speed recommended). System 7.0. QuickTime 2.0. 5MB RAM. 15MB hard disk. 640 x 480 pixel screen, 256-color monitor. $32.00. ISBN 0-679-76016-4.

This multimedia guide (6,000 screens with 2,100 bird photographs) contains an amazing amount of authoritative, accessible information in its three major sections (environment, birds, and notebook), plus an index/glossary and an on-screen instruction manual. The environment module illustrates 9 life zones and 62 typical habitats with probable birds. The bird module is the heart of the system, with a browser containing 723 species. Most are depicted in more than one view and available in normal or zoom form. Buttons provide about 700 vocalizations, distribution maps, and the (modified) texts of *The Audubon Society Field Guide to North American Birds* (rev. ed., Random House, 1994) and its 3-volume *Master Guide to Birding* (Random House, 1983). Another button adds the bird to the user's own "Life List."

The browser makes it possible to examine two (or more) birds simultaneously, but such comparisons are possible only with the smallest of the images. The bird identifier permits the user to choose features of color, shape, size, location, and life zone, and find any bird that matches the combination. Although most of the photographs are excellent, a few are dark or slightly off in the coloring (e.g., the yellow-throated vireo). The bird module also has five short videos on migration, flight, and the like. These are distinguished neither by content nor graphic quality. The third major component, the notebook, contains the "Life List," the "Trip Planner" (20-odd sites), and a bibliography. The nicely done "Life List" includes a zoomable picture of the bird with direct access to the full description, slots for place and date of sighting, and space for field notes. The package, which comes with the handsome, pocket-sized *Familiar Birds of Lakes and Rivers*, is attractively designed and easy to use, but then, so are its competitors—*Birds of North America CD-ROM* (Thayer Birding Software, 1996) and *Peterson's North American Birds* (Houghton Mifflin, 1996). Of the three discs, the National Audubon one is reportedly the best for Macintosh users.—**D. Barton Johnson**

Domestic Animals

1291. Hendricks, Bonnie L. **International Encyclopedia of Horse Breeds.** Norman, Okla., University of Oklahoma Press, 1995. 486p. illus. index. $65.00. ISBN 0-8061-2753-8.

This new encyclopedia claims to be the most complete collection of horse breeds ever attempted, with nearly 400 breeds of horses and ponies described. This is many more breeds than will be found in other recent offerings, such as *The Encyclopedia of the Horse* (see ARBA 95, entry 1582); *Horses* (see ARBA 94, entry 1707); and *An Illustrated International Encyclopedia of Horse Breeds & Breeding* (see ARBA 91, entry 1577). Although lacking the many attractive color illustrations of those volumes, *International Encyclopedia of Horse Breeds* does have a 16-page center section of color photographs, and one or more black-and-white photographs accompany most breed descriptions.

This volume's special strength is in the large number of uncommon breeds presented, and the amount of detail provided. Hendricks, a longtime horse breeder, has concentrated her efforts on identifying and describing breeds and has excluded more general horse topics, although she does provide a brief glossary of terms. Arrangement is strictly alphabetic by name of breed, both rare and common, from *Abtenaur* to *Zhemaichu*. Much of the information presented will be new to U.S. readers, as it was obtained directly from breed authorities around the world rather than taken from existing publications. More than 30 Chinese breeds are included, and many from the former Soviet Union, Turkey, and approximately 70 other countries. Some uncommon American breeds are described in addition to the familiar ones. There is a separate listing of worldwide horse breed organizations and their addresses.

Entries vary in length from a few short paragraphs to several pages. Each horse's history, description, and present status and uses are discussed. The author believes that many breeds still remain to be identified, and intends this new encyclopedia to be an ongoing project with future revisions. Both public and academic libraries should have this volume, as individual horse lovers may be discouraged by its high price. [R: Choice, May 96, p. 1450]—**William H. Wiese**

1292. Jackson, Frank. **Dictionary of Canine Terms.** Ramsbury, England, Crowood Press; distr., North Pomfret, Vt., Trafalgar Square, 1995. 256p. illus. $40.00. ISBN 1-85223-795-3.

Encompassing more than 15,000 words, this work provides definitions of myriad canine terms. Breed of dog, grooming, diseases, behavior, breeding, anatomy, scientific names, biologic deficiencies, genetics, and parasites are just some of the types of terminology abounding within the pages of this dictionary.

The terms are arranged alphabetically in bold typeface. The length of the entry varies depending upon the term being defined. For example, breed of dog constitutes the longest explanations, of approximately two or more paragraphs, while in other cases a sentence or two defines the term. In defining the breed, the height and weight are usually given as well. In some examples, more than one definition is given. Pen and ink drawings can be found throughout the definitions in order to clarify some of the terminology. In some cases, such as an explanation of the skeleton and parts of the body (points), a full labeled diagram of the dog is shown.

A preface discussing how the work was researched and a guide to the use of the dictionary begin the canine reference source. In addition to the definitions, a bibliography consisting of 500-plus citations can be found at the end of the work. It should be noted that a great deal of research was done in order to complete the dictionary, which is recommended for college, university, public, and high school libraries. [R: RBB, 1 Mar 96, p. 1208]—**George H. Bell**

Mammals

1293. Long, Kim. **Squirrels: A Wildlife Handbook.** Boulder, Colo., Johnson Books, 1995. 181p. illus. maps. index. $15.95pa. ISBN 1-55566-152-1.

As the author points out in his introduction, squirrels, as one of the less glamorous members of the animal kingdom, may be overlooked because they are so common. This popular treatment—part reference and part fun reading—is an attempt to remedy the situation. It covers the several species of tree squirrels (but not ground squirrels) common to North America, including the fox, gray, and red, and the Southern and Northern flying squirrels. Their folklore, food gathering and diet, nest building, reproduction, potential as pests, and assorted other topics are discussed in short, illustrated chapters that encourage browsing. A separate, 30-page section presents statistics and brief facts for each species with color drawings and North American range maps, excluding Mexico. For some reason, the map for Abert's squirrel is not shaded to show its home range, and no illustration or map is provided for the Arizona gray squirrel.

This handbook should add to the knowledge and enjoyment of squirrel watchers everywhere. It is not intended to be a comprehensive or scholarly study; those who require more scientific detail will be well served by *Grzimek's Encyclopedia of Mammals* (see ARBA 91, entry 1593) and *Walker's Mammals of the World* (5th ed.; see ARBA 93, entry 1572). *Squirrels* includes a five-page bibliography that directs readers to many other books.—**William H. Wiese**

1294. Whitaker, John O., Jr. **National Audubon Society Field Guide to North American Mammals.** rev. ed. New York, Alfred A. Knopf/Random House, 1996. 937p. illus. maps. index. $19.00pa. ISBN 0-679-44631-1.

The *National Audubon Society Field Guide to North American Mammals* is a fully revised and expanded edition of the 1st edition published in 1980 (see ARBA 82, entry 1497). The guide covers ". . . all the native land-dwelling or land-breeding species of wild mammals found in North America north of Mexico" (p. 15). The author, who is a professor of life sciences at Indiana State University, includes seals and sea lions because they breed on land, as well as some introduced and domesticated species. The criteria for inclusion of the latter are if the species "reproduce and maintain themselves under natural conditions, and interact with and influence native species" (p. 15). Inexplicably, the West Indian Manatee is discussed.

As with other books in this outstanding series of field guides, the book is divided into two main sections: a color photograph section depicting many of the species described in the other section, the species descriptions. There are color photographs for 265 of the 390 species covered in the volume. Some species are depicted by a small black-and-white drawing next to the species description when a good photograph was not available. Some species are not illustrated at all if they are almost identical to another illustrated species. One drawback to the Audubon field guide series is that they do not illustrate key field characteristics such as is done in William Burt's *A Field Guide to the Mammals: Field Marks of All North American Species Found North of Mexico* (3d ed.; see ARBA 77, entry 1392). This is a useful feature to aid in field identification.

The introduction to the work under review contains brief but valuable information on mammal measurement, dental patterns, and North American habitat. The classification of mammals and the sequence of presentation of the species are based on the *Revised Checklist of North American Mammals North of Mexico, 1991* (Occasional Papers no.146, Texas Tech University). The color plates, which comprise one-third of the book, are organized by a silhouette system that allows users to get to the right section for identification of a species. The color photographs are well reproduced. Each photograph caption includes the common name of the animal, total body length, and the page number of the full species description. Each well-written description contains the following information: common and scientific name; description; similar species; breeding; sign (e.g., nest, burrow—not all descriptions have this section); habitat; range (small map is included); and a brief paragraph on natural history. At the end of the volume there are appendixes, which include a glossary of terms, a list of endangered or threatened North American mammal species, range charts for smaller mammals to help in identification by geographic location, photograph credits, and an index that includes both scientific and common names.

This field guide will prove to be a valuable addition to all public, college, and university libraries. It is highly recommended. [R: Choice, Oct 96, pp. 259-60]—**James E. Bird**

Marine Animals

1295. Gosliner, Terence M., David W. Behrens, and Gary C. Williams. **Coral Reef Animals of the Indo-Pacific: Animal Life from Africa to Hawai'i Exclusive of the Vertebrates.** Monterey, Calif., Sea Challengers, 1996. 314p. illus. index. $45.00pa. ISBN 0-930118-21-9.

The authors, all associated with the California Academy of Sciences, have produced a useful reference book for those with an interest in coral reef animals in the Indo-Pacific area. As the subtitle of the book indicates, the Indo-Pacific encompasses the ocean area from the Indian Ocean coast of Africa to the Hawaiian Islands. This volume is restricted to invertebrate, benthic, and epibenthic coral reef animals, covering 1,103 of the most common species.

A detailed introduction sets the stage for the information presented, including the classification of animals, biotic communities in the Indo-Pacific area, biology of corals and reefs, and information on biogeography and biodiversity. This 14-page introduction is one of the highlights of the book, giving the reader a solid, concise background in the subject areas covered. The authors have organized the text into 32 chapters by major taxon or phylum. Each chapter has a short, general overview of the taxon or phylum, citing pertinent review article references. Each species account within the chapters gives concise information about the animal's identification, natural history, and distribution. All species accounts have an associated color photograph, showing the species in its natural habitat. These photographs are approximately $3\frac{1}{2}$-by-$2\frac{1}{4}$ inches in size and are beautifully reproduced.

As the authors state in the introduction, many of the animals outlined in this volume were unable to be identified to the species level. These animals are listed to genus only. This volume includes a glossary, a systematic list of genera, and an index that includes both scientific and common names. This volume will prove useful for all marine biologists studying coral reef animals. It should be a part of college and university library collections of those institutions with programs in marine biology and ecology.

—**James E. Bird**

32 Engineering

GENERAL WORKS

1296. **Information Sources in Engineering.** 3d ed. K. W. Mildren and P. J. Hicks, eds. New Providence, N.J., Bowker-Saur/Reed Reference Publishing, 1996. 772p. index. (Guides to Information Sources). $110.00. ISBN 1-85739-057-1.

The 3d edition of *Information Sources in Engineering* has maintained the same focus: to provide users of varying degrees of subject sophistication with an authoritative guide to the sources of high-quality information. At a time of expanding information sources, both in print and electronic, and the unedited material on the Internet, practitioners will want to consult this work.

The titles included seem to be exclusively those in English, with chiefly British and American imprints. The contributors, whose credentials are provided, are engineers familiar with the literature. There are brief sections on primary and secondary materials subdivided by format. Eighty percent of the work, however, consists of 27 subject essays, each subdivided by format. For the novice, a helpful introductory essay explains the parameters of the topic, something that is useful given the growing interdisciplinary nature of engineering fields. Completing each section is an alphabetic list by the author of all titles discussed. The work concludes with an index by author and by title.

Used in conjunction with larger, yet chiefly unannotated bibliographies, such as the *Encyclopedia of Physical Sciences and Engineering Information Sources* (see ARBA 90, entry 1424), this work is most useful. The effort of each contributor to give the user guidance as to which sources speak with greatest authority is most appreciated. [R: Choice, Nov 96, p. 432]—**John M. Robson**

1297. Kaplan, Steven M. **English-Spanish, Spanish-English Electrical and Computer Engineering Dictionary. Diccionario de Ingeniería Eléctrica y de Computadoras Inglés/Español, Español/Inglés.** New York, John Wiley, 1996. 792p. $59.95. ISBN 0-471-01037-5.

This reference contains almost 95,000 entries of both Spanish and English terms in electrical and computer engineering. Spanish-language terms have been checked by Spanish speakers in Puerto Rico, Mexico, and Spain. The lexicographer has written two other English-Spanish and Spanish-English dictionaries, one of legal terms and the other of psychology and psychiatry terms. As complex as dictionaries of technological terms go, this one is designed to be especially easy to use. Entries of words and phrases are listed side by side with their equivalent terms or phrases in the other language. Most entries are only one line long. Variations of a term are presented as separate entries. While the two-column page format is generous, the small typeface size of the entries is not; some users may need an amplification device to use the dictionary.

This reference would be useful to working professionals and students of computer and electrical engineering, but especially to translators and interpreters. It is highly recommended for large public and academic libraries in Spanish-speaking areas of the country. [R: Choice, Oct 96, p. 252]—**Edward Erazo**

AERONAUTICAL ENGINEERING

1298. **Jane's Aero-Engines.** Bill Gunston, ed. Alexandria, Va., Jane's Information Group, 1996. 1v. (unpaged). illus. $595.00 looseleaf w/binder. ISBN 0-7106-1405-5.

Building on the reputation of *Jane's All the World's Aircraft* (JAWA) (see entry 1440), the editors have created this semiannually updated looseleaf guide to all of the gas turbine aircraft engines currently in use around the globe. The information is based on data provided by the manufacturers, and clearly some have more information to share than others. There is an expansion of the number of illustrations and text describing each engine over that found in JAWA; the editors promise that half of the illustrations will not have been published in JAWA.

Each engine has a photograph and either a cutaway drawing or a longitudinal section of each major version of each type of engine. Pricing information has intentionally not been included because of the lack of meaningful, comparative information, although it may in the future. Preliminary sections include a glossary and seven concise overview essays on gas turbine engines—a textbook in brief. The data for each engine may include performance ratings, specific fuel consumption, weight, dimensions, starting, fuel and oil specifications, accessories, intake, compressor, combustion chamber, jetpipe, and so forth.

Those considering purchase may want to examine a copy or request the sheets for various engines to check for completeness. The coverage and convenience are commendable.—**John M. Robson**

ARCHITECTURAL ENGINEERING

1299. **Information Sources in Architecture and Construction.** 2d ed. Valerie J. Nurcombe, ed. New Providence, N.J., Bowker-Saur/Reed Reference Publishing, 1996. 489p. index. (Guides to Information Sources). $100.00. ISBN 1-85739-094-6.

This update of the 1983 edition is similar, but it is expanded in content. The 16 subject chapters have grown to 24 from 22 contributors overall. Each chapter covers varied aspects of architecture and construction; city planning; maps and geographic systems; visual information (e.g., slide library management); landscape; and interior design. Other sections on associations, libraries, computer databases, and trade literature offer tips for researchers. Most of the chapters are bibliographic essays describing resources, with a bibliography at the end of each that centralizes the citations mentioned. The remaining chapters review the management of the office or of resources.

With 75 percent of the contributors from British institutions, the work has a decidedly British accent. This limits its appeal somewhat for the North American marketplace by emphasizing materials not as germane to North American readers. European materials are also not emphasized. For example, such important staples for architecture collections as the Time-Saver Standards series (see ARBA 96, entry 1048), *Sweets Catalog*, and H. W. Wilson's *Art Index* (see ARBA 93, entry 1030, and ARBA 92, entry 992) (and *Art Abstracts*) are scarcely mentioned. The *Avery Index* is noted often in the text; it is comprehensive, but in CD-ROM format it is only published annually and does not have abstracts; *Art Abstracts* on CD-ROM, however, is updated monthly and covers the core journals. More of this type of evaluative assessment would improve the work.

For ready-reference, there is an alphabetic list of organizations and associations (60 percent British, 40 percent American or other) in appendix A, while acronyms and abbreviations are listed in appendix B. Bibliographic essays are not an ideal vehicle for the reference desk, but they are suitable for collection development and can be a useful supplement for the classroom. Unfortunately, the index is not as carefully structured as it needs to be if it is to be an effective entrée to the contents of this collection of independent contributors.

This work is suitable for sophisticated architecture, design, and construction collections, and for comprehensive research libraries. There are few competing reference works in this subject area, yet, despite the need for this type of information, the format and limited geographic scope may ultimately prove to be disappointing for some users. [R: Choice, July/Aug 96, p. 1774]—**Gary R. Cocozzoli**

ASTRONAUTICAL ENGINEERING

1300. Baker, David. **Spaceflight and Rocketry: A Chronology.** New York, Facts on File, 1996. 528p. illus. index. $65.00. ISBN 0-8160-1853-7.

Covering the period 360 B.C.E. through December 1993, Baker's chronology surveys the successes and failures of space exploration and rocketry. More than 7,000 entries tell the fascinating story of human rocket construction and exploration of space. Baker lists everything from rockets fired at Alexander the Great, through the "rockets red glare" over Fort McHenry in Baltimore Harbor in 1814, to modern space shuttle flights. Of special interest are the British rocket programs of the early 1800s, the German World War II rocket development at Peenemünde, the Soviet space flight program of the 1957-1993 period, and the U.S. space program managed by the National Aeronautics and Space Administration (NASA). Baker has worked for NASA as a consultant for 12 years and is the author of more than 50 books on space and aviation.

While chronologies rarely recommend themselves for casual reading, this one is hard to put down. Illustrated at occasional intervals with 130 black-and-white photographs, the work moves swiftly into the twentieth century to chronicle modern spaceflight. A few of these photographs claim to be the first ever published of the Soviet space program. (The Soviet photographs are generally smaller and inferior when compared to the U.S. space program illustrations.) There are some odd omissions in the text. On page 358, there is a rather poor photograph of the recovery of *Cosmos 1445* that was claimed to have been launched on March 15, 1983. This Soviet "space plane" flight is not listed in the chronology nor the index to the book. At best, this indicates sloppy editing; at worst, major omissions in the chronology.

The chronology is supplemented by a glossary and a list of abbreviations that contains interesting terms such as USN (for U.S. Navy), but not IRIS, STG, USMC, AAP, GMS, or DBS—all abbreviations used in the text. The author provides two indexes: a name index and a subject (general) index. Both indexes refer to the date of the entry in the chronology and not page numbers. The index is also plagued by blind references. For example, the *Apollo 13* entry refers to March 3, 1971, but there is no entry for that date. Similarly puzzling is the index entry "Application of Rockets to the Destruction and Capture of Whales" listed under "application" with no entry under the subject "Whales," which would appear more appropriate for a subject index of this type. Neither Robert Goddard nor Wernher von Braun are listed in the name or subject index, despite frequent sightings in the chronology. In fact, numerous names are listed in the chronology (such as John F. Kennedy, Laika [the first dog in space], Wright-Patterson Air Force Base, Allen Dulles, the Corona program) but do not turn up in the indexes. While the chronology itself is fascinating, the lack of adequate indexing frustrates the reader in the location of material. In addition, the index is in a rather small typeface, which further hampers its effective use. Most libraries with patrons interested in rocketry and space flight will want to own this chronology, even though serious reference use is hampered by the lack of an effective index scheme.—**Ralph Lee Scott**

1301. **Jane's Space Directory 1996-97.** 12th ed. Andrew Wilson, ed. Alexandria, Va., Jane's Information Group, 1996. 524p. illus. maps. index. $290.00. ISBN 0-7106-1357-1.

Jane's Space Directory provides an ideal platform from which one can launch a study of the year's activity in space. Using information that is purported to be unclassified, readers will be able to research the latest space missions and explorations as well as launch programs from the major national space players. Starting with a narrative chronological list of major launches (covering January 1995 to January 1996) the directory goes on to list additional "space logs," such as extravehicular astronaut events, manned flights, and geosynchronous satellites. The volume is then divided into sections covering such topics as national space programs, international programs, military aspects of space, launch vehicles, communications systems, ground/space stations, space navigation systems, earth observation devices, microgravity, earth space stations (cosmodromes), and an industry directory.

The entries in the directory make for interesting reading. They are well written and highly detailed. The volume has more than 600 illustrations, mostly photographs (some are actually concept drawings) and line illustrations. Some of the drawings are marked "classified" but contain no censor review. It is not clear if these are in fact uncleared classified drawings, or just an illustrator's attempt at adding authenticity to the work. Some illustrations are small and hard to examine without the aid of a magnifying glass.

The industry directory gives basic company data (name, address, telephone number), along with a short narrative of the company's space activity. This section includes such companies as Zeppelin Technologie Gesellschaft mit Beschraenkter Haftung and Thai Microsatellite Corporation. Most engineering collections will want to add this volume to their collections. While it makes for interesting reading for the general reader, its high cost will limit purchase.—**Ralph Lee Scott**

1302. **USA in Space.** Frank N. Magill and Russell R. Tobias, eds. Pasadena, Calif., Salem Press, 1996. 3v. illus. index. $210.00/set. ISBN 0-98356-924-0.

USA in Space consists of 197 articles on the major manned and unmanned space missions, as well as articles on space centers, launch sites, and issues of importance to the U.S. space program. The majority of the articles (160) were originally published in the *Magill's Survey of Science: Space Exploration Series* (see ARBA 90, entry 1582), which is now out-of-print. For the set under review, 37 new articles were written, each of the originals was reviewed for accuracy, and updated information was provided as needed.

The entire set is arranged in alphabetic order. As a result, all space shuttle missions are arranged together. A glossary of terms is included, as well as a time line of U.S. space events, and most interesting, a list of what the editors believe to be Websites that "will probably still exist when the next edition of this book is undertaken." A personage index, an alphabetic index, and a category index are furnished.

Each article supplies a bibliography and a head note that contains dates of the mission; type of mission; and a list of principal participants, along with their role. Each article consists of a summary of the mission, the context of the mission, and a description of the knowledge gained as a result. One of the most recent articles discusses the seven 1995 space shuttle flights, three of which involved a rendezvous with the Russian space station *Mir*.

Each article is signed, and at the end of the volume is a fairly comprehensive list of Web pages from astronauts (http://www.conveyor.com/space/astronaut.html) to White Sands Missile Range (http://sd-www.jsc.nasa.gove/wsmr.html). Overall, this is a fine reference set that should be of interest to public libraries, school libraries, and university collections. The writing is clear and not loaded with undefined jargon. The set is well worth the price—there is copious information presented here in one clear package.
—**Susan B. Ardis**

AUTOMOTIVE ENGINEERING

1303. Goodsell, Don. **Dictionary of Automotive Engineering.** 2d ed. Warrendale, Pa., Society of Automotive Engineers, 1995. 265p. illus. $49.00. ISBN 1-56091-683-4.

Jointly published in the United States and Great Britain, this work is international in scope. It is intended for a wide, English-speaking audience, from automotive engineers and students to enthusiasts. As such, it is a useful addition to the pertinent shelves of automotive, engineering, and public libraries.

More than 3,000 entries are included, along with 100-plus illustrations that are used to clarify meaning. While the text discusses words and informal and slang terms that have an automotive connotation, general terms relating to mechanical engineering, electronics, electricity, and fuels and lubricants are not listed, as they can be found in more specific works and related sources. A nice feature of this resource is the indication of the country of usage where the term is ingrained in the national consciousness and is unlikely to change, except where two terms are similar and they appear on the same page. Other useful features include *see also* references to other terms when the definition of terms may be made clearer by referring to other words, and the use of *see* references for the full definition of words that are neither preferred nor in mainstream usage.

This 2d edition (see ARBA 91, entry 1823, for a review of the 1st edition) expands coverage in seven subject areas: fuels and lubricants, materials such as plastics and elastomers, tires, construction and off-highway vehicles, testing, and electronics. The dictionary is easy to read and understand, with definitions that are brief and concise. The text concludes with a helpful appendix of abbreviations and acronyms.
—**James M. Murray**

CIVIL ENGINEERING

1304. **The Wiley Dictionary of Civil Engineering and Construction: English-Spanish/Spanish-English.** By Felicitas Kennedy. New York, John Wiley, 1996. 553p. $49.95. ISBN 0-471-12246-7.

This bilingual dictionary helps make current an area of reference that has not seen much updating in recent years. The specialized book contains more than 50,000 entries in both Spanish and English for the field of civil engineering, with some attention applied to the related fields of mechanical, industrial, and electrical engineering. The translations for the technical terms and phrases are provided, but rarely are definitions included. According to the preface, the terms and phrases were taken from a standard civil engineering reference book and from official publications, engineering specifications, and engineering textbooks.

The book is international in scope and terms belonging to a particular Spanish dialect are clearly labeled. Abbreviations used in the book are conveniently listed near the preface. As with most other language dictionaries, a reasonable knowledge of both languages is required to make good use of this book. The dictionary is recommended to libraries supporting engineering programs, especially civil engineering, as well as libraries supporting strong foreign-language programs. [R: Choice, Oct 96, p. 253]
—**Carl Pracht**

ELECTRIC ENGINEERING AND ELECTRONICS

1305. Graf, Rudolf F., and William Sheets. **Encyclopedia of Electronic Circuits. Volume 6.** New York, McGraw-Hill, 1996. 789p. illus. index. $60.00; $34.95pa. ISBN 0-07-011275-4; 0-07-011276-2pa.

This is the sixth installment of what has been a popular and well-received handbook. This volume should be equally well received, although it is not without at least one annoying characteristic. The inclusion in the index of all circuits found in the previous five volumes is laudable. The choice of typeface size is not. Handbooks are not meant to be tomes placed on a shelf and used rarely—they are nuts-and-bolts publications that receive high use. Three major access points identify handbooks: the contents list, the index, and the pieces of paper and dog-ears that users employ to personalize their searches. The contents list here is good, and the personalization is outside the control of the authors and publisher. The index, however, is a major component in any handbook. This one is technically done well. No matter how well made, any index with a typeface size as small as this one is flawed. The authors may well have had no say in the typesetting of the index, but they should know that it detracts seriously from an otherwise excellent handbook. It is even more critical because this is a cumulative index to this and the previous five volumes. McGraw-Hill can do and has done better.

The contents listing does have one interesting anomaly. There are two sections titled "Amateur Circuits" and "Amateur Television (ATV) Circuits." In reviewing these sections, it is not clear why they cannot and should not be merged into other categories. Certainly there are circuits in other categories that come from sources such as *Popular Electronics*. Someone seeking amplifier circuits (a category in this volume) would miss three amplifier circuits that are in the "Amateur Circuits" category. The index does bring these together; however, there appears to be no rationale as to why they were separated at all. The reader needs to be aware that there are overlaps in some of the first five volumes and this volume. In the cases examined, the duplicated circuits are not equivalent, except in function. The entry under "probes, logic probes," for example, shows entries for volumes 1, 4, and 6. Each of the circuits is different but each functionally defines a logic probe.

Unlike the index, the font size is readable and clear in the text. The authors and the publisher have done an excellent job of producing and publishing some fairly intricate line drawings without losing readability. A user can take this volume, prop it open on the bench, and build the circuit without a magnifying glass. The circuitry presented here is an excellent example of what a handbook should look like and how it should be presented. Overall, this is an excellent source for electronic circuits across a wide variety of categories. As with its predecessors, it is highly recommended and is truly an invaluable storehouse.—**C. D. Hurt**

1306. **INSPEC List of Journals and Other Serial Sources 1996/7.** Piscataway, N.J., Institution of Electric Engineers, 1996. 436p. $35.00pa. ISSN 0264-7508.

This list consists of publications scanned in physics, electrical engineering, electronics, and computers and control that are then input into the products forming the INSPEC database (both electronic and paper). Publications scanned include more than 3,981 journals, conference proceedings, books, reports, and theses. Entries are in either bold or regular typeface. Bold typeface denotes regularly received titles and regular typeface denotes cross-references, title changes, ceased titles, mergers, and the like. Coverage is broad and includes such diverse topics as navigation, library science, and banking. Not all titles are indexed completely; however, users can find out which are by referring to the section "Abstracted Completely Journals." Found there is a list of the 1,012 journals that are without exception abstracted completely. Some examples include at least 90 Institute of Electrical and Electronics Engineers journals, transactions, and magazines; American Institute of Physics journals, such as *Physical Reviews (A-E)*; and Institute of Physics journals, such as *Journal of Physics (A-D,* and *G)*. It would be nice if this information were coded into the main listing.

Aside from the above section, there is also a section called "Abbreviated Titles" that gives the abbreviated form of the periodical title as it generally appears in the INSPEC databases. Each entry is followed by the full title that is used in the *List of Journals and Other Serials Sources* section. They note that their abbreviations follow IS04-1984(E). Another section consists of the same titles listed by coden—followed by the complete title.

This is a useful addition to collections that have the INSPEC database, use it on Knight-Ritter or another service, or do many interlibrary loans. This is a wonderful source for verifying abbreviations of European, Chinese, and other less common serials. [R: Choice, April 96, p. 1288]—**Susan B. Ardis**

INDUSTRIAL ENGINEERING

1307. **Annual Bulletin of Steel Statistics for Europe. Volume XXI: 1991-1994.** By the Economic Commission for Europe. New York, United Nations, 1996. 254p. $37.00pa. ISBN 02-1-016312-5. ISSN 0250-9903. S/N E/F/R.96.II.E.10.

This is a standard, accepted source for production figures in the iron and steel industries worldwide. The basic language used is English, although notes are available in French and Russian as well. While the use of English is to the English speaker's advantage, some of the vocabulary is unusual, hindering a full-text mode of searching. For example, one notation discusses the "*Arisings* and Receipts of Iron and Steel Scrap in the Country" instead of the "*Accumulations* and Receipts . . . ."

There are seven main sets of tables on such topics as production of semifinished and finished steel products and consumption of energy in the steel industry. An added feature is the use of a table for "former Czechoslovakia" as well as for "Czech Republic" and "Slovak Republic," so that compilers can preserve integrity of older tables. Compilation credit is given to the Japan Iron and Steel Federation. This work would be useful in metallurgical and productivity libraries.—**Eugene B. Jackson**

MATERIALS SCIENCE

1308. Henry, Scott D., and others. **Fatigue Data Book: Light Structural Alloys.** Materials Park, Ohio, ASM International, 1995. 397p. $110.00. ISBN 0-87170-507-9.

ASM International is to be commended for its commitment to expand significantly the list of quality reference titles covering the properties of metals and other materials. This title greatly supplements the fatigue data for light structural alloys that is found in ASM's *Atlas of Fatigue Curves* (1985). The authors note that because of length considerations, the coverage of aluminum alloy fatigue was limited to stress-controlled data.

The work is divided into three alloy fatigue data sections: aluminum, magnesium, and titanium. Each begins with an overview of the current knowledge about the alloy, its metallurgy, fatigue and fracture properties, and applications. For each of the data sets, the authors have provided a useful source note for further information. The abundance of tables and figures for each alloy are clearly presented and easy to interpret. Researchers and students can use the data to benchmark their own work and lab findings and to assist in the selection of appropriate alloys. There is no comparable single-volume reference tool that so completely brings together such a mass of well-edited and -organized data.—**John M. Robson**

1309. **Worldwide Guide to Equivalent Nonferrous Metals and Alloys.** 3d ed. William C. Mack, ed. Materials Park, Ohio, ASM International, 1996. 1v. (various paging). index. $173.00. ISBN 0-87170-540-0.

Despite constant worldwide effort to arrive at uniform standards, several ways exist to identify each alloy, and many alloys that are similar must be given different designations because their content is not identical. This 3d edition of the guide produced by ASM lists nonferrous alloys alphabetically by the principal ingredient and in the sequence of decreasing content of that ingredient. In this way, alloys with slightly different composition are found next to one another. The first identifier for each alloy is the grade number and the Unified Numbering System notation, followed by the country of origin, other specifications, and the content as reported by the source. Indexes include standards organizations worldwide. This is an important resource for anyone who must specify alloys and for every technical library.—**Robert B. McKee**

MECHANICAL ENGINEERING

1310. Nayler, G. H. F. **Dictionary of Mechanical Engineering.** 4th ed. Warrendale, Pa., Society of Automotive Engineers, 1996. 454p. illus. $55.00. ISBN 1-56091-754-7.

For nearly 30 years Nayler has taken the responsibility for creating the standard English-language dictionary for mechanical engineering. Building on the content of the 3d edition (see ARBA 87, entry 1576), Nayler has kept the old and added new terms in the areas of micromaching, nanotechnology, and the manufacture of composites. Although British in orientation, more emphasis has been given to terms chiefly used in North America. The entries are models of clarity and brevity, with an abundance of cross-references that tie the terminology tightly together. The illustrations, although not numerous, are clear line drawings. Terms from such closely related fields as metallurgy, metrology, and welding are not given prominence. Well-known words that are not commonly found in contemporary engineering journals may not be included. The author has succeeded admirably in creating a compact, single-volume guide to the discipline that is useful to both students and practitioners.—**John M. Robson**

PLANT ENGINEERING

1311. **Comprehensive Dictionary of Measurement and Control.** 3d ed. Research Triangle Park, N.C., Instrument Society of America, 1995. 462p. $80.00pa. ISBN 1-55617-528-0.

The 3d edition of the *Dictionary of Measurement and Control* continues its tradition of excellence. Along with additional new material, each existing entry was reviewed by experts where needed. All Instrument Society of America standard terms are indexed; definitions are indicated by brackets, along with the standard number. Also included are thousands of general engineering terms, data processing terminology, 51 pages of symbols tables, and an abbreviations/acronyms index. The dictionary is highly recommended for academic libraries supporting engineering and technology programs.—**Barbara Delzell**

33 Health Sciences

GENERAL WORKS

Atlases

1312. **The Virtual Body.** [CD-ROM]. Minneapolis, Minn., IVI Publishing, 1995. Minimum system requirements: IBM or compatible 486/33MHz. Double speed CD-ROM drive. Windows 3.1. 8MB RAM. Hard disk. 256-color VGA monitor (640 x 480 mode). Mouse. Sound Blaster 16 or compatible sound card. Speakers or headphones. $59.95. ISBN 1-884899-11-0.

This animated view of the human body and its workings is well worth the price for libraries, schools, and families seeking quality software to enthrall and educate young thinkers. The basic menu offers eight choices—seven on the body's systems and an eighth as a multi-use browser. Self-explanatory instructions guide the user to full-color cutaway reproductions of human systems (e.g., the male and female reproductive organs). Choices of activities include straightforward presentation; for example, an animated view of a leg and a hip in action to demonstrate how muscles and joints move the limbs and trunk. The narrator describes the coordination of contracted muscles and hinged joints to produce basic motion. Other detailed data call up interactive screens and vernacular speech to explain the origin of goose bumps, how a sphygmomanometer measures both diastolic and systolic blood pressure, and why the stomach does not digest itself.

The editors of *The Virtual Body* tap into the kinds of information the beginning student of anatomy needs to know and the questions that are likely to evolve from intense study of body parts, digestion, nerves and brain, respiration, and reproduction. Narration avoids the cutesiness found in less serious programs. Instructions and use of multipurpose screens invite manipulation and study according to personal need, interest, and preference. One weakness is the pictorial browser, which displays unidentified close-ups of cells, bones, and tissue and halts the flow of access while the user decodes the small cells. Overall, *The Virtual Body* is a must for student health reference.—**Mary Ellen Snodgrass**

Bibliography

1313. **Health Industry QuickSource: A Complete Descriptive Reference to Health Care Information Resources.** Mary Jeanne Cilurzo, ed. Nanuet, N.Y., QuickSource Press, 1995. 1023p. $225.00pa. ISBN 1-886515-08-5. ISSN 1077-9469.

This text is a guide to the world of medical CD-ROMs, online databases, and printed periodicals. Presented in a user-friendly style, individuals involved in or who wish to know more about health care/medicine will find this text useful. One nice feature is that it provides the sources of information for more than 70 medical topics ranging from AIDS to sports medicine to women's health. The reader can look up a specific medical condition, and reference sources are provided, including addresses and telephone and fax numbers.

Throughout most of the text, hundreds of medical resources are provided and listed according to the categories of either CD-ROM, online databases, or printed periodicals. The reader simply looks up the name of the reference (e.g., *Journal of Emergency Medical Services*), and information such as number of persons subscribing, subscription cost, frequency of publication, address, and telephone contacts are provided. All material involving a computer discusses compatibility features (IBM, Macintosh) and gives a summary of the software. An extensive list of printed periodicals that may also be of use to the reader completes the text.

Overall, this reference is well presented and a valuable resource for gaining information regarding the health care field as a whole. Individuals involved in medicine (including practicing, teaching, or publishing) should find this text to be a valuable resource. [R: C&RL, Oct 95, p.661]]—**Paul M. Murphy III**

Dictionaries and Encyclopedias

1314. **Dictionary of Substances and Their Effects.** [CD-ROM]. Norwood, Mass., SilverPlatter, 1996. Minimum system requirements: IBM or compatible 386. CD-ROM drive with Microsoft CD-ROM Extensions 2.1. Windows 3.1. 4MB memory (8MB for Windows for Workgroups, Windows 95, Window NT, and OS/2). 14MB hard disk space. $1,795.00/stand-alone version.

These data represent information on more than 4,000 physiologically or ecologically active chemicals. Included are the basic uses, physiochemical properties, and toxicology/adverse effects. Also provided are short bibliographies. Chemicals selected for inclusion are listed on the dangerous substances and pollutant lists from the European Union, the United States, and Canada. Also evaluated were the legislative requirements of the European Union, the United States, and Japan. Information extends to the details of legislation, limit values, and references.

This compilation does not provide risk assessment, but offers pieces of information associated with the identification of chemical hazards. Examples include occupational exposure, ecotoxicity, mammalian toxicity, teratogenicity, and environmental fate. The authors indicate that this resource will benefit persons who are involved in a human or environmental risk assessment.—**Sue Lyon Mertl**

1315. Freudenheim, Ellen. **HealthSpeak: A Complete Dictionary of America's Health Care System.** New York, Facts on File, 1996. 310p. index. $30.00. ISBN 0-8160-3210-6.

This dictionary covers the language of health care and is not a medical/clinical dictionary. More than 2,000 terms are defined clearly and concisely, and they are referenced and cross-referenced for helping the user better understand a concept. Approximately 100 terms have longer essay definitions for clarity. The entries also include definitions for health care and health insurance organizations, economic terms related to health care, health care laws or acts, and compound terms. If an insurance company or health care provider uses a nonclinical term, it is probably in this book.

The book is arranged alphabetically, has a bibliography with more than 55 citations for further information, and contains an extensive index. The one deficiency is the font size of the index. The typeface is extremely small, making it difficult to read. There are half-a-dozen graphs that illustrate specific definitions. This book was written for the layperson and is highly recommended for all public libraries at this price. [R: RBB, 1 May 96, p. 1528]—**Betsy J. Kraus**

1316. **The Health Care Almanac: A Resource Guide to the Medical Field.** Lorri A. Zipperer, ed. Chicago, American Medical Association, 1995. 505p. index. $24.95pa. ISBN 0-89970-748-3.

This useful guide was assembled by the reference staff of the American Medical Association (AMA) library. Similar to its predecessor, *The Healthcare Resource and Reference Guide* (see ARBA 95, entry 1563), it is designed to address common queries by doctors and patients about a broad range of health and medical practice-related issues. The book contains a 360-page section of alphabetized entries, an extensive segment on the AMA itself, and a section containing display copies of the Principles of Medical Ethics, the Hippocratic Oath, and the Patient Bill of Rights. The entries are carefully edited and always readable. Coverage, however, is highly idiosyncratic: Breast feeding lists an address (for La Leche League International), while smoking covers seven pages, more than half of which is a list of magazines that will not accept tobacco advertising. Physicians will find detailed advice on how to close a practice, but there is no advice for patients who wish to find a doctor. A significant number of entries are distilled from AMA publications, particularly *JAMA* and the *AM News*. There is minimal cross-referencing, but an excellent index. The AMA section provides a comprehensive history and overview of association activities from 1846 to the present. Here are described the association's legal functions, business and management services, scientific and educational affairs, policy and political advocacy, and much more. On the whole, the volume is geared more to physicians than to patients, but it should be a popular general reference item in both academic and general libraries.—**Bruce Stuart**

1317. Modeste, Naomi N. **Dictionary of Public Health Promotion and Education: Terms and Concepts.** Newbury Park, Calif., Sage, 1996. 161p. $39.95; $18.95pa. ISBN 0-7619-0002-0; 0-7619-0003-9pa.

Some 240 books and journal articles were used as resources to select the range of terms in the dictionary. None was written after 1994. Terms relevant to the four settings of health promotion and education (community, workplace, primary care, and school) are emphasized (foreword). The terms, listed alphabetically, reflect the process of health promotion and education rather than focusing on disease-specific terminology, unlike most medical dictionaries. Approximately 130 additional sources provide broader coverage of the field. Also, 32 health and professional organizations are listed, with addresses, where more information can be sought.

The definitions vary in length, and many are cross-referenced. A brief example follows each entry to shed further light on the term. These may be of some assistance to the novice selector. Some terms and concepts may not meet standard public health, health promotion, and health education definitions, and one should keep that in mind when accessing a specific term. User frustration may arise due to the fact that the term one is searching for may not be within the parameters selected for inclusion. No firm criteria for selection are given. Although brief, this dictionary should be useful for public, medical, and health science reference collections, but probably not as an individual purchase. [R: Choice, May 96, p. 1454]
—**Judy Gay Matthews**

1318. Rinzler, Carol Ann. **Why Eve Doesn't Have an Adam's Apple: A Dictionary of Sex Differences.** New York, Facts on File, 1996. 200p. index. $25.95; $14.95pa. ISBN 0-8160-3352-8; 0-8160-3356-0pa.

Much has been written about the psychological and behavioral differences between men and women. In this new reference book, the author emphasizes physiological differences: For example, which sex is more likely to get heart disease, ulcers, and thumb pain? Do more men or women suffer from nightmares, cold hands, or headaches? Who is better at spatial reasoning? The entries, 232 in all, are presented in a straightforward alphabetic sequence. While most are short, some go on for a page or more, and some include tables. A nice feature is a section of "notes and references," which enables readers to see where the author found her information.

Much of that information is culled from such respected medical sources as the *Merck Manual* (16th ed., published by Merck); the *Physician's Desk Reference* (48th ed., published by Medical Economics Data); and publications from such organizations as the American Cancer Society, although in a few cases (e.g., AIDS, mathematical skills) the sources are popular publications, such as *The New York Times* and *Newsweek*. There is also a handy index, providing greater access to the information embedded in each entry. The book is physically attractive, with easy-to-read typeface and a provocative cover. This is an entertaining but hardly an exhaustive treatment of the subject. Its strength is its readability and the fact that the author brought together diverse information, making it a good jumping-off point for further research, a source for term paper topics, or even an inspiration for cocktail party conversation. [R: RBB, 1 Sept 96, p. 173]—**Hope Yelich**

1319. Slee, Vergil N., Debora A. Slee, and H. Joachim Schmidt. **Health Care Terms.** 3d ed. St. Paul, Minn., Tringa Press, 1996. 655p. $49.95pa. ISBN 0-9615255-8-4.

The 3d edition of *Health Care Terms* is an impressive compilation written for the key stakeholders in medicine today—clinical providers, administrators, health care purchasers, government bodies, social agencies, and patients. Clinical, business, and computer-specific entries range from a basic one or two sentences to several pages in length, depending upon the subject. The definitions are clearly stated. Acronyms and World Wide Web addresses are provided when appropriate. The authors include a comprehensive array of medical and technological terms in addition to lighter items, such as *parse analysis*: This term refers to a spoof published in the *New England Journal of Medicine* concerning multiple authorships of scholarly articles.

Far from being a dry glossary, this volume is a delight to browse, and the reader will discover unexpected gems throughout the book. For example, the first known discussion of patient empowerment, a current hot topic in medicine, appeared in 1747 when John Wesley published *Primitive Physic*. Wesley is better known as the founder of Methodism. This book is recommended for the general interest library as well as the health care institution. It is a strong resource for both health care professionals and general readers actively involved in their personal medical decisions.—**Adrienne Antink Bendel**

Directories

1320. **Canadian Medical Directory on CD-ROM, 1996.** [CD-ROM]. Don Mills, Ont., Southam, 1996. Minimum system requirements: IBM or compatible, Intel-compatible 386. CD-ROM drive. MS-DOS 3.0. Windows 3.1. 4MB RAM. 1MB hard disk space. VGA monitor. Microsoft-compatible mouse. $335.00/single user.

The disc under review is primarily a database of 56,000 Canadian physicians that can produce more than 20 categories of lists according to specialty, geographic location, hospital and other affiliations, and by year of graduation. These lists can be annotated and used to create personalized listings in a shadow file called an infobase. Furthermore, the infobase can be manipulated into word processing programs or printed directly from the program. The disc loads effortlessly (it was tested on a Windows 95 platform using a Pentium 75). The program was designed using Folio VIEWS, making it slick, powerful, and visually appealing. A brief 36-page pamphlet accompanies the disc and serves as an introductory self-training guide. In addition, the software help screens are useful and free of "dead end" information.

Hypertext features within the database records offer a variety of links. For example, a physician's affiliated hospital is linked to a database record for the hospital itself. Information is current and accurate in both records tested. Abbreviations for degrees and fellowships are hyperlinked to "pop-up" definitions. Shadow files created by the individual user are easy to tag and edit, especially for users familiar with Microsoft products or WordPerfect 6.1. Boolean operators and phrase searches are also easy to use once the user learns some of the necessary protocol through the help screens. The protocol, such as enclosing a phrase search in quotations, is easy to remember.

Printing results is an easy process. The software setup automatically detects printer configuration and accommodates color printing. Saving results to DOS files is also a simple process and within the menu prompts. Supporting 20-plus search criteria, this is a useful tool that produces defined subsets of Canadian physicians, as well as subsets of more than 1,300 hospitals.—**Mary Hemmings**

1321. **Directory of Health Grants: A Reference Directory Pinpointing Health, Hospital....** Loxahatchee, Fla., Research Grant Guides, 1996. 148p. index. $59.50pa. ISBN 0-945078-12-9.

This premier edition covers 761 sources in the United States and Puerto Rico for grants in health, hospitals, and other related areas. The main body of the book is arranged alphabetically by state, with the entries/funding agency numbered consecutively. Each entry consists of the organization name; address; telephone number; subject areas of funding; ranges of grants; and any conditions for funding, such as a specific local. The appendixes treat the Foundation Center, an independent national service organization established by foundations, and the Grantmanship Center, a training organization for the nonprofit sector. The indexes are an alphabetic list by foundation name with its entry number and a subject index. There are 15 broad subject areas, which include AIDS, cancer, hospice, medical research, nursing services, and youth. The three articles cover the topics of grantseeking and proposal writing and how to do both better for more success in receiving funding. This directory is recommended for medical and hospital libraries.—**Betsy J. Kraus**

1322. Gibbs, Tyson, comp. **A Guide to Ethnic Health Collections in the United States.** Westport, Conn., Greenwood Press, 1996. 139p. index. (Bibliographies and Indexes in Medical Studies, no.13). $49.95. ISBN 0-313-29740-1.

Archival repositories dealing with health care for U.S. minorities are described in varying detail in this guidebook. Organized by state jurisdiction, information is provided about the scope and contents of collections that have housed, for the most part, materials for African Americans, Native Americans, Asians, and Hispanics. Information for this guide was gleaned from respondents to a 4-page questionnaire mailed to nearly 400 institutions.

Although the index provides some access to collections according to ethnic group, the cross-references are not always dependable. Furthermore, the lack of reported resources in states such as Illinois, Wisconsin, and Minnesota suggests that a more vigorous investigative effort would have been appreciated. The uneven style and the hasty approach do not inspire scholarly confidence. This guide is not recommended.
—**Mary Hemmings**

1323. **HMO/PPO Directory 1996: U.S. Managed Healthcare Organizations in Detail Plus Key Decision Makers.** Montvale, N.J., Medical Economics Data, 1995. 1v. (various paging). index. $199.00. ISBN 1-56363-146-6. ISSN 0887-4484.

This reference source lists hundreds of health maintenance organizations (HMOs) and preferred provider organizations (PPOs) in the United States. The text is divided into six sections, any of which is easy to locate based on the black margin markings present. Section 1 is the largest part and provides users with a profile of each company. The information presented is summarized yet comprehensive enough to include topics such as the company's address, contact individuals, number of participating hospitals, number of physicians, fees, and claim compensation for the hospital and physician.

Sections 2 and 3 are similar in overall layout. Section 2 lists in alphabetic order the HMOs with reference to their location in section 1. Section 3 lists the PPOs in alphabetic order with reference to their (company) connection to section 2. Section 4 lists the names of the parent companies of vision, dental, and psychiatric care providers with section 1 reference. Section 5 provides a list of the personnel (e.g., medical director, president, administrator) from section 2 with page references to section 1. Section 6 lists the number of members each company/group has in descending order with reference to section 1 as well.

This text is designed for the adult reader and will be helpful to individuals requesting certain HMO/PPO issues such as co-payment costs, subscription costs, and patient complaints. Individuals concerned (or those with questions) about their insurance may find this text to be of use to them.—**Paul M. Murphy III**

1324. **National Health Directory, 1996.** Betty Ankrapp and Sara Nell Di Lima, eds. Gaithersville, Md., Aspen, 1996. 478p. maps. $99.00pa. ISBN 0-8342-0800-8.

Librarians working in a well-funded library that has a constant need for questions involving government officials at all levels may want to consider the *National Health Directory*. Otherwise, they should not spend $99 a year for a book that is probably out-of-date by the time it is received. The *National Health Directory* lists the names, titles, addresses, and telephone numbers of "key information sources on health programs and legislation at all levels" (p. v). The table of contents is extremely brief and lacking in detail and, worst of all, there is no index to the entire book.

Almost all the information on a national level can be found in the *United States Government Manual* (Bernan Press, annual) or the *Washington Information Directory* (see ARBA 96, entry 734; ARBA 93, entry 743; and ARBA 90, entry 702), both of which are easier to use. The maps of state congressional districts can also be found in many other places. The only information not available elsewhere would be that on the local or state level. For the occasional questions most public and academic libraries would get in this area, librarians are better off calling their local health departments rather than spending this amount of money on a book that is most likely valid for only nine months. Only government libraries need consider this directory.—**Natalie Kupferberg**

1325. **Tobacco and Health Network Directory 1996.** 4th ed. Ottawa, National Clearinghouse on Tobacco & Health, 1996. 1v (unpaged). index. $20.00 looseleaf (U.S.). ISBN 1-896025-12-9.

Tobacco-related health issues are major concerns for health professionals, policy-makers, and the general public. The intent of this looseleaf 4th edition reference work, created by the Canadian Council on Smoking and Health, is "to provide a resource which facilitates communication, collaboration, and cooperative action amongst organizations and individuals involved in the promotion of a tobacco-free Canada" (p. v). However, the information in this brief guide will also prove useful to the broader audience of antitobacco advocates and scholars.

The nonannotated listings are divided into six color-coded sections, followed by a comprehensive index of individuals mentioned in the preceding categories. The first three segments cover key personnel of the National Strategy to Reduce Tobacco Use, the tobacco-related offices of Canada's federal government, and the national nongovernmental organizations concerned with health and welfare. The largest section presents the health-related governmental infrastructure for each Canadian province, as well as major health associations (e.g., cancer and lung societies). The fifth category presents a useful survey of international contacts involved in the antitobacco crusade, from Albania to Zambia. This reference tool will be helpful for any patron seeking material on the worldwide antitobacco movement, especially for those focusing on Canadian activities in this area.—**Jonathon Erlen**

Handbooks and Yearbooks

1326. **The Complete Family Guide to Healthy Living.** By Stephen Carroll. Tony Smith, ed. New York, Dorling Kindersley, 1995. 320p. illus. index. $24.95; $15.95pa. ISBN 0-7894-0114-2; 0-7894-0120-7pa.

This book is beautifully laid out and illustrated with both diagrams and photographs. It is organized into chapters that focus on function, not on specific anatomic or physiological systems. The emphasis is on health and fitness, not on disease. Diet, fitness, disease prevention, stress, and weight control are the focus of the major sections of the book. However, some chapters do address common diseases, such as cancer, back pain, and heart disease. First aid, injury prevention, and safety are also covered.

The many photographs enhance the presentation of the material in this book. The illustrations of the exercises recommended, the foods discussed, and the lifestyle suggested complement the text well. Diagrams of anatomy, graphs, and diagrams and photographs of medical procedures are accurate and informative. Additional photographs set the mood and add a dimension: A depressed woman, a man in pain, or a distressed child contrast dramatically with the relaxed and confident people portrayed when interventions are discussed.

The book focuses on things people can do without medical intervention to improve and maintain their health. Yet the guide does not ignore the need for appropriate medical advice, and it provides plenty of examples of occasions when one should seek medical help, such as prenatal care, injury rehabilitation, heart attack treatment, and cancer diagnosis and treatment. There is a pertinent and clear section devoted to genetic testing. This book is a useful guide for everyone. [R: SLJ, April 96, p. 168]—**Margretta Reed Seashore**

1327. Cowles, C. McKeen. **Nursing Home Statistical Yearbook, 1995.** Tacoma, Wash., Cowles Research Group; distr., Baltimore, Md., Johns Hopkins University Press, 1995. 246p. index. $45.00. ISBN 0-8018-5378-8. ISSN 1085-0309.

In this book's introductory essay, one of the leaders of the American Health Care Association briefly describes the rapidly changing nature of the United States' long-term care industry. He continues by recommending that the consumers, health providers, and policy-makers involved with nursing homes use this reference tool when making decisions concerning these facilities. Regrettably, the highly technical nature of this volume's statistical tables, which are not accompanied by explanatory text, challenges this recommendation.

The data used to create the complex statistical tables have been taken from the July 3, 1995, version of the Health Care Financing Administration's Online Survey Certification and Reporting database, and the author has illuminated the duplicate records from this database and spot-checked the validity of entry information. These data are organized into six broad categories: acuity or case mix, special patient needs, unique health problems of patients, deficiencies found in nursing homes, number of nursing homes and their capacities, and staffing information. This information is arranged, primarily, by state, and there is no coverage of individual nursing homes or of chains of these facilities.

While this reference work may be of some limited value to long-term care policy-makers, the statistical complexity of the tables and the overall format will be of little or no assistance to health providers and will frustrate potential nursing home users. Individuals seeking information about specific long-term care facilities should use *The Directory of Nursing Homes* (see ARBA 96, entry 1731) published annually by HCIA.—**Jonathon Erlen**

1328. Ferguson, Tom. **Health Online: How to Find Health Information, Support Groups, and Self-Help Communities in Cyberspace.** Reading, Mass., Addison-Wesley Publishing, 1996. 308p. index. $17.00pa. ISBN 0-201-40989-5.

The information age has created a large number of options for those seeking medical information and other forms of health assistance without relying on the traditional doctor visit. This volume, written by one of the United States' leading self-help proponents, is intended to introduce both the computer novice, as well as the computer expert, to the ever-expanding world of online self-help medical resources. Special attention is given to online self-help communities that can provide information and support for individuals suffering health crises, as the author claims that the old standbys of families, friends, and caring physicians no longer exist, in many cases, in the United States today.

This reference guide is divided into three major parts. The first section, intended for beginning computer users, explains the ease of going online, the use of e-mail, and some of the basics of functioning online. The second segment presents in-depth information to help readers choose a commercial computer network for accessing online health resources (e.g., America Online, CompuServe, Prodigy). The last division lists and briefly describes some of the health-related Internet mailing lists, newsgroups, FAQ sites, computer bulletin boards, and Gopher and World Wide Web sites available to the public.

Libraries should be very cautious about acquiring this book. It is extremely anti-medical establishment in its orientation. The author fails to warn readers about the false information provided by some online health sites that could seriously mislead patrons. He also ignores the values that are the basis for the doctor/patient relationship. Libraries interested in providing reference tools discussing online health resources should purchase less biased reference works on this topic, such as *Dr. Tom Linden's Guide to Online Medicine* (see ARBA 96, entry 1709).—**Jonathon Erlen**

1329. **Plunkett's Health Care Industry Almanac.** Jack W. Plunkett, ed. Galveston, Tex., Plunkett Research, 1995. 699p. index. $125.00pa. ISBN 0-9638268-1-6.

Uniquely designed as part history book and part crystal ball, this volume is a comprehensive, one-stop source for researchers of all types. The guide opens with an overview of the health care industry. Chapter 1 presents a brief description of the 8 major trends contributing to the rapid changes in the health care industry. Chapter 2 explains current health care in the United States through the use of in-depth statistics on spending, utilization, patients, insurance coverage, diseases, and more. Chapter 3 examines the outlook for every major type of service in the health care industry, based on its annual volume, growth potential, and exports. Chapter 4 forecasts the future of the major technologies that are associated with increasing the quality of care. Chapter 5 provides an all-inclusive discussion on occupations and careers. Included are approximate salaries, training and education, projected employment growth, and licensing.

The second section is composed of one huge chapter that describes "The Health Care 500." Chosen specifically for their operational dominance, companies include insurance; manufacturers and distributors of pharmaceuticals, supplies, and products; all types of health care providers; specialized service companies; and many more. Criteria for inclusion involve U.S.-based, nongovernment corporations with $10 million annual sales and that are publicly traded. Companies are indexed by company name, industry, geographic location, and so on. This almanac provides great facts and great comparisons in an easy-to-understand format. Prepare to be amazed. [R: Choice, Feb 96, pp. 931-32]—**Sue Lyon Mertl**

MEDICINE

General Works

Dictionaries and Encyclopedias

1330. **Encyclopedia of U.S. Biomedical Policy.** Robert H. Blank and Janna C. Merrick, eds. Westport, Conn., Greenwood Press, 1996. 363p. index. $89.50. ISBN 0-313-28641-8.

Encyclopedia of U.S. Biomedical Policy is a compendium of U.S. biomedical policy since the early 1970s. The goal of the encyclopedia is to focus on subjects that relate directly to the array of issues on the public agenda raised by the use of biomedical technologies. The focus is on public policy. The purpose of this encyclopedia is to shed light on a range of public decisions that face society. Decision making has become more complex as an array of biomedical issues have been raised, such as human genetics and reproduction issues, prenatal and neonatal issues, biomedical issues within the life cycle, and death-related issues.

Entries are arranged alphabetically and are cross-referenced with an asterisk to related entries. The extensive index offers another means of cross-checking entries by subject. Entries vary in length. They include a mixture of legislation and court cases, as well as descriptions of key government agencies, private organizations, technologies, and issue areas. Each entry has a short, selected bibliography of key sources for further reading. Entries are authoritative. Entries include such subjects as egg donation, euthanasia, RU-486 (the abortion pill), the Human Genome Project, and HIV testing. Appendix A is a chronology of key events, court cases, and legislation and can be read as a summary of the cumulative development of policy activity in biomedicine. Appendix B provides a directory of key sources of information.

This easily accessible reference source describes court cases, legislation, public policies, technologies, issues, key government agencies, and private organizations dealing with the complex economic, cultural, social, and political context for biomedical decision making. The resource is recommended for students and professors; policy-makers; public administrators; college, university, and special libraries; and public libraries.—**Marilynn Green**

1331. Spilker, Bert, comp. **Medical Dictionary in Six Languages.** New York, Raven Press, 1995. 665p. $99.00. ISBN 0-7817-0182-1.

Among the 7,500 definitions in this English dictionary are translations for common phrases and multiword terms in French, Italian, Spanish, German, and Japanese. If one knows the English term, the front part of the book is the place to begin searching; other languages are cross-referenced to the main English listings by entry number. British and American spellings are used (e.g., aetiology, etiology; anaemia, anemia), but only universally understood abbreviations are included. Oriented vertically instead of horizontally, which is the most comfortable reference mode for many people, this book will not lie flat when opened, so handling the bulk of it could hamper reference use.

Two-, three-, and four-word phrases that cannot be translated word-for-word into languages other than English are listed, which could be helpful in conversations, at seminars, during patient examinations, and in writing reports. This is a book of considerable utility, and medical transcribers, in particular, are sure to applaud it.—**Judy Gay Matthews**

1332. Szycher, Michael. **Szycher's Dictionary of Medical Devices.** Lancaster, Pa., Technomic Publishing, 1995. 212p. $75.00. ISBN 1-56676-275-8.

Medical devices are among the most closely regulated of products; their names and definitions must also be closely monitored by the Food and Drug Administration (FDA). Title XXI of the Code of Federal Regulations publishes these definitions. Because they are spread over several medical specialties, they may be difficult to find. In this book, the author provides an alphabetic listing of officially defined devices in an attempt to ease this situation. However, if the searcher is unfamiliar with the device, or simply cannot recall it, finding the item may still be difficult as no cross-references have been added to the terms used by the government. When *braces* is not listed, who but sophisticated users would go directly to *limb orthosis* or *orthodontic band*?

Device is defined in the text as "any instrument, apparatus, implant, machine, contrivance, in vitro reagent, or similar or related article, including any component part or accessory" (p. 52). Such a broad definition reflects the great variety of regulated items, from tooth brush to some 26 devices listed under "cardiopulmonary bypass." Each entry gives the purpose or use of the device and its class. The text lists three classes. Class 1 devices are those that can be regulated by general controls, as they do not represent a health risk (e.g., a stethoscope). Class 2 devices require performance standards to ensure safety and effectiveness (e.g., cardiographs). Class 3 devices are the critical ones—life-supporting or -sustaining—requiring premarketing approval (e.g., pacemakers). This is not a catalog: There are no manufacturers, costs, and so forth. Specific statutes are not cited.

The author suggests using the book as a companion to his *Szycher's Dictionary of Biomaterials and Medical Devices*, also published by Technomic (see ARBA 93, entry 1639). Those interested in technology as applied to the medical field and the standards for its regulation should find this dictionary valuable, but it is not too useful for general readers, despite a possible familiarity with many medical devices and tests.

—**Harriette M. Cluxton**

1333. Turkington, Carol A., and Jeffrey S. Dover. **Skin Deep: An A-Z of Skin Disorders, Treatments, and Health.** New York, Facts on File, 1996. 404p. illus. index. $40.00. ISBN 0-8160-3071-5.

The skin is the body's largest, most visible organ. Caring for it properly and maintaining its health are major concerns. Finding reliable information about dermatology in lay language is difficult. *Skin Deep*, written by a medical writer and a dermatologist, is a source that fills this need.

The alphabetic entries range in length from a few lines to two pages. The subjects covered include anatomy (e.g., epidermis, hair anatomy); skin conditions (e.g., acne, vitiligo); systemic diseases that affect the skin (e.g., AIDS, lupus erythematosus); cosmetics; skin care; skin diseases (e.g., malignant melanoma, Hailey-Hailey disease); organizations (e.g., National Psoriasis Foundation, Plastic Surgery Research Council); medical/surgical treatments (e.g., phototherapy, skin graft); and drugs (e.g., nystatin, Retin-A). There is an entry for the Sjogrens Syndrome Foundation, but no entry for or information about the condition itself. This is a minor omission. Ample cross-references and a master index simplify access to the material. Small black-and-white line drawings illustrate anatomical entries. A glossary and an extensive bibliography of recent clinical and lay literature complete the text. Six appendixes list cosmetic ingredients, cosmetic ingredients to avoid, types of lesions, lay and professional organizations, and selected publications.

This is a useful source as it is the only comprehensive work on the skin written in lay language. It provides current, accurate information about skin care, diseases, and even scams related to cosmetics. It is a helpful, reasonably priced starting point for research. This book is an excellent addition to consumer health collections. [R: BR, May/June 96, p. 47; RBB, 1 May 96, pp. 1524-26; SLJ, June 96, p. 171]

—**Barbara M. Bibel**

1334. Turkington, Carol. **The Brain Encyclopedia.** New York, Facts on File, 1996. 316p. index. $40.00. ISBN 0-8160-3169-X.

Research in the neurological sciences has accelerated greatly in recent years. This book aims to summarize for the layperson the status of knowledge about the brain, the body's most important organ. The introduction claims the encyclopedia "provides a guided tour through the brain"—but provision of a map would greatly assist most readers: There are no diagrams or illustrations of any kind. The encyclopedic arrangement of articles of varying length makes browsing intriguing; the book is not a neurological text specifically about the brain.

Small topics alphabetically arranged cover aspects of the brain, its structure and function, disorders, their diagnosis and treatment, and its relationship with other parts of the neurological and endocrinologic systems. There are many terms from psychology and psychiatry, and discussions of drugs affecting the brain—in good or bad ways. Paragraphs under "the brain in history" provide interesting sidelights, as do those under important physiologists and philosophers. There is no entry for "mind," but it is mentioned under "thought," "emotions," "consciousness," and the like.

An appendix list supports organizations, many of which are also described under the entries. There is a glossary of neurological terms and an adequate index. The bibliography is a reading list of recent articles related to the general subject, often readily available in such magazines as *Science News*.

This book succeeds admirably in helping readers to understand what is now known about the brain, and some of what yet needs to be learned about its mysteries. The encyclopedia is highly recommended for school and public libraries and health care workers. [R: LJ, July 96, p. 106; RBB, 15 Sept 96, p. 280]
—**Harriette M. Cluxton**

1335. **The World Book Rush-Presbyterian-St. Luke's Medical Center Medical Encyclopedia: Your Guide to Good Health.** 7th ed. Chicago, World Book, 1995. 1072p. illus. index. $44.95. ISBN 0-7166-4202-6.

This medical encyclopedia updates and expands a 1991 edition (see ARBA 92, entry 1664) and provides a broad span of data written in uncomplicated English by a Chicago medical conglomerate, with assistance from the American Red Cross and the National Safety Council. Typeface is a clean sans serif with a minimum of italics and small capital letters. Spacing is generous and layout attractive and helpful, particularly the section on care of newborns. Arranged in alphabetic order with thumb indexing are 4,500 entries and 1,200 color photographs, charts, and line drawings. Appended to the text are two sections on symptoms; charts naming diseases and organ malfunctions common to specified age groups (e.g., glaucoma, kidney stones, stroke, and varicose veins among the middle-aged); preventive diet and exercise; and commentary on geriatrics, along with addresses of 80 social, legal, and medical agencies, including Gray Panthers, Foundation for Grandparenting, and Hospice.

Main entries begin with a simplified pronunciation guide that employs the schwa, macron, circumflex, and single accent mark to indicate major voice stress. Topics range from technical discussions of AIDS and toxic shock syndrome and advice on lifting and turning a patient to a Dick-and-Jane-level cartoon showing how to shampoo and dry hair. First aid instructions include a six-panel model of treatment for fainting, five panels on drug overdose, and four on convulsions. Useful adjuncts are symptom charts; names of medical specialties; advice on medical emergencies; and question-and-answer features on symptoms, treatment, and legal and ethical matters. Additional charts show a patient undergoing fluoroscopy, list menstrual problems and sources of saturated dietary fats, and describe a lengthy list of plant and chemical poisons. Generous cross-references assist the average user in locating specific topics.

Although well designed overall, the work has glaring faults. The cover, endpapers, and three prefatory pages are surprisingly devoid of an introduction, which may have established the mission and scope of the book or given advice on its use for general health advice or critical care and emergency needs. Illustrations focus on Caucasians. Line drawings are dismally shaded with heavy splotches of gray; color photographs are used sparingly. Coverage skimps on some topics—for instance, 12 lines on body odor, 12 lines on root canal, 10 lines on massage, 2 frail paragraphs on health maintenance organizations, 18 lines on posttraumatic shock disorder, and 5 lines on tendinitis. Some of the advice is unnecessarily simplistic and unsophisticated. Editors have neglected some current topics, notably athletic injury; racial circumstances; chronic pain; cost factors; and alternate medical treatment, such as herbs and aromatherapy. In contrast to current textbooks, television, newspapers, magazines, and online health information, this work is a dated, below-par source of medical information.—**Mary Ellen Snodgrass**

Handbooks and Yearbooks

1336. **Everything You Need to Know About Diseases.** Springhouse, Pa., Springhouse Publishing, 1996. 918p. index. $24.95. ISBN 0-87434-822-6.

1337. **Everything You Need to Know About Medical Tests.** Springhouse, Pa., Springhouse Publishing, 1996. 691p. illus. index. $24.95. ISBN 0-87434-823-4.

1338. **Everything You Need to Know About Medical Treatments.** Springhouse, Pa., Springhouse Publishing, 1996. 628p. illus. index. $24.95. ISBN 0-87434-821-8.

This series of books on diseases, medical tests, and medical treatments is similar to H. W. Griffith's trio of books *Complete Guide to Symptoms, Illness, & Surgery* (see ARBA 86, entry 1634); *Complete Guide to Pediatric Symptoms, Illness, & Medications* (Berkley, 1989); and *Complete Guide to Medical Tests* (see ARBA 90, entry 1667). *Everything You Need to Know About Diseases* is divided into 18 chapters by type of disorder (e.g., gynecologic, eye). With 100 leading doctors and medical experts, the book answers the following questions: What causes the condition? What are the symptoms? How is it diagnosed? and, What is the treatment? It also has special tips on prevention, self-help, and advice for caregivers.

Everything You Need to Know About Medical Tests details 400-plus tests in descriptions written by more than 70 physicians. The book answers these questions: Why are the tests done? What are the risks? What happens during and after the test? What are normal results? and, What do abnormal results mean? *Everything You Need to Know About Medical Treatments* covers more than 300 medically approved therapies. The book explains why these therapies are recommended, the risks, how doctors perform them, and what happens before and after treatments. It also includes practical advice for caregivers, self-help solutions, and straight answers to medical questions by 50 doctors and medical experts.

These are excellent new titles for the consumer health market. Few doctors today have the time or inclination to give consumers the how and why on medical disorders, treatments, and so forth. These books give consumers the opportunity to make more informed medical decisions. Springhouse Publishing has done an excellent job in preparing these informative medicine texts for the public. The series is highly recommended for small, medium, and large public libraries.—**Theresa Maggio**

1339. Rozario, Diane. **The Immunization Resource Guide: Where to Find Answers to All Your Questions About Childhood Immunizations.** 2d ed. Burlington, Iowa, Patter, 1995. 60p. index. $9.95pa. ISBN 0-9643366-2-6.

Although the author of this pamphlet-length guide claims impartiality, a glance at her work reveals she is deeply suspicious and critical of all vaccines and immunizations, childhood or otherwise. Almost all of the publications of established scientific merit are listed in a chapter title "Pro-vaccination" and are accompanied by the author's critical comments. Most other chapters are antivaccination, and are composed of publications from the popular press and various religious and alternative medical publishers. These (including publications of the Natural Hygiene movement, which denies the importance of bacteria and viruses in causing disease) are treated much less critically.

Many worthwhile publications and national and international organizations are listed in this pamphlet. Most, however, are well known and accessible through many other sources, available in any basic reference library. Parents who legitimately want more information on the dangers and side effects of childhood immunizations should consult these. This publication is for those who have already made up their mind and want a listing of all antivaccination literature, no matter how dubious the source. —**Carol L. Noll**

1340. Tremaine, M. David, and Elias M. Awad. **The Foot & Ankle Sourcebook: Everything You Need to Know.** Los Angeles, Calif., Lowell House, 1995. 324p. illus. index. $26.00. ISBN 1-56565-150-2.

In today's world, with people living longer and more active lives, the phrase "oh, my aching feet" can be heard more and more often. The authors (an orthopedic surgeon and an information specialist) set out to write a user's guide to the human foot, as much to prevent foot problems as to help sufferers treat them. The 18 chapters in this book discuss normal feet and the mechanics of walking and running, describe a variety of congenital problems that can appear in infants and children, and cover in detail the numerous ailments that can beset the feet of adults as they age. There is particular emphasis on sports injuries, occupational foot problems, and especially diabetic foot problems, which are the third leading cause of hospital admissions in the United States.

Throughout the text, the authors give excellent, practical advice in lay terms. They cover both self-help suggestions and advice on when it is best to consult a professional. For most injuries and problems, possible courses of treatment are discussed, and typical recovery times are given. Also included are a glossary of terms and an extensive list of agencies and support groups concerned with foot and ankle problems.—**Carol L. Noll**

1341. **The Women's Complete Healthbook.** Roselyn Payne Epps and Susan Cobb Stewart, eds. New York, Delacorte Press/Bantam Doubleday Dell, 1995. 708p. illus. index. $29.95. ISBN 0-385-31382-9.

This peerless reference book was written by women doctors, many of them specialists, for women patients and health care consumers. As medical research on women's problems is recent and quite incomplete, the authors of the separate chapters provide much information from their practices and personal experience, as well as what is generally know about a disease or condition, including up-to-date medical information. Because each contributor writes from her own point of view, there is some intentional repetition of information, so the user can also review it from another approach (e.g., osteoporosis is discussed in the excellent overview chapter on aging, as well as under the musculoskeletal system).

Material is organized into chapters under four main headings: "Being a Savvy Consumer of Healthcare"; "Keeping Yourself Healthy"; "Reproductive Healthy"; and the longest section called "The Healthy Body: Symptoms, Diagnosis, and Treatments." Each chapter begins with an outline of its topics, so it is easy to locate specific information. The detailed index is also helpful. There are many clear figures and charts. An appendix describes common diagnostic tests. A list of associations keyed to the chapters provides access to further resources.

The aim of this large handbook is to provide an authoritative resource that empowers women who make health care decisions for themselves and their families. Its scope, clarity, and quality is incredible. It reflects most favorably on the American Medical Women's Association, who presented it. All kinds of libraries should find it valuable, and it is recommended for widespread individual purchase.—**Harriette M. Cluxton**

Alternative Medicine

1342. Callinan, Paul. **Family Homeopathy: A Practical Handbook for Home Treatment.** New Canaan, Conn., Keats Publishing, 1995. 343p. index. $24.95. ISBN 0-87983-687-3.

In recent years, a number of books have been published concerning the practice of homeopathy, a system of alternative medicine that uses natural remedies to treat common and chronic ailments. Add *Family Homeopathy* to this growing list. The arrangement of this book is similar to other recent works on the topic. An introductory chapter describes how homeopathy works, and scientific evidence is cited to support the effectiveness of homeopathic treatments. Some of the author's examples are quite convincing. For instance, he cites a source that claims that a 10 percent mortality rate during the European cholera epidemic of 1832 was recorded for patients treated with homeopathy, compared to a 70 percent mortality rate for patients who received traditional medical treatment.

The balance of the work consists of two major sections: a list of treatments for common problems (e.g., acne, headache, indigestion and heartburn, gout, hair loss, constipation) and a *materia medica* of common remedies. Added information includes a chapter on the Bach flower remedies, a home medicine kit, a resource guide of suppliers, and a short bibliography. *Family Homeopathy* is a suitable purchase for the library circulating collection, or the home library. [R: RQ, Summer 96, pp. 557-58]—**Elaine F. Jurries**

1343. Chevallier, Andrew. **The Encyclopedia of Medicinal Plants.** New York, DK Publishing, 1996. 336p. illus. index. $39.95. ISBN 0-7894-1067-2.

Featuring more than 550 plants that are put to therapeutic use around the world, this book introduces readers to the rich traditions and resources of herbal medicine. With a refreshing combination of folkloric and scientific material, it brings together each plant's history and tradition with research-based information about its active constituents, key actions, and potential new uses.

After a general overview of the global development of herbal medicine, the book's focus shifts to major continents, tracing traditions within each. A colorful and well-illustrated index of herbs follows. This is divided into two broad sections—"Key Medicinal Plants" (which covers 100 herbs) and "Other Medicinal Plants" (which covers more than 400 herbs). Within the sections, herbs are listed alphabetically by their scientific name, below which appear—in large typeface—their common name or names. The following information is given for each herb: name (scientific and common), habitat and cultivation, related species, key constituents, key actions, traditional and current uses (including self-help uses), parts used, and key preparations and their uses. This same type of information is offered in each section, but it is given in greater detail in the first section. Final chapters in the book are devoted to growing, harvesting, and processing herbs; making herbal remedies; and consulting an herbal practitioner. A glossary, a bibliography, a general index, and an index of ailments conclude the book.

If this book has a weakness, it is in the sheer ambition of covering the globe with a rather slippery language. Because general readers are for the most part unaware of scientific names of herbs, they may have difficulty locating specific plants. A thorough index could make up for this problem, but although this book's index does list common names, it does not always list *all* common names for an individual herb. Hence, the Chinese herb *Angelica Senensis*, commonly known as dong quai in the United States, is listed under its Latin name and under a variation of the common name that one supposes is used in the United Kingdom, dang gui. Other herbs seem simply to be excluded. Osha root (or chuchupate), a Native American remedy for cough relief, does not appear, nor does the Asian Indian digestive ajwain (or ajawan).

Another fine work on this topic is *Rodale's Illustrated Encyclopedia of Herbs* (see ARBA 88, entry 1535), which focuses more on North American and Western European herbs and traditions. The Rodale volume also emphasizes cultivation and herb lore, rather than modern herbal medicine. In fact, these two books complement one another and should not be considered substitutes.

In spite of inevitable omissions and weaknesses of this book, it is a rare find. Used in conjunction with other herbal guides, it is a worthwhile reference book. One can always hope that in subsequent editions, the author will expand the index to provide easier access to this abundant information. For collections covering this subject area, the book is highly recommended. [R: BL, 1 Dec 96, p. 629]—**Barbara Ittner**

1344. Elkins, Rita. **The Complete Home Health Advisor.** Pleasant Grove, Utah, Woodland Publishing, 1995. 388p. index. $17.95pa. ISBN 0-913923-96-6.

The author depends on the cover description, "A Guide to Combining Standard Medical Treatments with Wholistic Alternatives," to convey the purpose of the book; there is no preface. Although her credentials are not stated, the text material would seem to indicate careful preparation. More than 100 common health concerns or "ailments" are described, their standard medical treatment discussed, and alternative treatments and other remedies suggested.

Alphabetically listed topics are treated according to the following formula: definition, causes, symptoms, emergency alerts, standard medical treatments (and side effects), home self-care, nutritional approach, herbal remedies, and prevention. Each of these sections is marked by a black symbol in the margin. For example, a stylized plant design indicates herbal remedies and what they are supposed to do. Some topics are actual disease names; most are common descriptions, such as fever. Earache and backache are listed, but strangely, the most common complaint, headache—which is often treated by home remedies—is not. Also, *hantavirus* is hardly a "common" complaint or ailment.

Using regular medical resources is always recommended. The alternatives discussed are presented as auxiliaries rather than substitutes, and medical advice should be sought before using them. The approach is interpretive, explaining how to understand the condition and seek help, not how to self-treat. Dosages or specific directions are not given. This perhaps justifies placing this oversized work in the consumer health collection as well as considering it as a home handbook. It contains much practical and interesting health information.—**Harriette M. Cluxton**

1345. **The Encyclopedia of Alternative Medicine: A Complete Family Guide to Complementary Therapies.** Jennifer Jacobs, ed. Boston, Journey Editions/Charles E. Tuttle, 1996. 320p. illus. index. $24.95pa. ISBN 1-885203-36-5.

Consumer interest in alternative medicine is at an all-time high in the United States, with the traditional medical establishment gradually, if reluctantly, recognizing and accepting its value. Publishers have responded to the public's enthusiasm for alternative medicine with a bevy of books to help consumers educate themselves. What distinguishes this volume from several others on the same subject are the format and attractive layout. The book begins with a short, clear introduction on what alternative therapies have in common and is followed by a useful section entitled "Finding the Right Therapy." Six charts of disorders list individual medical problems, such as asthma or back problems. A quick look at the chart tells the reader which alternative therapy to consider for each medical problem.

Rather than the classic A to Z format, this encyclopedia groups each of the 30 alternative or complementary treatment modalities into 7 related groupings. For example: Part 1, "Natural Healing," includes a chapter each on color therapy, homeopathy, iridology, and polarity therapy; part 7, "Eastern Therapies," has chapters on acupuncture, acupressure, shiatsu, tai chi, and Chinese herbal medicine. Because authorship is not given, the reader must assume that each chapter is written by 1 of the 30 contributors (leading practitioners, experts, authors) listed under each alternative treatment at the front of the book.

On the verso of the title page the publisher strongly disclaims: "The information and opinions contained herein, which should not be used or relied upon without consultation and advice of a physician, are those solely of the authors and not those of the publishers who disclaim any responsibility for the accuracy of such information and opinions and any responsibility for any consequences that may result from any use or reliance thereon by the reader." Despite the lack of confidence caused by reading the fine print, the reader gets a clear, easy-to-read understanding of almost all available alternative medical treatments. Most chapters include a history of the therapy, recent developments, case studies, and what conditions are best treated with the therapy. Many sidebars and lavish illustrations make the book a pleasure to read. A glossary and a list of addresses conclude the book.

Consumers of alternative health care will welcome this quick fix on their coffee tables. Public librarians will find the book useful as well and can feel confident referring patrons to it because, as the back cover states, this encyclopedia is "endorsed by a Member of the Program Advisory Council of the National Institutes of Health Office of Alternative Medicine."—**Georgia Briscoe**

1346. Lawless, Julia. **The Illustrated Encyclopedia of Essential Oils: The Complete Guide to the Use of Oils in Aromatherapy and Herbalism.** Rockport, Mass., Element Books, 1995. 256p. illus. index. $18.95pa. ISBN 1-85230-721-8.

This attractive, well-organized compendium offers schools, libraries, health workers, merchants, and consumers a colorful, economic guide to the use of fragrant and stimulating oils for health treatments and stress relief. Clearly explained and generously illustrated with photographs, the work opens with a preface expressing the author's aim in upgrading the 1992 edition. A two-page users' guide explains textual divisions and lists types of information found in the botanical index. A six-page spread models the entry arrangement, including ailments, methods of application, vital safety data, Latin and common names for plants, herbal and folk traditions, uses, related species and varieties, and where to find the plants.

Part 1 introduces the concept and history of aromatherapy, along with portraits of its founder. Guidelines stress the types of oils that are toxic and hazardous, such as arnica, mustard, and wormwood, and differentiate between natural and synthetic oils. Part 2 lists specific ills—dry skin, upset stomach, sore throat—and simples (herbal preparations) that combat or alleviate each. The author highlights with italics the oils that are most effective and readily available (e.g., benzoin for arthritis). A letter code indicates method of application, as in "F" for flower water, "M" for massage, "V" for vaporization, and "N" for neat application.

The highlight of this book is part 3, an examination of each oil, which appears in alphabetic order. A fresh, inviting layout juxtaposes data on plant names, traditions, and safety data. For example, marigold is the common name for *Calendula*, which is safe to use. A photograph shows the plant in the wild; a drawing illustrates stem, flower, leaves, and root. Back matter covers general terms, botanical classification by family, and botanical indexing, which the author codes with boldfaced numbers for major entry and italics for Latin plant name. She concludes with sources and with worldwide addresses that link consumers with sellers of oils, aromatherapists, training programs, medical herbalism, and holistic treatment. This work is well worth having.—**Mary Ellen Snodgrass**

1347. Lockie, Andrew, and Nicola Geddes. **The Complete Guide to Homeopathy.** New York, Dorling Kindersley, 1995. 240p. illus. index. $29.95. ISBN 0-7894-0148-7.

This book describes 150 homeopathic remedies arranged in 3 sections: key remedies (15), remedies commonly prescribed by homeopaths (30), and minor remedies (105). Descriptions include common names, sources, parts of sources used, and ailments treated. The selection of remedies in the system of homeopathy presented is based on the patient's "constitutional type," which is determined by a 16-page questionnaire assessing the "inherited or acquired physical, emotional and intellectual makeup" of the patient. The constitutional type associated with each remedy is given.

The latter portion of the book is composed of tables describing symptoms, causes, and remedies (including dosages) for specific diseases and conditions. These are arranged by categories of ailments. The book also includes an excellent short history of homeopathy, a brief discussion of homeopathic theory, and chapters on nutrition and special diets. A directory provides addresses of suppliers of homeopathic remedies. There is also a useful index. The guide is profusely, even excessively, illustrated with exceptionally fine color photographs.

This is an attractive book with solid, basic information for the general reader. However, many potential users will find the theory of constitutional types difficult to accept and may find the questionnaire difficult to use. Consequently, the guide may be a better candidate for circulation than for reference. Further, the questionnaire presents the usual risk of loss of pages or defacing of the book in a library setting.—**Gari-Anne Patzwald**

1348. **The Medical Advisor: The Complete Guide to Alternative & Conventional Treatments.** By the Editors of Time-Life Books. Alexandria, Va., Time-Life Books, 1996. 1152p. illus. index. $39.95. ISBN 0-8094-6737-2.

The Medical Advisor covers 300 diagnoses ranging from common mishaps, such as bee stings and sprains, to such serious problems as diabetes or heart disease. For each condition, there is a short description of the complaint, what causes it, the conventional medical treatment, and alternative therapies, plus prevention suggestions. This book is designed to provide a general understanding of specific illnesses to promote discussions between patients and their physicians. This guide is unusual in that it gives both conventional medical treatments and alternative therapies, such as meditation, yoga, acupuncture, homeopathic preparations, and the like. The editors caution that the natural remedies are not intended to replace traditional allopathic medicine but rather to complement it.

Other notable features of the guide are an index with references to 3,000 ailments, treatments, and medicines, as well as a first aid section with procedures for 21 frequent emergencies. There is also an appendix listing 350 commonly used drugs and herbal remedies, with a notation if it is a prescription or over-the-counter drug, a Chinese or Western herb, or a homeopathic remedy, and any precautions to be taken.

Weighing 7 pounds and encompassing 1,152 pages, this tome is intimidating at first glance. However, it is easy to use, with attractive tables and illustrations. The text is well written and avoids overly technical explanations. This book is a good general reference for individuals with no medical training. At $39.95, it is affordable for both the home and the general library. [R: LJ, 1 Oct 96, p. 68; RBB, 1 Sept 96, pp. 167-68]
—**Adrienne Antink Bendel**

1349. Murray, Michael T. **Encyclopedia of Nutritional Supplements: The Essential Guide for Improving Your Health Naturally.** Rocklin, Calif., Prima Publishing, 1996. 564p. illus. index. $19.95pa. ISBN 0-7615-0410-9.

Written to help users make sense of the voluminous information available on nutritional supplements, this book includes detailed profiles of all the major ones—vitamins, minerals, essential fatty acids, accessory nutrients, and glandular extracts—and tells how they can help one live longer, feel better, and fight the effects of aging. A concluding section counsels which nutritional supplements to take for a host of conditions, including high cholesterol, depression, and fatigue. A doctor of naturopathy, Murray, also the coauthor of *An Encyclopedia of Natural Medicine* (see ARBA 93, entry 1634), advocates supplementing with nutrients that the body needs anyway instead of or in addition to taking synthetic drugs. Murray's advice to everyone regarding supplements is a one-two-three punch of taking a multivitamin daily, supplementing with extra antioxidants, and taking a daily tablespoon of flaxseed oil, which is rich in essential fatty acids.

The 1,388 references to nutrition articles in medical journals are evidence of fine documentation (there are 95 references to carnitine alone), yet they are located at the back of the book endnote-style, a choice of format that makes the book more readable. The references at the end of each chapter constitute minibibliographies that could make a search of the journal literature on a topic unnecessary.

The book is written at a level that straddles the academic and the popular, making it suitable for academic or public libraries. It is considerably more scholarly than *The Complete Book of Natural & Medicinal Cures* (see ARBA 95, entry 1670). It is in softcover, which is not optimal for an encyclopedia, but which was probably the right choice because nutrition will probably change tremendously in the next five years, making a new edition necessary.—**Penny Papangelis**

1350. Stillerman, Elaine. **The Encyclopedia of Bodywork: From Acupressure to Zone Therapy.** New York, Facts on File, 1996. 320p. illus. index. $35.00. ISBN 0-8160-3187-8.

To fully appreciate this book, one must look beyond its title. Replace the word "bodywork" with "alternative (a.k.a. unconventional or complementary) medical therapies" and this volume becomes a reference for the most rapidly growing class of medical interventions in the United States. Studies indicate that 1 in 3 patients uses these therapies routinely, 7 in 10 do not inform their doctors of these practices, and most pay for these services out of their own pockets—sobering statistics for a struggling traditional health care system.

The author states that this book was written to "provide in-depth descriptions, explanations and historical backgrounds of common, esoteric, and sacred bodywork systems to people who are unfamiliar to them." In fact, the term *bodywork* is expanded to include all the "hands-on therapies, movement reeducation systems, psychological techniques and metaphysical and energetic modalities, which recognize the unity of the body/mind/spirit/emotions." Explanations of herbal therapies are limited to aromatherapy, body wraps, and moxibustion; however, short bibliographies are included.

Appendix 1 is a comprehensive resource list of names, addresses, and telephone and fax numbers for various providers, clinics, and professional associations. Appendix 2 is a repeat format for all states and provinces (in the United States and Canada) that require a license/board certification to practice massage therapy. Patient provider education is the focus—improved communication is the goal. Within these pages are clear and concise definitions that provide the critical first step.—**Sue Lyon Mertl**

Dentistry

1351. **Oxford Handbook of Clinical Dentistry.** 2d ed. By David A. Mitchell and Laura Mitchell. New York, Oxford University Press, 1995. 799p. illus. index. $36.50pa. ISBN 0-19-262602-7.

The cover of this work touts, "Dental students are going to love this book." This reviewer would agree and would add, "*Dentists* are going to love this book." The handbook is divided into the more or less traditional subspecialties of dentistry, for example, paedodontics and periodontology, but it also has sections on practice management and syndromes of the neck and head. A clever graphic in the table of contents allows one to flip directly to the primary sections without looking at page numbers. The book also contains two bound bookmarks to aid in use, and is in a convenient pocket-sized format.

The work is comprehensive in scope, but necessarily limited in detail and depth. It is presented in a logical, well-written manner, with an index and several useful reference sections. As dentistry continues to specialize and dentists are increasingly finding it necessary to revise and professionalize their practice, this work provides a crucial reference. Specialists can use it for finding information on practice and theory outside their area of expertise, general practitioners can use it for finding information in detail they cannot always be expected to know, and students should find it invaluable for surviving the rigors of an increasingly complex profession. The complications of the treatment of older patients, those living with AIDS or other severe illnesses, and the explosion of new pharmacology have come together to force dentists to become sophisticated diagnosticians, subtle and knowledgeable drug therapists, and adept referral consultants. A good reference work can aid in enhancing professionalism.

The handbook's only drawback for U.S. dentists and students is its political and clinical orientation toward U.K. dentistry. That orientation will prove especially confusing because the book does not use the American tooth numbering system. A suggestion to the authors and publishers would be an appendix or side-by-side comparison of the two systems. The value of the book, however, overcomes these drawbacks. All students, dentists, and dental schools will find this a useful and well-used reference.—**Luiz Alberto Cardoso**

Endocrinology

1352. Martin, Constance R. **Dictionary of Endocrinology and Related Biomedical Sciences.** New York, Oxford University Press, 1995. 785p. $75.00. ISBN 0-19-50633-4.

Noting that it is impossible for many professionals to keep up with the changing concepts and terminology of the many facets of endocrinology and related sciences, the author conceived this dictionary as a reference tool fostering mutual understanding, no matter which subspecialty or scientific discipline is being practiced. Much of the same information is of value to both.

Among the areas covered are endocrine physiology; hormones, neurotransmitters, and other regulatory factors; and terms relating to endocrinology drawn from other biomedical sciences. Although human physiology is emphasized, considerable attention is given to other species. Acronyms are numerous. The definitions are designed to be readily understood by readers who may be unfamiliar with specific terms, but are composed in highly technical language. Frequently, entries are accompanied by diagrams of chemical structure. These were produced by an ISIS/Draw program from Molecular Design Limited.

Considerable scientific acumen is needed for effective use of this scholarly, highly detailed, and extensive dictionary on endocrinology and aspects of biology, biochemistry, immunology, genetics, and the like, interrelated with this complicated subject. The book should be a valuable resource for many medical and research institutions, but it is not for general libraries. [R: Choice, Feb 96, p. 930]—**Harriette M. Cluxton**

Nursing

1353. Sparks, Sheila M., Cynthia M. Taylor, and Janyce G. Dyer. **Nursing Diagnosis Pocket Manual: A Timesaving Guide to Better Patient Care.** Springhouse, Pa., Springhouse Publishing, 1996. 494p. index. $21.95 spiralbound. ISBN 0-87434-827-7.

This pocket manual is a condensation of the *Nursing Diagnosis Reference Manual* (3d ed., Springhouse Publishing, 1994). Designed to serve in a clinical setting, it gives brief guides to the physiological and psychosocial problems that nurses may legally diagnose and treat. This manual offers updated methods for physiological care, but also recommends approaches to geriatric, pediatric, psychosocial, and family-centered care. When appropriate, alternative medical approaches are described as acceptable treatments.

The manual offers 139 care plans approved by the North American Nursing Diagnosis Association (NANDA). Each plan puts forth a diagnostic statement with etiology, definitions, assessments to validate the diagnoses, defining characteristics including known risk factors, associated disorders, expected outcomes, interventions arranged according to time frame, and evaluation guidelines.

The appendixes contain a complete table of NANDA taxonomy, some selected reference works, and a clear and accurate index. This manual is highly recommended for nursing practitioners.

—**Mary Hemmings**

Pediatrics

1354. Markel, Howard, and Frank A. Oski. **The Practical Pediatrician: The A to Z Guide to Your Child's Health, Behavior, and Safety.** New York, W. H. Freeman, 1996. 364p. index. $16.95pa. ISBN 0-7167-2897-4.

Books on child care are among the most popular and useful items in public library collections. *The Practical Pediatrician*, a new source written by two professors of pediatrics, is a fine addition to the literature. Arranged alphabetically by subject and written in lay language, it is reassuring and easy to use. The authors emphasize the positive aspects of parenthood and encourage mothers and fathers to trust their instincts, ask questions, and love their children.

Entries range in length from one paragraph to several pages. They cover both medical (ear infections, abdominal pain) and behavioral subjects (aggression, toilet training). They also offer practical advice on shopping with young children and choosing health care providers. The major strengths of the book include an emphasis on safety, with detailed first aid information and a foldout chart on child-proofing the home, and discussions of important contemporary issues, such as computers/the Internet, television, latchkey children, divorce, and firearms in the home. Black-and-white illustrations supplement the text. There are also detailed growth charts and tables of what should be included in well-child examinations from birth to eight years of age.

Although this book lacks the depth of the American Academy of Pediatrics's *Caring for Your Baby and Young Child: Birth to Age 5* (Bantam Books, 1993), it is an excellent ready-reference source. *The Practical Pediatrician* is a good choice for circulating parenting collections as well. [R: LJ, 1 Nov 96, p. 62; RBB, 1 Sept 96, p. 170]—**Barbara M. Bibel**

Psychiatry

1355. Copel, Linda Carman. **Nurse's Clinical Guide to Psychiatric and Mental Health Care.** Springhouse, Pa., Springhouse Publishing, 1996. 378p. index. $24.95 spiralbound. ISBN 0-87434-720-3.

It is a pleasure to review such a book as *Nurse's Clinical Guide to Psychiatric and Mental Health Care*, which so ably fulfills its stated purpose. According to the preface, the book was written as a guide for practicing nurses and students in designing individualized plans of care for psychiatric patients. This purpose is executed by taking the various pathological conditions (e.g., delirium) from the *Diagnostic and Statistical Manual of Mental Disorders* (4th ed., American Psychiatric Press, 1996) and listing the various North American Nursing Diagnosis Association (NANDA) nursing diagnoses for each. Goals for the client (Copel refers to patients as "clients") are then spelled out (e.g., "The client will maintain a safe and optimal level of functioning").

Following the statement of goals, therapies, medications, and family care are treated. Copel covers the gamut of disorders and aberrations encountered by nurses in the mental health field, including attention deficit/hyperactivity disorder, Alzheimer's disease, partner abuse, and even rape. She has also included chapters on the special needs of homeless people with mental illness, of abuse victims, and of persons with HIV/AIDS. Her description of AIDS is beautifully clear and concise. Also refreshing to see is spiritual well-being discussed as a goal in the HIV/AIDS chapter.

Copel writes at the professional level; some terms, such as *dyspnea* and *diaphoresis*, are defined in the text, but some, such as *anoxia* and *extrapyramidal*, are not. The book is handy (the size of a thick paperback), and, owing to its spiral binding, has a back cover that folds around to provide a spine when it is placed on a shelf. It is highly recommended for nursing collections.—**Penny Papangelis**

1356. **The Encyclopedia of Psychiatry, Psychology, and Psychoanalysis.** Benjamin B. Wolman, ed. New York, Henry Holt, 1996. 649p. index. $135.00. ISBN 0-8050-2234-1.

This single-volume resource is a product of the same editorial team that produced the *International Encyclopedia of Psychiatry, Psychology, Psychoanalysis, and Neurology* (see ARBA 78, entry 1367), which won the Dartmouth Medal from the American Library Association. That 12-volume set was lauded for its comprehensiveness and currentness. The volume under review not only abridges the larger work but also revises and updates the entries, and it endeavors to cover the advancements of the past 20 years of the topics at hand. Neurology has been omitted from this encyclopedia but will be the topic of a separate volume.

Adhering to the A to Z format found in the larger encyclopedia, this volume provides articles on a variety of topics, from abortion to human immunodeficiency virus and acquired immunodeficiency syndrome to stimulus-response theories in social psychology. The entries are signed by one of the nearly 700 contributing authors, many of whom hold Ph.D.s or M.D.s. Scope of the articles covers studies conducted (with the year), important statistics, people active in that particular study, and related concepts. They cover basic ground without delving too deeply into complex ideas. Much of the biographical information is brief, so brief as to be of little value to most users. A useful bibliography complements the body of the encyclopedia. The index is functional, providing *see also* references to related terms.

The intended audience for this one-volume encyclopedia is professionals in the fields discussed and graduate students or postdoctoral scholars. For its ready-reference value, one can easily see that audience making good use of the volume. It is doubtful that professional psychiatrists or psychologists would have a need for this volume beyond ready-reference; the same holds true for students. The articles are not in-depth enough for the book to serve as a textbook or as an answer-all encyclopedia. However, for quick answers to questions involving psychology, psychiatry, and psychoanalysis, this somewhat reasonably priced encyclopedia will be helpful to that audience not having access to the full 12-volume set.—**Melissa Rae Root**

Sports Medicine

1357. Potparic, O., and J. Gibson. **A Dictionary of Sports Injuries and Disorders.** Pearl River, N.Y., Parthenon, 1996. 155p. $35.00. ISBN 1-85070-686-7.

This text is presented in traditional dictionary form. Overall, the print is easy to read. Topics defined/discussed range from "abstinence syndrome" to the "Glasgow Coma Scale" and "zygoma fractures." Some of the definitions will require the reader to have a medical terminology background in order to understand them.

Unfortunately, there are no pictures or illustrations in the text. Having them would have enhanced some of the definitions or conditions mentioned in the text. In addition, there is no table of contents and no index, either of which would probably make this text easier to use.

The work is designed to be used primarily by individuals with a medical background or by athletes themselves. However, adult readers who are involved or interested in sports will probably find this text to be of benefit as a reference source in conjunction with other texts. It is a good reference for general sports injuries.—**Paul M. Murphy III**

PHARMACY AND PHARMACEUTICAL SCIENCES

1358. Friedman, J. M., and Janine E. Polifka. **The Effects of Drugs on the Fetus and Nursing Infant: A Handbook for Health Care Professionals.** Baltimore, Md., Johns Hopkins University Press, 1996. 648p. $49.95pa. ISBN 0-8018-5345-1.

This reference text is well written and presented in an easy-to-read format. Readers should be advised that the text uses medical terminology and deals with such topics as "teratogen." The work deals directly with medications, their effects on the fetus, and complications associated with the use of certain medications while pregnant or nursing an infant. Although medical terminology is used, the authors do define some of these terms so that the adult reader can follow the material. Having a medical background may be of benefit when using the text.

The introduction explains the purpose and goals and offers suggestions on how to apply the material in a clinical setting. The body of the text reviews hundreds of medications and their effects on the fetus, potential complications with breast feeding, and developmental issues associated with the use of medications. The medications are summarized with the following information: defining the drug and how it works, what the drug is used for, and its dosage. Teratogenic risk is also discussed in detail. Additional topics, such as reports of fetal malformation, impact on breast feeding, and pregnancy complications, are also included. A reference list for each medication is present, which allows the reader to consult other resources.

As indicated in the handbook, a majority of this information has been obtained through various computer systems or programs, such as TERIS, MEDLINE, TOXLINE, and DART. This text may be most useful to those in the medical field (especially obstetrics) or those interested in learning more about the effects of medications on pregnancy, fetal development, and the nursing of infants.—**Paul M. Murphy III**

1359. Graedon, Joe, and Teresa Graedon. **The People's Guide to Deadly Drug Interactions: How to Protect Yourself....** New York, St. Martin's Press, 1995. 434p. index. $25.95. ISBN 0-312-13243-3.

The People's Pharmacy (rev. ed., St. Martin's Press, 1996) authors expand their concern for consumers into the arcane world of substance interactions: food/drug, vitamin/drug, vitamin/mineral, drug/alcohol, and drug/drug (both prescription and over-the-counter). Three types of interactions are discussed: additive (one substance increasing the effectiveness of another), antagonistic (one canceling the effectiveness of the other), and unpredictable. Graphs, charts, and a heedful narrative are used to inform readers of thousands of potentially deadly chemical combinations. Sample interactions range from those commonly documented, such as grapefruit juice and calcium channel blockers, to others that are only remotely possible. Half the book is composed of a convenient listing of drugs, by type and by name, with possible interactions charted. It is this feature that should appeal to reference desk staff.

So that they may propose that timely mechanisms do not exist for determining the potential for drug interactions and for notifying doctors of such dangers, the authors do not discuss the communication that routinely takes place between pharmaceutical companies and the medical community. Yet such written notifications routinely crossed this reviewer's desk as a hospital librarian. The book makes many unsubstantiated criticisms of both the private and governmental wings of the health care community; studies are referred to but not cited and statistical evidence is rarely used to support conclusions. Contradictions also undermine the credibility of the text—for example, "Since the FDA does not have a system for gathering interaction data. . . ." (p. 2), and "Reports of dizziness attacks and heart palpitations began trickling in to the Food and Drug Administration (FDA)" (p. 5). A subtler flaw is raised by the authors' view that an improbable and minor risk is as worthy of concern and attention as a likelier, major risk. Treating all contraindications equally dilutes the jeremiad's impact.

Unexpected substance interactions do occur, and reasonable caution should be exercised in the consumption of foods, medicines, and supplements. However, it is difficult to take seriously a purported reference source that opens with the statement "Would you want to play Russian Roulette?" (p. 1). The book's graphs and charts offer a good deal of valuable information. It is unfortunate that the tone of the narrative is inclined to be pejorative, distrustful, and alarmist. Reference librarians are advised to preface their quoting of the book with the phrase, "In the opinion of the authors. . . ." [R: RBB, Jan 96, p. 890]—**Ed Volz**

1360. **Nursing96 Drug Handbook.** Springhouse, Pa., Springhouse Publishing, 1996. 1333p. illus. index. $29.95pa. ISBN 0-87434-817-X. ISSN 0273-320X.

This paperback text is a valuable drug reference designed to be used by the adult reader. The handbook offers several features that make it user friendly. Overall, the typeface is easy to read, and the contents of the book are easy to follow. The publishers have designed a section in the beginning of the text that users may find helpful when looking up specific topics or drugs, such as topical agents, general information, and cardiac medications.

Drugs presented in this text contain the following information: how the drug is supplied, its action, the onset/peak/duration, the indication and dosage, any adverse reactions (by system), interaction precautions, contraindications, and nursing considerations. If users know the drug name, all they need to do is look in the index. If the drug classification is known, the beginning of the book will refer the user to the section of the text in which to look. Each section lists the medications found there. The middle of the handbook has colored pictures of commonly encountered drugs, which can assist the user in identifying the pill if it is unknown.

This text may be most useful to adult readers, especially those involved in the health care field. It is large enough to be included in the home library, yet compact enough that medical personnel may be able to use it while on the job (e.g., emergency medical technicians, paramedics, nurses, physicians).

—**Paul M. Murphy III**

1361. **PharmFacts for Nurses.** Springhouse, Pa., Springhouse Publishing, 1996. 728p. illus. index. $34.95pa. ISBN 0-87434-803-X.

The administration of medication is one of a nurse's most important responsibilities. The rapid development of new drugs and increasingly complex delivery systems make the task more demanding than ever and require a highly comprehensive resource. This title organizes drug information into four sections. The first is "Drug Essentials," which explores common fallacies, legal considerations, errors, and conversions and calculations. The "Drug Alerts" section covers cautions and warnings, side effects and interactions, and the treatment of overdose. Part 3, "Drug Administration Tips and Techniques," describes the methods of delivery. Finally, the "Drug Therapy" section briefly discusses the most common medications used in common conditions and addresses the needs of special patients. Black-and-white photographs, which are rather small, and line drawings illustrate techniques, and tables serve to compress voluminous information into readily accessible form. A comprehensive index provides instant access to particular drugs or medical conditions.

This title is aimed at nursing professionals and will be of limited use to lay readers. The chapter on common conditions provides some information, but public libraries will do better with the American Hospital Formulary Service's annual *Drug Information*. Nursing schools and medical libraries, however, will want the title under review.—**Susan B. Hagloch**

34 High Technology

GENERAL WORKS

1362. **Multimedia: The Complete Guide.** New York, DK Publishing, 1996. 192p. illus. index. $24.95. ISBN 0-7894-0422-2.

In unique DK Publishing style, this beautifully designed book introduces readers to what multimedia is, how it is done, and where it is going. The guide is filled with vibrant color photographs and illustrations that make it just plain fun to look at. In comprehensible language, the book provides a history of the technologies that comprise multimedia, including software and hardware, the process of putting them all together to create a multimedia experience, and the future of consumer multimedia. The book's arrangement mimics multimedia by using pink "hot spots" such as those on Webpages for concepts that the book expands upon in other sections. The guide's discussion of multimedia focuses on its uses in education and entertainment and covers both Internet-based and interactive approaches to multimedia. At worst, its upbeat, advocative tone reads like an advertisement, but this does not deflect from the useful information given. The general public will appreciate this title, as will any undergraduate technology major. [R: LJ, 1 April 96, p. 76; RBB, 15 April 96, p. 1396]—**Glynys R. Thomas**

1363. **The Multimedia Directory.** 4th ed. Jon Samsel and Clancy Fort, eds. San Francisco, Calif., Carronade Group, 1995. 342p. index. $85.00pa. ISBN 1-885452-06-3.

By some estimates, multimedia will be a trillion-dollar industry before the end of this decade. The 4th edition of *The Multimedia Directory* profiles more than 1,000 of the principal players in this important convergence of the computer, communications, and contents industries. In addition to the information one would typically expect to find in a business directory—telephone number, fax number, address, company status, years in business, number of employees, gross annual sales, and names and titles of management—there are some very useful technology-specific categories. For example, most of these companies have e-mail addresses, and many have World Wide Web pages. The directory also indicates if the company is engaged in any joint ventures, the types of markets it produces products for; the computer platforms its products run on; the media (e.g., CD-ROM, floppy disk) they publish on; and key titles in their catalog. Of particular interest to jobseekers is information on the authoring and other multimedia creation tools used to produce a company's products. Most of this information is accessible through the eight indexes that supplement the main alphabetic arrangement by company name.—**Robert Skinner**

COMPUTING

General Works

1364. Cortada, James W., comp. **Second Bibliographic Guide to the History of Computing, Computers, and the Information Processing Industry.** Westport, Conn., Greenwood Press, 1996. 416p. index. (Bibliographies and Indexes in Science and Technology, no.9). $89.50. ISBN 0-313-29542-5.

This bibliography is a monumental feat. In the introduction, the author speculates that computers and the computing industry may be the most written-about industry in history. Given the fact that in just 15 years he has compiled nearly 7,000 titles—2,500 titles in this supplement to the original bibliography (see ARBA 91, entry 1721), which contained 4,500 titles—he may well be correct in his assessment. Research in this exciting, ever-changing industry is confounded by its own mass of available materials. The present bibliography is a significant contribution to the field that provides the researcher with an accessible, well-organized, and timely collection of what are the significant materials published on the topic.

This book was meant to serve as a supplement to the 1st edition, not as a substitute or a replacement for it. While the present volume is filled with useful references, a researcher will make a mistake to consult this bibliography alone. The same may be said about the original volume: In a sense, it, too, is a supplement to this second volume, and it is not recommended for a library to only possess the 1st edition. Together, both volumes provide a near-comprehensive look at the literature that describes the history of computing and computers.

The bibliography is well structured and well laid out. Every entry is annotated and is indexed by both author name and subject. The material in the book is organized around six different chapters that adequately define the subject. Each of the 6 chapters is further broken down into subtopics of as many as 20 or 30. The users of the bibliography therefore should have more than an adequate number of access points for identifying articles or books that are relevant to their research.

The only limitation that this book apparently has is that it does not cover some topics that may be of great interest to people in the information profession, such as materials on database performance, integration of electronic materials into a traditional library collection, or evaluation of automation packages. In this respect, the bibliography is focused on the hardware side of computing, but perhaps rightly so, because the history of computing is certainly most seen through the development of the technology itself. Overall, this book is a valuable contribution to its field and one that is suitable for inclusion in the collections of all libraries that may have patrons interested in the history of the most important technology of the modern age. [R: Choice, Sept 96, p. 94]—**Richard A. Leiter**

1365. Cortada, James W., comp. **A Bibliographic Guide to the History of Computer Applications, 1950-1990.** Westport, Conn., Greenwood Press, 1996. 278p. index. (Bibliographies and Indexes in Science and Technology, no.10). $85.00. ISBN 0-313-29876-9.

This work is a selective annotated bibliography on how computers were used between 1950 and 1990. The bibliography is divided into two parts. Part 1 covers the period between 1950 and 1966, when most software applications were run in batch mode. Part 2 covers the period between 1966 and 1990, when applications were increasingly run in online mode. The entries treat reference books, articles, and pamphlets, and are divided into categories such as accounting, agriculture, and weather. Broad headings, such as "commercial" and "science," contain citations to applications that do not fit clearly into any one category. Each entry includes a full bibliographic citation and a brief annotation. The volume concludes with an author and a subject index.

Included in the work is a good introductory essay in which the compiler briefly defines computer applications and discusses the importance of studying the history of software applications to enhance knowledge of technology development. The bibliography aims to support the work of researchers and technology historians. For this purpose, it is useful. However, it is not clear what criteria were used for items selected for inclusion or what sources were used in the compilation. [R: Choice, June 96, p. 1612]
—**Linda Main**

1366. **Elsevier's Dictionary of Computer Science and Mathematics in English, German, French, and Russian.** K. Peeva and B. Delijska, comps. New York, Elsevier Science, 1995. 785p. index. $220.50. ISBN 0-444-81816-2.

Polyglot dictionaries necessarily blur distinctions between individual languages to offer purported equivalencies across several. For a field as young as computer science, where words are likely to have been adapted from a single language, this may be less important than for the humanities, as evidenced in many of the 9,594 entries herein, illustrated by the English "cassette," the German *Kassette*, the French *cassette*, and the Russian (transliterated) *Kasseta*. The volume is organized as a basic table, with entries arranged alphabetically by the English term (with cross-references to English synonyms) followed by synonyms in German, French, and Russian. Full indexes referring back to the basic table follow for each of the languages. Concluding is an appendix of mathematical symbols.

The presentation is clear (although inflated by numerous irrelevant terms, such as "forest" and "sanity"), but the alphabetic organization places variations on a root term, such as "complete tree" and "tree structure," 400 pages apart. Although targeted at specialists, entries can also be instructive for the nonspecialist. An arcane term such as "login" or "logon" is meaningless outside of computer usage. In contrast, the Russian synonyms (transliterated) *nachalo seansa*—beginning of session—or *vkhod v sistemu*—entry into (or enter) the system—require no particular computer expertise. Despite a potential broader audience, the lexicon's price dictates recommending it only for larger research or appropriate special libraries. Claimed by the publisher to be the first such dictionary covering both computer science and mathematics, the primary use will be for promoting international cooperation and communications in those fields.—**K. Mulliner**

1367. **Encyclopedia of Computer Science and Technology. Volume 34, Supplement 19.** Allen Kent and James G. Williams, eds. New York, Marcel Dekker, 1996. 392p. $195.00. ISBN 0-8247-2287-6.

This volume contains 17 articles on computer science ranging from technical topics, such as fuzzy logic, computer performance, nonmonotonic reasoning, and database theory, to more human-related topics, such as artificial intelligence in education, computer security, electronic music, and resource management. The editors have engaged an impressive set of qualified computer scientists from around the world to write the articles. The level of expected reader expertise varies greatly, as is usually the case with a multiauthor, multitopic work such as this. Some technical articles assume prior knowledge of the field; others covering human and management aspects tend to be more along the lines of surveys or reviews. There seems to be no coherent pattern in the choice of topics or intended audience. A preface or introductory essay synthesizing the articles and explaining the volume's scope and purpose would have helped. There is no index. (See ARBA 90, entries 1711-1712; ARBA 78, entry 1523; and ARBA 76, entry 1626, for previous reviews.)—**A. Neil Yerkey**

1368. Farace, Joe. **The Digital Imaging Dictionary.** New York, Allworth Press, 1996. 223p. illus. index. $19.95pa. ISBN 1-880559-46-3.

This addition to the already voluminous collection of computer dictionaries has as its focus artists manipulating photographs and other graphic images via computers. The dictionary includes more than 500 related words, acronyms, phrases, and jargon. Farace aims his definitions at the relatively unsophisticated computer user. He includes many general computer terms (e.g., *boot, GUI, hacker*) in addition to those specifically related to graphics and digital imaging (e.g., *bitmap, CMS* for color management system, *photo CD*). Farace writes well and is not afraid to advance his own opinions, which gives a good personal touch to the book. Photographs and screen displays are used to illustrate some definitions, but more could have been used to advantage.

Two appendixes, one a guide to selecting an appropriate computer and the other a directory of companies mentioned in the dictionary, end the work. This dictionary will be useful on an individual artist's reference shelf in addition to being a helpful supplemental volume in all library reference collections (public, special, and academic). Because of continuing rapid technological changes, the effective shelf life for this book will be unfortunately fairly short. However, the price is right.

—**Richard D. Johnson**

1369. Freedman, Alan. **The Computer Desktop Encyclopedia.** New York, AMACOM, 1996. 1005p. illus. maps. $39.95pa. ISBN 0-8144-0010-8. [Also available with a CD-ROM for $59.95.]

This encyclopedic dictionary contains more than 8,500 terms on computer applications, commands, functions, programming languages, hardware, operating systems, standards, and people. Many acronyms are explained and there is much historical material. The entries are well written, informative, accurate, and well cross-referenced. They range in length from one-sentence definitions to four-page articles. Many are accompanied by excellent line drawings, tables, diagrams, and black-and-white photographs. A hypertext version is also available on CD-ROM.

The author's stated goal was to make sense of the computer industry. He does it with clear, readable definitions and an abundance of humor, including a few disarming tidbits, such as the article on "How to Find a Computer Book" under "H." Longer articles have marginal notes that provide an outline to the topic or act as sidebar explanations. Some marginal notes are humorous observations, such as "Drivers can drive you crazy!" The article on peripheral installation has its own marginal acronym concerning the benefits of reading the manual: RTFM (we will let the reader figure it out).

This reviewer could find no errors or obvious omissions; this is one dictionary that is fun to read. It is the best choice among several recently reviewed. Barron's Educational Series's *Dictionary of Computer Terms* (4th ed.; see ARBA 96, entry 1755) is not as comprehensive but has the advantage of being pocket size; *Dictionary of Computer Words* from Houghton Mifflin (rev. ed.; see ARBA 96, entry 1754) is not as comprehensive but is a worthy alternative; *Microsoft Press Computer Dictionary* (2d ed., Microsoft Press, 1993) is smaller and less interesting; *Prentice Hall's Illustrated Dictionary of Computing* (see ARBA 94, entry 1902) seems dated; Robin Williams's *Jargon: An Informal Dictionary of Computer Terms* (see ARBA 94, entry 1905) contains long, informal articles that are sometimes more clever than helpful; and *IBM Dictionary of Computing* (see ARBA 95, entry 1695) is large (20,000 terms) but draws most of its words from an IBM mainframe environment, limiting its usefulness.—**A. Neil Yerkey**

1370. Harris, Robert L. **Information Graphics: A Comprehensive Illustrated Reference.** Atlanta, Ga., Management Graphics, 1996. 448p. illus. maps. $60.00. ISBN 0-9646925-0-3.

This book is a reviewer's delight: a resource that is not only well done but an unexpected treatment of a mainstream topic. Charts, graphs, maps, diagrams, and tables are ubiquitous in society as tools for communicating information visually, but this is the first publication that provides an in-depth treatment of their practical application. For example, the entry on "Pie Chart" is six pages in length and covers description and terminology; general characteristics; methods for incorporating descriptive and quantitative information; reference angles used for plotting; methods for showing changes over time; size of circles proportional to overall value; methods for highlighting selected segments; methods for improving legibility; groupings of segments; use as histograms; encoding an additional quantitative variable; adding depth; overlapping; and examples of three less common variations on the pie chart—the decagraph, the belt chart, and the circle graph. Arrangement of the book is alphabetic, starting with "Abscissa" and ending with "Zigzag graph." In spite of the technical nature of the topic, the entries are surprisingly accessible. There is no index, but the author uses four types of cross-referencing. Every page has a half-dozen or more illustrations, and the page size of 8½-by-11 inches makes for good legibility. The reference is highly recommended. [R: Choice, Nov 96, p. 430]—**Robert Skinner**

Microcomputing

1371. **Encyclopedia of Microcomputers. Volume 18: Teaching Critical Thinking and Problem Solving to Truth-Functional Logic.** Allen Kent and James G. Williams, eds. New York, Marcel Dekker, 1996. 372p. illus. $175.00. ISBN 0-8247-2716-9.

This volume mainly consists of two types of articles. The first type deals with topics directly related to microcomputers, such as query languages and databases, scanning technology for imaging and optical character recognition, structured programming methods, the reorganization of information systems organizations to improve efficiency, the replacement product cycle in the computer industry, and transducers. A second group of articles focuses on specific applications, including the use of library workstations, the automation of astronomical telescopes, imaging technology that provides 3-D volume visualizations for medical analysis, and using neural network models to predict potential business failures. One particularly interesting application article reviews the use of computers in the various roles of tutor, tutee, and tool for the teaching of critical thinking and problem solving.

If there is a common theme to the articles in this volume, it may be best represented by Steven C. Lotz's contribution, which argues that the development of an effective telecommunications planning model is essential if organizations are to fully realize the strategic advantages that can result from the use of microcomputers. This volume does, indeed, bring together a significant amount of background material, and it should be helpful to those concerned with developing an organizational plan for the use of microcomputers.

—Harry E. Pence

1372. **McGraw-Hill Encyclopedia of Personal Computing.** Stan Gibilisco, ed. New York, McGraw-Hill, 1995. 1216p. illus. index. $89.95. ISBN 0-07-023718-2.

This encyclopedia is written for laypeople yet has broad enough coverage to interest experienced computer users. The range of topics covered is comprehensive, including operating systems, hardware, types of software, networking, and Internet terms. The more than 1,200 articles each run from nearly a full page to two pages in length. The book is thoroughly illustrated with clean line drawings, charts, and tables. The writing is concise and highly readable, with jargon kept to a minimum. Because the articles are so short, serious techies may find the lack of depth unappealing. For most users, however, the presentation is informative and interesting.

The work has some minor shortcomings. While various kinds of hardware are covered, including name brands (e.g., Pentium processor, Macintosh), few specific software programs are covered, and coverage is uneven (e.g., Adobe Illustrator has an entry, but similar programs do not). The cross-references are thorough, but not exhaustive. To find many acronyms, the user must look through the appendix of acronyms and abbreviations. For instance, FAT (file allocation table) cannot be found in the body or the index but was in the appendix. GIF, a common graphics file type on the Internet, did not have an entry and was not in the index or appendix, but was found only in the entry "Filename extensions" and only with the single word *graphics*.

These really are minor drawbacks. In a field as varied and dynamic as personal computing, a comprehensive resource is a near impossibility. There is enough here to provide answers to a wide range of questions on personal computing. Librarians will find it a useful work for patron questions and their own. It is recommended for that purpose. [R: RBB, 15 May 96, p. 1620]—**Stephen Haenel**

Software

1373. Levine, John, and others. **The UNIX Dictionary of Commands, Terms, and Acronyms.** New York, McGraw-Hill, 1996. 314p. $39.50; $24.95pa. ISBN 0-07-037643-3; 0-07-047644-1pa.

First developed in 1969, UNIX is a powerful computer operating system that exists in several versions. The infrastructure of the Internet resides on (mainly) UNIX systems; UNIX terms now appear in the popular press. Written for new and experienced users of the UNIX operating system, *The UNIX Dictionary of Commands, Terms, and Acronyms* offers a glimpse at a strange world where language has been compressed into a string of unpronounceable characters. The original developers of UNIX apparently disliked vowels: Most have been stripped from the UNIX command syntax. The UNIX dictionary includes definitions and copious cross-references for terms such as *fcntl*, *ismpx*, and *pptophys*. The definitions are largely readable, with frequent consultation to a regular dictionary for terms included within the definitions. The dictionary also treats many terms that can be found in the popular press, such as *network mask*, *netiquette*, *login*, and *packet*. Although there is considerable overlap with *UNIX—An Open Systems Dictionary* by William H. Holt and Rockie J. Morgan (Resolution Business Press, 1994), both dictionaries can be used side by side to gain perspective on the meaning of an individual term.

The dictionary occasionally includes a blind cross-reference, and cross-references from an acronym to the complete term are sometimes inconsistent: The entry for "PPP" (point-to-point protocol) includes the definition; the entry for "SLIP" consists of a cross-reference to "Serial Line Internet Protocol." With its copious cross-references, relatively easy-to-read definitions, and labeling of commands that are specific to a version of UNIX, this dictionary is a useful tool for libraries serving a large population of UNIX users. It should be used in conjunction with the Holt and Morgan book. Although many terms can be found in both dictionaries, both works contain terms not found in the other. [R: RBB, 1 Oct 96, p. 373]

—**Peggy Jobe**

TELECOMMUNICATIONS

1374. CyberHound's Internet Guide to the Coolest Stuff Out There. Detroit, Visible Ink Press/Gale, 1996. 384p. illus. index. $24.95pa. ISBN 0-7876-0688-X.

CyberHound's Internet Guide is a "Webliography": a highly selective, annotated listing of resources on the World Wide Web intended to provide a starting point for Web exploration, thereby saving readers both connect time and money. As an Internet counterpart to the publisher's *VideoHound's Golden Movie Retriever* (see ARBA 95, entry 1399), this guide emphasizes the entertainment value of the Internet. *CyberHound's* editors do not disclose their criteria for selecting sites, but admit to scanning existing lists of "cool sites," consulting Web users, and "receiving strong vibes from certain URLs." The result is a somewhat eclectic assortment of homepages spanning the landscape of popular culture, from Alien Nation to ZAM! the game. Although the guide also includes a smattering of serious sites, such as AskERIC and the Library of Congress's American Memory Project, the preponderance of resources relate to entertainment, trivia, games, and personalities.

Each entry contains a homepage title and uniform resource locator (URL); a paragraph-long description; an excerpt from the page; and a rating denoted by up to four steaming coffee mugs. The four-mug sites inspected by this reviewer are indeed remarkable in design or content. The one-mug sites, on the other hand, are considered "substandard" by the book's own editors. Why a highly selective Webliography of this nature would waste precious print space on lukewarm sites is a mystery.

The format of the book, with sites arranged alphabetically by title, favors leisurely browsing over quick lookups. The index does organize all sites under topical categories, but with such headings as "Eye Candy," it is doubtful that one could actually locate a desired site in a hurry. The guide also contains a Windows/Macintosh CD-ROM with some Internet software and an automatic dialer program for an Internet Service Provider. While a convenient perk, this disc is identical to those ubiquitous freebies distributed in computer magazines, retail stores, and other outlets. The one notable feature missing from *CyberHound's*, and common among other Webliographies, is a corresponding online site that provides updates to the information printed in the guide. Lacking this feature, the contents of an annual title such as this one are prone to go out-of-date before the next edition.

Given its lighthearted focus and entertaining, if somewhat hackneyed, writing style, this guide will likely appeal to Web users looking for amusement, humor, and perhaps a bit of spectacle. It may also be a helpful tool for librarians and Internet trainers hoping to attract and assuage wary new users by highlighting the Internet's lighter side.—**Gail Clement**

1375. Directory of Electronic Journals, Newsletters, and Academic Discussion Lists. 6th ed. Compiled by Dru Mogge and the ARL Directory Staff and Diane K. Kovacs and the Directory Team. Dru Mogge, ed. Washington, D.C., Association of Research Libraries, 1996. 1111p. index. $79.00pa. ISSN 1057-1337.

Directory of Electronic Journals, Newsletters, and Academic Discussion Lists contains printed copies of two directories that are also accessible for free via the World Wide Web. The electronic journals list identifies Internet-based publications, mainly in the form of Websites and FTP archives, while the academic discussions list mainly covers Usenet newsgroups and listserv-distributed discussion groups. For both, the range is wide, and the indexing good.

The lists themselves, unfortunately, are not that good. Although the directory has a June 1996 publication date and claims to be accurate as of March 1996, a test in December 1996 found an extraordinary percentage of obsolete information. Of nine WWW listings tried, only two were valid. Of the other seven, one pointed to a nonexistent host, two to hosts that referred to different sites (one of these referrals had a December 1995 date posted), two to sites where the journal in question no longer existed in any form, one unreachable host, and one where the journal was present but in a different (and hard-to-find) directory. The one FTP site checked did not have the identified directory, and one listserv group yielded a "host not found" reply.

Keeping up to date with the Internet and the Web is a challenge, but this failure rate, in a list that claims to be only nine months old, is high enough to make the publication useless as a reference. Any organization that wants to make this information available should use the more current version of the lists that are available electronically. The electronic journals list (which had updated link information for the outdated ones in the print list) is at http://arl.cni.org/scomm/edir, and the academic discussion list is at http://www.n2h2.com/KOVACS. [R: Choice, Jan 96, p. 754]—**Ray Olszewski**

1376. Morrow, Blaine Victor. **Dial Up! Gale's Bulletin Board Locator.** Detroit, Gale, 1996. 1081p. index. $49.00pa. ISBN 0-7876-0364-3. ISSN 1085-3189.

Dial Up! describes more than 10,000 bulletin board systems (BBSs) in the United States that are accessible with a computer and modem. Bulletin boards offering unrestricted dial-up access and a forum for sharing messages, files, and opinions are eligible for inclusion. The directory is arranged by state and then by area code within a state. Each entry includes name of the bulletin board, telephone number, sponsoring individual or organization, modem speeds and settings, and times the bulletin board is available. The entries also provide a brief description of the contents of the bulletin board; the target audience; the bulletin board software used; computer platforms supported; and subscription fees, if any. Separate sections supply the same information for bulletin boards available from online services such as America Online, CompuServe, Delphi, GEnie, and Prodigy.

Dial Up! also furnishes a glossary of terms, an area code table, and two indexes. The master index is an alphabetic listing of bulletin boards and organizations mentioned in the entries and contains an inversion on significant keywords appearing in BBS names. The topic index groups the bulletin boards into 29 subject headings. The subject headings are broad and add little to the usefulness of the volume. Federally sponsored bulletin boards providing regulatory information are grouped into the "government/politics" topic, along with bulletin boards that offer forums "related to political issues." The directory also provides information about Internet access to selected bulletin boards, but the information is spotty and incomplete. Although the introduction states that "great editorial effort has been made to verify all information," many entries in the directory lack some descriptive elements. The author seems to have relied on descriptions furnished by the sponsoring individual or organization without soliciting additional information as needed to fully complete each entry.

Libraries serving large populations of computer users will want to purchase the directory and future updates. For noncomputer users, the descriptive entries in the directory provide a look at a rapidly growing slice of American life. [R: RBB, 15 May 96, p. 1618]—**Peggy Jobe**

1377. **Web Site Source Book 1996: A Guide to Major U.S. Businesses....** Darren L. Smith and others, eds. Detroit, Omnigraphics, 1996. 522p. $65.00pa. ISBN 0-7808-0095-8. ISSN 1089-4861.

Web Site Source Book 1996 combines alphabetic and classified listings of the Uniform Resource Locators (URLs) of the World Wide Web sites of about 7,000 businesses, universities, nonprofit organizations, and government entities. Released in July 1996, it is, as of this writing, a complete and accurate guide to the Web locations of about every major organization with an Internet presence. Yet the rapid growth and shifting of sites on the Web, and the Internet generally, show little sign of slowing. As a result, any reference such as this one will become dated fairly quickly, so purchasers should watch for updates.

The alphabetic listings are the more useful. Every listing checked was accurate, and one would be hard-pressed to think of a major organization that was not listed (including a few listed as having no public Web site). Moreover, from a sample of listings, about 40 percent of the site names are not obvious: While someone familiar with the form of URLs could easily guess, for example, Microsoft's Web address (http://www.microsoft.com), about 4 out of 10 listings in a sample checked were considerably less obvious, such as Media General (http://www.gateway-va.com). So the alphabetic listing serves a useful purpose.

The categorized listings are considerably less useful. Only 54 main classifications are used, with education subdivided into 2-year and 4-year colleges, and government subdivided into 17 groupings. These are far too few categories to provide the "yellow pages" utility that readers need in guides such as this one. [R: LJ, 1 Oct 96, p. 70; RBB, 1 Sept 96, pp. 172-73]—**Ray Olszewski**

35 Physical Sciences and Mathematics

PHYSICAL SCIENCES

Chemistry

Dictionaries and Encyclopedias

1378. **Encyclopedia of Chemical Processing and Design. Volume 56: Supercritical Fluid Technology....** John J. McKetta and Guy E. Weismantel, eds. New York, Marcel Dekker, 1996. 508p. illus. maps. $175.00. ISBN 0-8247-2607-3.

Even though the chemical industry is central to the economy of developed countries, references such as this encyclopedia are most likely to be of interest to those who work professionally in the field or to investors and other analysts who are concerned with industrial performance. There are, however, a number of articles in this particular volume that should be of interest to general readers. For example, there are nine articles concerned with the sources and production of synthetic fuels. Interest in new energy sources in this country has vacillated with changing levels of governmental commitment, but it is clear that this topic must ultimately be significant. Some of the possible alternatives include oil shale, coal tar, tar and heavy oil sands, coal liquefaction, and syngas. Each of these topics is reviewed in enough detail to provide a good overview of the important issues. There are also articles on other subjects of general interest, including the theory and applications of supercritical fluids and a review of high-intensity sweeteners. This volume contains enough information on topics of widespread concern to justify purchase by libraries that maintain an extensive collection in the sciences.—**Harry E. Pence**

1379. **A Glossary of Plastics Terminology in 5 Languages: English, Deutsch, Français, Español, Italiano.** 3d ed. W. Glenz and others, eds. New York, Carl Hanser Verlag; distr., Cincinnati, Ohio, Hanser/Gardner, 1995. 304p. index. $24.00pa. ISBN 3-446-18491-0.

This latest edition contains 1,383 terms and phrases connected with the chemistry, properties, testing, and other technologies related to plastics—an increase of 35 percent over the previous edition. The largest portion of text is arranged in tabular form, alphabetized by the English word. Access to words in the other four languages is provided through word lists by language. Therefore, if users are looking for the English (or French) equivalent for the Spanish word *tobera*, they would be referred to entry 774, which shows "nozzle" as the English equivalent. Here one also finds another possible Spanish word, *boquilla*, along with the gender of both words and the equivalent words in the other three languages.

As with the previous editions, the 3d consists of word-to-word translations, without any explanation or interpretation. Obviously, this glossary does not take the place of even a concise technical dictionary. Rather, it provides quick lookup for words found in brochures, catalogs, and short technical texts. This would be of primary interest to salespeople, international researchers, and translators.—**Susan B. Ardis**

Directories

1380. Chemical Research Faculties: An International Directory. Washington, D.C., American Chemical Society, 1996. 1248p. index. $199.95. ISBN 0-8412-3301-2.

The American Chemical Society (ACS) has published the *Directory of Graduate Research* (see ARBA 87, entry 342) since 1953. The directory, now biennial, has been long established as an indispensable reference source for academic science collections. It provides information on North American university departments and faculty in chemistry, chemical engineering, biochemistry, and related fields. *Chemical Research Faculties* fills the same function for information on universities outside of North America. It is much harder to cover the rest of the world; this directory has so far had only three editions—in 1984 (see ARBA 86, entry 1754); in 1988 (see ARBA 90, entry 1755); and now in 1996. Comparing faculty indexes shows about 50 percent more names in *Chemical Research Faculties*.

This work is similar in organization and content to the *Directory of Graduate Research*. The main part is divided into biochemistry, chemistry, chemical engineering, and nine other areas. Each discipline is subdivided by country, and within each country, individual university departments are listed (giving address, telephone and fax numbers, e-mail address, World Wide Web address if available, department head, degrees offered, fields of specialization, and so forth). Under departments are listed faculty with rank, date of birth, source of degrees, telephone number, e-mail address, fields of specialization, and citations of a few recent publications. Some listings are relatively brief—departments may be listed without faculty, or faculty without additional information. Also provided are a section giving information on chemical societies by country and an index by country of all departments. The directory is a valuable resource for any library called upon for information on scientists or departments outside of North America. Perhaps this work will become biennial, alternating with the *Directory of Graduate Research*. The ACS makes both available, together with *College Chemistry Faculties* and *Chemical Sciences Graduate School Finder*, on the CD-ROM *Directories on Disc*.—**Robert Michaelson**

1381. Directory of Chemical Producers and Products. Volume I, Part I: Chemical Enterprises in Central and Eastern Europe. 2d ed. By the Secretariat of the Economic Commission for Europe. New York, United Nations, 1995. 218p. index. $110.00pa. ISBN 92-1-116620-9. ISSN 1020-0444. S/N E.95.II.E.2.

This directory consists of the names, addresses, telephone numbers, and principal products for chemical producers in 20 countries of Central and Eastern Europe. The companies are arranged by country, and there is also an alphabetic index listing all of them. The information is relatively up-to-date, as this 2d edition was completed in October 1994. This work is intended to be used in combination with *Volume II*, which identifies the companies that produce each major chemical product. Together, these two publications represent a helpful resource for anyone who wishes to establish contacts and take advantage of the commercial opportunities that have developed in this part of the world. For more quantitative information about this region, however, resources such as *The Chemical Industry in 1993* published by the United Nations Economic Commission for Europe (see ARBA 96, entry 222) and the annual reports published by chemical journals, such as *Chemical and Engineering News*, may well be more useful.

—**Harry E. Pence**

1382. Lee, C. C. **Chemical Guide to the Internet.** Rockville, Md., Government Institutes, 1996. 295p. index. $69.00pa. ISBN 0-86587-519-7.

Despite what the title may indicate, this book is more than just a manual on electronic wizardry. In fact, it contains a virtual plethora of communication tips on the subject of chemicals and its associated fields. The first chapter provides an A to Z account of selected organizations. Each entry, whether government or private, foreign or domestic, can be accessed via the Internet, e-mail, telephone, fax, or regular mail. Also included is a brief description of each organization's subject emphasis and target audience.

Next is a chapter describing World Wide Web (WWW) resources by subject. Entries include chemical and instrumentation manufacturers, computer software, chemical information and services, and professional and trade organizations. The format repeats on the subjects of environmental protection, P2 information, PLI, PLM, PLS, recycling, and the WWW virtual library. Chapter 3 is a who's who list of academic programs (chemical and environmental). Chapter 4 lists electronic discussion groups and bulletin boards. Chapter 5 provides descriptions and sample subjects on newsgroups. The last chapter focuses on Gopher resources. Clear, concise, and comprehensive, this volume is an excellent tool for anyone (layperson or professional) requiring chemical and environmental information.—**Sue Lyon Mertl**

1383. **World Databases in Chemistry.** C. J. Armstrong, ed. New Providence, N.J., Bowker-Saur/Reed Reference Publishing, 1996. 1200p. index. (World Databases Series). $235.00. ISBN 1-85739-101-2.

This volume presents worldwide coverage of nonprint databases in chemistry, including applied areas, such as agrochemistry, forensic chemistry, thermochemistry, pharmacology, materials science, chemical engineering, and manufacturing chemistry. These areas are divided into 9 sections, with the 10th section covering databases that include chemical patents. Within each section, entries are ordered alphabetically by database name (e.g., Agricola), followed by factual data from fields in the master records in the file, a description of the database service, and media on which the data are available. Media include direct online or Internet access, as well as CD-ROM, diskette, tape, e-mail, and other formats. Names, addresses, and telephone/telex/fax numbers of publishers or other information providers are available. For some entries, a brief bibliography of published reviews of the database service is also provided. Access to the main portion of the volume is through a subject index, which supplies a list of database providers under broad subject terms (e.g., *adhesives*, *beverages*, and *solid state physics*).

To the credit of the compilers, the volume is a tremendous undertaking. One of its chief benefits is the international coverage. A CD-ROM version of the index may be preferred for better access. The scope of the work may be one of its biggest drawbacks. The subject fields are much too broad, preventing comprehensive coverage, and the inclusion of such terms as *social welfare*, *sociolinguistics*, and *social work* detracts from its credibility. More specific and comprehensive database directories are available for the myriad fields attempted in the book's coverage. The audience for this publication is also unclear, described by the publishers as "users and potential users of electronic information." People working in a specific technical field will have little need for this volume. One could envision a use for beginning researchers, or perhaps for marketing purposes. [R: Choice, July/Aug 96, p. 1780]—**Andrew G. Torok**

Handbooks and Yearbooks

1384. **Annual Bulletin of Trade in Chemical Products.** By the Economic Commission for Europe. New York, United Nations, 1995. 429p. $47.00pa. ISBN 92-1-016300-1. ISSN 0251-0081. S/N E/F/R.94.II.E.32.

This book primarily consists of tables of data for trade in chemicals and chemical products. Tables for both value and quantity of chemical products are presented. Standard International Trade Classification categories are used. These include specific chemicals such as ethylene, methanol, or polypropylene, and broad categories such as organic chemicals, synthetic fibers, or carboxylic acids. The value tables present 85 commodities or chemical groups in terms of dollar values. The quantity tables list 22 categories by metric tonnage. Fifty-three countries and six regional and world geographic totals are included. The table of contents, definitions, and introductory material are in three languages (English, French, and Russian). This volume covers the year 1992. Both export and import data are included. Unfortunately, the reader is likely to be confused by the terminology used in the table headings. Tables are arranged according to country of origin or destination. The same arrangement is then given to both import and export tables, leaving the reader to decipher which is which.—**T. McKimmie**

1385. Ash, Michael, and Irene Ash, comps. **Handbook of Plastic and Rubber Additives: An International Guide to More Than 13,000 Products....** Brookfield, Vt., Gower/Ashgate Publishing, 1995. 1322p. $195.00. ISBN 0-566-07594-6.

Additives play an important role in the production of plastic and rubber products. This broad group of specialty chemicals includes compounds added to improve processing or to enhance the characteristics of the final merchandise. Choosing the best additive can be difficult, both because of the large number of possible combinations as well as the environmental, safety, and health effects that must be taken into consideration. The editors of this volume have done an outstanding job of collecting information on more than 13,000 additives and arranging the data in a readily accessible format.

A section of trade names gives the chemical composition, properties, and applications, in addition to toxicological and regulatory information. The section is complemented by an alphabetic listing of chemical names and a catalog of functional categories. Both these sections contain cross-references to the trade names. For further convenience, appendixes allow easy searching using Chemical Abstracts Service (CAS) or European Inventory of Existing Commercial Chemical Substances (EINECS) numbers. Finally, a manufacturers' directory provides the addresses for obtaining the compounds. A CD-ROM version is also available.

This is a well-designed and comprehensive resource. Although it is somewhat specialized, it should be valuable for institutions that serve technical people working in the plastic or rubber industries.

—**Harry E. Pence**

1386. Furr, A. Keith. **CRC Handbook of Laboratory Safety.** 4th ed. Boca Raton, Fla., CRC Press, 1995. 783p. illus. index. $125.00. ISBN 0-8493-2518-8.

The 4th edition of this excellent laboratory safety handbook has been thoroughly revised, article by article. The topical outline reflected by the table of contents appears much the same as previous editions, but content has been completely updated. Material on all standards changes occurring since the 3d edition (1989) has been added, along with any new regulations and guidelines impacting laboratory safety. This is a resource highly recommended for laboratories and all types of libraries.—**Barbara Delzell**

1387. Prager, Jan C. **Environmental Contaminant Reference Databook: Volume I.** New York, Van Nostrand Reinhold, 1995. 1240p. index. $129.95. ISBN 0-442-01918-1.

1388. Prager, Jan C. **Environmental Contaminant Reference Databook: Volume II.** New York, Van Nostrand Reinhold, 1996. 1292p. index. $129.95. ISBN 0-442-01969-6.

In a break from precedence with the usual handbooks offered by major engineering handbook publishers, this projected four-volume work has been compiled from public databases by a retired Environmental Protection Agency biologist with the only human assistance provided by two engineering undergraduate students from the University of Rhode Island. "These data are intended for environmental regulators in federal, state, and local governments, as well as for conservation officers, emergency response personnel, public safety personnel, and chemical manufacturers, transporters and sellers . . . . It is not a primary source of research information . . . . This work is for quick reference only" (introduction). The databases include CESARS, CHRIS, Hazardous Substances Data Bank, IRIS, and OHM/TADS.

An example of an entry follows: "Acetic Acid, Copper (2+) Salt" is the green discoloration on the surfaces of statues and copper roofs. In addition to its American Chemical Society (ACS) number of 142-71-2, its Czech name of *octan mednaty*, and its "Acute Hazard Level," there are 40 other factual topic notes plus 20 references. Both volumes have synonym and ACS number indexes. There is no statement as to how the two volumes' contents differ, and it would seem that 1,000-odd paged volumes were considered the limit for handy use. There is no indication of the content planned for volumes 3 and 4.

This set will be needed for both special and public libraries in locales hosting chemical facilities, chemicals transportation, or chemicals' exposure to the surrounding elements. Academic libraries supporting chemical engineering programs and environmental programs may need multiple copies.

—**Eugene B. Jackson**

1389. Verschueren, Karel. **Handbook of Environmental Data on Organic Chemicals.** 3d ed. New York, Van Nostrand Reinhold, 1996. 2064p. index. $199.95. ISBN 0-442-01916-5.

This volume provides in-depth coverage of dangerous organic compounds and provides control measures for mitigating their destructive impact on the ecosystem. The chemicals are listed alphabetically, including generic names and synonyms, molecular and structural formulas, and Chemical Abstracts Service registry numbers. The 2d edition was reviewed in-depth (see ARBA 84, entry 1288). The 3d edition has grown considerably in size from the 2d edition, which consisted of 1310 pages. While considerably more chemicals are treated, no major indexing changes have occurred. The volume remains a valuable authoritative source of preventive information for occupational hygienists, toxicologists, biochemists, and others.—**Andrew G. Torok**

Indexes

1390. **Chemistry Citation Index: A CD-ROM Database with Abstracts.** [CD-ROM]. Philadelphia, Institute for Scientific Information, 1995. Minimum system requirements: IBM PC, XT, AT or compatible. ISO 9660 CD-ROM drive with MS-DOS CD-ROM Extensions 2.0. MS-DOS 3.1. 640K RAM. 3MB hard disk space. Expanded Memory Specification 3.2 (recommended). $1,950.00/single user; $2,925.00/1-5 users; $3,900.00/6-10 users/yr. ISSN 1057-6088.

This is one of five specialty indexes on CD-ROM offered by the Institute for Scientific Information (ISI) (the others being *Biochemistry & Biophysics*, *Biotechnology*, *Neuroscience*, and *Materials Science*). Each new subscription includes all annuals back to 1991. An unlimited access, networked version is available for $4,290. Each disc contains up to one year of data, and is updated six times per year.

The DOS-based search engine is easy to load and runs smoothly. A context-sensitive help feature is user friendly. Search software supports keyword and author searching using Boolean operators. A "KeyWords Plus" feature permits searching for words or phrases that frequently appear in the titles of an article's cited references, but not in the title of the article itself. In addition to cited reference searching, ISI's CD-ROM products feature a bibliographic coupling mechanism that permits retrieval of articles having one or more references in common with a displayed/highlighted article. Abstracts are included for articles when provided with the original publication. Abstracts are also searchable. A printed quick reference guide documents searching features. A toll-free telephone number is also provided.

More than 1,000 journals in organic, inorganic, physical, and analytical chemistry are indexed, with about half covered in their entirety. Publisher and proceedings information are provided for all records, as are authors' addresses. ISI's Genuine Article document delivery service allows ordering of reprints. The combination of award-winning search software with the unique features of citation indexes makes this a most desirable product.—**Andrew G. Torok**

Earth and Planetary Sciences

General Works

1391. **Macmillan Encyclopedia of Earth Sciences.** E. Julius Dasch, ed. New York, Macmillan Library Reference/Simon & Schuster Macmillan, 1996. 2v. illus. maps. index. $190.00/set. ISBN 0-02-883000-8.

This reference work covers the broad area of earth sciences, the scientific study of the Earth and the other planets in our solar system. The articles bring together material from atmospheric sciences, hydrology, geology, oceanography, and planetary sciences. During the past few decades, there have been many dramatic discoveries in these disciplines, ranging from the exploration of our solar system to the improved understanding of the processes that shape the Earth. Thus, the topics covered are of broad and current interest to many readers.

The 360 individual entries are primarily organized around 5 categories: "Solid Earth Processes," "Surface Earth Processes," "Earth Resources and Stewardship," "Earth Sciences in the Public Eye," and "Earth in Space." Additional articles deal with careers in the various disciplines comprising the earth sciences, brief histories of these disciplines, and biographies of well-known scientists from these fields. The articles are complemented by a good selection of photographs and diagrams, and an extensive index makes the information more readily accessible.

The various articles are written at a uniform level, and the intended audience of advanced high school students and university undergraduates should find the presentations to be clear and interesting. This is a well-planned, comprehensive survey of a field that is of continuing interest to nonscientists, and so a general reference book of this type will be a valuable resource for many readers. [R: RBB, 1 Nov 96, p. 538]

—**Harry E. Pence**

Astronomy and Space Sciences

1392. **Cambridge Astronomy Dictionary.** New York, Cambridge University Press, 1996. 238p. illus. maps. $29.95; $14.95pa. ISBN 0-521-58007-2; 0-521-58991-6pa.

A search of OCLC's WorldCat database reveals at least two dozen general astronomical dictionaries published in the past three decades. The question, then, is why yet another work of this type has appeared. The *Cambridge Astronomy Dictionary* has two things in its favor. First, it is more up-to-date than its predecessors, an important quality in a field that changes rapidly, thanks to regular discoveries and revised data provided by orbiting telescopes and interplanetary spacecraft. Second, and more important, it is a high-quality work.

As with its first cousins, the *Cambridge Encyclopedia of Astronomy* (see ARBA 79, entry 1313) and *The Cambridge Star Atlas* (see entry 1393), the dictionary is well written and professionally done. True, this Cambridge title has far fewer entries than other works, for example *The Facts on File Dictionary of Astronomy* (3d ed.; see ARBA 95, entry 1721), but it makes up for this by focusing on the most important topics and presenting them clearly and concisely. In addition to standard definitions, the book includes biographical data on more than 100 astronomers, descriptions of major observatories, and a number of tables and more than 50 black-and-white diagrams. Aimed at the intelligent layperson, this work would be a sensible purchase for academic and larger public libraries.—**Robert A. Seal**

1393. **The Cambridge Star Atlas.** 2d ed. By Wil Tirion. New York, Cambridge University Press, 1996. 90p. illus. maps. $19.95. ISBN 0-521-56098-5.

This compact but highly useful star atlas belongs on the reference shelf of the beginning backyard astronomer as well as of the experienced observer of the heavens. Now in its 2d edition, this work consists primarily of 24 sky charts (white stars on a blue background) for the amateur astronomer and 20 detailed atlas charts (black celestial objects on a white sky). The former depict the constellations and show stars down to the fifth magnitude. Arranged for easy use according to the time of year and one's location (Northern and Southern Hemispheres), they are just right for the casual observer.

The far more detailed atlas star charts show a wide variety of celestial objects: stars (regular, variable, and binary); star clusters; nebulae; and galaxies. They are accompanied by a list of objects on each chart with right ascension, declination, magnitude, diameter, and so forth. The atlas concludes with six "all-sky maps" that show the constellations and present the distribution of specific celestial objects, for example galaxies, on the night sky. Well written on a beginning level, this inexpensive atlas would be appropriate for any type of library, from school to university. [R: RBB, 1 Dec 96, p. 684]—**Robert A. Seal**

1394. Cocks, Elijah E., and Josiah C. Cocks. **Who's Who on the Moon: A Biographical Dictionary of Lunar Nomenclature.** Greensboro, N.C., Tudor, 1995. 600p. illus. maps. $45.00. ISBN 0-936389-27-3.

The moon is the second brightest object in the Earth's sky, next to the Sun. The fact that variations of its surface are visible to the unaided eye has made the moon a source of lore and fascination. Some of the largest features were given names by various mapmakers of Europe beginning early in the seventeenth century, reflecting mostly European interests. With the development of the telescope, these features were seen in greater detail, and the lunar nomenclature became more confused. The International Astronomical Union (IAU), established in 1921, set out to standardize the naming of lunar features, resulting in 681 names. With the early lunar orbiters of the 1960s, the number of identifiable features dramatically increased. The United Nations, working with the IAU, sanctioned the naming of 1,993 lunar features. Of these, 1,586 are named for historical individuals.

The authors have compiled in this single volume a collection of biographical sketches of these 1,586 individuals. Included is the type, size, and location of the feature on the moon's surface. A section of photographs of the moon, with coordinates and features labeled, is provided, although the names are difficult to read. The five different lists found in the appendix are particularly helpful. The first is a list of women honorees. The next two lists are sorted, first by professions, and then by countries of origin. The last two are lists sorted by location and by size. The biographies provide only the very briefest information, which is reasonable within the purpose of this book. This resource would be an asset in any general reference collection. [R: Choice, Feb 96, pp. 924-26]—**Margaret F. Dominy**

1395. **Eyewitness Encyclopedia of Space and the Universe.** [CD-ROM]. New York, DK Multimedia, 1996. Minimum system requirements: IBM or compatible 486DX/33MHz. MPC-compatible double-speed CD-ROM drive. Windows 3.1. 4MB RAM (8MB recommended). SVGA 256-color monitor. Mouse. MPC-compatible sound card. Loudspeakers or headphones. $39.95. ISBN 0-7894-0881-3. [Also available in Macintosh version.]

Appropriate for public and school libraries, as well as home use, this multimedia encyclopedia is aimed at young people with an interest in outer space exploration and astronomy. It is not an in-depth reference work, but rather it has a little bit of everything at an elementary level. As with similar works, it combines text, sound, animation, still photographs and drawings, and videos in an attempt to make the subject "come alive." Entries consist of short paragraphs accompanied by color graphics and links to video clips, numerical facts, and related topics; coverage is rather superficial.

When the CD-ROM boots up, the user is presented with the "console," a screen of objects that one clicks on to go to various parts of the encyclopedia. For example, clicking on the antique telescope takes one to the chapter on observational astronomy, with entries on famous telescopes and observatories, X-ray astronomy, radio astronomy, and so on. Other sections include cosmology, space exploration, satellites and space probes, the history of astronomy, biographies of famous astronomers and space explorers, and more. The section called "Quiz Master" offers a trivia game. A list of astronomy and space World Wide Web addresses is also provided, although this information could quickly become dated.

The work's best feature is the Star Dome, a sort of miniplanetarium in which users can view the night skies at any time and from any location on Earth. The constellations can be turned on and off, planets and galaxies and other celestial objects can be highlighted, and the heavens rotate manually or by the passage of time. It is not overly sophisticated but would be instructive for young and older backyard or armchair astronomers.

There are a few negatives. For instance, moving around often requires backing out of a given section to return to the console, and to make matters worse, the escape key cannot be used for this. One has to guess how to move around by clicking the mouse. A user's manual, if there was one, may help here. Finally, the number of video clips and animated sequences is rather small, surprising given the vast numbers of such materials available from the National Aeronautics and Space Administration and other sources. [R: BL, 15 Oct 96, pp. 450-51]—**Robert A. Seal**

Climatology and Meteorology

1396. **Encyclopedia of Climate and Weather.** Stephen H. Schneider, ed. New York, Oxford University Press, 1996. 2v. illus. maps. index. $195.00/set. ISBN 0-19-509485-9.

Reference books, like large public buildings, are often imposing and intimidating. The size and mass are signs of serious purpose and authority. So it comes as a shock when city hall has a hot pink interior with turquoise ceilings. Even more surprising is when that city government works well. This is the case with the *Encyclopedia of Climate and Weather* from Oxford University Press. The encyclopedia is an effective and readable reference tool that successfully mixes adiabatic processes with the Mamas and the Papas. As the preface indicates, "No longer is the weather simply about clouds, rain, and temperature."

This encyclopedia reaches from the disciplines of climatology to the realm of music in its efforts to explain the weather. There are maps, charts, tables, a table of contents, and an index, but what this work really does is to teach. Its audience encompasses the layperson, the high school student, and the university student. The intended readers are a diverse lot rather than a narrow academic group. There certainly are pages filled with the sort of mathematics that normally frightens the calculus-deprived masses, but there are articles that draw one on past an initial visit. At the end of 2 volumes and 929 pages, the editor has proven that it is possible to assemble a reference book that lives up to its promise and then delivers clarity and a sense of wonder as well. The *Encyclopedia of Climate and Weather* is recommended for any library beyond the elementary-school level. [R: Choice, Oct 96, p. 250; LJ, 1 June 96, p. 94; RBB, Aug 96, p. 1924]
—**George M. Cumming Jr.**

1397. **Weather America: The Latest Detailed Climatological Data for Over 4,000 Places.** Alfred N. Garwood, ed. Milpitas, Calif., Toucan Valley, 1996. 1412p. $99.95. ISBN 1-884925-60-X.

This title is recommended both for its currency and its format. The book presents 13 types of climatological data for the years 1965 through 1994 for each of 4,158 locations in all 50 states. The narrative description of each state's physical features and climate are copied from a dated governmental report but are still valid. The state maps should have been redrawn to emphasize the contents of this book, and it would help to show which are the 280 first-order stations that operate 24 hours a day as opposed to cooperative sites that record information once a day.

The book states that "*Weather America* is not intended for climatologists or atmospheric scientists." This admits the inaccuracies due to inhomogeneities caused by the time of day observations are taken. Occasionally stations move and equipment is changed or upgraded. If 1 to 4 of the 30 data values are missing, the reader cannot ascertain that any are missing. The book states cooling degree days were not available until 1980. It would have been simple to calculate these for prior years.

At the end of each state's section, there are four ranking tables showing stations with the coldest average January temperature, warmest average July temperature, annual precipitation, and annual snowfall. It should have been stated that the coldest January minimum does not mean the record low; similarly the July maximum does not indicate the record high. The book concludes with nationwide ranking tables. This is a useful, current book in a unique format. Due to inhomogeneities and factors common in climatological data, readers should be warned that accuracy is within approximately a degree Fahrenheit rather than the tenths of a degree shown. [R: BL, 15 Oct 96, p. 453]—**Allen E. Staver**

1398. **Weather of U.S. Cities: A Guide to the Recent Weather Histories of 268 Key Cities....** 5th ed. Richard A. Wood, ed. Detroit, Gale, 1996. 1075p. $210.00. ISBN 0-8103-5525-6.

This compilation of local climatological data is comprehensive and easy to use. The statistics come from 268 "key cities" and include the usual items, such as precipitation, temperatures, wind speeds, and the like, as well as more derived measurements (e.g., heating and cooling degree days and mean sky cover). For most sites, about 30 years of data are presented, with a summary page of normals, means, and extremes. Each location is introduced with a brief description of geography and general weather patterns.

The data are ideal for CD-ROM products, and there are indeed weather data discs available. Computerization of these statistics enables quick and useful graphic comparisons and the compilation of summary tables involving several locations. Some of this type of data is already available on the World Wide Web, which can provide almost instantaneous weather information as well. Still, students of meteorology, climatology, and other environmental sciences often need a paper copy on hand for ready-reference. This book will fill that need, although its cost may give librarians pause.—**Mark A. Wilson**

Geology

1399. **Earthquakes and the Built Environment Index: 1984 - July 1995.** [CD-ROM]. Baltimore, Md., National Information Services Corporation, 1995. Minimum system requirements: IBM or compatible 386. CD-ROM drive. 150K RAM (512K without extended memory). Color or monochrome monitor. $295.00/yr. ISSN 1082-4588.

Earthquakes and the Built Environment Index consists of three research library databases: Quakeline (National Center for Earthquake Engineering at the State University of New York at Buffalo) Earthquake Engineering Abstracts (National Service for Earthquake Engineering at the University of California at Berkeley), and Newcastle Earthquake Database (Newcastle Region Library of Australia). Some 100,000 citations are provided on earthquakes, earthquake engineering, and related topics. All items are available through document delivery from the appropriate above-cited agencies. Coverage is from 1984 to the present. Semiannual updates are planned. Duplicate records from the three databases are combined by the publisher's software into a single composite record when it is loaded on the CD-ROM.

Standard topics in the field that are covered extensively in the index are earthquakes; natural hazard mitigation; seismology; seismometry; tsunamis; volcanoes; structural dynamics; hurricanes; tornadoes; earthquake prediction; wind engineering; flooding; and properties of soils, rocks, and foundations. Standard sources include periodicals; conference proceeding; technical reports; theses; books; government documents (including building codes, reports, and surveys); newspaper articles; software; tapes; and archival records. A typical entry includes the title; the author; the source; the series; notes; keywords; an abstract; and added index entries for major topics, language, publication type, availability, local call number, and database source. Entries are quite extensive. For example, abstractors often summarize the importance of the work and note local phenomena cited (e.g., atmosphere, seismoluminescence, and effluvia). Notes are also detailed, in most cases including complete bibliographic information.

Installation of the CD-ROM was menu driven and easy. The only trick is that the product code is required at one point to complete the install. This product code is a four-letter, case-sensitive security code that could be tricky to a novice computer user. The search engine is a proprietary National Information Services Corporation (NISC) software program called ROMWright. Users can choose from three search levels: novice, advanced, and expert. While NISC claims that the software features "unparalleled search speed," information seemed to be retrieved at the average rate one would expect from a CD-ROM index. The standard Boolean, proximity, truncation, and field-specific search modes are available. Output can be customized for user needs. Single site, concurrent user, and local and wide area network licensing is available. The publisher offers a 30-day free trial. Discs must be returned (or destroyed) at the end of the license period.

Most engineering and all geology libraries will want to own this index. Libraries in earthquake-prone areas may wish to consider purchasing it.—**Ralph Lee Scott**

1400. **Multilingual Thesaurus of Geosciences: Deutsch • English • Español • Français • Italiano • Russkij.** 2d ed. J. Gravesteijn and others, eds. Medford, N.J., Information Today, 1995. 645p. index. $99.00pa. ISBN 1-57387-009-9.

The 2d edition of the *Multilingual Thesaurus of Geosciences*, in English, Spanish, German, French, Italian, and Russian, contains 575 new key terms and many new terms in specific field divisions. These additions were based on frequency and use analysis in major international databases. Frequency and use analysis was also used to "weed" the 1st edition (see ARBA 89, entry 1664); 12.8 percent of general and nonsystematic terms were deleted, resulting in a polished, up-to-date product. On the other side of the coin, it will be necessary to keep the 1st and all subsequent editions in order to have comprehensive historical coverage for obsolete terms.

Overall, there are 5,823 key terms classed into 37 groups or field divisions, reflecting all major subdivisions of geoscience, concepts, and selected classification domains such as fossil groups and the like. A new section has been added for geographic terms, which contains 1,298 entries. The *Multilingual Thesaurus* is an excellent resource, essential for online and general literature searching in this subject area. It is highly recommended for academic and special librarians worldwide that support geoscience research and curriculums.—**Barbara Delzell**

1401. **The New Penguin Dictionary of Geology.** By Philip Kearey. New York, Penguin Books, 1996. 365p. $13.95pa. ISBN 0-14-051277-2.

Structural, physical, and biological processes and mechanisms that affect the surface and interior of the Earth define the field of geology. That said, this distinctly British dictionary contains some 7,600 entries broadened to include geomorphology, sedimentology, paleontology, and biology, which border on the field of geology.

Entries and synonyms are presented in bold typeface; terms that appear in the entries and that are entries themselves appear in italic typeface. All the common terms are here: *batholith*, *cirque*, *kame*, *loess*, and *sial*, with ample cross-references; British spelling predominates. A unit and conversion chart and a table of stratigraphic information precede the entries, but the typeface is too small for easy perusal. Stratigraphic ages are given according to *A Geologic Timescale 1990* (Cambridge University Press).

The supplemental bibliography is divided by subject, such as economic geology, mineralogy, crystallography, volcanology, plate tectonics, and so on. Most entries date from the mid- to the late 1980s. At its price, this compact, up-to-date dictionary offers a profusion of geologic terms that will be of use to amateur geologists and students in need of a ready-reference tool.—**Judy Gay Matthews**

1402. Sarjeant, William A. S. **Geologists and the History of Geology: An International Bibliography from the Origins to 1978. Supplement 2: 1985-1993 and Additions, Volume 1.** Malabar, Fla., Krieger Publishing, 1996. 815p. $365.00. ISBN 0-89464-880-2.

This 2d supplement to Sarjeant's *Geologists and the History of Geology* (see ARBA 81, entry 1522) continues the thorough and unique work that has covered the history of geologic science and practice from the origins to 1978 in the original 5-volume set and 1979-1984 in supplement 1 (see ARBA 89, entry 1665). The 2d supplement, intended, as was the first, to cover a 6-year span, instead covers 9 years, up through 1993, and extends to 3 volumes. The bibliography itself is categorized into the same sections as the original work (general works; historical accounts of societies and museums; histories of the petroleum industry; accounts of significant events in the history of geology; individual geologists, prospectors, diviners, and mining engineers; and indexes), and covers books, book chapters, articles, letters, and obituaries. Coverage has expanded in this latest supplement to include more than 100 new periodicals, comprehensively searched, which brings the total number of periodicals to nearly 350. Sarjeant has also added previously missed obituaries and brief biographies.

Many of the citations included here may be found in periodical databases, such as GeoRef and GeoBase. However, the many special features of this print bibliography make it a valuable reference source for a more specific audience. The scope of the work is well defined, covering those aspects of the history of geology and geologists noted above, yet the author has searched broadly for these citations in the literature of related scientific fields, and he should be commended for even attempting to achieve comprehensive coverage of this subfield. Specialized indexes, such as the index of women geologists and the index of geologists by specialty, provide unique access points. Annotations for biographical entries also add value to this bibliography. The convenience of having these citations on the history of geology and geologists extracted from the larger literature and so carefully compiled should make this supplement, with its predecessor volumes, a valuable addition, if budget allows, to collections serving the history of science and geology.—**Jean C. McManus**

Paleontology

1403. **Dinosaur Hunter.** [CD-ROM]. New York, DK Multimedia, 1996. (Eyewitness Virtual Reality). Minimum system requirements: IBM or compatible 486DX/33MHz. Double-speed CD-ROM drive. Windows 3.1. 8MB RAM. 10MB hard disk space. 640 x 480, 256-color monitor. Mouse. 8 bit sound card. Loud speakers or headphones. $29.95. ISBN 0-7894-0901-1.

DK Multimedia's *Dinosaur Hunter* demonstrates a thriving company's major strength—the ability to invite, intrigue, and challenge the curious young mind. This smorgasbord of graphics, maps, diagrams, text, and animation stalks about the Jurassic, Triassic, and Cretaceous periods with agility and expertise. Users can access dinosaurs by name or period and can unearth, reconfigure, and activate their finds. Historic annotations name important digs, locators, and data around the world. Voices narrate the story of dinosaurs site by site. Snarls and growls, rotating shin bones, and lush backdrops brighten the dark corners of the past. Colors and sounds create a virtual feast of old bones, all with the young mouse-clicker in mind.

Unfortunately, the beauties of this program cannot balance the heavy baggage of weaknesses and faults. Balky software, demands for memory, obscure abbreviations (e.g., MYA), glacier-slow backtracking, murky instructions, and frequent crashes derive from an attempt to showcase too slick and too complicated a program in a limited framework. The module that allows young diggers to reconstruct specific dinosaurs creaks along at a snail's pace and offers too little demonstration of how to access its mechanism. The i-box begins the process of tutelage, but fails to enliven the activity. Voices are staid and sonorous, better suited to undertakers than docents. Yes, the pictures lure the hand to click more choices, yes, the virtual reality sparks the imagination; but the clunky movement is antediluvian. Sorry, DK. It was a good idea.

—**Mary Ellen Snodgrass**

1404. Frickhinger, Karl Albert. **Fossil Atlas: Fishes.** Blacksburg, Va., Tetra Press, 1995. 1088p. illus. index. $79.95. ISBN 1-56465-115-0.

Fossils of all kinds have become objects of increasing interest to the general public. Not only are they featured in action movies, but large numbers of actual specimens are sold through galleries and boutiques around the world as objets d'art. Fossils appear in coffee-table books and numerous textbooks. This atlas is essentially a fossil handbook, in some ways similar to a field guide, albeit a heavy one. It resembles a picture book of fossil fishes wherein representatives of all groups are shown in generally good, but small, photographs. Some of these are too dark or the specimen, as preserved, is too difficult for a nonspecialist to recognize.

The book is a little more than 7 inches high, 5 inches wide, and 2 inches thick. Approximately 900 species are shown. Each photograph caption lists the name of the fossil, who named it, where it is from geologically and geographically, and the museum that owns it. Other information provided on the same page covers geologic range, geographic distribution, and a features section of a few lines with general characteristics of the fish. These are often difficult to observe from the small photographs. Other information includes "remarks," which primarily note whether the fish is a predator or where it lived, and "recent relatives" notes existence of living forms, if any, or when the genus became extinct. Aside from the photographs and brief text that comprise the overwhelming majority of the book, there are sections on collecting and photographing fossils, evolution of fishes, fish anatomy, a classification, nearly 30 pages of references, a systematic index, and a locality index.

Overall, the pictures provide a sense of the material on which paleoicthyology is based. However, for most readers, two other books primarily about fossil fishes also have been published recently, one by John Maisey, *The Hall of Vertebrate Origins* (American Museum of Natural History, 1996), the other by John Long, *The Rise of Fishes* (Johns Hopkins University Press, 1996). These, too, include many photographs but provide a much more extensive text that introduces a reader to the complex history and evolution of fishes. [R: RBB, Aug 96, pp. 1924-25]—**David Bardack**

1405. **The Penguin Historical Atlas of Dinosaurs.** By M. J. Benton. New York, Penguin Books, 1996. 144p. illus. maps. index. $16.95pa. ISBN 0-14-0-51336-1.

For the informed adult reader, this brief historical atlas may be of some help in understanding dinosaurs that have so captured popular imagination. The main thrust of the text is to trace the history of the dinosaurs and to illustrate the great success and diversity that they enjoyed during their reign on land and in the seas. Understanding dinosaur diversity, exploring evidence for life in its minutest prehistoric forms, and learning how shifting continents have affected the evolution of all life forms are the major themes of this book.

The geographically subdivided essays (e.g., England, China, the prehistoric supercontinent Gondwanaland, Germany, the Morrison Formation in Colorado, the American Midwest) explore the dinosaur forms of the Triassic, Jurassic, and Cretaceous eras. The Cretaceous period, lasting some 80 million years, witnessed fresh evolution among the dinosaurs, and their ranges during this time are highlighted on outline maps. Map keys provide clues to ancient continents, mountain chains, modern coastlines for comparison, and icons for the various dinosaurs represented. Newer discoveries of Alaskan and Australian dinosaurs that lived in the polar regions have sparked debate about their thermoregulation mechanisms and their unique adaptation to living in winter darkness. Similar skeletons unearthed in North America and North Africa, now a hotbed of dramatic new discoveries, have turned up intriguing evidence of a possible land link between the two continents, even though they previously have been thought to have always been separated.

The extinction of the dinosaurs has always been of interest to paleontologists and to the general public. It was not only dinosaurs that disappeared 65 million years ago, but also several families of birds and marsupial mammals. The asteroid impact hypothesis will continue to be explored well into the twenty-first century in an attempt to explain how selective extinctions could occur, because some dinosaurs showed an apparent reduction in numbers over a long time period.

The distinctly British tone and spellings may not appeal to American readers. The small typeface chosen and light screened material could cause eye fatigue during sustained reading. A brief bibliography, primarily for specialists, and an index conclude the volume. High school and public libraries may want to consider purchasing this entertaining work on the most fascinating giants to ever roam the land.—**Judy Gay Matthews**

Physics

1406. Cohen, E. Richard. **The Physics Quick Reference Guide.** Woodbury, N.Y., AIP Press, 1996. 209p. illus. index. $30.00 spiralbound. ISBN 1-56396-143-1.

Even before entering the age of information explosion, the world of science has been amassing data on every conceivable topic. In the field of physics, formulas galore have been accumulated over the centuries. From time to time people try to put them all together, neatly and concisely, for quick reference. The booklet under review is one such attempt.

The guide provides a complete listing of the Systeme International d'Unites (SI) units, formulas from basic dynamics to general relativity, definitions in engineering physics, even the Periodic Table of elements, with electron configuration, boiling and melting points, density, and all. The book also includes results from all the mathematics that serve physics: from decimal notation and the Einstein convention for dummy indexes to the roots of the quadratic, spherical Bessel functions, and more. Also, there are many essential results of probability and statistics.

This is the kind of book that students may find useful to have. The sheer range of material, besides attempting completeness in the survey, may attract a wide audience. More compact than the *Handbook of Physics* (2d ed., McGraw-Hill, 1967), less unwieldy than the *CRC Handbook of Chemistry and Physics* (see ARBA 95, entry 1711), this slender compilation can be carried and handled with little effort. Any library should have this ready-reference book; it is a useful tool in handling the data explosion. [R: BL, July 96, p. 1847]—**Varadaraja V. Raman**

1407. **Encyclopedia of Applied Physics. Volume 15: Power Electronics to Raman Scattering.** George L. Trigg and others, eds. New York, VCH, 1996. 619p. illus. $300.00. ISBN 1-56081-074-2.

1408. **Encyclopedia of Applied Physics. Volume 16: Raman Spectroscopy to Schottky Barriers.** George L. Trigg and others, eds. New York, VCH, 1996. 600p. illus. $300.00. ISBN 1-56081-075-0.

The latest two volumes of the *Encyclopedia of Applied Physics* continue their march through the alphabet and applied physics. Begun in 1991 (see ARBA 92, entry 1750), the encyclopedia continues to be a work in progress. The articles are signed by recognized authorities and are directed to the professional scientist. Each article begins with a detailed outline of the topic. This outline gives researchers an opportunity to quickly determine the contents of the article and its relevancy to their needs. Extensive illustrative and mathematical treatments are included. References cited and guides to further reading conclude each article.

The encyclopedic treatment of such rapidly changing topics as found in applied physics tends to be most useful as a resource for establishing a ground base of knowledge, rather than providing an up-to-the-minute statement of the topic. Therefore, the extended period over which this set is being produced should have minimal impact on its usefulness. The depth of the topics and the extensive mathematics make the *Encyclopedia of Applied Physics* appropriate for research-level science and engineering libraries. The set is highly recommended for those libraries wishing to build up a research-level science reference collection.—**Margaret F. Dominy**

1409. Kantha, Sachi Sri. **An Einstein Dictionary.** Westport, Conn., Greenwood Press, 1996. 298p. index. $75.00. ISBN 0-313-28350-8.

This book is an enigma, starting with the title. The arrangement of the material in the work is indeed alphabetic, but that is where the resemblance to a dictionary stops. The work is a compilation of trivia, short vignettes of one or two paragraphs, and miscellany. The glue that binds them all together is the fact that they all have something to do with Albert Einstein.

In addition to the entries, there are other facets to the book. There is a standard chronology of Einstein's life that continues with events related to Einstein in 1993. There is a short "Readers' Guide" to biographies and other sources consulted. There is an awkwardly done and graphically ugly genealogy chart. The chart appears to have been done partly by a distinctly unsteady hand and on a typewriter. There is a section listing all of Einstein's scientific publications. A further section lists journal articles. In this case, "journal articles" means *popular* articles about or by Einstein. A curious section follows, entitled

"Books." This runs the gamut from writings by Einstein through politics and public issues to Einsteiniana. These facets are, however, only tangential to the main body of the work. Nonetheless, a reader will be able to make use of these sections for additional or corollary information by or about Einstein. In doing so, the reader will have to interpret the categories and intentions of the author.

The foreword to the book suggests that there are two "riddles" to the book. The first is why it was written by a biochemist and second, why the foreword was written by a chemist. Neither is a real riddle, because the work Einstein began moved quickly into chemistry and biochemistry via quantum chemistry and other avenues. The riddle of the book is what audience it is supposed to address. If this is a scholarly work, then it falls short simply because the entries are not as replete as they should be. If this is intended as an entrée to Einstein, it misses the mark because to use the book at all, one needs to have some prior knowledge of Einstein. On the scholarly to popular continuum, this book falls closer to the popular. It is not clear at all that this is where the author intended this book to fall.

The majority of the book is a series of entries arranged in alphabetic order. For each of the entries there is varying information given, ranging in length from a couple of lines to substantive paragraphs. The problem with the intended audience of the book makes for curious entries. Max Planck is listed with a reasonable five-paragraph entry; Planck's constant is not mentioned except inside the entry on Planck—black body radiation, the genesis of Planck's work, is not mentioned at all. Curiously, there is no mention of tensor calculus, which was a major factor in allowing Einstein to place all space-time coordinate systems on an equal footing, leading to the general theory of relativity. This was critical to Einstein's concept of general covariance (which also is not among the entries in this book). For the entries that are missing, there are entries that stretch the connection to Einstein. *Einstein on the Beach*, an opera in four acts, is listed. There is an entry for Archibald MacLeish, the poet and later Librarian of Congress, who wrote a fairly lengthy poem, "Einstein."

On the production side, the inequalities in the typeface fonts between the main text and the tables are disconcerting. In some cases, the tables could have been more carefully integrated into the text or placed with the entry that references them. In a book short on so many important aspects, the typography and composition are unfortunate victims. On the plus side, the index is useful.

This is a book that is difficult to recommend. It has some features that make it interesting, but only if it is a part of a larger collection of Einsteiniana. Even then, the price is out of line with the benefit of owning the book. With so much other material on Einstein available, this work suffers. If the goal is to have everything published on Einstein, then this is a candidate for purchase. With any less aggressive collection development strategy, this work cannot be recommended. [R: Choice, Oct 96, p. 253]

—C. D. Hurt

1410. **Macmillan Encyclopedia of Physics.** John S. Rigden, ed. New York, Macmillan Library Reference/ Simon & Schuster Macmillan, 1996. 4v. illus. index. $400.00/set. ISBN 0-02-897359-3.

This is the first Macmillan encyclopedia to cover the mature and expansive science of physics, and the result is a successful and solid reference set appropriate for the advanced high school-level student and beyond. Useful for both quick-reference and concepts review, it is an especially valuable and appropriate tool for an undergraduate-level study of physics.

Four volumes provide access to a broad coverage of physics topics, arranged alphabetically. Each entry includes a bibliography, and many are illustrated. A helpful list of common abbreviations and mathematical symbols embedded in these black-and-white illustrations and in formulas is contained in each volume, as is a journal title abbreviation key. Structurally, the encyclopedia is prefaced by a reader's guide of key entries, an alphabetic list of articles, and a contributors list. Entries are cross-referenced. The 4th volume in the set concludes with a short glossary and a comprehensive index.

Coverage is broad in scope, encompassing essential concepts and principles, theories and laws, phenomena and effects, but there is also excellent coverage of the many physics subdisciplines as well as physics history and philosophy. Also of note is the thorough coverage of space and astronomy topics, from black holes to solar winds to descriptions of selected observatories. A section on the Nobel prize-winners in both physics and chemistry was wisely included, prefaced by an explanatory section covering the history, selection procedures, demographics, and politics of the Nobel prize. It should be noted that while the set includes biographical entries for such significant contributors to the field of physics as Niels Bohr, Enrico Fermi, Richard Feynman, Edwin Hubble, Robert Oppenheimer, and Max Planck, living physicists are not covered. Overall, this is a welcome addition to science reference shelves.—**Judith A. Matthews**

1411. Smith, Roger. **Popular Physics and Astronomy: An Annotated Bibliography.** Lanham, Md., Scarecrow and Pasadena, Calif., Salem Press, 1996. 507p. index. (Magill Bibliographies). $64.00. ISBN 0-8108-3149-X.

The allure and fascination with astronomy and its close relative, physics, are as much a part of popular culture as they are of academia. Historically, these sciences were studied by amateurs, so that literature authored by the professionals for public consumption is a natural byproduct of research. Smith has organized the vast array of twentieth-century popular literature on these two sciences in six subject groupings: "Classical Physics," "Relativity," "Atomic Physics," "Astronomy and Cosmology," "From Chaos to Superconductors: Subspecialties," and " 'Meta' Physics." He also devotes a chapter to materials suitable for young readers and another to nonprint materials. The indexing is extensive.

Within each chapter, the author arranges the entries alphabetically by author, followed by standard bibliographic information. For each entry, Smith provides a thorough description of the book or item, with commentary on the author or context in which the original publication was written. Each entry also includes a statement on the level of math presented in each book. In the chapter for young readers, Smith gives the appropriate age group for each entry.

This book could be useful in collection development in a public library, where building a science section is desirable. However, most of the entries are more than 10 years old—some more than 50 years old—so the availability of a majority of the entries will be questionable. It may have been better to arrange the entries chronologically, thereby clustering the more recent and in-print material. This would have given a better overview of the evolution of popular science through the years. Smith's commentaries are insightful and a delight to read. The book stands alone as a good read and is appropriate for any science collection.—**Margaret F. Dominy**

MATHEMATICS

1412. **Combined Membership List 1996-1997: American Mathematical Society, American Mathematical Association of Two-Year Colleges, Mathematical Association of America, [and] Society for Industrial and Applied Mathematics.** Providence, R.I., American Mathematical Society, 1996. 389p. $60.00pa. ISBN 0-8218-0186-4.

The organizations represented in this directory include members of the American Mathematical Society (29,210), the Mathematical Association of America (29,689), the Society for Industrial and Applied Mathematics (8,344), and the American Association of Two-Year Colleges (2,778). The names are broken into two lists. The first is a complete alphabetic list of all members in all four organizations. This section contains the full member entries, which include name, address, title, department, institution, telephone number, electronic address, and in which organizations memberships are held. The second section lists members' names, but organized within geographic categories. There is no categorization by area of specialization.

This will be a valuable resource to anyone interested in identifying and contacting professional mathematicians throughout the United States. However, the typeface size used in the directory is so painfully small that one should be prepared for some serious eyestrain while using it.—**G. Kim Dority**

1413. **CRC Standard Mathematical Tables and Formulae.** 30th ed. Daniel Zwillinger, ed. Boca Raton, Fla., CRC Press, 1996. 812p. index. $39.95. ISBN 0-8493-2479-3.

The *CRC Standard Mathematical Tables* is an old friend to librarians: a compact source of basic mathematical information, priced low enough to be included in any science or technology library or in the personal collection of any serious student. The title was changed for the 29th (1991) edition to *CRC Standard Mathematical Tables and Formulae*, and for this 30th edition (under a new editor), the contents have been significantly reworked. Tables of numerical values readily available on inexpensive pocket calculators (trigonometric functions, logarithms, and the like) are truncated or eliminated. Typeface is larger and more easily read. Many chapters now include a list of references (although perhaps emphasizing publications of CRC Press). More significantly, topics have been somewhat reorganized in the chapters, and many have been added or substantially enlarged, including control theory, group theory, integral equations, queuing theory, and wavelets. Taken together, these changes give the book a more modern feel and in many cases, make it easier to use.

Most libraries will want to add this new edition, although they will probably want to retain earlier edition(s) as well. If there is a quibble, it is that some information not available on pocket calculators has also been truncated. For example, the prime numbers less than 10,000 are listed in this edition, instead of primes under 100,000; it would have been desirable to include a reference to a source of longer listings. Nonetheless, this is a useful set of tables.—**Robert Michaelson**

1414. **MathSci Disc.** [CD-ROM]. Norwood, Mass., SilverPlatter, 1989-1996. 4 discs. Minimum system requirements: IBM or compatible 386. ISO 9660-compatible CD-ROM drive and controller card. 4MB RAM. 8MB hard disk space. VGA monitor. Windows-compatible printer. $4,915.00/yr. (1940+). [Network pricing also available.]

Since January 1996, the American Mathematical Society (AMS) has provided access, via the World Wide Web, to the information available on this CD-ROM. The service, called MathSciNet, is the preferred method of retrieving this indexing of mathematics research literature. It is updated more frequently than *MathSci Disc* and the printed *Mathematical Reviews Annual Index* (American Mathematical Society). The entire database is searchable at once, from the period 1940 to the present. Neither *MathSci Disc* nor MathSciNet has the full text of reviews from 1940-1979 available yet, but the AMS is working on retrospectively adding to the text of the older reviews on the database.

MathSci Disc would still be a valid purchase for institutions that do not have the technical infrastructure to provide access to Internet services. It is also available for online searching via DIALOG for libraries that cannot invest in onsite access. Some institutions have continued their subscriptions to the *MathSci Disc*s as well as MathSciNet because their users have grown accustomed to the SilverPlatter interface. Any institution that grants advanced degrees in mathematics should have access to this index, either on the disc or via the Internet. A demonstration version of the MathSciNet file can be seen at http://msn.mr.arms.org. The site includes a suggestion box.—**Molly White**

36 Resource Sciences

ENERGY RESOURCES

Directories

1415. Crowley, William R. **Oil and Gas on the Internet.** Houston, Tex., Gulf Publishing, 1996. 166p. index. $49.00pa. (with disk). ISBN 0-88415-155-7.

The author has listed more than 700 World Wide Web sites on the Internet that cover the worldwide oil and gas industry with emphasis on the exploration side. These sites include oil and gas companies, service and supply companies, petroleum-related associations and societies, government agencies, and universities and research institutes. Each site listing includes the title of the Webpage along with its specific URL for accessing the page, a description of the information found at each page, and additional links on the page to other similar information. An alphabetic index lists the site titles.

This book is a starting point for either experienced or novice Internet users. The introduction discusses what the Internet is and gives some directions for using it. The author has included chapters on other resources, such as books, journals, newsletters, libraries, Usenet newsgroups, and search engines on the Internet so that the user can pursue other related information. A computer disk containing a "hotlist" of the 740 oil and gas sites is furnished for use through an Internet browser.

No book could possibly list all of the sites for the oil and gas industry. This is a selective directory of the many Webpages on the Internet. It has limited coverage of natural gas sites; petroleum is more emphasized. Every day, new Webpages are added, and it is difficult to keep up with the new sites. The author's inclusion of the search engines for locating items by keywords or subjects is helpful, but there are many other search engines that are not listed. A novice Internet user may find some of the items listed confusing because not all items are defined in the glossary (e.g., search engines and Usenet). This book should be used as a stepping-stone to those oil and gas industry sources on the Internet. [R: Choice, Sept 96, p. 94]—**Anne C. Roess**

1416. **Directory of Power Plant Equipment & Processes, 1996.** Kharma Amos and others, eds. Tulsa, Okla., PennWell Publishing, 1995. 237p. index. $225.00pa.

This directory lists more than 700 turbines. In addition to information about turbines, this directory includes information about boilers, generators, gas turbine frames, Nox controls, burners, cooling systems, instrumentation and control equipment, and other pertinent data items. The purpose of this directory is to provide a complete listing of the types of equipment and processes being used in today's utility and nonutility plants.

The first section of this directory, on utility plants, is organized alphabetically by company name. Each entry includes company addresses, telephone and fax numbers, names of key executives, plant information, and power plant equipment details. The second section, on non-utility plants, is organized alphabetically by state and then by plant name. There is a company index and a personnel index. The page layout is a neat, two-column format, and the typeface is bold and clear. The publisher promises that this directory will be continuously updated. This is a useful reference tool for the power engineering industry.
—**Marilynn Green**

1417. **European Oilfield Service, Supply, & Manufacturers Directory, 1996.** 2d ed. Paul Lewin and others, eds. Tulsa, Okla., PennWell Publishing, 1995. 492p. index. $195.00pa. ISSN 1079-364X.

This directory provides a list of service, supply, and manufacturing companies active in Europe in the ever-changing oil industry. Companies are listed alphabetically within industry segments, such as associations, drilling, exploration, production, or technical services. Most entries consist of a brief company history; contact personnel and addresses; subsidiaries; and branch, district, or division offices. Although the table of contents provides some subject access, a topical index would enhance this source. An alphabetic company index and a domestic and international geographic index help the user find specific firms or locations. The clear layout and use of bold typeface make this an easy-to-use reference. As with many of PennWell's publications, this directory can also be purchased on diskette for personalizing mailing lists. This work will be valuable to any public, academic, or special library providing information on the international oil and petroleum industry.—**Diane J. Turner**

1418. **U.S. Electric Industry Phone and Fax Directory, 1996.** Kharma Amos and others, eds. Tulsa, Okla., PennWell Publishing, 1995. 227p. index. $110.00pa.

Telephone and fax numbers in this new annual from PennWell Publishing are for all companies included in its U.S. Electric Directories database. These same companies are covered in PennWell's much more detailed *Electric Light & Power U.S. Electric Utility Industry Directory* (see ARBA 96, entry 1651) and *Electric Light & Power U.S. Non-Utility Power Directory* (ARBA 96, entry 1652). Utilities, cooperatives, power plants, and electric associations are included here, as are companies of all types that service the electric industry.

Arrangement is alphabetic by state (Guam, Puerto Rico, and the Virgin Islands are also listed), then alphabetic by company name within each state. There are two indexes: a company name index in strict alphabetic order and a hierarchical index. The latter lists parent companies alphabetically, with divisions, branches, or plant sites shown underneath the parent name.

The work is strictly a telephone and fax directory. The city is indicated for each company, but street address and zip code are not provided. Organizations and individuals involved in various aspects of the electric industry should find this publication to be a useful and handy reference. Subscribers to the other PennWell directories mentioned above, however, may not feel the need for this new directory of reformatted information.—**William H. Wiese**

1419. **Worldwide Offshore Contractors & Equipment Directory, 1996.** 28th ed. Jonelle Guy and Pat Jackson, eds. Tulsa, Okla., PennWell Publishing, 1996. 587p. index. $165.00pa. ISSN 0475-1310.

This work is among 20 directories published and updated by PennWell Publishing on the subjects of oil, gas, and electrical companies and resources. The fairly high price tag and limited audience somewhat narrow the immediate usefulness of this reference resource specifically to petroleum corporations and equipment manufacturers. However, this guide may also have a place in specialized academic, business, and larger public libraries serving patrons who either work in or study the offshore petroleum industry and who may also be concerned with the industry's impact upon the environment. The clearly stated purpose of the directory is to provide a complete listing of all contractors and equipment involved in the petroleum industry. Coverage is worldwide and appears comprehensive, thereby providing an excellent snapshot of all players in the industry.

Ten kinds of firms are listed: drilling contractors and rig owners, workover and well servicing, construction contractors, geophysical contractors, diving contractors, transportation, exploration and production, service companies, supply companies, and manufacturers. Firms are alphabetically arranged under each of these listings with key information such as telephone, fax, and telex numbers; cable; key personnel; brief descriptions of company activities; and company equipment included. The text is followed by three useful, alphabetically arranged indexes listing companies, geographic location, and equipment.

—**James M. Murray**

Handbooks and Yearbooks

1420. **Electric Power in Asia and the Pacific, 1991 and 1992.** By the Economic and Social Commission for Asia and the Pacific. New York, United Nations, 1995. 108p. $25.00pa. ISBN 92-1-119715-5. ISSN 0252-4406. S/N E.96.II.F.23.

This highly specialized serial focuses on electric power capabilities and resources of responding countries in Asia and the Pacific for the years 1991 and 1992. It was initially published annually from 1951 to 1970, and since 1971 it has been published biennially, covering two-year increments. The limited focus of this resource likely makes it more useful to larger, urban public or academic library collections, with holdings that may include the complete set of this document, and that serve users with an ongoing interest in the subject of the international uses of electric power sources. Specialists such as economists, researchers, historians, and electrical engineers with an emphasis in the area of international electric resources may also find that this work is most helpful. However, the dated nature of the statistical information may require some researchers to acquire more up-to-date information elsewhere from, for example, the contributing organizations mentioned below, or by searching the Internet for any publicly available information.

The work is detailed and statistical. It begins with explanatory notes and exchange rates. The text consists of 17 statistical tables covering such matters as major power plants completed, voltages and frequencies employed, generation of electricity by type and ownership of power plants, revenue, water power potential development, and comparative electricity bills. The tables are followed by a helpful list of contributing organizations and their authorities, which are arranged under an alphabetic list of countries in which the information has been made available.—**James M. Murray**

1421. **Electric Power Industry Yearbook, 1996.** Tulsa, Okla., PennWell Publishing, 1996. 204p. illus. $95.00. ISBN 0-87814-475-7.

This work is intended to provide an overview of the major issues facing the electric power industry. It consists primarily of reprints of articles from power industry trade journals. The major themes of the 39 articles include technological developments, trends in the power industry related to deregulation, utility spending, management, and financial performance. International topics encompass power demand and construction of new dams and generators. There are many tables, graphs, and figures that provide useful information on industry economics and technological issues. Despite being written for trade journals, this compilation will be of interest to a variety of readers and will answer many questions regarding regulation, key industry players, markets, and engineering and pollution control.—**T. McKimmie**

1422. **Electric Power Statistics Sourcebook.** 3d ed. Sandra Meyer and others, eds. Tulsa, Okla., PennWell Publishing, 1995. 672p. $263.00pa. ISSN 1070-843X.

From the publisher of a wide variety of energy journals, directories, and other energy-related statistical references, Electric Power Statistics Sourcebook is a relatively new annual that began in 1993. Related publications from PennWell Publishing include *Electric Light & Power U.S. Electric Utility Industry Directory* (see ARBA 96, entry 1651) and *Electric Light & Power U.S. Non-Utility Power Directory* (see ARBA 96, entry 1652). Statistics on electric power generation, consumption, sales, prices, and facilities are provided for the United States as a whole, as well as for individual states, by way of several hundred tables. A few charts are also included. Little information is furnished for countries other than the United States. For many of the tables, 10, 20, or more years of data are reported, allowing the user to readily make comparisons and spot trends. Statistics are derived from PennWell's own database and from government sources.

As an example of the information available, one can find figures for total electricity generated by New York in January 1995 and compare them with January 1994, and compare these in turn with Pennsylvania or Florida for the same months and years. One can see how much of this generated electricity came from coal, petroleum, natural gas, nuclear, and hydroelectric power, and can find expenditures by the states in each of these categories from 1970 to the present.

This publication should serve as a valuable and handy reference for the electric power industry and anyone else needing the information. The statistical tables can also be purchased individually on diskette in Lotus 1-2-3 format.—**William H. Wiese**

1423. **Energy Balances for Europe and North America, 1992, 1993-2010. Balances Energetiques pour L'Europe et L'Amerique du Nord.** By the Economic Commission for Europe. New York, United Nations, 1996. 268p. $54.00pa. ISBN 92-1-000053-6. S/N GV.E/F.96.0.5.

This book gives statistics and projections for energy production and consumption for the countries of Europe and North America for the years 1992, 1993, 1995, and projected for 2000, 2005, and 2010. It also provides four regional balances for Western Europe, Central and Eastern Europe, North America, and the Economic Commission for Europe (ECE) region as a whole. As such, it will be of interest to larger business, science, and environment collections. The introduction indicates tersely that the figures in this document are based on a database containing information on energy use and consumption from 1960 to 1990 for developed countries, and from 1965 to 1990 for the transition countries of the former Iron Curtain region as supplemented by other (unspecified) sources of information. This seems to imply that most or all of the figures provided are projections, without explicitly saying so.

After detailed explanatory notes, the main body of the work is divided into an alphabetic grouping of tables by country for the six years projected. After the country balance tables, the same information is given by region. Then there is a series of summary tables listing consumption and production in all the countries treated. Each balance table lists imports, exports, consumption, and production, and breaks the figures down into type of energy source from solid fuels through steam, hot water, and other sources of energy. For 12 countries (mostly within the former Soviet Union and Yugoslavia) and the regions except North America, figures for 1995 and beyond are not included.

This is a useful work, although the apparent basing of the projections on relatively old statistics will obviously diminish its authority. Still, it should be considered by larger collections in science, business, and environment as a potentially useful acquisition.—**Nigel Tappin**

ENVIRONMENTAL SCIENCE

Bibliography

1424. Dwyer, Jim. **Earth Works: Recommended Fiction and Nonfiction About Nature and the Environment for Adults and Young Adults.** New York, Neal-Schuman, 1996. 507p. index. $39.95pa. ISBN 1-55570-194-9.

This annotated bibliography contains 2,601 entries for books relating to the environment and nature. These are separated by reading level for adults and young adults. There are seven categories of nonfiction works. "Specific Environments" includes titles on climate, biomes, parks, and land use issues. "Activities and Issues" contains books on agriculture, energy, waste, and water issues. "Cultural Factors" covers politics, Native Americans, and developing countries. Other sections are "General Works," such as encyclopedias, dictionaries, almanacs, and texts; "Philosophy and Nature Writing"; "Environmental Action"; and "Natural History." Approximately one-third of the entries are works of fiction. Here, the categories include "Literary Anthologies," "Animals," "Frontier and Pioneer Life," "The New West," "Ecofeminist Fiction," "Fantasy," and "Environmental Action."

The introduction to *Earth Works* recognizes the environmental crises facing the planet and the large number of books appearing on the subject. Following sections include preliminary statements placing that section in context. Annotations are brief but informative. The author, a librarian, wished to assist readers in finding relevant information and encourage environmental responsibility. About two-thirds of the works were published in the 1990s, but many classic works are included as well. The author considers all the books listed here to be recommended reading. Some works were excluded as being too technical, obsolete, or inaccurate. Author, title, and subject indexes are furnished. The work is thorough, and the author has succeeded in providing access to important books. [R: Choice, Sept 96, p. 95; EL, May/June 96, p. 42; LJ, 15 May 96, p. 53; RBB, 15 April 96, p. 1458; SLMQ, Summer 96, p. 221]—**T. McKimmie**

Dictionaries and Encyclopedias

1425. Coffel, Steve. **Encyclopedia of Garbage.** New York, Facts on File, 1996. 311p. illus. index. $60.00. ISBN 0-8160-3135-5.

Intended for general readers and students from middle school to the undergraduate level, this reference tool is a useful addition to public, school, and academic libraries. It serves as a broad but brief and straightforward introduction to the subject of waste in all its forms, the hazards of waste, and the current and proposed methods for handling it. Researchers and specialists in the field of waste management and the environment, however, will have to rely on other, more specialized reference tools and detailed works, because this work merely provides the reader with a general understanding of the subject matter.

The text is easy to read and understand, and subjects are alphabetically arranged. *See* and *see also* references are used to assist the reader in expanding upon an inquiry. Occasional diagrams, sketches, tables, and charts are interspersed throughout the text in order to enhance the definitions and the explanation and meaning of the various subjects. The body of this resource is preceded by a helpful introduction, and it is followed by a useful index.—**James M. Murray**

1426. **Conservation and Environmentalism: An Encyclopedia.** Robert Paehlke, ed. New York, Garland, 1995. 771p. index. $95.00. ISBN 0-8240-6101-2.

This is an excellent general reference work that covers a broad range of environmental topics at a technical level appropriate for those with relatively little background in science. The editor has done a fine job of organizing comprehensive coverage of environmental problems, especially the philosophical and ethical aspects. There are more than 500 entries offering concise discussions of important environmental issues; brief histories of many governmental offices, publications, and private organizations concerned with environmental problems; the individuals who have played an important role in these organizations; and locations that have special environmental significance. The main geographic focus is on North America, Great Britain, Australia, and New Zealand.

Many environmental books have a narrow focus or go into too much detail for nonprofessionals. Thus, this approach should be especially welcome as a resource for the general public. The presentation is well organized to help those wishing to pursue further information about a topic. Each entry includes further readings and cross-references, and there is a helpful index at the end of the book. This encyclopedia is a useful resource, and it should be seriously considered for purchase. [R: RBB, 15 Feb 96, pp. 1040-42]
—**Harry E. Pence**

1427. **The Grolier Library of Environmental Concepts and Issues.** Danbury, Conn., Grolier, 1996. 8v. illus. maps. index. $249.00/set. ISBN 0-7172-7518-3.

The Grolier Library of Environmental Concepts and Issues is not really an encyclopedia but more of a series of mini-textbooks, each dealing with a specific segment of the environment. Starting with the broad topic "Ecosystem Earth" and going through various resources such as water, air, and energy, the reader can learn about the Earth and its people. Within each volume, readers will find chapters on specific aspects of that particular resource. For example, in the volume on living resources, chapters dealing with topics such as farming techniques and soil are found. This method provides for an interdisciplinary approach and makes the text very readable. It also allows an educator to work on a specific topic from a number of angles, providing students with the opportunity to see the whole picture. The final volume pulls all the topics together, showing the interrelations between all parts of the environment.

There is an index in each volume, and the final volume has a cumulative index as well as a glossary of selected terms. Photographs and diagrams illustrate various concepts, and "envirobits" provide interesting sidebars of information. The series should prove a useful springboard for a school's environmental program. [R: BR, Sept/Oct 96, p. 58; SLJ, Aug 96, p. 181]—**Angela Marie Thor**

Directories

1428. **Co-op America's National Green Pages: A Directory of Products and Services for People and the Planet.** 1996 ed. Washington, D.C., Co-op America, 1995. 152p. illus. index. $5.95pa.; free with membership ($20.00/individual; $60.00/business). ISSN 1064-8729.

Co-op America's National Green Pages 1996 edition is the 4th and largest directory of socially and environmentally responsible businesses. Co-op America, a nonprofit, tax-exempt corporation devoted to promoting social justice and environmental responsibility, compiles this directory. Members receive the directory free of charge, while nonmembers can purchase it for $5.95. Co-op America screens all of the businesses and products in the directory according to their commitment to solving environmental issues and creativity in working with employees, consumers, and government toward a healthy quality of life. Co-op America clearly states its mission and organizational structure at the beginning of the directory.

Suggestions for living and working in a manner that will sustain the planet follow the introduction. All of the information is attractively arranged with appropriate graphics enhancing the text. Further planet-saving tips appear throughout the directory in the listings. All listings are arranged alphabetically under similarly organized subjects. Cross-references refer the reader to other listings. Each entry includes the business name in bold typeface, followed by a short description of the product, and ends with its complete address and telephone number. Alphabetic and state/city indexes finish the directory. All businesses are included. It would assist the reader to have the subject headings in the alphabetic index. A table of contents at the front of the directory showing the subject headings would also be useful.

Co-op America's National Green Pages is a practical resource for the environmentally concerned consumer. Even the advertisements in this directory relate to environmental issues.—**Marjorie H. Jones**

1429. **A Directory of Environmental Electronic Mail Users in Eurasia.** 4th ed. Petersham, Mass., Sacred Earth Network, 1996. 81p. index. $20.00 spiralbound.

A project of the Sacred Earth Network (SEN), a nonprofit educational organization of environmentalists founded in 1985, this directory is intended as a comprehensive reference to help organizations and individuals communicate with like-minded souls in Eurasia. To this end, the work identifies and provides the e-mail address, other contact information, and areas of interest for some 425 environmental groups found in such locales as Murmansk, Dzhambul, and Magnitogorsk, as well as the better-known Moscow and Saint Petersburg.

The directory provides extended entries for 160 of these groups, noting the "approaches" taken to further the goals of the organization (e.g., what publications, outreach efforts, teaching programs, and so forth are supported by each). The entries are organized alphabetically by country, with alternative access provided by the group name and individual contact names listed in the index. Unfortunately, the index does not include subject access. Nevertheless, the compilers are to be commended for undertaking what is obviously a labor of love born out of a commitment to saving the Earth.—**G. Kim Dority**

1430. **Environmental Telephone Directory.** 1996 ed. Edited by the Editorial Staff of Government Institutes. Rockville, Md., Government Institutes, 1996. 281p. $65.00pa. ISBN 0-86587-504-9.

Environmental Telephone Directory lists names, addresses, and telephone numbers for thousands of U.S. federal and state officials who are involved, to one extent or another, with environmental issues. Most of the information in this directory can be found in such standard sources as *The Federal Yellow Book* (see ARBA 95, entry 727) and *State Administrative Officials Classified by Function* (National Council of State Governments), but having so much information all in one volume will be useful for environmental researchers in academia, government, and business. One especially useful feature of *Environmental Telephone Directory* is its listing of the sometimes hard-to-find names and addresses for Senate and House environmental aides. While the directory is well organized, more imaginative use of running headings would make it easier to find one's place when flipping pages. The editors have scattered a few URLs throughout the directory, but the 1997 edition would be much improved by the inclusion of e-mail addresses and more URLs. Libraries with heavy traffic in environmental questions will want the directory. Other libraries can get along without it, especially if they have a good selection of general government directories or access to the Internet.—**Donald A. Barclay**

1431. **The Sierra Club Green Guide: Everybody's Desk Reference to Environmental Information.** By Andrew J. Feldman. San Francisco, Calif., Sierra Club Books; distr., New York, Random House, 1996. 282p. index. $25.00pa. ISBN 0-87156-402-5.

Green is a growing trend, but finding information can be difficult. With *The Sierra Club Green Guide*, users can find some of the best sources for greening their life, all in one spot. Information on all aspects of the environment and green living is given. Each chapter covers a different topic, from agriculture to green travel. A brief abstract of what's covered starts a chapter, then lists of government clearinghouses, organizations, Internet sites, commercial online services, bulletin boards, directories, and other printed reference materials are presented. There is a description for each of the 1,200 entries, along with directory information.

The information sought is easy to find. The index lists the organizations and subjects, and the table of contents acts as a broad subject index for those who like to browse. There are also cross-references from the entries to help expand the search.

This is not a comprehensive listing. Sources were evaluated and chosen as being vital or leading to other sources of relevant information. Also, with online sites being so volatile, some of the entries were obsolete before this book was even published. Nevertheless, it should prove to be a handy tool at the reference desk. [R: RBB, Aug 96, p. 1926]—**Angela Marie Thor**

1432. **World Directory of Country Environmental Studies: An Annotated Bibliography of Natural Resource Profiles, Plans, and Strategies.** 3d ed. Sean Gordon and Daniel B. Tunstall, eds. Washington, D.C., World Resources Institute, 1995. 272p. index. $24.95pa. ISBN 1-56973-095-4.

The introduction to the *World Directory of Country Environmental Studies* notes that "virtually every country of the world has prepared at least one report on its environment." However, the compilers also comment that these reports often do not make their way to commercial publishers for widespread distribution. This volume, the 3d edition since 1990, covers 181 countries and territories in 414 country and regional environmental studies. Reports selected for inclusion had to: be countrywide or regional in coverage; address environment and natural resource issues; include supporting numerical, tabular, and map data; be useful to policy-makers and development planners; be timely (issued since 1990); and be available publicly. Some countries are represented by less timely reports if no others were available.

The organization mainly responsible for the preparation of this annotated bibliography is the World Resources Institute (WRI). WRI helped to establish the International Environmental and Natural Resource Assessment Information Service (INTERAISE), the project that has planned for gathering and disseminating environmental information to policy-makers around the world, in part by maintaining the database on which this directory is based. The project will continue to expand the database of country environmental studies, and may make more use of electronic communications in the future. In addition to this print version, the database of the directory, comprising all three editions, is available on CD-ROM with keyword search capability for IBM-compatible machines, and on the Internet at WRI's Website (http://www.wri.org).

The bibliography entries cover reports in multiple languages and give basic bibliographic information and a thorough 150- to 200-word annotation. Information on availability is supplied for all reports, and in the event of a report being out-of-print, details are given for ordering copies from the United States Agency for International Development (USAID). The annotations highlight the environmental findings and proposed actions described in the reports, and thus are extremely useful in providing brief sketches of material not widely available. The *World Directory of Country Environmental Studies* is recommended as a useful ready-reference tool for locating international environmental reports, but also as a source of brief information on environmental profiles, plans, and strategies in the countries and regions described. The audience for this work will include environment and development policy professionals and graduate students and faculty in these areas.—**Jean C. McManus**

Handbooks and Yearbooks

1433. **Book of Lists for Regulated Hazardous Substances 1996.** By the Editorial Staff of Government Institutes. Rockville, Md., Government Institutes, 1996. 1v. (various paging). $99.00pa. ISBN 0-86587-520-0.

The recognition, regulation, and control of hazardous substances, as well as the mitigation of their environmental impacts, have become a major U.S. industry. This is especially true since both federal and state governments have accepted a mandate for responsibility for such regulation and have produced a comprehensive body of often-amended legislation. The resultant complexities have created a veritable jungle of chemical terms and environmental, health, and safety data through which the "regulated community" must wander in search of factual information crucial to ensuring compliance.

This volume attempts to simplify the process by providing under one cover the various relevant lists frequently referenced in compliance and implementation literature. Lists attached to such key federal legislation as the Resource Conservation and Recovery Act; the Comprehensive Environmental Response, Compensation, and Liability Act (or "Superfund"); the Clean Air Act; the Clean Water Act; the Safe Drinking Water Act; the Occupational Safety and Health Act; the Toxic Substances Control Act; and the Federal Insecticide, Fungicide, and Rodenticide Act are included, as are the hazardous chemicals listed in California's Proposition 65. The lists are provided exactly as they appear in the various publications, without editorial comment, but with appropriate references (for example, Chemical Abstracts numbers). This is scarcely a book of general interest, but it should prove an invaluable resource for any industries and agencies struggling to comply with current environmental law. [R: Choice, June 96, p. 1626]—**James R. McDonald**

1434. **Cooper's Comprehensive Environmental Desk Reference.** André R. Cooper Sr., comp and ed. New York, Van Nostrand Reinhold, 1996. 1039p. index. $99.95. ISBN 0-442-02159-3.

Cooper's Comprehensive Environmental Desk Reference, by the president of a national environmental consulting firm, is a good handbook of environmental information. The book is divided into eight sections. The first 2 sections contain definitions for more than 10,000 words, phrases, acronyms, and abbreviations. The definitions of the words and phrases are clear and concise. The other sections contain a sample Phase 1 environmental site assessment, the Hazardous Air Pollutants list (including CAS number), data conversion factors, a list of chemical elements, information on the offices of the Environmental Protection Agency (EPA) (both national and regional) and its programs, and an environmental jargon finder by topic. The book also comes with a spell check disk (WordPerfect for Windows 5.0) that includes the terminology covered in the volume.

Although a useful volume, there are some drawbacks. In the brief introduction, the author notes that a wide variety of references were used in the compilation of the book. However, no references are cited. The author also notes that many acts were consulted; however, he only lists the various acts by acronym. The complete name of the act is found in the acronyms and abbreviations section, but proper citation should have been given. The information on the EPA's offices and programs does not contain e-mail addresses or reference to an Internet location. Both would have been useful additions.

The book is recommended for college, university, and special libraries that support programs on environmental concerns. An earlier volume by the author, Cooper's Pocket Environmental Compliance Dictionary (Van Nostrand Reinhold, 1995), covers much of the same material (more than 4,500 definitions and acronyms) and would be an adequate substitution for many libraries. [R: Choice, Oct 96, p. 249]
—**James E. Bird**

1435. Newton, David E. **Environmental Justice: A Reference Handbook.** Santa Barbara, Calif., ABC-CLIO, 1996. 271p. index. (Contemporary World Issues). $39.50. ISBN 0-87436-848-0.

The coincidences of environmental degradation and poverty are numerous and often obvious: Migrant farmworkers and agricultural chemicals; urban blight and the toxic wastes of deteriorating industries; health problems and the pollution of local water supplies. Yet much mainstream environmental interest seems concerned with the preservation of wilderness areas and species diversity; as usual, few voices speak for the poor. This contradiction has given rise to the environmental justice movement in the United States, whose aims and approaches are summarized in this latest contribution to the Contemporary World Issues series.

This is an advocacy book, rather than a purely reference volume. Its first third consists of a modestly documented history and chronology of the environmental justice idea, along with biographical sketches of 19 pioneering activists in the field. What should be the heart of the work, a section on relevant laws, treaties, bills, and executive orders, is in fact only a series of selected excerpts and quotations from the vast body of such materials. Of much greater value are the directory of organizations concerned with environmental justice (including contact information) and the annotated bibliographies of print and nonprint resources. There are also a glossary, a list of acronyms, and an overall index.

The author's style is light and accessible, if often abrasive, while the various recommendations and "calls to action" are painfully simplistic. Nonetheless, for groups or individuals interested in understanding the background of the environmental justice movement, and perhaps working toward its goals, this book may be a useful starting point.—**James R. McDonald**

1436. Pohanish, Richard P., and Stanley A. Greene. **Hazardous Materials Handbook.** New York, Van Nostrand Reinhold, 1996. 1792p. index. $149.95. ISBN 0-442-02212-3.

This handbook covers approximately 1,300 hazardous chemicals found in the industrial workplace and frequently transported in bulk. Entries are arranged alphabetically by common chemical name and average a little more than one page in length. Each chemical record contains 15 data fields.

The synonyms field lists various scientific and trade names, as well as identification numbers such as RTECS or RCRA, that would be useful to safety personnel. These names are conveniently indexed for cross-referencing. The identification field lists the proper shipping name according to 49 CFR as well as the CAS number and DOT ID number. A labeling field describes label requirements, and a shipping information field discusses the normal procedures for bulk shipping. The hazard classifications field denotes the hazard rating for fire, health, water pollution, and reactivity hazards. Separate fields for each of these hazards describe the type of danger posed by the chemical, symptoms of exposure, and protective equipment required. Emergency response and response to discharge fields describe the proper authorities to notify, treatment of exposure, and other steps to be taken when discharge occurs.

Other fields include physical and chemical properties, chemical reactivity, environmental data, and observable characteristics. A section, "Guide to Compatibility of Chemicals," divides chemicals into reactivity groups and features a table that allows determination of the relative hazard when one group is accidentally mixed with another. A CAS number index and bibliography are included. While not intended to be a comprehensive source, this handbook provides important data, is easy to use, and the information is accessible. It is recommended.—**T. McKimmie**

37 Transportation

GENERAL WORKS

1437. **The ABC-CLIO Companion to Transportation in America.** By William L. Richter. Santa Barbara, Calif., ABC-CLIO, 1995. 653p. illus. index. (ABC-CLIO Companions to Key Issues in American History and Life). $55.00. ISBN 0-87436-789-1.

Part of the ABC-CLIO Companions to Key Issues in American History and Life series, *Transportation in America* presents hundreds of entries on all sorts of transportation modes and issues. Using a two-column format, entries range in length from a short paragraph (e.g., Big Medicine Trail, National Rail Passenger Act of 1971, Route 66) to several pages (Russell, Majors, and Waddell Company; intermodal freight; roads and highways, divided into pre- and post-World War I sections). The introduction (some 18 pages, plus 7 pages of bibliographic notes) gives an overview of transportation development. There are brief *see also* references after each entry, and a 46-page bibliography. There is also an 18-page chronology, from prehistory to 1994. The index is useful, but not really comprehensive. The few illustrations are of poor quality for the most part. The biographical entries emphasize the person's major contribution to the development of transportation in the United States. There are some curious omissions: The Van Swerengen brothers and Charles F. Kettering are missing, but Alfred P. Sloan Jr. and Ralph Nader are included. In sum, this is truly a companion, not an encyclopedia, well written and generally interesting. The details of many governmental policies and actions, here placed in context, should make the work useful in larger collections. [R: Choice, Mar 96, p. 1104; SLJ, May 96, p. 146]
—**Walter C. Allen**

AIR

1438. **Brassey's World Aircraft & Systems Directory 1996/97.** Michael Taylor and others, eds. McLean, Va., Brassey's (U.S.), 1996. 672p. illus. index. $99.95. ISBN 1-57488-063-2.

The aircraft coverage in this expansive international directory is not limited to standard jet and propeller airplanes, but includes the full range of combat and reconnaissance aircraft, helicopters and autogiros, general and recreational aircraft and gliders, and buoyant airships (dirigibles). Under each of these major groupings, the aircraft are arranged first by country of origin, then by company, then by model. In most cases, the company is described briefly; then for each model, data such as the developmental history, first flight and certification, first delivery, sales, crew required, passenger configurations or other capacities, and the many details and variations possible for the model are detailed. The listings include aircraft no longer manufactured but that are still in service, as well as previews and descriptions of proposed aircraft. Because the majority of entries are for currently manufactured aircraft, it is a disadvantage that a still-popular U.S. aircraft such as the Boeing 727 merits only a paragraph and the wide-body Lockheed L-1011 is not even mentioned. This work is not an encyclopedia but rather a directory of what is available or what will be available. There are numerous photographs and other illustrations on every page, and the tables that compare features of related models help clarify similarities and differences.

In addition to the expected aircraft types, a separate section lists missiles and airborne radar under country and manufacturer. An extensive table of engines, again arranged by country, then manufacturer, provides data and specifies the common uses of each engine. The alphabetic index to the contents is an essential feature and is reasonably complete; on occasion, the user needs to hunt for the exact entrée point, but it is otherwise effective. Two bonus features are a worldwide directory of airports noting the [weight] bearing capacity, length, and directional orientation of the longest runway, and the color insignias of the world's air forces on the endpapers.

This work will be well received in any library where there is an interest in aviation on a range of levels from the engineer to the hobbyist. The similarity to *Jane's All the World's Aircraft* (see entry 1440) is apparent; there are few differences. Either could be improved by broadening the scope to include more information on aircraft that are no longer manufactured but are still in service.—**Gary R. Cocozzoli**

1439. **Jane's Air Traffic Control 1996-97.** 3d ed. David F. Rider, ed. Alexandria, Va., Jane's Information Group, 1996. 324p. illus. maps. index. $295.00. ISBN 0-7106-1371-7.

Jane's Air Traffic Control is a reference on the technology, equipment, and companies involved in air traffic control (ATC). It covers every aspect of ATC in an easy-to-use format, including ATC systems, training equipment, communication, navigational and landing aids, airfield lighting, management hardware and software, and more than 500 suppliers of ATC-related technology. Each system or piece of equipment is described with manufacturer information, specifications, and evaluations. Many entries have illustrations and a "status" section that lists who the product was sold to recently, making it a valuable tool for researching equipment to purchase. The index allows the reader to find specific companies or equipment quickly. This reference also provides information on current worldwide trends in the field, and is a usable resource for students and aviation/ATC professionals.—**John Kirton**

1440. **Jane's All the World's Aircraft 1996-97.** 87th ed. Paul Jackson and others, eds. Alexandria, Va., Jane's Information Group, 1996. 838p. illus. index. $335.00. ISBN 0-7106-1377-6.

1441. **Jane's Avionics 1996-97.** 15th ed. Chris Johnson, ed. Alexandria, Va., Jane's Information Group, 1996. 658p. illus. index. $290.00. ISBN 0-7106-1367-9.

The world's aircraft and aerospace industry is never static. New companies with newly designed aircraft continue to appear, whereas older, classic companies such as Fokker Aviation have declared bankruptcy. *Jane's All the World's Aircraft*, however, continues to go on reflecting in detail the commercial production of all known powered aircraft. Now in its 87th year of issue, this book is also changing, adding, revising, and subtracting new entries, photographs, drawings, and diagrams. Approximately 85 percent of the entries have been updated in this edition. A major change to be noted this year has been the removal of the section on aeroengines to be placed in its own separate directory (see entry 1298). The detailed data on individual aircraft, as well as the inclusion of commercial and military aircraft, lighter-than-air, and air-launched missiles continues. While the target for this work is aircraft/aerospace companies and businesses, aviation buffs may want this edition for the last appearance of venerable Fokker aircraft as well as the introduction of new Uninhabited Tactical Aircraft (UTA), such as the McDonnell Douglas unmanned X-36 whose technology may someday revolutionize aviation as it is now known.

As aircraft become increasingly sophisticated and greater demands for safety are heard, reliance on electronics for communications, data processing, management, and displays is increasing. Many of the older electronic systems are becoming obsolete and newer systems have been introduced to meet present-day needs. *Jane's Avionics* is published as a directory of what is currently available off the shelf. This edition has undergone a comprehensive weeding-out of items now out of production but still in service. So that users can still have ready-reference to them, a complete list of deletions is given. With the initiative of the new Communication, Navigation and Surveillance/Air Traffic Management system (CNS/ATM) or so-called Free Flight concept, major changes and upgrades in avionics are expected, and this series will be the primary source for all new and upgraded equipment. Both volumes are available in CD-ROM format.—**Robert J. Havlik**

1442. **Jane's Helicopter Markets and Systems.** Günter Endres, ed. Alexandria, Va., Jane's Information Group, 1996. 1v. (various paging). illus. index. $750.00 looseleaf w/binder. ISBN 0-7106-1363-6.

In an effort to recover from a major slump in both civil and military helicopter sales, the world's primary helicopter operating nations—the United States, Russia, Canada, Japan, and France—are increasingly allocating their dollars to the helicopter industry. As the editor notes, "The United States and Canada are now considered a mature market, with future sales forecast to be almost entirely geared to meeting the demand for replacement machines." According to the Aerospace Industries Association (AIA), U.S. helicopter manufacturers have suffered declines in both civil and military markets. At the same time, the number of workers employed in the helicopter industry are diminishing. The editor focuses on two issues facing the world today: the wholesale establishment of nationwide heliports and a major revival of offshore oil and gas exploration activities. Endres concludes that the overall market decline has dissipated and that technological advancements will provide the industry with a considerable boost.

Country-by-country, *Jane's Helicopter Markets and Systems* provides a consistent and comparable guide to civil and military helicopters, speed, dimensions, design, and sales potential, plus new structural developments, manufacturing systems, and operational status. On the manufacturing side, major programs have been implemented to overhaul, repair, and refurbish several older models. A manufacturer's directory puts the reader in contact with more than 70 companies. Entries include contact names; titles; senior personnel; addresses; and telephone, fax, and telex numbers. An alphabetic index is included as well. *Jane's Helicopter Markets and Systems* is a complete guide to the global helicopter industry. This new reference source is divided into 10 main sections illustrated with more than 1,000 photographs and line drawings. It is recommended for engineers, marketing consultants, NASA scientific and technical libraries, medical libraries in hospitals supporting an EMS unit, and technical libraries connected to air force bases.—**Marilynn Green**

GROUND

1443. **The Eurail Guide to Train Travel in the New Europe, 1996.** New York, Houghton Mifflin, 1996. 668p. maps. index. $14.95pa. ISBN 0-395-75658-8. ISSN 0085-0330.

Designed to suit the needs of rail travelers in Eastern and Western Europe, Great Britain, and Ireland, this compact, geographically arranged guide provides descriptions and prices for more than 800 trips. Sight-seeing notes on hundreds of cities, information on pass options and Eurail pass combinations, international rail connections, and outlines of scenic journeys in 36 countries are all here in a user-friendly format. Key features for safe and uncomplicated rail travel warn travelers to check and recheck departure and arrival times, prices, station information, and so on. Divided into nine chapters, the book includes short essays on how to appreciate train travel, Eurail route charts, how to plan an itinerary and secure hotel reservations, car-sleeper accommodations, tips on overcoming jet lag, recovering lost money and passports, how to travel in non-Eurail pass European countries, and many other gems for world travelers. Route charts; pricing information; and an index of cities, resorts, and places of interest conclude the volume. Occasional illustrations amplify the text. Translation guides for key terms relating to rail travel in several countries and customs and duty-free shopping tips are a welcome addition.

Schedule information is clear and well presented for easy reading, and the route charts and fares are essential. Order forms to secure European rail passes conclude the book. Clearly suitable for all travel collections, and particularly for public libraries, this book is highly recommended.—**Judy Gay Matthews**

1444. **The Eurail Guide to World Train Travel, 1996.** 26th ed. New York, Houghton Mifflin, 1996. 972p. maps. $18.95pa. ISBN 0-395-75657-X. ISSN 0085-0330.

Although geographic coverage of this guidebook has long expanded from those Western European countries whose national railroad systems participate in the Eurail pass program (an outstanding bargain for travelers from outside the region) to encompass the passenger trains of the whole world, there is still a strong emphasis on the 17 Eurail pass countries, with approximately half the book treating that region. After a short introductory section covering the basics of rail travel, the majority of the book consists of geographically arranged, country-by-country accounts, including brief general tourist information on the country and a few selected major cities; an overview of the railroad system (including summary information on fare structures, but not precise dollars and cents data); and itineraries (including condensed timetables and descriptive text) for major intercity routes and suggested excursions. The emphasis is on the national systems, but in such countries as Switzerland, where there are numerous independent lines serving major tourist destinations, these lines are included. Urban rapid transit and commuter services are excluded; however, some information on bus and boat connections is provided. While not every passenger train in the world is treated, coverage is extensive and as timely as is possible in an annual publication; however, schedules do change without warning. Reasonably priced and compact enough to fit into any traveler's luggage, this guide is suitable for all popular travel collections.—**Paul B. Cors**

1445. Foster, Gerald L. **A Field Guide to Trains of North America.** New York, Houghton Mifflin, 1996. 146p. illus. index. $14.95pa. ISBN 0-395-70112-0.

A Field Guide to Trains of North America is a railroad fan guide to diesel locomotives and to their visual identification. Publications of this type are important because many of the numerous models of diesel locomotives used in the United States during the past 60 years are difficult to distinguish from one another. The book is organized on the basis of the appearance of the locomotives rather than by manufacturer or date. For example, all road switchers with high hoods and six axles are grouped together. This approach vastly simplifies the job of identifying unknown engines. Entries for individual types of locomotives (or groups of nearly identical models) include brief technical and historical data, plus clues to identification. The locomotives are illustrated with unusually fine drawings, including illustrations both of entire engines and of details essential to identification.

The book is in some ways similar to a pocket bird guide, with arrows used to call attention to key features on the drawings, and a "life list" checklist at the rear. In addition to covering diesels, the book contains a few pages of material on electric locomotives, passenger cars, and freight cars. The coverage of cars in particular is painfully superficial and completely out of keeping with the rest of the book; it gives the impression of having been added after the book was written merely to justify calling it *A Field Guide to Trains* rather than *A Field Guide to Diesel Locomotives*.

Louis Marre's *The Contemporary Diesel Spotter's Guide* (2d ed.; see ARBA 96, entry 1889) and *Diesel Locomotives: The First Fifty Years* (Kalmbach Publishing, 1996) cover similar ground. These volumes are vastly more detailed and complete than Foster's. Marre is the expert in the field, and his books form the standard reference work on U.S. diesel locomotives. However, Foster's book has several strong points. In particular, his use of simplified drawings rather than photographs may help to clarify essential details, and his concentration on pointing out key "spotting" characteristics should prove helpful.
—**Frederick A. Schlipf**

1446. Norris, John R., and Joann Norris. **The Historic Railroad: A Guide to Museums, Depots, and Excursions in the United States.** Jefferson, N.C., McFarland, 1996. 207p. illus. index. $28.50pa. ISBN 0-7864-0040-4.

The Historic Railroad is a guidebook for people who wish to visit the many railroad museums and operating tourist railroads in the United States. It provides useful information on approximately 300 of these sites. The book is organized alphabetically by state, and within states, alphabetically by the name of the attraction. Entries for individual attractions range from approximately 50 to 600 words in length. They contain brief historical comments, lists of equipment, descriptions of excursions, information on opening times and costs, and addresses and telephone numbers. The entries combine interesting narratives with useful tourist information. A short index provides access by site name, by railroad name, by associated tourist events, and by films shot at the site, but not by place-name.

This publication has much the same focus as George Drury's *Guide to Tourist Railroads and Railroad Museums* (4th ed.; see ARBA 96, entry 1886), which lists nearly 350 tourist railroads and museums in the United States and Canada. Because each book contains material not found in the other, both are worth owning. Drury, however, remains the standard work. Although it is less expensive than the Norris and Norris volume, it is substantially longer, with more information and clearer presentation of data. The former also has greater consistency in criteria for selecting sites to list. For example, Norris and Norris include 17 sites for North Dakota but only 3 for Illinois, while Drury lists 1 for North Dakota and 7 for Illinois, a far better balance of coverage. [R: RBB, 15 April 96, p. 1460]—**Frederick A. Schlipf**

1447. **Official License Plate Book: How to Read and Decode Current United States & Canadian Plates.** By Thomson C. Murray. Michael C. Wiener, ed. Jericho, N.Y., Interstate Directory Publishing, 1996. 128p. illus. maps. $16.95; $12.95pa. ISBN 0-9629962-9-7; 0-9629962-8-9pa.

Published somewhat erratically (9 editions between 1978 and 1996), the *Official License Plate Book* presents more information on current plates than can be found easily elsewhere. Included, for each state or province, are a page of illustrations of representative categories (all for some states, most or some for others); brief notes on dates for current basic plates; distinctive captions (e.g., "Dismantler"); numeric codes; prefixes for special groups (e.g., disabled veterans, POWs); special state office plates; and instructions for getting personalized plates and for tracing registered vehicles. At the end of the volume are four pages of miscellaneous information, including trends in numbering systems, special plates, collecting plates, a quiz on plate facts, and several games based on license plates and their numbers.—**Walter C. Allen**

WATER

1448. Ritchie, David. **Shipwrecks: An Encyclopedia of the World's Worst Disasters at Sea.** New York, Facts on File, 1996. 292p. illus. index. $40.00. ISBN 0-8160-3163-0.

A useful, attractive encyclopedia of major maritime disasters, Ritchie's volume seeks out the best-known shipwrecks, including the *Principessa Iolanda*, an Italian liner that sank upon launching. In addition to entries on ships, the text discusses reefs, radar, storms, shipbuilding, and data concerning the environmental impact of capsized nuclear submarines and oil tankers. Literary references include the wreck of the *Sea Venture*, from which William Shakespeare developed the play *The Tempest*, and the life of Alexander Selkirk, inspiration for Daniel Defoe's *Robinson Crusoe*. Reasonably priced and accessible to the student, teacher, librarian, historian, researcher, and general reader, the book documents ship size, passenger and casualty lists, weather and sea conditions, locales, and causes of loss. Ritchie adds an appendix on fatalities, a chronology of major shipwrecks from Christopher Columbus's time to the present, a brief bibliography, and an ample index that indicates main entries with boldfaced page numbers.

Ritchie's style is straightforward and unembellished as exemplified in his brief discussion of rescues, lifeboats, sharks, the Bermuda Triangle, and supernatural events. Cross-references make useful connections, for example, between the *Lusitania* and the Cunard Line, explosions, submarines, the social impact of shipwrecks, and torpedoes. Sketches clarify such difficult concepts as how a tsunami lifts a ship out of water and deposits it on land. Other illustrations (e.g., a murky shot on page 178 of a rescuer suspended from ship by lifeline) are uneven, often lacking clarity and substantive cutlines. Overall, the book would profit from more drawings, photographs, and maps, and a clearer explanation of difficult terms, such as *cargo hold*, *conning tower*, and *rigging*. [R: LJ, Jan 96, p. 90]—**Mary Ellen Snodgrass**

1449. Stern, Steven B. **Stern's Guide to the Cruise Vacation.** 6th ed. Gretna, La., Pelican Publishing, 1995. 492p. illus. index. $17.95pa. ISBN 1-56554-125-1.

The fact that this cruise guide is in its 6th edition is testimony to its usefulness and popularity. More than 195 ships in the cruising trade are examined, evaluated, and priced. A rating scheme of ribbon awards is used. Photographs of the ships and their interiors are included, along with deck plans, shipboard menus, and activity plans. The chapter "Where to Cruise and How Long" delves into the itineraries of various cruise ships and gives positive and negative aspects of their ports of call. The major portion of the book deals with the cruise lines and their vessels. Back matter consists of an alphabetic list of cruise ships, their size, the cost, and ratings. There is a table rating the ships in such various categories as food, service, activities, accommodations, and so forth. An index is also provided. The author, a Chicago attorney, has sailed on more than 450 cruise ships, has been to every major port in the world, and has inspected most of the ships in current operation, so he writes out of practical experience.—**Frank J. Anderson**

Author/Title Index

Reference is to entry number.

ABC-CLIO companion to ...
   American reconstruction, 1862-77, 420
   the Native American rights movement, 341
   transportation in America, 1437
Abortion, 2d ed, 666
Abortion policies, v.3, 665
Abstract expressionist women painters, 808
Abuov, Zhoumagaly, 876
Accessing US govt info, rev ed, 54
Acronyms, initialisms, & abbrevs dict 1997, 21st ed, 1
Adamec, Ludwig W., 106
Adelman, Alan, 310
Adler, Laura, 693
Adloff, Richard, 95
Adventures in video, 314
Affirmative action, 484
African American hist in the press 1851-99, 412
African American voices, 328
African-American yellow pages, 329
African ethnonyms, 315
AIDS funding, 4th ed, 683
Aitchison, Jean, 705
Akiyama, Carol, 859
Akiyama, Nobuo, 859
Alampi, Gary, 279
Alban Berg: a gd to research, 1045
Albert, Richard N., 944
Alcohol in the British Isles from Roman times to 1996, 441
Aldighieri, Anne Marie, 3
Alexander, Harriet Semmes, 1015
Algeria, rev ed, 93
All music bk of hit albums, 1066
All music bk of hit singles, 1067
All music gd to the blues, 1072
Allen Sapp: a bio-bibliog, 1038
Allsopp, Richard, 834
Almanac of American employers 1996-97, 259
Almanac of European pols 1995, 605
Alphabetical gd to the lang of name studies, 824
Alternative press index, 58
Amell, Samuel, 1014
American & British poetry, 1015
American art colonies, 1850-1930, 800
American bibliog of Slavic & E European studies for 1993, 114
American business locations dir, 157
American Civil War, 421
American decades 1900-09, 422
American decades 1910-19, 423
American decades 1920-29, 424
American decades 1980-89, 425
American drama criticism: suppl 4 to the 2d ed, 1146
American film personnel & co credits, 1908-20, 1142
American first ladies, 407

American folklore, 1088
American humanities index for 1995, v.21, 744
American Indian quotations, 345
American Indian reservations & trust areas, 342
American Jewish yr bk 1996, v.96, 1220
American nature writers, 965
American reform & reformers, 408
American song, 2d ed, 1077
American synagogue, 1221
American theatre, 1150
American women historians, 1700s-1990s, 411
American women's track & field, 664
American writers, suppl 4, 961
America's corporate families 1995, 158
Amory, Hugh, 39
Amos, Kharma, 1416, 1418
Ancell, R. Manning, 409
Ancient Peruvian art, 794
Anders CD-ROM gd, 2d ed, 15
Anderson, Lorin W., 298
Anderson, Sarah, 383
Anderson's travel companion: a gd to the best non-fiction & fiction for travelling, 383
Angels A to Z, 1176
Anglim, Christopher, 480
Ankrapp, Betty, 1324
Ann Radcliffe: a bio-bibliog, 998
Annotated bibliog of Jane Austen studies 1984-94, 988
Annotated bibliog of jazz fiction & jazz fiction criticism, 944
Annotated catalog, S Texas College of law, special collections, 480
Annotations: a dir of pers listed in the Alternative Press Index, 1996 ed, 63
Annual bulletin of steel stats for Europe, v.21: 1991-94, 1307
Annual bulletin of trade in chemical products, 1384
Annual register 1995, 581
Apostolos-Cappadona, Diane, 797
Apple, Hope, 946
Applegate, Edd, 977
Apte, Vasudeo Govind, 868
Arab-Israeli dispute, 457
Arav, Rami, 1213
Archaeology of the Mississippian culture, 398
Argentina business, 245
Argentina co hndbk, 246
ARL stats 1994-95, 527
Armenian (Eastern)-English dict, 844
Armstrong, C. J., 78, 172, 1241, 1247, 1383
Arnold, Guy, 568, 615
Arnold, John, 112
Art, truth, & high pols: a bibliographic study of the official lives of Queen Victoria's ministers in Cabinet, 1843-1969, 608

Artists & writers colonies, 745
Ash, Irene, 1385
Ash, Michael, 1385
Asian American chronology, 326
Asian Americans: social, economic, & pol aspects, 327
Asian markets, 4th ed, 234
Atkinson, David J., 1209
Atkinson, W. Patrick, 1155
Atlas of ...
　　American agriculture, 1246
　　English dialects, 839
　　holy places & sacred sites, 1167
　　human hist, 458
　　industrial protest in Britain, 1750-1990, 146
　　US economy, tech, & growth, 714
Attwater, Donald, 1174
Audi, Robert, 1159
Audiovisual resources for family programming, 313
Auerbach, Alan J., 627
Austin, Mary C., 142
Australia: a reader's gd, 112
Australia business, 237
Authentic Jane Williams' home school mrkt gd, 280
Avallone, Susan, 767
Avato, Rose M., 1203
Awad, Elias M., 1340
Awards almanac 1996, 701
Awesome almanac—N.Y., 85
Awesome almanac—Ohio, 86
Awesome almanac—Tex., 89
Axelrod, Alan, 415, 504
Azemoun, Youssef, 876
Azikiwe, Uche, 725

Bachtler, John, 243
Bacon's intl media dir 1996, 760
Baetjer, Katherine, 804
Baghdasarian, Louisa, 844
Baker, Christopher, 796
Baker, David, 1300
Baker, Janet, 112
Baker, Mark Allen, 775
Baker, William, 880
Balay, Robert, 8
Baldwin, David, 663
Baldwin, Louis, 733
Bales, Barbara A., 55
Ball perennial manual, 1275
Bamberger, Michelle, 1261
Bantas, Andrei, 865
Bardwell, Rebecca, 735
Barnard, Alan, 317
Barnard, Timothy, 1124
Barnes, Rik, 385
Barnhart concise dict of etymology, 825
Barnhart, Robert K., 825
Baron, Deborah G., 326
Baroque art, 798
Barron's business thesaurus, 178
Barry, Ines, 206

Barteau, Harry C., 119
Bartlett, Johnathan, 1248
Bartlett, Laurence, 991
Baseball by the nos, 650
Baskin, Ellen, 1104
Bassett, John E., 976
Bataille, Gretchen M., 322
Battles of the Somme, 1916, 561
Bauer, David G., 684
Baughman, Judith S., 424
Bauman, Richard W., 492
Baumgartner, James, 683
Baumgartner, James E., 300, 531, 697, 698, 1184
Baumgartner, Walter, 1198
Baxter, Colin F., 460
BBC Music Mag top 1000 CDs gd, 1055
Beach, Cecilia, 943
Beall, Julianne, 535
Beam, Joan, 958
Beaumont, J. Graham, 626
Beer-Taster's log, 1252
Beers, G. Kylene, 925
Behrens, David W., 1295
Benjamin Britten: a gd to research, 1040
Benjamin Rush, M.D.: a bibliographic gd, 403
Bennett, Alice, 755
Bennett, Matthew, 557
Benny Goodman: wrappin' it up, 1071
Benson, Marjorie, 86
Bentley, Elizabeth Petty, 354
Benton, M. J., 1405
Berger, Klaus, 1201
Berney, K. A., 468
Berryman-Fink, Cynthia, 265
Bertram, Anne, 837
Bertuca, David J., 404
Bessette, Alan E., 1278
Bessette, Arleen R., 1278
Best dir of recruiters, 4th ed, 253
Best dir of recruiters on-line, 254
Better buys for business, 187
Beyond the hill, 598
BHA: bibliog of the hist of art: subject headings/English, 790
BHA: bibliog of the hist of art 1996 [CD-ROM], 791
Bianculli, David, 1110
Bible baby names, 368
Bibliographic gd to the hist of computer applications, 1950-90, 1365
Bibliographical gd to the study of Western American lit, 2d ed, 959
Bibliography of ...
　　African lits, 1001
　　Fla., v.2: 1846-80, 84
　　sources in Christianity & the arts, 1206
　　the Caribbean, 128
　　the Soviet Union, it predecessors & successors, 124
Biddle, Stanton F., 329
Biebuyck, Daniel P., 315
Biggs, Mary, 72
Biggs, Melissa E., 1115

Billboard bk of ...
    no.1 albums, 1060
    top 40 albums, 3d ed, 1061
    top 40 hits, 6th ed, 1062
Billboard's hottest hot 100 hits, rev ed, 1080
Binns, Margaret, 97
Biographical dict of ...
    European labor leaders, 151
    the hist of tech, 1236
    the US Secretaries of the Treasury, 1789-1995, 587
    transcendentalism, 962
    20th-century philosophers, 1158
    WW II, 463
    WW II generals & flag officers: the US armed forces, 409
Biographical dir of Native American painters, 807
Birren, James E., 667
Bishop, Chris, 579
Black heritage sites, 330
Black, Jeremy, 556
Blackfoot dict of stems, roots, & affixes, 2d ed, 872
Blackhurst, Hector, 90
Blackwell dict of evangelical biog, 1730-1860, 1208
Blackwell dict of neuropsychology, 626
Blackwell ency of writing systems, 811
Blalock, Susan E., 970
Blank, Robert H., 1330
Bleiler, David, 1125
Blevins, Carolyn DeArmond, 731
Bliss, Marilyn, 1026
Blom, F., 1204
Blom, J., 1204
Bloom, Ken, 1077
Blum, Laurie, 189
Boarding school gd, 297
Boatner, Mark M., III, 463
Boccaccio in English: a bibliog of eds, adaptations, & criticism, 1011
Bock-Weiss, Catherine C., 805
Bogart, Dave, 528
Bogdanov, Vladimir, 1072
Bohlman, Philip V., 1073
Boles, Janet K., 735
Bolozky, Shmuel, 854
Bonavita, Mark, 656, 658
Bond, Mary E., 19
Bond, W. H., 39
Bondanella, Julia Conaway, 1010
Bondanella, Peter, 1010
Bondi, Victor, 425
Bond's franchise gd, 1996, 180
Bonk, Mary Rose, 1
Bonsai survival manual, 1256
Book of ...
    Ephesians, 1188
    European forecasts, 2d ed, 238
    Jeremiah, 1194
    lists for regulated hazardous substances 1996, 1433
    Revelation, 1191
Books in print 1996-97, 49th ed, 18
Borcherding, David H., 754

Borchert, Donald M., 1160
Borders, Rebecca, 598
Bordman, Gerald, 1150
Boring, M. Eugene, 1201
Boritt, Gabor S., 67
Boritt, Jakob B., 67
Born this day, 41
Borne, Barbara Wood, 543
Bosworth, Clifford Edmund, 135
Botterweck, G. Johannes, 1200
Bottorf, Paula, 228
Boultbee, Paul G., 131
Bowker annual lib & bk trade almanac, 1996, 41st ed, 528
Bowler, Gail Hellund, 745
Boyne, Walter J., 562
Bracken, James K., 553
Bradley, Edwin M., 1116
Brady, Clark A., 969
Brain ency, 1334
Brandes, Rand, 1008
Branstad, Barbara, 958
Branton, Ann, 1033
Brass, Ken, 392
Brass music of black composers, 1041
Brassey's world aircraft & systems dir 1996/97, 1438
Bray, Charles, 787
Brelin, Christa, 703
Brennan, Shawn, 1131
Brent, Ruth, 1094
Brereton, Mary M., 529
Bressett, K. E., 778
Brewster, Nancy Peterson, 1285
Bricault, Giselle C., 233
Bridgham, Fred, 849
Briggs, Virginia L., 252
Bright, William, 816
British archives, 3d ed, 440
British children's writers, 1800-80, 934
British children's writers, 1914-60, 935
British children's writers since 1960, 1st series, 936
British cinema source bk, 1109
British economic & social hist, 3d ed, 443
British empire, 444
British film studios, 1139
British imprints relating to N America, 1621-1760, 40
British literary bk trade, 1700-1820, 553
British playwrights, 1880-1956, 985
British playwrights, 1956-95, 986
British reform writers, 1789-1832, 977
British short-fiction writers, 1800-80, 978
British short-fiction writers, 1880-1914, 979
British short-fiction writers, 1915-45, 980
British travel writers, 1837-75, 981
British women's hist, 726
British writers, suppl 3, 982
Broadway, movie, TV, & studio cast musicals on record, 1030
Broadway sheet music, 1069
Brochstein, Martin, 165
Brockman, Terra Castiglia, 363

Brogan, T. V. F., 1019
Bromley, Debra J., 1153
Bronson, Fred, 1080
Brostrom, Jennifer, 901
Brostrom, Jennifer Allison, 902, 903, 904
Brothers, Barbara, 981
Broude, Gwen J., 708
Brown, Kathleen, 147
Brown, Stuart, 1158
Browne, Peter, 112
Browning, W. R. F., 1195
Brownstone, David, 640
Bruce-Young, Doris Marie, 302
Brune, Lester H., 431
Brunvand, Jan Harold, 1088
Bryan, John, 1276
Bryan, Mary Lynn McCree, 706
Bucher, Ward, 801
Buckley, John F., 257
Bulbs for the rock garden, 1255
Bulliet, Richard W., 136
Bunch, Bryan, 1242
Bunson, Margaret R., 453
Bunson, Stephen M., 453
Burchfield, R. W., 756
Burgess, Philip M., 248
Burroughs cyclopaedia, 969
Burrows, Elaine, 1109
Burton, Virgil L., III, 160
Business A to Z source finder, 147
Business & economic research dir, 159
Business lib & how to use it, 6th ed, 530
Business orgs, agencies, & pubns dir, 8th ed, 160
Business stats of the US, 1995 ed, 176
Bussmann, Hadumod, 812
Butler, Diane, 220, 244
Buttlar, Lois J., 522
Byers, Clive, 1288
Byers, Paula K., 367

Callaham, John R., 1237
Callaham, Ludmilla Ignatiev, 1237
Callaham's Russian-English dict of sci & tech, 4th ed, 1237
Callinan, Paul, 1342
Cambridge astronomy dict, 1392
Cambridge biogl dict, 20
Cambridge dict of philosophy, 1159
Cambridge gazetteer of the US & Canada, 381
Cambridge gd to American theatre, updated ed, 1151
Cambridge illus atlas of warfare: Renaissance to Revolution, 1492-1792, 556
Cambridge illus atlas of warfare: the Middle Ages, 768-1487, 557
Cambridge pa gd to lit in English, 894
Cambridge star atlas, 2d ed, 1393
Campbell, George L., 813
Campus-free college degrees, 7th ed, 292
Canadian almanac & dir 1997, 3
Canadian bed & breakfast gd, 12th ed, 393

Canadian ency plus, 1997 [CD-ROM], 42
Canadian medical dir on CD-ROM, 1996 [CD-ROM], 1320
Canadian ref sources, 19
Canadian sourcebk, 1997, 32d ed, 4
Canadian who's who 1996: v.31, 37
Canadian writers & their works: fiction series, v.12, 1003
Canadian writers & their works: poetry series, v.11, 1004
Cantor, George, 386, 387, 645
Capela, John J., 203
Carmichael, Cathie, 122
Carnes, Mark C., 402
Caron, Martine M., 19
Carper, James C., 301
Carr, Ian, 1076
Carranza, Miguel A., 322
Carrington, Vee Friesner, 8
Carroll, Stephen, 1326
Carter, Craig, 648, 655, 657
Casey, Marion R., 346
Cassell cluefinder, 832
Cassidy, Frederic G., 833
Catalog of music for the cornett, 1051
Catalogue of ...
    choral music arranged in biblical order, 2d ed, 1053
    forbidden German feature & short film productions held in Zonal Film Archives..., English lang ed, 764
    medieval & Renaissance mss in the Houghton Lib, Harvard Univ, v.1, 546
    the 15th-century printed bks in the Harvard Univ Lib, v.4, 547
Cayman Islands, 131
CD-ROMs in print 1995 [CD-ROM], 16
CD-ROMs in print 1996, 17
CDs, super glue, & salsa, series 2, 193
Center: a gd to genealogical research in the natl capital area, 358
Central European folk music, 1073
Cernea, Ruth Fredman, 307
Cerrito, Joann, 795, 908
Chabran, Rafael, 337
Chabran, Richard, 337
Chadwick, Bruce A., 718
Chai, Alan, 182
Challenge of urbanization, 722
Chaloner, W. H., 443
Chambliss, J. J., 287
Charismatic movement, pts.1-4, 1205
Charles Dickens on the screen, 1121
Charles, Jill, 1152, 1153
Charles-Maurice de Talleyrand 1754-1838, 447
Charlesworth, Andrew, 146
Charlton price gd to Canadian clocks, 777
Charteris, Richard, 1034
Chase's calendar of events 1997, 40th ed, 5
Chase's sports calendar of events 1997, 639
Chatfield, Michael, 179
Chaucer's pilgrims, 989
Chemical gd to the Internet, 1382

Chemical research faculties, 1380
Chemistry citation index [CD-ROM], 1390
Chevallier, Andrew, 1343
Chevrefils, Marlys, 1005
Children's bks & their creators, 939
Children's bks: awards & prizes, 1996 ed, 932
Children's rights, 515
Children's song index, 1978-93, 1033
China environmental report, 223
Choral music by African American composers, 1054
Christensen, Karen, 470
Christianson, Stephen G., 600
Chronicle of ...
    American music, 1700-1995, 1025
    the Olympics 1896-1996, 660
    the world, rev ed, 464
    the yr 1995, 465
Chronology & glossary of propaganda in the US, 595
Cicarelli, James, 150
Cicarelli, Julianne, 150
Cilurzo, Mary Jeanne, 1313
Cimbala, Paul A., 408
City profiles USA 1996, 388
Civil War CD-ROM [CD-ROM], 401
Claghorn, Gene, 1035
Clark, Jerome, 632, 638
Clark, Thomas L., 841
Clarke, Paul Barry, 73
Clarkson, J. Shannon, 1177
Classical studies, 461
Classification plus [CD-ROM], 533
Clement, Russell T., 806
Clements, Frank A., 140
Clinkscale, Martha Novak, 1050
Clynes, Tom, 1029
Cocks, Elijah E., 1394
Cocks, Josiah C., 1394
Coffel, Steve, 1425
Coger, Dalvan, 98
Cohen, E. Richard, 1406
Cohen, Morris L., 493
Cohn-Sherbok, Dan, 1222
Cohn-Sherbok, Lavinia, 1222
Cold War ency, 473
Cole Porter discography, 1068
Cole, Robert, 618
Coleman, J. A., 832
Colin, Wilson, 1167
Collector's gd to celebrity autographs, 775
College chemistry faculties 1996, 10th ed, 303
Collegeville pastoral dict of biblical theology, 1196
Collier, Clifford Duxbury, 351
Collins nations of the world atlas, 372
Collinson, Diane, 1158
Collver, Michael, 1051
Colonial wars of N America, 1512-1763, 413
Colpe, Carsten, 1201
Columbia Granger's index to poetry in collected & selected works, 1016
Columbia Granger's world of poetry [CD-ROM], 1017
Columbia world of quotations [CD-ROM], 68

Combined membership list 1996-97, 1412
Command performance, USA! a discography, 772
Commins, David, 141
Compact music dict, 1026
Compact up-to-date English-Hebrew dict, 856
Companies intl [CD-ROM], 209
Companion to the characters in the fiction & drama of W. Somerset Maugham, 996
Compendium of human settlements stats 1995, 5th ed, 715
Competitions: maximizing your abilities, 299
Complete family gd to healthy living, 1326
Complete grants sourcebk for higher educ, 3d ed, 684
Complete gd to American bed & breakfast, 4th ed, 385
Complete gd to homeopathy, 1347
Complete home health advisor, 1344
Comprehensive, annot bibliog on Mahatma Gandhi, 430
Comprehensive dict of measurement & control, 3d ed, 1311
Computer desktop ency, 1369
Concise compendium of the world's langs, 813
Concise dict of lib & info sci, 525
Concise ency biology, 1266
Concise ency of psychology, 2d ed, 627
Concise histl atlas of Eastern Europe, 446
Concise Oxford dict of music, 4th ed, 1027
Concise Oxford Russian dict, 866
Concordance to the complete poems & plays of T. S. Eliot, 971
Confessions of Saint Augustine, 1207
Connell, James E., 777
Connor, D. Russell, 1071
Conroy, Thomas F., 276
Conservation & environmentalism, 1426
Consultants & consulting orgs dir 1996 suppl, 16th ed, 161
Consumer Canada 1996, 268
Consumer Mexico 1996, 269
Consumer protection & the law, 487
Consumer South Africa 1995, 270
Consumer USA 1996, 271
Consumers index to product evaluations & info sources, v.24, no.2, April-June 1996, 188
Contemporary American folk art, 783
Contemporary artists, 4th ed, 795
Contemporary Australian women 1996/97, 734
Contemporary literary criticism, v.86, 895
Contemporary literary criticism, v.87, 896
Contemporary literary criticism, v.88, 897
Contemporary literary criticism, v.89, 898
Contemporary Spanish novel, 1014
Cook, Kevin L., 711
Cook's dict & culinary ref, 1248
Co-op America's natl green pages, 1996 ed, 1428
Cooper, Adam Merton, 359
Cooper, Andre R., Sr.,1434
Cooper, J. C., 1210
Cooper's comprehensive environmental desk ref, 1434
Copel, Linda Carman, 1355
Coppell, Bill, 643
Cops, crooks, & criminologists, 504

Coral reef animals of the Indo-Pacific, 1295
Cornfield, Daniel B., 250
Corporate affiliations plus, spring/summer 1995 [CD-ROM], 162
Corporate dir of US public cos [CD-ROM], 163
Corporate dir of US public cos 1996, 164
Corporate 500, 13th ed, 685
Corsini, Raymond J., 627
Cortada, James W., 1364, 1365
Cosman, Madeleine Pelner, 838
Cosner, Shaaron, 411
Cossolotto, Matthew, 605
Costa, Marie, 666
Cote d'Ivoire, 96
Coulmas, Florian, 811
County & city extra, 1995, 4th ed, 712
Covenants not to compete, 2d ed, 494
Cowie, Leonard W., 439
Cowles, C. McKeen, 1327
Cox, Elizabeth M., 601
Cox, Harold E., 446
Cragg, Dan, 562
Crampton, Luke, 1081
Crawford, Ann M., 990
Crawford, Walter B., 990
CRC hndbk of lab safety, 4th ed, 1386
CRC standard mathematical tables & formulae, 30th, 1413
Creaton, Heather, 116
Creber, Geoffrey, 1273
Crime in America, 508
Crisostomo, Isabelo T., 332
Critical gd to mgmt training videos & selected multimedia, 1996, 266
Critical legal studies, 492
Crowley, William R., 1415
Cruisers of WW II, 574
Crystal, David, 20
Cuba, 132
Cullen-DuPont, Kathryn, 736
Current issues sourcefile [CD-ROM], 59
Curson, Jon, 1288
Curtis, Nancy C., 330
Cushion plants for the rock garden, 1257
CyberHound's Internet gd to the coolest stuff out there, 1374
Cyberstocks, 182

D. H. Lawrence: a ref companion, 995
Dabrishus, Michael J., 1046
Dahl, Henry Saint, 486
Dahl's law dict: an annot legal dict, Spanish-English/English-Spanish, 2d ed, 486
Dalzell, Tom, 842
Dance words, 1102
Dancers & choreographers, 1100
Dane, Suzanne G., 390
Dani, A. H., 479
Daniel, LaNelle, 1146
Daniels, Morna, 96
Daniels, Peter T., 816

Danilov, Victor J., 62
Darch, Colin, 102
Darnay, Arsen J., 197, 279
Darnay, Brigitte T., 161
Dasch, E. Julius, 1391
David, Jack, 1003, 1004
Davis, Cynthia J., 738
Davis, Elisabeth B., 1264, 1272
Davis, Paul K., 564
Davis, Todd M., 311
Dawson, J. L., 971
Dawson, Jeff, 676
Day, Alan, 13, 133
Day, Alan J., 581
Day, Lance, 1236
Deane, Bill, 1127
de Angury, Maree, 706
Dear, I. C. B., 571
Dearling, Robert, 1052
Decalo, Samuel, 95, 103
Decca lables: a discography, 1031
Definitive Andy Griffith show ref, 1134
DeGraaf, Richard M., 1289
de Grummond, Nancy Thomson, 397
Delaney, John, 963
Delaware-English/English-Delaware dict, 845
Del Conte, Anna, 1280
Delijska, B., 1366
Dell Orto, Arthur E., 670
DeLong, Thomas A, 762
Del Vecchio, Deborah, 1119
Demastes, William W., 985, 986
De Mente, Boye Lafayette, 107, 109, 134
DenBoer, Gordon, 371
Dennis, Peter, 565
Denoeu, Francois, 846
Derbyshire, Ian, 582
Derbyshire, J. Denis, 582
Dervaes, Claudine, 384
Detecting women 2, 1996-97 ed, 947
De Vries, Mary A., 178
Dewey decimal classification & relative index, 21st ed, 535
Dewey for Windows [CD-ROM], 536
Dial up! Gale's bulletin board locator, 1376
Diamant, Anita, 368
Dickey, Bruce, 1051
Dickinson, W. Calvin, 435
Dickson, Paul, 369
Dictionary of ...
   Afghan wars, revolutions, & insurgencies, 106
   American biog, comprehensive index, 32
   American children's fiction, 1990-94, 938
   American hist, 419
   American hist suppl, 414
   American penology, rev ed, 506
   American regional English, v.3: I-O, 833
   Australian colloquialisms, 4th ed, 829
   automotive engineering, 2d ed, 1303
   bldg preservation, 801
   canine terms, 1292

Caribbean English usage, 834
Christianity, 1210
Cleveland biog, 87
contemporary French connectors, 847
cultural & critical theory, 746
dvlpmtl psychology, 629
economics, 156
endocrinology & related biomedical scis, 1352
ethics, theology, & society, 73
euphemisms, 827
European hist & pols, 1945-95, 438
feminist theologies, 1177
glass, 787
Hispanic biog, 334
insurance terms, 3d ed, 201
intl biog 1996, 24th ed, 21
intl business terms, 203
intl human rights law, 516
Irish lit, rev ed, 1007
Islamic architecture, 803
Italian lit, rev ed, 1010
Judaism in the biblical period, 1223
literary biog documentary series, v.13, 963
literary biog yrbk: 1995, 899
mechanical engineering, 4th ed, 1310
natl biog, 1986-90, 38
1000 Spanish proverbs with English equivalents, 1089
philosophy, 3d ed, 1164
phonetics & phonology, 819
Portuguese-African civilization, v.2, 427
public health promotion & educ, 1317
South African English on histl principles, 830
sports injuries & disorders, 1357
substances & their effects [CD-ROM], 1314
teleliteracy, 1110
the Bible, 1195
the British Empire & Commonwealth, 117
the 1st World War, 474
the Middle East, 138
the modern US military, 566
the Turkic langs, 876
20th century culture: Hispanic culture of Mexico, Central America, & the Caribbean, 348
US intelligence servs, 597
word origins, 826
Diefendorf, Elizabeth, 882
Dietrich, Gerhard, 1266
Digital imaging dict, 1368
Di Lima, Sara Nell, 1324
Dillon, Kim, 12
Dinosaur hunter [CD-ROM], 1403
Dintrone, Charles V., 1144
Directory of ...
    African American religious bodies, 2d ed, 1181
    American firms operating in foreign countries, 14th ed, 210
    American poets & fiction writers, 1995-96 ed, 749
    chemical producers & products, v.1, pt.1, 2d ed, 1381
    college & univ librarians in Canada, 2d ed, 550
    college cooperative educ programs, 304
    corp & fndn givers 1996, 686
    designated members, 1996, 282
    electronic journals, newsletters, & academic discussion lists, 6th ed, 1375
    environmental electronic mail users in Eurasia, 4th ed, 1429
    EU info sources 1995-96, 7th, 606
    family assns, 3d ed, 354
    fed jobs & employers, 258
    health grants, 1321
    intl orgs, 617
    Japanese-affiliated cos in the EU, 1996-97, 211
    overseas catalogs, 1997, 212
    power plant equipment & processes, 1996, 1416
    research grants 1996, 687
    social serv grants, 688
    the steel industry & the environment, 194
    trade & investment related orgs of developing countries & areas in Asia & the Pacific, 7th ed, 235
DISCovering authors modules [CD-ROM], 900
DISCovering multicultural America [CD-ROM], 323
Dissertation abstracts [CD-ROM], 60
Distinguished African American scientists of the 20th century, 1230
DK ency of rock stars, 1081
DK geography of the world, 379
Dobrin, Adam, 507
Docherty, James C., 251
Dockery, C. C., 598
Doctrine of the Holy Spirit, 1193
Dodd, Mary Ann, 1036
Dogra, Ramesh Chander, 1225
Domestic violence, 675
Dominic, Catherine C., 909, 910, 911
Doniach, N. S., 855
Dorling Kindersley world ref atlas, 2d ed, 373
Douglas, Krystan V., 987
Dover, Jeffrey S., 1333
Dow Jones averages, 1885-1995, 183
Dow, James W., 318
Drew, Bernard A., 941
Drowne, Kathleen Morgan, 890
Dubester's US census bibliog with SuDocs class nos & indexes, 711
Due, Andrea, 458
Dumouchel, J. Robert, 689
Durham, Jennifer L., 508
Durkan, Michael J., 1008
Dutch modernism, 802
Duvvuri, Raj, 817
Duxbury, John, 649
Dwyer, Jim, 1424
Dwyer, Philip G., 447
Dyer, Janyce G., 1353

Earls, Irene, 798
Earth works, 1424
Earthquakes & the built environment index, 1984-July 1995 [CD-ROM], 1399
East & NE Africa bibliog, 90

Economic & social progress in Latin America 1995 report, 127
Economic & social survey of Africa, 1994-95, 231
Economic survey of Europe in 1995-96, 239
Economics, trade, & dvlpmt: English-Spanish general terminology, 272
Edmonds, Beverly C., 515
Education & the law, 491
Educational media & tech yrbk 1995/96, v.21, 312
Educators index of free materials 1995, 104th ed, 294
Educator's word frequency gd, 817
Edwards, Adrian, 121
Edwards, Bill, 784, 785
Effects of drugs on the fetus & nursing infant, 1358
Einstein dict, 1409
Eis, Arlene L., 498
Elder, John, 965
Electric power in Asia & the Pacific, 1991 & 1992, 1420
Electric power industry yrbk, 1996, 1421
Electric power stats sourcebk, 1422
Elementary school lib collection, 20th ed, 544
Elementary school lib collection, 20th ed [CD-ROM], 545
Elias, Stephen, 520
Elkins, Rita, 1344
Ellet, William, 266
Elliott, Clark A., 1235
Elliott, Doreen, 704
Elliott, Jack, 1255
Elsevier's dict of ...
    computer sci & math in English, German, French, & Russian, 1366
    financial & economic terms, 153
    fundamental & applied biology, 1267
    plant names, 1273
Elwell, Walter A., 1197
Ely, Donald P., 312
Ember, Melvin, 316
Emerson, Isabelle, 1103
Emil Brunner: a bibliog, 1172
Employee benefits desk ency, 252
Employee duty of loyalty, 495
Employee duty of loyalty, 1996 suppl covering 1994, 496
Employment/Unemployment & earnings stats, 249
Encyclicals of John Paul II on CD-ROM [CD-ROM], 1217
Encyclopaedia Africana dict of African biog, v.3, 91
Encyclopaedia of Sikh religion & culture, 1225
Encyclopedia Americana [CD-ROM], 43
Encyclopedia of ...
    African-American culture & hist, 331
    African-American educ, 285
    allegorical lit, 890
    alternative medicine, 1345
    American biog, 2d ed, 33
    American educ, 288
    American prisons, 505
    American religious hist, 1180
    ancient Mesoamerica, 453
    apocalyptic lit, 893
    applied physics, v.15, 1407
    applied physics, v.16, 1408
    assns: natl orgs of the US [CD-ROM], 49
    bodywork, 1350
    British humorists, 984
    business, 155
    business info sources suppl, 10th ed, 177
    chemical processing & design, v.56, 1378
    claims, frauds, & hoaxes of the occult & supernatural, 637
    Cleveland hist, 2d ed, 88
    climate & weather, 1396
    computer sci & tech, v.34, suppl 19, 1367
    constitutional amendments, proposed amendments, & amending issues, 1789-1995, 596
    cultural anthropology, 316
    democracy, 612
    disability & rehabilitation, 670
    drugs & alcohol, 707
    electronic circuits, v.6, 1305
    European cinema, 1111
    garbage, 1425
    gerontology, 667
    global industries, 204
    human rights, 2d ed, 517
    invasions & conquests from ancient times to the present, 564
    Latin American hist & culture, 349
    lib & info sci, v.58, suppl 21, 524
    life scis, 1268
    literary epics, 889
    medicinal plants, 1343
    microcomputers, v.18, 1371
    molecular biology & molecular medicine, v.1, 1269
    molecular biology & molecular medicine, v.2, 1270
    molecular biology & molecular medicine, v.3, 1271
    Native American healing, 340
    N American eating & drinking traditions, customs, & rituals, 1250
    nutritional suppls, 1349
    occultism & parapsychology, 4th ed, 633
    philosophy suppl, 1160
    psychiatry, psychology, & psychoanalysis, 1356
    relationships across the lifespan, 631
    revolutions & revolutionaries, 477
    rhetoric & composition, 840
    satirical lit, 892
    social & cultural anthropology, 317
    the American West, 415
    the ancient Greek world, 450
    the bk, 2d ed, 554
    the Enlightenment, 475
    the future, 44
    the hist of classical archaeology, 397
    the McCarthy era, 591
    the modern Middle East, 136
    the paranormal, 634
    the Persian Gulf War, 454
    the Reagan-Bush yrs, 593
    the US in the 20th century, 416
    the Vietnam War, 433
    transcendentalism, 964

TV game shows, 2d ed, 1113
US biomedical policy, 1330
values & ethics, 1163
vitamins, minerals, & suppls, 1265
war & ethics, 1161
women & sports, 644
women in religious art, 797
women's hist in America, 736
world cultures, v.8: Middle America & the Caribbean, 318
world cultures, v.9: Africa & the Middle East, 319
world cultures, v.10: indexes, 320
Encyclopedia USA, v.22, 417
Encyclopedia USA, v.23, 418
Endres, Gunter, 1442
Endres, Kathleen L., 743
Energy balances for Europe & N America, 1992, 1993-2010, 1423
Engholm, Christopher, 168
Engle, Ron, 1147
English castles, 394
English Catholic bks, 1701-1800, 1204
English lang scholarship, 809
English-Spanish, Spanish-English electrical & computer engineering dict, 1297
English-Russian economics glossary, 154
Engquist, Jayson Rod, 1036
Enos, Theresa, 840
Entertainment awards, 1099
Environment & the law, 514
Environmental contaminant ref databk, v.1, 1387
Environmental contaminant ref databk, v.2, 1388
Environmental grantmaking fndns 1996, 4th ed, 690
Environmental justice, 1435
Environmental racism & the environmental justice movement, 513
Environmental telephone dir, 1430
EPM licensing letter sourcebk, 1997 ed, 165
Epps, Roselyn Payne, 1341
Epstein, Lee, 497
Erdman, David V., 884
ERIC on CD-ROM [CD-ROM], 293
Erickson, John, 558
Erickson, Ljubica, 558
Ericson, Margaret D., 1020
Erlewine, Michael, 1072
Eskind, Andrew H., 789
Essential ASL, 871
Esteban, H. Bartolome, 1279
Ethnic & vernacular music, 1898-1960, 1075
Ethnic cuisines, 1253
Ethnic studies in the US, 322
Etulain, Richard W., 959
Eurail gd to train travel in the new Europe, 1996, 1443
Eurail gd to world train travel, 1996, 26th ed, 1444
European drinks mktg dir, 4th ed, 240
European mktg data & stats 1996, 31st ed, 273
European oilfield serv, supply, & manufacturers dir, 1996, 2d ed, 1417
European paintings in the Metropolitan Museum of Art by artists born before 1865, 804

European powers in the 1st World War, 467
European private label dir, 241
European regional incentives, 1996-97, 243
European Union ency & dir 1996, 2d ed, 607
Europe's medium-sized cos dir, 242
Evangelical dict of biblical theology, 1197
Evangelical sectarianism in the Russian Empire & the USSR, 1173
Every manager's gd to business processes, 267
Every thing in Dickens, 992
Everyone in Dickens, 993
Everything you need to know about diseases, 1336
Everything you need to know about medical tests, 1337
Everything you need to know about medical treatments, 1338
Everything you pretend to know & are afraid someone will ask, 57
Exegetical bibliog of the N.T., v.4, 1185
Exhaustive concordance to the Greek N.T., 1199
Export financing & insurance vocabulary, 206
Exporting to the USA & the dict of intl trade, 1996-97 ed [CD-ROM], 205
Eyewitness ency of nature [CD-ROM], 1287
Eyewitness ency of space & the universe [CD-ROM], 1395
Eyston, Felice, 662

Fabry, Heinz-Josef, 1200
Facts about the Congress, 600
Fagan, Thomas K., 286
Fairweather, Digby, 1076
Falkland Islands, S Georgia, & the S Sandwich Islands, 133
Family archive viewer [CD-ROM], 355
Family homeopathy, 1342
Family studies database [CD-ROM], 674
Family wisdom, 69
Far East & Australasia 1997, 28th ed, 143
Farace, Joe, 1368
Fargnoli, A. Nicholas, 1009
Farr, David F., 1279
Fashion & costume in American popular culture, 1093
Fatigue data bk, 1308
Faulkner, Keith, 577
Feldman, Andrew J., 1431
Feminism & postmodern theory, 727
Feminist jurisprudence, 739
Feminist writers, 886
Fenton, R. R., 78, 172, 1241
Ferguson, Tom, 1328
Fernandes, David, 1134
Fernekes, William R., 515
Ferrara, Miranda H., 701
Ferrell, Robert H., 414
Feuer, Bryan, 448
Feuerhahn, Ronald R., 1168
Ficher, Miguel, 1042
Fiction catalog, 13th ed, 945
Field gd to common animal poisons, 1262
Field gd to trains of N America, 1445

Field, David H., 1209
Filby, P. William, 367
Filipino achievers in the USA & Canada, 332
Film actors gd, 1997, 3d ed, 1143
Film composers gd, 3d ed, 1037
Film producers, studios, agents, & casting directors gd, 5th ed, 766
Film writers gd, 6th ed, 767
Financial resources for intl study, 2d ed, 309
Finding help: a ref gd for personal concerns, 55
Findlay, Scott, 1002
Findling, John E., 661
Fink, Charles B., 265
First century of film, 1112
First dict of cultural literacy, 2d ed, 296
First Hollywood musicals, 1116
Fischer, Clare B., 1169
Fischer-Schreiber, Ingrid, 1226
Fiske, Robert Hartwell, 759
Fitzroy Dearborn dir of the world's banks, 11th ed, 190
Fitzroy Dearborn intl dir of venture capital funds, 2d ed, 181
501 Hebrew verbs, 854
Flappers 2 rappers: American youth slang, 842
Flavell, Linda, 826
Flavell, Roger, 826
Fleming, Michael C., 716
Floring, John, 1246
Following The Fugitive: an episode gd & hndbk to the 1960s TV series, 1127
Food & beverage market place, 1996, 1249
Food & drink in lit, 881
Foot & ankle sourcebk, 1340
Foot, M. R. D., 571
Ford, Simon, 792
Former major league teams, 646
Fort, Clancy, 1363
Foss, Christopher F., 575, 576
Fossil atlas: fishes, 1404
Foster, Gerald L., 1445
Foster, Janet, 440
Four French symbolists, 806
Fowler, H. W., 756
Fox, Claire G., 403
Fox, Franklin W., III, 2
Foy, Felician A., 1203
Fradkin, Robert A., 1056
Franck, Irene, 640
Frank, Ben G., 436
Franklin, D., 219
Frankovich, Nicholas, 1016
Franks, Don, 1099
Frantz, Donald G., 872
Frantz, Pollyanne, 1033
Frasier, David K., 503
Fred Waring discography, 1049
Free money from the fed govt for small businesses & entrepreneurs, 2d ed, 189
Freedman, Alan, 1369
Freedom of religion decisions of the US Supreme Court, 1183
Freedom of speech decisions of the US Supreme Court, 541
Freedom of the press decisions of the US Supreme Court, 761
French films, 1945-93, 1115
French women playwrights of the 20th century, 943
Freudenheim, Ellen, 1315
Frickhinger, Karl Albert, 1404
Friedl, Vicki L., 559
Friedman, J. M., 1358
Friendly German-English dict, 849
Fritze, Ronald H., 442
Fujie-Winter, Kumiko, 860
Fund raiser's gd to religious philanthropy 1996, 9th ed, 691
Funding for US study, 2d ed, 305
Funding sources for community & economic dvlpmt 1996, 692
Fungi on rhododendron, 1279
Furman, John M., 1042
Furr, A. Keith, 1386
Fuss, Charles J., 1074

Galbraith, Stuart, IV, 1117
Gale ency of psychology, 628
Gale ency of sci, 1238
Gale, Steven H., 984
Gale's ready ref shelf [CD-ROM], 50
Gall, Susan, 628
Gall, Susan B., 326
Gall, Susan Bevan, 79
Gall, Timothy L., 79, 511, 512
Gallagher, Michael G., 223
Gallay, Alan, 413
Gander, Terry J., 570
Gangs, 509
Gangster films, 1114
Garden trees, 1282
Gardner Read: a bio-bibliog, 1036
Gariepy, Jennifer, 919, 920, 921, 922
Garraty, John A., 33, 402
Garwood, Alfred N., 1397
Gastrow, Shelagh, 611
Gatten, Jeffrey N., 1082
Gauthier, Mark A., 529
Gay almanac, 677
Gay & lesbian literary heritage, 888
Gay & lesbian movement, 681
Gay & lesbian online, 676
Gay, Kathlyn, 22, 1250
Gay, Martin K., 22, 538, 1250
Geddes, Nicola, 1347
Gee, Robin, 753
Gems, Gerald R., 642
Genealogical & local hist bks in print, 5th ed, 350
Genealogical research in England's public record office, 357
Genealogy & local hist to 1900, 351
General bibliog for music research, 3d ed, 1022

Generals in muddy boots: a concise ency of combat commanders, 562
Geologists & the hist of geology, suppl 2, v.1, 1402
Gergits, Julia, 981
German baroque writers, 1580-1660, 1006
German-English dict of idioms, 852
German poetry in song, 1032
Gerring, Anthony L., 170
Getz, Leslie, 1100
Gibbs, Tyson, 1322
Gibilisco, Stan, 1372
Giblin, Nan J., 55
Gibson, J., 1357
Gibson, John S., 516
Gilber, Nedda, 169
Gilbert, Steve, 541, 761, 1183
Gilchrist, J. Brian, 351
Gillaspy, Mary L., 537
Gillespie, Michael Patrick, 1009
Gillon, Margaret, 678
Ginsberg, Susan, 69
Giovanni Gabrieli (ca.1555-1612): a thematic catalogue of his music...., 1034
Giroux, Christopher, 895, 896, 897, 898
Glaister, Geoffrey Ashall, 554
Glassman, Bruce S., 7
Glenz, W., 1379
Glickman, Simon, 339
Glickman, Sylvia, 1047, 1048
Global dvlpmt, 228
Global village companion, 470
Global voices, global visions: a core collection of multicultural bks, 10
Glock, Hans-Johann, 1162
Glossary of insurance & risk mgmt terms, 6th ed, 200
Glossary of plastics terminology in 6 langs, 3d ed, 1379
Gneuss, Helmut, 809
Gobbledygook bk: dict of acronyms, abbrevs, initializations, & estoric terminology, 2
Goehlert, Robert U., 584, 585, 586
Golden horrors: an illus critical filmography of terror cinema, 1931-39, 1122
Goldoftas, Lisa, 520
Golitzin, Alexander, 1212
Good skiing gd 1997, 662
Goodrick, Edward W., 1199
Goodsell, Don, 1303
Gordon, Sean, 1432
Gosliner, Terence M., 1295
Goslinga, Marian, 128
Gottlieb, Richard, 1249
Gould, Lewis L., 407
Gove, Thomas P., 253, 254
Government assistance almanac 1996-97, 10th ed, 689
Grabowski, John, 85
Grabowski, John J., 87, 88
Graedon, Joe, 1359
Graedon, Teresa, 1359
Graf, Rudolf F., 1305
Graff, Gary, 1084
Graff, Henry F., 589

Grant seekers gd, 4th ed, 693
Grant, Tina, 214, 215, 216
Grants & awards available to American writers 1996-97, 19th ed, 694
Grants on disc [CD-ROM], 695
Gravesteijn, J., 1400
Gray, Sharon A., 338
Graying of America: an ency of aging, health, mind, & behavior, 668
Great dates in Islamic hist, 137
Great events: the 20th century, suppl, 478
Great rock discography, 1085
Greek-English lexicon, 853
Green, Alan, 1038
Green, Scott E., 968
Greenberg, Gerald S., 747
Greenberg's gd to marbles, 2d ed, 786
Greene, Stanley A., 1436
Greenfield, John R., 978
Greenfieldt, John, 945
Grieve, James, 847
Grimes, Scott, 168
Grolier lib of environmental concepts & issues, 1427
Grolier lib of intl biogs, 23
Grolier student ency of sci, tech, & the enviroment, 1239
Groseclose, David A., 973
Gross, David C., 878
Gross, Liza, 609
Grossman, John, 755
Grossman, Mark, 341, 454
Growing up: a cross-cultural ency, 708
Gruber, Mayer I., 1186
Guide to ...
  America's sex laws, 499
  British drama explication, v.1, 987
  ethnic health collections in the US, 1322
  info resources in ethnic museum, lib, & archive collections in the US, 522
  info sources in the botanical scis, 2d ed, 1272
  ref bks, 11th ed, 8
  serial bibliogs for modern lits, 2d ed, 885
  the early reports of the Supreme Court of the US, 493
  the secular poetry of T. S. Eliot, 970
Guinea, 97
Gun control, 510
Gunston, Bill, 1298
Gunter, Wagner, 1185
Gunzenhauser, Margot, 1101
Gutt-Mostowy, Jan, 864
Gutzke, David W., 441
Guy, Jonelle, 1419

Hadamitzky, Wolfgang, 860
Haines, Lila, 132
Haines, Meic F., 132
Hale, Constance, 758
Hall, Carolyn M., 524
Hall, Charles J., 1025
Hall, George E., 712
Hall, Joan Houston, 833

Hall, Sarah M., 917
Hamilton, Neil A., 613
Hammer films: an exhaustive filmography, 1119
Hammond atlas of the 20th century, 459
Hammond Citation world atlas, 374
Hammond new century world atlas, 375
Handbook of ...
   American military hist, 569
   ancient Greek & Roman coins, 778
   current sci & tech, [2d ed], 1242
   environmental data on organic chemicals, 3d ed, 1389
   leftist guerrilla grps in Latin America & the Caribbean, 609
   plastic & rubber additives, 1385
Hannam, June, 726
Hansan, John E., 669
Hansen, Gladys, 83
Hardaway, Roger D., 405
Hardin, James, 1006
Hardy, Peter, 662
Harkness, Linda, 650
Harmon, Robert B., 975
Harris, Robert L., 1370
Harrison, Maureen, 541, 761, 1183
Harrod's librarians' glossary, 8th ed, 526
Hart, James D., 966
Hartman, Donald K., 404
Hartman, Stephen W., 203
Harvard biogl dict.of music, 1024
Hauck, Dennis William, 635
Haunted places: the natl dir, rev ed, 635
Havel, James T., 588
Hawkins-Dady, Mark, 915
Hazardous materials hndbk, 1436
Health care almanac, 1316
Health care terms, 3d ed, 1319
Health industry quicksource, 1313
Health of native people of N America, 338
Health online, 1328
HealthSpeak, 1315
Heaton, Tim B., 718
Hebrew & Aramaic lexicon of the O.T., v.2, 1198
Heising, Willetta L., 947
Helander, Brock, 1083
Helbig, Alethea K., 938
Hellebust, Lynn, 602, 622
Hellenistic commentary to the N.T., 1201
Help! the quick gd to first aid for your cat, 1261
Henderson, Kathy, 751
Henderson, Lesley, 917
Hendricks, Bonnie L., 1291
Hendrickson, Robert, 835
Henri Matisse: a gd to research, 805
Henry, Scott D., 1308
Henry, Tom, 796
Herbert, Kevin, 779
Hermann Sasse: a bibliog, 1168
Heroes of conscience: a biogl dict, 22
Herron, Nancy L., 76
Hester, Joseph P., 1163
Hettinga, Donald R., 935

Hey, David, 352
Heyman, Neil M., 1118
Hicks, P. J., 1296
Higbee, Joan F., 437
High strangeness: UFOs from 1960 through 1979, 632
Higher educ money bk for women & minorities, 1997 ed, 302
Highlander Polish-English/English-Highlander Polish dict, 864
Hile, Kevin S., 926, 927, 928, 929, 930
Hillerbrand, Hans J., 1211
Hinkelman, Edward G., 236, 245
Hinnells, John R., 1179
Hipp, James W., 899
Hippocrene concise Hungarian-English, English-Hungarian dict, 857
Hippocrene concise Sanskrit-English dict, 868
Hippocrene concise Yoruba-English, English-Yoruba dict, 879
Hippocrene practical English-Yiddish, Yiddish-English dict, expanded ed, 878
Hiro, Dilip, 138
Hirsch, E. D., Jr., 296
Hispanic American chronology, 335
Hispanic resource dir, 3d ed, 336
Hispanic surnames & family hist, 356
Historic festivals, 386
Historic railroad, 1446
Historical atlas of SE Asia, 429
Historical atlas of the Vietnam War, 434
Historical dict of ...
   aid & dvlpmt orgs, 615
   Albania, 113
   Botswana, 3d ed, 94
   Congo, 95
   feminism, 735
   India, 108
   Luxembourg, 119
   Mali, 3d ed, 99
   Mauritania, 2d ed, 100
   Methodism, 1214
   Mongolia, 111
   multinatl peacekeeping, 616
   New Zealand, 144
   organized labor, 251
   Romania, 120
   Spain, 452
   Stuart England, 1603-89, 442
   Syria, 141
   the modern Olympic movement, 661
   the orthodox church, 1212
   Togo, 3d ed, 103
Historical ency of school psychology, 286
Historical ency of the Arab-Israeli conflict, 455
Historical stats 1960-94, 1996 ed, 225
History of accounting, 179
History of American classical music, 1059
History of humanity, v.2, 479
History of sci in the US, 1235
Hitchcock, Eloise R., 435
Hitchens, Susan Hayes, 1039

HIV/AIDS & HIV/AIDS-related terminology, 537
HMO/PPO dir 1996, 1323
Hobbes dict, 1165
Hobson, Archie, 381
Hodgson, Peter J., 1040
Hoeveler, Diane Long, 735
Hoff, Joan, 414
Hoffman, Marian, 350
Hoffman, Verena, 581
Hogan, Robert, 1007
Holder, R. W., 827
Holland, Francis Schmid, 739
Holland, P. D., 971
Hollywood & the foreign touch, 1108
Hollywood Reporter bk of box office hits, rev ed, 1128
Hollywood war films, 1937-45, 1123
Holmberg, Erin E., 17
Holmes, Roger, 1259
Holtze, Sally Holmes, 937
Homa, Linda L., 544
Home herbal, 1281
Honderich, Ted, 1166
Hooper, Nicholas, 557
Hoover's dir of human resources executives 1996, 255
Hoover's masterlist of major US cos 1996-97, 166
Horne, Aaron, 1041
Hostelling USA, 1996, 389
Hostetter, Edwin C., 1187
How to research Congress, 585
How to research the presidency, 586
Howard, Carol, 982
Howard Keel: a bio-bibliog, 1078
Howard, N. Jill, 959
Howlett, Colin, 866
Huber, Jeffrey T., 537
Hughes, Ann, 726
Hughes, James, 46
Humling, Virginia, 1215
Hunt, Caroline C., 936
Hunt, Thomas C., 301
Hupchick, Dennis P., 446
Huso, Deborah R., 67
Hutcheson, Polly, 304
Hutchings, Raymond, 113
Huxford's old bk value gd, 8th ed, 776

Iceland, rev ed, 118
Ilko, John "Jake" A., Jr., 343
Illustrated bk of questions & answers, 56
Illustrated dict of constitutional concepts, 594
Illustrated ency of ...
    essential oils, 1346
    handguns, 782
    musical instruments, 1052
Immunization resource gd, 2d ed, 1339
Imperato, Pascal James, 99
Importers manual USA & the dict of intl trade, 1996-97 ed [CD-ROM], 274
Independent study catalog, 6th ed, 290

Index to American Jewish Histl Quarterly/American Jewish Hist: vols. 51-80, 347
Index to American photographic collections, 3d ed, 789
Indigenous langs of the Americas, 810
Industrial commodity stats yrbk 1994, 195
Information graphics, 1370
Information please almanac, atlas, & yrbk, 1996, 49th ed, 6
Information sources in ...
    architecture & construction, 2d ed, 1299
    engineering, 3d ed, 1296
    finance & banking, 191
Injury prevention for young children, 710
Inside Sports world series factbk, 645
INSPEC list of jls & other serial sources 1996/7, 1306
Instat: intl stats sources, 716
Intellectual freedom manual, 5th ed, 542
International biblog of theatre, 1148
International dict of ...
    historic places, v.4, 468
    historic places, v.5, 469
    psychology, 2d ed, 630
    theatre-3: actors, directors, & designers, 1149
International dir of ...
    business info sources & servs 1996, 2d ed, 213
    co hists, v.12, 214
    co hists, v.13, 215
    co hists, v.14, 216
International educ quotations ency, 289
International ency of ...
    horse breeds, 1291
    teaching & teacher educ, 2d ed, 298
    violin-keyboard sonatas & composer biogs, 2d ed, 1043
International fndn dir 1996, 7th ed, 696
International hndbk on social work educ, 704
International motion picture almanac, 1996, 67th ed, 770
International relations, 5th ed, 620
International relations research dir, 619
International student's gd to Mexican univs, 310
International TV & video almanac, 1996, 41st ed, 771
International thesaurus of refugee terminology, 2d ed, 705
International who's who in music, v.2: popular music, 1063
International yrbk of industrial stats 1996, 196
Introduction to US govt info sources, 5th ed, 53
Iordanskaja, Lidija, 867
Irish experience in NYC, 346
Isaac Asimov: an annot bibliog of the Asimov collection at Boston Univ, 968
Islamic economics & finance, 232
Italy, 395
Ivens, Stephen H., 817

Jackson, Frank, 1292
Jackson, Guida M., 889
Jackson, Keith, 144
Jackson, Pat, 1419
Jackson, Paul, 1440

Jacob, Merle, 946
Jacobs, Arthur, 1028
Jacobs, Jennifer, 1345
Jacobson, Arthur Lee, 1283
Jacquet-Francillon, Vincent, 1037
Jaffe, Jerome H., 707
Jakubiak, Joyce, 262
James A. Michener: a bibliog, 973
James Joyce A to Z, 1009
Jane Addams papers, 706
Jane's aero-engines, 1298
Jane's air traffic control 1996-97, 3d ed, 1439
Jane's aircraft upgrades, 1996-97, 4th ed, 572
Jane's all the world's aircraft 1996-97, 87th ed, 1440
Jane's armour & artillery 1995-96, 16th ed, 575
Jane's avionics 1996-97, 15th ed, 1441
Jane's fighting ships 1996-97, 99th ed, 573
Jane's helicopter markets & systems, 1442
Jane's intl ABC aerospace dir 1996, 46th ed, 217
Jane's intl defence dir 1997, 218
Jane's NBC protection equipment 1996-97, 9th ed, 570
Jane's sentinel: Central America & the Caribbean security assessment, 1996 ed, 129
Jane's space dir 1996-97, 12th ed, 1301
Jane's tank & combat vehicle recognition gd, 576
Jane's warship recognition gd, 577
Jankowski, Bernard, 691
Jankowski, Katherine E., 686
Japan & the Japanese, 110
Japan ency, 109
Japanese filmography, 1117
Jaszczak, Sandra, 701
Jawed, Mohammed Jawed, 81
Jayawardene, S. A., 1227
Jazz: the rough gd, 1076
Jenkins, Carol A., 142
Jenkins, Esther C., 142
Jenkins, Everett, Jr., 426
Jenkins, Fred W., 461
Jesus & his world, 1213
Joan Baez: a bio-bibliog, 1074
Joan Robinson: a bio-bibliog, 150
Joel Whitburn's top pop albums 1955-96, 1070
Joel Whitburn's top R&B singles 1942-1995, 1079
John, Catherine Rachel, 1174
John Max Wulfing collection in Washington Univ, v.3: Roman imperial coins...., 779
John Metcalf papers, 1005
John Steinbeck: an annot gd to biogl sources, 975
Johnson, Anne E., 359, 360
Johnson, Chris, 1441
Johnson, Dale A., 1170
Johnson, Jean E., 682
Johnson, Otto, 6
Johnson, Tom, 1119
Johnson, Yolanda A., 51
Johnston-Des Rochers, Janeen, 206
Jones, Charles Edwin, 1205
Jones, Constance, 702
Jones, David L., 1284
Jones, Donald D., 646

Jones, Henry Stuart, 853
Jones, Marie F., 63
Jones-Wilson, Faustine C., 285
Jordan, Barbara, 313
Jordan, William Chester, 471
Jost, Kenneth, 603
Jules Verne ency, 952
Julien, Nadia, 636
Junior worldmark ency of the nations, 79

Kahane, A., 855
Kalasky, Drew, 954, 955, 956, 957
Kalasky, Kyung Lim, 193
Kambarov, Nasir, 876
Kanellos, Nicholas, 335
Kanji dict, 860
Kantha, Sachi Sri, 1409
Kaplan, Steven M., 1297
Kari, Daven Michael, 1206
Karnes, Frances A., 299
Karp, Rashelle, 940
Kascus, Marie A., 521
Kasinec, Denise, 918
Katz, Bernard S., 587
Katzner, Kenneth, 814
Kausler, Barry C., 668
Kausler, Donald H., 668
Kavasch, E. Barrie, 366
Kazzazi, Kerstin, 812
Kearey, Philip, 1401
Keen, Peter G. W., 267
Keenan, Stella, 525
Kelliher, Susan, 315
Kelly, Gary, 977
Kelly, Katherine E., 985
Kelly, Michael, 248
Kelson, John F., 764
Kemper, Kurt, 504
Kenealy, Pamela M., 626
Kennedy, Felicitas, 1304
Kennedy, Michael, 1027
Kent, Allen, 524, 1367, 1371
Kentucky: atlas of histl county boundaries, 371
Kenya, rev ed, 98
Kermode, Frank, 916
Kern, Robert W., 451
Kerr, Donald, 567
Kerschner, Helen K., 669
Kessler, James H., 1230
Kester-Shelton, Pamela, 886
Khan, Javed Ahmad, 232
Khorana, Meena, 934
Kiefer, Peter T., 1049
Kiell, Norman, 881
Kim, Sun-Jin, 659
Kimmens, Andrew C., 887
King, J. E., 148
Kingfisher 1st ency, 45
Kings of medieval England, c. 560-1485, 445
Kinnear, Karen L., 509

Kipen, David M., 766
Klawans, Zander H., 778
Klein, William W., 1188
Klemp, P. J., 997
Klepper, Robert K., 1120
Klingaman, William K., 591
Knapp, Ellen M., 267
Knight, Paul, 852
Koda, Cub, 1072
Koehler, Ludwig, 1198
Kofmel, Kim G., 550
Kohlenberger, John R., III, 1199
Kohler, Dayton, 906
Korean War, 431
Korsten, F., 1204
Krannich, Caryl Rae, 258
Krannich, Ronald L., 258
Krantz, Les, 74, 263
Krause, Chester L., 780
Krohn, Lauren, 487
Krstovic, Jelena O., 909
Kruschke, Earl R., 510
Kuper, Adam, 75
Kuper, Jessica, 75
Kurian, George Thomas, 44
Kuroff, Barbara, 753
Kurz, Kenneth Franklin, 592
Kushner, Michael G., 252
Kutler, Stanley I., 416, 433
Kutzer, M. Daphne, 942
Kuwait, rev ed, 140
Kwacz, Jose Daniel, 153
Kyrillidou, Martha, 527

Lacey, A. R., 1164
Lackmann, Ron, 765
Ladusaw, William A., 815
Laessoe, Thomas, 1280
Laird, Ross, 1064
Lambdin, Laura C., 989
Lambdin, Robert T., 989
Lance, Steven, 1129
Landmarks of American presidents, 391
Lane, A. Thomas, 151
Langer, Howard J., 345
Langley, Andrew, 56
Langmead, Donald, 802
Languages of the world, new ed, 814
Lao-English dict, 861
Larousse desk ref, 46
Larousse dict of sci & tech, 1240
Larousse English-Spanish, Spanish-English dict, new ed, 873
Larousse mini French-English, English-French dict, new ed, 848
Larousse mini German-English, English-German dict, new ed, 850
Larousse mini Italian-English, English-Italian dict, new ed, 858
Larousse mini Spanish-English, English-Spanish dict, new ed, 874
Laster, James, 1053
Latin American classical composers, 1042
Latin American women artists, 793
Latinas in the US, 728
Latino ency, 337
Laughlin, Kay, 1033
Lavin, Michael R., 713
Law & pols, 490
Law bks & serials in print 1996, 481
Law lib ref shelf, 3d ed, 482
Law, Joe, 284
Lawless, Julia, 1346
Lawless, Richard I., 93
Lawson, Edward, 517
Lawson, Edwin D., 370
Lazzari, Marie, 908, 909, 910, 911, 912
Lea, Peter W., 13
Lecker, Robert, 1003, 1004
Leckie, Gloria J., 550
Lee, C. C., 1382
Leed, Richard L., 867
Leeming, David Adams, 890
Left gd: a gd to left-of-center orgs, 614
Left index: a quarterly index to pers on the Left, 61
Legal researcher's desk ref 1996-97, 498
Leiby, Bruce R., 1078
Leininger, Phillip W., 966
Lems-Dworkin, Carol, 1145
Lentz, Harris M., 1130
Lentz, Harris M., III, 1097, 1098
Leonard, Patt, 114
Lesbian almanac, 679
Lesbian & gay liberation in Canada, 680
Lesbians in print, 678
Lester, Patrick D., 807
Lester, Ray, 191
Lever, Richard, 1002
Leverington, Karen, 580
Levi, Erik, 1055
Levine, John, 1373
Levinson, David, 316, 320, 470, 1178
Levy, Peter B., 593
Lewin, Paul, 1417
Lewis, Colin, 1256
Lewis, Donald M., 1208
Lewis, James R., 1176
Librarian's companion, 2d ed, 532
Libraries Unltd professional collection CD 1995 [CD-ROM], 523
Library lit 1995, 529
Library of Congress subject headings, 19th ed, 534
Library servs for off-campus & distance educ, 521
Liddell, Henry George, 853
Lieberman, Philip A., 763
Liebman, Roy, 1105
Light, Laura, 546
Lignor, Amy, 1249
Limb, Peter, 1001
Lincoff, Gary, 1280

Lind, Beth Beutler, 933
Lindfors, Bernth, 1012
Linzey, Andrew, 73
Lipkowitz, Myron A., 1265
Lippy, Charles H., 1171
Lipset, Seymour Martin, 612
Lisa, Laurie, 322
Liska, Theresa I., 250
Lissauer, Robert, 1065
Lissauer's ency of popular music in America, 1065
Literally entitled, 891
Literary-critical approaches to the Bible, 1190
Literary index to American mags, 1850-1900, 960
Literature criticism from 1400 to 1800, v.28, 901
Literature criticism from 1400 to 1800, v.29, 902
Literature criticism from 1400 to 1800, v.30, 903
Literature criticism from 1400 to 1800, v.31, 904
Literature for children & YAs about Oceania, 142
Literature of American music 3, 1983-92, 1021
Literature of the nonprofit sector, v.7, 682
Lithuanian dict, 862
Litz, A. Walton, 961
Living with low vision, 671
Lockie, Andrew, 1347
Lomer, Cecile, 552
London, 116
Long, John H., 371
Long, Kim, 1293
Longman, Tremper, 1189
Look of the century, 788
Lord, Mary E., 700
Lowe, Duncan, 1257
Lubin, Bernard, 623
Lucas, Daniel M., 511, 512
Lueck, Therese L., 743
LuKanic, Steven A., 1143
Lumley, Elizabeth, 37
Lundquist, Gunnar, 1142
Lynch, Richard Chigley, 1030
Lyon, William S., 340

Mabunda, L. Mpho, 334
MacDonald, Calum, 1055
Mack, William C., 1309
Mackenzie, Harry, 772
Macmillan color atlas of the states, 82
Macmillan ency of earth scis, 1391
Macmillan ency of physics, 1410
Maddex, Robert L., 594
Maggio, Rosalie, 70
Magill, Frank N., 905, 906, 953, 1302
Magill's cinema annual 1995, 14th ed, 1131
Magill's gd to sci fiction & fantasy lit, 948
Magill's survey of world lit, 905
Magoulias, Michael, 901
Mahar, Mary, 1216
Maier, Ernest L., 530
Major business orgs of Eastern Europe & the Commonwealth of Independent States 1995/96, 5th ed, 244

Major cos of ...
   Africa S of the Sahara 1996, 219
   Central & Eastern Europe & the Commonwealth of Independent States 1996/97, 6th ed, 220
   Latin America 1996, 247
   the Arab world 1996/97, 20th ed, 233
Makers of the piano, 1700-1820, 1050
Makino, Yasuko, 110
Malinowski, Sharon, 339
Malsberger, Brian M., 494, 495, 496
Maman, Marie, 1245
Mammoth dict of symbols, English lang ed, 636
Manager's desk ref, 2d ed, 265
Manela, Stewart S., 495
Mansingh, Surjit, 108
Mansukhani, Gobind Singh, 1225
Mantran, Robert, 137
Manual for writers of term papers, theses, & dissertations, 6th ed, 755
Manual of bulbs, 1276
Manufacturing worldwide, 197
Mapping America's past, 402
Marco, Guy A., 1021
Marinelli, Robert P., 670
Marjorie Kinnan Rawlings: a descriptive bibliog, 974
Markel, Howard, 1354
Market gd for young writers, 5th ed, 751
Market info 1995/96, 275
Markets of the US for business planners, 276
Martin, Constance R., 1352
Martin, Fenton S., 584, 585, 586
Martin Heidegger (2): a bibliog, 1156
Martin, Murray S., 8
Martin, Suzanne, 89
Martinich, A. P., 1165
Mason, Wendy H., 204
Mastering Spanish vocabulary, 875
Masterplots, 2d ed, 906
Masterplots 2: short story series suppl, 953
MathSci Disc [CD-ROM], 1414
Mattar, Philip, 136
Matthews, Elizabeth W., 482
Matthews, Winton E., Jr., 535
Mattson, Mark T., 82
Maturi, Richard J., 226
Maurer, John G., 155
Maximov, Andrei, 610
Maximov's companion to who governs the Russian Federation, summer 96, v.2, no.1, 610
Maxwell Anderson on the European stage 1929-92, 1147
Maxwell, Kimberley A., 527
Mayadas, Nazneen S., 704
Mays, Terry M., 616
Mazzeno, Laurence W., 906, 1000
McAleer, Dave, 1066, 1067
McBride, Francis R., 118
McCarter, Joan, 123
McCarthy, J. Thomas, 519
McCarthy's desk ency of intellectual property, 2d ed, 519
McCormick, Jim, 74

McCue, Margi Laird, 675
McDonald, Lee M., 1192
McEvedy, Colin, 428
McGraw-Hill ency of personal computing, 1372
McGraw-Hill yrbk of sci & tech 1996, 1243
McIlwaine, John, 92
McKenna, Erin, 365
McKenty, Elizabeth J., 682
McKenzie, Kirsty, 392
McKetta, John J., 1378
McKim, Mark G., 1172
McKitterick, D. J., 971
McLeish, Kenneth, 1091
McLeod, Donald W., 680
McNeil, Alex, 1132
McNeil, Ian, 1236
McRae, Linda, 315
McRobie, Alan, 144
McShane, Marilyn D., 505
Media review digest, v. 26, 1996, 9
Medical advisor, 1348
Medical dict in 6 langs, 1331
Medieval art, 799
Medieval wordbk, 838
Meek, Kerry Lynne, 730
Melton, J. Gordon, 633
Members of Congress, 584
Mercer, Derrik, 464
Merriam, Louise A., 406
Merriam-Webster dict, home & office ed, 820
Merriam-Webster's crossword puzzle dict, 2d ed, 836
Merriam-Webster's dict of law, 488
Merriam-Webster's pocket biogl dict, 24
Merriam-Webster's pocket geographical dict, 380
Merrick, Janna C., 1330
Mertvago, Peter, 1089
Metter, Ellen, 752
Mexico environmental report, 224
Meyer, Sandra, 1422
Meyers, Robert A., 1269, 1270, 1271
Michaelides, Chris, 121
Michaluk, Stephen, Jr., 952
Michell, Simon, 572
Middle Ages, 471
Middle East & N Africa 1997, 43d ed, 139
Middle level educ, 295
Middleton, John, 319
Miki, Mihoko, 110
Mildren, K. W., 1296
Militias in America, 613
Millard, Robert T., 817
Miller, Christine M., 409
Miller, E. Willard, 621
Miller, Gordon L., 403
Miller, Hope H., 1278
Miller, J. Michael, 1217
Miller, Jacquelyn C., 403
Miller, Orson K., Jr., 1278
Miller, Randall M., 408
Miller, Ruby M., 621
Miller, Tice L., 1151

Miller-Lachmann, Lyn, 10
Mills, Jerry Leath, 924
Minahan, James, 583
Minor, Barbara B., 312
Minor, Mark, 1190
Mischler, Clifford, 780
Mitchell, Bruce M., 283
Mitchell, David A., 1351
Mitchell, Joan S., 535
Mitchell, Laura, 1351
Mitchell, Susan, 717
Mixter, Keith E., 1022
Moanin' low: a discography of female popular vocal recordings, 1920-33, 1064
Modern American popular religion, 1171
Modern women writers, 907
Modeste, Naomi N., 1317
Moeng, Sao Tern, 869
Moffat, Riley, 723
Mogge, Dru, 1375
Mohen, J. -P., 479
Molitor, Graham T. T., 44
Momsen, Janet Henshall, 145
Monush, Barry, 770, 771
Moore, Jean M., 1005
More names & naming, 370
Morehead, Joe, 53
Morgan, Bill, 972
Morkot, Robert, 449
Morris, James McGrath, 693
Morrison, Elizabeth, 112
Morrow, Blaine Victor, 1376
Morton, Barry, 94
Morton, Fred, 94
Moser, James D., 770
Moss, Joyce, 472
Mott, Wesley T., 962, 964
MSA profile, 1996, 724
Mullay, Marilyn, 1229
Multicultural children's lit, 933
Multicultural educ, 283
Multilingual thesaurus of geosciences, 1400
Multimedia: the complete gd, 1362
Multimedia dir, 4th ed, 1363
Multistate payroll gd, 257
Murder cases of the 20th century, 503
Murphy, C. Edward, 683
Murphy, Christina, 284
Murphy, Justin D., 467
Murphy, Michael J., 1262
Murray, Michael T., 1349
Murray, Thomson C., 1447
Muschell, David, 823
Muse, Robert L., 1191
Mushroom bk, 1280
Mushrooms of N America in color, 1278
Music & dance of the world's religions, 1087
Music festivals from Bach to blues, 1029
Music of Francis Poulenc (1899-1963), 1044
Musical anthologies for analytical study, 1023
MusicHound rock: the essential album gd, 1084

Musiker, Naomi, 101
Musiker, Reuben, 101, 551
Muslim almanac, 1219
Mycenaean civilization, 448
Myth: myths & legends of the world explored, 1091

Nanji, Azim A., 1219
Narrative bibliog of the African American frontier, 405
National Audubon Society field gd to N American mammals, rev ed, 1294
National Audubon Society interactive CD-ROM gd to N American birds [CD-ROM], 1290
National dir of grantmaking public charities, 697
National fax dir, 1996, 51
National 5-digit zip code & post office dir 1996, 52
National Gallery complete illus catalogue, 796
National gd to ...
    funding for children, youth, & families, 3d ed, 698
    funding for community dvlpmt, 699
    funding for elem & secondary educ, 300
    funding for libs & info servs, 531
    funding in religion, 1184
National health dir, 1996, 1324
National storytelling dir, 1996, 549
National Trust gd to historic bed & breakfasts, inns, & small hotels, 4th ed, 390
Nations without states: a histl dict of contemporary natl movements, 583
Native American in long fiction, 958
Native American issues, 344
Native N American biog, 339
Nau, Jim, 1275
Nauffus, William F., 980
Navarra, Tova, 1265
Navarro, Jose Maria, 875
Nayler, G. H. F., 1310
Naylor, Lynne, 769
NCAA basketball, 652
NCAA Final Four, 653
NCEA/Ganley's Catholic schools in America 1995, 23d ed, 1216
Nellis, Joseph G., 716
Nelson, Richard Alan, 595
Neotropical migratory birds, 1289
Netzorg, Morton J., 432
Neumeister, Susan M., 404
Neusner, Jacob, 1223
New Beacon bk of quotations by women, 70
New dict of Christian ethics & pastoral theology, 1209
New dict of religions, rev ed, 1179
New Fowler's modern English usage, 3d ed, 756
New, George R., 535
New info revolution: a ref hndbk, 538
New Islamic dynasties, 135
New parents sourcebk, 709
New Penguin dict of geology, 1401
New Testament intro, 1192
New view almanac, 7
New York Public Lib's bks of the century, 882
New York Times film reviews, v.19: 1993-94, 1133
New York Times theater reviews, v.28: 1993-94, 1154
Newlin, George, 992, 993
Newman, Patricia E., 1237
Newton, David E., 748, 1435
Nguyen, Dinh-hoa, 877
Nicholls, C. S., 38
Nietzsche canon, 1157
1990-91 Gulf War, 456
Nineteenth century baseball, 651
Nineteenth-century lit criticism, v.47, 908
Nineteenth-century lit criticism, v.48, 909
Nineteenth-century lit criticism, v.49, 910
Nineteenth-century lit criticism, v.50, 911
Nineteenth-century lit criticism, v.51, 912
Nineteenth-century lit criticism, v.52, 913
Nineteenth-century lit criticism annual cum title ind for 1996, 914
Noble, Keith Allan, 289
Noble, Scott, 483
Noble's intl gd to the law reports, 483
Nolan, James L., 237
Nordquist, Joan, 327, 484, 513, 727, 728, 729, 1156
Norris, Joann, 1446
Norris, John R., 1446
North American brewers resource dir 1996-97, 13th ed, 1251
North American landscape trees, 1283
North American shortwave frequency gd, v.3, 768
Northcutt, Wayne, 115
Notable black American women, bk.2, 34
Notable women in the life sciences, 1231
Novel & short story writer's market, 1996, 753
Nowlan, Robert A., 41
NTC's dict of ...
    folksy, regional, & rural sayings, 837
    China's cultural code words, 107
    Mexican cultural code words, 134
NTC's multilingual dict of American Sign Lang, 870
NTC's Romanian & English dict, 865
NTC's Vietnamese-English dict, 877
Nuclear test ban: glossary in English, French, & Arabic, 578
Nunez, Benjamin, 427
Nurcombe, Valerie J., 1299
Nurse's clinical gd to psychiatric & mental health care, 1355
Nursing diagnosis pocket manual, 1353
Nursing home statl yrbk, 1995, 1327
Nursing96 drug hndbk, 1360
Nyeko, Balam, 104

Oberly, James W., 406
Obituaries in the performing arts, 1994, 1097
Obituaries in the performing arts, 1995, 1098
O'Connor, Sharon Hamby, 493
O'Daly, Anne, 1268
Ody, Penelope, 1281
OECD statl compendium 1996/1 [CD-ROM], 227
Of spirituality, 1169

Of the people, by the people, for the people, & other quotations by Abraham Lincoln, 67
Official gd to ...
    American attitudes, 717
    household spending, 278
    racial & ethnic diversity, 324
Official license plate bk, 1447
Official 1996 NFL record & fact bk, 654
Ofosu-Appiah, L. H., 91
Ogilvie, Marilyn Bailey, 730
Oil & gas on the Internet, 1415
Ojibwa chiefs, 1690-1890, 343
Old Testament commentary survey, 2d ed, 1189
Old Testament intro, 1187
Olitzky, Kerry M., 1221
Oliver, Evelyn Dorothy, 1176
Oliver, Valerie Burnham, 1093
Olson, James S., 321
Olson, Jenni, 1126
Olsson, Urban, 1288
Olton, Roy, 620
O'Meara, John, 845
100 best mutual funds you can buy, 1995, 185
100 most popular YA authors, 941
100 research topic gds for students, 543
105 best investments for the 21st century, 226
Open doors 1994/95, 311
Orchestration theory, 1057
Orgill, Andrew, 456
Orthodox Judaism in America, 1224
Ortolani, Benito, 1148
Oski, Frank A., 1354
O'Sullivan, Marie, 305, 309
Our Sunday Visitor's 1997 Catholic almanac, 1203
Ousaka, Yumi, 1202
Ousby, Ian, 894
Oxford atlas of the world, 4th ed, 376
Oxford companion to ...
    American lit, 6th ed, 966
    Australian military hist, 565
    local & family hist, 352
    philosophy, 1166
    WW II, 571
Oxford dict of current English, 821
Oxford dict of humorous quotations, 71
Oxford ency of the Reformation, 1211
Oxford encyclopedic world atlas, 3d ed, 377
Oxford English dict on CD, 2d ed [CD-ROM], 843
Oxford English-Hebrew dict, 855
Oxford hndbk of clinical dentistry, 2d ed, 1351
Oxford large print dict, 2d ed, 818
Oztopcu, Kurtulus, 876

Pacific Coast League: statl hist, 1903-57, 647
Pada index & reverse Pada index to early Jain canons, 1202
Paddock, Lisa Olson, 364
Padwa, Lynette, 57
Paehlke, Robert, 1426
Palm, Mary E., 1279

Palmer, Alan, 117
Palms throughout the world, 1284
Pan-African chronology, 426
Pandiri, Ananda M., 430
Pantel, Gerda, 393
Paperno, Slava, 867
Paradise Lost: an annot bibliog, 997
Pare, Michael A., 641
Parent, Mary P., 294
Parker, Helen, 1274, 1277
Parker, Peter, 916
Parrish, Thomas, 473
Passenger & immigration lists index, 1996 suppl, 367
Patent, copyright, & trademark, 520
Patricia Smith's doll values, 12th ed, 781
Patterson, William L., 861
Patton-Hulce, Vicki R., 514
Payne, Jennifer, 746
Payne, Michael, 746
Payne, Wardell J., 1181
Pazzanita, Anthony G., 100, 105
Pear, Nancy, 638
Pederson, Jay P., 951
Pedigo, Alan, 1043
Pedowitz, Arnold H., 494, 495, 496
Peeva, K., 1366
Pelle, Kimberly D., 661
Penguin atlas of African hist, new ed, 428
Penguin dict of music, 6th ed, 1028
Penguin dict of saints, 3d ed, 1174
Penguin histl atlas of ancient Greece, 449
Penguin histl atlas of dinosaurs, 1405
Peoplepedia: the ultimate ref on the American people, 74
People's gd to deadly drug interactions, 1359
Peoples of Africa, 321
Peregrine, Peter N., 398
Perennials, 1274
Peretz, Don, 457
Periodicals in print: Australia, New Zealand, & the S Pacific 1996, 13th ed, 64
Perkins, Agnes Regan, 938
Perone, James E., 1023, 1057
Perry, William, 129
Person, James E., Jr., 901, 911, 913
Petersen, Andrew, 803
Peterson, Michael D., 1212
Peterson's distance learning 1997, 291
Peterson's internships 1996, 16th ed, 256
Peterson's summer opportunities for kids & teenagers 1996, 13th ed, 167
Peterson's top colleges for sci, 306
Petren, Suzanne, 623
Pettifer, Adrian, 394
PharmFacts for nurses, 1361
Phenix, Katharine Joan, 741
Philippines business, 236
Philippines in WW II & to independence (Dec. 8, 1941-July 4, 1946), 2d ed, 432
Phillips, Charles, 415, 504
Philosophy of educ, 287

Phonetic symbol gd, 2d ed, 815
Physics quick ref gd, 1406
Pickard, James D., 768
Pickering, David, 1149
Pierce, Phyllis S., 183
Piesarskas, Bronius, 862
Pilger, Mary Anne, 1244
Pillsbury, Richard, 1246
Placenames of Russia & the former Soviet Union, 382
Plano, Jack C., 620
Plants that merit attention, v.2: shrubs, 1285
Platt, Lyman D., 356
Plays for children & YAs, suppl 1, 1989-94, 940
Plumb, Donald C., 1263
Plunkett, Jack W., 259, 539, 1329
Plunkett's health care industry almanac, 1329
Plunkett's infotech industry almanac, 539
Pluvier, Jan M., 429
Pocket factfile of 20th century events, 466
Pocket factfile of 20th century people, 25
Poem finder 95 [CD-ROM], 1018
Pohanish, Richard P., 1436
Pointer, Michael, 1121
Polifka, Janine E., 1358
Political systems of the world, 582
Polk, Alicia, 623
Pollard, Elaine, 818
Polling & survey research methods, 1935-79, 77
Ponnuswami, Meenakshi, 746
Poor, Janet Meakin, 1285
Pop culture landmarks, 387
Popa, Marcel, 120
Pope, Stephen, 474
Poplawski, Paul, 995
Popular American housing, 1094
Popular dict of Judaism, 1222
Popular physics & astronomy, 1411
Population hist of W US cities & towns, 1850-1990, 723
Porter, Stanley E., 1192
Posner, Richard A., 499
Post-Colonial lits in English: Australia, 1970-92, 1002
Post-Colonial lits in English: SE Asia, New Zealand, & the Pacific, 1970-92, 1013
Post Keynesian economics, 148
Post-Soviet hndbk, 123
Potparic, O., 1357
Powell, John, 608
Practical pediatrician, 1354
Prager, Jan C., 1387, 1388
Prentice Hall dir of online business info 1997, 168
Presidents: a ref hist, 2d ed, 589
Preston-Dunlop, Valerie, 1102
Prices & financial stats in the ESCWA region, 192
Priestly, Brian, 1076
Princeton hndbk of multicultural poetries, 1019
Princeton Review Hillel gd to Jewish life on campus, 1996 ed, 307
Princeton Review student access gd to the best business schools, 169
Pringle, David, 949, 950

Printed catalogues of the Harvard College Lib, 1723-90, 39
Proctor, Claude O., 870
Profile of western N America, 248
Profiles in business & mgmt [CD-ROM], 221
Profiles in world hist, 472
Prokurat, Michael, 1212
Prominent women of the 20th century, 26
Propaganda in 20th century war & pols, 618
Prothero, Stephen R., 1180
Prunckun, Henry W., Jr., 501
Prytherch, Ray, 526
Psychology: an introductory bibliog, 624
Psychotronic video gd, 1140
PsycLit [CD-ROM], 625
Public interest profiles 1996-97, 599
Publishers, distrs, & wholesalers of the US 1996-97, 555
Publishing & bk dvlpmt in Sub-Saharan Africa, 552
Puerto, Cecilia, 793
Pullum, Geoffrey K., 815
Pumroy, Eric L., 333
Puniello, Francoise S., 808
Punjab, 126
Purvis, Thomas L., 399, 419
Pym, John, 1136

Queen, Edward L., II, 1180
Quigley, Ellen, 1003, 1004
Quigley, Martin S, 1112
Quin, Carolyn L., 1046
Quinlan, David, 1106
Quinlan's illus dir of film character actors, new ed, 1106

Racism in contemporary America, 325
Radio stars, 762
Radio's morning show personalities, 763
Radovich, Don, 1096
Ramil, Axel J. Navarro, 875
Rampelmann, Katja, 333
Ramsay, Jeff, 94
Randel, Don Michael, 1024
Randi, James, 637
Random House concise ency, 47
Raphael, Marc Lee, 1221
Rappole, John H., 1289
Rasor, Eugene L., 462
Rassam, Amal, 319
Rate ref gd to the US treasury market 1984-95, 184
Rawson, Hugh, 828
Rawson's dict of euphemisms & other doubletalk, rev ed, 828
Reader's adviser on CD-ROM [CD-ROM], 11
Reader's gd to lit in English, 915
Reader's gd to 20th-century writers, 916
Ready ref: American justice, 489
Reagan yrs A to Z, 592
Realization & suppression of the Situationist Intl, 792
Recent work in critical theory, 1989-95, 880
Recommended reading: 500 classics reviewed, 883

Rees, Dafydd, 1081
Reference bks bulletin 1994-95, 12
Reference gd for botany & horticulture, 1258
Reference gd to world lit, 2d ed, 917
Reference sources hndbk, 4th ed, 13
Regional theatre dir 1996-97, 1152
Regions of France, 115
Regions of Spain, 451
Reich, Bernard, 455
Reid, Judith Prowse, 357
Reill, Peter Hanns, 475
Religion: a cross-cultural ency, 1178
Religious higher educ in the US, 301
Religious right, 1218
Rentschler, Cathy, 529
Research gd to the Turner movement in the US, 333
Research on group treatment methods, 623
Research servs dir, 170
Resources for elders with disabilities, 3d ed, 672
Resources for people with disabilities & chronic conditions, 3d ed, 673
Response to Allen Ginsberg 1926-94, 972
Revolutionary America 1763-1800, 399
Rhoden, David, 85
Rhyne, George N., 476
Ricchiuto, Steven R., 184
Rich, Elizabeth H., 699
Richardson, David A., 983
Richardson, R. C., 443
Richter, William L., 420, 1437
Rider, David F., 1439
Ridinger, Robert B. Marks, 681
Rigden, John S., 1410
Riley, Tracy L., 299
Rimler, Walter, 1068
Ring, Trudy, 468
Ringgren, Helmer, 1200
Rinzler, Carol Ann, 1318
Rist, Peter, 1124
Ritchie, David, 1448
Robert, Maguy, 206
Robertson, James D., 1252
Robinson, Dale, 1134
Robinson, Lillian S., 907
Robison, William B., 442
Robl, Gregory, 362
Rock music scholarship, 1082
Rock who's who, 2d ed, 1083
Rogal, Samuel J., 996, 1086
Rogers, Deborah D., 998
Rogers, John H., 979
Rogers, Marcus J. C., 626
Rogers, Pat, 994
Rogg, Carla S., 297
Rogg, Oskar H., 297
Rollyson, Carl Sokolnicki, 364
Romance writer's sourcebk, 754
Romantic movement, 884
Room, Adrian, 382, 824, 891
Roots of the Republic, 410
Rose, Carol, 1090

Rosen, Craig, 1060
Rosenak, Chuck, 783
Rosenak, Jan, 783
Roses, 1277
Ross Lee Finney: a bio-bibliog, 1039
Ross, John M., 249
Ross, Leslie, 799
Rossi, Renzo, 458
Roth, Barry, 988
Rousseau, John J., 1213
Routh, Rebecca, 114
Routledge dict of lang & linguistics, 812
Routledge German technical dict, 851
Rowland, William G., Jr., 296
Rowlands, John, 353
Rowlands, Sheila, 353
Rozario, Diane, 1339
Rubin, Harvey W., 201
Rubin, Louis D., Jr., 924
Ruffin, M. Holt, 123
Ruppli, Michel, 1031
Rusak, Halina R., 808
Russell, Cheryl, 324
Russell, Letty M., 1177
Russell, Norma Jean, 872
Russian-English collocational dict of the human body, 867
Rust, E. Gardner, 1087
Ryan, Bryan, 335
Ryan, Steve, 1113

Saari, Peggy, 26
Sackett, Susan, 1128
Sacks, David, 450
St. James gd to fantasy writers, 950
St. James gd to sci fiction writers, 4th ed, 951
St. Lucia, 145
Salazar, Sylvia Ortega, 310
Salkin, Robert M., 469
Salokar, Rebecca Mae, 485
Salsbury, Robert E., 283
Salzman, Jack, 331
Same time ... same station: an A-Z gd to radio from Jack Benny to Howard Stern, 765
Samsel, Jon, 1363
Samuel Johnson ency, 994
Samuel Taylor Coleridge: an annot bibliog of criticism & scholarship, v.3, 990
Samuels, Barbara G., 925
San Francisco almanac, rev ed, 83
San Marino, 121
Sander, Reinhard, 1012
Sanders, Alan J. K., 111
Sarjeant, William A. S., 1402
Savitt, William, 228
Sawinski, Diane M., 204
Sayre, John R., 584
Scanlon, Jennifer, 411
Schaberg, William H., 1157
Schaefer, Christina K., 358

Schaffner, Bradley L., 124
Schandorff, Esther Dech, 1193
Schellinger, Paul E., 469
Schemann, Hans, 852
Schilit, W. Keith, 181
Schinabeck, Michael J., 252
Schlager, Neil, 193
Schleifer, Martha Furman, 1042, 1047, 1048
Schlessinger, Bernard S., 30, 940
Schlessinger, June H., 30, 940
Schlicke, Priscilla, 1229
Schmidt, Carl B., 1044
Schmidt, Diane, 1264, 1272
Schmidt, Gary D., 935
Schmidt, H. Joachim, 1319
Schneider, Stephen H., 1396
Schomberg Center gd to black lit from the 18th century to the present, 918
Schorr, Alan Edward, 336
Schraepler, Hans-Albrecht, 617
Schreck, Ann L., 544
Schwartz, David, 1113
Schwarz, Benyamin, 1094
Science & tech: a purchase gd for libs 1995, 1234
Science experiments index for young people, 2d ed, 1244
Scientific revolution, 1227
SciTech ref plus 1995-96 [CD-ROM], 1228
Scott, G., 1204
Scott, Robert, 853
Scott, Thomas A., 1266
Scott, William, 1223
Scouton, William O., 230
Seamus Heaney: a ref gd, 1008
Search for economics as a sci, 149
Search for security: fndns in intl affairs, 700
Second bibliographic gd to the hist of computing, computers, & the info processing industry, 1364
Secrist-Schmedes, Barbera, 1058
Segal, Jeffrey A., 497
Selden, Holly M., 160
Seldin, Ruth R., 1220
Sendero Luminoso: an annot bibliog of the Shining Path guerrilla movement, 1980-93, 502
Senn, Bryan, 1122
Sennitt, Andrew G., 773
Serials on British TV 1950-94, 1104
Servies, James A., 84
Servies, Lana D., 84
Seventh bk of jr authors & illustrators, 937
Severson, Richard, 1207
Sexton, Donal J., Jr., 560
Sexual harassment, 702
Seymore, Bruce, II, 700
Seymour-Smith, Martin, 887
Shadow of death: an analytic bibliog on pol violence, terrorism, & low-intensity conflict, 501
Shakespeare's lang, 999
Shambhala dict of Taoism, 1226
Shan-English dict, 869
Sharpe, Richard, 573
Shattuck, Gardiner H., Jr., 1180

Shave, D., 247
She, Colleen, 361
Shea, Ann M., 346
Shearer, Barbara S., 1231
Shearer, Benjamin F., 1231
Sheets, William, 1305
Sheppard, Julia, 440
Sherman, Moshe D., 1224
Sherrin, Ned, 71
Sherrow, Victoria, 563, 644
Sherwood, Steve, 284
Shewmaker, Eugene F., 999
Shifflett, Crandall, 400
Shiffman, Jody Robin, 1010
Shim, Jae K., 156
Shipp, Steve, 800
Shippey, T. A., 948
Shipwrecks, 1448
Short, K. R. M., 764
Short story criticism, v.18, 954
Short story criticism, v.19, 955
Short story criticism, v.20, 956
Short story criticism, v.21, 957
Short-title catalogue of Hungarian bks printed before 1851 in the British Lib, 14
Shortwave listening on the road, 774
Shrubs & climbers, 1286
Shull, Michael S., 1123
Sices, David, 846
Sices, Jacqueline B., 846
Siegel, Joel G., 156
Sienkewicz, Thomas J., 1092
Sierra Club green gd, 1431
Sight and Sound film review v.: Jan. 1994 to Dec. 1994, 1135
Signals intelligence in WW II, 560
Sikkel, Robert W., 494, 496
Silbaugh, Katharine B., 499
Silent film performers, 1105
Silent films on video, 1120
Silva, Penny, 830
Silver, Joel, 553
Silverman, Helaine, 794
Silvey, Anita, 939
Simmons, R. C., 40
Simms, Bryan R., 1045
Simon, Reeva S., 136
Simon, Ronald G., 1258
Sing glory & hallelujah! histl & biogl gd to Gospel Hymns nos.1-6 Complete, 1086
Singer, David, 1220
Singerman, Robert, 810
Sir Robert Peel 1788-1850: a bibliog, 439
Sirotof, Gene, 1153
Sisung, Kelle S., 1176
Sixteenth-century British nondramatic writers, 3d series, 983
Skin deep: an A-Z of skin disorders, treatments, & health, 1333
Slade, Alexander L., 521
Slater, Courtenay M., 176, 712

Slavin, Sarah, 737
Slee, Debora A., 1319
Slee, Vergil N., 1319
Slide, Anthony, 1107
Sloan, Dave, 648, 655
Slote, Nancy, 706
Slovenia, 122
Smirnov, A. N., 1267
Smirnov, N. N., 1267
Smith, Angel, 452
Smith, Darren L., 1377
Smith, David Lionel, 331
Smith, Jessie Carney, 34
Smith, Patricia, 781
Smith, Roger, 1411
Smith, Tony, 1326
Snelling, Dennis, 647
Snodgrass, Mary Ellen, 892
Snyder, Lawrence D., 1032
Sobczak, A. J., 948
Social sci ency, 2d ed, 75
Social scis, 2d ed, 76
Some Joe you don't know: an American biogl gd to 100 British TV personalities, 1107
Something about the author, v.81, 926
Something about the author, v.82, 927
Something about the author, v.83, 928
Something about the author, v.84, 929
Something about the author, v.85, 930
Sourcebook of fed courts, 2d ed, 500
Sourcebook of online public record experts, 540
Sources & methods: labour stats, v.2, 260
Sources of London English, 831
South African bibliog, 3d ed, 551
South America, Central America, & the Caribbean 1997, 6th ed, 130
South American cinema, 1124
Southern Africa bibliog, 101
Southwest Pacific campaign, 1941-45, 462
Soviet armed forces, 1918-92, 558
Spaceflight & rocketry, 1300
Spaeth, Harold J., 497
Spahn, Mark, 860
Spain, 396
Sparks, Sheila M., 1353
Sparrows & buntings, 1288
Spears, Richard A., 837
Specialty occupational outlook: trade & tech, 262
Spehr, Paul C., 1142
Spencer, Jonathan, 317
Spilker, Bert, 1331
Spirits, fairies, gnomes, & goblins, 1090
Sporting News baseball gd, 1996 ed, 648
Sporting News hockey gd, 1996-97 ed, 657
Sporting News hockey register, 1996-97 ed, 658
Sporting News official baseball register, 1996 ed, 649
Sporting News pro football gd, 1996 ed, 655
Sporting News pro football register, 1996 ed, 656
Sports in N America, v.5, 642
Sports people in the news 1996, 640
Sports stars: series 2, 641

Sports style gd & ref manual, 757
Sportspeak: an ency of sport, 643
Square dance & contra dance hndbk, 1101
Squirrels, 1293
Stackpole, Noreen, 313
Stade, George, 982
Stafford, Pauline, 726
Stamm, Johann Jakob, 1198
Standard & Poor's insurance co ratings gd, 1995 ed, 202
Standard & Poor's smallcap 600 gd, 1996 ed, 171
Standard carnival glass price gd, 10th ed, 784
Standard catalog of world coins 1601-1700, 780
Standard ency of carnival glass, 5th ed, 785
Standard per dir, 1997, 20th ed, 65
Standish, Peter, 348
Stanford, Michael, 296
Stang, Mark, 650
State legislative sourcebk 1996, 602
Statistical hndbk of social & economic indicators for the former Soviet Union, 125
Statistical hndbk on ...
  adolescents in America, 718
  violence in America, 507
  women in America, 2d ed, 740
Statistics on crime & punishment, 511
Statistics on weapons & violence, 512
Steel market in 1995 & prospects for 1996, 198
Steele, Apollonia, 1005
Steen, Sara J., 305, 309
Stein, Gordon, 634
Stephens, Michael L., 1114
Stern, Peter A., 502
Stern, Robert N., 250
Stern, Steven B., 1449
Sternberg, Martin L. A., 871
Stern's gd to the cruise vacation, 6th ed, 1449
Sternstein, Jerome L., 33
Stewart, John, 444
Stewart, Sean, 649, 656, 658
Stewart, Susan Cobb, 1341
Still, Judith Anne, 1046
Stillerman, Elaine, 1350
Stocker, Friedrich W., 1266
Storey, John W., 1218
Strange & unexplained happenings, 638
Straub, Deborah Gillan, 328, 967
Strength in numbers: a lesbian, gay, & bisexual resource, 703
Strickler, Dave, 1095
Strong, M. C., 1085
Strouthes, Daniel P., 490
Struble, John Warthen, 1059
Stuart-Hamilton, Ian, 629
Stubblebine, Donald J., 1069
Stubbs, Jean, 132
Stubbs, Kendon, 527
Student's gd to ...
  African American genealogy, 359
  British American genealogy, 360
  Chinese American genealogy, 361
  German American genealogy, 362

Student's gd to ... (*continued*)
   Irish American genealogy, 365
   Italian American genealogy, 363
   Native American genealogy, 366
   Scaninavian American genealogy, 364
Stuhlmueller, Carroll, 1196
Stych, F. S., 1011
Subject gd to women of the world, 741
Summer theatre dir 1996, 1153
Summers, Claude J., 888
Summers, Harry G., Jr., 434
Supplement to The Modern Ency of Russian, Soviet, & Eurasian Hist, v.1, 476
Supreme Court compendium, 2d ed, 497
Supreme Court yrbk 1995-96, 603
Surnames of Wales, 353
Sutherland, Stuart, 630
Sutton, Walter, 442
Svecevicius, Bronius, 862
Swan, Jennifer, 757
Swanson, James A., 1199
Sweeney, Jerry K., 569
Sydney, 392
Syndicated comic strips & artists, 1924-95, 1095
Szycher, Michael, 1332
Szycher's dict of medical devices, 1332

Tabloid journalism, 747
Taeuber, Cynthia M., 740
Takacs, Geza, 857
Talbot, Ian, 126
Tambini, Michael, 788
Tandy, Ian, 217
Tanzania, rev ed, 102
Tardiff, Joseph C., 334
Tarr, Rodger L., 974
Tate, Thelma H., 1245
Tatla, Darshan Singh, 126
Taves, Brian, 952
Taylor, Bonnie B., 491
Taylor, Cynthia M., 1353
Taylor, Michael, 1438
Taylor's gd to fruits & berries, 1259
Taylor's gd to heirloom vegetables, 1260
Te Matatiki: contemporary Maori words, 863
Television program master index, 1144
Television writers gd, 4th ed, 769
Tenenbaum, Barbara A., 349
Tesar, Jenny, 7
Theatrical design in the 20th century, 1155
Theological dict of the O.T., v.7, 1200
Think tank dir, 622
This is a Thriller: an episode gd, hist, & analysis of the classic 1960s TV series, 1138
Thomas Wolfe: an annot critical bibliog, 976
Thompson, Della, 821
Thompson, Henry O., 1194
Thompson, Virginia, 95
Thompson, William N., 344
Thorson, Marcie Kisner, 292

365 ways...retirees' resource gd for productive lifestyles, 669
Thurmond, Molly E., 207
Tiller, Veronica E. Velarde, 342
Time Out film gd, 5th ed, 1136
Tirion, Wil, 1393
TLA film & video gd 1996-97, 1125
To be continued: an annot gd to sequels, 946
Tobacco & health network dir 1996, 4th ed, 1325
Tobias, Russell R., 1302
Tomajczyk, S. F., 566
Tompkins, Vincent, 422, 423
Tony Richardson: a bio-bibliog, 1096
Total TV, 4th ed, 1132
Totten, Samuel, 295
Townsend, Kiliaen V. R., 297
Track & field record holders, 663
Trade data elements dir v.3, 277
Tran, Hoai Huong, 278
Trask, R. L., 819
Trauth, Gregory, 812
Travel dict, new ed, 384
Travel gd to Jewish Europe, 2d ed, 436
Travers, Bridget, 1238
Tremaine, M. David, 1340
Trends in Europe & N America 1995, 719
Treptow, Kurt W., 120
Tricard, Louise Mead, 664
Trigg, George L., 1407, 1408
Trilingual vocabulary of road transport vehicles, 229
Tucker, Spencer C., 467
Tunstall, Daniel B., 1432
Turabian, Kate L., 755
Turgeon, Lynn, 149
Turkington, Carol, 1334
Turkington, Carol A., 1333
Turner, Jeffrey S., 631
Tuttle dict of the martial arts of Korea, China, & Japan, 659
Twentieth-century American music for the dance, 1103
Twentieth-century Caribbean & black African writers, 3d series, 1012
Twentieth-century literary criticism, v.58, 919
Twentieth-century literary criticism, v.59, 920
Twentieth-century literary criticism, v.60, 921
Twentieth-century literary criticism, v.61, 922
Twentieth-century literary criticism annual cum title index for 1996, 923
2001 French & English idioms, 2d ed, 846
2001 Japanese & English idioms, 859
Tyler, Sean, 1063

Uganda, rev ed, 104
Ulrich's intl pers dir 1997, 35th ed, 66
Ultimate gd to lesbian & gay film & video, 1126
Ultimate gd to sci fiction, 2d ed, 949
Understanding the census, lib ed, 713
Unger, Harlow G., 288
U.S. Catholic sources, 1215
U.S. electric industry phone & fax dir, 1996, 1418

United States govt manual 1996/97, 604
United States hist, 406
United States immigration, 621
U.S. labor movement, 250
U.S. presidential candidates & the elections, 588
U.S. women's interest groups, 737
University & college museums, galleries, & related facilities, 62
UNIX dict of commands, terms, & acronyms, 1373
Upjohn, Richard, 123
Upton, Clive, 839
Uriona, Martha, 153
Urwin, Derek W., 438
USA in space, 1302
Usilton, Larry W., 445
Using the biological lit, 2d ed, 1264
Utter, Glenn H., 1218
U*X*L biogs [CD-ROM], 27

Valade, Roger M., III, 918
van Creveld, Martin, 477
Vandivier, Elizabeth Louise, 147
Vangermeersch, Richard, 179
van Hartesveldt, Fred R., 561
Van Kemper, Robert, 318
Van Tassel, David D., 87, 88
Vassilian, Hamo B., 1253
Veltrop, Kyle, 649
Vencill, C. Daniel, 587
Vermilyea, Peter C., 67
Vernon, Paul, 1075
Verschueren, Karel, 1389
Veterinary drug hndbk, 2d ed, 1263
Veutro, Martina, 458
Vice presidents, 590
Victorian America, 1876 to 1913, 400
Victorian poetry, 1000
VideoHound's complete gd to cult flicks & trash pics, 1137
Videos of African & African-related performance, 1145
Vile, John R., 596
Vincendeau, Ginette, 1111
Violence & the media, 748
Virtual body [CD-ROM], 1312
Vital gd to combat guns & infantry weapons, 579
Vital gd to fighting aircraft of WW II, 580
Voices of multicultural America, 967
Volcansek, Mary L., 485
Volet, Jean-Marie, 1001

Wagner, Hilory, 709
Walden, Graham R., 77
Waldman, Harry, 1108
Waldrup, Carole Chandler, 590
Walford's gd to ref material, v.1: sci & tech, 7th ed, 1229
Walker, Bonnie L., 710
Walker, Peter M. B., 1240
Walker, Thomas G., 497
Wall, C. Edward, 9, 188

Walsh, James E., 547
Walter, John, 782
War in N Africa, 1940-43, 460
War of the Spanish Succession, 1702-13, 435
Warden, Paul G., 286
Wardin, Albert W., Jr., 1173
Warmath, Dee Anne, 250
Warren, Alan, 1138
Warren, Patricia, 1139
Warrick, Susan E., 1214
Wars in the Third World since 1945, 2d ed, 568
Washington almanac of intl trade & business, 1995/96, 230
Watson, Benjamin, 1260
Watson, Lia M., 157
Watts, Thomas D., 704
Weather America, 1397
Weather of US cities, 5th ed, 1398
Web site source bk 1996, 1377
Webb, Dennis, 786
Webster, Valerie J., 157
Webster's new American dict, 822
Weigel, Molly, 961
Weinberg, Meyer, 325
Weismantel, Guy E., 1378
Weldon, Michael J., 1140
Well-tempered announcer: a pronunciation gd to classical music, 1056
Wells, Daniel A., 960
Wells, Donald A., 1161
Wendling, Patricia A., 314
Wertsman, Vladimir F., 532, 1254
West, Cornel, 331
West, Kathryn, 738
Western & frontier film & TV credits 1903-95, 1130
Western civilization: a critical gd to documentary films, 1118
Western Europe since 1945, 437
Western lore & lang, 841
Western Sahara, 105
What in the word? origins of words dealing with people & places, 823
What's cooking in multicultural America, 1254
What's in a name, 369
Wheal, Elizabeth-Anne, 474
Wheeless, Carl, 391
Whisenhunt, Donald W., 417, 418
Whitaker, John O., Jr., 1294
Whitburn, Joel, 1061, 1062, 1070, 1079
White, Evelyn Davidson, 1054
Whiteley, Sandy, 12
Whitley, M. J., 574
Who was who v.9: who was who 1991-95, 28
Who's who in finance & industry, 1996-97, 152
Who's who in the world 1996, 13th ed, 29
Who's who in theology & sci, 1996 ed, 1175
Who's who in ...
    Polish America, 1996-1997 ed, 35
    sci & engineering 1996-97, 3d ed, 1232
    sci in Europe, 9th ed, 1233
    South African pols, no.5, 611

Who's who in ... (continued)
   the South & Southwest 1995-96, 36
Who's who of Australian children's writers, 2d ed, 931
Who's who of Nobel prize winners 1901-95, 3d ed, 30
Who's who on the Moon, 1394
Wholesale & retail trade USA, 279
Why Eve doesn't have an Adam's apple: a dict of sex differences, 1318
Widdowson, J. D. A., 839
Wieland, James, 1002
Wiener, Michael C., 1447
Wierzbianski, Boleslaw, 35
Wilcox, Derk Arend, 614
Wiley dict of civil engineering & construction: English-Spanish/Spanish-English, 1304
Wilkes, G. A., 829
Wilkinson, Robert, 1158
William Congreve: an annot bibliog, 1978-94, 991
William Grant Still: a bio-bibliog, 1046
Williams, Frank P., III, 505
Williams, Gary C., 1295
Williams, James G., 1367, 1371
Williams, Jane A., 280
Williams, Mark, 1013
Williams, Patrick, 402
Williams, Vergil L., 506
Williamson, Gordon K., 185
Willig, John T., 181
Wilmeth, Don B., 1151
Wilson, Andrew, 1301
Wilson, C. Dwayne, 623
Wilson, Ellen Judy, 475
Wilson, George, 472
Wilson, William, 597
Wilt, David Edward, 1123
Wind chamber music, 1058
Winig, Laura, 266
Wired style, 758
Wishlade, Fiona, 243
Witman, Kathleen L., 193
Wittgenstein dict, 1162
Wolfson, Paulette S., 224
Wolman, Benjamin B., 1356
Womack, Kenneth, 880
Women & men in Europe & N America 1995, 720
Women & music, 1020
Women & religion in Britain & Ireland, 1170
Women & sci, 730
Women & the military, 563
Women composers & songwriters, 1035
Women composers, v.1, 1047
Women composers, v.2, 1048
Women in ...
   agriculture, 1245
   Christian hist, 731
   law, 485
   Nigeria, 725
   the biblical world, v.1, 1186
   the US military, 1901-95, 559
Women of color: feminist theory, 729
Women of strength, 733

Women state & territorial legislators, 1895-1995, 601
Women workers, 732
Women writers in the US, 738
Women's complete healthbk, 1341
Women's periodicals in the US, 743
Women's studies on disc [CD-ROM], 742
Women's words, 72
Wood, Laura Matysek, 467
Wood, Richard A., 1398
Woodstra, Chris, 1072
Woodworth, Steven E., 421
Working stiffs, union maids, reds, & riffraff: an organized gd to films about labor, 1141
World academic database [CD-ROM], 308
World Afghanistan to Zimbabwe, 378
World Almanac job finders gd 1997, 263
World authors 1900-50, 887
World biogl index, 2d ed [CD-ROM], 31
World Bk ency, [1996 ed], 48
World Bk Rush-Presbyterian-St. Luke's medical center medical ency, 7th ed, 1335
World databases in ...
   agriculture, 1247
   bioscis & pharmacology, 1241
   chemistry, 1383
   co info, 172
   social scis, 78
World dir of ...
   business info libs, 548
   country environmental studies, 3d ed, 1432
   defence & security, 567
   human rights research & training insts, 3d ed, 518
   trade & business assns, 173
   trade & business journals, 174
World engineering industries & automation, 199
World factbk 1996-97, 80
World gd to religious & spiritual orgs 1996, 1182
World gd to trade assns, 4th ed, 175
World mktg data & stats 1996 on CD-ROM, 2d ed [CD-ROM], 281
World mythology, 1092
World radio TV hndbk, 1996 ed, 773
World retail dir & sourcebk, 2d ed, 222
World stats pocketbk, 721
World stock exchange fact bk, 186
World trade almanac 1996-97, 207
World trade almanac & the dict of intl trade, 1997 ed [CD-ROM], 208
World's Columbian Exposition, 404
World's writing systems, 816
Worldwide gd to equivalent nonferrous metals & alloys, 3d ed, 1309
Worldwide offshore contractors & equipment dir, 1996, 28th ed, 1419
Wortman, William A., 885
Wostbrock, Fred, 1113
Woy, James, 177
Wright, Laura, 831
Wright, Marshall D., 651
Writer's companion, 924
Writer's Digest dict of concise writing, 759

Writer's ency, 3d ed, 750
Writers of multicultural fiction for YAs, 942
Writer's ultimate research gd, 752
Writing centers, 284
Writings on African archives, 92
Written out of TV, 1129
Wrobel, Murray, 1273
Wynar, Lubomyr R., 522

Yaakov, Juliette, 945
Yai, Olabiyi Babalola, 879
Yamazaki, Moriichi, 1202
Yankee talk: a dict of New England expressions, 835
Year bk of the Muslim world 1996, 81
Yearbook of labour stats 1995, 54th ed, 261
Yoder, Andrew, 774
Young person's occupational outlook hndbk, 264
Young, William C., 302
Your reading, 1995-96 ed, 925
Yrigoyen, Charles Jr., 1214
Yuill, Douglas, 243

Zaniello, Tom, 1141
Zell, Hans M., 552
Zeno, Susan M., 817
Zhuk, A. B., 782
Zilberman, Shimon, 856
Zils, Michael, 175
Zimbaro, Valerie P., 893
Zipperer, Lorri A., 1316
Ziring, Lawrence, 620
Zorc, R. David, 844
Zwillinger, Daniel, 1413
Zwirn, Jerrold, 54

Subject Index
Reference is to entry number.

ABBREVIATIONS. *See also* **ACRONYMS**
Acronyms, initialisms, & abbrevs dict 1997, 21st ed, 1
Gobbledygook bk: a dict of acronyms, abbrevs, initializations, & esoteric terminology, 2

ABORTION
Abortion, 2d ed, 666
Abortion policies, v.3, 665

ABSTRACT EXPRESSIONISM
Abstract expressionist women painters, 808

ACCIDENTS—PREVENTION
Injury prevention for young children, 710

ACCOUNTING
History of accounting, 179

ACRONYMS
Acronyms, initialisms, & abbrevs dict 1997, 21st ed, 1
Gobbledygook bk: dict of acronyms, abbrevs, initializations, & estoric terminology, 2

ACTORS. *See also* **MOTION PICTURE ACTORS & ACTRESSES**
International dict of theatre-3: actors, directors, & designers, 1149
Quinlan's illus dir of film character actors, new ed, 1106

ADDAMS, JANE
Jane Addams papers, 706

ADMINISTRATIVE AGENCIES
Business orgs, agencies, & pubns dir, 8th ed, 160

ADVENTURE STORIES
Burroughs cyclopaedia, 969

AERONAUTICS
Jane's aero-engines, 1298

AEROSPACE INDUSTRIES
Jane's intl ABC aerospace dir 1996, 46th ed, 217

AFFIRMATIVE ACTION PROGRAMS
Affirmative action, 484

AFGHANISTAN
Dictionary of Afghan wars, revolutions, & insurgencies, 106

AFRICA
Dictionary of Portuguese-African civilization, v.2, 427
Economic & social survey of Africa, 1994-95, 231
Encyclopaedia Africana dict of African biog, v.3, 91
Encyclopedia of world cultures, v.9: Africa & the Middle East, 319
Guinea, 97
Historical dict of Botswana, 3d ed, 94
Historical dict of Congo, 95
Historical dict of Mali, 3d ed, 99
Historical dict of Togo, 3d ed, 103
International dict of historic places, v.4, 468
Kenya, rev ed, 98
Major cos of Africa S of the Sahara 1996, 219
Pan-African chronology, 426
Penguin atlas of African hist, new ed, 428
Videos of African & African-related performance, 1145
Writings on African archives, 92
Year bk of the Muslim world 1996, 81

AFRICA, EAST
East & NE Africa bibliog, 90

AFRICA, NORTH
Algeria, rev ed, 93
Encyclopedia of the modern Middle East, 136
Middle East & N Africa 1997, 43d ed, 139
War in N Africa, 1940-43, 460
Western Sahara, 105

AFRICA—SOCIAL LIFE & CUSTOMS
Peoples of Africa, 321

AFRICA, SOUTHERN
Southern Africa bibliog, 101

AFRICAN LITERATURE
Bibliography of African lits, 1001
Twentieth-century Caribbean & black African writers, 3d series, 1012

AFRO-AMERICAN CHURCHES
Directory of African American religious bodies, 2d ed, 1181

AFRO-AMERICAN WOMEN
Notable black American women, bk.2, 34

AFRO-AMERICANS
African American hist in the press 1851-99, 412
African American voices, 328
African-American yellow pages, 329
Black heritage sites, 330
Choral music by African American composers, 1054
Directory of African American religious bodies, 2d ed, 1181
DISCovering multicultural America [CD-ROM], 323
Distinguished African American scientists of the 20th century, 1230
Encyclopedia of African-American culture & hist, 331
Encyclopedia of African-American educ, 285
Libraries Unltd prof collection CD 1995 [CD-ROM], 523
Narrative bibliog of the African American frontier, 405

Pan-African chronology, 426
Student's gd to African American genealogy, 359

AGED. *See also* **GERONTOLOGY**
Graying of America: an ency of aging, health, mind, & behavior, 668
Resources for elders with disabilities, 3d ed, 672
365 ways...retirees' resource gd for productive lifestyles, 669

AGRICULTURE
Atlas of American agriculture, 1246
Who's who in sci in Europe, 9th ed, 1233
Women in agriculture, 1245
World databases in agriculture, 1247

AIDS (DISEASE)
AIDS funding, 4th ed, 683
HIV/AIDS & HIV/AIDS-related terminology, 537

AIR TRAFFIC CONTROL
Jane's air traffic control 1996-97, 3d ed, 1439

AIRCRAFT INDUSTRY
Brassey's world aircraft & systems dir 1996/97, 1438

AIR-ENGINES
Jane's aero-engines, 1298

AIRPLANES
Brassey's world aircraft & systems dir 1996/97, 1438
Jane's all the world's aircraft 1996-97, 87th ed, 1440

AIRPLANES, MILITARY
Jane's aircraft upgrades, 1996-97, 4th ed, 572
Vital gd to fighting aircraft of WW II, 580

ALBANIA
Historical dict of Albania, 113

ALCOHOLIC BEVERAGES
Alcohol in the British Isles from Roman times to 1996, 441

ALGERIA
Algeria, rev ed, 93

ALLEGORY
Encyclopedia of allegorical lit, 890

ALLOYS
Fatigue data bk, 1308
Worldwide gd to equivalent nonferrous metals & alloys, 3d ed, 1309

ALMANACS
Awesome almanac—N.Y., 85
Awesome almanac—Ohio, 86
Awesome almanac—Tex., 89
Canadian almanac & dir 1997, 3
Canadian sourcebk, 1997, 32d ed, 4
Chase's calendar of events 1997, 40th ed, 5
Chase's sports calendar of events 1997, 639

Information please almanac, atlas, & yrbk, 1996, 49th ed, 6
New view almanac, 7
San Francisco almanac, rev ed, 83

ALPINE GARDEN PLANTS
Cushion plants for the rock garden, 1257

ALTERNATIVE MEDICINE. *See also* **MEDICINE, POPULAR**
Complete gd to homeopathy, 1347
Complete home health advisor, 1344
Encyclopedia of alternative medicine, 1345
Encyclopedia of bodywork, 1350
Encyclopedia of nutritional suppls, 1349
Medical advisor, 1348

ALTERNATIVE PRESS INDEX
Alternative Press index, 58
Annotations: a dir of pers listed in the Alternative Press Index, 1996 ed, 63

AMERICAN FILM INDEX
American film personnel & co credits, 1908-20, 1142

AMERICAN JEWISH HISTORICAL SOCIETY
Index to American Jewish Histl Quarterly/American Jewish Hist: vs.51-80, 347

AMERICAN LITERATURE
American nature writers, 965
American writers, suppl 4, 961
Bibliographical gd to the study of Western American lit, 2d ed, 959
Cambridge pa gd to lit in English, 894
Encyclopedia of transcendentalism, 964
James A. Michener: a bibliog, 973
Literally entitled, 891
Literary index to American mags, 1850-1900, 960
Oxford companion to American lit, 6th ed, 966
Voices of multicultural America, 967

AMERICAN POETRY
Concordance to the complete poems & plays of T. S. Eliot, 971
Guide to the secular poetry of T. S. Eliot, 970
Response to Allen Ginsberg, 1926-94, 972

AMERICAN SIGN LANGUAGE
Essential ASL, 871
NTC's multilingual dict of American Sign Lang, 870

AMERICAN TURNERS
Research gd to the Turner movement in the US, 333

AMERICANISMS
Dictionary of American regional English, v.3: I-0, 833
NTC's dict of folksy, regional, & rural sayings, 837
Western lore & lang, 841
Yankee talk: a dict of New England expressions, 835

ANDERSON, MAXWELL
Maxwell Anderson on the European stage 1929-92, 1147

ANGELS
Angels A to Z, 1176

ANIMAL BREEDS
International ency of horse breeds, 1291

ANIMALS
Field gd to common animal poisons, 1262

ANKLE
Foot & ankle sourcebk, 1340

ANTHROPOLOGY
Encyclopedia of cultural anthropology, 316
Encyclopedia of social & cultural anthropology, 317
Encyclopedia of world cultures, v.8: Middle America & the Caribbean, 318
Encyclopedia of world cultures, v.9: Africa & the Middle East, 319
Encyclopedia of world cultures, v.10: indexes, 320

ANTI-COMMUNIST MOVEMENTS
Encyclopedia of the McCarthy era, 591

APOCALYPTIC LITERATURE
Encyclopedia of apocalyptic lit, 893

ARAB COUNTRIES
Major cos of the Arab world 1996/97, 20th ed, 233

ARAMAIC LANGUAGE
Hebrew & Aramaic lexicon of the O.T., v.2, 1198

ARCHAEOLOGY
Archaeology of the Mississippian culture, 398
Encyclopedia of the hist of classical archaeology, 397

ARCHITECTURE
Dictionary of bldg preservation, 801
Dictionary of Islamic architecture, 803
Dutch modernism, 802
Information sources in architecture & construction, 2d ed, 1299

ARCHIVES
British archives, 3d ed, 440
Guide to info resources in ethnic museum, lib, & archive collections in the US, 522
Writings on African archives, 92

ARGENTINA
Argentina business, 245
Argentina co hndbk, 246

ARMENIAN LANGUAGE—DICTIONARIES—ENGLISH
Armenian (Eastern)-English dict, 844

ARMORED VEHICLES (MILITARY)
Jane's tank & combat vehicle recognition gd, 576

ART
African ethnonyms, 315
Baroque art, 798
BHA: bibliog of the hist of art 1996 [CD-ROM], 791
BHA: bibliog of the hist of art: subject headings/English, 790
Four French symbolists, 806
Latin American women artists, 793
Medieval art, 799

ART & RELIGION
Bibliography of sources of Christianity & the arts, 1206
Encyclopedia of women in religious art, 797

ART, MODERN
Abstract expressionist women painters, 808
American art colonies, 1850-1930, 800
Contemporary artists, 4th ed, 795
Realization & suppression of the Situationist Intl, 792

ART MUSEUMS
National Gallery complete illus catalogue, 796

ARTILLERY
Jane's armour & artillery 1995-96, 16th ed, 575

ARTIST COLONIES
American art colonies, 1850-1930, 800
Artists & writers colonies, 745

ARTISTS
Contemporary artists, 4th ed, 795

ARTS
Bibliography of sources in Christianity & the arts, 1206
Reader's adviser on CD-ROM [CD-ROM], 11

ASIA
Asian markets, 4th ed, 234
Directory of trade & investment related orgs of developing countries & areas in Asia & the Pacific, 7th ed, 235
Electric power in Asia & the Pacific, 1991 & 1992, 1420
International dict of historic places, v.5, 469
Prices & financial stats in the ESCWA region, 192
Supplement to The Modern Ency of Russian, Soviet, & Eurasian Hist, v.1, 476
Year bk of the Muslim world 1996, 81

ASIA, SOUTHEASTERN
Historical atlas of SE Asia, 429

ASIAN AMERICANS
Asian American chronology, 326
Asian Americans: social, economic, & pol aspects, 327
DISCovering multicultural America [CD-ROM], 323
Student's gd to Chinese American genealogy, 361

ASIAN LITERATURE. *See* **ORIENTAL LITERATURE**

ASIMOV, ISAAC
Isaac Asimov: an annot bibliog of the Asimov collection at Boston Univ, 968

ASSOCIATIONS, INSTITUTIONS, ETC. *See also* TRADE & PROFESSIONAL ASSOCIATIONS
Business orgs, agencies, & pubns dir, 8th ed, 160
Encyclopedia of assns: natl orgs of the US [CD-ROM], 49
Post-Soviet hndbk, 123
World gd to religious & spiritual orgs 1996, 1182

ASTRONAUTICS
Spaceflight & rocketry, 1300
USA in space, 1302

ASTRONOMY
Cambridge astronomy dict, 1392
Cambridge star atlas, 2d ed, 1393
Eyewitness ency of space & the universe [CD-ROM], 1395
Popular physics & astronomy, 1411
Who's who on the moon, 1394

ATHLETES
Sports people in the news 1996, 640
Sports stars: series 2, 641

ATLASES
Cambridge illus atlas of warfare: Renaissance to Revolution, 1492-1792, 556
Cambridge illus atlas of warfare: the Middle Ages, 768-1487, 557
Collins nations of the world atlas, 372
Dorling Kindersley world ref atlas, 2d ed, 373
Hammond atlas of the 20th century, 459
Hammond Citation world atlas, 374
Hammond new century world atlas, 375
Historical atlas of SE Asia, 429
Historical atlas of the Vietnam War, 434
Kentucky: atlas of histl county boundaries, 371
Macmillan color atlas of the states, 82
Mapping America's past, 402
Oxford atlas of the world, 4th ed, 376
Oxford encyclopedic world atlas, 3d ed, 377
Penguin atlas of African hist, new ed, 428
Penguin histl atlas of ancient Greece, 449
Penguin histl atlas of dinosaurs, 1405
World Afghanistan to Zimbabwe, 378

ATTITUDE (PSYCHOLOGY)
Official gd to American attitudes, 717

AUDIO-VISUAL MATERIALS
Audiovisual resources for family programming, 313
Elementary school lib collection, 20th ed, 544
Elementary school lib collection, 20th ed [CD-ROM], 545

AUGUSTINE, SAINT
Confessions of Saint Augustine, 1207

AUSTEN, JANE
Annotated bibliog of Jane Austen studies 1984-94, 988

AUSTRALIA
Australia: a reader's gd, 112
Australia business, 237
Contemporary Australian women 1996/97, 734
Far East & Australasia 1997, 28th ed, 143
Oxford companion to Australian military hist, 565
Periodicals in print: Australia, New Zealand, & the S Pacific 1996, 13th ed, 64

AUSTRALIAN LITERATURE
Post-Colonial lits in English: Australia, 1970-92, 1002
Who's who of Australian children's writers, 2d ed, 931

AUSTRALIANISMS
Dictionary of Australian colloquialisms, 4th ed, 829

AUTHORS
Contemporary literary criticism, v.87, 896
Contemporary literary criticism, v.88, 897
Contemporary literary criticism, v.89, 898
DISCovering authors modules [CD-ROM], 900
Feminist writers, 886
James Joyce A to Z, 1009
Literature criticism from 1400 to 1800, v.28, 901
Literature criticism from 1400 to 1800, v.29, 902
Literature criticism from 1400 to 1800, v.30, 903
Literature criticism from 1400 to 1800, v.31, 904
Magill's survey of world lit, 905
Nineteenth-century lit criticism, v.47, 908
Nineteenth-century lit criticism, v.48, 909
Nineteenth-century lit criticism, v.49, 910
Nineteenth-century lit criticism, v.50, 911
Nineteenth-century lit criticism, v.51, 912
Nineteenth-century lit criticism, v.52, 913
Nineteenth-century lit criticism annual cum title index for 1996, 914
100 most popular YA authors, 941
Reader's gd to lit in English, 915
Reader's gd to 20th-century writers, 916
St. James gd to sci fiction writers, 4th ed, 951
Seventh bk of jr authors & illustrators, 937
Short story criticism, v.18, 954
Short story criticism, v.19, 955
Short story criticism, v.20, 956
Short story criticism, v.21, 957
Something about the author, v.81, 926
Something about the author, v.82, 927
Something about the author, v.83, 928
Something about the author, v.84, 929
Something about the author, v.85, 930
Television writers gd, 4th ed, 769
Twentieth-century literary criticism, v.59, 920
Twentieth-century literary criticism, v.60, 921
Twentieth-century literary criticism, v.61, 922
Twentieth-century literary criticism annual cum title index for 1996, 923
Who's who of Australian children's writers, 2d ed, 931
World authors 1900-50, 887

AUTHORS, AMERICAN
American nature writers, 965

American writers, suppl 4, 961
Biographical dict of transcendentalism, 962
Burroughs cyclopaedia, 969
Dictionary of literary biog documentary series, v.13, 963
Directory of American poets & fiction writers, 1995-96 ed, 749
Isaac Asimov: an annot bibliog of the Asimov collection at Boston Univ, 968
James A. Michener: a bibliog, 973
John Steinbeck: an annot gd to biogl sources, 975
Marjorie Kinnan Rawlings: a descriptive bibliog, 974
Thomas Wolfe: an annot critical bibliog, 976

AUTHORS, CANADIAN
Canadian writers & their works: fiction series, v.12, 1003
John Metcalf papers, 1005

AUTHORS, ENGLISH
Ann Radcliffe: a bio-bibliog, 998
Annotated bibliog of Jane Austen studies 1984-94, 988
British children's writers, 1800-80, 934
British children's writers, 1914-60, 935
British children's writers since 1960, 1st series, 936
British reform writers, 1789-1832, 977
British short-fiction writers, 1800-80, 978
British short-fiction writers, 1880-1914, 979
British short-fiction writers, 1915-45, 980
British travel writers, 1837-75, 981
British writers, suppl 3, 982
Chaucer's pilgrims, 989
Companion to the characters in the fiction & drama of W. Somerset Maugham, 996
D. H. Lawrence: a ref companion, 995
Encyclopedia of British humorists, 984
Every thing in Dickens, 992
Every one in Dickens, 993
Samuel Johnson ency, 994
Samuel Taylor Coleridge: an annot bibliog of criticism & scholarship, v.3, 990
Sixteenth-century British nondramatic writers, 3d series, 983
William Congreve: an annot bibliog, 991

AUTHORS, GERMAN
German baroque writers, 1580-1660, 1006

AUTHORS, ITALIAN
Boccaccio in English: a bibliog of eds, adaptations, & criticism, 1011

AUTHORSHIP. See also PUBLISHERS & PUBLISHING
Artists & writers colonies, 745
Grants & awards available to American writers 1996-97, 19th ed, 694
Market gd for young writers, 5th ed, 751
Novel & short story writer's market, 1996, 753
Romance writer's sourcebk, 754
Writer's Digest dict of concise writing, 759
Writer's ency, 3d ed, 750
Writer's ultimate research gd, 752

AUTOGRAPHS
Collector's gd to celebrity autographs, 775

AUTOMOBILES
Dictionary of automotive engineering, 2d ed, 1303

AUTOMOBILES—LICENSES
Official license plate bk, 1447

AVANT-GARDE
Realization & suppression of the Situationist Intl, 792

AVIATION
Jane's avionics 1996-97, 15th ed, 1441

AWARDS
Children's bks: awards & prizes, 1996 ed, 932
Contemporary literary criticism, v.87, 896
Entertainment awards, 1099
Grants & awards available to American writers 1996-97, 19th ed, 694

BAEZ, JOAN
Joan Baez: a bio-bibliog, 1074

BALLET DANCERS
Dancers & choreographers, 1100

BANKRUPTCY
Sourcebook of fed courts, 2d ed, 500

BANKS & BANKING. See also ECONOMICS; FINANCE
Fitzroy Dearborn dir of the world's banks, 11th ed, 190
Information sources in finance & banking, 191
Prices & financial stats in the ESCWA region, 192

BAROQUE LITERATURE
German baroque writers, 1580-1660, 1006

BASEBALL
Baseball by the nos, 650
Former major league teams, 646
Inside Sports world series factbk, 645
Nineteenth century baseball, 651
Pacific Coast League: statl hist, 1903-57, 647
Sporting News baseball gd, 1996 ed, 648
Sporting News official baseball register, 1996 ed, 649

BASKETBALL
NCAA basketball, 652
NCAA Final Four, 653

BED & BREAKFAST ACCOMMODATIONS
Canadian bed & breakfast gd, 12th ed, 393
Complete gd to American bed & breakfast, 4th ed, 385
National Trust gd to historic bed & breakfasts, inns, & small hotels, 4th ed, 390

BEER
Beer-taster's log, 1252
North American brewers resource dir 1996-97, 13th ed, 1251

BERG, ALBAN
Alban Berg: a gd to research, 1045

BEST BOOKS
Dictionary of American children's fiction, 1990-94, 938
Earth works, 1424
New York Public Lib's bks of the century, 882
Recommended reading: 500 classics reviewed, 883
Ultimate gd to sci fiction, 2d ed, 949

BEVERAGE INDUSTRY
European drinks mktg dir, 4th ed, 240
Food & beverage market place, 1996, 1249

BEVERAGES IN LITERATURE
Food & drink in lit, 881

BIBLE
Bible baby names, 368
Catalog of choral music arranged in biblical order, 2d ed, 1053
Hermann Sasse: a bibliog, 1168
Literary-Critical approaches to the Bible, 1190
Women in the biblical world, v.1, 1186

BIBLE—DICTIONARIES
Collegeville pastoral dict of biblical theology, 1196
Dictionary of the Bible, 1195
Evangelical dict of biblical theology, 1197

BIBLE, N.T.
Book of Ephesians, 1188
Book of Revelation, 1191
Exegetical bibliog of the N.T., v.4, 1185
Exhaustive concordance to the Greek N.T., 1199
Hellenistic commentary to the N.T., 1201
New Testament intro, 1192

BIBLE, O.T.
Book of Jeremiah, 1194
Hebrew & Aramaic lexicon of the O.T., v.2, 1198
Old Testament commentary survey, 2d ed, 1189
Old Testament intro, 1187
Theological dict of the O.T., v.7, 1200

BIBLIOGRAPHY
Anders CD-ROM gd, 2d ed, 15
Audiovisual resources for family programming, 313
Bibliography of sources in Christianity & the arts, 1206
Books in print 1996-97, 49th ed, 18
British imprints relating to N America, 1621-1760, 40
Business A to Z source finder, 147
Catalogue of medieval & Renaissance mss in the Houghton Lib, Harvard Univ, v.1, 546
Catalogue of the 15th-century printed bks in the Harvard Univ Lib, v.4, 547
CD-ROMs in print 1995 [CD-ROM], 16
CD-ROMs in print 1996, 17
Classical studies, 461
English Catholic bks, 1701-1800, 1204
General bibliog for music research, 3d ed, 1022
Global voices, global visions: a core collection of multicultural bks, 10
Guide to ref bks, 11th ed, 8
Law bks & serials in print 1996, 481
1990-91 Gulf War, 456
Noble's intl gd to the law reports, 483
Printed catalogues of the Harvard College Lib, 1723-90, 39
Reader's adviser on CD-ROM [CD-ROM], 11
Reference sources hndbk, 4th ed, 13
Science & tech: a purchase gd for libs 1995, 1234
Short-Title catalogue of Hungarian bks printed before 1851 in the British Lib, 14
South African bibliog, 3d ed, 551
Soviet armed forces, 1918-92, 558
Women & music, 1020

BIG BANDS
Command performance, USA! a discography, 772

BIOGRAPHY
Art, truth, & high pols: a bibliographic study of the Official Lives of Queen Victoria's ministers in Cabinet, 1843-1969, 608
Biographical dict of European labor leaders, 151
Biographical dict of transcendentalism, 962
Biographical dict of 20th-century philosophers, 1158
Biographical dir of Native American painters, 807
British children's writers, 1800-80
British children's writers, 1914-1960, 935
British children's writers since 1960, 1st series, 936
British short-fiction writers, 1800-80, 978
British short-fiction writers, 1880-1914, 979
British short-fiction writers, 1915-45, 980
British women's hist, 726
Cambridge biogl dict, 20
Canadian who's who 1996: v.31, 37
Contemporary Australian women 1996/97, 734
Dictionary of Hispanic biog, 334
Dictionary of intl biog 1996, 24th ed, 21
Dictionary of literary biog documentary series, v.13, 963
Dictionary of natl biog, 1986-90, 38
Distinguished African American scientists of the 20th century, 1230
Encyclopaedia Africana dict of African biog, v.3, 91
Encyclopedia of American biog, 2d ed, 33
German baroque writers, 1580-1660, 1006
Grolier lib of intl biogs, 23
Harvard biogl dict of music, 1024
Heroes of conscience: a biogl dict, 22
International who's who in music, v.2: popular music, 1063
Members of Congress, 584
Merriam-Webster's pocket biogl dict, 24
Notable black American women, bk.2, 34
Notable women in the life scis, 1231
Pocket factfile of 20th century people, 25
Subject gd to women of the world, 741
Who was who v.9: who was who 1991-95, 28
Who's who in finance & industry, 1996-97, 152
Who's who in the world 1996, 13th ed, 29

Who's who in sci & engineering 1996-97, 3d ed, 1232
Who's who in sci in Europe, 9th ed, 1233
Who's who in South African pols, no.5, 611
Who's who in the South & Southwest 1995-96, 36
Who's who of Nobel prize winners 1901-95, 3d ed, 30
Women of strength, 733
World authors 1900-50, 887
World biographical index, 2d ed [CD-ROM], 31

BIOGRAPHY—JUVENILE LITERATURE
Native N American biog, 339
Profiles in world hist, 472
Prominent women of the 20th century, 26
Sports people in the news 1996, 640
Sports stars: series 2, 641
U*X*L biogs [CD-ROM], 27

BIOLOGICAL WARFARE
Jane's NBC protection equipment 1996-97, 9th ed, 570

BIOLOGY
Concise ency biology, 1266
Elsevier's dict of fundamental & applied biology, 1267
Encyclopedia of molecular biology & molecular medicine, v.1, 1269
Encyclopedia of molecular biology & molecular medicine, v.2, 1270
Encyclopedia of molecular biology & molecular medicine, v.3, 1271
Using the biographical lit, 2d ed, 1264

BIRDS
National Audubon Society interactive CD-ROM gd to N American birds [CD-ROM], 1290
Neotropical migratory birds, 1289
Sparrows & buntings, 1288

BIRTHDAY BOOKS
Born this day, 41

BISEXUALS
Strength in numbers: a lesbian, gay, & bisexual resource, 703

BLACKS IN LITERATURE
Schomberg Center gd to black lit from the 18th century to the present, 918

BLACKS—MUSIC
Brass music of black composers, 1041

BLIND—REHABILITATION
Living with low vision, 671

BLUES (MUSIC)
All music gd to the blues, 1072

BOARDING SCHOOLS
Boarding school gd, 297

BOCCACCIO, GIOVANNI
Boccaccio in English: a bibliog of eds, adaptations, & criticism, 1011

BODY, HUMAN
Russian-English collocational dict of the human body, 867
Virtual body, 1312

BONSAI
Bonsai survival manual, 1256

BOOK COLLECTING
Huxford's old bk value gd, 8th ed, 776

BOOK INDUSTRIES & TRADE. See also
PUBLISHERS & PUBLISHING
Harrod's librarians' glossary, 8th ed, 526
Librarian's companion, 2d ed, 532

BOOKS
Encyclopedia of the bk, 2d ed, 554

BOOKSELLERS & BOOKSELLING. See also
PUBLISHERS & PUBLISHING
Authentic Jane Williams' home school mrkt gd, 280
Bowker annual lib & bk trade almanac, 1996, 41st ed, 528
Publishers, distrs, & wholesalers of the US 1996-97, 555

BOTANY
Elsevier's dict of plant names, 1273
Guide to info sources in the botanical scis, 2d ed, 1272
Reference gd for botany & horticulture, 1258

BOTSWANA
Historical dict of Botswana, 3d ed, 94

BRAIN
Brain ency, 1334

BRASS INSTRUMENTS
Brass music of black composers, 1041

BREAST MILK
Effects of drugs on the fetus & nursing infant, 1358

BREWING
North American brewers resource dir 1996-97, 13th ed, 1251

BRITISH AMERICANS
Student's gd to British American genealogy, 360

BRITISH LITERATURE
D. H. Lawrence: a ref companion, 995
Magill's survey of world lit, 905
Reader's gd to lit in English, 915
Reader's gd to 20th century writers, 916
World authors 1900-50, 887

BRITTEN, BENJAMIN
Benjamin Britten: a gd to research, 1040

BRUNNER, EMIL
Emil Brunner: a bibliog, 1172

BUDDHISM
Pada index & reverse Pada index to early Jain canons, 1202

BUILDING
Dictionary of bldg preservation, 801

BULBS
Bulbs for the rock garden, 1255
Manual of bulbs, 1276

BUNTINGS (BIRDS)
Sparrows & buntings, 1288

BURROUGHS, EDGAR RICE
Burroughs cyclopaedia, 969

BUSINESS. *See also* BANKS & BANKING; CORPORATIONS; ECONOMICS; FINANCE; MANAGEMENT; MARKETING
America's corporate families 1995, 158
Barron's business thesaurus, 178
Book of European forecasts, 2d ed, 238
Business & economic research dir, 159
Business stats of the US, 1995 ed, 176
Companies intl [CD-ROM], 209
Economic & social survey of Africa, 1994-95, 231
Economics, trade, & dvlpmt: English-Spanish general terminology, 272
Encyclopedia of business, 155
Encyclopedia of business info sources suppl, 10th ed, 177
Encyclopedia of global industries, 204
Every manager's gd to business processes, 267
Profiles in business & mgmt [CD-ROM], 221
World trade almanac 1996-97, 207
World trade almanac & the dict of intl trade, 1997 ed [CD-ROM], 208

BUSINESS—DIRECTORIES
American business locations dir, 157
Asian markets, 4th ed, 234
Business A to Z source finder, 147
Business orgs, agencies, & pubns dir, 8th ed, 160
International dir of co hists, v.12, 214
International dir of co hists, v.13, 215
International dir of co hists, v.14, 216
Hoover's masterlist of major US cos 1996-97, 166
Major business orgs of Eastern Europe & the Commonwealth of Independent States 1995/96, 5th ed, 244
World dir of trade & business assns, 173
World dir of trade & business jls, 174
World retail dir & sourcebk, 2d ed, 222

BUSINESS EDUCATION
Princeton Review student access gd to the best business schools, 169

BUSINESS INFORMATION SERVICES
Asian markets, 4th ed, 234
Encyclopedia of business info sources suppl, 10th ed, 177
International dir of business info sources & servs 1996, 2d ed, 213
Prentice Hall dir of online business info 1997, 168
World dir of business info libs, 548

BUSINESS LIBRARIES
Business lib & how to use it, 6th ed, 530

CALENDARS
Chase's calendar of events 1997, 40th ed, 5
Chase's calendar of sports events 1997, 639

CANADA
Canadian almanac & dir 1997, 3
Canadian bed & breakfast gd, 12th ed, 393
Canadian ency plus, 1997 [CD-ROM], 42
Canadian sourcebk, 1997, 32d ed, 4
Canadian who's who 1996: v.31, 37
Consumer Canada 1996, 268
Profile of western N America, 248

CANADA. BIBLIOGRAPHY
Canadian ref sources, 19

CANADA—HISTORY
Genealogy & local hist to 1900, 351

CANADIAN FICTION
Canadian writers & their works: fiction series, v.12, 1003

CANADIAN POETRY
Canadian writers & their works: poetry series, v.11, 1004

CARIBBEAN AREA
Bibliography of the Caribbean, 128
Cayman Islands, 131
Dictionary of Caribbean English usage, 834
Encyclopedia of world cultures, v.8: Middle America & the Caribbean, 318
Jane's sentinel: Central America & the Caribbean security assessment, 1996 ed, 129

CARIBBEAN LITERATURE
Twentieth-century Caribbean & black African writers, 3d series, 1012

CARNIVAL GLASS
Standard carnival glass price gd, 10th ed, 784
Standard ency of carnival glass, 5th ed, 785

CASTLES
English castles, 394

CATALOGING
Classification plus [CD-ROM], 533
Dewey decimal classification & relative index, 21st ed, 535
Dewey for Windows [CD-ROM], 536
Libraries Ultd prof collection CD 1995 [CD-ROM], 523
Library of Congress subject headings, 19th ed, 534

CATALOGS
Printed catalogues of the Harvard College Lib, 1723-90, 39

CATALOGS, COMMERCIAL
Directory of overseas catalogs, 1997, 212

CATHOLIC CHURCH
English Catholic bks, 1701-1800, 1204
Our Sunday Visitor's 1997 Catholic almanac, 1203
U.S. Catholic sources, 1215

CATHOLIC CHURCH—DOCTRINES
Encyclicals of John Paul II on CD-ROM [CD-ROM], 1217

CATHOLIC SCHOOLS
NCEA/Ganley's Catholic schools in America 1995, 23d ed, 1216

CATS
Help! the quick gd to first aid for your cat, 1261

CAYMAN ISLANDS
Cayman Islands, 131

CD-ROM BOOKS
Anders CD-ROM gd, 2d ed, 15
CD-ROMs in print 1995 [CD-ROM], 16
CD-ROMs in print 1996, 17
Media review digest, v. 26, 1996, 9
Multimedia dir, 4th ed, 1363

CD-ROMs
BHA: bibliog of the hist of art 1996 [CD-ROM], 791
Canadian ency plus, 1997 [CD-ROM], 42
Canadian medical dir on CD-ROM, 1996 [CD-ROM], 1320
CD-ROMs in print 1995 [CD-ROM], 16
Chemistry citation index [CD-ROM], 1390
Civil War CD-ROM [CD-ROM], 401
Classification plus [CD-ROM], 533
Columbia Granger's world of poetry [CD-ROM], 1017
Columbia world of quotations [CD-ROM], 68
Companies intl [CD-ROM], 209
Corporate affiliations plus, spring/summer 1995 [CD-ROM], 162
Corporate dir of US public cos [CD-ROM], 163
Current issues sourcefile [CD-ROM], 59
Dewey for Windows [CD-ROM], 536
Dictionary of substances & their effects [CD-ROM], 1314
Dinosaur hunter [CD-ROM], 1403
DISCovering authors modules [CD-ROM], 900
DISCovering multicultural America [CD-ROM], 323
Dissertation abstracts [CD-ROM], 60
Earthquakes & the built environment index, 1984-July 1995 [CD-ROM], 1399
Elementary school lib collection, 20th ed [CD-ROM], 545
Encyclicals of John Paul II on CD-ROM [CD-ROM], 1217
Encyclopedia Americana [CD-ROM], 43
Encyclopedia of assns: natl orgs of the US [CD-ROM], 49
ERIC on CD-ROM [CD-ROM], 293
Exporting to the USA & the dict of intl trade, 1996-97 ed [CD-ROM], 205
Eyewitness ency of nature [CD-ROM], 1287
Eyewitness ency of space & the universe [CD-ROM], 1395
Family archive viewer [CD-ROM], 355
Family studies database [CD-ROM], 674
Gale's ready ref shelf [CD-ROM], 50
Grants on disc [CD-ROM], 695
Importers manual USA & the dict of intl trade, 1996-97 ed [CD-ROM], 274
Libraries Unltd prof collection CD 1995 [CD-ROM], 523
MathSci disc [CD-ROM], 1414
National Audubon Society interactive CD-ROM gd to N American birds [CD-ROM], 1290
OECD statl compendium 1996/1 [CD-ROM], 227
Oxford English dict on CD, 2d ed [CD-ROM, 843
Poem finder 95 [CD-ROM], 1018
Profiles in business & mgmt [CD-ROM], 221
PsycLit [CD-ROM], 625
Reader's adviser on CD-ROM [CD-ROM], 11
SciTech ref plus 1995-1996 [CD-ROM], 1228
U*X*L biogs [CD-ROM], 27
Virtual body [CD-ROM], 1312
Women's studies on disc [CD-ROM], 742
World academic database [CD-ROM], 308
World biogl index, 2d ed [CD-ROM], 31
World mktg data & stats 1996 on CD-ROM, 2d ed [CD-ROM], 281
World trade almanac & the dict of intl trade, 1997 ed [CD-ROM], 208

CELEBRITIES
Collector's gd to celebrity autographs, 775

CENSORSHIP
Intellectual freedom manual, 5th ed, 542

CENTRAL AMERICA. See also CARIBBEAN AREA
Dictionary of 20th century culture: Hispanic culture of Mexico, Central America, & the Caribbean, 348
Encyclopedia of ancient Mesoamerica, 453
Encyclopedia of world cultures, v.8: Middle America & the Caribbean, 318
Jane's sentinel: Central America & the Caribbean security assessment, 1996 ed, 129

CHAMBER MUSIC
Wind chamber music, 1058

CHARACTERS & CHARACTERISTICS IN LITERATURE
Companion to the characters in the fiction & drama of W. Somerset Maugham, 996

CHARITABLE USES, TRUSTS, & FOUNDATIONS. See also ENDOWMENTS; FUND RAISING; GRANTS-IN-AID
AIDS funding, 4th ed, 683
Awards alamanac 1996, 701
Complete grants sourcebk for higher educ, 3d ed, 684

Directory of social serv grants, 688
Fund raiser's gd to religious philanthropy 1996, 9th ed, 691
Grant seekers gd, 4th ed, 693
International fndn dir 1996, 7th ed, 696
National gd to funding for community dvlpmt, 699
Search for security: fndns in intl affairs, 700

CHARITIES
Corporate 500, 13th ed, 685
Fund raiser's gd to religous philanthropy 1996, 9th ed, 691
Literature of the nonprofit sector, v.7, 682
National dir of grantmaking public charities, 697

CHARTS, DIAGRAMS, ETC.
Information graphics, 1370

CHAUCER, GEOFFREY
Chaucer's pilgrims, 989

CHEMICAL INDUSTRY
Annual bulletin of trade in chemical products, 1384
Encyclopedia of chemical processing & design, v.56, 1378

CHEMICAL LABORATORIES
CRC hndbk of lab safety, 4th ed, 1386
Jane's NBC protection equipment 1996-97, 9th ed, 570

CHEMICALS
Directory of chemical producers & products, v.1, pt.1, 2d ed, 1381
Encyclopedia of chemical processing & design, v.56, 1378
Environmental contaminant ref databk, v.1, 1387
Environmental contaminant ref databk, v.2, 1388

CHEMISTRY
Chemical gd to the Internet, 1382
Chemical research faculties, 1380
Chemistry citation index [CD-ROM], 1390
Handbook of environmental data on organic chemicals, 3d ed, 1389
World databases in chemistry, 1383

CHEMISTRY—STUDY & TEACHING
College chemistry faculties 1996, 10th ed, 303

CHILD DEVELOPMENT
Growing up: a cross-cultural ency, 708

CHILDREN
National gd to funding for children, youth, & families, 3d ed, 698
Practical pediatrician, 1354

CHILDREN—BOOKS & READING
Dictionary of American children's fiction, 1990-94, 938

CHILDREN'S ATLASES
Atlas of human hist, 458

CHILDREN'S ENCYCLOPEDIAS & DICTIONARIES
Encyclopedia of life scis, 1268
First dict of cultural literacy, 2d ed, 296
Gale ency of sci, 1238
Grolier student ency of sci, tech, & the enviroment, 1239
Junior worldmark ency of the nations, 79
Kingfisher 1st ency, 45
Middle Ages, 471

CHILDREN'S LITERATURE
British children's writers, 1800-80
British children's writers, 1914-1960, 935
British children's writers since 1960, 1st series, 936
Literature for children & YAs about Oceania, 142
Multicultural children's lit, 933
Your reading, 1995-96 ed, 925

CHILDREN'S LITERATURE—BIBLIOGRAPHY
Elementary school lib collection, 20th ed, 544
Elementary school lib collection, 20th ed [CD-ROM], 545

CHILDREN'S LITERATURE—BIOGRAPHY
Children's bks & their creators, 939
Seventh bk of jr authors & illustrators, 937
Something about the author, v.81, 926
Something about the author, v.82, 927
Something about the author, v.83, 928
Something about the author, v.84, 929
Something about the author, v.85, 930
Who's who of Australian children's writers, 2d ed, 931

CHILDREN'S PLAYS—INDEXES
Plays for children & YAs, suppl 1, 1989-94, 940

CHILDREN'S RIGHTS
Children's rights, 515

CHILDREN'S SONGS
Children's song index, 1978-93, 1033

CHINA
China environmental report, 223

CHINA—SOCIAL LIFE & CUSTOMS
NTC's dict of China's cultural code words, 107

CHINESE CHARACTERS—JAPAN
Kanji dict, 860

CHINESE LANGUAGE
NTC's dict of China's cultural code words, 107

CHORAL MUSIC
Catalogue of choral music arranged in biblical order, 2d ed, 1053
Choral music by African American composers, 1054

CHOREOGRAPHY
Dancers & choreographers, 1100

CHRISTIAN ANTIQUITIES
Jesus & his world, 1213

CHRISTIAN ART & SYMBOLISM
Medieval art, 799

CHRISTIAN BIOGRAPHY
Blackwell dict of evangelical biog, 1730-1860, 1208

CHRISTIAN ETHICS
New dict of Christian ethics & pastoral theology, 1209

CHRISTIAN PILGRIMS & PILGRIMAGES IN LITERATURE
Chaucer's pilgrims, 989

CHRISTIAN SECTS
Evangelical sectarianism in the Russian Empire & the USSR, 1173
Historical dict of the Orthodox Church, 1212

CHRISTIANITY
Bibliography of sources in Christianity & the arts, 1206
Dictionary of Christianity, 1210
Oxford ency of the Reformation, 1211

CHRISTIANITY & POLITICS
Religious right, 1218

CHRONICALLY ILL
Resources for people with disabilities & chronic conditions, 3d ed, 673

CHRONOLOGY, HISTORICAL
African American hist in the press 1851-99, 412
American decades 1900-09, 422
American decades 1910-19, 423
American decades 1920-29, 424
American decades 1980-89, 425
Asian American chronology, 326
Chronicle of the Olympics 1896-1996, 660
Chronicle of the world, rev ed, 464
Chronicle of the yr 1995, 465
Hispanic American chronology, 335
History of sci in the US, 1235
Lesbian & gay liberation in Canada, 680
Pan-African chronology, 426
Pocket factfile of 20th century events, 466
Women writers in the US, 738

CHURCH COLLEGES
Religious higher educ in the US, 301

CHURCH HISTORY
Women in Christian hist, 731

CHURCH MUSIC
Catalogue of choral music arranged in biblical order, 2d ed, 1053

CITIES & TOWNS
Challenge of urbanization, 722
City profiles USA 1996, 388
County & city extra, 1995, 4th ed, 712
MSA profile, 1996, 724
Population hist of western US cities & towns, 1850-1990, 723

CITY PLANNING
Challenge of urbanization, 722

CIVIL RIGHTS
Encyclopedia of human rights, 2d ed, 517
World dir of human rights research & training insts, 3d ed, 518

CIVIL SERVICE POSITIONS
Directory of fed jobs & employers, 258

CIVILIZATION
American bibliog of Slavic & E European studies for 1993, 114
Global voices, global visions: a core collection of multicultural bks, 10
Medieval wordbk, 838
Western civilization: a critical gd to documentary films, 1118

CLASSICAL ANTIQUITIES
Encyclopedia of the hist of classical archaeology, 397

CLASSICAL PHILOLOGY
Classical studies, 461

CLASSIFICATION, DEWEY DECIMAL
Dewey decimal classfication & relative index, 21st ed, 535
Dewey for Windows [CD-ROM], 536
Libraries Unltd prof collection CD 1995 [CD-ROM], 523

CLASSIFICATION, LIBRARY OF CONGRESS
Classification plus [CD-ROM], 533
Libraries Unltd prof collection CD 1995 [CD-ROM], 523
Library of Congress subject headings, 19th ed, 534

CLEVELAND (OHIO)
Dictionary of Cleveland biog, 87
Encyclopedia of Cleveland hist, 2d ed, 88

CLIMATOLOGY
Encyclopedia of climate & weather, 1396
Weather America, 1397
Weather of US cities, 5th ed, 1398

CLIMBING PLANTS
Shrubs & climbers, 1286

CLOCKS & WATCHES
Charlton price gd to Canadian clocks, 777

COINS
Handbook of ancient Greek & Roman coins, 778
John Max Wulfing collection in Washington Univ, v.3: Roman imperial coins...., 779
Standard catalog of world coins 1601-1700, 780

COLD WAR
Cold War ency, 473

COLERIDGE, SAMUEL TAYLOR
Samuel Taylor Coleridge: an annot bibliog of criticism & scholarship, v.3, 990

COLLECTIBLES
Charlton price gd to Canadian clocks, 777
Greenberg's gd to marbles, 2d ed, 786
Handbook of ancient Greek & Roman coins, 778
Huxford's old bk value gd, 8th ed, 776
Patricia Smith's doll values, 12th ed, 781
Standard carnival glass price gd, 10th ed, 784
Standard ency of carnival glass, 5th ed, 785

COLLEGE CHOICE
Peterson's top colleges for sci, 306
Princeton Review Hillel gd to Jewish life on campus, 1996 ed, 307
World academic database [CD-ROM], 308

COLLEGE LIBRARIANS
Directory of college & univ librarians in Canada, 2d ed, 550

COLLEGE MUSEUMS
University & college museums, galleries, & related facilities, 62

COLLEGE STUDENTS—EMPLOYMENT
Directory of college cooperative educ programs, 304

COMIC BOOKS, STRIPS, ETC.
Syndicated comic strips & artists, 1924-95, 1095

COMMAND PERFORMANCE (RADIO SHOW)
Command performance, USA! a discography, 772

COMMERCE. See also BUSINESS
Annual bulletin of trade in chemical products, 1384
Economics, trade, & dvlpmt: English-Spanish general terminology, 272
Energy balances for Europe & N America, 1992, 1993-2010, 1423

COMMONWEALTH COUNTRIES
Dictionary of the British Empire & Commonwealth, 117

COMMUNICATION
Encyclopedia of rhetoric & composition, 840

COMMUNITY
Dictionary of ethics, theology, & society, 73

COMMUNITY DEVELOPMENT
Funding sources for community & economic dvlpmt 1996, 692

COMPENSATION MANAGEMENT
Multistate payroll gd, 257

COMPETITION (PSYCHOLOGY)
Competitions: maximizing your abilities, 299

COMPOSERS
Alban Berg: a gd to research, 1045
Allen Sapp: a bio-bibliog, 1038
Benjamin Britten: a gd to research, 1040
Cole Porter discography, 1068
Film composers gd, 3d ed, 1037
Gardner Read: a bio-bibliog, 1036
Giovanni Gabrieli (ca.1555-1612): a thematic catalogue of his music...., 1034
Harvard biogl dict of music, 1024
International ency of violin-keyboard sonatas & composer biogs, 2d ed, 1043
Music of Francis Poulenc (1899-1963), 1044
Ross Lee Finney: a bio-bibliog, 1039
Sing glory & hallelujah! histl & biogl gd to Gospel Hymns nos.1-6 Complete, 1086
William Grant Still: a bio-bibliog, 1046
Women composers & songwriters, 1035
Women composers, v.1, 1047
Women composers, v.2, 1048

COMPOSERS—LATIN AMERICA
Latin American classical composers, 1042

COMPUTER BULLETIN BOARDS
Gay & lesbian online, 676

COMPUTER GRAPHICS
Information graphics, 1370

COMPUTER SCIENCE
Elsevier's dict of computer sci & math in English, German, French, & Russian, 1366

COMPUTER SOFTWARE
Multimedia dir, 4th ed, 1363

COMPUTERS
Bibliographic gd to the hist of computer applications, 1950-90, 1365
Computer desktop ency, 1369
Digital imaging dict, 1368
Encyclopedia of computer sci & tech, v.34, suppl 19, 1367
English-Spanish, Spanish-English electrical & computer engineering dict, 1297
Second bibliographic gd to the hist of computing, computers, & the info processing industry, 1364
UNIX dict of commands, terms, & acronyms, 1373

COMPUTING
Plunkett's infotech industry almanac, 539

CONGO (BRAZZAVILLE)
Historical dict of Congo, 95

CONGREVE, WILLIAM
William Congreve: an annot bibliog, 1978-94, 991

CONSERVATION OF NATURAL RESOURCES
Conservation & environmentalism, 1426

CONSERVATISM—RELIGIOUS ASPECTS
Religious right, 1218

CONSTRUCTION
Information sources in architecture & construction, 2d ed, 1299
Wiley dict of civil engineering & construction: English-Spanish/Spanish-English, 1304

CONSULTANTS
Consultants & consulting orgs dir 1996 suppl, 16th ed, 161

CONSUMER BEHAVIOR
Consumer Canada 1996, 268
Consumer Mexico 1996, 269
Consumer South Africa 1995, 270
Consumer USA 1996, 271
Official gd to household spending, 278

CONSUMER EDUCATION
Better buys for business, 187
Consumers index to product evaluations & info sources, v.24, no.2, April-June 1996, 188

CONSUMER PROTECTION
Consumer protection & the law, 487

CONTESTS
Competitions: maximizing your abilities, 299

CONTRACTORS
Worldwide offshore contractors & equipment dir, 1996, 28th ed, 1419

COOKERY
Cook's dict & culinary ref, 1248
Ethnic cuisines, 1253
Mushroom bk, 1280
What's cooking in multicultural America, 1254

COPYRIGHT
McCarthy's desk ency of intellectual property, 2d ed, 519
Patent, copyright, & trademark, 520

CORAL REEF FAUNA
Coral reef animals of the Indo-Pacific, 1295

CORNETT MUSIC
Catalog of music for the cornett, 1051

CORPORATIONS. *See also* BUSINESS
Almanac of American employers 1996-97, 259
America's corporate families 1995, 158
Companies intl [CD-ROM], 209
Corporate affiliations plus, spring/summer 1995 [CD-ROM], 162
Corporate dir of US public cos [CD-ROM], 163
Corporate dir of US public cos 1996, 164
Corporate 500, 13th ed, 685

Directory of American firms operating in foreign countries, 14th ed, 210
Directory of corp & fndn givers 1996, 686
Directory of Japanese-affiliated cos in the EU, 1996-97, 211
Encyclopedia of global industries, 204
European regional incentives, 1996-97, 243
Europe's medium-sized cos dir, 242
Hoover's masterlist of major US cos 1996-97, 166
International dir of co hists, v.12, 214
International dir of co hists, v.13, 215
International dir of co hists, v.14, 216
Major cos of Africa S of the Sahara 1996, 219
Major cos of Latin America 1996, 247
Major cos of the Arab world 1996/97, 20th ed, 233
U.S. electric industry phone & fax dir, 1996, 1418
World databases in co info, 172
World mktg data & stats 1996 on CD-ROM, 2d ed [CD-ROM], 281

CORRECTIONS
Dictionary of American penology, rev ed, 506

CORRESPONDENCE SCHOOLS & COURSES
Independent study catalog, 6th ed, 290

COST & STANDARD OF LIVING
Sources & methods: labour stats, v.2, 260
Yearbook of labour stats 1995, 54th ed, 261

COSTUME—UNITED STATES
Fashion & costume in American popular culture, 1093

COTE D'IVOIRE
Cote d'Ivoire, 96

COUNSELING
Research on group treatment methods, 623

COUNTRY LIFE
NTC's dict of folksy, regional, & rural sayings, 837

COURTS—UNITED STATES
Sourcebook of fed courts, 2d ed, 500

COVENANTS (LAW)
Covenants not to compete, 2d ed, 494

CRIME
Crime in America, 508
Statistical hndbk on violence in America, 507
Statistics on crime & punishment, 511
Statistics on weapons & violence, 512

CRIMINAL JUSTICE
Dictionary of American penology, rev ed, 506

CRIMINALS
Cops, crooks, & criminologists, 504

CRIMINOLOGY
Cops, crooks, & criminologists, 504

Encyclopedia of American prisons, 505
Murder cases of the 20th century, 503
Statistics on crime & punishment, 511

CRITICAL THEORY
Dictionary of cultural & critical theory, 746
Recent work in critical theory, 1989-95, 880

CRITICISM
Contemporary literary criticism, v.86, 895
Contemporary literary criticism, v.87, 896
Contemporary literary criticism, v.88, 897
Contemporary literary criticism, v.89, 898
Literature criticism from 1400 to 1800, v.28, 901
Literature criticism from 1400 to 1800, v.29, 902
Literature criticism from 1400 to 1800, v.30, 903
Literature criticism from 1400 to 1800, v.31, 904
Modern women writers, 907
Nineteenth-century lit criticism, v.47, 908
Nineteenth-century lit criticism, v.48, 909
Nineteenth-century lit criticism, v.49, 910
Nineteenth-century lit criticism, v.50, 911
Nineteenth-century lit criticism, v.51, 912
Nineteenth-century lit criticism, v.52, 913
Nineteenth-century lit criticism annual cum title index for 1996, 914
Short story criticism, v.18, 954
Short story criticism, v.19, 955
Short story criticism, v.20, 956
Short story criticism, v.21, 957
Twentieth-century literary criticism, v.58, 919
Twentieth-century literary criticism, v.59, 920
Twentieth-century literary criticism, v.60, 921
Twentieth-century literary criticism, v.61, 922
Twentieth-century literary criticism annual cum title index for 1996, 923

CROSSWORD PUZZLES
Cassell cluefinder, 832
Merriam-Webster's crossword puzzle dict, 2d ed, 836

CUBA
Cuba, 132

CULTURE
Dictionary of cultural & critical theory, 746
Global voices, global visions: a core collection of multicultural bks, 10

CURIOSITIES & WONDERS
Encyclopedia of claims, frauds, & hoaxes of the occult & supernatural, 637
Strange & unexplained happenings, 638

DANCE
Bibliography of sources in Christianity & the arts, 1206
Dance words, 1102
Music & dance of the world's religions, 1087
Square dance & contra dance hndbk, 1101

DANCE MUSIC
Twentieth-century American music for the dance, 1103

DANCERS
Dancers & choreographers, 1100

DATABASES
Chemistry citation index [CD-ROM], 1390
ERIC on CD-ROM [CD-ROM], 293
Gale's ready ref shelf [CD-ROM], 50
Health industry quicksource, 1313
Sourcebook of online public record experts, 540
World databases in agriculture, 1247
World databases in bioscis & pharmacology, 1241
World databases in chemistry, 1383
World databases in co info, 172
World databases in social scis, 78

DECCA RECORDS (FIRM)
Decca labels: a discography, 1031

DEFENSE INDUSTRIES
Jane's intl defence dir 1997, 218
World dir of defence & security, 567

DEGREES, ACADEMIC
Campus-free college degrees, 7th ed, 292

DELAWARE LANGUAGE—DICTIONARIES—ENGLISH
Delaware-English/English-Delaware dict, 845

DEMOCRACY
Encyclopedia of democracy, 612

DEMOGRAPHICS
County & city extra, 1995, 4th ed, 712
Statistical hndbk on adolescents in America, 718

DENTISTRY
Oxford hndbk of clinical dentistry, 2d ed, 1351

DERMATOLOGY
Skin deep: an A-Z of skin disorders, treatments, & health, 1333

DESIGN
Look of the century, 788

DESIGNERS
International dict of theatre-3: actors, directors, & designers, 1149

DESTROYERS (WARSHIPS)
Jane's fighting ships 1996-97, 99th ed, 573

DETECTIVE & MYSTERY FILMS
Gangster films, 1114

DETECTIVE & MYSTERY STORIES
Detecting women 2, 1996-97 ed, 947

DEVELOPING COUNTRIES
Global dvlpmt, 228
Historical dict of aid & dvlpmt orgs, 615
Wars in the Third World since 1945, 2d ed, 568

DEVELOPMENTAL PSYCHOLOGY
Dictionary of dvlpmtl psychology, 629
Encyclopedia of relationships across the lifespan, 631
Growing up: a cross-cultural ency, 708

DIARIES
Contemporary literary criticism, v.86, 895
Nineteenth-century lit criticism, v.48, 909
Nineteenth-century lit criticism, v.51, 912
Nineteenth-century lit criticism annual cum title index for 1996, 914

DICKENS, CHARLES
Charles Dickens on the screen, 1121
Every thing in Dickens, 992
Everyone in Dickens, 993

DICTIONARIES, POLYGLOT
Elsevier's dict of computer sci & math in English, German, French, & Russian, 1366
Export financing & insurance vocabulary, 206
Larousse desk ref, 46
Medical dict in 6 langs, 1331
Multilingual thesaurus of geoscis, 1400
NTC's multilingual dict of American Sign Lang, 870
Trilingual vocabulary of road transport vehicles, 229

DICTIONARY OF AMERICAN BIOGRAPHY
Dictionary of American biog, comprehensive index, 32

DIETARY SUPPLEMENTS
Encyclopedia of vitamins, minerals, & suppls, 1265

DINNER THEATER
Regional theatre dir 1996-97, 1152

DINOSAURS
Dinosaur hunter [CD-ROM], 1403
Penguin histl atlas of dinosaurs, 1405

DISABLED. *See* HANDICAPPED

DISSERTATIONS
Dissertation abstracts [CD-ROM], 60
Indigenous langs of the Americas, 810
Manual for writers of term papers, theses, & dissertations, 6th ed, 755

DISTANCE EDUCATION
Library servs for off-campus & distance educ, 521
Peterson's distance learning 1997, 291

DISTRIBUTIVE JUSTICE
Environmental justice, 1435

DOCUMENTARY FILMS
Western civilization: a critical gd to documentary films, 1118

DOGS
Dictionary of canine terms, 1292

DOLLS
Patricia Smith's doll values, 12th ed, 781

DOMESTIC VIOLENCE. *See* FAMILY VIOLENCE

DOW JONES INTERNATIONAL AVERAGE
Dow Jones averages, 1885-1995, 183

DRAMA
American drama criticism: suppl 4 to the 2d ed, 1146
American theatre, 1150
Bibliography of sources in Christianity & the arts, 1206
Concordance to the complete poems & plays of T. S. Eliot, 971
New York Times theater reviews, v.28: 1993-94, 1154

DRAMATISTS
British playwrights, 1880-1956, 985
British playwrights, 1956-95, 986
Contemporary literary criticism, v.88, 897
DISCovering authors modules [CD-ROM], 900
French women playwrights of the 20th century, 943
Guide to British drama explication, v.1, 987
Literature criticism from 1400 to 1800, v.28, 901
Literature criticism from 1400 to 1800, v.30, 903
Maxwell Anderson on the European stage 1929-92, 1147
Nineteenth-century lit criticism, v.51, 912
Nineteenth-century lit criticism annual cum title index for 1996, 914
Reader's gd to 20th-century writers, 916
Twentieth-century literary criticism, v.60, 921
William Congreve: an annot bibliog, 1978-94, 991

DRINKING CUSTOMS
Encyclopedia of N American eating & drinking traditions, customs, & rituals, 1250

DRINKING OF ALCOHOLIC BEVERAGES
Alcohol in the British Isles from Roman times to 1996, 441

DRUG INTERACTIONS
People's gd to deadly drug interactions, 1359

DRUGS. *See also* PHARMACOLOGY
Dictionary of substances & their effects [CD-ROM], 1314
Nursing96 drug hndbk, 1360
PharmFacts for nurses, 1361

DRUGS—SIDE EFFECTS
Effects of drugs on the fetus & nursing infant, 1358
People's gd to deadly drug interactions, 1359

EARTH SCIENCES. *See also* GEOLOGY
Macmillan ency of earth scis, 1391

EARTHQUAKES
Earthquakes & the built environment index, 1984-July 1995 [CD-ROM], 1399

EAST ARMENIAN DIALECT
Armenian (Eastern)-English dict, 844

EAST ASIA
Far East & Australasia 1997, 28th ed, 143

ECOLOGY
Co-op America's natl green pages, 1996 ed, 1428
Grolier lib of environmental concepts & issues, 1427
Grolier student ency of sci, tech, & the enviroment, 1239

ECONOMIC ASSISTANCE
Government assistance almanac 1996-97, 10th ed, 689
Historical dict of aid & dvlpmt orgs, 615

ECONOMIC DEVELOPMENT
Economic & social progress in Latin America 1995 report, 127
Funding sources for community & economic dvlpmt 1996, 692
Global dvlpmt, 228

ECONOMICS. See also **BANKS & BANKING; BUSINESS; FINANCE; INDUSTRY**
Atlas of US economy, tech, & growth, 714
Book of European forecasts, 2d ed, 238
Business & economic research dir, 159
Business stats of the US, 1995 ed, 176
Dictionary of economics, 156
Economic & social survey of Africa, 1994-95, 231
Economics, trade, & dvlpmt: English-Spanish general terminology, 272
Elsevier's dict of financial & economic terms, 153
English-Russian economics glossary, 154
Islamic economics & finance, 232
Junior worldmark ency of the nations, 79
Post Keynesian economics, 148
Profile of western N America, 248
Search for economics as a sci, 149
Trends in Europe & N America 1995, 719

ECONOMISTS
Joan Robinson: a bio-bibliog, 150

EDUCATION
Adventures in video, 314
Boarding school gd, 297
Education & the law, 491
Educator's word frequency gd, 817
Encyclopedia of African-American educ, 285
Encyclopedia of American educ, 288
ERIC on CD-ROM [CD-ROM], 293
International educ quotations ency, 289
Philosophy of educ, 287
Religious higher educ in the US, 301

EDUCATION, ELEMENTARY
International ency of teaching & teacher educ, 2d ed, 298
National gd to funding for elem & secondary educ, 300

EDUCATION, HIGHER
Campus-free college degrees, 7th ed, 292
Directory of college cooperative educ programs, 304
Peterson's distance learning 1997, 291
Princeton Review student access gd to the best business schools, 169
World academic database [CD-ROM], 308

EDUCATION, SECONDARY
International ency of teaching & teacher educ, 2d ed, 298
National gd to funding for elem & secondary educ, 300

EDUCATIONAL EXCHANGES
International student's gd to Mexican univs, 310
Open doors 1994/95, 311

EDUCATIONAL LITERATURE
Educators index of free materials 1995, 104th ed, 294

EDUCATIONAL PSYCHOLOGY
Historical ency of school psychology, 286

EDUCATIONAL TECHNOLOGY
Educational media & tech yrbk 1995/96, v.21, 312

EINSTEIN, ALBERT
Einstein dict, 1409

ELECTIONS
U.S. presidential candidates & the elections, 588

ELECTRIC INDUSTRIES
U.S. electric industry phone & fax dir, 1996, 1418

ELECTRIC POWER
Electric power industry yrbk, 1996, 1421
Electric power stats sourcebk, 1422

ELECTRIC POWER-PLANTS
Electric power in Asia & the Pacific, 1991 & 1992, 1420

ELECTRONIC CIRCUITS
Encyclopedia of electronic circuits, v.6, 1305

ELECTRONIC JOURNALS
Directory of electronic jls, newsletters, & academic discussion lists, 6th ed, 1375

ELECTRONIC MAIL
Directory of environmental electronic mail users in Eurasia, 4th ed, 1429

ELECTRONIC PUBLISHING
Anders CD-ROM gd, 2d ed, 15
CD-ROMs in print 1995 [CD-ROM], 16
CD-ROMs in print 1996, 17

ELECTRONICS
Encyclopedia of electronic circuits, v.6, 1305
Jane's avionics 1996-97, 15th ed, 1441

ELEMENTARY SCHOOL LIBRARIES
Elementary school lib collection, 20th ed, 544
Elementary school lib collection, 20th ed [CD-ROM], 545

ELIOT, T. S.
Concordance to the complete poems & plays of T. S. Eliot, 971
Guide to the secular poetry of T. S. Eliot, 970

EMPLOYEE FRINGE BENEFITS
Employee benefits desk ency, 252

EMPLOYEE LOYALTY
Employee duty of loyalty, 495
Employee duty of loyalty, 1996 suppl covering 1994, 496

EMPLOYEES—RECRUITING
Best dir of recruiters, 4th ed, 254
Best dir of recruiters on-line, 253

ENCYCLICALS
Encyclicals of John Paul II on CD-ROM [CD-ROM], 1217

ENCYCLOPEDIAS & DICTIONARIES. See also CHILDREN'S ENCYCLOPEDIAS & DICTIONARIES
Canadian ency plus, 1997 [CD-ROM], 42
Encyclopedia Americana [CD-ROM], 43
Encyclopedia of the future, 44
Encyclopedia of world cultures, v.8: Middle America & the Caribbean, 318
Encyclopedia of world cultures, v.9: Africa & the Middle East, 319
Encyclopedia of world cultures, v.10: indexes, 320
Encyclopedia USA, v.22, 417
Encyclopedia USA, v.23, 418
Larousse desk ref, 46
Merriam-Webster dict, home & office ed, 820
Oxford dict of current English, 821
Oxford English dict on CD, 2d ed [CD-ROM], 843
Oxford large print dict, 2d ed, 818
Random House concise ency, 47
World Afghanistan to Zimbabwe, 378
World Bk ency, [1996 ed], 48
Writer's companion, 924

ENDOCRINOLOGY
Dictionary of endocrinology & related biomedical scis, 1352

ENDOWMENTS. See also CHARITABLE USES, TRUSTS, & FOUNDATIONS; GRANTS-IN-AID
Awards alamanac 1996, 701
Complete grants sourcebk for higher educ, 3d ed, 684
Directory of corp & fndn givers 1996, 686
International fndn dir 1996, 7th ed, 696
National gd to funding for elem & secondary educ, 300
National gd to funding for libs & info servs, 531
National gd to funding in religion, 1184

ENERGY INDUSTRY
Electric power industry yrbk, 1996, 1421
Energy balances for Europe & N America, 1992, 1993-2010, 1423

ENGINEERING
Callaham's Russian-English dict of sci & tech, 4th ed, 1237
Encyclopedia of applied physics, v.15, 1407
Encyclopedia of applied physics, v.16, 1408
English-Spanish, Spanish-English electrical & computer engineering dict, 1297
Information sources in engineering, 3d ed, 1296
Who's who in sci & engineering 1996-97, 3d ed, 1232
Wiley dict of civil engineering & construction: English-Spanish/Spanish-English, 1304
World engineering industries & automation, 199

ENGINEERING—PERIODICALS
INSPEC list of jls & other serial sources 1996/7, 1306

ENGLISH DRAMA
British playwrights, 1880-1956, 985
British playwrights, 1956-95, 986
Companion to the characters in the fiction & drama of W. Somerset Maugham, 996
Guide to British drama explication, v.1, 987

ENGLISH FICTION
British short-fiction writers, 1800-80, 978
British short-fiction writers, 1880-1914, 979
British short-fiction writers, 1915-45, 980
Companion to the characters in the fiction & drama of W. Somerset Maugham, 996

ENGLISH IMPRINTS
English Catholic bks, 1701-1800, 1204

ENGLISH LANGUAGE—AUSTRALIA
Dictionary of Australian colloquialisms, 4th ed, 829

ENGLISH LANGUAGE—DIALECTS
Atlas of English dialects, 839
Sources of London English, 831

ENGLISH LANGUAGE—DIALECTS—UNITED STATES
NTC's dict of folksy, regional, & rural sayings, 837
Western lore & lang, 841

ENGLISH LANGUAGE—DICTIONARIES
Cassell cluefinder, 832
Merriam-Webster dict, home & office ed, 820
Oxford dict of current english, 821
Oxford English dict on CD, 2d ed [CD-ROM, 843
Oxford large print dict, 2d ed, 818
Rawson's dict of euphemisms & other doubletalk, rev ed, 828
Webster's new American dict, 822

ENGLISH LANGUAGE—DICTIONARIES—DELAWARE
Delaware-English/English-Delaware dict, 845

ENGLISH LANGUAGE—DICTIONARIES—FRENCH
Larousse mini French-English, English-French dict, new ed, 848
2001 French & English idioms, 2d ed, 846

ENGLISH LANGUAGE—DICTIONARIES—GERMAN
Larousse mini German-English, English-German dict, new ed, 850
Routledge German technical dict, 851

ENGLISH LANGUAGE—DICTIONARIES—HEBREW
Compact up-to-date English-Hebrew dict, 856
Oxford English-Hebrew dict, 855

ENGLISH LANGUAGE—DICTIONARIES—HUNGARIAN
Hippocrene concise Hungarian-English, English-Hungarian dict, 857

ENGLISH LANGUAGE—DICTIONARIES—ITALIAN
Larousse mini Italian-English, English-Italian dict, new ed, 858
Medical dict in 6 langs, 1331

ENGLISH LANGUAGE—DICTIONARIES—JAPANESE
2001 Japanese & English idioms, 859

ENGLISH LANGUAGE—DICTIONARIES—LITHUANIAN
Lithuanian dict, 862

ENGLISH LANGUAGE—DICTIONARIES—POLISH
Highlander Polish-English/English-Highlander Polish dict, 864

ENGLISH LANGUAGE—DICTIONARIES—ROMANIAN
NTC's Romanian & English dict, 865

ENGLISH LANGUAGE—DICTIONARIES—RUSSIAN
Concise Oxford Russian dict, 866
English-Russian economics glossary, 154
Russian-English collocational dict of the human body, 867

ENGLISH LANGUAGE—DICTIONARIES—SIKSIKA
Blackfoot dict of stems, roots, & affixes, 2d ed, 872

ENGLISH LANGUAGE—DICTIONARIES—SOUTH AFRICAN
Dict of South African English on histl principles, 830

ENGLISH LANGUAGE—DICTIONARIES—SPANISH
Dahl's law dict: an annot legal dict, Spanish-English/English-Spanish, 2d ed, 486
Elsevier's dict of financial & economic terms, 153
English-Spanish, Spanish-English electrical & computer engineering dict, 1297
Larousse English-Spanish, Spanish-English dict, new, 873
Larousse mini Spanish-English, English-Spanish dict, new ed, 874
Wiley dict of civil engineering & construction: English-Spanish/Spanish-English, 1304

ENGLISH LANGUAGE—DICTIONARIES—TURKISH
Dictionary of the Turkic langs, 876

ENGLISH LANGUAGE—DICTIONARIES—YIDDISH
Hippocrene practical English-Yiddish, Yiddish-English dict, expanded ed, 878

ENGLISH LANGUAGE—DICTIONARIES—YORUBA
Hippocrene concise Yoruba-English, English-Yoruba dict, 879

ENGLISH LANGUAGE—EPONYMS
What in the word? origins of words dealing with people & places, 823

ENGLISH LANGUAGE—ETYMOLOGY
Barnhart concise dict of etymology, 825
Dictionary of word origins, 826

ENGLISH LANGUAGE—EUPHEMISM
Dictionary of euphemisms, 827
Rawson's dict of euphemisms & other double talk, rev ed, 828

ENGLISH LANGUAGE—IDIOMS
Dictionary of American regional English, v.3: I-O, 833
Dictionary of Caribbean English usage, 834

ENGLISH LANGUAGE—MIDDLE ENGLISH
Sources of London English, 831

ENGLISH LANGUAGE—OBSOLETE WORDS
Medieval wordbk, 838

ENGLISH LANGUAGE—REGIONALISMS
Dictionary of American regional English, v.3: I-O, 833
NTC's dict of folksy, regional, & rural sayings, 837
Yankee talk: a dict of New England expressions, 835

ENGLISH LANGUAGE—STYLE
Wired style, 758

ENGLISH LANGUAGE—WORD FREQUENCY
Educator's word frequency gd, 817

ENGLISH LITERATURE
Cambridge pa gd to lit in English, 894
Literally entitled, 891
Sixteenth-century British nondramatic writers, 3d series, 983

ENGLISH LITERATURE—19TH CENTURY
British children's writers, 1800-1880, 934
British reform writers, 1789-1832, 977
British travel writers, 1837-75, 981
Every thing in Dickens, 992
Everyone in Dickens, 993

ENGLISH LITERATURE—HISTORY & CRITICISM
Reader's gd to lit in English, 915

ENGLISH PHILOLOGY
English lang scholarship, 809

ENGLISH POETRY
Victorian poetry, 1000

ENGLISH WIT & HUMOR
Encyclopedia of British humorists, 984

ENLIGHTENMENT
Encyclopedia of the Enlightenment, 475

ENTERTAINERS
Radio stars, 762

ENTREPRENEURSHIP
Free money from the fed govt for small businesses & entrepreneurs, 2d ed, 189

ENVIRONMENTAL POLICY
China environmental report, 223
Mexico environmental report, 224
Environmental justice, 1435
Environmental racism & the environmental justice movement, 513
Environmental telephone dir, 1430
Grolier lib of environmental concepts & issues, 1427
World dir of country environmental studies, 3d ed, 1432

ENVIRONMENTAL PROTECTION
Book of lists for regulated hazardous substances 1996, 1433
Cooper's comprehensive environmental desk ref, 1434
Environment & the law, 514
Environmental contaminant ref databk, v.1, 1387
Environmental contaminant ref databk, v.2, 1388

ENVIRONMENTAL SCIENCE
Conservation & environmentalism, 1426
Cooper's comprehensive environmental desk ref, 1434
Earth works, 1424
Sierra Club green gd, 1431

ENVIRONMENTALISM
Co-op America's natl green pages, 1996 ed, 1428
Directory of environmental electronic mail users in Eurasia, 4th ed, 1429
Environment & the law, 514
Environmental grantmaking fndns 1996, 4th ed, 690

EPIC LITERATURE
Encyclopedia of literary epics, 889

ESSAY
Contemporary literary criticism, v.86, 895
Literature criticism from 1400 to 1800, v.30, 903
Nineteenth-century lit criticism, v.48, 909
Nineteenth-century lit criticism, v.49, 910
Nineteenth-century lit criticism, v.50, 911
Nineteenth-century lit criticism, v.51, 912
Nineteenth-century lit criticism annual cum title index for 1996, 914
Twentieth-century literary criticism, v.59, 920
Twentieth-century literary criticism annual cum title index for 1996, 923

ESSENCES & ESSENTIAL OILS
Illustrated ency of essential oils, 1346

ETHICS
Dictionary of ethics, theology, & society, 73
Encyclopedia of values & ethics, 1163
Encyclopedia of war & ethics, 1161

ETHNIC GROUPS.—UNITED STATES See also MINORITIES
Ethnic studies in the US, 322
Voices of multicultural America, 967

ETHNOLOGY
Encyclopedia of cultural anthropology, 316
Encyclopedia of world cultures, v.8: Middle America & the Caribbean, 318
Encyclopedia of world cultures, v.9: Africa & the Middle East, 319
Encyclopedia of world cultures, v.10: indexes, 320
Ethnic studies in the US, 322
Guide to info resources in ethnic museum, lib, & archive collections in the US, 522
Peoples of Africa, 321

ETYMOLOGY
Alphabetical gd to the lang of name studies, 824

EUPHEMISM
Dictionary of euphemisms, 827
Rawson's dict of euphemisms & other doubletalk, rev ed, 828

EUROPE
Book of European forecasts, 2d ed, 238
Directory of chemical producers & products, v.1, pt.1, 2d ed, 1381
Energy balances for Europe & N America, 1992, 1993-2010, 1423
Eurail gd to train travel in the new Europe, 1996, 1443
Eurail gd to world train travel, 1996, 26th ed, 1444
European drinks mktg dir, 4th ed, 240
European mktg data & stats 1996, 31st ed, 273
European oilfield serv, supply, & manufacturers dir, 1996, 2d ed, 1417
European private label dir, 241
Europe's medium-sized cos dir, 242

Major cos of Central & Eastern Europe & the Commonwealth of Independent States 1996/97, 6th ed, 220
Trends in Europe & N America 1995, 719
World mktg data & stats 1996 on CD-ROM, 2d ed [CD-ROM], 281

EUROPE, EASTERN
American bibliog of Slavic & E European studies for 1993, 114
Concise histl atlas of Eastern Europe, 446
Directory of chemical producers & products, v.1, pt.1, 2d ed, 1381
Major business orgs of Eastern Europe & the Commonwealth of Independent States 1995/96, 5th ed, 244
Slovenia, 122

EUROPE—ECONOMIC CONDITIONS
Economic survey of Europe in 1995-96, 239

EUROPE—HISTORY
Dictionary of European hist & pols, 1945-95, 438
Supplement to The Modern Ency of Russian, Soviet, & Eurasian Hist, v.1, 476
Travel gd to Jewish Europe, 2d ed, 436
War of the Spanish Succession, 1702-13, 435
Western Europe since 1945, 437

EUROPE—POLITICS & GOVERNMENT
Almanac of European pols 1995, 605

EUROPEAN COMMUNITIES
Directory of EU info sources 1995-96, 7th, 606
Directory of Japanese-affiliated cos in the EU, 1996-97, 211
European Union ency & dir 1996, 2d ed, 607

EUROPEAN ECONOMIC COMMUNITY
European regional incentives, 1996-97, 243

EVANGELICALISM
Blackwell dict of evangelical biog, 1730-1860, 1208
Evangelical dict of biblical theology, 1197
Evangelical sectarianism in the Russian Empire & the USSR, 1173

EXECUTIVES
Critical gd to mgmt training videos & selected multimedia, 1996, 266
Hoover's dir of human resources executives 1996, 255

EXPERIMENTS
Science experiments index for young people, 2d ed, 1244

EXPLORERS
Literature criticism from 1400 to 1800, v.31, 904

EX-PRESIDENTS
How to research the presidency, 586

FACSIMILE TRANSMISSION
National fax dir, 1996, 51

FAIRIES
Spirits, fairies, gnomes, & goblins, 1090

FALKLAND ISLANDS
Falkland Islands, S Georgia, & the S Sandwich Islands, 133

FAMILY
Audiovisual resources for family programming, 313
Family studies database [CD-ROM], 674
National gd to funding for children, youth, & families, 3d ed, 698

FAMILY VIOLENCE
Domestic violence, 675

FANTASTIC FICTION
Magill's gd to sci fiction & fantasy lit, 948
St. James gd to fantasy writers, 950

FASHION
Fashion & costume in American popular culture, 1093
Look of the century, 788

FEDERAL GOVERNMENT
Directory of fed jobs & employers, 258

FEMINISM. *See also* **WOMEN**
Encyclopedia of women's hist in America, 736
Historical dict of feminism, 735
U.S. women's interest groups, 737
Women & music, 1020

FEMINIST JURISPRUDENCE
Feminist jurisprudence, 739

FEMINIST THEOLOGY
Dictionary of feminist theologies, 1177

FEMINIST THEORY
Feminism & postmodern theory, 727
Women of color: feminist theory, 729

FEMINISTS
Feminist writers, 886

FESTIVALS
Historic festivals, 386
Music festivals from Bach to blues, 1029

FETUS
Effects of drugs on the fetus & nursing infant, 1358

FICTION
Annotated bibliog of jazz fiction & jazz fiction criticism, 944
Detecting women 2, 1996-97 ed, 947
Fiction catalog, 13th ed, 945
Jules Verne ency, 952
Masterplots 2: short story series suppl, 953
Native American in long fiction, 958
Short story criticism, v.18, 954
Short story criticism, v.19, 955
Short story criticism, v.20, 956

Short story criticism, v.21, 957
To be continued: an annot gd to sequels, 946
Writers of multicultural fiction for YAs, 942

FILIPINOS
Filipino achievers in the USA & Canada, 332

FINANCE
Elsevier's dict of financial & economic terms, 153
Export financing & insurance vocabulary, 206
Information sources in finance & banking, 191
Islamic economics & finance, 232
Prices & financial stats in the ESCWA region, 192
Search for economics as a sci, 149
Who's who in finance & industry, 1996-97, 152

FINANCE, PERSONAL
Official gd to household spending, 278

FINANCIAL MINISTERS
Biographical dict of the US Secretaries of the Treasury, 1789-1995, 587

FINNEY, ROSS LEE
Ross Lee Finney: a bio-bibliog, 1039

FIREARMS
Gun control, 510
Vital gd to combat guns & infantry weapons, 579

FISHES
Fossil atlas: fishes, 1404

FLORIDA
Bibliography of Fla., v.2: 1846-80, 84

FOLK ART
Contemporary American folk art, 783

FOLK MUSIC
Central European folk music, 1073
Ethnic & vernacular music, 1898-1960, 1075

FOLKLORE
American folklore, 1088

FOOD
Cook's dict & culinary ref, 1248
Encyclopedia of N American eating & drinking traditions, customs, & rituals, 1250
Food & beverage market place, 1996, 1249

FOOD IN LITERATURE
Food & drink in lit, 881

FOOT
Foot & ankle sourcebk, 1340

FOOTBALL—UNITED STATES
Official 1996 NFL record & fact bk, 654
Sporting News pro football gd, 1996 ed, 655
Sporting News pro football register, 1996 ed, 656

FORECASTING
Encyclopedia of the future, 44

FORMER SOVIET REPUBLICS. *See also* RUSSIA; SOVIET UNION
Bibliography of the Soviet Union, it predecessors & successors, 124
Major cos of Central & Eastern Europe & the Commonwealth of Independent States 1996/97, 6th ed, 220
Placenames of Russia & the former Soviet Union, 382
Post-Soviet hndbk, 123
Statistical hndbk of social & economic indicators for the former Soviet Union, 125

FOSSILS
Fossil atlas: fishes, 1404

FRANCE
Battles of the Somme, 1916, 561
Charles-Maurice de Talleyrand 1754-1838, 447
Regions of France, 115

FRANCHISES (RETAIL TRADE)
Bond's franchise gd, 1996, 180

FREE MATERIAL
Educators index of free materials 1995, 104th ed, 294

FREEDOM OF INFORMATION
Intellectual freedom manual, 5th ed, 542

FREEDOM OF RELIGION
Freedom of religion decisions of the US Supreme Court, 1183

FREEDOM OF SPEECH
Freedom of speech decisions of the US Supreme Court, 541

FREEDOM OF THE PRESS
Freedom of the press decisions of the US Supreme Court, 761

FRENCH LANGUAGE—DICTIONARIES—ENGLISH
Dictionary of contemporary French connectors, 847
Larousse mini French-English, English-French dict, new ed, 848
2001 French & English idioms, 2d ed, 846

FRUIT
Taylor's gd to fruits & berries, 1259

FUGITIVE (TELEVISION PROGRAM)
Following The Fugitive: an episode gd & hndbk to the 1960s TV series, 1127

FUNCTION TESTS (MEDICINE)
Everything you need to know about medical tests, 1337

FUND RAISING
AIDS funding, 4th ed, 683

National gd to funding for community dvlpmt, 699
National gd to funding for elem & secondary educ, 300
National gd to funding for libs & info servs, 531
National gd to funding in religion, 1184

FUNGI
Fungi on rhododendron, 1279
Mushroom bk, 1280
Mushrooms of N America in color, 1278

GABRIELI, GIOVANNI
Giovanni Gabrieli (ca.1555-1612): a thematic catalogue of his music...., 1034

GANDHI, MAHATMA
Comprehensive, annot bibliog on Mahatma Gandhi, 430

GANGS
Gangs, 509

GANGSTER FILMS
Gangster films, 1114

GARBAGE. *See* **ORGANIC WASTES**

GARDENING
Bulbs for the rock garden, 1255
Garden trees, 1282

GAS INDUSTRY
Oil & gas on the Internet, 1415

GAYS. *See also* **LESBIANS**
Gay almanac, 677
Gay & lesbian literary heritage, 888
Gay & lesbian movement, 681
Gay & lesbian online, 676
Lesbian & gay liberation in Canada, 680
Strength in numbers: a lesbian, gay, & bisexual resource, 703
Ultimate gd to lesbian & gay film & video, 1126

GAZETTEERS
Cambridge gazetteer of the US & Canada, 381

GENEALOGY
Center: a gd to genealogical research in the natl capital area, 358
Directory of family assns, 3d ed, 354
Family archive viewer [CD-ROM], 355
Genealogical & local hist bks in print, 5th ed, 350
Genealogical research in England's public record office, 357
Genealogy & local hist to 1900, 351
Hispanic surnames & family hist, 356
Oxford companion to local & family hist, 352
Passenger & immigration lists index, 1996 suppl, 367
Student's gd to African American genealogy, 359
Student's gd to British American genealogy, 360
Student's gd to Chinese American genealogy, 361
Student's gd to German American genealogy, 362
Student's gd to Irish American genealogy, 365

Student's gd to Italian American genealogy, 363
Student's gd to Native American genealogy, 366
Student's gd to Scaninavian American genealogy, 364
Surnames of Wales, 353
U.S. Catholic sources, 1215

GENETIC COUNSELING
Effects of drugs on the fetus & nursing infant, 1358

GEOGRAPHY
DK geography of the world, 379
Hammond Citation world atlas, 374
Junior Worldmark ency of the nations, 79
Merriam-Webster's pocket geographical dict, 380
World Afghanistan to Zimbabwe, 378

GEOLOGISTS
Geologists & the hist of geology, suppl 2, v.1, 1402

GEOLOGY. *See also* **EARTH SCIENCES**
Geologists & the hist of geology, suppl 2, v.1, 1402
Multilingual thesaurus of geoscis, 1400
New Penguin dict of geology, 1401

GERMAN AMERICANS
Research gd to the Turner movement in the US, 333
Student's gd to German American genealogy, 362

GERMAN LANGUAGE—DICTIONARIES—ENGLISH
Friendly German-English dict, 849
German-English dict of idioms, 852
Larousse mini German-English, English-German dict, new ed, 850
Routledge German technical dict, 851

GERMAN LITERATURE
German baroque writers, 1580-1660, 1006

GERONTOLOGY. *See also* **AGED**
Encyclopedia of gerontology, 667
Graying of America: an ency of aging, health, mind, & behavior, 668

GINSBERG, ALLEN
Response to Allen Ginsberg 1926-94, 972

GLASS
Dictionary of glass, 787

GOODMAN, BENNY
Benny Goodman: wrappin' it up, 1071

GOSPEL MUSIC
Sing glory & hallelujah! histl & biogl gd to Gospel Hymns nos.1-6 Complete, 1086

GOVERNMENT FINANCIAL INSTITUTIONS
Government assistance almanac 1996-97, 10th ed, 689

GOVERNMENT PUBLICATIONS
Accessing US govt info, rev ed, 54
Introduction to US govt info sources, 5th ed, 53

GRANTS-IN-AID. *See also* **CHARITABLE USES, TRUSTS, & FOUNDATIONS; ENDOWMENTS; FUND RAISING**
Directory of health grants, 1321
Environmental grantmaking fndns 1996, 4th ed, 690
Financial resources for intl study, 2d ed, 309
Funding for US study, 2d ed, 305
Funding sources for community & economic dvlpmt 1996, 692
Government assistance almanac 1996-97, 10th ed, 689
Grant seekers gd, 4th ed, 693
Grants & awards available to American writers 1996-97, 19th ed, 694
Grants on disc [CD-ROM], 695
National dir of grantmaking public charities, 697
National gd to funding for children, youth, & families, 3d ed, 698

GRAPHIC METHODS
Information graphics, 1370

GREAT BRITAIN
Atlas of industrial protest in Britain, 1750-1990, 146
British imprints relating to N America, 1621-1760, 40
Dictionary of natl biog, 1986-90, 38
English castles, 394

GREAT BRITAIN—COLONIES
British empire, 444
Dictionary of the British Empire & Commonwealth, 117

GREAT BRITAIN—HISTORY
British archives, 3d ed, 440
British economic & social hist, 3d ed, 443
British empire, 444
British women's hist, 726
Historical dict of Stuart England, 1603-89, 442
Kings of medieval England, c. 560-1485, 445

GREAT BRITAIN—LIBRARY RESOURCES
Short-title catalogue of Hungarian bks printed before 1851 in the British Lib, 14

GREAT BRITAIN—POLITICS & GOVERNMENT
Art, truth, & high pols: a bibliographic study of the official lives of Queen Victoria's ministers in Cabinet, 1843-1969, 608
Sir Robert Peel 1788-1850: a bibliog, 439

GREECE
Encyclopedia of the ancient Greek world, 450
Penguin histl atlas of ancient Greece, 449

GREECE—ANTIQUITIES
Mycenaean civilization, 448

GREEK LANGUAGE
Exhaustive concordance to the Greek N.T., 1199
Greek-English lexicon, 853

GREEK LITERATURE
Hellenistic commentary to the N.T., 1201

GROUP COUNSELING
Research on group treatment methods, 623

GUERRILLAS
Handbook of leftist guerrilla grps in Latin America & the Caribbean, 609
Sendero Luminoso: an annot bibliog of the Shining Path guerrilla movement, 1980-93, 502

GUINEA
Guinea, 97

GUN CONTROL
Gun control, 510

HAMMER FILM PRODUCTIONS
Hammer films: an exhaustive filmography, 1119

HANDBOOKS, VADE-MECUMS, ETC.
Everything you pretend to know & are afraid someone will ask, 57
Writer's companion, 924

HANDICAPPED
Encyclopedia of disability & rehabilitation, 670
Resources for elders with disabilities, 3d ed, 672
Resources for people with disabilities & chronic conditions, 3d ed, 673

HARVARD UNIVERSITY
Printed catalogues of the Harvard College Lib, 1723-90, 39

HAZARDOUS SUBSTANCES
Book of lists for regulated hazardous substances 1996, 1433
Environmental contaminant ref databk, v.1, 1387
Environmental contaminant ref databk, v.2, 1388
Hazardous materials hndbk, 1436

HEALING
Encyclopedia of Native American healing, 340

HEALTH
Complete family gd to healthy living, 1326
Health care almanac, 1316
Health care terms, 3d ed, 1319
Health industry quicksource, 1313
Health online, 1328
HealthSpeak, 1315
Plunkett's health care industry almanac, 1329
Tobacco & health network dir 1996, 4th ed, 1325
Why Eve doesn't have an Adam's apple: a dict of sex differences, 1318

HEALTH & RACE
Guide to ethnic health collections in the US, 1322

HEALTH MAINTENANCE ORGANIZATIONS
HMO/PPO dir 1996, 1323

HEANEY, SEAMUS
Seamus Heaney: a ref gd, 1008

HEBREW LANGUAGE
Compact up-to-date English-Hebrew dict, 856
501 Hebrew verbs, 854
Hebrew & Aramaic lexicon of the O.T., v.2, 1198
Oxford English-Hebrew dict, 855
Theological dict of the O.T., v.7, 1200

HEIDEGGER, MARTIN
Martin Heidegger (2): a bibliog, 1156

HELICOPTERS
Jane's all the world's aircraft 1996-97, 87th ed, 1440
Jane's helicopter markets & systems, 1442

HERBS
Home herbal, 1281

HEROES
Heroes of conscience: a biogl dict, 22

HISPANIC AMERICANS
Dictionary of Hispanic biog, 334
DISCovering multicultural America [CD-ROM], 323
Hispanic American chronology, 335
Hispanic resource dir, 3d ed, 336
Latino ency, 337

HISTORIANS
American women historians, 1700s-1990s, 411

HISTORIC SITES
Black heritage sites, 330
International dict of historic places, v.4, 468
International dict of historic places, v.5, 469
Landmarks of American presidents, 391

HISTORICAL FICTION
Nineteenth-century lit criticism, v.48, 909

HISTORICAL GEOGRAPHY
Atlas of human hist, 458
Historical atlas of SE Asia, 429
Historical atlas of the Vietnam War, 434
Mapping America's past, 402

HISTORY
Dictionary of American hist suppl, 414
Encyclopedia of invasions & conquests from ancient times to the present, 564
Encyclopedia of the hist of classical archaeology, 397
Illustrated bk of questions & answers, 56
Junior Worldmark ency of the nations, 79
Oxford companion to local & family hist, 352

HISTORY, ANCIENT
Atlas of human hist, 458
Dictionary of Judaism in the biblical period, 1223
History of humanity, v.2, 479

HISTORY MATERIALS
Genealogical & local hist bks in print, 5th ed, 350

HISTORY, MODERN
American decades 1980-89, 425
Chronicle of the yr 1995, 465
Current issues sourcefile [CD-ROM], 59
Global village companion, 470
Great events: the 20th century, suppl, 478
Pocket factfile of 20th century events, 466

HOBBES, THOMAS
Hobbes dict, 1165

HOCKEY
Sporting News hockey gd, 1996-97 ed, 657
Sporting News hockey register, 1996-97 ed, 658

HOLY SPIRIT
Doctrine of the Holy Spirit, 1193

HOME EDUCATION. *See* **SELF-CULTURE**

HOME SCHOOLING
Authentic Jane Williams' home school mrkt gd, 280

HOMEOPATHY
Complete gd to homeopathy, 1347
Family homeopathy, 1342

HOMOSEXUALITY. *See* **GAYS; LESBIANS**

HORSES
International ency of horse breeds, 1291

HORTICULTURE
Reference gd for botany & horticulture, 1258

HOSPITALS
Canadian medical dir on CD-ROM, 1996 [CD-ROM], 1320

HOTELS
Complete gd to American bed & breakfast, 4th ed, 385
National Trust gd to historic bed & breakfasts, inns, & small hotels, 4th ed, 390

HOUSING
Popular American housing, 1094

HUMAN ANATOMY
Russian-English collocational dict of the human body, 867
Virtual body [CD-ROM], 1312

HUMAN CAPITAL
Hoover's dir of human resources executives 1996, 255

HUMAN RIGHTS
Dictionary of intl human rights law, 516
Encyclopedia of human rights, 2d ed, 517
World dir of human rights research & training insts, 3d ed, 518

HUMAN SETTLEMENTS
Compendium of human settlements stats 1995, 5th ed, 715

HUMANITIES
American humanities index for 1995, v.21, 744
Libraries Unltd prof collection CD 1995 [CD-ROM], 523

HUMORISTS
Encyclopedia of British humorists, 984

HUNGARIAN LANGUAGE—DICTIONARIES—ENGLISH
Hippocrene concise Hungarian-English, English-Hungarian dict, 857

HUNGARY
Short-title catalogue of Hungarian bks printed before 1851 in the British Lib, 14

HYMNS
Sing glory & hallelujah! histl & biogl gd to Gospel Hymns nos.1-6 Complete, 1086

ICELAND
Iceland, rev ed, 118

IDIOMS
German-English dict of idioms, 852
2001 French & English idioms, 2d ed, 846
2001 Japanese & English idioms, 859

ILLUSTRATED BOOKS, CHILDREN'S
Seventh bk of jr authors & illustrators, 937

IMAGING SYSTEMS
Digital imaging dict, 1368

IMMIGRANTS
Passenger & immigration lists index, 1996 suppl, 367

IMMUNIZATION OF CHILDREN
Immunization resource gd, 2d ed, 1339

IMPORTS. See also MARKETING
Importers manual USA & the dict of intl trade, 1996-97 ed [CD-ROM], 274

INCOME
Markets of the US for business planners, 276
Multistate payroll gd, 257

INCUNABULA
Catalogue of the 15th-century printed bks in the Harvard Univ Lib, v.4, 547

INDEXES
Alternative Press index, 58
Annotations: a dir of pers listed in the Alternative Press Index, 1996 ed, 63
Children's song index, 1978-93, 1033
Left index: a quarterly index to pers on the Left, 61

INDIA
Comprehensive, annot bibliog on Mahatma Gandhi, 430
Historical dict of India, 108

INDIAN ART
Ancient Peruvian art, 794

INDIAN RESERVATIONS
American Indian reservations & trust areas, 342

INDIANS
Encyclopedia of ancient Mesoamerica, 453
Indigenous langs of the Americas, 810

INDIANS IN LITERATURE
Native American in long fiction, 958

INDIANS OF NORTH AMERICA
ABC-CLIO companion to the Native American rights movement, 341
American Indian quotations, 345
American Indian reservations & trust areas, 342
Biographical dir of Native American painters, 807
DISCovering multicultural America [CD-ROM], 323
Encyclopedia of Native American healing, 340
Health of native people of N America, 338
Native N American biog, 339
Native American issues, 344
Ojibwa chiefs, 1690-1890, 343
Student's gd to Native American genealogy, 366

INDUSTRIAL STATISTICS
International yrbk of industrial stats 1996, 196

INDUSTRIAL SURVEYS
Markets of the US for business planners, 276

INDUSTRIES. See also MANUFACTURES
Industrial commodity stats yrbk 1994, 195
Manufacturing worldwide, 197

INDUSTRY
American business locations dir, 157
America's corporate families 1995, 158
Business orgs, agencies, & pubns dir, 8th ed, 160
Business stats of the US, 1995 ed, 176
Encyclopedia of global industries, 204
European regional incentives, 1996-97, 243
Multimedia dir, 4th ed, 1363
Who's who in finance & industry, 1996-97, 152
World engineering industries & automation, 199

INFANTS
Effects of drugs on the fetus & nursing infant, 1358
New parents sourcebk, 709

INFORMATION SCIENCE
Concise dict of lib & info sci, 525
Encyclopedia of lib & info sci, v.58, suppl 21, 524
Harrod's librarians' glossary, 8th ed, 526

INFORMATION SERVICES
Business A to Z source finder, 147
Directory of EU info sources 1995-96, 7th, 606
Research servs dir, 170

INFORMATION TECHNOLOGY
New info revolution: a ref hndbk, 538
Plunkett's infotech industry almanac, 539

INSTRUCTIONAL MATERIALS CENTERS
Audiovisual resources for family programming, 313
Educational media & tech yrbk 1995/96, v.21, 312

INSURANCE
Dictionary of insurance terms, 3d ed, 201
Export financing & insurance vocabulary, 206
Glossary of insurance & risk mgmt terms, 6th ed, 200
Standard & Poor's insurance co ratings gd, 1995 ed, 202

INTELLECTUAL PROPERTY
McCarthy's desk ency of intellectual property, 2d ed, 519
Patent, copyright, & trademark, 520

INTELLIGENCE SERVICE
Dictionary of US intelligence servs, 597

INTERNATIONAL AGENCIES
International fndn dir 1996, 7th ed, 696
Search for security: fndns in intl affairs, 700

INTERNATIONAL BUSINESS ENTERPRISES
Argentina co hndbk, 246
Dictionary of intl business terms, 203
Directory of American firms operating in foreign countries, 14th ed, 210
Directory of overseas catalogs, 1997, 212
Export financing & insurance vocabulary, 206
Fitzroy Dearborn dir of the world's banks, 11th ed, 190
International yrbk of industrial stats 1996, 196
Major cos of Central & Eastern Europe & the Commonwealth of Independent States 1996/97, 6th ed, 220
Major cos of Latin America 1996, 247
Major cos of the Arab world 1996/97, 20th ed, 233
OECD statl compendium 1996/1 [CD-ROM], 227
World retail dir & sourcebk, 2d ed, 222

INTERNATIONAL ECONOMIC RELATIONS
Directory of the steel industry & the environment, 194
Global dvlpmt, 228
Historical stats 1960-94, 1996 ed, 225

INTERNATIONAL EDUCATION
Financial resources for intl study, 2d ed, 309
Open doors 1994/95, 311

INTERNATIONAL ORGANIZATIONS
Directory of intl orgs, 617
Historical dict of aid & dvlpmt orgs, 615
Major business orgs of Eastern Europe & the Commonwealth of Independent States 1995/96, 5th ed, 244

INTERNATIONAL RELATIONS
Historical dict of multinatl peacekeeping, 616
International relations, 5th ed, 620
International relations research dir, 619

INTERNATIONAL TRADE
Argentina business, 245
Dictionary of intl business terms, 203
Exporting to the USA & the dict of intl trade, 1996-97 ed [CD-ROM], 205
International dir of business info sources & servs 1996, 2d ed, 213
Philippines business, 236
Trade data elements dir v.3, 277
Washington almanac of intl trade & business, 1995/96, 230
World trade almanac 1996-97, 207
World trade almanac & the dict of intl trade, 1997 ed [CD-ROM], 208

INTERNET (COMPUTER NETWORK)
Best dir of recruiters on-line, 253
Chemical gd to the Internet, 1382
CyberHound's Internet gd to the coolest stuff out there, 1374
Cyberstocks, 182
Gay & lesbian online, 676
Health online, 1328
Oil & gas on the Internet, 1415
Post-Soviet hndbk, 123
Prentice Hall dir of online business info 1997, 168
Web site source bk 1996, 1377

INTERNSHIP PROGRAMS
Higher educ money bk for women & minorities, 1997 ed, 302
Peterson's internships 1996, 16th ed, 256

INTERPERSONAL RELATIONS
Encyclopedia of relationships across the lifespan, 631

INVESTMENTS
Cyberstocks, 182
Fitzroy Dearborn intl dir of venture capital funds, 2d ed, 181
100 best mutual funds you can buy, 1995, 185
105 best investments for the 21st century, 226
Rate ref gd to the US treasury market 1984-95, 184
Standard & Poor's smallcap 600 gd, 1996 ed, 171
World stock exchange fact bk, 186

INVESTMENTS, FOREIGN
Australia business, 237

IRELAND IN LITERATURE
James Joyce A to Z, 1009

IRISH AMERICANS
Irish experience in NYC, 346
Student's gd to Irish American genealogy, 365

IRISH LITERATURE
Dictionary of Irish lit, rev ed, 1007
James Joyce A to Z, 1009
Seamus Heaney: a ref gd, 1008

ISLAMIC COUNTRIES
Dictionary of Islamic architecture, 803
Great dates in Islamic hist, 137
Islamic economics & finance, 232
Muslim almanac, 1219
New Islamic dynasties, 135
Year bk of the Muslim world 1996, 81

ISRAEL—ANTIQUITIES
Jesus & his world, 1213

ISRAEL-ARAB CONFLICTS
Arab-Israeli dispute, 457
Historical ency of the Arab-Israeli conflict, 455

ITALIAN AMERICANS
Student's gd to Italian American genealogy, 363

ITALIAN LANGUAGE—DICTIONARIES—ENGLISH
Larousse mini Italian-English, English-Italian dict, new ed, 858

ITALIAN LITERATURE
Boccaccio in English: a bibliog of eds, adaptations, & criticism, 1011
Dictionary of Italian lit, rev ed, 1010

ITALY
Italy, 395

IVORY COAST
Cote d'Ivoire, 96

JAINA ANTIQUITIES
Pada index & reverse Pada index to early Jain canons, 1202

JAPAN
Directory of Japanese-affiliated cos in the EU, 1996-97, 211
Japan & the Japanese, 110
Japan ency, 109
Philippines in WW II & to independence (Dec. 8, 1941-July 4, 1946), 2d ed, 432

JAPANESE LANGUAGE—DICTIONARIES—ENGLISH
Kanji dict, 860
2001 Japanese & English idioms, 859

JAZZ
Annotated bibliog of jazz fiction & jazz fiction criticism, 944
Benny Goodman: wrappin' it up, 1071
Command performance, USA! a discography, 772
Harvard biogl dict of music, 1024
Jazz: the rough gd, 1076

JESUS CHRIST—BIOGRAPHY
Jesus & his world, 1213

JEWISH-ARAB RELATIONS
Arab-Israeli dispute, 457

Historical ency of the Arab-Israeli conflict, 455

JEWISH COLLEGE STUDENTS
Princeton Review Hillel gd to Jewish life on campus, 1996 ed, 307

JEWS. *See also* JUDAISM
Index to American Jewish Histl Quarterly/American Jewish Hist: vs.51-80, 347
Orthodox Judaism in America, 1224
Travel gd to Jewish Europe, 2d ed, 436

JOB HUNTING
Almanac of American employers 1996-97, 259
Best dir of recruiters, 4th ed, 254
Best dir of recruiters on-line, 253
Directory of fed jobs & employers, 258
Specialty occupational outlook: trade & technical, 262
World Almanac job finders gd 1997, 263

JOHNSON, SAMUEL
Samuel Johnson ency, 994

JOURNALISM
Sports style gd & ref manual, 757
Tabloid journalism, 747

JOYCE, JAMES
James Joyce A to Z, 1009

JUDAISM. *See also* JEWS
American Jewish yr bk 1996, v.96, 1220
Dictionary of Judaism in the biblical period, 1223
Index to American Jewish Histl Quarterly/American Jewish Hist: vs.51-80, 347
Popular dict of Judaism, 1222
Princeton Review Hillel gd to Jewish life on campus, 1996 ed, 307

JURISPRUDENCE
Feminist jurisprudence, 739

JUSTICE
Ready ref: American justice, 489

KEEL, HOWARD
Howard Keel: a bio-bibliog, 1078

KENTUCKY
Kentucky: atlas of histl county boundaries, 371

KENYA
Kenya, rev ed, 98

KINGS & RULERS
Kings of medieval England, c. 560-1485, 445
New Islamic dynasties, 135

KOREAN WAR, 1950-1953
Korean War, 431

KUWAIT
Kuwait, rev ed, 140

LABOR
Biographical dict of European labor leaders, 151
Employment/unemployment & earnings stats, 249
Sources & methods: labour stats, v.2, 260
Working stiffs, union maids, reds, & riffraff: an organized gd to films about labor, 1141
Yearbook of labour stats 1995, 54th ed, 261

LABOR COSTS
Employee benefits desk ency, 252
Multistate payroll gd, 257
Sources & methods: labour stats, v.2, 260
Yearbook of labour stats 1995, 54th ed, 261

LABOR DISPUTES
Atlas of industrial protest in Britain, 1750-1990, 146

LABOR LAWS & LEGISLATION
Covenants not to compete, 2d ed, 494
Employee duty of loyalty, 495
Employee duty of loyalty, 1996 suppl covering 1994, 496

LABOR MOVEMENT
Historical dict of organized labor, 251
U.S. labor movement, 250

LANDSCAPE PLANTS
Plants that merit attention, v.2: shrubs, 1285

LANGUAGE & LANGUAGES
Blackwell ency of writing systems, 811
Concise compendium of the world's langs, 813
Encyclopedia of rhetoric & composition, 840
Languages of the world, new ed, 814
Routledge dict of lang & linguistics, 812
World's writing systems, 816

LAO LANGUAGE—DICTIONARIES—ENGLISH
Lao-English dict, 861

LARGE TYPE BOOKS
Oxford large print dict, 2d ed, 818

LATIN AMERICA
Economic & social progress in Latin America 1995 report, 127
Encyclopedia of Latin American hist & culture, 349
Handbook of leftist guerrilla grps in Latin America & the Caribbean, 609
Major cos of Latin America 1996, 247
South America, Central America, & the Caribbean 1997, 6th ed, 130

LATIN AMERICANS
Dictionary of 20th century culture: Hispanic culture of Mexico, Central America, & the Caribbean, 348
Encyclopedia of Latin American hist & culture, 349
Latin American classical composers, 1042
Latinas in the US, 728

LAW
Consumer protection & the law, 487
Critical legal studies, 492
Dahl's law dict: an annot legal dict, Spanish-English/English-Spanish, 2d ed, 486
Education & the law, 491
Guide to the early reports of the Supreme Court of the US, 493
Law bks & serials in print 1996, 481
Law lib ref shelf, 3d ed, 482
Legal researcher's desk ref 1996-97, 498
Merriam-Webster's dict of law, 488
Noble's intl gd to the law reports, 483
Ready ref: American justice, 489
World dir of human rights research & training insts, 3d ed, 518

LAW & POLITICS
Law & pols, 490

LAW LIBRARIES
Annotated catalog, S Texas College of Law, special collections, 480

LAWRENCE, D. H. (DAVID HERBERT)
D. H. Lawrence: a ref companion, 995

LEFT INDEX
Left index: a quarterly index to pers on the Left, 61

LEGAL RESEARCH
Critical legal studies, 492

LEGENDS
Myth: myths & legends of the world explored, 1091

LEGISLATIVE BODIES
How to research Congress, 585
State legislative sourcebk 1996, 602
Women state & territorial legislators, 1895-1995, 601

LESBIANS. *See also* **GAYS**
Gay & lesbian movement, 681
Gay & lesbian online, 676
Lesbian almanac, 679
Lesbian & gay liberation in Canada, 680
Lesbians in print, 678
Strength in numbers: a lesbian, gay, & bisexual resource, 703
Ultimate gd to lesbian & gay film & video, 1126

LIBRARIES
Business lib & how to use it, 6th ed, 530
Librarian's companion, 2d ed, 532

LIBRARIES & STUDENTS
Library servs for off-campus & distance educ, 521

LIBRARIES—CENSORSHIP
Intellectual freedom manual, 5th ed, 542

LIBRARIES, CHILDREN'S
Dictionary of American children's fiction, 1990-94, 938

LIBRARIES—SPECIAL COLLECTIONS
World dir of business info libs, 548

LIBRARY CATALOGS
Science & tech: a purchase gd for libs 1995, 1234

LIBRARY SCIENCE
ARL stats 1994-95, 527
Bowker annual lib & bk trade almanac, 1996, 41st ed, 528
Concise dict of lib & info sci, 525
Encyclopedia of lib & info sci, v.58, suppl 21, 524
Libraries Unltd prof collection CD 1995 [CD-ROM], 523
Library lit 1995, 529
National gd to funding for libs & info servs, 531

LIBRARY SCIENCE—TERMINOLOGY
Harrod's librarians' glossary, 8th ed, 526

LIBRETTISTS
Nineteenth-century lit criticism, v.50, 911
Nineteenth-century lit criticism annual cum title index for 1996, 914

LICENSES
EPM licensing letter sourcebk, 1997 ed, 165

LIFE SCIENCES
Encyclopedia of life scis, 1268
Notable women in the life scis, 1231
World databases in bioscis & pharmacology, 1241

LIFE SKILLS
Finding help: a ref gd for personal concerns, 55

LINCOLN, ABRAHAM
Of the people, by the people, for the people, & other quotations by Abraham Lincoln, 67

LINGUISTICS
Dictionary of phonetics & phonology, 819
Educator's word frequency gd, 817
Routledge dict of lang & linguistics, 812

LINGUISTS
Twentieth-century literary criticism, v.61, 922

LITERACY
First dict of cultural literacy, 2d ed, 296

LITERARY MOVEMENTS
Contemporary literary criticism, v.87, 896
Nineteenth-century lit criticism, v.52, 913
Twentieth-century literary criticism, v.58, 919

LITERARY PRIZES
Children's bks: awards & prizes, 1996 ed, 932
Contemporary literary criticism, v.87, 896

LITERARY THEORY
Recent work in critical theory, 1989-95, 880

LITERATURE
Bibliographical gd to the study of Western American lit, 2d ed, 959
Bibliography of sources in Christianity & the arts, 1206
Chaucer's pilgrims, 989
Classical studies, 461
Dictionary of Irish lit, rev ed, 1007
Dictionary of Italian lit, rev ed, 1010
Dictionary of literary biog yrbk: 1995, 899
Encyclopedia of allegorical lit, 890
Encyclopedia of apocalyptic lit, 893
Encyclopedia of literary epics, 889
Encyclopedia of satirical lit, 892
Literally entitled, 891
Literature criticism from 1400 to 1800, v.28, 901
Literature criticism from 1400 to 1800, v.29, 902
Literature criticism from 1400 to 1800, v.30, 903
Literature criticism from 1400 to 1800, v.31, 904
Magill's survey of world lit, 905
Masterplots, 2d ed, 906
New York Public Lib's bks of the century, 882
Reader's adviser on CD-ROM [CD-ROM], 11
Recommended reading: 500 classics reviewed, 883
Reference gd to world lit, 2d ed, 917
Romantic movement, 884
Writer's companion, 924

LITERATURE—BLACK AUTHORS
Schomberg Center gd to black lit from the 18th century to the present, 918

LITERATURE—ENGLISH
Paradise Lost: an annot bibliog, 997

LITERATURE, MODERN
Contemporary literary criticism, v.86, 895
Contemporary literary criticism, v.87, 896
Contemporary literary criticism, v.88, 897
Contemporary literary criticism, v.89, 898
Contemporary Spanish novel, 1014
Guide to serial bibliogs for modern lits, 2d ed, 885
Isaac Asimov: an annot bibliog of the Asimov collection at Boston Univ, 968
Modern women writers, 907
Nineteenth-century lit criticism, v.47, 908
Nineteenth-century lit criticism, v.48, 909
Nineteenth-century lit criticism, v.49, 910
Nineteenth-century lit criticism, v.50, 911
Nineteenth-century lit criticism, v.51, 912
Nineteenth-century lit criticism, v.52, 913
Nineteenth-century lit criticism annual cum title index for 1996, 914
Post-Colonial lits in English: Australia, 1970-92, 1002
Post-Colonial lits in English: SE Asia, New Zealand, & the Pacific, 1970-92, 1013
Reader's gd to 20th-century writers, 916
Twentieth-century literary criticism, v.58, 919
Twentieth-century literary criticism, v.59, 920
Twentieth-century literary criticism, v.60, 921
Twentieth-century literary criticism, v.61, 922

Twentieth-century literary criticism annual cum title index for 1996, 923

LITHUANIAN LANGUAGE—DICTIONARIES—ENGLISH
Lithuanian dict, 862

LONDON (ENGLAND)
London, 116
Sources of London English, 831

LUTHERAN CHURCH
Hermann Sasse: a bibliog, 1168

LUXEMBOURG
Historical dict of Luxembourg, 119

MALI
Historical dict of Mali, 3d ed, 99

MAMMALS
National Audubon Society field gd to N American mammals, rev ed, 1294

MAN
History of humanity, v.2, 479

MANAGEMENT. *See also* **BUSINESS**
Critical gd to mgmt training videos & selected multi-media, 1996, 266
Every manager's gd to business processes, 267
Manager's desk ref, 2d ed, 265
Profiles in business & mgmt [CD-ROM], 221

MANUFACTURES. *See also* **INDUSTRIES**
Business stats of the US, 1995 ed, 176
CDs, super glue, & salsa, series 2, 193
European private label dir, 241
Industrial commodity stats yrbk 1994, 195
International yrbk of industrial stats 1996, 196
Jane's intl defence dir 1997, 218
Manufacturing worldwide, 197
World engineering industries & automation, 199

MANUSCRIPTS
Catalogue of medieval & Renaissance mss in the Houghton Lib, Harvard Univ, v.1, 546

MAORI LANGUAGE
Te Matatiki: contemporary Maori words, 863

MARBLES
Greenberg's gd to marbles, 2d ed, 786

MARINE FAUNA
Coral reef animals of the Indo-Pacific, 1295

MARKET SURVEYS
Markets of the US for business planners, 276

MARKETING. *See also* **BUSINESS**
Asian markets, 4th ed, 234
Authentic Jane Williams' home school mrkt gd, 280

Book of European forecasts, 2d ed, 238
Consumer Canada 1996, 268
Consumer Mexico 1996, 269
Consumer South Africa 1995, 270
Consumer USA 1996, 271
European drinks mktg dir, 4th ed, 240
European mktg data & stats 1996, 31st ed, 273
Food & beverage market place, 1996, 1249
Trade data elements dir v.3, 277
World mktg data & stats 1996 on CD-ROM, 2d ed [CD-ROM], 281
World trade almanac 1996-97, 207
World trade almanac & the dict of intl trade, 1997 ed [CD-ROM], 208

MARKETING RESEARCH
Market info 1995/96, 275

MARTIAL ARTS
Tuttle dict of the martial arts of Korea, China, & Japan, 659

MASS MEDIA
Bacon's intl media dir 1996, 760
Violence & the media, 748
Writer's ency, 3d ed, 750

MATERIALS—FATIGUE
Fatigue data bk, 1308

MATHEMATICS
CRC standard mathematical tables & formulae, 30th, 1413
Elsevier's dict of computer sci & math in English, German, French, & Russian, 1366
MathSci Disc [CD-ROM], 1414

MATHEMATICIANS
Combined membership list 1996-97, 1412

MATISSE, HENRI
Henri Matisse: a gd to research, 805

MAUGHAM, W. SOMERSET
Companion to the characters in the fiction & drama of W. Somerset Maugham, 996

MAURITANIA
Historical dict of Mauritania, 2d ed, 100

MCCARTHY, JOSEPH
Encyclopedia of the McCarthy era, 591

MECHANICAL ENGINEERING
Dictionary of mechanical engineering, 4th ed, 1310

MEDIA PROGRAMS (EDUCATION)
Media review digest, v. 26, 1996, 9

MEDICAL CARE
Health industry quicksource, 1313
HMO/PPO dir 1996, 1323

National health dir, 1996, 1324
Plunkett's health care industry almanac, 1329

MEDICAL INSTRUMENTS & APPARATUS
Szycher's dict of medical devices, 1332

MEDICAL POLICY
Encyclopedia of US biomedical policy, 1330
National health dir, 1996, 1324

MEDICAL REHABILITATION
Encyclopedia of disability & rehabilitation, 670
Living with low vision, 671
Resources for elders with disabilities, 3d ed, 672
Resources for people with disabilities & chronic conditions, 3d ed, 673

MEDICAL STATISTICS
Nursing home statl yrbk, 1995, 1327

MEDICINAL PLANTS
Encyclopedia of medicinal plants, 1343

MEDICINE
Dictionary of substances & their effects [CD-ROM], 1314
Encyclopedia of molecular biology & molecular medicine, v.1, 1269
Encyclopedia of molecular biology & molecular medicine, v.2, 1270
Encyclopedia of molecular biology & molecular medicine, v.3, 1271
Health care almanac, 1316
Health online, 1328
HealthSpeak, 1315
Medical dict in 6 langs, 1331
Nursing diagnosis pocket manual, 1353
PsycLit [CD-ROM], 625
World Bk Rush-Presbyterian-St. Luke's medical center medical ency, 7th ed, 1335

MEDICINE, POPULAR. *See also* **ALTERNATIVE MEDICINE**
Complete home health advisor, 1344
Encyclopedia of alternative medicine, 1345
Encyclopedia of bodywork, 1350
Encyclopedia of medicinal plants, 1343
Everything you need to know about diseases, 1336
Everything you need to know about medical tests, 1337
Everything you need to know about medical treatments, 1338
Family homeopathy, 1342
Foot & ankle sourcebk, 1340
Illustrated ency of essential oils, 1346
Immunization resource gd, 2d ed, 1339
Medical advisor, 1348
People's gd to deadly drug interactions, 1359
Skin deep: an A-Z of skin disorders, treatments, & health, 1333
Women's complete healthbk, 1341

MEN
Women & men in Europe & N America 1995, 720

MENTAL HEALTH
Nurse's clinical gd to psychiatric & mental health care, 1355

MERCHANDISE LICENSING
EPM licensing letter sourcebk, 1997 ed, 165

METAL TRADE
Annual bulletin of steel stats for Europe, v.21: 1991-94, 1307

METALS
Fatigue data bk, 1308
Worldwide gd to equivalent nonferrous metals & alloys, 3d ed, 1309

METCALF, JOHN
John Metcalf papers, 1005

METEOROLOGY
Encyclopedia of climate & weather, 1396

METHODIST CHURCH
Historical dict of Methodism, 1214

METROPOLITAN AREAS
MSA profile, 1996, 724

METROPOLITAN MUSEUM OF ART
European paintings in the Metropolitan Museum of Art by artists born before 1865, 804

MEXICO
Consumer Mexico 1996, 269
Dictionary of 20th century culture: Hispanic culture of Mexico, Central America, & the Caribbean, 348
Encyclopedia of ancient Mesoamerica, 453
Encyclopedia of world cultures, v.8: Middle America & the Caribbean, 318
Mexico environmental report, 224
NTC's dict of Mexican cultural code words, 134
Profile of western N America, 248

MICHENER, JAMES A.
James A. Michener: a bibliog, 973

MICROCOMPUTERS. *See also* **COMPUTERS**
Encyclopedia of microcomputers, v.18, 1371
McGraw-Hill ency of personal computing, 1372

MIDDLE AGES
Cambridge illus atlas of warfare: the Middle Ages, 768-1487, 557
Medieval wordbk, 838
Middle Ages, 471

MIDDLE EAST
Dictionary of the Middle East, 138
Encyclopedia of the modern Middle East, 136
Encyclopedia of the Persian Gulf War, 454
Encyclopedia of world cultures, v.9: Africa & the Middle East, 319

Historical dict of Syria, 141
International dict of historic places, v.4, 468
Middle East & N Africa 1997, 43d ed, 139
1990-91 Gulf War, 456

MIDDLE SCHOOLS
Middle level educ, 295

MILITARY ART & SCIENCE
Cambridge illus atlas of warfare: Renaissance to Revolution, 1492-1792, 556
Cambridge illus atlas of warfare: the Middle Ages, 768-1487, 557
Dictionary of the modern US military, 566

MILITARY BIOGRAPHY
Generals in muddy boots: a concise ency of combat commanders, 562

MILITARY HISTORY
Battles of the Somme, 1916, 561
Cambridge illus atlas of warfare: Renaissance to Revolution, 1492-1792, 556
Cambridge illus atlas of warfare: the Middle Ages, 768-1487, 557
Dictionary of Afghan wars, revolutions, & insurgencies, 106
Encyclopedia of the Persian Gulf War, 454
European powers in the 1st World War, 467
Handbook of American military hist, 569
Oxford companion to Australian military hist, 565
Oxford companion to WW II, 571
Soviet armed forces, 1918-92, 558
War in N Africa, 1940-43, 460

MILITARY INTELLIGENCE
Dictionary of US intelligence servs, 597
Signals intelligence in WW II, 560

MILITARY OCCUPATION
Encyclopedia of invasions & conquests from ancient times to the present, 564

MILITARY READINESS
Jane's sentinel: Central America & the Caribbean security assessment, 1996 ed, 129
World dir of defence & security, 567

MILITARY SUPPLIES
Jane's NBC protection equipment 1996-97, 9th ed, 570

MILITIA MOVEMENTS
Militias in America, 613

MILTON, JOHN
Paradise Lost: an annot bibliog, 997

MIND & BODY THERAPIES
Encyclopedia of bodywork, 1350

MINERAL INDUSTRIES
Industrial commodity stats yrbk 1994, 195

MINERALS IN HUMAN NUTRITION
Encyclopedia of nutritional suppls, 1349
Encyclopedia of vitamins, minerals, & suppls, 1265

MINOR LEAGUE BASEBALL
Pacific Coast League: statl hist, 1903-57, 647

MINORITIES. *See also* **ETHNIC STUDIES**
Ethnic studies in the US, 322
Guide to ethnic health collections in the US, 1322
Official gd to racial & ethnic diversity, 324
Voices of multicultural America, 967
Women of color: feminist theory, 729

MISSIONS
World gd to religious & spiritual orgs 1996, 1182

MISSISSIPPIAN CULTURE
Archaeology of the Mississippian culture, 398

MODERN DANCE
Dancers & choreographers, 1100

MOLECULAR BIOLOGY
Encyclopedia of molecular biology & molecular medicine, v.1, 1269
Encyclopedia of molecular biology & molecular medicine, v.2, 1270
Encyclopedia of molecular biology & molecular medicine, v.3, 1271

MONGOLIA
Historical dict of Mongolia, 111

MOON
Who's who on the Moon, 1394

MOTION PICTURE ACTORS & ACTRESSES. *See also* **ACTORS**
Film actors gd, 1997, 3d ed, 1143
Howard Keel: a bio-bibliog, 1078
Quinlan's illus dir of film character actors, new ed, 1106
Silent film performers, 1105
Some Joe you don't know: an American biogl gd to 100 British TV personalities, 1107
Western & frontier film & TV credits 1903-95, 1130

MOTION PICTURE INDUSTRY
American film personnel & co credits, 1908-20, 1142
Encyclopedia of European cinema, 1111
Film producers, studios, agents, & casting directors gd, 5th ed, 766
First century of film, 1112
International motion picture almanac, 1996, 67th ed, 770

MOTION PICTURE MUSIC
Film composers gd, 3d ed, 1037

MOTION PICTURE PRODUCERS & DIRECTORS
Contemporary literary criticism, v.89, 898
Hollywood & the foreign touch, 1108

Tony Richardson: a bio-bibliog., 1096
Western & frontier film & TV credits 1903-95, 1130

MOTION PICTURE STUDIOS
British film studios, 1139

MOTION PICTURES
American film personnel & co credits, 1908-20, 1142
British film studios, 1139
Charles Dickens on the screen, 1121
Encyclopedia of European cinema, 1111
Film writers gd, 6th ed, 767
First century of film, 1112
French films, 1945-93, 1115
Gangster films, 1114
Golden horrors: an illus critical filmography of terror cinema, 1931-39, 1122
Hammer films: an exhaustive filmography, 1119
Hollywood Reporter bk of box office hits, rev ed, 1128
International motion picture almanac, 1996, 67th ed, 770
International TV & video almanac, 1996, 41st ed, 771
Japanese filmography, 1117
South American cinema, 1124
Working stiffs, union maids, reds, & riffraff: an organized gd to films about labor, 1141

MOTION PICTURES—ARCHIVAL RESOURCES
British cinema source bk, 1109
Catalogue of forbidden German feature & short film productions held in Zonal Film Archives..., English lang ed, 764

MOTION PICTURES—REVIEWS
Magill's cinema annual 1995, 14th ed, 1131
New York Times film reviews, v.19: 1993-94, 1133
Psychotronic video gd, 1140
Sight & Sound film review v.: Jan. 1994 to Dec. 1994, 1135
Time Out film gd, 5th ed, 1136
TLA film & video gd 1996-97, 1125
Ultimate gd to lesbian & gay film & video, 1126
VideoHound's complete gd to cult flicks & trash pics, 1137

MULTICULTURAL EDUCATION
Multicultural educ, 283

MULTICULTURALISM
DISCovering multicultural America [CD-ROM], 323
Global voices, global visions: a core collection of multicultural bks, 10
Multicultural children's lit, 933
Official gd to racial & ethnic diversity, 324
Princeton hndbk of multicultural poetries, 1019
What's cooking in multicultural America, 1254
Writers of multicultural fiction for YAs, 942

MULTIMEDIA SYSTEMS
Multimedia: the complete gd, 1362
Multimedia dir, 4th ed, 1363

MURDER
Murder cases of the 20th century, 503

MUSEUMS
Historic railroad, 1446
University & college museums, galleries, & related facilities, 62

MUSHROOMS
Mushroom bk, 1280
Mushrooms of N America in color, 1278

MUSIC
BBC Music Mag top 1000 CDs gd, 1055
Brass music of black composers, 1041
Broadway sheet music, 1069
Chronicle of American music, 1700-1995, 1025
Compact music dict, 1026
Concise Oxford dict of music, 4th ed, 1027
Ethnic & vernacular music, 1898-1960, 1075
Film composers gd, 3d ed, 1037
General bibliog for music research, 3d ed, 1022
Harvard biogl dict of music, 1024
History of American classical music, 1059
Jazz: the rough gd, 1076
Literature of American music 3, 1983-92, 1021
Music & dance of the world's religions, 1087
Penguin dict of music, 6th ed, 1028
Twentieth-century American music for the dance, 1103
Well-tempered announcer: a pronunciation gd to classical music, 1056
Women & music, 1020
Women composers & songwriters, 1035
Women composers, v.1, 1047
Women composers, v.2, 1048

MUSIC FESTIVALS
Music festivals from Bach to blues, 1029

MUSIC—LATIN AMERICA
Latin American classical composers, 1042

MUSIC THEORY
Orchestration theory, 1057

MUSICAL ANALYSIS
Musical anthologies for analytical study, 1023

MUSICAL INSTRUMENTS
Catalog of music for the cornett, 1051
Illustrated ency of musical instruments, 1052
Makers of the piano, 1700-1820, 1050

MUSICALS
American song, 2d ed, 1077
Broadway, movie, TV, & studio cast musicals on record, 1030
Broadway sheet music, 1069
First Hollywood musicals, 1116

MUSLIMS
Muslim almanac, 1219
Year bk of the Muslim world 1996, 81

MUTUAL FUNDS
100 best mutual funds you can buy, 1995, 185

MYCENAE (EXTINCT CITY)
Mycenaean civilization, 448

MYSTERY & DETECTIVE STORIES. *See* **DETECTIVE & MYSTERY STORIES**

MYTHOLOGY
Myth: myths & legends of the world explored, 1091
World mythology, 1092

NAMES
Alphabetical gd to the lang of name studies, 824
What in the word? origins of words dealing with people & places, 823

NAMES, ETHNOLOGICAL
African ethnonyms, 315

NAMES, GEOGRAPHICAL
Merriam-Webster's pocket geographical dict, 380
Placenames of Russia & the former Soviet Union, 382

NAMES, PERSONAL
Bible baby names, 368
Directory of family assns, 3d ed, 354
Hispanic surnames & family hist, 356
More names & naming, 370
Surnames of Wales, 353
Well-tempered announcer: a pronunciation gd to classical music, 1056
What's in a name, 369

NATIONAL GALLERY (ENGLAND)
National Gallery complete illus catalogue, 796

NATIONALISM
Nations without states: a histl dict of contemporary natl movements, 583

NATURAL HISTORY
Illustrated bk of questions & answers, 56

NATURE
American nature writers, 965
Eyewitness ency of nature [CD-ROM], 1287

NEUROLOGY
Brain ency, 1334

NEUROPSYCHOLOGY
Blackwell dict of neuropsychology, 626

NEW ENGLAND
Yankee talk: a dict of New England expressions, 835

NEW LEFT
Left gd: a gd to left-of-center orgs, 614
Left index: a quarterly index to pers on the Left, 61

NEW YORK
Awesome almanac—N.Y., 85

NEW YORK PUBLIC LIBRARY
New York Public Lib's bks of the century, 882

NEW ZEALAND
Historical dict of New Zealand, 144
Periodicals in print: Australia, New Zealand, & the S Pacific 1996, 13th ed, 64
Post-Colonial lits in English: SE Asia, New Zealand, & the Pacific, 1970-92, 1013

NEWSLETTERS
Directory of electronic jls, newsletters, & academic discussion lists, 6th ed, 1375

NEWSPAPERS
Bacon's intl media dir 1996, 760

NIETZSCHE, FRIEDRICH WILHELM
Nietzsche canon, 1157

NIGERIA
Women in Nigeria, 725

NOBEL PRIZES
Who's who of Nobel prize winners 1901-95, 3d ed, 30

NORTH AMERICA
American folklore, 1088
Profile of western N America, 248
Trends in Europe & N America 1995, 719

NUCLEAR ARMS CONTROL
Nuclear test ban: glossary in English, French, & Arabic, 578

NUCLEAR WARFARE
Jane's NBC protection equipment 1996-97, 9th ed, 570

NURSING
Nurse's clinical gd to psychiatric & mental health care, 1355
Nursing diagnosis pocket manual, 1353
Nursing96 drug hndbk, 1360
PharmFacts for nurses, 1361

NURSING HOMES
Nursing home statl yrbk, 1995, 1327

OCCULTISM
Encyclopedia of occultism & parapsychology, 4th ed, 633
Mammoth dict of symbols, English lang ed, 636

OCCUPATIONS
Peterson's internships 1996, 16th ed, 256
Specialty occupational outlook: trade & technical, 262
Young person's occupational outlook hndbk, 264

OCEANIA
Far East & Australasia 1997, 28th ed, 143
International dict of historic places, v.5, 469
Literature for children & YAs about Oceania, 142

OCEAN TRAVEL
Stern's gd to the cruise vacation, 6th ed, 1449

OFFICE EQUIPMENT & SUPPLIES
Better buys for business, 187

OFFSHORE OIL INDUSTRY
Worldwide offshore contractors & equipment dir, 1996, 28th ed, 1419

OHIO
Awesome almanac—Ohio, 86

OIL INDUSTRIES
European oilfield serv, supply, & manufacturers dir, 1996, 2d ed, 1417

OLYMPICS
Chronicle of the Olympics 1896-1996, 660
Historical dict of the modern Olympic movement, 661

ONOMASTICS
Alphabetical gd to the lang of name studies, 824

ORCHESTRAL MUSIC
Orchestration theory, 1057

ORGANIC COMPOUNDS
Handbook of environmental data on organic chemicals, 3d ed, 1389

ORGANIC WASTES
Encyclopedia of garbage, 1425

ORIENTAL LITERATURE (ENGLISH)
Post-Colonial lits in English: SE Asia, New Zealand, & the Pacific, 1970-92, 1013

ORNAMENTAL CLIMBING PLANTS
Shrubs & climbers, 1286

ORNAMENTAL TREES
North American landscape trees, 1283

ORTHODOX EASTERN CHURCH
Historical dict of the orthodox church, 1212

ORTHODOX JUDAISM
Orthodox Judaism in America, 1224

OUTER SPACE. *See also* **ASTRONOMY**
Eyewitness ency of space & the universe [CD-ROM], 1395
Illustrated bk of questions & answers, 56

PACIFIC
Electric power in Asia & the Pacific, 1991 & 1992, 1420

PACIFIC ISLAND LITERATURE
Post-Colonial lits in English: SE Asia, New Zealand, & the Pacific, 1970-92, 1013

PAINTERS
Abstract expressionist women painters, 808
Biographical dir of Native American painters, 807
Henri Matisse: a gd to research, 805

PAINTING
European paintings in the Metropolitan Museum of Art by artists born before 1865, 804

PALEONTOLOGY
Dinosaur hunter [CD-ROM], 1403
Fossil atlas: fishes, 1404
Penguin histl atlas of dinosaurs, 1405

PALMS
Palms throughout the world, 1284

PARAPSYCHOLOGY. *See also* **OCCULTISM**
Encyclopedia of claims, frauds, & hoaxes of the occult & supernatural, 637
Encyclopedia of occultism & parapsychology, 4th ed, 633
Encyclopedia of the paranormal, 634
Haunted places: the natl dir, rev ed, 635

PARENTING. *See also* **SAFETY EDUCATION**
Family wisdom, 69
Growing up: a cross-cultural ency, 708
New parents sourcebk, 709

PASTORAL THEOLOGY
New dict of Christian ethics & pastoral theology, 1209

PATENTS
McCarthy's desk ency of intellectual property, 2d ed, 519
Patent, copyright, & trademark, 520

PEDIATRICS
Practical pediatrician, 1354

PEEL, ROBERT
Sir Robert Peel 1788-1850: a bibliog, 439

PENTACOSTALISM
Charismatic movement, pts.1-4, 1205

PERENNIALS
Ball perennial manual, 1275
Perennials, 1274

PERFORMING ARTS
Artists & writers colonies, 745
Entertainment awards, 1099
Music festivals from Bach to blues, 1029
Obituaries in the performing arts, 1994, 1097
Obituaries in the performing arts, 1995, 1098

PERIODICALS
Alternative Press index, 58
Annotations: a dir of pers listed in the Alternative Press Index, 1996 ed, 63
Bacon's intl media dir 1996, 760
International relations research dir, 619

Literary index to American mags, 1850-1900, 960
Novel & short story writer's market, 1996, 753
Periodicals in print: Australia, New Zealand, & the S Pacific 1996, 13th ed, 64
Standard per dir, 1997, 20th ed, 65
Ulrich's intl pers dir 1997, 35th ed, 66
Women's pers in the US, 743
World dir of trade & business jls, 174

PERSIAN GULF WAR, 1991
Encyclopedia of the Persian Gulf War, 454
1990-91 Gulf War, 456

PERSONAL COMPUTERS. *See* **MICROCOMPUTERS**

PERSONNEL MANAGEMENT. *See also* **MANAGEMENT**
Manager's desk ref, 2d ed, 265

PERU
Ancient Peruvian art, 794
Sendero Luminoso: an annot bibliog of the Shining Path guerrilla movement, 1980-93, 502

PETROLEUM INDUSTRY & TRADE. *See also* **OIL INDUSTRIES**
Geologists & the hist of geology, suppl 2, v.1, 1402
Oil & gas on the Internet, 1415
Worldwide offshore contractors & equipment dir, 1996, 28th ed, 1419

PETS
Help! the quick gd to first aid for your cat, 1261

PHARMACOLOGY
PharmFacts for nurses, 1361
World databases in bioscis & pharmacology, 1241

PHILIPPINES
Philippines business, 236
Philippines in WW II & to independence (Dec. 8, 1941-July 4, 1946), 2d ed, 432

PHILOLOGY
English lang scholarship, 809

PHILOSOPHERS
Biographical dict of 20th-century philosophers, 1158
Contemporary literary criticism, v.86, 895
Hobbes dict, 1165
Martin Heidegger (2): a bibliog, 1156
Nietzsche canon, 1157
Nineteenth-century lit criticism, v.51, 912
Nineteenth-century lit criticism annual cum title index for 1996, 914
Oxford companion to philosophy, 1166
Twentieth-century literary criticism, v.59, 920
Twentieth-century literary criticism, v.61, 922
Twentieth-century literary criticism annual cum title index for 1996, 923
Wittgenstein dict, 1162

PHILOSOPHY
Cambridge dict of philosophy, 1159
Dictionary of philosophy, 3d ed, 1164
Encyclopedia of philosophy suppl, 1160
Encyclopedia of the Enlightenment, 475
Oxford companion to philosophy, 1166

PHONETICS
Dictionary of phonetics & phonology, 819
Phonetic symbol gd, 2d ed, 815

PHOTOGRAPHY
Index to American photographic collections, 3d ed, 789

PHYSICIANS
Canadian medical dir on CD-ROM, 1996 [CD-ROM], 1320

PHYSICS
Einstein dict, 1409
Encyclopedia of applied physics, v.15, 1407
Encyclopedia of applied physics, v.16, 1408
Macmillan ency of physics, 1410
Physics quick ref gd, 1406
Popular physics & astronomy, 1411

PIANO
Makers of the piano, 1700-1820, 1050

PIANO MUSIC
International ency of violin-keyboard sonatas & composer biogs, 2d ed, 1043

PISTOLS
Illustrated ency of handguns, 782

PLANTS
Bonsai survival manual, 1256
Elsevier's dict of plant names, 1273
Plants that merit attention, v.2: shrubs, 1285

PLASTICS
Glossary of plastics terminology in 6 langs, 3d ed, 1379
Handbook of plastic & rubber additives, 1385

PLAYWRIGHTS
British playwrights, 1880-1956, 985
British playwrights, 1956-95, 986
French women playwrights of the 20th century, 943
Nineteenth-century lit criticism, v.52, 913

POETRY
American & British poetry, 1015
Columbia Granger's index to poetry in collected & selected works, 1016
Columbia Granger's world of poetry [CD-ROm], 1017
Poem finder 95 [CD-ROM], 1018
Princeton hndbk of multicultural poetries, 1019
Victorian poetry, 1000

POETS
Canadian writers & their works: poetry series, v.11, 1004
Contemporary literary criticism, v.86, 895

Contemporary literary criticism, v.88, 897
Contemporary literary criticism, v.89, 898
Directory of American poets & fiction writers, 1995-96 ed, 749
DISCovering authors modules [CD-ROM], 900
Literature criticism from 1400 to 1800, v.28, 901
Literature criticism from 1400 to 1800, v.30, 903
Literature criticism from 1400 to 1800, v.31, 904
Nineteenth-century lit criticism, v.47, 908
Nineteenth-century lit criticism, v.49, 910
Nineteenth-century lit criticism, v.50, 911
Nineteenth-century lit criticism, v.51, 912
Nineteenth-century lit criticism, v.52, 913
Nineteenth-century lit criticism annual cum title index for 1996, 914
Reader's gd to 20th-century writers, 916
Twentieth-century literary criticism, v.59, 920
Twentieth-century literary criticism, v.60, 921
Twentieth-century literary criticism annual cum title index for 1996, 923

POISONS
Field gd to common animal poisons, 1262

POLICE
Cops, crooks, & criminologists, 504

POLISH AMERICANS
Who's who in Polish America, 1996-1997 ed, 35

POLISH LANGUAGE—DICTIONARIES—ENGLISH
Highlander Polish-English/English-Highlander Polish dict, 864

POLITICAL SCIENCE
Illustrated dict of constitutional concepts, 594
Law & pols, 490
Political systems of the world, 582
Propaganda in 20th century war & pols, 618
Public interest profiles 1996-97, 599
World factbk 1996-97, 80

POLITICIANS
Beyond the hill, 598
Vice presidents, 590

POLLUTION
Encyclopedia of garbage, 1425
Environment & the law, 514

POPULAR CULTURE
Fashion & costume in American popular culture, 1093
Pop culture landmarks, 387

POPULAR MUSIC
All music bk of hit albums, 1066
All music bk of hit singles, 1067
Billboard bk of no.1 albums, 1060
Billboard bk of top 40 albums, 3d ed, 1061
Billboard bk of top 40 hits, 6th ed, 1062
Broadway sheet music, 1069
Cole Porter discography, 1068
Command performance, USA! a discography, 772
DK ency of rock stars, 1081
Fred Waring discography, 1049
Harvard biogl dict of music, 1024
International who's who in music, v.2: popular music, 1063
Joan Baez: a bio-bibliog, 1074
Joel Whitburn's top pop albums 1955-96, 1070
Joel Whitburn's top R&B singles 1942-1995, 1079
Lissauer's ency of popular music in America, 1065
Moanin' low: a discography of female popular vocal recordings, 1920-33, 1064

POPULATION
Atlas of US economy, tech, & growth, 714
Population hist of western US cities & towns, 1850-1990, 723

PORTER, COLE
Cole Porter discography, 1068

POSTAL SERVICE
National 5-digit zip code & post office dir 1996, 52

POSTMODERNISM
Feminism & postmodern theory, 727

POULENC, FRANCIS
Music of Francis Poulenc (1899-1963), 1044

POWER RESOURCES
Directory of power plant equipment & processes, 1996, 1416

PRESIDENTIAL CANDIDATES
U.S. presidential candidates & the elections, 588

PRESIDENTS' SPOUSES
American first ladies, 407

PRESIDENTS—UNITED STATES
Encyclopedia of the Reagan-Bush yrs, 593
How to research the presidency, 586
Landmarks of American presidents, 391
Presidents: a ref hist, 2d ed, 589
Reagan yrs A to Z, 592

PRESSURE GROUPS
Post-Soviet hndbk, 123
Public interest profiles 1996-97, 599

PRISONS
Dictionary of American penology, rev ed, 506
Encyclopedia of American prisons, 505

PROCESS CONTROL
Comprehensive dict of measurement & control, 3d ed, 1311

PROFESSIONAL SPORTS
Sporting News pro football gd, 1996 ed, 655
Sporting News pro football register, 1996 ed, 656

PROGRAMMING LANGUAGES
UNIX dict of commands, terms, & acronyms, 1373

PROPAGANDA
Chronology & glossary of propaganda in the US, 595
Propaganda in 20th century war & pols, 618

PROVERBS
Dictionary of 1000 Spanish proverbs with English equivalents, 1089

PSYCHIATRY
Encyclopedia of psychiatry, psychology, & psychoanalysis, 1356
Nurse's clinical gd to psychiatric & mental health care, 1355
PsycLit [CD-ROM], 625

PSYCHOLOGISTS
Twentieth-century literary criticism, v.61, 922

PSYCHOLOGY
Blackwell dict of neuropsychology, 626
Concise ency of psychology, 2d ed, 627
Dictionary of dvlpmtl psychology, 629
Encyclopedia of psychiatry, psychology, & psychoanalysis, 1356
Gale ency of psychology, 628
International dict of psychology, 2d ed, 630
Psychology: an introductory bibliog, 624
PsycLit [CD-ROM], 625

PUBLIC HEALTH
Dictionary of public health promotion & educ, 1317

PUBLIC OPINION
Official gd to American attitudes, 717

PUBLIC OPINION POLLS
Polling & survey research methods, 1935-79, 77

PUBLIC RECORDS
Genealogical research in England's public record office, 357
Sourcebook of online public record experts, 540

PUBLISHERS & PUBLISHING. See also BOOK INDUSTRIES & TRADE; BOOKSELLERS & BOOKSELLING
Authentic Jane Williams' home school mrkt gd, 280
British literary bk trade, 1700-1820, 553
Dictionary of literary biog documentary series, v.13, 963
Encyclopedia of the bk, 2d ed, 554
Harrod's librarians' glossary, 8th ed, 526
Market gd for young writers, 5th ed, 751
Novel & short story writer's market, 1996, 753
Publishers, distrs, & wholesalers of the US 1996-97, 555

PUNJAB
Punjab, 126

QUESTIONS & ANSWERS
Illustrated bk of questions & answers, 56

QUOTATIONS
American Indian quotations, 345
Born this day, 41
Columbia world of quotations [CD-ROM], 68
Family wisdom, 69
International educ quotations ency, 289
New Beacon bk of quotations by women, 70
Of the people, by the people, for the people, & other quotations by Abraham Lincoln, 67
Oxford dict of humorous quotations, 71
Women's words, 72

RACE RELATIONS
Ethnic studies in the US, 322

RACISM
Environmental racism & the environmental justice movement, 513
Racism in contemporary America, 325

RADCLIFFE, ANN
Ann Radcliffe: a bio-bibliog, 998

RADICALISM IN LITERATURE
Alternative Press index, 58

RADIO
North American shortwave frequency gd, v.3, 768
Radio stars, 762
Radio's morning show personalities, 763
Same time ... same station: an A-Z gd to radio from Jack Benny to Howard Stern, 765
World radio TV hndbk, 1996 ed, 773

RAILROADS
Eurail gd to train travel in the new Europe, 1996, 1443
Eurail gd to world train travel, 1996, 26th ed, 1444
Field gd to trains of N America, 1445
Historic railroad, 1446

RAWLINGS, MARJORIE K.
Marjorie Kinnan Rawlings: a descriptive bibliog, 974

READ, GARDNER
Gardner Read: a bio-bibliog, 1036

REAGAN, RONALD
Encyclopedia of the Reagan-Bush yrs, 593
Reagan yrs A to Z, 592

REAL ESTATE BUSINESS
Directory of designated members, 1996, 282

RECONSTRUCTION
ABC-CLIO companion to American reconstruction, 1862-77, 420

REFERENCE BOOKS
Canadian ref sources, 19

Guide to info sources in the botanical scis, 2d ed, 1272
Guide to ref bks, 11th ed, 8
Law lib ref shelf, 3d ed, 482
Reference bks bulletin 1994-95, 12
Reference sources hndbk, 4th ed, 13
Social scis, 2d ed, 76
Walford's gd to ref material, v.1: sci & tech, 7th ed, 1229
Writer's ultimate research gd, 752

REFORMATION
Oxford ency of the Reformation, 1211

REFUGEES
International thesaurus of refugee terminology, 2d ed, 705

REFUSE
Encyclopedia of garbage, 1425

RELIGION
Angels A to Z, 1176
Book of Ephesians, 1188
Charismatic movement, pts.1-4, 1205
Doctrine of the Holy Spirit, 1193
Fund raiser's gd to religous philanthropy 1996, 9th ed, 691
Modern American popular religion, 1171
Music & dance of the world's religions, 1087
Of spirituality, 1169
Religion: a cross-cultural ency, 1178
Religious higher educ in the US, 301
Women & religion in Britain & Ireland, 1170
Women in the biblical world, v.1, 1186

RELIGION & SCIENCE
Who's who in theology & sci, 1996 ed, 1175

RELIGIONS
Encyclopedia of American religious hist, 1180
National gd to funding in religion, 1184
New dict of religions, rev ed, 1179
Shambhala dict of Taoism, 1226

RELIGIOUS EDUCATION
NCEA/Ganley's Catholic schools in America 1995, 23d ed, 1216

RELIGIOUS INSTITUTIONS
World gd to religious & spiritual orgs 1996, 1182

REPERTORY THEATER
Regional theatre dir 1996-97, 1152

REPORT WRITING
Manual for writers of term papers, theses, & dissertations, 6th ed, 755
100 research topic gds for students, 543

RESEARCH
Business & economic research dir, 159
International relations research dir, 619

Profiles in business & mgmt [CD-ROM], 221
Research servs dir, 170
Writer's ultimate research gd, 752

RESEARCH GRANTS
Directory of research grants 1996, 687
Higher educ money bk for women & minorities, 1997 ed, 302

RESEARCH INSTITUTES
Think tank dir, 622

RESEARCH LIBRARIES
ARL stats 1994-95, 527

RETAIL TRADE
European private label dir, 241
Wholesale & retail trade USA, 279
World retail dir & sourcebk, 2d ed, 222

RETIREMENT. *See also* **AGED**
365 ways...retirees' resource gd for productive lifestyles, 669

REVOLUTIONS
Encyclopedia of revolutions & revolutionaries, 477

REVOLVERS
Illustrated ency of handguns, 782

RHETORIC
Encyclopedia of rhetoric & composition, 840
New Fowler's modern English usage, 3d ed, 756
Wired style, 758
Writing centers, 284

RHODODENDRON
Fungi on rhododendron, 1279

RHYTHM & BLUES MUSIC
All music gd to the blues, 1072
Joel Whitburn's top R&B singles 1942-1995, 1079

RICHARDSON, TONY
Tony Richardson: a bio-bibliog., 1096

RIGHT & LEFT (POLITICAL SCIENCE)
Left gd: a gd to left-of-center orgs, 614
Left index: a quarterly index to pers on the left, 61

RIGHT-WING EXTREMISTS
Militias in America, 613

RISK MANAGEMENT
Glossary of insurance & risk mgmt terms, 6th ed, 200

ROBINSON, JOAN
Joan Robinson: a bio-bibliog, 150

ROCK GARDENS
Bulbs for the rock garden, 1255
Cushion plants for the rock garden, 1257

ROCK MUSIC
All music bk of hit albums, 1066
All music bk of hit singles, 1067
Billboard's hottest hot 100 hits, rev ed, 1080
Great rock discography, 1085
MusicHound rock: the essential album gd, 1084
Rock music scholarship, 1082
Rock who's who, 2d ed, 1083

ROCK PLANTS
Cushion plants for the rock garden, 1257

ROCKETRY
Spaceflight & rocketry, 1300

ROMANCE FICTION
Romance writer's sourcebk, 754

ROMANIA
Historical dict of Romania, 120

ROMANIAN LANGUAGE—DICTIONARIES—ENGLISH
NTC's Romanian & English dict, 865

ROMANTICISM
British short-fiction writers, 1880-1914, 979
Romantic movement, 884

ROSES
Roses, 1277

RUBBER
Handbook of plastic & rubber additives, 1385

RUSH, BENAJMIN
Benjamin Rush, M.D.: a bibliographic gd, 403

RUSSIA. See also FORMER SOVIET REPUBLICS; SOVIET UNION
Maximov's companion to who governs the Russian Federation, summer 96, v.2, no.1, 610
Placenames of Russia & the former Soviet Union, 382
Supplement to The Modern Ency of Russian, Soviet, & Eurasian Hist, v.1, 476

RUSSIAN LANGUAGE—DICTIONARIES—ENGLISH
Concise Oxford Russian dict, 866
English-Russian economics glossary, 154
Russian-English collocational dict of the human body, 867

SACRED SPACE
Atlas of holy places & sacred sites, 1167

SACRED VOCAL MUSIC
Music & dance of the world's religions, 1087

SAFETY EDUCATION
CRC hndbk of lab safety, 4th ed, 1386
Injury prevention for young children, 710

ST. LUCIA
St. Lucia, 145

SAINTS
Penguin dict of saints, 3d ed, 1174

SAN FRANCISCO (CALIFORNIA)
San Francisco almanac, rev ed, 83

SAN MARINO
San Marino, 121

SANSKRIT LANGUAGE—DICTIONARIES—ENGLISH
Hippocrene concise Sanskrit-English dict, 868

SAPP, ALLEN
Allen Sapp: a bio-bibliog, 1038

SASSE, HERMANN
Hermann Sasse: a bibliog, 1168

SATIRE
Encyclopedia of satirical lit, 892

SCANDINAVIAN AMERICANS
Student's gd to Scaninavian American genealogy, 364

SCHOLARSHIPS
Funding for US study, 2d ed, 305
Government assistance almanac 1996-97, 10th ed, 689
Higher educ money bk for women & minorities, 1997 ed, 302

SCHOOL MEDIA CENTERS. See INSTRUCTIONAL MATERIALS CENTERS

SCHOOL PSYCHOLOGY
Historical ency of school psychology, 286

SCIENCE
Callaham's Russian-English dict of sci & tech, 4th ed, 1237
Encyclopedia of life scis, 1268
Gale ency of sci, 1238
Grolier student ency of sci, tech, & the enviroment, 1239
Handbook of current sci & tech, [2d ed], 1242
History of sci in the US, 1235
Illustrated bk of questions & answers, 56
Larousse dict of sci & tech, 1240
Macmillan ency of earth scis, 1391
MathSci disc [CD-ROM], 1414
McGraw-Hill yrbk of sci & tech 1996, 1243
Peterson's top colleges for sci, 306
Reader's adviser on CD-ROM [CD-ROM], 11
Routledge German technical dict, 851
Science & tech: a purchase gd for libs 1995, 1234
Science experiments index for young people, 2d ed, 1244
Scientific revolution, 1227
SciTech ref plus 1995-1996 [CD-ROM], 1228
Walford's gd to ref material, v.1: sci & tech, 7th ed, 1229
Women & sci, 730

SCIENCE FICTION
Burroughs cyclopaedia, 969
Jules Verne ency, 952
Magill's gd to sci fiction & fantasy lit, 948
St. James gd to fantasy writers, 950
St. James gd to sci fiction writers, 4th ed, 951
Ultimate gd to sci fiction, 2d ed, 949

SCIENTISTS
Distinguished African American scientists of the 20th century, 1230
Who's who in theology & sci, 1996 ed, 1175
Who's who in sci & engineering 1996-97, 3d ed, 1232
Who's who in sci in Europe, 9th ed, 1233

SCOTTISH LITERATURE
Literature criticism from 1400 to 1800, v.29, 902

SCREENWRITERS
Contemporary literary criticism, v.86, 895
Film writers gd, 6th ed, 767

SEARCHING, BIBLIOGRAPHICAL
100 research topic gds for students, 543

SECURITIES
Rate ref gd to the US treasury market 1984-95, 184
World stock exchange fact bk, 186

SELF-CULTURE
Adventures in video, 314

SELF-HELP TECHNIQUES
Finding help: a ref gd for personal concerns, 55

SEQUELS (LITERATURE)
To be continued: an annot gd to sequels, 946

SERIAL PUBLICATIONS. See also PERIODICALS
Standard per dir, 1997, 20th ed, 65
Ulrich's intl pers dir 1997, 35th ed, 66

SEX & LAW
Guide to America's sex laws, 499

SEX DIFFERENCES
Why Eve doesn't have an Adam's apple: a dict of sex differences, 1318

SEXUAL HARASSMENT
Sexual harassment, 702

SHAKESPEARE, WILLIAM
Shakespeare's lang, 999

SHAMANS
Encyclopedia of Native American healing, 340

SHAN LANGUAGE—DICTIONARIES—ENGLISH
Shan-English dict, 869

SHINING PATH (GUERRILLA MOVEMENT)
Sendero Luminoso: an annot bibliog of the Shining Path guerrilla movement, 1980-93, 502

SHIPS
Jane's fighting ships 1996-97, 99th ed, 573

SHIPWRECKS
Shipwrecks, 1448

SHORT STORIES
British short-fiction writers, 1800-80, 978
British short-fiction writers, 1880-1914, 979
British short-fiction writers, 1915-45, 980
Masterplots 2: short story series suppl, 953
Short story criticism, v.18, 954
Short story criticism, v.19, 955
Short story criticism, v.20, 956
Short story criticism, v.21, 957

SHORTWAVE RADIO STATIONS
Shortwave listening on the road, 774

SHRINES
Atlas of holy places & sacred sites, 1167

SIGN LANGUAGE
Essential ASL, 871
NTC's multilingual dict of American Sign Lang, 870

SIGNS & SYMBOLS
Mammoth dict of symbols, English lang ed, 636
Phonetic symbol gd, 2d ed, 815

SIKHISM
Encyclopaedia of Sikh religion & culture, 1225

SIKSIKA LANGUAGE—DICTIONARIES—ENGLISH
Blackfoot dict of stems, roots, & affixes, 2d ed, 872

SILENT FILMS
Silent film performers, 1105
Silent films on video, 1120

SITUATIONIST INTERNATIONAL
Realization & suppression of the Situationist Intl, 792

SKIN
Skin deep: an A-Z of skin disorders, treatments, & health, 1333

SKIS & SKIING
Good skiing gd 1997, 662

SLANG
Flappers 2 rappers: American youth slang, 842

SLAVERY
Pan-African chronology, 426

SLAVIC COUNTRIES
American bibliog of Slavic & E European studies for 1993, 114

SLOVENIA
Slovenia, 122

SMALL BUSINESS
Bond's franchise gd, 1996, 180
Free money from the fed govt for small businesses & entrepreneurs, 2d ed, 189

SOCIAL HISTORY
Profile of western N America, 248
Women writers in the US, 738

SOCIAL INSTITUTIONS
Family studies database [CD-ROM], 674

SOCIAL INTERACTIONS
Encyclopedia of relationships across the lifespan, 631

SOCIAL MOVEMENTS
ABC-CLIO companion to the Native American rights movement, 341

SOCIAL REFORMERS
American reform & reformers, 408
British reform writers, 1789-1832, 977
Jane Addams papers, 706

SOCIAL SCIENCES
Reader's adviser on CD-ROM [CD-ROM], 11
Social sci ency, 2d ed, 75
Social scis, 2d ed, 76
World databases in social scis, 78

SOCIAL SERVICE
Directory of social serv grants, 688

SOCIAL SURVEYS
Polling & survey research methods, 1935-79, 77

SOCIAL WORK EDUCATION
International hndbk on social work educ, 704

SOCIALIZATION
Growing up: a cross-cultural ency, 708

SOCIOLOGY
Dictionary of ethics, theology, & society, 73

SOMME, FIRST BATTLE OF THE, FRANCE, 1916
Battles of the Somme, 1916, 561

SONATAS
International ency of violin-keyboard sonatas & composer biogs, 2d ed, 1043

SONGS
American song, 2d ed, 1077

Children's song index, 1978-93, 1033
German poetry in song, 1032

SOUTH AFRICA
Consumer South Africa 1995, 270
Dict of South African English on histl principles, 830
South African bibliog, 3d ed, 551
Who's who in South African pols, no.5, 611

SOUTH AMERICA
South America, Central America, & the Caribbean 1997, 6th ed, 130
South American cinema, 1124

SOUTHERN STATES
Who's who in the South & Southwest 1995-96, 36

SOVIET UNION. *See also* **FORMER SOVIET REPUBLICS; RUSSIA**
Bibliography of the Soviet Union, it predecessors & successors, 124
Evangelical sectarianism in the Russian Empire & the USSR, 1173
Soviet armed forces, 1918-92, 558
Statistical hndbk of social & economic indicators for the former Soviet Union, 125

SPACE FLIGHT
Jane's space dir 1996-97, 12th ed, 1301
Spaceflight & rocketry, 1300
USA in space, 1302

SPACE SCIENCES
Eyewitness ency of space & the universe [CD-ROM], 1395

SPAIN
Historical dict of Spain, 452
Regions of Spain, 451
Spain, 396

SPANISH FICTION
Contemporary Spanish novel, 1014

SPANISH LANGUAGE—DICTIONARIES—ENGLISH
Dahl's law dict: an annot legal dict, Spanish-English/English-Spanish, 2d ed, 486
Dictionary of 1000 Spanish proverbs with English equivalents, 1089
Economics, trade, & dvlpmt: English-Spanish general terminology, 272
Elsevier's dict of financial & economic terms, 153
English-Spanish, Spanish-English electrical & computer engineering dict, 1297
Larousse English-Spanish, Spanish-English dict, new, 873
Larousse mini Spanish-English, English-Spanish dict, new ed, 874
Mastering Spanish vocabulary, 875
Wiley dict of civil engineering & construction: English-Spanish/Spanish-English, 1304

SPANISH LANGUAGE—PROVINCIALISM
NTC's dict of Mexican cultural code words, 134

SPANISH SUCCESSION, WAR OF
War of the Spanish Succession, 1702-13, 435

SPARROWS
Sparrows & buntings, 1288

SPEECHES, ADDRESSES, ETC., AMERICAN
African American voices, 328
Voices of multicultural America, 967

SPIRITS
Spirits, fairies, gnomes, & goblins, 1090

SPIRITUALISM
Angels A to Z, 1176

SPORTS
Chase's sports calendar of events 1997, 639
Chronicle of the Olympics 1896-1996, 660
Encyclopedia of women & sports, 644
Historical dict of the modern Olympic movement, 661
Sports in N America, v.5, 642
Sports stars: series 2, 641
Sportspeak: an ency of sport, 643

SPORTS JOURNALISM
Sports style gd & ref manual, 757

SPORTS MEDICINE
Dict of sports injuries & disorders, 1357

SPORTS RECORDS
Track & field record holders, 663

SPORTS UNIFORMS
Baseball by the nos, 650

SQUARE DANCING
Square dance & contra dance hndbk, 1101

STARS
Cambridge astronomy dict, 1392
Cambridge star atlas, 2d ed, 1393

STATE GOVERNMENT
State legislative sourcebk 1996, 602

STATISTICS
Atlas of US economy, tech, & growth, 714
Business stats of the US, 1995 ed, 176
Compendium of human settlements stats 1995, 5th ed, 715
County & city extra, 1995, 4th ed, 712
Historical stats 1960-94, 1996 ed, 225
Instat: intl stats sources, 716
OECD statl compendium 1996/1 [CD-ROM], 227
Peoplepedia: the ultimate ref on the American people, 74
Statistical hndbk of social & economic indicators for the former Soviet Union, 125
Statistical hndbk on adolescents in America, 718
Statistical hndbk on violence in America, 507
Statistical hndbk on women in America, 2d ed, 740
Trends in Europe & N America 1995, 719
Women & men in Europe & N America 1995, 720
World stats pocketbk, 721

STEEL INDUSTRY & TRADE
Annual bulletin of steel stats for Europe, v.21: 1991-94, 1307
Directory of the steel industry & the environment, 194
Steel market in 1995 & prospects for 1996, 198

STEINBECK, JOHN
John Steinbeck: an annot gd to biogl sources, 975

STILL, WILLIAM GRANT
William Grant Still: a bio-bibliog, 1046

STOCK EXCHANGES
Standard & Poor's smallcap 600 gd, 1996 ed, 171
World stock exchange fact bk, 186

STOCKS
Dow Jones averages, 1885-1995, 183

STORYTELLING
National storytelling dir, 1996, 549

SUBJECT HEADINGS. *See also* **CATALOGING**
BHA: bibliog of the hist of art: subject headings/English, 790
Classification plus [CD-ROM], 533
Library of Congress subject headings, 19th ed, 534
HIV/AIDS & HIV/AIDS-related terminology, 537
Libraries Unltd prof collection CD 1995 [CD-ROM], 523

SUBMARINES
Jane's fighting ships 1996-97, 99th ed, 573

SUBSIDIARY CORPORATIONS
America's corporate families 1995, 158

SUBSIDIES
European regional incentives, 1996-97, 243

SUBSTANCE ABUSE
Encyclopedia of drugs & alcohol, 707

SUBVERSIVE ACTIVITIES
Encyclopedia of the McCarthy era, 591

SUMMER EMPLOYMENT
Peterson's summer opportunities for kids & teenagers 1996, 13th ed, 167
Summer theatre dir 1996, 1153

SUPERNATURAL
Encyclopedia of claims, frauds, & hoaxes of the occult & supernatural, 637
Haunted places: the natl dir, rev ed, 635
Strange & unexplained happenings, 638

SYDNEY
Sydney, 392

SYMBOLISM
Mammoth dict of symbols, English lang ed, 636

SYMBOLISM (ART MOVEMENT)
Four French symbolists, 806

SYNAGOGUES
American synagogue, 1221

SYRIA
Historical dict of Syria, 141

TABLOID NEWSPAPERS
Tabloid journalism, 747

TALLYRAND, CHARLES-MAURICE DE
Charles-Maurice de Talleyrand 1754-1838, 447

TALMUD
Dictionary of Judaism in the biblical period, 1223

TANKS (MILITARY)
Jane's tank & combat vehicle recognition gd, 576

TANZANIA
Tanzania, rev ed, 102

TAOISM
Shambhala dict of Taoism, 1226

TEACHERS
International ency of teaching & teacher educ, 2d ed, 298

TEACHING—AIDS & DEVICES
Media review digest, v. 26, 1996, 9

TECHNOLOGY
Atlas of US economy, tech, & growth, 714
Biographical dict of the hist of tech, 1236
Callaham's Russian-English dict of sci & tech, 4th ed, 1237
Encyclopedia of computer sci & tech, v.34, suppl 19, 1367
Grolier student ency of sci, tech, & the enviroment, 1239
Handbook of current sci & tech, [2d ed], 1242
Illustrated bk of questions & answers, 56
Larousse dict of sci & tech, 1240
McGraw-Hill yrbk of sci & tech 1996, 1243
Routledge German technical dict, 851
Science & tech: a purchase gd for libs 1995, 1234
Scientific revolution, 1227
SciTech ref plus 1995-1996 [CD-ROM], 1228
Walford's gd to ref material, v.1: sci & tech, 7th ed, 1229
Who's who in sci in Europe, 9th ed, 1233

TEENAGERS—UNITED STATES
Statistical hndbk on adolescents in America, 718

TELEVISION
International TV & video almanac, 1996, 41st ed, 771
Tabloid journalism, 747
Television writers gd, 4th ed, 769
Western & frontier film & TV credits 1903-95, 1130
World radio TV hndbk, 1996 ed, 773

TELEVISION ACTORS & ACTRESSES
Some Joe you don't know: an American biogl gd to 100 British TV personalities, 1107
Television program master index, 1144
Western & frontier film & TV credits 1903-95, 1130
Written out of TV, 1129

TELEVISION MUSIC
Broadway, movie, TV, & studio cast musicals on record, 1030

TELEVISION PROGRAMS
Charles Dickens on the screen, 1121
Definitive Andy Griffith show ref, 1134
Dictionary of teleliteracy, 1110
Encyclopedia of TV game shows, 2d ed, 1113
Following The Fugitive: an episode gd & hndbk to the 1960s TV series, 1127
Serials on British TV 1950-94, 1104
Television program master index, 1144
This is a Thriller: an episode gd, hist, & analysis of the classic 1960s TV series, 1138
Total TV, 4th ed, 1132
Written out of TV, 1129

TERRORISM
Shadow of death: an analytic bibliog on pol violence, terrorism, & low-intensity conflict, 501

TEXAS
Awesome almanac—Tex., 89

THEATER
American drama criticism: suppl 4 to the 2d ed, 1146
American theatre, 1150
British playwrights, 1880-1956, 985
British playwrights, 1956-95, 986
Cambridge gd to American theatre, updated ed, 1151
International biblog of theatre, 1148
International dict of theatre-3: actors, directors, & designers, 1149
Maxwell Anderson on the European stage 1929-92, 1147
New York Times theater reviews, v.28: 1993-94, 1154
Regional theatre dir 1996-97, 1152
Summer theatre dir 1996, 1153

THEATERS—STAGE SETTING
Theatrical design in the 20th century, 1155

THEATRICAL PRODUCERS & DIRECTORS
International dict of theatre-3: actors, directors, & designers, 1149
Tony Richardson: a bio-bibliog., 1096

THEOLOGIANS
Who's who in theology & sci, 1996 ed, 1175

THEOLOGY
Collegeville pastoral dict of biblical theology, 1196
Confessions of Saint Augustine, 1207
Dictionary of ethics, theology, & society, 73

Dictionary of feminist theologies, 1177
Emil Brunner: a bibliog, 1172
Evangelical dict of biblical theology, 1197
Hermann Sasse: a bibliog, 1168

THESAURI
Barron's business thesaurus, 178
Multilingual thesaurus of geoscis, 1400

THRILLER (TELEVISION PROGRAM)
This is a Thriller: an episode gd, hist, & analysis of the classic 1960s TV series, 1138

TITLES OF BOOKS
Literally entitled, 891

TOBACCO
Tobacco & health network dir 1996, 4th ed, 1325

TOGO
Historical dict of Togo, 3d ed, 103

TRACK & FIELD ATHLETICS
American women's track & field, 664
Track & field record holders, 663

TRADE. See also BUSINESS; MARKETING
World dir of trade & business jls, 174

TRADE & PROFESSIONAL ASSOCIATIONS
Business orgs, agencies, & pubns dir, 8th ed, 160
Directory of designated members, 1996, 282
Directory of trade & investment related orgs of developing countries & areas in Asia & the Pacific, 7th ed, 235
Gale's ready ref shelf [CD-ROM], 50
World dir of trade & business assns, 173
World gd to trade assns, 4th ed, 175

TRADE SECRETS
Employee duty of loyalty, 495
Employee duty of loyalty, 1996 suppl covering 1994, 496

TRADEMARKS
McCarthy's desk ency of intellectual property, 2d ed, 519
Patent, copyright, & trademark, 520

TRADE-UNIONS
Historical dict of organized labor, 251

TRANSCENDENTALISM
Biographical dict of transcendentalism, 962
Encyclopedia of transcendentalism, 964

TRANSPORTATION
ABC-CLIO companion to transportation in America, 1437
Trilingual vocabulary of road transport vehicles, 229

TRAVEL
Anderson's travel companion: a gd to the best non-fiction & fiction for travelling, 383
British travel writers, 1837-75, 981
City profiles USA 1996, 388
Complete gd to American bed & breakfast, 4th ed, 385
Eurail gd to train travel in the new Europe, 1996, 1443
Eurail gd to world train travel, 1996, 26th ed, 1444
Haunted places: the natl dir, rev ed, 635
Historic festivals, 386
Italy, 395
Landmarks of American presidents, 391
Pop culture landmarks, 387
Stern's gd to the cruise vacation, 6th ed, 1449
Sydney, 392
Travel dict, new ed, 384
Travel gd to Jewish Europe, 2d ed, 436

TREES
Garden trees, 1282
Palms throughout the world, 1284

TRUCKING
Trilingual vocabulary of road transport vehicles, 229

TURKISH LANGUAGE—DICTIONARIES—ENGLISH
Dictionary of the Turkic langs, 876

TUTORS
Writing centers, 284

TWENTIETH CENTURY
American decades 1900-09, 422
American decades 1910-19, 423
American decades 1920-29, 424
American decades 1980-89, 425
Encyclopedia of the US in the 20th century, 416

UGANDA
Uganda, rev ed, 104

UNEMPLOYMENT
Employment/unemployment & earnings stats, 249

UNIDENTIFIED FLYING OBJECTS
Haunted places: the natl dir, rev ed, 635
High strangeness: UFOs from 1960 through 1979, 632
Strange & unexplained happenings, 638

UNITED NATIONS
Historical dict of multinatl peacekeeping, 616

UNITED STATES—ARMED FORCES
Biographical dict of WW II generals & flag officers, 409
Dictionary of the modern US military, 566
Women in the US military, 1901-95, 559

UNITED STATES—ARMED FORCES RADIO SERVICE
Command performance, USA! a discography, 772

UNITED STATES—BIOGRAPHY
Dictionary of American biog, comprehensive index, 32

Encyclopedia of American biog, 2d ed, 33
Who's who in Polish America, 1996-1997 ed, 35

UNITED STATES—CENSUS
Dubester's US census bibliog with SuDocs class nos
    & indexes, 711
Understanding the census, lib ed, 713

UNITED STATES—CIVILIZATION
Encyclopedia USA, v.22, 417
Encyclopedia USA, v.23, 418
Revolutionary America 1763-1800, 399
Victorian America, 1876 to 1913, 400

UNITED STATES—CLIMATE
Weather America, 1397
Weather of US cities, 5th ed, 1398

UNITED STATES. CONGRESS
Accessing US govt info, rev ed, 54
Beyond the hill, 598
Facts about the Congress, 600
How to research Congress, 585
Members of Congress, 584

UNITED STATES CONSTITUTION
Encyclopedia of constitutional amendments, proposed
    amendments, & amending issues, 1789-1995, 596

UNITED STATES. DECLARATION OF INDEPENDENCE
Roots of the Republic, 410

UNITED STATES DEPARTMENT OF TREASURY
Biographical dict of the US Secretaries of the
    Treasury, 1789-1995, 587

UNITED STATES—DESCRIPTION & TRAVEL
Hostelling USA, 1996, 389

UNITED STATES EMIGRATION & IMMIGRATION
United States immigration, 621

UNITED STATES—GOVERNMENT
Introduction to US govt info sources, 5th ed, 53

UNITED STATES—GUIDE BOOKS
Complete gd to American bed & breakfast, 4th ed, 385

UNITED STATES—HISTORY
ABC-CLIO companion to American reconstruction,
    1862-77, 420
Colonial wars of N America, 1512-1763, 413
Dictionary of American hist, 419
Dictionary of American hist suppl, 414
Encyclopedia of the US in the 20th century, 416
Encyclopedia of women's hist in America, 736
Encyclopedia USA, v.22, 417
Encyclopedia USA, v.23, 418
Historic festivals, 386

Korean War, 431
Revolutionary America 1763-1800, 399
United States hist, 406
Victorian America, 1876 to 1913, 400
World's Columbian Exposition, 404

UNITED STATES—HISTORY—CHRONOLOGY
African American hist in the press 1851-99, 412
American decades 1900-09, 422
American decades 1910-19, 423
American decades 1920-29, 424
American decades 1980-89, 425

UNITED STATES—HISTORY—CIVIL WAR, 1861-1865
American Civil War, 421
Civil War CD-ROM [CD-ROM], 401

UNITED STATES—HISTORY—MILITARY
Handbook of American military hist, 569

UNITED STATES—MAPS
Macmillan color atlas of the states, 82

UNITED STATES—POLITICS & GOVERNMENT
American first ladies, 407
Chronology & glossary of propaganda in the US, 595
Encyclopedia of the Reagan-Bush yrs, 593
Illustrated dict of constitutional concepts, 594
Presidents: a ref hist, 2d ed, 589
Reagan yrs A to Z, 592
Religious right, 1218
United States govt manual 1996/97, 604

UNITED STATES—RELIGION
Modern American popular religion, 1171

UNITED STATES—SOCIAL LIFE & CUSTOMS
Revolutionary America, 1763-1800, 399
Victorian America, 1876 to 1913, 400

UNITED STATES—STATISTICS
New view almanac, 7
Statistical hndbk on adolescents in America, 718
Statistical hndbk on violence in America, 507
Statistical hndbk on women in America, 2d ed, 740

UNITED STATES. SUPREME COURT
Freedom of religion decisions of the US Supreme
    Court, 1183
Freedom of speech decisions of the US Supreme
    Court, 541
Freedom of the press decisions of the US Supreme
    Court, 761
Guide to the early reports of the Supreme Court of the
    US, 493
Supreme Court compendium, 2d ed, 497
Supreme Court yrbk 1995-96, 603

UNIVERSITIES & COLLEGES
College chemistry faculties 1996, 10th ed, 303
Peterson's top colleges for sci, 306

UNIVERSITY EXTENSION
Library servs for off-campus & distance educ, 521

UNIX
UNIX dict of commands, terms, & acronyms, 1373

URBAN CLIMATOLOGY
Weather of US cities, 5th ed, 1398

URBANIZATION
Challenge of urbanization, 722

VALUES
Dictionary of ethics, theology, & society, 73
Encyclopedia of values & ethics, 1163

VEGETABLE GARDENING
Taylor's gd to heirloom vegetables, 1260

VENTURE CAPITAL
Fitzroy Dearborn intl dir of venture capital funds, 2d ed, 181

VERNE, JULES
Jules Verne ency, 952

VETERINARY DRUGS
Veterinary drug hndbk, 2d ed, 1263

VICE-PRESIDENTS
Vice presidents, 590

VIDEO RECORDINGS
Adventures in video, 314
Charles Dickens on the screen, 1121
Critical gd to mgmt training videos & selected multimedia, 1996, 266
International TV & video almanac, 1996, 41st ed, 771
Media review digest, v. 26, 1996, 9
Psychotronic video gd, 1140
Silent films on video, 1120
Time Out film gd, 5th ed, 1136
TLA film & video gd 1996-97, 1125
Videos of African & African-related performance, 1145

VIETNAMESE CONFLICT, 1961-1975
Encyclopedia of the Vietnam War, 433
Historical atlas of the Vietnam War, 434

VIETNAMESE LANGUAGE
NTC's Vietnamese-English dict, 877

VIOLENCE
Shadow of death: an analytic bibliog on pol violence, terrorism, & low-intensity conflict, 501
Statistical hndbk on violence in America, 507
Statistics on weapons & violence, 512
Violence & the media, 748

VIOLIN MUSIC
International ency of violin-keyboard sonatas & composer biogs, 2d ed, 1043

VISUALLY HANDICAPPED
Living with low vision, 671

VITAMINS
Encyclopedia of nutritional suppls, 1349
Encyclopedia of vitamins, minerals, & suppls, 1265

VOCAL MUSIC
Giovanni Gabrieli (ca.1555-1612): a thematic catalogue of his music...., 1034

VOCATIONAL GUIDANCE
Young person's occupational outlook hndbk, 264

WAGES
Employment/unemployment & earnings stats, 249

WALES
Surnames of Wales, 353

WAR
Dictionary of Afghan wars, revolutions, & insurgencies, 106
Propaganda in 20th century war & pols, 618
War of the Spanish Succession, 1702-13, 435
Wars in the Third World since 1945, 2d ed, 568

WAR & SOCIETY
Cambridge illus atlas of warfare: Renaissance to Revolution, 1492-1792, 556
Cambridge illus atlas of warfare: the Middle Ages, 768-1487, 557

WAR FILMS
Hollywood war films, 1937-45, 1123

WAR—MORAL & ETHICAL ASPECTS
Encyclopedia of war & ethics, 1161

WARING, FRED
Fred Waring discography, 1049

WARSHIPS
Cruisers of WW II, 574
Jane's fighting ships 1996-97, 99th ed, 573
Jane's warship recognition gd, 577

WEAPONS
Jane's armour & artillery 1995-96, 16th ed, 575
Statistics on weapons & violence, 512
Vital gd to combat guns & infantry weapons, 579

WEATHER
Encyclopedia of climate & weather, 1396
Weather America, 1397
Weather of US cities, 5th ed, 1398

WEST INDIES
St. Lucia, 145

WEST (U.S.)
Bibliographical gd to the study of Western American lit, 2d ed, 959

Encyclopedia of the American West, 415
Narrative bibliog of the African American frontier, 405
Population hist of western US cities & towns, 1850-1990, 723
Profile of western N America, 248
Western lore & lang, 841

WESTERN FILMS
Western & frontier film & TV credits 1903-95, 1130

WESTERN SAHARA
Western Sahara, 105

WHOLESALE TRADE
Wholesale & retail trade USA, 279

WIND QUINTETS
Wind chamber music, 1058

WIT & HUMOR
Oxford dict of humorous quotations, 71

WITTGENSTEIN, LUDWIG
Wittgenstein dict, 1162

WOLFE, THOMAS
Thomas Wolfe: an annot critical bibliog, 976

WOMAN SINGERS
Moanin' low: a discography of female popular vocal recordings, 1920-33, 1064

WOMEN
British women's hist, 726
Contemporary Australian women 1996/97, 734
Detecting women 2, 1996-97 ed, 947
Encyclopedia of women's hist in America, 736
Latinas in the US, 728
New Beacon bk of quotations by women, 70
Notable black American women, bk.2, 34
Notable women in the life scis, 1231
Statistical hndbk on women in America, 2d ed, 740
Subject gd to women of the world, 741
U.S. women's interest groups, 737
Women & men in Europe & N America 1995, 720
Women & religion in Britain & Ireland, 1170
Women in law, 485
Women in Nigeria, 725
Women of color: feminist theory, 729
Women of strength, 733
Women's pers in the US, 743
Women's studies on disc [CD-ROM], 742
Women's words, 72

WOMEN & LITERATURE
French women playwrights of the 20th century, 943
Marjorie Kinnan Rawlings: a descriptive bibliog, 974

WOMEN & RELIGION
Of spirituality, 1169
Women in Christian hist, 731

WOMEN & THE MILITARY
Women & the military, 563
Women in the US military, 1961-95, 559

WOMEN ARTISTS
Abstract expressionist women painters, 808
Latin American women artists, 793

WOMEN ATHLETES
American women's track & field, 664
Encyclopedia of women & sports, 644

WOMEN AUTHORS
Literature criticism from 1400 to 1800, v.30, 903
Modern women writers, 907
Women writers in the US, 738

WOMEN—BIOGRAPHY
Prominent women of the 20th century, 26

WOMEN COMPOSERS
Women composers & songwriters, 1035
Women composers, v.1, 1047
Women composers, v.2, 1048

WOMEN—EMPLOYMENT
Women workers, 732

WOMEN—HEALTH & HYGIENE
Women's complete healthbk, 1341

WOMEN HISTORIANS
American women historians, 1700s-1990s, 411

WOMEN IN AGRICULTURE
Women in agriculture, 1245

WOMEN IN ART
Encyclopedia of women in religious art, 797

WOMEN IN SCIENCE
Women & sci, 730

WOMEN IN THE BIBLE
Women in the biblical world, v.1, 1186

WOMEN LEGISLATORS
Women state & territorial legislators, 1895-1995, 601

WOMEN MUSICIANS
Women & music, 1020

WOMEN'S PERIODICALS
Women's pers in the US, 743

WOMEN'S RIGHTS
U.S. women's interest groups, 737

WOMEN'S STUDIES INDEX
Women's studies on disc [CD-ROM], 742

WORKING CLASS
Working stiffs, union maids, reds, & riffraff: an organized gd to films about labor, 1141

WORLD HISTORY
Chronicle of the world, rev ed, 464
Classical studies, 461
Hammond atlas of the 20th century, 459
Pocket factfile of 20th century events, 466
Profiles in world hist, 472

WORLD POLITICS
Annual register 1995, 581
Cold War ency, 473
Encyclopedia of revolutions & revolutionaries, 477
Nations without states: a histl dict of contemporary natl movements, 583
Political systems of the world, 582
Wars in the Third World since 1945, 2d ed, 568
World dir of defence & security, 567
World factbk 1996-97, 80

WORLD SERIES (BASEBALL)
Inside Sports world series factbk, 645

WORLD WAR, 1914-1918
Dictionary of the 1st world war, 474
European powers in the 1st World War, 467

WORLD WAR, 1939-1945
Biographical dict of WW II, 463
Biographical dict of WW II generals & flag officers, 409
Cruisers of WW II, 574
Hollywood war films, 1937-45, 1123
Oxford companion to WW II, 571
Philippines in WW II & to independence (Dec. 8, 1941-July 4, 1946), 2d ed, 432
Signals intelligence in WW II, 560
Southwest Pacific campaign, 1941-45, 462
Vital gd to fighting aircraft of WW II, 580
War in N Africa, 1940-43, 460

WORLD'S COLUMBIAN EXPOSITION
World's Columbian Exposition, 404

WOUNDS & INJURIES
Injury prevention for young children, 710

WRITING
Blackwell ency of writing systems, 811
World's writing systems, 816

WRITING CENTERS
Writing centers, 284

YEARBOOKS
American Jewish yr bk 1996, v.96, 1220
Industrial commodity stats yrbk 1994, 195
International yrbk of industrial stats 1996, 196
Library lit 1995, 529
Magill's cinema annual 1995, 14th ed, 1131
McGraw-Hill yrbk of sci & tech 1996, 1243
Reference bks bulletin 1994-95, 12
Sources & methods: labour stats, v.2, 260
United States govt manual 1996/97, 604
Yearbook of labour stats 1995, 54th ed, 261

YIDDISH LANGUAGE—DICTIONARIES—ENGLISH
Hippocrene practical English-Yiddish, Yiddish-English dict, expanded ed, 878

YORUBA LANGUAGE—DICTIONARIES—ENGLISH
Hippocrene concise Yoruba-English, English-Yoruba dict, 879

YOUNG ADULT LITERATURE
100 most popular YA authors, 941
Literature for children & YAs about Oceania, 142
Writers of multicultural fiction for YAs, 942
Your reading, 1995-96 ed, 925

YOUTH
National gd to funding for children, youth, & families, 3d ed, 698
Peterson's summer opportunities for kids & teenagers 1996, 13th ed, 167

YOUTH HOSTELS
Hostelling USA, 1996, 389

YUGOSLAVIA
Slovenia, 122

ZIP CODE
National 5-digit zip code & post office dir 1996, 52

ZONAL FILM ARCHIVES
Catalogue of forbidden German feature & short film productions held in Zonal Film Archives..., English lang ed, 764